FOUR MARTYRDOMS
FROM THE PIERPONT MORGAN
COPTIC CODICES

Four Martyrdoms from the Pierpont Morgan Coptic Codices

Edited by

E. A. E REYMOND

and

J. W. B. BARNS

OXFORD
AT THE CLARENDON PRESS

Oxford University Press, Great Clarendon Street, Oxford OX2 6DP

Oxford New York

Athens Auckland Bangkok Bogotá Buenos Aires Calcutta
Cape Town Chennai Dar es Salaam Delhi Florence Hong Kong Istanbul
Karachi Kuala Lumpur Madrid Melbourne Mexico City Mumbai
Nairobi Paris São Paulo Singapore Taipei Tokyo Toronto Warsaw
and associated companies in
Berlin Ibadan

Oxford is a registered trade mark of Oxford University Press

Published in the United States by
Oxford University Press Inc., New York

© Oxford University Press 1973

Special edition for Sandpiper Books Ltd., 1998

ISBN 0-19-815448-8

1 3 5 7 9 10 8 6 4 2

Printed in Great Britain
on acid-free paper by
Bookcraft (Bath) Ltd.,
Midsomer Norton.

IN MEMORIAM

P. E. KAHLE, 1923–1955

CONTENTS

BIBLIOGRAPHY (SELECT) AND
ABBREVIATIONS

The following list confines itself to literary material cited in abbreviated form.

Abd el-Latif. See Sacy (de).

AI. & Pt. = Apaioule & Pteleme.

Amélineau, E. *La géographie de l' Égypte à l'époque copte* (Paris, 1893), (*Géogr.*)

Annales du Service des Antiquités de l' Égypte (Cairo, 1900–   ). (*Ann. Serv.*)

Apophthegmata Patrum. See Chaîne, M.

Balestri, I. & Hyvernat, H. *Acta Martyrum* I–II (Corpus Scriptorum Christianorum Orientis (CSCO), ser. 3., tom. 1, 2. Paris, 1907–50). (Bal.-Hyv. *AM*)

Ball, J. *Egypt in the Classical Geographers* (Survey of Egypt, Cairo, 1942).

Basset, R. *Le synaxaire arabe jacobite* (rédaction copte):
    I: P(*atrologia*) O(*rientalis*), t.i, pp. 217 (1907)
    I–III: ibid. t. iii, pp. 243 ff. (1909)
    IV–V: ibid. t. xvi, pp. 185 ff. (1922)
    (*Synax.*: ref. under month name)

Bell, H. I. *Cults and Creeds in Graeco-Roman Egypt, being the Forwood Lectures for 1952* (Liverpool Monographs in Archaeology and Oriental Studies. Liverpool, 1953).

BIFAO = Bulletin de l' Institut Français d'Archéologie Orientale du Caire.

BSAC = Bulletin de la Société d' Archéologie Copte.

Budge, Sir Ernest Alfred Thompson Wallis. *Coptic Martyrdoms, etc. in the Dialect of Upper Egypt* (London, 1914). (*Mart.*)

––– *The Martyrdom of Isaac of Tiphre, as contained in a Coptic Manuscript of the tenth century in the collection of Lord Zouche* (London, 1886).

––– *The Martyrdom & Miracles of St. George of Cappadocia* (Oriental Text Series I, London, 1888). (*St. George*)

––– *Miscellaneous Coptic Texts in the Dialect of Upper Egypt* (London, 1915). (*Misc.*)

Bulletin de l'Institut Français d'Archéologie Orientale du Caire (Cairo, 1901–   ). (*BIFAO*)

Bulletin de la Société d'Archéologie Copte (Cairo, 1936–   ). (*BSAC*)

Byzantinische Zeitschrift (Leipzig, 1892–   ). (*Byz. Ztschr.*)

Calderini, A. *Dizionario dei nomi geografici e topografici dell' Egitto greco-romano* (Cairo, 1935–   ). (*Diz. geogr.*)

Chaîne, M. *Le manuscrit de la version copte en dialecte sahidique des 'Apophthegmata Patrum'* (Cairo, 1960).

Coluthus I = P.M. Cod. M. 591, t. 28, fols. 88 V–92.

Coluthus II = MS. Paris copte 78, fols. 16 f. (See Appendix, pp. 139-143)

Crum, W. E. *Catalogue of the Coptic Manuscripts in the British Museum* (London, 1905). (*Cat. Copt. B.M.*)

––– *Catalogue of the Coptic Manuscripts in the Collection of the John Rylands Library, Manchester* (Manchester, etc., 1909). (*Cat. Copt. Ryl.*)

––– 'Colluthus, the Martyr and his Name', *Byz. Ztschr.* XXX (1929/30), 323 ff. ('Colluthus')

––– *A Coptic Dictionary* (Oxford, 1939). (*CD*)

––– *Short Texts from Coptic Ostraca and Papyri* (London, 1921). (*Short Coptic Texts*)

——— *Theological Texts from Coptic Papyri* (*Anecdota Oxoniensia*, Semitic Series 12, Oxford, 1913).

Delehaye, H. *Les Martyrs de l'Égypte* (Analecta Bollandiana, t. 40, pp. 5 ff. Brussels, 1923). (*Mart. Ég.*)

——— *Les passions des martyrs et les genres littéraires*, ed. [2] (Subsidia Hagiographica 13 B. Brussels, 1966). (*Pass. Mart.*)

Drescher, J. *Apa Mena: a selection of Coptic Texts relating to St. Menas* (Cairo 1946). (*Mena*)

——— 'Graeco-Coptica', *Le Muséon*, 82 (1969), 85 ff.

Epima. See Mina, T.

Evelyn White, H.G. *New Texts from the Monastery of St. Macarius*, (*The Monasteries of the Wadi 'n Natrûn*, Part I. Metropolitan Museum of Art Expedition. New York, 1926). (E. W. *Macarius*)

Frend, W. H. C. *Martyrdoms and Persecutions in the Early Church: a study of conflict from the Maccabees to Donatus* (Oxford, 1965).

Gardiner, Sir Alan Henderson, *Ancient Egyptian Onomastica* (London, 1947). (*AEO*)

Georgi, A. A. *De miraculis Sancti Coluthi, et reliquiis actorum Sancti Panesnii* (Rome, 1791).

Girgis, W. 'Greek loan words in Coptic', *BSAC* 17 (1963–4), 63 ff; 18 (1965–6), 71 ff; 19 (1967–8), 51 ff.

Hagedorn, D. & Weber, M. 'Die griechisch-koptische Rezension der Menander-Sentenzen', *Ztschr. f. Papyrologie u. Epigraphik*, 3 (1968), 15 ff.

Hyvernat, H. *Les actes des Martyrs de L'Égypte* i (only). (Paris, 1886). (*Actes*)

——— *Bibliothecae Pierpont Morgan codices coptici photographice expressi* (Rome, 1922). (*P.M.*)
    See also under Balestri.

JEA = Journal of Egyptian Archaeology.

Jones, A. H. M., Martindale, J. R., and Morris, J. *The Prosopography of the Later Roman Empire*, I (Cambridge, 1971).

Journal of Egyptian Archaeology (London, 1914–   ). (*JEA*)

Journal of Theological Studies (London, 1900–   ), (*JTS*)

Kiessling, E. *Wörterbuch des griechischen Papyrusurkunden*, vol. IV (Berlin-Marburg, 1944).

Lallemand, J. *L'administration civile de l'Égypte, 284–382* (Brussels, 1964).

Lampe, G. M. H. *A Patristic Greek Lexicon* (Oxford, 1961–8). (*Patr. Gr. Lex.*)

Leipoldt, J. *Sinuthii Archimandritae Vita et Opera Omnia* (Corpus Scriptorum Christianorum|Orientis. Paris, 1906–13).

Lemm, O. von, *Bruchstücke Koptischer Martyrerakten* (Mém. de l'Acad. Impér. des Sciences de St.-Petersbourg, 1913).

——— *Das Martyrium des H. Victor und des H. Stephanon* (printed, but undated and unpublished).

Liddell, H. G., & Scott, R. *Greek Lexicon*, ed. [9] (Oxford, 1925–40) (L&S[9])

Martin, V. *P. Bodmer XX: Apologie de Philéas évêque de Thmouis* (Bibliotheca Bodmeriana. Geneva, 1964). (*Phileas*)

Migne. *Patrologia Graeca*. (*PG*)

Mina, T. *Le martyre d'Apa Epima* (Service des Antiquités de L'Égypte, Cairo, 1937). (*Epima*)

Munier, H. 'Fragment des actes du martyre de l'Apa Chnoubé', *Ann. Serv.* 17 (1917), 145 ff.

——— '*La géographie de L'Égypte d'après les listes copto-arabes*', *BSAC* 5 (1939), 201 ff.

——— *Recueil des listes épiscopales de l'Egypte copte'* (Soc. d'arch. copte, Textes et documents. Cairo, 1943). (*Recueil*)
Muséon, Le: revue d'études orientales (Louvain, 1881–).
O'Leary, de Lacy. *The Saints of Egypt* (London, 1937). (*Saints*)
Oxyrhynchus Papyri, ed. Grenfell, B. P., Hunt, A. S., and others (London, 1898–)
P. & T. = Paēse and Thecla.
Patrologia Graeca (Migne). (*PG*)
Patrologia Orientalis (Paris, 1907–). (*PO*)
P. Bodmer XX. See Martin, V.
P. Herm. Rees. See Rees, B. R.
Phileas. See Martin, V.
P. Lond. = *Greek Papyri in the British Museum*, ed., F. Kenyon and others (London, 1893–1917).
P. M. = Pierpont Morgan.
P. Merton = *The Merton Papyri*, ed. Bell, H. I., Roberts, C. H., and others (London, Dublin, 1948–67).
PO = Patrologia Orientalis.
P. Oxy. = *The Oxyrhynchus Papyri.*
Preisigke, F. *Berichtigungsliste der griechischen Papyrusurkunden aus Ägypten* (Berlin, Leipzig, Heidelberg, 1922–).
——— *Namenbuch*, etc. (Heidelberg, 1922). (*Nb.*)
——— *Sammelbuch griechischer Urkunden aus Ägypten* (Strassburg, 1913–), (*Sb.*)
——— *Wörterbuch der griechischen Papyrusurkunden*, vols. I–III (Berlin, 1925–) (*Wb.*)
  See also Kiessling, E.
Proceedings of the Society of Biblical Archaeology (London, 1872–1918). (*PSBA*)
PSBA. See the last entry.
Ranke, H. *Die ägyptischen Personennamen* (Glückstadt, etc., 1935–).
Rees, B. R. 'The curator civitatis in Egypt', *Journal of Juristic Papyrology* VII (Warsaw, 1953/4), 83 ff.
——— *Papyri from Hermopolis* (London, 1964). (P. Herm. Rees)
Revue égyptologique (Paris, 1880–1924). (*Rev. ég.*)
Rossi, F. *Un nuovo codice copto del museo egizio di Torino* (R. Accad. dei Lincei. Rome, 1893).
——— *I papiri copti del museo egizio di Torino* (Turin, 1887–8).
Rouillard, G. *L'administration civile de l'Égypte byzantine*, ed.[2] (Paris, 1928).
Sacy, Baron Silvestre de. *Relation de l'Égypte par Abd-Allatif: traduit et enrichi de notes historiques et critiques* (Paris, 1810).
Sb. See Preisigke.
Sh. = Shenoufe and his Brethren.
Sin.= Sinuthius (Shenoute).
Sobhy, G. *Le martyr de St. Hélias, et l'encomium de l'évêque Stéphanos de Hnès sur St Hélias* (Bibl. des études coptes, I, Cairo, 1919).
Sophocles, E. A. *A Greek Lexicon of the Roman and Byzantine Periods* (Cambridge, 1914). (*Lex. Byz. Gr.*)
Sottas, H. 'Compte-rendus bibliographiques', *Revue égyptologique*, N. S. I (1919), 264 ff.
Stud. Pal. See Wessely, C.
Synax(ary). See Basset, R.

Till, W. *Koptische Dialektgrammatik*, ed.[2] (Munich, 1961).
——— *Koptische Grammatik* (Sahidischer Dialekt), ed.[3] (Leipzig, 1966).
——— *Koptische Heiligen- und Martyrerlegende*, (*Orientalia christiana analecta* 102. Rome, 1935–6). (*KHML*)
Vandersleyen, C. *Chronologie des préfets de l'Égypte de 284 à 395* (Brussels, 1962).
Vergote, J. 'Eculeus, Rad- und Pressefolter in den ägyptischen Martyrerakten', *Ztschr. f. NT. Wiss.* 37 (1938), 239 ff.
——— 'Le texte sous-jacent du palimpseste Berlin no. 9755', *Le Muséon* 48 (1935), 275 ff.
Wb. See Preisigke.
Wessely, C. *Studien zur Palaeographie und Papyruskunde* (Leipzig, 1901–24). (*Stud. Pal.*)
Winstedt, E. O. *Coptic texts on St. Theodore the Eastern, Chamoul and Justus* (London, 1910). (*CTST*)
ZAS. See the next entry.
Zeitschrift für ägyptische Sprache und Altertumskunde (Leipzig, 1863–   ). (*ZÄS*)
Zeitschrift für die Neutestamentliche Wissenschaft (Giessen, Berlin, 1900–   ). (*Ztschr. f. NT. Wiss.*)
Zeitschrift für Papyrologie und Epigraphik (Bonn, 1967–   ).
Zoëga, G. *Catalogus codicum copticorum qui in Museo Borgiano Velitris adservantur* (Rome, 1810). (Zoëga)

INTRODUCTION

The four works edited in this volume come from the great collection
of Coptic codices containing Biblical, theological and liturgical texts
from the monastery of S. Michael in Phantow, found at Hamouli in
the Fayûm in 1910, and mostly acquired by the Pierpont Morgan
Library in New York in 1911. Professor H. Hyvernat's check list of
their contents, produced in 1919, was followed in 1922 by the
publication of admirable photographic reproductions of the whole
of the material in a limited edition of fifty-six volumes; this was made
more generally available in an edition reproduced from the last in
1957. Of the four texts selected by us for publication, with the kind
permission of the Pierpont Morgan Trustees, two each are from vols.
28 and 41 respectively. They all purport to record the *Acta* of
Egyptian martyrs at the time of the great persecutions at the beginning
of the fourth century, and thus belong to a category of literature
plentifully represented in Coptic. Three at any rate—*Shenoufe,
Apaioule and Pteleme* and *Paēse and Thecla* (cited hereinafter as
Sh., AI. & Pt., and *P. & T.* respectively) exemplify the characteristics
which have won Egyptian martyrologies in particular the low
estimation in which they are held by the scholar and the historian;
thus such an authority as Delehaye can speak of 'cette misérable
littérature';[1] his general study of the martyrology, *Les passions des
martyrs*, in a chapter devoted to the fictional or 'epic' type of martyr
act and its analysis, has a special word of disapproval for examples of
this genre from Egypt.[2]

    Considered as literature, some at least of the Egyptian martyr acts
seem hardly as contemptible as the outraged sensibilities of the
historian would make them; there are moments in *P. & T.*, for instance
in the narrative of Thecla's voyage to Alexandria (68 R i ff.), which
achieve something like poetic imagination. One of the permanent
features of the Egyptian mind was its taste and talent for romantic
story-telling.[3] In one martyrdom at least, that of *Eustathius and
Theopistē* (Migne, *PG* 105, 375 ff.; Budge, *Mart.*, pp. 102 ff.; 356 ff.),
the influence of the Greek romance, with many of its favourite
motifs, situations and devices, is unmistakable. It would perhaps be
not over-fanciful to see in the martyrologies from Egypt points of

---

[1] *Mart. Ég.*, p. 148.   [2] *Pass. Mart.*, pp. 173 ff. Cf. O'Leary, *Saints*, pp. 12 ff.
[3] See Barns, 'Egypt and the Greek Romance', *Mitt. a. d. Papyrussammlung d. österr.
Nationalbibliothek*, N. F. 5 (*Akt. d. viii. intern. Kongresses f. Papyrologie, Wien 1955*),
pp. 29 ff., where a case is put for Egyptian connections with that latecomer among Greek
literary forms, the prose romance.

resemblance, not only to the romance, but also to Greek drama, in
the tendency for stock character types to recur from piece to piece;[4]
not only the martyr hero and the villainous persecuting governor,
but minor characters such as the gaoler converted by the saint's
miracles, and the governor's wife, modelled upon Pilate's, who
sympathizes with the martyr and counsels her husband, wisely but
in vain, to have nothing to do with this just man. The appearances of
the Lord and His angels may be compared with theophanies in drama,
though they are more frequent; one may also see an analogy with the
rôle of the Chorus in the intervention, by sympathetic word or action,
of the city populace which witnesses the proceedings. The character
type of the martyr hero of the piece will of course vary from case to
case, but they tend to fall into a few familiar categories; those
represented in the present texts include a recusant soldier, an
anchorite, and two examples of the favourite type of the prosperous
farmer, merchant or man of property, in each case supported by a
sister whose constancy matches his own. (The accompaniment of
one of them, Shenoufe, by ten like-minded brothers is an unusual
feature in the Egyptian martyr acts.) The situations tend to follow
the stereotyped pattern summarized by Delehaye.[5] *Sh., Al. & Pt.*
and *P. & T.* are hardly to be outdone by any in extravagance,
improbability or, in places, sheer absurdity; they abound in Divine
and angelic visions and visitations and miracles of healing and
resuscitation. The Governor's stupidity, malevolence and irascibility[6]
are alike excessive. As to the tortures employed, while few of them
are individually incredible,[7] when heaped upon the same individual
they become merely ridiculous.[8] The martyr himself, having earned
severe treatment by fantastic feats of provocative rudeness, is made
to display superhuman fortitude under torture; his repeated recovery
from it by supernatural means leaves the mind surfeited with improbability. The reader's opinion of the authenticity of Coptic martyr acts
is not improved when he compares the texts in detail. They abound
in passages which may be matched word for word elsewhere, so that
it is often possible to emend a phrase from its doublet in another
martyrology. Such correspondences with other martyr acts are too
common in these three Pierpont Morgan texts to be exhaustively

---

[4] Delehaye, *Mart. Ég.*, pp. 138 ff.
[5] *Pass. Mart.*, ch. iii (pp. 171 ff.); cf. O'Leary., *Saints*, p. 19 f.
[6] Cf. Delehaye, *Pass. Mart.*, p. 178. In *Sh.* the words 'The Governor was angry; he
ordered . . .' occur, with small variations, sixteen times.
[7] Neither, we may be sure, is their repertoire exhaustive. Obscene tortures are obviously
favourites with those who devise or employ them, and offer high entertainment value to
the spectator; but we should not expect to hear much of them in this context, since they
are hardly conducive to the dignity of a saint; see, however, our note on *Sh.* 125 R i 9 ff.
[8] Cf. Delehaye, *Mart. Ég.*, p. 141; *Pass. Mart.*, pp. 197 ff.

recorded, but for the sake of illustration we have noted the numerous
and close correspondences between *Sh.* and the equally complete
martyrdom of *Epima*.[9] Everything seems to point to the existence
of scriptoria[10] where martyrologies were produced to order, and, one
suspects, paid for by the yard; they were padded out with stock
passages to the requisite size.[11] Another feature of this class of
literature, itself useful as a padding device, is the way in which the
stories are made to interconnect by the introduction of the same
characters; thus in *Sh.* we have subsidiary narratives about Eusebius
son of Basilides (104 R i 3–105 R i 8); Pamoun and Elias (112 V ii
19–113 V ii 7); Astratolē (119 R ii 23–V ii 23); there is also an
interesting mention (105 V ii 5) of Philemon, bishop of Thmuis (see
below, p. 8 f.); in *P. & T.*, Victor (55 R ii 27–56 R ii 18); Hēraei
(70 V ii 3–71 R i 3); Apa Arē (Arius) (88 R i 6–ii 23); and Paul and
Apollonius, both prominent in this story, were the heroes of individual martyrdoms (see below).[12] Two other recurrent factors have been
noted as links by which the Egyptian martyrdoms may be grouped
into cycles: the participation or mention in them of members of the
family of Basilides, or the attribution of the piece in question to the
authorship of Julius of Kbahs (Aqfaḥs), who also features in the
narratives.[13] In *Sh.* and *P. & T.* both these elements are found. The
representation of evidently identical characters recurring from one
martyrdom to another is not always consistent. For instance, the
story of Paēse and Thecla has wide variations. In the *Synaxary* (Kihak
8th) the account is much as in our text, except that the son of
Romanus whose example inspires Paēse is not Victor but Justus, and
the priest of Shetnoufe who preserves the bodies of P. and T. is not
Arē (Arius) but Macarius.[14] Elsewhere in the *Synaxary*, however
(Amshir 9th) we find the story of Paul the Syrian, who is described
as a merchant of Shmoun and a friend of Abaisi (Paēse) and Thecla;
here all three are martyred in a different order. A widely different
story is found in the martyrology of Justus,[15] where Justus is the

[9] Available in the admirable publication of T. Mina, *Le Martyre d' Apa Epima*, Service des
Antiquités de l'Égypte, Cairo 1937. For correspondence between *Sh.* and other texts see
our note on *Sh.* 115 V i 17, where there is evidence of a curious reading apparently
repeated from text to text.
[10] Cf. Delehaye, *Mart. Ég.*, p. 152; O'Leary, *Saints*, p.14.
[11] See Delehaye, *Mart Ég.*, pp. 171 ff.; O'Leary, *Saints*, p. 19.
[12] It is to be noted, as an indication of the lengths to which forgiveness could go in the stern
and uncompromising Christianity of Egypt, that hagiographical legend makes Arianus
himself a Christian convert and martyr; see the Arabic *Synaxary* (ed. Basset, *PO* xvi, p. 210),
Barmahat 8th; O'Leary, *Saints*, p. 86.; Rossi, *Un nuovo codice copto . . . Torino*, pp. 77 ff.
[13] See Delehaye, *Mart. Ég.*, p. 137 f.; O'Leary, *Saints*, p. 19.
[14] For a Macarius (a son of Basilides) connected with Shetnoufe, see *Synaxary*, Abib 22nd
(O'Leary, *Saints*, p. 181).
[15] See Evelyn White, *Macarius*, pp. 79 ff.; O'Leary, *Saints*, p. 175 f.

husband of Theocleia (doubtless = Thecla)[16] and father of Apoli
(= Apollonius); the three are martyred, apparently simultaneously,
but in different places. There is also a martyrdom devoted to Apoli
himself, a boy, son of Justus.[17]

Another tendency may be suspected rather than demonstrated—
the association in one story of two or more martyrs not originally
connected. This seems very likely in the case of the Latin martyrdom of *Phileas and Philoromus*, part of which is found in an early
and evidently more authentic form, concerning Phileas alone (see
below, p. 8 f.). We venture to suggest that something similar
happened in the case of one of the present martyrdoms, that of
Apaioule and Pteleme; and that here a romantic story has been
written round two individuals of whom no traditions were preserved,
other than that the one was a recusant soldier and the other an
anchorite; the former would belong to the time of the great persecution, but the latter might not be connected or contemporary
with him; their combination in one composition being contrived for
the convenience of two neighbouring localities.

The abundant evidence for romantic and imaginary treatment gives
a bad enough impression of the historical value of martyr acts from
Egypt. This is intensified not only by individual cases of evident
misstatement about dates and the careers and titles of officials, but
by misrepresentations of a more general kind. We know that the great
persecutions of the beginning of the fourth century were instigated
by a series of edicts, and were not immediately, but only progressively
general in their application. Among the martyrologies themselves the
earlier stages seem reflected in the accounts of the martyrdoms of
soldiers whose refusal to obey and sacrifice was punished as a breach
of military discipline. But the picture most often presented by the
Egyptian martyrologies—those at any rate which record the acts of
martyrs who had been farmers or merchants—is of a peaceful and
prosperous life rudely disrupted by a single act of wanton tyranny
and cruelty by the highest authority of the State; whereas it is plain
from the wealth of documentary evidence which we have from Egypt,
particularly from the third century, that the great persecutions were
not only themselves phases of increasing severity as the results of
successive edicts, but were the culmination of a long period of
increasing economic trouble and social unrest. This simplication
serves to show, however, the deep impression which the general order
to sacrifice made upon the people of Egypt.

[16] In our text she is the widow of an unnamed husband.
[17] See references cited by O'Leary, *Saints*, p. 81; Evelyn White, *Macarius*, pp. 87 ff.

It seems often to be taken for granted by historians that between Alexandria and the other centres of Greek culture in Egypt on the one hand, and the native masses on the other there must have been a deep division in sympathy. In fact it would be hard to substantiate this from any source; it certainly does not emerge from the martyrologies, where there is no trace of opposition or contrast between (for instance) the behaviour of the populace of Alexandria and that of a community in the Fayûm or Upper Egypt. The charge of 'nationalism' is often brought against the Egyptian Church. Now it cannot be denied that the Egyptian had always regarded the land of the Nile, and his own native part of it especially, as the centre of the universe, and that this mental fixation of local patriotism persisted in the Christian era.[18] It is also true that when the persecutions were over, Egypt was to show itself implacably opposed to the high-handed imposition of foreign patriarchs by imperial Constantinople; but its obdurate pride was founded as much on the theological achievements of Alexandria as upon the spiritual achievements of Egyptian monastic asceticism. And, in fact, the crudest manifestations of national and racial prejudice are not to be found in the native literature about Egyptian martyrs, provincial as it is. There we shall find only one superior race of men, 'the race of Christians', and the 'fatherland' which claims their allegiance is 'the heavenly Jerusalem'. Indeed, the Coptic martyrologies seem to go out of their way to glorify saints of foreign origin who fulfil their martyrdom in exile in Egypt, thus setting an example to the faithful there. So of the works edited here one has as one of its two heroes Pteleme, said to be a Phoenician of Antioch; the opening narrative of another, which has no obvious connection with the rest of the story, is another Antiochene martyrdom, that of Eusebius son of Basilides; in a third the celebrated Victor, also of Antioch, not only serves to inspire its hero by his example, but is said to excel the latter in merit and glory as much as a king excels a mere magistrate (*P. & T.* 78 V ii 18 ff.; 81 R i 9 ff.). One of the ways in which a really nationalistic spirit, had it flourished in Christian Egypt, could hardly have failed to manifest itself would have been the glorification of Egypt's pagan past. But of this there is no trace; Pharaoh is the type of the tyrant here as with Christians in general, and his gods are vain and abominable. It might at first sight seem that Diocletian's gods, to whom sacrifice is demanded—Apollo, Artemis, Zeus, Aphrodite—were alien importations from the Greek world, and that only Serapis had any Egyptian connection. But such

---

[18] It is significant that in the martyrologies one of the tribulations which won their heroes most merit was the pain of separation from their native place, 'the condition of a stranger'; cf. *Sh.* 107 R i 15 f.; *P. & T.* 80 V ii 32 f.

a conclusion could hardly be maintained; purely Greek cults never had any substantial influence in Egypt, and it is incredible that any emperor would have attempted anything as hopeless as their introduction, priesthoods and all, at this time. These seemingly Greek divinities must be taken to be basically Egyptian ones, here found wearing the names of the Greek deities with whom they had been identified, as far as the Greek-speaking world was concerned, for centuries,[19] though their representations may well have been in a blend of Egyptian and classical styles. This may also have been true of the pagan religious buildings of the period; but despite the frequent statement that the persecuting emperor built (or rebuilt) pagan temples, buildings from this period devoted to pagan worship are hardly to be found in Egypt; perhaps because the Christians were at especial pains to destroy pagan temples whose erection they had witnessed with their own eyes. For by the fourth century it seems evident that the great majority of Egypt's people hated not only their Roman oppressors, but the traitorous gods who are represented on the temple walls as supporting the tyrant power, and the craven priesthood which served them. And whatever derogatory terms the Romans might use to describe the fanatical passive or active resistance of the Egyptians, they had in fact the courage which characterizes a people with an absolute conviction of the reality of the world to come; belief in this, and preoccupation with it, was in part a legacy from the discarded pagan religion, and it was now intensified by intolerable earthly hardship into a positive longing to be free from the body and to inherit the joys of eternal life in the heavenly Jerusalem, to which martyrdom for the name of Christ was the surest way.

It may be said of the Coptic martyr acts in general that the blatantly unhistorical manner of their presentation has tended to make the historian dismiss them as unworthy of serious consideration.[20] This

---

[19] This is the normal practice in Coptic writings; apart from the furtive and disreputable world of the magical texts, the native names of Egyptian deities rarely occur except as components of proper names. Even there they were sometimes given up (see Frend, *Martyrdom and Persecution in the Early Church*, p. 476, n. 191). This may be because the very pronunciation of the true name of a pagan abomination was felt to be dangerous. So we find Shenoute (*Sinuthii Archimandritae Vita et Opera Omnia* (ed. Leipoldt) iii, pp. 77 ff.) referring to the patron god of his pagan adversary as Kronos; in another place by the epithet Petbe, 'The Avenger'; see Crum, *Copt. Dict.*, p. 399a; the actual identity of this divinity is uncertain. He elsewhere (iii 89, 12) mentions 'the Pan who is ours'; the allusion is to an image of Min, prominent in the district of Panopolis/Akhmim; a reference there to his ἀσχημοσύνη no doubt alludes to the fact that representations of him are ithyphallic.

[20] One of the things which the historian must find especially hard to forgive is the deliberate and conscious untruth of the statement, occurring regularly in martyr acts purporting to be from the pen of Julius of Aqfahs (e.g., *P. & T.* 87 V i 7 ff.; *Sh.* 136 V ii 32 ff.), that the writer has neither omitted anything of the truth nor added to it.

has perhaps in the past been carried too far. The martyrdoms would not be valueless as evidence of the psychological state of early Christianity in Egypt even if none of the statements contained in them could be substantiated. In fact, however, there are several respects in which their evidence is not to be discounted. Even their most sceptical critics must admit that they contain topographical information of some value;[21] some of the localities which they name are not mentioned elsewhere, or if they are, are not identified; the fact that in these narratives they occur in the course of an itinerary is often an indication of their location.[22]

With regard to the personalities named in the martyrologies, the tendency in the past seems to have been to excessive scepticism. This is demonstrable in the cases of some of the Roman officials; more recent evidence tends to indicate that although their designation is often wildly inaccurate, and the accounts of their words and works highly imaginative, they must not lightly be assumed to have been invented. An example of an official previously taken to be legendary, but now attested as a real personality, and an important one, is the man whose name is spelt in the martyrologies, with some variations, as Hrokēllianos (see below, p. 185, n. 7). The most notorious persecutor of all, Arianus, has long been known from Greek documents as a historical figure, Satrius Ar(r)ianus, *praeses* of the Thebaid; to P. Florence I 33, 10 and P. Grenfell II 78, 1 we must now add P. Oxy. 2665, 15, which shows Arianus in a characteristically grim light.[23] Another document in the same volume, No. 2673 (dated A.D. 304) should dispel any doubt about the truth of the statement so often repeated in the martyr acts that the Roman

---

[21] This is admitted by Delehaye, whose judgment on the Egyptian martyrology tends to excessive severity.

[22] E.g., in the present texts, Pousire (*P. & T.* 49 R i 5; 29); Tepôt (ib. 86 V i 22); Chortasa (*Sh.* 105 V i 17; ii 14); Poubaste (Bubastis) in the Fayûm, = Kamē polis (ib. 124 V i 22 f.; 138 V i 12 f.); Empaiat 'of the Plainland' (ib. 108 R ii 24 ff.); Psoutoumēt (*Al. & Pt.* 168 V ii 18 ff.); Hanepioor (ib. 171 R i 13).

[23] See *Oxy. Pap.* xxiii, pp. 87 ff. On this person, see Lallemand, *L' administration*, p. 141, n. 2; 250; Vandersleyen, *Chronologie*, pp. 85 ff.; 104 f., a work which, while assessing the evidence of all sources with care, caution and judgment, gives due and serious consideration to the hagiographical ones; and Jones–Martindale–Morris, *Prosopography* I, p. 14. It should be noted that the spelling of his name adopted in the last named work as 'Adrianus' is probably mistaken. It rests upon the reading of Vitelli in P. Flor. 33, where the editor himself marks the δ as doubtful, thou he later maintained it; see Preisigke, *Berichtigungsliste d. gr. Papyrusurk.* I, p. 455. In view not only of the consensus of Coptic Mss., but of the writings 'Arianus' and 'Arrianus' in the other Greek papyri we should doubtless take Vitelli's δ as a miswriting or a misreading. The form with doubled ρ may be significant; it may represent a parvenu's attempt to dignify an original name Ἄρειος by not only adding the ending -*anus* (cf. Eutychianus, Hierocleianus, Diocletianus), but by suggesting a derivation from the Latin gentile name Arrius. For further particulars about Arianus, see below, p. 145.

authorities destroyed Christian churches and confiscated their possessions. Here it is stated that the only furnishing of the demolished
church of the village of Chysis worthy of salvage was its bronze gate;
this itself suggests a building of some size. The church described in
Sh. 106 R ii 3 ff may well be a 'house church' devoted to private
worship by a family and their intimate friends; in a time of persecution such a private, modest and inconspicuous institution will
have had much to commend it;[24] another way of avoiding notice
will have been to place a building for public worship in a secluded
spot.[25]

Our remarks have so far been principally concerned with the type
of martyrology represented by *P. & T.*, *Sh.* and *Al. & Pt.*; the great
majority of those from Egypt fall into this category—dramatic,
romantic, or (to use Delehaye's euphemistic term) 'epic'. But in
1922 this scholar had already noted (*Mart. Ég.*, pp. 154 ff.) a writing
concerning Egyptian martyrs with special claims to be taken seriously.
This was the Acta of *Phileas and Philoromus*, up to then extant only
in Latin versions.[26] This judgment was confirmed by the publication
by Prof. V. Martin, in 1964, of P. Bodmer xx, a Greek text corresponding to part of the Latin *Acta*, recording the hearing of the case of
Phileas alone, with a brief but informative introduction. This text,
which is early—its editor remarks that the MS. should be dated before
350—is evidently more original and authentic. Its subject, Phileas,
bishop of Thmuis (evidently identical with 'Philemon the bishop of
Thmoui' in *Sh.* 105 V ii 5, Φιλέας being presumably the hypocoristic
form of the name) is tried at Alexandria by Clodius Culcianus, prefect
of Egypt A.D. 302–308,[27] another notorious persecutor; the piece is
very different in style from the 'epic' martyrologies, consisting as it
does simply of a dialogue between the bishop and the governor, the
only other interlocutors being the advocates (δικολόγοι)[28] In *Phileas*,

[24] When the tables were turned upon the pagans and they became subject to persecution,
we find them thrown back upon domestic worship of their gods; the raids of Shenoute
and his monks upon pagan households produced a variety of cult objects to be held up
to their condemnation. Such private worship, however, was nothing new; we hear of
altars in private houses as early as the third century B.C. See Bell, *Cults and Creeds*,
p. 68; Otto, *Priester und Tempel* I, pp. 169 ff.

[25] See Till, *KHML*, p. 61 (Panine and Panew), where the faithful are found building one
in a desert place.

[26] For a similarly favourable verdict upon it, see Frend, pp. 495; 528.

[27] See Vandersleyen, pp. 73 ff.; 87 ff.; 93.

[28] The form of this text is plentifully represented among Greek documents of the Roman
period from Egypt; see R.A. Coles, *Reports of Proceedings in Papyri* (*Papyrologica
Bruxellensia* 4, 1966), where a large number of such texts are analysed, and such topics
as the conventions of reporting and the use of shorthand discussed. The same form is
imitated with varying degrees of verisimilitude by the Alexandrian patriotic pamphlet
literature known as the *Acta Alexandrinorum*; see Musurillo, *The Acts of the Pagan
Martyrs*, pp. 236 ff.

although the verbal exchange between the protagonists touches upon theological and philosophical matters, there is nothing to suggest that the body of the text is other than a literal transcription of the actual proceedings in court; a convincing detail is its description in its introduction as the *fifth* hearing of the case.

Now up to the present this has been regarded as unique among martyr literature from Egypt; thanks, perhaps, to the low historical reputation of Coptic martyrologies it would hardly have occurred to any one to look for a close parallel in that language. But this we believe we have in the other piece whose text we publish here. *Coluthus* is one of the more famous Egyptian martyrs; an account of the traditions about him and a summary of the literary sources are given by W.E. Crum in his article 'Colluthus the Martyr and his name'.[29] His status and profession are not specified in the body of our text, but its introduction describes him as a physician; this description is a commonplace elsewhere in Coptic literature, which also makes him a presbyter (see Crum, art. cit.). The dramatic date of the piece is given in the introductory part of our text as May 304,[30] but in the other redaction, *Coluthus* II (see below, pp. 11 ff.) as May 305. The piece ends with a conventional, one might almost say obligatory, account of Coluthus' reception into heavenly company of the saints. But between these two sections in the usual martyrological style the resemblance of our piece to the 'epic' martyrdoms ends. Like *Phileas* the body of the text is simply an account, with a minimum of comment or extraneous matter, and no evident abbreviation or alteration, of the verbal exchange between the martyr and the magistrate who is trying him, Arianus; and this is all, except for a couple of interpositions by two advocates (ῥήτορες) and members of the governor's suite. Whether, as in the case of *Phileas*, it was preceded by other hearings is not expressly stated; but it seems certain that this was so; this, however, was the only hearing of which a transcript was available. How this might have been obtained is a matter for conjecture; it seems unlikely that any one would in the circumstances have ventured openly to consult the public records of the trial, but an official may have been bribed[31] or

---

[29] *Byz. Ztschr.* xxx (1929/30), 323 ff. Greek and Coptic variations of the name are discussed there; in our text it is spelt Ⲕⲟⲗⲁ(ⲗ)ⲟⲑⲟⲥ, in its duplicate, the palimpsest Berl. 9755 (see below, p.20), ⲅⲟⲗⲗⲟⲩⲑⲟⲥ. For hieroglyphic writings, see Ranke, *Äg. Personnamen*, s.n. Ḳrṯ. For further particulars about the saint and the literature devoted to him, see Vergote, *Le Muséon*, 48, 276 ff. P. Antinoopolis 109 (6th cent.) is now seen to refer to the celebration of this saint's commemoration. See also P. Ant. 190 (6th–7th cent.) (a) 18; (b) 41.

[30] The equation of this with the 'third year of Constantine' does not inspire confidence in its writer's chronology.

[31] Cf. a case cited by Delehaye, *Pass. Mart.*, p. 130.

(since the trial was plainly held in public) someone may have surreptitiously transcribed the proceedings himself.[32]

Now the fact that we have here a record of a single session, in a single place, is itself a feature which inspires confidence. The narrative in the 'epic' martyrologies generally extends over long periods and involves long journeys and changes of scene.[33] These things are not of course improbable in themselves; indeed they were doubtless normal in the cases of notable prisoners; but the complete recording of their cases was obviously impossible without the supposition of a sympathetic scribe accompanying the journey, and having access to confidential matters[34] —hence the need for such a character as Julius of Aqfahs. Furthermore, other usual features which make accounts of martyrs' trials unrealistic are here notably absent. There are no Divine or angelic appearances, and no miracles; various tortures are threatened, but not applied until the martyr is finally taken out to execution by burning (see below, p. 149), which is not described. And instead of those impossible feats of rudeness[35] and sermons and copious quotations of Holy Scripture[36] on the part of the martyr, he is reluctant to speak at all; his only quotation is probably to be traced to the Greek New Comedy (see below, p. 146), and his demeanour is positively deferential until his final outburst of irritation is answered by an immediate sentence of death. The Governor is even more unlike the stock type of villain who out-Herods Herod in the 'epic' martyrologies. He is loquacious, conciliatory and flattering; he loses his temper only once, but that is the end of the trial. The general impression with which we are left by this piece is of a dialogue so full of small convincing details that it is simply impossible to believe it to be a literary fiction from the milieu which produced the other three writings edited here. Not only has it the ring of literal authenticity; there is one reference in it which seems to support this impression. This is the mention (90 R ii 1 ff.) of Apollonius, bishop of Siout, who, with another bishop, otherwise unknown, is warmly praised by the Governor as a shining example of good sense for complying with the imperial order to sacrifice.[37] This wretch is the recipient of a letter attributed to Peter of Alexandria, the beginning of which is preserved in Ms. Paris Copte 131.[38]

---

[32] The statement in the martyrologies attributed to the authorship of Julius of Aqfahs (e.g. *Sh.* 138 R ii 7 ff.) that he 'planted' trusty official scribes in courts throughout Egypt to record martyrs' trials is by no means wholly absurd.

[33] Cf. Delehaye, *Mart. Ég.*, pp. 138 ff.   [34] Cf. Delehaye, *Pass. Mart.*, pp. 181 f.

[35] Cf. Delehaye, *Pass. Mart.*, p. 191.   [36] Cf. Delehaye, *Pass. Mart.*, pp. 192 ff.

[37] Cf. Pierius in Martin, *Phileas*, pp. 26 f.

[38] To be published by H. Chadwick and J. Barns in *Journal of Theological Studies*, October 1973.

If one were determined to contest the genuineness of our *Coluthus* document, it might perhaps be objected that some of the arguments and observations of the governor, and some of the replies of the martyr himself, are plainly echoed in one or other of the 'epic' martyrologies. These cases will be found noted in our marginal comments at the following places: 89 R ii 19–22; V ii 19 ff.; 90 R i 15 ff., V ii 8 ff.; 91 V ii 7 ff.; 92 R ii 5 ff. To this we may reply (a) that one like Arianus who has conducted many similar trials will naturally repeat the same words of argument and persuasion from case to case; and since the trials are conducted in public, his stock arguments and clichés will be remembered and reproduced; (b) that the answers of the martyrs themselves will tend to be stereotyped; any predictable question will be met with a preconsidered reply, such as *verbum sapienti satis* (see below, p. 146), with which, as an evasive answer to an impertinent, absurd or awkward question, we may compare the modern 'No comment'; (c) Coluthus was a prominent saint, and the *Acta* which we have here may have been so well known as to inspire not only compositions about him, but martyrologies written for other saints. We have at any rate a fragment of another text of the present form of *Coluthus*, the Berlin palimpsest 9755 (see below, p. 20); its variations from the text of the Morgan codex are somewhat wide, but not abnormally so for a category of literature which tends to considerable textual fluidity.[39] Our text, with the Berlin fragment, will hereinafter be designated *Coluthus* I. There is another version of the story, however, which is very different. It is plainly secondary, and a complete rewriting of it, though its debt to *Coluthus* I is everywhere apparent in numerous echoes which we shall note in our comments on our translation of the latter. Of this text, which we designate *Coluthus* II, the beginning is preserved in Ms. Paris Copte 78, fols. 16 f. (apparently of the ninth century). It was published by Peyron in his *Grammatica Linguae Copticae*, pp. 165 ff.; we give a collated and corrected text in an Appendix (below, pp. 142 ff.). The translation is as follows:
'The *martyrdom* of the revered *martyr*, the *holy* Apa Coluthus, which he fulfilled in fortitude on the twenty-fourth day of the month Pashons.

It befell in the twenty-first year of the emperors Diocletian and Maximinianus (*sic*) the *transgressors*, when they were *persecuting* the *Christians*, on the twenty-first (*sic*) day of the month Pashons, that the *holy* Apa Coluthus was *produced* before Arianus the *governor* as he sat on the *tribunal* in Shmoun (Hermopolis). Arianus the *governor* of the Thebaid said to Apa Coluthus, 'Wilt thou obey?

[39] See Delehaye, *Mart. Ég.*, p. 148.

For [all] these who stand here are praying for thee that thou mayest be wise. If therefore it is shame which restrains thee, *by reason of* vanity and *by reason of* the *law* of the *Christians*, well, now let a proper shame come to thee, so that thou worship the Emperor's gods.' The *holy* Apa Coluthus answered, 'May it not befall that I should forsake my God and worship *idols* which are the works of men's hands; eyes have they and see not, ears have they and hear not, mouths have they and speak not, noses have they and smell not; their hands handle not, their feet walk not; they speak not through their throat; for there is no *spirit* in them; they who have made them are like unto them, and all such as put their trust in them.[40] *For* as for thee and thy *lawless* emperors, the *Devil* has shut up all the *perceptions* of your *souls* like those things which you worship.' Arianus was angry, and *ordered* the soldiers to lay before the *holy* Apa Coluthus all the things with which people are *tortured*, if perchance through the fear of them he should be able to prevail on him and *persuade* him to *sacrifice* to the *idols*. And he brought into the midst fire, and a great stone to be hung upon the neck of the *blessed* man, and a sack full of sand, and a *helmet*,[41] and the rest of the *instruments of torture*. And when he had laid all these in his sight, the *governor* said to him, 'O Coluthus, fear all these *torments* and pains which are laid before thee, and *sacrifice*; all these *torments* are for those who disobey the Emperors.' And Apa Coluthus answered, 'It is written, "Fear not them which kill your *body*, but are not able to kill your *soul*; but rather fear him which is able to destroy your *soul* and your *body* in the *Gehenna* of fire."[42] And [again] it is written, "Whosover [shall] *confess* Me before men, him will I *confess* also before My Father Which is in heaven, and His holy *angels*";[43] and again, "Whosoever shall *deny* Me before men, him will I also *deny* before My Father Which is in heaven, and His holy *angels*." '[44]

[40] Ps. cxv 4 ff.; ib. cxxxv 15 ff.

[41] Ⲕⲁⲥⲓⲥ = *cassis*, 'helmet', used (heated) as an instrument of torture; so Crum, *Theological Texts from Coptic Papyri*, p. 77 (Apa Moui); Rossi, *P. Copt. Torin.* I v, p. 28 (Djoore); Budge, *St. George*, p. 24; ib. *Mart.* p. 23 (Victor); von Lemm, *Victor & Stephanou*, p. 29; similarly περικεφαλαία in *Sh.* 121 V ii 26; 122 R i 10; Bal. - Hyv., *AM*, p. 131 (Epima). In the present text Ⲕⲁⲥⲓⲥ is used again: fol. 17, V ii 24 ff.: ⲛ̄ⲧⲥⲉⲍⲱⲱⲕⲉ ⲙ̄[ⲙ]ⲟⲟ ⲍ̄ⲛ̄ⲟⲩ]ⲕⲁⲥⲓⲥ. If ⲍⲱⲱⲕⲉ is understood as 'scrape', as no doubt ⲍⲱⲕⲉ must be in fol. 2, V ii 7, it would hardly suit the latter passage; we believe, however, that it is a less correct (though not unexampled) spelling of ⲍⲱⲱⲕ, 'fit out', which might well be used of a helmet. Sophocles, *Lex. Byz. Gr.*, cites κάσις as a misspelling of κασσίς (*cassis*) with this meaning. We should therefore delete the entry κάσις, 'whip', in Lampe, *Patr. Gr. Lex.*, p. 704, which is cited from Cyr. Alex. *Hom. Div.* xiv, ed. Aubert, vol. V (2) 411 (= Migne, *PG* 77, 1084), in a passage describing infernal torments: βαρεῖαι αἱ κασίδες αἱ τιμωρητικαὶ ἐκεῖναι, where Aubert's translation, '*scuticae*', is evidently a mere guess.

[42] Mt. x 28.   [43] Mt. x 32; Lk. xii 9.
[44] Mt. x 33; Lk. xii 9.

Arianus answered and said to Apa Coluthus, 'Thou hast not been called upon to make long speeches; if thou *darest* to speak again in my presence, I will have thy tongue torn out. *For* all [these] who stand here [*grieve*] for thy sake [. . . .] .' Apa Coluthus [answered], 'My pride and my crown is the Lord. *For* it is written, 'Our *conversation* is in heaven, from whence we look for our *Saviour*, the Lord Jesus, Who shall change the *body* of our low estate into the likeness of the *body* of His glory;[45] that the eyes of our heart may be enlightened.'[46] Arianus answered and said to him, 'Art thou a *deacon* or a *presbyter*, that thou utterest these words? And tell me too, what is thy calling?' Apa Coluthus said to him, '*Before* this *world* I am a physician from my youth up, [for] by God I have been *granted* [the power of] *healing* [(men?)] ; *but before* God I am a *Christian*, worshipping Jesus *Christ* my Lord.' Arianus said to him, '*Sacrifice*, O Coluthus, and have pity on thyself; let every one look upon thee *favourably*, and regard thee in a good light. *For* thou hast not had any of the *advocates* who are present here contend for thee; they are all together (?) and thou hast not availed thyself of their favour to speak for thee.' Apa Coluthus answered, 'I do not *need* them, *for* I have my Lord Jesus *Christ* fighting for me. *For* all thy *torments* which are laid (before me) are nothing in my sight. Therefore every *torment* which thou pleasest, give them to me . . . [. . . . . . it is written?], 'An athlete is not crowned *except* he strive *well*.'[47] The *governor* straightway *ordered* him to be set upon the *rack* and scraped and stabbed. *But* when he was set up on the *rack*, the *holy* Apa Coluthus *signed* himself[48] (with the Cross) straightway, and the *rack* fell in two pieces. *And* Arianus said, 'See the *magic* of the *Christians*, how great it is!' *And* the *governor ordered* another *rack* to be brought, and Apa Coluthus to be set upon it and fitted [with a] *helmet* [. . . Apa] Coluthus [. . .'

Here we see the process by which a convincing and apparently genuine document can develop into an 'epic' martyrology. Although *Coluthus* II as a mere fragment we observe several significant alterations from its evident original. The martyr himself is no longer reticent or deferential, but prolix, sententious and insolent. The governor, though his remarks in *Coluthus* I are sometimes echoed, is more like the twopence coloured villain of the average martyrology. Tortures are not merely shown and threatened, but inflicted; and at least one miracle takes place. In the Sermons of Phoebammon (Till, *KHML* I, pp. 169 ff.) and Isaac of

---

[45] Phil. iii 20 f.   [46] Eph. i 18.
[47] Cf. II Tim. ii 5.
[48] Or possibly 'signed *it*' (the rack); but if so the expression here is somewhat clumsy and misleading.

Antinoē (Pierpont Morgan Copt. Cod. xxviii, 93 ff.; unpublished) on S. Coluthus, and in the *Synaxary* under the names of Abadîyûn (Apa Dion?) (Amshir 1st), and Coluthus (Bashons 25th) we find the development of the legend complete. We are presented with the whole early history of Coluthus; he is the son of a Christian governor, Heraclamon, and a close friend of Philip, the son of Apa Dion (?), bishop of Antinoē, who like him is a physician, and is ordained deacon with him. Arianus is represented as Coluthus' brother-in-law, having married Coluthus' sister before the accession and legislation of Diocletian prompted him to declare himself a pagan. He subsequently arrests Coluthus and keeps him in custody. (In the Sermon of Isaac Arianus has him executed; but in the *Synaxary* it is not he, but his successor who is responsible for his death.) Although these romantic details are palpably fictitious, it is sometimes possible to suggest reasons for their invention. For instance, it may be that those who worked over *Coluthus* I noted with some surprise the affable and even familiar way in which Arianus addresses Coluthus until the end; they can only account for this by supposing a previous relationship between the two men. In fact, the governor's apparent genial familiarity and fair and reasonable words imply no such thing; they are simply part of the stock in trade of the professional authoritarian inquisitor, to be used on any prisoner notable enough for the full individual treatment. This glimpse of Arianus at work affords us a most convincing impression of the man and his personal technique. Unlike Culcianus, who is seen in *Phileas* as a brusque and peremptory inquisitor, asking short, theologically well-informed questions, Arianus has a smooth tongue.[49] The flatteries and temptations which the 'epic' martyrologies labour to represent on such a heroic scale by making the governor promise the martyr riches or high office or the hand of his only child in marriage are here also, but on a realistic worldly level; not only immunity, but public respect is the promised prize. The lawcourt is for common criminals, and no place for respectable men; to testify to this we have the figures of two eminent bishops, no less, who have chosen the prudent and decorous course of compliance with the Emperor's edict and now exercise their episcopal office with authority's approval (which will no doubt have been true) and to the satisfaction of every one (which will certainly not have been).[50] This passage illustrates a point which the

[49] The fact that he appeals to worldly common sense rather than to theology is perhaps partly due to the fact that, unlike Culcianus, he is not dealing with a bishop.

[50] Apollonius, we note, is bishop of Siout, the diocese of Meletius. Did Apollonius precede or supplant the latter? The division of feeling in that place may be imagined. The Rev. Dr. Henry Chadwick suspects that *Coluthus* I may owe its preservation to the rigorist faction which supported Meletius.

'epic' martyrologies, by exaggerating the villainy of the governor, tend
to obscure—that the Roman authority was not concerned to stamp
out the Christian faith as the personal conviction of its subjects, or
even to force them to abjure it, but only to enforce the formal and
physical gesture of sacrifice as a token of its own supremacy. This
seems to be illustrated by Eusebius' quotation (*Martyrs of Palestine*,
i. 4. 5) of the case of a Christian who was discharged after his hands
had been put through the motions of sacrifice by main force. Those
who were responsible for doing this to him probably did so with
genuinely kind intentions; and we should not discount this in
Arianus' own case; his geniality is not all false. He simply cannot see
any point in defying an imperial order, or understand how any human
being can prefer death to the delights of life in this world, the beauties
of nature and the pleasure of a sunny day; such an unnatural choice
can only come from perverse vanity. The martyr for his part, though
his heaven-directed longing for freedom from the body and the world
is as far removed from the governor's mentality as the gulf between
Dives and Lazarus, shows more understanding of his mind, and even
sympathy with it, than any literary martyrologist would allow us to
think; when he speaks of Arianus' 'kindness', he does so only half in
irony; realizing that Arianus would rather save his life than take it, he
gives him credit for this kind intention, without wavering for a
moment from the course upon which he was firmly set before he
came into court. His instructions from his heavenly King are as plain
and as inflexible as Arianus' orders from his earthly emperor; the
outcome was never in doubt. We may be sure that Arianus went home
after a trying day's work tired, and perhaps even a little depressed, as
no doubt he usually did when duty required him to burn a rather
likeable Christian alive. He had tried so hard; Coluthus had been one
of his failures. The exchange between the governor and his victim,
short as it is, conveys the horror of the former's corruption by the
brutal authority which employs him, and the glory of the martyr's
constancy, so perfectly that one cannot but ask how even the
naïveté of the Egyptian Church public can have thought the 'epic'
type of martyrology an improvement upon it. One reason for this
might be deduced from references often found near the end of a
martyrology, which indicate the purpose for which it is designed; it
is meant to be read on the appropriate day in places of worship, and
particularly in the shrine of the martyr whom it celebrates.[51] Such an
occasion calls for a composition of some length, which no doubt a
professional writer of such literature will be commissioned to produce.

[51] See O'Leary, *Saints*, p. 32 f.

If, as no doubt often happened, those responsible for the cult of the
saint in question have no biographical details about him with which
to furnish the writer, the martyrology will be wholly imaginary or
stereotyped.[52] In many cases, however, the writing which has come
down to us has at least some distinctive features which suggest that
its writer had some kind of draft to work from. This might well be
supplied by the community of the place where the martyr had his
shrine. One of the present editors has been working upon an unpublished Coptic papyrus from Oxyrhynchus, written in a coarse semi-
literate hand which may be tentatively dated in the fourth century.
The text, which fills one side of a small sheet of papyrus and half of
the other, is in an unfamiliar Middle Egyptian dialect, and abominably
spelt, so that the following translation[53] is in places doubtful.
'In the sixth year of Severus,[54] after the *persecution* had come to pass,
before the *blessed* Dionysius, the *bishop* of Alexandria, the emperor
Severus arose and came down to the great *city* of Alexandria, which
was the *metropolis* of Egypt, and a *persecution* was raised up against the
Christians. (Of) every one *therefore* who had *believed* in *Christ*, many
of them feared and *sacrificed* to the *idols*; others *withdrew* from the
city, having been unable to bear the foul worship to which (men)
came; *for* there were altars set up in the *market-place*, and any one
whom it pleased to receive indulgence (?) from the emperor would
go secretly (?) and *sacrifice*, and he would then be allowed a *gratuity*.
It was a great *persecution* which took place in the *country* of Egypt;
the *Christians* were being put to death, and the temples of the so-
called gods were being built; some of the *Christians withdrew* from
the *city*. Some *virgins* moreover had fled for refuge into a *suburb* two
miles to the east side of the *city*, which was (under the care) of a
presbyter named John. They stayed in that place, dwelling in peace,
after having *endured* (?) these numerous (?) terrors in the places
whence they came (?), and *persevering* in their prayer, while the
blessed John, the *presbyter* of whom we have already told you, was
like a good father (?) to them.'
Apart from the difficulties presented by the writer's chronology, this
looks like an attempt at sober and factual narrative. Although the story
begins at Alexandria, it may concern a saint whose career ended (in
martyrdom?) in the district from which the papyrus comes; if so, it
might well be just such a draft as we have postulated as the nucleus of a

---

[52] Cf. Delehaye, *Pass. Mart.*, p. 222.
[53] Given in advance of the publication of the papyrus, by courtesy of its owners, the
Egypt Exploration Society.
[54] For Septimius Severus as a persecutor, see P. Keresztes, 'The Emperor Septimius
Severus: a precursor of Decius', *Historia*, 19 (1970), 565 ff.

good many Lives and martyrdoms. We should not, we believe, conclude that the piece (which ends in the middle of the leaf) is incomplete; on our assumption, it contains all that this particular informant knew of the early history of the presbyter John. In cases (which will probably have been unusual) where a document as solid as *Coluthus* I was available, it will have been greatly expanded and altered,[55] but, as we are able to trace in the case of *Coluthus* I and its successors, something may be expected to remain of the original document. One alteration which we find in the story of Coluthus is, we believe, significant. We see that in *Coluthus* I the martyr is executed by being burned alive. (The end of *Coluthus* II is missing.) The Sermon of Isaac also makes this the manner of the saint's execution.[56] In the *Synaxary*, however, (Bashons 25th) it is said to have been decapitation—the usual form of death for a martyr. Successful execution by burning, as Crum remarks ('Colluthus', p. 326), is rare in the martyr acts. Two possible reasons for the alteration occur to us: (a) A favourite Scriptural prototype with the martyrologists is the story of the Three Holy Children in the fiery furnace. The hero of a martyrology of any length will certainly find himself shut in a furnace at least once; but since Ananias, Azarias and Misael emerged from the furnace unscathed, so should he; anything an Old Testament character can do a Christian martyr can do as well, or better. Decapitation, however, is a treatment from which S. John the Baptist himself failed to recover. (b) Incineration, properly carried out, leaves little of the martyr's body for subsequent veneration by the pious. The martyr shrines, however, made much of saintly relics and their healing power.[57] For this reason, no doubt, in the martyrologies great stress is laid by the martyr himself, or his Divine or angelic helpers, upon the preservation of his mortal remains (see, e.g., *Sh.* 134 R i 3 ff.; *P. & T.* 79 R i 23 ff.; 85 V i 1 ff.), and meaningful emphasis is laid upon the maintenance of the shrine of the martyr and his proper veneration there; one of the activities which merit the promise of heavenly reward is the writing of a book for the shrine, presumably the martyrology itself.

[55] Or, as perhaps in the case of *Phileas*, 'contaminated' with another martyrdom; the need for a longer composition being the motive for the interpolation of *Philoromus*. It must be noted, however, that the mention of Phileas and Philoromus in the same chapter of Eusebius (*H. E.* ii 2, 79) might suggest some real connection between them.

[56] So also in the Greek *Basilii Imperatoris Menologium* cited in Georgi, *Coluthi Miracula*, p. 4.

[57] The attitude of Egyptian church authority to attendance at the shrines of saints and martyrs and the veneration of their relics was variable; we find no less a person than Shenoute expressing his disapproval of festivals held there, which seem to have tended to be riotous, in no uncertain terms; see Delehaye, *Mart. Ég.*, pp. 36 ff.; Pachomius also clearly disapproved, see Lefort, *Les vies coptes de Saint Pachôme*, p. 49 f.; but the tendency was evidently ineradicable.

The final impression with which we are left is that, hard as it is to extract history from a literary form which has overlaid whatever factual foundations it may have had with pious and romantic fiction, there may still be enough to make the attempt worth while. If we may be permitted to draw an analogy from art, we may compare the treatment of icons in the Eastern Orthodox Church. The more venerable and valuable the picture, the more likely it is for all but the saintly or Divine features and hands to be overlaid with rich silver or golden ornamentation by the pious. However much this practice may offend Western taste and antiquarian standards, no one will be tempted to impute to it motives of falsification, or to suspect the authenticity of the painting underneath. We believe that the embroidery of romantic narrative, however much it may obscure the facts of a martyr's story, is likewise innocent enough in intention; and that such a sceptical judgment on Egyptian martyr literature as O'Leary's (*Saints*, p. 20) that 'many, or most, of the characters are fictitious' is unjustified. Our *Coluthus* I affords us a unique glimpse of the truth underlying a legend, and enables us to trace the pattern of its mutation.

As a last general question about the texts edited here, it may be asked whether they were composed in Coptic or represent a version of a text originally Greek. In the case of *Coluthus* I, on our assumption that it is in fact a true record of a martyr's trial, the latter must be the case, since as with *Phileas* the proceedings will certainly have been conducted in Greek, or partly in Latin. The other cases may be thought to be more disputable. In *Sh.* 138 R ii 18 ff. Julius of Aqfaḥs is made to state that he wrote the memoirs of the saints 'in Roman characters'; in *John and Simeon* (Hyv. *Actes*, p. 198) he adds that he had the *notarius* Menas translate them into Egyptian. We are not, of course, obliged to believe this—indeed, the occurrence of this statement in such a mendacious context might well decide some of us in the contrary direction. But in fact it seems to us more likely that many of such works were regularly composed in Greek, though they will have been translated straightway into Coptic. In a country as bilingual as Byzantine Egypt the language employed reflects the purpose of the writing rather than the antecedents or sympathies of the writer. We may suggest a general criterion in such questions as this. If a writing is not intended to have any circulation or interest outside Egypt, it may well be composed in Coptic; but if it is intended for a wider public it may be assumed to have been originally in Greek. An example of this is the *Apophthegmata Patrum*, of which we have versions in Greek, Coptic, Latin, Syriac and Ethiopic; the Sa'idic text which we have at any rate is certainly secondary, for there are places where the Coptic is demonstrably a mistranslation of a Greek original. The case of our Egyptian martyrs is more doubtful; many of them will have had little interest for any but Egyptians, and it would not be hard for a Coptic writer to produce a martyrology for a local martyr in the native language by borrowing from other examples, with the substitution of a few names. Such a composition, however, could scarcely be called original.[58]

Notes on the method of publication

Our presentation of these texts is something of a compromise. The spellings are exactly as in the originals, corrections being noted below; but since the published reproductions are complete and admirably clear, and so can readily be consulted, we have not felt it necessary to reproduce the points, etc., found in the originals, but have introduced modern punctuation, consistent superlineation and word division.[59] The text is immediately followed by textual remarks and corrections; the latter are reduced to a minimum, and generally confined to cases in which the scribe's Coptic or Greek orthography might be misleading or ambiguous. Where duplicate texts in Sa'idic exist, their variants are given below this; the P. M. Ms. in each case is cited as A, and others by the following letters of the alphabet according to the order in which their texts (in every case incomplete) begin. In the case of *P. & T.* the Bohairic text is given below this again, in full.

In our translations we have ventured to represent the contrast between *Coluthus* (I), which we believe (see Introduction, pp. 9 ff.) to be a transcript of real court proceedings, and the other three, by making the former in colloquial modern English, and for the latter employing an artificial idiom appropriate to the pretentious literary style to which they aspire. We dispense with full commentaries; such remarks as seemed necessary will be found in footnotes to the translations, together with references to Biblical citations and allusions, and to some parallel passages in other martyrologies.

Each martyrology is indexed individually. The commonest words are not as a rule exhaustively enumerated, though there are exceptions to this; e.g., $\kappa\epsilon\lambda\epsilon\acute{\upsilon}\epsilon\iota\nu$, which generally marks a fresh action on the part of the Governor. Coptic and Greek words are of course indexed separately, but in the case of the indices of proper names, place names and ethnics, in which the two languages had to be combined, it was found necessary to give the primary spelling in English characters and alphabetic order.

[58] See Delehaye, *Mart. Ég.*, p. 152.
[59] We regard the division fashionable at the present day (see Till, *BIFAO* 60 (1950)) as unrepresentative of the Coptic writers' own ideas of what constituted indivisible compounds of words.

The Manuscripts

The Pierpont Morgan codices containing the texts published here are expressly dated in the middle of the ninth century: see Lantschoot, *Recueil des Colophons des manuscrits chrétiens d' Égypte* I: *Les colophons coptes des manuscrits sahidiques*: fasc. 1, 2. (Bibl. du *Muséon* I, Louvain, 1929), pp. 10; 20.

Coluthus

A = P. M. Codex M. 591, t. 28, fols. 88 V–92.

B = Berl. 9755 (palimpsest): published by Vergote, *Le Muséon* 48 (1935), 275 ff. Apparently tenth century; ibid., p. 284, n. 24. (Corresponding to P. M. 92 V i 5 to end (the text of the conclusion is different.))

Paēse and Thecla

A = P. M. Codex M. 591, t. 28, fols. 49–88 R.

B = Borg. Copt. 109, fasc. 144: Zoëga, p. 238; Till, *KHML* I, pp. 71–74. Date not specified by editors. (Corresponding to P. M. 51 R i 30–57 V i 1.)

C = Vienna K 9437; Wessely, *Stud. Pal.* 15, 147 f. (No. 247). Ninth century. (Corresponding to P. M. 56 V ii 20–58 R i 4.)

D = Borg. Copt. 109, fasc. 143: Zoëga, p. 238; Till, *KHML*, pp. 74–84. Date not specified by editors. (Corresponding to P. M. 60 V i 1–75 R i 19.)

Boh. = Evelyn White, *Macarius*, pp. 113–118 (No. 21).

We have been unable to obtain reproductions of the Cairo fragments of this text, and so any suggestions of ours about their reading (apart from the portion illustrated in *Macarius*, Plate V) must be a matter of conjecture; but we have been fortunate enough to get excellent photographs of Tischendorf's leaves, thanks to the Leipzig University authorities, which have enabled us to modify their reading considerably. The page listed by ed. pr. as Fr. 1 does not belong to this martyrology. With regard to the others, we have the impression that, despite the opinion expressed by him on p. 113 f., fr. 5 is from the same manuscript as the others, and indeed probably by the same hand; the forms of the letters are identical, and the variation in size and thickness may be accounted for by changes of pen. Tenth century. (Frs. 2 and 3 correspond to P. M. 60 V i 12–62 R ii 30; fr. 5 to 77 V ii 4–78 V i 5; fr. 4 to 81 V ii 9–82 V i 8.)

Shenoufe and his Brethren

A = P. M. Codex M. 583, t. 41, fols. 103–138.

B = Ms. published by H. Munier in *Ann. Serv.* 17 (1917), 145–159.

Extensive corrections and comments by Sottas, *Rev. Ég.*, N. S. 1 (1919), 264–267. A very fragmentary text whose re-edition would have been desirable; ed. pr., however, only says that it came from Hamouli; its present whereabouts cannot be traced. If it was part of the main Hamouli find it will probably belong to the ninth century. (Corresponding to P. M. 119 V ii 29–127 V i 32.)

Apaioule and Pteleme

P. M. Codex M. 583, t. 41, fols. 168–173. No duplicate texts.

MARTYRDOM OF S. COLUTHUS
FROM PIERPONT MORGAN CODEX M 591
T. 28, FF. 88V–92

(88 V i) ⲡⲙⲁⲣⲧⲏⲣⲟⲗⲟⲅⲓⲟⲛ ⲙ̄ⲡⲙⲁⲣⲧⲩⲣⲟⲥ ⲉⲧⲟⲩⲁⲁⲃ ⲙ̄ⲡⲉ ⲭ̄ⲥ̄ ⲕⲟⲗⲟⲑⲟⲥ ⲁⲩⲱ ⲡⲥⲁⲉⲓⲛ ⲛ̄ⲣⲉϥⲑⲉⲣⲁⲡⲉⲩⲉ ⲛⲟⲩⲟⲛ ⲛⲓⲙ ⲉⲧϫⲓ ⲉⲃⲟⲗ ϩⲙ̄ⲡⲉⲥⲱ-
ⲙⲁ ⲙⲛ̄ⲡⲉⲥⲛⲟϥ ⲙ̄ⲡⲉ ⲭ̄ⲥ̄ ϩ̄ⲛⲟⲩⲧⲃ̄ⲃⲟ· ⲛ̄ⲧⲁⲩϫⲱⲕ ⲇⲉ ⲉⲃⲟⲗ ⲙ̄ⲡⲉϥⲁⲅⲱⲛ
ⲛ̄ⲥⲟⲩϫⲟⲩⲧⲁϥⲧⲉ ⲙ̄ⲡⲁϣⲟⲛⲥ̄, ϩⲛ̄ⲟⲩⲉⲓⲣⲏⲛⲏ ⲛ̄ⲧⲉⲡⲛⲟⲩⲧⲉ, ϩⲁⲙⲏⲛ·
ⲁⲥϣⲱⲡⲉ ⲇⲉ ϩⲛ̄ⲧⲙⲉϩϫⲟⲩⲱⲧⲉ ⲛ̄ⲣⲟⲙⲡⲉ ⲛ̄ⲇⲓⲟⲕⲗⲏⲧⲓⲁⲛⲟⲥ ⲙⲛ̄ⲙⲁⲝⲓ-
ⲙⲓⲛⲓⲁⲛⲟⲥ ⲛ̄ⲣ̄ⲣⲱⲟⲩ ⲙ̄ⲡⲁⲣⲁⲛⲟⲙⲟⲥ, ⲁⲩⲱ ϩⲛ̄ⲧⲙⲉϩϭⲟⲙⲧⲉ ⲛ̄ⲣⲟⲙⲡⲉ
ⲛ̄ⲕⲟⲥⲧⲁⲛⲧⲓⲛⲟⲥ, ⲛ̄[ⲥⲟⲩ]ϫⲟⲩⲧⲁϥⲧⲉ [ⲙ̄ⲡⲁ]ϣⲟⲛⲥ̄, ⲁⲩⲧⲁϩⲉ ⲡⲁⲅⲓⲟⲥ
ⲕⲟⲗⲗⲟⲑⲟⲥ ⲉⲣⲁ(ⲧϥ̄)ⲧϥ̄ ⲉϫⲙ̄ⲡⲃⲏⲙⲁ ⲛ̄ⲁⲛⲧⲓⲛⲟⲟⲩ· ⲡⲉⲁⲣⲓⲁⲛⲟⲥ ⲡϩⲏⲅⲉⲙⲱⲛ ⲙ̄ⲡⲁⲅⲓⲟⲥ ⲕⲟⲗⲗⲟⲑⲟⲥ ϫⲉ ⲉϣⲱⲡⲉ ⲕⲟⲩⲱϣ ⲉⲟⲩϫⲁⲓ, ⲁⲣⲓⲑⲩⲥⲓⲁ ⲧⲁⲣⲉⲕⲱⲛϩ̄· ⲛⲁⲓ ⲇⲉ ⲧⲏⲣⲟⲩ ⲉⲧⲁϩⲉⲣⲁⲧⲟⲩ ⲥⲉⲩⲗⲏⲗ ⲉⲧⲣⲉⲕ-
ⲣⲥⲁⲃⲉ· ⲉϣϫⲉ ⲟⲩϣⲓⲡⲉ ⲡⲉⲧⲁⲙⲁϩⲧⲉ ⲙ̄ⲙⲟⲕ ⲕⲁⲧⲁⲟⲩⲙ̄ⲛ̄ⲧϣⲟⲩϣⲟ,
ⲧⲉⲛⲟⲩ ⲇⲉ ϩⲱⲱϥ ϣⲓⲡⲉ ⲙ̄ⲡⲁⲙ̄ⲧⲟ ⲉⲃⲟⲗ· ⲁⲣⲓⲑⲩⲥⲓⲁ ⲧⲁⲣⲉⲕⲟⲩϫⲁⲓ·
ϣⲁⲧⲉⲛⲟⲩ ⲅⲁⲣ ⲙ̄ⲡⲁⲧⲉⲕϭⲛ̄ⲡⲉ ϩⲏⲧϥ̄ ⲛ̄ⲗⲁⲁⲩ ⲛ̄ⲣⲱⲙⲉ ⲛ̄ϣⲟⲩ̣ϣⲓ ⲡⲉ ϩⲏ-
ⲧⲟⲩ· ⲱ ⲕⲟⲗⲟⲑⲟⲥ, ⲟⲩⲱϣⲧ̄ ⲛ̄ⲛ̄ⲛⲟⲩⲧⲉ ⲙ̄ⲡⲣ̄ⲣⲟ ϫⲉ ⲛ̄ⲛⲉⲕⲙⲟⲩ ⲕⲁⲕⲱⲥ·
ⲁϥⲟⲩⲱϣⲃ̄ ⲛ̄ϭⲓ ⲡϩⲁⲅⲓⲟⲥ ⲕⲟⲗⲟⲑⲟⲥ ⲡⲉϫⲁⲩ ϫⲉ ⲡⲉⲟⲟⲩ ⲙ̄ⲡⲉⲓⲕⲟⲥⲙⲟⲥ
ⲟⲩⲡⲣⲟⲥⲟⲩ(89 R i)ⲉⲓϣ ⲡⲉ· ⲡⲉⲟⲟⲩ ⲇⲉ ⲛ̄ⲧⲟϥ ⲛ̄ⲧⲙⲛ̄ⲧⲉⲣⲟ ⲛ̄ⲙ̄ⲡⲏⲩⲉ
ⲟⲩⲱⲛϩ̄ ϣⲁⲉⲛⲉϩ ⲡⲉ· ⲡⲉϫⲉ ⲡϩⲏⲅⲉⲙⲱⲛ ⲛⲁⲩ ϫⲉ ⲛⲁ̣ϣ ⲉⲛⲃⲁⲥⲁⲛⲟⲥ
ⲙ̄ⲡⲇⲓⲕⲁⲥⲧⲏⲣⲓⲟⲛ, ⲁⲩⲱ ⲉⲣⲉⲟⲩⲁ ⲙ̄ⲡⲟⲟⲩ ⲁϩⲉⲣⲁⲧϥ̄ ⲉϥⲕⲁⲧⲏⲅⲟⲣⲉ ⲙ̄-
ⲙⲟⲕ, ⲛⲉⲕⲛⲁⲣ̄ ⲧⲉⲕϭⲟⲙ ⲡⲉ ⲉⲧⲙ̄ⲧⲣⲉⲩⲃⲟⲧⲕ̄ ϩⲛ̄ⲗⲁⲁⲩ ⲛ̄ϣⲁϫⲉ· ⲛ̄ⲧⲟⲕ
ⲇⲉ ⲙ̄ⲡⲉⲣⲕⲁⲧⲏⲅⲟⲣⲓ ⲙ̄ⲙⲟⲕ ⲙⲁⲩⲁⲁⲕ ⲛ̄ⲅϫⲟⲧⲃⲉⲕ ⲙⲁⲩⲁⲁⲕ· ⲛⲉⲕⲣⲱⲙⲉ
ⲅⲁⲣ ⲧⲏⲣⲟⲩ ⲉⲧⲁϩⲉⲣⲁⲧⲟⲩ ⲥⲉⲗⲏⲡⲏ ⲉⲧⲃⲏⲏⲧⲕ̄· ⲙⲁⲣⲟⲩⲛⲁⲩ ⲉⲣⲟⲕ ⲉⲕ-
ⲑⲩⲥⲓⲁⲍⲉ ⲛ̄ⲥⲉⲣⲁϣⲉ ⲛⲙ̄ⲙⲁⲕ· ⲡⲣⲉϥϯϩⲁⲡ ⲇⲉ ⲟⲛ ⲉⲧⲉⲛⲟⲕ ⲡⲉ ⲙ̄ⲡⲉϥ-
ϯⲉⲟⲟⲩ ⲙ̄ⲡⲉϥⲙⲁⲛϯϩⲁⲡ ⲉⲧⲃⲉⲡⲁⲓ· ⲙⲁⲣⲉ ⲟⲩⲟⲛ ⲛⲓⲙ ⲛⲁⲩ ⲉⲧⲉⲕⲙⲛ̄ⲧⲥⲁⲃⲉ
ⲛ̄ⲥⲉⲣϣⲡⲏⲣⲉ ⲉϩⲣⲁⲓ (R ii) ⲉϫⲱⲕ. ⲏ ⲉϣϣ̄ⲡⲉ ⲇⲉ ⲟⲛ ⲟⲩⲛⲟⲩϩⲱⲃ ⲏ ⲟⲩ-
ϣⲁϫⲛⲉ ϩⲛ̄ⲧⲉⲕⲙⲏⲧⲉ ⲙ̄ⲛⲟⲩⲁ, ⲡⲁⲛⲧⲟⲥ ⲡⲉⲓⲕⲉⲟⲩⲁ ⲁϩⲉ̣ⲣⲁⲧϥ̄ ⲉϥⲗⲩⲡⲏ
ⲙ̄ⲙⲟⲕ· ⲛ̄ⲧⲟⲕ ⲇⲉ ⲙ̄ⲡⲉⲣⲙⲉⲥⲧⲱⲕ ⲙⲁⲩⲁⲁⲕ· ⲡⲙⲟⲩ ⲅⲁⲣ ⲉϣⲁϥⲉⲓ ⲙⲁⲩⲁⲁⲩ ϩⲛ̄ⲟⲩϭⲣ̄ϩⲏ, ϣⲁⲣⲉ ⲛ̄ⲣⲱⲙⲉ ⲥⲗ̄ⲥⲱⲗⲟⲩ, ⲉⲩⲙⲟⲩⲧⲉ ⲅⲁⲣ ⲉⲣⲟϥ ϫⲉ
ⲁⲛⲑⲣⲟⲡⲟⲓⲛⲟⲛ, ϫⲉ ⲧⲁⲓ ⲡⲁϣⲟⲩⲟⲛ ⲛⲓⲙ ⲡⲉ· ϩⲙ̄ⲡⲉⲓⲙⲁ ⲇⲉ ϩⲱⲱϥ ⲉⲧⲕ̄-
ⲁϩⲉⲣⲁⲧⲕ̄ ⲛ̄ϩⲏⲧϥ̄, ⲉⲩⲁⲛⲧⲁⲡⲟⲫⲁⲥⲓⲥ ⲉⲛⲉⲫⲟⲛⲉⲩⲥ ⲛ̄ϩⲏⲧϥ̄ ⲙ̄ⲡⲛⲉ ϣⲁⲗ-

---

88 V i 13. ϫⲟⲩⲧⲁϥⲧⲉ : ⲟ corr. from ⲁ.   ii 3. ℓ. ⲡⲉϫⲉ-   89 R ii 3. ℓ. ϣⲟⲩϣⲉ
(or ϣⲁϫⲉ?)   16 f. ℓ. ⲁⲛⲑⲣⲱⲡⲓⲛⲟⲛ   18. ℓ. ⲡⲁⲓ.   20 ⲇⲉ added in margin

ⲡⲉ ⲙⲁⲛ'ⲣⲉⲩⲃⲉⲣⲃⲉⲣⲕⲱ'ⲱⲥ ⲙⲛⲛⲉⲙⲡⲟⲣ'ⲛⲟⲥ ⲙⲛⲁⲛⲟⲉⲓⲕ' ⲙⲛⲛⲉⲩϣⲁⲩⲧⲉ· ³⁰
ⲙⲉⲩϣⲓⲗⲁⲁⲩ ⲉⲃ[ⲟ]ⲗ' ⲍⲙⲡⲉⲓⲙⲁ ⲉⲩϩⲁⲕ' ⲡⲉ ⲛⲥⲉⲧⲁⲕⲟⲩ·' ⲁⲩⲱ ⲉⲩϣⲱⲡⲉ ⲟⲩⲁ
ⲡⲉ (89 V i) ⲉⲁⲩⲕⲁⲧⲁⲫⲣⲟ'ⲛⲉⲓ ⲙⲡⲛⲟⲙⲟⲥ, 'ϣⲁⲣⲉⲡⲁⲓ ϣⲱⲡⲉ'ⲉⲩⲟⲩⲟⲛⲍ
ⲉⲃⲟⲗ⁵ ⲛⲟⲩⲟⲛ ⲛⲓⲙ ϫⲉ'ⲛⲧⲁⲩⲡⲁⲣⲁⲇⲓ'ⲇⲟⲩ ⲙⲙⲟⲩ ⲁⲛ'ⲉⲧⲃⲉⲧⲉⲩⲥⲟⲫⲓⲁ,'ⲁⲗⲗⲁ ϩⲁⲟⲩⲙⲁ'ⲛⲓⲁ ¹⁰ⲙⲙⲛⲧⲩⲟⲩ'ϣⲟ, ⲛⲑⲉ ⲛⲩⲁ'ⲣⲉⲛⲥⲟⲟⲛⲉ ⲕⲁⲧⲁ'ⲫⲣⲟⲛⲉⲓ ⲙ-
ⲡⲙⲟⲩ' ⲉⲧⲃⲉⲧⲉⲩⲙⲛⲧ ¹⁵'ⲥⲟⲟⲛⲉ. ⲁⲛⲟⲕ' ⲅⲁⲣ ϯⲟ ⲛϩⲁⲣϣ ϩⲏⲧ 'ⲉϫⲱⲕ ϣⲁⲛⲧⲉ'ⲛⲟⲩ ⲉⲧⲣⲉⲕϣⲱ'ⲡⲉ ⲛⲥⲁⲃⲉ ⲛⲧⲅⲱⲛⲍ ²⁰ϩⲛⲟⲩⲱⲛⲍ ⲛⲉ'ⲗⲉⲩⲑⲉⲣⲟⲥ ⲛⲑⲉ ⲛ-'
ⲣⲱⲙⲉ ⲛⲓⲙ ⲛⲣⲙϩⲉ·' ²⁵ ⲱ ⲕⲟⲗⲟⲑⲟⲥ, ⲉⲧⲃⲉⲟⲩ ⲛⲧⲅϣⲁϫⲉ ⲛⲙ'ⲙⲁⲓ ⲁⲛ ⲉⲓϣⲁϫⲉ'
ⲛⲙⲙⲁⲕ; 'ⲡⲉϫⲉⲡϩⲁⲅⲓⲟⲥ ⲕⲟ'ⲗⲟⲑⲟⲥ ϫⲉ ⲙⲡⲉ'ⲧⲉⲩϣⲉ ⲉⲣⲟⲓ ⲁⲛ' ³⁰ ⲡⲉ ⲉϫⲉ-
ⲛⲟϭ ⲛⲩⲁ'ϫⲉ ϩⲓⲑⲏ ⲛⲟⲩϩⲅ'ⲧⲉⲙⲱⲛ. 'ⲡⲉϫⲉⲡϩⲏⲅⲉⲙⲱ(ⲛ) (V ii) ⲛⲁⲩ ϫⲉ
ⲁⲣⲓⲑⲩⲥⲓⲁ' ⲱ ⲕⲟⲗⲟⲑⲟⲥ. ⲡⲉ'ϫⲉ ⲡϩⲁⲅⲓⲟⲥ ϫⲉ ⲛϯⲛⲁⲑⲩⲥⲓⲁⲍⲉ ⲁⲛ. ⁵'ⲡⲉϫⲉ-
ⲡϩⲏⲅⲉⲙⲱ(ⲛ)' ⲛⲁⲩ ϫⲉ ⲁⲗⲏⲑⲱⲥ' ⲙⲡⲉⲕⲥⲱⲧⲙ ⲛ'ϭⲱⲓ ⲛⲧⲅⲑⲩⲥⲓⲁⲍⲉ'ⲛⲛⲟⲩ-
ⲧⲉ ⲛⲧⲁ¹⁰ⲡⲣⲣⲟ ⲥϩⲁⲓ ⲛⲁⲓ'ⲉⲧⲃⲏⲏⲧⲟⲩ· ϯⲛⲁ'ⲁⲛⲍⲁⲗⲓⲥⲕⲉ ⲙ'ⲡⲉⲕⲥⲱⲙⲁ ϩⲛ-'
ⲟⲩⲕⲱϩⲧ. ⲁⲗ¹⁵ⲗⲁ ⲙⲡⲁⲓ ⲛⲁϣⲱ'ⲡⲉ ⲁⲛ ⲧⲉⲛⲟⲩ,'ⲙⲏⲡⲱⲥ ⲕⲟⲩⲱϣ'ⲉⲥⲕⲏⲡⲧⲉⲓ
ⲙⲙⲟⲕ.' ⲁⲩⲟⲩⲱϣⲃ ²⁰ⲛϭⲓ ⲡϩⲁⲅⲓⲟⲥ ϫⲉ ⲁⲓⲟⲩⲱ'ⲉⲓⲥⲕⲏⲡⲧⲉⲓ ⲙⲙⲟⲓ' ⲙⲡⲁⲧⲉⲓ
ⲉⲛⲉⲓⲙⲁ' ϣⲁⲣⲟⲕ. ' ²⁵ ⲛⲉϩⲣⲏⲧⲱⲣ ⲇⲉ ⲡⲉ'ϫⲁⲩ ⲛⲁⲩ ϫⲉ ϯⲍⲛ'ⲕⲟⲛⲓ ⲛϩⲟⲟⲩ
ⲛⲁⲩ,'ⲉϣⲱⲡⲉ ⲉϩⲛⲁⲕ' ⲡⲉ. ³⁰ⲁⲣⲓⲁⲛⲟⲥ' ⲇⲉ ⲡⲉϫⲁⲩ ⲛⲛⲉϩ'ⲣⲏⲧⲱⲣ ϫⲉ ϯⲛⲁⲩ
ⲉⲣⲟⲩ ϩⲱⲥ ⲉⲁⲩⲟⲩ'ⲱϣ ⲁⲩⲱ ⲁⲩⲣϩⲅ'ⲧⲏⲩ. ⲡⲉϫⲉ(90 R i)ⲡϩⲏⲅⲉⲙⲱⲛ ⲛⲁⲩ'
ϫⲉ ⲕⲟⲩⲱϣ ⲉⲕⲁ'ⲁⲕ ⲛϩⲉⲛⲕⲉⲕⲟⲛⲓ' ⁵ⲛϩⲟⲟⲩ ⲉⲧⲣⲉⲕϣⲁϫⲛⲉ ⲉⲣⲟⲕ; ϫⲉ ⲛⲁⲩ'
ⲉⲡⲉⲕϩⲟ ⲉⲩⲟⲩⲱⲛⲍ ⲙⲙⲟⲕ ⲉⲃⲟⲗ' ⲉⲧⲣⲉⲕⲟⲩϫⲁⲓ.' ¹⁰ⲡϩⲁⲅⲓⲟⲥ ⲇⲉ ⲙⲡⲉⲩ'ⲟⲩⲱϣⲃ
ⲛⲁⲩ ⲉⲡⲧⲏⲣϥ. ⲡⲉϫⲉ'ⲡϩⲏⲅⲉⲙⲱⲛ ⲛⲁⲩ 'ϫⲉ ⲙⲏ ⲉⲕϣⲓⲡⲉ 'ⲛⲅϩⲟⲙⲟⲗⲟⲅⲉⲓ; ¹⁵'
ⲡⲉϫⲉⲡϩⲁⲅⲓⲟⲥ ⲛⲁⲩ' ϫⲉ ϣⲁⲣⲉⲟⲩⲅⲁ'ϫⲉ ⲣⲉⲩⲧⲟⲩⲥⲁⲃⲉ. 'ⲡϩⲏⲅⲉⲙⲱⲛ ⲇⲉ'
ⲁⲩⲧⲣⲉⲩⲕⲱ ²⁰ⲉϩ'ⲣⲁⲓ ⲙⲡⲕⲱϩⲧ 'ϩⲓⲑⲏ ⲙⲡⲙⲁⲕⲁ'ⲣⲓⲟⲥ ⲕⲟⲗⲟⲑⲟⲥ, 'ⲡⲉϫⲉⲡ-
ϩⲏⲅⲉⲙⲱ(ⲛ) ²⁵'ⲛⲁⲩ ϫⲉ ϭⲱ, ⲙⲡⲣ'ⲣ ⲗⲁⲁⲩ ⲛϩⲉⲃⲣⲏⲥⲓⲥ' ⲛⲁⲩ ⲧⲉⲛⲟⲩ.' ⲧⲟⲧⲉ ⲁ-
ⲡϩⲏⲅⲉⲙⲱ(ⲛ)' ⲕⲟⲧϥ ⲉⲡϩⲁⲅⲓⲟⲥ' ⲕⲟⲗⲟⲑⲟⲥ, ⲡⲉϫⲁⲩ ³⁰'ⲛⲁⲩ ϫⲉ ϣⲱⲡⲉ'ⲛⲥⲁⲃⲉ
ⲧⲉⲛⲟⲩ ⲛⲅ'ⲉⲓⲣⲉ ⲛⲛⲧⲁⲩϫⲟ(R ii)ⲟⲩ ⲛⲁⲕ. ⲁⲡⲟⲗ'ⲗⲟⲛⲓⲟⲥ ⲇⲉ ⲡⲉⲡⲓⲥ'ⲕⲟⲡⲟⲥ ⲛ-
ⲥⲓⲟⲟⲩⲧ,'ⲛⲉⲣⲉⲡⲉϥⲙⲏⲏ ⁵'ϣⲉ ⲟ ⲛⲣⲙⲥⲃⲱ 'ⲛⲛⲁϩⲣⲁⲩ ⲉⲙⲁⲧⲉ' ⲡⲉ ⲁⲩⲱ ⲛⲥⲏⲙ·
ⲛⲟⲥ ⲉⲧⲃⲉⲧⲉⲩⲥⲟ'ⲫⲓⲁ, ⲉⲡⲉⲓⲇⲏ ¹⁰ⲙ'ⲡⲉⲩⲟⲩⲱϣ ⲉⲣⲁⲧ'ⲥⲱⲧⲙ, ⲟⲩⲇⲉ ⲉ'ⲉⲛⲧⲅ ⲉ-
ⲡⲇⲓⲕⲁⲥⲧⲏⲣⲓⲟⲛ· ⲟⲩⲇⲉ'ⲙⲡⲉⲩⲟⲩⲱϣ ⲉⲥⲱ'ⲧⲙ ⲉⲧⲓⲁϣⲉ ⲛϣⲁϫⲉ· ⲁⲗⲗⲁ ⲛⲧⲟⲩ
ⲙⲁⲩⲁⲁⲩ ⲁⲩ'ϯⲡⲉⲩⲟⲩⲟⲓ ⲉϩⲟⲩⲛ' ¹⁵ⲉⲛⲡⲉ, ⲁⲩⲑⲉⲥⲓ'ⲁⲍⲉ ²⁰ⲉⲣⲉⲟⲩⲟⲛ ⲛⲓⲙ'ⲑⲱⲣⲉⲓ

---

90 R i 4. l. -ϣⲟϫⲛⲉ. 24. l.ⲛⲁⲩ. 25 =-ⲍⲩⲑⲣⲓⲁⲥ (sic). ii 7 l.-ⲥⲉⲕⲛⲟⲥ

ⲘⲘⲞⲨ, ⲈⲢⲈⲚⲈⲤⲔⲈⲨⲎ Ⲙ̅ⲠⲞⲨⲰⲦⲚ̅ ⲈⲂⲞⲖ Ⲛ̅ⲦⲞⲞⲦⲨ̅, ⲈⲨⲀⲌⲈⲢⲀ̅²⁵ⲦⲨ̅ ⲈⲨⲦⲀⲖⲈⲨⲤⲒⲀ
ⲈⲌⲢⲀⲒ̈· Ⲛ̅ⳤⲨϢⲒⲠⲈ ⲀⲚ ⲈⲠⲦⲎⲢϤ̅, ⲈⲢⲈⲞⲨⲞⲚ ⲚⲒⲘ ⳁⲈⲞⲞⲨ ⲚⲀⳤ·³⁰ ⲖⲞⲒⲠⲞⲚ ϢⲀϪⲈ
ⲚⲘⲀⲒ̈ ⳌⲰⲰⲔ, Ⲱ ⲔⲞⲖⲞⲐⲞⲤ, Ⲛ̅Ϥ(90 Vi)ϢⲰⲠⲈ Ⲍ̅ⲚⲞⲨ ϮⲘⲎ ⲈⲤⲤⲞⲦⲠ̅· ⲠⲞⲨ-
ⲦⲀⲢⲬⲞⲤ ⲞⲚ ⲠⲈ ⲠⲒⲤⲔⲞⲠⲞⲤ Ⲛ̅Ⲥ̅ⲂⲈⳌⲦ, ⲠⲀⲒ̈ ⲈⲦⲂⲈⲠ ⲦⲀⲒ̈Ⲟ Ⲛ̅ⲦⲈⲨ ⲤⲞⲪⲒⲀ ⲀⲨⲰ ϥ̅-
Ⲙ̅ⲠϢⲀ Ⲛ̅ϢⲒⲠⲈ Ⲛ̅ⳌⲎⲦϤ̅, ⲀϤ ϢⲰⲠⲈ Ⲛ̅ⲤⲞⲪⲞⲤ, ¹⁰Ⲁ ⲞⲨⲰϢⲦ̅ Ⲛ̅Ⲛ̅ⲚⲞⲨ ⲦⲈ Ⲁ̅Ⲛ̅ⲢⲢⲞ,
ⲀⲨⲦⲀ̅ⲖⲈⲐⲨⲤⲒⲀ ⲚⲀⲨ ⲈⳌⲢⲀⲒ̈, ⲀⲨⲰ ⲈⲒⲤϨⲎⲎⲦⲈ ⲦⲈⲚⲞⲨ ϤⲞⲚ̅Ⳍ Ⲙ̅¹⁵ⲞⲨⲞⲚ ⲚⲒⲘ
Ⲛ̅ⲦⲀⲨ ⲐⲨⲤⲒⲀⲌⲈ ⲚⲘⲀⲨ, ⲈϤⲞ Ⲛ̅ⲈⲠⲒⲤⲔⲞⲠⲞⲤ ⲈⳌⲢⲀⲒ̈ ⲈϪⲰⲞⲨ· Ⲛ̅ⲦⲞⲔ Ⲱ ⲔⲞⲖⲞ-
ⲐⲞⲤ ²⁰ⲞⲨ ϨⲈⲘⲰⲚ ⲠⲈⲦ ⲔⲰ Ⲣⳏ ⲈⲢⲞⲔ, ⲀⲨⲰ ⲈϤⲤⲨⲘⲂⲞⲨⲖⲈⲨⲈ ⲚⲀⲔ· ⲦⲘⲚ̅Ⲧ ⳌⲎ-
ⲄⲈⲘⲰⲚ ⲀⲤⲐ̅Ⲃ̅²⁵ⲂⲒⲞⲤ ⲚⲀⲔ· ⳌⲰ ⲈⲢⲞⲔ ⲈⲠϨⲰⲂ Ⲛ̅ⲦⲀⲔⲀ̅ⲀⲨ ⲈⲦⲂⲈⲚⲈϪⲰ ⲘⲈ,
ⲈⲀⲔ ⲠⲒⲐⲈ Ⲙ̅ⲠⲈⲔⲚⲞⲨⲦⲈ Ⲙ̅ⲠⲈⲔ ⲢⲞⲔ ⲌⲞⲨ· ⲀⲨⲰ ⲚⲈ ⲢⲈⲞⳄⲀ Ⲙ̅ⲠⲈⲒ̈ⲘⲀ Ⲙ̅ⲠⲞⲞⲨ
ⲈⲨⲌ̅ⲚⲞⲨⲈ(Vii)ⲦⲒⲀ Ⲛ̅ⲢⲈϤⳌⲰⲦⲂ̅· ⲠⲀⲒ̈ ⲆⲈ ⲈϤⲞⲨⲰϢ ⲈⲰⲚⳍ· Ⲛ̅ⲦⲞⲔ ⲆⲈ, Ⲱ
ⲔⲞⲖⲞⲐⲞⲤ, ⲞⲨ ϨⲰⲂ ⁵ ⲈϤ ϨⲞⲞⲨ ⲠⲈⲦⲀⲘⲀⳌ ⲦⲈ Ⲙ̅ⲘⲞⲔ ϨⲰⲤ ⲦⲈ ⲈⲦⲀⲔⲞⲔ Ⲙ̅Ⲛ̅ⲚⲈⲚ-
ⲢⲈϤⳌⲰⲦⲂ̅· Ⲛ̅Ϥ̅ⲚⲀⲨ Ⲛ̅ⲦⲞⲔ ⲀⲚ ⲈⲠⲤⲀ Ⲙ̅ⲠⲒⲀⲎⲢ ⲈⲦⲚⲀⲚⲞⲨϤ· ¹⁰ⲘⲚ̅ ⲠⲈⲦⲚⲀⲚⲞⲨϤ
ⲚⲀⲦⲀⳌⲞⲔ ⲈⲔ ϢⲀⲚ ⲘⲞⲞⲨⲦⲚ̅ ⲘⲀⲨⲀⲀⲔ· ⲀⲖⲖⲀ ⲤⲰⲦⲘ̅ Ⲛ̅ⲤⲰⲒ̈ ¹⁵ Ⲛ̅ⲦⲀⲢⲈⲔ ⲞⲨϪⲀⲒ̈·
ⲠⲈϪⲈ ⲠϨⲀⲄⲒⲞⲤ ⲔⲞⲖⲞⲐⲞⲤ ⲚⲀⲨ ϪⲈ· ⲚⲀⲚⲞⲨ ⲚⲘⲞⲨ ⲈⲦ ⲚⲎⲨ ⲚⲀⲒ̈ Ⲙ̅ⲠⲀⲢⲀ̅ ²⁰ ⲠⲰ-
Ⲛ̅Ⳍ ⲈⲦⲈⲔⲚⲀ̅ ⲦⲀⲀⲨ ⲚⲀⲒ̈· ⲠⲈϪⲈ ⲠⳌⲎ ⲄⲈⲘⲰⲚ ⲚⲀⲨ ϪⲈ ⲈⲒ̈Ⲉ Ⲛ̅Ϥ̅ ⲤⲞⲞⲨⲚ ⲀⲚ
ϪⲈ ⲞⲨⲚ̅ ⲦⲀⲒ̈ⲦⲈ ²⁵ ⳌⲞⲨⲤⲒⲀ Ⲙ̅ⲘⲀⲨ ⲈⲠⲈⲆⲈⲨ Ⲙ̅ⲘⲞⲔ; ⲦⲈⲚⲞⲨ ⲆⲈ ϪⲒ ⲚⲀⲔ Ⲛ̅-
ⲞⲨⳖⲞⲠ ⲤⲘⲞⲤ Ⲙ̅ⲘⲚ̅ⲦⲤⲀⲂⲈ ³⁰ Ⲛ̅ϤⲤⲰⲦⲘ̅ Ⲛ̅ⲤⲰⲒ̈· ⲠⲈϪⲈ ⲠϨⲀⲄⲒⲞⲤ ⲔⲞ̅ⲖⲞⲐⲞⲤ ⲚⲀⲨ
ϪⲈ ⲠⲈⲦ(91Ri)ⲚⲀⲤⲰⲦⲘ̅ Ⲛ̅ⲤⲰⲔ ⲈϤⲚⲀⲈⲒⲚⲈ ⲈϪⲰⲨ Ⲙ̅ⲠⲘⲞⲨ ⲘⲀⲨⲀⲀⲨ·
ⲀⲚⲞⲔ ⲆⲈ Ⲛ̅ϮⲚⲀⲔⲰ ⁵ Ⲛ̅ⲤⲰⲒ̈ ⲀⲚ Ⲙ̅ⲠⲀϪⲞⲈⲒⲤ ⲒⲤ̅ ⲠⲈⲬⲤ̅· ⲠⲈϪⲈ ⲠⳌⲎ ⲄⲈⲘⲰ(Ⲛ)
ⲚⲀⲨ ϪⲈ ϬⲰϢⲦ̅ Ⲛ̅Ϥ̅ⲚⲀⲨ ⲈⲠⲈⲒ̈ⲢⲰⲘⲈ ¹⁰ ⲦⲎⲢⲞⲨ ⲈⲢⲈⲚⲈⲨ Ⲣ̅ⲘⲈⲒⲞⲞⲨⲈ ϢⲞⲨⲞ Ⲉ-
ⲠⲈⲤⲎⲦ ⲈⲨⲚⲀⲨ ⲈⲢⲞⲔ ⲈⲔⲀⳌⲈ ⲈⲢⲀ̅ⲦⲔ̅ ϨⲒϪⲘ̅ⲠⲂⲎⲘⲀ· ¹⁵ ⲀⲨⲰ Ⲛ̅ⲦⲞⲔ Ⲙ̅ⲠⲈⲔ
Ϣ̅Ⲛ̅Ⳍ ⲦⲎⲔ ϨⲀⲢⲞⲔ Ⲙ̅ⲘⲒⲚ Ⲙ̅ⲘⲞⲔ, ⲀⲖⲖⲀ Ⲕ̅Ⲱ Ⲛ̅Ⲁ ⲦⲤⲰ̅ⲦⲘ̅· ⲖⲞⲒⲠⲞⲚ ⲤⲰ̅ⲦⲘ̅
Ⲛ̅ⲤⲰⲒ̈ Ⲛ̅ⲄⲐⲨ ⲤⲒⲀⳀⲈ Ⲛ̅ⲦⲀⲢⲈⲔ ⲰⲚⳍ· ⲠⲈϪⲈ ⲠϨⲀⲄⲒⲞⲤ ⲚⲀⲨ ϪⲈ ⲠⲒ ⲰⲚⳍ ⲢⲰ
Ⲛ̅ⲞⲨⲰ ²⁵ Ⲛ̅Ⳍ ⲀⲚ ⲠⲈ ⲚⲀⳌⲢⲀⲒ̈, ⲀⲖⲖⲀ ⲞⲨⲘⲞⲨ ⲠⲈ· ⲀⲨⲰ Ⲛ̅ⲦⲈⲨⲚⲞⲨ ⲀϤ ⲔⲈⲖⲈⲨⲈ
ⲈⲦⲀⲖⲞⲨ ⲈⲠⳌⲈⲢⲘⲎⲦⲀⲢⲒⲞⲚ· ³⁰ ⲠⲈϪⲈ ⲠⳌⲎ ⲄⲈⲘⲰ(Ⲛ) ⲚⲀⲨ ϪⲈ Ⲛ̅Ⲅ̅ Ⲣ̅ ⲬⲢⲒⲀ
ⲀⲚ ϪⲈⲔⲀⲤ ⲈⲢⲈⲞⳄⲀ (Rii) ⳀⲚⲞⲨⲔ· ϪⲞⲨⲰϢ ⲈⲦⲢⲀ Ⲧ ⲚⲀⲔ Ⲛ̅ⳌⲈⲚ ⲔⲈ-
ⳌⲞⲞⲨ; ⲠⲈϪⲈ ⲂⲎ ⲤⲀⲘⲰⲚ ⲠⲈϨ̅ ⁵ ⲢⲎⲦⲰⲢ ϪⲈ ⲤⲈ, ⲠⲀⲒ̈ ⲠⲈ ⲠⲈϤⲞⲨⲰϢ· ⲠⲈϪⲈ
Ⲡ ⳌⲎ ⲄⲈⲘⲰ(Ⲛ) ⲚⲀⲨ ϪⲈ ⲞⲨ ⲠⲈⲦⲔ̅ ⲞⲨⲀϢϤ̅; ⲀⲨⲰ ⲀⲚⲞⲔ ¹⁰ ϮⲚⲀⲀⲀⲨ ⲚⲘⲘⲀⲔ·

---

90 Vi 3. l. ⲡⲗⲟⲩⲧⲁⲣⲭⲟⲥ.   ii 21. Final letter looks like N; but this is
probably due to offset or alteration.   91 Ri 18. l. Ko

ⲡⲉϫⲉⲉⲓⲏⲣⲏⲙⲓⲁⲥ ′ⲡⲛⲟϭ ⲛ̄ⲍⲣⲏⲧⲱⲣ′ ϫⲉ ⲡⲁϫⲟⲉⲓⲥ, ⲡⲁⲓ ′ⲣⲱ ⲡⲉⲧϥⲟⲩⲁ¹⁵ϣⲩ,′
ϫⲉ ⲉⲕⲉⲁⲛⲉⲭⲉ ⲙ̄ⲙⲟⲩ ⲛ̄ⲍⲉⲛⲕⲉϩⲟⲟⲩ· ′ⲡⲉⲩⲕⲁⲣⲱⲟⲩ ⲅⲁⲣ ′ⲧⲁⲙⲟ ⲙ̄ⲙⲟⲛ ⲉ′ⲡⲁⲓ
ϩⲓⲧⲙ̄ ⲡⲉⲩⲥ̄ⲙⲟⲧ. ⲡⲉϫⲉ′ⲡϩⲏⲅⲉⲙⲱⲛ ⲇⲉ′ ⲱ ⲕⲟⲗⲟⲑⲟⲥ, ⲁ ⲍⲣⲟⲕ ′ⲛ̄ϥϫⲁϫⲉ ⲁⲛ·′
ⲕ̄ⲟⲩⲱϣ ⲉⲧⲣⲁⲧⲁ′ⲡⲟⲫⲁⲥⲓⲥ ⲉⲣⲟⲕ′ ϫⲓⲛ ⲙ̄ⲙⲟⲛ ⲧⲁϫ′ⲣⲟⲩ ⲛ̄ϩⲏⲧ ⲉϩⲣⲁⲓ ′ⲉϫⲱⲕ;
ⲡⲉϫⲉ′ⲡⲇⲓⲕⲁⲓⲟⲥ ⲛⲁϥ′ ϫⲉ ⲡⲉⲧⲉⲕⲟⲩⲱϣ′ⲉⲁⲁⲩ, ⲁⲣⲓϥ. ⲡⲉϫⲉⲡϩⲏⲅⲉⲙⲱⲛ
(91 Vi) ⲛⲁϥ ϫⲉ ϣⲁⲧⲉⲛⲟⲩ ′ⲧⲉ ⲱⲥ ϯϩⲣⲟⲩ ′ⲛ̄ϩⲏⲧ ⲉϩⲣⲁⲓ ⲉϫⲱⲕ· ′ⲉϣ ⲱⲡⲉ
ϩⲱⲱ⁵ⲕ ′ⲕ̄ⲛⲁϩⲣⲁⲩ ⲛ̄ϩⲏⲧ′ ⲉϫⲱⲕ, ⲉⲓⲉ ϯⲛⲁ′ⲣⲁⲩϣⲉ ⲉ ⲡⲉϩⲟⲩⲟ. ′ⲡⲉϫⲉⲡⲡⲉⲧⲟⲩⲁ′
ⲁⲃ ⲛⲁϥ ϫⲉ ⲧⲉⲕⲙⲛ̄ⲧ¹⁰ⲙⲁⲓⲣⲱⲙⲉ ⲁⲙⲁϩ′ⲧⲉ ⲙ̄ⲙⲟⲓ ⲉ ⲧⲣⲁ′ϫⲱ ⲛ̄ⲟⲩϫⲁϫⲉ ⲛ̄ϩⲟⲩⲟ.
ⲡⲉϫⲉ ⲡ′ϩⲏⲅⲉⲙⲱⲛ ⲛⲁϥ¹⁵ ϫⲉ ⲧⲉⲛⲟⲩ ⲁ ⲓⲁⲣ′ⲭⲉⲓ ⲉⲥⲱⲧⲙ̄ ⲉⲛ ⲅⲁ′ϫⲉ ⲉⲛⲁⲛⲟⲩ
ⲉⲃⲟⲗ′ ϩⲓⲧⲟⲟⲧⲕ̄. ⲡⲉⲓϩ′ⲣⲟⲟⲩ ⲅⲁⲣ ⲛ̄ⲧⲉⲓⲙⲓ′ⲛⲉ ⲧⲁⲙⲟ ⲙ̄ⲙⲟⲓ′ ϫⲉ ⲕ̄ⲟⲩⲱϣ
ⲉⲧ′ⲣⲁ ⲕⲁⲁⲕ ⲛ̄ϩⲉⲛ′ⲕⲉⲕⲟⲩⲓ ⲛ̄ϩⲟⲟⲩ.′ ⲡⲉϫⲉ ⲡϩⲁⲅⲓⲟⲥ ⲕⲟ²⁵ⲗⲟⲑⲟⲥ ⲙ̄ⲡϩⲏⲅⲉ′ⲙⲱⲛ
ϫⲉ ⲟⲩ ⲛⲉ ⲛⲓ′ϫⲁϫⲉ ⲛ̄ⲥⲟⲗⲥⲗ̄ ⲉ′ⲧⲉⲕϫⲱ ⲙ̄ⲙⲟⲟⲩ; ′ⲟⲩⲕⲉⲧⲓ ⲛ̄ⲧⲛⲁ³⁰ⲥⲱⲧⲙ̄ ⲛ̄
ⲥⲱⲕ ⲁⲛ′ ⲧⲁⲡⲗⲁⲛⲁ ϩⲱⲥ′ⲧⲉ ⲛ̄ⲧⲁⲕⲱ ⲛ̄ⲥⲱⲓ (Vii) ⲙ̄ⲡⲁⲛⲟⲩⲧⲉ· ⲁⲗⲗⲁ ⲙⲁⲗ′
ⲗⲟⲛ ϯⲧⲁϫⲣⲏⲩ ϩⲛ̄ ⲧⲉⲩ ⲡⲓⲥ′ⲧⲓⲥ· ⲁⲩⲱ ϯⲥ̄ⲃ̄ⲧⲱⲧ⁵ ′ⲉϩⲓ ϩⲁϩ ⲱⲃ ⲛⲓⲙ ⲉⲧⲃⲉ ⲡⲉⲩ′
ⲣⲁⲛ ⲉⲧⲟⲩⲁⲁⲃ·′ ϫⲉ ⲛ̄ⲃⲁⲥⲁⲛⲟⲥ ⲙ̄ⲡⲉⲓⲕⲟⲥⲙⲟⲥ ϩⲉⲛ′ⲗⲁⲁⲩ ⲛⲉ· ⲛ̄ⲃⲁⲥⲁ¹⁰ⲛⲟⲥ
ⲇⲉ ⲙ̄ⲡⲛⲟⲩⲧⲉ ′ϩⲉⲛⲛⲟϭ ⲛⲉ ⲁⲩⲱ ′ϩⲉⲛϣⲁⲉⲛⲉϩ ⲛⲉ,′ ⲁⲩⲱ ⲙⲛ̄ⲗⲁⲁⲩ ′ⲛⲁϣⲱⲡ
ⲙ̄ⲡⲉⲩ¹⁵ⲙ̄ⲧⲟ ⲉⲃⲟⲗ. ′ⲁⲩⲕⲉⲗⲉⲩⲉ ⲛ̄ϭⲓ ⲡϩⲏⲅⲉⲙⲱⲛ ⲉⲧⲣⲉⲩ′ⲉⲓ ϣⲉ ⲛ̄ⲟⲩⲛⲟϭ ′ⲛ̄′
ⲱⲛⲉ ⲉ ⲡⲉⲩⲙⲁⲕϩ̄.²⁰ ′ⲡⲉϫⲉ ⲡϩⲏⲅⲉ ⲛⲁϥ ′ϫⲉ ⲱ ⲕⲟⲗⲟⲑⲟⲥ, ⲙ̄′ⲡⲉⲣ ϫⲉⲗⲁⲁⲩ ⲛ̄′
ϣⲁϫⲉ ⲛⲁⲓ ⲛ̄ⲥⲁ′ⲃⲏⲗ ⲉ ⲡⲧⲱϣ ⲉ′ⲧⲉⲧⲛ̄ϫⲉⲗⲡⲓϫⲉ ⲉ′ⲣⲟⲩ, ϫⲉⲕⲁⲥ ⲉⲕⲉ′ⲥⲱⲧⲙ̄ ⲛ̄
ⲥⲁ ⲡⲛⲟ′ⲙⲟⲥ ⲛ̄ⲡⲣ̄ⲣⲟⲟⲩ.′ ⲡⲡⲉⲧⲟⲩⲁⲁⲃ ⲇⲉ ⲙ̄ⲡⲉⲩϫⲉⲗⲁⲁⲩ ⲛ̄ϣⲁϫⲉ ⲉ ⲡ′
ⲧⲏⲣϥ̄.′ ⲡⲉϫⲉ ⲡϩⲏⲅⲉⲙⲱⲛ (92 Ri) ⲛⲁϥ ϫⲉ ⲕⲁⲧⲁⲫ′ⲣⲟⲛⲉⲓ ⲙ̄ⲡⲉⲓⲉⲟⲟⲩ′ ⲉⲧ
ϣⲟⲩⲉⲓⲧ, ⲡⲁⲓ ′ⲉⲧⲉ ⲛ̄ϥⲛⲁ ϯϩⲏⲩ ′ⲙ̄ⲙⲟⲕ ⲁⲛ· ⲕⲁ′ⲧⲕ̄ ⲇⲉ ⲱ ⲡⲣⲱⲙⲉ, ′ϫⲓ ⲛⲁⲕ
ⲛ̄ⲟⲩⲉⲟⲟⲩ ′ⲛ̄ϣⲟⲩ ϣⲓⲡⲉ ⲛ̄′ϩⲏⲧϥ̄. ⲡⲉϫⲉ¹⁰ ⲡϩⲁⲅⲓⲟⲥ ⲛⲁϥ ϫⲉ′ⲡⲉⲟⲟⲩ ⲙ̄ⲡⲁϫⲟ′
ⲉⲓⲥ′ ⲓ̄ⲥ̄ ⲡⲉⲭ̄ⲥ̄ ⲡⲉⲧⲛⲁ′ⲧⲟⲩϫⲟⲓ ϣⲁ ⲉⲛⲉϩ. ′ ⲡⲉϫⲉ ⲡϩⲏⲅⲉⲙⲱ(ⲛ)¹⁵′ⲛⲁϥ ϫⲉ
ⲉ ⲛⲉⲛⲕⲁ′ⲗⲉⲓ ⲙ̄ⲙⲟⲕ ⲁⲛ ⲉⲧ′ⲣⲉⲕ ϯ ⲧⲱⲛ ⲛⲙ̄′ⲙⲁⲛ ϩⲛ̄ ϩⲉⲛⲯⲁ′ϫⲉ, ⲁⲗⲗⲁ ⲉⲛ′
ⲉⲛ²⁰ⲕⲁⲗⲉⲓ ⲙ̄ⲙⲟⲕ ⲉⲩϩⲱⲃ ⲡⲁⲛⲁⲅⲕⲁⲓⲟⲛ, ⲉⲧⲣⲉⲕⲗⲓⲃⲉ ′ⲙ̄ⲙⲟⲛ ⲛ̄ⲑⲩⲥⲓⲁϫⲉ
ⲛ̄ⲛ̄ⲛⲟⲩⲧⲉ·²⁵ ′ⲗⲟⲓⲡⲟⲛ ⲇⲉ ⲥⲕⲉⲡ′ⲧⲉⲓ ⲙ̄ⲙⲟⲕ. ′ⲡⲉϫⲉ ⲡϩⲁⲅⲓⲟⲥ ⲕⲟ′ⲗⲟⲑⲟⲥ ⲛⲁϥ
ϫⲉ ⲙ̄′ⲡⲉⲣ ⲕⲁⲧⲉⲭⲉ ⲙ̄′ⲙⲟⲓ ϫⲓⲛ ⲧⲉⲛⲟⲩ.′ ⲡⲉϫⲉ ⲡϩⲏⲅⲉⲙⲱ(ⲛ) (R ii) ⲛⲁϥ ϫⲉ ⲛ̄
ⲧⲁ ⲩⲕⲉⲗⲉⲩⲉ ⲛⲁⲕ ⲉ ϩⲣⲁⲃⲉ′ ⲛ̄ϥⲧⲙ̄ ⲕⲁⲧⲁⲫⲣⲟ′ⲛⲉⲓ ⲙ̄ⲡⲇⲓⲕⲁⲥ′ⲧⲏⲣⲓⲟⲛ. ⲡⲉϫⲉ ′
ⲡϩⲁⲅⲓⲟⲥ ⲕⲟⲗⲟⲑⲟⲥ′ ⲛⲁϥ ϫⲉ ⲁⲛⲟⲕ ϯ ′ⲟ ⲛ̄ⲥⲁⲃⲉ ⲛ̄ⲟⲩⲟⲉⲓϣ ′ⲛⲓⲙ, ⲁⲩⲱ ⲛ̄ⲧⲁⲓ′

ει επεϊμα ειϥιϊΝε Ν̄cατΜ̄Ντcaϊβε Μ̄παϫοεις Ϊ̄c ̇ πεϫε ̇ ̇ πεϫεπ̄ηγε-
μω(ν)¹⁵ Ν̄ναττα⳽ις ⳽ε ̇ εις⳽ηητε αϊρ̇cμοτ ΝΙΜ Ν̄Μ̄μαγ ειογωϥϊε-
τρεγογⳉαϊ,²⁰ ̇ αγω εις⳽ηητε ̇ Μ̄πεγcωτΜ̄ Ν̄ϥ̄ογⳉαϊ. ωΝτοċ Ν̄Τ̄Νααανε-
ϫε Μ̄Μογ αν Ν̄κεογ̇Ν̄νογ Ν̄ογωτ.²⁵ ̇ πεϫεΝαττα⳽ις ̇ ⳽ε ϯαποϕαcιċ ε-
ρογ, ⳽ε ϥ̄π̄λ̄πϳα ̇ Μ̄Μογ, αγ³⁰ τολμα γαρ επ̇λανα Μ̄Μον, (92Vi)
αγω Ν̄ταγcΜ̄Ν̄τε̄ ΝΜ̄Μαν επ̇ϫιΝ⳽η, εαγcω̇βε Μ̄Μον Μ̄πεγ̄⳽γ̄⁵-
ciαⳲε. πεϫε̇πⳉαγιοc κολοβοċ ναγ ⳽ε Μ̄πεϊ⳺ε̇λααγ Ν̄ϥατε̄ Ν̄-
ϣϳγε αν εχοογ.¹⁰ πεϫεπ̄ηγεμω(ν) ̇ ναγ ⳽ε θγciαⳲε ̇ Ν̄ϯ̄cαβε.
πε⳺ε̇πⳉαγιοc ναγ ⳽ε Ν̄ϯ̄ναθγciαⳲε αν, ̇¹⁵ ογ⳺ε Ν̄ϯ̄ναcωτΜ̄ αν Ν̄-
canεκα̇πολογiα Μ̄Ν̄Τ̄̇cοϥ. πⳉηγεμω(ν)̇ ⳽ε αγⳗωΝ̄τ, πε̇ϫαγ
ναγ ⳽ε εγ̇⳽ε Ν̄ϥ̄ναθγciα̇Ⳳε αν, cωτΜ̄ ετεκ̇αποϕαcιc, ταϊ ̇ε-
τεκΜ̄π̄λⳳγα²⁵ Μ̄̇λοc· ϯκελεγε ̇ Ν̄cερωκ⳽̄Μ̄ εκωΝⳉ. ̇ πε⳺επⳉαγιοċ κολοβοc ⳽ε ϯεγ̇ⲭαριcτει νακ ̇ παϫοεις Ϊ̄c πε⳯̄c (Vii) ⳽ε αϊπ̄λⳳγα
Μ̄̇πεκⳉμοτ ετρα̇μογ Ⳳι⳺Μ̄πεκ̇ραν ετογααβ.⁵ ̇ αγω αγⳗιτ̄γ ε̇βολ
ετρεγρωκⳳ̄.̇ Νεcογ⳽ογτⲁγτε̇ γαρ Μ̄πεβοτ πα̇γονⳲ πε πεⳉο̇ογ¹⁰
ετ̄Μ̄μαγ. ̇ αγω αγⳗωκ εβολ ̇ Ν̄τεγμαρτγ̇ρiα Ν̄⳼ι πⳉαγιοċ κολοβοc,
αγω̇¹⁵ αγⳳι Ν̄τεγⳳγ̇ⲭη εⳉραϊ ε̄Μ̄πηγε̇Ⳡ̄Νογεοογ, αγρ̇ⳳⲁ Μ̄Ν̄Ναг-
γε̇λοc, αγω ανετογ̇ααβ τηρογ ραϣε̇ ΝΜ̄Μαγ, ⳲιⲦ̄Ν̄τε̇ⲭαριc Μ̄Ν̄Τ̄-
Μ̄Ν̄τ̇μαϊρωμε Μ̄πε(Ν)̇⳺οεic Ϊ̄c πε⳯̄c,²⁵ ̇ παϊ πεοογ Μ̄πεϊ̈ωτ ΝΜ̄Μαγ
Μ̄Ν̄πεπ̄ν̄α ετογααβ ϣαενε⳺ Ν̄ενε⳺, ̇ ⳲαμηΝ.

---

92 R ii 22. l. οΝτωc

---

92 Vi. B begins with two lines ending Ϳμοc; ϳογεΝνε, which seem not to
correspond with anything in A. 5–7. πεϫεΝⳉ. ⳽ε A;]ατεγΝογ α[το]λλογ-
θοc ογωΝ ερωϥ εϥ⳺ω Μ̄μοc ⳽ε B. 9. Ν̄ϣϳγε A; εⳳϳγε B. 10–12. πεϫεΝⳉ.
—Ν̄ϯ̄cαβε A; απιανοc ⳺ε πⳉηγεμων πε⳺αγ Ν̄ⲧⲟⲗλογθοc ⳽ε Ν̄ναθγciαⳲε
⳺ε Ν̄τοογⲛ̄ B. 12f. πεϫεΝⳉ. ναγ A; om. B. 18–20. ⳂⳲ. —ναγ ⳽ε A; απιανοc ⳺ε ⳂⳲ.
πε⳺αγ Ν̄τολλογθοc ⳽ε B. 21f. Ν̄ϯ̄ναθγciαⳲε A; ϥναθ. B. 22. After cωτΜ̄, +
τεΝογ B. 22–5. ετεκαπ. — Μ̄μοc A; ετκολαcic Μ̄ⲧⲁⲇγμωⲣⲓⲁ κ̄π̄λⳳγα Μ̄π[ⲟ]γ]
B. 25f. ϯκελεγε — εκω⳯⳽̄ A; α⳷κελεγε ετρεⲩτεικⲱ⳽⳽̄ Μ̄μογ ε⳷⳽Ⳡ̄ Ν̄cερω-
κ⳽̄ Μ̄μογ B. 27–1i 4: B omits the martyr's final words.
In place of 92 Vii 5–29, B has the following conclusion: αγω ταϊ τε θε εⲛ-
ταγⳳωκ εβολ Ν̄τεγμαρτηⲣⲓⲁ Ν̄cογⳳογτⲁγⲧε Μ̄πεβοτ παⲅⲟⲛⳲ Ν̄⳼ι πⲙⲁⲣ-
τηⲣⲟⲥ ετⲟⲩⲁⲁⲃ απα ⲅⲟ⳻⳺ⲟ[ⲩ]θⲟⲥ αⲅⲱ Ν̄⳽[ⲱ]ⲣⲉ αⲅⲱ Ν̄ⲅⲟⲉⲓⲕ ⲛⲁⲙⲉ Μ̄πε⳯̄c,
ⲡⲁⲓ̈ πⲉⲟⲟⲩ ⲛⲁⲩ Μ̄ⲡⲉⲩⲉⲓ̈ⲱⲧ Ν̄ⲁ⳷ⲁⲑⲟⲥ Μ̄ⲡⲉⲡ̄ⲛ̄ⲁ ⲉⲧⲟⲩⲁⲁⲃ ϣⲁⲉⲛⲉ⳺ ⲉⲛⲉⲛⲉ⳺,
Ⳳⲁⲙⲏⲛ.

MARTYRDOM OF SS. PAESE AND THECLA
FROM PIERPONT MORGAN CODEX M 591
T. 28, FF. 49–88R

(ⲙ̅ⲑ Ri) ⲧⲙⲁⲣⲧⲩⲣⲓⲁ ⲙ̄ⲡ̄ϩⲁⲅⲓⲟⲥ ⲙ̄ⲙⲁⲣⲧⲩⲣⲟⲥ ⲁⲡⲉⲭⲥ̄ ⲡϩⲁ'ⲅⲓⲟⲥ ⲁⲡⲁ ⲡⲁⲏⲥⲉ
ⲡⲣ̄ⲙ̄ⲡⲟⲩⲥⲓⲣⲉ' ⲙⲛ̄ⲑⲁⲅⲓⲁ ⲑⲉⲕⲗⲁ' ⲧⲉϥⲥⲱⲛⲉ· ⲛ̄ⲧⲁⲩϫⲱⲕ ⲇⲉ ⲉⲃⲟⲗ ⲛ̄ⲧⲁⲑⲗⲏⲥⲓⲥ
ⲙ̄ⲡⲉⲩⲁⲅⲱⲛ ⲛ̄ⲥⲟⲩⲛⲙⲟⲩⲛ ⲙ̄ⲡⲉⲃⲟⲧ' ⲭⲓⲁⲕ, ϩⲛ̄ⲟⲩⲉⲓ'ⲣⲏⲛⲏ ⲛ̄ⲧⲉⲡⲛⲟⲩⲧⲉ, ϩⲁⲙⲏⲛ'
ⲁⲥϣⲱⲡⲉ ⲇⲉ ϩⲛ̄ⲧ'ⲙⲛ̄ⲧⲉⲣⲟ ⲛ̄ⲇⲓⲟⲕⲗⲏⲧⲓⲁⲛⲟⲥ ⲡ̄ⲣ̄ⲣⲟ' ⲛ̄ⲁⲛⲟⲙⲟⲥ, ⲡⲁⲓ ⲛ̄ⲧⲁⲩⲧⲟⲩ-
ⲛ̄ⲧ ⲉⲡ̄ⲛⲟⲩⲧⲉ ⲙ̄ⲛ̄ⲛⲉϥⲁⲅⲅⲉⲗⲟⲥ, ⲉⲣⲉϩⲁⲣⲙⲉⲛⲓⲟⲥ ⲟ ⲛ̄ⲇⲟⲩⲝ ϩⲛ̄ⲣⲁⲕⲟⲧⲉ, ⲉⲣⲉ'ⲉⲩ-
ⲧⲉⲭⲓⲁⲛⲟⲥ ⲟ ⲛ̄ⲇⲟⲩⲝ ⲉⲑⲏⲃⲁⲉⲓⲥ,' ⲛⲉⲩⲛ̄ⲟⲩⲣⲱⲙⲉ' ⲇⲉ ⲙ̄ⲡⲉϫⲓⲧ ⲛ̄ⲩⲙⲟⲩⲛ ϩⲛ̄
ⲟⲩⲧⲟⲟⲩ ϫⲉ ⲡⲟⲩⲥⲓⲣⲉ, ⲉⲡⲉⲩ'ⲣⲁⲛ ⲡⲉ ⲡⲁⲏⲥⲉ·' ⲡⲁⲓ ⲇⲉ ⲉⲛⲉⲩⲣⲱ(R ii)ⲙⲉ ⲛ̄ⲁⲅⲁ-
ⲑⲟⲥ ⲡⲉ' ⲉϥⲉⲓⲣⲉ ⲛ̄ϩⲉⲛⲛⲟⲃ' ⲙⲛ̄ⲧⲛⲁ ⲙⲛ̄ⲛⲉⲛϩⲏⲕⲉ ⲙⲛ̄ⲛ̄ⲟⲣⲫⲁⲛⲟⲥ ⲙⲛ̄ⲛⲉⲭⲏⲣⲁ
ⲉⲧϩⲙ̄'ⲡⲙⲁ ⲉⲧⲙ̄ⲙⲁⲩ.' ⲁⲩⲱ ⲡⲣⲱⲙⲉ ⲉⲧⲙ̄'ⲙⲁⲩ ⲛⲉⲩⲛ̄ⲧϥ̄ ⲟⲩⲛⲟϭ ⲛ̄ϩⲏⲡⲏ'ⲣⲉⲥⲓⲁ
ϩⲙ̄ⲡⲉⲓ'ⲕⲟⲥ'ⲙⲟⲥ, ⲙ̄ⲡⲟⲩⲙⲏ'ⲛⲉ ⲛ̄ⲥⲟⲩ'ⲱϥⲉ ⲙⲛ̄ϩⲉⲛⲧⲃⲛⲟⲟⲩⲉ' ⲉⲛⲁϣⲱⲟⲩ ⲙⲛ̄ϩⲉⲛ-
ⲉⲟⲟⲩ ⲙⲛ̄ϩⲛ̄'ϭⲁⲙⲟⲩⲗ ⲙⲛ̄ϩⲉⲛⲉⲥⲟⲟⲩ ⲙⲛ̄ⲟⲩⲛⲟϭ ⲙ̄ⲙⲛ̄ⲧ'ⲣⲙ̄ⲙⲁⲟ.' ⲡⲣⲱⲙⲉ ⲇⲉ
ⲉⲧⲙ̄'ⲙⲁⲩ ⲉϥϭⲁⲛ'ϩⲱⲱⲕⲉ ⲛ̄ⲛⲉϥⲉ'ⲥⲟⲟⲩ ⲉⲧⲉⲣⲟⲙⲡⲉ,' ϣⲁϥⲧ ⲛ̄ⲩϥ ⲛ̄ⲉ'ⲥⲟⲟⲩ ⲛ̄-
ⲥⲁⲣⲧ ⲛ̄ⲛⲉⲭⲏⲣⲁ ⲙⲛ̄ⲛⲟⲣ'ⲫⲁⲛⲟⲥ ⲙⲛ̄ⲛⲉⲛ'ϩⲏⲕⲉ ⲙⲛ̄ⲛⲉⲧ'ϭⲁⲁⲧ ⲉⲧⲙ̄ⲡⲉⲩ ⲧⲙⲉ·
ⲁⲩⲱ ⲟⲛ' ϩⲙ̄ⲡⲙⲉϩⲥⲉⲡⲥⲛⲁⲩ' ⲛ̄ϩⲱⲱⲕ ⲛ̄ⲛⲉⲩ(Vi)ⲉⲥⲟⲟⲩ ϣⲁϥⲧ ⲛ̄'ⲕⲉⲩϥ ⲛ̄ⲉⲥⲟⲟⲩ
ⲛ̄'ⲥⲁⲣⲧ ⲛ̄ⲛⲉⲧϩⲙ̄'ⲡⲉϥⲧⲙⲉ, ⲛ̄ϩⲏ'ⲕⲉ ⲙⲛ̄ⲛⲉⲧⲕⲱ ⲉⲣⲟⲩ.' ⲁⲩⲱ ⲟⲛ ϩⲙ̄ⲡⲉⲅⲟ'ⲉⲓⲩ
ⲙ̄ⲡⲉⲅⲟⲉⲓⲩ' ⲙ̄ⲡⲱϩⲥ̄ ⲛⲉ''ϣⲁϥⲧ ⲛ̄ⲟⲩⲕⲛⲁ'ⲁⲩ ⲛ̄ⲧⲟⲅⲉⲓ ⲧⲟⲅⲉⲓ' ⲛ̄ⲛⲉⲭⲏⲣⲁ ⲙⲛ̄ⲛ̄ϩⲙ̄ⲙⲟ
ⲉⲧϩⲙ̄'ⲡⲉϥⲱϩⲥ̄ ⲕⲁⲧⲁ'ϩⲟⲟⲩ ⲥⲛⲁⲩ.' ⲁⲩⲱ ⲡⲉϫⲉⲉⲓⲱⲧ' ϩⲏⲗⲓⲁⲥ ⲙⲛ̄ⲧⲉϥ'ⲙⲁⲁⲩ ⲙⲁ-
ⲣⲓϩⲁⲙ' ⲉⲛⲉⲩϣ̄ⲡⲁⲣⲁⲕⲁ'ⲗⲉⲓ ⲙ̄ⲙⲟⲩ ϫⲉ' ⲕⲁⲁⲛ ⲛ̄ⲧⲛ̄ϫⲓ'ⲥϩⲓⲙⲉ ⲛⲁⲕ, ϫⲉⲕⲁⲥ ⲉ-
ⲛⲉⲛⲁⲩ ⲉⲩϣⲏⲣⲉ ⲛ̄ⲧⲁⲕ ⲙ̄'ⲡⲁⲧⲉⲛⲙⲟⲩ·' ⲛ̄ⲧⲟϥ ⲇⲉ ⲉⲙⲉϥⲁ'ⲛⲉⲭⲉ ⲉⲡⲧⲏⲣϥ̄,' ⲉϥϫⲱ
ⲙ̄ⲙⲟⲥ ϫⲉ' ⲙ̄ⲡⲁⲣⲟⲟⲩⲧ ⲁⲛ' ⲡⲉ ϩⲁϫ̄ⲥϩⲓⲙⲉ.' ⲧⲁⲥⲱⲛⲉ ⲅⲁⲣ ⲁⲥ'ϫⲓϩⲁⲓ, ⲁⲩⲱ ⲉⲓⲥϩⲏⲏⲧⲉ ⲁⲥⲣ̄ⲭⲏⲣⲁ, (Vii) ⲁⲥϫⲡⲟ ⲅⲁⲣ ⲛ̄ⲟⲩ'ϣⲏⲣⲉ, ϯⲛⲁⲣⲱ'ϣⲉ ⲙ̄ⲙⲟⲓ ⲛ̄ⲙⲁⲥ.' ⲁⲩⲱ
ⲙⲛ̄ⲛ̄ⲥⲁϩⲉⲛ'ⲕⲟⲩⲓ ⲛ̄ϩⲟⲟⲩ ⲁ'ⲡⲉϥⲉⲓⲱⲧ ⲙ̄ⲧⲟⲛ' ⲙ̄ⲙⲟⲩ ϩⲛ̄ⲟⲩⲙⲛ̄ⲧ'ϩⲗ̄ⲗⲟ ⲉⲛⲁⲛⲟⲩⲥ.'
ⲁⲩⲱ ⲧⲉϥⲕⲉⲙⲁⲁⲩ' ⲁⲥⲙ̄ⲧⲟⲛ ⲙ̄ⲙⲟⲥ' ⲉϥϩⲛ̄ⲥⲉⲧⲏ ⲛ̄ⲣⲟⲙ'ⲡⲉ ⲙ̄ⲡⲁⲧⲉⲡ'ⲇⲓⲱⲅⲙⲟⲥ
ϣⲱ'ⲡⲉ. ⲛ̄ⲧⲉⲣⲉϥ'ⲣ̄ⲣⲟ ⲇⲉ ⲛ̄ϭⲓ ⲡⲁ'ⲛⲟⲙⲟⲥ ⲛ̄ⲣ̄ⲣⲟ ⲇⲓⲟⲕⲗⲏⲧⲓⲁⲛⲟⲥ,' ⲁϥϫⲁⲓ ⲛ̄ⲟⲩ-
ⲇⲓ'ⲁⲧⲁⲅⲙⲁ ⲉⲃⲟⲗ ϩⲛ̄'ⲛⲉⲭⲱⲣⲁ ⲧⲏⲣⲟⲩ' ⲉϥϫⲱ ⲙ̄ⲙⲟⲥ ϫⲉ' ⲡⲉⲧⲛ̄ⲛⲁⲑⲩⲥⲓⲁ'ⲍⲉ ⲁⲛ
ⲛ̄ⲛⲁⲛⲟⲩⲧⲉ, ϯⲛⲁⲙⲟⲩ ϩⲛ̄'ⲧⲥⲏϥⲉ.' ⲁⲥϣⲱⲡⲉ ⲇⲉ ⲛ̄ⲧⲉ'ⲣⲉⲛⲉⲥϩⲁⲓ ⲉⲓ ⲉϩⲟⲩ(ⲛ) ⲉ
ⲣⲁⲕⲟⲧⲉ, ⲁⲩⲧⲁⲁⲩ ⲛ̄ϩⲁⲣⲙⲉⲛ'ⲓⲟⲥ ⲡⲕⲟⲙⲓⲥ ⲛ̄ⲣⲁⲕⲟⲧⲉ· ⲁⲩⲟ'ⲅⲟⲩ· ⲁⲧⲡⲟⲗⲓⲥ' ⲧⲏⲣⲟ
ⲩⲧⲟⲣⲧⲣ̄ (50 Ri) ⲉⲧⲃⲉⲡⲉⲛⲧⲁⲩ'ϣⲱⲡⲉ. ⲁⲩⲱ'ⲁϩⲁϩ ϩⲛ̄ⲛⲉⲭⲣⲏⲥ'ⲧⲓⲁⲛⲟⲥ ⲡⲁⲣϫⲉ'ⲧⲁ

First hand continues to 74 Vi b; from there it alternates with a second, less care-
ful and elegant, apparently, that of a novice, showing many mistakes in spelling
and some lapses into non-Sahidic dialect forms. 49 R i 10 = -ϩⲩⲡⲏⲣⲉⲥⲓⲁ. 11. ℓ. ϩⲱⲛⲉ-
ⲥⲟⲟⲧ. 23; 32: traces of ink above end of line. V ii 33. ℓ. ⲧⲏⲣⲉ̄

ⲛⲛⲉⲩⲥⲱⲙⲁ ⲉⲡⲙⲟⲩ ⲙ̄ⲡⲕⲱϩⲧ̄ ⲙⲛ̄ⲧⲥⲏϥⲉ ⲙⲛ̄ϩⲉⲛⲕⲉⲙⲟⲩ ⲉⲩϭⲟⲃⲉ· ⲁⲩⲱ ⲛⲉⲩⲧⲉ-
ⲕⲱⲟⲩ ⲁⲩⲙⲁϩⲟⲩ ⲕⲁⲧⲁⲙⲁ ⲛ̄ϩⲟⲟⲩⲧ· ϩⲓⲥϩⲓⲙⲉ ⲉⲧⲃⲉⲡⲣⲁⲛ ⲙ̄ⲡⲉⲭ̄ⲥ̄· ⲁⲩⲱ ⲛⲉⲥⲁ̄
ⲁⲩⲛ̄ⲧⲟⲩ ⲉⲣⲏⲥ ⲉⲑⲏⲃⲁ ⲉⲓⲥ, ⲁⲩⲧⲁⲁⲩ ⲛⲉⲩⲧⲉⲭⲓⲁⲛⲟⲥ ⲡϫ̄ⲏⲅⲉⲙⲱⲛ, ⲁⲩⲱ ⲁⲩⲇⲓⲱ-
ⲕⲉⲓ ⲛⲥⲁ ⲛⲉⲭⲣⲏⲥⲧⲓⲁⲛⲟⲥ· ⲁⲩⲱ ϩⲉⲛⲛⲟϭ ⲙ̄ⲙⲏⲏϣⲉ ⲁⲩⲛⲟ ϩⲟⲩ ⲉⲛⲉⲩⲧⲉⲕⲱ ⲟⲩ ⲕⲁ-
ⲧⲁⲙⲁ· ⲁⲩⲱ ⲡⲁⲛⲥⲉ ⲡⲣⲙ̄ ⲡⲟⲩⲥⲓⲣⲉ ⲉⲛⲉ ⲩⲁⲩⲧⲱⲟⲩⲛ ⲛϥ̄ⲃⲱⲕ ⲉϩⲟⲩⲛ ⲉϥ̄ⲙⲟⲩⲛ
ⲙ̄ⲙⲁⲛ̄ ⲧⲛ̄ⲟⲟⲩ ⲛ̄ⲡⲓⲥⲉ ⲛ̄ϩⲉⲛⲛⲟϭ ⲛ̄ϭⲓⲛⲟⲩⲱⲙ· ⲁⲩⲱ ⲛϥ̄ⲥⲟⲃⲧⲉ   (50 R ii) ⲛ̄ϩⲉⲛ-
ⲏⲣⲡ̄ ⲛϥ̄ⲧⲁⲗⲟⲟⲩ ϩⲓϫⲛ̄ ⲛⲉⲩⲅⲣⲅⲁⲧⲏⲥ· ⲙ̄ⲛⲉⲩϩⲙ̄ϩⲁⲗ ⲛϥ̄ⲙⲟⲟⲩϣⲉ ⲛϥ̄ⲃⲱⲕ ⲉⲛⲉ-
ⲩⲧⲉ ⲕⲱⲟⲩ ⲛϥ̄ⲡⲁ ⲣⲁⲕⲁⲗⲉⲓ ⲛ̄ⲛⲉⲧⲟⲩⲁⲁⲃ ϣⲁⲛⲧⲟⲩ ⲱⲙ ⲉⲃⲟⲗ ϩⲙ̄ⲡⲉϥ ⲁⲣⲓⲥⲧⲟⲛ.
ⲛⲉⲧⲟⲩⲁⲁⲃ ⲇⲉ ⲉ ⲛⲉⲩⲁⲩⲛⲁⲩ ⲉⲩⲕⲗⲟⲙ ⲛ̄ⲟⲩⲟⲉⲓⲛ ⲉϥ̄ⲁϫⲉ ⲙⲡⲉ ⲧⲡⲉ ⲛ̄ⲧⲉϥⲁⲡⲉ·
ⲁⲩⲱ ϣⲁⲩⲉⲓⲙⲉ ϫⲉ ⲟⲩⲡⲉⲧⲟⲩⲁⲁⲃ ϩⲱⲱϥ ⲡⲉ ⲛ̄ⲧⲉϩⲉ. ⲉⲧⲃⲉ ⲡⲁⲓ ϣⲁⲩϭⲓ ⲉⲃⲟⲗ
ϩⲙ̄ⲡⲉϥⲁⲣⲓⲥⲧⲟⲛ· ⲛ̄ⲥⲉⲟⲩⲱⲙ· ⲁⲩⲱ ⲥⲉⲛⲁⲥⲙⲟⲩ ⲉⲣⲟⲩ ⲉⲩϫⲱ ⲙ̄ⲙⲟⲥ ϫⲉ ⲉⲣⲉⲡ̄ϫⲟ
ⲉⲓⲥ ⲭⲁⲣⲓⲍⲉ ⲛⲁⲕ ⲙ̄ⲡⲉⲕⲗⲟⲙ· ⲛ̄ⲁⲧⲧⲁⲕⲟ ϩⲛ̄ ⲑⲓⲗⲏⲙ ⲛ̄ⲧⲡⲉ· ⲉⲓⲥϩⲏⲏⲧⲉ ⲅⲁⲣ· ⲙ̄
ⲡⲟⲟⲩ ⲁⲕ ϫⲱⲕ ⲉⲃⲟⲗ ⲛ̄ⲧⲙ̄(ⲟⲓ)ⲡⲟⲗⲏ ⲙ̄ⲡⲉⲭ̄ⲥ̄ ⲉϥ̄ϫⲱ ⲙ̄ⲙⲟⲥ ϫⲉ ⲛⲓ ⲩϣⲟⲛⲉ ⲡⲉ, ⲁ-
ⲧⲉⲧⲛ̄ ϭⲙ̄ⲡⲁϣⲓⲛⲉ· ⲛⲉⲓ ϩⲙ̄ⲡⲉⲩⲧⲉⲕⲟ· ⲁⲧⲉⲧⲛ̄ⲉⲓ ϣⲁⲣⲟⲓ· ⲁⲩⲱ ⲟⲛ ϫⲉ ⲡⲉⲧ ⲛⲁ-
ⲧⲥⲉⲟⲩⲁ ⲛ̄ⲛⲉⲓ ⲕⲟⲩⲓ ⲛ̄ⲟⲩⲕⲱ ⲙ̄ⲙⲟⲩ ⲛ̄ⲱⲣϫ̄ ⲙ̄ⲙⲁⲧⲉ ⲉⲡⲣⲁⲛ ⲛⲟⲩⲙⲁⲑⲏⲧⲏⲥ· ϩⲁⲙⲏⲛ ϯϫⲱ ⲙ̄ⲙⲟⲥ ⲛⲏⲧⲛ̄ ϫⲉ ⲛ̄ⲛⲉⲩⲥⲱⲣⲙ̄ ⲙ̄ⲡⲉϥ ⲃⲩⲕⲉ· ⲧⲁⲓ ⲅⲁⲣ ⲧⲉ ⲑⲉ ⲉⲛⲉⲩⲉⲓⲣⲉ
ⲙ̄ⲙⲟⲥ ⲛⲟⲩ ⲙⲏⲏϣⲉ ⲛ̄ϩⲟⲟⲩ· ⲉⲩⲃⲏⲕ ⲉⲩⲙⲟⲩⲛ ⲙ̄ⲡⲁⲛ ⲧⲛ̄ⲟⲟⲩ· ⲉⲩⲟⲩⲱⲙ ⲙ̄ⲛⲉ-
ⲧⲟⲩⲁⲁⲃ. ⲛⲉⲩⲛ̄ ⲧⲁⲩ ⲇⲉ ⲙ̄ⲙⲁⲩ ⲛⲟⲩ ⲥⲱⲛⲉ ⲛ̄ⲥϩⲓⲙⲉ· ⲉⲡⲉⲥⲣⲁⲛ ⲡⲉ ⲑⲉⲕⲗⲁ, ⲉⲁⲥ
ϩⲙⲟⲟⲥ· ⲙ̄ⲡⲟⲩϩⲁⲓ ϩⲛ̄ⲁⲛ̄ ⲧⲛ̄ⲟⲟⲩ ⲧⲡⲟⲗⲓⲥ· ⲁⲥϫⲡⲟ ⲇⲉ ⲛⲟⲩ ϣⲏⲣⲉ, ⲁⲥⲙⲟⲩⲧⲉ
ⲉⲡⲉⲩⲣⲁⲛ ϫⲉ ⲁ ⲡⲱⲗⲗⲱⲛⲓⲟⲥ· ⲁⲥ(V ii)ⲧⲁⲁⲩ ⲉⲧⲁⲛϩⲏⲃ ⲙ̄ⲡⲁⲧⲉⲡⲇⲓⲱⲕⲙⲟⲥ·
ϣⲱⲡⲉ· ⲁⲩⲱ ⲡ̄ϩⲁⲓ ⲛ̄ⲑⲉⲕⲗⲁ ⲁϥⲙ̄ⲧⲟⲛ ⲙ̄ⲙⲟϥ. ⲛⲉⲩ ⲣⲙ̄ⲙⲁⲟ ⲉⲙⲁⲧⲉ ⲡⲉ· ⲁϥⲙ̄-
ⲧⲟⲛ ⲙ̄ⲙⲟϥ ⲉϥⲟ ⲛ̄ⲩⲏⲣⲉ ϣⲏⲙ· ⲁⲥϣⲱⲡⲉ ⲗⲟⲓⲡⲟⲛ· ⲉⲥⲟ ⲛ̄ⲭⲏⲣⲁ ⲛ̄ϭⲓ ⲑⲉⲕⲗⲁ·
ⲁⲩⲱ ⲧⲁⲓ· ⲉⲛⲉⲥⲱⲥ ⲉⲙⲁⲧⲉ· ϩⲛ̄ⲡⲉⲥⲥⲁ. ⲉⲛⲉ ⲩⲁⲥⲃⲱⲕ ⲉϩⲟⲩⲛ ⲉⲧⲉⲕⲕⲗⲏⲥⲓⲁ
ⲛ̄ⲥⲥⲱⲧⲙ̄ ⲉⲛⲅⲁϫⲉ ⲛ̄ⲧⲉⲅⲣⲁⲫⲏ ⲙ̄ⲡⲉⲥϣⲏⲣⲉ· ⲁⲩⲱ ⲉⲛⲉⲩⲁⲥⲧⲛ̄ⲛⲟⲟⲩ ⲛ̄ϭⲓ ⲑⲉⲕ-
ⲗⲁ· ⲛⲉ ⲩϣⲡ ⲛ̄ϩⲉⲛ ϩⲟⲓⲧⲉ ⲉⲛⲁⲩⲟⲩⲟⲩ· ⲙ̄ⲛ̄ⲍⲉⲙ ⲡⲣⲏⲩ· ⲛ̄ⲉⲧⲁⲗⲟⲟⲩ ⲉⲛⲉⲥ ϩⲙ̄ϩⲁⲗ
ⲛ̄ⲧⲛ̄ⲛⲟⲟⲩⲥⲟⲩ ⲉⲃⲟⲗ ϩⲛ̄ⲡⲟⲗⲓⲥ ⲧⲏⲣϥ̄· ⲛ̄ⲉⲥⲟⲣⲟⲩ ⲛ̄ⲛⲍⲏⲕⲉ· ⲙ̄ⲛ̄ⲛⲉⲧϣⲁⲁⲧ· ⲁⲩⲱ
ⲧⲁⲓ ⲧⲉ ⲧⲃⲉ ⲉⲛⲉⲥ ⲉⲓⲣⲉ ⲙ̄ⲙⲟⲥ ϣⲁ ⲡϫⲱⲕ ⲉⲃⲟⲗ ⲛ̄ϣⲟⲙ ⲧⲉ ⲛ̄ⲣⲟⲙⲡⲉ. (51 R i)
ⲁⲩⲱ ϫⲓⲛⲧⲁⲛ̄ ⲇⲓ ⲟⲩ ⲙⲟⲥ ϣⲱⲡⲉ· ⲉⲛⲉⲥⲇⲓⲁⲕⲟⲛⲉⲓ· ⲡⲉ ⲉⲛⲉⲧⲟⲩⲁⲁⲃ ⲡⲉ· ⲉⲥⲑⲁⲗⲡⲉⲓ
ⲙ̄ⲙⲟⲩ· ⲁⲩⲱ ⲧⲉⲥⲁⲅⲁⲡⲏ· ⲛⲉⲥⲙⲏⲛ ⲉⲃⲟⲗ ϩⲙ̄ⲛⲉⲩⲧⲉⲕⲱⲟⲩ, ⲉⲥ ⲡⲓⲥⲉ ⲛ̄ϭⲓⲛⲟⲩⲱⲙ,
ⲉⲥϫⲓ ⲙ̄ⲙⲟⲩ ⲉϩⲟⲩⲛ ϣⲁⲛⲉⲧⲟⲩ ⲁⲁⲃ, ⲉⲩⲟⲩⲱⲙ ⲉⲃⲟⲗ ϩⲛ̄ⲛⲉⲥϭⲓϫ· ⲁⲩⲱ ⲉⲥϩⲁⲛ-

---

50 R i 6. l. ⲉⲡⲙⲟⲟⲩ? ii 9 f. = ϣⲁⲛⲧⲟⲩⲟⲩⲱⲙ. V i 2. l. ⲛⲉⲓϣ. 10. l. -ⲙⲟⲟⲩ. 16
l. -ⲃⲉⲕⲉ. ii 30. l. ⲑⲉ; ⲧⲑ for ⲑ elsewhere in this ms. 51 R i 4 ⲡⲉ - ⲡⲉ, sic.

ⲚⲀⲨ[15]ⲈⲞⲨⲀ ⲈⲨⲔⲎ ⲔⲀ·ⲌⲎⲨ, ⲈⲚⲈⲨⲀⲤ·ϤⲒⲧϤ ⲈⲌⲞⲨⲚ ⲈⲠⲈⲤ·ⲎⲒ ⲚⲈϤ ⲌⲒⲰⲰⲨ, ⲀⲨⲰ
ⲈⲚⲈⲨⲀⲤϮ[20]ⲚⲀⲨ Ⲛ̄ⲦⲞⲨⲰⲘ. ⲀⲨⲰ ⲈⲚⲈⲨⲀⲢⲈⲠⲀⲅ·ⲄⲈⲖⲞⲤ Ⲙ̄ⲠⲬⲞⲈⲒⲤ· ⲞⲨⲞⲚϨϤ ⲈⲢⲞⲤ
Ⲛ̄·ⲌⲀ2 Ⲛ̄ⲤⲞⲠ ⲚϤ·ϤⲀ[25]ϨⲈ Ⲛ̄ⲘⲘⲀⲤ. Ⲛ̄ⲦⲞⲤ ⲆⲈ ⲈⲚⲈⲨⲀⲤ·ϢⲀϪⲈ Ⲛ̄ⲘⲘⲀⲨ· Ⲛ̄ϨⲀⲌ
Ⲛ̄ⲤⲞⲠ ϪⲈ· ⲠⲀϪⲞⲈⲒⲤ, ⲂⲞⲎⲐⲒⲀ·[30]ⲈⲢⲞⲒ· ⲀⲨⲰ Ⲉ·ⲚⲈⲨϢϪⲞⲞⲤ ⲚⲀⲤ· ϪⲈ Ⲛ̄ⲐⲈ Ⲛ̄ⲦⲀ-
Ⲣ2Ⲱ̄ⲂⲈ Ⲛ̄ⲚⲈⲦⲔⲎ ⲔⲀ(51 Rii)2ⲎⲨ, ϮⲚⲀⲦⲢⲈⲨ·ϨⲰⲂⲈ[5] ϨⲰⲰⲦⲈ Ⲙ̄·ⲠⲞⲨⲤⲰⲘⲀ Ⲙ̄Ⲛ̄·
ⲦⲞⲨⲮⲨⲬⲎ Ϩ̄Ⲙ̄ⲠⲈⲚ·ⲦⲎⲘⲀ Ⲙ̄ⲠⲞⲨⲞ·ⲈⲒⲚ· ⲀⲨⲰ ⲠⲈⲦ·ⲚⲀⲨ Ⲛ̄ⲞⲨⲔⲀⲒⲤⲈ Ⲉ·ⲠⲈⲦⲚ̄ⲤⲰ-
ⲘⲀ, ϮⲚⲀⲤ·ⲔⲎⲠⲀⲌⲈ Ⲛ̄ⲚⲈⲨ[10]ⲮⲨⲬⲎ Ϩ̄Ⲙ̄ⲠⲈⲚ·ⲦⲎⲘⲀ Ⲙ̄ⲠⲞⲨⲞⲈⲒⲚ· ϪⲈ Ⲙ̄Ⲛ̄ⲖⲀⲀⲨ Ⲛ̄-
ⲆⲨⲚⲀⲘⲒⲤ Ⲛ̄ⲦⲈⲠ·ⲔⲀⲔⲈ Ϭ̄Ⲙ̄ϬⲞⲘ Ⲉ·ⲢⲞⲞⲨ. ⲐⲈⲔⲖⲀ· ⲆⲈ ⲚⲈⲤⲘⲞⲔⲘⲈⲔ· Ϩ̄ⲢⲀⲒ Ⲛ̄ϨⲎ-
ⲦⲈ ⲈⲦⲂⲈ·ⲠⲈϢⲀϪⲈ Ⲙ̄ⲠⲀⲄ·ⲄⲈⲖⲞⲤ Ⲛ̄ⲦⲀⲨϪⲞ·ⲞⲨ ⲚⲀⲤ ϪⲈ ⲤⲈⲚⲀ·ϨⲰⲂⲈ[25] Ⲙ̄ⲠⲈⲦⲚ̄·ⲤⲰ-
ⲘⲀ, ⲈⲤϪⲰ· Ⲙ̄ⲘⲞⲤ ϪⲈ ⲞⲨ ⲀⲢⲀ· ⲠⲈⲦⲚⲀϢⲰⲠⲈ· Ⲙ̄ⲘⲞⲒ; ⲀⲢⲎⲨ· ⲈⲢⲈⲞⲨⲘⲚ̄Ⲧ2Ⲏ-
ⲔⲈ· ⲚⲎⲨ ⲈϪⲰⲒ, Ⲏ Ⲉ·ⲢⲈⲚⲈⲐⲎⲢⲒⲞⲚ ⲚⲀ·ⲞⲨⲞⲘⲦ, Ⲛ̄ⲤⲈ·[30]ⲔⲰⲰⲤ Ⲙ̄ⲠⲀⲤⲰ·ⲘⲀ Ⲛ̄ϨⲀ·ϨⲀ-
ⲠⲎ· ⲀⲖⲖⲀ ⲠⲞⲨⲰϢ Ⲙ̄·ⲠⲚⲞⲨⲦⲈ ⲠⲈⲦ(Vi)ⲚⲀⲨϢⲰⲠⲈ· ⲀⲌⲀϨ ⲆⲈ Ⲛ̄ⲢⲘ̄ⲘⲀⲞ·Ⲛ̄-
ⲦⲈⲦⲠⲞⲖⲒⲤ ⲠⲀ·ⲢⲀⲔⲀⲖⲈⲒ Ⲙ̄ⲘⲞⲤ[5] ϪⲈ ⲈⲚⲞⲨⲰϢ ⲈϪⲒ·ⲦⲞⲨ Ⲛ̄ϬⲒ·ⲌⲒⲘⲈ· Ⲛ̄ⲦⲞⲤ· ⲆⲈ Ⲙ̄-
ⲠⲈⲤⲠⲒⲐⲈ ⲚⲀⲨ,· ⲀⲖⲖⲀ ⲚⲈⲤⲠⲢⲞⲤⲔⲀⲢ·ⲦⲎⲢⲈⲒ ⲈⲚⲈⲦⲞⲨⲀⲀⲂ,[10] ⲈⲤⲘⲞⲨⲢ Ⲛ̄ⲚⲈⲨⲤⲀϢ·
ⲚⲈⲨⲤⲰⲘⲀ ⲆⲈ ⲈⲦϨ̄Ⲁ·ⲂⲀⲤⲀⲚⲞⲤ ⲈⲚⲈⲤϮ·ⲚⲈ2 ϨⲒϨⲢ̄Ⲡ̄ Ⲉ̄ϪⲰⲞⲨ·· ⲚⲈⲦⲞⲨⲀⲀⲂ ⲆⲈ
ⲈⲚⲈ·ⲨⲀⲨⲤⲰⲦ̄Ⲙ̄ Ⲉ·ⲢⲞⲤ ⲈⲤϪⲰ Ⲙ̄ⲘⲞⲤ· ϪⲈ ⲈⲢⲈⲠϪⲞⲈⲒⲤ· ⲚⲈϨⲘ̄Ⲧ̄ⲎⲨⲦⲚ̄·Ⲛ̄ⲦⲞ Ⲙ̄Ⲛ̄-
ⲠⲞⲨ·ⲔⲞⲨⲒ Ⲛ̄ϢⲎⲢⲈ· Ⲙ̄ⲠⲖⲞⲨⲤⲞⲚ,· Ⲛ̄ⲦⲈⲦⲚ̄ⲈⲒ Ⲉ2ⲞⲨ(Ⲛ̄) ⲈⲠⲀⲢⲒⲐⲘⲞⲤ Ⲛ̄·ⲚⲈⲦⲞⲨⲀⲀⲂ,
ⲀⲨⲰ[25] Ⲛ̄ⲦⲈⲦⲚ̄ϪⲒⲔⲖⲎⲢ·ⲞⲚⲞⲘⲒⲀ Ϩ̄Ⲛ̄Ⲑ̄·Ⲗ̄Ⲙ̄Ⲡ̄ Ⲛ̄ⲦⲠⲈ.· ⲀⲤϢⲰⲠⲈ ⲆⲈ Ⲙ̄Ⲛ̄·Ⲛ̄ⲤⲀⲚⲀⲒ
ⲚⲈⲨⲚ̄·ⲞⲨⲢⲰⲘⲈ Ϩ̄Ⲛ̄ϢⲨ·ⲘⲞⲨⲚ ⲦⲠⲞⲖⲒⲤ· ⲈⲨⲚⲞϬ Ⲙ̄ⲠⲢⲀⲔ·ⲘⲀⲦⲈⲨⲦⲎⲤ ⲠⲈ (Vii)Ϩ̄Ⲙ̄-

---

51 R i 15 f. ⲈⲨⲔⲎ ⲔⲞϨⲎⲨ· from other occurrences in this MS. This is seen to be the division assumed by the present writer. 29. ⲂⲞⲎⲐⲒⲀ: noun used as verb, as often in
this text. ii 4 f. = -ⲈⲚⲆⲨⲘⲀ. 29. ℓ. ⲞⲨⲞⲘⲦ. V i 5 f. ℓ. ⲈϪⲒⲦⲈ. 114-16. ℓ.
ⲈⲚⲈⲨⲀⲨⲤⲘⲞⲨ ⲈⲢⲞⲤ ⲈⲨϪⲰ (So B.)

---

51 R i 30 ff. The fragmentary lines at the beginning of B might be ⲀⲨⲰ ⲚⲈ[ⲨⲀⲨ]-
ϪⲞⲞⲤ, but [. . .]ⲘⲘⲞⲞⲨ after this is puzzling. ii 2 f. ϨⲰⲰⲦⲈ Ⲙ̄ⲠⲞⲨⲤⲰⲘⲀ A; Ⲙ̄-
2. B 3-6. Ⲙ̄Ⲛ̄ⲦⲞⲨϤ. - Ⲙ̄ⲠⲞⲨⲞⲈⲒⲚ A; om. B. 6 f. ⲀⲨⲰ —Ⲛ̄ⲞⲨⲔⲀⲒⲤⲈ Ⲙ̄- A; ⲔⲀⲦⲰ
(sic) ⲠⲈⲦⲚⲀϨⲰⲂⲈ Ⲙ̄- B. 9. Ⲛ̄ⲚⲈⲨϤ A; Ⲛ̄ⲦⲈⲨϤ. B. 10-15. 2Ϩ̄Ⲙ̄ⲠⲈⲚⲦⲎⲘⲀ — ⲈⲢⲞⲞⲨ; om. B.
16 f. ⲚⲈⲤⲘⲞⲔⲘⲈⲔ ϨⲢⲀⲒ Ⲛ̄ϨⲎⲦⲈ A; ⲚⲈⲤⲘⲀⲔϨ̄ Ⲛ̄ϨⲎⲦ B. 18. ⲠϢⲀϪⲈ A; ⲠⲈⲒ·Ⲩ·B. 18.
-20. Ⲙ̄ⲠⲀⲄⲄⲈⲖⲞⲤ Ⲛ̄ⲦⲀⲨϪⲞⲞⲨ A; Ⲛ̄ⲦⲀⲠⲀⲄⲄⲈⲖⲞⲤ ϪⲞⲞⲨ B. 26 f. ⲚⲀ2ⲦⲞⲨ B as A. 27. Ⲏ
A; ⲈⲒⲈ B. 32 - V i 1. ⲀⲖⲖⲀ — ⲚⲀⲨϢⲰⲠⲈ A; om. B. 2. ⲀⲌⲀϨ ⲆⲈ A; ⲀⲨⲰ ⲀⲌⲀϨ B.
3 f. ⲠⲀⲢⲀⲔⲀⲖⲈⲒ Ⲙ̄ⲘⲞⲤ A; ϪⲞⲞⲨ ⲨⲀⲢⲞⲤ B. 5 f. ϪⲈ ⲈⲚⲞⲨⲰϢ ⲈϪⲒⲦⲞⲨ(sic) A;
ⲈⲦⲞⲨⲰϢ ⲈϪⲒⲦⲈ ⲚⲀⲨ B. 6 f. Ⲛ̄ⲦⲞⲤ —ⲚⲀⲨ A; ⲀⲨⲰ Ⲙ̄ⲠⲈⲤⲞⲨⲰϢ B. 8. ⲀⲖⲖⲀ A;
om. B. 10-13. ⲈⲤⲘⲞⲨⲢ— ⲈϪⲰⲞⲨ A; ⲈⲤⲆⲒⲀⲔⲞⲚⲈⲒ ⲈⲢⲞⲞⲨ B. 14-16. ⲈⲚⲈⲨⲀⲨⲤⲰⲦⲘ̄
(sic) ⲈⲢⲞⲤ ⲈⲤϪⲰ (sic) Ⲙ̄ⲘⲞⲤ A; ⲚⲈⲨⲤⲘⲞⲨ ⲈⲢⲞⲤ ⲈⲨϪⲰ Ⲙ̄ⲘⲞⲤ B. 17-21. ϪⲈ ⲈⲢⲈⲠϪⲞⲈⲒⲤ—Ⲙ̄Ⲛ̄ⲠⲞⲨⲤⲞⲚ A; ϪⲈ ⲈⲢⲈⲠⲚⲞⲨⲦⲈ ⲤⲘⲞⲨ ⲈⲢⲞ Ⲙ̄ⲠⲞⲨⲤⲞⲚ (sic) Ⲙ̄Ⲛ̄ⲠⲞⲨⲔⲞⲨⲒ Ⲛ̄-
ϢⲎⲢⲈ B. 32- ii 2. ⲈⲨⲚⲞϬ - ⲠⲈ A;]Ⲧ̄Ⲙ̄[±7]ⲒⲤ (Ⲙ̄ⲠⲢⲀ]ⲅ̄Ⲙ̄[ⲀⲦⲈⲨⲦ]Ⲏ̄Ⲥ?) Ⲛ̄ⲢⲘ̄-

πεγγενος, εγ'ρ̄ρα˙ϊτε πε· παϊ' ⲇⲉ ⲛⲉⲩ̄ⲧ̄ϥ̄ⲟⲩ'ⲛⲟϭ ⲛ̄ⲭⲣⲏⲙⲁ ⲙ̄'ⲙⲁⲩ, ⲁⲩⲱ
ⲛ̄ⲧⲟⲩ' ⲡⲉ ⲛⲉⲩⲩⲱⲡ' ⲙ̄ⲡⲉⲓⲡⲡⲟⲛ ⲙ̄'ⲡⲧⲟⲩ ⲧⲏⲣϥ̄ ⲉⲧⲙ̄'ⲙⲁⲩ· ⲡⲣⲁⲛ ⲇⲉ' ⲙ̄ⲡ̄-
ⲣⲱⲙⲉ ⲉⲧⲙ̄'ⲙⲁⲩ ⲡⲉ ⲡⲁⲩⲗⲟⲥ·' ⲡⲁⲓ ⲇⲉ ⲉⲛⲉⲩⲣⲱ'ⲙⲉ ⲡⲉ ⲉⲩⲣ̄ϩⲟⲧⲉ ϩⲏ'ⲧϥ̄ ⲙ̄-
ⲡⲛⲟⲩⲧⲉ,' ⲉϥⲉⲓⲣⲉ ⲛ̄ϩⲛ̄ⲛⲟϭ' ⲙ̄ⲙⲛ̄ⲧⲛⲁ ϩⲛⲟⲩ' ⲡⲉⲑⲏⲡ· ⲁⲩⲱ' ⲡⲣⲱⲙⲉ ⲉⲧⲙ̄ⲙⲁⲩ'
ⲉⲛⲉϥⲟ ⲛ̄ϣⲃⲏⲣ' ⲉⲡⲁⲛⲥⲉ, ⲉⲡⲓ'ⲇⲏ ⲛ̄ⲧⲟϥ ⲡⲉ ⲛⲉⲩ'ϥⲓ ⲡⲥⲓⲡⲡⲟⲛ ⲧⲏ'ⲣϥ̄ ⲛ̄ⲧⲉⲩⲥⲱ-
ⲩⲉ·' ⲉⲡⲓⲇⲏ ⲛⲉⲣⲉⲡⲁ'ⲏⲥⲉ ϫⲟ ⲛⲟⲩⲛⲟϭ' ⲛ̄ⲥⲱⲩⲉ ⲙ̄ⲙⲁϩⲉ·' ⲡⲁⲛⲥⲉ ⲇⲉ ⲛⲉⲩⲉ-
ⲩⲅⲉⲛⲏⲥ ⲡⲉ ⲙ̄ⲡ'ⲗⲟⲩⲥⲓⲟⲥ ⲉϥⲟ ⲛ̄'ⲥⲁⲉⲓⲧ ϩⲙ̄ⲡⲧⲟⲩ' ⲧⲏⲣϥ̄ ⲉⲧⲙ̄ⲙⲁⲩ' ⲉⲛⲉ-
ⲩⲁⲩⲱⲡ̄' ⲛ̄ⲡⲥⲁⲙⲟⲩⲗ ⲛⲁⲛ (52 Ri) ϩⲟⲗⲟⲙⲁ ⲛⲩ̄ⲧⲱ'ⲟⲩⲛ ⲛϥ̄ⲃⲱⲕ ⲉⲧ'ⲡⲟⲗⲓⲥ
ⲩⲙⲟⲩⲛ' ϩⲁⲧⲙ̄ⲡⲁⲩⲗⲟⲥ' ⲡⲉⲡⲣⲁⲕⲙⲁⲧⲉⲩ'ⲧⲏⲥ· ⲁⲩⲱ ⲉⲛⲉ'ⲩⲁⲩⲣⲁⲩⲉ ⲛ̄ϭⲓ'
ⲡⲁⲩⲗⲟⲥ ⲉϥⲩⲁⲛ'ⲛⲁⲩ ⲉⲡⲁⲛⲥⲉ, ⲁⲩⲱ ⲉⲛⲉⲩⲁⲩⲁ'ⲙⲁϩⲧⲉ ⲙ̄ⲙⲟⲩ'ϩⲁϩⲧⲏⲩ
ⲛ̄ⲟⲩⲉ'ⲃⲟⲧ ⲛ̄ϩⲟⲟⲩ, ⲉⲧⲟⲩ'ⲱⲙ ⲉⲧⲥⲱ ⲙ̄ⲛⲛⲉⲩ'ⲉⲣⲏⲩ, ⲉⲩⲣⲁⲩⲉ ⲉ'ⲙⲁⲧⲉ ⲉⲩⲩⲁϫⲉ'
ⲙ̄ⲛⲛⲉⲩⲉⲣⲏⲩ ϩⲙ̄'ⲡϣⲁϫⲉ ⲙ̄ⲡⲛⲟⲩⲧⲉ· ⲁⲥⲩⲱⲡⲉ' ⲇⲉ ϩⲣⲁ̈ⲓ ϩⲙ̄ⲡⲉⲃⲟⲧ' ⲡⲁⲣⲙ̄ϩⲟⲧ
ⲁϥ'ⲧⲱⲟⲩⲛ ⲛ̄ϭⲓ ⲡⲁⲩ'ⲗⲟⲥ ⲡⲉⲡⲣⲁⲅⲙⲁ'ⲧⲉⲩⲧⲏⲥ, ⲁϥ'ⲃⲱⲕ ⲛⲁⲩ ⲉⲣⲁⲕⲟⲧⲉ ⲙ̄-
ⲧⲉϥⲡ'ⲣⲁⲅⲙⲁⲧⲓⲁ·' ϩⲙ̄ⲡⲧⲣⲉϥⲃⲱⲕ' ⲇⲉ ⲉϩⲟⲩⲛ ⲉⲧⲡⲟ'ⲗⲓⲥ ⲁϥⲩⲱⲡⲉ (Rii) ⲁⲩⲱ
ⲁϥⲗⲟϩⲗⲉϫ̄' ⲁϥⲉⲓ ⲉϥⲛⲁⲙⲟⲩ·' ⲁϥⲥϩⲁⲓ ⲉⲣⲏⲥ ⲉⲛⲉⲩ'ϩϩⲁⲗ ⲉϥϫⲱ'ⲙ̄ⲙⲟⲥ ⲇⲉ
ⲧⲁⲭⲏ' ⲧⲁϩⲟⲓ· ⲙ̄ⲙⲟⲛ ⲉⲓⲥ'ⲍⲏⲏⲧⲉ ϯⲩⲱ'ⲛⲉ· ⲙⲏⲡⲟⲧⲉ ⲧⲁ'ⲙⲟⲩ· ⲁⲩⲱ ⲁ'ϫⲓⲥ ⲉⲡⲁ-
ⲥⲟⲛ ⲡⲁⲏⲥⲉ ϫⲉ ⲉⲩⲩⲱⲡⲉ ⲕⲟⲩⲱⲩ ⲉⲉⲓ'ⲧⲁⲛⲁⲩ ⲉⲣⲟⲕ' ⲙ̄ⲡⲁⲧⲙⲟⲩ, ⲉⲓⲉ' ⲁⲙⲟⲩ·
ⲉⲩⲩⲱⲡⲉ' ⲙ̄ⲙⲟⲛ, ϯⲩⲓⲛⲉ 'ⲉⲣⲟⲕ· ⲁⲥⲩⲱ'ⲡⲉ ⲇⲉ ⲛ̄ⲧⲉⲣⲉⲛⲉⲥ'ϩⲁⲓ ⲉⲓ ⲉⲣⲏⲥ, ⲁⲩⲧⲁ-'
ⲙⲉⲡⲁⲛⲥⲉ· ⲛ̄'ⲧⲉⲩⲛⲟⲩ ⲇⲉ ⲛ̄ⲧⲁⲩ'ⲥⲱⲧⲙ̄ ⲛ̄ϭⲓ ⲡⲁⲏⲥⲉ, ⲁⲡⲉϥϩⲏⲧ ⲙ̄'ⲕⲁϩ ⲉⲙⲁⲧⲉ,
ⲁϥ'ⲧⲱⲟⲩⲛ, ⲁϥϥⲓ ⲛ̄ⲁ'ⲡⲛⲁⲩ ⲛ̄ⲟⲩⲗⲓⲧ'ⲣⲁ ⲛ̄ⲛⲟⲩⲃ ⲙ̄ⲛ̄ϩⲉⲛⲁⲛϩⲟⲗⲟⲙⲁ,' ⲁⲩⲁⲗⲉ
ⲉⲡϫⲟⲓ·' ⲁϥⲕⲱ ⲙ̄ⲡⲉⲩⲉ'ⲡⲓⲧⲣⲟⲡⲟⲥ ϩⲓϫⲛ̄'ⲛⲉϥϭⲱⲩⲉ, ⲁⲩⲱ (Vi) ⲛ̄ⲟⲓⲕⲟⲛⲟⲙⲟⲥ'
ϩⲓϫⲙ̄ⲡⲉϥⲏⲓ, ⲁϥ'ⲃⲱⲕ ⲉϩⲟⲩⲛ ⲉⲁⲛ'ϯⲛⲱⲟⲩ, ⲁϥⲃⲱⲕ' ⲉϩⲟⲩⲛ ⲉⲡⲏⲓ ⲛ̄ⲑⲉⲕⲗⲁ
ⲧⲉϥⲥⲱ'ⲛⲉ, ⲡⲉϫⲁⲩ ⲛⲁⲥ' ϫⲉ ⲑⲉⲕⲗⲁ ⲧⲁⲥⲟ'ⲛⲉ, ⲉⲓⲥϩⲏⲏⲧⲉ' ⲁⲡⲁⲩⲃⲏⲣ ⲡⲁⲩ'

---

51 V ii 1. l. ϩⲁⲡⲉⲩⲅⲉⲛⲟⲥ? 22. l. -ϥⲓ ⲙ̄ⲡⲥⲓⲡⲡⲟⲛ 33–52 Ri 1. °ⲛ̄ⲁⲛⲁⲗⲱⲙⲁ

Ⲉⲣⲁⲓ̈ⲧⲉ ⲡⲉ B. 3 f. ⲛⲉⲩⲛ̄ⲧϥ̄ⲟⲩⲛⲟϭ A; ⲉⲛⲉⲟⲩⲛ̄ⲧⲁⲩ ⲙ̄ⲙⲟⲟⲩ (sic; l. ⲙ̄ⲙⲁⲩ) ⲟⲩⲛⲟϭ B.
4 f. ⲙ̄ⲙⲁⲩ A; om. B. 5 f. ⲁⲩⲱ ⲛ̄ⲧⲟⲩ ⲡⲉ ⲛⲉⲩⲩⲱⲡ A; ⲁⲩⲱ ⲡⲉⲩⲣⲁⲛ ⲡⲉ ⲡⲁⲩⲗⲟⲥ,
ⲁⲩⲱ ⲛⲉⲩⲩⲱⲡ B. 9–11. ⲡⲣⲁⲛ — ⲡⲁⲩⲗⲟⲥ A; om. B (sec above). 13 f. ϩⲏⲧϥ̄ A;
ⲛ̄ϩ̄ⲍ̄ B. 15 f. ⲉϥⲉⲓⲣⲉ — ⲙ̄ⲙⲛ̄ⲧⲛⲁ A; ⲉϥⲉⲓ̄ⲙ: B 17–19. ⲁⲩⲱ—ⲉⲛⲉⲟⲩ A; ⲁⲩⲱ
ⲛⲉϥⲟ B. 21 f. ⲡⲉ ⲛⲉⲩϥⲓ ⲡⲥⲓⲡⲡⲟⲛ (sic) A; ⲡⲉⲧⲩⲱⲡ ⲙ̄ⲡⲥ B. 25. ⲛⲟⲩⲛⲟϭ ⲛ̄-
ⲥⲱⲩⲉ A; ⲛ̄ϩⲁϩ ⲛ̄ⲥⲱ[ⲩⲉ B. 52 Ri 10–19. ⲁⲩⲱ — ⲙ̄ⲡⲛⲟⲩⲧⲉ A; om. B. 20.
ϩⲣⲁⲓ̈ A; om. B. 24 f. ⲁⲩⲃⲱⲕ ⲛⲁⲩ A; ⲁⲩⲉⲓ B. 27. ϯⲧⲏⲣ B. 30 – ii 1. ⲁⲩ-
ⲩⲱⲛⲉ ⲁⲩⲱ A; om. B. 1. ⲁϥⲗⲟϩⲗⲉϫ̄ A; ⲁⲩϩⲁⲗϩⲉⲗ (sic) B (– ⲗⲟϩⲗ ⲉϫ̄ corr. Jernstedt). 2. ⲁⲩⲉⲓ A; om. B.   The loss indicated by Till (p. 72) as 'min-
destens 8 Zeilen' in fact amounts to many pages.

ⲗⲟⲥ ⲉϥϫⲓ ⲛⲁⲛ· ϫⲉ ⲁⲙⲟⲩ ⲛⲧⲁ'ⲛⲁⲩ ⲉⲣⲟⲕ ⲙⲡⲁ'ϯⲙⲟⲩ. ⲧⲉⲛⲟⲩ ⲇⲉ[15] ⲧⲁⲥⲱⲛⲉ[20]
ⲁⲣⲓ ⲡⲁ'ⲙⲉⲉⲩⲉ ϩⲁ ⲛⲟⲩ'ⲩⲗⲏⲗ, ϫⲉ ⲛⲧⲉ'ⲟⲩⲁ ⲕⲓⲧⲏⲥ ⲛϭ'ϩⲓⲙⲉ. ⲡⲉϫⲁⲥ'ⲛⲁⲩ ϫⲉ
ⲡⲁⲥⲟⲛ, 'ϯⲥⲟⲟⲩⲛ ϫⲉ ⲉⲕ'ϣⲁⲛⲃⲱⲕ ⲉⲃⲟⲗ ϩⲓⲧⲟⲟⲧ ⲧⲁ'ⲧⲙⲉⲓ ⲛⲙⲙⲁⲕ,' ⲛ̄ϯⲛⲁⲉⲩ[25]
ϭⲙϭⲟⲙ' ⲁⲛ ⲉϭⲱ ⲉⲧⲃⲏⲏⲧⲕ' ⲉⲓⲙⲉⲉⲩⲉ ⲉⲃⲟⲗ ⲉ'ⲣⲟⲕ. ϩⲱⲗⲟⲥ ⲣⲱ' ⲉⲓϣⲁⲛⲣⲟⲩϩⲏⲃ[30]
ⲇⲱⲙⲁⲥ ⲙⲡⲉⲓ'ⲛⲁⲩ ⲉⲣⲟⲕ, ϣⲁⲓ'ⲑⲗⲓⲃⲉ ⲉⲙⲁⲧⲉ, (52 Vii) ⲁⲩⲱ ϣⲁⲓ ⲧⲛ̄ⲛⲟⲟⲩ' ⲛ̄-
ⲁⲡⲟⲗⲗⲱⲛⲓⲟⲥ' ⲡⲁϣⲏⲣⲉ ⲛⲁⲕ ⲉ'ⲡⲟⲩⲥⲓⲣⲉ ⲛ̄ϩⲁⲡⲉⲕ'ⲟⲩⲱ ⲛⲁⲓ. ⲉⲕϣⲁ(ⲛ)'ⲃⲱⲕ ⲉ-[5]
ⲡⲉⲓⲙⲁ ⲉⲧⲟⲩⲏⲩ ⲧⲁⲧⲙ̄ⲥⲱⲧⲙ̄' ⲉⲡⲉⲕⲟⲩⲱ, ϯⲛⲁ'ⲙⲟⲩ ⲉⲧⲃⲏⲏⲧⲕ.' ⲕⲥⲟⲟⲩⲛ ϩⲱⲱⲕ'[10]
ⲱ ⲡⲁⲥⲟⲛ ϫⲉ' ⲙⲛ̄ⲧⲁⲓ ⲥⲟⲛ ⲟⲩ'ⲇⲉ ⲥⲱⲛⲉ ϩⲓⲃⲙ̄'ⲡⲕⲁϩ ⲛ̄ⲥⲁ ⲃⲏⲗ ⲗⲁⲕ. ⲛ̄ⲧⲟⲩ ⲇⲉ'[15]
ⲡⲉϫⲁⲩ ⲛⲁⲥ ϫⲉ ⲙ̄'ⲡⲉⲣⲕⲟⲩⲓ ⲛ̄ϩⲏⲧ' ⲱ ⲧⲁⲥⲱⲛⲉ· ⲁⲗⲗⲁ ϯⲛⲁⲃⲱⲕ ⲧⲁ'ⲧⲉⲧ ⲡⲉⲩ-[20]
ϩⲏⲧ,' ϫⲉ ⲡⲁϣ[B]ⲏⲣ ⲡⲉ·' ⲁⲩⲱ ⲉϣⲱⲡⲉ' ⲡⲟⲩⲱϣ ⲙ̄ⲡⲛⲟⲩ'ⲧⲉ ⲡⲉ, ⲧⲛⲏⲩ ϣⲁ'ⲣⲟ[25]
ϩⲛ̄ⲟⲩⲉⲓⲣⲏⲛⲏ' ⲑⲉⲕⲗⲁ ⲇⲉ ⲉⲛⲉⲥ'ⲙⲉ ⲙ̄ⲙⲟⲩ ⲉⲙⲁⲧⲉ. ⲡⲉϫⲁⲥ ⲛⲁⲩ' ϫⲉ ⲉϣⲱⲡⲉ ⲧⲁⲓ[30] ⲛ̄ⲧⲟⲟⲩⲛ ⲧⲉ ⲑⲉ,' ⲃⲱⲕ ϩⲛ̄ⲟⲩⲉⲓⲣⲏ(53 Ri)ⲛⲏ, ⲛ̄ϥⲉⲓ ⲟⲛ ϩⲛ̄'ⲟⲩⲉⲓⲣⲏⲛⲏ ⲛ̄ⲧⲁ'ⲛⲁⲩ ⲉⲣⲟⲕ ⲙⲡⲁϯ'ⲙⲟⲩ. ⲁⲩⲱ ⲙ̄ⲡⲉⲕ'ⲟⲩϣⲁⲓ ⲡⲁⲥⲟⲛ· ϯⲥⲟⲟⲩⲛ ⲅⲁⲣ ϫⲉ ⲕ-[5]
ⲛⲁⲃⲱⲕ ⲉϩⲟⲩⲛ ⲉ'ⲡⲉⲩⲧⲉⲕⲟ ⲛ̄ⲣⲁ'ⲕⲟⲧⲉ ⲉⲣⲁⲧⲟⲩ' ⲛ̄ⲛⲉⲧⲟⲩⲁⲁⲃ·' ⲁⲣⲓ ⲧⲁⲅⲁⲡⲏ[10]
ⲁⲣⲓ'ⲡⲁⲙⲉⲉⲩⲉ ⲙⲛ̄'ⲡⲁⲕⲟⲩⲓ ⲛ̄ϣⲏⲣⲉ,' ⲁⲣⲏⲩ ⲛ̄ⲧⲉⲡⲛⲟⲩ'ⲧⲉ ⲟⲡⲧ ϩⲱ ⲉ'ⲡⲉⲩⲁⲣⲓ-[15]
ⲑⲙⲟⲥ.' ⲁϥⲟⲩⲱϣⲃ̄ ⲛ̄ϭⲓ' ⲡⲁⲏⲥⲉ ϫⲉ ϥ̄ⲟⲛϩ̄' ⲛ̄ϭⲓ ⲡϫⲟⲉⲓⲥ ⲧⲁ'ⲥⲱⲛⲉ ϫⲉ ϯⲛⲁ-[20]
ϯ'ⲣⲉⲩⲥⲙⲟⲩ ⲉⲣⲟ ⲛ̄'ϣⲟⲣⲡ̄ ⲉⲣⲟⲓ. ⲁⲩⲱ'ⲁⲥⲑⲛⲟⲩ ⲉⲃⲟⲗ' ⲉⲥⲧⲡ ⲉⲣⲟⲩ.' ⲡⲁⲏⲥⲉ ⲇⲉ[25]
ⲁⲩ'ⲃⲱⲕ ⲉϩⲟⲩⲛ ⲉ'ⲡⲉⲩⲧⲉⲕⲟ ⲛⲁⲛ'ϯⲧⲛⲟⲟⲩ ⲉⲡⲙⲁ'ⲉⲧⲉⲣⲉⲛⲉⲧⲟⲩⲁ'ⲁⲃ ⲛ̄ϩⲏⲧϥ. ⲁⲩ[30]
ⲉ'ⲙⲟⲩ ⲉⲣⲟⲩ ⲉⲩϫⲱ' ⲙⲙⲟⲥ ϫⲉ ⲃⲱⲕ (R ii) ϩⲛ̄ⲟⲩⲉⲓⲣⲏⲛⲏ ⲡⲉ(ⲛ)ⲥⲟⲛ ⲙ̄ⲙⲉⲣⲓⲧ.'
ⲡⲉϫⲉ ⲟⲩⲁ ⲛⲁⲩ ⲉ'ⲃⲟⲗ ϩⲛ̄ⲛⲉⲧⲟⲩ'ⲁⲁⲃ ϫⲉ ⲡⲁⲥⲟⲛ' ⲡⲁⲏⲥⲉ, ⲛ̄ϣⲁⲛ'ⲃⲱⲕ ⲛ̄ϣⲟⲣⲡ̄[5]
ⲉ'ⲣⲟⲕ, ⲧⲛ̄ⲛⲁⲉⲓ' ϣⲁⲣⲟⲕ· ⲉⲕ'ϣⲁⲛⲃⲱⲕ ⲛ̄ϣⲟ'ⲣⲡ̄ ⲉⲣⲟⲛ, ⲁⲙⲟⲩ' ϣⲁⲣⲟⲛ ϩⲱⲱⲛ'[10]
ⲧⲛ̄ⲩⲓⲛⲉ ⲉⲣⲟⲕ.' ⲙ̄ⲙⲟⲛ ⲛ̄ⲧⲛ̄ⲛⲁⲕ'ⲧⲟⲛ ⲁⲛ ⲉⲛⲁⲩ ⲉ'ⲛⲉⲛⲉⲣⲏⲩ ϩⲛ̄ⲧ'ⲥⲁⲣⲝ ϣⲁⲛⲧⲉⲛ'[15]
ⲃⲱⲕ ⲉⲑⲓⲗⲏⲙ̄' ⲛ̄ⲧⲡⲉ. ⲡⲁⲏⲥⲉ'ⲇⲉ[20] ⲙ̄ⲡⲉϥⲉⲓⲙⲉ ⲉⲡ'ϣⲁϫⲉ ⲛ̄ⲧⲁⲩϫⲟ'ⲟⲩ ⲛⲁⲩ ⲁⲩⲱ
ⲛ̄'ⲧⲉⲓϩⲉ ⲁϥⲉⲓ ⲉⲃⲟⲗ' ⲛ̄ϭⲓ ⲡⲁⲏⲥⲉ,' ⲁⲩⲱ ⲛ̄ⲧⲉⲣⲉϥⲉⲓ' ⲉⲃⲟⲗ ⲁϥⲁⲗⲉ ⲉⲡ'ϫⲟⲓ, ⲁⲩ-[25]
ⲥϩⲏⲣ ⲉϩⲣⲏⲧ ϣⲁⲛⲧⲉϥⲉⲓ'ⲉⲣⲁ ⲕⲟⲧⲉ. ⲛ̄ϩⲱ'ⲥⲟⲛ ⲇⲉ ⲉⲩϩⲛ̄ⲧⲉ'ⲍⲓⲏ, ⲁⲡⲛⲟⲩⲧⲉ' ϯ-[30]
ⲡⲟⲩ ϫⲁⲓ ⲙ̄ⲡⲁⲩ(Vi)ⲗⲟⲥ ⲉⲡⲓⲇⲏ ⲅⲁⲣ' ⲛ̄ⲧⲁ ⲡⲉⲓ ϩⲱⲃ' ϣⲱⲡⲉ ⲉⲃⲟⲗ ϩⲓ ϯⲡⲛⲟⲩⲧⲉ'[5]
ϫⲉ ⲉⲩⲉⲥⲉⲣ ⲡⲥⲱ'ⲙⲁ ⲛ̄ⲛⲉⲧⲟⲩⲁⲁⲃ' ⲛ̄ⲥⲁ ⲃⲟⲗ ⲙ̄ⲡⲉⲩ'ⲏⲓ· ⲁⲩⲱ ⲛ̄ⲧⲉ'ⲣⲉϥⲉⲓ ⲉϩⲟⲩⲛ
ⲉⲣⲁ'ⲕⲟⲧⲉ ⲙⲛ̄ⲛϩ̄ϩⲁⲗ ⲙ̄ⲡⲁⲩⲗⲟⲥ,' ⲁⲩⲃⲱⲕ ⲉϩⲟⲩⲛ' ⲉⲡ ⲏ ⲓ, ⲁⲩϭⲉ ⲉⲣⲟⲩ' ⲉⲁⲩ-[10]
ⲟⲩϫⲁⲓ ϩⲙ̄'ⲡⲉⲩϣⲱⲛⲉ· ⲁ'ⲡⲉⲩϩⲏⲧ ⲙ̄ⲧⲟⲛ' ⲉⲣⲟⲩ, ⲁⲩⲱ ⲁⲩ'ⲁⲥⲡⲁⲍⲉ ⲛ̄ⲛⲉⲩⲉⲣⲏⲩ'[15]
ⲛ̄ⲧⲟⲩ ⲙⲛ̄ⲛⲉⲩϩ̄'ϩⲁⲗ· ⲁⲩⲱ ⲡⲉϫⲁⲩ' ⲛⲁⲩ[20] ϫⲉ ⲉⲛⲉ ϥⲟⲩ'ⲟϣ ⲛ̄ϭⲓ ⲡⲁⲩ'ⲃⲏⲣ ⲡⲁⲏⲥⲉ

---

52 V i 28 = ϩⲟⲗⲟⲥ. ii 21. λ (or possibly Δ) altered to B.

ⲙⲛ̄ⲑⲉⲕⲗⲁ ⲧⲉⲩⲥⲱⲛⲉ ⲙ̄ⲙⲁⲓⲛⲟⲩⲧⲉ; ⲛ̄ⲧⲟⲟⲩ ⲇⲉ ⲡⲉϫⲁⲩ ϫⲉ ⲉⲓⲥ ⲡⲁⲏⲥⲉ ⲙ̄ⲡⲃⲟⲗ
ⲙ̄ⲡⲣⲟ. ⲁϥⲟⲩⲱⲛⲧ ⲉⲛⲉϥ ⲍ̄ⲍ̄ⲁⲗ, ⲁϥⲧⲱⲟⲩⲛ, ⲁϥⲉⲓ ⲉⲃⲟⲗ, ⲁϥⲡⲁϩⲧϥ̄ ϩⲓϫⲙ̄ (53
Vii) ⲡⲕⲁϩ, ⲁϥⲟⲩⲱϣⲧ ⲛⲁⲩ ⲉⲝ̄ⲙ̄ⲡⲉϥϩⲟ. ⲡⲁⲏⲥⲉ ⲇⲉ ⲁϥⲕⲁϩ ⲛ̄ϩⲏⲧ ⲉⲙⲁⲧⲉ
ⲁⲩⲱ ⲁϥⲡⲁϩⲧⲟⲩ ⲉ ϫⲙ̄ⲡⲙⲁⲕϩ̄ ⲛ̄ⲛⲉϥⲉⲣⲏⲩ, ⲁϥⲣⲓⲙⲉ ⲛⲟⲩⲛⲟϭ ⲛ̄ⲛⲁⲩ. ⲡⲉϫⲉⲡⲁⲩⲗⲟⲥ
ⲙ̄ⲡⲁⲏⲥⲉ ϫⲉ ⲁⲙⲟⲩ ⲉϩⲟⲩⲛ· ⲉⲧⲃⲉⲟⲩ ⲕⲁϩⲉⲣⲁⲧⲕ̄ ϩⲓⲡ̄ⲥⲁ ⲛ̄ⲃⲟⲗ; ⲁⲙⲟⲩ ⲉϩⲟⲩⲛ,
ⲡⲣⲱⲙⲉ ⲛ̄ϣⲟⲩⲁⲩϥ ϩⲓⲧⲙ̄ ⲡⲛⲟⲩⲧⲉ ⲙⲛ̄ⲛ̄ⲣⲱⲙⲉ. ⲡⲁⲏⲥⲉ ⲇⲉ ⲡⲉϫⲁⲩ ϫⲉ ⲁⲗⲏⲑⲱⲥ
ⲡⲁⲥⲟⲛ ⲁⲓⲣⲁⲩϥⲉ ⲛ̄ⲧⲁⲓⲍⲉ ⲉⲣⲟⲕ ⲉⲕⲟⲩⲟⲕ. ⲡⲉϫⲉⲡⲁⲩⲗⲟⲥ ⲛⲁⲩ ϫⲉ ⲛ̄ⲧⲁⲡⲛⲟⲩⲧⲉ ϯ
ⲛⲁⲓ ⲛⲟⲩⲕⲟⲩⲓ ⲛ̄ⲥⲃⲱ ⲉⲧⲃⲉⲛⲁⲛⲟⲃⲉ. ϯⲩⲡⲟⲙⲟⲛⲧ ⲛ̄ⲧⲉⲡⲛⲟⲩⲧⲉ ⲙⲛ̄ⲛⲉⲩϣⲗⲏⲗ ⲛ̄ⲛⲉ
ⲧⲟⲩⲁⲁⲃ ⲛ̄ⲧⲁⲩϯϭⲟⲙ ⲛⲁⲓ, ⲁϥⲧⲁⲗϭⲟⲓ. ⲁⲩⲱ ⲁϥϫⲓⲧϥ̄ ⲉϩⲟⲩⲛ ⲉⲡⲉϥ (54 Ri) ⲏⲓ,
ⲁϥⲣⲁⲩϥⲉ ⲛⲙ̄ⲙⲁⲩ, ⲁⲩⲟⲩⲱⲙ ⲁⲩⲥⲱ ⲙⲛ̄ⲛⲉⲩⲉⲣⲏⲩ. ⲙ̄ⲡⲉϥⲣⲁⲥⲧⲉ ⲇⲉ ⲁϥⲉⲓ ⲉ
ⲃⲟⲗ ϩⲛ̄ⲧⲡⲟⲗⲓⲥ ⲛ̄ϭⲓ ⲡⲁⲏⲥⲉ ⲙⲛ̄ⲡⲉϥϩ̄ⲙ̄ϩⲁⲗ, ⲁⲩⲱ ⲁϥⲃⲱⲕ ⲉϩⲟⲩ(ⲛ) ⲉⲡⲉⲩⲧⲉ
ⲕⲟ, ⲁϥ ϭⲓⲛⲉ ⲛ̄ⲥⲁⲛⲉⲧⲟⲩⲁⲁⲃ. ⲁⲩⲱ ⲡⲉϫⲉⲟⲩⲁ ⲛⲁⲩ ϩⲛ̄ⲛⲉⲧⲟⲩⲁⲁⲃ ϫⲉ ⲭⲁⲓ
ⲣⲉ ⲡⲁⲏⲥⲉ ⲡⲣⲱⲙⲉ ⲙ̄ⲡⲛⲟⲩⲧⲉ ⲙⲛ̄ ⲧⲙⲁⲕⲁⲣⲓⲁ ⲑⲉⲕⲗⲁ ⲧⲉⲕⲥⲱⲛⲉ ⲙ̄ⲙⲁⲓ
ⲛⲟⲩⲧⲉ ⲙⲛ̄ⲁⲡⲟⲗⲗⲱⲛⲓⲟⲥ ⲡⲉⲥⲕⲟⲩⲓ ⲛ̄ϣⲏⲣⲉ, ⲕⲁⲧⲁⲡⲁⲛⲁⲩ ⲛ̄ⲧⲁⲕⲱⲣⲕ̄ ⲙ̄ⲙⲟϥ
ⲛⲁⲥ ⲉⲕⲛⲏⲩ ⲉⲃⲟⲗ ϩⲓⲧⲟⲟⲧϥ̄ ϫⲉ ϯⲛⲁⲣⲡⲟⲩⲙⲉⲉⲩⲉ ⲁⲩⲱ ϫⲉ ϯⲛⲁⲧⲣⲉⲩⲥⲙⲟⲩ
ⲉⲣⲟ ⲛ̄ϣⲟⲣⲡ̄ ⲉⲣⲟⲓ. ⲉⲣⲉⲡϫⲟⲉⲓⲥ ⲣ̄ⲡⲉⲥⲙⲉⲉⲩⲉ ⲛϥ̄ⲥⲙⲟⲩ ⲉⲣⲟⲥ ⲙⲛ̄ⲡⲉⲥⲕⲟⲩⲓ ⲛ̄
ϣⲏⲣⲉ, (Rii) ⲁⲩⲱ ⲛϥ̄ⲉⲡⲧⲏⲩ ⲧⲛ̄ ⲉⲡⲁⲣⲓⲑⲙⲟⲥ ⲛ̄ⲛⲉⲧⲟⲩⲁⲁⲃ. ⲁⲥϣⲱⲡⲉ ⲇⲉ ⲛ̄
ⲧⲉ ⲣⲉϥⲥⲱⲧⲙ̄ ⲉⲛⲉⲓ ϣⲁϫⲉ, ⲁϥⲣ̄ ⲡ̄ϣⲡⲏⲣⲉ ⲉⲙⲁⲧⲉ ⲉ ϫⲙ̄ⲛⲉⲛⲧⲁϥⲥⲱⲧⲙ̄ ⲉⲣⲟⲟⲩ ⲛ̄
ⲧⲟ̄ⲟⲧⲟⲩ ⲛ̄ⲛⲉⲧⲟⲩⲁⲁⲃ ⲙ̄ⲙⲁⲣⲧⲩⲣⲟⲥ. ⲡⲉϫⲉ ⲡⲁⲏⲥⲉ ⲙ̄ⲡⲉⲧϣⲁϫⲉ ⲛⲙ̄ⲙⲁⲩ ϫⲉ
ⲉⲕⲥⲟⲟⲩⲛ ⲙ̄ⲙⲟⲓ ⲧⲱⲛ ⲡⲁⲉⲓⲱⲧ ⲉⲧⲟⲩⲁⲁⲃ; ⲡⲉϫⲁⲩ ⲛⲁⲩ ϫⲉ ϫⲓⲛⲧⲓⲟⲩⲛⲏ ⲛ̄
ⲧⲁⲓⲧⲱⲟⲩⲛ ⲉⲓⲉⲓⲣⲉ ⲛ̄ⲛⲁⲥⲩⲛⲁⲍⲓⲥ, ⲁⲡⲁⲅⲅⲉⲗⲟⲥ ⲙ̄ⲡϫⲟⲉⲓⲥ ⲧⲁⲙⲟⲓ ϫⲉ ⲕ̄ⲛⲏⲩ
ϣⲁⲣⲟⲓ, ⲁⲩⲱ ⲁⲩⲟⲡⲕ̄ ⲉⲧⲏⲡⲉ ⲛ̄ⲛⲉⲧⲟⲩⲁⲁⲃ ⲛ̄ⲧⲟⲕ ⲙⲛ̄ⲧⲉⲕⲥⲱⲛⲉ ⲙⲛ̄ⲡⲉⲕⲕⲟⲩⲓ
ⲛ̄ϣⲏⲣⲉ ⲙ̄ⲡⲡⲁⲩⲗⲟⲥ ⲡⲣⲱⲙⲉ ⲉⲧⲉⲕⲥⲁⲗⲱⲟⲩ ⲉⲣⲟⲩ. ⲁϥⲉⲓ (Vi) ⲉⲃⲟⲗ ϩⲓⲧⲟⲟⲧϥ̄
ⲙ̄ⲡⲉϥϩ̄ⲙ̄ϩⲁⲗ, ⲁϥⲡⲁϩⲧϥ̄ ⲇⲉ ⲛ̄ⲛⲉⲧⲟⲩⲁⲁⲃ, ⲁⲩⲥⲙⲟⲩ ⲉⲣⲟϥ, ⲁϥⲉⲓ ⲉⲃⲟⲗ ϩⲓ
ⲧⲟⲟⲧⲟⲩ ⲛ̄ⲧⲟϥ ⲙⲛ̄ⲡⲉϥϩ̄ⲙ̄ϩⲁⲗ ⲉⲩⲣ̄ϣⲡⲏⲣⲉ ⲉϩⲙ̄ⲡϣⲁϫⲉ ⲛ̄ⲧⲁⲡⲡⲉ ⲧⲟⲩⲁⲁⲃ
ϫⲟⲟⲩ ⲛⲁⲩ. ⲁⲩⲱ ⲁⲩⲃⲱⲕ ⲉϩⲟⲩⲛ ⲉⲡⲏⲓ ⲙ̄ⲡⲁⲩⲗⲟⲥ, ⲡⲉϫⲁⲩ ⲛⲁⲩ ϫⲉ ⲉⲓⲟⲩⲱϣ
ⲡⲁⲥⲟⲛ ⲉⲧⲣⲉⲕⲣ̄ ⲡⲉⲓⲕⲟⲩⲓ ⲛ̄ϩⲱⲃ ⲛⲙ̄ⲙⲁⲓ. ⲡⲉϫⲉⲡⲁⲩⲗⲟⲥ ⲛⲁⲩ ϫⲉ ⲡⲉⲧⲉⲕ
ⲟⲩⲁϣϥ̄ ⲁϫⲓϥ ⲉⲣⲟⲓ, ⲁⲩⲱ ⲁⲛⲟⲕ ϯⲛⲁⲁⲁⲩ ⲛⲙ̄ⲙⲁⲕ. ⲡⲉϫⲉⲡⲁⲏⲥⲉ ⲛⲁⲩ ϫⲉ
ⲟⲩⲱϣ ⲉⲧⲣⲉⲛⲉⲕϩ̄ⲙ̄ϩⲁⲗ ⲙⲟⲟϣⲉ ⲛⲙ̄ⲙⲁⲓ, ϫⲉ ⲁⲛⲟⲩ ⲅⲩⲙⲙⲟ ϩⲛ̄ⲧⲉⲓⲡⲟⲗⲓⲥ,
ϫⲉ ⲕⲁⲥ ⲉⲓⲉ ϣⲱⲡ ⲛⲟⲩ ⲩ ϩⲙ ⲛ̄ⲏⲣⲡ̄ ⲙ̄ⲛ̄ⲥⲉⲛ ⲕⲟⲩⲓ ⲛ̄ⲛ̄ⲕⲁ ⲛⲟⲩⲱⲙ, ⲛ̄ⲥⲉ (Vii)

53 Vii 20 ⲛ̄ⲧⲁⲓⲍⲉ: instead of correct Sahidic ⲛ̄ⲧⲉⲣⲉⲓⲍⲉ; cf. Till, _Koptische Dialekt grammatik_, ed. 2, p. 57.   54 Vi 11. l. ϫⲟⲟⲩ   25. l. ⲉⲓⲟⲩⲱⲛ

παстоγ ναϊ ταϳαλοογ εροογ ⲛⲥⲉⲉⲓ ⲛⲙⲙⲁⲓ ⲉⲡⲉⲩⲧⲉⲕⲟ ϫⲉ ⲉⲓⲉⲟⲩⲱⲙ ⲙⲛ
ⲛⲉⲧⲟⲩⲁⲁⲃ ⲙⲡⲁϥⲉⲓ ⲉⲣⲏⲥ ⲉⲡⲁⲏⲓ. ⲡⲁⲩⲗⲟⲥ ⲇⲉ ⲁϥⲣⲁϣⲉ ⲉⲙⲁⲧⲉ ⲛⲧⲉⲣⲉϥⲥⲱⲧⲙ
ⲉⲛⲁⲓ· ⲁϥⲟⲩⲉⲥⲥⲁϩⲛⲉ ⲛⲛⲉϥϩⲙϩⲁⲗ, ⲁⲩⲃⲱⲕ ⲛⲧⲉⲩⲛⲟⲩ, ⲁⲩϣⲱⲡ ⲛϩⲱⲃ ⲛⲓⲙ
ⲛⲧⲁϥⲟⲩⲉⲥⲥⲁϩⲛⲉ ⲙⲙⲟⲟⲩ ⲛⲁⲩ. ⲁⲩⲱ ⲡⲁⲛⲥⲉ ⲁϥϣⲱⲡ ⲛⲟⲩⲛⲟϭ ⲛⲁⲛϫⲟⲗⲟⲕⲙⲁ
ⲛⲟⲉⲓⲕ ϩⲓ ⲏⲣⲡ ϩⲓ ⲛⲉϩ ⲩⲁϩⲣⲁⲓ ⲉⲛⲕⲉⲩⲉ ⲛⲥⲁϣⲧⲉ ⲛⲧⲟⲩ ⲁⲩϣⲟⲗⲟⲩ. ⲁⲩⲱ ⲛⲧⲉ
ⲣⲉⲛ ϩⲙϩⲁⲗ ⲙⲡⲁⲩⲗⲟⲥ ⲡⲓⲥⲉ ⲛⲛϭⲓ ⲛⲟⲩⲱⲙ, ⲁⲩⲧⲁⲗⲟⲟⲩ ⲉϫⲱⲟⲩ, ⲁⲩϫⲓⲧⲟⲩ ⲉ
ϩⲟⲩⲛ ⲉⲛⲉⲩ ⲧⲉⲕⲱⲟⲩ ⲙⲡⲉ ϩⲟⲟⲩ ⲉⲧⲙⲙⲁⲩ, ⲁⲩⲱ ⲁⲩⲡⲁⲣⲁⲕⲁⲗⲉⲓ ⲛⲛⲉⲧⲟⲩⲁⲁⲃ ⲉ
ⲧⲣⲉⲩⲟⲩⲱⲙ ⲉ(55 Ri)ⲃⲟⲗ ϩⲛ ⲛⲉⲩⲥⲓⲝ. ⲁⲩⲱ ⲡⲁⲛⲥⲉ ⲛⲉⲩ ⲙⲏⲣ ⲉϩⲛⲧⲉⲩⲧⲡⲉ ⲉϥ
ⲇⲓⲁⲕⲟⲛⲓ ⲉⲛⲉⲧⲟⲩⲁⲁⲃ. ⲙⲡⲉϥⲣⲁⲥⲧⲉ ⲟⲛ ⲁⲩⲃⲱⲕ ⲉϩⲟⲩⲛ ⲉⲕⲉⲟⲩⲁ ⲛⲛⲉⲩⲧⲉ
ⲕⲱⲟⲩ, ⲁⲩⲧⲁⲙⲟ(ⲛ) ⲉⲛⲉⲧⲟⲩⲁⲁⲃ ⲉⲧⲟⲧⲡ ⲉϩⲟⲩⲛ, ⲁⲩⲱ ⲁⲩⲧⲥⲟⲟⲩ. ⲁⲩⲱ ⲙⲛ ⲛ
ⲥⲁⲡϫⲱⲕ ⲙⲙⲛⲧⲏ ⲛϩⲟⲟⲩ ⲉϥϣⲟⲟⲡ ϩⲛ ⲣⲁⲕⲟⲧⲉ ⲉϥϭⲓⲛⲉ ⲙⲛ ⲩⲓⲛⲉ ⲛⲛⲉⲧⲩ ⲱⲛⲉ
ⲙⲛ ⲛⲉⲧⲟⲩⲁⲁⲃ ⲙⲙⲏⲛⲉ, ⲁⲩⲱ ⲡⲉϫⲁⲩ ⲙ ⲡⲁⲩⲗⲟⲥ ϫⲉ ⲕⲁⲁⲧ ⲉⲃⲟⲗ ⲧⲁⲃⲱⲕ ⲛⲁⲓ
ⲉⲙⲁⲣⲏⲥ. ⲙⲙⲟⲛ ⲕⲥⲟⲟⲩⲛ ϫⲉ ⲡⲕⲁⲓⲣⲟⲥ ⲡⲉ ⲛⲣ ϩⲱⲃ ⲉⲧⲥⲱⲩⲉ. ⲁⲩⲱ ϯⲟⲩⲱⲛ
ϫⲉ ⲧⲁⲥⲱⲛⲉ ⲩⲧⲣ ⲧⲱⲣ ⲉⲧⲃⲏⲏⲧ. ⲡⲉϫⲉ ⲡⲁⲩⲗⲟⲥ ⲛⲁⲩ ϫⲉ ⲁⲛⲟⲕ ϯⲛⲏⲩ ⲛⲙⲙⲁⲕ·
ⲉⲧⲃⲉ ⲟⲩ [ⲕ](Rⁱⁱ)ⲩⲧⲉⲣⲧⲱⲣ ⲛⲧⲉⲓ ϩⲉ ⲁⲩⲱ ⲕⲟ ⲛⲕⲟⲩⲓ ⲛϩⲏⲧ; ⲁⲗⲗⲁ ϩⲙⲟⲟⲥ ⲛⲁⲕ
ⲛⲧⲉⲓ ϩⲉⲃⲇⲱ ⲙⲁⲥ. ⲁⲩⲱ ⲩⲁ(ⲛ) ⲃⲱⲕ ⲛⲁⲛ ⲙⲛ ⲛⲉⲛⲉⲣⲏⲩ· ⲉⲧⲃⲉ ⲟⲩ ⲉⲕⲛⲁⲃⲱⲕ ⲛⲅ
ⲕⲁⲁⲧ; ⲁⲩⲱ ⲡⲁⲩⲗⲟⲥ ϩⲱⲱϥ ⲟⲛ ⲁϥⲣϩⲟⲟⲩ· ⲥⲛⲁⲩ ⲉⲛⲉⲧⲟⲩⲁⲁⲃ ϩⲙⲡⲉⲩⲧⲉⲕⲟ
ⲉⲣⲉⲡⲁⲛⲥⲉ ⲃⲏⲕ ⲛⲙⲙⲁⲩ ⲙⲛ ⲛⲉϥϩⲙϩⲁⲗ ⲉϥ ⲇⲓⲁⲕⲟⲛⲉⲓ ⲛⲁⲩ, ⲉⲃⲟⲗ ⲇⲉ ⲛⲉⲣⲉ
ⲡⲁⲩⲗⲟⲥ ⲣϩⲟⲧⲉ ⲉⲃⲱⲕ ⲉⲡⲉⲩⲧⲉⲕⲟ, ϫⲉ ⲛⲛⲉⲩ ϫⲟⲟⲥ ⲉⲛⲇⲟⲩⲝ ⲉⲧⲃⲏ ⲛⲧⲩ ⲛϥ
ⲁⲙⲁϩⲧⲉ ⲙⲙⲟⲩ ⲛϥ ⲑⲩⲥⲓⲁⲍⲉ. ⲙⲛⲥⲁ ⲛⲁⲓ ⲇⲉ ϩⲣⲁⲓ ϩⲛ ϩⲟⲟⲩ ϫⲟⲩⲱⲧ ⲙ ⲡⲁⲣ
ⲙⲟⲩⲧⲉ ⲁⲡⲣⲣⲟ ⲇⲓⲱⲕⲗⲏⲧⲓⲁⲛⲟⲥ ⲉϫⲱⲣⲓⲍⲉ ϩⲟⲣ(Vⁱ)ⲩⲏⲣⲉ ⲩⲏⲙ ⲉⲡⲉⲩⲣⲁⲛ
ⲡⲉ ⲃⲓⲕⲧⲱⲣ, ⲉⲛⲩⲣⲉ ⲡⲉ ⲛⲟⲩⲛⲟϭ ⲛⲥⲧⲣⲁⲧⲏⲗⲁⲧⲏⲥ ⲛⲧⲉ ⲡ ⲣⲣⲟ· ⲁⲩⲛⲧϥ ⲉ
ϩⲟⲩⲛ ⲉⲣⲁⲕⲟⲧⲉ ⲉϥⲥⲟⲛϩ ϩⲛ ϩⲉⲛ ϩⲁⲗⲏⲥⲓⲥ ⲙⲡⲉⲛⲓ ⲡⲉ ⲉⲛⲉⲩϭⲓϫ ⲙⲛ ⲛⲉⲩⲟⲩⲉ ⲣⲏ
ⲧⲉ, ⲁⲩⲱ ⲛⲉⲣⲉⲟⲩⲭⲁ ⲙⲟⲥ ϩⲛ ⲣⲱⲩ. ⲁⲡ ⲃⲉⲣⲉⲧⲁⲣⲓⲟⲥ ϯ ⲛⲛⲉϥϫⲁⲓ ⲙⲡ ⲇⲟⲩⲝ. ⲁⲩ
ⲧⲣⲉⲩ ⲟⲩ ϫⲟⲩ ⲉⲧⲡⲟⲗⲓⲥ ⲧⲏⲣⲥ, ⲁⲩⲕⲉⲗⲉⲩⲥⲉ ⲉⲧⲣⲉⲩ ⲭⲓⲧϥ ⲉⲡⲉⲩⲧⲉⲕⲟ. ⲛⲁⲧⲡⲟⲗⲓⲥ
ⲇⲉ ⲁⲩⲣⲩⲡⲏⲣⲉ ⲉⲩ ϫⲱ ⲙⲙⲟⲥ ϫⲉ ⲉⲩϭⲉ ⲙⲡⲉⲩ ϯⲥⲁ ⲉⲛⲩⲏⲣⲉ ⲙⲡ ⲛⲟϭ ⲛ
ⲥⲧⲣⲁⲧ ⲏⲗⲁⲧⲏⲥ ⲛⲧⲉⲩ ⲙⲏⲧⲉⲣⲟ, ⲉⲓⲉ ϭⲛⲁⲧⲥⲁ ⲉⲛⲉ ϩⲏⲕⲉ ⲛ ⲛⲡⲟⲗⲓⲕ, ⲁⲩⲱ ⲁⲡ
ⲙⲏⲏⲩⲉ ⲧⲏ ⲣϥ ⲛⲧⲡⲟⲗⲓⲥ (Vⁱⁱ) ⲩⲧⲟⲣⲧⲣ ⲉⲧⲃⲉⲡ ⲩⲏⲣⲉ ⲩⲏⲙ ⲉⲧⲟⲩⲁⲁⲃ ⲛ ϫⲁ
ⲅⲓⲟⲥ ⲃⲓⲕⲧⲱⲣ, ⲉⲡⲓ ⲇⲏ ⲉⲛⲉⲥⲱⲩ ⲉⲙⲁ ⲧⲉ ϩⲙ ⲡⲉⲩϩⲟ, ⲁⲩⲱ ⲛⲉⲩ ⲩⲏⲣⲉ ⲛⲟⲩ ⲱⲧ

---

55 Ri 9f. l. ⲁⲩⲧⲙⲙⲟ ⲛⲛⲉⲧⲟⲩⲁⲁⲃ. 20. ⲁⲩⲱ superfluous. Ti 25f. ⲛⲅ ⲗⲁⲛⲁⲧⲕⲁ-
ⲍⲉ ⲙⲙⲟⲩ ⲑⲑⲩⲥⲓⲁⲍⲉ? 31. Surface damaged at beginning of line, which is short
in consequence. Vi9. ⲙⲡⲉⲛⲓⲡⲉ: ⲃⲉⲛⲓⲡⲉ so regularly spelt in this MS.

ⲡⲉ ⲙ̄ⲡⲉⲩϭⲉⲓⲱⲧ. ⲙ̄ⲡⲉⲩⲣⲁⲥⲧⲉ ⲇⲉ ⲁⲩϩⲙⲟⲟⲥ ⲛ̄ϭⲓ ⲡⲗⲟⲩϫ ϩⲙ̄ⲡⲉⲑⲉⲁⲇⲣⲟⲛ, ϫⲉ-

ⲕⲁⲥ ⲉⲩⲉⲥⲱⲧⲙ̄ ⲉⲡⲡⲉⲧⲟⲩⲁⲁⲃ ⲁⲡⲁ ⲃⲓⲕⲧⲱⲣ. ⲁⲩⲥⲱⲧⲙ̄ ⲛ̄ϭⲓ ⲛⲁⲧⲡⲟⲗⲓⲥ, ⲁⲩ-

ⲥⲟⲟⲩϩ ϩⲓⲟⲩⲥⲟⲡ, ⲛ̄ϩⲟⲟⲩⲧ ⲙⲛ̄ⲛⲉϩⲓⲟⲙⲉ, ⲛⲉⲣⲙ̄ⲙⲁⲟ ⲙⲛ̄ϩⲏⲕⲉ ϫⲉⲕⲁⲥ ⲉⲩⲉ-

ⲛⲁⲩ ⲉⲡϣⲏⲣⲉ ⲙ̄ⲡⲉⲥⲧⲣⲁⲧⲏⲗⲁⲧⲏⲥ. ⲁⲥϣⲱⲡⲉ ⲇⲉ ⲛ̄ⲧⲉⲣⲉⲡⲁⲏⲥⲉ ⲥⲱⲧⲙ̄ ⲉ-

ⲛⲉⲩϣⲁϫⲉ ⲉ'ⲧⲉⲣⲉⲡⲙⲏⲏⲩⲉ ϫⲱ ⲙ̄ⲙⲟⲟⲩ, ⲁⲩⲣ̄ϣⲡⲏⲣⲉ. ⲁⲩⲱ ⲉⲛⲉⲩⲙⲟⲟⲩⲛⲉ ϩⲱ-

ⲟⲩ ⲙⲛ̄ⲛⲉⲣⲱⲙⲉ ⲉⲩ (56 R i) ⲟⲣⲱⲟⲩ ⲉⲛⲁⲩ ⲉⲡϣⲏⲣⲉ ⲩⲏⲙ ⲃⲓⲕⲧⲱⲣ, ⲁⲡⲗⲟⲩϫ'

ⲇⲉ ⲟⲩⲉϩⲥⲁϩⲛⲉ ⲉⲧ'ⲛⲁⲩ ⲛ̄ϩⲉⲛⲛⲟϭ ⲛ̄ⲇⲓⲙⲱⲣⲓⲁ ⲙⲛ̄ϩⲉⲛⲃⲁⲥⲁⲛⲟⲥ. ⲁⲩⲱ ⲙ̄-

ⲡⲉⲩⲁⲓⲥⲑⲁ'ⲛⲉ ⲉⲡⲧⲏⲣϥ̄. ⲁⲩⲱ ⲛ̄ⲧⲉⲩⲛⲟⲩ ⲁⲩⲟⲩⲱⲛ ⲛ̄ϭⲓ ⲛ̄'ⲃⲁⲗ ⲙ̄ⲡϩⲁⲅⲓⲟⲥ ⲁ-

ⲡⲁ ⲡⲁⲏⲥⲉ, ⲁⲩ'ⲛⲁⲩ ⲉⲡⲁⲅⲅⲉⲗⲟⲥ ⲙ̄ⲡϫⲟⲉⲓⲥ ⲉϥⲁϩⲉⲣⲁⲧϥ̄ ⲉⲣⲟⲩ ⲉϥϯⲅⲟⲙ ⲛⲁⲩ

ϣⲁⲛ'ⲧⲉⲩⲧⲱⲟⲩⲛ ϩⲁ'ⲛⲉⲃⲁⲥⲁⲛⲟⲥ. ⲁⲩⲕⲉⲗⲉⲩⲥ ⲇⲉ ⲛ̄ϭⲓ ⲡⲗⲟⲩϫ ⲉⲧ'ⲣⲉⲩⲛⲟⲩϫⲩ ⲉ-

ⲉⲟⲩ(ⲛ)'ⲉⲡⲙⲁ ⲛ̄ⲧⲱⲕ ⲛ̄ⲧ'ⲥⲓⲟⲟⲩⲛ. ⲁⲩⲧⲱⲕ'ⲉⲝⲟⲩ ⲛ̄ϩⲉⲛⲩϫⲉ ⲛ̄ⲁϫⲟⲛ ⲙⲛ̄ϩⲉⲛ'ⲩⲉ

ⲛ̄ⲉⲗⲟⲟⲗⲉ. ⲁⲩⲱ ⲁⲩⲉⲓ ⲉⲃⲟⲗ ϩⲛ̄ⲧ'ⲡⲉ ⲛ̄ϭⲓ ⲟⲩⲁⲅⲅⲉⲗⲟⲥ ⲛ̄ⲧⲉⲡϫⲟⲉⲓⲥ, ⲁⲩⲃⲱⲗ ⲉⲃⲟⲗ

ⲛ̄ⲛ̄'ϩⲁⲗⲏⲥⲓⲥ ⲙ̄ⲡⲉⲛⲓ'ⲡⲉ ⲉⲧϩⲁⲛⲉⲩϭⲓϫ (R ii) ⲙ̄ⲛⲉⲩⲟⲩⲉⲣⲏⲧⲉ, ⲁⲩϯⲅⲟⲙ ⲛⲁⲩ.

ⲛ̄ⲧⲉⲣⲉⲩⲛⲁⲩ ⲇⲉ ⲛ̄ϭⲓ ⲡⲗⲟⲩϫ, ⲁⲩⲟⲩⲛ̄ⲧ ⲉⲙⲁⲧⲉ, ⲁⲩ'ⲕⲉⲗⲉⲩⲉ ⲉⲧⲣⲉⲩϭⲓ'ⲛ̄ⲧⲉⲩⲁⲡⲉ.

ⲁⲩⲱ'ⲁⲡⲉⲛⲁⲧⲡⲟⲗⲓⲥ'ⲕⲁⲁⲩ, ⲉⲩⲥⲱ ⲙ̄ⲙⲟⲥ ϫⲉ ⲛ̄ⲧⲛ̄ⲛⲁ'ⲕⲁⲁⲧ ⲁⲛ ⲉϩⲱⲧⲃ̄'ⲙ̄ⲡϣⲏⲣ-

ⲣⲉ ⲙ̄ⲡⲉⲥ'ⲧⲣⲁⲧⲏⲗⲁⲧⲏⲥ'ϩⲛ̄ⲧⲉⲛⲡⲟⲗⲓⲥ. ⲁⲩⲕⲉⲗⲉⲩⲉ ϫⲉⲕⲁⲥ'ⲉⲩⲉϩⲟⲣⲓⲍⲉ ⲙ̄'ⲙⲟⲩ

ⲉⲣⲏⲥ ⲉⲑⲛ̄'ⲃⲁⲉⲓⲥ. ⲡⲁⲏⲥⲉ ⲇⲉ ϩⲱⲱϥ'ⲛ̄ⲧⲉⲣⲉⲩⲛⲁⲩ ⲉ'ⲛⲓⲛⲟϭ ⲛ̄ϭⲟⲙ'ⲉⲣⲉⲡⲡⲉⲧⲟⲩ-

ⲁⲁⲃ'ⲁⲡⲁ ⲃⲓⲕⲧⲱⲣ'ⲉⲓⲣⲉ ⲙ̄ⲙⲟⲟⲩ, ⲁⲡⲉⲡ̄ⲛ̄ⲁ ⲉⲧⲟⲩ'ⲁⲁⲃ ⲉⲓ ⲉϩⲣⲁⲓ ⲉⲝⲟⲩ, ⲁⲩⲱ

ⲡⲉϫⲁⲩ ϩ'ⲣⲁⲓ ⲛ̄ϩⲏⲧϥ̄ ϫⲉ'ⲉⲓⲥϩⲏⲏⲧⲉ ⲁⲡ'ϣⲏⲣⲉ ⲙ̄ⲡⲛⲟϭ'ⲛ̄ⲥⲧⲣⲁⲧⲏⲗⲁⲧⲏⲥ'ⲙ̄ⲡⲣⲣⲟ

ⲕⲱ ⲛ̄'ⲥⲱⲩ ⲙ̄ⲡⲉⲩⲛⲟϭ (V i) ⲛ̄ⲁⲝⲓⲱⲙⲁ ⲙⲛ̄'ⲛⲉⲩϩⲩⲡⲁⲣⲭⲟⲛ'ⲧⲁ ⲧⲏⲣⲟⲩ, ⲁⲩⲧⲁ'ⲗⲟ

ⲙ̄ⲡⲉⲩⲥⲱⲙⲁ'ⲛ̄ⲟⲩⲑⲩⲥⲓⲁ ⲙ̄ⲡⲉⲛ'ϫⲟⲉⲓⲥ ⲓ̄ⲥ̄ ⲡⲉⲭ̄ⲥ̄, ⲁⲩⲱ ⲙ̄ⲡⲉⲩⲥⲱⲧⲙ̄ ⲛ̄ⲥⲁⲡⲉ-

ⲡⲣⲟⲥ'ⲧⲁⲅⲙⲁ ⲙ̄ⲡⲣⲣⲟ, ⲁⲗⲗⲁ ⲁⲩϥⲓ ⲙ̄ⲡⲉⲩⲥϭⲣⲟⲥ ⲁⲩⲟⲩⲁϩⲩ ⲛ̄'ⲥⲁⲡⲉⲩϫⲟⲉⲓⲥ, ⲉ-

ⲁⲩϫⲱⲕ ⲉⲃⲟⲗ'ⲙ̄ⲡⲉⲧⲥⲏϩ ϩⲛ̄'ⲛⲉⲩⲁⲅⲅⲉⲗⲓⲟⲛ ⲉ'ⲧⲟⲩⲁⲁⲃ ⲉϥϫⲱ'ⲙ̄ⲙⲟⲥ ϫⲉ ⲡⲉⲧ'

ⲛⲁⲕⲁⲉⲓⲱⲧ ⲛ̄'ⲥⲱⲩ ϩⲓⲙⲁⲁⲩ ϩⲓ'ⲩⲉⲉⲣⲉ ϩⲓⲥϩⲓⲙⲉ ϩⲓϩⲓ ϩⲓⲥⲱϫⲉ, 'ϥⲛⲁϫⲓⲧⲟⲩ ⲛ̄-

ϩⲁϩ ⲛ̄ⲕⲱⲃ, ⲁⲩⲱ ⲛ̄ϥⲕⲗⲏⲣⲟⲛⲟ'ⲙⲉⲓ ⲙ̄ⲡⲱⲛ̄ϩ ϣⲁ'ⲉⲛⲉϩ. ⲧⲉⲛⲟⲩ ⲇⲉ ⲁⲛⲟⲕ'ⲉⲓ-

56 R ii 10 f. l. ⲛ̄ⲧⲛ̄ⲛⲁⲕⲁⲁⲕ, or -ⲕⲁⲁⲩ. V i 20. l. -ⲩⲏⲣⲉ

56 R ii 22-24 ⲉⲣⲉⲡⲡⲉⲧⲟⲩⲁⲁⲃ ⲁ. ⲃ. ⲉⲓⲣⲉ ⲙ̄ⲙⲟⲟⲩ A; ⲉⲩⲉⲓⲣⲉ ⲙ̄ⲙⲟⲟⲩ ⲛ̄ϭⲓ ⲛ̄ⲙⲁ[ⲕⲁ-
ⲣⲓⲟⲥ ⲁⲛ]ⲁ ⲃⲓⲕ[ⲧⲱⲣ? ⲃ. 27. ⲁⲩⲱ A; om. ⲃ. 30. ⲁ̄ⲛⲛⲟⲩ ⲛ̄ⲥⲧⲣ. A; om. ⲃ. 33–V i 1.
ⲛⲟϭ ⲛ̄- A; om. ⲃ. 34. ⲁⲩⲧⲁⲗⲟ A; ⲁⲩⲧⲁ (sic) ⲃ. 4. + ⲉϩⲣⲁⲓ ⲃ. 5. ⲛⲟⲩⲑⲩⲥⲓⲁ A;
ⲛ̄ⲟ̄. ⲃ. ⲙ̄ⲡⲉⲛϫⲟⲉⲓⲥ ⲓ̄ⲥ̄ ⲡⲉⲭ̄ⲥ̄ ⲁⲩⲱ A; ⲙ̄ⲡϫⲟⲉⲓⲥ ⲃ. 20 f. ϩⲓⲥⲓⲙⲉ ϩⲓϩⲓ ϩⲓⲥⲱϫⲉ A;
]ⲏ ⲥⲱ[ⲛⲉ ⲏ ϩϩⲓⲙ]ⲉ ⲏ ⲩⲏ[ⲣⲉ ⲓⲧ ⲥⲱ]ϫⲉ ⲃ. + ⲉⲧⲃⲏ[ⲏⲧ] ⲃ. 24 f. ⲛ̄ⲅⲕⲗⲏⲣⲟⲛⲟⲙⲉⲓ
A; ⲛ̄ⲥⲉⲕⲗ. ⲃ. 25 f. ⲙ̄ⲡⲱⲛ̄ϩ ⲩⲁⲉⲛⲉϩ A; ⲛ̄ⲧⲙⲛ̄ⲧⲣ̄ⲣⲟ ⲛ̄ⲙ̄ⲡⲏⲩⲉ ⲃ. 27. ⲧⲉⲛⲟⲩ ⲇⲉ
ⲁⲛⲟⲕ A; ⲉⲧⲃⲉⲟⲩ ⲇⲉ ⲧⲉⲛⲟⲩ ⲃ.

ⲍⲙⲟⲟⲥ ϣⲁⲧⲉⲛⲟⲩ ⲉⲓⲛⲁⲩ ⲉⲛⲉⲓⲛⲟϭ ⲛ̄ⲧⲁⲓⲟ ⲉⲣⲉⲛⲉⲧⲟⲩⲁⲁⲃ ϫⲓ ⲙ̄ⲙⲟⲟⲩ· ⲁⲗⲗⲁ ϯ
ⲛⲁⲧⲱⲟⲩⲛ(ⲛ) (56 V ii) ⲍⲱ ⲛ̄ⲧⲁⲩⲓ ⲙ̄ⲡⲁⲥϭⲟⲥ, ⲧⲁⲟⲩⲁⲍϯ ⲛ̄ⲥⲁⲡⲁϫⲟⲉⲓⲥ ⲓⲥ̄ ⲡⲉϫⲉ
ⲙⲏ ⲛⲁ̈ⲛⲟⲩⲓ ⲁⲛⲟⲕ ⲛ̄ⲑⲉ ⲙ̄ⲡⲉⲓϣⲏⲣⲉ ϣⲏⲙ̄ ⲁⲣⲣⲟ; ⲛⲁⲓ ⲇⲉ ⲉⲩϫⲱ ⲙ̄ⲙⲟⲟⲩ ⲍⲙ̄
ⲡⲉⲩⲍⲏⲧ ⲛ̄ϭⲓ ⲡ̄ⲙⲁⲕⲁⲣⲓⲟⲥ ⲁⲡⲁ ⲡⲁⲏⲥⲉ, ⲁϥⲉⲓ ⲉ̄ⲍⲟⲩⲛ ⲉⲡⲏⲓ ⲙ̄ⲡⲁⲩ̄ⲗⲟⲥ, ⲁⲅⲟⲩⲱⲙ
ⲙ̄ⲛⲛⲉⲩⲉⲣⲏⲩ ⲙ̄ⲡⲛⲁⲩ ⲙ̄ⲙⲉⲉⲣⲉ· ⲁⲩⲱ ⲡⲉϫⲉⲡⲁⲩⲗⲟⲥ ⲙ̄ⲡⲁⲏⲥⲉ ϫⲉ ⲕⲛⲁⲩ ⲡⲁⲥⲟⲛ
ⲉⲡⲉⲓⲛⲟϭ ⲛ̄ⲣⲱⲙⲉ ⲙ̄ⲡⲟⲟⲩ ⲛ̄ⲧⲁⲩⲧⲱⲟⲩⲛ ⲍⲁⲛⲉⲓⲛⲟϭ ⲛ̄ⲃⲁⲥⲁⲛⲟⲥ ⲉⲧⲃⲉⲡ̄ⲣⲁⲛ ⲙ̄
ⲡⲉⲭⲥ̄· ⲡⲉϫⲉⲡⲁⲏⲥⲉ ⲛⲁⲩ ϫⲉ ⲁⲍⲉ ⲡⲁⲥⲟⲛ· ⲁⲓ̈ⲙ̄ⲕⲁⲍ ⲛ̄ⲍⲏⲧ ⲉⲙⲁⲧⲉ· ⲁⲩⲱ ⲇⲉ
ⲉⲩϫⲁϫⲉ ⲙ̄ⲛⲛⲉⲩⲉⲣⲏⲩ ⲉⲧⲃⲉⲡⲉⲩⲧⲁⲓ̈ⲟ· ⲁⲩⲱ ⲁⲡⲉⲡ̄ⲡⲁ ⲉⲧⲟⲩⲁⲁⲃ ⲉⲓ ⲉⲍⲣⲁⲓ ⲉ
ϫⲙ̄ⲡⲉⲧⲟⲩⲁⲁⲃ ⲁⲡⲁ (57 R i) ⲡⲁⲏⲥⲉ· ⲁϥϣⲟⲣⲡ̄ ⲙ̄ⲡⲉⲩⲣⲁⲥⲧⲉ, ⲁϥⲉⲓ ⲉ
ⲃⲟⲗ ⲙ̄ⲡⲉⲩⲕⲟⲩⲓ ⲛ̄ⲍⲙ̄ⲍⲁⲗ, ⲁⲩϯ ⲛⲁⲩ ⲛ̄ⲅⲟⲩⲱⲧ ⲛ̄ⲍⲟⲗⲟ ⲕⲟⲧⲧⲓⲛⲟⲥ, ⲁⲩ ⲕⲁⲁⲩ
ⲉⲃⲟⲗ ⲉⲩⲟ ⲛ̄ⲣ̄ⲙ̄ⲍⲉ· ⲡⲉϫⲁⲩ ⲛⲁⲩ ϫⲉ ϥⲓ ⲛ̄ⲛⲁⲓ ⲛⲁⲕ ⲛ̄ⲅⲱⲛϫ ⲉⲣⲟⲟⲩ, ϫⲉ ⲛⲁⲓ
ⲙ̄ⲙⲁⲧⲉ ⲛⲉⲛⲧⲁⲩ ⲥⲉⲉⲡⲉ ⲍⲛ̄ⲛⲛⲟⲩⲃ ⲛ̄ⲧⲁⲓ̈ⲛⲧⲟⲩ ⲛⲙ̄ⲙⲁⲓ· ⲁⲩⲱ ⲍⲛ̄ⲧⲉⲩⲛⲟⲩ ⲉⲧⲙ̄
ⲙⲁⲩ ⲁⲩⲃⲱⲕ ⲉⲡⲉⲡⲣⲉ ⲧⲟⲣⲓⲟⲛ, ⲁⲩϫⲓ ⲩⲕⲁⲕ ⲉⲃⲟⲗ ⲉⲩϫⲱ ⲙ̄ⲙⲟⲥ ϫⲉ ⲁⲛⲟⲩ
ⲭⲣⲏⲥⲧⲓⲁⲛⲟⲥ ⲡⲁⲣⲣⲏⲥⲓⲁ· ⲡⲉϫⲉⲡⲇⲟⲩⲍ ⲛⲁⲩ ϫⲉ ⲕⲁⲕⲏ ⲕⲉⲫⲁⲗⲏ, ⲛ̄ⲧⲕⲟⲩ
ⲣⲙ̄ⲛⲧⲱⲛ, ⲏ ⲛⲓⲙ ⲡⲉ ⲡⲉⲕⲣⲁⲛ· ⲁⲩⲟⲩⲱϣⲃ ⲛ̄ϭⲓ ⲡⲙⲁⲕⲁⲣⲓⲟⲥ ϫⲉ ⲉϣⲱⲡⲉ ⲉⲕ
ϣⲓⲛⲉ ⲛ̄ⲥⲁⲡⲁⲣⲁⲛ· ⲡⲁⲏⲥⲉ ⲡⲉ ⲡⲁ (R ii) ⲣⲁⲛ, ⲁⲩⲱ ⲁⲛϥ̄ⲟⲩⲣⲙ̄ⲡⲟⲩⲥⲓⲣⲉ ⲍⲙ̄
ⲡⲧⲟϣ ⲩⲙⲟⲩⲛ· ⲡⲉϫⲉⲡⲇⲟⲩⲍ ⲛⲁⲩ ϫⲉ ⲁⲩⲱ ⲉⲧⲃⲉⲟⲩ ⲁⲕⲉⲓ ⲉⲡⲓⲙⲁ· ⲡⲉϫⲉ
ⲙⲁⲕⲁⲣⲓⲟⲥ ⲛⲁⲩ ϫⲉ ⲡⲛⲟⲩⲧⲉ ⲡⲉⲛⲧⲁⲩⲉⲓⲛⲉ ⲙ̄ⲙⲟⲓ̈ ⲉⲡⲉⲓⲙⲁ· ϫⲉⲕⲁⲥ ⲉⲓⲉⲉⲓ
ⲉⲍⲟⲩ(ⲛ) ⲉⲛⲉⲩⲁⲅⲱⲛ ⲉ̄ϫⲟⲩⲁⲁⲃ· ⲡⲉϫⲉⲡⲇⲟⲩⲍ ⲛⲁⲩ ϫⲉ ⲑⲩⲥⲓⲁⲍⲉ, ⲓⲡⲣ̄ⲙⲟⲩ
ⲕⲁⲕⲱⲥ· ⲉⲓⲉ ⲙ̄ⲡⲉⲕⲥⲱⲧⲙ̄ ⲛ̄ⲧⲟⲕ ⲉⲧⲃⲉⲡ̄ⲩϣⲏⲣⲉ ⲁⲡⲉⲥⲧⲣⲁ ⲧⲏⲗⲁⲧⲏⲥ ⲙ̄ⲡⲣ̄ⲣⲟ;

---

56 V i 28 f. l. ϣⲁⲧⲛ̄(ⲛ)ⲁⲩ. ii 17. l. ϫⲉ ⲁⲕⲛⲁⲩ?

56 V i 28 f. ϣⲁⲧⲉⲛⲟⲩ (sic) A; om. B. 29–32. ⲉⲛⲉⲓⲛⲟϭ —ⲙ̄ⲙⲟⲟⲩ A; ⲉⲛⲉⲧⲟⲩⲁⲁⲃ ⲉⲩ
ϫⲓ ⲙ̄ⲡⲉⲓⲛⲟϭ ⲛ̄ⲧⲁⲓ̈ⲟ B. 32 f. ⲁⲗⲗⲁ ϯⲛⲁⲧⲱⲟⲩⲛ A; ⲉⲙⲉⲓⲧ. B. ii 1. ⲍⲱ A; om. B.
3.–ⲡⲁϫⲟⲉⲓⲥ A; [ⲡ]ϫⲥ̄. B. 5. ⲁⲛⲟⲕ A; om. B. 5 f. ⲙ̄ⲡⲉⲓϣⲏⲣⲉ A; ⲛⲟⲩⲍⲙ̄ⲍⲁⲗ ⲛ̄ⲟⲩⲱⲧ ⲛ̄ⲧⲉ
ⲡⲉⲓϥ. B. 7. ⲁ̄ⲣⲣⲟ A; om B. 14. ⲙ̄ⲡⲛⲁⲩ A; so in B? 21. ⲍⲁⲛⲉⲓⲛⲟϭ A; ⲍⲁⲧⲁⲩⲏ C
22. +ⲙ̄ⲡⲟⲟⲩ C. 23. ⲙ̄ⲡⲉⲭⲥ̄ A; ⲉⲡⲉⲛϫⲟⲉ (sic) ⲓⲥ̄ ⲡⲉϫⲉ C. 24 f. ⲡⲉϫⲉⲡ. —ⲡⲁⲥⲟⲛ
AC; so probably B. 25. After ⲡⲁⲥⲟⲛ, +ⲁⲓ̈ⲛⲁⲩ ⲉⲣⲟⲩ ⲁⲩⲱ C; so probably B. 27. ⲁⲩ
ϭⲱ ⲇⲉ A; ⲁⲩⲱ ⲁⲩϭⲱ B; ⲁⲩϭⲱ C. 29 f. ⲉⲧⲃⲉⲛⲉⲩⲧⲁⲓ̈ⲟ ⲁⲩⲱ A; ⲉⲛⲉⲩⲧⲁⲓ̈ⲟ B; ⲉⲩⲙⲁ
ⲕⲁⲣⲓⲍⲉ ⲙ̄ⲙⲟⲩ C. 32–57 R i 1. ⲉϫⲙ̄ⲡⲡⲉⲧⲟⲩⲁⲁⲃ ⲁ.ⲡ. A; ⲉϫⲙ̄. BC. 1 f. ⲁϥϣⲟⲣ
ⲡⲏ ⲙ̄ⲡⲉⲩⲣⲁⲥⲧⲉ AB; ⲙ̄ⲡⲉⲩⲣ. ⲇⲉ C. 4 f. ⲙ̄ⲛⲡⲉⲩⲕⲟⲩⲓ ⲛ̄ⲍⲙ̄ⲍⲁⲗ AB; ⲙ̄ⲛⲛⲉⲩⲍ. C. 7 f.
ⲁⲩⲕⲁⲁⲩ ⲉⲃⲟⲗ ⲉⲩⲟ A; ⲁⲩⲁⲁⲩ BC. 10. ϥⲓ ⲛ̄ⲛⲁⲓ AC; ϥⲓⲛⲁⲓ̈ B. 12. After ⲉⲣⲟⲟⲩ, +ⲉ
ⲃⲟⲗ C. 12 f. ⲙ̄ⲙⲁⲧⲉ AC; om.B. 14. After–ⲥⲉⲉⲡⲉ, +ⲉⲣⲟⲓ̈ B. 16 f. ⲍⲛ̄ⲧⲉⲩⲛⲟⲩ ⲉⲧⲙ̄ⲙⲁⲩ AB;
+ϫⲉ C. 18. After ⲁⲩⲃⲱⲕ, +ⲉⲍⲟⲩⲛ BC. 19 f. ⲁⲩ ϫⲓ ⲩⲕⲁⲕ ⲉⲃⲟⲗ AB; ⲁⲩⲟⲩ ⲉⲃⲟⲗ? C. 20 f.
ⲉⲩϫⲱ ⲙ̄ⲙⲟⲥ om. C ⲁⲛⲟⲩⲭⲣ. AB; ⲁⲛⲟⲕ ⲟⲩⲭⲣ. C. 29. ⲁⲅⲟⲩⲱϣⲃ ⲛ̄ϭⲓ A; ⲡⲉϫⲉ–C. 32. +
ⲛ̄ⲧⲁⲛⲁⲓ̈ⲟⲧⲉ ⲧⲁⲁⲩ ⲉⲣⲟⲓ̈ C. ii 5. ⲁⲩⲱ A; om. C. 8–10. ⲡⲛⲟⲩⲧⲉ —ⲉⲡⲉⲓⲙⲁ A; ⲡⲁϫⲟⲉⲓⲥ ⲡⲉⲛ
ⲧⲁⲩ ⲧⲁⲍⲙⲉⲧ C; B fragmentary. 15. ⲑⲩⲥⲓⲁⲍⲉ om B. 19 f. ⲁⲡⲉⲥⲧⲣ AB; ⲁⲡⲛⲟϭ ⲛ̄ⲥⲧⲣ. C.

ⲉⲩϭⲉ ⲙ̄ⲡⲉⲓ̈ⲧⲥⲁ ⲉⲡⲉⲧⲙ̄ⲙⲁⲩ,' ⲉⲓⲉ ϯⲛⲁⲧⲥⲁ ⲉⲣⲟⲕ ⲛ̄ⲧⲟⲕ;' ⲡⲉϫⲉⲡⲙⲁⲕⲁⲣⲓⲟⲥ
ⲁⲡⲁ ⲡⲁⲛⲥⲉ' ⲛⲁⲩ ϫⲉ ⲕⲁⲗⲱⲥ' ⲁⲕϫⲟⲟⲥ· ⲉⲩϭⲉ ⲙ̄ⲡⲉⲡⲩⲙ̄ⲣⲉ' ⲙ̄ⲡⲉⲥⲧⲣⲁⲧⲏ-'
ⲗⲁⲧⲏⲥ ⲑⲩⲥⲓⲁⲍⲉ' ⲛ̄ⲛⲉⲕⲛⲟⲩⲧⲉ,'ⲁⲗⲗⲁ ⲁⲩⲥⲁϩⲟⲩ (57 Vi)ⲛ̄ⲥⲁⲡⲛⲟⲩⲧⲉ ⲁ̄ⲧ̄ⲡⲉ
ⲓ̄ⲥ̄ ⲡⲉⲭ̄ⲥ̄, ⲧⲁ'ⲣⲉⲕⲉⲓⲙⲉ ϫⲉ ⲛ̄ϩⲉⲛ'ⲛⲟⲩⲧⲉ ⲁⲛ ⲛⲉ' ⲛⲉⲕⲛⲟⲩⲧⲉ, ⲁⲗⲗⲁ ϩⲉⲛⲁⲯⲩ-
ⲭⲟⲛ' ⲛⲉ· ⲡⲁϫⲟⲉⲓⲥ ⲇⲉ' ⲛ̄ⲧⲟⲩ ⲓ̄ⲥ̄ ⲡⲉⲭ̄ⲥ̄' ⲟⲩⲛ̄ϭⲟⲙ ⲙ̄ⲙⲟⲩ' ϩⲛ̄ϩⲱⲃ ⲛⲓⲙ.' ⲡϫⲟⲩϫ
ⲇⲉ ⲛ̄ⲧⲉⲣⲉⲩ'ⲥⲱⲧⲙ̄ ⲉⲛⲁⲓ̈ ⲁⲩ'ϭⲱⲛⲧ ⲉⲙⲁⲧⲉ,' ⲡⲉϫⲁⲩ ⲛⲁⲩ' ϫⲉ ⲁⲕⲧⲥⲱⲩ' ⲛ̄ⲛ̄-
ϫⲓⲥⲟⲟⲩ ⲛ̄ⲣ̄'ⲣⲱⲟⲩ ⲙⲛ̄ⲛⲉⲩ'ⲛⲟⲩⲧⲉ ⲉⲧⲧⲁⲓ̈ⲏⲩ. ⲩⲉ ⲧⲧⲩⲭⲏ' ⲛ̄ⲛ̄ϫⲓⲥⲟⲟⲩ ⲛ̄ⲣ̄'ⲣⲱⲟⲩ
ⲙⲛ̄ⲛⲉⲩ'ⲛⲟⲩⲧⲉ ⲉⲧⲧⲁⲓ̈ⲏⲩ ⲙ̄ⲛ̄ⲟⲩⲕⲁⲓ̈' ⲙ̄ⲡⲁⲡⲱⲗⲗⲟⲛ,' ϯⲛⲁⲣ̄ⲡⲉⲕⲥⲱⲙⲁ' ⲛ̄-
ⲕⲉⲣⲙⲉⲥ, ⲧⲁ'ⲛⲟϫⲩ ⲉⲑⲁⲗⲁⲥⲥⲁ' ⲩⲁⲛⲧⲉⲓⲙⲉ ϫⲉ'ⲁⲩ ⲡⲉ ⲡⲛⲟⲩⲧⲉ' ⲉⲧⲉⲟⲩⲛ̄-
ϭⲟⲙ' ⲙ̄ⲙⲟⲩ ⲉⲛⲁϩⲙⲉⲕ' ⲉⲃⲟⲗ ϩⲛ̄ⲛⲁϭⲓϫ.' ⲁⲩⲟⲩⲱϣⲃ̄ ⲛ̄ϭⲓ (Vii) ⲡⲙⲁⲕⲁⲣⲓⲟⲥ ⲁ'ⲡⲁ ⲡⲁⲛⲥⲉ ⲡⲉϫⲁⲩ' ⲛⲁⲩ ϫⲉ ϯⲥⲟⲟⲩⲛ̄' ϫⲉ ϥϣⲟⲟⲡ ⲛⲙ̄'ⲙⲁⲓ̈ ⲛ̄ϭⲓ ⲡⲁϫⲟⲉⲓⲥ' ⲓ̄ⲥ̄ ⲡⲉⲭ̄ⲥ̄, ⲁⲩⲟ' ⲛ̄ⲧⲟⲕ ϩⲱⲱⲕ ϯ'ⲛⲁⲧ ⲛⲁⲕ ⲛ̄ϩⲉⲛ'ⲛⲟϭ ⲛ̄ⲕⲟⲗⲁⲥⲓⲥ' ϩⲁ-
ⲁⲙⲛ̄ⲧⲉ ϩⲙ̄ⲡⲉϩⲟⲟⲩ ⲙ̄ⲡϩⲁⲡ' ⲙ̄ⲙⲉ. ⲉⲩⲥⲱⲧⲙ̄ ⲇⲉ ⲉⲛⲁⲓ̈ ⲛ̄ϭⲓ ⲡ'ϫⲟⲩϫ, ⲁⲩⲕⲉⲗⲉⲩⲉ'
ⲉⲧⲣⲉⲩⲕⲁⲁⲩ ⲕⲁ'ϩⲏⲩ ⲛ̄ⲛⲉⲩϭⲟⲓ̈ⲧⲉ ⲛ̄ⲥⲉⲙⲟⲩⲣ' ⲛ̄ⲛⲉⲩϭⲓⲥ ⲙⲛ̄'ⲛⲉⲩⲟⲩⲉⲣⲏⲧⲉ' ⲛ̄ⲥⲉ-
ⲧⲁⲗⲟⲩ ⲉⲡ'ϩⲉⲣⲙⲏⲧⲁⲣⲓⲟⲛ' ⲛ̄ⲥⲉϩⲱⲕⲉ ⲙ̄ⲙⲟⲩ' ⲛ̄ϭⲓ ϥⲙⲟⲩⲛ ⲛ̄'ⲕⲉⲥⲧⲱⲛⲁⲣⲓⲟⲥ,' ϥⲧⲟⲟⲩ ϩⲓⲑⲏ ⲛ̄ϥ'ⲧⲟⲟⲩ, ⲩⲁⲛⲧⲉ'ⲛⲉⲕⲉⲉⲥ ⲙ̄ⲡⲉⲩ'ⲥⲱⲙⲁ ⲟⲩⲱⲛϩ̄'ⲉⲃⲟⲗ.' ⲙ̄ⲛ̄ⲛⲥⲱⲥ ⲁⲩ-
ⲧ'ⲣⲉⲩⲉⲓⲛⲉ ⲛ̄ⲥⲁ ⲛ̄'ⲗⲁⲙⲡⲁⲥ ⲛ̄ⲕⲱ'ϩⲧ̄ ⲛ̄ⲥⲉⲕⲁⲁⲩ ϩⲁ(58 Ri)ⲛⲉⲩⲥⲡⲓⲣⲟⲟⲩⲉ' ⲩⲁⲛ-
ⲧⲉⲡⲉⲥⲧⲟⲓ̈' ⲛ̄ⲛⲉⲩⲥⲁⲣⲝ̄ ⲩⲟⲩ'ⲉⲃⲟⲗ ⲉⲙⲁⲧⲉ.' ⲁⲩⲟ ⲛ̄ⲧⲉⲩⲛⲟⲩ'ⲁⲩϥⲓ ⲛ̄ⲛⲉⲩⲃⲟⲗ ⲉ-
ϩⲣⲁⲓ̈ ⲉⲧⲡⲉ, ⲁⲩ'ⲱϣ ⲉⲃⲟⲗ ⲉⲩϫⲱ' ⲙ̄ⲙⲟⲥ ϫⲉ ⲡⲁ'ϫⲟⲉⲓⲥ ⲓ̄ⲥ̄ ⲡⲉⲭ̄ⲥ̄' ⲡϫⲟⲉⲓⲥ ⲡⲛⲟⲩ'ⲧⲉ
ⲡⲡⲁⲛⲧⲱⲕ'ⲣⲁⲧⲱⲣ ⲡⲉⲧ'ⲛⲟⲩϩⲙ̄ ⲛ̄ⲛⲉⲧ'ϩⲉⲗⲡⲓⲍⲉ ⲉⲣⲟⲩ,' ⲥⲱⲧⲙ̄ ⲉⲣⲟⲓ̈ ⲛ̄ϯ'ⲧ̄ⲛⲛⲟⲟⲩ ⲛⲁⲓ̈
ⲛ̄'ⲡⲉⲕⲁⲅⲅⲉⲗⲟⲥ' ⲛ̄ϥϯϭⲟⲙ ⲛⲁⲓ̈' ⲩⲁⲛⲧϫⲱⲕ ⲉ'ⲃⲟⲗ ⲙ̄ⲡⲁⲁⲅⲱⲛ' ⲛ̄ⲧⲁⲩϫⲡⲉ ⲙ̄ⲡⲉⲓ̈-
ⲁⲛⲟⲙⲟⲥ ⲙⲛ̄'ⲡⲉⲩⲕⲉⲣⲣⲟ ⲙ̄'ⲡⲁⲣⲁⲛⲟⲙⲟⲥ.' ⲡⲉⲟⲟⲩ ⲛⲁⲕ ⲩⲁ'ⲉⲛⲉϩ ⲛ̄ⲉⲛⲉϩ, ϩⲁ'ⲙⲏⲛ.'
ⲛⲁⲓ̈ ⲇⲉ ⲉϥϫⲱ ⲙ̄'ⲙⲟⲟⲩ, ⲉⲓⲥ ϩⲣⲁ'ⲫⲁⲏⲗ ⲡⲁⲅⲅⲉ'ⲗⲟⲥ ⲁϥⲉⲓ ⲉⲃⲟⲗ' ϩⲛ̄ⲧⲡⲉ, ⲁⲩⲟⲩ-
(Rii)ⲱϣϥ ⲙ̄ⲡϩⲉⲣ'ⲙⲏⲧⲁⲣⲓⲟⲛ,' ⲁⲩⲟ ⲛ̄ϩⲁⲗⲏⲥⲓⲥ' ⲉⲧⲙⲏⲣ ⲛ̄ⲛⲉⲩ'ϭⲓⲥ ⲙ̄ⲛⲉⲩⲟ'ⲉ-

57 R ii 21. ⲉⲩϫⲉ A; ϫ(ⲉ)B; ⲁⲩⲟ C. 22. ⲉⲡⲉⲧⲙ̄ⲙⲁⲩ A; ⲉⲣⲟⲩ BC. 23 f. ⲉⲓⲉ ϯ-
ⲛⲁⲧⲥⲁ A; ⲙⲁⲗⲓⲥⲧⲁ B; ⲙⲁⲗⲓⲥ (sic)C. 28-31. ⲉⲩϫⲉ — ⲑⲩⲥⲓⲁⲍⲉ A; ϫⲉ ⲡⲩⲙⲣⲉ ⲙ̄ⲡⲉ-
ⲥⲧⲣ· ⲁⲡⲉⲩⲑ. BC. 32. ϯⲛ̄ⲃⲟⲧⲉ BC. V i 3 f. ⲛ̄ϩⲉⲛⲛⲟⲩⲧⲉ A; ϩⲛⲟⲩⲧⲉ (sic) C. 8. ⲓ̄ⲥ̄
ⲡⲉⲭ̄ⲥ̄ om. C. 10. ϩⲛ̄ϩⲱⲃ A; ⲛ̄ϩ. C. 15. ⲁⲕⲧⲥⲱⲩ A; ⲉⲕⲥⲱⲩ C. 17 f. ⲙ̄ⲛⲉⲩⲛⲟⲩⲧⲉ A;
ⲙⲛ̄ⲛ̄. C. 19-23. ⲩⲉ ⲧⲧⲩⲭⲏ — ⲙ̄ⲡⲟⲩⲕⲁⲓ̈ A; ⲩⲉⲡⲟⲩⲕⲁⲓ̈ C. 25. ϯⲛⲁⲣ̄ⲡⲉⲕⲥⲱⲙⲁ ⲛ̄ⲕⲉⲣ-
ⲙⲉⲥ A; ϯⲛⲁⲣ̄ⲡⲉ ⲉⲡⲉⲕⲥ. (sic) ⲧⲁⲁⲁⲩ ⲛ̄ⲕ. C. 29-31. ⲁⲩ ⲡⲉ ⲛⲟⲩⲧⲉ ⲉⲧⲉⲟⲩⲛ̄ϭⲟⲙ
ⲙ̄ⲙⲟⲩ A; ⲁⲩ ⲛ̄ⲛ̄. ⲡⲉⲧⲉⲩϭⲟⲙ ⲙⲟⲩ (sic) C. ii 2 f. ⲡⲉϫⲁⲩ ⲛⲁⲩ A; om. C. 10. ϩⲛ̄-
ⲁⲙⲛ̄ⲧⲉ A; om. C. 10 f. ϩⲙ̄ⲡⲉϩⲟⲟⲩ A; ⲙ̄ⲡ. C. 12 f. ⲉⲩⲥⲱⲧⲙ̄ ⲇⲉ ⲉⲛⲁⲓ̈ A; ⲛⲁⲓ̈ ⲇⲉ
ⲛ̄ⲧⲉⲣⲉⲩⲥⲱⲧⲙ̄ ⲉⲣⲟⲟⲩ C. 18 f. ⲙ̄ⲛⲉⲩⲟⲩⲉⲣⲏⲧⲉ A; ϩⲓⲡⲁϩⲟⲩ ⲙ̄ⲙⲟⲩ C. 23-26. ⲩⲙⲟⲩⲛ
ⲛ̄ⲕⲉⲥⲧⲱⲛⲁⲣⲓⲟⲥ ϥⲧⲟⲟⲩ ϩⲓⲑⲏ ⲛ̄ϥⲧⲟⲟⲩ A; ⲃⲧⲟⲟⲩ ⲙ̄ⲙⲁⲧⲟⲓ̈ C. 31. ⲛ̄ⲥⲁ (sic) A; ⲛ̄ϥⲧⲟ
(sic) C. 58 R i 3. ⲩⲟⲩ A; ⲩⲙ̄ⲩⲉ (sic) C. 4. ⲉⲙⲁⲧⲉ A; om. C.

ⲣⲏⲧⲉ ⲁⲩⲃⲱⲗ ⲉⲃⲟⲗ, ⲁⲩⲱ ⲁⲛⲗⲁⲙⲡⲁⲥ ⲱϣⲙ, ⲁⲛϭⲓⲝ ⲛ̄ⲛⲕⲉⲥⲧⲱⲛⲁⲣⲓⲟⲥ ⲧⲱⲥ, ⲁⲩⲣ-
ⲑⲉ ⲛ̄ⲟⲩⲱ̄ⲛⲉ. ⲡⲉⲭⲉⲡⲁⲅⲅⲉⲗⲟⲥ ⲛⲁⲩ ϫⲉ ⲙ̄ⲡⲣ̄ⲣϩⲟⲧⲉ ⲱ ⲡⲁϩⲥⲉ· ⲛ̄ⲧⲁⲡⲛⲟⲩⲧⲉ ⲧⲛ̄-
ⲛⲟⲟⲩⲧ ϣⲁⲣⲟⲕ ⲉⲧⲣⲁϯϭⲟⲙ ⲛⲁⲕ ⲧⲁⲛⲟⲩϩⲙ ⲙ̄ⲙⲟⲕ ϣⲁⲛⲧⲉⲕϫⲱⲕ ⲉⲃⲟⲗ ⲙ̄ⲡⲉⲕ-
ⲁⲅⲱⲛ ϩⲛ̄ⲟⲩⲉⲓⲣⲏⲛⲏ· ⲁⲩⲱ ⲟⲛ ⲡⲙⲁ ⲉⲧⲟⲩⲛⲁⲕⲱ ⲙ̄ⲡⲉⲕⲥⲱⲙⲁ ⲛ̄ϩⲏⲧϥ̄ ϯⲛⲁ-
ⲇⲓⲁⲕⲟⲛⲉⲓ ⲉⲣⲟⲩ ϣⲁⲉⲛⲉϩ. ⲁⲡⲁⲅⲅⲉⲗⲟⲥ ⲇⲉ ⲥⲟⲟⲩⲧⲛ̄ ⲉⲃⲟⲗ ⲛ̄ⲧⲉϥϭⲓⲝ, ⲁⲩⲥⲗⲁⲗ-
ⲗⲉⲥ ⲙ̄ⲡⲉϥⲥⲱⲙⲁ (58 V i) ⲧⲏⲣϥ̄· ⲁⲩⲱ ⲛ̄ⲧⲉⲩⲛⲟⲩ ⲁⲩⲧⲁⲗϭⲟ ϩⲱⲥ ⲉⲩϫⲉ ⲙ̄ⲡⲟⲩ-
ⲃⲁⲥⲁⲛⲓⲍⲉ ⲙ̄ⲙⲟⲩ ⲉⲡⲧⲏⲣϥ̄, ⲁⲩⲱ ⲁⲛϭⲓⲝ ⲛ̄ⲛ̄ⲕⲉⲥⲧⲱⲛⲁⲣⲓⲟⲥ ⲱⲗⲕ ⲉⲣⲟⲩ, ⲙ̄ⲡⲟⲩ-
ⲉⲩϭⲙϭⲟⲙ ⲉⲥⲟⲩⲧⲱⲛⲟⲩ ⲉⲃⲟⲗ· ⲁⲩⲱ ⲛ̄ⲕⲉⲥⲧⲱⲛⲁⲣⲓⲟⲥ ⲁⲩⲡⲁⲣⲁⲕⲁⲗⲉⲓ ⲙ̄ⲙⲟⲩ ϫⲉ
ⲁⲣⲓⲧⲁⲅⲁⲡⲏ ⲛ̄ⲧⲁⲗϭⲟ ⲛ̄ⲛ̄ϭⲓⲝ. ⲁⲩⲱ ⲛ̄ⲧⲉⲩⲛⲟⲩ ⲁⲩⲥⲫⲣⲁⲅⲓⲍⲉ ⲙ̄ⲙⲟⲟⲩ ⲉⲩϫⲱ
ⲙ̄ⲙⲟⲥ ϫⲉ ϩⲙ̄ⲡⲣⲁⲛ ⲙ̄ⲡⲉⲓⲱⲧ ⲙ̄ⲡϣⲏⲣⲉ ⲙ̄ⲡⲉⲡⲛ̄ⲁ̄ ⲉⲧⲟⲩⲁⲁⲃ ⲉⲩⲉⲭⲁⲣⲓⲍⲉ
ⲛⲏⲧⲛ̄ ⲙ̄ⲡⲧⲁⲗϭⲟ. ⲁⲩⲱ ⲛ̄ⲧⲉⲩⲛⲟⲩ ⲁⲩⲧⲁⲗϭⲟ. ⲡⲡⲉⲧⲟⲩⲁⲁⲃ ⲇⲉ ⲁⲡⲁ ⲡⲁϩⲥⲉ ⲡⲉϫⲁⲩ ⲙ̄ⲡⲟⲩϫ ϫⲉ ϭⲓϫⲡⲉ ⲛⲁⲕ ⲱ ⲡⲁⲛⲟⲙⲟⲥ ϫⲉ ϥ̄ϣⲟⲟⲡ ⲛⲙ̄(V ii)ⲙⲁⲓ ⲛ̄ϭⲓ ⲡⲁϫⲟⲉⲓⲥ ⲓ̄ⲥ̄ ⲡⲉϫⲉ· ⲁⲩⲱ ⲉⲓⲥϩⲏⲏⲧⲉ ⲁⲩⲧⲛ̄ⲛⲟⲟⲩ ⲙ̄ⲡⲉⲩⲁⲅⲅⲉⲗⲟⲥ ϣⲁⲣⲟⲓ, ⲁⲩⲧⲁⲗ-
ϭⲟⲓ ϩⲛ̄ⲛⲉⲕⲃⲁⲥⲁⲛⲟⲥ ⲛ̄ⲧⲁⲕⲧⲁⲁⲩ ⲛⲁⲓ. ⲁⲩϭⲱⲛⲧ ⲛ̄ϭⲉ ϩⲁⲣⲙⲏⲛⲓⲟⲥ ⲡⲇⲟⲩϫ,
ⲡⲉϫⲁⲩ ⲛⲁⲩ ϫⲉ ⲱ ⲡⲁϩⲥⲉ, ⲙⲏ ⲉⲕⲛⲁⲣϩⲱⲃ ϩⲱⲱⲕ ⲉⲅⲉⲛϩⲃⲏⲩⲉ ⲙ̄ⲙⲁⲅⲓⲁ
ⲛ̄ⲑⲉ ⲙ̄ⲡⲉⲓⲁⲛϩⲟⲥⲓⲟⲥ ϫⲉ ⲃⲓⲕⲧⲱⲣ, ⲡⲁⲓ ⲛ̄ⲧⲁⲩⲧⲟⲥⲉ ⲙ̄ⲡⲉⲩⲁⲝⲓⲱⲙⲁ· ⲁⲩⲱ ⲙ̄ⲡⲉ-
ⲛⲉⲩⲙⲁⲅⲓⲁ ⲉⲩⲛⲁϩⲙⲉϥ ⲉⲃⲟⲗ ϩⲛ̄ⲛⲁϭⲓⲝ· ⲡⲉⲭⲉⲡⲙⲁⲕⲁⲣⲓⲟⲥ ⲁⲡⲁ ⲡⲁϩⲥⲉ ⲛⲁⲩ
ϫⲉ ⲧⲱⲙ ⲉⲣⲟⲕ ⲱ ⲡⲁⲥⲉⲃⲏⲥ ⲛ̄ⲧⲗⲟ ⲉⲕϫⲓⲟⲩⲁ ⲉⲡⲛⲟⲩⲧⲉ ⲉⲧⲟⲛ̄ϩ̄· ϩⲁⲣⲙⲏⲛⲓⲟⲥ ⲇⲉ ⲁⲩϭⲱⲛⲧ ⲉⲙⲁⲧⲉ, ⲡⲉϫⲁⲩ ⲙ̄ⲡⲙⲁⲕⲁⲣⲓⲟⲥ ⲁⲡⲁ (59 R i) ⲡⲁϩⲥⲉ ϫⲉ
ⲩⲏ ⲡⲉⲩϭⲉ ⲛ̄ⲛⲟⲩⲧⲉ ⲉⲧⲧⲁⲓⲏⲩ ϯⲛⲁⲣⲡⲉⲕⲕⲁⲣϫ ⲛ̄ϣⲙ ϣⲙ. ⲁⲩⲕⲉⲗⲉⲩⲉ ⲇⲉ ⲛ̄-
ϭⲓ ⲡⲇⲟⲩϫ ⲛ̄ⲥⲉⲥⲟⲩϩϥ̄ ⲛ̄ⲥⲉⲛⲧϥ̄ ⲉϫⲛ̄ϩⲏⲧϥ̄, ⲁⲩⲱ ⲛ̄ⲥⲉⲥⲱⲕ ⲉϣⲱϥ ⲛ̄ϭⲓ ϫⲟⲩⲱⲧ ⲛ̄ⲣⲱⲙⲉ, ⲁⲩⲱ ⲁⲩⲧⲣⲉⲙⲙⲁⲧⲟⲓ ϩⲓⲟⲩⲉ ⲉⲣⲟⲩ ⲛ̄ϩⲉⲛⲩⲁⲁⲣ ⲉⲛⲟⲩⲱⲧ ϣⲁⲛⲧⲉ
ⲡⲕⲁϩ ϩⲱⲣⲡ ϩⲙ̄ⲡⲉⲩⲥⲛⲟⲩ, ⲁⲩⲱ ⲛ̄ⲧⲉⲡⲉⲩⲥⲱⲙⲁ ⲣ̄ⲡⲱϩ ⲡⲱϩ ⲁⲩⲱ ⲛ̄ⲧⲉⲕⲁⲥ
ⲛ̄ⲛⲉⲩⲕⲉⲗⲉⲛ̄ⲕⲉⲥ ⲙ̄ⲡⲉⲩⲥⲟⲓ ⲛⲟⲩϫⲉ ⲉⲃⲟⲗ ⲛ̄ⲛⲉⲩⲉⲣⲏⲩ ⲉⲩⲥⲱⲕ ϩⲓϣⲱϥ. ⲁⲩⲕⲉⲗ-
ⲗⲉⲩⲉ ⲟⲛ ⲛ̄ϭⲓ ⲡⲇⲟⲩϫ ⲉⲧⲣⲉⲩⲉⲓⲛⲉ ⲛⲟⲩⲕⲟⲛⲓⲁ ⲛ̄ⲁⲧⲱϥⲙ ⲛ̄ⲥⲉⲧⲁⲗⲟⲩ ⲉϫⲙ̄ⲡⲉⲩ-
ⲥⲱⲙⲁ ⲛ̄ⲥⲉⲡⲱϩⲧ (R ii) ⲉϫⲱⲩ ⲛ̄ⲟⲩϩⲙ̄ϫ· ⲛⲉⲁⲡⲉⲩⲥⲱⲙⲁ ⲧⲏⲣϥ̄ ⲉⲣⲕⲱϩⲧ ⲁⲩⲱ
ⲁⲩⲙⲟⲩϩ ⲛ̄ⲑⲉ ⲛ̄ⲟⲩⲗⲁⲙⲡⲁⲥ ϩⲱⲥⲧⲉ ⲛ̄ⲥⲉϫⲃⲟⲥ ϫⲉ ⲁⲩⲙⲟⲩ. ⲁⲩⲱ ⲉⲛⲉⲩⲛⲏϣ
ϩⲓϫⲙ̄ⲡⲕⲁϩ, ⲙ̄ⲡⲉⲩϭⲙϭⲟⲙ ⲉϥⲓϫⲱⲩ ⲉϩⲣⲁⲓ ⲉⲧⲃⲉⲡϫⲓⲥⲉ ⲛ̄ⲛ̄ⲃⲁⲥⲁⲛⲟⲥ ⲉⲧ-
ϩⲙ̄ⲡⲉⲩⲥⲱⲙⲁ, ⲁⲩⲱ ⲛⲉⲩⲣⲓⲙⲉ ⲉⲩϫⲱ ⲙ̄ⲙⲟⲥ ϫⲉ ⲡⲛⲟⲩⲧⲉ ⲡⲁⲛⲟⲩⲧⲉ, ⲉⲧⲃⲉⲟⲩ ⲁⲕ-
ⲕⲁⲁⲧ ⲛ̄ⲥⲱⲕ; ⲡⲇⲟⲩϫ ⲇⲉ ⲁⲩϫⲓ ⲩⲕⲁⲕ ⲉⲃⲟⲗ ϫⲉ ⲁⲕϫⲓϫⲡⲉ ⲱ ⲡⲁϩⲥⲉ· ⲉⲧⲃⲉ-

58 V i 15 f. l. ⲡⲛⲉⲛϭⲓⲝ. 23 f. l. ⲉⲩⲉⲭⲁⲣⲓⲍⲉ? ii 9. l. ⲛ̄ϭⲓ. 26. l. ⲉⲣⲟⲕ. 33. ⲁⲡⲁ: first a added. 59 R i 5. l. ⲩⲏⲙ ⲩⲏⲙ.

ⲟⲩ ⲙ̅ⲗⲉϥⲉⲓ ⲛ̅ϭⲓ 'ⲓ̅ⲥ̅ ⲛⲏⲃⲟⲏⲑⲓⲁ' ⲉⲣⲟⲕ ⲁⲩⲱ' ⲛⲏ̅ⲛⲁⲅⲙⲉⲕ ⲉ̄ⲃⲟⲗ ⲍⲛ̅ⲛⲁⲥⲓⲁ;'
ⲉⲡⲓⲇⲏ ⲙⲛ̅ⲛⲟⲩ'ⲧⲉ ⲉⲩⲛ̅ϭⲟⲙ ⲙ̄ⲙⲟⲩ ⲛ̅ⲑⲉ ⲙ̄ⲡⲁ'ⲡⲟⲗⲗⲟⲛ.' ⲛⲁⲓ ⲇⲉ ⲉϥϫⲱ ⲙ̄-'
ⲙⲟⲟⲩ ⲛ̅ϭⲓ ⲡⲇⲟⲩⲝ (59 V i) ⲉⲓⲥ ⲅⲣⲁⲫⲁⲏⲗ ⲡⲁⲣ'ⲭⲁⲅⲅⲉⲗⲟⲥ ⲁϥⲉⲓ' ⲉⲃⲟⲗ ⲍⲛ̅ⲧⲡⲉ,'
ⲁϥⲁϩⲉⲣⲁⲧϥ̅ ϩⲓ'ϫⲙⲡ̅ⲥⲱⲙⲁ ⲙⲡ̄'ⲙⲁⲕⲁⲣⲓⲟⲥ ⲁⲡⲁ' ⲡⲁⲛⲥⲉ, ⲡⲉϫⲁϥ 'ⲛⲁⲩ ⲇⲉ ϫⲣⲟ
ⲙ̄ⲙⲟⲕ' ⲱ ⲡⲁⲛⲥⲉ, ⲙ̄ⲡⲣ̄'ⲣ̄ϩⲟⲧⲉ· ϯϣⲟⲟⲡ' ⲛⲙ̄ⲙⲁⲕ· ⲧⲱⲟⲩ(ⲛ) ⲛ̅ⲅⲁϩⲉⲣⲁⲧⲕ̅ ϩⲓ-
ϫⲛ̅'ⲛⲉⲕⲟⲩⲉⲣⲏⲧⲉ' ⲛ̅ⲅⲃⲱⲕ ⲛ̅ⲅⲁϩⲉ'ⲣⲁⲧⲕ̅ ⲉⲡⲓⲁⲛⲟ'ⲕⲟⲥ ⲛ̅ϯⲩⲓⲡⲉ' ⲛⲁⲩ ⲙ̄ⲛⲛⲉϥ'
ⲙⲟⲩⲛⲅ̅ ⲛ̅ϭⲓⲝ.' ⲁⲡⲁⲅⲅⲉⲗⲟⲥ ⲇⲉ' ⲙ̄ⲡϫⲟⲉⲓⲥ ⲥⲟⲟⲩ'ⲧⲛ̅ ⲉⲃⲟⲗ ⲛ̅ⲧⲉϥϭⲓⲝ' ⲉϫⲙ̅ⲡⲥⲱ-
ⲙⲁ ⲙ̄'ⲡⲙⲁⲕⲁⲣⲓⲟⲥ ⲁ'ⲡⲁ ⲡⲁⲛⲥⲉ, 'ⲁⲱ ⲁⲩⲧⲱⲟⲩⲛ' ϩⲛ̅ⲟⲩⲙⲛ̅ⲧⲁⲱ'ⲱⲣⲉ ϩⲱⲥ ⲙ̄-
ⲡⲟⲩ'ⲃⲁⲥⲁⲛⲓⲍⲉ ⲙ̄ⲙⲟⲩ' ⲉⲡⲧⲏⲣϥ̅.' ⲡⲙⲏⲏϣⲉ ⲇⲉ ⲧⲏ'ⲣϥ̅ ⲛ̅ⲧⲉⲣⲟⲩⲛⲁⲩ' ⲉⲡⲉⲛⲧⲁϥ-
ϣⲱ'ⲡⲉ, ⲁⲩⲣⲩⲡⲏ(V ii)ⲣⲉ ⲉⲙⲁⲧⲉ ⲉⲩⲛⲁⲩ' ⲉⲡⲙⲁⲕⲁⲣⲓⲟⲥ' ⲁⲡⲁ ⲡⲁⲛⲥⲉ ⲉⲙⲛ̅'
ⲗⲁⲁⲩ ⲛ̅ⲧⲁⲕⲟ' ϣⲟⲟⲡ ϩⲙ̄ⲡⲉϥ'ⲥⲱⲙⲁ, ⲁⲩϫⲓϣ'ⲕⲁⲕ ⲉⲃⲟⲗ ⲉⲩϫⲱ' ⲙ̄ⲙⲟⲥ ϫⲉ
ⲟⲩⲛⲟϭ' ⲡⲉ ⲡⲛⲟⲩⲧⲉ ⲛ̄'ⲛⲉⲭⲣⲏⲥⲧⲓⲁⲛⲟⲥ,' ⲡⲁⲓ ⲉⲧⲧ̄ϭⲟⲙ' ⲛ̄ⲛⲉⲧϩⲉⲗⲡⲓⲍⲉ' ⲉⲣⲟϥ.'
ⲡⲇⲟⲩⲝ ⲇⲉ ⲛ̅ⲧⲉ'ⲣⲉϥⲛⲁⲩ ⲉⲡⲉⲛ'ⲧⲁϥϣⲱⲡⲉ, ⲁϥ'ϣⲧⲟⲣⲧⲣ̄ ⲉⲙⲁⲧⲉ' ⲁⲩⲱ ⲁⲩⲕⲉⲗⲉⲩⲉ' ⲉⲛⲟⲩϩ ⲙ̄ⲡⲙⲁ'ⲕⲁⲣⲓⲟⲥ ⲉⲡⲉϥ'ⲧⲉⲕⲟ ϣⲁⲛⲧⲉϥ'ⲥⲕⲉⲡⲧⲉ ⲙ̄ⲙⲟϥ' ϫⲉ ⲟⲩ
ⲡⲉⲧϥ̅ⲛⲁ'ⲁⲁϥ ⲛⲁϥ. ⲁⲩⲱ' ⲛ̅ⲧⲉⲩⲛⲟⲩ ⲁⲩϫⲓ'ⲧϥ̅ ⲉⲡⲉϥⲧⲉⲕⲟ' ⲉⲣⲉⲡⲉϥⲕⲟⲩⲓ ⲛ̄ϩⲙ̄-
ϩⲁⲗ ⲟⲩⲏϩ ⲛ̄'ⲥⲱϥ ⲉϥⲣⲓⲙⲉ.' ⲛ̅ⲧⲉⲣⲟⲩϫⲓⲧϥ̄' ⲇⲉ ⲉⲡⲉϥⲧⲉⲕⲟ' ⲁⲩⲛⲁⲩ ⲉⲣⲟϥ ⲛ̄-
ϭⲓ ⲛⲉⲧⲟⲩⲁⲁⲃ, (60 Ri) ⲁⲩⲁⲥⲡⲁⲍⲉ ⲙ̄ⲙⲟϥ' ⲉⲩϫⲱ ⲙ̄ⲙⲟⲥ ϫⲉ' ⲕⲁⲗⲱⲥ ⲁⲕⲉⲓ
ϣⲁ'ⲣⲟⲛ ⲙ̄ⲡⲟⲟⲩ· ⲧⲛ̅ⲛⲁⲩ ⲉⲣⲟⲕ ⲙ̄ⲙⲏ'ⲛⲉ, ⲁⲗⲗⲁ ⲙ̄ⲡⲟⲟⲩ' ⲛ̄ϩⲟⲩⲟ ⲧⲏⲣⲁϣⲉ' ⲛⲙ̄-
ⲙⲁⲕ ϫⲉ ⲁⲕ'ⲉⲓ ⲉϩⲟⲩⲛ ⲉⲡⲙⲁⲛ̄'ϣⲉⲗⲉⲉⲧ ⲙ̄ⲡⲉⲭ̄ⲥ̄' ϩⲙ̄ⲡⲉⲕϩⲏⲧ ⲧⲏ'ⲣϥ̅. ⲡⲁⲩⲗⲟⲥ'
ⲇⲉ ⲛⲉϥⲛ̄ϩⲟⲩⲛ ⲉ'ⲡⲉϥⲏⲓ ⲁⲩⲱ ⲙ̄'ⲡⲉϥⲉⲓⲙⲉ ⲉⲛⲉⲛ'ⲧⲁⲩϣⲱⲡⲉ ⲙ̄'ⲡⲁⲛⲥⲉ· ⲁϥ'ⲃⲱⲕ
ⲇⲉ ⲛ̄ϭⲓ ⲡⲉϥϩⲙ̄ϩⲁⲗ 'ⲉϥⲣⲓⲙⲉ', ⲁϥⲧⲁⲙⲟϥ ⲉⲛⲉⲛ'ⲧⲁⲩϣⲱⲡⲉ ⲙ̄ⲙⲟϥ. ⲡⲁⲩⲗⲟⲥ ⲇⲉ
ⲛ̄ⲧⲉⲣⲉϥⲥⲱⲧⲙ̄ ⲉⲛⲁⲓ, ⲁⲩⲧⲟⲟⲧϥ̄' ⲉⲛⲉϥϩⲟⲓⲧⲉ, ⲁϥ'ⲡⲁϩⲟⲩ, ⲁⲩⲱ ⲁϥ'ⲣⲓⲙⲉ ϩⲛ̅-
ⲟⲩⲛⲟϭ' ⲛ̄ⲣⲓⲙⲉ ⲉϥϫⲱ ⲙ̄'ⲙⲟⲥ ϫⲉ ⲱ ϩⲁ'ⲙⲟⲓ ⲉⲛⲉⲛⲧⲁⲓ'ⲕⲁⲁⲩ ⲉⲃⲟⲗ ⲛ̄ϥ̅'ⲃⲱⲕ
ⲉⲡⲉϥⲏⲓ·' ⲁⲩϩⲓⲥⲉ ⲅⲁⲣ ⲉⲩⲡⲁ(Rii)ⲣⲁⲕⲁⲗⲉⲓ ⲙ̄ⲙⲟⲓ' ϫⲉ ⲕⲁⲁⲧ ⲉⲃⲟⲗ ⲛ̄'ⲧⲁⲃⲱⲕ ⲛⲁⲓ, ⲁⲩⲱ' ⲙ̄ⲡⲉⲓⲕⲁⲁϥ.' ⲉⲛⲓⲟⲩϣⲁⲩ ⲙⲉⲛ' ⲉⲁⲓⲧⲟⲥⲉ ⲛ̄ϩⲟⲩ'ⲱⲧⲉ ⲛ̄ⲗⲓ-
ⲧⲣⲁ ⲛ̄'ⲛⲟⲩⲃ ⲙ̄ⲡⲟⲟⲩ ⲙ̄'ⲡⲉⲡⲁⲓ ϣⲱⲡⲉ.' ⲉⲓⲣⲟⲩ ⲛ̄ⲭⲣⲏⲙⲁ' ⲛ̄ⲛⲟⲩⲃ ϩⲓϩⲁⲧ' ⲛ̄-
ⲑⲉ ⲛ̄ⲟⲩⲩⲃⲏⲣ' ⲉϥϫⲁⲗ̄ ⲉⲛⲁⲛⲟⲩϥ;' ⲟⲩⲛ̄ⲕⲉⲛⲟϭ ⲛ̄ⲗⲩⲡⲏ ϩⲙ̄ⲡⲁϩⲏⲧ' ⲉⲧⲃⲉⲧⲉⲩ-
ϭⲱⲛⲉ.' ⲉⲛⲁϫⲟⲟⲥ ⲇⲉ ⲛ̄ⲧⲁⲡⲁⲓ ϣⲱⲡⲉ' ⲙ̄ⲙⲟⲩ ⲉⲧⲃⲏⲏⲧⲕ̄.' ⲛⲉϥϩⲙ̄ϩⲁⲗ ⲇⲉ'
ⲧⲏⲣⲟⲩ ⲁⲩϩⲉⲓ'ⲛⲉⲩϩⲟⲓⲧⲉ ⲁⲩⲣⲓⲙⲉ, ϫⲉ ⲛⲉⲩⲙⲉ ⲙ̄ⲙⲟϥ ⲉⲙⲁⲧⲉ.' ⲁⲩⲧⲱⲟⲩⲛ ⲇⲉ ⲛ̄'
ϭⲓ ⲡⲁⲩⲗⲟⲥ, ⲁϥ'ⲃⲱⲕ ⲉⲡⲉϥⲧⲉ'ⲕⲟ· ⲁϥⲛⲁⲩ ⲉⲡⲁⲛⲥⲉ ⲉⲣⲉⲛ̄ⲃⲁⲥⲁ'ⲛⲟⲥ ϩⲙ̄ⲡⲉϥ-

---

cⲱⲙⲁ, ⲁ ϥ ϭ ⲓⲛ ϭ ⲕⲁⲕ' ⲉⲃⲟⲗ ⲉϥ ⲣⲓ ⲙⲉ ⲉ ϥ' ϫ ⲱ ⲙ̄ⲙⲟⲥ ϫ ⲉ ⲟⲩ (ϭ ⲟ ϥ ⲓ) ⲛ ⲟ ⲥ ⲡⲉ ⲡⲁ -
ⲡ̄ⲕⲁ ϩ ' ⲛ̄ ϩⲏ ⲧ ⲙ̄ⲡ ⲟⲟⲩ ⲱ ' ⲡⲁ ⲥ ⲟⲛ · ϩⲁ ⲙⲟ ⲓ ' ⲉ ⲛ ⲉⲛ ⲧ ⲁⲓ ⲧ ⲟ ⲥ ⲉ ⲙ̄ⲡ ⲉ ⲧ ⲛ̄ⲧ ⲁⲓ ⲧⲏ -
ⲣ ϥ̄' ⲙ̄ⲡ ⲟⲟⲩ ⲙ̄ⲡⲉ ⲡⲁ ⲓ' ϣⲱ ⲡ ⲉ ⲙ̄ⲙ ⲟ ⲕ ·' ⲛ̄ ⲧ ⲥ ⲟⲟ ⲩ ⲛ̄ ⲁⲛ ' ϫ ⲉ ⲉ ⲓⲛⲁ ϫ ⲉ ⲟⲩ ⲛ̄ ⲧ ⲉⲕ -
ⲥⲱ ⲛⲉ ·' ⲡⲉ ϫ ⲉ ⲡ ⲁ ⲛⲥ ⲉ ⲛ ⲁ ⲩ ' ϫ ⲉ ⲟⲩ ⲕ ⲟⲩ ⲛ ⲉ ⲕ' ⲙ ⲟ ⲥⲧ ⲉ ⲙ̄ⲙ ⲟ ⲓ' ϫ ⲉ ⲁ ⲓⲱ ⲡ ⲉ ⲡⲉ ⲕ ⲗ ⲏ -
ⲣ ⲟ ⲥ ⲛ̄ⲛⲉ ⲧ ⲟⲩ ⲁ ⲁⲃ ; ' ⲡ ⲁ ⲓ ⲡⲉ ⲡⲁ ⲣ ⲁ ⲅ ⲉ' ⲉ ϥ ⲅ ⲓⲛ ⲉ ⲛ̄ ⲥ ⲱ ϥ,' ϫ ⲉ ⲁⲡⲛ ⲟⲩ ⲧ ⲉ ⲥ ⲱ ⲧ ⲉ
ⲙ̄ⲙ ⲟ ⲓ' ⲉⲃ ⲟⲗ ϩ ⲛ̄ ⲛ ⲁ ⲛ ⲟⲃ ⲉ. ⲁⲩ ⲱ' ⲛ̄ⲧ ⲉ ⲓ ϩ ⲉ ⲁ ϥ ⲥ ⲉ ⲗ ⲥ ⲱ ⲗ ϥ̄ ⲛ̄ⲧ ⲟ ϥ ⲙ̄ⲛ̄ ⲛ ⲉ ⲧ ⲟⲩ ⲁ ⲁⲃ ·
ⲁⲩ ⲃⲱ ⲕ' ⲉ ⲡⲉ ϥ ⲏ ⲓ ϩ ⲛ̄ ⲟⲩ ⲉⲓ ' ⲣ ⲏ ⲛ ⲏ. ⲙ̄ⲡ ⲉ ϥ ⲟⲩ ' ⲱ ⲙ ⲟⲩ ⲇ ⲉ ⲙ̄ⲡ ⲉ ϥ' ⲥ ⲱ ⲛ̄ ⲅ ⲟ ⲙ̄ⲛ ⲧ̄
ⲛ̄ ϩ ⲟ' ⲟⲩ ⲙ̄ⲛ̄ ⲅ ⲟ ⲙ ⲧ ⲉ' ⲛ̄ ⲟ ⲩ ϣ ⲏ, ⲁⲩ ⲱ' ⲁ ϥ ϣ ⲱ ⲛ ⲉ ⲛ̄ ϫ ⲱ' ⲗ ⲏ ⲉⲧ ⲃ ⲉ ⲡⲁ ⲛⲥ ⲉ.' ⲁ ⲅ ⲉ ⲓ ⲟⲛ
ⲛ̄ ϭ ⲓ ⲛⲉ ϥ 2 ⲡ̄ ϩ ⲁ ⲗ, ⲁ ⲣ ⲧ ⲁⲙ ⲉ (ⲛ̄ ⲓ ⲓ) ⲡⲁ ⲛ ⲥ ⲉ ϫ ⲉ ⲉ ⲣ' ϣ ⲁⲛ ⲡⲁ ⲩ ⲗ ⲟ ⲥ ⲉ ⲓ' ϣ ⲁ ⲣ ⲟ ⲕ ⲉ ϥ̄ⲛ ⲁⲡ ⲉ ⲕ'
ϣ ⲓⲛ ⲉ, ⲙ ⲁ ⲣ ⲉ ϥ' ⲟⲩ ⲱ ⲙ ⲛ̄ⲙ ⲙ ⲁ ⲕ,' ϫ ⲉ ⲉ ⲓ ⲥ ϣ ⲟ ⲙ̄ⲛ ⲧ̄' ⲛ̄ ϩ ⲟ ⲟⲩ ⲙ̄ⲡ ⲉ ϥ ⲟⲩ ' ⲱ ⲙ ⲟⲩ ⲇ ⲉ ⲙ̄
ⲡ ⲉ ϥ' ⲥ ⲱ ⲉ ⲧ ⲃ ⲏ ⲏ ⲧ ⲕ̄.' ⲁⲩ ⲱ ⲛ̄ⲧ ⲉ ⲣ ⲉ ϥ ⲉ ⲓ' ⲉ ⲡ ⲉ ⲩ ⲧ ⲉ ⲕ ⲟ ⲛ̄ ϭ ⲓ ⲡⲁ ⲩ ⲗ ⲟ ⲥ ⲉ ϥ ⲛ̄' ⲡ ϣ ⲓⲛ ⲉ
ⲙ̄ⲡ ⲉ ϥ' ϣ ⲃ ⲏ ⲣ ⲡⲁ ⲛ ⲥ ⲉ,' ⲡⲉ ϫ ⲉ ⲡⲁ ⲛ ⲥ ⲉ ⲙ̄' ⲡⲁ ⲩ ⲗ ⲟ ⲥ ϫ ⲉ ϫ ⲓ ⲧ ⲕ̄ ⲛ̄ ϭ ⲟ ⲛ ⲉ ⲛ̄ ⲅ' ⲟⲩ ⲱ ⲙ
ⲛ̄ ⲟⲩ ⲕ ⲟⲩ ⲓ' ⲛ̄ ⲟ ⲉ ⲓ ⲕ ⲙ̄ⲛ̄ ⲛ ⲉ ⲧ ⲟⲩ' ⲁ ⲁⲃ ⲙ̄ⲡ ⲟⲟⲩ.' ⲡⲁ ⲩ ⲗ ⲟ ⲥ ⲇ ⲉ ⲛ̄ⲧ ⲉ' ⲣ ⲉ ϥ ⲥ ⲱ ⲧ ⲙ̄ ⲉ -
ⲛⲁ ⲓ' ⲁⲩ ⲃⲱ ⲕ ϩ ⲛ̄ ⲟⲩ' ϭ ⲉ ⲡ ⲏ ⲉ ⲡⲉ ϥ ⲏ ⲓ,' ⲁ ϥ ⲥ ⲟⲃ ⲧ ⲉ ⲛ̄ ⲟⲩ ⲁ' ⲣ ⲓⲥ ⲧ ⲟⲛ, ⲁ ϥ ⲛ̄ⲧ ϥ̄ ⲉ ⲡⲉ
ⲩ ⲧ ⲉ ⲕ ⲟ,' ⲁ ⲅ ⲟⲩ ⲱ ⲙ ⲙ̄ⲛ̄ ⲛ ⲉ ⲧ ⲟⲩ ⲁ ⲁⲃ ⲧⲏ' ⲣ ⲟⲩ. ⲛ̄ⲧ ⲉ ⲣ ⲟⲩ' ⲱ ⲇ ⲉ ⲉ ⲩ ⲟⲩ ⲱ ⲙ' ⲡⲉ ϫ ⲉ ⲡⲁ -

---

60 V ii. Offsets of ink from ll. 1 f. of 61 i. 30 f. = ⲛ̄ⲧ ⲉ ⲣ ⲟⲩ ⲟ ⲩ ⲱ

60 V i 3-6. ϩ ⲁ ⲙ ⲟ ⲓ — ⲙ̄ⲡ ⲟ ⲟ ⲩ A; om. D. 6. ⲙ̄ⲡ ⲉ ⲡⲁ ⲓ A; ⲟ ⲩ ⲡ ⲉ ⲛ ⲧ ⲁ ⲩ - D. 9. ⲉ ⲓ ⲛ ⲁ -
ϫ ⲉ ⲟ ⲩ A; ⲉ ⲓ ⲛ ⲁ ⲭ ⲟ ⲟ ⲥ ϫ ⲉ ⲟ ⲩ D. 17-20. ⲉ ϥ ϭ ⲓ ⲛ ⲉ — ⲁ ⲩ ⲱ A (cf. Boh.); om. D. 21. After
ⲛ̄ⲧ ⲉ ⲓ ϩ ⲉ, + ⲇ ⲉ D. 24 f. ϩ ⲛ̄ ⲟⲩ ⲉ ⲓ ⲣ ⲏ ⲛ ⲏ A (cf. Boh.); om. D. 27-29. ⲛ̄ ϩ ⲟ ⲙ̄ⲛ ⲧ̄ ⲛ̄ ϩ ⲟ ⲟ ⲩ (cf.
Boh.) ⲙ̄ⲛ̄ ⲅ ⲟ ⲙ ⲧ ⲉ ⲛ̄ ⲟ ⲩ ϣ ⲏ A; ⲛ̄ ϩ ⲟ ⲟⲩ ⲉ ⲛ ⲁ ⲩ D. 29 f. ⲁ ⲩ ⲱ ⲁ ϥ ϣ ⲱ ⲛ ⲉ A; ⲉ ϥ ϥ. D. 32 ⲟ ⲛ A;
om. D. ii 1 - ⲡ ⲁ ⲛ ⲥ ⲉ A; ⲡ ⲡⲉ ⲧ ⲟ ⲩ ⲁ ⲁⲃ ⲁ ⲡ ⲁ ⲡ. D. 6. ϫ ⲉ A; ⲙ̄ⲙ ⲟ ⲛ D. 6 f. ϣ ⲟ ⲙ ⲛ ⲧ̄ ⲛ̄-
ϩ ⲟ ⲟ ⲩ A (cf. Boh.); ϣ ⲟ ⲩ ⲉ ⲛ ⲁ ⲩ D. 8 f. ⲟ ⲩ ⲇ ⲉ ⲙ̄ⲡ ⲉ ϥ ⲥ ⲱ (cf. Boh.) A; om. D. 10. ⲁ ⲩ ⲱ ⲛ̄-
ⲧ ⲉ ⲣ ⲉ ϥ ⲉ ⲓ A; ⲛ̄ⲧ ⲉ ⲣ ⲉ ϥ ⲅ ⲓ ⲇ ⲉ D. 11. ⲉ ⲡ ⲉ ⲩ ⲧ ⲉ ⲕ ⲟ A; om. D. 12-14. ⲉ ϥ̄ⲡ ϣ ⲓ ⲛ ⲉ ⲙ̄ⲡ ⲉ ϥ ϣ ⲃ ⲏ ⲣ
A; ⲉ ⲛ ⲁ ⲩ ⲉ - D. 17 f. ⲛ̄ ⲅ ⲟ ⲩ ⲱ ⲙ A; ϫ ⲉ ⲉ ⲛ ⲉ ⲟ ⲩ ⲱ ⲙ D. 18. - ⲕ ⲟ ⲩ ⲓ ⲛ̄ - A; om. D (cf. Boh.).
21 - 24. ⲛ̄ⲧ ⲉ ⲣ ⲉ ϥ ⲥ ⲱ ⲧ ⲙ̄ ⲉ ⲛ ⲁ ⲓ ⲁ ⲩ ⲃⲱ ⲕ ϩ ⲛ̄ ⲟ ⲩ ϭ ⲉ ⲡ ⲏ (cf. Boh.) ⲉ ⲡ ⲉ ϥ ⲏ ⲓ A; ⲁ ϥ ⲡ ⲁ ⲣ ⲁ ⲅ ⲉ (cf. Boh.)
ⲉ ⲙ ⲁ ⲧ ⲉ D. 28-30. ⲁ ⲅ ⲟⲩ ⲱ ⲙ — ⲧ ⲏ ⲣ ⲟ ⲩ A (cf. Boh.); om. D. 31 ⲇ ⲉ A; om. D.

Boh. Evelyn White, Macarius, No. xxi, fr. 2 (p. 115). (Lines 1-17 Cod. Cairo.)
(R)] ⲧ ⲉ ⲕ ⲥ ⲱ ⲛ ⲓ . ⲟ ⲩ ⲟ ϩ ⲡ ⲉ ϫ ⲉ [ⲡ ⲁ ⲛ ⲥ ⲓ] ⲛ ⲁ ϥ ϫ ⲉ ⲉ ⲕ ⲙ ⲟ ⲥ ⲧ ⲙ̄ⲙ ⲟ ⲓ ⲡ ⲁ [ⲥ ⲟ ⲛ] ϫ ⲉ ⲁ ⲓ̈ ⲉ ϩ ⲟ ⲩ ⲛ ⲉ -
ⲡ ⲓ ⲕ ⲗ ⲏ ⲣ ⲟ ⲥ ' (ⲛ̄ ⲉ) ⲙ ⲙ ⲏ ⲛ ⲉ ⲑ ⲟ ⲩ ⲁ ⲃ ; ⲫ ⲁ ⲓ ⲅ ⲁ ⲣ ⲡ ⲉ ⲡ ⲁ [ⲣ] ⲁ ⲅ ⲓ ⲉ ϥ ⲣ ⲁ ⲩ ⲓ ⲙ ⲙ ⲟ ϥ, ϫ ⲉ ⲁ ϥ ⲧ̄ ⲥ ⲱ ⲧ̄ ⲙ ⲙ ⲟ ⲓ
ⲉ ⲃ ⲟ ⲗ ϧ ⲉ ⲛ ⲛ ⲁ ⲛ ⲟ ⲃ ⲓ ' ⲟ ⲩ ⲟ ϩ ⲁ ϥ ⲥ ⲉ ⲗ ⲥ ⲱ ⲗ ϥ ⲛ ⲉ ⲙ ⲏ ⲛ ⲉ ⲑ ⲟ ⲩ' ⲁ ⲃ ' ⲁ ϥ ϣ ⲉ ⲛ ⲁ ϥ ⲉ ⲡ ⲉ ϥ ⲏ ⲓ ϧ ⲉ ⲛ ⲟ ⲩ'
ϩ ⲓ ⲣ ⲏ ⲛ ⲏ, ⲁ ϥ ⲛ ⲕ ⲟ ⲧ . ⲙ ⲡ ⲉ ϥ ⲟ ⲩ ⲱ ⲙ ' ⲟ ⲩ ⲇ ⲉ ⲙ ⲡ ⲉ ϥ ⲥ ⲱ ⲛ ϥ̄ ⲛ ϩ ⲟ ⲟ ⲩ.' ⲉ ⲧ ⲁ ⲩ ⲓ ⲇ ⲉ ⲛ ϫ ⲉ ⲡ ⲁ ⲩ ⲗ ⲉ ϫ ⲉ
ⲛ ⲧ ⲉ ϥ ϣ ⲓ ⲛ ⲓ ' ⲛ ⲥ ⲁ [ⲡ ⲁ] ⲛ ⲥ ⲓ, ⲁ ⲛ ⲓ ⲁ ⲗ ⲱ ⲟ ⲩ ⲓ ⲛ ⲧ ⲉ ⲡ ⲁ ⲩ ⲗ ⲉ ϫ ⲱ ⲙ ⲡ ⲁ ⲛ ⲥ ⲓ ϫ ⲉ ⲉ ϣ ⲱ ⲡ ⲛ ⲧ ⲉ ' ⲡ ⲁ ⲩ ⲗ ⲉ
ϣ ⲁ ⲣ ⲟ ⲕ ⲙ ⲫ ⲟ ⲟ ⲩ, ⲁ ⲣ ⲓ ⲁ ⲛ ⲁ ϣ ' ⲕ ⲁ ϩ ⲓ ⲛ ⲙ ⲙ ⲟ ⲩ ⲛ ⲧ ⲉ ϥ ⲟ ⲩ ⲱ ⲙ ⲛ ⲉ ⲙ ⲁ ⲕ,' ϫ ⲉ ⲓ ⲥ ⲅ̄ ⲛ ⲉ ϩ ⲟ ⲟ ⲩ ⲙ ⲡ ⲉ ϥ
ⲟ ⲩ ⲱ ⲙ' ⲟ ⲩ ⲇ ⲉ ⲙ ⲡ ⲉ ϥ ⲥ ⲱ .' (Cod. Tisch. to end of page.) . . . . . . ⲉ [. . . . .] ⲙ ⲡ ⲁ ⲩ ⲗ ⲉ [ϫ ⲉ] ⲡ ⲁ '
ⲥ ⲟ ⲛ ⲡ ⲁ ⲩ ⲗ ⲉ, ϭ ⲓ ⲧ ⲉ ⲕ ⲛ ϭ ⲟ ⲛ ⲥ ϩ ⲓ ⲛ ⲁ ⲛ ⲧ ⲉ ⲛ ⲟ ⲩ ⲱ ⲙ ⲛ ⲟ ⲩ ⲱ ⲓ ⲕ ⲛ ⲉ ⲙ ⲏ ⲛ ⲉ ⲑ ⲟ ⲩ ⲁ ⲃ ⲧ ⲏ ⲣ ⲟ ⲩ. ' [ⲁ] ϥ
ⲣ ⲁ ⲩ ⲓ ⲛ ϫ ⲉ ⲡ ⲁ ⲩ ⲗ ⲉ, ⲁ ϥ ϣ ⲉ ⲛ ⲁ ϥ ⲛ ⲭ ⲱ' ⲗ ⲉ ⲙ, ⲁ ϥ ⲥ ⲟ ⲃ ⲧ̄ ⲛ ⲟ ⲩ ⲁ ⲣ ⲓⲥ ⲧ ⲟ ⲛ, ⲁ ϥ [ⲉ ⲛ ϥ ⲉ] ⲡ ⲓ ⲟ ⲩ ⲧ ⲉ -
ⲕ ⲟ, ⲁ ϥ ⲟ ⲩ ⲱ ⲙ ⲛ ⲉ ⲙ [ⲡ ⲁ ⲛ ⲥ ⲓ] ⲛ ⲉ ⲙ ⲏ ⲛ ⲉ ⲑ ⲟ ⲩ ⲁ ⲃ ⲧ ⲏ ⲣ ⲟ ⲩ. ' [ⲁ ⲥ] ϣ ⲱ ⲡ ⲓ ⲇ ⲉ ⲉ ⲩ ⲟ ⲩ ⲱ ⲙ, ⲡ [ⲉ ϫ ⲉ ⲡ ⲁ] '

 нсе м̄'паγλос ϫε ει(61 Ri)ογωγ εναγ ε'ѳεκλα τасωне'м̄паϯмоγ.' пеϫε-
паγλос наγ' ϫε пасон, εις пεκ'ϩ̄ϫϫαλ м̄пειма·'анок ϫω ϯна'τ̄ннооγ н̄-
κεϫ̄'ϫαλ ̄νϫι ̄ν̄μμαγ' ̄νсεвωκ εрнс' ̄νсεταμοκ επε(ν)'ταγγωπε м̄'μοκ.
пεϫε'пансε наγ ϫε м̄'мон пасон,' т̄ναϫμοос м̄пειμα γαντε'п̄ϫοεις
̄ντε нан' επειμα· αγω εγωπε ноγωγ' м̄п̄ϫοεις он пε'επορϫ̄ ενενε'рнγ,
ειε пεγоγ'ωγ μαрεγ'γωπε. ϩ̄н'τεγγн ϫε ετ̄μμαγ αγογωνϩ̄'наγ εвоλ н̄-
ϭι ϩ'раφанλ паг'гελος, пεϫαγ' наγ ϫε хαιрε п'рωμε ̄νγoγ'αγγ ϩιτ̄μ-
ноγ(Rii)τε м̄̄νрωμε.'асγωпε ϫε ̄ντε'репансε наγ επαг'гελос м̄п̄ϫо-
εις'αγϩε εϩрαι εϫ̄μ'πεγϩο· αγω αγ'τоγносγ, αγϭоμ' наγ· αλεγτε'κо тнрγ роγоειν' ̄нѳε м̄прн· а'нετоγααв наγ ε'поγоειν, αγγ'торт̄р̄· пεϫαγ' наγ
̄ν̄ϭι пагге'λος ϫε ϯρннм̄' ̄нмт̄н тнрт̄н·'αγω αγпαϫτоγ,' αγоγωγτ м̄паγ-'

61 Ri 11. ℓ. ̄нсεταμοс (with D). Omission here; see D.

60 Vii 32 f. м̄паγλос A (cf.Boh.); om. D. 61 Ri 2. ѳεκλα A; om. D. 4. наγ A;
om. D. 5. пасон A; om. D. 5–10. εις – εрнс D; εις паϫ̄ϫαλ м̄пнωκ ̄нт̄нт̄н-
нооγсоγ D. 11– таμок (sic) A; - таμос D. 12 f. επεнταγγωπε м̄мок A; ε-
пεнтαγγωπε· αγω εςγανсωт̄μ ϫε αναι γωπε м̄мок εναλоγ D; evidently
omission (by haplography) in A. 13 f. пεϫεпансε наγ ϫε A; αγоγωγ̄ᵇ н̄ϭι п-
μακαριос αпансε (sic) εγϫω м̄мос м̄паγλос ϫε D. 14–21. м̄мон – он пε A;
εγγωπε п̄ϫоεις κελεγε (cf. Boh.), т̄ναϫω ̄ноγεγ̄ⁿт̄ннооγ ̄нсωс γαнтεп̄ϫоεις
̄ντε επειма ϭоγωγ он D. 23. ειε A; om. D. 26. ϫε A; om. D. 28. наγεвоλ A;
εроγ D. 31. After хαιрε, ϯпансε D. 33–ii 2. ϩιτ̄ппноγτε – ϫε A (cf Boh.); om.
D. 2 f. ̄нтεрепансε A; ̄нтереγ- D. 3 f. επαггεлос м̄п̄ϫоεις A(cf·Boh.); επар-
хаггελос D. 5 f. αγϩε εϩрαι εϫ̄мпεγϩо (cf Boh.) αγω A; αγпαϫт̄γ αγоγωγτ
наγ D. 7 f. αγτϭоμ наγ A; om. D. 8 f. αλεγτεκо тнрγ A (cf· Boh.); αγω αпεγϩо
D. Rϫ f. αγγторт̄р̄ A (cf·Boh.); αγ̄rϭoтε αγоγωγτ м̄пархаггελос D. 14 f. н̄ϭι
пагге̄λос A; om. D. 16. тнрт̄н A; om. D. 17–19. αγω – αγϭмоγ A; αϩраφанλ
ϭмоγ εроογ εγϫω м̄мос ϫε εрετ̄ϭом м̄п̄ϫоεις ϭмоγ ερωτ̄н ̄нтεт̄нϯγιпε м̄-

Boh.'[нсι м̄паϫγλε [ϫε ειω]γωγ [ϫ'[·]···[··]γ···········н'[·]···ϭωνι
а······[··]···³⁰[·]·············анок ϫ····'[···](illegible traces)'[···](illegible
traces)γ····тεϭ'[····](illegible traces)сна'[········ γαμναι·? ϫ' (V)
(Cod. Cairo ℓ. 18)[а]рεγανпϭε оγαϫϭαϫνι ϯ[на]'ϫεμϭι (тλεннαϫ'ϫεμϭι?) γαнтε-
пϭε ενϭ нан· εγωп ϫε ϭоγωγ εφ[ωϫϫ] [εϩо[ϫрϫн]?]'εвоλ ннεнεрноγ. пεγоγ[γ]'
марεγγωпι.'ϩεнпιεϫωрϩ ϫε ετεммαγ αγоγ'онϩγ εроγ нϫε гαврнλ пιαрхн-
аггελος, пεϫαγ наγ ϫε хεрε' пιрωμι нγоγμενрιτ ϩιτεн'φϯ нεмпιрωμι.'ас-
γωпι ϫε εταγναγ нϫε пансι ε'пιаггελос ̄нтε'пϭε, αγϭε ϩι'ϫεнпεγϩо, αγεр-
ϩоϯ εμαγω,'ϫε αпιγτεκо тнрγ εроγωιнι'м̄фрнϯ м̄пιεϩооγ· анн εѳоγ'αв
наγ επιογωινι, αγγѳε[рт̄]εр̄, αγϭε ϩιϫεнпоγϩо· αγ[ϭωγтεн]тε[γ] ϫιϫ εвоλ
нϫε пιаг'гελος, αγαмоні м̄мωоγ, αγтоγ'носоγ, пεϫαγ нωоγ ϫε ϭро м̄'мωтεн,
εрετϫоμ ̄нтεніапос'тоλос γωпι κεмωтεн ̄нтεт̄н'ϯγιпι м̄паιаномос, ̄нтεγ-

λος, αϥϭⲙⲟⲧ·²⁰ ⲡⲉϫⲉⲡⲅⲁⲅⲓⲟⲥ· ⲁⲡⲁ ⲡⲁⲛⲥⲉ ⲙ̄·ⲡⲁⲅⲅⲉⲗⲟⲥ ϫⲉ· ⲡⲁϫⲟⲉⲓⲥ. ⲉⲓⲟⲩⲱϣ
ⲉⲛⲁⲩ ⲉⲧⲁ·²⁵ⲥⲱⲛⲉ ⲙ̄ⲡⲁⲧ·ⲙⲟⲩ. ⲡⲉϫⲉ·ⲡⲁⲅⲅⲉⲗⲟⲥ ⲛⲁⲩ·ϫⲉ ⲉⲧⲓ ⲕⲉⲥⲁⲩϥ·ⲛ̄ϩⲟⲟⲩ
ⲛⲉ ϣⲁⲛ·ⲧⲉⲧⲉⲕⲥⲱⲛⲉ· ⲉⲓ ⲛⲁⲕ ⲉⲡⲉⲓⲙⲁ·ⲛ̄ⲅⲛⲁⲩ ⲉⲣⲟⲥ· ⲁⲩⲱ·ϯⲛⲁⲙⲁϫⲉ (61Vi)
ⲛ̄ϭⲟⲙ ϩⲓⲧⲟⲟⲙ· ⲙ̄ⲡⲉⲭ̅ⲥ̅, ⲁⲩⲱ ⲛⲉ·ⲧⲁ̄ⲯⲩⲭⲏ ⲙⲛ̄ⲛⲉ·ⲧⲛ̄ⲥⲱⲙⲁ ⲛ̄ⲛⲉⲩ·ⲡⲱⲣ̄ϫ ⲉ-
ⲛⲉⲩⲉⲣⲏⲩ· ⲉⲕϣⲁⲛⲧⲱⲟⲩⲛ· ⲇⲉ ⲛ̄ϩⲧⲟⲟⲩⲉ, ⲡ·ⲇⲟⲩ̄ⲝ ⲛⲁⲧⲛ̄ⲛⲟ·ⲟⲩ ⲛ̄ⲥⲱⲕ ⲛ̄ϥⲧⲁ·¹⁹ⲗⲟⲕ
ⲉⲡⲉⲥⲗⲟϥ ⲙ̄·ⲡⲉⲛⲓⲡⲉ ⲛ̄ϥⲥⲁϫ·ⲧⲉ ϩⲁⲣⲟⲕ· ⲁⲩⲱ·ⲁⲛⲟⲕ ϯⲛⲁⲱ̄ϣⲙ̄·ⲙ̄ⲡⲕⲱϩⲧ ϩⲁ-
ⲣⲟⲕ·¹⁵ ⲧⲁⲉⲣϩⲁⲓⲃⲉ̄ ⲉⲡⲉⲕ·ⲥⲱⲙⲁ ϫⲉ ⲛ̄ⲛⲉ·ⲡ̄ϣⲁϩ ⲙ̄ⲡⲕⲱϩⲧ· ⲉⲛⲟⲭⲗⲉⲓ ⲛⲁⲕ· ⲟⲛ̄·
ϭⲟⲙ ⲛ̄ⲅϣⲱ·ⲡⲉ ⲛ̄ⲟⲩⲣⲱⲙⲉ· ⲛ̄ϫⲱⲱⲣⲉ, ϫⲉ· ⲕⲛⲁϣⲱⲡⲉ ϩⲓ·ⲡⲇⲓⲕⲁⲥⲧⲏⲣⲓⲟⲛ ⲙ̄-
ⲡⲉⲓ·ⲁⲛⲟ·ⲙⲟⲥ ⲛ̄ϥⲧ̄ϣⲓⲡⲉ· ⲛⲁⲩ ⲛ̄ⲥⲁⲩϥ ⲛ̄ⲉ·ⲃⲟⲧ· ⲁⲩⲟⲩⲱϣⲃ̄ ⲛ̄ϭⲓ ⲡ·ⲙⲁⲕⲁⲣⲓⲟⲥ
ⲁⲡⲁ· ⲡⲁⲛⲥⲉ ⲡⲉϫⲁⲩ·ⲙ̄ⲡⲁⲅⲅⲉⲗⲟⲥ· ϫⲉ ϯⲥⲃ̄ⲧⲱⲧ ⲡⲁϫⲟⲉⲓⲥ ⲉⲧⲣⲁ(Vii)ϥⲓ ϩⲁⲍⲓ-
ⲥⲉ ⲛⲓⲙ· ⲉⲧⲃⲉⲡⲣⲁⲛ ⲙ̄ⲡⲁ·ϫⲟⲉⲓⲥ ⲓ̅ⲥ̅ ⲡⲉⲭ̅ⲥ̅. ⲁⲩⲱ ⲡⲁⲅⲅⲉⲗⲟⲥ· ⲁⲥⲡⲁϫⲉ ⲙ̄-

---

61 R ii 33. ϯⲛⲁⲙⲁϫⲉ̄ apparently a correction from ϯⲛⲁⲛⲁϫⲏⲉ̄. The corrupt reading of D.

ⲡⲭⲁϫⲉ ⲛ̄ϥⲕⲓⲑⲟⲟⲩ ⲛ̄ϭⲓ ⲡⲣⲁⲛ ⲙ̄ⲡⲱⲟⲛⲧⲉ D (cf. partly, Boh.) 20. -ⲙⲁⲅⲓⲟⲥ A; om. D. 21.
ⲙ̄ⲡⲁⲅⲅⲉⲗⲟⲥ A; om. D. 23. ⲡⲁⲭⲟⲉⲓⲥ A (cf. Boh.); om. D. 27. ⲛⲁⲩ A; om D. 28. ⲉⲧⲓ
A; ⲱ ⲡⲁⲛⲥⲉ D (cf. Boh.). -ⲥⲁⲩϥ A (cf. Boh.); -ϣⲟⲙⲛⲧ D. 31f. ⲉⲡⲉⲓⲙⲁ ⲛ̄ⲅⲛⲁⲩ ⲉⲣⲟⲥ A;
om. D. 33. ϯⲛⲁⲙⲁϫⲉ̄ A (cf. Boh.); ϯⲛⲁⲛⲁϫⲙⲉⲥ (sic) D. Vi 1. ⲛ̄ϭⲟⲙ A; om. D (cf. Boh.).
2. ⲙ̄ⲡⲉⲭ̅ⲥ̅ A; ⲙ̄ⲡⲁϫⲟⲉⲓⲥ D. 2-7. ⲛⲉⲧⲙ̄ⲯⲩⲭⲏ — ⲛ̄ϩⲧⲟⲟⲩⲉ A (cf. Boh.); ⲧⲉⲕⲯⲩⲭⲏ ⲛⲁⲡⲱ-
ⲣϫ̄ ⲁⲛ ⲉⲧⲉⲧⲩⲭⲏ ⲛ̄ⲧⲉⲕⲥⲱⲛⲉ ⲁⲩⲱ ⲡⲉⲕⲥⲱⲙⲁ ⲛⲁⲡⲱⲣϫ̄ ⲁⲛ ⲉⲡⲱⲥ. (cf. Boh.) ⲁⲩⲟⲛ D.
9. Aϥⲧⲛ̄ ⲛ̄ⲥⲱⲕ, ϯ ⲛ̄ⲣⲁⲥⲧⲉ ⲉⲡⲃ̄ⲛⲏⲙⲁ D (cf. Boh.) 11f. ⲛ̄ϥⲥⲁϫⲧⲉ A (cf. Boh.); ⲛ̄ⲥⲉⲗ. D.
12. ⲁⲩⲱ A; om. D. 13-18. ϯⲛⲁⲱϣⲙ̄ — ⲛⲁⲕA (cf. Boh.); ϯⲛⲁⲣϩⲟⲣⲡ̄ ⲉⲣⲟⲕ ⲉⲧⲣⲉ-
ⲡⲕⲱϩⲧ ϫⲱϩ ⲉⲣⲟⲕ ⲉⲛⲧⲏⲣϥ̄ D. 22-27. ⲕⲛⲁϣⲱⲡⲉ — ⲛ̄ϥⲧ̄ϣⲓⲡⲉ ⲛⲁⲩ (cf Boh.) ⲛ̄ⲥⲁⲩϥ
ⲛ̄ⲉⲃⲟⲧ A; ⲧⲉⲕⲙⲁⲣⲧⲩⲣⲓⲁ ⲛⲁϣⲱⲡⲉ (cf. Boh.) ⲛ̄ⲥⲁⲩϥ ⲛ̄ⲉⲃⲟⲧ ϩⲓⲧⲙ̄ⲡⲉⲓⲁⲛⲟⲙⲟⲥ ⲛ̄ⲁⲟⲩϥ
D. 28. ⲁⲩⲟⲩⲱϣⲃ̄ ⲛ̄ϭⲓ A; ⲡⲉϫⲉ- D. 30f. ⲡⲉϫⲁϥ ⲙ̄ⲡⲁⲅⲅⲉⲗⲟⲥ A; om. D. 32-ii 4 ϯ ⲥⲃ̄-
ⲧⲱⲧ — ⲁⲩⲱ A; ϯⲟⲩⲙ ⲛⲁⲓ ⲱ ⲡⲁϫⲟⲉⲓⲥ ⲡⲉⲓⲱⲧ ⲁⲩⲱ ⲁⲛⲟⲕ ϯⲛⲁⲧ ⲙ̄ⲡⲁⲥⲱⲙⲁ ⲉⲛ̄ⲃⲁ-
ⲥⲁⲛⲟⲥ ⲉ̄ⲛⲡⲇⲓⲕⲁⲥⲧⲏⲣⲓⲟⲛ D (cf. Boh.) 5f. ⲙ̄ⲡⲙⲁⲕⲁⲣⲓⲟⲥ a. ⲡ.; ⲙ̄ⲙⲟⲩ D (cf. Boh)

Boh.-ϥⲓ·ⲱⲟⲩ ⲛ̄ϫⲉ ϥ̄ϯ ⲛⲉⲙⲛⲉϥⲁⲅⲅⲉⲗⲟⲥ·²⁵ⲉⲑⲟⲩⲁⲃ· ⲡⲉϫⲉⲡⲁⲛⲥⲓ ⲙ̄ⲡⲓⲁⲅⲅⲉⲗⲟⲥ ϫⲉ ⲡⲁ-
[ϭ̅ⲥ̅,ϯ]·ⲟⲩⲱϣ ⲉⲛⲁⲩ ⲉⲑⲉⲕⲗⲁ ⲧⲁ[ⲥ]ⲱⲛⲓ ⲙ̄ⲡⲁⲧ·ⲙⲟⲩ. ⲡⲉϫⲉ·ⲡⲓⲁⲅⲅⲉⲗⲟⲥ ⲛ̄ⲧⲉⲡⲟⲥ̅ ⲛⲁⲩ
ϫⲉ ⲡⲁ·ⲏⲥⲓ, ⲕⲉⲍ ⲛⲉϩⲟⲟⲩ ⲛⲉ ϣⲁⲧⲉⲕⲛⲁ[ⲧ]·ⲉⲑⲉⲕⲗⲁ ⲧⲉⲕⲥⲱⲛⲓ, ⲟⲩⲟϩ ⲉⲓ̈ⲉ·ⲙⲁ̀ϫ̀ϭ ϧⲉⲛ·
ϯϫⲟⲙ ⲛ̄ⲧⲉⲡⲟⲥ̅ ⲧⲉ[ⲕⲯⲩ]ⲭⲏ ⲛ̄ⲛⲉⲥϥⲱⲣⲝ ⲛ̄ⲃⲱⲥ, ⲟⲩⲇⲉ ⲡⲉⲕ·ⲥⲱⲙⲁ ⲛⲛⲉϥϥⲱⲣⲝ ⲉ-
ⲃⲟⲗ ⲛ̄ϥⲱⲥ·]· ⲓⲥⲕⲉ (blank?) ⲭⲟⲩⲱϣ [·]ⲉϣ
E.W. fr. 3 (p.116) (Cod. Cairo) (R = E.W., pl. V̲) [·ⲡⲓⲇⲟⲩ]ⲝ̄ ⲛⲁⲉⲛⲕ ϩⲓⲝⲉⲛⲡⲓ-
ⲃⲏⲙⲁ ⲛ̄ⲧⲟ·[ⲣⲓ], ⲩⲛⲁⲑⲣⲟⲩⲧⲁⲗⲟⲕ ϩⲓⲝⲉⲛⲟⲩ·[ⲥⲗⲟ]ϫ ⲙ̄ⲃⲉⲛⲓⲡⲓ ⲛⲧⲉⲩⲥⲁ̀ϫ̀ϯ ϩⲁ-
ⲣⲟⲕ· [ⲟⲩⲟ]ϩ ϯⲛⲁⲉⲣ·ϧⲟⲣⲡ ⲉⲣⲟⲕ ⲉⲡⲓⲥⲗⲟⲭ, [ϯ]ⲛⲁⲱϣⲉⲙ ⲙ̄ⲡⲓⲭⲣⲱⲙ ϩⲁⲣⲟⲕ,·
ⲟⲩⲟϩ ϯⲛⲁⲉⲣ·ϧⲏⲓⲃⲓ ⲉϫⲱⲕ ⲛⲧⲉⲩⲧⲉⲙⲡⲓⲭⲣⲱⲙ, ⲟⲩⲱⲙ ⲛⲟⲩⲕⲁⲛ ⲛ̄ϣⲱ ⲛⲧⲉ-
ⲧⲉⲕⲁϥⲉ. ϫⲉⲙϫⲟⲙ, ⲟⲩⲟϩ ϣⲱⲡⲓ ⲛⲟⲩⲣⲱⲙⲓ ⲛ̄¹⁰ϫⲱⲣⲓ, ϫⲉ ⲟⲩⲏⲓ ⲧⲉⲕⲙⲁⲣⲧⲩⲣⲓⲁ
ⲛⲁ·ϣⲱⲡⲓ ⲉⲥⲧⲩⲡⲓ ⲙ̄ⲡⲁⲓ·ⲁⲛⲟⲙⲟⲥ ⲛ̄ⲍ̄ ⲛⲁⲃⲟⲧ· ⲧⲟⲧⲉ ⲡⲉϫⲉⲡⲁⲛⲥⲓ ⲛⲁⲩ ϫⲉ
ⲡⲁⲧⲉ, ⲙⲁ·ϫⲟⲙ ⲛⲏⲓ, ⲟⲩⲟϩ ϯⲛⲁⲧ ⲙ̄ⲡⲁⲥⲱⲙⲁ· ⲉⲛⲓⲃⲁⲍⲁⲛⲟⲥ ⲧⲏⲣⲟⲩ ⲛ̄ⲧⲉⲡⲓⲇⲩⲕⲁⲥ·ⲧⲏ-
ⲣⲓⲟⲛ.·ⲡⲓⲁⲅⲅⲉⲗⲟⲥ ⲇⲉ ⲛ̄ⲧⲉⲡⲟⲥ̅ ⲁⲩⲉⲣⲁⲥⲡⲁϫⲉ·ⲑⲉ ⲙ̄ⲙⲟϥ, ⟶

ⲛⲙⲁ'ⲕⲁⲣⲓⲟⲥ ⲁⲡⲁ ⲡⲁ'ⲏⲥⲉ, ⲁⲩⲃⲱⲕ ⲉⲍ'ⲣⲁⲓ̈ ⲉⲙⲡⲏⲩⲉ ⲍ̄ⲛ̄'ⲟⲩⲉⲟⲟⲩ. [10] ⲙ̄ⲡⲉⲩⲣⲁⲥⲧⲉ
ⲇⲉ' ⲁⲩⲙⲟⲟⲥ ⲍⲓⲡ'ⲃⲏⲙⲁ ⲛ̄ⲟⲓ ⲅⲁⲣ'ⲙⲏⲛⲓⲟⲥ ⲍ̄ⲡⲉ'ⲑⲉⲁⲇⲣⲟⲛ, ⲁⲩ[15]'ⲕⲉⲗⲉⲩⲉ ⲉ-
ⲧⲣⲉⲩ'ⲉⲓⲛⲉ ⲛⲁⲩ ⲙ̄ⲡ'ⲙⲁⲕⲁⲣⲓⲟⲥ ⲁⲡⲁ' ⲡⲁⲏⲥⲉ ⲙ̄ⲛⲛⲉ'ⲧⲟⲩⲁⲁⲃ ⲧⲏⲣⲟⲩ[20] ⲉⲩⲥⲟⲛⲍ̄
ⲛ̄ⲧⲟⲟ'ⲧⲟⲩ ⲙ̄ⲛ̄ⲣⲁⲧⲟⲩ' ⲍ̄ⲛ̄ⲍⲉⲛⲍⲁⲗⲏⲥⲓⲥ' ⲙ̄ⲡⲉⲛⲓⲡⲉ, ⲉⲣⲉ'ⲍ̄ⲛ̄ⲕⲟⲗⲗⲁⲣⲓⲟⲛ[25] ⲍ̄ⲛ̄-
ⲛⲉⲩⲙⲁⲕⲍ̄,' ⲉⲩⲡⲏⲧ ⲛⲙ̄ⲙⲁⲩ' ⲛ̄ⲟⲓ ⲛ̄ⲕⲉⲥⲧⲱ'ⲛⲁⲣⲓⲟⲥ ϣⲁⲛ'ⲧⲟⲩⲛ̄ⲧⲟⲩ ⲍⲓϫⲙ̄'ⲡ[30]-
ⲃⲏⲙⲁ.' ⲛ̄ⲇⲟⲩⲍ ⲇⲉ ⲛ̄ⲧⲉⲣⲉϥ'ⲛⲁⲩ ⲉⲣⲟⲩ ⲡⲉ'ϫⲁⲩ ⲙ̄ⲡ̄ⲙⲁⲕⲁ(62 Ri)ⲣⲓⲟⲥ
ⲁⲡⲁ ⲡⲁⲏⲥⲉ' ϫⲉ ⲱ ⲛ̄ⲙⲁⲅⲟⲥ,'ⲁⲕ̄ϫⲓⲧⲡⲉ ⲛ̄ⲛ̄'ⲃⲁⲥⲁⲛⲟⲥ[5] ⲙ̄ⲡⲇⲓ'ⲕⲁⲥⲧⲏⲣⲓⲟⲛ,'
ⲁⲕⲉⲓⲙⲉ ϫⲉ ⲥⲉⲍⲟⲩ· ⲧⲉⲛⲟⲩ ⲇⲉ' ⲑⲩⲥⲓⲁⲍⲉ ⲛ̄ⲛ̄ⲛⲟⲩ'ⲧⲉ ⲉⲧⲧⲁⲓ̈ⲏⲩ,'[10] ⲙ̄ⲡⲉⲣⲙⲟⲩ
ⲕⲁⲕⲱⲥ.' ⲡⲉϫⲉⲡⲙⲁⲕⲁ'ⲣⲓⲟⲥ ⲛⲁⲩ ϫⲉ ⲁⲕ'ϫⲓ ϣⲓⲡⲉ ⲛ̄ⲧⲟⲕ' ⲙ̄ⲛ̄ⲛⲉⲕⲛⲟⲩ'ⲧⲉ[15] ⲛ̄-
ⲃⲟⲧⲉ.' ⲉⲩⲥⲱⲧⲙ̄ ⲇⲉ ⲉ'ⲛⲁⲓ̈ ⲛ̄ⲟⲓ ⲛⲇⲟⲩⲍ,' ⲁⲩϭⲱⲛⲧ ⲉⲙⲁ'ⲧⲉ· ⲁⲩⲕⲉⲗⲉⲩⲉ'[20] ⲉ-
ⲧⲣⲉⲩⲧⲁⲗⲟⲩ ⲉ'ⲡⲉϭⲗⲟϭ ⲙ̄ⲡⲉⲛⲓⲡⲉ ⲛ̄ⲥⲉⲥⲁⲍⲧⲉ'ⲍⲁⲣⲟⲩ ⲛ̄ⲟⲓ ϣ'ⲙⲟⲩⲛ ⲛ̄ⲕⲉⲥⲧⲱ'[25]
ⲛⲁⲣⲓⲟⲥ· ⲁⲩⲱ' ⲛ̄ⲧⲉⲩⲛⲟⲩ ⲁⲩⲉⲓ' ⲉⲃⲟⲗ ⲍⲓⲧⲡⲉ ⲛ̄ⲟⲓ ⲍⲣⲁⲫⲁⲏⲗ ⲡⲁⲅ'ⲅⲉⲗⲟⲥ, ⲁⲩⲣ̄
ⲍⲁⲓ̈'ⲃⲉ̄ ⲉⲣⲟⲩ ⲍⲁⲛⲉⲩ'ⲧⲛ̄ⲛ̄ⲍ̄ ⲛ̄ⲟⲩⲟⲉⲓⲛ,'[30] ⲁⲩⲱ ⲉⲩϣⲁϫⲉ'ⲛⲙ̄ⲙⲁⲩ ⲍⲛ̄ⲡ̄ⲕ̄(Rii)-

---

61 V ii 8. ⲍ̄ⲛ̄ⲟⲩⲉⲟⲟⲩ A (cf. Boh.); ⲟⲙ. D. 1ⲁ ⲇⲉ A; ⲟⲙ. D. 11f.ⲍⲓⲡⲃⲏⲙⲁ A; ⲉⲛ B.
D. 15f. ⲉⲧⲣⲉⲩⲉⲓⲛⲉ A; ⲉⲓⲛⲉ D. 16. ⲙ̄ⲡⲙⲁⲕⲁⲣⲓⲟⲥ ⲁ. ⲛ. A; ⲛⲁ. ⲛ. D. 20. ⲛ̄-
ⲧⲟⲟⲧⲟⲩ ⲙ̄ⲛ̄ⲣⲁⲧⲟⲩ A; ⲉⲛⲉⲩϭⲓⲝ ⲙ̄ⲛⲉⲩⲉⲣⲏⲧⲉ D. 22 f. ⲍ̄ⲛ̄ⲍⲉⲛⲍⲁⲗⲏⲥⲓⲥ ⲙ̄ⲡⲉ-
ⲛⲓⲡⲉ A (cf. Boh.); ⲟⲙ. D. 24. -ⲍ̄ⲛ̄ⲕⲟⲗⲗⲁⲣⲓⲟⲛ A; - ⲟⲩⲕ D. 25. ⲍ̄ⲛ̄ⲛⲉⲩⲙⲁⲕⲍ̄
A; ⲍ̄ⲛ̄ⲛⲉⲩⲙ D. 27-30. ⲛ̄ⲟⲓ -ⲍⲓϫⲙ̄ⲡⲃⲏⲙⲁ A (cf. Boh.); ⲟⲙ. D. 31f. ⲛ̄ⲧⲉⲣⲉϥ-
ⲛⲁⲩ ⲉⲣⲟⲟⲩ A (cf. Boh.); ⲟⲙ. D. 33 – 62 R i 1. ⲙ̄ⲡⲙⲁⲕⲁⲣⲓⲟⲥ ⲁ. ⲛ. A; ⲛⲁ. ⲛ.
D. 2. ⲛ̄ⲙⲁⲅⲟⲥ A; ⲛⲉⲫⲁⲣⲙⲁⲅⲟⲥ D (cf. Boh.). 3. ⲁⲕϫⲓⲧⲡⲉ A; ⲁⲕ̄ϫⲉⲛⲧⲁⲣ-
ⲭⲏ D. 4. ⲙ̄ⲡⲇⲓⲕⲁⲥⲧⲏⲣⲓⲟⲛ A (cf. Boh.); ⲟⲙ. D. 6f. ⲥⲉⲍⲟⲩⲛ A; ⲥⲉⲍⲟⲥⲉ D.
8. ⲑⲩⲥⲓⲁⲍⲉ A; ⲁⲣⲓⲑⲩⲥⲓⲁⲍⲉ D (cf. Boh.) 9. ⲉⲧⲧⲁⲓ̈ⲏⲩ A; ⲟⲙ. D. (cf. Boh.). 12.
ⲛⲁⲩ A; ⲁⲡⲁ ⲡⲁⲏⲥⲉ D. 13. ⲛ̄ⲧⲟⲕ A; ⲟⲙ. D. 17. ⲛ̄ⲟⲓ ⲛⲇⲟⲩⲍ A (cf. Boh.); ⲟⲙ.
D. 20. ⲉⲧⲣⲉⲩⲧⲁⲗⲟⲩ A; ⲉⲧⲁⲗⲟⲩ D (cf. Boh.)

Boh. ⲁⲩϭⲱⲗ ⲉⲍⲣⲏⲓ̈ ⲉⲛⲓⲫⲏ'ⲟⲧⲓ ϩⲉⲛⲟⲩⲱⲟⲩ. ⲉⲧⲁⲧⲟⲟⲩⲓ̈[20] ⲇⲉ ϣⲱⲡⲓ, ⲁⲩϩⲉⲙⲥⲓ ⲍⲓⲡⲓⲃⲏ-
ⲙⲁ ⲛ̄ϫⲉ ⲁⲣⲙⲉⲛⲓⲟⲥ ⲡⲓⲇⲟⲩⲍ ⲛ̄ⲧⲉⲣⲁⲕⲟⲧ ϩⲟⲛ'ⲛⲓⲑⲉⲁⲧⲣⲟⲛ,' ⲁϥⲟⲩⲁⲍⲥⲁϩⲛⲓ ⲉⲑⲣⲟⲩⲓⲛⲓ
ⲛⲁⲩ ⲙ̄ⲡ[ⲓ]'ⲁⲅⲓⲟⲥ ⲡⲁⲏⲥⲓ ⲛⲉⲙⲛⲏ ⲉⲑⲟⲩⲁⲃ· [5]ⲁⲩⲅⲉⲛⲟⲩ ⲉⲩⲥⲟⲛⲍ̄ ⲛ̄ⲛⲟⲩϭⲓⲝ ⲛⲉⲙ'ⲛⲟⲩ-
ϭⲁⲗⲁⲩϫ ⲛ̄ϫⲁⲛⲁⲗⲩⲥⲓⲥ ⲙ̄ⲃⲉⲛ'ⲓⲡⲓ, ⲉⲣⲉⲟⲩⲟⲛⲟⲩⲕⲟⲗⲗⲁⲣⲓⲟⲛ ⲧⲟⲓ' ⲉⲛⲉⲩⲙⲟⲩⲧ, ⲉⲩⲇⲟϣⲓ
ⲛ̄ⲥⲱⲩ' [ⲛ]ⲉⲙⲛⲏ ⲉⲑⲟⲩⲁⲃ ⲧⲏⲣⲟⲩ ⲛ̄ϫⲉⲛⲓ'[ⲕ]ⲉⲥⲧⲟⲛⲁⲣⲓⲟⲥ ⲉⲩⲃⲟⲣⲃⲉⲣ ⲙ̄'[ⲉ]ⲱⲟⲩ ⲉⲃⲟⲗ
ϣⲁⲛⲧⲟⲩⲉⲛⲟⲩ ⲍⲓϫⲉⲛ'[ⲡ]ⲓⲃⲏⲙⲁ. '[ⲉⲧⲁ]ⲡⲓ ⲛ̄ⲇⲟⲩⲍ ⲛⲁⲩ ⲉⲣⲱⲟⲩ, [ⲡ]ⲉϫⲁⲩ ⲙ̄'[ⲡⲁⲏⲥⲓ]
ϫⲉ ⲡⲓⲫⲁⲣⲙⲁⲅⲟⲥ, ⲁⲕϫⲉⲙⲧ[ⲓ] ⲛ̄ⲛⲓⲃⲁⲍⲁⲛⲟⲥ ⲛ̄ⲧⲉⲡⲓⲇⲓⲕⲁⲥ(V)ⲧⲏⲣⲓⲟⲛ, ⲁⲕⲉⲙ[ⲓ]
ϫⲉ ⲥⲉϩⲟⲩⲧ ...(-ϩⲟⲥⲓ?)· ⲧ]ⲛⲟⲩ ⲇⲉ (ϫⲉ?) ⲁⲣⲓ(ⲑ)ⲩⲥⲓⲁ ⲛ̄ⲛⲓⲛⲟⲩⲧ, ⲙ̄ⲡⲉⲣⲙⲟⲩ'ⲛ̄ⲕⲁⲕⲗⲱⲥ.'
ⲡⲓⲁⲅ[ⲓⲟ]ⲥ ⲇⲉ [ⲡ]ⲉϫⲁⲩ ϫⲉ ⲁⲕⲉ·[...]ϫ[.......]ⲛ̄ⲉⲙⲛ[ⲉ]ⲕⲁⲡⲟⲗⲗⲱⲛ(-ⲡⲉⲕ-?) [ⲛⲉ]ⲁ'[ⲧ-
ⲁⲣⲧⲉⲙⲓⲥ](?)ⲍⲟⲥ ⲟⲩⲟⲍ ⲡⲉⲕⲟⲩ'[ⲣⲱ ⲇⲓⲟⲕⲗⲏ[ⲧ[ⲓⲁⲛ]ⲟⲥ(?) ⲉⲧⲟⲁϩⲉⲙ' ⲁ[ⲩϣⲱ]ⲛ[ⲧ] ⲛ̄-
ϫⲉ ⲡⲓⲇⲟⲩⲍ, ⲁⲩⲉⲣⲕⲉ'[ⲗ]ⲉⲩⲓⲛ ⲉⲧⲁⲗⲟⲩ ⲉⲟⲩⲟⲗⲟϫ ⲙ̄ⲃⲉⲛⲓ'[ⲡⲓ] ⲛ̄ⲥⲉⲥⲁⲍⲧ ⲉⲣⲟⲩ (ϩⲁ-
ⲣⲟⲩ?) ⲛ̄ϫⲉ ⲛⲓ[ⲕ]ⲉⲥⲧⲟⲛⲁⲣⲓⲟⲥ.' ⲟⲩⲟⲍ ⲛ̄ⲧⲟⲩⲛⲟⲩ ⲁⲩ ⲉⲡⲉⲥⲏⲧ ⲉⲃⲟⲗ' ϩⲉⲛⲧⲫⲉ ⲛ̄ϫⲉ
ⲅⲁⲃⲣⲓⲏⲗ ⲡⲓⲁⲣⲭⲏ'ⲁ[ⲅⲅ]ⲉⲗⲟⲥ ···ⲍⲉ[......]ⲛⲁⲩ, ⲁⲩⲉⲣ[15]ⲏⲓⲃⲓ ⲉϫⲱⲩ ϩⲉⲛⲛⲉⲩⲧⲉ-
ⲛ̄ⲍ,' ⲁⲩⲥⲁϫⲓ ⲛⲉⲙⲁⲩ ϩⲉⲛⲛⲓ- →

ⲙⲏⲥⲧⲏⲣⲓⲟⲛ ⲛ̄ⲧ'ⲡⲉ· ⲁⲩⲱ ⲙ̄ⲡⲉⲡ'ⲕⲱϯ ⲃⲗⲁⲡⲧⲓ' ⲙ̄ⲙⲟⲩ ⲉⲛⲗⲁⲁⲩ⁵ ⲉⲡⲧⲏⲣϥ. ⲛⲉⲩ'ⲥⲁⲍ
ⲧⲉ ⲍⲁⲣⲟⲩ ⲡⲉ'ⲛ̄ϭⲓ ⲁⲕⲉⲥⲧⲱⲛⲁ'ⲣⲓⲟⲥ ϫⲓⲛⲁ̄ⲛ̄'ⲥⲛ̄ⲧⲉ ⲙ̄ⲡⲉⲍⲟⲟⲩ¹⁰ ⲩⲁⲧⲭ̄ⲛⲥⲁ.'ⲛ̄ⲧⲉⲣⲉⲩ
ⲧⲱⲟⲩⲛ(ⲛ) ⲇⲉ ⲛ̄ϭⲓ ⲡⲗⲟⲩϫ' ϫⲉ ⲉⲩⲛⲁⲁⲛⲁⲭⲱ'ⲣⲉⲓ, ⲁⲩⲕⲉⲗⲉⲩⲉ¹⁵ ϫⲉ ϥⲓ ⲙ̄ⲡⲉⲩⲕⲉⲣⲙⲉⲥ
ⲛ̄ⲧⲉⲧⲛ̄ⲛⲟ'ϫϥ̄ ⲉⲑⲁⲗⲁⲥⲥⲁ.' ⲛⲉⲩⲙⲉⲉⲩⲉ ⲅⲁⲣ' ϫⲉ ⲁⲩⲟⲩⲱ ⲉϥ'ⲙⲟⲩ.' ⲡⲍⲁⲅⲓⲟⲥ ⲇⲉ ⲁⲡⲁ'
ⲡⲁⲏⲥⲉ ⲟⲩⲉⲓ ⲉⲃⲟⲗ' ϩⲛ̄ⲧⲙⲏⲧⲉ ⲙ̄ⲡ'ⲕⲱϯ ϩⲛ̄ⲧϭⲟⲙ' ⲙ̄ⲡⲉⲡⲛ̄ⲁ ⲉⲧⲟⲩ'ⲁⲁⲃ, ⲉⲣⲉⲡⲁⲅ'
ⲅⲉⲗⲟⲥ ⲙ̄ⲡϫⲟⲉⲓⲥ' ⲁⲍⲉⲣⲁⲧⲩ̄ ⲉϥ'ⲙⲁⲍⲧⲉ ⲛ̄ⲧⲉϥ'ϭⲓϫ, ⲉϥⲁⲍⲉⲣⲁ'ⲧϥ̄ ϩⲛ̄ⲧⲙⲏⲧⲉ' ⲙ̄
ⲡⲙⲏⲏⲩⲉ ⲉ'ⲙ̄ⲡⲗⲁⲁⲩ ⲛ̄ⲧⲁ(62 Vi)ⲕⲟ ⲩⲟⲟⲡ ⲙ̄ⲙⲟⲩ.' ⲛ̄ⲧⲉⲣⲉⲩⲛⲁⲩ ⲇⲉ ⲛ̄ϭⲓ ⲡⲙⲏⲏ
ⲩⲉ' ⲉⲧⲉⲓ̈ⲛⲟϭ ⲛ̄ⲩⲡⲏ'ⲣⲉ ⲛ̄ⲧⲁⲥⲩⲱ'ⲡⲉ, ⲁⲩⲱⲱⲩ' ⲉⲃⲟⲗ ⲉⲩϫⲱ ⲙ̄'ⲙⲟⲥ ϫⲉ ⲟⲩⲁ ⲡⲉ
ⲡ'ⲛⲟⲩⲧⲉ ⲙ̄ⲡⲉⲧⲟⲩ'ⲁⲁⲃ ⲁⲡⲁ ⲡⲁⲏ'ⲥⲉ ⲉⲙⲛ̄ⲕⲉⲟⲩⲁ' ⲛ̄ⲃⲗ̄ⲗⲁⲩ. ⲁⲩⲱ'ⲧⲏⲡⲉ ⲛ̄ⲛⲉⲣⲱ
ⲙⲉ' ⲛ̄ⲧⲁⲩⲡⲓⲥⲧⲉⲩⲉ' ⲙ̄ⲡⲉⲍⲟⲟⲩ ⲉⲧⲙ̄'ⲙⲁⲩ ⲥⲉⲉⲓⲣⲉ ⲛ̄'ϣⲟⲩⲧⲁⲩⲧⲉ ⲙ̄'ⲯⲩⲭⲏ·ⲁⲩⲁⲍⲉ'
ⲣⲁⲧⲟⲩ ⲁⲩⲧⲥⲱⲟⲩ' ⲙ̄ⲡⲗⲟⲩϫ ⲙⲛ̄'ⲡⲕⲉⲣⲣⲟ ⲛ̄ⲁⲛⲟ'ⲙⲟⲥ ⲙ̄ⲛⲉⲩ'ⲛⲟⲩⲧⲉ ⲛ̄ⲃⲁⲧⲉ.' ⲁⲩ
ⲕⲉⲗⲉⲩⲉ ⲇⲉ' ⲛ̄ϭⲓ ⲡⲗⲟⲩϫ ⲛ̄'ⲥⲉϥⲓⲧⲟⲩ ⲉⲡ'ⲃⲟⲗ ⲛ̄ⲧⲡⲟⲗⲓⲥ' ⲛ̄ⲥⲉϥⲓ ⲛ̄ⲧⲉⲩ'ⲁⲡⲉ. ⲁⲩⲱ
ⲧⲁⲓ̈' ⲧⲉ ⲑⲉ ⲛ̄ⲧⲁⲩϫⲱⲕ' ⲉⲃⲟⲗ ⲛ̄ⲧⲉⲩⲙⲁⲣ'ⲧⲩⲣⲓⲁ ⲛ̄ⲥⲟⲩⲥⲛⲁⲩ (Vii) ⲙ̄ⲡⲉⲃⲟⲧ ⲡⲁⲩⲟ'
ⲛⲉ̄, ϩⲛ̄ⲟⲩⲉⲓⲣⲏ'ⲛⲏ, ϩⲁⲙⲏⲛ.' ⲡⲗⲟⲩϫ ⲇⲉ ⲁⲩ'ⲕⲟⲧϥ̄ ⲉⲡⲙⲁ'ⲕⲁⲣⲓⲟⲥ ⲁⲡⲁ ⲡⲁ'ⲏⲥⲉ,

---

62 V i 6. l. ⲁⲩⲱⲩ

---

62 R ii 1f. ⲛ̄ⲧⲡⲉ A (cf Boh.); ⲉⲧϩⲛ̄ⲙ̄ⲡⲏⲩⲉ D. 2–5. ⲁⲩⲱ – ⲉⲡⲧⲏⲣϥ A; om. D (cf. Boh.)
5f. ⲛⲉⲩⲥⲁⲍⲧⲉ ⲍⲁⲣⲟⲩ ⲡⲉ A; ⲛ̄ⲧⲉⲣⲟⲩⲧⲱ ⲇⲉ ⲉⲩⲥⲁⲍⲧⲉ ⲍⲁⲣⲟⲩ D. 7f. ⲛ̄ϭⲓ ⲁⲕⲉⲥⲧⲱⲛⲁⲣⲓ-
ⲟⲥ A (cf. Boh.); om. D. 9. ⲁ̄ⲡⲉⲍⲟⲟⲩ A; om. D. 10. ⲩⲁⲧⲭ̄ⲛⲥⲁ A; ⲩⲁⲭ̄ⲛ̄ⲥⲟⲉ D. 11f.
ⲛ̄ⲧⲉⲣⲉⲩⲧⲱⲟⲩⲛ ⲇⲉ A; ⲁⲩⲧⲱⲟⲩⲛ D. 15. ϫⲉ ϥⲓ A; ⲉϥⲓ D. 15f. ⲙ̄ⲡⲉⲩⲕⲉⲣⲙⲉⲥ A (cf. Boh.);
ⲙ̄ⲡⲉⲩⲥⲱⲙⲁ ⲉⲩⲩⲁⲛⲣ̄ⲕⲉⲣⲙⲉⲥ D. 16f. ⲛ̄ⲧⲉⲧⲛ̄ⲛⲟϫϥ̄ A; ⲛ̄ⲥⲉⲛⲟϫϥ̄ D. 18–20. ⲛⲉⲩⲙⲉⲉⲩⲉ — ⲉϥⲙⲟⲩ A; ⲁⲩϫⲟⲟⲥ ⲅⲁⲣ ϫⲉ ⲉⲩϫⲉ ⲓ̄ⲥ̄ ⲕⲁⲛⲁⲍⲧⲩ̄ ⲙⲁⲣⲉϥⲓ ⲧⲉⲛⲟⲩ ⲛ̄ϥⲛⲁⲍⲙⲉϥ
ϩⲛ̄ⲛⲁϫⲓϫ ϫⲉ ⲙ̄ⲛ̄ⲛⲟⲩⲧⲉ ⲛ̄ⲥⲁⲡⲁⲡⲟⲗⲗⲱⲛ ⲙ̄ⲛ̄ⲧⲁⲣⲧⲉⲙⲓⲥ D (cf. Boh.) 26f. ⲉⲣⲉⲡⲁⲅⲅⲉⲗⲟⲥ A; ⲉⲣⲉⲡⲁⲣⲭⲁⲅⲅⲉⲗⲟⲥ D. 27f. ⲙ̄ⲡϫⲟⲉⲓⲥ (cf. Boh.) ⲁⲍⲉⲣⲁⲧϥ̄ ⲉϥ – A; om. D.
30f. ⲉϥⲁⲍⲉⲣⲁⲧϥ̄ A; ⲁⲩⲁⲍ. D. 32. ⲙ̄ⲡⲙⲏⲏⲩⲉ D. 32 –V i 1. ⲉⲙ̄ⲛ̄
ⲗⲁⲁⲩ — ⲙ̄ⲙⲟⲩ A; om. D. 2–6. ⲛ̄ⲧⲉⲣⲉⲩⲛⲁⲩ — ⲛ̄ⲧⲁⲥⲩⲱⲡⲉ A; ⲉⲣⲉⲡⲙⲏⲏⲩⲉ ⲧⲏ-
ⲣϥ̄ ⲑⲉⲱⲣⲉⲓ ⲙ̄ⲙⲟⲩ D. 6. ⲁⲩⲱⲱⲩ (sic) A; ⲉⲣⲱⲩ D. 7f. ⲁⲩⲭⲱ ⲙ̄ⲙⲟⲥ A; om. D.
9f. ⲙ̄ⲡⲉⲧⲟⲩⲁⲁⲃ a. n. A; ⲛ̄ⲁ. п. D. 11f. ⲉⲙ̄ⲛ̄ⲕⲉⲟⲩⲁ ⲛ̄ⲃⲗ̄ⲗⲁⲩ A; ⲁⲩⲱ ⲙ̄ⲛ̄-
ⲕⲉⲟⲩⲁ ⲛ̄ⲥⲁⲃⲗ̄ⲗⲁⲩ D. 12f. ⲁⲩⲱ ⲧⲏⲡⲉ ⲛ̄ⲛⲉⲣⲱⲙⲉ A; ⲛ̄ⲣⲱⲙⲉ D. 18f. ⲁⲩⲁⲍⲉⲣⲁⲧⲟⲩ ⲁⲩⲧⲥⲱⲩ A; ⲉⲩⲁⲍ. ⲁⲩⲧⲥⲱⲩ D. 21. – ⲡⲕⲉⲣⲣⲟ A; – ⲡⲣ̄ⲣⲟ D. 22f. ⲙ̄ⲛⲉⲩⲛⲟⲩⲧⲉ ⲛ̄ⲃⲁ-
ⲧⲉ A; om. D. 24. ⲇⲉ A; om. D. 25f. ⲛ̄ⲥⲉϥⲓⲧⲟⲩ A; ⲉⲧⲣⲉⲩϥⲓⲧⲟⲩ D. 26. ⲉⲡⲃⲟⲗ A; ⲡⲃ̄ D.

Boh. – ⲙⲩⲥⲧⲏⲣⲓⲟⲛ ⲛ̄ⲧϫⲉⲧⲫⲉ· ⲟⲩⲟϩ ⲁⲩⲥⲁϯ ϩⲁ'ⲣⲟⲩ [ⲛ̄]ϫⲉ ⲛⲓⲕⲉⲥⲧⲓⲟⲛⲁⲣⲓⲟⲥ ⲓⲥϫⲉⲛ'
ⲁϫⲡⲉ̄ϯ (–ⲟ̄ϯ?) ⲙ̄ⲡⲓⲉϩⲟⲟⲩ ⲩⲁⲁϫⲡⲅ̄.⁷ ⲟⲩⲟϩ ⲁⲩⲧⲱⲛϥ ⲛ̄ϫⲉ ⲡⲓⲗⲟⲩϫ, ⲁϥ'ⲉⲣⲕⲉⲗⲉⲩⲓⲛ
ⲉϥϫⲱ ⲙ̄ⲙⲟⲥ ϫⲉ ⲁ'ⲛⲓⲟⲩⲓ ⲛ̄ⲧⲉⲩⲕⲉⲣⲙⲓ, ⲥⲁⲧϭ ⲉϥⲓⲟⲙ.' ϫⲉ ϫⲟⲥ ..ⲣ (ⲁⲩϫⲟⲥ ⲅⲁⲣ?) ϫⲉ
ⲡⲭ̄ⲥ̄ ⲛⲁ̄ⲛⲁϩⲙⲉⲧ' ⲉϣⲁⲣⲉϥ ϯⲛⲟⲩ ⲛ̄ⲧⲉⲩⲛⲁϩⲙⲉⲩ ⲉ[ⲃ]ⲟⲗ⁷ ϩⲉⲛⲡⲁⲓ̈ⲃⲁⲥⲁⲛⲟⲥ (–ⲛⲁⲓ̈?)
ⲓⲥϫⲉ ⲟⲩⲟⲛ'[ⲩ]ϫ[ⲟ]ⲙ ⲙ̄ⲙⲟⲩ' ⲉⲡⲓⲇⲏ ⲙ̄ⲙⲟⲛⲛⲟ[ⲩ]ϯ ⲉⲟⲩⲟⲛⲩϫ[ⲟⲙ]' ⲙ̄ⲙⲟⲩ ⲙ̄ⲫⲣⲏϯ ⲙ̄ⲡⲓ-
ⲁⲡⲟⲗⲗⲱⲛ' ⲛⲉⲙ̄ⲧⲁⲣⲧⲉⲙⲓⲥ.' ϩⲉⲛⲧⲟⲩⲛⲟⲩ ⲉⲧⲓ ⲉϥϫⲱ ⲙ̄ⲙⲟⲥ, ⲁϥⲓ' ⲉⲃⲟⲗ ϩⲉⲛ ⲡⲓⲭⲣⲱⲙ ⲛ̄
ⲧⲉⲡ[ⲓⲑⲗⲟⲝ ⲛ̄ϫⲉ] ⲡⲁⲏⲥⲓ [ⲛ̄ϫⲉ ⲡ[ⲓⲁⲅⲓⲟⲥ] ⲡ.?) ϩⲉⲛⲧⲇⲟⲙ (–ϯϫ.?) ⲙ̄ⲡⲓⲡⲛ̄ⲁ ⲉⲑⲟⲩⲁⲃ,
ⲉⲣⲉ ⲡⲓⲁⲅⲅⲉⲗⲟⲥ ⲛ̄ⲧⲟⲡⲟϭ ⲁⲙⲟⲛⲓ ⲛ̄ⲧⲉⲩϫⲓϫ ..ⲉⲛⲓϫ[

πεχαγ ναγ' χε απεκϭητ ⲙ̄ⲧⲟⲛ ⲧⲉⲛⲟⲩ ⲛ̄'ⲧⲁ̄ⲛⲁ̈ⲓ ⲭⲱⲡⲉ' ⲉⲁⲛⲁ̈ⲓ ⲧⲏⲣⲟⲩ' ⲙⲟⲩ ⲛ̄-
ⲧⲉⲕⲁⲫⲟⲣ'ⲙⲏ; ⲁⲩⲟⲩⲱ̀ⲭⲃ̄ ⲛ̄ϭⲓ ⲡⲙⲁⲕⲁ̄'ⲣⲓⲟⲥ ⲁⲡⲁ ⲡⲁⲏ'ⲥⲉ, ⲡⲉⲭⲁⲩ ναγ' χε ⲉⲕⲩⲁⲛⲃⲱⲕ' ⲉⲣⲁⲧϥ̄ ⲙ̄ⲡⲉⲕⲣ̄'ⲣⲟ ⲛ̄ⲁⲛⲟⲙⲟⲥ, ⲙⲏ ⲙⲉⲕⲭⲟⲟⲩ' ⲍⲓⲑⲏ ⲙ̄ⲙⲟⲕ ⲛ̄'ⲍⲉⲛⲧⲁⲓⲟ; ⲧⲁⲓ
ⲧⲉ' ⲧⲁⲍⲉ ⲍⲱ· ⲛ̄ⲧⲁⲓ'ⲧⲛ̄ⲛⲟⲟⲩ ⲙ̄ⲛⲁ̈ⲓ' ⲍⲓⲑⲏ ⲙ̄ⲙⲟⲓ̈ ⲛ̄'ⲧⲁⲓⲟ ⲙ̄ⲡⲁⲣⲣⲟ ⲡⲉⲭⲥ̄. ⲡⲉⲭⲉ-
ⲛ'ⲇⲟⲩⲝ ναγ χε' ⲡⲁⲗⲓⲛ ⲟⲛ ⲉⲕϯ'ⲥⲱⲟⲩ ⲛ̄ⲛⲭⲓ'ⲥⲟⲟⲩⲉ ⲛ̄ⲣⲣⲱⲟⲩ.' ⲩⲉ ⲡⲟⲩⲭⲁⲓ̈ ⲙ̄'ⲡⲁⲡⲱⲗⲗⲟⲛ (63 R i) χε ⲛ̄ϯⲛⲁⲟⲩⲱⲙ' ⲁⲛ ⲛ̄ϯⲛⲁⲥⲱ' ⲁⲛ ⲩⲁⲛⲧⲁⲃⲱⲗ' ⲉⲃⲟⲗ ⲛ̄ⲛⲉⲕⲙⲉⲗ[...]
ⲁⲩⲱ ⲁⲩⲕⲉⲗⲉⲩⲉ ⲉⲧⲣⲉⲩⲧⲱⲕ' ⲉⲩⲧⲣⲓⲣ ⲭⲓⲛⲉⲡ'ⲛⲁⲩ ⲙ̄ⲡⲉⲉⲣⲉ' ⲩⲁⲡⲛⲁⲩ ⲛ̄ⲣⲟⲩⲍⲉ· ⲁⲩ-
ⲧⲣⲉⲩⲉⲓ'ⲛⲉ ⲛ̄ⲟⲩⲗⲁⲙⲭⲁⲧⲏ̄.' ⲁⲣⲧⲱⲍⲉ̄ ⲙ̄ⲡⲉⲩ'ⲥⲱⲙⲁ ⲧⲏⲣϥ̄' ⲩⲁϩⲣⲁⲓ ⲉⲧⲉⲩⲁⲡⲉ·' ⲁⲩⲱ
ⲁⲩⲧⲣⲉⲩⲥⲁ'ⲛⲍϥ̄ ⲛ̄ⲍⲉⲛⲍⲁⲗⲏ'ⲥⲓⲥ ⲙ̄ⲡⲉⲛⲓⲡⲉ,' ⲁⲩⲱ ⲁⲩⲙⲟⲩⲣ ⲛ̄ⲛⲉⲩⲟⲩⲉⲣⲏⲧⲉ ⲉ'ⲡⲉⲩⲙⲁ-
ⲕⲍ̄, ⲁⲩ'ⲛⲟⲩⲭⲉ ⲙ̄ⲙⲟⲩ ⲉ'ⲡⲉⲥⲏⲧ ⲛ̄ⲧⲉⲧⲣⲓⲣ ⲛ̄'ⲕⲱⲍⲧ̄, ⲁⲩⲱ ⲉⲛⲉⲥⲙⲟⲩⲍ ⲉⲙⲁⲧⲉ̄ ⲡⲉ,
ⲉⲥϩⲍⲟⲧⲉ ⲉⲃⲟⲗ' ϩⲓⲩⲧⲟⲣⲧⲣ̄.' ⲁⲩⲕⲉⲗⲉⲩⲉ ⲛ̄ϭⲓ ⲡ'ⲇⲟⲩⲝ ⲉⲧⲣⲉⲩⲍⲱ'ⲃⲉ ⲛ̄ⲧⲉⲧⲣⲓⲣ ⲛ̄ⲥⲉ-
ⲧⲱⲱⲃⲉ ⲙ̄'ⲙⲟⲥ ⲛ̄ⲥⲉⲁⲛⲁ'ⲭⲱⲣⲉⲓ ναγ ⲩⲁ'ⲡⲉⲩⲣⲁⲥⲧⲉ. (R ii) ⲡⲙⲁⲕⲁⲣⲓⲟⲥ ⲇⲉ' ⲁⲡⲁ
ⲡⲁⲏⲥⲉ ⲁⲩⲩⲗⲏⲗ ⲙ̄ⲡⲉⲥⲏⲧ' ⲛ̄ⲧⲉⲧⲣⲓⲣ ⲉⲩⲕⲱ' ⲙ̄ⲙⲟⲥ χε ⲥⲱⲧⲙ̄ ⲉⲣⲟⲓ ⲙ̄ⲡⲟⲟⲩ' ⲡⲁⲭⲟⲉⲓⲥ ⲓⲥ̄ ⲡⲉⲭ' ⲛ̄ⲃⲟⲏⲑⲓ ⲉⲣⲟⲓ,'ⲡⲉⲛⲧⲁⲩⲛⲟⲩⲍⲙ̄' ⲙ̄ⲡⲓⲩⲟⲙⲛ̄ⲧ ⲛ̄ϩⲁⲅⲓⲟⲥ ϩⲛ̄ⲧⲉⲣⲱ'
ⲛ̄ⲥⲁⲧⲉ ⲉⲧⲙⲟⲩⲍ,' ⲉⲕⲉⲥⲱⲧⲙ̄ ⲉⲣⲟⲓ' ϩⲱ, ⲁⲛⲟⲕ ⲡⲉⲕ'ϩⲙ̄ϩⲁⲗ ϩⲛ̄ⲧⲉⲓ'ⲟⲩⲛⲟⲩ ⲛ̄ⲁ-
ⲛⲁⲅⲕⲏ· ⲡⲉⲛⲧⲁⲩ'ⲥⲱⲧⲙ̄ ⲉⲡⲉⲡⲣⲟ'ⲫⲏⲧⲏⲥ ⲇⲁⲛⲓ'ⲏⲗ ⲉⲩϩⲙ̄ⲡⲩⲏⲓ' ⲛ̄ⲛⲉⲙⲙⲟ̈ⲓ,
ⲉⲕⲉ'ⲥⲱⲧⲙ̄ ⲉⲣⲟⲓ ϩⲱ'ⲙ̄ⲡⲟⲟⲩ·' ⲡⲉⲛⲧⲁⲩⲧⲛ̄ⲛⲟⲟⲩ' ⲙ̄ⲡⲉⲩⲁⲅⲅⲉⲗⲟⲥ' ⲁⲩⲛⲟⲩⲍⲙ̄ ⲙ̄'
ⲡⲉⲩϩⲙ̄ϩⲁⲗ ⲃⲓⲕ'ⲧⲱⲣ ⲉⲃⲟⲗ ϩⲙ̄'ⲡⲙⲁⲛⲧⲱⲕ ⲛ̄ⲧ'ⲥⲓⲟⲟⲩⲛ, ⲉⲕⲉ'ⲧⲛ̄ⲛⲟⲟⲩ ⲟⲛ ⲧⲉ-'

---

62 V ii 26. l. ⲙ̄ⲡⲁⲣⲣⲟ

62 V ii 9. ⲧⲉⲛⲟⲩ A; om. D. 10 f. ⲩⲱⲡⲉ ⲉⲁⲛⲁⲓ A; om. D. 12 f. ⲛ̄ⲧⲉⲕⲁⲫⲟⲣⲙⲏ A;
ⲉⲧⲃⲏⲏⲧⲕ̄ D. 16. ⲡⲉⲭⲁⲩ ναγ A; om. D. 17–19. ⲉⲕⲩⲁⲛⲃⲱⲕ ⲉⲣⲁⲧϥ̄ ⲙ̄ⲡⲉⲕⲣⲣⲟ A;
ⲙ̄ⲡⲛⲁⲩ ⲉⲕⲛⲁⲃⲱⲕ ⲩⲁⲡⲣⲣⲟ D. 20. ⲙⲏ A; om. D. 21. ⲍⲓⲑⲏ ⲙ̄ⲙⲟⲕ A; om. D. 22.
-ⲧⲁⲓⲟ A; -ⲇⲱⲣⲟⲛ ϩⲁⲧⲉⲕϭⲏ D. 22 f. ⲧⲁⲓ ⲧⲉ ⲧⲁⲍⲉ ⲍⲱ A; ⲧⲁⲓ ⲍⲱⲱⲧ ⲧⲉ ⲑⲉ D.
24. -ⲧⲛ̄ⲛⲟⲟⲩ A; -ⲭⲟⲟⲩ D. 25. ⲍⲓⲑⲏ ⲙ̄ⲙⲟⲓ A; om. D. 26. -ⲧⲁⲓⲟ A; -ⲇⲱⲣⲟⲛ D.
ⲡⲉⲭⲉ A; ⲧⲁⲍⲏ D. 29. ⲡⲁⲗⲓⲛ ⲟⲛ A; om. D. 29 f. ⲉⲕϯⲥⲱⲩ A; ⲉⲕⲥⲱⲩ D. 30.
ⲛ̄ⲛⲭⲓⲥⲟⲟⲩⲉ ⲛ̄ A; om. D. 63 R i 1. χε A; om. D. 2. After ⲁⲛ, + ⲟⲩⲇⲉ D. 9.
ⲩⲁⲡⲛⲁⲩ ⲛ̄ⲣⲟⲩⲍⲉ A; ⲅⲁⲣ D. 10 f. ⲁⲩⲧⲣⲉⲩⲉⲓⲛⲉ A; ⲁⲩⲕⲉⲗⲉⲩⲉ ⲉⲧⲣⲉⲩⲉⲓⲛⲉ D.
12 f. ⲁⲣⲧⲱⲍⲉ̄ ⲙ̄ⲡⲉⲩⲥⲱⲙⲁ A; ⲛ̄ⲥⲉⲗⲁⲗⲱⲡⲉⲩϭ D. 14 f. ⲩⲁϩⲣⲁⲓ - ⲁⲣⲱⲁⲓ om.
D. 18. ⲁⲩⲙⲟⲩⲣ A; ⲛ̄ⲥⲉⲙ. D. 20 f. ⲁⲩⲛⲟⲩⲭⲉ ⲙ̄ⲙⲟⲩ A; ⲁⲩⲛⲟⲭϥ̄ D. 21 f. ⲉ-
ⲡⲉⲥⲏⲧ A; om. D. 22. ⲛ̄ⲧⲉⲧⲣⲓⲣ A; ⲉⲧⲉⲧ. D. 22–26. ⲁⲩⲱ - ϩⲓⲩⲧⲟⲣⲧⲣ̄ A; om.
D. 28–31. ⲉⲧⲣⲉⲩⲍⲱⲃⲉ ⲛ̄ⲧⲉⲧⲣⲓⲣ ⲛ̄ⲥⲉⲧⲱⲱⲃⲉ ⲙ̄ⲙⲟⲥ A; ⲉⲧⲣⲉⲩⲍⲟⲃⲥⲉ̄ ⲛ̄ⲥⲉⲧⲟⲟ-
ⲃⲉⲥ D. 31 f. ⲛ̄ⲥⲉⲁⲛⲁⲭⲱⲣⲉⲓ ναγ A; om. D. ii 4 f. ⲉⲩⲕⲱ ⲙ̄ⲙⲟⲥ A; om. D. 5. After χε, + ⲛ̄ⲭⲟⲉⲓⲥ D. 7 f. ⲡⲁⲭⲟⲉⲓⲥ - ⲉⲣⲟⲓ A; om. D. 11. After ⲛ̄ϩⲁⲅⲓⲟⲥ, + ⲉⲃⲟⲗ D.
12. ⲉⲧⲙⲟⲩⲍ A; om. D. 14. ϩⲱ A; ϩⲱⲱⲧ D. 14 f. ⲁⲛⲟⲕ ⲡⲉⲕϩⲙ̄ϩⲁⲗ A; ⲙ̄ⲡⲟⲟⲩ D.
20 f. ⲉⲩϩⲙ̄ⲡⲩⲏⲓ ⲛ̄ⲛⲉⲙⲙⲟⲓ A; om. D. 22. ϩⲱ A; ϩⲱⲱⲧ D. 26–29. ⲁⲩⲛⲟⲩⲍⲙ̄
- ϩⲛ̄ⲡⲙⲁⲛⲧⲱⲕ A; ⲩⲁⲡⲉⲩϩⲙ̄ϩⲁⲗ ⲃⲓⲕⲧⲱⲣ ⲁⲩⲛⲁϩⲙⲉⲩ ϩⲙ̄ⲡⲉⲛⲧⲱⲕ D. 30–32.
ⲉⲕⲉⲧⲛ̄ⲛⲟⲟⲩ - ⲙ̄ⲡⲟⲟⲩ A; ⲉⲕⲉⲭⲟⲟⲩ ⲙ̄ⲡⲉⲕⲁⲅⲅⲉⲗⲟⲥ ⲩⲁⲣⲟⲓ D

ΝΟΥ ⲙ̄ⲙⲟⲟⲩ ⲛϥ̄'ⲛⲟⲩⲍ̄ⲙ ⲉⲙⲟⲓ ⲉ(63 Vi)ⲃⲟⲗ ⲍⲛ̄ⲛⲉⲓⲛⲟⲥ' ⲛ̄ⲃⲁⲥⲁⲛⲟⲥ.' ⲛⲁⲓ̈ ⲇⲉ ⲉϥϫⲱ
ⲙ̄'ⲙⲟⲟⲩ ⲛ̄ϭⲓ ⲡⲙⲁ̄ⲕⲁⲣⲓⲟⲥ ⲁⲡⲁ ⲡⲁ̄ⲏⲥⲉ, ⲁϥⲉⲓ ⲉⲡⲉⲥⲏⲧ' ⲉⲃⲟⲗ ⲍⲛ̄ⲧⲡⲉ ⲛ̄'ⲟ̄ⲓ ⲍⲣⲁⲫⲁⲏⲗ ⲡⲁⲅ'ⲅⲉⲗⲟⲥ ⲙ̄ⲡⲭⲟⲉⲓⲥ,[19] ⲁϥⲁⲍⲉⲣⲁⲧϥ̄ ⲍⲓⲟⲩ'ⲛⲁⲙ ⲙ̄ⲙⲟⲩ, ⲁϥ'ⲧⲣⲉⲡⲓⲩⲁⲍ ⲛ̄-
ⲧⲉⲧ̄'ⲣⲓⲣ ⲣ̄ⲑⲉ ⲛ̄ⲟⲩⲧⲏⲩ' ⲛ̄ⲓ̈ⲱⲧⲉ ⲉϥⲥⲱⲕ[15] ⲙ̄ⲡⲛⲁⲩ ⲛ̄ⲍⲧⲟⲟⲩⲉ 'ⲍⲓⲕⲙ̄ⲡⲕⲁⲍ.' ⲡⲉⲧⲟⲩⲁⲁⲃ ⲇⲉ' ⲁⲡⲁ ⲡⲁⲏⲥⲉ ⲉⲛⲉϥ'ⲍ̄ⲙⲟⲟⲥ ⲍⲛ̄ⲧⲏⲛ[20]'ⲧⲉ ⲙ̄ⲡⲕⲱⲍⲧ̄ ⲛ̄'ⲑⲉ ⲛ̄ⲟⲩⲁ ⲛ̄ⲧⲁⲩ-
ⲉⲓ' ⲉⲃⲟⲗ ⲍⲙ̄ⲡⲕⲁⲩ'ⲙⲁ ⲁϥⲕⲟⲟⲥ ⲍⲓ'ⲭ̄ⲛⲟⲩⲡⲗⲁⲍ[25] ⲉⲥⲟ'ⲟ̄ⲃ ⲉⲧⲃⲉⲧⲟⲟⲙ' ⲙ̄ⲡⲁⲅⲅⲉ-
ⲗⲟⲥ ⲉⲧ'ⲣⲟⲉⲓⲥ ⲉⲣⲟϥ· ⲁⲩⲱ'ⲁⲛ̄ϫⲁⲗⲏⲥⲓⲥ ⲉⲧ'ⲙⲏⲣ ⲙ̄ⲙⲟⲩ ⲃⲱⲗ[30] ⲉⲃⲟⲗ, ⲁⲩⲱ ⲁⲡⲗⲁⲙ-
ⲇⲁⲧⲛ̄ ⲉⲓ ⲉ'ⲡⲉⲥⲏⲧ ⲍⲙ̄ⲡⲉϥ'ⲥⲱⲙⲁ, ⲁϥⲕⲁⲑⲁ(Vii)ⲣⲓⲍⲉ ⲛ̄ⲑⲉ ⲛ̄ⲟⲩⲁ' ⲛ̄ⲧⲁⲩϫⲱⲕⲙ̄
ⲍⲛ̄ⲟⲩⲥⲓⲟⲧⲛ̄, ⲉϥⲛⲁ'ⲃⲱⲕ ⲉⲩⲁⲣⲓⲥⲧⲟⲛ.[5] ⲡⲁⲅⲅⲉⲗⲟⲥ ⲇⲉ ⲙ̄'ⲡⲭⲟⲉⲓⲥ ⲁϥⲧⲣⲉ'ⲭⲟ ⲛ̄ⲧⲉ-
ⲧⲣⲓⲣ ⲡⲱⲍ,' ⲁϥⲉⲓⲛⲉ ⲙ̄ⲡⲇⲓ'ⲕⲁⲓⲟⲥ ⲁⲡⲁ ⲡⲁ̄ⲏⲥⲉ ⲉⲃⲟⲗ ⲍⲛ̄ⲧ'ⲙⲏⲧⲉ ⲛ̄ⲧⲉⲧⲣⲓⲣ'ⲛ̄ⲕⲱ-
ⲍⲧ̄ ⲉⲙⲛ̄'ⲗⲁⲁⲩ ⲛ̄ⲧⲁⲕⲟ'ⲩϣⲟⲟⲡ ⲙ̄ⲙⲟⲩϥ[15] ⲉⲡⲧⲏⲣϥ̄.' ⲡⲉϫⲉⲡⲁⲅⲅⲉⲗⲟⲥ' ⲙ̄ⲡⲭⲟⲉⲓⲥ ⲛⲁⲩ
ϫⲉ' ⲙ̄ⲡⲣ̄ⲣⲍⲟⲧⲉ ⲱ̄ ⲡⲁⲙⲉⲣⲓⲧ ⲡⲁⲏ'ⲥⲉ[20] ⲍⲏⲧⲟⲩ ⲛ̄ⲛⲉⲓ̈'ⲃⲁⲥⲁⲛⲟⲥ ⲙ̄ⲡⲣⲟⲥ'ⲟⲩⲟⲉⲓϣ,
ϫⲉ ⲁⲛⲟⲕ' ϯϣⲟⲟⲡ ⲛⲙ̄ⲙⲁⲕ' ⲉⲓ̈ϯⲟ̄ⲙ ⲛⲁⲕ.[25] ⲡⲁⲅⲅⲉⲗⲟⲥ ⲇⲉ ⲙ̄'ⲡⲭⲟⲉⲓⲥ ⲁϥⲙⲟⲟⲩϣⲉ
ⲛⲙ̄ⲙⲁϥ. ⲉⲛⲉⲧⲡⲁϥⲉ ⲛ̄'ⲧⲉⲩⲩⲏ ⲧⲉ· ⲁϥ'ϫⲓⲧϥ̄[30] ⲉⲍⲟⲩⲛ ⲉ'ⲡⲏⲓ̈ ⲙ̄ⲡⲁⲩⲗⲟⲥ' ⲉⲛⲕⲟⲓⲧⲱⲛ
ⲉϥ'ⲛ̄ⲕⲁⲧⲕ̄ ⲛ̄ⲍⲏⲧϥ̄· (64Ri) ⲁⲩⲱ ⲁⲡⲁⲅⲅⲉⲗⲟⲥ' ⲁⲥⲡⲁⲍⲉ ⲙ̄ⲙⲟϥ, ⲁϥ'ⲃⲱⲕ ⲉⲍⲣⲁⲓ̈
ⲉⲙⲡⲏⲩⲉ' ⲍⲛ̄ⲟⲩⲉⲟⲟⲩ.[5] ⲛⲉϥⲛ̄ⲕⲁⲧⲕ̄ ⲅⲁⲣ ⲛ̄ⲟ̄ⲓ ⲡⲁⲩⲗⲟⲥ ⲉϥⲙⲁⲕⲍ̄'ⲛ̄ⲍⲏⲧ ⲉⲧⲃⲉⲡⲁ'ⲏⲥⲉ,

---

63 Vi 33. Omission here; see D.   ii 6 f. l. ⲁⲩⲧⲣⲉⲡ̄ⲍⲟ (superlineation omitted).

---

63 Vi 33–ii 1. ⲉⲃⲟⲗ A; om. D.   1. ⲍⲛ̄ⲛⲉⲓⲛⲟⲟ̄ A; ⲍⲛ̄ⲧⲉⲓⲛⲟⲟ̄ D.   6. ⲉⲡⲉⲥⲏⲧ A; om. D.
8 f. ⲡⲁⲅⲅⲉⲗⲟⲥ ⲙ̄ⲡⲭⲟⲉⲓⲥ A; ⲡⲁⲣⲭⲁⲅⲅⲉⲗⲟⲥ D.   10 f. ⲍⲓⲟⲩⲛⲁⲙ A; ⲛ̄ⲥⲁⲟⲩⲛⲁⲙ D.   11. ⲙ̄-
ⲙⲟⲩ A; ⲙ̄ⲡⲙⲁⲕⲁⲣⲓⲟⲥ ⲁⲡⲁ ⲡⲁⲏⲥⲉ D.   12 f. ⲛ̄ⲧⲉⲧⲣⲓⲣ A; ⲛ̄ⲧⲉⲣⲣⲱ D.   15. ⲛ̄ⲍⲧⲟⲟⲩⲉ A;
ⲛ̄ⲩϣⲣ̄ D.   16. ⲍⲓⲕⲙ̄ⲡⲕⲁⲍ A; om. D.   18. ⲁⲡⲁ ⲡ. A; om. D.   18 f. ⲉⲛⲉϥⲍⲙⲟⲟⲥ A;
ⲁϥⲍ. D.   20. ⲙ̄ⲡⲕⲱⲍⲧ̄ A; ⲛ̄ⲧⲉⲧⲣⲓⲣ D.   22. ⲉⲃⲟⲗ A; om. D.   22 f. ⲍⲙ̄ⲡⲕⲁⲩⲙⲁ A;
ⲍⲛ̄ⲟⲩⲕ. D.   23–25. ⲍⲓⲭ̄ⲛⲟⲩⲡⲗⲁⲍ ⲉⲥⲟⲟ̄ⲃ A; ⲍⲛ̄ⲟⲩⲙⲁ ⲉϥⲕⲏⲃ D.   25–27. ⲉⲧⲃⲉⲧⲟⲟⲙ
—ⲉⲣⲟϥ A; om. D.   33. After ⲍⲛ̄ⲡⲉϥⲥⲱⲙⲁ, + ⲛ̄ⲑⲉ ⲛ̄ⲟⲩⲙⲟⲟⲩ ⲉϥⲕⲏⲃ, ⲁⲩⲱ ⲁⲡⲉⲩⲥⲱⲙⲁ
D; om. in A by haplography?   33–ii 1. ⲁϥⲕⲁⲑⲁⲣⲓⲍⲉ A; ⲕⲁⲑⲁⲣⲓⲍⲉ D.   3 f. ⲉϥⲛⲁⲃⲱⲕ
A; ⲉϥⲕⲏⲃ (sic; l. ⲉϥⲃⲏⲕ) D.   5–7. ⲡⲁⲅⲅⲉⲗⲟⲥ — ⲡⲱⲍ A; ⲍⲛ̄ⲧⲡⲁⲩϥⲉ ⲇⲉ ⲛ̄ⲧⲉⲩⲩⲏ ⲉⲓⲥ
ⲙⲓⲭⲁⲏⲗ ⲡⲁⲣⲭⲁⲅⲅⲉⲗⲟⲥ ⲁϥⲡⲱⲍ ⲛ̄ⲧⲭⲟⲉ ⲛ̄ⲧⲉⲧⲣⲓⲣ D.   8 f. ⲙ̄ⲡⲇⲓⲕⲁⲓⲟⲥ A; ⲙ̄ⲡⲙⲁ-
ⲕⲁⲣⲓⲟⲥ D.   10–12. ⲍⲛ̄ⲧⲙⲏⲧⲉ —ⲛ̄ⲕⲱⲍⲧ̄ A; ⲛ̄ⲍⲏⲧⲉ D.   12–15. ⲉⲙⲛ̄ⲗⲁⲁⲩ — ⲉⲡⲧⲏ-
ⲣϥ̄ A; om. D.   16 f. ⲡⲉϫⲉⲡⲁⲅⲅⲉⲗⲟⲥ ⲙ̄ⲡⲭⲟⲉⲓⲥ A; ⲡⲉϫⲁⲩ D.   18. ⲙ̄ⲡⲣ̄ⲣⲍⲟⲧⲉ ⲱ A; om.
D.   After ⲡⲁⲏⲥⲉ, + ⲙ̄ⲡⲣ̄ⲣⲍⲟⲧⲉ D.   20 f. ⲛ̄ⲛⲉⲓ̈ⲃⲁⲥⲁⲛⲟⲥ A; ⲛ̄ⲛ̄ⲃ. D.   21 f. ⲙ̄ⲡⲣⲟⲥ-
ⲟⲩⲟⲉⲓϣ A; om. D.   24. ⲉⲓ̈ϯⲟ̄ⲙ ⲛⲁⲕ A; om. D.   After this, + ⲡⲉϫⲉⲡⲙⲁⲕⲁⲣⲓⲟⲥ
ϫⲉ ⲁⲛⲟⲕ ϯⲥⲃ̄ⲧⲱⲧ ⲉϯ ⲙ̄ⲡⲁⲥⲱⲙⲁ ⲉⲛⲃⲁⲥⲁⲛⲟⲥ ⲉⲧⲃⲉⲡⲣⲁⲛ ⲛ̄ⲧⲉ ⲡⲉⲭⲥ D.   27–
29. ⲉⲛⲉⲧⲡⲁϥⲉ — ⲧⲉ A; om. D.   30. ⲉⲍⲟⲩⲛ A; om. D.   31. After ⲙ̄ⲡⲁⲩⲗⲟⲥ, + ⲁϥ-
ϫⲓⲧϥ̄ ⲉⲍⲟⲩⲛ D.   32. After ⲉⲛⲕⲟⲓⲧⲱⲛ, + ⲡⲙⲁ D.   32 f. ⲉⲧϥ̄ⲛ̄ⲕⲁⲧⲕ̄ A; ⲡⲙⲁ ⲉ-
ⲛⲉϥⲛ̄ⲕⲟⲧⲕ̄ D.   64 Ri 1–5. ⲁⲩⲱ — ⲅⲁⲣ A; om. D. (by haplography).   7 f. ⲉⲧⲃⲉ-
ⲡⲁⲏⲥⲉ A; om. D.

εῆ<u>ς</u>cooүῆˈ αν ῆπενταуˈ¹⁰ψωπε ῆμοчˈˈ πμακαριος Δε αˈπα παнсε αуˈнεζcε
ῆπαγλοсˈˈ παγλοс Δε εν¹⁵ˈτερεуoγωνˈνεуβωλ αуˈναγ επεуψγβнρˈ παнсε,αу-
γτορῖρ εβολ ζε νεˈ²⁰ρεoγφανος моγζˈ ερογ ῆζoγν εˈπεуκoιτων ῆναγ νιμˈ
αγωˈεπιδн ῆπεуειˈ²⁵με επζωβ ῆταуˈψωπε ῆμoчˈˈ πεχεπμακαριˈoс απα
παнсεˈ ναγ ζε ῆπῆρˈ³⁰ζoтε πасονˈ αˈνok πε παнсεˈˈ асуωπε Δε ῆтеˈρε-
παγλoс сωтῆ (64 R ii) ετεсмн ῆπεуˈψγβнρ παнсε,ˈαуτωoυν ῆтеγˈνoγ
ζῆoγδεπнˈˈ⁵ αуπαζтῆ ζανεуˈoγερнтε, αγoγˈωψτ ναγ ζῆˈoγραψε· αγωˈ ῆ-
τεγνoγ αγτoγˈ¹⁰нoсч, αγωλῆˈ εζoγν ῆνεγεˈρнγ ῆπεсναγˈˈ πεχεπαγλoсˈ
ῆπαнсε ζε αïˈ¹⁵ειμε ῆπooγ ζεˈ πνoγтε νoγˈζῆ ῆνετζελπιˈζε ερογ· αγωˈ
αγζμoос αγγαˈ²⁰ζε μῆνεγερнγˈ ζῆῆμῆτνoδˈ ῆπνoγτεˈ μῆῆδoм ετγ-
ειρε ῆμooγˈ²⁵μῆνεγπετoγˈaaв. πεχεπˈмакариос απаˈπансε ῆπαγˈλoс
ζε ψε πεkˈ³⁰oγζαïˈ πасoνˈ ενεῆταïειμεˈ ζε πνoγтε γˈζoπ μῆνεγπε(Vi)-
тoγааβ ῆχρнсˈтιανoс ῆτειˈζε,ˈεγχπε αïωπˈεροoγ χινεπˈ⁵ˈγoρπ ῆζoογ ῆˈ-
тапδιωkмoсˈ ψωπε· αλλαˈ ῆναγ πε παï ῆˈταςπαναγ ῆπαˈ¹⁰χoειс ῑ͞с πε-
χ͞с, αγˈταζмет επεγˈмαῆγελεετ εˈтoγааβˈ ϥснζ ϝар ζε πε(ν)ˈтaγει ῆ-
ζῆμῆˈтoγε αγχι ῆπˈвγkε ῆπεζooγˈтнрῆˈˈ πεχεπαγλoс ναγˈζε ψε π<u>ε</u>ˈ^{ek}oγ-
oγˈζaï πасoν, χιν<u>ε</u>ˈπναγ ῆταуˈχιтῆ επвнма ῆсαγ,ˈῆπειoγˈ²⁵ˈεμoειk oγδε
ῆπειcεмoογˈˈ αγω ῆτεγνoγˈ αγνεζcε ῆνεγˈζῆζαλ· αγωˈ ῆτερογναγ επ-ˈ
мaкариoс апaˈ παнсε αγoγˈωψτ ναγ εζρaï (Vii)εζῆπkαζ, αγωˈαγ<u>α</u>-ˈ
спaζε ῆмoчˈˈ παγλoс Δε αγoγˈεζcaζνε ῆνεγˈ⁵ζῆζαλ, αγсoвтεˈ ῆoγтρα-
πεζa,ˈ αγoγωμ αγcωˈ μῆνεγερнγ, αγˈῆkaтῆ ψαντεˈ¹⁰ˈoγoειν сωρ εβoλˈˈ

64 R i 16. ℓ. ῆνεγβωλ. Vi 17. ℓ. -βεkε

64 R i 8. εῆ<u>ς</u>cooγῆ A; νεγc. D. 9 f. ῆπενταγψωπε A; ζε oγ πενταγч. D. 11-
26 om. D, by haplography. 27. -πμακαριoс A; om. D. 29 f. ῆπῆρ̄ζoτε A; ῆπῆρ̄-
ρωπнρε αγω ῆπεργτoρῖρ D. 31. After παнсε, † πενταγνoδχ ετετριρ D. ii 2.
παнсε A; om. D. 3 f. ῆτεγνoγ A; om. D. 4. ζῆoγδεπн A; ζῆoγνoδ ῆραψε D.
6-12. αγoγωγῖ — ῆπεсναγ A; αγωλῆ εζoγν ερογ αγω D. 16 f. νoγζῆ A;
ναν. D. 17 f. ῆνετζελπιζε A; ῆoγoν νιμ ετζ. D. 23-26. μῆῆδoм — μῆ-
νεγπετoγααβ A; om. D. 30. Before πασoν, † ω D. 31. After ενεῆταïειμε,
† ζaвн ῆπooγ D. 32. πνoγтε A; νειδoм тнρoγ D. 33-V i 2. μῆνεγπετoγ-
ααβ ῆχρнстιανoс A; ῆνεχρ. D. 2-4. ῆτειζε — εροoγ A; om. D. 7. After
ψωπε, † aïωπ ετнπε ῆνετoγααβ D (cf. A 3 f., above). 8. πναγ πε παï A;
πaï πε πναγ D. 9 f. ῆπαχoειс ῑ͞с πεχ͞с A; ῆπνoγтε D. 10-13. αγταζмет
— ετoγααβ A; om. D. 21. Before πασoν, † ω D. 23. - χιтῆ A; -чιтῆ D.
27. αγω A; om. D. 28-ii 3. αγνεζcε — Δε A; om. D(by haplography). 7. αγcω
A; om. D. 10. сωρ εβoλ A; ει εζρaï D.

ⲁⲩⲧⲱⲟⲩⲛ ⲛ̄ϭⲓ ⲛ̄'ⲡⲉⲧⲟⲩⲁⲁⲃ ⲁⲡⲁ' ⲡⲁⲏⲥⲉ, ⲁⲩⲃⲱⲕ'ⲉⲡⲉⲩⲧⲉⲕⲟ· ⲁⲛⲉ¹⁵ⲧⲟⲩⲁⲁⲃ
ⲛⲁⲩ ⲉⲣⲟϥ,' ⲁⲩⲣⲁϣⲉ, ⲁⲩⲁⲥⲡⲁⲍⲉ ⲙ̄ⲙⲟϥ· ⲁϥ'ⲧⲁⲙⲟⲟⲩ ⲇⲉ ⲉⲑⲉ ⲛ̄'ⲧⲁⲡⲁⲅⲅⲉⲗⲟⲥ
ⲙ̄²⁰ⲡϫⲟⲉⲓⲥ ⲛⲁϩ'ⲙⲉϥ ⲉⲃⲟⲗ ϩⲓⲧⲉⲧ'ⲣⲓⲣ ⲛ̄ⲕⲱϩⲧ̄.' ⲡⲣⲱⲙⲉ ⲇⲉ ⲉⲧⲓ̈ϫⲓⲡⲉⲩⲧⲉⲕⲟ
ⲛ̄²⁵ⲧⲉⲣⲉⲩⲛⲁⲩ ⲉⲡⲡⲉ'ⲧⲟⲩⲁⲁⲃ ⲁⲡⲁ ⲡⲁ'ⲏⲥⲉ, ⲁⲩⲧⲱⲟⲩⲛ,' ⲁⲩⲡⲁϩⲧ̄ϥ, ⲁⲩⲟⲩ'ⲱϣⲧ
ⲛⲁⲩ ⲉⲩϫⲱ³⁰ ⲙ̄ⲙⲟⲥ ϫⲉ ⲁⲗⲏⲑⲱⲥ ⲙ̄ⲛ̄ϭⲉ ⲛⲟⲩ'ⲧⲉ ϣⲟⲟⲡ ⲉϥⲥⲟ'ϭⲟⲙ ⲛ̄ⲥⲁⲓ̈ⲥ ⲡⲉϫⲉ·
(65 R i) ⲁⲣⲓⲡⲁⲙⲉⲉⲩⲉ ϩⲱ' ⲛ̄ⲧⲉⲡⲉⲧⲛ̄ϩⲙⲟⲧ' ⲧⲁϭⲟⲓ̈. ⲁⲛⲉⲧⲟⲩ'ⲁⲁⲃ ⲥⲙⲟⲩ ⲉⲣⲟϥ⁵
ⲉⲩϫⲱ ⲙ̄ⲙⲟⲥ ϫⲉ' ⲉⲣⲉⲡϫⲟⲉⲓⲥ ⲧⲁϩ'ⲙⲉⲕ ⲉⲡⲁⲣⲓⲑⲙⲟⲥ' ⲛ̄ⲛⲉⲧⲟⲩⲁⲁⲃ ⲉⲧ'ϩⲛ̄ⲛⲉⲙ-
ⲡⲏⲩⲉ.¹⁰ ⲥⲧⲟⲟⲩⲉ ⲇⲉ ⲛ̄ⲧⲉ'ⲣⲉⲩϣⲱⲡⲉ ⲙ̄ⲡⲉϥⲣⲁⲥⲧⲉ,' ⲡⲉϫⲉⲛⲇⲟⲩⲝ ⲛ̄ⲛⲁⲧ'ⲧⲁⲝⲓⲥ
ϫⲉ ⲃⲱⲕ' ⲛ̄ⲧⲉⲧⲛ̄ⲛⲁⲩ¹⁵ ⲛ̄ⲧⲉ'ⲧⲣⲓⲣ ϫⲉ ⲥⲧⲟⲟⲃⲉ'ⲛ̄ⲧⲉⲥϩⲉ ⲛ̄ⲧⲉ'ⲧⲛ̄ⲟⲩⲱⲛ ⲙ̄ⲙⲟⲥ' ⲛ̄ⲧⲉⲧⲛ̄-
ⲛⲁⲩ ϫⲉ' ϥⲟⲛϩ̄ ⲛ̄ϭⲓ ⲡⲉⲓ̈ⲁ'ⲛⲟⲙⲟⲥ ⲛ̄ⲭⲣⲏⲥⲧⲓⲁⲛⲟⲥ· ⲁⲩϫⲟⲟⲥ ⲅⲁⲣ' ϫⲉ ⲟⲩⲛ̄ϭⲟⲙ ⲙ̄-
ⲡⲁ'ⲛⲟⲩⲧⲉ ⲉⲛⲁϩⲙⲉⲧ²⁵ ⲉⲃⲟⲗ ϩⲛ̄ⲛⲉⲕϭⲓϫ.' ⲛ̄ⲧⲟⲟⲩ ⲇⲉ ⲁⲩⲃⲱⲕ,' ⲁⲩⲉⲓⲣⲉ ⲕⲁⲧⲁⲑⲉ'
ⲛ̄ⲧⲁⲩⲥⲧⲉ³⁰ϩⲥⲁ'ⲛⲉ ⲛⲁⲩ ⲛ̄ϭⲓ ⲡ'ⲇⲟⲩⲝ· ⲁⲩϩⲉ ⲉⲧⲉⲧ'ⲣⲓⲣ ⲉⲥⲧⲟⲟⲃⲉ ⲛ̄ⲧⲉⲥϩⲉ· ⲁⲩ-
ⲥⲟⲗⲡⲥ̄' ⲉⲃⲟⲗ· ⲁⲡⲉⲥⲉⲗ(R ii)ϩⲱⲃ ⲃⲱⲧⲉ ⲉϩⲣⲁⲓ̈,' ⲁⲩⲣⲱⲕϩ̄ ⲛ̄ⲧⲁⲡⲉ' ⲛ̄ⲛⲕⲉⲥ-
ⲧⲟⲛⲁⲣⲓⲟⲥ' ⲉⲧⲙ̄ⲛ̄ⲕⲱⲧⲉ ⁵ ⲛ̄'ⲧⲉⲧⲣⲓⲣ, ⲁⲩⲱ ⲁⲩⲙⲟⲩ ⲙ̄ⲡⲉⲩϣⲟ'ⲙⲛⲧ· ⲁⲩⲱ ⲙ̄'ⲡⲉⲗⲁⲁⲩ
ⲉⲩϫⲱⲛ' ⲉϩⲟⲩⲛ ⲉⲧⲉⲧⲣⲓⲣ,¹⁰ ϫⲉ ⲛⲉⲥⲙⲟⲩϩ ⲅⲁⲣ' ⲉⲙⲁⲧⲉ ⲡⲉ.' ⲁⲩⲧⲁⲙⲉⲛⲇⲟⲩⲝ' ⲇⲉ
ⲉⲡⲉⲛⲧⲁⲩ'ϣⲱⲡⲉ· ⲡⲉϫⲁϥ¹⁵ ϫⲉ ⲅⲉ ⲡⲁⲡⲱⲗ'ⲗⲟⲛ ⲡⲛⲟϭ ⲛ̄ⲛⲟⲩⲧⲉ, ⲁⲡⲕⲱϩⲧ̄'ⲁⲛ-
ϫⲁⲗⲓⲥⲕⲉ ⲛ̄ⲛⲉⲩⲕⲉⲉⲥ· ⲙⲁ'ⲣⲉϥⲉⲓ ⲧⲉⲛⲟⲩ ⲛⲓ̈'ϭⲱⲛ ⲛ̄ⲛϫⲓⲥⲟ'ⲟⲩⲉ ⲛ̄ⲣⲣⲱⲟⲩ ⲙ̄'ⲛⲉⲩ-
ⲕⲉⲛⲟⲩⲧⲉ' ⲉⲧⲧⲁⲓ̈ⲏⲩ. ϩⲟ'ⲥⲟⲛ ⲇⲉ ⲉϥϣⲁϫⲉ' ⲉⲓⲥ ⲟⲩⲁ ⲛ̄ⲛⲕⲉⲥ'ⲧⲟⲛⲁⲣⲓⲟⲥ ⲁϥⲉⲓ,'
ⲡⲉϫⲁϥ ϩⲓⲑⲏ ⲙ̄ⲡⲇⲟⲩⲝ³⁰ ϫⲉ ⲡⲁ'ϫⲟⲉⲓⲥ, ⲉⲓⲥ ⲡⲁ'ⲏⲥⲉ ⲛ̄ϩⲟⲩⲛ ⲉⲡⲉ'ⲩⲧⲉⲕⲟ ⲉⲙ̄ⲡ-
ⲗⲁ'ⲁⲩ ⲛ̄ⲧⲁⲕⲟ ϣⲟⲟⲡ (V i) ⲙ̄ⲙⲟϥ ⲉⲡⲧⲏ'ⲣϥ̄, ⲁⲗⲗⲁ ⲉϥⲟ ⲛ̄'ⲑⲉ ⲛ̄ⲟⲩⲁ ⲉϥⲉⲧϥ̄'ⲣⲁ-
ⲛⲉ ϩⲛ̄ⲟⲩϩⲣⲃ̄⁵ ⲉⲛⲁⲛⲟⲩϥ.' ϩⲁⲣⲙⲏⲛⲓⲟⲥ ⲇⲉ ⲁϥ'ϭⲱⲛⲧ, ⲡⲉϫⲁϥ ⲙ̄ⲡⲕⲉⲥⲧⲱ-'
ⲛⲁⲣⲓⲟⲥ ϫⲉ ⲕⲁⲕⲏ¹⁰ ⲕⲏⲫⲁⲗⲏ, ⲁⲣⲏⲩ' ⲟⲩⲁ ⲡⲉ ⲉϥⲉⲓⲛⲉ' ⲙ̄ⲙⲟϥ· ⲁϥⲕⲉⲉⲥ' ⲙ̄ⲡⲉ-
ⲧⲙ̄ⲙⲁⲩ ⲣ̄'ⲕⲉⲣⲙⲉⲥ ⲉⲡⲧⲏⲣϥ̄.¹⁵ ⲡⲉϫⲁϥ ⲛ̄ϭⲓ ⲡⲕⲉⲥ'ⲧⲟⲛⲁⲣⲓⲟⲥ ϫⲉ ⲕⲟⲩ'ⲱϣ ⲉⲧⲣⲁ-
ⲃⲱⲕ' ⲧⲁⲛ̄ⲧϥ̄ ⲉⲡⲉⲕⲙ̄'ⲧⲟ ⲉⲃⲟⲗ, ⲛ̄ⲅⲉⲓⲙⲉ²⁰ ϫⲉ ⲛ̄ⲧⲟϥ ⲡⲉ ϫⲛ̄'ⲟⲩⲙⲉ; ⲡⲉϫⲁϥ' ⲛⲁϥ
ϩⲛ̄ⲟⲩϭⲱⲛⲧ' ϫⲉ ⲃⲱⲕ, ⲁⲛⲓϥ.' ϭⲉ ⲡⲟⲩϫⲁⲓ̈ ⲙ̄ⲡⲁ'ⲡⲱⲗⲗⲟⲛ,²⁵ ⲉϣⲱⲡⲉ ⲛ̄ⲧⲟϥ ⲁⲛ ⲡⲉ'
ϯⲛⲁϥⲉⲉⲧⲡⲉⲕ'ⲗⲁⲥ ⲉⲃⲟⲗ, ϫⲉⲕⲁⲥ ⲛ̄ⲛⲉⲕⲧⲟⲗⲟ'ⲙⲁ ⲛ̄ⲕⲉⲥⲟⲡ ⲉ'ⲧⲁⲩⲉⲩϫⲁϣⲉ ⲙ̄'ⲡⲁ-
ⲙ̄ⲧⲟ ⲉⲃⲟⲗ.' ⲁⲩⲱ ⲛ̄ⲧⲉⲓ̈ϩⲉ ⲁϥ(V ii)ⲃⲱⲕ ⲉⲡⲉⲩⲧⲉⲕⲟ' ⲛ̄ϭⲓ ⲡⲕⲉⲥⲧⲟⲛⲁ'ⲣⲓⲟⲥ, ⲁϥ-
ⲡⲁϩⲧϥ̄' ⲛ̄ⲙⲁⲕⲁⲣⲓⲟⲥ ⁵ ⲁⲡⲁ ⲡⲁⲏⲥⲉ, ⲁϥⲡⲁ'ⲣⲁⲕⲁⲗⲉⲓ ⲙ̄ⲙⲟϥ ϫⲉ'ⲙⲁⲣⲉⲡⲉⲕ-

---

64 V ii 31f. l. ⲙ̄ⲛ̄ⲕⲉⲛⲟⲩⲧⲉ   65 R i 6f. l. ⲉⲧⲁϩⲙⲉⲕ.   ii 4. l. ⲉⲧⲥⲙ̄ⲛ̄ⲕⲱⲧⲉ

64 V ii 15f. ⲛⲁⲩ ⲉⲣⲟϥ ⲁⲩⲣⲁϣⲉ ⲁⲩ- A; om. D. 17f. ⲁⲩⲧⲁⲙⲟⲟⲩ A; ⲁⲩϫⲱ ⲉⲣⲟⲟⲩ
D. ⲇⲉ A; om. D. 19.- ⲡⲁⲅⲅⲉⲗⲟⲥ ⲙ̄- A; om. D. 20f. ⲛⲁϩⲙⲉϥ A; ⲛⲟⲩϩⲙ̄ ⲙ̄ⲙⲟϥ D.

ⲛⲁⲧⲁ⳿ⲍⲟⲓ ⲱ ⲡⲁⲭⲟⲉⲓⲥ ⲛ̄ⲓ̈ⲱⲧ ⲛ̄ϥⲉⲓ ⲛ̄ⲙⲁⲓ̈¹⁰ ⲩⲁⲡⲉⲓ̈ⲁⲛⲟⲙⲟⲥ⳿ ⲛ̄ⲇⲟⲩⲍ ⲛ̄ϯ⳿ⲩⲓⲡⲉ
ⲛⲁⲩ· ⲁⲛⲟⲕ⳿ ⲅⲁⲣ ϯⲡⲓⲥⲧⲉⲩⲉ⳿ ⲁⲩⲱ ϯⲟⲙⲟⲗⲟ̄¹⁵ⲅⲉⲓ ⲭⲉ ⲙ̄ⲛ̄ⲟⲩ⳿ⲧⲉ ϣⲟⲟⲡ ⲛ̄ⲥⲁ ⲓ̈ⲉ⳿
ⲡⲉⲭⲥ. ⲛⲁⲓ̈ ⲇⲉ⳿ ⲉϥϫⲱ ⲙ̄ⲙⲟⲟⲩ⳿ ²⁰ⲁⲩⲧⲱⲟⲩⲛ ⲛ̄ϭⲓ⳿ ⲡⲍⲁⲅⲓⲟⲥ ⲁⲡⲁ⳿ ⲡⲁⲛⲥⲉ, ⲁⲩⲙⲟⲟ⳿
ⲩⲉ ⲛ̄ⲙⲙⲁⲩ, ⲁⲩⲉⲓ,⳿ ⲁⲩⲁⲍⲉⲣⲁⲧϥ̄ ⲙ̄ⲡⲙ̄⳿ⲧⲟ ⲉⲃⲟⲗ ⲙ̄ⲛ̄ⲇⲟⲩⲍ⳿ ²⁵ⲛ̄ⲇⲟⲩⲍ ⲇⲉ ⲛ̄ⲧⲉ⳿ⲣⲉϥ
ⲛⲁⲩ ⲉⲣⲟϥ ⲁϥϯ ⲛ̄ⲟⲩⲛⲟϭ ⲛ̄ϩ̄⳿ⲣⲟⲟⲩ ⲍ̄ⲛ̄ⲩⲁⲁⲛ⳿ⲧϥ̄, ⲁⲩϫⲁ ⲍ ³⁰ⲛ̄ⲛⲉϥϭⲓⲝ ϩⲓ ⲭⲛ̄⳿
ⲛⲉⲩⲉⲣⲏⲩ, ⲡⲉ⳿ϫⲁⲩ ⲛ̄ⲛⲉⲧⲕⲱⲧⲉ ⲉⲣⲟϥ ⲭⲉ ⲁⲗⲏ(66 R i)ⲑⲱⲥ ⲁⲓ̈ⲥⲱⲧⲙ̄ ⲉ⳿ⲍⲁⲍ
ⲛ̄ⲭⲣⲏⲥⲧⲓⲁ⳿ⲛⲟⲥ, ⲙ̄ⲡⲉⲓ̈ⲛⲁⲩ⳿ ⁵ⲉⲙⲁⲅⲓⲁ ⲉϥϭⲙ̄⳿ϭⲟⲙ ⲛ̄ⲑⲉ ⲛ̄ⲧⲙⲁⲅⲓⲁ ⲙ̄ⲡⲁⲓ̈ ⲭⲉ⳿ ⲃⲓⲕ
ⲧⲱⲣ ⲙ̄ⲡⲁ⳿ⲏ̄ⲥⲉ ⲡⲉⲓ̈ⲙⲁⲅⲟⲥ ⲛ̄⳿ⲭⲣⲏⲥⲧⲓⲁⲛⲟⲥ,¹⁰⳿ ⲁⲩⲟⲩⲱϣⲃ̄ ⲛ̄ϭⲓ ⲡⲍⲁⲅⲓⲟⲥ ⲁⲡⲁ ⲡⲁ
ⲏ̄ⲥⲉ ⲭⲉ ⲛ̄ⲅⲥⲟⲟⲩⲛ̄ ⲁⲛ ⲭⲉ ⲛⲉⲕⲃⲁⲥⲁ⳿ⲛⲟⲥ ⲛⲁⲉϥϭⲙ̄¹⁵ϭⲟⲙ ⲉⲣⲟⲓ̈ ⲁⲛ, ⲉϥ⳿ⲩⲟⲟⲡ
ⲛ̄ⲙⲙⲁⲓ̈⳿ ⲛ̄ϭⲓ ⲡⲁⲭⲟⲉⲓⲥ ⲓ̄ⲥ̄⳿ ⲡⲉⲭⲥ̄.⳿ ²⁰ⲡⲇⲟⲩⲍ ⲇⲉ ⲡⲉϫⲁϥ⳿ ⲛⲁϥ ϩ̄ⲛ̄ⲟⲩϭⲱⲛ̄ⲧ⳿ ⲭⲉ
ⲉⲓⲥ ⲍⲏⲏⲧⲉ ⲁⲕ⳿ⲧⲟⲗⲟⲙⲁ ⲉϥⲥⲱϥ⳿ ⲛⲁⲓ̈· ⲩⲉ ⲡⲟⲩϫⲁⲓ̈⳿ ²⁵ⲙ̄ⲡⲁⲡⲟⲗⲗⲱⲛ⳿ ϯⲛⲁⲉⲓⲣⲉ
ⲛ̄ⲛⲉⲕ⳿ⲥⲁⲣ ⲝ ⲛ̄ⲩⲏⲙ ⲩⲏⲙ.⳿ ϯⲥⲟⲟⲩⲛ̄ ⲅⲁⲣ ⲭⲉ ⲛ̄⳿ⲧⲁⲕⲛⲟⲩⲍⲙ̄ ⲉⲧⲉⲧ⳿ⲣⲓⲣ ⲉⲧⲃⲉⲛⲉⲕ
³⁰ⲙⲁ⳿ⲅⲓⲁ· ⲁⲗⲗⲁ ϯⲛⲁ⳿ⲡⲉⲇⲉⲩⲉ ⲙ̄ⲙⲟⲕ⳿ ⲕⲁⲕⲱⲥ. ⲡⲇⲟⲩⲍ (R ii) ⲇⲉ ⲉⲛⲉϥϫⲱ ⲙ̄ⲙⲟⲥ⳿
ⲭⲉ ⲉⲓ̈ⲩⲁⲛⲃⲁⲥⲁ⳿ⲛⲓⲍⲉ ⲙ̄ⲙⲟⲩ ⲛ̄ⲕⲉ⳿ⲥⲟⲡ ⁵ⲛ̄ⲩⲛⲟⲩⲍⲙ̄,⳿ ϥⲛⲁϯ ⲩⲓⲡⲉ ⲛⲁⲓ̈⳿ ϩ̄ⲛ̄ⲧ
ⲙⲏⲧⲉ ⲙ̄ⲡ⳿ⲙⲏⲏⲩⲉ.⳿ ⲡⲇⲟⲩⲍ ⲇⲉ ⲁϥⲕⲉ⳿ⲗⲉⲩⲉ ⲉⲛⲟϫϥ ⲉⲡⲉ¹⁰ⲩⲧⲉⲕⲟ ⲩⲁⲛ̄ⲧⲉϥ
ⲉⲓⲙⲉ ⲭⲉ ⲉϥ⳿ⲛⲁⲣⲟⲩ ⲛⲁϥ.⳿ ϩ̄ⲛ̄ⲧⲉⲩⲩⲏ ⲇⲉ ⲉⲧⲙ̄ⲙⲁⲩ ⲁϥⲉⲓ̈⳿¹⁵ⲩⲁⲣⲟϥ ⲛ̄ϭⲓ ⲡⲁⲅ⳿
ⲅⲉⲗⲟⲥ ⲙ̄ⲡϭⲟⲉⲓⲥ,⳿ ⲁϥⲩⲁϫⲉ ⲛ̄ⲙⲙⲁϥ⳿ ⲉϥϫⲱ ⲙ̄ⲙⲟⲥ ⲭⲉ⳿ ²⁰ⲭⲁⲓⲣⲉ ⲡⲣⲱⲙⲉ ⲛ̄⳿ⲟⲩ
ⲁⲩϥ̄. ⲡⲡⲉ⳿ⲧⲟⲩⲁⲁⲃ ⲇⲉ ⲁⲡⲁ⳿ⲡⲁⲛⲥⲉ ⲛ̄ⲧⲉⲣⲉϥ⳿ⲛⲁⲩ ⲉⲡⲁⲅⲅⲉⲗⲟⲥ⳿ ⲁϥⲟⲩⲱϣⲧ̄ ⲛⲁϥ.⳿²⁵
ⲁⲩⲱ ⲁϥⲧⲟⲟⲧϥ̄⳿ ⲛ̄ϭⲓ ⲡⲁⲅⲅⲉⲗⲟⲥ,⳿ ⲁϥⲧⲟⲩⲛⲟⲥϥ̄·⳿ ³⁰ⲡⲉϫⲁϥ ⲭⲉ ϭⲙ̄⳿ϭⲟⲙ ⲛ̄ϥⲩⲱ
ⲡⲉ ⲛ̄ⲟⲩⲣⲱⲙⲉ⳿ ⲛ̄ϫⲱⲱⲣⲉ ⲛ̄ϯ⳿ⲙⲓϣⲉ ⲉϫⲙ̄ⲡⲉⲕ(V i)ϫⲟⲉⲓⲥ, ⲁⲩⲱ ⲕⲉ⳿ϥⲧⲟⲟⲩ ⲛ̄
ϩⲟⲟⲩ⳿ ⲛⲉ ⲩⲁⲛⲧⲁⲉⲓ̈⳿ⲛⲉ ⲛⲁⲕ ⲛ̄ⲑⲉⲕⲗⲁ ⁵ⲧⲉⲕⲥⲱⲛⲉ, ⲧⲉⲓ̈⳿ϫⲱⲱⲣⲉ ϩ̄ⲛ̄ⲧⲉⲥ⳿ϥⲩ
ⲭⲏ, ⲁⲩⲱ ⲉ⳿ⲛⲁⲡⲗⲏⲣⲟⲫⲟⲣⲉⲓ̈⳿ ⲙ̄ⲡⲉⲕϩⲏⲧ,¹⁰⳿ ⲁⲩⲱ ⲛ̄ϯ ⲩⲓⲡⲉ⳿ ⲙ̄ⲡⲇⲟⲩⲍ ⲙ̄ⲛ̄ⲡⲉϥ
ⲇⲓⲕⲁⲥⲧⲏ⳿ⲣⲓⲟⲛ ⲙ̄ⲛ̄ⲛⲉϥ⳿ⲛⲟⲩⲧⲉ ⲛ̄ⲃⲁⲧⲉ,¹⁵⳿ ⲁⲩⲱ ⲉ̄ⲛⲁⲣ ⲍⲉⲛ⳿ⲛⲟϭ ⲛ̄ϭⲟⲙ, ⲛ̄ⲧⲉⲍⲉⲛ
ⲛⲟϭ ⲙ̄ⲙⲏ̄⳿ⲩⲉ ⲕⲟⲧⲟⲩ ²⁰ⲉⲡ⳿ⲛⲟⲩⲧⲉ ⲉⲧⲃⲏ̄⳿ⲏⲧⲉ. ⲡⲉϫⲉⲁ⳿ⲡⲁ ⲡⲁⲛⲥⲉ ⲙ̄ⲡⲁⲅ⳿ⲅⲉ
ⲗⲟⲥ ⲭⲉ ⲡⲁϫⲟ⳿ⲉⲓⲥ, ⲁⲕ⳿ⲙ̄ⲧⲟⲛ⳿ ²⁵ⲛⲁⲓ̈ ⲉⲩϫⲉ ⲛ̄ⲧⲁ⳿ⲥⲱⲛⲉ ⲛⲁⲡⲱ⳿ⲣ ⲝ ⲉⲣⲟⲓ̈ ⲁⲛ.⳿
ⲡⲉϫⲉⲡⲁⲅⲅⲉⲗⲟⲥ⳿ ⲛⲁϥ ⲭⲉ ϯⲛⲁⲃⲱⲕ⳿ ⲩⲁⲡⲉⲓ̈ⲁⲛⲟⲙⲟⲥ⳿ ³⁰ⲛ̄ⲇⲟⲩⲍ, ⲧⲁⲉⲓ̈⳿ⲛⲉ ⲉϫⲱⲩ
ⲛⲟⲩ⳿ⲛⲟϭ ⲛ̄ⲩⲱⲛⲉ (V ii)ⲭⲉ ⲛ̄ⲛⲉϥⲩⲓⲛⲉ⳿ ⲛ̄ⲥⲱⲕ ⲩⲁⲛⲧⲉ⳿ⲧⲉⲕⲥⲱⲛⲉ ⲉⲓ,⳿ ⲁⲩⲱ ⲛ̄
ⲛⲉϥⲗⲟ⳿⁵ⲉⲃⲟⲗ ϩⲙ̄ⲡϣⲱ⳿ⲛⲉ ⲩⲁⲛⲧⲉⲕⲃⲱⲕ⳿ ⲉϩⲟⲩⲛ ⲩⲁⲣⲟϥ⳿ ⲛ̄ⲅⲧⲁⲗϭⲟϥ.⳿ ⲛⲁⲓ̈ ⲇⲉ
¹⁰ⲛ̄ⲧⲉⲣⲉϥ⳿ϫⲟⲟⲩ ⲛ̄ϭⲓ ϩⲣⲁ⳿ⲫⲁⲏⲗ ⲡⲁⲅⲅⲉ⳿ⲗⲟⲥ, ⲁϥϯ ⲛⲁϥ⳿ ⲛ̄ϯⲣⲏⲛⲏ, ⲁϥⲉⲓ̈⳿ⲉⲃⲟⲗ ϩⲓ
ⲧⲟⲟⲧϥ̄,¹⁵⳿ ⲁϥⲃⲱⲕ, ⲁϥⲉⲓⲛⲉ⳿ⲉϫⲙ̄ⲡⲇⲟⲩⲍ⳿ ⲛ̄ⲟⲩⲛⲟϭ ⲛ̄ⲩⲱ⳿ⲛⲉ, ⲁϥⲃⲱⲕ ⲉϩ⳿ⲣⲁⲓ̈ ⲉⲙ̄

---

66 R i 4ϥ. l. ⲉⲥⲟ̄ⲙ̄ϭⲟⲙ.

ⲡⲏⲅⲉ ⲍⲛ̄'ⲟⲩⲉⲟⲟⲩ.' ϣⲱⲡⲏ ⲇⲉ ⲛ̄ⲧⲉ'ⲣⲉϥϣⲱⲡⲉ ⲁⲛⲉ'ⲧⲟⲩⲁⲁⲃ ⲧⲱⲟⲩⲛ'ⲉⲉⲓⲛⲉ ⲛ̄-
ⲛⲉⲩⲥⲩ'ⲛⲁⲍⲓⲥ· ⲁⲩⲛⲁⲩ' ⲉⲡⲡⲉⲧⲟⲩⲁⲁⲃ ⲁ'ⲡⲁ ⲡⲁⲏⲥⲉ ⲉⲣⲉⲟⲩ'ⲛⲟϭ ⲛ̄ⲭⲁⲣⲓⲥ ⳩ⲓ'ⲣ̄-
ⲡⲉⲩⲍⲟ, ⲁⲩ'ⲉⲓⲙⲉ ⲧⲏⲣⲟⲩ ϫⲉ'ⲟⲩⲁⲅⲅⲉⲗⲟⲥ ⲛ̄ⲧⲉⲡϫⲟⲉⲓⲥ ⲡⲉⲛ(67 Ri)ⲧⲁϥⲟⲩⲱⲛ̄
ⲛⲁⲩ' ⲉⲃⲟⲗ. ⲙ̄ⲡⲉⲩ'ⲣⲁⲥⲧⲉ ⲇⲉ ⲁϥϣⲱ'ⲡⲉ ⲛ̄ϭⲓ ⲡⲗⲟⲩⲍ' ⲍⲛ̄ⲟⲩⲛⲟϭ ⲛ̄ϣⲱⲡⲉ· ⲁϥⲱϣ ⲉ'ⲃⲟⲗ ⲉϥϫⲱ ⲙ̄ⲙⲟⲥ' ϫⲉ ⲡⲉⲓⲁⲛⲟⲙⲟⲥ' ϫⲉ ⲡⲁⲏⲥⲉ ⲡⲉⲛ'ⲧⲁⲩⲣ̄ϫⲓⲕ ⲉⲣⲟⲓ'ⲍⲛ̄-
ⲛⲉⲩⲙⲁⲅⲓⲁ' ϣⲁⲛⲧϣⲱⲡⲉ.' ⲡⲉϫⲉⲧⲉϥⲥϩⲓⲙⲉ' ⲛⲁⲩ ϫⲉ ⲁⲓ̈ϫⲟⲟⲥ' ⲛⲁⲕ ϫⲉ ⲥⲁ-
ϩⲱ'ⲕ ⲉⲃⲟⲗ ⲛ̄ⲛⲉⲭ'ⲣⲏⲥⲧⲓⲁⲛⲟⲥ,' ⲁⲩⲱ ⲙ̄ⲡⲉⲕⲥⲱ'ⲧⲙ̄ ⲛ̄ⲥⲱⲓ· ⲡⲉⲩ'ⲛⲟⲩⲧⲉ ⲅⲁⲣ
ⲡⲉⲧ'ⲙⲓϣⲉ ⲉϫⲱⲟⲩ,' ⲟⲩⲛ̄ϭⲟⲙ ⲙ̄ⲙⲟⲩ' ⲉⲛⲁϩⲙⲟⲩ.' ⲁϥⲟⲩⲱϣⲃ̄ ⲡⲉ'ϫⲁⲩ ⲛⲁⲥ ϫⲉ
ⲉⲣ'ϣⲁⲛⲡⲁⲡⲱⲗ'ⲗⲱⲛ ⲡⲛⲟϭ ⲛ̄'ⲛⲟⲩⲧⲉ ϯ ⲛⲁⲓ' ⲙ̄ⲡⲧⲁⲗϭⲟ ⲧⲁ'ⲧⲱⲟⲩⲛ, ϯⲛⲁⲉⲓⲙⲉ
ϫⲉ ⲉⲓ̈ⲣⲟⲩ ⲙ̄ⲡⲉⲓ̈'ⲁⲛⲍⲟⲥⲓⲟⲥ ⲉⲧⲙ̄(Rii)ⲙⲁⲩ. ⲁⲩⲱ ⲁϥ'ⲕⲉⲗⲉⲩⲉ ⲛ̄ϭⲓ ⲡⲗⲟⲩⲍ'
ⲉⲧⲣⲉⲩⲧⲱⲟⲩ(ⲛ)' ⲙ̄ⲙⲟⲩ ⲛ̄ⲥⲉⲧ'ⲩⲧⲟⲩ ϩⲁⲧⲃⲁⲥⲓⲥ' ⲙ̄ⲡⲁⲡⲱⲗⲗⲟⲛ,' ⲁⲩⲱ ⲁⲩⲟⲩⲉϩⲥⲁϩⲛⲉ ⲉⲧⲣⲉⲩⲧⲱϭ' ⲙ̄ⲙⲟⲩ ϩⲛ̄ⲟⲩⲛⲉϩ ⲛ̄ⲧⲛⲟⲩ'ⲃⲉ.' ⲙⲛ̄ⲛⲥⲱⲥ ⲁⲩ'ⲣⲉⲩⲧⲁⲗⲉ-
ⲗⲃⲁⲛⲟⲥ ⲉϩⲣⲁⲓ̈ ⲉϫⲛ̄'ⲧⲩϩⲏⲉ, ⲁⲩⲱ' ⲁⲩⲉⲣⲏⲧ ⲛⲁⲩ ⲛ̄ⲟⲩ'ⲉⲣⲏⲧ ⲉϥϫⲱ ⲙ̄ⲙⲟⲥ ϫⲉ
ⲡⲁⲡⲱⲗ'ⲗⲱⲛ, ⲉϣⲱⲡⲉ' ϣⲁⲕⲧⲁⲗϭⲟⲓ̈ ⲉⲃⲟⲗ' ϩⲛ̄ⲧⲙⲁⲅⲓⲁ ⲙ̄ⲡⲉⲓ̈'ⲙⲁⲅⲟⲥ ϫⲉ ⲡⲁⲏⲥⲉ,'
ϯⲛⲁⲭⲁⲣⲓⲍⲉ ⲛ̄ϩⲉⲛ'ⲛⲟϭ ⲛ̄ⲇⲱⲣⲟⲛ ⲉ'ⲡⲉⲕⲣ̄ⲡⲉ. ϯⲥⲟⲟⲩ(ⲛ̄)' ⲅⲁⲣ ϫⲉ ⲟⲩⲛ̄ϭⲟⲙ
ⲙ̄'ⲙⲟⲕ ⲉⲡⲁⲇⲉⲩⲉ' ⲙ̄ⲙⲟⲩ. ⲁⲥϣⲱⲡⲉ ⲇⲉ' ⲙⲛ̄ⲛⲥⲁⲛⲁⲓ̈ ⲧⲏ'ⲣⲟⲩ ⲁⲑⲉⲕⲗⲁ ⲉⲣ'ⲕⲟⲩⲓ̈
ⲛ̄ϩⲏⲧ ⲉⲙⲁⲧⲉ ⲉⲧⲃⲉⲡⲉⲥⲥⲟⲛ (Vi) ⲡⲁⲏⲥⲉ· ⲡⲉϫⲁⲥ' ϫⲉ ⲁⲣⲏⲩ ⲙ̄ⲡⲁ'ⲥⲟⲛ ϣⲟⲟⲡ
ⲁⲛ.' ⲉⲓⲥ ⲟⲩⲉⲃⲟⲧ ⲟⲩ'ϭⲟⲥ ⲁ̄ϩⲟⲟⲩ ϫⲓⲛ'ⲧⲁⲩⲃⲱⲕ, ⲙ̄'ⲡⲉⲩϫⲉⲓ, ⲟⲩⲇⲉ ⲙ̄'ⲡⲉⲩⲧⲛ̄-
ⲛⲟⲟⲩ' ⲙ̄ⲡⲉⲩϣⲟⲩⲱ'ⲛⲁⲓ̈· ϯⲛⲁ'ⲧⲱⲟⲩⲛ ⲛ̄ⲧⲁ'ⲃⲱⲕ ϣⲁⲛⲉⲧⲟⲩ'ⲁⲁⲃ ϩⲛ̄ⲡⲉⲩⲧⲉ'ⲕⲟ
ⲧⲁϣⲓⲛⲉ ⲛ̄'ⲥⲱϥ ⲉⲃⲟⲗ ϩⲓⲧⲟⲟ'ⲧⲟⲩ. ⲁⲥⲧⲱⲟⲩ(ⲛ)' ⲇⲉ ⲛ̄ϭⲓ ⲧⲙⲁⲓ̈ⲛⲟⲩⲧⲉ ⲑⲉⲕⲗⲁ,
ⲁⲥ'ⲃⲱⲕ ⲉⲡⲉⲩⲧⲉ'ⲕⲟ ⲉϫⲓⲥⲙⲟⲩ ⲉ'ⲃⲟⲗ ϩⲓⲧⲟⲟⲧⲟⲩ ⲛ̄'ⲛⲉⲧⲟⲩⲁⲁⲃ.' ⲡⲉϫⲉⲟⲩⲁ
ⲛⲁⲥ ⲉ'ⲃⲟⲗ ϩⲛ̄ⲛⲉⲧⲟⲩⲁⲁⲃ' ϫⲉ ⲑⲉⲕⲗⲁ· ⲛ̄ⲧⲟⲥ ⲇⲉ ⲡⲉϫⲁⲥ ϫⲉ' ⲥⲙⲟⲩ ⲉⲣⲟⲓ̈
ⲡⲁⲉⲓ̈ⲱⲧ· ⲡⲉϫⲁⲩ' ⲛⲁⲥ ϫⲉ ⲉⲧⲃⲉⲟⲩ ⲙ̄'ⲡⲉⲃⲱⲕ ⲉⲡϩⲟ'ⲟⲡ ⲙ̄ⲡⲟⲩⲥⲟⲛ' ⲡⲁⲏⲥⲉ;
ⲉⲓⲥϩⲏⲏ(Vii)ⲧⲉ ⲅⲁⲣ ⲥⲉⲣϩⲟⲟⲡ' ϩⲛ̄ⲟⲩⲛⲟϭ ⲛ̄ⲣⲁ'ϣⲉ· ⲟⲩⲁⲅⲅⲉⲗⲟⲥ ⲅⲁⲣ ⲛ̄ⲧⲉⲡ-
ϫⲟⲉⲓⲥ ⲡⲉⲛⲧⲁⲩ'ϫⲟⲟⲥ ⲛⲁⲓ̈ ϫⲉ ⲁ'ϫⲓⲥ ⲛⲉ ϫⲉ ⲃⲱⲕ' ⲉⲡϩⲟⲟⲡ ⲙ̄ⲡⲟⲩ'ⲥⲟⲛ. ⲑⲉⲕⲗⲁ ⲇⲉ' ⲡⲉϫⲁⲥ ⲛⲁⲩ ϫⲉ ⲁ'ⲣⲏⲩ ⲛ̄ⲧⲁⲡⲁ'ⲥⲟⲛ ⲙⲟⲩ, ⲡⲁⲉⲓ̈ⲱⲧ· ⲉϣⲱⲡⲉ' ⲉϩⲉ,
ⲙⲁⲧⲁⲙⲟⲛ,' ϫⲉ ⲉⲓ̈ⲉⲃⲱⲕ ⲧⲁⲛ̄ⲡⲉⲩⲥⲱⲙⲁ ⲉ'ⲡⲁⲏⲓ̈ ϫⲉ ⲙⲛ̄'ⲧⲁⲓⲥⲟⲛ ⲟⲩⲇⲉ
ⲥⲱⲛⲉ ⲉⲓⲙⲏⲧⲉⲓ ⲛ̄'ⲧⲟϥ ⲙ̄ⲡⲁⲕⲟⲩⲓ̈' ⲛ̄ϣⲏⲣⲉ.' ⲡⲉϫⲉⲡⲉⲧⲟⲩⲁ'ⲁⲃ ⲛⲁⲥ ϫⲉ
ϥ̄ⲟⲛϩ̄ ⲛ̄ϭⲓ ⲡϫⲟⲉⲓⲥ ϫⲉ' ⲙ̄ⲡⲉϥⲙⲟⲩ, ⲁⲗ'ⲗⲁ ϥ̄ⲟⲛϩ̄, ⲁⲩⲱ' ϥ̄ϩⲛ̄ⲟⲩⲛⲟϭ ⲛ̄ⲣⲁ'ϣⲉ
ⲙ̄ⲡⲟⲟⲩ ⲧⲉ'ⲛⲟⲩ, ⲁⲩⲱ ⲉⲓⲥ' ⲟⲩⲙⲏⲏϣⲉ ⲛ̄ⲣⲱⲙⲉ ⲁⲩⲥⲱⲟⲩϩ' ⲉⲧⲉⲩϣⲉⲓⲉⲉⲧ. (68 Ri)

---

66 V ii 24. l. ⲉⲉⲓⲣⲉ

λοιπον τωογ(ν)· ΝτεΒωκ ζΝογ'ειρηνη· αγω'εψωπε πογ'ωψ ΜπΝογτε
πε, ειε τΝααει· ζωων επραψε'Μπογσον, χε'πενψΒηρ πε·[10]ΤΜαϊνογτε
Δε'θεκλα ΑπεσειˈΜε εταγμΒια'Μπχαχε,' αλλα αστωογν,'[15] ασει ε-
Βολ εχΝ'ΤΗρω Ναντιˈνοογ, ασσινε'Νογκογι ΝΧαϊˈερεζραφαηλ'[20]παγγε-
λος αζεˈρατϥ ζιχωϥ,' ερεγαΒριηλ ζˈΜοος, ερεθαγια' μαρια τπαρθεˈνος
ετογααΒ' ΜπελιζαΒετ' τμααγ Νιωˈζαννης πΒαπ'τιστης ετζˈΜοος ζιθη
Μπˈχοϊ· νεσΜεεγε' γαρ χε Ννεεϥ' νε Ναγγελος, (68 R ii) αγω χε ζΝ-
αρˈχων νε νεχιοˈμε· Ντος Δε' πεχας χε νασˈνηγ, ετετΝΒηκ' ετων Ν-
τειζε;' αγογωψΒ χε' ζΝπογωψ Μπˈνογτε ενΒηκ·[10] ετπολις ρακοˈτε·
πεχεθεκ'λα ναγ χε τετΝαˈγ̄ρταγαπη' ΝτετΝταλοϊ'[15] ΝΜΜητΝ, χε'κας
ειεγψινε Ν'σαπασον;' πεχαγ νας χε' Βωκ Ντεειν̄ε'[20]Ννογσκεγη'ταχμ
αμη Ντ̄νγψΒηρ ζ̄'πεϊτογρης.' θεκλα Δε πεχας' ναγ χε νασνηγ,' μα-
ρεογα Νζητ'θητ̄ν ει Νϳˈναγ ενασκεγε.' Ντοογ Δε πεχαγˈ[30] νας χε
Βωκ, ανιˈσογ· τΝναπωˈλϳ Ν̄με·' ειc νικεζιομε (Vi) Ναρχων ταμην'
Ν̄μαν· Νθε εˈτογναˈτζ̄με,'† ζωωτε·[5] θεκλα Δε ασταˈλο Ν̄νεσκεγη'
εξΝ̄νεсζ̄ζαλ,' ασειˈνε Ν̄απˈγαγ Ν̄ογλιτρα'[10]Ν̄νογΒ, εсχω'Μμос χε
†ναˈχεογκογι εΒολˈ ενετογααΒ,' αγω Ντατκε'[15]κογι Μπасον' Ν̄ταϊο.'
ασχι Ν̄ψογτ'Μπεсηϊ, αстα'αγ Ν̄απωλλωνιˈос πεσκογι Ν̄ψη̄ρε, πεχας ναγ' χε λαγηρε, Μ'πΡ̄ρκογι Ν̄ζητ' ψανταει·[25] αγω'Απ̄Ρκανε-
τογα'αΒ Ν̄сωκ, αλλα' ψωκ Ν̄Βιπεγ'ροογγ· καταˈθε ετεκναγ εροϊ·[30]
ειˈειρε Μμος, αρισ' ζωωκ ον.' πεχεαπωλλωνιος (Vii) νας χε Μπογ'
ογχαϊ ω ταμαˈαγ, εργανΒωκ' εΡατογ Ν̄νετογ'ααΒ ετοτπ εζογ(ν)' Ν̄-
τεγϳνε Ν̄εω'ογ, μαρογσμογ' εροϊ ζω· Ντος' Δε πεχαс ναγ χε'[10] ψε
πεκογχαϊ' ω λαγηρε, ερˈγαννογτε' Μ̄νεγχηλ Ν̄νετογααΒ ναϳ-[15]
μετ ψαντˈναγ επαнсε πaˈсон εϥογοϳ,' †νατρεγсμογ' εροκ Ν̄-
ψορπ'[20] εροϊ· αγω αс'асπαζε Μμοϥ,' ασει εΒολ ζιτοоˈτϥ ερενεс-
ζ̄ζαλ ογηζ Ν̄ˈсωс εγθπο Μμос εΒολ.' αγω αˈναγγελος' ταλο Ν̄-
νεσκηγε' τηρογ· αγω'[30]асαλε Ντос Μ̄ν̄'ογζ̄ζαλ Ν̄сζιˈμε Ν̄ταс Μ̄-
ματε. (69 R i) αΝαγγελος δεγ'Νχοϊ εΒολ, αγ'νεзтλαγο εζητ,'χε
νερεπτογ'[5]ρης сωκ πε·' θεκλα Δε νεс'μεεγε χε ζΝ'νεεϥ νε Ναγγε-

---

68 V i 27. l. Βωκ νϥϥι-   ii 28. l. Ν̄νεσκεγη (-νεсск.?)

ⲗⲟⲥ, ⲁⲩⲱ ⲡⲉⲝⲁⲥ ⲛⲁⲩ ⲝⲉ ⲛⲁⲥⲛⲏⲩ, ϥⲓⲟⲩ̄ⲩⲏⲙ ⲛ̄ϩⲣ̄ⲡ̄ ⲛ̄ⲏⲧ̄ⲛ ⲙ̄ⲛ̄ϩⲉⲛ ⲕⲟⲩⲓ̈ ⲛ̄ⲟⲉⲓⲕ
ⲙⲛ̄ ⲟⲩⲩⲏⲙ ⲛ̄ⲧⲃ̄ⲧ̄ ⲛ̄ⲧⲉⲧⲛ̄ⲟⲩⲱⲙ, ⲝⲉ ⲁⲧⲉⲧⲛ̄ⲍⲉ ⲥⲉ ⲛ̄ⲙ̄ⲙⲁⲓ̈ · ⲛ̄ⲧⲟⲟⲩ ⲇⲉ ⲡⲉⲝⲁⲩ ⲛⲁⲥ
ⲝⲉ ⲡⲉⲧⲣⲟⲩⲱⲩ ⲉⲧⲁⲁⲩ ⲛ̄ⲧⲟ ϩⲛ̄ ⲛⲟⲩⲟⲓⲝ, ⲧⲁⲁⲩ ⲛⲁⲛ · ⲙ̄ⲙⲟⲛ ⲛ̄ⲧⲛ̄ⲛⲁⲕⲱⲍ ⲁⲛ
ⲉⲗⲁⲁⲩ ⲉⲃⲟⲗ ϩⲛ̄ ⲛⲟⲩⲥⲕⲉⲩⲏ, ⲝⲉ ⲕⲁⲥ ⲛ̄ⲛⲉⲭⲟⲟⲥ ⲝⲉ ⲁⲛⲁⲓ̈ ⲃⲱⲗ ⲉⲃⲟⲗ ⲛ̄ⲛⲁⲥⲛⲏⲩⲉ
ⲑⲉⲕⲗⲁ ⲇⲉ ⲁⲥⲟⲩⲉⲓⲥⲁϩⲛⲉ ⲛ̄ⲧⲉⲥϩⲙ̄ϩⲁⲗ ϭⲧ ⲛⲁⲩ ⲛ̄ⲧⲉⲩ ⲭⲣⲓⲁ · ⲉⲛⲉⲥⲙⲉⲉⲩⲉ (69Rii)
ⲅⲁⲣ ⲝⲉ ϩⲛ̄ⲣⲱⲙⲉ ⲛⲉ ⲉⲩϩⲛ̄ⲧⲥⲁⲣⲍ · ⲛ̄ⲧⲉⲣⲉⲟⲩϩⲉ ⲇⲉ ⲩⲱⲡⲉ, ⲁⲥⲛⲁⲩ ⲉⲛⲉⲍⲓⲟ-
ⲙⲉ ⲉⲩϩⲙⲟⲟⲥ ⲉⲣⲉⲡⲉⲩϩⲟ ⲟⲕⲙ̄ · ⲡⲉⲝⲁⲥ ⲛⲁⲩ ⲛ̄ϭⲓ ⲑⲉⲕⲗⲁ ⲝⲉ ⲛⲁⲥⲛⲏⲩ, ⲁϩⲣⲱ-
ⲧⲛ̄ ⲉⲣⲉⲛⲉⲧⲛ̄ϩⲟ ⲟⲕⲙ̄ ⲛ̄ⲧⲓ ϩⲉ; ⲁⲥⲟⲩⲱⲩⲃ ⲛ̄ϭⲓ ⲉⲗⲓⲥⲁⲃⲉⲧ ⲇⲉ ⲧⲁⲥⲱⲛⲉ, ⲛ̄ⲧ
ⲟⲩⲱⲩ ⲁⲛ ⲉⲧ ⲣⲁⲩⲕⲙ̄ · ⲛ̄ⲧⲁⲩ ϥⲓ ⲛ̄ⲧⲁⲡⲉ ⲙ̄ⲡⲁ ϩⲁⲓ̈ ⲙ̄ⲛ̄ⲧⲁⲡⲉ ⲙ̄ⲡⲁⲩⲏⲣⲉ ⲉⲧ ⲃⲉ-
ⲡⲉⲓ̈ⲣⲁⲛ ⲝⲉ ⲓ̅ⲥ̅ · ⲁⲩⲱ ⲉⲓⲥϫⲏⲧⲉ ⲁⲅⲉⲓ ⲛ̄ⲥⲱⲓ̈ ⲝⲉ ⲙⲁ ⲣⲟⲛ ⲉⲩ ϭⲗⲉⲉⲧ ϩⲛ̄ⲣⲁⲕⲟⲧⲉ
ⲡⲉⲝⲉⲑⲉⲕⲗⲁ ⲝⲉ ⲉⲓⲉ ⲧⲉⲓ̈ⲕⲉⲥⲱⲛⲉ ϩⲱⲱⲥ; ⲡⲉⲝⲉⲙⲁⲣⲓⲁ ⲧⲡⲁⲣⲑⲉⲛⲟⲥ ⲉⲧⲟⲩⲁⲁⲃ
ⲛⲁⲥ ⲝⲉ ⲛ̄ⲧⲁⲩ ⲧⲁⲗⲟ ⲙ̄ⲡⲁⲩⲏⲣⲉ ⲉⲝⲛ̄ⲟⲩϭⲏⲙ ⲛ̄ⲥ̄ⲧⲟⲥ ⲉⲧⲃⲉⲡⲅⲉ(ⲛⲓ)ⲛⲟⲥ ⲛ̄ⲛ̄ⲣⲱⲙⲉ
ⲡⲉⲝⲉⲑⲉⲕⲗⲁ ⲛⲁⲩ ⲝⲉ ⲁⲗⲏⲑⲱⲥ ⲛⲁⲥⲛⲁⲩ ⲁⲧⲉⲧⲛ̄ ϫⲓ ⲛⲟⲩⲛⲟϭ ⲛ̄ⲕⲁϩ ⲛ̄ϩⲏⲧ
ⲛ̄ⲧⲱⲧⲛ̄ ⲛⲁⲁⲩ ⲙ̄ ⲡⲟⲗⲓⲥ; ⲁⲛⲟⲕ ⲣⲱ ⲛ̄ⲧⲥⲟⲟⲩⲛ̄ ⲙ̄ⲙⲱⲧⲛ̄ ⲁⲛ · ⲡⲉⲝⲁⲩ ⲛⲁⲥ ⲝⲉ
ⲁ̄ⲙⲟⲛ ⲁⲛⲟⲛ ϩⲛ̄ⲣ̄ⲑⲓⲗⲏ̄ⲙ · ⲡⲉⲝⲉ ⲧⲡⲁⲣⲑⲉⲛⲟⲥ ⲉⲧⲟⲩⲁⲁⲃ ⲙⲁⲣⲓⲁ ⲛⲁⲥ ⲝⲉ
ⲉⲛⲉⲓ̈ ⲩⲟⲟⲛ ⲡⲉ ϩⲛ̄ⲧⲡⲟⲗⲓⲥ ⲩⲙⲟⲩⲧⲛ, ⲁ̄ⲛⲟⲕ ⲙ̄ⲛ̄ⲡⲁⲕⲟⲩⲓ̈ ⲛ̄ⲩⲏⲣⲉ ⲉⲩϫⲓⲉ ⲕⲓⲃⲉ
ⲙ̄ⲙⲟⲓ̈, ⲁⲩⲱ ⲁⲓ̈ⲕⲧⲟⲓ̈ ⲉⲃⲟⲗ ϩⲛ̄ ⲡⲙⲁ ⲉⲧⲙ̄ⲙⲁⲩ · ⲁⲩⲱ ⲁⲡⲁⲩⲏⲣⲉ ⲣⲛⲟϭ ⲩⲁⲛⲧⲉϥ
ⲣ̄ⲙⲁⲁⲃⲉ ⲛ̄ⲣⲟⲙ̄ⲡⲉ, ⲁⲩⲱ ⲁⲩⲥϥⲟⲩ ⲙ̄ⲙⲟϥ ⲛ̄ϭⲓ ⲛ̄ⲓⲟⲩ ⲇⲁⲓ̈ · ⲁⲩⲱ ⲉⲓⲥϫⲏⲧⲉ ϯⲃⲏⲕ
ⲉⲩ ϭⲗⲉⲉⲧ ϩⲛ̄ⲣⲁⲕⲟⲧⲉ · ⲡⲉⲝⲉⲑⲉⲕⲗⲁ ⲛⲁⲩ ⲝⲉ ⲛⲉⲥⲛⲏⲩ, ⲙⲁ(Vⅱ)ⲧⲁⲙⲟⲓ̈ ⲝⲉ
ⲉⲧⲉⲧⲛ̄ ⲃⲏⲕ ϩⲁⲧⲛ̄ⲛⲓⲙ ϩⲛ̄ⲣⲁⲕⲟⲧⲉ; ⲡⲉⲭⲁⲩ ⲝⲉ ⲉⲛⲃⲏⲕ ϩⲁⲧⲙ̄ⲡⲁⲩⲗⲟⲥ ⲡⲉⲡ ⲣⲁⲅ-
ⲙⲁⲧⲉⲩⲧⲏⲥ · ⲉⲩⲉⲣⲩⲉⲗⲉⲉⲧ ⲛ̄ⲟⲩⲣⲱⲙⲉ ⲝⲉ ⲡⲁⲛⲥⲉ ⲡⲣⲏⲙⲟⲩ ⲥⲓⲣⲉ · ⲡⲉⲝⲉⲅⲣⲁⲫⲁ-
ⲏⲗ ⲛⲁⲥ ⲝⲉ ϯⲥⲟⲟⲩⲛ̄ ⲝⲉ ⲛ̄ⲧⲟ ⲡⲉ ⲑⲉⲕⲗⲁ ⲧⲩ ⲧⲉⲣⲉ ⲛ̄ϩⲏⲗⲓⲁⲥ · ⲛ̄ⲧⲁⲛⲧⲁⲗⲟ ⲣⲱ
ⲉⲧⲃⲉⲡⲉⲓ̈ϩⲱⲃ, ⲙ̄ⲙⲟⲛ ⲛ̄ⲧⲛ̄ⲛⲁⲧⲁ ⲗⲟ ⲁⲛ ⲡⲉ · ⲛⲉⲍⲓⲟⲙⲉ ⲇⲉ ⲁⲩⲁ ⲙⲁϩⲧⲉ ⲛ̄ⲑⲉⲕⲗⲁ
ⲁⲩⲧⲡⲓ ⲉⲣⲱⲥ ⲙ̄ⲛ̄ⲧⲉⲥⲁⲡⲉ, ⲁⲩⲱ ⲡⲉⲝⲁⲩ ⲛⲁⲥ ⲝⲉ ⲉⲩⲝⲉ ⲛ̄ⲧⲟ ⲡⲉ ⲧⲥⲱⲛⲉ ⲙ̄ⲡⲁ-

---

69 R ii 31. Aϥⲉⲓ ⲛ̄ⲧⲁⲩⲧⲁⲗⲟ, + ⲙ̄ⲡⲥⲱⲙⲁ D. 33–V i 1. ⲉⲧⲃⲉⲡⲅⲉⲛⲟⲥ ⲛ̄ⲡⲣⲱⲙⲉ A; ⲉⲧ-
ⲃⲉⲡⲉⲓⲧ. ⲝⲉ ⲣ. D. 4. ⲛⲁⲥⲛⲁⲩ (sic) A; om. D. 12. ⲙ̄ⲙⲟⲛ A; om. D. 12f. ϩⲛ̄ⲣ̄ⲑⲓⲗⲏ̄ⲙ
A; ⲛⲁⲑ. D. 13. + ⲁⲩⲱ D. 14f. -ⲧⲡⲁⲣⲑⲉⲛⲟⲥ ⲉⲧⲟⲩⲁⲁⲃ A; om. D. 16f. ⲉⲛⲉⲓ̈ⲩⲟⲟⲛ A;
ⲛⲉⲓ̈ⲩ. D. 17. ⲡⲉ A; om. D. 17f. -ⲧⲡⲟⲗⲓⲥ A; 18f. ⲁⲛⲟⲕ A; om. D. 21.
ⲙ̄ⲙⲟⲓ̈ ⲁⲩⲱ A; om. D. 22–24. ⲉⲃⲟⲗ —ⲁⲡⲁⲩⲏⲣⲉ A; ⲟⲛ ⲉⲙⲁⲩ ⲩⲁⲛⲧⲉⲡⲁⲩ. D. 25f.
ⲩⲁⲛⲧⲉⲩ ⲣ̄ⲙⲁⲁⲃⲉ A; ⲛⲩ̄ⲣ̄ⲙⲁⲁⲃ D. ii 3f. ⲡⲉⲝⲁⲩ ⲝⲉ ⲉⲛⲃⲏⲕ A; om. D. 8. ⲛ̄ⲟⲩ-
ⲣⲱⲙⲉ A; ⲉⲩⲣ. + ⲉⲩⲁⲩⲙⲟⲩⲧⲉ ⲉⲣⲟ D. 11. ⲛⲁⲥ A; om. D. 12. ⲝⲉ A; ⲙ̄ⲙⲟ ⲱⲧⲉ-
ⲥⲍⲓⲛⲉ D. 13. ⲡⲉ (sic) A; ⲧⲉ D. 15. ⲣⲱ A; 16–18 ⲙ̄ⲙⲟⲛ — ⲡⲉ A; om. D.
21f. ⲙ̄ⲛ̄ⲧⲉⲥⲁⲡⲉ A; ⲙ̄ⲛ̄ⲧⲉⲥⲧⲁⲡⲣⲟ (sic) D. 23–25. ⲉⲩⲝⲉ — ⲙ̄ⲡⲁⲛⲥⲉ A; om. D.

ΗϹΕ, ΤΝ ραϥε ΝΑΜΗ. Ντοϲ ΔΕ αϲτω ογν ϲπογΔΕΠΗ, αϲϲαβτε Νογτραπεζα,
αγω αϲκω ϲιϲωϲ Νϩαϩ ΝαγαθοΝ ΜΝογΗρπ, ε(70 Ri)νεϲΜεεγε γαρ ϫε
ϩνρωΜε νε εγΝτϲαρϫ· θεκλα ΔΕ ενεϲαϩερατϲ εϲΔιακονει Ναγ· νεγο
γαρ πε ΜπεϥΜοτ ϩωϲ εγογωΜ. πεϫαγ ναϲ ϫε ϲωτΜ εροϊ ω θεκλα, ΤΝ-
ϥαΔε ΝαΜε Νθε γαρ Νταραϩερατε εροΝ, αϥΔιακονει εροΝ ενο ΝϩγΜ-
Μο ετεϲοογΝ ΜΜοΝ αν, ϩοπε εροΝ ϩωω(Ν) πε ΝΤΝαϩερα ΤΝ еро ΜΝογ-
ϲοΝ ΜΝογκογι Νϣμρε. πεϫαϲ ναγ ϫε κω ναϊ εβολ ναϲ ΝΗΥ, ΝΤΑΠ-
ϥα αν ϩωλοϲ εϩΜοοϲ εϩραϊ ΝΑΜΗ ΤΝ. ενετεγγΗ γαρ τε ετε ΜΝογοειΝ
Νοοϲ εβολ, αγω νερε πογοειΝ ΜΠΝογτε Μοϩϩ (Rii) ΜΠϫοϊ ΤΗΡϥ, αγω
νερετλαγο ϲωκ ΜΠϫοϊ ΤΗ Ρϥ εΜατε. πεϫε θεκλα ναγ ϫε αληθωϲ Μ-
πεϊναγ εογγΗ ενεϩ Νθε ΝΤαϊ. πεϫαγ ΔΕ ναϲ ϫε Μ ΠεϲωΤΝ ΝΤο ϫε
τεγγΗ ΝαρογοειΝ Νθε ΜΠεϩοογ; αγω ον Ν τερεπϲωτΗρ αλε ΕΠϫοϊ ΜΝ-
νεγΜαθΗτΗϲ, αγνοϭ Νκμτο γωπε αγτωογν Νϭι πϲωτΗρ, αγε πιτιΜα
ΝΝΤΗΥ ΜΝθαλαϲϲα, αγω αϲϣωπε Νϭι ογνοϭ Νϫαμη. ανον ϩΝ Μα-
θΗΤΗϲ γαρ Ν τε πετΝΜΜαγ. αγω απαρθενοϲ Μαρια εινε εβολ Νογ-
ϲκεγϲ ναγ αν Νϩοϥ εϥΜεϩ ΝΝεϩ Νϲτ ΝογΒε εναγε ϲογΝΤϥ, αϲπαϩΤϥ
(Vi) εϩραϊ εϫΝ ταπε Νθεκλα, αϲτωϩϲ ΜπεϲϲωΜα ΤΗ Ρϥ. πεϫαϲ ναϲ

---

70 Ri 10. l. εροΝ. 26. = ϩωλοϲ. 31. αγω: l. αλλα? ii 3 f. ΤΗΡϥ: probably repeated from l. 8. A long passage evidently omitted; see D. 29. l. -ϲκεγοϲ

70 Rii 1. γαρ Α; om. D. 2 f. ϩνρωΜε νε εγΝτϲαρϫ Α; ϩ[ε]νρΝκοϲμοϲ νε D.
4 f. ενεϲαϩερατϲ Α; νεϲα. D. 6. ναγ Α; εροογ D. 6–9. νεγο – εγογωΜ Α; νε-
αγρογϲμοτ γαρ ϫε νεγογωΜ D. 9. + αγω νεγω D. 10. ϲωτΜ εροϊ ω Α; om. D. 11 f.
ΤΝϥα ϫε ΝαΜε Α; πεϫαϲ ϫε ϲΜογ εροϊ πεϫαγ ναϲ ϫε D. 13. γαρ Α; om. D. 13–15.
Νταραϩερατε εροΝ αϥΔιακονει Α; Νταρ Διακονει D. 15 f. ενο ΝϩγΜΜο Α; om. D.
16 f. ετεϲοογΝ Α; Ντεϲ. D. 18. εροΝ ϩωων Α; ον D. 19 f. ΝΤΝαϩερα ΤΝ Α; ΑΤΝ-
Διακονει D. 21 f. -κογι Ν- Α; om. D. 26. ϩωλοϲ Α; om. D. 26 f. εϩΜοοϲ εϩραϊ Α;
εϲοογΝ εβολ εογωΜ D. 28 f. ενετεγγΗ Α; νετ. D. 29–31. ετεΜΝογοειΝ Νοοϲ
εβολ Α; ογΔε ΜΠΛ· ΙΝβολ[...] ΔΕ νεγοϲ D. ii 7. After ενεϩ, + εϥο Νογοειν D.
8. After Νταϊ, + ερετλαγο ϲωκ ΜΠϫοϊ· αγω νερεΝαγγελοϲ ϩμοοϲ ϩιϫΝ ΜΠϫοϊ
Μπογϭιοττωρε επϫιχΝ ογΔε εθη· αγω νερεπϫοϊ Ρϩωτ εϩΗτ ϩΝογμοτνεϲ. πεϫε
θεκλα ναγ ϫε αληθωϲ Μπεϊναγ εϫοϊ ενεϩ Νθε Μπεϊϫοϊ ϸ; A's omission
no doubt due to partial homoeoteleuton. 9. ΔΕ Α; om. D. 9 f. ΜπεϲωΤΝ Α; Μ-
πρϲ·(sic) D. 10. ΝΤο Α; om. D. 13. After ον, + ϫε D. 17. Νκμτο Α; Νκαμη (sic) D.
22–24. αγω αϲϣωπε – Νϫαμη Α; αγνοϭ Νϫαμη γωπε D. 24. After ανον, + γαρ
ανον D. 25. γαρ Α; om. D. 27. αγω Α; om. D. απαρθενοϲ Α; αθαγια D. 28.
εβολ Α; om. D. 29–31. ναγ αν – ΝΝεϩ Α; om. D. 32 f. εναγε ϲογΝΤϥ Α; om. D.
Vi 1. εϩραϊ Α; om. D. 4–6. πεϫαϲ – θεκλα Α; πεϫε θεκλα ναϲ D.

ⲛ̄ϭⲓ ⲧⲙⲁⲓⲛⲟⲩⲧⲉ ⲑⲉⲕⲗⲁ ϫⲉ ⲕⲱ ⲛⲁⲓ ⲉⲃⲟⲗ ⲧⲁϫⲟⲉⲓⲥ ⲙ̄ⲙⲁⲁⲩ· ⲛ̄ⲧⲡ̄ⲥⲡ̄ⲥ̄ⲡⲁ ⲁⲛ ⲙ̄ⲡⲉⲓ-
ⲛⲟⲥ ⲛ̄ⲧⲁⲓⲟ ⲛ̄ⲧⲁⲣⲧⲁⲁⲩ ⲛⲁⲓ. ⲡⲉϫⲉⲧⲡⲁⲣⲑⲉⲛⲟⲥ ⲉⲧⲟⲩⲁⲁⲃ ⲛⲁⲥ ϫⲉ ⲉⲛⲉⲛ̄ⲧⲉ-
ⲉⲙⲡ̄ⲡϫⲁ ⲙ̄ⲙⲟⲩ ⲁⲛ ⲡⲉ ⲛⲉⲩⲛⲁ ⲡⲁϫⲧⲩ̄ ⲁⲛ ⲉϫⲱ ⲡⲉ· ⲡⲁⲓ ⲅⲁⲣ ⲡⲉ ⲡⲛⲉϩ ⲛ̄ⲧⲩ-
ⲗⲉⲉⲧ ⲙ̄ⲡⲁⲩϣⲏⲣⲉ ⲛ̄ⲧⲁⲓ ⲛ̄ⲧⲩ̄ ⲉⲧⲩⲗⲉⲉⲧ ⲙ̄ⲡⲟⲩⲥⲟⲛ. ⲡⲉϫⲉ ⲑⲉⲕⲗⲁ ϫⲉ ⲛ̄ⲧⲁⲣⲧ ⲟⲛ
ⲉⲡⲉⲓⲛⲉϩ; ⲁⲗⲏⲑⲱⲥ ⲙ̄ⲡⲉⲓⲛⲁⲩ ⲉ ⲟⲩⲟⲛ ⲉⲛⲉϩ ⲛ̄ⲑⲉ ⲙ̄ⲡⲁⲓ. ⲡⲉϫⲉ ⲡⲁⲣⲑⲉⲛⲟⲥ
ⲉⲧⲟⲩⲁ ⲁⲃ ⲛⲁⲥ ϫⲉ ⲙ̄ⲛ̄ ⲗⲁⲁⲩ ⲛⲁϫⲉ ⲉⲡⲉⲓ ⲉⲛⲉϩ ⲛ̄ⲥⲁⲛⲉ ⲧⲙ̄ⲡ̄ⲡϫⲁ ⲙ̄ⲡⲙⲁ ⲛ̄ ⲑⲩⲗⲉⲉⲧ
ⲙ̄ⲡⲁⲩϣⲏⲣⲉ. ⲑⲉⲕⲗⲁ ⲇⲉ ⲁⲥⲛ̄(70 VII)ⲕⲁⲧⲕ̄, ⲁⲥⲱⲩⲃ̄ ⲉⲧⲃⲉ ⲡⲉⲥⲧⲟⲓ̈ ⲙ̄ⲡ̄ⲛⲉϩ. ⲡⲉϫⲉ ⲡⲁⲣⲑⲉⲛⲟⲥ ⲉⲧⲟⲩⲁⲁⲃ ⲙⲁⲣⲓⲁ ⲛ̄ⲅⲁⲃⲣⲓⲏⲗ ⲙ̄ⲛ̄ ϩⲣⲁⲫⲁⲏⲗ ϫⲉ ⲙⲁⲛⲉⲛ ϫⲟⲓ ⲉ-
ϩⲟⲩⲛ ⲉⲡⲉⲓ ⲙⲁ ⲛ̄ⲧⲛ̄ⲧⲱϣ̄ⲙ̄ ⲛ̄ⲧⲉⲓ ⲕⲉⲩⲃⲉⲉⲣⲉ ⲉⲧⲩⲗⲉⲉⲧ. ⲁⲩⲱ ⲁⲩⲙⲁⲛⲉⲛ ϫⲟⲓ ⲉ-
ϩⲟⲩⲛ ⲉⲧⲁⲙⲙⲁϩ ϩⲙ̄ ⲡⲧⲟⲩ ⲙ̄ⲙ̄ⲃ̄ⲃⲉ, ⲁⲩⲃⲱⲕ ⲉϩⲟⲩⲛ ⲉ ⲡⲏⲓ ⲙ̄ⲡⲛⲟϭ ⲙ̄ⲡⲣⲉⲥⲃⲩ-
ⲧⲉⲣⲟⲥ ⲙ̄ⲡ̄ⲧⲙⲉ, ⲁⲩⲛⲁⲩ ⲉ ⲧⲉⲩϣⲏⲣⲓ ⲛ̄ϣⲩⲉⲉⲣⲉ ⲉⲥϩⲛ̄ ⲙⲛ̄ⲧⲥⲛⲟⲟⲩⲥⲉ ⲛ̄ⲣⲟⲙⲡⲉ, ⲉ-
ⲡⲉⲥⲣⲁⲛ ⲡⲉ ϩⲏⲣⲁⲉⲓ. ⲁⲩⲱ ⲁⲧⲉ ⲑⲉⲟⲇⲟⲕⲟⲥ ⲧⲁⲗⲟ ⲛ̄ⲧⲉⲥϫⲓϫ ⲉϫⲛ̄ ⲧⲉⲥⲁⲡⲉ, ⲁⲥⲥⲙⲟⲩ ⲉⲣⲟⲥ ⲉⲥϫⲱ ⲙ̄ⲙⲟ ϫⲉ ⲥⲉⲡⲏ, ⲧⲁϫⲟⲓ ⲉⲧⲩⲗⲉⲉⲧ· ⲁⲓ ⲟ ⲩⲱ ⲅⲁⲣ ⲉ ⲓⲥⲟⲩ ⲧⲉ
ⲛⲏ ⲙ̄ⲡⲟⲩⲛⲩⲙ̄ ⲫⲓⲟⲥ. ⲛⲁⲓ ⲇⲉ ⲛ̄ⲧⲉⲣⲉⲥϫⲟⲟⲩ, ⲁⲩ(71 R i)ⲉⲓ ⲉⲃⲟⲗ ϩⲙ̄ ⲡⲏⲓ ⲉⲩⲙⲉϩ
ⲛ̄ⲣⲁϣⲉ ⲛ̄ⲧⲉ ⲡⲉⲡⲛ̄ⲁ ⲉⲧⲟⲩⲁⲁⲃ, ⲁⲩⲥⲏⲣ ⲉϩⲏⲧ· ⲡⲉϫⲉ ⲑⲉⲕⲗⲁ ϫⲉ ⲧⲁϫⲟⲉⲓⲥ, ⲉⲧⲃⲉ
ⲟⲩ ⲁⲡⲉϫⲟⲟⲥ ⲛ̄ⲛⲉⲥ ⲉⲓⲟⲧⲉ ⲛ̄ⲥⲉ ⲧⲛ̄ⲛⲟ ⲟⲩⲥ ⲛⲙ̄ⲙⲁⲛ; ⲛⲁ ⲩ ⲛ̄ϫⲉ ⲉⲣⲉ ⲧⲩⲉⲉⲣⲉ ⲩⲏⲙ
ⲛⲁⲉⲓ ⲙⲁⲩ ⲁⲁⲥ; ⲡⲉϫⲉ ⲡⲁⲣⲑⲉⲛⲟⲥ ⲉⲧⲟⲩⲁ ⲁⲃ ⲙⲁⲣⲓⲁ ⲛⲁⲥ ϫⲉ ⲡⲉⲥⲱⲧⲙ̄ ⲉⲧⲟ
ⲉⲡⲉⲧ ⲥⲏϩ ϩⲙ̄ ⲡⲉⲩⲁⲅⲅⲉ ⲗⲓⲟⲛ ϫⲉ ⲡⲉⲧⲛ̄ⲩ̄ ⲛⲁⲕⲁ ⲓ̈ⲱⲧ ⲛ̄ⲥⲱⲩ ⲁⲛ ϩⲓ ⲙⲁⲁⲩ ϩⲓ ⲥⲟⲛ ϩⲓ-
ⲥⲱⲛⲉ, ⲙⲛ̄ ⲥⲟⲙ̄ ⲙ̄ⲙⲟⲩ ⲉ ⲩϣⲱⲡⲉ ⲛⲁⲓ ⲙ̄ⲙⲁⲑⲏⲧⲏⲥ; ⲑⲉⲕⲗⲁ ⲇⲉ ⲙ̄ⲡⲉ ⲡⲉⲥ ⲛⲟⲩⲥ

70 V i 29 f. ⲗ. ⲉⲡⲉⲓⲛⲉϩ (so D). ii 1. ⲗ. ⲁⲥⲱⲃ̄ⲩ̄. 26. ⲁⲥⲥⲙⲟⲩ: first c added. 71 R i
15. ⲗ. ⲙ̄ⲡⲉⲥⲱⲧⲙ̄ ⲛ̄ⲧⲟ.

70 V i 10 f. ⲛ̄ⲧⲁⲣⲧⲁⲁⲩ ⲛⲁⲓ A; om. D. 11 f. -ⲧⲡⲁⲣⲑⲉⲛⲟⲥ ⲉⲧⲟⲩⲁⲁⲃ A; -ⲧⲉⲑⲉⲟⲇⲱⲕⲟⲥ D.
13 f. ⲉⲛⲉⲛ̄ⲧⲉⲉⲙⲡ̄ⲡϫⲁ ⲙ̄ⲙⲟⲩ ⲁⲛ ⲡⲉ A; ⲉⲛⲉⲣ̄ⲉⲙⲡ̄ϫⲁ ⲁⲛ ⲙ̄ⲙⲟⲩ D. 17 ⲡⲉ A; om. D. ⲅⲁⲣ
A; om. D. 22. After ⲑⲉⲕⲗⲁ, + ⲛⲁⲥ] D. After ϫⲉ, + ⲧⲁ[ϫⲟⲉⲓⲥ] D. 27 f. ⲉⲧⲟⲩⲁⲁⲃ A; om.
D. 29. -ⲗⲁⲁⲩ A; -ⲟⲩⲟⲛ ⲛⲓⲙ D. 30. -ⲉⲛⲉϩ (sic) A; -ⲛⲉϩ ⲛⲁⲓ D. 31-33. ⲙ̄ⲡⲙⲁⲛ̄ ⲑⲩⲉ-
ⲗⲉⲉⲧ ⲙ̄ⲡⲁⲩϣⲏⲣⲉ A; ⲙ̄ⲙⲟⲩ D. ii 1. ⲁⲥⲱⲩ̄ⲃ̄ (sic) A; ⲁⲥⲱⲃ̄ⲩ̄ D. 2 f. -ⲡⲉⲥⲧⲟⲓ̈ ⲙ̄ⲡ̄ⲛⲉϩ
A; -ⲛⲉⲥⲧⲟⲓ̈ ⲙ̄ⲡⲥⲟϥⲛ̄ D. After this, + ⲩⲱϣⲛ̄ ⲇⲉ ⲛ̄ⲧⲉⲣⲉⲩⲱⲡⲉ ⲁⲩⲉⲓ ⲙ̄ⲡ̄ⲁⲧⲟ ⲉⲃⲟⲗ
ⲛ̄ⲟⲩⲕⲟⲓ ⲛ̄ⲧⲙⲉ ⲉⲩⲁⲩⲙⲟⲩⲧⲉ ⲉⲣⲟⲩ ϫⲉ ⲧⲁⲙⲙⲁϩ D. 4. ⲉⲧⲟⲩⲁⲁⲃ A; om. D. 5-7.
ⲛ̄ⲅ̄ ⲙ̄ϩⲣ̄ⲡ̄ A; ⲛ̄ϩⲣ̄ⲡ̄ D. 7 f. ⲙⲁⲛⲉⲡϫⲟⲓ A; ⲙⲟⲟⲛⲉ ⲙ̄ⲡϫⲟⲓ̈ D. 10. ⲛ̄ⲧⲉⲓ ⲕⲉⲩⲃⲉⲉⲣⲉ
A; ⲉⲛⲧⲉⲓ ⲩⲉⲉⲣⲉ ⲩⲏⲙ D. 11. ⲁⲩⲱ A; om. D. 12. ⲁⲩⲙⲁⲛⲉⲡϫⲟⲓ A; ⲁⲩⲙⲟⲟⲛⲉ ⲙ̄
ⲡϫⲟⲓ̈ D. 12-14. ⲉϩⲟⲩⲛ — ⲙ̄ⲙ̄ⲃ̄ⲃⲉ A; ⲉⲡⲉⲕⲣⲟ D. Then + ⲁⲩⲧⲓ ⲛ̄ⲑⲉⲕⲗⲁ ⲛ[ⲉ-
ⲙⲁⲩ?] D. 23. ⲁⲩⲱ A; om. D. 27. + ⲛⲁⲥ D. 33. ⲛ̄ⲧⲉⲣⲉⲥϫⲟⲟⲩ A; ⲉⲩⲕⲱ (sic) ⲙ̄
ⲙⲟⲟⲩ D. 71 R i 1. ϩⲙ̄ ⲡⲏⲓ A; om. D. 5. + ⲛⲁⲥ D. 6. ⲧⲁϫⲟⲉⲓⲥ A; ⲧⲁⲥⲱⲛⲉ D.
7. ⲁⲡⲉϫⲟⲟⲥ A; ⲙ̄ⲡⲉⲣ̄ϫⲟⲟⲥ D. 8 f. ⲛ̄ⲥⲉⲧⲛ̄ⲛⲟⲟⲩⲧⲉ ⲛⲙ̄ⲙⲁⲛ A; ⲛ̄ⲥⲉⲉⲓ ⲛⲙ̄ⲙⲁⲥ D.
13 f. ⲉⲧⲟⲩⲁⲁⲃ A; om. D. 14-16. In D the text can probably be restored from A
as far as ⲡⲉⲧⲥ]ⲏϩ 2. 20. ⲙⲛ̄ ⲥⲟⲙ A; ⲙ̄ⲛ̄ ⲩ̄ⲥⲟⲙ D. 24. ⲙ̄ⲡⲉⲡⲉⲥ ⲛⲟⲩⲥ A; ⲙ̄ⲡⲉ
ⲡⲉⲥϩⲏⲧ D.

ϭⲱⲧⲍ̄ ⲉⲛⲉⲓ̈·²⁵ⲅⲁϫⲉ. ⲁⲩⲛⲱϩ'ⲇⲉ ⲉⲩⲕⲟⲩⲓ̈ ⲛ̄ⲧ̄ⲙⲉ'ⲉⲩⲁⲩⲙⲟⲩⲧⲉ ⲉⲣⲟⲩ' ϫⲉ ⲩⲉⲣⲉⲙⲟⲩⲛ,'
ⲉⲁⲩⲛⲁⲩ ⲉⲡⲓⲉⲣⲟ'³⁰ ⲉⲩϯ2ⲓⲥⲉ ⲛⲁⲩ.' ⲡⲉϫⲉⲧⲡⲁⲣⲑⲉⲛⲟⲥ' ⲛⲁⲩ ϫⲉ ⲥⲁϫⲱϫⲕ'ⲉⲃⲟⲗ ⲙ̄
ⲡⲉⲓ̈ⲧ̄ⲙⲉ, (71 Rii)ⲙ̄ⲡⲉⲣϯ2ⲓⲥⲉ ⲛⲁⲩ.' ⲩ̄ⲥⲛ2 ⲅⲁⲣ ϫⲉ ⲉⲩⲅⲁ(ⲛ)'ⲍⲉ ⲉⲩⲃⲉⲗⲃⲓⲗⲉ 2ⲙ̄
ⲡⲉⲥⲙⲁ2, ⲩⲁⲧⲕⲟ̄ⲟⲥ ϫⲉ ⲙ̄ⲡⲉⲣⲧⲁⲕⲟⲩ,' ϫⲉ ⲟⲩⲛ̄ⲟⲩⲥⲙⲟⲩ ⲛ̄ⲧⲉⲛ̄ϫⲟⲉⲓⲥ ⲛ̄2ⲏⲧ̄ⲩ̄·' ⲡϫⲟ
ⲉⲓⲥ ⲥⲙⲁⲙⲁ̈ⲁⲧ ⲩⲁⲉⲛⲉ2. ⲁⲩⲱ'ⲉⲓⲥ ⲟⲩⲥⲙⲏ ⲁⲥⲩⲱⲡⲉ 2ⲛ̄ⲧⲡⲉ 2ⲛ̄ⲡⲉⲓⲉⲣⲟ ϫⲉ ⲙ̄ⲛ̄'
ⲕⲟⲣⲓⲟⲥ ⲕⲱⲧⲉ' ⲉⲣⲟⲩ· ⲁⲥⲟⲩⲱ̈¹⁵ⲩ̄ⲃ̄ ⲛ̄ϭⲓ ⲧⲡⲁⲣⲑⲉ'ⲛⲟⲥ ⲉⲧⲟⲩⲁⲁⲃ ⲙⲁ'ⲣⲓⲁ ϫⲉ ⲁⲡⲁⲩⲛ'
ⲣⲉ ⲟⲩⲱ ⲉⲩⲥⲟⲃⲧⲉ' ⲛ̄ⲛ̄ⲧⲱⲃⲉ. ⲉⲓⲥ ⲕⲉ²⁰ⲩ̄ⲧⲟⲟⲩ ⲛ̄ⲉⲃⲟⲧ' ⲛ̄ⲥⲉⲕⲱⲧ ⲉⲣⲟⲩ' ⲛ̄ⲟⲩⲕⲟⲣⲓⲟⲥ ⲙⲛ̄
ⲟⲩⲥⲁⲃⲧ̄ ⲛ̄ⲩⲟ⳽ⲙ̄ⲛ̄ⲧ̄ ⲛ̄ϫⲟⲟⲩ.²⁵ ⲁⲩⲱ ⲛ̄ⲧⲉⲓϩⲉ ⲁⲩⲥ'ϭⲏⲣ ⲉ2ⲏⲧ. ⲩⲱ'ⲣⲡ̄ ⲇⲉ ⲙ̄ⲡⲉⲩⲣⲁⲥ'ⲧⲉ
ⲁⲩⲙⲟⲟⲛⲉ ⲉⲧ'ⲡⲟⲗⲓⲥ ⲣⲁⲕⲟⲧⲉ,³⁰ ⲁⲩⲧⲱⲟⲩⲛ, ⲁⲩⲉⲓ' ⲉⲡⲉⲕⲣⲟ· ⲡⲉϫⲉⲑⲉⲕⲗⲁ ⲛⲁⲩ ϫⲉ'
ⲛⲁⲥⲛⲏⲩ, ⲧⲉⲧⲛ̄(Vi)ⲥⲟⲟⲩⲛ̄ ⲙ̄ⲡⲏⲓ̈ ⲙ̄'ⲡⲁⲩⲗⲟⲥ; ⲉⲩϫⲉ'ⲥⲉ, ⲃⲱⲕ ⲛ̄ⲧⲉⲧⲛ̄ⲣ̄'ⲧⲁⲅⲁⲡⲏ
ⲛ̄ⲧⲉ'ⲧⲛ̄ⲙⲟⲩⲧⲉ ⲉⲡⲁ'ⲥⲟⲛ ⲛ̄ⲩⲧⲁⲗⲟ ⲛ̄'ⲛⲁⲥⲕⲏⲩⲉ· ⲙⲁⲟ(ⲛ)' ⲛ̄ⲧⲥⲟⲟⲩⲛ̄ ⲁⲛ ⲙ̄ⲡⲙⲁ ⲉⲃⲟⲗ
ϫⲉ ⲙ̄ⲡⲉⲓ̈'ⲉⲓ ⲉⲧⲉⲓ̈ⲡⲟⲗⲓⲥ ⲉⲛⲉ2.' ⲡⲉϫⲁⲩ ⲛⲁⲥ ϫⲉ ⲕⲱ [ⲛ̄]ⲛ̄ⲧⲟⲩ2ⲙ̄ϫⲁⲗ'2ⲁⲧⲛ̄ⲛⲟⲩ
ⲥⲕⲏⲩⲉ·'ⲁⲙⲏ ⲛ̄ⲧⲛ̄ⲧⲁⲙⲟ'¹⁵ⲉⲡⲙⲁ ⲙ̄ⲡⲟⲩⲥⲟⲛ.' ⲁⲩⲱ ⲁⲥⲙⲟⲟⲩⲉ' ⲛ̄ⲙⲁⲩ, ⲁⲩⲧⲥ̄'
ⲉⲡⲙⲁ ⲙ̄ⲡⲉⲩ'ⲧⲉⲕⲟ, ⲁⲩⲁⲍⲉⲣⲁ'ⲧⲟⲩ, ⲁⲩⲱ ⲡⲉϫⲉ'ⲧⲡⲁⲣⲑⲉⲛⲟⲥ ϫⲉ'ⲑⲉⲕⲗⲁ, ⲙ̄ⲡⲉⲣ'
ⲥⲟⲩⲱⲛⲧ̄; ⲡⲉϫⲁⲥ ϫⲉ ⲙ̄ⲡⲉ ⲧⲁ'ϫⲟⲉⲓⲥ. ⲡⲉϫⲁⲥ ⲇⲉ ⲁⲛⲟⲕ ⲡⲉ ⲙⲁ'ⲣⲓⲁ ⲧⲡⲁⲣⲑⲉ
ⲛⲟⲥ' ⲉⲧⲟⲩⲁⲁⲃ, ⲧⲉⲛ̄'ⲧⲁⲥϫⲡⲟ ⲙ̄ⲡⲛⲟⲩ'ⲧⲉ ⲡⲗⲟⲅⲟⲥ ⲡⲉⲛ'ⲧⲁⲛ̄ⲓ̈ⲟⲩⲇⲁⲓ̈' ⲥ̄ⲣⲟⲩ ⲙ̄ⲙⲟⲩ,'
ⲁⲩⲱ ⲧⲁⲓ̈ ⲉⲧⲣⲛ̄ⲁⲩ (Vii) ⲉⲣⲟⲥ ⲧⲉ ⲉ̄ⲛⲥⲁⲃⲉⲧ' ⲧⲙⲁⲁⲩ ⲛ̄ⲓ̈ⲱ2ⲁⲛ̄ⲛⲏⲥ ⲡⲃⲁⲡⲧⲓⲥ'
ⲧⲏⲥ, ⲁⲩⲱ ⲡⲉⲓ̈'ⲕⲉⲣⲱⲙⲉ ⲥⲛⲁⲩ ⲉ'ⲧⲉⲣⲛ̄ⲁⲩ ⲱⲣⲟⲟⲩ'ⲉⲧⲧⲁⲗⲏⲩ ⲉⲡ'ϫⲟⲓ ⲡⲉ ⲥⲁⲩⲣⲓ
ⲏⲗ' ⲙ̄ⲛ̄ⲅⲣⲁⲫⲁⲏⲗ'¹⁰ⲛⲉⲧⲁ2ⲉⲣⲁⲧⲟⲩ' ⲙ̄ⲡⲙ̄ⲧⲟ ⲉⲃⲟⲗ ⲙ̄ⲡⲛⲟⲩⲧⲉ.' ⲛⲁⲓ̈ ⲇⲉ ⲛ̄ⲧⲉⲣⲉⲥ'ⲥⲱ
ⲧⲙ̄ ⲉⲣⲟⲟⲩ ⲛ̄ϭⲓ ⲑⲉⲕⲗⲁ, ⲁⲥϫⲉ'ⲉ2ⲣⲁⲓ̈ ⲉⲕ̄ⲡⲕⲁ2' ⲉⲕ̄ⲡⲉⲥ2ⲟ, ⲁⲥⲩⲱⲡⲉ ⲛ̄ⲑⲉ ⲛ̄
ⲛⲉⲧ'ⲙⲟⲟⲩⲧ. ⲁⲥⲥⲟⲟⲩ²⁰ⲧⲛ̄ ⲉⲃⲟⲗ ⲛ̄ϭⲓ ⲧⲡⲁⲣ'ⲑⲉⲛⲟⲥ ⲉⲧⲟⲩⲁⲁⲃ' ⲙⲁⲣⲓⲁ, ⲁⲥⲧⲟⲩ'ⲛⲟⲥⲥ̄,'
ⲡⲉϫⲁⲥ'ⲛⲁⲥ ϫⲉ ⲙ̄ⲡⲉⲥⲱⲧⲙ̄ ⲉⲡ·²⁵ⲃⲟ ⲉⲛⲉⲧ'ⲥⲛ2 2ⲙ̄ⲡⲉⲩⲁⲅⲅⲉ'ⲗⲓⲟⲛ ⲉⲧⲟⲩⲁⲁⲃ,' ⲉⲣⲉ
ⲡⲁⲩ2ⲣⲉ ϫⲱ'ⲙ̄ⲙⲟⲥ ⲛ̄ⲛⲉⲩⲁ³⁰ⲡⲟⲥⲧⲟⲗⲟⲥ ϫⲉ'ⲛ̄ⲧⲱⲧⲛ̄ ⲁⲛ ⲡⲉⲛ'ⲧⲁⲧⲉⲧⲛ̄ⲥⲟⲧⲡ̄,' ⲁⲗ
ⲗⲁ ⲁⲛⲟⲕ ⲡⲉⲛ(72 Ri)ⲧⲁⲓ̈ⲥⲉⲧⲡ̄ⲧⲏⲩⲧⲛ̄;'ⲧⲉⲛⲟⲩ ϭⲉ ⲡⲁⲩⲏ'ⲣⲉ ⲡⲉⲛⲧⲁⲩⲥⲉⲧⲡ̄'
ⲧⲏⲩⲧⲛ̄· ⲙ̄ⲡⲉⲣ'ⲩⲱⲡⲉ ⲛ̄ⲃⲁⲃ2ⲏⲧ,'ⲁⲗⲗⲁ ⲛ̄ϩⲁⲣ2ⲏⲧ,' ⲁⲩⲱ ⲉⲓⲥ2ⲏⲏⲧⲉ'ⲁⲓ̈ⲥⲟⲃⲧⲉ
ⲛⲏⲧⲛ̄' ⲛ̄ⲛⲉⲧⲛ̄ⲏⲓ̈ ⲙ̄ⲛ̄'ⲛⲉⲧⲛ̄ⲑⲣⲟⲛⲟⲥ' ⲙ̄ⲛ̄ⲛⲉⲧⲛ̄ⲕⲗⲟⲙ' 2ⲛ̄ⲧⲡⲟⲗⲓⲥ ⲉⲧⲟⲩ'ⲁⲁⲃ ⲙ̄
ⲡⲁⲩ2ⲣⲉ ⲑⲓⲗⲏⲙ̄ ⲛ̄ⲧⲡⲉ.'¹⁵ ⲉⲓⲥ2ⲏⲏⲧⲉ ⲅⲁⲣ ⲁⲓ̈'ⲧⲉ2ⲥⲉ ⲙ̄ⲡⲛⲉ2' ⲉⲧⲟⲩⲁⲁⲃ, ⲛⲁⲓ̈' ⲉⲧ

---

71 Vi 13. ⲧ added. ii 6. *l*.ⲉⲣⲟⲟⲩ. 25. *l*.ⲛ̄ⲧⲟ. 31 *f*. *l*.ⲡⲉⲛⲧⲁⲧⲉⲧⲛ̄ⲥⲟⲧⲡ̄.

---

71 R i 25. After-ⲅⲁϫⲉ, ϯ ⲛ̄2ⲟⲥⲟⲛ ⲉⲩⲅⲁϫⲉ ⲙ̄ⲛⲉⲩⲉⲣⲏⲩ D. 26. ⲇⲉ A; ⲙ.D. 28.'
ⲩⲉⲣⲉⲙⲟⲩⲛ A; ⲩⲉⲙⲙⲟⲩⲛ D. 29. ⲉⲁⲩⲛⲁⲩ A; ⲁⲩⲛⲁⲩ D. ii 11 *f*. 2ⲛ̄ⲧⲡⲉ 2ⲛ̄ⲡⲉⲓⲉⲣⲟ ϫⲉ
A; if Till's estimate of the number of letters lost before ϫⲉ is correct, we should
probably restore 2ⲛ̄ⲡⲉⲓⲉⲣⲟ (rather than 2ⲛ̄ⲧⲡⲉ) in D.

ϩⲁⲧⲉ ⲉⲡⲉⲥⲏⲧ ⲉⲧⲁⲩⲭⲛⲓⲁ ⲛ̄ⲛⲓⲩⲣ̄ⲡⲙⲓⲥⲉ· ⲁⲩⲱ ⲁⲓⲧ̄ⲥⲟⲙ ⲛⲉ ⲛ̄ⲧⲟ·Ⲁⲩ ⲉⲓⲥ ⲅⲣⲁⲫⲁⲏⲗ
ⲡⲁⲣⲭⲁⲅⲅⲉⲗⲟⲥ· ⲁⲓⲧⲟⲩϥ ⲉⲧⲣⲉϥ ⲣⲟⲉⲓⲥ ⲉⲣⲱⲧⲛ̄·Ⲁⲁⲩⲱ ⲛ̄ϥ̄ⲧ̄ⲥⲟⲙ ⲛⲏ ⲧⲛ̄ ϣⲁⲛⲧⲉⲧⲛ̄ ⲃⲱⲕ
ⲉⲃⲟⲗ ⲙ̄ⲡⲉ ⲧⲛ̄ⲁⲅⲱⲛ· ⲙⲟⲟϣⲉ ϩⲛ̄ ⲟⲩⲉⲓⲣⲏⲛⲏ· ϭⲙ̄ϭⲟⲙ· ⲙ̄ⲡ ⲉⲣⲅ ⲟⲧⲉ· ⲁⲩⲱ ⲁⲥⲁⲥⲡⲁⲍⲉ
ⲙ̄ⲙⲟⲥ· (72 R ii) ⲁⲥⲃⲱⲕ ⲉϩⲟⲩⲛ· ⲉⲡⲉϣⲧⲉⲕⲟ· ⲁⲧⲉⲑⲉⲟⲇⲟⲕⲟⲥ ⲉⲧⲟⲩⲁⲁⲃ ⲙⲁⲣⲓⲁ
ⲙⲛ̄ ⲉⲗⲓⲥⲁⲃⲉⲧ· ⲃⲱⲕ ⲉϩⲣⲁⲓ ⲉⲧ ⲡⲏⲅⲉ· ⲉⲣⲉⲑⲉⲕⲗⲁ· ϭⲱϣⲧ ⲛ̄ⲥⲱⲟⲩ·Ⲁⲛ̄ⲧⲉⲣⲉⲥⲃⲱⲕ ⲉ-
ϩⲟⲩⲛ ⲉⲡⲉϣⲧⲉⲕⲟ· ⲁⲥⲣⲟⲩⲛⲟϭ ⲛ̄ⲇⲓⲡⲛⲟⲛ ⲉⲛⲉⲧⲟⲩⲁⲁⲃ· ⲁⲥ ϣⲓⲛⲉ ⲛ̄ⲥⲁ ⲡⲉⲥⲥⲟⲛ·
ⲁⲥϭⲉ ⲉⲣⲟⲩ ⲉϥⲥⲁ ⲛ̄ϩ̄ ⲙⲛ̄ ⲛⲉⲧⲟⲩⲁⲁⲃ· ⲉⲣⲉⲟⲩⲛⲟϭ ⲛ̄ϩⲁ ⲣⲓⲥ ϩⲓⲣⲛ̄ ⲡⲉϩⲟ· ⲛ̄ⲑⲉ ⲛ̄-
ⲟⲩⲁⲅⲅⲉⲗⲟⲥ· ⲛ̄ⲧⲉ ⲡⲛⲟⲩⲧⲉ· ⲁⲩⲱ ⲁⲥ ⲡⲉⲥⲟⲩⲟⲓ ⲉⲣⲟⲩ· ⲁⲥⲧ̄ⲡⲓ ⲉⲣⲟϥ· ⲡⲉⲭⲁⲥ ⲛⲁϥ
ϫⲉ ⲡⲁϫⲟⲉⲓⲥ· ⲁⲩⲱ ⲡⲁⲥⲟⲛ· ⲉⲕⲟⲩⲱϣ ⲉⲃⲱⲕ ⲉⲧ ⲙ̄ⲛ̄ⲧⲉⲣⲟ ⲛ̄ⲙ̄ⲡⲏⲩⲉ· ⲛ̄ⲅⲕⲁⲧⲉⲕ-
ⲧⲁⲗⲁⲓⲡⲟⲣⲟⲥ ⲛ̄ⲥⲱⲛⲉ· ϩⲛ̄ ⲛ̄ⲕⲟⲗⲁⲥⲓⲥ· ⲉⲧⲃⲉⲟⲩ ⲙ̄ⲡⲉⲕ ⲧⲛ̄ⲛⲟⲟⲩ ⲛ̄ⲥⲱⲓ (V i) ⲙ̄ⲛ̄-
ⲗⲁⲕⲟⲛ ⲓ̄ⲛ̄ϣⲏⲣⲉ· ⲉⲛⲉⲁⲛⲟⲕ· ⲡⲉⲛⲧⲁⲓ ϣⲓⲛⲉ· ⲛ̄ⲟⲩ ⲙ̄ⲛ̄ⲧⲛⲟϭ· ⲉⲛⲉⲓ ⲛⲁⲧⲁⲙⲟⲕ· ⲛ̄ϣⲟⲣⲡ̄
ⲡⲉ· ⲁⲅⲟⲩⲱϣⲃ̄ ⲛ̄ϭⲓ· ⲡⲁϩⲥⲉ ⲡⲉⲭⲁϥ· ϫⲉ ϣϫⲉ ⲡⲉⲟⲩϥⲁⲓ· ⲱ ⲧⲁⲥⲱⲛⲉ· ⲁⲓ ⲃⲱⲕ ϫⲉ
ⲉⲓⲛⲁ ⲧⲛ̄ⲛⲟⲟⲩ ⲛ̄ⲥⲱ· ⲙ̄ⲡⲉ ⲡⲁⲅⲅⲉⲗⲟⲥ ⲙ̄ⲡ ϫⲟⲉⲓⲥ ⲕⲁⲁⲧ· ⲁϥϫⲟⲟⲥ ⲅⲁⲣ ⲛⲁⲓ ϫⲉ ⲁ-
ⲛⲟⲕ ⲡⲉⲧⲛⲁ ⲁⲧ̄ⲥ ⲛⲁⲕ ⲉ ⲡⲉⲓ ⲙⲁ· ⲁⲩⲱ ⲁⲅⲟⲩ ⲱⲛϩ̄ ⲉⲣⲟⲓ ⲛ̄ⲧⲓ ⲟⲩϣⲏ ⲉϥϫⲱ ⲙ̄ⲙⲟⲥ
ϫⲉ ϣⲁⲣⲓ ⲉⲡⲉⲓⲙⲁ ⲙ̄ⲡⲟⲟⲩ· ⲛⲁⲓ ⲇⲉ ⲛ̄ⲧⲉ ⲣⲉⲥⲭⲟⲟⲩ ⲁⲥⲉⲓ ⲉⲃⲟⲗ ϩⲓⲧⲟⲟⲧⲥ̄· ⲁⲥ-
ⲃⲱⲕ· ⲁⲥⲧⲁⲗⲟ· ⲛ̄ⲛⲉⲥⲕⲉⲩⲉ ⲉϩⲣⲁⲓ· ⲁⲥϫⲓⲧⲟⲩ ⲉⲡⲉϣⲧⲉⲕⲟ· ⲁⲥⲣ̄ⲟⲩⲛⲟϭ ⲛ̄ⲇⲓⲡⲛⲟⲛ·
ⲉⲧⲟⲩⲁⲁⲃ ⲙ̄ⲡⲉ ϩⲟⲟⲩ ⲉⲧⲙ̄ⲙⲁⲩ· (V ii) ⲁⲩⲱ ⲁⲥϫⲱ ⲉ ⲣⲟⲟⲩ ⲛ̄ϩⲱⲃ ⲛⲓⲙ· ⲛ̄ⲧⲁⲥ-
ⲛⲁⲩ ⲉⲣⲟⲟⲩ· ϩⲛ̄ ⲡϫⲟⲓ ⲙ̄ⲁⲛⲉ(ⲛ)ⲧⲁ ⲡⲁⲣⲑⲉⲛⲟⲥ· ⲉⲧⲟⲩⲁⲁⲃ ⲙⲁⲣⲓⲁ ϫⲟⲟⲩ ⲉⲣⲟⲥ·
ⲁⲅⲣ̄ϩⲏⲣⲉ ⲧⲏⲣⲟⲩ ⲛ̄ϭⲓ ⲛⲉⲧⲟⲩⲁⲁⲃ ⲙ̄ⲡⲛⲟⲩⲧⲉ· ⲁⲩⲱ ⲁⲣⲧⲉⲟⲟⲩ ⲙ̄ⲡⲉⲭⲥ̄ ⲓⲥ̄·
ⲑⲉⲕⲗⲁ ⲇⲉ ⲡⲉⲭⲁⲥ ⲙ̄ⲡⲉⲥⲥⲟⲛ· ⲡⲁϩⲥⲉ ϫⲉ ⲡⲁⲥⲟⲛ· ⲉⲕⲟⲩⲱϣ· ⲉⲧⲣⲁⲣⲟⲩ ⲛ̄ⲧⲓ ⲕⲟⲩⲓ
ⲛ̄ⲉⲩⲗⲟⲅⲓⲁ· ⲛ̄ⲧⲁⲓⲛ̄ⲧ̄ⲥ ⲛⲁ ⲙⲁⲓ; ⲛ̄ⲧⲟϥ ⲇⲉ· ⲡⲉϫⲁϥ ϫⲉ ϫⲟⲟⲩⲥ· ⲉⲣⲏⲥ ⲛ̄ⲁⲡⲱⲗ-
ⲗⲟⲛⲓⲟⲥ ⲡⲟⲩϣⲏⲣⲉ· ⲁⲩⲱ ϥ̄ⲛⲁ ⲁⲥ· ⲉⲃⲟⲗ ⲉⲛⲉϩⲥⲏⲕⲉ· ⲙ̄ⲛ̄ ⲛⲉⲧⲟⲩⲁⲁⲃ· ⲉⲓⲥ ⲡⲁⲩⲗⲟⲥ ⲛⲁ ⲃⲱⲕ ⲉⲣⲏⲥ· ⲁⲩⲱ ⲥⲅⲁⲓ ⲛⲁⲩ ⲉⲧⲣⲉϥ ϥⲓⲡⲣⲟⲟⲩϣ ⲙ̄ⲡⲉϥϩⲏ· ⲙ̄ⲙⲟⲛ ⲧⲁⲓ
ⲧⲉ ⲑⲉ ⲛ̄ⲧⲁⲡ ϫⲟⲉⲓⲥ ⲧⲟⲩϫ ⲛⲁⲛ· (73 R i) ⲁⲥϣⲱⲡⲉ ⲇⲉ ⲙ̄ⲛ̄ⲛⲥⲁⲛⲁⲓ· ⲁⲩϫⲓⲥⲉ·
ⲛ̄ϭⲓ ⲡⲗⲟⲩϩ· ⲉϥⲛ̄ⲕⲁⲧⲕ̄ ϩⲙ̄ⲡⲣ̄ⲡⲉ ⲙ̄ⲁⲡⲟⲗⲗⲱ(ⲛ)· ⲙ̄ⲡⲉϥⲗⲟ· ⲁⲧⲉϥⲥϩⲓⲙⲉ ⲃⲱⲕ
ϣⲁⲣⲟϥ· ⲡⲉϫⲁⲥ ⲛⲁϥ ϫⲉ ϣⲁⲧⲛⲁⲩ ⲉⲕⲛ̄ⲕⲁⲧⲕ̄ ⲙ̄ⲡⲉⲓⲙⲁ; ⲉⲓⲉϩⲏⲏⲧⲉ ⲅⲁⲣ ⲙ̄-
ⲡⲉⲕⲗⲟ ⲉⲕϣⲱⲛⲉ· ⲧⲱⲟⲩⲛ ⲛ̄ⲅⲉⲓ ⲉⲡⲉⲕ ⲏⲓ· ⲁⲩⲱ ϯⲛⲁ ⲧⲛ̄ⲛⲟⲟⲩ ⲛ̄ⲥⲁⲡ ⲡⲉⲧⲟⲩⲁⲁⲃ
ⲁⲡⲁ ⲡⲁϩⲥⲉ ⲛ̄ϥⲥⲗⲏⲗ ⲉϫⲱⲕ ⲁⲩⲱ ⲕ̄ⲛⲁ ⲗⲟ· ⲁϥⲧⲱⲟⲩⲛ ⲛ̄ϭⲓ ⲡⲗⲟⲩϩ· ⲡⲉϫⲁϥ·
ϫⲉ ⲁⲙⲏ ⲛ̄ⲧⲉⲑⲩⲥⲓⲁⲍⲉ ⲙ̄ⲁⲡⲟⲗⲗⲱⲛ ⲛ̄ⲧⲉ ⲡⲁⲣⲁ ⲕⲁⲗⲉⲓ ⲙ̄ⲙⲟϥ· ⲁⲩⲱ ϥ̄ⲛⲁ ⲭⲁⲣⲓⲍⲉ ⲛⲁⲓ ⲙ̄ⲡⲧⲁⲗϭⲟ· ⲛ̄ⲧⲟⲥ ⲇⲉ ⲡⲉⲭⲁⲥ ⲛⲁⲩ ϫⲉ ⲛ̄ϯⲛⲁ ⲑⲩⲥⲓⲁⲍⲉ ⲁⲛ· ⲟⲩⲇⲉ

---

72 V i 21. l. ϣⲁⲣⲟⲉⲓ. 31. l. ⲛ̄ⲛⲉⲧⲟⲩⲁⲁⲃ. 73 R i 11. l. ⲉⲓⲥϩⲏⲏⲧⲉ

ⲛ̄ϥ²ᴣⲏⲩ ⲁⲛ ᴣⲁⲣⲟⲕ. ⲁⲧⲉⲣⲉϥⲛⲁⲩ ⲇⲉ ⲛ̄ϭⲓ ⲡⲇⲟⲩᴣ ϫⲉ ⲙ̄ (73 R ii) ⲡⲉⲗⲁⲁⲩ ⲛ̄ⲧⲟⲛ
ϣⲱⲡⲉ ⲛⲁϥ, ⲁϥ'ⲧⲣⲉⲩϫⲓⲧϥ̄ ⲉⲡⲉϥ'ⲏⲓ; ⲁϥ⁵ⲡⲁⲣⲁⲕⲁ'ⲗⲉⲓ ⲛ̄ⲧⲉϥⲥϩⲓⲙⲉ' ⲉϥϫⲱ ⲙ̄ⲙⲟⲥ
ϫⲉ' ⲧⲛ̄ⲛⲟⲟⲩ ⲛ̄ⲥⲁⲡⲓ'ⲭⲣⲏⲥⲧⲓⲁⲛⲟⲥ ϫⲉ'ⲡⲁⲏⲥⲉ· ⲁⲣⲏⲩ ⲉ¹⁰ⲛⲁⲧⲁⲗϭⲟⲓ ⲉⲃⲟⲗ ϩⲛ̄-
ⲛⲉϥⲙⲁⳡⲓⲁ.'ⲛ̄ⲧⲟⲥ ⲇⲉ ⲁⲥⲧⲛ̄ⲛⲟ'ⲟⲩ ⲛ̄ⲥⲁⲡⲡⲉⲧⲟⲩ'ⲁⲁⲃ ⲁⲡⲁ ⲡⲁ¹⁵ⲏ'ⲥⲉ, ⲁⲩⲱ ⲛ̄ⲧⲉ-'
ⲣⲉϥⲉⲓ ⲁⲧⲉϥⲥϩⲓ'ⲙⲉ ⲉⲓ ⲉⲃⲟⲗ ϩⲓⲧⲛ̄, ' ⲁⲥⲡⲁϫ²ⲧⲉ̄ ϩⲁⲛⲉϥ'ⲟⲩⲉⲣⲏⲧⲉ· ⲛ̄ⲧⲟⲥ ⲇⲉ·²⁰ⲁⲥ-
ⲧⲟⲩ²ⲛⲟⲥϥ, ⲁⲥ'ⲡⲁⲣⲁⲕⲁⲗⲉⲓ ⲙ̄'ⲙⲟϥ ⲉⲥϫⲱ ⲙ̄ⲙⲟⲥ· ϫⲉ ⲡⲁϫⲟⲉⲓⲥ, ϣⲛ̄²⁵ϩⲧⲏⲕ ϩⲁ-
ⲡⲉⲓ²ⲧⲁ'ⲗⲁⲓⲡⲱⲣⲟⲥ ⲛ̄ϥ'ⲥⲩⲛⲭⲱⲣⲉⲓ ⲛⲁϥ' ϩⲙ̄ⲡⲉⲓ'ϣⲱⲛⲉ' ϣⲁⲡⲉ²⁰ϩⲟⲟⲩ ⲉⲧⲉ'ⲉⲡⲛⲟⲉⲓⲥ
ⲛⲁ³⁰ϭⲓⲛⲉ ⲛ̄ⲥⲱϥ ⲙⲛ̄'ⲡⲉⲩⲕⲉⲣ̄ⲣⲟ ⲛ̄ⲁⲛⲟ'ⲙⲟⲥ ⲛ̄ϥ̄ⲧ ⲛⲁⲩ' ⲕⲁⲧⲁⲛⲉⲩϩⲃⲏⲩⲉ. (V i)
ⲡⲇⲟⲩᴣ ⲇⲉ ⲡⲉϫⲁϥ'ⲙ̄ⲡⲡⲉⲧⲟⲩⲁⲁⲃ' ⲁⲡⲁ ⲡⲁⲏⲥⲉ ϫⲉ ϯ'ⲥⲟⲟⲩⲛ̄.ϫⲉ ⲕ̄ϭⲟⲛⲧ̄⁵'ⲉⲣⲟⲓ'
ϫⲉ ⲁⲓ̈ⲧ ⲛⲁⲕ' ⲛ̄ⲛⲉⲓ̈ⲃⲁⲥⲁⲛⲟⲥ' ⲧⲏⲣⲟⲩ· ⲁⲗⲗⲁ ϯ'ⲥⲟⲟⲩⲛ̄ ϫⲉ ⲛ̄ⲧⲕⲟⲩ'ⲛⲁϩⲧ ⲙ̄-
ⲛⲉⲕ¹⁰'ⲥ̄ⲛⲏⲩ ⲧⲏⲣⲟⲩ· ⲁ'ⲙⲟⲩ ⲛ̄ⲅ̄ⲧⲁⲗⲟ ⲛ̄ⲧⲉⲕ'ϭⲓϫ ⲉϩⲣⲁⲓ̈ ⲉϫⲱⲓ̈' ⲁⲩⲱ ϯⲛⲁⲟⲩϫⲁⲓ.'
ⲡⲡⲉⲧⲟⲩⲁⲁⲃ ⲇⲉ ⲁ'ⲡⲁ¹⁵ ⲡⲁⲏⲥⲉ ⲁϥⲧⲁ'ⲗⲟ ⲛ̄ⲧⲉϥϭⲓϫ ⲉϩⲣⲁⲓ̈'ⲉϫⲱϥ, ⲡⲉϫⲁϥ ϫⲉ'ϩⲙ̄-
ⲡⲣⲁⲛ ⲙ̄ⲡⲁϫⲟ'ⲉⲓⲥ ⲓ̄ⲥ̄ ⲡⲉⲭ̄ⲥ̄ ⲉⲕⲉⲥⲛ̄²⁰'ⲭⲱⲣⲉⲓ ⲙ̄ⲡⲉⲓ'ⲧⲁⲗⲉ'ⲡⲱⲣⲟⲥ ⲉⲃⲟⲗ ϩⲙ̄'ⲡⲉϥϣⲱⲛⲉ
ϣⲁ(ⲛ)'ⲧⲉϥⲉⲓ ⲉⲛⲉⲕϭⲓϫ,' ⲁⲩⲱ ⲕ̄ⲛⲁϯⲥⲃⲱ²⁵' ⲛⲁϥ. ⲁⲩⲱ ⲁⲩϥ'ⲣⲁⲥⲓ²ⲍⲉ ⲙ̄ⲙⲟϥ, ⲁϥ'ⲉⲓ
ⲉⲃⲟⲗ ϩⲓⲧⲟⲟⲧϥ̄,' ⲁⲩⲃⲱⲕ ⲉⲡⲉϥ'ⲧⲉⲕⲟ.'³⁰ⲁϥⲕⲉⲗⲉⲩⲉ ⲛ̄ϭⲓ ⲡ'ⲇⲟⲩᴣ ⲉⲧⲣⲉⲩϫⲓ'ⲛⲟⲩⲛⲟϭ
ⲛ̄ⲧⲁⲓ̈ⲟ' ϩⲓⲡⲁϩⲟⲩ ⲛ̄ⲁⲡⲁ (V ii) ⲡⲁⲏⲥⲉ ⲉⲡⲉϥⲧⲉ'ⲕⲟ· ⲁⲩⲱ ⲙ̄ⲡⲉ'ⲛⲉⲧⲟⲩⲁⲁⲃ ⲟⲩⲱⲙ'ⲉⲃⲟⲗ
ⲛ̄ϩⲏⲧⲟⲩ ϫⲉ'⁵ϩⲉⲛϣⲱⲱⲧ ⲛⲓ̈'ⲇⲱⲗⲟⲛ ⲛⲉ· ⲁⲩ'ⲧⲁⲁⲩ ⲛ̄ⲛⲉⲧⲟⲧ̄¹⁰'ⲉϩⲟⲩⲛ· ⲛⲉⲧⲟⲩⲁⲁⲃ'ϩⲱⲟⲩ ⲁⲩⲟⲩⲱⲙ ⲉ'ⲃⲟⲗ ϩⲙ̄ⲡⲁⲅⲁⲑⲟ(ⲛ)' ⲛ̄ⲧⲁⲑⲉⲕⲗⲁ ⲛ̄ⲧⲟⲩ' ⲛⲙ̄ⲙⲁⲥ.' ⲙ̄ⲡⲉϥⲣⲁⲥⲧⲉ ⲇⲉ
ⲁϥ'ⲧⲱⲟⲩⲛ ⲛ̄ϭⲓ ⲡ'ⲇⲟⲩᴣ¹⁵ ⲉⲃⲟⲗ ϩⲙ̄ ⲡⲉϥ'ϣⲱⲛⲉ· ⲡⲉϫⲉ'ⲧⲉϥⲥϩⲓⲙⲉ ⲛⲁϥ ϫⲉ' ⲉⲓⲥϩⲏⲏⲧⲉ ⲁⲡⲛⲟⲩⲧⲉ ⲛ̄ⲛⲉⲭⲣⲏⲥⲧⲓ²⁰'ⲁⲛⲟⲥ ϯⲡⲟⲩϫⲁⲓ̈'ⲛⲁⲕ· ⲕⲁⲁϥ ⲉⲃⲟⲗ,' ⲙ̄ⲛ̄ⲧⲁⲕϩⲱⲃ ⲛⲙ̄-
ⲙⲁϥ, ⲙⲏⲡⲟⲧⲉ' ⲛ̄ⲥⲉⲛⲟⲩϫ²⁵ ⲉⲣⲟⲕ' ⲛ̄ⲙⲟϥ ⲛ̄ⲑⲉ ⲙ̄'ⲡⲉⲕⲕⲉϣⲏⲣⲉ' ⲛ̄ⲧⲁϥⲙⲟⲩ ⲛ̄ⲧⲉⲕ-'
ⲁⲫⲟⲣⲙⲏ.' ⲁϥⲟⲩⲱⲛ̄ϩ̄ ⲛ̄ϭⲓ ⲡ'ⲇⲟⲩᴣ, ⲡⲉϫⲁϥ 'ⲛⲁⲥ ϫⲉ ⲕⲁⲕⲏ' ⲕⲉⲫⲁⲗⲏ, ⲟⲩ'ⲕⲟⲩⲛ
ⲉⲛⲛⲁⲟⲩ(74 R i)ⲉⲥϥ̄ⲧⲕⲉⲗⲉⲩⲥⲓⲥ' ⲙ̄ⲡⲣ̄ⲣⲟ ⲉⲧⲃⲉϩⲛ̄'ⲙⲁⲧⲟⲥ; ⲧⲉϥⲥϩⲓⲙⲉ ⲇⲉ ⲁⲥⲱ-
ⲛ̄ⲧ̄⁵ ϫⲉ ⲉⲛⲉⲍⲧⲏⲥ ⲅⲁⲣ' ϩⲙ̄ⲡⲛⲟⲩⲧⲉ ⲡⲉ, 'ⲁⲩⲱ ⲡⲉϫⲁⲥ ⲛⲁϥ ϫⲉ ϯⲛⲁⲛⲁⲩ ⲟⲛ ⲉ-
ⲣⲟⲕ ⲉⲣⲉⲛⲉⲭⲣⲏⲥ¹⁰'ⲧⲓⲁⲛⲟⲥ ϯⲙⲓⲛⲉ'ⲛⲁⲕ. ⲡⲇⲟⲩᴣ' ⲇⲉ ⲁϥⲧⲛ̄ⲛⲟⲟⲩ ⲛ̄ⲥⲁⲡⲙⲁⲕⲁⲣⲓⲟⲥ'
ⲁⲡⲁ ⲡⲁⲏⲥⲉ, ⲡⲉ¹⁵ϫⲁⲩ ⲛⲁⲩ ϫⲉ ⲉⲓⲥⲧⲁ(ⲛ)'ⲧⲛ̄ⲛⲟⲟⲩ ⲛ̄ⲥⲱⲕ· ϫⲉ ⲑⲩⲥⲓⲁⲍⲉ ⲛ̄ⲛ̄'ⲛⲟⲩⲧⲉ,
ⲁϫⲓⲥ ϫⲉ'ⲧⲛⲁⲑⲩⲥⲓⲁⲍⲉ, ⲛ̄ϥ̄'ϯⲉⲟⲟⲩ ⲛⲁⲓ̈ ⲙ̄ⲡⲙ̄'ⲧⲟ ⲉⲃⲟⲗ ⲙ̄ⲡⲙⲏⲏ'ϣⲉ ⲧⲏⲣϥ̄ ⲙⲛ̄ⲧ-'
ⲧⲁᴣⲓⲥ, ⲁⲩⲱ ⲧⲛⲁ'ⲗⲟ ⲉⲓ̈ϭⲟⲛⲧ²⁵ ⲉⲣⲟⲕ' ⲉⲧⲃⲉⲡⲉⲓ̈ϣⲁϫⲉ' ⲙ̄ⲙⲁⲧⲉ, ⲉⲕϣⲁⲛ'ⲙ̄ⲙⲟⲓ̈ ⲙ̄-
ⲡⲙ̄ⲧⲟ ⲉⲃⲟⲗ' ⲛ̄ⲧⲧⲁᴣⲓⲥ· ⲙ̄ⲙⲟⲛ' ϣⲉ ⲡⲟⲩϫⲁⲓ̈ ⲙ̄ⲡⲁ'ⲡⲱⲗⲗⲟⲛ ⲧⲙⲉ'ⲙ̄ⲙⲟⲕ ϩⲛ̄ⲧⲁⲯⲩ·

73 R ii 19 f. ℓ. ⲛ̄ⲧⲟⲩ ⲇⲉ ⲁⲩⲧⲟⲩⲛⲟⲥ.   29. ℓ. -ⲡⲛⲟⲉⲓⲥ   V ii 24. ℓ. ⲛ̄ⲥⲉⲛⲟⲩϫ̄

74 R i 28. ⲛ̄ⲧⲧⲁᴣⲓⲥ A; ⲛ̄ⲛⲁⲧⲧ- D. After this, + ⲙ̄ⲡⲙⲙⲏⲏϣⲉ ϯⲛⲁⲗⲟ ⲉⲓ̈ϭⲟⲛⲧ ⲉⲣⲟⲕ D.
29. ⲡⲟⲩϫⲁⲓ̈ ⲙ̄ⲡⲁⲡⲟⲗⲗⲱⲛ A; ⲡⲛⲟϭ ⲛ̄ⲛⲟⲩⲧⲉ ⲡⲁⲡ. D.   31 f. ϩⲛ̄ⲧⲁⲯⲩⲭⲏ A; ⲉⲙⲁⲧⲉ D.

ⲭⲏ· ⲁⲩⲱ ϯⲛⲁⲥϩⲁⲓ' ⲉⲣⲏⲥ ⲙ̄ⲡⲇⲟⲩϩ ⲛ̄(74 Rⲏ)ⲑⲙⲃⲁⲉⲓⲥ ⲉⲧⲃⲙ̄ⲏⲧⲕ̄ ⲛ̄ⲅⲧⲁϩⲟⲕ'
ⲉⲣⲁⲧⲕ̄ ⲉⲭⲙⲏⲧ' ⲛ̄ϯⲙⲉ ⲭⲱⲣⲓⲥ ⲡⲱⲕ·' ⲁⲩⲱ ⲛⲉⲕϭⲱⲣⲉ' ⲧⲏⲣⲟⲩ ϯⲛⲁⲧⲣⲉⲩ'ⲕⲁⲛⲉⲩⲕⲁⲛⲉⲩⲇⲁⲓ'ⲙⲟⲥⲓⲟⲛ ⲛⲁⲕ ⲉⲃⲟⲗ' ⲁⲩⲧⲁⲙⲟⲓ̈ ⲅⲁⲣ ϫⲉ ⲛ̄ⲧⲕⲟⲩⲛⲟϭ ⲛ̄ϩⲙ̄ϩⲁⲟ ⲛ̄-
ⲃⲁⲓ'ⲇⲁⲓⲙⲟⲥⲓⲟⲛ ⲙ̄'ⲡⲗⲟⲩⲥⲓⲟⲥ ⲁⲩⲱ' ⲛ̄ⲉⲩⲅⲉⲛⲏⲥ ⲁⲩⲱ' ⲛ̄ⲅⲉⲛⲟⲥ ⲉⲩⲧⲁⲓ̈ⲏⲩ' ⲙ̄ⲙⲁ-
ⲧⲉ. ⲡⲉϫⲉ'ⲡⲙⲁⲕⲁⲣⲓⲟⲥ ⲛⲁⲩ' ϫⲉ ϯⲛⲁⲥⲱⲧⲙ̄ ⲛ̄'ⲥⲱⲕ ⲛ̄ⲑⲉ ⲛ̄ⲧⲁⲕ'ϫⲟⲟⲥ. ⲁⲩⲉⲓ ⲉ-
ⲃⲟⲗ' ϩⲓⲧⲟⲟⲧϥ̄, ⲁⲩⲃⲱⲕ' ⲉⲡⲉⲩⲧⲉⲕⲟ· ⲁⲩⲉⲓ'ⲛⲉ ⲛⲁⲩ ⲛ̄ϩⲉⲛⲧⲁⲓ̈ⲟ' ⲉⲃⲟⲗ ϩⲓⲧⲟⲟⲧϥ̄
ⲙ̄'ⲡⲗⲟⲩϩ, ⲁⲩⲱ ⲁⲩ'ⲧⲁⲙⲉⲛⲉⲧⲟⲩⲁⲁⲃ' ⲉⲧⲃⲉⲧⲁⲡⲟⲗⲟⲅⲓⲁ' ⲙ̄ⲡⲛⲁϫⲉ· ⲁⲩⲧ'ⲉⲟⲟⲩ
ⲙ̄ⲡⲛⲟⲩⲧⲉ,' ⲡⲁⲓ̈ ⲉⲧⲛⲟⲩϩⲙ̄ ⲛ̄ⲛⲉⲧϩⲉⲗⲡⲓⲍⲉ' ⲉⲣⲟⲩ. ⲙ̄ⲡⲉⲩ'ⲣⲁⲥⲧⲉ ⲇⲉ ⲁⲩⲙⲟⲟⲥ
(Vⲓ)ⲉⲡⲃⲏⲙⲁ ⲛ̄ϭⲓ'ⲡⲇⲟⲩϩ· ⲁⲩⲕⲉ'ⲗⲉⲩⲉ ⲉⲧⲣⲉⲩⲉⲓ'ⲛⲉ ⲛⲁⲩ ⲙ̄ⲡⲙⲁ'ⲕⲁⲣⲓⲟⲥ ⲁ-
ⲡⲁ ⲡⲁ'ⲏⲥⲉ. ⲁⲩⲱ ⲛⲉⲥⲧⲱ'ⲛⲁⲣⲓⲟⲥ ⲁⲩⲉⲱⲛ̄' ⲙ̄ⲙⲟⲩ ⲛ̄ⲛⲉⲩϭⲓϫ' ⲙ̄ⲙⲛⲉⲩⲟⲩⲉⲣⲏⲧⲉ,'
ⲁⲩϯ ⲛ̄ⲟⲩⲕⲟⲗⲁ'ⲣⲓⲟⲛ ⲉⲡⲉⲩⲙⲟⲕϩ̄,' ⲁⲩⲉⲛⲧϥ̄ ⲉⲃⲟⲗ ⲉ'ⲡⲉⲩⲧⲉⲕⲟ. ' ⲁⲥⲧⲱⲟⲩⲛ ⲇⲉ
ⲛ̄ϭⲓ'ⲧⲉⲩⲥⲱⲛⲉ, ⲁⲥⲡⲱⲣϣ̄ ⲛ̄ⲛⲉⲥϭⲓϫ ⲉϩ'ⲣⲁⲓ̈ ⲉⲧⲡⲏ, ⲁⲥϣ'ⲗⲏⲗ ⲉⲥϫⲱ ⲙ̄ⲙⲟⲥ'ϫⲉ
ⲡⲛⲟⲩⲧⲉ ⲡⲡⲁⲛ'ⲧⲱⲕⲣⲁⲧⲱⲣ,' ⲡⲉⲛⲧⲁⲩⲧⲛ̄ⲛⲟⲟ'ⲟⲩ ⲙ̄ⲡⲉⲩϣⲏⲣⲉ' ⲙⲙⲉⲣⲓⲧ ⲙ̄ⲡⲕⲟⲥ-'
ⲙⲟⲥ ϣⲁⲛⲧⲉϥ'ⲥⲱⲧⲉ ⲙ̄ⲙⲟⲛ ϩⲓ'ⲧⲙ̄ⲡⲉϥⲥⲱⲙⲁ' ⲙ̄ⲛ̄ⲡⲉϥⲥⲛⲟⲩ ⲉ'ⲧⲟⲩⲁⲁⲃ, ⲁⲩⲱ'
ⲁⲩⲁⲁⲛ ⲛ̄ⲣⲙ̄ϩⲉ' ⲉⲃⲟⲗ ϩⲛ̄ⲧⲙⲛ̄ⲧ'ϩⲙ̄ϩⲁⲗ ⲙ̄ⲡⲇⲓⲁ'ⲃⲟⲗⲟⲥ, ⲉⲕⲉⲧϭⲟⲙ (Vⲓⲓ) ⲛⲁⲓ;
ⲁⲛⲟⲕ ⲙ̄ⲡⲁ'ⲥⲟⲛ, ⲧⲛ̄ϫⲱⲕ ⲉ'ⲃⲟⲗ ⲙ̄ⲡⲉⲕⲟⲩϣⲁⲓ̈' ⲙ̄ⲡⲉⲕⲟⲩⲱϣ,' ϫⲉ ⲡⲱⲕ ⲡⲉ
ⲡⲉⲟⲟⲩ ⲙ̄ⲡⲁⲛⲁϩ'ⲧⲉ ⲙ̄ⲡⲉⲕⲙⲉⲣⲓⲧ' ⲛ̄ϣⲏⲣⲉ ⲓ̅ⲥ̅ ⲡⲉϫⲉ' ⲡⲉⲛϫⲟⲉⲓⲥ ⲙ̄ⲛ̄'ⲡⲉⲕ-

---

74 Rii 7. -ⲕⲁⲛⲉⲩⲕⲁⲛⲉⲩ-: dittography. 7f. =-ⲇⲏⲙⲟⲥⲓⲟⲛ. 11. l. ⲛ̄ⲅⲁⲓ̈-. Vi 6.
After ⲡⲁ'ⲏⲥⲉ, 2nd hand (to l. 20). 6 f. l. ⲛ̄ⲕⲉⲥⲧⲱⲛⲁⲣⲓⲟⲥ ⲁⲩⲉⲱⲛ̄. 11. l. ⲉⲡⲉⲩ-
ⲙⲟⲕϩ. 12 f. l. ⲙ̄ⲡⲉⲩⲧⲉⲕⲟ (or 2ⲙ̄ⲡ.); probably the former, ⲉ- for ⲙ̄- being a
favourite error of this scribe. 17. l. ⲉⲧⲡⲉ; so often below. 21. 1st h. (to ii 14).
ii 2. l. ⲛ̄ⲧⲛ̄ϫⲱⲕ. 10. l. ⲡⲉⲡⲡⲁ (so D).

---

74 Ri 33. ⲉⲣⲏⲥ A; om. D. ii 4. ⲡⲱⲕ A; ⲡⲉⲕⲧⲕⲉ ⲙ̄ⲙⲓⲛ ⲙ̄ⲙⲟⲕ D. 6.ⲧⲏⲣⲟⲩ
A; om. D. 6f.ϯⲛⲁⲧⲣⲉⲩⲕⲁ- A; ϯⲛⲁⲕⲁ-D. 10-13. ⲛ̄ⲧⲕⲟⲩⲛⲟϭ—ⲙ̄ⲡⲗⲟⲩⲥⲓⲟⲥ A;
ⲛ̄ⲧⲕⲟⲩⲣⲉⲛⲟⲥ ⲉⲩⲧⲁⲓ̈ⲏⲩ D. 14-16. ⲁⲩⲱ ⲛ̄ⲅⲉⲛⲟⲥ ⲉⲩⲧⲁⲓ̈ⲏⲩ ⲙ̄ⲙⲁⲧⲉ A; om. D (but
see above). 17. ⲡⲙⲁⲕⲁⲣⲓⲟⲥ A; ⲡⲡⲉⲧⲟⲩⲁⲁⲃ D. 18. ϯⲛⲁⲥⲱⲧⲙ̄ A; ⲛ̄ⲧⲁⲥⲱⲧⲙ̄
D. 18f. ⲛ̄ⲥⲱⲕ A; ⲛ̄ⲥⲱ(sic)ⲁⲛ D. 19-22. ⲛ̄ⲑⲉ — ⲉⲡⲉⲩⲧⲉⲕⲟ A; om. D. 22.
Before ⲁⲩⲉⲓⲛⲉ, +ⲁⲩⲱ D. 23-25. ⲛⲁⲩ — ⲙ̄ⲡⲗⲟⲩϩ A; ⲙ̄ⲙⲟⲩ ⲉⲧⲉϥⲫⲩⲗⲁⲕⲏ D.
25f. ⲁⲩⲱ ⲁⲩⲧⲁⲙⲉ- A; ⲁⲩⲧ. D. 27. ⲉⲧⲃⲉⲧⲁⲡⲟⲗⲟⲅⲓⲁ A; ⲉⲧⲁ. D. 28. After
ⲙ̄ⲡⲛⲁϫⲉ, +ⲙ̄ⲡⲗⲟⲩϩ ⲁⲩⲩϩⲙ̄ⲣⲉ ⲛ̄ϭⲓ ⲛⲉⲧⲟⲩⲁⲁⲃ D. 30. ⲡⲁⲓ̈ ⲉⲧⲛⲟⲩϩⲙ̄ A; ⲡⲉⲧⲛ.
D. 31. ⲛ̄ⲛⲉⲧϩⲉⲗ ⲡⲓⲍⲉ A; ⲛ̄ⲟⲩⲟⲛ ⲛⲓⲙ ⲉⲧⲉ. D. Vi 1f. ⲉⲡⲃⲏⲙⲁ ⲛ̄ϭⲓ ⲡⲇⲟⲩϩ A;
om. D. 2f. ⲁⲩⲕⲉⲗϭⲩⲉ ⲉⲧⲣⲉⲩⲉⲓⲛⲉ A; ⲁⲩⲧⲣ. D. 8. ⲙ̄ⲙⲟⲩ A; om. D. 9. ⲙ̄ⲙⲛⲉⲩⲟⲩⲉⲣ-
ⲣⲏⲧⲉ A; ϩⲓⲡⲁϩⲟⲩ ⲙ̄ⲙⲟⲩ D. 12f. ⲉⲡⲉⲩⲧⲉⲕⲟ A; ϩⲁⲡⲉⲩ. D. 14.ⲇⲉ A; om. D. 16.
After ⲁⲥⲡⲱⲣϣ̄, +ⲉⲃⲟⲗ D. 19. After ϫⲉ, +ⲡϫⲟⲉⲓⲥ D. 23. ⲙ̄ⲡⲕⲟⲥⲙⲟⲥ A; ⲉⲡⲕ. D. 24f.
ϣⲁⲛⲧⲉϥⲥⲱⲧⲉ A; ⲁ-ϥⲥ. D. 27f. ⲉⲧⲟⲩⲁⲁⲃ A; om. D. ii 1. ⲁⲛⲟⲕ A; ⲁⲛⲟⲛ D. 2. (ⲛ̄)-
ⲧⲛ̄ϫⲱⲕ A; [ϣⲁ]ⲛⲧⲉⲛⲭ. D. 3f. ⲙ̄ⲡⲉⲕⲟⲩϣⲁⲓ̈ ⲙ̄ⲡⲉⲕⲟⲩⲱϣ A; ⲙ̄ⲡⲉⲛⲁⲧⲱⲛ D. 6f.
ⲙ̄ⲡⲁⲛⲁϩⲧⲉ A; ⲙ̄ⲡⲧⲁⲉⲓⲟ D. 8f. ⲓ̅ⲥ̅ ⲡⲉϫⲉ ⲡⲉⲛϫⲟⲉⲓⲥ; om. D. 9f. ⲙ̄ⲛ̄ⲡⲉⲕ ⲡⲛⲁ(sic)

ⲡ̄ⲛⲁ ⲉⲧⲟⲩⲁⲁⲃ ϣⲁⲉⲛⲉϩ ⲇⲉ'ⲛⲉϩ, ϩⲁⲙⲏⲛ.' ⲁⲥⲧⲱⲟⲩⲛ ⲇⲉ ⲛ̄ϭⲓ'ⲧⲙⲁⲕⲁⲣⲓⲁ ⲑⲉⲕⲗⲁ,¹⁵
ⲁⲥⲙⲟⲟϣⲉ ⲙ̄ⲡⲉⲥ'ⲥⲟⲛ ϩⲛ̄ⲛⲟⲩⲛⲟϭ' ⲙ̄ⲙⲛ̄ⲧⲭⲁⲣϩⲏⲧ·'ⲛ̄ⲧⲉⲣⲟⲩⲡⲱϩ ⲇⲉ' ⲉⲡⲃⲏⲙⲁ,
ⲁⲩⲁ²⁰ϩⲉⲣⲁⲧⲟⲩ ⲉⲡⲏⲧⲟ' ⲉⲃⲟⲗ ⲉⲛⲇⲟⲩϩ.' ⲡⲉϫⲉⲡⲇⲟⲩϩ ⲛⲁⲩ'ϫⲉ ⲱ ⲡⲁⲛⲥⲉ, ⲁ'ⲙⲟⲩ
ⲛ̄ⲅⲑⲩⲥⲓⲁϩⲉ²⁵' ⲙ̄ⲡⲁⲡⲟⲗⲗⲱⲛ' ⲡⲛⲟϭ ⲛ̄ⲛⲟⲩⲧⲉ' ⲛ̄ⲅⲃⲱⲕ ⲉⲡⲉⲕⲏⲓ' ϩⲛ̄ⲛⲟⲩⲉⲓⲣⲏⲛⲏ.'
ⲁⲥⲟⲩⲱϣⲃ̄ ⲛ̄ϭⲓ ⲧⲉⲓ̈³⁰ϣⲱⲣⲉ ϩⲛ̄ⲧⲉⲥ'ⲯⲩⲭⲏ ϫⲉ ⲉϣϫⲉ' ⲟⲩⲛ̄ϭⲟⲙ ⲙ̄ⲡⲉⲕ'ⲛⲟⲩⲧⲉ, ⲉⲧⲃⲉⲟⲩ (75 R i)ⲗ̄...ⲛⲉ ⲉϥϣⲟ⳿ϭⲙ̄ϭⲟⲙ' ⲉⲧⲁⲗϭⲟⲕ ⲉⲃⲟⲗ ϩⲙ̄'ⲡⲉⲕϣⲱⲛⲉ;' ⲡⲇⲟⲩϩ
ⲇⲉ ⲁϥⲁⲡⲟ⁵'ⲣⲉⲓ ⲉⲧⲃⲉⲡⲉⲓ̈ϩⲁ'ϫⲉ, ⲡⲉϫⲁⲩ ϫⲉ' ⲛⲓⲙ ⲧⲉ ⲧⲁⲓ̈ ⲉⲧⲁ'ⲡⲟⲗⲟⲅⲓⲍⲉ ⲛⲁⲓ
ⲛ̄'ⲧⲉⲓϩⲉ; ⲡⲉϫⲁⲩ¹⁰ ⲛⲁⲩ ϫⲉ ⲧⲥⲱⲛⲉ' ⲙ̄ⲡⲁⲛⲥⲉ ⲧⲉ.' ⲡⲉϫⲉⲡⲇⲟⲩϩ ϫⲉ' ⲁⲓ̈ϫⲟⲟⲥ
ϩⲱ ϫⲉ ⲟⲩ'ⲅⲉⲛⲟⲥ ⲛ̄ⲁⲧϣⲓⲡⲉ¹⁵' ⲡⲉ· ⲁⲩⲱ ⲡⲉϫⲁⲩ'ⲛⲁⲥ ϫⲉ ⲑⲩⲥⲓⲁⲍⲉ,' ⲙ̄ⲡⲉⲣⲙⲟⲩ
ⲕⲁⲕⲱⲥ.' ⲁⲥⲟⲩⲱϣⲃ̄ ϫⲉ ⲛ̄ϯ'ⲛⲁⲑⲩⲥⲓⲁⲍⲉ ⲁⲛ.' ⲁⲩⲕⲉⲗⲉⲩⲉ ⲉⲧⲣⲉⲩ'ⲧⲁⲗⲟⲥ ⲉⲡ-
ϩⲉⲣⲙⲏ'ⲧⲁⲣⲓⲟⲛ ⲛ̄ⲥⲉϩⲱⲕⲉ' ⲙ̄ⲙⲟⲥ ϣⲁⲛⲧⲉⲛ'ⲕⲁⲥ ⲛ̄ⲛⲉⲥⲡⲓ²⁵'ⲣⲟⲟⲩⲉ ⲟⲩⲱⲛϩ̄'ⲉⲃⲟⲗ.
ⲧⲉⲓⲙⲁ'ⲕⲁⲣⲓⲁ ⲇⲉ ⲁⲥⲧⲱ'ⲟⲩⲛ ϩⲁⲧⲉⲓ̈ⲃⲁⲥⲁ'ⲛⲟⲥ ϩⲛ̄ⲛⲟⲩⲛⲟϭ ³⁰ⲛ̄'ⲙⲛ̄ⲧϣⲱⲣⲉ.' ⲙⲛ̄-
ⲥⲱⲥ ⲁⲩϯ'ⲣⲉⲛⲟⲩⲧⲉ ⲛ̄ⲧⲉⲥ'ⲉⲕⲓⲃⲉ ⲥⲛ̄ⲧⲉ, ⲁⲩ(R ⲓⲓ)ⲧⲣⲉⲩϭⲓⲛⲉ ⲛ̄ⲕⲉⲩ'ⲧⲟ ⲛ̄ⲗⲁⲙⲡⲁⲥ ⲉⲩ-'
ⲙⲟⲩϩ, ⲁⲩⲕⲁⲁⲩ ϩⲁ'ⲛⲉⲥⲡⲓⲣⲟⲟⲩⲉ·⁵'ⲧⲙⲁⲕⲁⲣⲓⲁ ⲑⲉⲕⲗⲁ ⲁⲥⲧⲱⲟⲩⲛ ϩⲁ'ϩⲁⲛⲉⲓ̈ⲃⲁ-
ⲥⲁⲛⲟⲥ' ϩⲛ̄ⲛⲟⲩⲙⲛ̄ⲧϣⲱ'ⲱⲣⲉ, ⲁⲥϭⲓ ⲛ̄ⲛⲉⲥ'ⲃⲟⲗ ⲉϩⲣⲁⲓ̈ ⲉⲧⲡⲏ,' ⲡⲉϫⲁⲥ ϫⲉ ⲧⲁⲭⲟ'ⲉⲓⲥ
ⲙⲁⲣⲓⲁ ⲧⲡⲁⲣ'ⲑⲉⲛⲟⲥ ⲉⲧⲟⲩⲁⲁⲃ,' ⲛ̄ⲧⲟ ⲙⲛ̄ⲡⲟⲩϭⲙ̄¹⁵'ⲣⲉ ⲙ̄ⲙⲉⲣⲓⲧ ⲓ̄ⲥ̄ ⲡⲉⲭ̄ⲥ̄' ⲁⲧⲉⲧⲛ̄ⲧⲁϩ-
ⲙⲛ̄ ⲉ'ⲉϩⲟⲩⲛ ⲉⲡⲉⲓ̈ⲁⲕⲱⲛ,' ⲁⲩⲱ ⲁⲣ̄ⲥⲙ̄ⲛ̄ⲧⲉ' ⲛ̄ⲙ̄ⲙⲁⲛ ⲉⲧⲓϭⲟⲙ²⁰'ⲛⲁⲛ ϣⲁⲛⲧⲉⲛϫⲱⲕ ⲉ-'
ⲃⲟⲗ ⲉⲡⲉⲛⲁⲕⲱ(ⲛ).' ⲧⲉⲛⲟⲩ ⲇⲉ ⲧⲓϭⲟⲙ' ⲛⲁⲛ ϩⲁⲧⲉⲓ̈ⲉⲛⲟⲭ' ⲛ̄ⲁⲛⲁⲅⲕⲏ.'²⁵ ϩⲛ̄ⲧⲉⲩⲛⲟⲩ
ⲇⲉ ⲉⲧⲙ̄'ⲙⲁⲩ ⲁϥⲉⲓ ⲉⲃⲟⲗ' ϩⲛ̄ⲧⲡⲏ ⲛ̄ϭⲓ ϩⲣⲁ'ⲫⲁⲏⲗ ⲡⲁⲣⲭⲁⲅ'ⲅⲉⲗⲟⲥ, ⲁⲩⲁϩⲉⲣⲁⲧϥ³⁰
ϩⲓⲟⲩⲛⲟⲙ ⲙⲟⲥ,' ⲡⲉϫⲁϥ ⲛⲁⲥ ϫⲉ' ⲙ̄ⲡⲉⲣϩⲟⲧⲉ· ⲁⲩⲱ ⲁϥⲱϣⲙ̄ ⲛ̄ⲗⲁⲙ(V i)ⲡⲁⲥ
ⲉⲧϩⲁⲛⲉⲥⲡⲓ'ⲣⲟⲟⲩⲉ, ⲁⲩⲱ ⲁⲩ'ⲧⲁⲗϭⲟ ⲛ̄ⲛⲉⲥⲉⲕⲓ'ⲃⲉ ϩⲱⲥ ⲉⲩϣϫⲉ ⲙ̄'ⲡⲟⲩⲃⲁⲥⲁⲛⲓⲍⲉ'⁵ ⲙ̄-
ⲙⲟⲥ ⲉⲡⲧⲏⲣϥ̄,' ⲁⲩⲱ ⲁϥⲟⲩⲱϣⲛ̄ ⲙ̄'ⲡϩⲉⲣⲙⲏⲧⲁⲣⲓⲟⲛ,' ⲁϥⲣ̄ⲛⲁⲩ. ⲁⲥⲁϩⲉ'ⲣⲁⲧⲥ̄ ϩⲛ̄ⲟⲩ-¹⁰

---

74 V ii 15. 2nd h. (to 75 R i 3). 16. l. ϩⲛ̄ⲛⲟⲩⲛⲟϭ; another favourite error of 2nd h. 20.
l. ⲙ̄ⲡⲏⲧⲟ. 21. l. ⲙ̄ⲛⲇⲟⲩϩ. 29. ϥ added. 75 R i 4. 1st h. (to ii 5). 24 f. l.
ⲛ̄ⲛⲉⲥⲡⲓⲣⲟⲟⲩⲉ. ii 5. 2nd h. (ⲕⲁⲣⲓⲁ) to 33. 6 f. Dittography. 16 f. Dittography. 17. l.
-ⲁⲅⲱⲛ. 19. l. ⲉⲧⲓϭⲟⲙ; so often in 2nd h. 21. l. ⲉⲡⲉⲛⲁⲅⲱⲛ. 23. ϩⲁⲧⲉⲓ̈ⲉⲛⲟϭ. 30.
l. ϩⲓⲟⲩⲛⲁⲙ ⲙ̄ⲙⲟⲥ. V i 1. 1st h. (to 19). 1 f. ⲉⲧϩⲁⲛⲉⲥⲡⲓⲣⲟⲟⲩⲉ.

A; ⲙ̄ⲡⲉⲡ̄ⲛⲁ D. 11 f. ⲛ̄ⲉⲛⲉϩ A; om. D. 14. ⲧⲙⲁⲕⲁⲣⲓⲁ A; ⲧⲙⲁⲓ̈ⲛⲟⲩⲧⲉ D. 20 f. ⲉⲡⲏⲧⲟ
(sic) ⲉⲃⲟⲗ ⲉⲛⲇⲟⲩϩ (sic) A; ⲙ̄ⲡ.ⲉⲃ. ⲙ̄ⲡⲛ̄ϩⲓⲉⲙⲱⲛ D. 22. ⲡⲉϫⲉⲡⲇⲟⲩϩ ⲛⲁⲩ A; ⲡⲉϫⲉϩⲁⲣ-
ⲙⲉⲛⲓⲟⲥ ⲛ̄ⲁⲗⲁ ⲡⲁⲛⲥⲉ D. 23. ⲱ ⲡⲁⲛⲥⲉ A; om. D. 25 f. ⲙ̄ⲡⲁⲡⲟⲗⲗⲱⲛ ⲡⲛⲟϭ ⲛ̄ⲛⲟⲩⲧⲉ A;
ⲙ̄ⲡ ⲛ̄ⲛ̄ ⲡⲁⲡ. D. 29 f. ⲧⲉⲓ̈ϣⲱⲣⲉ A; ⲧ.ϣ. D. 75 R i 1 f. ⲙ̄ⲡⲉϥⲉⲩϣϭⲙ̄ϭⲟⲙ ⲉⲧⲁⲗϭⲟⲕ
A; ⲙ̄ⲡⲉϥϯ D. 2. ⲉⲃⲟⲗ A; om. D. 5 f. ⲉⲧⲃⲉⲡⲉⲓ̈ϩⲁϫⲉ A; om. D. 7. ⲛⲓⲙ A; ⲧⲁⲧⲱⲛ
D. 7 f. ⲉⲧⲁⲡⲟⲗⲟⲅⲓⲍⲉ A; ⲉⲥⲁ. D. 8. ⲛⲁⲓ̈ A; om. D. 12. ⲡⲉϫⲉⲡⲇⲟⲩϩ A; ⲡⲇⲟⲩϩ
ⲇⲉ ⲡⲉϫⲁⲩ D. 13. ϩⲱ A; ϩⲱⲧ D. 15. ⲡⲉ A; ⲧⲉ (sic) D. 18. After ⲁⲥⲟⲩⲱϣⲃ̄, +
ⲛ̄ϭⲓ ⲑⲉⲕⲗⲁ D.

ⲛⲟⲥ ⲙ̄ⲙⲟⲧⲭⲱⲱⲣⲉ ⲙ̄ⲡ̄ⲧⲟ ⲉⲃⲟⲗ ⲙ̄ⲡⲗⲟⲩⲍ̄ ⲡⲉϫⲁⲥ ⲛⲁⲩ ϫⲉ ⲛⲁⲓ ⲛⲉ ⲛⲉⲕⲃⲁⲥⲁⲛⲟⲥ
ⲉⲣⲉⲡⲭⲟⲉⲓⲥ ⲓ̄ⲥ̄ ⲡⲉϫ̄ϫⲉ ϯϣⲓⲡⲉ ⲛⲁⲕ ⲙ̄ⲡⲉⲕⲉⲣⲣⲟ ⲛ̄ⲁⲛⲟⲙⲟⲥ ⲡⲗⲟⲩⲍ̄ ⲇⲉ ⲁϥϭⲱⲛⲧ̄
ⲙ̄ⲙⲁⲧⲉ ⲡⲉϫⲁⲩ ⲛⲁⲥ ϫⲉ ⲩⲉ ⲡⲉⲕⲕⲣⲁⲧⲟⲥ ⲛ̄ϩ̄ⲣⲱⲙⲁⲓⲟⲥ ϯⲛⲁⲉⲣⲡⲟⲩⲥⲱⲙⲁ ⲛ̄-
ϣⲁⲩ ϣⲁⲩ ⲧⲁⲧⲁ ⲁⲩ ⲛ̄ⲛⲉⲑⲏⲣⲓⲟⲛ ⲙ̄ⲛ̄ⲛⲉϩⲁⲗⲁⲧⲉ ϣⲁⲛ ϯ ⲛⲁⲩ ϫⲉ ⲁⲩ ⲛ̄ⲛⲟⲩⲧⲉ ⲡⲉⲧⲛⲁ ⲉⲩⲛⲁϩⲙⲉ ϩⲛ̄ⲛⲁ ϭⲓϫ ⲁⲥⲟⲩⲱϣⲃ̄ ⲛ̄ϭⲓ ⲑⲉⲕⲗⲁ ⲡⲉϫⲁⲥ ⲛⲁⲩ ϫⲉ ⲡⲉⲛⲧⲁⲃ (75 V ii)
ϯϭⲟⲙ ⲛⲁⲓ ⲙ̄ⲡ ϣⲟⲣⲡ ⲛ̄ⲥⲟⲡ ⲛ̄ⲧⲟϥ ⲟⲛ ⲡⲉⲧⲛⲁ ⲛⲁϩⲙⲉⲧ ⲉⲃⲟⲗ ϩⲛ̄ ⲛⲉⲕⲃⲁⲥⲁⲛⲟⲥ
ⲛⲁⲧⲧⲁϫⲓⲥ ⲇⲉ ⲛ̄ⲧⲉⲣⲟⲩ ⲛⲁⲩ ⲉⲣⲟⲥ ⲉⲙ̄ⲡⲗⲁⲁⲩ ⲛ̄ⲧⲁ ⲅⲟ ϣⲟⲟⲡ ⲙ̄ⲙⲟⲥ ϩⲙ̄ ⲡⲉⲥⲥⲱⲙⲁ
ⲁⲩⲱ ⲉⲃⲟⲗ ⲉⲣⲧⲉ ⲟⲩ ⲙ̄ⲡⲛⲟⲩⲧⲉ ⲛ̄ⲛⲉⲭⲣⲏⲥⲧⲓⲁⲛⲟⲥ ⲡⲁⲓ ⲉⲧⲛⲟⲩϩ̄ⲙ̄ ⲛ̄ⲛⲉⲧ ϩⲉⲗⲡⲓⲍⲉ
ⲉⲣⲟϥ ⲡⲗⲟⲩⲍ̄ ⲇⲉ ⲡⲉϫⲁⲩ ⲙ̄ⲙⲁⲕⲁⲣⲓⲟⲥ ⲁⲗⲁ ⲡⲁⲛⲥⲉ ϫⲉ ⲛ̄ⲧⲟⲕ ⲇⲉ ⲁⲕ ϯ ⲛ̄ⲟⲩⲗⲟⲅⲟⲥ
ⲛⲁⲓ ⲙ̄ⲛ̄ϭⲟⲙ ⲙ̄ⲙⲟⲕ ⲉⲡⲗⲁⲛⲁ ⲙ̄ⲙⲟⲓ ⲡⲉϫⲉⲡⲁⲅⲓⲟⲥ ⲛⲁⲩ ϫⲉ ⲛ̄ⲧⲕ ⲟⲩⲁⲧ ⲛⲟⲩⲧⲉ ⲛ̄-
ⲧⲟⲕ ⲙ̄ⲡⲉⲕⲉⲓⲱⲧ ⲡ ⲇⲓⲁⲃⲟⲗⲟⲥ ⲁⲩⲕⲉⲗⲉⲩⲉ ⲛ̄ϭⲓ ⲡ ⲇⲟⲩⲍ̄ ⲉⲧⲣⲉⲩⲥⲱⲧ̄ϩ̄ ⲛ̄ⲛⲉⲩⲧⲃ̄ⲥ̄ ⲛ̄-
ⲥⲉ ϯ ⲛ̄ϩⲉⲛϩⲁⲗⲏⲥⲓⲥ ⲉⲃⲟⲗ ⲛ̄ϩⲏⲧⲟⲩ ⲛ̄ⲥⲉⲙⲟⲩⲣ ⲛⲟⲟⲩ (76 R i) ⲛⲉ ⲉⲡⲉⲩⲙⲁⲕϩ̄ ⲛ̄ⲥⲉ-
ⲁⲩⲧⲟⲩ ⲉϩⲣⲁⲓ ⲛ̄ⲥⲁ ϫⲱⲟⲩ ϣⲁⲛ ⲧⲉⲡⲉⲩⲥⲛⲟϥ ϩⲁⲧ ϫⲉⲗ ⲉⲃⲟⲗ ϩⲙ̄ ⲡ ⲣⲱ ⲟⲩ ⲙ̄ⲛϣⲁⲁⲛⲧⲟⲩ
ⲡⲗⲟⲩⲍ̄ ⲇⲉ ⲁϥⲁⲛⲁ ⲭⲱⲣⲉⲓ ⲛⲁⲩ ⲁϥⲕⲁⲁⲩ ⲉⲧⲁ ⲩ ⲉ ⲉϩⲣⲁⲓ ⲉϩⲛ̄ ⲍⲁⲃⲁⲥⲁⲛⲟⲥ ⲁⲩⲱ ⲉⲓⲥ
ϩⲣⲁϥⲁⲏⲗ ⲡ ⲁⲅⲅⲉⲗⲟⲥ ⲁϥⲉⲓ ⲉⲃⲟⲗ ϩⲛ̄ ⲧⲡⲉ ⲁϥⲉⲓ ⲛⲉ ⲛⲟⲩϩⲓⲏⲃ ⲉϩⲛ̄ ⲛⲉⲧⲣⲟⲉⲓⲥ ⲉⲛⲉⲧⲟⲩ ⲁⲁⲃ ⲁϥⲛ̄ⲧⲟⲩ ⲉ ⲡⲉⲥⲏⲧ ⲁⲩⲱ ⲁϥ ⲥⲱⲗⲡ̄ ⲛ̄ⲛⲉⲩⲙ̄ⲣ̄ⲣⲉ ⲁϥⲁⲙⲁϩⲧⲉ ⲛ̄ⲛⲉⲩ ϭⲓϫ ⲁⲩ-
ⲛ̄ⲧⲟⲩ ⲉ ⲡⲉⲩⲧⲉⲕⲟ ⲁⲩⲱ ⲁ ⲛⲉⲧⲟⲩⲁⲁⲃ ⲛⲁⲩ ⲉⲣⲟⲟⲩ ⲁⲩⲣⲁ ϣ ⲉ ⲙⲁⲧⲉ ⲉ ⲛⲉⲩ ϣ̄ⲗⲏⲗ
ⲅⲁⲣ ⲉⲩⲟⲩ ⲡⲉ ⲛ̄ⲧⲉⲣⲟⲩ ⲧⲱⲟⲩⲛ ⲇⲉ ⲛ̄ϭⲓ ⲙ̄ⲙⲁⲧⲟⲓ ⲁ̄ⲡⲟⲩ ⲛⲁⲩ ⲉ ⲛⲉⲧⲟⲩⲁⲁⲃ ⲁⲩ-
ϣⲧⲟⲣⲧ̄ⲣ̄ ⲁⲩⲱ ⲁⲩ ⲡⲱϩ ⲛ̄ⲛⲉⲩϩⲟⲓⲧⲉ ⲁⲩⲃⲱⲕ ⲁⲩⲧⲁⲙⲉ (R ii) ⲡ ⲗⲟⲩⲍ̄ ⲉⲩϫⲱ ⲙ̄ⲙⲟⲥ
ϫⲉ ⲡϫⲟⲉⲓⲥ ⲁⲛⲓ ⲙⲁⲅⲟⲥ ⲉⲓⲛⲉ ⲛ̄ⲟⲩϩⲓⲏⲃ ⲉⲃⲱ(ⲛ) ⲉⲛⲉⲛⲕⲁⲧ ⲁ ϥ ⲡⲱⲧ ⲁⲩⲱ ⲛ̄ⲧⲛ̄
ⲥⲟⲟⲩⲛ ⲁⲛ ϫⲉ ⲛ̄ⲧⲁⲩ ⲃⲱⲕ ⲉ ⲧⲱⲛ ⲁⲩϭⲱⲛⲧ ⲇⲉ ⲛ̄ϭⲓ ⲡ ⲗⲟⲩⲍ̄ ⲁⲩⲱ ⲁϥ ⲧⲛ̄ⲛⲟⲟⲩ ⲉ-
ⲡⲉⲩ ⲧⲉⲕⲟ ⲁⲩϭⲓⲛⲉ ⲛ̄ ⲛⲉⲧⲟⲩⲁⲁⲃ ⲉ ⲙ̄ⲡ̄ ⲗⲁⲁⲩ ⲛ̄ⲧⲁⲕⲟ ϣⲟⲟⲡ ϩⲙ̄ ⲡⲉⲩⲥⲱⲙⲁ ⲉ ⲡⲧⲏ-
ⲣ̄ϥ̄ ⲙ̄ⲡⲉⲩⲣⲁⲥⲧⲉ ⲇⲉ ⲁϥⲕⲉⲗⲉⲩⲉ ⲛ̄ϭⲓ ⲡ ⲗⲟⲩⲍ̄ ⲉⲧⲣⲉⲩⲉⲓⲛⲉ ⲛ̄ ⲛⲉⲧⲟⲩⲁⲁⲃ ⲛⲁⲩ ⲉⲭⲛ̄
ⲡⲃⲏⲙⲁ ⲡⲉϫⲉ ⲡ ⲗⲟⲩⲍ̄ ⲛⲁⲩ ϫⲉ ⲛ̄ⲛⲉⲓ ϩⲃⲏⲩⲉ ϩⲙⲁⲅⲓⲁ ⲛⲁⲉⲩ ⲛⲉϩⲛ̄ ⲧⲏⲩⲧⲛ̄ ⲁⲛ ⲉ-
ⲃⲟⲗ ϩⲛ̄ ⲛⲁ ϭⲓϫ ⲗⲟⲓⲡⲟⲛ ⲑⲩⲥⲓⲁⲍⲉ ⲛ̄ⲛⲉⲩⲧⲉ ⲉⲧ ⲧⲁⲓⲏⲩ ⲡⲉϫⲉ ⲧⲙⲁⲕⲁⲣⲓⲁ ⲑⲉⲕⲗⲁ
ⲙ̄ⲡ ⲗⲟⲩⲍ̄ ϫⲉ ⲙⲁⲣⲉ ⲡⲁ ⲡⲱⲗ (V i) ⲗⲱⲛ ⲙⲟⲟⲩⲉ ⲛ̄ϥ ⲉⲓ ⲛⲁⲓ ⲉⲡⲉⲓⲙⲁ ⲁⲩⲱ ⲁⲛⲟⲕ ϯ-
ⲛⲁ ⲟⲩ ⲱϣⲧ ⲛⲁϥ ⲡⲉϫⲉ ⲡ ⲗⲟⲩⲍ̄ ⲛⲁⲥ ϫⲉ ϯ ⲛⲁ ⲧⲣⲉ ⲡ ⲟⲩ ϩⲓⲏⲃ ⲧⲱⲟⲩⲛ ⲙ̄ⲙⲟϥ ⲛ̄ⲥⲉ ⲛ̄ⲧ̄
ⲉⲣⲁⲧϥ̄ ⲁⲥⲟⲩⲱϣⲃ̄ ⲛ̄ϭⲓ ⲧⲉ ⲧ ⲟⲩⲁⲁⲃ ⲑⲉⲕⲗⲁ ϫⲉ ⲙ̄ⲡⲉⲓ ⲛⲁⲩ ⲉ ⲛⲟⲩ ⲧⲉ ⲉⲛⲉϩ ⲉⲩ ⲧⲟⲩⲟ(ⲩⲛ)
ⲙ̄ⲙⲟ ⲩ ⲉⲩⲉⲓⲛⲉ ⲙ̄ⲙⲟ ⲩ ⲉⲣⲁⲧ ⲩ ⲛ̄ⲣⲱ ⲙⲉ ⲡⲉⲛ ϫⲟⲉⲓⲥ ⲇⲉ ⲛ̄ⲧⲟ ⲩ ⲓ̄ⲥ̄ ⲡⲉϫ̄ ϣⲁ ⲩ ⲃⲱⲕ
ϣⲁ ⲟⲩⲟⲛ ⲛⲓⲙ ⲛ̄ ⲩ ⲛⲟⲩ ϩ̄ⲙ̄ ⲛ̄ⲛⲉⲧϩⲉⲗⲡⲓⲍⲉ ⲉ ⲣⲟ ⲩ ⲉ ⲩϣ ⲉ ⲟⲩ ⲛⲟⲩ ⲧⲉ ⲡⲉ ⲡⲁⲡⲱⲗ ⲗⲱⲛ

PAESE AND THECLA 76 V i 22–77 V i 23

ⲙⲁⲣⲉⲩⲥⲉⲩⲧ’ⲡⲣⲏ ⲙⲁⲡⲟⲟⲩ ⳿ⲥⲛⲧⲡⲉ ⲛⲩⲭⲟⲟⲥ ⲛ̄²⁵ⲑⲁⲗⲁⲥⲥⲁ ⳿ⲍⲉ ⲡⲱⲣⲝ̄ ⲛ̄ⲡⲱⲣⲝ̄.’
ⲉⲩⲥⲱⲧⲙ̄ ⲇⲉ ⲉⲛⲁⲓ’ⲛ̄ϭⲓ ⲡⲇⲟⲩⲍ, ⲁⲩⲙⲟⲩⲍ ⲛ̄ϭⲱⲛⲧ̄.’³⁰ ⲡⲉⳍⲁⲩ ⲛⲁⲥ ⳿ⲍⲉ’ ⲟⲩⲙⲁ⳿ⲟⲥ
ⲍⲱⲟⲩ’ ⲡⲉ ⲡⲁⲡⲱⲗⲗⲟⲛ (76 V ii) ⲛ̄ⲑⲉ ⲛ̄ⲛⲉⳍⲣⲏⲥⲧⲓ’ⲁⲛⲟⲥ· ⲟⲩⲛⲟⲩⲧⲉ’ ⲅⲁⲣ ⲛ̄ⲕⲱⲥ.
ⲙⲱⲕⲣⲁ’ⲧⲱⲣ ⲡⲉ. ⲡⲉⳍⲁⲥ⳿ ⲛⲁⲩ ⲛ̄ϭⲓ ⲧⲉⲧⲟⲩⲁⲁⲃ’ ⳿ⲍⲉ ⲉⲩⳍⲉ ⲟⲩⲛⲟⲩⲧⲉ ⲉⲩⲟⲛⲍ̄ ⲡⲉ
ⲡⲁ’ⲡⲱⲗⲗⲟⲛ, ⲉⲕⲩⲁⲗ(ⲛ)’ⳡⲱⲛⲉ ⲟⲛ ⲙⲁⲣⲉⳡ¹⁹ⲧⲁⲗϭⲟⲕ. ⲁⳡⳍⲱⲛⲧ̄’ ⲛ̄ϭⲓ ⲡⲇⲟⲩⲍ, ⲡⲉⳍⲁⲩ’
⳿ⲍⲉ ⲕⲁⲕⲏ ⲕⲏⲫⲁ’ⲗⲏ, ⲟⲩⲕⲟⲩⲛ ⲉⲣⲟⳡ’ⲉⲩⲧⲣⲁⳡⳡⲱⲛⲉ ⲟⲛ;¹⁵ ⲕⲁⲓ ⲅⲁⲣ ⲛ̄ⲧⲟ ⲙⲛ̄’ⲡⲟⲩⲥⲟⲛ
ⲁⲧⲉⲧⲛ̄’ⲣ̄ⲍⲓⲕ ⲉⲣⲟⳓ ⳡⲁⲛⲧ’ⳡⲱⲛⲉ. ⲁⲗⲗⲁ’ ⲁⲡⲛⲟϭ ⲛ̄ⲛⲟⲩⲧⲉ’²⁰ ⲡⲁⲡⲱⲗⲗⲟⲛ ⲃⲟ’ⲏⲑⲓⲁ
ⲉⲣⲟⳓ, ⲁⲩⲧⲁⲗ’ϭⲟⳓ. ⲡⲇⲟⲩⲍ ⲇⲉ ⲁⳡ’ⲕⲉⲗⲉⲩⲉ ⲉⲧⲣⲉⲩⲑⲙ̄’ⲛ̄ⳑⲟⲟⲩ ⲍⲓ⳿ⲭⲛⲟⲩⲕⲁ’²⁵ⲑⲉⲇⲣⲁ ⲙ̄-
ⲡⲉⲛⲓⲡⲉ,’ⲁⲩⲧⲣⲉⲩⲍⲓⲧⲉ ⲙ̄’ⲡⲩⲁⲁⲣ ⲛ̄ⲧⲉⲩⲁⲡⲉ.’ ⲁⳡⲕⲉⲗⲉⲩⲉ ⲇⲉ ⲟⲛ’ ⲉⲧⲣⲉⲩⲥⲱⲧⲍ̄ ⲛ̄-
ⲛⲉⲩ’ⲁⲡⲏⲩⲉ ⲛ̄ⲟⲩⲛⲁ⳿ⳍⲉ’³⁰ⲛ̄ⳍⲁⲙⳡⲉ ⲛ̄ⲥⲉ’ⳡⲟⲅⲉⲁⳑⳍⲉⲧⲛ̄ (77 R i) ⲉⲩⲃⲣ̄ⲃⲣ̄ ⲉⲡⲉⲥⲏⲧ’
ⲉⲡⲉⲩⲁⲛⲕⲉⲫⲁⲗⲟⲥ.’ ⲡⲁⲗⲓⲛ ⲟⲛ ⲁⳡⲕⲉ’ⲗⲉⲩⲉ ⲛ̄ϭⲓ ⲡⲇⲟⲩⲍ⳿ ⲉⲧⲣⲉⲩⲉⲓⲛⲉ ⲛ̄⳿ⲍⲉⲱ(ⲛ)’ⲩⲉ ⲛ̄-
ⳍⲟⲉⲓⲧ ⲉⳡ’ⲗⲁⲗⲏ ⳡⲁⲙⲣⲏⳍⲉ,’ ⲁⲩⲧⲣⲉⲩⲥⲟⲛⲧⲱ’ⲛⲟⲩ ⲍⲓ⳿⳿ⳍⲛⲡⲕⲁⳍ¹⁰’ ⳡⲁⲛⲧⲟⲩⳍⲓⲥⲉ’ ⲉ-
ⲧⲉⲩⲁⲡⲉ ⲙ̄ⲙⲁⳍⲉ’ ⲥⲛⲁⲩ. ⲁⳡⲕⲉⲗⲉⲩⲉ’ ⲉⲧⲣⲉⲩⳍⲉⲣⲱⲟⲩ’ ⲍⲛ̄ⲟⲩⲕⲱⲍⲧ̄, ⲁⲩⲱ’¹⁵ⲁⲩⲙⲟⲩⲍ
ⲉⲙⲁⲧⲉ’ ⳍⲱⲥⲧⲉ ⲛ̄ⲧⲉⲟⲩⲛⲟ⳿ⳡ ⲛ̄ⳡⲁⳍ ⳡⲱⲡⲉ’ ⲛ̄ⲧⲉⲧⳑ̄ⲗⲁⲁⲩ ⲉⲩⳍⲛ̄ⳍⲟⲙ ⲉⳡⲱ ⲙ̄ⲡⲉⳡ²⁰ⲕⲱⲧⲉ. ⲁⲩⲱ ⲉⲓⲥ’ ⲧⲡⲁⲣⲑⲉⲛⲟⲥ ⲉⲧⲟⲩ’ⲁⲁⲃ ⲙⲁⲣⲓⲁ ⲁⲥⲉⲓ’ ⲉⲃⲟⲗ ⳍⲁⲧⲡⲉ ⲙⲛ̄’ⲅⲁⲃⲣⲓⲏⲗ ⲙⲛ̄²⁵’ⲣⲁⲫⲁⲏⲗ, ⲁⲩⲉⲓ’ ⳡⲁⲛⲉⲧⲟⲩⲁⲁⲃ.’ ⲡⲉⳍⲁⲥ ⲛⲁⲩ ⳿ⲍⲉ ⳿ⳍⲣⲟ ⲛ̄ⲧⲉⲧⳑ̄ⳍⲟⲙ,
ⲡⲁ⳿ⳡⲏⲣⲉ ⳡⲟ’ⲟⲡ ⲛⲉⲙⲏⲧⲛ̄.’³⁰ ⲁⲩⲱ ⲁⳡⲫⲣⲁⲅⲓⲍⲉ’ ⲙ̄ⲙⲟⲟⲩ ⳍⲙ̄ⲡⲣⲁ(ⲛ) (77 R ii) ⲙ̄ⲡⲉⳍⳍ̄·
ⲁⳑ̄ⲃⲁⳍⲁ’ⲛⲉⲥ ⲧⲏⲣⲟⲩ ⲉⲧⳍⲙ̄’ⲡⲉⲩⲥⲱⲙⲁ ⲧⲱⳑⲟ,’ ⲁⲩⲱ ⲁⳡⲧⲣⲉⲡⲕⲱⳍⲧ̄⳿ ⳿ⲣ̄ⲑⲉ ⲛ̄ⲟⲩⲧⲏⲩ
ⲛ̄ⳓ’ⲱⲧⲉ ⲉⳡⳍⲱⲕ ⲙ̄ⲡⲛⲁⲩ ⲛ̄ⳡⲱⲣⲡ̄. ⲁⲥ’ⲥⲙⲟⲩ ⲉⲣⲟⲟⳡ, ⲁⲥⲃⲱⲕ’ ⲉⳍⲣⲁⳓ ⲉⳑ̄ⲡⲏⲩⲉ ⳍⲛ̄¹⁰’
ⲟⲩⲛⲟϭ ⲛ̄ⲉⲟⲟⲩ.’ ⲡⲉⳍⲉⲛⲁⲧⲧⲁⳍⲓⲥ’ ⲙ̄ⲡⲇⲟⲩⲍ ⳿ⲍⲉ ⲡⲉⲛ’⳿ⳍⲟⲉⲓⲥ, ⲁⲛⲉⲩⲕⲉⲉⳓ’ ⲣⲱⲕⳍ̄. ⲁⲩⲱ¹⁵
ⲁⳡⲥⲱⲃⲉ, ⲡⲉⳍⲁⲩ’⳿ⲍⲉ ⲙⲁⲣⲉⲥⲉⲓ ⲧⲉⲛⲟⲩ’ ⲛ̄ϭⲓ ⲧⲓⲁⲧⲩⲁⲛ’ ⲛ̄ⲉⲁⲡⲟⲗⲟⲅⲓⲍⲉ ⲛⲁⲓ’ ⲛ̄ⲕⲉ-
ⲥⲟⲡ· ⲙ̄ⲛⲛⲟ’ⲧⲉ²⁰ ⲅⲁⲣ ⲉⲟⲩⲛ̄ϭⲟⲙ’ ⲙ̄ⲙⲟⳡ ⲛ̄ⲑⲉ ⲙ̄ⲡⲁ’ⲡⲱⲗⲗⲟⲛ ⲙⲛ̄’ⲧⲁⲣⲧⲩⲙⲓⲥ. ⲛ̄-
ⳍⲟ’ⲥⲟⲛ ⲇⲉ ⲉⳡⳍⲱ ⲛ̄’ⲛⲁⳓ²⁵, ⲉⲓⲥ ⳿ⳍⲣⲁⲫⲁ’ⲏⲗ ⲡⲁⲅⲅⲉⲗⲟⲥ ⲁⳡ’ⲉⲓ ⲉⲃⲟⲗ ⳍⲛ̄ⲧⲡⲉ,’ⲁⳡⲉⲓ-
ⲛⲉ ⲛ̄ⲛⲉⲧⲟⲩⲁⲁⲃ ⲉⲃⲟⲗ ⳍⲛ̄³⁰ⲡⲕⲱⳍⲧ̄ ⲉⲙ̄’ⳑⲁⲁⲩ ⲛ̄ⲧⲁⲕⲟ ⳡⲟⲟⲡ ⲙ̄ⲙⲟⲟⲩ, ⲟⲩⲇⲉ (77 V i) ⟦ⲟⲩⲇⲉ⟧ ⲙ̄ⲡⲉⲡⲉⲩⲥⲱ’ⲙⲁ ⲉⲣⲥⲧⲟⳓ ⲛ̄ⲕⲱⳍⲧ̄.’ ⲁⲧⳓⳡⳍⳡ ⲉⲃⲟⲗ ⲉⳡⳍⲱ ⲙ̄ⲙⲟⲥ
⳿ⲍⲉ ⳿ⲁⳡⳡⲓⲡⲉ’ ⲛⲁⲕ ⲛ̄ⲧⲟⲕ ⲙⲛ̄’ⲡⲉⲕⲁⲡⲟⲗⲗⲟⲛ’ ⲛ̄ⲁⳡⲩⳍⲟⲛ. ⲁⲩⲱ’ ⲁⲡⳑ̄’¹⁰⟦ⳑ̄⟧ⲏⲏⳡⲉ ⲧⲏ-
ⲣⲉⳡ ⲛⲁⲩ ⲉⲡⲉⲛ’ⲧⲁⳡⳡⲱⲡⲉ, ⲁⲩⲧⲓ’ⲉⲟⲟⲩ ⲉⲡⲛⲟⲩⲧⲉ’ ⲛ̄ⲛⲉⳍⲣⲏⲥⲧⲓⲁ’ⲛⲟⲥ ⲡⲉⳍⳓ ⲓ̄ⲥ̄’
ⲡⲉⲧⲛⲟⲩⳍⲙ̄ ⲛ̄ⲛⲁⲧ’ⳍⲉⲗⲡⲓⲍⲉ ⲉⲣⲟⳡ.’¹⁵ ⲁⲩⲱ ⲧⲏⲡⲉ ⲛ̄ⲛⲧⲁⲩ’ⲡⲓⲥⲧⲉⲩⲉ ⲙ̄ⲡⲉⳍⲟⲟⲩ ⲉⲧⲙ̄-
ⲙⲁⳡ’ ⲥⲉⲉⲓⲣⲉ ⲕ̄... ⳑ̄ⳑⲍ̄ⳑⲉ ⲛ̄ⲣⲱⲙⲉ ⲙⲛ̄’ⳡⲙⲟⲩⲛ ⲙ̄ⲙⲁ’ⲧⲟⳓ ⲛ̄ⲧⲉⲧⲧⲁⳍⲓⲥ.’²⁰ ⲁⲩⲱ ⲁⳡ-

---

76 V ii 32. ⲗ. -ⲗⲁⲩⳡⲁⲧⲏ. 77 R i 2. ⲗ. ⲉⲧⲕⲉⲫⲁⲗⲟⲥ. 31. ⲗ. ⲁⲥⲥⲫⲣⲁⲅⲓⳍⲉ. ii 29 f.
Dittography. V i 1. After ⟦ⲟⲩⲇⲉ⟧, 2nd ⲗ. (to ii 31). 14 f. ⲗ. ⲛ̄ⲛⲉⲧ⳿ⳍⲉⲗⲡⲓⳍⲉ. 16 f. ⲗ. ⲛ̄-
ⲛⲉⲛⲧⲁⲩⲡⲓⲥⲧⲉⲩⲉ. 19. ⲗ. ⲥⲉⲉⲓⲣⲉ.

ⲕⲉⲗⲉⲩⲉ ⲛ̄ϭⲓ ⲡⲗⲟⲩϫ ⲉⲧⲣⲉⲩⲃⲓⲧⲟⲩ ⲉⲡ'ⲃⲟⲗ ⲉⲧⲡⲟⲗⲓⲥ' ⲛ̄ⲥⲩⲃⲓ ⲛ̄ⲧⲉⲩⲁ'ⲡⲏ, ⲁⲩⲭⲱⲕ' ⲉ-
ⲃⲟⲗ ⲛ̄ⲧⲉⲩⲙⲁⲣ'ⲧⲉⲣⲓⲁ ⲛ̄ⲥⲟⲩⲭⲟⲩ'ⲱⲧ ⲁ̄ⲗⲉⲃⲟⲧ ⲉ'ⲡⲏⲡ, ⲍ̄ⲛ̄ⲟⲩ(77 V ii)ⲉⲓⲣⲏⲛⲏ ⲛ̄ⲧⲉ-
ⲡⲛ̄'ⲟⲩⲧⲉ, ⲍⲁⲙⲏⲛ.' ⲡⲗⲟⲩϫ ⲇⲉ ⲁⲩⲕⲉ'ⲗⲉⲩⲉ ⲉⲧⲧⲣⲉⲩϫⲓ ⲛ̄'ⲛⲉⲧⲟⲩⲁⲁⲃ ⲉⲡⲉⲩ'ⲧⲉⲕⲟ
ⲩⲁⲡⲉⲩⲣⲁⲥ'ⲧⲉ. ⲁⲥⲱⲡⲉ ⲇⲉ'ⲛ̄ⲧⲁⲩϣⲉ ⲛ̄ⲧⲉⲩⲩⲙ' ⲁⲩⲉⲓ ⲩⲁⲣⲟⲩ ⲛ̄ϭⲓ ⲡⲁⲅⲅⲉⲗⲟⲥ
ⲉⲡⲥ̄,' ⲁⲩⲧⲁⲗⲟ ⲁ̄ⲡⲉⲧⲟⲩ'ⲁⲁⲃ ⲁⲗⲁ ⲡⲁⲛⲥⲉ ϩⲓ'ⲭ̄ⲛ̄ⲛⲉⲩⲧⲏⲛ̄ϫ̄ ⲛ̄ⲟⲩⲃⲉⲓⲛ, ⲁⲩⲭⲓⲧⲩ̄
ⲙ̄'ⲙ̄ⲡⲏⲩⲉ, ⲁⲩⲧⲥⲁ'ϥⲟⲩ ⲉⲧⲡⲟⲗⲓⲥ ⲉ'ⲧⲟⲩⲁⲁⲃ ⲑⲓⲗ̄ⲙ̄' ⲛ̄ⲧⲡⲉ· ⲁⲩⲱ ⲁⲛⲉ'ⲧⲟⲩⲁⲁⲃ ⲧⲏⲣⲟⲩ'
ⲉⲓ ⲉⲃⲟⲗ ϩⲁⲭⲱⲩ,' ⲁⲩⲁⲥⲡⲁⲍⲉ ⲙ̄ⲙⲟⲩ,' ⲁⲩⲧⲥⲁⲃⲟⲩ ⲉⲧⲡⲟ'ⲗⲥ̄ ⲙ̄ⲡⲉⲭ̄ⲥ̄, ⲉⲣⲉ'ⲛⲉⲥⲡⲗⲁ-
ⲧⲓⲁ ⲧⲁⲧⲥ̄' ⲛ̄ⲟⲩⲛⲏ ⲙ̄ⲙⲏ,' ⲉⲥⲉⲣⲟⲩⲟⲉⲓⲛ ⲛ̄ⲍⲟⲩⲉ'ⲡⲣⲏ. ⲁⲩⲭⲓⲧⲩ̄'ⲛ̄ϭⲓ ⲡⲁⲛⲅⲉⲗⲟⲥ ⲉ̄'ⲡϫⲟⲉⲓⲥ, ⲁⲩⲧⲥⲁ'ⲃⲟⲩ ⲉⲩⲛⲏⲓ' ⲉⲩⲟⲩ'ⲁⲩϫ̄ ⲉⲃⲟⲗ (78 R i) ⲉⲙⲁⲧⲉ· ⲡⲏⲓ ⲇⲉ' ⲉⲧⲙ̄ⲙⲁⲩ ⲛⲉⲩ-
ⲧⲟⲥⲉ' ⲁ̄ⲱⲛⲉ ⲛ̄ⲁⲩⲉⲓ ⲁⲩ'ⲁⲛ, ⲉⲩⲛⲏⲭⲁⲕ'ⲧⲓⲛ ⲛ̄ⲟⲩⲟⲉⲓⲛ ⲉⲃⲟⲗ,' ⲉⲣⲉⲛⲉⲥⲧⲩⲗⲗⲟⲥ' ⲧⲁ-
ⲭⲣⲏⲩ· ⲁⲩⲱ' ⲛⲉⲣⲉⲡⲏⲓ ⲉⲧⲙ̄ⲙⲁⲩ' ⲟ ⲛ̄ⲥⲧⲟⲁ ⲥⲧⲟⲁ, ⲉⲣⲉ'ⲭⲟⲩⲱⲧ ⲛ̄ⲥⲧⲩⲗ'ⲗⲟⲥ ϩⲁⲧⲟⲩⲉⲓ
ⲧⲟⲩⲉⲓ' ⲛ̄ⲛⲉⲥⲧⲟⲁ, ⲉⲩⲛⲏⲭ'ⲁⲕⲧⲓⲛ ⲛ̄ⲟⲩⲟⲉⲓⲛ' ⲉⲃⲟⲗ, ⲉⲣⲉⲛⲉⲥⲧⲩⲗⲗⲟⲥ ⲉⲧⲥⲁⲣⲏⲥ ⲙ̄'
ⲡⲏⲓ ⲉⲓⲣⲉ ⲛ̄ⲥⲉⲧⲏ,' ⲁⲩⲱ ⲡⲕⲉⲥⲉⲉⲡⲉ ϩⲓ'ⲡⲥⲁ ⲙ̄ⲡⲙ̄ϩⲓⲧ,' ⲁⲩⲱ ⲡⲕⲉⲙⲁⲁⲃ'ⲛ̄ⲥⲧⲩⲗⲗⲟⲥ
ϩⲓⲡⲥⲁ ⲙ̄ⲡⲉⲙⲛ̄ⲧ·' ⲁⲩⲱ ϩⲓⲧⲡⲉ ⲙ̄ⲡⲏⲓ' ⲉⲩⲧⲁⲭⲣⲏⲧ ⲉⲭⲱⲩ' ⲛ̄ϭⲓ ⲩⲉ ⲛ̄ⲥ̄'ⲧⲩⲗⲗⲟⲥ ⲉⲧ-
ⲧⲁⲓ'ⲏⲩ ⲉⲙⲁⲧⲉ, ⲉⲩ'ⲕⲏⲧ ⲅⲁⲣ ⲛ̄ⲑⲉ ⲛ̄ⲟⲩ'ⲉⲕⲕⲗⲏⲥⲓⲁ. ⲁⲓ'ϭⲱϣⲧ ⲉⲡⲓⲏ̄ⲃⲧ,' ⲡⲉϫⲁⲩ,
ⲁⲓ'ⲛⲁⲩ ⲉⲩ'ⲛⲟϭ ⲛ̄ⲑⲣⲟⲛⲟⲥ' ⲉⲣⲉⲙⲛ̄ⲧⲥⲛⲟⲟⲩⲥ (R ii) ⲛ̄ⲧⲟⲣⲧⲣ̄ ⲁ̄ⲛ̄ϫⲏⲧⲩ̄' ⲩⲁⲛⲧⲉⲕⲡⲱϩ
ⲉ'ⲡⲉⲑⲣⲟⲛⲟⲥ· ⲟⲩⲛⲟϭ' ⲅⲁⲣ ⲡⲉ ⲡⲧⲁⲓⲟ ⲙ̄ⲡⲉⲑⲣⲟⲛⲟⲥ ⲉⲧⲙ̄ⲙⲁⲩ,' ⲉⲣⲉⲍⲉⲛⲛⲟϭ ⲛ̄ⲩⲩⲙ(ⲛ)'

---

77 V i: 25. ℓ. -ϥⲓⲧⲟⲩ. 26. ℓ. ⲛ̄ⲧⲡⲟⲗⲓⲥ. 27. ℓ. ⲛ̄ⲥⲉⲩⲓ. ii 4. ℓ. ⲉⲧⲣⲉⲩϫⲓ. 10.ℓ. Ⲓ̄ⲡⲭⲟⲉⲓⲥ; the form ⲥⲉ̄ presumably shows the scribe lapsing into his native dialect. 14 f. ℓ. ⲉⲙ̄ⲙⲡⲏⲩⲉ. 15 f. ℓ. ⲁⲩⲧⲥⲁⲃⲟⲩ. 24.=ⲧⲁⲕⲉ. 78 R i: 1. 1st ℓ. (+ ii 33). 4 f. ℓ. ⲉⲩⲛⲉⲭ-
ⲁⲕⲧⲓⲛ. 17. ℓ. ⲡⲕⲉⲥⲉⲧⲏ (cf. Boh.) 19. ℓ. ⲕⲉⲙⲁⲁⲃ. 22. See commentary. 31. ℓ. ⲛ̄ⲑⲣⲟ-
ⲛⲟⲥ. ii 1. ℓ. ⲛ̄ϫⲏⲧⲩ̄.

Ⲃⲟⲏ. E.W. fr. 5 (p. 118) (Cod. Tisch.)

(R) [ⲉ]ⲑⲣⲟⲩⲱⲗⲓ ⲛ̄ⲛⲏ ⲉⲑⲟⲩⲁⲃ ⲉⲡⲓⲩ'[ⲧⲉ]ⲕⲟ ⲩⲁⲡⲉⲩⲣⲁⲥⲧ. ⲟⲩⲟϩ'[ϩ]ⲉⲛⲧϥⲁⲩϣ ⲛ̄ⲡⲓⲉ-
ϫⲱⲣϩ ⲁⲩϥ' ⲛ̄ϫⲉ ⲡⲓⲁⲅⲅⲉⲗⲟⲥ ⲛ̄ⲧⲉⲡⲥ̄, [ⲁ]ϥ̄ⲱⲗⲓ ⲙ̄ⲡⲓⲁⲅⲓⲟⲥ ⲡⲁⲛⲥⲉ ⲉⲡϣⲱⲓ'[ⲉⲧ]ϥⲉ, ⲁⲩⲧⲁⲙⲟⲩ ⲉⲓⲭⲏⲙ ⲉⲧ'[ϣ]ⲉⲛⲧϥⲉ, ϯⲃⲁⲕⲓ ⲛ̄ⲧⲉ'ⲡⲓⲟⲩ̄ⲗ̄(?)· ⲟⲩⲟϩ ⲁⲛⲏ ⲉⲃⲟⲗ ⲓ ⲉⲃⲟⲗ ϩⲁ-
ϫⲟⲩ ⲉⲩⲉⲣⲁⲥⲡⲁⲥⲉⲥⲑⲉ [ⲙ̄]'ⲙⲟⲩ, ⲁⲩⲧⲁⲗⲟⲩ ⲉϩⲣⲟⲗⲓ(ⲥ) ⲛ̄ⲧⲉⲛ̄ⲏ ⲉⲑⲟⲩⲁⲃ ⲉⲥⲧⲟⲧⲉ ⲛ̄-
ⲛⲟⲩⲃ ϩⲓⲱⲛⲓ ⲙ̄ⲙⲏⲓ, ⲉⲥ'ⲉⲣⲟⲩⲱⲓⲛⲓ ⲉϩⲟⲧⲉⲫⲣⲏ ⲛ̄ⲟⲩ'ⲑ̄ⲃⲁ ⲛ̄ⲕⲱⲃ ⲛ̄ⲥ[ⲟⲡ]· ⲟⲩⲟϩ ⲁⲩ-
ⲟⲗϥ̄ ⲛ̄ϫⲉ ⲡⲓⲁⲅⲅⲉⲗⲟⲥ,' ⲁⲩⲧ[ⲁ]ⲙⲟϥ ⲉⲟⲩⲛⲓⲩⲧ ⲛ̄ⲏⲓ ⲉϥ'ⲧⲁⲓⲏ̄[ⲟ]ⲩⲧ ⲙ̄ⲙⲁⲩϣⲟ, ⲉⲩⲧⲟ-
ⲧⲥ̄ ⲛ̄ⲱⲛⲓ ⲛⲁⲑⲟⲓ ⲛⲁⲃⲁⲛ, ⲉⲩ'ⲥⲧ̄[ⲏ]ⲧⲁⲕⲧⲓⲛ ⲛ̄ⲟⲩⲱⲓⲛⲓ ⲉ'ⲃⲟⲗ,' ⲉⲣⲉⲡⲓⲏⲓ ⲉⲧⲉⲙ̄ⲙⲁⲩ
ⲟⲓ ⲛ̄ⲥⲧⲟ'ⲁ ⲥⲧⲟⲁ, ⲉⲩⲥⲉⲧⲁⲕⲧⲓⲛ' ⲛ̄ⲟⲩⲱⲓⲛⲓ ⲉⲃⲟⲗ, ⲉⲣⲉⲛⲓ'ⲥⲧⲩⲗⲗⲟⲥ ⲉⲧⲥⲁⲣⲏⲥ ⲙ̄ⲡⲓⲏⲓ'
ⲉⲩⲟⲓ ⲛ̄ⲥ̄ⲉ· ⲟⲩⲟⲛ ⲕⲉⲥ̄ⲉ' ⲥⲁⲩⲏⲧ ⲙ̄ⲡⲓⲏⲓ, ⲟⲩⲟϩ ⲕⲉ'ⲥ̄ⲉ ⲛ̄ⲥⲧⲩⲗⲗⲟⲥ ⲥⲁⲡⲉⲓⲉⲃⲧ ⲙ̄ⲡⲓ-
ⲏⲓ· ⲥⲁⲩⲣⲏⲓ ⲇⲉ ⲙ̄ⲡⲓⲏⲓ ⲉⲩ'ⲧⲁⲭⲣⲏⲟⲩⲧ ⲛ̄ϫⲉ ⲣ̄ ⲛ̄ⲥⲧⲩⲗⲗⲟⲥ' ⲉⲩⲧⲁⲓⲏⲟⲩⲧ· ⲛⲁⲩⲕⲏⲧ
ⲡⲉ' ⲙ̄ⲫⲣⲏⲧ ⲛ̄ⲟⲩⲉⲕⲕⲗⲏⲥⲓⲁ.' (V) ⲁⲓϫⲟⲩⲱⲧ ⲥⲁⲡⲉⲓⲉⲃⲧ, ⲡⲉϫⲁⲩ.' ⲁⲓⲛⲁⲩ ⲉⲟⲩⲛⲓⲩⲧ ⲛ̄ⲑⲣⲟⲛ[ⲟⲥ]' ⲉⲩⲟⲥⲓ ⲙ̄ⲙⲁⲩϣⲟ, ⲉⲣⲉ[ⲟⲩ]ⲟⲛ ⲓ̄ⲃ ⲛ̄ⲧⲱⲧⲉⲣ ⲙ̄ⲙⲟⲩ ⲩⲁ'ⲧⲉⲕϫⲉ
ⲉⲡⲓϣⲱⲓ ⲉⲡⲓⲑⲣⲟⲛⲟⲥ·' ⲟⲩⲛⲓⲩⲧ ⲅⲁⲣ ⲡⲉ ⲡⲧⲁⲓⲟ ⲙ̄[ⲡⲓⲑⲣⲟ]ⲛⲟⲥ ⲉⲧⲉⲙ̄ⲙⲁⲩ ⲛⲉⲙ-
ⲥⲛ̄ϫⲉⲩ'[ⲧ]ⲱⲧⲉⲣ· ⲟⲩⲟϩ ⲛⲉ[ⲟ]ⲩⲟⲛⲟⲩ'[ⲛ̄]ⲛⲓⲩⲧ ⲛ̄ⲱⲟⲩ ⲕⲱⲧ ⲉⲣⲟⲩ· ⲉ'ⲣⲉⲟⲩⲟⲛ ϩⲁⲛⲛⲓⲩ-
ϯ ⲛⲓϣⲏⲛ' ➝

ο Ñογκλοм ερογ' ελκωτε εγοτπ' Ñκαρπος, αγω¹⁰ερεπεϲτνογΒε' ωωγ εΒολ
εмате. αϊναγ εγσ'ρηπε Ñρρο μπετ'πε μπεθρονος.¹⁵αγω αϊναγ εΝ̄ΖΒ̄' cω
Ñγπε, ερε'νεγπλακιν α'ωε μμαρκαρι'της, εγΖι'χμπεθρονος.' αϊναγ εγτο-
ογ Ñθρονος Ζαπε'εϲητ μπεϲτγλ'λεϲ πεϲτγλλος,²⁵ογα κατας'πιρ, εγπορÿ
Ζñ'ογνοσ Ñταϊο, ερε'ογκλοм μμαρ'καριτης Ζιϫμ̄'πετθρονος πεθ'ρονος,
ερεογ'ωιτν ρητ κατα'ϲτγλλος, ερε(78 Vi)νεκλατος μπογα' πογα πορεγ
εΒολ' εχñνεθρονος.' αϊναγ αΝακ παηϲε⁵εγνοσ Ñλογτηρ μπαγαν μπ-
κωτ̄', ερεογϲτηλλος Ñ'νογΒ Ζαρογ, ερε'γτοογ Ñϲογλην Ñ'νογΒ Ζαπλογ-
τηρ' κατασπιρ· αγω ερε'πεγτοογ Ñϲογλην' Ζατε εΒολ Ñναγ'νιм Ñθη
Ñογπγ'γη μμογ, ερεΖñ'φιαλη ÑνογΒ Ζι'μαρκαριτης Ζραϊ'Ζñπλογτηρ,
ερε'ΖÑματοϊ²⁰ Ζñπηϊ' ψατηπε Ñγη'μματοϊ εγφορει' ÑογνογΒ Ζιϣγñε,'
αγω ερεΖñμανι'ακης ÑνογΒ' Ζιπεγμακϩ', ερεΖñμοσϩ ÑνογΒ' мηρ Ζι-
χñνεντι'πε, ερεπογα πογα Ñ'Ζητογ ειρε Ñτογ' μμαϩε Ñγηϩ,' εмπ-
ρεμκαϩ εγ'φορει Ñτεγ Ζη. (Vii)ογγπηρε πε ναγ' εροογ. πεχαϊ μπαγ'-
γελος χε παχοεις,' ογπε πτωϣ μπεϊ'Ηϊ; μ̄λααγ Ñρρο' Ñτεπεϊκοϲмος'
ναεγκωτ Ñογηϊ' Ñτεϊϩη. πεχεπεαγ'γελος ναϊ χε ωε γε πεκογ'χαϊ ω πα-
мεριτ πα'ηϲε, μμÑτρροογ' τηρογ μπκοϲмος' εкπωϣα ωΝ Νογϲ'τηλλος Ñ-
ογωτ Ζñ'πιηϊ. αϊσωωΒ' πεχαϊ χε παχοεις,' πανιм πε πεϊηϊ;'πεχαγ
ναϊ Ñσι παγ'γελος χε παϊ πε²⁰ πηϊ Ñαπα Βικτωρ' πϣηρε Ñϩρωма'νος πε-
ϲτρατελα'της, πενταγ'κω Ñϲωγ²⁵ μπεγαϩιωм'μα μÑνεγϩγ'παρχωντα
τηρ'ογ, εαγϭι μπεγ'ϲταγρος αγογαϩγ̄'³⁰ Ñϲαπεγϫοεις·' ετΒεπαϊ αγτι
ναγ' μπιταϊο Ñτϭοτ. (79 Ri)αΝοκ δε πεχαϊ 'ναγ χε παχοεις,'ταмοϊ
επτωϣ'μπεϊηϊ μÑνιθ'ρονος τηρογ μÑ'νεϊγην ετπο'ρϣ εΒολ εϣωογ' εγοτπ Ñκαρπος.' πεχαγ ναϊ χε κ̄'ναγ ενιθρονος'τηρογ μÑνιγη(ν)' ετπο-

78 V i. 2nd h. (to ii 32). 9. l. -cwλHn. ii 1. l. εNaγ. 8. Second πε superfluous.
29. γ added. 32. l. μπειταειο. 79 R i i. 1st h. (to ii 33).

Boh. οϊ νχλοм εροϥ μπκωτ' εγοπτ νκαρπος εγνα'νεγ·'' ογοζ ερεπεϲθοινογ-
ϥι νΝιϣ'γην νοτεμ μμαγω. ογο'Ζ' αϊναγ εογϲρηπι νο[γρ]ω' χη Ζιϫενπιθρονο[ϲ], ογ[οϩ]'αϊναγ εχλοϊ Β̄ μμαργαριτηϲ'' χιτ Ζιϫενπιθρονο[ϲ] αϊ-'
χογνϥ ον αϊναγ ενιϲτγ'λλοϲ Ñτενιϲτοα ερεογ'ον νθρονοϲ ϲαπεϲιεΒτ (l. Ᾱ
νθρονοϲ ϲαπεϲΗτ?) μπιϲτγλλοϲ πιϲτγλοϲ, ογαϊ' καταϲϥιρ μπιϲτγλ'λοϲ.'
ναγφορϣ πε ϩενογταϊ[ο] ογο'Ζ' ερεογχλοм μμαργαριτηϲ'ϩενπιθρονοϲ νιθρο-
νοϲ,'' ογοϩ ναρεογνιϣϯ νψγην ρητ πε κατεθρονοϲ, ερεφογαι φογαι ννιταρ
φορÿ' εΒολ Ζιϫεννιθρονοϲ.'ανοκ παηϲι αϊναγ εογλογτηρ'[

ⲣⲱ ⲉⲃⲟⲗ ϩⲓⲧⲟⲟⲧ· ⲛⲁⲓ ⲛⲉ ⲙ̄ⲙⲁⲛⲧⲟⲛ ⲛ̄ⲣⲱⲙⲉ ⲛⲓⲙ ⲉⲧⲛⲁϯⲉⲟⲟⲩ ⲛ̄ⲟⲩⲡⲉⲧⲟⲩⲁ-
ⲁⲃ ϩⲓⲭⲙ̄ⲡⲕⲁϩ· ⲁⲛⲟⲕ ⲇⲉ ⲡⲉϫⲁⲓ ⲛⲁⲩ ϫⲉ ⲡⲁϫⲟⲉⲓⲥ ⲛⲁⲩ ⲛ̄ϫⲉ ⲙⲁⲧⲁⲙⲟⲓ ⲉ-
ⲡⲉⲓⲧⲱⲩ· ⲁϥⲟⲩⲱϣⲃ ⲡⲉϫⲁϥ ⲛⲁⲓ ϫⲉ ⲉⲣϣⲁⲛⲟⲩⲣⲱⲙⲉ ⲕⲱⲧ ⲛ̄ⲟⲩⲙⲁⲣⲧⲩⲣⲓⲟⲛ
ϩⲁⲡⲣⲁⲛ ⲛ̄ⲟⲩⲡⲉⲧⲟⲩⲁⲁⲃ· ⲏ ⲛ̄ⲧⲉⲟⲩⲁ ϩⲱⲃ· ϩⲡⲥⲱⲙⲁ ⲛ̄ⲟⲩⲁ ϩⲛ̄ⲟⲩⲕⲁⲓⲥⲉ· ⲏ ⲛ̄-
ⲧⲉⲟⲩⲁ ϯ ⲛ̄ⲟⲩⲡⲣⲟⲥⲫⲟⲣⲁ ⲙ̄ⲡⲉϩⲟⲟⲩ ⲛ̄ⲟⲩⲡⲉⲧⲟⲩⲁⲁⲃ, (79 Rii) ⲏ ⲛ̄ϥϯ ⲛ̄ⲟⲩⲙⲛ̄ⲧ-
ⲛⲁ ⲛ̄ϩⲏⲕⲉ ⲙⲛ̄ⲛⲉⲛϫⲙⲟ ϩⲙ̄ⲡⲉϩⲟⲟⲩ ⲙ̄ⲡⲉϥⲣ̄ⲡⲙⲉⲉⲩⲉ, ⲏ ⲛ̄ⲧⲉⲟⲩⲁ ⲧⲟⲩⲇⲱⲣⲟⲛ ⲉ-
ⲡⲏⲓ ⲛ̄ⲟⲩⲡⲉⲧⲟⲩⲁⲁⲃ, ⲏ ⲛ̄ϥⲧⲁⲙⲓⲟ ⲛ̄ⲟⲩϫⲱⲱⲙⲉ ⲉⲡⲏⲓ ⲙ̄ⲡⲛⲟⲩⲧⲉ ϩⲁⲡⲉⲩⲣⲁⲛ, ⲏ ⲛ̄ϥ-
ⲱⲡ ⲛ̄ⲟⲩⲉⲩⲁⲅⲅⲉⲗⲓⲟⲛ ⲛ̄ϥⲕⲁⲁϥ ϩⲙ̄ⲡⲉϥⲙⲁⲣⲧⲩⲣⲓⲟⲛ ⲉⲩⲣ̄ⲡⲙⲉⲉⲩⲉ ⲛⲁϥ, ϩⲁⲡ-
ⲗⲱⲥ ⲩⲁϩⲣⲁⲓ ⲉⲩⲟⲉⲓⲕ ⲛ̄ⲟⲩⲱⲧ ⲉⲧⲉⲣⲉⲡⲣⲱⲙⲉ ⲛⲁⲧⲁⲁϥ, ⲩⲁⲩϩⲉ ⲉⲣⲟϥ ⲉⲩⲩⲁⲛⲉⲓ
ⲉⲃⲟⲗ ϩⲛ̄ⲥⲱⲙⲁ ϩⲓⲧⲛ̄ⲛⲉⲛⲥⲱⲙⲁ ⲛ̄ⲛⲉⲧⲟⲩⲁⲁⲃ· ⲕⲁⲓ ⲅⲁⲣ ⲩⲁⲣⲉⲙⲁⲣⲧⲩⲣⲟⲥ ⲃⲱⲕ ⲉ-
ϩⲟⲩⲛ· ⲩⲁⲡⲡⲁⲛⲧⲱⲕ̄ⲣⲁⲧⲱⲣ ⲛ̄ϥⲡⲁϩⲧϥ̄ ⲛ̄ϥⲟⲩⲱϣⲧ̄ ⲉϥϫⲱ ⲙ̄ⲙⲟⲥ ϫⲉ ⲡⲁϫⲟⲉⲓⲥ,
ⲭⲁⲣⲓⲍⲉ ⲛⲁⲓ ⲛ̄ⲧⲉⲓⲯⲩⲭⲏ, ϫⲉ ⲁⲥⲧⲙ̄ⲧⲟⲛ ⲛⲁⲓ ϩⲙ̄ⲡⲉⲓⲕⲟⲥⲙⲟⲥ· ⲉⲩⲱⲡⲉ ⲙⲉⲛ
ⲉⲧⲟ(ⲩⲓ)ⲗⲙ̄ ϩⲛ̄ϩⲁϩ ⲛ̄ⲛⲟⲃⲉ, ⲩⲁⲣⲉⲧⲉⲥⲙⲏ ⲉⲓ ⲉⲃⲟⲗ ϩⲛ̄ⲧⲁⲡⲣⲟ ⲙⲓⲭⲁⲏⲗ ϫⲉ ⲙⲉ-
ⲭⲉⲡ̄ϫⲟⲉⲓⲥ ⲡⲁⲛⲧⲱⲕ̄ⲣⲁⲧⲱⲣ ϫⲉ ϯ ⲛⲁⲥ ⲛ̄ϩⲉⲛⲕⲟⲩⲓ ⲛ̄ⲕⲟⲗⲁⲥⲓⲥ ⲉⲩⲛⲁϣⲧ, ⲙⲛ̄ⲛⲉⲥⲱⲥ
ⲛ̄ⲧⲁⲭⲁⲣⲓⲍⲉ ⲙ̄ⲙⲟⲥ ⲛⲁⲕ· ⲁⲩⲱ ⲛ̄ⲧⲉⲩⲛⲟⲩ ⲩⲁⲛⲧⲁⲁⲥ ⲉⲧⲟⲟⲧⲟⲩ ⲛ̄ⲛⲉⲃⲁⲥⲁⲛⲓⲥ·
ⲧⲏⲥ ⲛ̄ⲥⲩⲟⲕⲥ ϩⲛ̄ϩⲛ̄ⲕⲟⲗⲁⲥⲓⲥ ⲉⲩⲛⲁϣⲧ· ⲙⲛ̄ⲛⲉⲥⲱⲥ ⲛ̄ⲥⲩⲉⲓⲛⲉ ⲙ̄ⲙⲟⲥ ⲉϩⲣⲁⲓ
ⲉⲥⲟⲃⲩ̄ ⲛ̄ⲑⲉ ⲛ̄ⲟⲩⲭⲓⲟ(ⲛ), ⲁⲩⲱ ⲩⲁⲛⲧⲁⲁⲥ ⲉⲧⲟⲟⲧϥ̄ ⲙ̄ⲡⲡⲉⲧⲟⲩⲁⲁⲃ ⲛ̄ⲧⲁⲩ ϫⲓ ϩⲙⲟⲧ
ⲉϩⲱⲥ· ⲩⲁϥϫⲓⲧⲥ̄ ⲉϩⲟⲩ(ⲛ) ⲉⲡⲉϥⲏⲓ ⲛ̄ϥϯ ϩⲓⲱⲱⲥ ⲛ̄ⲟⲩϩⲃⲥⲱ ⲉⲥⲧⲁⲓⲏⲩ ⲛ̄ϥⲑⲙ̄ⲥⲟⲥ
ϩⲓϩⲙ̄ⲡⲉⲑⲣⲟⲛⲟⲥ ⲛ̄ϥⲧ ⲉϩⲱⲥ· ⲙ̄ⲡⲉⲕⲗⲟⲙ ⲛ̄ⲁⲧⲧⲁⲕⲟ, ⲛ̄ⲥⲟⲩⲱⲙ ⲉⲃⲟⲗ ϩⲛ̄ⲛⲁⲅⲁⲑⲟⲛ
ⲛ̄ⲛⲏⲩⲛ (Vii) ⲛ̄ⲥⲉⲙⲧⲟⲛ ⲙ̄ⲙⲟⲥ ⲩⲁⲉⲛⲉϩ· ⲧⲁⲓ ⲧⲉ ⲑⲉ ⲛ̄ⲟⲩⲟⲛ ⲛⲓⲙ ⲉⲧⲛⲁⲧⲉⲟⲟⲩ
ⲛ̄ⲟⲩⲡⲉⲧⲟⲩⲁⲁⲃ ϩⲓⲭⲙ̄ⲡⲕⲁϩ· ⲉⲧⲃⲉⲡⲁⲓ ⲛⲓⲑⲣⲟⲛⲟⲥ ⲙ̄ⲛⲓⲩⲏⲛ ⲥⲉϩⲛ̄ⲛⲏⲓ ⲛ̄ⲛⲉⲧⲟⲩ-
ⲁⲁⲃ ⲧⲏⲣⲟⲩ, ⲁⲩⲱ ⲧⲉⲓϥⲧⲟ ⲙ̄ⲡⲩⲏ ⲙ̄ⲙⲟⲟⲩ· ⲉⲧϩⲁⲇⲉ ⲉⲡⲉⲓⲗⲟⲩⲧⲏⲣ ⲉⲧϩⲛ̄ⲛⲏⲓ·
ⲛ̄ⲛⲉⲧⲟⲩⲁⲁⲃ ⲉⲧⲣⲉⲩⲥⲱ ⲉⲃⲟⲗ ⲛ̄ϩⲏⲧⲟⲩ. ⲁⲛⲟⲕ ⲇⲉ ⲡⲉϫⲁⲓ ⲙ̄ⲡⲁⲅⲅⲉⲗⲟⲥ ϫⲉ ⲡⲁϫⲟⲉⲓⲥ, ⲥⲉⲙⲁϣⲧ ⲙ̄ⲛⲛⲉⲣⲉⲏⲩ. ⲛ̄ⲧⲟⲩ ⲇⲉ ⲡⲉϫⲁⲩ ⲛⲁⲓ ϫⲉ ⲙⲛ̄ⲃⲟⲙ ⲉⲧⲣⲉⲩⲙⲁⲕⲧⲟⲩ, ⲁⲗⲗⲁ ⲡⲉⲧⲉⲣⲉⲡⲟⲩⲁ ⲡⲟⲩⲁ ⲟⲩⲁⲩϥ ϭⲛⲏⲩ ⲩⲁⲣⲟϥ. ⲁⲛⲟⲕ ⲇⲉ ⲡⲉϫⲁⲓ ⲛⲁⲩ ϫⲉ ⲡⲁϫⲟⲉⲓⲥ,
ⲛⲓⲙ ⲛⲉ ⲛⲓⲙⲁⲧⲟⲓ ⲉⲧϥⲟⲣⲉⲓ ⲡⲛⲓ ⲛⲁϩ ⲛ̄ⲧⲁⲓⲟ ⲛ̄ⲧⲉⲓϭⲟⲧ; ⲡⲉϫⲁⲩ (80 Ri) ⲛⲁⲓ ⲛ̄ϭⲓ
ⲡⲁⲅⲅⲉⲗⲟⲥ· ϫⲉ ⲕ̄ⲛⲁⲩ ⲉⲛⲓⲙⲁⲧⲟⲓ· ⲛⲁⲓ ϩⲉⲛⲁⲅⲅⲉⲗⲟⲥ ⲛⲉ ⲉⲩⲁϩⲉⲣⲁⲧⲟⲩ ⲉⲩⲇⲓⲁⲕⲟⲛⲉⲓ
ⲉⲛⲉⲧⲟⲩⲁⲁⲃ· ⲁⲩⲱ ⲉⲣⲩⲁⲛⲡⲣⲟⲉⲓⲥ ⲙ̄ⲡⲏⲓ ⲉⲓ ⲉⲃⲟⲗ ϩⲛ̄ⲧⲡⲟⲗⲓⲥ, ⲩⲁⲙ̄ⲙⲟⲟⲩⲉ ϩⲓⲑⲏ
ⲙ̄ϩⲓⲡⲁϩⲟⲩ ⲙ̄ⲙⲟϥ ⲉⲩⲧⲉⲟⲟⲩ ⲛⲁϥ· ⲁⲛⲟⲕ ⲇⲉ ⲁⲓⲣ̄ϣⲡⲏⲣⲉ ⲉⲙⲁⲧⲉ, ϫⲉ ⲩⲁⲣⲉ-

79 Ri 16. ℓ. ⲛ̄ⲟⲩⲡⲉⲧⲟⲩⲁⲁⲃ. ii 21. ℓ. ϩⲓⲧⲛ̄ⲛ̄ⲥⲱⲙⲁ. V i 1. 2nd ℓ. (ⲧⲟ 18). 3. ℓ. ϩⲛ̄ⲧⲁⲡ-
ⲧⲣⲟ ⲙ̄ⲙⲓⲭⲁⲏⲗ. 4–6. ℓ. ⲡⲉⲭⲉⲡϫⲟⲉⲓⲥ ⲡⲡⲁⲛⲧⲟⲕⲣⲁⲧⲱⲣ. 8 f. ℓ. ⲙ̄ⲛ̄ⲥⲱⲥ. 14. ℓ. ⲛ̄ⲥⲉ-
ⲟⲙⲥⲉ. 16 f. ⲛ̄ⲥⲉⲉⲓⲛⲉ. 19. 1st ℓ. (ⲧⲟ 81 R i 6).

ⲣⲱⲙⲉˈ ⲛ̄ⲥⲁⲣⲝ ⳿ ⲍⲓ ⲥⲛⲟⲩˈ ⲕⲗⲏⲣⲟⲛⲟⲙⲉⲓ ⲛ̄ⲛⲉⲓⲛⲟϭ ⲛ̄ⲧⲁⲓⲟˈ ⲉⲧⲃⲉ ⲟⲩⲕⲟⲧⲓ ⁲ⲛ̄ˈⲍⲓⲥⲉ ⲉⲧⲛ̄
ⲛⲁⲩ ⲟⲛ ϥˈ ⲍⲓ ⲥⲛ̄ⲡⲕⲁⲍ ⲍⲁ⳿ⲡⲣⲁⲛ ⲙ̄ⲡϫⲟⲉⲓⲥ.ˈ ⲡⲉϫⲁⲓ ⲛⲁⲩ ⲟⲛ ϫⲉˈ ⲡⲁϫⲟⲉⲓⲥ, ⲙⲁ
ⲧⲁ⳿ⲙⲟⲓ ⲉⲡⲉⲓⲕⲉϩⲱⲃ.ˈ ⲉⲣϣⲁⲛ ⲟⲩ ⲡⲣⲉⲥ⳿ⲃⲩⲧⲉⲣⲟⲥ ⲏ ⲟⲩ ⲇⲓ⳿ⲁⲕⲟⲛⲟⲥ ϣⲱⲡⲉˈ ⲍ̄ⲡⲏⲓ ⲛ̄
ⲟⲩⲡⲉˈⲧⲟⲩⲁⲁⲃ ⲛ̄ϥⲧⲁ⳿ⲕⲟ ⲛ̄ⲧⲉ ⲡⲣⲟⲥⲫⲟ⳿ⲣⲁ ⲉⲧⲟⲩ⳿ϥ ⲙ̄ⲙⲟⲥ̇ ⲉⲡⲧⲟⲡⲟⲥ ⲍ̄ⲛⲟⲩ (80 Rii) ⲙⲛ̄ⲧ
ϣⲛⲁ, ⲟⲩ⳿ⲡⲉ ⲡⲉϥϩⲱⲃ; ⲡⲉˈϫⲉ ⲡⲁⲅⲅⲉⲗⲟⲥ ⲛⲁⲓ⳿ ϫⲉ ⲥⲱⲧⲙ̄ ⲧⲁⲧⲁ⳿ⲙⲟⲕ· ⲉⲣϣⲁⲛ ⲟⲩ⳿ⲣⲱ
ⲙⲉ ⲍ̄ⲛ ⲧⲡⲟⲗⲓⲥˈ ⲏ ⲍ̄ⲛ ⲧⲙⲉ ϯ ⲛⲟⲩ⳿ⲡⲣⲟⲥⲫⲟⲣⲁ ⲉ ⲡⲧⲟ⳿ⲡⲟⲥ ⲛ̄ⲟⲩ ⲡⲉ ⲧⲟⲩⲁⲁ⳿ⲃ ϩⲁ ⲡ ⲥⲱⲧⲉ
ⲛ̄ⲧ ⲉϥⲯⲩⲭⲏ, ϣⲓⲛⲁ⳿ ⲉϥ ϣⲓⲛⲉ ⲛ̄ⲥⲱⲥ ⲛ̄ⲧⲟⲟⲧϥ̄ ⲛ̄ ⲡ ⲟⲓⲕⲟ⳿ⲛⲟⲙⲟⲥ· ⲉⲩⲧⲁ⳿ⲅⲁⲡⲏ ⲅⲁⲣ ϩⲛ̄ ⲟⲩ⳿
ⲙ̄ⲛ̄ⲧⲁⲧ ϩⲟⲧ ϩ̄ⲧ.ˈ ⲉϣⲱⲡⲉ ⲇⲉ ⲡⲉ⳿ⲡⲣⲉⲥⲃⲩⲧⲉⲣⲟⲥˈ ⲏ ⲡ ⲇⲓⲁⲕⲟⲛⲟⲥ ˈⲏ ⲡ ⲟⲓⲕⲟⲛⲟⲙⲟⲥˈ
ⲉⲓⲣⲉ ⲙ̄ⲡⲩⲛ̄ ϩⲩⲉˈ ⲙ̄ ⲡ ⲡⲉ ⲧⲟⲩⲁⲁⲃˈ ⲕⲁⲗⲱⲥ ⲁ ϩⲛ̄ⲕⲁ⳿ⲧⲁ ⲫⲣⲟⲛⲉⲓ, ⲁⲩⲱ ⲛ̄ϥ ⲥⲡⲟⲩⲇⲁⲍⲉ
ⲉⲣⲟϥ ϩⲛ̄ ⲟⲩ ⲥⲡⲟ⳿ⲇⲏ, ⲉϥϣⲁⲛⲉⲓ⳿ ⲉⲃⲟⲗ ϩⲛ̄ ⲥⲱⲙⲁˈ ϣⲁⲣⲉ ⲡ ⲡⲉ ⲧⲟⲩ⳿ⲁⲁⲃ ϫⲓⲧϥ̄ ⲉϩⲟⲩ(ⲛ)
ⲉⲡⲉϥ ⲏⲓ ⲛ̄ϥⲃ̄ⲙ⳿ⲥⲟⲩ ϩⲓ ⲃ̄ⲛⲟⲩ ⲑ⳿ⲣⲟⲛⲟⲥ ⲛ̄ϥ ϯ ⲉ ⲁ ⲭϥ (Vi) ⲛ̄ⲟⲩⲕⲗⲟⲙ ⲛ̄ϥ ⲧ⳿ⲣⲉⲩ ⲇⲓ
ⲁⲕⲟⲛⲉⲓ ⲉ⳿ⲣⲟϥ ⲕⲁⲗⲱⲥ.ˈ ⲉϣⲱⲡⲉ ⲇⲉ ϩ ⲱⲟ ⲩˈ ⲉϥϣⲁⲛ ⲃⲱ ⲉϥⲟⲩ⳿ⲱⲙ ⲉϥ ⲥⲱ ⲍ̄ⲛ
ⲟⲩ⳿ⲙⲛ̄ⲧ ϣⲛⲁ ⲉϥ ⲧⲁ⳿ⲕⲟ ⲛ̄ⲛⲉ ⲡⲣⲟⲥⲫⲟⲣⲁˈ ⲉⲧⲟⲩ ϯ ⲙ̄ⲙⲟⲟⲩ ϩⲙ̄ ⳿ⲡⲣⲁⲛ ⲙ̄ ⲡ ⲡⲉ ⲧⲟⲩ⳿ⲁⲁⲃ,
ϣⲁⲣⲉ ⲡ ⲡⲉ⳿ⲧⲟⲩⲁⲁⲃ ⲧⲣⲉⲩ ϫⲓⲧϥ̄ˈ ⲉ ϩⲉⲛ ⲕⲟⲗⲁⲥⲓⲥ ⲉⲩ⳿ⲛⲁ ϣⲧ̄ ⲛ̄ⲁⲧ ⲃ̄ⲙ ⲡⲉ ⲩˈ ϣⲓⲛⲉ· ⲛⲁⲓ
ⲛⲉⲧ⳿ⲛⲁⲧⲁⲝⲉ ⲡ ⲟⲓⲕⲟⲛⲟ⳿ⲙⲟⲥ ⲉⲧⲉⲛϥ̄ ϣⲓ ⲣⲉˈ ⲁⲛ ⲙ̄ ⲡⲉⲧⲥⲟⲩⲧⲱ(ⲛ) ϩⲁ ⲡ ⲏⲓ ⲙ̄ ⲡ ⲛⲟⲩⲧⲉˈ
ⲛ̄ⲧⲉⲣⲉⲓ ⲥⲱⲧⲙ̄ ⲇⲉˈ ⲉⲛⲁⲓ, ⲁⲛⲟⲕ ⲡⲁ ⲏ ⲥⲉ ⲁⲓ ⲩⲧⲟⲣⲧⲣ̄ ⲉⲙⲁⲧⲉ, ⲁⲩⲱ ⲁⲓˈⲣ̄ ϩⲩⲡ ⲏⲣⲉ. ⲡⲉ
ϫⲁⲩˈ ⲛⲁⲓ ⲛ̄ϭⲓ ⲡ ⲁⲅⲅⲉⲗⲟⲥ; ˈϫⲉ ⲙ̄ ⲡⲉⲕ ⲥⲱⲧⲙ̄ ⲛ̄ⲧⲟⲕ ⲉⲧⲃⲉ ⲛ̄ϣⲩ⳿ⲏⲣⲉ ⲛ̄ ϫⲏⲗ ϫⲉ ⲛ̄ⲧⲁ⳿
ⲟⲩ ϣⲱⲡⲉ ⲙ̄ⲙⲟⲟⲩ; ˈ ⲁ ⲩ ⲁ ⲙⲁ ϫⲧⲉ ⲟⲛ ⲛ̄ⲧⲁ ϭⲓⲝ ⲛ̄ϭⲓ ⲡⲁⲅ⳿ⲅⲉⲗⲟⲥ, ⲁ ϥⲭⲓⲧ⳿ ⲁ ϥ ⲧⲥⲁⲃⲟⲓ
ⲉ ⲕⲉ (Vii) ⲏⲓ ⲛ̄ⲑⲉ ⲛ̄ ⲩ ⲟⲣⲡ̄, ˈⲉⲣⲉ ⲩϥ ⲛ̄ ⲥⲧⲩⲗⲗⲟⲥˈ ϩ ⲁ ⲡ ⲏ ⲓ ⲉⲧ ⲙⲙⲁⲩ, ⲁⲩⲱ ⲩ ⲧⲟⲟⲩ ⲛ̄ ⲑⲣⲟ
ⲛⲟⲥ ⲕⲁⲧⲁ ⲥⲧⲩⲗⲗⲟⲥ, ˈ ⲁⲩⲱ ⲟⲩ ⲗⲟⲩⲧ ⲏⲣˈ ⲉ ⲩ ϩ ⲛ̄ⲧ ⲙ ⲏⲧⲉ ⲙ̄ ⲡ ⲏ ⲓ, ˈ ⲁⲩⲱ ⲉⲣⲉ ⲟ ⲩ ϣ ⲏ ⲛ̄ˈ ⲣⲏⲧ
ⲕⲁⲧⲁ ⲥⲧⲩⲗⲗⲟⲥ, ˈ ⲁⲩⲱ ⲛ̄ ⲉⲣⲉ ⲡ ⲗ ⲟⲩⲧⲏⲣ ⲉⲧ ϩ ⲛ̄ ⲧ ⲙⲏⲧⲉˈ ⲙ̄ ⲡ ⲏⲓ ⲙⲉϩ ⲉⲃⲟⲗ ϩ ⲁ ⲡⲉⲩ ⲧⲟⲟⲩ
ⲛ̄ ⲓ ⲣ̄⳿ⲣ ⲟ· ⲁⲩⲱ ⲁ ⲓ ⲛⲁⲩ ˈ ⲉ ϥ ⲟ ⲙ ⲛ̄ ⲧ ⲛ̄ ⲑ ⲣ ⲟ ⳿ ⲛⲟⲥ ⲉⲩ ϫ ⲟⲥⲉ ⲉⲙ ⲁ ⲧ ⲉ ⲁ ⲩ ⲱ ⲉ ⲩ ⲧ ⲁ ⲏⲩ, ˈ ⲉ ⲣⲉ
ϩ ⲉ ⲛ ⲩ ⲏ ⲛ ⲕ ⲱ ⳿ ⲧ ⲉ ⲣ ⲟ ⲟ ⲩ ⲉ ⲩ ⲧ ⲏ ⳿ ⲛ̄ ⲕ ⲁ ⲣ ⲡ ⲟ ⲥ, ⲁⲩⲱ ˈ ⲉ ⲣ ⲉ ⲟ ⲩ ⲕ ⲗ ⲟ ⲙ ⲙ̄ ⲙ ⲁ ⲣ ⳿ ⲕ ⲁ ⲣ ⲓ ⲧ ⲏ ⲥ
ϩ ⲓ ⲃ ⲙ̄ ⳿ ⲛ ⲟ ⲩ ⲁ ⲡ ⲟ ⲩ ⲁ ⲛ̄ ⲛ ⲉ ⲑ ⳿ ⲣ ⲟ ⲛ ⲟ ⲥ. ⲡ ⲉ ϫ ⲉ ˈ ⲡ ⲁ ⲅ ⲅ ⲉ ⲗ ⲟ ⲥ ⲛ ⲁ ⲓ ϫ ⲉ ˈ ⲕ ⲛ ⲁ ⲩ ⲉ ⲡ ⲉ ⲓ ⲏ ⲓ · ˈ ⲡ ⲱ ⲕ
ⲡⲉ ⲙⲛ̄ ⲧⲉⲕ⳿ⲥⲱⲛⲉ ⲙ̄ⲡⲗⲁⲩ⳿ⲗⲟⲥ ⲡⲉⲕϫⲃⲏⲣ.ˈ ⲉⲓⲥ ⲡⲉⲧⲛ̄ ⲟ ⲙ ⲛ̄ⲧ ˈ ⲛ̄ ⲕⲗⲟⲙ ⲥ ⲃ ⲧⲱ ⲧ
ⲛⲏⲧⲛ̄, ⲟ ⲩ ⲁ ϩ ⲁ ⲧ ⲉ ⳿ ⲧ ⲛ̄ ⲙ ⲛ̄ ⲧ ⲯ ⲩ ⲙ ⲟ (81 Ri) ⲟ ⲩ ⲁ ϩ ⲁ ⲡ ⲉ ⲧ ⲛ̄ ⲥ ⲛ ⲟ ⲩ ˈ ⲉ ⲧ ⲟ ⲩ ⲛ ⲁ ⲡ ⲁ ϩ
ⲧ ϥ̄ ˈ ⲉ ⲃ ⲟ ⲗ ⲉ ϫ ⲙ̄ ⲡ ⲣ ⲁ ⲛ ˈ ⲙ̄ ⲡ ⲉ ⲭ ̄ ⲥ · ⲁ ⲩ ⲱ ⲕ ⲉ ⲟ ⲩ ⲁ ⲉ ⲧ ⲃ ⲉ ⲧ ⲉ ⲧ ⲛ̄ ϩ ⲁ ⲕ ⳿ ⲛ ⲓ ⲁ. ⲛ ⲉ ⲧ ⲛ̄ ⲥ ⲱ ⲙ ⲁ ˈ
ⲇ ⲉ ⲥ ⲉ ⲛ ⲁ ϣ ⲱ ⲡ ⲉ ϩ ⲛ̄ ⲛ ⲟ ⲩ ⲧ ⲟ ⲡ ⲟ ⲥ ⲛ̄ ⲟ ⲩ ⲱ ⲧ ϩ ⲓ ϫ ⲙ̄ ⳿ ⲡ ⲕ ⲁ ϩ. ⲁ ⲩ ⲱ ⲡ ⲉ ϫ ⲁ ⲓ ⲙ̄ ⲡ ⲁ ⲅ ⳿ ⲅ ⲉ ⲗ ⲟ ⲥ
ϫ ⲉ ⲡ ⲁ ϫ ⲟ ⲉ ⲓ ⲥ, ⲁ ⲕ ˈ ϯ ⲉ ⲟ ⲟ ⲩ ⲛ ⲁ ⲓ ⲙ̄ ⲙ ⲁ ⲧ ⲉ ⲡ ⲁ ⳿ ⲣ ⲁ ⲡ ϥ ⲓ · ⲁ ⲗ ⲗ ⲁ ⲟ ⲩ ⲕ ⲟ ⲩ ⲓ ˈ ⲡ ⲉ ⲡ ⲁ ⲏ ⲓ ⲡ ⲁ ⲣ ⲁ
ⲡ ⳿ ⲉ ϣ ⲟ ⲣ ⲡ̄. ⲁ ϥ ⲟ ⲩ ⲱ ϣ ⲃ ̄ ⲡ ⲉ ϫ ⲁ ⲩ ⲛ ⲁ ⲓ ϫ ⲉ ⲛ̄ ⲉ ⲕ ⳿ ⲥ ⲟ ⲟ ⲩ ⲛ ⲁ ⲛ ϫ ⲉ ⲟ ⲩ ⲉ ⲧ ⳿ ⲡ ⲉ ⲟ ⲟ ⲩ ⲛ ⲟ ⲩ ⲉ ⲣ ⲣ ⲟ,

ⲟⲩⲉⲧ ⲛⲉⲩⲟⲩ ⲛⲟⲩⲁⲣⲭⲱ(ⲛ);' ⲙⲛⲛⲉⲥⲁⲛⲁⲓ ⲇⲉ ⲁⲩⲁ'ⲙⲁⲍⲧⲉ ⲛⲧⲁⲥⲓⲝ, ⲁⲩ'ⲉⲓⲛⲉ ⲙⲙⲟⲓ
ⲉⲡⲕⲁ ⲛ'ⲧⲁⲩⲭⲓⲧ ⲛⲍⲏⲧϥ.' ⲁⲩⲱ ⲛⲉⲓⲣⲩⲡⲏⲣⲉ ⲛⲛⲁ'ⲕⲁⲑⲟⲛ ⲉⲧⲉⲣⲉⲡⲛⲟⲩ'ⲧⲉ ⲛⲁⲧⲁⲁⲩ
ⲛⲛⲉⲩ'ⲡⲉⲧⲟⲩⲁⲁⲃ ⲛⲩⲉⲃⲓⲱ' ⲛⲛⲉⲍⲓⲥⲉ ⲉⲧⲟⲩⲛⲁ'ⲩⲁⲗⲟⲩ ⲍⲓⲕⲛⲕⲁⲍ.' ⲁⲥⲩⲱⲡⲉ ⲇⲉ
ⲛⲧⲉⲣⲉⲡⲁⲅⲅⲉⲗⲟⲥ ⲉⲓⲛⲉ ⲛⲁⲗⲁ' ⲡⲁⲛⲥⲉ ⲉⲍⲟⲩⲛ ⲉⲡⲉⲩ'ⲧⲉⲕⲟ, ⲁⲩⲁⲥⲡⲁⲥⲉ ⲙⲙⲟϥ,'
ⲁⲩⲃⲱⲕ ⲉⲍⲣⲁⲓ ⲉⲙⲛ (81 R ii) ⲏⲩⲉ ⲉⲣⲉⲡⲙⲁⲕⲁ'ⲣⲓⲟⲥ ϭⲱⲩⲧ ⲛⲥⲱⲩ.' ⲁⲥⲩⲱⲡⲉ ⲇⲉ ⲛ-
ⲧⲉⲣⲉ'ⲛⲉⲧⲟⲩⲁⲁⲃ ⲧⲱⲟⲩⲛ (ⲛ) ϩⲧⲟⲟⲩⲉ, ⲁⲩⲛⲁⲩ ⲉⲛ'ⲡⲉⲧⲟⲩⲁⲁⲃ ⲁⲡⲁ' ⲡⲁⲛⲥⲉ ⲉⲣⲉⲡⲉⲩ-
ⲍⲟ ⲙⲍ' ⲛⲣⲁⲩⲉ, ⲁⲩⲱ ⲛⲉⲩϭⲟⲓ' ⲛⲉⲩⲩⲉⲩϭⲛⲟⲩⲩⲉ' ⲉⲃⲟⲗ· ⲁⲩⲉⲓⲙⲉ ⲭⲉ ⲟⲩ'ⲥⲱⲗⲡ
ⲉⲃⲟⲗ ⲛⲧⲁⲩ'ⲛⲁⲩ ⲉⲣⲟϥ. ⲁⲩⲱ ⲁⲩ'ⲣⲉⲕ ⲉⲣⲟϥ ⲭⲉ ⲉⲕⲉ'ⲧⲁⲙⲟⲛ ⲉⲛⲉⲛⲧⲁⲕ'ⲛⲁⲩ
ⲉⲣⲟⲟⲩ ⲧⲏⲣⲟⲩ' ⲛϥⲧⲙ̄ϩⲉⲡⲗⲁⲁⲩⲉ' ⲉⲣⲟⲛ. ⲡⲡⲉⲧⲟⲩⲁⲁⲃ ⲇⲉ ⲁⲡⲁ ⲡⲁⲛⲥⲉ' ⲁⲩⲧⲁⲙⲟⲟⲩ ⲉⲛⲛⲧⲁⲩ'ⲛⲁⲩ ⲉⲣⲟⲟⲩ ⲧⲏⲣⲟⲩ·' ⲛⲉⲧⲟⲩⲁⲁⲃ ⲇⲉ ⲛⲧⲉⲣⲟⲩ'ⲥⲱⲧⲙ̄ ⲉⲛⲁⲓ,
ⲁⲩⲧⲉ'ⲟⲟⲩ ⲉϩⲛⲟⲩⲧⲉ ⲉⲍⲛ̄'ⲛⲁⲕⲁⲑⲟⲛ ⲉⲧⲟⲩ'ⲛⲁⲭⲓⲧⲟⲩ ⲉⲃⲟⲗ' ϩⲓⲧⲟⲟⲧϥ ⲙ̄ⲡϫⲟⲉⲓⲥ.'
ⲁⲥⲩⲱⲡⲉ ⲇⲉ ⲙⲛ̄'ⲥⲁⲛⲁⲓ ⲁⲩⲙⲟⲟⲥ' ⲉⲡⲃⲏⲙⲁ ⲛϭⲓ ⲡ'ⲇⲟⲩⲝ ϩⲙ̄ⲡⲉⲑⲉⲁ'ⲇⲣⲟⲛ· ⲁⲩⲕⲉⲗⲉⲩⲉ' ⲉⲧⲣⲉⲩⲉⲓⲛⲉ ⲛⲛⲉⲧⲟⲩ'ⲁⲁⲃ ⲛⲁⲩ· ⲡⲉⲭⲁⲩ (V i) ⲭⲉ ⲧⲉⲧⲛⲁⲑⲩⲥⲓⲁ'ⲍⲉ ⲭⲓⲛ-
ⲙ̄ⲙⲟⲛ;' ⲁⲩⲟⲩⲱϣⲃ ⲛϭⲓ' ⲛⲉⲧⲟⲩⲁⲁⲃ ⲭⲉ' ⲩⲁⲣⲉⲟⲩⲩⲁⲭⲉ' ⲛⲟⲩⲱⲧ ⲣⲉⲩⲧⲟⲩ'ⲥⲁⲃⲉ·
ⲡⲁⲑⲏⲧ ⲇⲉ' ⲛⲧⲟϥ ⲩⲁⲕϩⲓⲥⲉ ⲉⲕ'ϯⲥⲃⲱ ⲛⲁϥ. ⲙⲉⲩⲁⲓⲥ'ⲑⲁⲛⲉ. ⲩⲁϥϫⲟⲟⲥ'ⲅⲁⲣ ⲛϭⲓ
ⲡⲥⲟⲫⲟⲥ' ⲥⲟⲗⲟⲙⲱⲛ ⲭⲉ ⲭ'ⲡⲓⲉⲩⲥⲁⲃⲉ ⲧⲁⲣⲉϥ'ⲙⲉⲣⲓⲧⲕ̄· ⲙ̄ⲡⲉⲣϯ'ⲥⲃⲱ ⲛⲟⲩⲁⲑⲏⲧ.'
ⲡⲗⲏⲛ ⲉⲛⲉⲛⲧⲟⲕ' ⲟⲩⲥⲁⲃⲉ ⲉⲛⲉⲕⲛⲁ'ⲭⲉⲉⲓⲩⲁⲭⲉ ⲁⲛ'ⲛⲕⲉⲥⲟⲡ ⲡⲉ·' ⲡⲇⲟⲩⲝ ⲇⲉ
ⲛⲧⲉⲣⲉϥ'ⲥⲱⲧⲙ̄ ⲉⲛⲁⲓ, ⲡⲉⲭⲁⲩ' ⲭⲉ ⲟⲩⲕⲟⲩⲛ ⲛⲧ'ⲕⲟⲩⲥⲟϭ ⲁⲩⲱ ⲛⲁ'ⲑⲏⲧ; ⲁⲩⲕⲉⲗⲉⲩⲉ'
ⲛⲧⲉⲩⲛⲟⲩ ⲉⲧⲣⲉⲩ'ⲩⲱⲱⲧ ⲛⲛⲉⲩⲗⲁⲥ' ⲁⲩⲱ ⲛⲥⲉⲡⲱⲣⲕ̄' ⲛ̄ⲛⲉⲩⲃⲁⲗ ⲛⲥⲉⲧⲁ'ⲁⲩ ⲉⲍⲣⲁⲓ
ⲉⲛⲉⲩϭⲓⲝ.' ⲁⲩⲱ ⲁⲩⲧⲣⲉⲩⲉⲓⲛⲉ' ⲛ̄ⲍⲉⲛϩⲩⲙⲟⲩ ⲛ'ⲥⲉⲧⲟⲕⲥⲟⲩ ⲉⲡⲕⲁⲍ' ⲛⲥⲉϫⲱⲗⲕ ⲛ̄-
ⲛⲉ (V ii) ⲟⲩⲁⲁⲃ ⲉⲣⲟⲟⲩ ⲩⲁ(ⲛ)'ⲧⲉⲛⲉⲩⲕⲉⲉⲥ ⲛⲟⲩⲍⲉ' ⲉⲃⲟⲗ ⲛⲛⲉⲩⲉⲣⲏⲩ.' ⲙⲛ̄-
ⲥⲱⲥ ⲟⲛ ⲁⲩⲕⲉ'ⲗⲉⲩⲉ ⲉⲧⲣⲉⲩⲉⲓⲛⲉ' ⲛⲟⲩⲥⲓⲃⲉ ⲙⲛⲟⲩ'ⲗⲁⲙϫⲁⲧⲛ̄ ⲙⲛ̄'ⲟⲩⲁⲥⲫⲁⲗ-
ⲧⲟⲛ' ⲙⲛⲟⲩⲕⲟⲛⲓⲁ, ⲁⲩ'ⲛⲁϣⲟⲩ ⲉⲩⲭⲁⲗⲭⲓⲟⲛ, ⲁⲩⲥⲁⲍⲧⲉ ϩⲁ'ⲣⲟⲟⲩ ⲩⲁⲛⲧⲉ ⲡⲉⲩ'
ⲃⲣⲃⲣ ⲭⲓⲥⲉ ⲉⲙⲁⲧⲉ,' ⲁⲩⲧⲣⲉⲩⲟⲩⲱⲛ ⲉ'ⲣⲱⲟⲩ ⲛⲛⲉⲧⲟⲩⲁ'ⲁⲃ ϩⲛⲟⲩⲁⲭⲱ ⲙ̄ⲡⲉ ⲛⲓⲡⲉ,
ⲁⲩⲡⲱⲍⲧ' ⲉⲍⲣⲁⲓ ⲉⲣⲱⲟⲩ. ⲁⲩⲱ' ⲛⲧⲉⲩⲛⲟⲩ ⲁϥⲉⲓ ⲉⲃⲟⲗ' ϩⲛⲧⲡⲉ ⲛϭⲓ ϩⲣⲁ'ⲫⲁⲏⲗ

---

81 R ii 8. l. ⲛⲉⲩϩⲟⲓⲧⲉ. 10. l. ⲉⲃⲟⲗ. 16. l. -ⲗⲁⲁⲩ. 19 f. l. ⲉⲛⲉⲛⲧⲁⲩⲛⲁⲩ. V i 1.
l. ϩⲗ. (ϯⲟ 82 R ii 2). 1 f. l. ⲧⲉⲧⲛⲁⲑⲩⲥⲓⲁⲍⲉ. 22 f. l. ⲁⲛⲧⲟⲩⲥⲟϭ. lib. l. ⲛⲟⲩⲥⲓⲩⲉ

ⲃⲟⲗ. E. W. f. 4 (p. 117) (Cod. Tisch.)
(R) ⲕⲟⲛⲓⲁ ⲛⲁⲧⲱⲩⲉϩ, ⲟⲧⲟϩ ⲁⲩϫⲓⲧⲟⲩ' ⲉϩⲣⲏⲓ ⲉⲩⲭⲁⲗⲕⲓⲟⲛ, ⲁⲩⲥⲁϯ ϩⲁ'ⲣⲟⲩ
ⲩⲁⲛⲧⲉ ⲡⲉⲩⲃⲉⲣⲃⲉⲣ ϭⲓⲥⲓ ⲉⲡ'ⲩⲱⲓ ⲉⲙⲁⲩⲱ. ⁵ ⲁ[ⲩⲟⲩⲁ]ⲥⲁϩⲛⲓ ⲛ[ⲭⲉ ⲡⲓⲇⲟⲩⲝ]
ⲉⲑⲣⲟⲩ'ⲟⲩⲱⲛ ⲛⲣⲱⲟⲩ ⲛⲛⲏ ⲉⲑⲟⲩⲁⲃ ⲛⲥⲉ'[. . . . .] (illegible traces of c. 15 letters)
ⲩⲟⲣ.'[. . . . .]ⲉⲥ ⲣⲁⲫⲁⲏⲗ →

ⲡⲁⲅⲅⲉⲗⲟⲥ·ⲁϥⲧⲣⲉⲡⲉⲭⲁⲗⲭⲓⲱⲛ ⲉⲣⲑⲉ ⲛ̅ⲟⲩⲙⲟ'ⲟⲩ ⲉⲩⲕⲏⲃ, ⲁⲩⲱ ⲁϥⲧⲣⲉⲩϭⲗⲟϭ ⲍ̅ⲛ̅'ⲣⲱⲩ
ⲛ̅ⲛⲉⲧⲟⲩ'ⲁⲁⲃ ⲛ̅ⲑⲉ ⲛ̅ⲟⲩⲉⲃⲓⲱ·ⲁϥⲧⲱⲟⲩⲛ ⲁⲉ ⲛ̅ϭⲓ ⲡⲁⲟⲩϩ, ⲁⲩⲁ'ⲛⲁⲭⲱⲣⲉⲓ, ⲁϥ'ⲕⲁⲛⲉ-
ⲧⲟⲩⲁⲁⲃ ⲉⲩ'ⲛⲏⲭ ⲉⲃⲟⲗ ⲍ̅ⲙ̅ⲡⲉ'ⲑⲉⲁⲇⲣⲟⲛ. ⲡⲁⲅ(82 R ii)ⲅⲉⲗⲟⲥ ⲁⲉ ⲙ̅ⲡⲛⲟⲉⲓⲥ'ⲁⲩ ϣⲱⲍ
ⲉⲛⲉⲧⲟⲩ'ⲁⲁⲃ, ⲁϥⲧⲟⲩⲛⲟⲥⲟⲩ·ⲁⲩⲱ ⲁⲩⲧⲁⲗϭⲟⲟⲩ ⲉ'ⲃⲟⲗ ⲍ̅ⲛ̅ⲛⲉⲩⲃⲁⲥⲁ'ⲛⲟⲥ·ⲁⲩⲱ ⲁⲩⲧⲣⲉ-/
ⲛⲉⲩⲃⲁⲗ ⲛⲁⲩ ⲉⲃⲟⲗ·ⲁⲛⲉⲩⲗⲁⲥ ⲥⲟⲟⲩⲧⲛ̅·ⲁ'ⲩⲅⲁϣⲉ, ⲁⲩⲥⲙⲟⲩ ⲉⲡⲛⲟⲩⲧⲉ·ⲁⲩⲱ'ⲁϥⲥⲫⲣⲁ-
ⲅⲓⲍⲉ ⲙ̅'ⲙⲟⲟⲩ, ⲁⲩⲃⲱⲕ ⲉϩ'ⲣⲁⲓ ⲉⲡⲏⲩⲉ ⲍ̅ⲛ̅'ⲟⲩⲉⲟⲟⲩ.·ⲡⲛⲉⲧⲟⲩⲁⲁⲃ ⲁⲉ ⲁ'ⲡⲁ ⲡⲁⲛⲥⲉ
ⲙ̅ⲛ̅ⲑⲉⲕ'ⲗⲁ ⲧⲉϥⲥⲱⲛⲉ ⲁⲩ'ⲡⲱⲧ ⲁⲩⲧⲁⲍⲉⲡ'ⲇⲟⲩⲍ ⲉⲩⲛⲏⲩ ⲉⲃⲟⲗ·ⲍ̅ⲛ̅ⲧⲥⲓⲟⲟⲩⲛ ⲉⲩⲛⲁ-/
ⲃⲱⲕ ⲉⲡⲁⲣⲓⲥⲧⲟ(ⲛ).·ⲡⲉⲭⲁⲩ ⲛⲁⲩ ϫⲉ ⲛⲉⲕ'ⲃⲁⲥⲁⲛⲟⲥ ⲁⲩⲭⲓ'ϣⲓⲡⲉ·ⲉⲓⲥϩⲏⲏⲧⲉ ⲁⲩⲉⲓ
ⲩⲁⲣⲟⲛ ⲛ̅ϭⲓ ⲡⲁⲅⲅⲉⲗⲟⲥ ⲙ̅'ⲡⲛⲟⲉⲓⲥ, ⲁⲩⲭⲁ'ⲣⲓⲍⲉ ⲛⲁⲛ ⲙ̅ⲡⲧⲁⲗ'ϭⲟ ⲛ̅ⲛⲉⲙⲙⲉⲗⲟⲥ'ⲧⲏⲣⲟⲩ.
ⲡⲓⲕⲏⲏ'ⲩϣⲉ ⲁⲉ ⲛ̅ⲧⲉⲣⲟⲩ'ⲛⲁⲩ ⲉⲙ̅[ⲙⲉ]ⲗⲟ]ⲥ'ⲛ̅ⲛⲉⲧⲟⲩⲁⲁⲃ ⲉⲩ(R ii)ⲧⲁⲗϭⲏⲩ, ⲉⲣⲉⲛⲉⲩ'ⲃⲁⲗ
ⲟⲩⲏⲛ, ⲁⲩⲱ'ⲉⲣⲉⲛⲉⲩⲗⲁⲥ ⲩⲁϫⲉ,'ⲁⲩⲱ ⲩ ⲉⲃⲟⲗ ⲉⲩϫⲱ ⲙ̅ⲙⲟⲥ ϫⲉ ⲟⲩⲛⲟϭ'ⲡⲉ ⲡⲛⲟⲩⲧⲉ
ⲛ̅ⲁⲡⲁ'ⲡⲁⲛⲥⲉ. ⲁⲩⲃⲱⲕ ⲁⲉ'ⲉⲡⲉϥⲏⲓ ⲛ̅ϭⲓ ⲡⲁⲟⲩⲍ,'ⲙ̅ⲡⲉϥⲟⲩⲱⲙ'ⲟⲩⲁⲉ ⲙ̅ⲡⲉϥⲥⲱ
ⲉⲃⲟⲗ·ⲍ̅ⲛ̅ⲧⲉϣⲱⲭⲏ.·ⲧⲉϥⲥⲍⲓⲙⲉ ⲁⲉ ⲡⲉϫⲁⲥ'ⲛⲁϥ ϫⲉ ⲉⲧⲃⲉⲟⲩ'ⲛ̅ⲉⲕⲟⲩⲱⲙ ⲁⲛ ⲟⲩ'ⲁⲉ
ⲛ̅ⲅ̅ⲥⲱ ⲁⲛ; ⲧⲁⲭⲁ'ⲅⲁⲣ ⲛ̅ⲧⲁⲛⲉⲕⲭ'ⲣⲏⲥⲧⲓⲁⲛⲟⲥ ⲉⲣⲍ̅'ⲥ̅ⲟⲙ ⲙ̅ⲡⲉⲕ̅ⲙ̅ⲧⲟ'ⲉⲃⲟⲗ, ⲁⲕⲧⲓ-
ⲁ̅ⲧⲣⲏⲡ'.·ⲡ̅ⲁ̅ⲟⲩⲍ ⲁⲉ ⲡⲉϫⲁⲩ'ⲛⲁⲥ ϫⲉ ⲕⲁⲕⲏ ⲕⲏⲫⲁ'ⲗⲏ·ϯⲥⲟⲟⲩⲛ ⲅⲁⲣ'ϫⲉ ⲉⲣⲩ̅ⲙ̅-

---

82 R i 18 f. l. ⲁⲩⲧⲁⲍⲉⲡ'ⲇ. 29. l. ⲛ̅ⲛⲉⲛⲙⲉⲗⲟⲥ. ii 2. After ⲟⲩⲏⲛ, 2nd l. (to 31). omission here; xu Boh. 9. l. ⲙ̅ⲡⲉϥ-. 11. l. -ⲭⲟⲗⲏ. 16 f. l. ⲛ̅ⲧⲁⲛⲉⲭⲣ-. 21. Ka added.

Boh. ⲡⲓⲁ[ⲣⲭ]ⲏⲁⲅⲅⲉ'ⲗⲟⲥ··]····ⲁⲗⲏ····[···]·ⲛ̅'ⲡⲓⲭⲁⲗⲕⲓⲟⲛ, ⲁⲩⲑⲣⲉⲩ-
ⲁⲣ[ⲩ ⲙ̅ⲫ]ⲣⲏϯ[ⲛ̅ⲟⲩⲙ̅]ⲱ[ⲟ]ⲩ ⲉⲩⲁⲣⲉ··ⲛⲟ[··]ⲍⲱ·'[····] ⲁⲩⲑⲣⲉⲩϩⲗⲟϭ ϩⲉⲛ-
ⲣⲱⲟⲩ ⲛ̅'ⲛⲏ ⲉⲑⲟⲩⲁⲃ ⲙ̅ⲫⲣⲏϯ ⲛ̅ⲟⲩⲉⲃⲓⲱ·ⲛⲓⲟⲡⲓ [ⲛ̅ⲕⲟⲛⲧⲓⲧⲟⲛ. ⲁⲩⲧ[ⲱⲛϥ]'ⲛ̅-
ϫⲉ ⲡ[ⲓⲟ]ⲩϫ, ⲁⲩϩⲱⲗ ⲉⲡⲉϥⲏⲓ ⲉⲁϥⲭⲱ'ⲛ̅ⲛⲏ ⲉ[ⲑⲟ]ⲩⲁⲃ (sic) ϩⲉⲛⲛⲓⲑⲉⲁⲧⲣ[ⲟⲛ
]'····(further traces?)'····λ (ⲣⲁⲫⲁⲏⲗ?) ⲡⲓⲁⲣⲭⲏⲁⲅⲅⲉⲗⲟⲥ λ̅'··
ⲙ̅····ⲛⲏ ⲉⲑⲟⲩⲁⲃ, ⲁⲩⲧⲟⲩ'ⲛⲟⲥⲟⲩ, ⲁⲩ ϩⲓⲧⲉϥ[ϫ]ⲓϫ ϩⲓϫⲉⲛⲛⲟⲩ'ⲍⲟ·ⲥⲁⲧⲟ-
ⲧⲟⲩ ⲁⲩⲛⲁⲩ ⲙ̅ⲃⲟⲗ, ⲁⲛⲟⲩ'ⲃⲁⲗ ⲥⲁⲧⲁⲕⲧⲓⲛ ⲛⲟⲩⲱⲓⲛⲓ ⲉⲃ[ⲟⲗ ⲙ̅]ⲫⲣⲏϯ ⲙ̅ⲡⲓⲥⲓⲟⲩ
ⲛ̅ⲧⲉϩⲁⲛⲁ[ⲗ]ⲧⲱⲟⲩⲓ]'ⲉⲩⲁⲩϩⲁ ⲙ̅ⲫⲛⲁⲩ ⲙ̅ⲡⲓⲟⲩⲱⲓⲛⲓ.'ⲁⲡⲓⲁⲅⲅⲉⲗⲟⲥ ϯ ⲙ̅ⲡⲉⲩⲗⲁⲥ
ⲉⲣⲱⲟⲩ, ⲁⲩⲥⲁϫⲓ ⲛⲉⲙⲁⲩ ⲉⲩϫⲱ ⲙ̅ⲙⲟⲥ ϫⲉ ⲙⲁ'ϣⲁⲙ (sic) ⲛⲁⲛ ⲡⲉⲛ⳪·ⲁ ⲩϯ-
ⲧⲉⲩⲭⲓϭ ⲉ'ⲃⲟⲗ ϩⲓϫⲉⲛ ⲡⲟⲩⲥⲱⲙⲁ ⲧⲏⲣϥ, ⲟⲩⲟ2'ⲁⲩⲥⲉⲙⲛⲭⲟⲙ ⲙ̅ⲙⲁϣⲱ ⲙ̅ⲫⲣⲏϯ ⲛ̅-
ⲥⲁⲩ·ⲟⲩⲟⲍ ⲉⲁⲩⲟⲣⲡ[··]ⲉⲛⲛ·ⲟⲁⲉ'[·]ⲧ̅ⲙⲟⲥ·'ⲁ···ⲛ·ⲟ·[·]·ⲟⲟ··ⲁⲩϩⲱⲗ ⲉ-
ⲡ̅ⲓ'ϣⲱⲓ ⲉⲛⲓⲫ[ⲏⲟⲩⲓ ϩⲉ]ⲛ̅ⲟⲩⲟⲟⲩ.'ⲁ ⲛ̅ⲏ ⲉⲑⲟⲩⲁⲃ ⲫⲓⲱⲧ ⲉⲃⲟⲗ], ⲁⲩⲧⲁⲍⲉⲡ'ⲇⲟⲩⲍ
ⲉⲩⲛⲏⲟⲩ [ⲉ]ⲃ[ⲟⲗ] ϩⲉⲛⲧⲥⲓⲱⲟⲩⲛⲓ (V) ⲉⲩϩⲏⲗ ⲉⲟⲩⲱⲙ. ⲡⲉϫⲱⲟⲩ ⲛⲁⲩ ⲁⲉ (sic)'
ⲁⲛⲉⲕⲃⲁⲥⲁⲛⲟⲥ ϭⲓϣⲓⲡⲓ·ϩⲏⲡⲡⲉ'ⲓⲥ ⲡⲉⲛⲗⲁⲥ ⲛⲉⲙⲛⲉⲛⲃⲁⲗ ⲧⲟⲓ [ⲛⲁⲛ],'ⲟⲩⲟⲍ
ⲡⲉⲛⲥⲱⲙⲁ ⲟⲩⲟⲍ.'ⲉⲧⲁ ⲡⲓⲙⲏⲩ ⲁⲉ ⲛⲁⲩ ⲉⲛⲏ ⲉⲑⲟⲩⲁⲃ ⲉⲣⲉ'ⲡⲟⲩⲥⲱⲙⲁ ⲟⲩⲟⲍ, ⲁⲩⲱⲩ ⲉⲃⲟⲗ'ⲉⲩⲭⲱ ⲙ̅ⲙⲟⲥ ϫⲉ ⲟⲩⲛⲓ ϯ ⲡⲉ ⲫϯ'ⲛ̅ⲡⲓⲁⲅⲓⲟⲥ ⲡⲁⲛⲥⲓ ⲛⲉⲙⲑⲉⲕⲗⲁ ⲧⲉϥⲥⲱⲛⲓ. [10]ⲁ ⲩϭⲉ ⲛⲁⲩ ⲁⲉ ⲛ̅ϫⲉ ⲡⲓⲁⲅⲓⲟⲥ ⲡⲁⲛⲥⲓ'ⲛⲉⲙⲑⲉⲕⲗⲁ ⲧⲉϥⲥⲱⲛⲓ ⲉⲡⲓϣⲧⲉ'ⲕⲟ,
ⲟⲩⲟⲍ ⲁⲩϭⲉ ⲛⲁⲩ ⲉⲡⲉϥⲏⲓ ⲛ̅ϫⲉ ⲡⲓⲁⲟⲩⲍ, ⲙ̅ⲡⲉϥⲟⲩⲱⲙ ⲟⲩⲁⲉ ⲙ̅ⲡⲉϥⲥⲱ, ⲉϥⲭⲟⲛⲧ
ⲉⲑⲃⲉ'ⲛⲓϣⲓⲡⲓ ⲉⲧⲁⲛⲏ ⲉⲑⲟⲩⲁⲃ ⲧⲏⲓⲧⲟⲩ ⲛⲁϥ.'ⲟⲩⲟⲍ ⲁⲱⲣⲟⲑⲉⲁ ⲧⲉϥⲥⲍⲓⲙⲓ ⲁⲥⲓ ⲉ-
ϩⲟⲩⲛ ⲉⲡⲓⲇⲣⲓⲕⲗⲓⲛⲟⲥ, ⲡⲉϫⲁⲥ ⲛⲁϥ'ϫⲉ ⲉⲑⲃⲉⲟⲩ ⲕⲟⲗ[ⲩ]ⲱⲙ ⲙ̅ⲫⲟⲟⲩ ⲁⲛ,[20] ⲟⲩⲁⲉ ⲕⲥⲱ
ⲁⲛ; [ⲧ]ⲁⲭⲁ ⲉⲧⲁⲛⲓⲭⲣⲏⲥ'ⲧⲓⲁⲛⲟⲥ ϯ ⲛ̅ϩⲁⲛ[ⲕ]ⲟⲩϫⲓ ⲛ̅ϣⲓⲡⲓ'ⲛⲁⲕ ⲟⲛ.'ⲁⲩϭⲱⲛⲧ ⲛ̅-
ϫⲉ ⲡⲓⲁⲟⲩⲍ, ⲡⲉϫⲁϥ ⲛⲁⲥ'ϫⲉ ⲕⲁⲕⲏ ⲕⲉⲫⲁⲗⲏ, ⲟⲩⲕⲟⲩⲛ'ⲁⲣⲉ'ⲩⲉⲙ — →

ϥⲉ ⲛ̅ⲓⲥ̅· ⲉⲧⲃⲉⲡⲁⲓ̈ ⲧⲉⲛⲁ²⁵ϫⲉ ⲉⲭⲛ̅ⲛⲉⲓ̈ⲙⲁ·ⲕⲟⲥ ⲛ̅ⲭⲣⲏⲥⲧⲁ·ⲛⲟⲥ. ϥⲉ ⲡⲟⲩϫⲁⲓ̈ ⲛ̅ⲡⲁ-
ⲡⲟⲗⲗⲱⲛ· ⲡⲛⲟϭ ⲛ̅ⲛⲟⲩⲧⲉ,³⁰ ⲧⲓⲛⲁⲃⲓ ⲛ̅ⲧⲟⲩⲁ·ⲡⲉ ⲍⲱⲧⲥⲉϥⲉ ⲛ̅ⲧⲉⲩ(82 Vi)ⲁⲫⲟⲣⲙⲏ.
ⲁⲥⲟⲩ·ⲱϣⲃ̅ ⲡⲉϫⲁⲥ ϫⲉ· ⲍⲁⲙⲟⲓ ⲣⲱ ⲉⲓⲛⲁ·ⲁⲡⲓⲩⲁ ⲙ̅ⲡⲉⲓⲛⲟϭ·ⲛ̅ⲧⲁⲓⲟ. ⲡⲁⲟⲩⲉ·
ⲇⲉ ⲁⲩⲧⲣⲉⲩϫⲓ ⲛ̅ⲛⲉⲧⲟⲩⲁⲁⲃ ⲉⲧⲉ·ⲫⲉⲗⲗⲁⲕⲏ. ⲑⲉⲕⲗⲁ ⲇⲉ ⲉⲛⲉⲥϭⲓ ²⁰ⲍⲁ·ⲛⲉⲃⲁⲥⲁ-
ⲛⲟⲥ ⲉⲧⲍⲛ̅·ⲡⲉⲥⲥⲱⲙⲁ, ⲁⲩⲱ· ⲉⲛⲉⲥⲇⲓⲁⲕⲟⲛⲉⲓ· ⲉⲛⲉⲧⲟⲩⲁⲁⲃ ⲍⲛ̅·ⲡⲉⲧⲛ̅ⲧⲁⲥ. ⲡ-
ⲡⲉ¹⁵ⲧⲟⲩⲁⲁⲃ ⲇⲉ ⲁⲗⲁ·ⲡⲁⲛϭⲉ ⲡⲉϫⲁⲩ ⲛ̅·ⲑⲉⲕⲗⲁ ϫⲉ ⲉⲧⲃⲉⲟⲩ· ⲧⲉⲛⲉⲍⲁⲓ ⲛ̅ⲟⲩⲉⲡⲓ-
ⲥ·ⲧⲟⲗⲓⲧ ⲧⲡⲟⲩ·ⲩⲙⲣⲉ ²⁰ⲁⲡⲱⲗⲗⲱⲛⲓⲟⲥ, ·ϫⲉⲕⲁⲥ ⲉϥⲉϭⲓ ⲡⲣⲟ·ⲟϥⲩ ⲙ̅ⲡⲉϥⲏⲓ̈, ϫⲉ· ⲁ̅-
ⲛⲉϥϭⲱ ⲉϥϭⲱϣⲧ· ⲉⲃⲟⲗ ⲍⲏⲧⲛ̅; ⲁⲛⲟⲕ· ⲣⲱ ⲁⲓ̈ϯ ⲙ̅ⲡⲉⲧⲛ̅ⲧⲁⲓ̈· ⲛ̅ⲧⲟⲟⲧϥ̅ ⲙ̅ⲡⲁⲩⲗⲟⲥ·
ϫⲉⲕⲁⲥ ⲉϥⲉⲧⲁⲁⲩ· ⲙ̅ⲙⲛ̅ⲧⲛⲁ· ϫⲉ ⲛ̅ϯⲥⲟⲟⲩⲛ ⲁⲛ ⲙ̅ⲡⲉ³⁰ⲍⲟⲟⲩ ⲉⲧⲉⲣⲉⲡϫⲟ·ⲉⲓⲥ ⲛⲁ-
ϥⲓⲛⲉ ⲛ̅ⲥⲱⲓ̈·ⲁⲩⲱ ⲁⲥϯ ⲛⲁⲥ ⲛⲟⲩ·ⲭⲁⲣⲧⲏⲥ ⲛ̅ϭⲓ ⲧⲑⲉⲕ(Vⅱ)ⲗⲁ, ⲁⲥⲥⲍⲁⲓ̈ ⲙ̅ⲡⲉⲥ·
ϣⲏⲣⲉ ⲉⲥϫⲱ ⲙ̅ⲙⲟⲥ ⲛ̅ⲧⲉⲓϩⲉ· ⲛ̅ϣⲟⲣⲡ̅ ⲙⲉⲛ ⲛ̅ⲍⲱⲃ· ⲛⲓⲙ ϯϣⲓⲛⲉ ⲉⲡⲉⲕ·ⲟⲩϫⲁⲓ̈
ⲱ ⲁⲡⲱⲗⲗⲱⲛⲓⲟⲥ ⲡⲁⲕⲟⲩⲓ̈· ⲛ̅ϣⲏⲣⲉ ⲉⲧⲍⲟⲗϫ̅· ⲕⲁⲧⲁⲑⲉ ⲛ̅ⲧⲁⲓ̈ⲉⲓ ⲉⲃⲟⲗ· ⲍⲓⲧⲟⲟ-
ⲧⲕ̅ ⲉⲓⲃⲏⲕ· ⲉⲣⲁⲕⲟⲧⲉ, ⲧⲉⲛⲟⲩ· ϭⲉ ⲉⲓⲥ ⲡⲉⲛϫⲟⲉⲓⲥ· ⲁⲩⲧⲁⲍⲙⲉⲛ ⲉⲍⲟⲩⲛ· ⲉⲡⲉⲩ-
ⲁⲅⲱⲛ ⲉⲧⲟⲩ·ⲁⲁⲃ. ⲙ̅ⲡⲉⲣⲣ̅ⲕⲟⲩⲓ̈· ⲛ̅ⲍⲏⲧ ⲱ ⲡⲁϣⲏⲣⲉ· ϯⲥⲟⲣⲙ̅ ⲉⲃⲟⲗ ⲍⲙ̅·ⲡⲩⲙⲗⲟ,
ⲁⲩⲱ· ⲁⲛⲉⲛⲉⲓⲟⲧⲉ ⲧⲏⲣⲟⲩ· ²⁰ⲣ̅ⲩⲙⲟ· ⲁⲩϫⲟ·ⲟⲥ ⲅⲁⲣ ⲛ̅ϭⲓ ⲡⲉⲛⲉⲓⲱⲧ ⲇⲁⲇ ϫⲉ ⲁⲛⲅ̅⁻¹
ⲟⲩⲣⲙ̅ⲛ̅ϭⲟⲓⲗⲉ ⲉⲓ̈·ϭⲁⲗⲱⲟⲩ ⲕⲁⲧⲁⲑⲉ²⁵ ⲛ̅ⲛⲁⲉⲓⲟⲧⲉ ⲧⲏⲣⲟⲩ· ⲙ̅ⲡⲣ̅ϫⲟⲟⲥ ϫⲉ ⲁⲓ̈·ⲙⲟⲩ·
ⲛ̅ⲧⲁⲓ̈ⲙⲟⲩ ⲍⲙ̅·ⲡⲙⲟⲩ ⲛ̅ⲛ̅ⲁⲡⲟⲥ·ⲧⲟⲗⲟⲥ ⲙⲛ̅ⲛⲉⲡⲣⲟ·ⲫⲏⲧⲏⲥ. ⲙ̅ⲡⲉⲕ·ⲟⲩϫⲁⲓ̈ ⲱ ⲡⲁϣⲏⲣⲉ,
ⲙ̅ⲡⲉⲣⲕⲱ ⲛ̅ⲥⲱⲕ· ⲛ̅ⲧⲡⲓⲥⲧⲓⲥ ⲙ̅ⲡⲉϫⲥ̅ (83 Rⅰ) ⲓ̅ⲥ̅ ⲡⲉⲛϫⲟⲉⲓⲥ· ⲁⲩⲱ· ϯⲍ̅ⲧⲏⲕ ⲉ-
ⲛⲉⲧⲟ·ⲁⲁⲃ ϫⲉⲕⲁⲥ ⲉⲩⲛⲁ·ⲩⲗⲏⲗ ⲉϫⲱⲕ ⲛ̅ϯ⁵·ⲛⲟⲩϫⲙ̅. ⲍⲉⲛⲥⲍⲁⲓ̈· ⲅⲁⲣ ⲉⲩⲟⲩⲁⲁⲃ ⲛⲉ-
ⲧⲟⲩ·ⲛⲁⲛⲧⲟⲩ ⲛⲁⲕ· ⲙ̅ⲡⲉⲕⲟⲩϫⲁⲓ̈ ⲱ ⲡⲁϣⲏⲣⲉ ⲁⲛⲁⲩ ⲉⲛⲉⲕ·ⲕⲟⲩⲓ̈ ⲛ̅ϩⲙ̅ϩⲁⲗ· ⲛⲉϯ
ⲛⲁⲩ ⲛⲟⲩⲟϯ·ⲧⲓⲁ ⲛ̅ⲛⲟⲩⲃ ⲉⲡⲟⲩⲁ· ⲉⲧⲃⲉⲧⲉⲩϭⲓⲛⲱⲛϩ̅,· ¹⁵ⲁⲩⲱ ⲛ̅ϭⲱⲣ ⲛ̅ⲛⲁ·ϩ̅ⲟⲓⲧⲉ
ⲙ̅ⲛⲉⲧⲕⲏ· ⲕⲁⲍⲏⲩ. ⲁⲣⲏⲩ ⲛ̅·ⲧⲉⲡⲛⲟⲩⲧⲉ ⲧⲁⲁⲥ· ⲙ̅ⲡⲍⲏⲧ ⲛ̅ⲟⲩⲁ ⲛϥ̅·ⲍⲱⲃⲉ ⲙ̅ⲡⲁ-
ⲥⲱⲙⲁ·²⁰ⲍⲱ ⲉⲣϥ̅ⲁⲛⲡϫⲟ·ⲉⲓⲥ ⲟⲩⲗⲁϥⲓⲛⲉ· ⲁⲩⲱ ⲃⲱⲕ ⲉⲡⲉⲥⲏⲧ· ⲉⲡⲉⲥⲡⲏⲗⲁⲓⲟⲛ,·
ⲕ̅ⲛⲁϭⲓⲛⲉ ⲙ̅ⲡⲉⲓ̈ⲛ̅ⲧⲁⲩ ⲙ̅ⲡⲉⲕⲉⲓ̈·ⲱⲧ. ϥⲉ ⲡⲉⲕⲟⲩ·ϫⲁⲓ̈ ⲱ ⲡⲁϣⲏⲣⲉ· ϫⲉ ⲙ̅ⲡⲉⲓ̈ⲧⲁ-
ⲕⲉ·ⲗⲁⲁⲩ ⲍⲛ̅ⲡⲉⲧⲛ̅²⁵·ⲧⲁⲩ ⲙ̅ⲡⲉⲕⲉⲓⲱⲧ,· ⲁⲗⲗⲁ ⲟⲩⲟⲛ ⲛⲓⲙ ⲛ̅·ⲧⲁⲓ̈ⲭⲟⲩ ⲉⲃⲟⲗ ⲍⲙ̅(Rⅱ)-

---

82 R ii 30. l. ϯⲛⲁϥⲓ. 31. l. ⲍⲱⲧⲥⲏϥⲉ. Vi 1. 1st h. (to 83 R i 31). 5. Omission probable here (see Boh.) 6. l. ⲁϥⲧⲣⲉϥϫⲓ. 8. l. ϯⲫⲩⲗⲁⲕⲏ. 33–ii 1. l. ⲑⲉⲕⲗⲁ. 83 R i 31. 2nd
h. (to ii 33). ⲟⲩⲟⲛ: l. ⲍⲱⲃ? 32. ⲉⲟⲩϫⲉⲃⲟⲗ?

Boh. -ϥⲓ ⲙ̅ⲡⲁⲓ̈ⲣⲁⲛ ϫⲉ ⲓ̅ⲏ̅ⲥ̅, ⲉⲑⲃⲉ·ⲫⲁⲓ̈ ⲁⲣⲉⲥⲁϫⲓ ⲉϫⲉⲛⲛⲁⲓ̈ⲫⲁⲣⲙⲁⲅⲟⲥ· ϥⲉ ⲡⲟⲩϫⲁⲓ̈ ⲙ̅-
ⲡⲓⲁⲡⲟⲗⲗⲱⲛ ⲡⲓⲛⲓϣϯ· ⲛ̅ⲛⲟⲩϯ ϫⲉ ϯⲛⲁϯ ⲙ̅ⲗⲉⲙⲟⲩ ⲧⲏⲣϥ̅ (sic) ⲉϥ̅ⲃⲏⲧⲟⲩϥ. ⲛⲉϫⲁⲥ ⲛⲁⲩ
ϫⲉ ⲁⲙⲟⲓ̈· ⲣ̅ⲱ ⲛ̅ⲧⲁⲙⲩⲁ ⲙ̅ⲡⲁⲓ̈ⲧⲁⲓⲟ·· ⲡⲉϫⲁⲥ ⲛⲁⲩ ⲟⲛ ϫⲉ ⲁⲓ̈ϩⲓⲥⲓ ⲉⲓ̈ϯⲍⲟ ⲉⲣⲟ·ⲕ ϫⲉ
ⲍⲉⲛⲕ ⲥⲁⲃⲟⲗ ⲛ̅ⲛⲓⲭⲣⲏⲥⲧⲓⲁⲛⲟⲥ,· ⲙⲙⲟⲛ ϥ̅ϯ ⲉⲍⲣⲏⲓ̈ ⲉϫⲱⲟⲩ ⲛ̅ϫⲉ ⲡⲟⲩ·ⲛⲟⲩϯ· ⲟⲩⲟⲛⲩⲙ̅-
ϫⲟⲙ ⲙ̅ⲙⲟϥ ⲉϩⲟ·ⲧⲉ ⲡⲉⲕⲁ ⲡⲟⲗⲗⲱⲛ ⲛ̅ⲱⲛⲓ ⲛ̅ⲕⲟⲩⲣ· [

ⲡⲁⲛⲁⲓⲟⲧⲉ ⲡⲉ. ⲁ̅ⲡⲉⲕⲕⲧⲉⲡⲥⲕⲟ' ⲉⲃⲟⲗ ⲛ̅ⲟⲩϩ̅ⲙⲙⲟ' ⲙ̅ⲛ̅ⲟⲩⲭⲏⲣⲁ ⲙ̅ⲛ̅ⲟⲩⲟⲣⲫⲁ-
ⲛⲟⲥ, ' ϫⲉⲕⲁⲁⲥ ⲉⲣⲉⲡⲛⲟⲩ'ⲧⲉ ⲛⲁⲉⲣⲥⲟⲃⲧ ⲉⲣⲟⲕ' ⲉⲃⲟⲗ ϩ̅ⲛ̅ⲉϭⲟⲣⲉϭ' ⲙ̅ⲡⲇⲓⲁⲃⲟ-
ⲗⲟⲥ· ⲁⲩⲱ ' ⲉⲓ̈ϣⲁⲛⲟ̅ⲗⲁⲁⲩ' ⲙ̅ⲡⲁⲣϩⲉⲥⲓⲁ ϩⲁⲧⲙ̅'ⲡϫⲟⲉⲓⲥ, ⲛ̅ⲧⲟⲕ' ⲡⲉ ⲡϣⲟⲣⲡ̅ ⲛ̅-
ⲩⲁⲓ̈'ϫⲓ ϩⲙⲟⲧ ⲉⲧⲱⲕ. ' ⲙ̅ⲡⲉⲣⲉⲙⲕⲁϩ ⲛ̅ϩⲏⲧ ⲱ ⲡⲁϣⲏⲣⲉ' ϫⲉ ⲛⲉⲛ̅ⲛ̅ⲥⲱⲙⲁ' ⲡⲟ-
ⲣϫ̅ ⲉⲃⲟⲗ ⲛ̅ⲛⲉⲛⲉ'ⲣⲏⲩ· ⲛⲁⲛⲟⲩⲥ ⲅⲁⲣ ' ⲛⲁⲛ ⲉⲛⲛⲟⲣⲉϫ' ⲉⲛⲉ̅ⲛⲉⲣⲏⲩ ϩⲙ̅ⲡⲉⲓ̈ⲕⲟⲥ-
ⲙⲟⲥ ϫⲉ ⲉⲛⲉ'ϣⲱⲡⲉ ϩⲁⲧⲉⲛⲛⲉ'ⲛⲉⲣⲏⲩ ϩ̅ⲛ̅ⲑⲓⲗⲏ̅ⲙ' ⲧⲡⲟⲗⲓⲥ ⲙ̅ⲡⲉⲭ̅ⲥ̅·' ϯϣⲓⲛⲉ ⲉ-
ⲣⲟⲕ ⲡⲁϣⲟⲩⲓ' ⲛ̅ϣⲏⲣⲉ, ϫⲉ ⲛ̅ϯ'ⲛⲁⲕⲧⲟⲓ̈ ⲁⲛ ⲉ'ⲛⲁⲩ ⲉⲣⲟⲕ ϩⲁⲧ'ⲥⲁⲣϫ̅. ⲁⲩⲱ ⲡⲉⲕ-'
ⲓ̈ⲱⲧ ⲡⲁϩⲥⲉ ϣⲓⲛⲉ ⲉⲣⲟⲕ. ⲇⲓⲁⲥⲡⲁ'ⲍⲉ ⲙ̅ⲙⲟⲕ ϩ̅ⲛ̅ⲧⲁ (83 V i) ⲯⲩⲭⲏ ⲙ̅ⲛ̅ⲡⲁⲡⲛⲁ·'
ⲟⲩϫⲁⲓ̈ ϩⲙ̅ⲡϫⲟ'ⲉⲓⲥ ⲡⲁⲙⲉⲣⲓⲧ ⲛ̅'ϣⲏⲣⲉ. ' Ⲛ̅ⲧⲉⲣⲉⲥⲟⲩⲱ ⲇⲉ' ⲉⲥϩⲁⲓ̈ ⲛ̅ⲧⲉⲓ̈ⲉ ⲡⲓⲥ-'
ⲧⲟⲗⲏ ⲛ̅ϭⲓ ⲑⲉⲕⲗⲁ' ⲁⲥⲧⲁⲁⲥ ⲛ̅ⲟⲩⲕⲟⲩⲓ' ⲛ̅ϣⲏ̅ϫⲁⲗ ⲛ̅ⲧⲁⲥ,' ⲁⲥϫⲟⲟⲩⲥ ⲉⲁⲛⲧ'ⲛⲟⲟⲩ.
ⲙ̅ⲛ̅'ⲥⲁⲛⲁⲓ̈ ⲇⲉ ⲁⲩⲱϭⲕ̅ ⲛ̅ϭⲓ ⲡⲇⲟⲩϫ ⲙ̅'ⲡⲉⲩϣⲓⲛⲉ ⲛ̅ⲥⲁ'ⲛⲉⲧⲟⲩⲁⲁⲃ ϩⲙ̅ⲡⲉⲩⲧⲉⲕⲟ·
ⲛⲉⲩ'ⲙⲉⲉⲩⲉ ⲅⲁⲣ ⲡⲉ ϫⲉ'ⲙ̅ⲡⲇⲟⲩϫ ⲛⲁⲃⲁ'ⲥⲁⲛⲓⲍⲉ ⲙ̅ⲙⲟⲟⲩ' ⲁⲛ ⲁ̅ⲕⲉⲥⲟⲡ.' ⲁⲥϣⲱⲡⲉ
ⲇⲉ ⲙ̅ⲛ̅'ⲥⲁϣⲟⲩⲱⲧ ⲛ̅'ϩⲟⲟⲩ ⲁ̅ⲩⲉⲓ ⲛ̅ϭⲓ'ⲛⲟⲩⲏⲏⲃ ⲙ̅ⲡⲣ̅ⲡⲉ,' ⲡⲉϫⲁⲩ ⲙ̅ⲡⲇⲟⲩϫ' ϫⲉ ⲁ-
ⲧⲡⲟⲗⲓⲥ ⲧⲏ'ⲣϫ̅ ⲟⲩⲁϩϥ̅ ⲛ̅ⲥⲁⲡⲉⲓ̈'ⲙⲁⲅⲟⲥ ⲥⲛⲁⲩ· ⲁⲩⲱ' ⲥⲉⲧⲁⲗϭⲟ ⲛ̅ⲛⲉⲧ'ϣⲱⲛⲉ ϩⲓⲧⲛ̅-
ⲛⲉⲩ'ⲙⲁⲅⲓⲁ, ⲁⲩⲥⲉⲕⲧ'ⲡⲟⲗⲓⲥ ⲉⲣⲟⲟⲩ ⲧⲏ'ⲣϫ̅, ⲁⲩⲗⲟ ⲉⲩⲕⲱ (V ii) ⲛ̅ⲉⲣⲱⲙⲉ ⲉⲉⲓ ⲉ-'
ⲡⲣ̅ⲡⲉ.' ⲁⲩϭⲱⲛⲧ ⲛ̅ϭⲓ ⲡ'ⲇⲟⲩϫ, ⲡⲉϫⲁⲩ ⲛⲁⲩ' ϫⲉ ϣⲓⲛⲉ ⲛ̅ⲧⲟⲟⲧⲟⲩ' ⲛ̅ⲛⲛⲟⲩⲧⲉ, ⲙⲁ-'
ⲣⲟⲩⲧⲁⲙⲟⲓ̈ ⲉϩⲉⲛ'ⲃⲁⲥⲁⲛⲟⲥ ⲉⲩⲛⲁⲩϯ'ⲧⲁⲧⲁⲁⲩ ⲛⲁⲩ. ⲙ̅ⲙⲟⲛ ⲙ̅ⲡⲉⲩ̅ϭⲙ̅'ϭⲟⲙ
ⲉⲣⲟⲟⲩ· ⲁⲩⲱ' ⲁⲩⲑⲗⲓⲃⲉ ⲙ̅ⲙⲟⲓ̈ ⲉ'ⲙⲁⲧⲉ· ⲁⲩⲱ ⲉⲓ̈'ϣⲁⲛⲕⲁⲁⲩ ⲛ̅ⲧⲉⲓ̈'ϩⲉ, ⲧⲡⲟⲗⲓⲥ ⲧⲏ-'
ⲣϫ̅ ⲛⲁⲧⲱⲟⲩⲛ ⲉϩ'ⲣⲁⲓ̈ ⲉϫⲱⲓ̈· ⲁⲩⲱ' ⲧⲁⲕⲉⲥϩⲓⲙⲉ ⲁⲩⲙⲁ'ⲅⲉⲩⲉ ⲙ̅ⲙⲟⲥ, ⲁⲥ'ⲁⲣⲛⲁ
ⲛ̅ⲛⲛⲟⲩⲧⲉ.' ⲛⲟⲩⲏⲏⲃ ⲇⲉ ⲁⲩ'ⲃⲱⲕ, ⲁⲩⲣⲟⲩⲅⲁ'ϫⲛⲉ ⲛ̅ⲟⲩⲱⲧ' ⲁⲩⲉⲓ ϣⲁ̅ⲡⲇⲟⲩϫ,' ⲡⲉϫⲁⲩ ⲛⲁⲩ ϫⲉ' ⲁ̅ⲛⲉⲛⲛⲟⲩⲧⲉ ⲧⲁ'ⲙⲟⲛ ⲉϩⲉⲛⲃⲁⲥⲁ'ⲛⲟⲥ ⲉⲩⲛⲁⲩϯ, ⲁⲩ'ϫⲟⲟⲥ ⲅⲁⲣ ⲛⲁⲛ
ϫⲉ' ϫⲓ ⲛ̅ⲛⲉⲓ̈'ⲙⲁⲅⲟⲥ,' ⲙⲁⲣⲟⲩ ⲛ̅ϫⲉⲛⲍⲁ'ⲗⲏⲕⲓⲥ ⲙ̅ⲡⲉⲛⲓⲡⲉ,' ⲧⲁⲗⲟⲟⲩ ⲉⲩⲥⲕⲁ (84 R i)-
ⲫⲟⲥ, ⲙⲁⲫⲟⲩⲛⲟϭ'ⲛ̅ⲱⲛⲉ ⲉⲡⲉⲩⲙⲁⲕϩ̅' ⲛ̅ⲥⲉϥⲓⲧⲟⲩ ⲉⲃⲟⲗ' ⲛ̅ⲥⲉⲛⲟϫⲟⲩ ⲉⲡ'ⲛⲩⲗⲁ-
ⲅⲟⲥ ⲛ̅ⲧⲉ'ⲑⲁⲗⲁⲥⲥⲁ, ⲛ̅ⲧⲉ'ⲧⲙ̅ⲣⲱⲙⲉ ⲛⲁⲩ ⲉ'ⲣⲟⲟⲩ ⲛ̅ϣⲁⲉⲛⲉϩ.' ⲛⲁⲓ̈ ⲇⲉ ⲛ̅ⲧⲉⲣⲉϥ-'
ⲥⲱⲧⲙ̅ ⲉⲣⲟⲟⲩ ⲛ̅ϭⲓ ⲡ'ⲇⲟⲩϫ, ⲁⲩⲕⲉ'ⲗⲉⲩⲉ ⲉⲧⲣⲉⲩⲉⲓⲛⲉ' ⲛⲁⲩ ⲛ̅ⲛⲉⲧⲟⲩ'ⲁⲁⲃ ⲙ̅ⲡⲉϥ-
ⲣⲁⲥ'ⲧⲉ· ⲛⲉⲩϫⲱ' ⲇⲉ ⲙ̅ⲙⲟⲥ ϫⲉ ⲁⲗⲏⲑⲱⲥ ⲧⲁⲓ̈ ⲧⲉ ⲧⲃⲁ'ⲥⲁⲛⲟⲥ ⲉⲧⲛⲁⲉⲩ̅ϭⲙ̅ϭⲟⲙ
ⲉⲣⲟⲟⲩ ⲛ̅ϩⲏⲧⲥ̅. ⲁⲩⲙⲟⲟⲥ ⲉⲛⲉⲧⲟⲩⲁⲁⲃ' ⲡⲣⲟⲃⲏⲙⲁⲧⲟⲥ,' ⲡⲉϫⲁⲩ ⲛⲁⲩ ϫⲉ' ⲁⲡⲉⲧⲛ̅-
ⲥⲕⲩⲡ'ⲧⲉⲓ ⲉ̅ⲙⲱⲧⲛ̅' ⲛ̅ⲛⲉⲓ̈ϩⲟⲟⲩ ⲧⲏ'ⲣⲟⲩ, ϫⲉⲕⲁⲥ ⲉ'ⲧⲉⲧⲛⲁⲑⲩⲥⲓⲁⲍⲉ ' ⲛ̅ⲛⲛⲟⲩⲧⲉ ⲉⲧ-'
ⲧⲁⲓ̈ⲏⲩ. ⲁⲥⲟⲩⲱϣⲃ̅ ⲛ̅ϭⲓ ⲑⲉⲕⲗⲁ' ⲡⲉϫⲁⲥ ⲛⲁⲩ ϫⲉ (R ii) ⲛ̅ⲑⲉ ⲛ̅ⲟⲩⲥϩⲓⲙⲉ 'ⲉⲥⲛⲁ̅ⲣ-

---

83 R ii 1 f. l. ⲙ̅ⲡⲣ̅ⲕ̅ⲧⲉ-. 7. l. ⲛⲁⲣϩ̅ⲟⲩⲃⲧⲉ-. 8. l. ϩⲛ̅ⲡϭⲟⲣϭ̅. 11. l. ⲧ̅ⲡⲁⲣⲣⲏⲥⲓⲁ. 27. l.
ⲛ̅ⲧⲛⲁⲕⲧⲟⲓ̈. 32 f. l. ⲧⲁⲥⲡⲁⲍⲉ. V i. 1st h. (to 86 R i 13). 6. l. ⲉⲥⲥϩⲁⲓ̈. ii 22 f. =
-ⲩⲟϫⲛⲉ (rather than -ⲩⲁϫⲉ).

ϭοϥ ⲛ̄ⲧⲉ ⲛⲉⲥⲉⲓⲟⲧⲉ ⲙⲛ̄ ⲛⲉⲥⲣⲱⲙⲉ ϩⲓⲥⲉ ⲉⲩⲧⲥⲃⲱ ⲛⲁⲥ ⲛ̄ⲧⲙ̄ⲥⲱⲧⲙ̄ ⲛ̄ⲥⲱⲟⲩ ⲛⲉ-
ⲩⲡⲉ, ⲁⲩⲱ ⲛ̄ⲑⲉ ⲛ̄ⲟⲩϭⲟⲣ ⲛ̄ⲩⲁⲩⲕⲟⲧϥ̄ ⲉ ⲡⲉⲩⲕⲁⲃⲟⲗ ⲛ̄ⲥⲉ ⲙⲉⲥⲧⲱⲥ, ⲧⲁⲓ ⲧⲉ ⲧⲉⲕ-
ⲥⲉ ϩⲱⲱⲕ. ⲡⲇⲟⲩⲝ ⲇⲉ ⲛ̄ⲧⲉ ⲣⲉⲩⲥⲱⲧⲙ̄ ⲉⲛⲁⲓ ⲁⲩϭⲱⲛⲧ̄ ⲉⲙⲁⲧⲉ, ⲁⲩⲱ ⲁⲩⲙⲟⲩϩ
ⲛ̄ⲑⲉ ⲛ̄ⲟⲩⲕⲱϩⲧ̄, ⲁⲩⲣⲟⲝⲣⲉⲝ ⲛ̄ⲛⲉⲩⲟϩⲃⲉ· ⲡⲉϫⲁⲩ ⲛ̄ⲛⲁⲧⲧⲁϩⲓⲥ ϫⲉ ⲛ̄ⲧⲉⲧⲛ̄-
ⲥⲱⲧⲙ̄ ⲁⲛ ⲉⲧⲓ ⲁⲧⲩⲁⲩ ⲉⲥⲧⲟⲛ̄ⲧⲛ̄ ⲙ̄ⲙⲟⲓ ⲉⲛⲉⲙ̄ ⲡⲟⲣⲛⲏ ⲙⲛ̄ ⲛⲉⲩϩⲟⲟⲣ; ⲁⲥⲟⲩ-
ⲱϣⲃ̄ ⲛ̄ϭⲓ ⲧⲉⲧⲟⲩⲁⲁⲃ ϫⲉ ⲁⲣⲏⲩ ⲣⲱ ⲕ̄ϫⲟⲟⲩ ⲉⲛⲉⲩ ϩⲟⲟⲣ, ϫⲉ ⲛⲉⲑⲏⲣⲓⲟⲛ ⲙⲉⲛ
ⲥⲉ ⲥⲟⲟⲩⲛ ⲙ̄ⲡⲛⲟⲩⲧⲉ· ⲛ̄ⲧⲟⲕ ⲇⲉ ⲙ̄ (84 V i) ⲡⲉⲕⲥⲟⲩⲱⲛϥ̄. ⲡⲇⲟⲩⲝ ⲇⲉ ⲁⲩⲟⲛⲧ̄
ⲉϩⲣⲁⲓ ϩⲛ̄ ⲟⲩϭⲱⲛⲧ̄, ⲁⲩⲧⲣⲉⲩ ⲥⲟⲛϩⲟⲩ ⲛ̄ϩⲉⲛ ϩⲁⲗⲏⲥⲓⲥ ⲙ̄ⲡⲉⲥ ⲛⲓⲡⲉ, ⲁⲩⲧⲣⲉⲩ ⲙⲟⲩⲣ
ⲛ̄ⲟⲩⲛⲟϭ ⲛ̄ⲱⲛⲉ ⲉⲡⲉⲩ ⲙⲁⲕϩ̄, ⲁⲩⲧⲁⲗⲟ ⲟⲩ ⲉⲩⲥⲕⲁⲫⲟⲥ, ⲁⲩϫⲓⲧⲟⲩ ⲉⲃⲟⲗ ⲉ-
ⲑⲁⲗⲁⲥⲥⲁ, ⲁⲩ ⲛⲟϫⲟⲩ ⲉⲡ ⲡⲩⲗⲁⲅⲟⲥ. ⲁⲩⲱ ⲛ̄ⲧⲉⲩ ⲛⲟⲩ ⲁϥⲉⲓ ⲉⲃⲟⲗ ϩⲓ ⲧⲡⲉ
ⲛ̄ϭⲓ ⲅⲣⲁⲫⲁⲏⲗ ⲡⲁⲣⲭⲁⲅⲅⲉⲗⲟⲥ, ⲁⲩⲣ ϩⲁⲓⲃⲉ ⲉⲣⲟ ⲟⲩ, ⲁⲩⲱ ⲁⲩⲃⲟⲗ ⲟⲩ ⲉⲃⲟⲗ ϩⲛ̄
ⲛⲉⲙ̄ ⲙ̄ⲣⲣⲉ ⲉⲧⲙⲏⲣ ⲙ̄ⲙⲟⲟⲩ· ⲁⲩⲱ ⲁⲩ ⲉⲓ ⲛ̄ϭⲓ ⲟⲩⲛⲟϭ ⲛ̄ⲕⲏ ⲇⲟⲥ, ⲁⲩⲧⲁⲗⲟ ⲟⲩ,
ⲁϥⲉⲓⲛⲉ ⲙ̄ⲙⲟⲟⲩ ⲉⲡⲉⲕⲣⲟ. ⲗⲓⲙⲏ ⲛ̄ⲩⲉ ⲇⲉ ⲛ̄ⲧⲉⲣⲟⲩ ⲛⲁⲩ ⲉⲛⲉⲧⲟⲩⲁⲁⲃ ⲉⲙⲛ̄
ⲗⲁⲁⲩ ⲛ̄ⲧⲁ ⲕⲟ ϣⲟⲟⲡ ⲙ̄ⲙⲟ ⲟⲩ, ⲁⲩϫⲓ ⲩ ⲕⲁⲕ (V ii) ⲉⲃⲟⲗ ⲧⲏⲣⲟⲩ ϫⲉ ⲟⲩⲁ ⲡⲉ ⲡ-
ⲛⲟⲩⲧⲉ ⲛ̄ⲁⲡⲁ ⲡⲁⲏⲥⲉ ⲙⲛ̄ ⲑⲉⲕⲗⲁ ⲧⲉϥ ⲥⲱⲛⲉ ⲡⲉϫⲉ ⲓ̄ⲥ̄. ⲡⲇⲟⲩⲝ ⲇⲉ ⲛ̄ⲧⲉ ⲣⲉⲩ-
ⲥⲱⲧⲙ̄ ⲉⲛⲉⲕ ⲣⲁⲩⲕⲏ ⲙ̄ⲡⲙⲏⲏ ϣⲉ, ⲁⲩ ⲩⲓⲛⲉ ϫⲉ ⲟⲩ ⲡⲉⲧ ϣⲟⲟⲡ· ⲁⲩⲧⲁⲙⲟⲩ ⲇⲉ
ⲛⲉⲧⲟⲩⲁⲁⲃ ⲛⲉⲛ ⲧⲁⲩⲉⲓ ⲉⲡⲉⲕⲣⲟ. ⲡⲇⲟⲩⲝ ⲇⲉ ⲛ̄ⲧⲉ ⲣⲉⲩⲥⲱⲧⲙ̄, ⲁⲩⲣ ϣⲡⲏⲣⲉ,
ⲁⲩⲁ ⲛⲁⲭⲱⲣⲉⲓ ⲉⲩ ⲣϩⲟⲧⲉ ϩⲓⲧⲟⲩ ⲛ̄ⲛⲉⲙ̄ ⲙⲏⲏ ϣⲉ. ⲛⲉⲧⲟⲩ ⲁⲁⲃ ⲇⲉ ϩⲱⲟⲩ ⲁⲩⲃⲱⲕ ⲉⲡⲉⲩⲧⲉⲕⲟ, ⲁⲩⲁⲥⲡⲁⲍⲉ ⲛ̄ⲛⲉⲩ ϣⲃⲏⲣ ⲙⲁⲣⲧⲩⲣⲟⲥ, ⲁⲩⲱ ⲁⲩⲧⲁⲙⲟⲟⲩ ⲉ-
ⲑⲉ ⲛ̄ⲧⲁⲡϫⲟⲉⲓⲥ ⲛⲁϫⲕⲟⲩ ⲉⲃⲟⲗ ϩⲛ̄ ⲑⲁⲗⲁⲥⲥⲁ. ⲙ̄ⲡⲉⲩⲣⲁⲥⲧⲉ ⲇⲉ ⲁⲩⲕⲉⲗⲉⲩⲉ
ⲉⲧ ⲣⲉⲩⲉⲓⲛⲉ ⲛⲁⲩ ⲛ̄ⲛⲉⲧⲟⲩⲁⲁⲃ· ⲁⲩⲱ ⲛⲉⲣⲉ ⲡⲙⲏ ⲛ̄ⲩⲉ ⲧⲏⲣϥ̄ ϫⲓ (85 Ri) ⲩ ⲕⲁⲕ
ⲉⲃⲟⲗ ϫⲉ ⲟⲩⲁ ⲡⲉ ⲡⲛⲟⲩⲧⲉ ⲛ̄ⲁⲡⲁ ⲡⲁⲏⲥⲉ ⲙⲛ̄ ⲑⲉⲕⲗⲁ ⲧⲉⲩ ⲥⲱⲛⲉ. ⲁⲩⲕⲉⲗⲉⲩⲉ
ⲛ̄ϭⲓ ⲡⲇⲟⲩⲝ ϩⲛ̄ ⲟⲩ ϭⲱⲛⲧ̄ ⲉⲧⲣⲉⲩϫⲓ ⲧⲟⲩ ⲡ̄ⲃⲟⲗ ⲛ̄ⲧⲡⲟⲗⲓⲥ ⲛ̄ⲥⲉ ϭⲓ ⲛ̄ⲧⲉⲩⲁⲡⲉ.
ⲁⲩⲱ ⲁⲩϩⲱⲧⲃ̄ ⲙ̄ⲡⲉ ϩⲟⲟⲩ ⲉⲧⲙ̄ⲙⲁⲩ ⲛ̄ⲩⲉ ⲙ̄ⲡⲁⲩⲧⲉ ⲙ̄ⲯⲩⲭⲏ, ⲁⲩ ϫⲱⲕ ⲉⲃⲟⲗ
ⲛ̄ⲧⲉⲩ ⲙⲁⲣⲧⲩⲣⲓⲁ ⲛ̄ⲥⲟⲩ ⲙⲟⲩⲛ ⲙ̄ⲡⲉⲃⲟⲧ ϩⲁⲑⲱⲣ, ϩⲛ̄ ⲟⲩ ⲉⲓⲣⲏⲛⲏ, ϩⲁⲙⲏⲛ. ⲡⲇⲟⲩⲝ
ⲇⲉ ⲁⲩⲧⲣⲉⲩϫⲓ ⲛ̄ⲛⲉⲧⲟⲩ ⲁⲁⲃ ⲉⲡⲉⲩⲧⲉⲕⲟ ϣⲁⲛ ⲧⲉⲩ ⲥⲕⲉⲡ ⲧⲉⲓ ⲙ̄ⲙⲟ ϫⲉ ⲟⲩ ⲡⲉⲧ ⲛⲁ
ⲁⲁⲩ ⲛⲁⲩ. ⲁⲥ ϣⲱⲡⲉ ⲇⲉ ϩⲓⲧⲛ̄ ⲡⲁⲩϣ ⲛ̄ⲧⲉⲩ ϣⲏ· ⲉⲓⲥ ⲡϫⲟⲉⲓⲥ ⲓ̄ⲥ̄ ⲡⲉ ϫⲉ ⲁϥⲉⲓ ⲉⲡⲉⲥ-
ⲥⲏⲧ ⲉⲃⲟⲗ ϩⲓ ⲧⲡⲉ ⲙⲛ̄ ⲛⲉϥⲁⲅⲅⲉⲗⲟⲥ ⲉ ⲧⲟⲩⲁⲁⲃ, ⲁϥⲉⲓ (R ii) ⲩ ⲁⲛⲉⲧⲟⲩⲁⲁⲃ ⲁⲡⲁ
ⲡⲁⲏⲥⲉ ⲙⲛ̄ ⲧⲉⲩ ⲥⲱⲛⲉ, ⲡⲉϫⲁⲩ ⲛⲁⲩ ϫⲉ ⲭⲁⲓⲣⲉ ⲛⲁ ⲩ ϣⲃⲏⲣ ⲕⲗⲏ ⲣⲟⲛⲟⲙⲟⲥ ⲛ̄ⲧ ⲙ̄ⲛⲧⲉⲣⲟ-
ⲣⲟ ⲛ̄ⲙ̄ ⲡⲏⲩⲉ· ⲭⲁⲓⲣⲉ ⲛⲉⲛ ⲧⲁⲩ ⲁⲅⲱⲛⲓ ⲍⲉ ⲕⲁⲗⲱⲥ ⲉⲕⲙ̄ ⲡⲉⲩ ϫⲟⲉⲓⲥ· ⲭⲁⲓⲣⲉ ⲛⲉⲧ ⲉⲙⲁ-

84 R ii 8. l. ⲛ̄ⲟⲩ ⲟⲩϩⲟⲣ. 18f. l. ⲡⲛⲉⲩⲟϩⲃⲉ. V i 24. l. ⲁⲩⲟⲛⲧϥ̄

ⲙⲁⲁⲧ ⲛ̄ⲧⲉⲡⲁⲉⲓⲱⲧ, ⲛⲉⲧⲛⲁⲕⲗⲏⲣⲟⲛⲟⲙⲉⲓ ⲛ̄ⲁⲅⲁⲑⲟⲛ ⲛ̄ⲛ̄ⲕⲁⲣⲡⲟⲥ ⲙ̄ⲡⲩⲏ(ⲛ)' ⲙ̄ⲡⲱ-
ⲛⲉ̄.' ⲛⲁⲓ ⲇⲉ ⲛ̄ⲧⲉⲣⲉϥⲥⲱⲧⲙ̄ ⲉⲣⲟⲟⲩ ⲛ̄ϭⲓ ⲡⲁⲅⲓⲟⲥ ⲁⲡⲁ ⲡⲁⲛϭⲉ ⲙ̄ⲧⲉϥⲥⲱⲛⲉ ⲑⲉⲕⲗⲁ',
ⲁⲗⲉⲩϩⲏⲧ ⲟⲩⲛⲟϭ' ⲉⲣⲟⲟⲩ ⲙ̄ⲙⲁⲧⲉ.' ⲡⲉϫⲉⲡⲕⲟⲉⲓⲥ ⲛⲁⲩ' ϫⲉ ⲙ̄ⲡⲉⲣⲣ̄ϩⲟⲧⲉ,' ⲁⲗⲗⲁ ϭⲣⲟ
ⲛ̄ⲧⲉ̄ⲧⲛ̄ϭⲟⲙ. ⲁⲛⲟⲕ ⲅⲁⲣ ϯϣⲟⲟⲡ ⲛⲙ̄ⲙⲏⲧⲛ̄. ⲑⲉⲕⲗⲁ' ⲇⲉ ⲁⲥⲡⲁⲍ ϩⲁ'ⲛⲉⲟⲩⲉ-
ⲣⲏⲧⲉ ⲙ̄(85 Vi)ⲡⲥⲱⲧⲏⲣ, ⲡⲉϫⲁⲥ' ⲛⲁⲩ ϫⲉ ⲡⲁϫⲟⲉⲓⲥ,' ⲙⲁⲣⲉⲡⲉⲕⲛⲁ' ⲧⲁϫⲟⲛ ⲛ̄ϥ-
ⲥⲕⲩⲡⲁⲍⲉ ⲛ̄ⲛ̄ⲥⲱⲙⲁ' ϫⲉ ⲙ̄ⲡⲉⲛⲓⲁⲥⲉⲃⲏⲥ' ⲛⲟϫⲟⲩ ⲛ̄ⲛⲉⲑⲏⲣⲓⲟⲛ ⲛ̄ⲥⲉⲧⲙ̄ϫⲉ ⲉ'ⲛⲉⲛ-
ⲕⲉⲉⲥ. ⲡⲉϫⲉ'ⲡⲥⲱⲧⲏⲣ ⲛⲁⲩ ϫⲉ' ⲙ̄ⲡⲣ̄ϩⲟⲧⲉ· ⲁⲛⲟⲕ' ⲡⲉⲧⲛⲁⲥⲕⲩⲡⲁⲍⲉ' ⲛ̄ⲛⲉⲧⲛ̄ⲥⲱⲙⲁ',
ⲁⲩⲱ ϯⲛⲁⲧⲣⲉⲩ'ⲕⲱⲧ ⲉⲣⲱⲧⲛ̄ ⲛ̄ⲟⲩ'ⲙⲁⲣⲧⲏⲣⲓⲟⲛ ϩⲙ̄'ⲡⲁⲣⲁⲛ· ⲁⲩⲱ ⲡⲉⲧ'ⲛⲁⲕⲱⲧ ⲉⲣⲱⲧⲛ̄'
ⲛ̄ⲟⲩⲙⲁⲣⲧⲏⲣⲓⲟⲛ.' ϯⲛⲁϣⲁⲣⲓⲍⲉ ⲙ̄ⲙⲟϥ' ⲛⲏⲧⲛ̄ ⲛ̄ⲟⲩϩⲙ̄ⲣⲉ' ϩⲛ̄ⲧⲁⲙⲛ̄ⲧⲉⲣⲟ·' ⲁⲩⲱ ⲡⲉⲧⲛⲁⲧ ⲛ̄ⲟⲩ'ⲡⲣⲟⲥⲫⲟⲣⲁ ⲉⲡⲉ'ⲧⲟⲡⲟⲥ, ϯⲛⲁ'ⲙⲉϫⲗⲉⲩϩⲓ' ⲛ̄ⲁⲅⲁⲑⲟⲛ ⲛⲓⲙ ϩⲓϫⲙ̄'ⲡⲕⲁϩ,
ⲁⲩⲱ ϯ'ⲛⲁⲧⲣⲉⲛⲁⲅⲅⲉⲗⲟⲥ ⲥⲕⲩⲡⲁⲍⲉ ⲙ̄ⲡⲉⲩⲥⲱⲙⲁ ⲙⲛ̄'ⲧⲉⲩⲯⲩⲭⲏ ϩⲛ̄ⲛⲉ'ⲱⲛ ⲙ̄ⲡ-
ⲟⲩⲟⲉⲓⲛ· (V ii) ⲛⲉⲧⲛⲁⲥϩⲁⲓ̈ ⲙ̄ⲡ'ϫⲱⲱⲙⲉ ⲛ̄ⲧⲉ'ⲧⲁⲙⲁⲣⲧⲩⲣⲓⲁ,' ϯⲛⲁⲥϩⲁⲓ̈ ⲙ̄ⲡⲉⲩ'ⲣⲁⲛ
ⲉⲡⲭⲱⲱⲙⲉ' ⲙ̄ⲡⲱⲛⲉ̄· ⲁⲩⲱ' ϯⲛⲁⲕⲱ ⲙ̄ⲡⲁⲥ'ⲙⲟⲩ ⲙⲛ̄ⲧⲁⲉⲓⲣⲏ'ⲛⲏ ϩⲛ̄ⲡⲙⲁ ⲉⲧⲟⲩ'ⲛⲁ-
ⲕⲱ ⲛ̄ⲛⲉⲧⲛ̄'ⲥⲱⲙⲁ ⲛ̄ϩⲏⲧϥ̄·' ⲁⲩⲱ ⲉⲓⲥϩⲏⲏⲧⲉ' ⲁⲓ̈ⲕⲱ ⲛ̄ϩⲣⲁϥⲁⲏⲗ ⲡⲁⲅⲅⲉⲗⲟⲥ ⲉϥ-
ⲇⲓⲁⲕⲟⲛⲉⲓ ⲉⲡⲉⲧⲛ̄ⲧⲟⲡⲟⲥ,' ⲁⲩⲱ ⲟⲩⲛ̄ϩⲉⲛⲛⲟⲟ' ⲙ̄ⲙⲏⲏⲩⲉ ⲉⲧⲩ'ⲛⲉ ϩⲛ̄ϩⲉⲛ'ⲩ'ⲛⲉ
ⲉⲩϫⲟⲃⲉ ⲛⲁⲉⲓ ⲉⲡⲉⲧⲛ̄ⲧⲟⲡⲟⲥ ⲛ̄ⲥⲉⲙⲁⲧⲉ ⲙ̄ⲡⲧⲁⲗϭⲟ' ⲛ̄ⲥⲉⲃⲱⲕ ⲉⲛⲉⲩⲏⲓ̈' ϩⲛ̄ⲟⲩⲉⲓ-
ⲣⲏⲛⲏ·' ⲁⲩⲱ ⲡⲉⲧⲛⲁⲧ ⲛ̄ⲟⲩ'ⲙⲁⲧⲛⲁ ⲛ̄ⲟⲩϩⲛ̄ⲕⲉ, ⲟⲩⲅⲁⲗⲟ' ⲏ ⲟⲩⲭⲏⲣⲁ ⲙ̄ⲡⲉ'ϩⲟⲟⲩ
ⲙ̄ⲡⲉⲧⲛ̄ⲣ̄'ⲙⲉⲉⲩⲉ, ⲏ̄ⲛⲁ ⲕⲁ'ⲁⲩ ⲁⲛ ⲉⲩϫⲁⲁⲧ' ⲛ̄ⲗⲁⲁⲩ ⲛ̄ⲁⲅⲁⲑⲟⲛ' ϣⲁⲉⲛⲉϩ.(86 Ri)
ⲙ̄ⲡⲣ̄ⲣ̄ϩⲟⲧⲉ, ⲁⲗⲗⲁ ϭⲣⲟ ⲛ̄ⲧⲉⲧⲛ̄ϭⲙ̄ϭⲟⲙ·' ⲁⲛⲟⲕ ⲅⲁⲣ ϯϣⲟ'ⲟⲡ ⲛⲙ̄ⲙⲏⲧⲛ̄·' ⲕⲉⲃⲟⲧ
ⲅⲁⲣ ⲛ̄ϩⲟⲟⲩ' ⲡⲉⲧⲉⲟⲩⲛ̄ⲧⲏⲧⲛ̄ⲉⲩ ϩⲓϫⲙ̄ⲡⲕⲁϩ' ϣⲁⲛⲧⲉⲧⲛ̄ⲉⲓ ϩⲁⲍ'ⲧⲏⲓ̈ ⲛ̄ⲧⲉⲧⲛ̄ⲙ̄ⲧⲟⲛ·
ⲙ̄ⲙⲱⲧⲛ̄ ⲉⲃⲟⲗ ϩⲛ̄ⲛⲉⲧⲛ̄ϩⲓⲥⲉ ⲛ̄ⲧⲉⲧⲛ̄ϫⲓ ⲙ̄ⲡⲉⲧⲛ̄ⲙ̄ⲧⲟⲛ' ϣⲁⲉⲛⲉϩ·' ⲛⲁⲓ̈ ⲧⲉ ⲛ̄-
ⲧⲉⲣⲉϥϫ'ⲟⲟⲩ ⲛⲁⲩ ⲛ̄ϭⲓ ⲡⲥⲱⲧⲏⲣ, ⲁϥⲁⲥ'ⲡⲁⲍⲉ ⲙ̄ⲙⲟⲟⲩ,' ⲁϥⲃⲱⲕ ⲉϩⲣⲁⲓ̈ ⲉ'ⲛⲙ̄-
ⲡⲏⲩⲉ ϩⲛ̄ⲛⲟⲩⲉⲟⲟⲩ.' ⲁⲥϣⲱⲡⲉ ⲇⲉ ⲙ̄ⲛ̄ⲥⲁⲛⲁⲓ̈ ⲁϥⲉⲓ ⲉϩⲟⲩ(ⲛ)' ⲉⲣⲁⲕⲟⲧⲉ ⲛ̄ϭⲓ
ⲟⲩⲥ'ⲕⲣⲓⲃⲱⲛ ⲛ̄ⲧⲉ'ⲡⲉⲣⲣⲟ ⲉⲁⲩⲧⲉⲛ'ⲛⲟⲟⲟⲩϥ ⲉⲃⲟⲗ ϩⲛ̄ⲕⲏⲙⲉ ⲧⲏⲣⲉϥ,' ⲁϥⲉⲓⲛⲉ ⲛ̄ⲛ̄-
ⲁⲣⲭⲱ(ⲛ)' ⲧⲏⲣⲟⲩ ⲕⲁⲧⲁⲡⲟ'ⲗⲓⲥ ϫⲉⲕⲁⲁⲥ ⲉϥⲉ'ⲱϣ ⲉⲣⲟⲟⲩ ⲙ̄ⲡⲉ'ⲡⲣⲟⲥⲧⲁⲅⲙⲁ' ⲙ̄ⲡⲣ̄ⲣⲟ·
ⲁϥⲉⲓ ⲇⲉ (R ii) ϩⲱⲱϥ ⲟⲛ ⲛ̄ϭⲓ ⲉⲩ'ⲧⲩⲭⲓⲁⲛⲟⲥ ⲡⲇⲟⲩⲍ' ⲛ̄ⲟⲩⲃⲁⲉⲓⲥ, ⲁⲩⲱ' ⲁⲩⲱϣ
ⲉⲣⲟⲟⲩ ⲛ̄'ⲛⲉⲥϩⲁⲓ̈ ⲙ̄ⲡⲣ̄ⲣⲟ·' ⲁⲩⲱ ⲙⲛ̄ⲛ̄ⲥⲁⲙ̄'ⲧⲁⲥⲉ ⲛ̄ϩⲟⲟⲩ ⲉⲩ ϩⲛ̄'ⲣⲁⲕⲟⲧⲉ, ⲁⲡⲉⲥⲧⲣⲁ-
ⲧⲉⲗⲁⲧⲏⲥ ⲕⲁ'ⲁⲩ ⲉⲃⲟⲗ ⲉⲧⲣⲉ'ⲡⲟⲩⲁ ⲇⲉ ⲡⲟⲩⲁ ⲃⲱⲕ ⲛⲁⲩ ⲉⲧⲉϥⲡⲟⲗⲓⲥ·' ϩⲁⲣⲙⲉⲛⲓⲟⲥ
ⲇⲉ' ⲡⲕⲟⲙⲓⲥ ⲛ̄ⲡⲣⲁ'ⲕⲟⲧⲉ ⲁⲩⲡⲁⲣⲁ'ⲕⲁⲗⲉⲓ ⲛ̄ⲉⲩⲧⲩ'ⲭⲓⲁⲛⲟⲥ ⲡⲇⲟⲩⲍ' ⲛ̄ⲑⲏⲃⲁⲉⲓⲥ ⲉϥ'

---

85 R ii 32 f. l. ϩⲁⲛⲉⲩⲅⲟⲩⲉⲣⲏⲧⲉ. Vis. l. ⲛ̄ⲛⲉⲛⲥⲱⲙⲁ. 24 f. l. ⲉⲡⲉⲧⲛ̄ⲧⲟⲡⲟⲥ. 32 f.
l. ϩⲛ̄ⲛⲁⲓⲱⲛ. ii 1. l. ⲛⲉⲧⲛⲁⲥϩⲁⲓ̈. 86 R i 14: 2nd l. (to V ii 23). l. ⲇⲉ. 18 f. l.
ⲛ̄ⲁⲡⲏⲩⲉ. 25 f. l. ⲉⲁⲩⲧⲛ̄ⲛⲟⲟⲩ. ii 11. a of first ⲛⲟⲩⲁ added. ⲇⲉ superfluous.

ϫⲱ ⲙ̄ⲙⲟⲥ ϫⲉ ϫⲓ ⲙ̄ⲡⲉⲓ̈ⲙⲁⲧⲟⲥ· ⲉⲛⲁⲩ· ⲁⲣⲓⲡⲉⲓ̈ϩⲙⲟⲧ ⲛⲉⲙⲟⲓ̈ ⲛ̄ⲅ̄ϫⲓⲧⲟⲩ ⲉⲣⲏⲥ
ⲛⲙ̄ⲙⲁⲕ ⲛ̄ⲅⲕⲱⲣⲓⲍⲉ ⲙ̄ⲙⲟⲟⲩ·' ⲏ ⲛ̄ⲥⲉⲑⲩⲥⲓⲁⲍⲉ· ⲏ ⲛ̄ⲅⲛⲟϫⲟⲩ ⲉⲛⲉⲑⲏⲣⲓⲟⲛ· ⲙ̄
ⲙⲟⲛ· ⲁⲩⲧⲓⲥⲱⲩ ⲙ̄ⲡⲇⲓⲕⲁⲥⲧⲏⲣⲓⲟⲛ· ⲁⲩⲱ ⲁⲓ̈ϫⲓⲥⲉ ⲉⲓ̈ⲟⲩⲱⲛ ⲉⲧⲁⲕⲟⲟⲩ·' ⲁⲩⲱ ⲙ̄
ⲡⲉⲓ̈ϭ̄ⲙ (86 V i) ϭⲟⲙ· ⲁⲩⲱ ⲁⲩⲧⲟⲩⲛⲉⲧⲡⲟⲗⲓ ⲧⲏⲣϥ̄ ϩⲓ ϩⲱⲓ̈ ⲁⲩⲱ ⲁⲩϫⲓ ⲛ̄ⲟⲩⲁⲏⲛ-
ϭⲉ ⲛ̄ⲣⲱⲙⲉ· ⲛ̄ⲧⲟⲟⲧ ϩⲛ̄ⲛⲉⲩⲙⲁⲕⲓⲁ· ⲛⲁⲓ ⲇⲉ· ⲉϥϫⲱ ⲙ̄ⲙⲟⲟⲩ· ⲛ̄ϭⲓ ϩⲁⲣⲙⲉⲛⲓⲟⲥ· ⲡⲕⲟⲙⲓⲥ, ⲁⲩⲟⲩⲉϩⲥⲁϩⲛⲉ ⲉⲧⲣⲉⲩⲉⲓⲛⲉ ⲛ̄ⲛⲉⲧⲟⲩⲁⲁⲃ· ⲉⲃⲟⲗ ϩⲙ̄ⲡⲉⲩⲧⲉⲕⲟ· ⲁⲩⲡⲁⲣϫⲓ-
ⲥ̄ⲧⲁ ⲙ̄ⲙⲟⲟⲩ ⲉⲧⲟⲟⲧϥ̄ ⲛ̄ⲉⲩⲧⲩⲭⲓⲁⲛⲟⲥ· ⲡⲇⲟⲩϫ, ⲁⲩⲧⲣⲉⲩⲛⲟϫⲟⲩ ⲉⲡⲉⲥⲏⲧ ⲉⲡⲟⲩⲏⲛⲧ
ⲙ̄ⲡϫⲟⲓ̈,' ⲁⲩⲧⲁⲗⲉ, ⲁⲩⲉⲣϩⲱⲧ· ⲉⲣⲏⲥ· ⲁⲩⲧⲁⲍⲉⲟⲩ ⲕⲟⲧⲉ ϩⲙ̄ⲡⲉⲓⲁⲣⲟ· ⲛ̄ⲥⲁϩⲏⲧ ⲛ̄ⲧⲉ-
ⲡⲱⲧ· ⲁⲡⲧⲏⲩ· ⲕⲁⲁⲩ, ⲁⲩⲙⲁⲛⲉ· ⲡϫⲟⲓ̈ ⲉⲡⲉⲕⲣⲟ, ⲉⲩⲟⲩⲱϩ· ⲉⲛⲉⲥⲟⲩ ϭⲩⲙⲟⲩⲛ ⲛ̄ϫⲟⲓ̈·
ⲁϫⲕ ⲡⲉ ⲡⲉϫⲟⲟⲩ· ⲉⲧⲙ̄ⲙⲁⲩ· ⲁⲩⲕⲉⲗⲉⲩⲉ ⲛ̄ϭⲓ ⲉⲩⲧⲩⲭⲓⲁⲛⲟⲥ ⲉⲩⲱⲣϫ̄ ⲙ̄ⲡⲃⲏⲙⲁ,
ⲁⲩⲧⲣⲉⲩⲉⲓⲛⲉ ⲛ̄ⲛⲉⲧⲟⲩ (V ii) ⲁⲁⲃ ⲉⲡⲉⲕⲣⲟ· ⲁⲩⲱ ⲁⲩⲉⲛⲧⲟⲩ ⲉϩⲣⲁⲓ̈ ϩⲙ̄ⲡⲟⲩⲏⲛⲧ· ⲙ̄
ⲡϫⲟⲓ̈, ⲉⲣⲉⲟⲩⲛⲟϭ ⲛ̄ϩⲁⲣⲓⲥ ϩⲓ ⲣⲙ̄ⲡⲉⲩϩⲟ· ⲉⲛⲉ ⲛⲉⲩⲙ̄ϭⲩⲙⲟⲩⲛ· ⲛ̄ϩⲟⲟⲩ ⲡⲉ ⲙ̄ⲡⲉⲩⲟⲩ-
ⲱⲙ ⲟⲩⲇⲉ ⲙ̄ⲡⲉⲩⲥⲱ· ⲡⲉϫⲉ ⲉⲩⲧⲩⲭⲓⲁⲛⲟⲥ ⲛⲁⲩ· ϫⲉ ⲁⲙⲏⲓⲧⲛ̄ ⲛ̄ⲧⲉⲧⲛ̄ⲑⲩⲥⲓⲁⲍⲉ ⲛ̄
ⲛ̄ⲛⲟⲩⲧⲉ ⲙ̄ⲡⲣⲣⲟ·' ⲉⲓⲥϩⲏⲏⲧⲉ ⲅⲁⲣ· ⲙ̄ⲡⲣⲱⲙⲉ ⲛⲁⲛⲁⲩ· ⲉⲣⲟⲧⲛ̄ ϩⲙ̄ⲡⲉⲓ̈ⲙⲁ· ⲡⲉϫⲉⲡⲙⲁⲕⲁⲣⲓⲟⲥ ⲁⲡⲁ ⲡⲁⲛϩⲥⲉ ⲛⲁⲩ ϫⲉ ϥ̄ⲥⲏϩ· ϫⲉ ⲡⲉⲧⲛⲁϩⲟⲙⲟⲗⲟⲅⲓ ⲙ̄ⲙⲟⲓ̈ ⲙ̄ⲡⲉⲙⲧⲟ
ⲉⲃⲟⲗ ⲛ̄ⲛⲉⲛⲣⲱⲙⲉ, ϯⲛⲁϩⲟⲙⲟⲗⲟⲅⲓ ϩⲱ· ⲛ̄ϩⲏⲧϥ̄ ⲙ̄ⲡⲁⲧⲟ· ⲉⲃⲟⲗ ⲙ̄ⲡⲁⲉⲓⲱⲧ· ⲉⲧ-
ϩⲛ̄ⲛⲉⲙⲡⲏⲩⲉ· ⲙ̄ⲛ̄ⲛⲉϥⲁⲅⲅⲉⲗⲟⲥ ⲉⲧⲟⲩⲁⲁⲃ·' ϥ̄ⲥⲏϩ ⲟⲛ ϫⲉ ⲡⲙⲁ· ⲉⲧⲉⲣⲉⲥⲛⲁⲩ ⲏ ϣⲟ-
ⲙⲛ̄ⲧ ⲥⲟⲟⲩϩ (87 R i) ⲛ̄ϩⲏⲧϥ̄ ϩⲙ̄ⲡⲁⲣⲁ(ⲛ),' ϯⲅⲟⲟⲡ ⲛⲙ̄ⲙⲁⲩ·' ⲟⲩⲕⲟⲩⲛ ⲉⲛⲡⲣⲟ·ⲧⲉ
ⲉⲍⲏⲧⲟⲩ ⲛ̄ⲛⲉ·ⲣⲱⲙⲉ; ⲙ̄ⲙⲟⲛ,' ⲁⲗⲗⲁ ⲉⲛⲉⲣϩⲟⲧⲉ ⲉϩⲏⲧϥ̄ ⲙ̄ⲡⲛⲟⲩⲧⲉ,' ⲡⲁⲓ ⲉⲧⲛⲁ-
ⲧⲟⲩϫⲟⲛ ⲉⲃⲟⲗ ϩⲛ̄ⲛⲉⲕ·ⲃⲁⲥⲁⲛⲟⲥ. ⲉϥⲥⲱⲧⲙ̄ ⲉⲛⲁⲓ ⲛ̄ϭⲓ ⲉⲩⲧⲩⲭⲓⲁⲛⲟⲥ ⲡⲇⲟⲩϫ,' ⲁⲩ-
ϭⲱⲛⲧ̄, ⲁⲩⲧⲓⲁⲡⲟⲫⲁⲥⲓⲥ ⲉⲣⲟⲟⲩ· ⲉⲩⲧⲣⲉⲩϭⲓ ⲛ̄ⲧⲉⲩⲁⲡⲉ. ⲁⲩⲱ ⲁⲩⲧⲣⲉⲩϫⲓⲧⲟⲩ ⲉϩⲟⲩⲛ·
ⲉϩⲛ̄ⲕⲁⲙ ⲙ̄ⲡⲍⲛ̄ⲥⲟⲩⲣⲉ ϫⲉⲕⲁⲁⲥ ⲉⲣⲉ·ⲛⲉⲑⲏⲣⲓⲟⲛ ⲛⲁⲟⲩⲱⲙ ⲛ̄ⲛⲉⲩⲥⲁⲣϫ·' ⲁⲩⲱ ⲛ̄
ⲧⲉⲣⲟⲩϫⲓ· ⲛ̄ⲛⲉⲧⲟⲩⲁⲁⲃ· ⲉⲡⲙⲁ ⲛ̄ⲧⲉⲩⲁⲡⲟⲫⲁⲥⲓⲥ, ⲁⲩ·ⲕⲧⲟ ⲙ̄ⲡⲉⲩϩⲟ ⲉ·ⲡⲓ̈ⲏⲃⲧ ⲉⲩ-
ϫⲱ· ⲙ̄ⲙⲟⲥ ϫⲉ ⲡϫⲟⲉⲓⲥ ⲡⲛⲟⲩⲧⲉ ⲡⲁⲛⲧⲱⲕⲣⲁⲧⲱⲣ,' ⲡⲉⲓⲱⲧ ⲙ̄ⲡⲛ̄ϫⲟⲉⲓⲥ ⲓ̄ⲥ̄ ⲡⲉ
ⲭ̄ⲥ̄, ⲡⲉⲛⲧⲁⲩϯϭⲟⲙ ⲛ̄ⲛⲉϥ (R ii) ⲡⲣⲟⲫⲏⲧⲏⲥ ⲙ̄ⲛ̄ⲛⲉϥⲁⲡⲟⲥⲧⲟⲗⲟⲥ ⲉⲧⲟⲩⲁⲁⲃ, ⲡⲛ̄-
ⲧⲁⲩϯϭⲟⲙ ⲛ̄ⲛϥ̄·ⲙⲁⲣⲧⲩⲣⲟⲥ [ⲉⲧⲟⲩ] ⲉⲧⲟⲩⲁⲁⲃ, ⲉⲕⲉϯ·ϭⲟⲙ ⲛⲁⲛ [. .] ϩⲱ·ⲱⲛ, ⲁⲩⲱ
ⲛ̄ⲧⲥ·ⲕⲉⲛⲁϩϭ ⲛ̄ⲥⲱⲙⲁ· ⲁⲩⲱ ⲛ̄ϥ̄ϫⲱⲡ ⲉ·ⲣⲟⲕ ⲛ̄ⲛⲯⲩⲭⲏ· ϩⲙ̄ⲛⲟⲩϩⲟ ⲉⲙⲉϥⲓⲏⲉ ⲛ̄
ϩⲏⲧϥ̄. ⲡⲉ·ⲟⲟⲩ ⲛⲁⲕ ⲙ̄ⲛ̄·ⲡⲉⲕⲙⲉⲣⲓⲧ· ⲛ̄ϣⲏⲣⲉ ⲉⲧⲟⲩⲁⲁⲃ· ⲓ̄ⲥ̄ ⲡⲉϫⲉ ⲡⲁϫⲟⲉⲓⲥ· ⲙ̄ⲡⲉ-

---

86 R ii 22. l. ⲛⲁ̄ⲙⲁⲓ̈. 24. 1st l. (to V ii 33). 24 f. l. ⲛ̄ⲅⲉϫⲱⲣⲓⲍⲉ. V ii. ⲛⲥ ⲁⲇⲇⲉⲇ
in margin. l. -ⲧⲡⲟⲗⲓⲥ. ii 17. l. ⲉⲣⲱⲧⲛ̄. 23 f. l. ⲁ̄ⲛ̄ⲣⲱⲙⲉ. 87 R i 1. 2nd l. (to end).
3-5. l. ⲉⲛⲉⲣϩⲟⲧⲉ ϩⲏⲧⲟⲩ ⲁ̄ⲛ̄ⲣⲱⲙⲉ. 9. l. ϩ̄ⲛⲉⲕ-. 12. l. ⲡⲇⲟⲩϫ. 15. l. ⲉⲧⲣⲉⲩϭⲓ. 21. l.
ⲛ̄ⲛⲉⲩⲥⲁⲣϫ. 24. l. ⲉⲡⲙⲁ. 29 f. l. ⲡⲡⲁⲛⲧ. ii 9; 11. l. ⲛ̄ⲛⲉⲛ-. 12 f. l. ϩ̄ⲛⲟⲩϩⲟ ⲉⲙⲁϩⲓⲛⲉ.

ΠⲚⲀ ⲈⲦⲞⲨⲀⲀⲂ ⲨⲀⲒⲚⲌⲚⲈⲌ, ⳋ²⁰ⲀⲘⲎⲚ.ⳋ ⲐⲀⲄⲒⲀ ⲐⲈⲔⲖⲀ ⲀⲤⳋⲀⲒⲨⲔⲀⲔ ⲈⲂⲞⲖⳋ ⲈⲤⳊⲰ
ⲘⲘⲞⲤ ⳋⲈⳋ ⲦⳋⲒⲚⲈ ⲈⲢⲞⲔ ⲠⲀⳋⲔⲞⲨⲒ ⲈⲨⲎⲢⲈ, ⳋⲈⳋ ⲚⲦⲚⲀⲔⲦⲞⲒ ⲀⲚⳋ ⲈⲚⲀⲨ ⲈⲢⲞⲔ Ⲛ-
ⲔⲈⳋⲤⲞⲠ ⳋⲚⲦⳋⲤⲀⲢⲈⳋ.ⳋ ⲚⲀⲒ ⲆⲈ ⲚⲦⲈⲢⲞⲨⳋⲞⲞⲨ ⲚϬⲒ ⲚⲈⲦⲞⲨⲀⲀⲂ, ⲀⲚⲔⲈⲤⲦⲞⳋⲚⲀⲢⲒⲞⲤ
ⲌⲈⲔⲠⲈⳋⳋⲀⲘⲞⲤ ⲈⲢⲞⲨ,ⳋ (87 Vi) ⲀⲨ ⲚⲦⲈⲨⲀⲠⲈ.ⳋ ⲀⲚⲞⲔ ⲠⲈ ⲒⲞⲨⲖⲒⲞⲤⳋ ⲈⲚⲈⳋⲒⳋⲞⲞⲠ
ⳋⳋ ⲚⲢⲀⳋⲔⲞⲦⲈ ⲈⲒⳋⳋⲀⲒ ⲚⲚⲈⳋⳋ ⲨⲠⲞⲘⲚⲎⲘⲀⳋ ⲚⲚⲈⲦⲞⲨⲀⲀⲂ.ⳋ ⲠⲚⲞⲨⲦⲈ ⲠⲈⲦⲤⲞⲞⲨ(Ⲛ)ⳋ ⳋⲈ
ⲚⲚⲦⲀⲒⲚⲀⲨⳋ ⲈⲢⲞⲞⲨ ⳋⲀⲚⲒⲠⲈⳋⲦⲞⲨⲀⲀⲂ, ⲘⲠⲒⲞⲨⳋⲰ ⲈⲢⲞⲞⲨ ⲞⲨⲆⲈⳋ ⲀⲠⲈⲒϤⲒ ⲚⳋⲎⲦⲞⲨ.ⳋ
ⲀⲨⲰ ⲈⲚⲈⲒⲦⲀⲖⲎⲨⳋ ⲘⲠⲠⲖⲞⲨⳋ ⲨⲀⲚⲦⲞⲨⳋⳋⲞⲔ ⲈⲂⲞⲖ ⲘⲠⲈⳋⲀⲔⲞⲚ ⲚϬⲒ ⲚⲈⲒⲠⲈ-
ⲦⲞⲨⲀⲀⲂ ⲚⲤⲞⲨⳋⲨⳋⲘⲞⲨⲚ ⲘⲠⲈⳋ²⁰ⲂⲞⲦ ⳋ ⲒⲀⳋ Ⲕ· ⲀⲒⲚⲀⲨⳋ ⲈⲈⳋⲢⲀⲪⲀⲎⲖ ⲠⲀⲄⳋⲄⲈⲖⲞⲤ ⲈⲀⲨ-
ⲤⲞⲞⲨⲦⲈⲚ ⲈⲂⲞⲖ ⲚⲚⲈϤⳋⲤⲒⳋ, ⲀⲨⳋⲰⲖ ⲘⳋⲠⲈⲤⲚⲞⲨ ⲚⲚⲈⲒⳋⲠⲈⲦⲞⲨⲀⲀⲂ,ⳋ ⲘⲠⲈⲨⲔⲀⲀϤ Ⲉ-
ⲂⲰⲔ ⳋⲒ ⳋⲨⳋⲚⳋ ⲔⲀⳋ· ⲀⲨⲰ ⲀⲒⲚⲀⲨⳋ ³⁰ⲈⲠⲈⲤⲦⲈⲢⲈⲰⲘⲀ ⲦⲎⲢϤ ⲈⲀϤⲘⲞⲨⳋ ⳋⲚⲀⲄⲄⲈⲖⲞⲤ,
(Vii) ⲀⲨⲰ ⲀⲒⲚⲀⲨ ⲈⳋⳋⲚⳋ ⲔⲖⲞⲘ ⲘⳋⲚⳋⳋⳋ ⳋⲦⲞⲖⲎ ⲈⲚⲀⳋⲨⲈⲚⲤⲞⲨⲎⲚⲦⲞⲨⳋ ⲈⲀⲨⲦⲀⲀⲨ ⳋⲒ-ⳋ
ⳋⳋⲚⲚⲈⲦⲞⲨⲀⲀⲂ.ⳋ ⲚⲈⲨⳋⳋⲈⲚⲞⳋⲈ ⲆⲈⳋ ⲚⲈⲤⲟⲟⲨ ⲈⲨⲘⲞⲞ·ⲚⲈ ⲘⲘⲞⲞⲨ ⳋⳋⳋⲠⲞⲨⳋⳋ ⲈⲦⲘⳋ
ⲘⲀⲨ, ⲈⲢⲈⲤⲞⲞⲨ ⲚⲚⲞϬ ⲚⲞⲨⳋⲞⲢ ⳋ Ⲛⳋ ⲎⲦⲞⲨ ⲈⲨⳋⳋⳋⲞⲘ ⲘⲀⲦⲈ.ⳋ ⲀⲨⲈⲢⲦⲈⲨ ⳋⲎ ⲦⲎⲢⲈ
ⲈⲦⲘⳋⲘⲀⲨ ⲈⲨⳋⲢⲞⲈⲒⲤ ⲚⲚⲈⲤⲰⲘⲀⳋ ⲚⲚⲈⲦⲞⲨⲀⲀⲂ,ⳋ ⲘⲠⲈⲨⲔⲀⲖⲀⲀⲨⳋ²⁰ ⲈⳋⲰⳋ ⲈⲢⲞⲞⲨ.ⳋ
ⲠⲖⲞⲨⳋ ⲆⲈ ⲀⲨⳋⲦⲞⲢⳋⲦⲢ ⲘⲚⲚⲈⲦⲚⲈⲘⳋⲘⲀⲨ· ⲀⲨⲔⲈⲖⲈⲨⲈⳋ ⲈⲈⲦⲢⲈⲚⲔⲈⳋ²⁵ⲦⲰⲚⲀⲢⲒⲞⲤⳋ
ⲂⲰⲔ ⲚⲤⲈⲚⲞⲨⳋ ⲚⲚⲈⲤⲰⲘⲀ ⲚⲚⲈⲦⲞⲨⲀⲀⲂⳋ ⲈⲠⲘⲞⲞⲨ· ⲚⲔⲈⳋ³⁰ⲦⲰⲚⲀⲢⲒⲞⲤ ⲆⲈⳋ ⲚⲦⲈ-
ⲢⲞⲨ ⳋ ⲰⲚ (88 Ri) ⲈⳋⲞⲨⲚ ⲚⳋⲤⲰⲘⲀⳋ ⲚⲚⲈⲦⲞⲨⲀⲀⲂ, ⲀⲨⳋ ⲞⲚ ⲄⲞⲨ ⲈⳋⲢⲀⲒ Ⲛ ⳋ Ⲥⲓ ⲚⲈⲨ-
ⳋⲞⲞⲢ, ⲀⲨⳋⲠⲖⲎⲔⲈ ⲘⲘⲞⲞⲨⳋ ⲈⲘⲀⲦⲈ. ⲚⲈⲨⳋⲞⲨⳋⲚⳋⳋⲈⲖⲖⲟ ⲆⲈⳋ ⲚⲢⲰⲘⲈⳋ ⳋ Ⲛ ⳋ ⲈⲦⲚⲞⲨϬⲈ·ⳋ
ⲠⲀⲒ ⲆⲈ ⲈⲚⲈⲞⲨⲠⲈⳋⲦⲞⲨⲀⲀⲂ ⲠⲈ ⲈⲠⳋⲈϤⲢⲀⲚ ⲠⲈ ⲀⲢⳋ.ⳋ ⲀⲨⲰ ⲀⲠⲀⲄⲄⲈⲖⲞⲤⳋ ⲘⲠⳋⳋⲞⲈⲒⲤ
ⲞⲨⲰⳋⲚⳋ ⳋ·ⳋ ⲈⲢⲞϤ ⲚⲦⲈϤⳋ¹⁵Ⲩⳋ, ⲠⲈⳋⲀϤ ⲚⲀϤ ⳋ Ⲉ ⲀⲢⳋⲈⲢⳋ ⲀⲢⳋ· ⲀⳋⲨⲞⲨⲰⳋⲂ ⳋⲈ ⲈⲒⲤ-
ⳋⲎⳋⲦⲈ ⲀⲚⲀⲔⳋ ⲠⳋⲞⲈⲒⲤ. ⲠⲈⳋⲀϤⳋ ⲚⲀϤ ⲚϬⲒ ⲠⲀⲄⲄⲈⲖⲞⲤ ⲘⲠⳋⳋⲞⲈⲒⲤⳋ ⳋⲈ ⲦⲰⲞⲨⲚ,
Ⲁ ⲘⲞⲨⳋ ⲚϤⲈⲔⲈⲖⲀⳋⲈ ⲚⲚⳋⲤⲰⲘⲀ ⲚⲚⲈⲒⲠⲈⳋ²⁵ⲦⲞⲨⲀⲀⲂ. ⲠⲈⳋⲀϤ ⲚⲀϤ ⳋⲈ ⲠⳋⳋⳋⲞ-ⳋ
ⲈⲒⲤ, ⲚⲦⲒⲤⲞⲞⲨⳋ ⲀⲚ ⲈⲠⲈⲨⲘⲀ.ⳋ ⲀⲠⲀⲄⲄⲈⲖⲞⲤ ⲘⳋⲠⳋⳋⲞⲈⲒⲤ ⲘⲞⲞⳋⲨⲈⳋ ⲚⲈⲘⲘⲀϤ· ⲀⲨ·ⳋ
ⲈⲒⲚⲈ ⲆⲈ ⲚϬⲒ ⲠⲢⲰ(R ii)ⲘⲈ ⲈⳋⳋⲚ ⲔⲞⲨⲒ Ⲛ ⳋ ⲔⲀⲒⳋⲈ· ⲀⲨⲰ Ⲛ ⳋ ⲦⲈⲢⲞⲨ ⲈⲒ Ⲉⳋⳋⳋⳋⳋ ⳋⲤⲰⲘⲀ
ⲚⲚⲈⳋⲦⲞⲨⲀⲀⲂ, ⲀⲨⲚⲀⲨ ⲈⲢⲞⲞⲨ ⲚϬⲒ ⲠⲢⲰⳋⲘⲈ ⲘⲠⲚⲞⲨⲦⲈ,ⳋ ⲠⲈⳋⲀⲨ ⳋⲈ ⲦⳋⲒⳋⲈⲠⳋⲘⲟⲦ
ⲚⲦⲟⲟⳋⲔ, ⲠⲚⲞⲨⲦⲈ,ⳋ ⳋⲈ ⲔⲀⲀⲦ Ⲛ ⳋ ⲠⳋⲠⲚⳋⲨⲀ ⲀⲒⲚⲀⲨ ⲈⳋⲤⲰⲘⲀ ⲚⲚⲈⲒⲠⲈⳋⲦⲞⲨⲀⲀⲂ. ⲀⲨⲰ
ⲀⲨⳋⲤⲞⲨⲖⲞⲖⲞⲨ ⲚⳋⲚⳋ ⲔⲀⲒⳋⲈ, ⲀⲨⳋⲒⳋⲦⲟⲩ ⲈⳋⲚⲚⲟⲩⳋⲘⲀ ⲈⲨⳋⲞⲈⳋ, ⲀⲨⳋⲦⲀⳋⲤⲟⲩ ⲨⲀ-

_____

87 R ii 19. ℓ. ⲨⲀⲈⲚⲈⳋ ⲚⲈⲚⲈⳋ. 25. ℓ. ⲚⲨⲎⲢⲈ. 29. ⲚⲦⲈⲢⲞⲨ-:Ⲉ ⲁⲇⲇⲉⲇ. 33. ℓ. ⲈⲢⲞⲞⲨ.
Vi 8. ℓ. ⲚⲈⲚⲦⲀⲒⲚⲀⲨ. 10. ℓ. ⲘⲠⲚⲈⲒ-. 16. ℓ. ⳋⲰⲔ. 17. ℓ.-ⲀⳋⲰⲚ. 21. ℓ. ⲈⳋⲢ. ℓℓ 34. ℓ.
ⲈⲚⲀⲨⲈⲤⲞⲨⲚⲀⲦⲞⲨ. 14. ℓ. ⲈⲘⲀⲦⲈ. 26f. ℓ. ⲚⲤⲈⲚⲞⲨⳋⲈ ⲚⲤⲰⲘⲀ. 88 R i 1. ℓ. ⲈⲚⲤⲰⲘⲀ.
7. Ⲛ ⲱⲣⲟⲛⲅⲗⲩ ⲁⲇⲇⲉⲇ ⲓⲛ ⲙⲁⲣⲅⲓⲛ. ℓℓ 1. ℓ. ⳋⳋⲈⲚⲔⲞⲨⲒ. 3f. ℓ. ⲈⳋⳋⳋⲤⲰⲘⲀ ⲚⲚⲈⲦⲞⲨⲀⲀⲂ.
11f. ℓ. ⲀⲔⲀⲀⲦ Ⲛ ⳋ ⲠⲚⲨⲀ. 18. ℓ. ⲈⲨⳋⲞⲤⲈ.

ⲡⲉ²⁰ϩⲟⲟⲩ ⲛ̄ⲧⲁⲥⲉⲣϩ'ⲛⲟⲩ ⲛ̄ϭⲓ ⲡⲛⲟⲩ'ⲧⲉ ⲉⲟⲩⲟⲛϩⲟⲩ ⲉ'ⲃⲟⲗ. ⲁⲩⲱ ⲧⲏⲡⲉ' ⲛ̄ⲛ̄ⲣⲱⲙⲉ
ⲛ̄ⲧⲁⲩ²⁵'ⲉⲣⲙⲁⲣⲧⲩⲣⲟⲥ' ⲙ̄ⲡⲉϩⲟⲟⲩ ⲉⲧⲙ̄'ⲙⲁⲩ ⲙ̄ⲛ̄ⲛⲉⲧⲟⲩ'ⲁⲁⲃ ⲥⲉⲉⲓⲣⲉ ⲛ̄ϣⲉ'ⲙⲁⲁⲃ
ⲥⲁϣϥⲉ ⲛ̄'ⲯⲩⲭⲏ. ⲡⲉⲟⲟⲩ' ⲙ̄ⲡⲓⲱⲧ ⲙ̄ⲛ̄ⲡϣⲏⲣⲉ ⲙ̄ⲛ̄ⲡⲉ'ⲡⲛⲁ ⲉⲧⲟⲩⲁⲁⲃ' ϣⲁⲉⲛⲉϩ,
ϩⲁⲙⲏⲛ.

---

88 R ii, 20 f. l. ⲛ̄ⲧⲁⲥⲣ̄ϩ̄ⲛⲁⲩ.

MARTYRDOM OF S. SHENOUFE AND HIS BRETHREN
FROM PIERPONT MORGAN CODEX M 583
T. 41, FF. 103–138

(103 R i) ⲧⲁⲓ ⲧⲉ ⲧⲙⲁⲣⲧⲩⲣⲓⲁ ' ⲙ̄ⲡⲁⲅⲓⲟⲥ ⲉⲧⲟⲩⲁⲁⲃ ' ⲁⲡⲁ ⲯⲩⲟⲩⲅⲉ ⲙⲛ̄ ' ⲛⲉϥ-
ⲥⲛⲏⲩ ⲛ̄ⲥⲟⲩ ' ⲥⲁϣϥ̄ ⲙ̄ⲡⲁⲟⲡⲉ, ⲍ̄ⲛ̄ ⲟⲩ ' ⲉⲓⲣⲏⲛⲏ, ⲍⲁⲙⲏⲛ. ' ⲧⲁⲓ ⲧⲉ ⲧⲩ̄ⲟⲣⲡⲉ ' ⲛ̄ⲁⲡⲟ-
ⲅⲣⲁⲫⲏ ' ⲛ̄ⲧⲁⲥϣⲱⲡⲉ ⲍ̄ⲙ̄ ' ⲡⲕⲁϩ ⲛ̄ⲕⲏⲙⲉ ' ⲉⲧⲃⲉⲛⲉⲧⲟⲩⲁⲁⲃ ' ⲍ̄ⲛ̄ⲛⲉⲍⲟⲟⲩ ⲛ̄ⲇⲓⲟⲕⲗⲏ-
ⲧⲓⲁⲛⲟⲥ ⲡⲣ̄ⲣⲟ ⲛ̄ⲁⲛⲟⲙⲟⲥ ⲉ ⲩⲟ ⲛ̄ⲣ̄ⲣⲟ ⲍ̄ⲛ̄ⲧⲁⲛⲧⲓⲟⲭⲓⲁ, ' ⲉⲣⲉⲁⲛⲇⲓⲟⲭⲟⲥ ⲟ ⲛ̄ⲍⲏ-
ⲅⲉⲙⲱⲛ ⲉⲧⲉⲫⲩⲛⲉⲓ ' ⲕⲏ, ⲉⲣⲉⲕⲟⲩⲗⲕⲓⲁ ' ⲛⲟⲥ ⲟ ⲛ̄ⲍⲏⲅⲉⲙⲱⲛ ' ⲉⲣⲁⲕⲟⲧⲉ, ' ⲉⲣⲉⲡⲟⲙ-
ⲡⲉⲓⲟⲥ ⲟ ⲛ̄ⲍⲏ ' ⲅⲉⲙⲱⲛ ⲉⲡⲉⲣⲉⲙⲟⲩ(ⲛ), ' ⲉⲣⲉⲍⲣⲟⲕⲗⲉⲓⲁⲛⲟⲥ ' ⲟ ⲛ̄ⲍⲏⲅⲉⲙⲱⲛ ⲉⲧ- '
ⲡⲟⲗⲓⲥ ⲍ̄ⲏⲣⲁⲕⲗⲁⲓⲟⲥ ' ⲙⲛ̄ⲧ̄ⲡⲟⲗⲓⲥ ⲁⲣⲥⲓⲛⲟⲛ ' ⲙⲛ̄ⲧⲕⲉⲡⲟⲗⲓⲥ ⲝⲉ ' ⲣⲓⲭⲟⲥ, ⲉⲣⲉⲁⲣⲓ-
ⲁⲛⲟⲥ ' ⲟ ⲛ̄ⲍⲏⲅⲉⲙⲱⲛ ⲉⲑⲩ ' ⲃⲁⲉⲓⲥ. ⲡⲣ̄ⲣⲟ ⲇⲉ ' ⲇⲓⲟⲕⲗⲏⲧⲓⲁⲛⲟⲥ ' ⲛⲉ ⲩ ⲍ̄ⲙⲟⲟⲥ ⲍ̄ⲛ̄-
ⲧⲙⲏ(R ii)ⲧⲉ ⲙ̄ⲡⲉⲩⲡⲁⲗⲗⲁⲧⲓ ' ⲟⲛ, ⲉⲩⲕⲱⲧⲉ ⲉⲣⲟ ⲩ ' ⲛ̄ϭⲓ ⲛⲉ ⲩ ⲡⲁⲗⲗⲁⲧⲓⲛⲟⲥ ' ⲙ̄ⲛ̄ⲛⲉ ⲩ-
ⲕⲱⲙⲏⲥ ' ⲧⲏⲣⲟⲩ, ⲙⲛ̄ⲛⲉ ⲩⲥⲕⲟⲩ ' ⲃⲓⲧⲱⲣ ⲙ̄ⲛ̄ⲛⲉ ⲩ ' ⲡⲣⲟⲧⲏⲕⲧⲱⲣ. ' ⲡⲣ̄ⲣⲟ ⲇⲉ ⲇⲓⲟⲕⲗⲏ-
ⲧⲓⲁ ' ⲕⲟⲥ ⲁ ⲩ ϣⲁⲭⲉ ⲙ̄ⲛ̄ ' ⲛⲉ ⲩ ⲛⲟϭ ⲉ ⲩ ϫⲱ ⲙ̄ⲙⲟⲥ ϫⲉ ⲥⲱⲧⲙ̄ ⲉⲣⲟⲓ ' ⲧⲏⲣⲧⲛ̄ ⲱ ⲛⲁⲩⲃⲉⲉⲣ. ' ⲧⲉⲧⲛ̄ⲥⲟⲟⲩⲛ ⲅⲁⲣ ⲧⲏⲣ ' ⲧⲛ̄ ϫⲉ ϯⲙⲉ ⲙ̄ⲙⲱⲧⲛ̄. ' ⲡⲉⲭⲁ ⲩ ⲛⲁ ⲩ ϫⲉ ⲩⲁⲭⲉ '
ⲡⲉⲛⲭⲟⲉⲓⲥ. ⲡⲉⲭⲁ ⲩ ' ⲛⲁ ⲩ ϫⲉ ⲧⲉⲧⲛ̄ⲥⲟⲟⲩⲛ ' ϫⲉ ⲙⲉⲣⲉⲡⲣ̄ⲣⲟ ϫⲓϭⲟⲗ. ' ⲁⲓⲧⲉⲓ ⲉ ⲓ-
ⲛ̄ⲕⲟⲧⲕ̄ ⲛ̄ ' ⲧⲉⲓⲟ ⲩϣⲏ, ⲁ ϥ ⲉⲓ ⲉ ⲍⲟⲩⲛ ⲩⲁⲣⲟⲓ ⲛ̄ϭⲓ ⲡⲛⲟϭ ' ⲛ̄ⲛⲟ ⲩⲧⲉ ⲡⲁⲡⲟⲗ ' ⲗⲱⲛ
ⲙ̄ⲛ̄ⲕⲉⲯⲩⲅⲉ ' ⲛ̄ⲛⲟ ⲩⲧⲉ, ⲡⲉⲭⲁ ⲩ ' ⲛⲁⲓ ⲍ̄ⲛ̄ⲧⲉ ⲩⲁⲥⲡⲉ ⲉⲧ ' ⲛⲟⲧⲙ̄ ϫⲉ ⲉⲓⲥⲍⲏⲏⲧⲉ '
ⲁⲛⲧⲁⲉⲓⲟⲕ, ⲁⲛϯ ' ⲛⲁⲕ ⲙ̄ⲡⲉⲭⲣⲟ ⲍ̄ⲙ̄ ' ⲡⲟⲗⲁⲓⲙⲟⲥ, ⲁ ⲩⲱ ' ⲁⲛϯ ⲛⲁⲕ ⲙ̄ⲡⲉⲕ-
ⲕⲗⲟⲙ ' ⲛ̄ⲧⲃⲓⲕⲧⲱⲣⲓⲁ. ' ⲛ̄ⲧⲟⲕ ⲍⲱⲱⲕ ⲧⲁ(V i)ⲉⲓⲟⲛ ⲍ̄ⲛ̄ⲧⲉⲕⲙⲛ̄ⲧ ' ⲣ̄ⲣⲟ ⲧⲏⲣⲥ̄. ⲟ ⲩ
ⲇⲉ ⲡⲉⲧⲉ ' ⲧⲛ̄ⲟ ⲩⲱϣ ⲉⲧⲣⲁⲁ ⲩ ' ⲛⲁ ⲩ; ⲁ ⲩⲟ ⲩⲱϣⲃ̄ ' ⲛ̄ϭⲓ ⲍⲣⲱⲙⲁⲛⲟⲥ ⲡⲉⲥⲧⲣⲁⲧⲏ-
ⲗⲁⲧⲏⲥ, ⲉⲧⲉ ' ⲡⲉⲓ ⲩⲧ ⲡⲉ ⲛ̄ⲁⲡⲁ ' ⲃⲓⲕⲧⲱⲣ, ⲡⲉⲭⲁ ⲩ ' ⲛⲁ ⲩ ϫⲉ ⲥⲱⲧⲙ̄ ⲉⲣⲟⲓ ' ⲱ
ⲡⲣ̄ⲣⲟ. ⲛ̄ⲑⲉ ⲉⲧⲉ ' ⲩⲟⲟⲡ ⲍ̄ⲛ̄ⲡⲕⲁϩ ' ⲛ̄ⲕⲏⲙⲉ ⲍ̄ⲛ̄ⲛⲉⲍⲟⲟⲩ ' ⲙ̄ⲫⲁⲣⲁⲱ ⲉⲧⲟⲩ- '
ⲕⲱ ⲛ̄ⲍⲧⲏⲩ ⲉ ⲛ̄ⲛ̄ⲟ ⲩⲧⲉ ⲛ̄ⲧⲁ ⲩⲧⲁⲙⲓⲟⲟ ⲩ, ' ⲛ̄ⲧⲉⲓ ϩⲉ ⲙⲁⲣⲟ ⲩⲁⲁⲥ ⲟⲛ. ' ⲧⲱⲟ ⲩⲛ,
ⲡⲣ̄ⲣⲟ, ⲛⲅ̄ⲍⲁⲓ ⲛ̄ⲟ ⲩⲇⲓⲁⲧⲁⲅⲙⲁ ' ⲉ ⲍ ⲣⲁⲓ ⲉⲕⲏⲙⲉ ϫⲓⲛ ' ⲧⲉⲍⲣⲱⲙⲁⲛⲓⲁ ' ⲧ ⲩⲟⲣⲡⲉ
ⲛ̄ⲡⲟⲗⲓⲥ ' ⲩⲁⲧϩⲁⲉ ⲛ̄ⲡⲟⲗⲓⲥ ' ϩⲓⲡⲣⲏⲥ ⲙ̄ⲡⲓⲗⲁⲭ ' ϩⲁⲧⲛ̄ⲡⲉⲇⲟⲟ ⲩ. ' ⲙⲁⲣⲟ ⲩⲕⲱⲧ
ⲙ̄ⲛⲉ ' ⲣ̄ⲡⲉ ⲛ̄ⲥⲉⲕⲱ ⲛ̄ⲛ̄ ' ⲛⲟ ⲩⲧⲉ ⲉⲧⲧⲁⲓⲏ ⲩ ' ⲛ̄ⲍⲏⲧⲟ ⲩ, ⲉⲧⲣⲉ ⲩ ' ⲧⲁⲙⲓⲟ ⲛⲁ ⲩ ⲛ̄ϩⲉⲛ- '
ⲛⲟ ⲩⲧⲉ ⲛ̄ⲛⲟ ⲩⲃ ϩⲓ ' ϩⲁⲧ ⲛ̄ⲥⲉ ⲩⲙϣⲉ ' ⲛⲁ ⲩ ⲛ̄ϭⲓ ⲛⲉⲟ ⲩⲏⲏⲃ (V ii) ⲁ ⲩⲱ ⲛ̄ⲥⲉϥⲉⲓ
ⲙ̄ⲡⲉ ⲩ ⲣⲟ ' ⲟ ⲩ ⲛ̄ⲥⲉⲧⲁⲗⲉ ⲑ ⲩⲥⲓⲁ ' ⲛⲁ ⲩ ⲉ ⲍ ⲣⲁⲓ ϩⲓⲡⲣⲡ̄ ⲛⲁ ' ⲅ ⲣⲁⲧⲱⲛ ϩⲓⲥⲁⲙⲓⲧ '
ⲉ ϥⲟ ⲩⲱ ⲩ ⲙ̄, ⲁ ⲩⲱ ' ⲛⲟ ⲩⲏⲏⲃ ⲙⲁⲣⲟ ⲩⲣⲡⲉ ⲩ ' ⲕⲁϩ ⲛ̄ⲁⲧⲧⲏⲗⲥ ⲛⲁ ⲩ ' ⲧⲁⲣⲟ ⲩ-

---

103 R i 13. At end of line, apparently a correction.   23. = -ⲍⲓⲉⲣⲟⲕⲗⲏⲓⲁⲛⲟⲥ. 25.
= ⲍⲏⲣⲁⲕⲗⲉ ⲩⲥ. 27f. = ⲟⲝⲩⲣⲩⲅⲭⲟⲥ. ii 5f. = ⲉⲝⲕⲟ ⲩⲃⲓⲧⲱⲣ, *excubitor*.
19. *l.* ⲉⲧⲓ. V i 3. *l.* ⲉⲧⲣⲁⲁ ⲩ. 4. *l.* ⲁ ⲩⲟ ⲩⲱϣⲃ̄; so frequently in this MS., where
B and Ϥ freely interchanged. 13f. *l.* ⲉ ⲩⲕⲱ? So *Epima* .(Or ⲛ̄ⲧⲁⲩ-?) 23. In *Epima*
more correctly ⲉⲧⲉⲡⲓⲗⲁⲕ ⲡⲉ. ii 7. ⲛ̄ mistakenly added; *l.* ⲛ̄ⲁⲧⲉⲗⲏⲥ

ⲱⲛ̄ϩ ⲕⲁⲗⲱⲥ ' ⲛ̄ⲥⲉϥⲓ ⲡⲣⲟⲟⲩϣ ⲛ̄ⲛⲉⲛⲟⲩⲧⲉ ⲉⲧⲧⲁⲓⲏⲩ ' ⲁⲩⲱ ⲛ̄ⲥⲉⲧⲁϩⲟ ⲉⲣⲁⲧⲟⲩ '
ⲛ̄ⲛⲁⲣⲭⲱⲛ ⲙⲛ̄ ⲛ̄ϩⲏⲅⲉⲙⲱⲛ ⲕⲁⲧⲁ ' ⲡⲟⲗⲓⲥ ⲁⲩⲱ ⲕⲁⲧⲁ ⲉⲡⲁⲣⲭⲓⲁ, ϫⲉⲕⲁⲥ
ⲉⲣⲉ ⲡⲟⲩⲁ ⲡⲟⲩⲁ ⲱⲡⲉ ⲛ̄ⲛⲉⲭⲣⲏⲥⲧⲓⲁⲛⲟⲥ ⲉⲧ ϩⲙ̄ ⲡⲉϥⲧⲟⲩ ⲛ̄ⲥⲉⲉⲓ ' ⲛ̄-
ⲥⲉⲟⲩⲱϣⲧ ⲛ̄ⲛⲉⲛⲟⲩⲧⲉ ⲙ̄ⲡⲣ̄ⲣⲟ, ⲛ̄ⲥⲉ ⲧⲁⲗⲉ ⲑⲩⲥⲓⲁ ⲉϩⲣⲁⲓ ·· ⲛⲉⲧⲛⲁⲣ̄ ⲁⲧ-
ⲥⲱⲧⲙ̄ ⲛ̄ⲥⲉ ⲛⲁϩⲟⲧⲃⲟⲩ ϩⲙ̄ ⲡⲕⲱϩⲧ ' ⲙⲛ̄ ⲧⲥⲏⲃⲉ ⲙⲛ̄ ϩⲉⲛ ⲙⲟⲩ ⲉⲩϭⲟⲥⲉ.
ⲁⲩⲱ ' ⲛ̄ϩⲏⲅⲉⲙⲱⲛ ⲉⲧ ϩⲛ̄ ⲛⲙ̄ⲡⲟⲗⲓⲥ ⲉⲧ ϩⲛ̄ ⲕⲏ ⲙⲉ ⲥϩⲁⲓ ⲉⲣⲁⲓ ⲉⲕⲏⲙⲉ ' ⲛ̄-
ⲥⲱⲟⲩ· ⲙⲁⲣⲟⲩϭⲛ̄ ⲧⲟⲩ ⲛⲁⲕ ⲉϩⲣⲁⲓ ⲉⲡⲉⲓⲙⲁ · † ⲛⲁⲩ ⲙ̄ⲡⲉⲡⲣⲟⲥⲧⲁⲅ ⲙⲁ,
ⲙⲁⲣⲉ ⲡⲟⲩⲁ ⲡⲟⲩⲁ (104 R i) ϫⲓⲧϥ̄ ⲉϩⲣⲁⲓ ⲉⲧⲉϥⲡⲁⲧⲣⲓⲥ ' ⲙⲛ̄ ⲧⲉϥ ⲉⲡⲁⲣⲭⲓⲁ ' ⲁⲩⲱ ϩⲱⲛ ⲉⲧⲟⲟⲧⲟⲩ, ' ⲙⲁⲣⲟⲩⲉⲓⲣⲉ ⲕⲁⲧⲁ ⲡⲉⲕ ⲟⲩⲉϩⲥⲁϩⲛⲉ. ⲁϥⲟⲩⲱ ϣϥ̄ ⲛ̄ϭⲓ ⲇⲓⲟⲕⲗⲏⲧⲓ ⲁⲛⲟⲥ ⲉϥϫⲱ ⲙ̄ⲙⲟⲥ ' ϫⲉ ϣϫⲉ ⲡⲟⲩϫⲁⲓ ⲙ̄ⲡ ⲛⲟϭ
ⲛ̄ⲛⲟⲩⲧⲉ ⲡⲁⲡⲟⲗ ⲗⲱⲛ ϯⲛⲁⲉⲓⲣⲉ ⲛ̄ ⲧⲉⲓ ϩⲉ, ⲁⲩⲱ ⲛ̄ϯⲛⲁⲣⲁ ⲙⲉⲗⲏⲥ ⲁⲛ.
ⲇⲓⲟⲕ ⲗⲏⲧⲓⲁⲛⲟⲥ ⲇⲉ ⲁϥⲥϩⲁⲓ ' ⲛ̄ϩⲉⲛ ⲥϩⲁⲓ, ⲁϥⲧⲟϭⲟⲩ ' ⲉⲃⲟⲗ ϩⲙ̄ ⲡⲡⲁⲗ-
ⲗⲁⲧⲓⲟⲛ ϫⲉ ⲣⲱⲙⲉ ' ⲛⲓⲙ ⲙ̄ⲙⲁⲧⲟⲓ ϩⲓ ⲥⲧⲣⲁ ⲧⲏⲗⲁⲧⲏⲥ, ⲅⲉⲛⲟⲥ ' ⲛⲓⲙ
ⲛ̄ⲣⲱⲙⲉ ⲉⲧϣⲟⲟⲡ ϩⲛ̄ ⲧⲁ ⲙⲛ̄ⲧⲣ̄ⲣⲟ ⲧⲏⲣⲥ̄, ' ⲙ̄ⲡⲣ̄ⲧⲣⲁⲥⲱⲧⲙ ⲉⲡⲉⲓ ' ⲣⲁⲛ
ϫⲉ ⲓ̅ⲥ̅, ⲁⲗⲗⲁ ⲙⲁ ' ⲣⲟⲩⲕⲱⲧⲉ ⲙ̄ⲡⲉⲩϩⲟ ' ⲉⲡⲉⲙⲛ̄ⲧ ⲛ̄ⲥⲉⲟⲩⲱϣⲧ ⲛ̄ⲛⲟⲩⲧⲉ
ⲉⲧⲧⲁⲓⲏⲩ ' ⲛ̄ⲥⲉⲧⲁⲗⲉ ⲗⲓⲃⲁⲛⲟⲥ ' ⲛⲁⲩ ⲉϩⲣⲁⲓ · ⲁⲩⲱ ⲁⲩ ' ⲧⲱⲃⲉ ⲙ̄ⲡⲇⲓⲁⲧⲁⲅ-
ⲙⲁ ' ⲉⲃⲟⲗ ϩⲙ̄ ⲡⲡⲁⲗ ⲗⲁⲧⲓⲟⲛ. ' ⲛⲉⲩⲛ̄ ⲟⲩϣⲏⲣⲉ ' ϣⲏⲙ ⲇⲉ, ⲉⲡⲉϥⲣⲉ ' ⲡⲉ
ⲛⲟⲩⲥⲧⲣⲁⲧⲏⲗⲁⲧⲏⲥ (R ii) ⲉⲡⲉϥⲣⲁⲛ ⲡⲉ ⲃⲁⲥⲓⲗⲓⲧⲏⲥ, ' ⲁⲩⲱ ⲡⲣⲁⲛ ⲙ̄ⲡ-
ϣⲏⲣⲉ ' ⲕⲟⲩⲓ ⲡⲉ ⲉⲩⲥⲉⲃⲓⲟⲥ. ' ⲛ̄ⲧⲉⲣⲉϥⲛⲁⲩ ⲉⲛⲉⲥϩⲁⲓ ⲉⲩⲧⲏⲅ ⲉⲃⲟⲗ ϩⲙ̄
ⲡⲡⲁⲗ ⲗⲁⲧⲓⲟⲛ, ⲁϥⲗⲩⲡⲓ ⲉⲙⲁⲧⲉ, ' ⲁϥⲱϣ ⲉⲃⲟⲗ ϫⲉ ⲓ̅ⲥ̅ ' ⲡⲉⲭ̅ⲥ̅ ⲃⲟⲏⲑⲉⲓ
ⲉⲣⲟⲓ ' ⲛ̄ϥϫⲉⲣⲟ ⲙ̄ⲡⲁϩⲏⲃⲥ̄ ϩⲓ ϩⲟⲩⲛ ⲙ̄ⲙⲟⲓ ϣⲁⲛⲧ ϥϯ ϭⲟⲙ ⲉϣⲁϫⲉ ⲙⲛ̄ '
ⲡⲉⲓ ⲁⲧϭⲓⲡⲉ ⲛ̄ϩⲏⲅⲉⲙⲱⲛ, ⲡⲁⲓ ⲉⲧ ⲥⲱϣϥ̄ ⲙ̄ⲡⲉⲕ ⲣⲁⲛ ' ⲉⲧⲟⲩⲁⲁⲃ. ⲛⲁⲓ ⲇⲉ '
ⲛ̄ⲧⲉⲣⲉϥϫⲟⲟⲩ, ⲁϥⲕⲁⲩ ' ⲕⲁ ϩⲏⲩ ⲙ̄ⲡⲉϥϩⲟⲕ, ' ⲁϥⲕⲁ ⲡⲉϥ ⲫⲓⲕⲁⲗⲓ ⲟⲛ ⲙ̄-
ⲙⲁⲧⲉ ϩⲓ ϫⲱϥ, ' ⲁϥ ⲃⲱⲕ ⲉϩⲟⲩⲛ ϣⲁ ⲡ ⲣⲣⲟ, ⲁϥⲁϩⲉ ⲣⲁⲧϥ̄ ϩⲓ ϩⲏ ⲙ̄ⲙⲟϥ.
ⲡⲉϫⲉ ⲡⲣⲣⲟ ⲛⲁϥ ϫⲉ ⲛⲓⲙ ⲡⲉ ' ⲡⲁⲓ; ⲡⲉϫⲁⲩ ⲛⲁϥ ' ϫⲉ ⲁⲛⲟⲕ ⲡⲉ ⲉⲩⲥⲉ-
ⲃⲓ ⲟⲥ ⲡϣⲏⲣⲉ ⲛ̄ⲃⲁⲥⲓⲗⲓ ⲧⲏⲥ. ⲡⲉϫⲉ ⲡⲣⲣⲟ ⲛⲁϥ ' ϫⲉ ⲁⲩⲱ ⲉⲧⲃⲉⲟⲩ ⲕⲁϩⲉ '
ⲣⲁⲧⲕ̄ ⲙ̄ⲡⲉⲓⲙⲁ ⲉⲡⲉ ϩⲏⲕ ⲁⲛ; ⲁⲕⲧⲁⲕⲟ ⲙ̄ⲡⲁϫⲓⲱⲙⲁ ⲙ̄ⲡⲉⲕ ⲉⲓⲱⲧ. ⲡⲉϫⲉ ⲡϣⲏ(ⲣ)ⲣⲉ ⲕⲟⲩⲓ ⲛⲁϥ ϫⲉ ⲛ̄ϯ ⲛⲁⲣ̄ ⲙⲁⲧⲟⲓ ⲛⲁⲕ ⲁⲛ ' ⲛ̄ϫⲓ ⲉ̄ ⲛ̄ⲛⲉⲓⲛⲁⲩ,

---

103 Vii 22. ⲥⲉ added, perhaps as correction of ⲛ̄ without cancellation of latter.
28. l. ⲉϩⲣⲁⲓ. 104 R i 29–31: lines short, since there is a hole in the parchment. ii 3. ⲉ added. 12 f. l. ⲛ̄ⲣ̄ⲣⲟ. 16. l. ⲁⲩⲕⲁⲁⲩ. 18 f. = -ⲫⲁⲕⲓⲁⲗⲓⲟⲛ?
But Epima has -ⲫⲉⲙⲓⲛⲁⲣⲓⲟⲛ.

ⲭⲉ ⲁⲧⲛⲟⲩⲛⲉ ⲙ̄ⲡⲇⲓⲁⲃⲟⲗⲟⲥ ⲭⲉⲛⲟⲩⲛⲉ ⲉⲃⲟⲗ ⲛ̄ϩⲏⲧⲕ̄. ⲁⲗⲗⲁ ⲉⲓⲛⲁⲣⲙⲁⲧⲟⲓ
ⲙ̄ⲡⲁϫⲟⲉⲓⲥ ⲓ̄ⲥ̄ ⲡⲉϫⲉ, ⲡⲉ(ⲛ)ⲧⲁⲩⲧⲁⲙⲓⲉⲧⲡⲉ ⲙⲛ̄ ⲡⲕⲁϩ ⲙ̄ⲛ̄ⲑⲁⲗⲁⲥⲥⲁ ⲙ̄ⲛ̄
ⲛ̄ⲉⲓⲉⲣⲣⲱⲟⲩ ⲙ̄ⲛⲉⲧⲛ̄ϩⲏⲧⲟⲩ ⲧⲏⲣⲟⲩ· ⲁⲩⲱ ⲛ̄ⲧⲟⲩ ⲡⲉⲛⲧⲁⲩⲧⲁⲙⲉⲓⲟⲓ̈ ϩⲱ,
ⲁⲩⲱ ⲉⲣⲉⲡⲁⲛⲓⲃⲉ ϩⲛ̄ⲛⲉⲩϭⲓⲭ. ⲛ̄ⲧⲉⲣⲉⲩⲭⲉⲛⲁⲓ̈ ⲛ̄ϭⲓ ⲡϣⲏⲣⲉ ⲕⲟⲩⲓ̈, ⲁⲩ-
ⲟⲩⲱϣϥ̄ ⲟⲛ ⲡⲉϫⲁⲩ ⲙ̄ⲡⲣ̄ⲣⲟ ϫⲉ ⲗⲟⲓⲡⲟⲛ ⲇⲉ ⲉⲕⲟⲩⲱϣ ⲉⲧⲣⲁⲕⲱ ⲛ̄ⲥⲱⲓ̈
ⲙ̄ⲡⲛⲟⲩⲧⲉ ⲉⲧⲟⲛϩ̄, ⲧⲁⲩⲙ̄ϣⲉ ⲛ̄ⲛⲓⲙ̄ ⲛ̄ⲛⲟⲩⲧⲉ; ⲡⲉϫⲉⲡⲣ̄ⲣⲟ ⲛⲁⲩ ϫⲉ ⲉⲓⲟⲩⲱϣ
ⲉⲧⲣⲉⲕⲩⲙ̄ϣⲉ ⲙ̄ⲡⲁⲡⲟⲗⲗⲱⲛ ⲡⲛⲟϭ ⲛ̄ⲛⲟⲩⲧⲉ. ⲡⲉϫⲉⲡϣⲏⲣⲉ ⲕⲟⲩⲓ̈ ⲛⲁⲩ ϫⲉ
ⲙ̄.ϫⲁⲣⲟⲩⲛ̄ⲧϥ̄ ⲛⲁⲓ̈ ⲉⲡⲉⲓⲙⲁ ⲛ̄ⲧⲁ (104 V ii) ⲛⲁⲩ ⲉⲣⲟϥ ϩⲱ ϫⲉⲕⲁⲥ ⲉⲣⲉⲡⲉⲟⲟⲩ ⲛ̄ⲓ̄ⲥ̄ ⲟⲩⲱⲛϩ̄ ⲉⲃⲟⲗ, ⲛⲁⲛⲓⲉⲟⲟⲩ ⲧⲏⲣⲟⲩ ⲙ̄ⲛ̄ⲓϭⲟⲙ ⲧⲏⲣⲟⲩ. ⲡⲣ̄ⲣⲟ ⲇⲉ
ⲁⲩⲕⲉⲗⲉⲩⲉ ⲛ̄ⲛ̄ⲟⲩⲏⲏⲃ, ⲁⲩⲉⲓⲛⲉ ⲙ̄ⲡⲁⲡⲟⲗⲗⲟⲛ, ⲁⲩⲧⲁϩⲟⲩ ⲉⲣⲁⲧϥ̄ ⲙ̄ⲡⲉϥⲙⲧⲟ
ⲉⲃⲟⲗ. ⲡϣⲏⲣⲉ ⲕⲟⲩⲓ̈ ⲇⲉ ⲁⲩⲧⲱⲟⲩⲛ, ⲁⲩⲁϩⲉⲣⲁⲧϥ̄, ⲁⲩⲡⲣ̄ϣ̄ⲛⲉⲩϭⲓⲭ ⲉⲃⲟⲗ ⲙ̄-
ⲡⲧⲩⲡⲟⲥ ⲙ̄ⲡⲉⲥ̄ⲣ̄ⲟⲥ, ⲁⲩⲥⲙⲟⲩ ⲉⲡⲛⲟⲩⲧⲉ ⲉϥ ϫⲱ ⲙ̄ⲙⲟⲥ ϫⲉ ⲡⲁⲭⲟ ⲉⲓⲥ ⲓ̄ⲥ̄ ⲡⲉ-
ⲭ̄ⲥ̄, ϥⲧⲟⲟⲧⲕ̄ ⲛⲙ̄ⲙⲁⲓ̈, ϫⲉ ⲡⲛⲁⲩ ⲡⲉ ⲡⲁⲓ̈ ⲛ̄ⲧⲉⲡⲉⲕⲣⲁⲛ ϫⲓ ⲉⲟⲟⲩ, ⲡⲙⲟⲛⲟⲅⲉⲛⲏⲥ
ⲙ̄ⲡⲉⲓⲱⲧ. ⲛ̄ⲧⲉⲩ ⲛⲟⲩ ⲁⲩⲧ ⲛⲟⲩⲩ̄ⲛⲟⲩⲉ ⲣⲏⲧⲉ ⲙ̄ⲡⲁⲡⲟⲗⲗⲱⲛ, ⲁⲩⲥⲕⲟⲣⲕ̄ⲣ̄ ⲉⲡⲉⲥⲏⲧ ϩⲓϫⲙ̄ⲡⲕⲁϩ ϣⲁⲛ ⲧⲉϥⲉⲓ ⲉⲡⲙⲁ ⲙ̄ⲡⲉⲑⲣⲟ ⲛⲟⲥ ⲛ̄ⲇⲓⲟⲕⲗⲏⲧⲓⲁⲛⲟⲥ. ⲁⲩϣⲱⲡⲉ ⲛ̄ⲟⲩⲥⲏⲃⲉ ⲉⲥϩⲛ̄ⲧϭⲓⲭ ⲛ̄ⲟⲩⲙⲁⲧⲟⲓ̈, ⲁⲩⲧⲁⲁⲥ ⲉϩⲟⲩⲛ ⲉⲧ ⲕⲁⲗⲁϩⲏ ⲙ̄ⲡϣⲏⲣⲉ
ⲕⲟⲩⲓ̈, ⲁⲩⲡⲉϩϩⲏⲧϥ̄ · ⲁⲩⲛⲁⲩ ⲇⲉ ⲛ̄ϭⲓ ⲙ̄ⲙⲁⲧⲟⲓ̈, ⲁⲩ (105 R i) ⲕⲱⲧⲉ ⲉⲡϣⲏⲣⲉ ⲕⲟⲩⲓ̈, ⲁⲩⲁⲁⲩ ⲙ̄ⲙⲉⲗⲟⲥ ⲙⲉⲗⲟⲥ ϩⲛ̄ⲧⲥⲏⲃⲉ· ⲁⲩϫⲱⲕ ⲉⲃⲟⲗ ⲛ̄ⲧⲉϥⲙⲁⲣ-
ⲧⲩⲣⲓⲁ ⲛ̄ⲥⲟⲩⲙⲛ̄ⲧⲁⲩⲧⲉ ⲛ̄ⲉ̄ⲡⲏⲡ, ⲁⲩϫⲓ ⲙ̄ⲡⲉⲕ ⲗⲟⲙ ⲛ̄ⲓ̄ⲥ̄ ⲡⲉϫⲉ ϩⲛ̄ⲟⲩ ⲉⲓⲣⲏⲛⲏ,
ϩⲁⲙⲏⲛ. ⲁⲥϣⲱⲡⲉ ⲇⲉ ⲙ̄ⲛ̄ⲛ̄ⲥⲁⲛⲁⲓ̈ ⲁⲇⲓⲟⲕⲗⲏⲧⲓⲁⲛⲟⲥ ϫⲉⲩⲡⲉⲛ ⲡⲣⲟⲥⲧⲁⲅⲙⲁ
ⲉϩⲟⲩⲛ ⲉⲣⲁⲕⲟⲧⲉ ⲛ̄ϣⲟⲣⲡ̄ ⲉⲧ ⲣⲟⲩⲧⲁⲁⲩ ⲛ̄ⲉⲩⲧⲏⲭⲓ ⲁⲛⲟⲥ ⲡⲕⲱⲙⲏⲥ ⲛ̄ⲣⲁ-
ⲕⲟⲧⲉ ϫⲉⲕⲁⲥ ⲉϥⲉ ⲧⲛ̄ⲛⲟⲟⲩⲩ ⲉϩⲣⲁⲓ̈ ⲉⲕⲙ̄ⲉ ⲛ̄ⲥⲉⲉⲓⲛⲉ ⲛⲁⲩ ⲛ̄ⲛ̄ϩⲏⲅⲉⲙⲱⲛ
ⲕⲁⲧⲁ ⲉⲡⲁⲣⲭⲓⲁ ⲛ̄ⲥⲉϫⲓⲧⲟⲩ ⲉⲣⲁⲧϥ̄ ⲛ̄ϩⲁⲣⲙⲉⲛⲓⲟⲥ· ⲁⲩⲱ ⲁⲩⲥⲱⲟⲩϩ ⲛ̄ϭⲓ ⲛ̄
ϩⲏⲅⲉⲙⲱⲛ ⲕⲁⲧⲁ ⲉⲡⲁⲣⲭⲓⲁ ⲁⲩⲱ ⲕⲁⲧⲁ ⲡⲟⲗⲓⲥ, ⲁⲩⲃⲱⲕ ⲉϩⲟⲩ(ⲛ) ⲉⲧⲁⲛⲧⲓ-
ⲟⲭⲓⲁ ⲉⲣⲁⲧϥ̄ ⲛ̄ⲇⲓⲟⲕⲗⲏⲧⲓⲁⲛⲟⲥ, ⲁⲩⲧⲣⲟⲩⲑⲩⲥⲓⲁⲍⲉ ⲧⲏⲣⲟⲩ ⲛ̄ⲛⲉⲛⲟⲩⲧⲉ.
ⲁⲩⲱ ⲛⲉⲛⲧⲁⲩⲟⲩⲱϣⲧ̄ ⲧⲏⲣⲟⲩ ⲙ̄ⲡⲉϩⲟⲟⲩ ⲉⲧⲙ̄ⲙⲁⲩ ⲁⲩⲙⲟⲩⲛ ⲛ̄ (R ii) ⲩⲟ
ⲙ̄ⲙⲁⲧⲟⲓ̈ ⲟⲩⲱϣⲧ̄ ⲙ̄ⲡⲩⲟⲙⲛ̄ⲧ ⲛ̄ⲧⲃⲁ ⲙ̄ⲡⲁⲅⲁⲛⲟⲥ· ⲛ̄ⲕⲟⲩⲓ̈ ⲙ̄ⲛ̄ⲛⲟϭ, ⲛ̄
ϩⲟⲟⲩⲧ ⲙ̄ⲛ̄ⲛⲉϩⲓⲟⲙⲉ, ⲣⲱⲙⲉ ⲛⲓⲙ ⲉⲧϩⲛ̄ⲧⲡⲟⲗⲓⲥ ⲉⲣⲉⲡⲁ ⲛⲓⲙ ⲟⲛϩ̄ ⲛ̄
ϩⲏⲧⲟⲩ, ⲁⲩⲧⲣⲉⲩⲟⲩⲱϣⲧ̄ ⲧⲏⲣⲟⲩ, ⲉⲩⲉⲓⲣⲉ ⲛ̄ϫⲟⲩⲧⲥⲁϣϥ̄ ⲛ̄ⲧⲃⲁ. ⲙ̄ⲛ̄ⲛ̄ⲥⲱⲥ

---

104 V i 4. ⲗ. ⲁⲛϩⲏⲧ? Cf. Epiph. 11. ⲗ. ⲙ̄ⲛ̄ⲧⲉⲓⲉⲣⲱⲟⲩ. 29 f. lines short;

ⲁⲩⲥⲁⲓ ⲛ̄ⲍ̄ⲛ̄ⲉϩⲁⲓ, ⲁⲩⲧⲁⲁⲩ ⲛ̄ⲁⲣⲓⲁⲛⲟⲥ ⲡ̄ϩⲏⲅⲉⲙⲱⲛ ¹⁵ⲛ̄ⲑⲉⲃⲁⲉⲓⲥ, ⲁⲩⲭⲟⲟⲩϥ
ⲉϩⲟⲩⲛ ⲉⲣⲁⲕⲟⲧⲉ ⲛ̄ⲩⲟⲣⲡ̄, ⲁⲩⲧⲁⲁⲩ ⲛⲉⲩⲧⲩⲭⲓⲁⲛⲟⲥ ⲡⲇⲟⲩⲝ ⲛ̄ⲣⲁⲕⲟⲧⲉ ²⁰
ⲁⲩⲕⲉⲗⲉⲩⲉ ⲛⲁⲩ ⲉⲧⲣⲉϥϯ ⲛ̄ⲟⲩⲛⲟϭ ⲛ̄ⲃⲟⲏⲑⲓⲁ ⲛ̄ⲛ̄ⲙⲁⲧⲟⲓ ⲙⲛ̄ ⲡⲉⲡⲣⲟⲥⲧⲁ
ⲅⲙⲁ, ²⁵ ϫⲉⲕⲁⲥ ⲉϥⲉϫⲓⲧⲟⲩ ⲉϩⲣⲁⲓ ⲉⲕⲏⲙⲉ ⲛ̄ϥⲡ̄ⲣⲁⲥⲥⲉ ⲙ̄ⲙⲟⲟⲩ ⲕⲁⲧⲁ ⲡⲟ
ⲗⲓⲥ · ⲉⲩⲧⲩⲭⲓⲁⲛⲟⲥ ⲇⲉ ⲡⲇⲟⲩⲝ ⲛ̄ⲣⲁ ⲕⲟⲧⲉ ⲁⲩⲙⲟⲩⲧⲉ ³⁰ ⲉⲓⲟⲩⲗⲓⲟⲥ ⲡⲃⲟⲏ
ⲑⲟⲥ ⲡⲕⲱⲙⲙⲏⲛⲧⲁⲛⲏⲥⲓⲟⲥ, ⲁⲩⲧ ⲛⲁⲩ ϩⲟⲩ(105 Vi)ⲃⲟⲏⲑⲉⲓⲁ ⲙⲙⲁⲧⲟⲓ
ⲉⲧⲣⲟⲩⲙⲟⲟⲩϣⲉ ⲙⲛ̄ ⲁⲣⲓⲁⲛⲟⲥ ⲡⲛ̄ϩⲅⲉⲙⲱⲛ ⲛ̄ⲥⲉⲉⲓⲣⲉ ⲕⲁ ⁵ⲧⲁ ⲧⲕⲉⲗⲉⲩⲉⲥⲓⲥ
ⲛ̄ⲇⲓⲟⲕⲗⲏⲧⲓⲁⲛⲟⲥ. ⲁⲩⲁⲗⲉ ⲇⲉ ⲉⲟⲩϫⲟⲓ ⲛ̄ϭⲓ ⲁⲣⲓⲁⲛⲟⲥ, ⲛ̄ⲧⲟϥ ⲙⲛ̄ ⲓⲟⲩⲗⲓⲟⲥ
ⲡⲃⲱⲏⲑⲟⲥ ¹⁰ ⲙⲛ̄ ⲧⲕⲟⲩⲥⲇⲟⲧⲓⲁ ⲛ̄ⲙ̄ⲙⲁⲧⲟⲓ, ⲁⲩⲉⲓ ⲉⲣⲏⲥ ⲉⲕⲏⲙⲉ ϩⲛ̄ⲛⲉⲓⲉⲣⲱ
ⲙⲛ̄ⲛ̄ϩⲟⲣⲙⲟⲥ ⲕⲁⲧⲁ ⲡⲟⲗⲓⲥ ¹⁵ⲁⲩⲱ ⲕⲁⲧⲁ ϯⲙⲉ ⲩⲁⲛⲧⲉϥⲉⲓ ⲉⲟⲩⲡⲟⲗⲓⲥ ϫⲉ
ⲭⲟⲣⲧⲁⲥⲁ. ⲁⲩⲙⲟⲟⲛⲉ ⲉⲡⲙⲁ ⲉⲧⲙⲙⲁⲩ ²⁰ⲛ̄ϭⲓ ⲡⲛ̄ϩⲅⲉⲙⲱⲛ. ⲁⲩⲱ ⲁⲩ?ⲁⲍ ⲛ̄
ⲣⲱⲙⲉ ϩⲓⲥϩⲓⲙⲉ ϩⲓ ⲩⲏⲣⲉ ⲕⲟⲩⲓ ⲁⲩⲕⲱ ⲛ̄ⲥⲱⲟⲩ ⲛ̄ϩⲱⲃ ⲛⲓⲙ ²⁵ⲉⲧⲩⲟⲟⲡ ⲛⲁⲩ,
ⲁⲩⲃⲱⲕ ⲩⲁ ⲡⲛ̄ϩⲅⲉⲙⲱⲛ, ⲁⲩⲱ ⲩⲡ ⲉⲃⲟⲗ ϫⲉ ⲁⲛⲟⲛ ϩⲉⲛ ⲭⲣⲏⲥⲧⲓⲁⲛⲟⲥ ⲡⲁⲣ
ⲣⲏⲥⲓⲁ. ⲁⲩϩⲙ̄ ³⁰ ⲟⲟⲥ ⲉⲣⲟⲟⲩ ⲙ̄ⲡⲣⲟⲃⲏ ⲙⲁⲧⲟⲥ ϩⲙ̄ ⲡⲉⲓⲣⲣⲟ ⲉⲧⲙ̄ⲙⲁⲩ· ⲁⲩⲱ ⲡⲉ
(Vii) ⲛⲁⲩ ⲛ̄ⲛⲉⲡⲣⲟⲉⲓⲥⲧⲟⲥ ⁵ⲧⲏⲣⲟⲩ ⲉⲧϩⲙ̄ⲡⲧⲟⲩ ⲉⲧⲙ̄ⲙⲁⲩ, ⲛⲉⲉⲡⲓⲥⲕⲟ ⲡⲟⲥ
ⲙⲛ̄ ⲛⲉⲡⲣⲉⲥⲃⲉⲧⲉⲣⲟⲥ, ⲫⲓⲗⲏⲙⲱⲛ ⲡⲉⲡⲓⲥⲕⲟⲡⲟⲥ ⲛ̄ⲑⲕⲟⲩⲓ ⲙⲛ̄ ⲁⲛⲧⲟⲛⲓ
ⲟⲥ ⲡⲉⲡⲓⲥⲕⲟⲡⲟⲥ ⲛ̄ⲁⲑⲱ ⲙⲛ̄ ⲡⲗⲁⲥⲥⲉ ⲡⲉⲡⲓⲥⲕⲟⲡⲟⲥ ¹⁰ⲛ̄ⲁⲧⲣⲩⲡⲉⲓ ⲙⲛ̄
ⲉⲓⲥⲓⲇⲓⲙⲟⲥ ⲡⲉⲡⲓⲥⲕⲟⲡⲟⲥ ⲛ̄ⲧⲥⲓⲙⲓⲥⲉ ⲛ̄ⲧⲡⲁⲣ ⲙ̄ⲃⲟⲗⲏ, ⲛⲁⲓ ⲉⲧⲩϭⲟⲡ ϩⲙ̄
ⲡⲧⲟⲩ ⲛ̄ⲣⲁⲕⲟⲧⲉ, ¹⁵ⲁⲩϯ ⲛⲁⲩ ⲛ̄ϩⲉⲛⲙⲏⲏⲩϣⲉ ⲛ̄ⲃⲁⲥⲁⲛⲟⲥ· ϩⲛ̄ⲛⲟϭ ⲇⲉ ⲛ̄ⲧⲟⲙ
ⲙⲛ̄ ϩⲉⲛ ⲩⲡⲏⲣⲉ ⲁⲩⲩⲟ ⲡⲉ ⲉⲃⲟⲗ ϩⲓ ⲧⲟⲟⲧⲟⲩ. ²⁰ⲥⲱⲧⲙ̄ ϭⲉ ϩⲱⲱⲩ ⲧⲉⲛⲟⲩ ⲛⲉⲛ
ⲧⲁⲩⲧ ⲛⲁⲩ ⲙ̄ⲡⲥⲱⲧⲙ̄, ϯⲍ̄ⲧⲏⲧⲛ̄ ⲛⲉⲛⲧⲁⲩⲧ ⲛⲁⲩ ⲛ̄ⲧⲉⲥⲃⲱ, ⲉⲡⲓⲇⲏ ⲙⲛ̄ ²⁵
ⲡⲉⲧ ϩⲟⲗ ⲉⲡⲉⲓⲣⲁⲛ ϫⲉ ⲓⲥ, ⲁⲩⲱ ⲙⲛ̄ ⲡⲉⲧ ⲧⲁⲓⲏⲩ ⲉⲡⲉⲓⲣⲁⲛ ϫⲉ ⲭⲣⲏⲥⲧⲓ
ⲁⲛⲟⲥ, ⲕⲁⲧⲁ ⲑⲉ ⲛ̄ⲧⲁⲡⲥⲁϩ ³⁰ ⲛ̄ⲁⲡⲟⲥ ⲧⲟⲗⲟⲥ ϫⲟⲟⲥ ϫⲉ ⲟⲩⲛⲟⲩ ⲛⲟϭ ⲛ̄ϩⲱⲃ
ⲕⲏ ⲛⲁⲛ ⲉϩⲣⲁⲓ ⲉⲧⲃⲉⲛⲉⲓ ⲙⲁⲣⲧⲩ(106 R i)ⲣⲟⲥ. ⲛⲁⲓ ⲇⲉ ⲧⲏⲣⲟⲩ ⲛ̄ⲧⲁ ⲩⲅ ⲱ
ⲡⲉ ϫⲉⲕⲁⲥ ⲉⲣⲉⲡⲉⲟⲟⲩ ⲛ̄ⲧⲉⲕⲕⲗⲏⲥⲓⲁ ⲟⲩⲱⲛϩ ⲉⲃⲟⲗ. ⁵ⲛⲉⲟⲩⲛ̄ ⲙⲛ̄ⲧⲟⲩⲉ ⲛ̄ⲣⲱ
ⲙⲉ ⲉⲃⲟⲗ ϩⲛ̄ⲛⲁ ⲡⲁⲓⲁⲧ, ⲉⲍⲉⲛⲉⲃⲟⲗ ϩⲛ̄ⲟⲩ ⲥⲩⲅⲅⲉⲛⲉⲓⲁ ⲛ̄ⲟⲩⲱⲧ ⲧⲏⲣⲟⲩ ⲛⲉ,
ⲉⲧⲉⲛⲁⲓ ¹⁰ⲛⲉ ⲛⲉⲩⲣⲁⲛ. ⲩⲛⲟⲩϥⲉ ⲙⲛ̄ ⲫⲓⲗⲩ ⲙⲱⲛ ⲙⲛ̄ ⲁⲡⲁ ⲛⲓⲗⲉ ⲙⲛ̄ ⲡⲉⲧⲣⲟⲥ

---

105 R ii 22. l. ⲥⲙⲁⲧⲟⲓ. 25 f. l. -ⲡⲗⲁⲥⲥⲉ; so Erima. 31 f. = -ⲕⲟⲙⲙⲉⲛⲧⲁⲣⲏⲥⲓⲟⲥ,
commentarensis. V i 7. o added, unnecessarily. 12 f. l. ϩⲛ̄ⲛⲁⲡⲣⲱ ⲙⲛ̄ⲛ̄ϩⲟⲣⲙⲟⲥ.
31. l. ϩⲛ̄ⲡⲉⲓⲉⲣⲟ. ii 1. l. -ⲡⲣⲟⲉⲥⲧⲓⲥ. 8. l. ⲁⲛⲁⲑⲱ. 10. l. ⲛⲁⲧⲣⲏⲡⲉ. 12 f. l.
-ⲡⲁⲣⲉⲙⲃⲟⲗⲏ. 106 R i 6. l. ϩⲛ̄ⲛⲁ ⲡⲁⲓⲁⲧ. 11–18. Numerals added in margin : ⲁ/
ⲃ/ⲅ/ⲇ ⲉ̄ⲋ (sic; without superlineation)/ⲍ/ⲏ̄/ⲑ ⲓ̄ⲁ ⲓ̄ⲃⲓ

ⲙ̄ⲛ̄ⲓ̈ⲱⲁⲛⲛⲏⲥ, ¹⁵ⲁⲛⲇⲣⲉⲁⲥ, ⲫⲟⲓⲃⲁ'ⲙⲱⲛ, ⲁⲛⲇⲟⲛⲓ'ⲟⲥ, ⲫⲓⲗⲓⲡⲡⲟⲥ ⲙ̄ⲛ̄ⲭⲉⲣⲙⲱⲛ '
ⲙ̄ⲁ2ⲉⲣⲙⲓⲛⲓ ⲙ̄ⲛ̄ⲟⲩⲅⲱ'ⲛⲉ ⲁⲅ2ⲓⲙⲉ ⲛ̄ⲧⲁⲩ ²⁰ⲉⲡⲉⲥⲣⲁⲛ ⲡⲉ ⲥⲟⲫⲓⲁ 'ⲛ̄ⲛⲉ2ⲉⲛ-
ⲭⲣⲏⲥⲧⲓⲁⲛⲟⲥ'ⲛⲉ ⲉⲩⲥⲁ2ⲏ ⲉⲃⲟⲗ ⲙ̄'ⲡⲉⲑⲟⲟⲩ ⲛⲓⲙ, ⲉ2ⲉⲛⲥⲁ'ⲃⲉⲉⲩ ⲛⲉ ⲙ̄ⲙⲁⲓ̈-
ⲩⲙ̄'ⲙⲟ ⲙ̄ⲙⲁⲓ̈ⲣⲱⲙⲉ 'ⲉⲩⲙⲉ ⲛ̄ⲛⲉⲩⲥⲩⲛⲁ2ⲓⲥ,'ⲙⲁⲓ̈ⲡⲣⲟⲥⲫⲟⲣⲁ,'ⲉⲣⲉⲗⲉⲏⲏ o
ⲙ̄ⲙⲁⲛⲃⲟⲓ'ⲗⲉ ⲛ̄ⲛⲉⲛⲩⲙ̄ⲙⲟ.³⁰ⲛ̄ⲛⲉ2ⲉⲛⲣ̄ⲙⲙⲁⲟ ⲉⲙⲁ'ⲧⲉ ⲛⲉ ⲕⲁⲧⲁⲡⲓⲕⲟⲥ'ⲙⲟⲥ,
ⲉⲩⲟ ⲛ̄ⲛⲁⲩⲧⲉ (106 R ii) ⲛ̄ⲛⲉⲭⲏⲣⲁ ⲧⲏⲣⲟⲩ 'ⲙ̄ⲛ̄ⲟⲣⲫⲁⲛⲟⲥ ⲉⲧ2ⲙ̄ⲡⲉⲧⲟⲩ·
ⲉⲩⲛ̄'ⲧⲁⲩ ⲙ̄ⲙⲁⲩ ⲛ̄ⲟⲩⲛⲟ6 ⁵ⲛ̄ⲉⲕⲕⲗⲏⲥⲓⲁ, ⲉⲩⲟ ⲛ̄ⲁ'ⲡⲉ ⲉⲣⲟⲥ. ⲛ̄2ⲁⲅⲓⲟⲥ'ⲇⲉ ⲛ̄-
ⲅⲉⲛⲛⲁⲓⲟⲥ ⲛ̄ⲧⲉ'ⲣⲟⲩⲥⲱⲧⲙ̄ ⲉⲧⲃⲉⲛ̄6ⲟⲙ'ⲉⲧⲉⲣⲉⲛⲉⲧⲟⲩⲁⲁⲃ ⲉⲓ 'ⲣⲉ ⲙ̄ⲙⲟⲟⲩ 2ⲙ̄
ⲡⲃⲏ'ⲙⲁ ⲛ̄ⲁⲣⲓⲁⲛⲟⲥ, ⲁⲩ'ⲉⲡⲓⲑⲩⲙⲉⲓ 2ⲱⲟⲩ 'ⲉⲡⲉⲕⲗⲟⲙ ⲛ̄ⲧⲙ̄ⲛ̄'ⲙⲁⲣⲧⲩⲣⲟⲥ,
ⲁⲩⲱ 'ⲛⲉⲩⲩ̄ⲓⲛⲉ ¹⁵ⲙ̄ⲙⲏ'ⲛⲉ ϫⲉ ⲟⲩ ⲧⲉ ⲑⲉ ⲉⲧⲟⲩ'ⲛⲁ2ⲱⲕ ⲩⲁⲡ'2ⲏⲅⲉⲙⲱⲛ, ϫⲉ'
ⲕⲁⲥ ⲉⲩⲉϫⲓ ⲙ̄ⲡⲉⲕ'ⲗⲟⲙ ⲁⲡⲉⲭⲥ. 'ⲡ2ⲁⲅⲓⲟⲥ ⲇⲉ ⲁⲡⲁ ⲩ'ⲛⲟⲩϥⲉ ⲛⲉϥⲛ̄ⲕⲟ'ⲧⲕ̄
ⲛ̄2ⲟⲩⲛ ⲉⲧⲉϥⲉⲕ'ⲕⲗⲏⲥⲓⲁ ⲙ̄ⲡⲉⲓ̈2ⲟⲟⲩ ²⁵ⲉϥⲉⲅⲣⲁⲧⲉⲩⲉ ⲙ̄ⲙⲟϥ 'ⲥⲁⲃⲟⲗ ⲙ̄ⲡⲉϥ-
ⲙⲁ(ⲛ̄)'ⲉⲛⲕⲟⲧⲕ̄. ⲉⲓⲥ ⲟⲩ'ⲣⲱⲙⲉ ⲛ̄ⲟⲩⲟⲉⲓⲛ ⲁϥⲉⲓ 'ⲉⲣⲉⲟⲩ2ⲣⲁⲩⲧⲟⲥ 2ⲛ̄'ⲧⲉϥ-
6ⲓϫ ⲛ̄ⲟⲩⲛⲁⲙ,'ⲁϥⲁ2ⲉⲣⲁⲧϥ̄ 2ⲓϫⲱϥ,'ⲁϥⲕⲓⲙ ⲉⲡⲉϥⲥⲡⲓⲣ (V i) ⲛ̄ⲟⲩⲛⲁⲙ
ⲉϥⲭⲱ ⲙ̄ⲙⲟⲥ ϫⲉ ⲩ̄ⲛⲟⲩϥⲉ,'ⲩ̄ⲛⲟⲩϥⲉ, ⲁⲟⲩⲱⲛ 'ⲛ̄ⲛⲉⲕⲃⲁⲗ ⲛ̄ⲧⲥⲟⲩ'ⲱⲛⲧ ⲇⲉ
ⲁⲛ̄ⲅⲛⲓⲙ.'ⲁⲛⲟⲕ ⲡⲉ ⲓ̄ⲥ ⲡⲉⲛⲧⲁ'ⲡⲉϥⲥⲓⲟⲩ ⲩⲁ·ⲁⲛⲟⲕ'ⲡⲉⲛⲧⲁⲅⲁⲃⲣⲓⲏⲗ ⲧⲁ-'
ⲩⲉⲟⲉⲓⲩ ⲛ̄ⲛ̄ⲩⲟⲟⲥ ¹⁰ⲉⲧⲃⲏⲏⲧϥ̄.'ⲁⲛⲟⲕ'ⲡⲉ ⲓ̄ⲥ ⲡⲉⲛⲧⲁⲙⲁⲣⲓⲁ 'ⲧⲡⲁⲣⲑⲉⲛⲟⲥ
ϫⲡⲟⲩ.'ⲁⲛⲟⲕ ⲡⲉ ⲓ̄ⲥ ⲡⲩⲁⲓ̈'ⲩ̄ⲉⲛⲟⲩϥⲉ.'ⲉⲓⲥ2ⲏ'ⲏⲧⲉ ϯⲧⲁⲩⲉⲟⲉⲓⲩ'ⲛⲁⲕ ⲙ̄ⲛ̄-
ⲛⲉⲕⲕⲉ'ⲥⲛⲏⲩ.'ⲉⲧⲃⲉⲡⲁⲓ̈'ⲟⲩⲛ ⲧⲉⲧⲛ̄2ⲙⲟⲟⲥ 'ⲉⲧⲉⲧⲛ̄ⲟ ⲛ̄ⲁⲙⲉⲗⲏⲥ ²⁰ⲛ̄ⲧⲉⲓ̈2ⲉ,
ⲉⲣⲉⲡⲁⲩⲟ(ⲛ)'ⲡⲟⲣϫ̄ ⲉⲃⲟⲗ, ⲉⲣⲉⲛⲉ'ⲧⲛ̄ⲕⲗⲟⲙ ⲕⲏ ⲉ2ⲣⲁⲓ̈;'ⲉⲡⲉⲓⲇⲏ ⲅⲁⲣ ⲕ̄-
ⲛⲁϫⲓ 'ⲛ̄ⲟⲩⲛⲟ6 ²⁵ⲛ̄ⲕⲗⲏⲣⲟ'ⲛⲟⲙⲓⲁ. ⲛ̄ⲧⲟⲕ ⲙ̄ⲛ̄'ⲡⲉⲕⲕⲉⲙ̄ⲛ̄ⲧⲟⲩⲉ'ⲛ̄ⲥⲟⲛ, ⲁ-
ⲧⲉⲧⲛ̄'ϫⲓ 2ⲱⲧⲧⲏⲩⲧⲛ̄ ³⁰ⲙ̄'ⲡⲧⲩⲡⲟⲥ ⲙ̄ⲡⲁⲙ̄'ⲧⲥⲛⲟⲟⲩⲥ ⲙ̄ⲙⲁⲑⲩ'ⲧⲏⲥ· ⲛ̄ⲧⲟⲕ
ⲇⲉ '2ⲱⲕ ⲟⲛ, ⲱ ⲡⲁⲙⲉⲣⲓⲧ, (V ii) ⲛ̄ⲛⲉⲩⲙⲟⲩⲧⲉ 6ⲉ ⲉⲡⲉⲕ'ⲣⲁⲛ ϫⲓⲛⲉⲡⲉⲓ̈-
ⲛⲁⲩ 'ϫⲉ ⲩⲉⲛⲟⲩϥⲉ, ⲁⲗⲗⲁ 'ⲉⲩⲛⲁⲙⲟⲩⲧⲉ ⲉⲣⲟⲕ ϫⲉ ⁵'ⲩ̄ⲛⲟⲩϥⲉ, ϫⲉ ⲡⲁⲓ̈
ⲡⲉ'ⲡⲩⲟⲣⲡ̄ ⲛ̄ⲭⲁⲓⲣⲉ ⲛ̄'ⲧⲁⲅⲁⲃⲣⲓⲏⲗ ⲧⲁⲩⲉⲟⲉⲓ'ⲩ̄ ⲙ̄ⲙⲟϥ ⲙ̄ⲙⲁⲣⲓⲁ 'ⲧⲁⲗⲁⲁⲩ·
ⲁϥⲧⲁⲩⲉ'ⲟⲉⲓⲩ ¹⁰ⲛⲁⲥ ϫⲉ ⲉⲓⲥ ⲡⲩⲏ̄ⲣⲉ ⲙ̄ⲡⲛⲟⲩⲧⲉ ⲛⲏⲩ 'ⲛ̄ϥ̄ϫⲓⲥⲱⲙⲁ ⲛ̄2ⲏⲧⲉ 'ⲛ̄-
ⲧⲉⲙⲓⲥⲉ ⲙ̄ⲙⲟϥ, ⲛϥ̄'ⲩⲱⲡⲉ ⲛ̄ⲟⲩⲥⲱⲧⲏⲣⲓⲁ '¹⁵ⲙ̄ⲡⲕⲟⲥⲙⲟⲥ ⲧⲏⲣϥ̄.'ⲧⲱⲟⲩⲛ 6ⲉ,
ⲃⲱⲕ ⲩⲁ'ⲡ2ⲏⲅⲉⲙⲱⲛ, ⲛ̄ⲧⲟⲕ 'ⲙ̄ⲛ̄ⲛⲉⲕⲕⲉⲥⲛⲏⲩ, 'ⲙⲁⲣⲧⲩⲣⲓ2ⲉ ⲛ̄ⲛⲉⲧⲛ̄'²⁰ⲥⲱⲙⲁ

---

106 R i 16. l. αντωνιος. 17. ⲙ̄ⲛ̄ⲭⲉⲣⲙⲱⲛ (l. ⲙ̄ⲛ̄ⲭⲁⲓⲣⲏⲙⲱⲛ) added in another hand. 18. Elsewhere 2ⲉⲣⲙⲓⲁⲧⲥ). 21. l. ⲉⲛⲉ-. 30. α added.
ii 23 f. l. ⲛ̄ⲧⲉϥⲉⲕⲕⲗⲏⲥⲓⲁ; ⲉ for ⲏ frequent in this text. 25. l. ⲉϥⲉⲧⲕⲣⲁⲧⲉⲩⲉ.
29. = -2ⲣⲁⲃⲇⲟⲥ. V i 17 f. l. ⲉⲧⲃⲉⲟⲩ ⲥⲉ (so Erman)

ⲉϩⲣⲁⲓ̈ ⲉϫⲙ ⲡⲁⲣⲁⲛ· ⲟⲩϩⲉⲛⲛⲟϭ ⲛ̄ϭⲟⲙ ⲙ̄ϩⲉⲛϣⲡⲏⲣⲉ ·ⲛⲁϣⲱⲡⲉ ϩⲓⲧⲛ̄ⲧⲏⲩⲧ̄-
ⲧⲛ̄, ⲉⲡⲓⲇⲏ ⲁⲓ̈ⲧⲱⲛ ⲛⲏⲧⲛ̄ ⲙ̄ⲙⲓ̈ⲭⲁⲏⲗ ⲡⲁⲣⲭⲁⲅⲅⲉⲗⲟⲥ ·ⲉⲧⲣⲉϥϣⲱⲡⲉ ⲉϥϫⲓ-·
ⲁⲕⲱⲛⲉⲓ ⲉⲣⲱⲧⲛ̄, ·ⲉϥⲧϭⲟⲙ ⲛⲏⲧⲛ̄ ϣⲁ(ⲛ)ⲧⲉⲧⲛ̄ϫⲱⲕ ⲉⲃⲟⲗ ⲙ̄ⲡⲉⲧⲛ̄ⲁⲅⲱⲛ· ⲛⲉ-
ⲧⲛ̄ⲥⲱⲙⲁ ⲛⲁⲣⲟⲩⲛⲟϭ (107 Ri) ⲛ̄ⲟⲩⲟⲉⲓϣ ⲉⲩϩⲏⲡ ϩⲙ̄ⲡⲕⲁϩ· ⲙⲛ̄ⲛⲥⲱⲥ
ⲥⲉⲛⲁⲟⲩⲱⲛϩ̄ ·ⲉⲃⲟⲗ, ⲁⲩⲱ ⲡⲙⲁ ⲉ·ⲧⲟⲩⲕⲱ ⲛ̄ⲛⲉⲧⲛ̄ⲥⲱⲙⲁ ⲛ̄ϩⲏⲧϥ̄, ⲙⲓⲭⲁⲏⲗ ⲡⲁⲣⲭⲁⲅⲅⲉⲗⲟⲥ ·ⲛⲁϣⲱⲡⲉ ⲉϥⲇⲓⲁⲕⲱⲛⲉⲓ ⲉⲣⲟⲟⲩ· ⲉⲣⲉ·ⲡⲉⲧⲛ̄ϫⲱⲕ ⲅⲁⲣ ⲉⲃⲟⲗ ·ⲛⲁ-
ϣⲱⲡⲉ ϩⲛ̄ⲟⲩⲡⲟⲗⲓⲥ ⲛ̄ⲩⲙ̄ⲙⲟ, ϩⲛ̄ⲟⲩⲙⲁ ⲛ̄ϣⲁⲙⲙⲟⲛⲧⲉ ⲉⲣⲟϥ· ϫⲉ ⲡⲟⲩⲃⲁⲥⲧⲉ,
ϩⲟⲡⲟⲥ ·ⲛ̄ⲧⲉⲧⲛ̄ϫⲓ ⲛ̄ⲕⲗⲟⲙ ·ⲥⲛⲁⲩ· ⲟⲩⲁ ϩⲁⲧⲉⲧⲛ̄ⲙⲛ̄ⲧⲩⲙ̄ⲙⲟ, ⲕⲉⲟⲩⲁ ·ϩⲁⲧⲉ-
ⲧⲛ̄ⲙⲁⲣⲧⲩⲣⲓⲁ ·ⲉⲧⲉⲧⲛ̄ⲁⲕⲟⲕⲉ ⲉⲃⲟⲗ. ·ⲛⲉⲧⲛ̄ⲥⲱⲙⲁ ⲛⲁϣⲱⲡⲉ ϩⲛ̄ⲟⲩⲧⲟⲡⲟⲥ ⲛ̄-
ⲟⲩⲱⲧ ϩⲙ̄ⲡⲕⲟⲥⲙⲟⲥ, ·ⲛⲉⲧⲛ̄ⲯⲩⲭⲏ ⲇⲉ ⲟⲛ ·ⲛⲁϣⲱⲡⲉ ϩⲛ̄ⲟⲩⲙⲁ ·ⲛ̄ⲟⲩⲱⲧ ϩⲛ̄-
ⲑⲓⲗⲏⲙ̄ ⲛ̄ⲧⲡⲉ. ⲁⲓ̈ⲧⲱⲛ ·ⲅⲁⲣ ⲛ̄ⲛⲓⲟⲩⲗⲓⲟⲥ ⲡⲃⲟⲏⲑⲟⲥ ⲡⲕⲱⲙⲉⲛⲧⲁⲣⲏ·ⲥⲓⲟⲥ
ⲡⲣⲙ̄ⲕⲃⲁϩⲉ ⲉⲧⲣⲉϥϭⲉⲓ ⲙ̄ⲡⲉⲧⲛ̄ⲣⲟⲟⲩϣ· ϣⲁⲡⲉϩⲟⲟⲩ ⲉⲧⲉⲧⲛⲁ·ϫⲱⲕ ⲉⲃⲟⲗ
ⲙ̄ⲡⲉⲧⲛ̄ⲁⲅⲱⲛ· ⲁⲩⲱ ⲛⲉ(Rii)ⲧⲛ̄ϩⲟⲓⲡⲟⲙⲛⲏⲙⲁ·ⲛ̄ϥⲥϩⲁⲓⲥⲟⲩ ⲛϥ̄ⲕⲁⲁⲩ·ϩⲙ̄
ⲡⲉϥⲏⲓ̈ ϣⲁⲡⲉ·ϩⲟⲟⲩ ⲉⲧⲉⲣⲉⲡⲁⲉⲓⲱⲧ ·ⲛⲁⲣϩⲛⲁϥ ⲉⲩⲟⲛϩⲟⲩ·ⲉⲃⲟⲗ. ⲛⲁⲓ ⲇⲉ ⲛ̄·
ⲧⲉⲣⲉⲡⲥⲱⲧⲏⲣ ϫⲟⲟⲩ·ϩⲙ̄ϩⲁⲅⲓⲟⲥ ⲁⲡⲁ ⲯⲛ̄ⲟⲩϭⲉ, ⲁϥⲁⲥⲡⲁⲍⲉ ·ⲙ̄ⲙⲟϥ, ⲁϥϯ
ⲛⲁⲩ ⲛ̄ϯⲣⲏⲛⲏ, ⲁϥⲃⲱⲕ ⲉⲃⲟⲗ· ϩⲓⲧⲟⲟⲧϥ̄ ϣⲁⲛⲉϥ·ⲕⲉⲥⲛⲏⲩ ⲙ̄ⲙⲁⲣⲧⲩ·ⲣⲟⲥ,
ⲁϥⲟⲩⲱⲛϩ̄ ⲉⲣⲟⲟⲩ·ϩⲱⲟⲩ ϩⲛ̄ⲟⲩϩⲟⲣⲁⲙⲁ, ·ⲁⲩⲱ ⲁϥⲧⲁⲩⲉⲟⲉⲓϣ ·ⲛⲁⲩ ⲛ̄ⲛⲉⲓϣⲁ-
ϫⲉ, ·ⲁϥⲃⲱⲕ ⲉϩⲣⲁⲓ̈ ⲉⲧⲡⲏ·ⲩⲉ ⲉⲣⲉⲁⲅⲅⲉⲗⲟⲥ ⲙ̄·ⲡⲉⲟⲟⲩ ϩⲩⲙⲛⲉⲩⲉ ϩⲁ·ⲧⲉⲩϭⲉ,
ϩⲛ̄ⲟⲩⲉⲓⲣⲏⲛⲏ, ·ϩⲁⲙⲏⲛ. ·ⲡϩⲁⲅⲓⲟⲥ ⲇⲉ ⲁⲡⲁ ⲯⲛ̄ⲟⲩϭⲉ ⲙ̄ⲡⲉϥⲁⲙⲉⲗⲉⲓ·ⲉⲡ-
ⲧⲏⲣϥ̄, ⲁⲗⲗⲁ ⲁϥ·ⲧⲱⲟⲩⲛ, ⲁϥⲉⲓ ⲉⲃⲟⲗ ϩⲛ̄·ⲧⲉⲕⲕⲗⲏⲥⲓⲁ ⲉⲧⲙ̄ⲙⲁⲩ, ·ⲁϥⲉⲓ ⲉϩⲟⲩⲛ
ⲉⲡⲉϥⲏⲓ̈, ·ⲁϥϫⲟⲟⲩ, ⲁϥⲙⲟⲩⲧⲉ ⲉⲡⲉⲓ·ⲕⲉⲙⲏⲧ ⲛ̄ϩⲁⲅⲓⲟⲥ ⲙⲛ̄·ⲧⲉⲩⲕⲉⲥⲱⲛⲉ ⲛ̄-
ⲥϩⲓⲙⲉ, ·ⲁϥⲉⲓⲣⲉ ⲛ̄ⲟⲩⲛⲟϭ ⲛ̄ⲁⲣⲓⲥ(ⲧ)ⲟⲛ ⲉⲣⲟⲟⲩ ⲛ̄ϩⲟⲩⲛ ⲉⲡⲉϥⲏⲓ̈ ⲙ̄ⲡⲉϩⲟ-
ⲟⲩ ⲉⲧⲙ̄ⲙⲁⲩ· ·ⲛ̄ⲧⲉⲣⲟⲩⲟⲩⲱⲙ ⲇⲉ ⲛ̄ⲥⲉ·ⲥⲱ ⲛ̄ⲥⲉⲟⲩⲛⲟϥ ⲙ̄·ⲙⲟⲟⲩ, ⲡⲉϫⲉⲡϩⲁ-
ⲅⲓ·ⲟⲥ ⲁⲡⲁ ⲯⲛ̄ⲟⲩϭⲉ ⲛⲁⲩ· ϫⲉ ⲛⲁⲥⲛⲏⲩ, ⲁⲓ̈ⲛⲁⲩ ·ⲉⲣⲟⲓ̈ ϩⲛ̄ⲟⲩϩⲟⲣⲁⲙⲁ ⲛ̄ⲧⲉⲓ̈·
ⲟⲩⲛⲟⲩ ⲉⲣⲉⲓ̈ⲥ ⲧⲕⲗⲟⲙ ·ⲉϫⲱⲛ ⲙ̄ⲡⲙⲛ̄ⲧⲥ·ⲛⲟⲟⲩⲥ. ⲁⲩⲟⲩⲱϣⲃ̄ ·ⲛ̄ϭⲓ ⲡⲕⲉⲙⲛ̄-
ⲟⲩⲉ ⲛ̄ϩⲁⲅⲓⲟⲥ ϩⲛ̄ⲟⲩⲥⲙⲏ ⲛ̄ⲟⲩ·ⲱⲧ ϫⲉ ⲁⲗⲏⲑⲱⲥ ·ⲡⲉⲛⲧⲁⲕⲛⲁⲩ ⲉⲣⲟϥ · ⲁⲛ-
ⲛⲁⲩ ⲉⲣⲟϥ ϩⲱⲛ, ·ⲛ̄ϣⲁϫⲉ ⲛ̄ⲧⲁⲩϫⲟⲟⲩ·ⲛⲁⲕ ⲁⲩϫⲟⲟⲩ ⲉⲣⲟⲛ ·ϩⲱⲛ. ⲡⲉϫⲉ·
ⲡϩⲁⲅⲓⲟⲥ ⲁⲡⲁ ⲯⲛ̄ⲟⲩϭⲉ ⲛⲁⲩ· ϫⲉ ⲁⲩⲱ ·ⲟⲩ ⲡⲉⲧϩⲙ̄ⲡⲉⲧⲛ̄·ϩⲏⲧ ⲉⲧⲃⲉⲛ̄ϣⲁϫⲉ ·
ⲛ̄ⲧⲁⲩϫⲟⲟⲩ ⲛⲏⲧⲛ̄; ·ⲁⲩⲟⲩⲱϣⲃ̄ ⲛ̄ϭⲓ ⲛⲉⲧⲟⲩⲁⲁⲃ ϫⲉ ϥⲟⲛϩ̄ ·ⲛ̄ϭⲓ ⲡⲛⲟⲩⲧⲉ ϫⲉ·

---

107 Ri 1. -ⲟⲩⲟⲉⲓϣ: second o added. 2. -ⲟⲩⲱⲛϩ̄: ⲱ added. 13. l. ϩⲟⲡⲟⲥ. 26. l. ⲛ̄ⲓ̈
ii 1. = ϩⲩⲡ. 4. ⲉⲧⲉⲣⲉ-: second and third ⲉ added. 15. = -ϩⲟⲣⲁⲙⲁ. 21. l. -ϩⲙ
V i 1 f. l. ⲡⲉϥⲏⲓ̈. 8. -ϩⲟⲣⲟⲙⲁ; second o added.

ⲡⲙⲁ ⲉⲧⲉⲕⲛⲁⲃⲱⲕ 'ⲉⲣⲟⲩ, ⲧⲁⲛⲁⲟⲩⲁⲍⲉⲛ ⲛ̄ⲥⲱⲕ, ⲁⲩⲱ'ⲛⲙⲟⲩ ⲉⲧⲉⲕⲛⲁⲙⲟⲩ
ⲛ̄ⲍⲏⲧϥ, ⲧⲁⲛⲁⲙⲟⲩ (107 Vⁱⁱ) ⲛ̄ⲍⲏⲧϥ ⲍⲱⲛ, ⲇⲉ'ⲕⲁⲥ ⲛ̄ⲑⲉ ⲙ̄ⲡⲉⲡⲗⲱⲣⲉ̄'ⲉ
ⲛⲉⲛⲉⲣⲏⲩ ⲅⲓⲥⲙ̄ⲡⲕⲁⲍ 'ⲛ̄ⲧⲁ̄ⲧⲁⲡⲗⲱⲣⲉ̄ ⲟⲛ 'ⲍⲙ̄ⲡⲏ ⲙ̄ⲡⲛⲟⲩⲧⲉ. 'ⲁⲩⲧⲱⲟⲩⲛ ⲛ̄ϭⲓ
ⲛ̄ⲍⲁⲅⲓⲟⲥ, 'ⲁⲩⲁⲍⲉⲣⲁⲧⲟⲩ, ⲁⲩⲩⲗⲏⲗ 'ⲍⲓⲟⲩⲥⲟⲡ. ⲛ̄ⲧⲉⲣⲟⲩⲥⲱ 'ⲇⲉ ⲛ̄ⲥⲉⲟⲩⲛⲟⲩ ⲙ̄
ⲙⲟⲟⲩ, 'ⲁⲩⲃⲱⲗ ⲉⲃⲟⲗ ⲍⲙ̄ⲡⲁⲣⲓⲥ'ⲧⲟⲛ· ⲁⲡⲟⲩⲁ ⲡⲟⲩⲁ 'ⲃⲱⲕ ⲉⲡⲉⲩⲏⲓ, ⲁⲩⲧ'ⲡⲧⲱϣ
ⲙ̄ⲡⲉⲩⲏⲓ ⲉⲧⲟ'ⲟⲧⲟⲩ ⲛ̄ⲛⲉⲩⲣⲱⲙⲉ 'ⲙ̄ⲛⲛⲉⲩϣⲙ̄ⲣⲉ· ⲁⲗⲗⲁ 'ⲙ̄ⲡⲟⲩⲧⲁⲙⲉⲗⲁⲁⲩ ⲉⲡ'
ⲙⲩⲥⲧⲏⲣⲓⲟⲛ ⲉⲓⲙⲏⲧⲉ 'ⲛ̄ⲧⲟⲟⲩ ⲙⲁⲩⲁⲁⲩ. 'ⲡⲍⲁⲅⲓⲟⲥ ⲇⲉ ⲁⲡⲁ ⲩⲛⲟⲩⲅ̄ϭⲉ, ⲛ̄ⲧⲉ
ⲣⲉⲩⲛ̄ⲕⲟⲧⲕ̄ 'ⲛ̄ⲍⲟⲩⲛ ⲉⲡⲉⲩⲏⲓ,' ⲉⲓⲥ ⲡ̄ϫⲟⲉⲓⲥ ⲁϥⲉⲓ ϣⲁⲣⲟⲩ, 'ⲡⲉϫⲁⲩ ⲛⲁⲩ ϫⲉ
ⲭⲁⲓ'ⲣⲉ ⲩⲛⲟⲩⲅⲉ ⲡⲁⲩⲃⲣ̄'ⲙⲉⲗⲟⲥ· ⲁⲕⲡⲁⲣⲓⲥⲧⲟⲛ 'ⲙ̄ⲛⲛⲉⲕⲥⲛⲏⲩ ⲍⲙ̄'ⲡⲉⲓⲕⲟⲥ
ⲙⲁ· ⲧⲉⲛⲟⲩ' ϭⲉ ⲥⲃ̄ⲧⲱⲧⲕ̄ ϫⲉ ⲉⲕⲉⲁ'ⲁⲩ ⲉⲣⲟⲩ ⲍⲛ̄ⲧⲁⲡⲟⲗⲓⲥ 'ⲑⲓⲗⲏⲙ ⲛ̄ⲧⲡⲉ,
ⲉⲕⲟ'ⲛ̄ⲁⲡⲉ ⲉⲣⲟⲟⲩ ⲍⲛ̄ⲧⲁⲙⲛ̄'ⲧⲣ̄ⲣⲟ ⲉⲧⲍⲛ̄ⲙ̄ⲡⲏⲩⲉ. (108 Rⁱ) ⲧⲣⲏⲛⲏ ⲙ̄ⲡⲁ·
ⲉⲓⲱⲧ' ⲉⲥⲉϣⲱⲡⲉ ⲛ̄ⲙ̄ⲙⲏⲧⲛ̄' ⲩⲁⲉⲛⲉⲍ, ⲍⲁⲙⲏⲛ. 'ⲁⲩⲱ ⲁⲡⲥⲱⲧⲏⲣ ⲃⲱⲕ 'ⲉⲍⲣⲁⲓ
ⲙ̄ⲡⲏⲩⲉ ⲉⲣⲉⲡⲍⲁ'ⲅⲓⲟⲥ ⲁⲡⲁ ⲩⲛⲟⲩⲅⲉ 'ϭⲱϣⲧ̄ ⲛ̄ⲥⲱⲩ ⲩⲁ'ⲉⲍⲣⲁⲓ ⲉⲧⲡⲉ· ⲡⲍⲁⲅⲓ'
ⲟⲥ ⲇⲉ ⲁⲡⲁ ⲩⲛⲟⲩⲅⲉ 'ⲁⲩϣⲟⲣⲡϥ̄ ⲉⲍⲧⲟⲟⲩⲉ 'ⲙ̄ⲡⲁⲧⲉⲗⲁⲁⲩ ⲛ̄ⲣⲱ'ⲙⲉ ⲧⲱⲟⲩⲛ·
ⲁⲩⲃⲱⲕ,' ⲁⲩⲛⲉⲍⲥⲉ ⲙ̄ⲡⲕⲉⲗⲙ̄'ⲧⲟⲧⲉ ⲛ̄ⲍⲁⲅⲓⲟⲥ, ⲁⲧⲉⲓ 'ⲉⲡⲥⲁ ⲙ̄ⲡⲉⲓⲃⲉⲧ ⲙ̄'
ⲡⲉⲩⲏⲓ, ⲁⲩⲩⲗⲏⲗ 'ⲍⲓⲟⲩⲥⲟⲡ, ⲁⲩⲙⲟⲟⲩ⳥ 'ⲍⲓⲟⲩⲥⲟⲡ ⲩⲁⲛⲧⲟⲩ'ⲉⲓ ⲉⲍⲣⲁⲓ ⲉϫⲉⲛ
ⲧⲉⲙ̄'ⲣⲱ ⲛ̄ⲭⲟⲣⲧⲁⲥⲁ, ⲉⲡ'ⲙⲁ ⲉⲧⲉⲣⲉⲡⲍⲏⲅⲉⲙ'ⲱⲛ ⲛ̄ⲍⲏⲧϥ̄. 'ⲁⲩⲛⲁⲩ ⲉⲣⲟⲩ ⲉⲩ
ⲍⲙⲟⲥ 'ⲍⲙ̄ⲡⲣⲟⲃⲏⲙⲁⲧⲟⲥ, 'ⲉⲩⲧⲁⲕⲣⲓⲛⲉⲓ ⲙ̄ⲡⲙⲏ'ⲏⲩⲉ ⲛ̄ⲛⲉⲭⲣⲏⲥⲧⲓ'ⲁⲛⲟⲥ· ⲁⲩ
ⲧ̄ ⲙ̄ⲡⲉⲩ'ⲟⲩⲟⲓ ⲉⲍⲣⲁⲓ ⲉⲭⲙ̄ⲡⲃⲏ'ⲙⲁ, ⲁⲩⲱϣ ⲉⲃⲟⲗ 'ϫⲉ ⲱ ⲡⲁⲛⲟⲙⲟⲥ ⲛ̄'ⲍⲏⲅⲉ
ⲙⲱⲛ, ⲩⲁⲧ'ⲛⲁⲩ ϭⲉ ⲕ̄ϯⲍⲓⲥⲉ ⲛ̄ⲛⲉ(Rⁱⁱ)ⲛ̄ⲍⲙⲍⲁⲗ ⲙ̄ⲡⲉⲭ̄ⲥ̄, 'ⲉⲕⲁⲛⲁⲅⲕⲁⲍⲉ
ⲙ̄ⲙⲟⲟⲩ 'ⲉⲧⲟⲩⲕⲱ ⲛ̄ⲥⲱⲟⲩ 'ⲙ̄ⲡⲛⲟⲩⲧⲉ ⲉⲧⲟⲛⲍ̄ 'ⲛ̄ⲥⲉⲩⲙ̄ϣⲉ ⲛ̄ⲍⲉⲛ'ⲛⲟⲩⲧⲉ ⲉⲩ
ⲙⲟⲟⲩⲧ; ⲁⲛⲟⲛ ⲅⲁⲣ ⲍⲱⲛ, ⲁⲛⲟⲛ ⲍⲉⲛⲭⲣⲏⲥⲧⲓⲁⲛⲟⲥ,'ⲁⲩⲱ ⲁⲛⲟⲛ ⲍⲛ̄ⲍⲙ̄ⲍⲁⲗ
ⲛ̄'ⲧⲉⲡⲛⲟⲩⲧⲉ ⲉⲧⲟⲛⲍ̄' ⲓⲥ̄ ⲡⲉⲭⲥ̄. ⲡⲉϫⲉ'ⲡⲍⲏⲅⲉⲙⲱⲛ ⲛⲁⲩ 'ⲍⲓⲧⲛ̄ⲡⲍⲉⲣⲙⲏⲛⲉⲩ'
ⲧⲏⲥ ϫⲉ ⲛ̄ⲧⲉⲧⲛ̄'ⲍⲉⲛⲉⲃⲟⲗ ⲧⲱⲛ, ⲓⲉ 'ⲁⲩ ⲛ̄ⲭⲱⲣⲁ, ⲓⲉ ⲛ̄'ⲧⲁⲧⲉⲧⲛⲉⲓ ⲉⲡⲉⲓⲙⲁ'
ⲉⲃⲟⲗ ⲧⲱⲛ; ⲁⲩⲟⲩ'ⲱϣⲃ̄ ⲛ̄ϭⲓ ⲡⲍⲁⲅⲓⲟⲥ 'ⲁⲡⲁ ⲩⲛⲟⲩⲅⲉ ⲡⲉ'ⲭⲁⲩ ⲙ̄ⲡⲍⲏⲅⲉ
ⲙⲱ(ⲛ) 'ϫⲉ ⲉⲧⲃⲉⲟⲩ ⲣⲱ ⲕ̄ϫⲓⲛⲉ ⲛ̄ⲥⲁⲡⲉⲛⲧⲙⲉ;'ⲁⲛⲟⲛ ⲍⲉⲛⲉⲃⲟⲗ ⲍⲛ̄'ⲙ̄ⲡⲁ
ⲉⲓⲁⲧ ⲛ̄ⲧⲉⲡⲉ'ϯⲛⲏ· ⲁⲩⲱ ⲁⲛⲟⲛ 'ⲍⲉⲛⲥⲛⲏⲩ ⲙ̄ⲛⲉ'ⲛⲉⲣⲏⲩ, ⲁⲩⲱ ⲧⲛ̄'ⲡⲟⲗⲓⲥ ⲙ̄ⲙⲉ
ⲧⲉ ⲧⲑⲓ'ⲗⲏⲙ ⲛ̄ⲧⲡⲉ ϫⲓⲛ'ⲡⲟⲟⲩ ⲉⲃⲟⲗ, ⲧⲁⲓ ⲉⲙⲉ'ⲣⲉⲡⲉⲥⲣⲏ ⲍⲱⲧⲡ̄ ⲉⲛⲉⲍ,(V i)
ⲟⲩⲇⲉ ⲙⲉⲣⲉⲡⲉⲥⲟⲟⲍ 'ϫⲱⲕⲃ̄· ⲁⲗⲗⲁ ⲡⲉⲛ'ϫⲟⲉⲓⲥ ⲓⲥ̄ ⲡⲉⲧⲣ̄ⲟⲩⲟⲉⲓ(ⲛ) 'ⲉⲣⲟⲥ

---

107 Vⁱ 31. ⲗ. ⲉⲧⲉⲕⲛⲁⲙⲟⲩ. ⁱⁱ 27. ⲗ. -ⲕⲟⲥⲙⲟⲥ. 108 Rⁱ 5. ⲗ. ⲉⲙ̄ⲡⲏⲩⲉ. 23.
ⲗ. ⲉⲩⲍⲙⲟⲟⲥ. 25. = -ⲇⲓⲁⲕⲣⲓⲛⲉⲓ. ⁱⁱ 2. = -ⲁⲛⲁⲅⲕⲁⲍⲉ. 9. ⲁⲩⲱ added. 15ϥ.
=ⲏ. 25ϥ. = -ⲡⲉⲇⲓ(ⲉⲓ)ⲛⲏ. 29. ⲗ. ⲑⲓⲗⲏⲙ. Vⁱ 2. ⲗ. ϫⲱⲕⲃ̄.

ⲛ̅ⲛⲁⲩ ⲛⲓⲙ. ⲛ̅ⲧⲉⲣⲉϥⲥⲱⲧⲙ̅ ⲇⲉ ⲉⲛⲁⲓ̈ ⲛ̅ϭⲓ ⲁⲣⲓⲁⲛⲟⲥ ⲡϩⲏⲅⲉⲙⲱⲛ, ⲁϥϭⲱⲛⲧ
ⲉⲙⲁⲧⲉ, ⲁϥⲕⲉⲗⲉⲩⲉ ⲉⲧⲣⲟⲩⲕⲟⲩⲙ̅ⲡⲟⲥ ⲉϩⲟⲩⲛ ⲉⲣⲟⲟⲩ, ϣⲁⲛⲧⲉⲛⲉⲩⲟⲃϩⲉ ϫⲉ
ⲁⲡⲃⲉⲣⲉⲧⲱⲛ ⲱ̅ϣ ⲉⲃⲟⲗ ϫⲉ ⲧⲱⲙ ⲉⲣⲱⲧⲛ̅, ⲕⲁⲣⲱⲧⲛ̅, ⲙ̅ⲡⲣ̅ⲧⲣⲁⲥⲱⲧⲙ̅ ⲉ ⲡⲉⲓⲣⲁⲛ
ϫⲉ ⲓ̅ⲥ̅ ⲉⲃⲟⲗ ϩⲛ̅ ⲣⲱⲧⲛ̅. ⲁϥⲟⲩⲱϣⲃ̅ ⲛ̅ϭⲓ ⲡϣⲟⲉⲓⲭ ⲛ̅ⲧⲙⲛ̅ⲧⲉⲩⲥⲉⲃⲏⲥ, ⲡⲉ
ϫⲁϥ ⲙ̅ⲡϩⲏⲅⲉⲙⲱⲛ ϫⲉ ⲉⲧⲃⲉⲟⲩ ⲣⲱ ⲕ̅ϫⲓⲟⲩⲉ ⲉϩⲟⲩⲛ ϩⲛ̅ ⲣⲱⲛ; ⲡⲉϫⲉ ⲡϩⲏ
ⲅⲉⲙⲱⲛ ⲛⲁϥ ϫⲉ ⲉⲡⲓⲇⲏ ⲁⲕϫⲉϩⲁϩ ⲛ̅ϣⲁϫⲉ ⲙ̅ⲡⲁⲓ̈ⲧⲟ ⲉⲃⲟⲗ, ⲁⲕⲧⲁⲡⲟⲗⲟ
ⲅⲓⲁ ϩⲁ ⲛⲉⲓ̈ⲕⲟⲟⲩⲉ ⲛ̅ⲥⲉϣⲁϫⲉ ⲁⲛ. ⲁϥⲟⲩⲱϣⲃ̅ ⲛ̅ϭⲓ ⲛⲉⲧⲟⲩⲁⲁⲃ ϩⲛ̅ ⲟⲩⲥⲙⲏ
ⲛ̅ⲟⲩⲱⲧ ⲉⲩϫⲱ ⲙ̅(108 V ii)ⲙⲟⲥ ϫⲉ ⲛ̅ⲧⲁⲛⲉⲓ ⲉⲡⲉⲓ̈ⲙⲁ ϩⲛ̅ ⲟⲩϩⲏⲧ ⲛ̅ⲟⲩⲱⲧ, ⲉ
ⲧⲣⲉⲛⲡⲱⲣϫ̅ ⲉⲃⲟⲗ ⲙ̅ⲡⲉⲛⲥⲛⲟⲩ ⲉϫⲙ̅ ⲡⲣⲁⲛ ⲙ̅ⲡⲉϫⲥ̅ ⲓ̅ⲥ̅. ⲛ̅ⲧⲉⲩⲛⲟⲩ ⲁϥϭⲱ
ϣⲧ̅ ⲛ̅ϭⲓ ⲡϩⲏⲅⲉⲙⲱⲛ ⲉϫⲛ̅ ⲡⲙ̅ⲙⲏ ⲉ ⲉⲧⲕⲱⲧⲉ ⲉⲣⲟϥ, ⲁϥⲛⲁⲩ ⲉⲣⲟⲟⲩ ⲉⲩ
ⲥⲃ̅ⲧⲱⲧ ⲉⲣⲡⲟⲗⲩⲙⲟⲥ ⲛ̅ⲙⲙⲁⲩ ⲛ̅ⲥⲉϫⲓ ⲛ̅ⲛⲉϩⲁϩⲓⲟⲥ ⲛ̅ⲧⲟⲟⲧϥ̅, ⲁϥⲣ̅ϩⲟⲧⲉ, ⲁϥ
ⲕⲉⲗⲉⲩⲉ ⲉⲧⲣⲟⲩϣⲱⲡⲉ ⲛ̅ⲛⲁⲙⲁⲣⲧⲩⲣⲟⲥ ⲛ̅ⲥⲉⲛⲟϫⲟⲩ ⲉⲡⲉⲥⲏⲧ ⲉⲡⲟⲩⲛⲧ ⲙ̅ⲡ
ϣⲟⲓ, ⲁⲩⲱ ⲁⲩⲣ̅ϩⲱⲧ ⲉⲣⲏⲥ ϣⲁⲛⲧⲟⲩϩⲱⲛ ⲉϩⲟⲩⲛ ⲉⲧⲡⲟⲗⲓⲥ ⲙⲏⲃⲉ. ⲁϥⲕⲉ
ⲗⲉⲩⲉ ⲛ̅ϭⲓ ⲡϩⲏⲅⲉⲙⲱⲛ ⲉⲧⲣⲟⲩⲙⲁⲛⲟⲩ ⲡϣⲟⲓ̈ ⲉⲡⲉⲕⲣⲟ, ⲁϥⲃⲱⲕ ⲉϩⲟⲩⲛ ⲉⲡⲣⲉ
ⲛ̅ⲧⲡⲟⲗⲓⲥ, ⲁϥⲟⲩⲱϣⲧ̅, ⲁϥⲉⲓ ⲉⲃⲟⲗ, ⲁϥⲕⲉⲗⲉⲩⲉ ⲉⲧⲣⲟⲩⲛ̅ⲛⲉⲧⲟⲩⲁⲁⲃ ⲛⲁⲩ
ⲉϩⲟⲩⲛ ⲉⲡⲏⲓ̈. ⲛⲉⲩⲥⲱⲕ ϩⲓⲑⲏ ⲙ̅ⲙⲟⲟⲩ ⲛ̅ϭⲓ ⲡⲡⲉⲧⲟⲩⲁⲁⲃ ⲁⲡⲁ ⲯⲟⲩⲅⲉ,
ⲉϥⲧⲁⲟⲩⲟ ⲙ̅ⲡⲉⲓ̈ⲯⲁⲗⲙⲟⲥ ⲛ̅ⲧⲉⲓ̈ϩⲉ ϫⲉ ⲙⲁⲣⲉⲡⲛⲟⲩⲧⲉ (109 R i) ⲧⲱⲟⲩⲛ
ⲛ̅ⲧⲉⲛⲉⲩϣⲁϫⲉ ϫⲱⲱⲣⲉ ⲉⲃⲟⲗ. ⲛⲉⲩⲟⲩⲱϩⲙ̅ ⲛ̅ⲥⲱϥ ⲛ̅ϭⲓ ⲡⲙⲏⲏϣⲉ ⲛ̅ⲛⲉ
ⲧⲟⲩⲁⲁⲃ. ⲛ̅ϩⲟⲥⲟⲛ ⲉⲩⲙⲟⲟϣⲉ ϩⲛ̅ ⲧⲉⲡⲗⲁⲧⲓⲁ, ⲉⲓⲥ ⲛⲉⲧⲟⲩⲱⲧ ⲁⲩϫⲓ ⲛ̅ⲟⲩ
ⲥⲙⲏ ⲛ̅ⲣⲱⲙⲉ, ⲉⲩϫⲱ ⲙ̅ⲙⲟⲥ ϫⲉ ⲭⲁⲓⲣⲉ ⲁⲡⲁ ⲯⲟⲩⲅⲉ ⲡⲁⲡⲣⲁⲛ ⲛ̅ⲣⲁ ⲉ·
ⲭⲁⲓ̈ⲣⲉ ⲛⲉⲩⲕⲉⲥⲛⲏⲩ ⲉⲧⲧⲁⲓ̈ⲏⲩ· ⲛⲁⲓⲁⲧⲛ̅ ⲁⲛⲟⲛ ⲙ̅ⲡⲟⲟⲩ ϫⲉ ⲁⲕⲉⲓ ϣⲁⲣⲟ(ⲛ),
ⲁⲕⲛ̅ⲯⲩⲭⲉ ⲛⲟⲩϥⲉ ⲛⲁ(ⲛ) ⲉϩⲟⲩⲛ ⲉⲧⲛ̅ⲡⲟⲗⲓⲥ· ⲛⲁⲓⲁⲧϥ̅ ⲙ̅ⲙⲁ ⲛⲓⲙ ⲉⲧⲩⲛⲁϫⲓ
ⲧⲕ̅ ⲉⲣⲟϥ· ⲛⲁⲓⲁⲧϥ̅ ⲙ̅ⲡⲙⲁ ⲉⲧⲟⲩ ⲛⲁⲕⲁ ⲛⲉⲧⲛ̅ⲥⲱⲙⲁ ⲛ̅ϩⲏⲧϥ̅. ⲛ̅ⲧⲉⲣⲉ ⲡⲙ
ⲏⲏϣⲉ ⲇⲉ ⲥⲱⲧⲙ̅ ⲉⲛⲉⲧⲟⲩⲱⲧ ⲉⲩϫⲱ ⲛ̅ⲛⲁⲓ̈, ⲁⲩϯⲉⲟⲟⲩ ⲛ̅ⲧ ⲥⲓⲛ ⲡⲁⲣⲁⲅⲉ ⲛ̅
ⲛⲉⲧⲟⲩⲁⲁⲃ, ⲁⲩⲡⲁϩⲧⲟⲩ ⲉⲡⲉⲥⲏⲧ, ⲁⲩⲟⲩⲱϣⲧ̅ ⲛⲁⲩ ⲙ̅ⲡⲙⲁⲕⲁⲣⲓⲟⲥ ⲁⲡⲁ
ⲯⲟⲩⲅⲉ ⲉⲩϫⲱ ⲙ̅ⲙⲟⲥ ϫⲉ ⲛⲁⲓⲁⲧ ⲁⲛⲟ(ⲛ) ϫⲉ ⲁⲛⲏⲡϩⲁ ⲁⲧⲉ ⲧⲛ̅ⲡⲁⲣⲁⲅⲉ
ⲙ̅ⲙⲟⲛ. ⲛ̅ⲧⲉⲩⲛⲟⲩ ⲉⲓⲥ ⲟⲩⲣⲟ (R ii) ⲙⲉ ⲛ̅ⲃⲗ̅ⲗⲉ ⲉϥⲙⲟⲟⲥ ϩⲛ̅ ⲧⲉⲡⲗⲁⲧⲓⲁ ⲛ̅
ⲧⲡⲟⲗⲓⲥ, ⲛ̅ⲧⲉⲣⲉϥⲥⲱ ⲧⲙ̅ ⲉⲛⲉⲧⲉⲣⲉ ⲡⲙⲏ ⲩϣⲉ ϫⲱ ⲙ̅ⲙⲟⲟⲩ, ⲁⲩⲛⲉⲥ ⲛⲉϥϩⲟⲓⲧⲉ
ⲉⲃⲟⲗ ⲙ̅ⲡⲛⲉϥⲥⲕⲉⲟⲥ ⲉⲧϥ̅ ϫⲓ ⲙ̅ⲛ̅ⲧⲛⲁ ⲛ̅ϩⲏⲧⲟⲩ, ⲁⲩⲉⲓ ⲉϥⲡⲏⲧ, ⲁⲩⲡⲁϩⲧϥ̅
ϩⲁⲣⲁⲧⲟⲩ ⲛ̅ⲛⲉⲩⲟⲩⲉⲣⲏⲧⲉ ⲛ̅ⲛⲉⲧⲟⲩⲁⲁⲃ, ⲁⲩⲡⲁⲣⲁⲕⲁⲗⲉⲓ ⲙ̅ⲙⲟⲟⲩ ϫⲉⲕⲁⲥ ⲉⲩⲉ

---

108 V i 28 f. l. ⲉ ⲛ̅ⲥⲉϣⲁϫⲉ.   109 R ii 7. = -ⲥⲕⲉⲩⲟⲥ

ϯⲡⲟⲩⲟⲉⲓⲛ·ⲉⲛⲉⲩⲃⲁⲗ· ⲡϫⲁⲅⲓⲟⲥ ⲇⲉ ⲁⲡⲁ ⲩⲛⲟⲩϭⲉ·ⲁⲩⲱⲗⲏⲗ ⲉϥϫⲱ ⲙ̄ⲙⲟⲥ ϫⲉ
ⲥⲱⲧⲙ̄ ⲉⲣⲟⲓ·ⲡⲁϫⲟⲉⲓⲥ ⲓⲥ ⲡⲉϫⲥ̄,· ⲡⲉⲛⲧⲁⲩⲛⲉϫⲧⲉⲩⲡⲁϭⲥⲉ ⲉϫⲙ̄ⲡⲕⲁϩ,ⲁⲩⲧⲁ
ⲙⲓⲟ ⲛ̄ⲟⲩⲟⲙⲉ,ⲁⲩ·ⲗⲁⲗⲟⲟⲩ ⲉⲛⲉⲃⲁⲗ ⲙ̄·ⲡⲃⲗ̄ⲗⲉ ⲙ̄ⲙⲓⲥⲉ,ⲁⲩ·ⲛⲁⲩ ⲉⲃⲟⲗ·ⲉⲕⲉ
ⲟⲩⲱⲛ ⲛ̄ⲛ̄ⲃⲁⲗ ⲙ̄ⲡⲉⲓϩⲏⲕⲉ·ⲛ̄ⲣⲱⲙⲉ ⲛ̄ⲅ̄ⲉⲓⲣⲉ·ⲙ̄ⲡⲉϥϩⲱⲃ ⲛ̄ϭⲱⲛϩ̄·ϩⲁ
ⲡⲉⲕⲛⲁ· ⲛ̄ⲧⲉⲩⲛⲟⲩ ⲁⲩⲛⲉⲓⲃⲉ ⲉϩⲟⲩⲛ·ⲉϩⲣⲁⲩ ⲛ̄ϣⲟⲙⲛ̄ⲧ ⲛ̄ⲥⲟⲡ·ϩⲙ̄ⲡⲣⲁⲛ
ⲙ̄ⲡⲉⲓⲱⲧ·ⲙ̄ⲡⲗ̄ϣⲏⲣⲉ ⲙ̄ⲡⲉⲡⲛ̄ⲁ (109 V i) ⲉⲧⲟⲩⲁⲁⲃ· ⲁⲩⲱ ⲛ̄·ⲧⲉⲩⲛⲟⲩ
ⲁⲛⲉⲩⲃⲁⲗ·ⲟⲩⲱⲛ,ⲁⲩⲛⲁⲩ ⲉⲃⲟⲗ.·ⲉⲓⲥ ⲕⲉⲣⲱⲙⲉ ⲟⲛ ⲉⲣⲉ·ⲧⲉⲩϭⲓϫ ϣⲟⲩ
ⲱⲟⲩ·ⲙ̄ⲡⲉⲩⲥⲡⲓⲣ ⲛ̄ⲟⲩ·ⲛⲁⲙ ⲛⲉⲩⲙⲟⲟⲩϣⲉ·ϩⲛ̄ⲛⲉⲡⲗⲁⲧⲓⲁ ⲉϥ·ⲕⲱⲗϫ̄,ⲉ
ⲙ̄ⲡϣ̄ⲃⲟⲙ·ⲉϭⲟⲩⲧⲱⲛϭ ⲉϩⲣⲁⲓ,·ⲛ̄ⲧⲉⲣⲉϥⲛⲁⲩ ⲉⲧⲃⲟⲙ·ⲛ̄ⲧⲁⲥϣⲱⲡⲉ ⲙ̄·ⲡ
ⲃⲗ̄ⲗⲉ,ⲁⲩⲧⲡⲉϥ·ⲟⲩⲟⲓ ⲉⲡϫⲁⲅⲓⲟⲥ ⲁⲡⲁ·ⲩⲛⲟⲩϭⲉ,ⲁⲩⲡⲁⲣⲁ·ⲕⲁⲗⲉⲓ ⲙ̄·
ⲙⲟⲩ ϫⲉ·ⲕⲁⲥ ⲉϥⲉⲑⲉⲣⲁⲡⲉⲩⲉ·ⲙ̄ⲙⲟⲩ ϩⲱⲱϥ.·ⲡϫⲁⲅⲓⲟⲥ ⲇⲉ ⲁⲡⲁ ⲩⲛⲟⲩ
ϭⲉ ⲁϥⲥⲱⲕ·ⲛ̄ⲟⲩⲥⲧⲁⲩⲣⲟⲥ ϩⲛ̄ⲧⲉϥ·ϭⲓϫ ⲙ̄ⲡⲉⲩⲥⲡⲓⲣ·ⲉϥϫⲱ ⲙ̄ⲙⲟⲥ ϫⲉ ϩⲙ̄·
ⲡⲣⲁⲛ ⲙ̄ⲡⲁϫⲟⲉⲓⲥ·ⲓⲥ ⲡⲉϫⲥ̄,ⲡⲉⲧⲉⲣⲉ·ⲛ̄ⲧⲁⲗϭⲟ ⲙ̄ⲛ̄ⲡⲱⲛϩ̄·ϣⲟⲟⲡ ⲉⲃⲟⲗ
ϩⲓⲧⲟⲟⲧϥ̄,·ⲙⲁⲣⲉⲡⲉⲕⲉⲟⲟⲩ ⲙ̄ⲛ̄·ⲧⲉⲕϭⲟⲙ ⲟⲩⲱⲛϩ̄ ⲉⲃⲟⲗ·ϩⲛ̄ⲡⲉⲓⲣⲱⲙⲉ. ⲛ̄
ⲧⲉⲩⲛⲟⲩ ⲁⲧⲉⲩⲥⲁⲣⲝ ϣⲱ·ⲡⲉ ⲉⲥⲣⲟⲟⲩⲧ ⲛ̄ⲑⲉ ⲛ̄(V ii)ⲧⲁⲟⲩϣⲏⲣⲉ ⲕⲟⲩⲓ,·ⲁⲩ
ⲙⲟⲟϣⲉ ⲉⲡⲓⲥⲁ ⲙ̄ⲛ̄ⲡⲁⲓ ϩⲛ̄ⲧⲉⲡⲗⲁⲧⲓⲁ·ⲛ̄ⲧⲡⲟⲗⲓⲥ,ⲉⲩϯⲉⲟⲟⲩ ⲙ̄ⲛ̄ⲛⲟⲩⲧⲉ
ⲙ̄ⲡϫⲁⲅⲓⲟⲥ ⲁⲡⲁ ⲩⲛⲟⲩϭⲉ,ⲡⲏ·ⲉⲃⲟⲗ ϩⲛ̄ⲙⲡⲁⲓⲁⲧ·ⲙ̄ⲛ̄ⲛⲉⲩⲕⲉⲥⲛⲏⲩ.·ⲛ̄
ⲧⲉⲣⲟⲩⲭⲓⲧⲟⲩ ⲇⲉ ⲛⲁⲩ·ⲉⲕⲙ̄ⲡⲃⲏⲙⲁ,ⲡⲉ·ϫⲉⲡϩⲏⲅⲉⲙⲱⲛ·ⲛⲁⲩ ϫⲉ ⲛ̄ⲧⲟⲕ
ⲡⲉ·ⲩⲛⲟⲩϭⲉ ⲡⲉⲓⲉⲃⲟⲗ·ϩⲛ̄ⲙ̄ⲡⲁⲓⲁⲧ·ⲁⲙⲟⲩ,ⲟⲩⲱϣⲧ ⲛ̄ⲛ̄ⲛⲟⲩⲧⲉ ⲙ̄ⲛ̄
ⲛⲉⲕⲥⲛⲏⲩ·ⲕⲁⲧⲁⲡⲟⲩⲉϩⲥⲁϩⲛⲉ ⲛ̄ⲛ̄ⲣ̄ⲣⲱⲟⲩ.ⲡⲉϫⲉ·ⲡϫⲁⲅⲓⲟⲥ ⲁⲡⲁ ⲩⲛⲟⲩ·ϭⲉ
ⲛⲁⲩ ϫⲉ ϥⲥⲏϩ·ϫⲉ ⲛ̄ⲛⲉⲕⲟⲩⲱϣⲧ·ⲛ̄ⲗⲁⲁⲩ ⲉⲓⲙⲏⲧⲓ ⲉⲡ·ⲛⲟⲩⲧⲉ ⲙⲁⲩⲁⲁϥ,
ⲡⲉ·ⲧⲕ̄ⲛⲁϣⲙ̄ϣⲉ ⲛⲁϥ.·ⲧⲉⲛⲟⲩ ⲇⲉ ⲛ̄ⲛⲉⲥϣ·ⲡⲉ ⲛⲁⲛ ⲛ̄ⲧⲛⲟⲩ·ⲱϣⲧ ⲛ̄ⲕⲉ
ⲛⲟⲩⲧⲉ·ⲉⲓⲙⲏⲧⲓ ⲉⲡⲛⲟⲩⲧⲉ·ⲡⲉⲓⲱⲧ ⲙ̄ⲡⲉϥ·ϣⲏⲣⲉ ⲙ̄ⲙⲉⲣⲓⲧ ⲓⲥ ⲡⲉϫⲥ̄ ⲙ̄ⲛ̄
ⲡⲉⲡⲛ̄ⲁ·ⲉⲧⲟⲩⲁⲁⲃ. ⲁⲩϭⲱⲛⲧ̄ (110 R i) ⲛ̄ϭⲓ ⲡϩⲏⲅⲉⲙⲱⲛ,·ⲁϥⲕⲉⲗⲉⲩⲉ ⲉⲧⲣⲟⲩ
ⲕⲁ·ⲧⲉⲣⲓⲁⲍⲉ ⲙ̄ⲙⲟⲩ ϩⲛ̄·ϩⲉⲛⲥⲟⲩⲃⲗⲓⲛ ⲙ̄ⲡⲉ·ⲛⲓⲡⲉ ⲉⲩⲗⲟⲃⲛ̄ ϩⲛ̄ⲟⲩ·ⲕⲱϩⲧ
ϣⲁⲛⲧⲟⲩ·ϭⲱⲧϩ̄ ⲙ̄ⲡⲉⲩϩⲏⲧ·ⲙ̄ⲛ̄ⲛ̄ⲃⲏⲧ ⲛ̄ϩⲏⲧⲟⲩ·ϣⲁⲛⲧⲉⲛⲉⲩⲥⲡⲓⲣ·ⲟⲩⲉ
ϭⲱⲧϩ̄· ⲁⲩⲱ·ⲁⲩⲧⲣⲟⲩⲡⲁϩⲧⲟⲩ ⲉϫⲛ̄ϩⲏⲧⲟⲩ,ⲁⲩⲛⲱϩⲧ̄·ⲛ̄ⲟⲩⲛⲉϩ ⲉϥϩⲃ̄ⲣⲃ̄ⲣ ⲉ·
ϩⲣⲁⲓ ⲉϫⲛ̄ϩⲏⲧⲟⲩ·ϣⲁⲛⲧⲉⲗⲉⲩϣⲁⲁⲣ·ϭⲱⲗ.·ⲡⲙⲁⲕⲁⲣⲓⲟⲥ ⲇⲉ ⲁⲡⲁ·ⲩⲛⲟⲩϭⲉ
ⲛⲉⲩ·ϫⲱ ⲙ̄ⲡⲉⲓϣⲁⲗⲗⲟⲥ·ϫⲉ ⲁⲙⲛⲓⲧⲛ̄ ⲧⲛ̄ⲧⲉ·ⲗⲏⲗ ⲙ̄ⲡϫⲟⲉⲓⲥ, ⲧⲛ̄·ϯⲗⲟⲩⲗⲁⲓ ⲙ̄

ⲡⲛⲟⲩⲧⲉˈ ⲡⲉⲛⲟⲩⲝⲁⲓ˙ ⲝⲉ ⲡˈⲭⲟⲉⲓⲥ ⲡⲉⲛⲛⲟⲩⲧⲉ ²⁵ⲟⲩⲛⲟϭ ⲡⲉ, ⲁⲩⲱˈ ⲟⲩⲛⲟϭ ⲛ̄-
ⲣⲣⲟ ⲡⲉ ⲉⲝⲛ̄ⲛ̄ϫⲱⲱⲣⲉ ⲧⲏ'ⲣⲟⲩ ⲛ̄ⲧⲉⲡⲕⲁⲍ ˙ˈⲙ̄ⲛ̄ⲥⲱⲥ ⲁⲩⲕⲟⲧⲟⲩ̄ ³⁰ⲉⲛⲉⲧⲟⲩⲁ-
ⲁⲃ, ⲡⲉⲭⲁⲩˈ ⲛⲁⲩ ⲝⲉ ⲙ̄ⲡⲣ̄ⲣⲍⲟⲧⲉ ˈⲛⲁⲥⲛⲏⲩ ˙ ⲙ̄ⲡⲭⲟⲉⲓⲥ (ⲓⲓⲟ ⲣ ⲓⲓ) ⲛⲁⲕⲁⲁⲛ
ⲛ̄ⲥⲱⲩ ⲁⲛˈ ˙ϯⲛⲁⲩ ⲅⲁⲣ ⲉⲙⲓⲭⲁⲏⲗ ˈⲡⲁⲣⲭⲁⲅⲅⲉⲗⲟⲥ ⲉⲣⲉˈⲍⲉⲛⲕⲗⲟⲙ ⲍ̄ⲛ̄ⲉⲩ⁵ⲟⲓⲝ, ⲉⲩ-
ⲛⲁⲥⲧⲉⲫⲁⲛⲟⲩˈ ⲙ̄ⲙⲟⲛ ⲛ̄ⲍⲏⲧⲟⲩ ˙ ⲡⲉⲭⲉⲡϩⲏⲅⲉⲙⲱⲛˈ ⲛⲁⲩ ⲝⲉ ⲧⲉⲧⲛ̄ⲛⲁⲣ'ⲟⲩⲱ,
ⲝⲉⲛⲙ̄ⲙⲟⲛ ¹⁰ⲧⲉⲧⲛ̄ⲛⲁⲙⲟⲩ ⲕⲁⲕⲱⲥ ˙ ⲡⲉⲭⲉⲛⲉⲧⲟⲩⲁⲁⲃ ⲛⲁⲩˈ ⲝⲉ ⲛ̄ⲛⲉⲥⲱⲡⲉ ⲙ̄ˈ
ⲙⲟⲛ ⲛ̄ⲧⲉⲛⲕⲱ ⲛ̄'ⲥⲱⲛ ⲙ̄ⲡⲉⲛⲛⲟⲩⲧⲉ ¹⁵ⲛ̄ⲧⲉⲛⲟⲩⲱϣⲧ ⲛ̄ⲍⲉⲛˈⲛⲟⲩⲧⲉ ⲉⲩⲙⲟⲟⲩⲧ, ˈ
ⲉⲃⲟⲗ ⲝⲉ ⲁⲡⲉⲛⲭⲟⲉⲓⲥˈ ⲭⲟⲟⲥ ⲝⲉ ⲡⲉⲧⲛⲁⲁⲣ'ⲛⲁ ⲙ̄ⲙⲟⲓˈ ϯⲛⲁⲁⲣⲛⲁ ²⁰ⲙ̄ⲙⲟⲩ
ϩⲱ ˙ⲁⲩⲱˈ ⲡⲉⲧⲛⲁϩⲟⲙⲟⲗⲟⲅⲉⲓˈ ⲙ̄ⲙⲟⲓ̈ ϯⲛⲁϩⲟⲙⲟ'ⲗⲟⲅⲉⲓ ⲙ̄ⲙⲟⲩ ϩⲱ ⲙ̄ⲡⲉⲙⲧⲟ
ⲉⲃⲟⲗ ²⁵ⲙ̄ⲡⲁˈⲉⲓⲱⲧ. ⲡϩⲁⲅⲓⲟⲥ ⲇⲉˈ ⲁⲗⲁ ⲯⲛ̄ⲟⲩϭⲉ ⲉⲛⲟⲩˈⲕⲁⲓ̈ⲉ ⲡⲉ ⲟⲩⲇⲉ ⲛ̄ⲧⲟⲟⲩˈ
ⲧⲏⲣⲟⲩ ˙ⲉⲛⲉⲟⲩⲙ̄ⲣⲩ̄ϭˈ ⲡⲉ ⲉⲛⲉⲥⲉⲛⲉⲩⲃⲁⲗ, ³⁰ⲉⲣⲉⲡⲉⲩⲃⲱ ⲟⲗⲙ̄ ⲛ̄ⲑⲉ ⲛ̄ⲛⲉⲥⲙⲁϩ
ⲛ̄ⲕⲟⲩˈⲡⲉⲣ, ⲉⲩⲧⲣⲉⲩⲣⲱⲟⲩ (ⲩ ⲓ) ϩⲙ̄ⲡⲉⲩⲥⲱⲙⲁ ⲛ̄ⲑⲉˈ ⲛ̄ⲛⲉⲓ̈ⲟⲩⲏⲣⲧ, ⲉⲩˈⲧⲏⲩ
ⲕⲁⲗⲱⲥ ϩⲁⲧⲉⲩˈϭⲟⲧ ⲙ̄ⲛ̄ⲧⲉⲩϩⲉⲝⲓⲥ ˙ ⁵ⲁⲩⲧⲣⲟⲩⲙⲟⲩⲧⲉ ⲉⲣⲟⲩ, ˈ ⲡⲉⲭⲁⲩ ⲛⲁⲩ
ⲝⲉ ⲯⲛ̄ⲟⲩϭⲉ, ϯⲛⲁⲩ ⲅⲁⲣˈ ⲉⲧⲕⲁⲧⲁⲥⲧⲁⲥⲓⲥ ⲉⲧⲕ̄'ϩⲟⲟⲡ ⲛ̄ϩⲏⲧⲥ̄, ⲙ̄ⲛ̄'ⲧⲉⲕ-
ⲙⲛ̄ⲧⲥⲁⲃⲉ, ⲭⲉˈ ⲧⲁⲟⲩⲣⲱⲙⲉ ⲙ̄ⲫⲣⲟ'ⲛⲓⲙⲟⲥ ⲧⲉ ˙ ⲧⲉⲛⲟⲩˈ ⲥⲉ ⲥⲱⲧⲙ̄ ⲛ̄ⲧⲟⲩ-
ⲥⲓⲁ'ⲍⲉ ⲧⲁⲕⲁⲁⲕ ⲉⲃⲟⲗ ˈ¹⁵ⲁⲩⲱ ⲁⲓⲧⲉⲓ ⲙ̄ⲙⲟⲓ ˈⲛ̄ⲟⲩⲁⲓⲇⲏⲙⲁ ⲧⲁ'ⲧⲁⲁⲩ ⲛⲁⲕ
ⲉⲡⲉⲓ'ⲇⲏ ϯⲩⲉⲛϩⲧⲏ ϩⲁ'ⲣⲟⲕ ⲝⲉ ⲛ̄ⲧⲕ̄ⲟⲩⲥⲁⲃⲉ. ²⁰ⲡⲉⲭⲉⲡϩⲁⲅⲓⲟⲥ ⲛⲁⲩˈ ⲉⲩⲥⲱ-
ϭⲉ ⲝⲉ ⲟⲩ ϩⲱ'ⲱⲩ ⲡⲉ ⲡⲁⲓⲇⲏⲙⲁˈ ⲉⲧⲕ̄ⲛⲁⲧⲁⲁⲩ ⲛⲁⲓ̈; ⲡⲉⲭⲉⲡϩⲏⲅⲉⲙⲱⲛ ²⁵
ⲛⲁⲩ ⲝⲉ ϯⲛⲁⲥϩⲁⲓ̈ ⲙ̄ⲡⲁⲭⲟⲉⲓⲥ ⲛ̄ⲣⲣⲟˈ ⲇⲓⲟⲕⲗⲏⲧⲓⲁⲛⲟⲥ ˈⲉⲧⲃⲏⲏⲧⲕ̄, ⲛ̄ϥϯ
ⲛⲁⲕ ³⁰ⲛ̄ⲟⲩⲛⲟϭ ⲛ̄ⲁˈⲍⲓⲱⲙⲁ ⲛ̄ⲧⲉⲛ̄ⲣ̄'ⲣⲱⲟⲩ, ⲛ̄ϥ̄ⲭⲁⲣⲓⲍⲉ ⲛⲁⲕ ⲛ̄ϩⲉ ⲙ̄ⲙⲁⲧⲟⲓ̈
(ⲩⲓⲓ) ⲛ̄ⲥⲉⲱⲡⲉ ϩⲁⲧⲉⲕⲉⲍⲟⲩ'ⲥⲓⲁ, ⲉⲕⲧⲱⲩ ⲉϩⲣⲁⲓ̈ ⲉ'ⲭⲱⲟⲩ. ⲡⲉⲭⲉⲡϩⲁ-
ⲅⲓ'ⲟⲥ ⲛⲁⲩ ⲝⲉ ⲓ̈ⲉ ⲡⲁⲓ ⲡⲉ ⁵ⲡⲉⲕⲁⲓⲧⲏⲙⲁ ⲉⲧⲕ̄ⲛⲁ'ⲧⲁⲁⲩ ⲛⲁⲓ̈· ϥ̄ⲟⲛϩ̄ ⲛ̄ϭⲓ
ⲡⲁⲛⲟⲩⲧⲉ ⲓ̄ⲥ̄ ⲡⲉⲭ̄ⲥ̄ˈ ⲝⲉ ⲉⲕϣⲁⲛⲧ ⲛⲁⲓ̈ ⲛ̄ϩⲉ ⲙ̄ⲙⲁⲧⲟⲓ̈, ⲛ̄ⲥⲉⲉⲣ¹⁰ϣⲩⲉⲧⲁⲓ̈ⲟⲩ
ⲛ̄ⲣⲟⲙⲡⲉˈ ϩⲁⲣⲁⲧ ⲉⲛⲟⲩⲁ, ⲛ̄ⲥⲉⲛⲁˈϭⲉⲛⲟⲩϩⲟⲟⲩ ⲛ̄ⲟⲩⲱⲧ'ⲁⲛ ϩⲁⲧⲙ̄ⲛ̄ⲧ-
ⲣⲣⲟ ⲙ̄ⲡⲁⲭⲟⲉⲓⲥ ⲓ̄ⲥ̄ ⲡⲉⲭ̄ⲥ̄. ˈ¹⁵ⲁⲩϭⲱⲛⲧ ⲛ̄ϭⲓ ⲡϩⲏ'ⲅⲉⲙⲱⲛ, ⲁⲩⲕⲉⲗⲉⲩⲉ'
ⲉⲧⲣⲟⲩⲑⲃ̄ⲥⲟ ⲙ̄ⲡϩⲁⲅⲓ'ⲟⲥ ⲁⲡⲁ ⲯⲛ̄ⲟⲩϭⲉ ⲉˈⲝⲉⲛⲍⲉⲛⲙⲁⲛ̄ⲛ̄ⲕⲟⲧⲕ̄ ⲙ̄ⲡⲉⲛⲓ-²⁰
ⲡⲉ, ⲛ̄ⲧⲟⲩˈ ⲙ̄ⲛ̄ⲛⲉⲩⲕⲉⲥⲛⲏⲩ,ˈⲛ̄ⲥⲉⲥⲁϩⲧⲉ ϩⲁⲣⲟⲟⲩ. ˈ ⲡⲉⲭⲉⲡϩⲏⲅⲉⲙⲱⲛ ˈⲛⲁⲩ
ⲝⲉ ⲯⲛ̄ⲟⲩϭⲉ, ²⁵ⲥⲱⲧⲙ̄ ⲛ̄ⲥⲱⲓ̈, ⲙ̄ⲡⲣ̄ˈⲙⲟⲩ ⲕⲁⲕⲱⲥ. ⲁⲩⲟⲩˈⲱϣⲃ̄ ⲛ̄ϭⲓ ⲡⲙⲁ-
ⲕⲁⲣⲓ'ⲟⲥ ⲁⲡⲁ ⲯⲛ̄ⲟⲩϭⲉ ⲡⲉ'ⲭⲁⲩ ⲝⲉ ⲡⲉϩⲙⲟⲧ ⲙ̄ⲡⲛⲟⲩⲧⲉ ϣⲏⲡ, ˈ³⁰ⲡⲁⲓ ⲛ̄ⲧⲁⲩ-

---

ⲧⲁϩⲙⲉⲧ'ⲉϩⲟⲩⲛ ⲉⲡⲉⲩⲧⲱϣ̄ (ΙΙΙ R ï) ⲉⲧⲟⲩⲁⲁⲃ. ⲛ̄ⲧⲉⲩⲛⲟⲩ' ⲁⲡⲁⲣⲭⲁⲅⲅⲉⲗⲟⲥ
ⲙⲓⲭⲁ'ⲏⲗ ⲥⲟⲩⲧⲱⲛⲧⲉϥ'ϭⲓϫ ⲉⲃⲟⲗ ⲉϫⲛ̄ⲡⲕⲱϩ̄ⲧ', ⲁϥϣⲱⲡⲉ ⲛ̄ⲑⲉ ⲛ̄ⲟⲩ'ⲉⲓⲱⲧⲉ· ⲁⲩⲱ
ⲁⲡ'ⲥⲱⲙⲁ ⲛ̄ⲛⲉⲧⲟⲩⲁⲁⲃ' ⲣ̄ⲑⲉ ⲛ̄ⲟⲩⲁ ⲉⲩϩⲙⲟⲟⲥ ϩⲓ'ⲭⲏϩϫⲛ̄ⲡⲗⲁϩ ⲉⲩⲕⲏⲃ' ϩⲛ̄ⲛⲉ-
ϩⲟⲟⲩ ⲛ̄ⲧⲉⲡⲣⲱ.' ⲡϩⲁⲅⲓⲟⲥ ⲇⲉ ⲁⲡⲁ ϣⲛ̄ⲟⲩϥⲉ ⲛⲉⲩⲧⲁϭⲟ' ⲙ̄ⲡⲉⲓ̈ⲯⲁⲗⲙⲟⲥ ϫⲉ' ⲁⲓ̈-
ⲕⲁϩⲧⲏ ⲉⲣⲟⲕ ⲡ'ϫⲟⲉⲓⲥ, ⲙ̄ⲡⲣ̄ⲧⲣⲁϫⲓ'ϣⲓⲡⲉ ϣⲁⲉⲛⲉϩ·' ⲁⲩⲱ ⲛⲉⲩⲟⲩⲱϣ̄ⲙ̄ 'ⲛ̄ⲥⲱϥ
ⲛ̄ϭⲓ ⲛⲉϥⲥ'ⲛⲏⲩ ϩⲛ̄ⲧⲙⲏⲧⲉ ⲙ̄ⲡⲕⲱϩ̄ⲧ. 'ⲁⲩⲱ ⲡⲉϫⲁⲩ ⲛ̄ⲁⲣⲓⲁ'ⲛⲟⲥ ⲡϩⲏⲅⲉⲙⲱⲛ'
ϫⲉ ⲁϫⲓⲥ ⲛ̄ⲛⲉⲕⲙⲁ'ⲧⲟⲓ̈, ⲙⲁⲣⲟⲩⲧⲁⲙⲉⲓⲉ'ⲛⲉⲕⲃⲁⲥⲁⲛⲟⲥ ⲕⲁⲗⲱⲥ,' ⲉⲙⲙⲟⲛ ⲉⲩ-
ⲱⲟϭ.' ⲛ̄ⲧⲉⲣⲉϥⲥⲱⲧⲙ̄ ⲉⲛⲁⲓ̈ ⲛ̄ϭⲓ ⲡϩⲏⲅⲉⲙⲱⲛ,' ⲁϥϭⲱⲛⲧ ⲉⲛ̄ϩⲏⲗⲙ̄'ⲣⲏⲧⲏⲥ,
ⲉϥⲙⲉⲉⲩⲉ ϫⲉ' ⲧⲙⲉ ⲧⲉ· ⲁⲩⲧⲱⲟⲩⲛ' ⲙ̄ⲙⲓⲛ ⲙ̄ⲙⲟϥ, ⲁⲩ (R ïï) ⲃⲱⲕ ⲉϫⲛ̄ⲡⲕⲱ-
ϩ̄ⲧ' ⲉϥⲟⲩⲱϣ̄ ⲉⲉⲓⲙⲉ ⲉⲡ'ϩⲱⲃ· ⲡϩⲁⲅⲓⲟⲥ ⲇⲉ' ⲁⲡⲁ ϣⲛ̄ⲟⲩϥⲉ ⲁϥ'ⲙⲉϩⲧⲉϥ-
ϭⲓϫ ⲛ̄ⲕⲱϩ̄ⲧ,' ⲁϥⲛⲟϫⲥ̄ ⲉϩⲟⲩⲛ ϩⲙ̄'ⲡϩⲟ ⲙ̄ⲡϩⲏⲅⲉⲙⲱⲛ·' ⲛ̄ⲧⲉⲩⲛⲟⲩ ⲁⲡⲉϥ-
ϩⲟ'ⲟⲩⲱϣⲉ· ⲁⲡⲙ̄'ⲏϣⲉ ⲧⲏⲣϥ ⲱϣ ⲉ'ⲃⲟⲗ ϫⲉ ⲟⲩⲁ ⲡⲉ ⲡⲛⲟⲩⲧⲉ' ⲛ̄ⲛⲓϩⲁ-
ⲅⲓⲟⲥ, ⲉϥϭⲟⲙ' ⲛ̄ⲛⲉⲧⲥⲱⲧⲙ̄ ⲛ̄ⲥⲱϥ.' ⲛ̄ⲧⲉⲩⲛⲟⲩ ⲁⲩⲃⲟϭⲟⲩ ⲉ'ϩⲟⲩⲛ ⲛ̄ϭⲓ ⲙⲛ̄ⲧ-
ϣ̄'ⲙⲏⲛ ⲛ̄ⲣⲱⲙⲉ ⲉ'ⲃⲟⲗ ϩⲙ̄ⲡⲙⲏⲏϣⲉ,' ⲁⲩⲱ ⲉⲃⲟⲗ ϫⲉ ⲁⲛⲟⲛ' ϩⲛ̄ⲭⲣⲏⲥⲧⲓⲁⲛⲟⲥ'
ⲡⲁⲣⲣⲏⲥⲓⲁ·' ⲡⲙⲟⲩ ⲅⲁⲣ ⲉⲧⲉⲣⲉⲛⲉⲓ̈'ϩⲁⲅⲓⲟⲥ ⲙ̄ⲙⲁⲣⲧⲩⲣⲟⲥ' ⲛⲁⲙⲟⲩ ⲛ̄ϩⲏⲧϥ̄,
ⲧⲛ̄'ⲛⲁⲙⲟⲩ ⲛ̄ϩⲏⲧϥ̄ ϩⲱ(ⲛ).' ⲡⲉϫⲉ ⲡϩⲏⲅⲉⲙⲱⲛ' ⲛⲁⲩ ϫⲉ ⲥⲱⲧⲙ̄ ⲛ̄'ⲥⲱⲓ̈, ⲑⲩⲥⲓⲁⲍⲉ, ⲙ̄ⲡⲣ̄'ⲙⲟⲩ ⲕⲁⲕⲱⲥ. ⲁⲩⲟ'ⲩⲱϣϥ ϫⲉ ⲛ̄ⲧⲛ̄ⲛⲁⲑⲩ'ⲥⲓⲁⲍⲉ ⲁⲛ, ⲁⲗⲗⲁ' ⲉⲛⲏⲡ ⲉⲓⲥ ⲡⲉⲭⲥ̄. ⲁⲩⲱ' ⲁⲩⲥⲁϩⲟⲩ ⲙ̄ⲙⲟϥ ⲙⲛ̄(ⲛ̄)ⲛⲉϥⲉⲓⲇⲱⲗⲟⲛ ⲙⲛ̄'ⲛⲉϥⲉⲣ-
ⲣⲱⲟⲩ. ⲁϥϭⲱⲛⲧ̄ ⲛ̄ϭⲓ ⲡϩⲏⲅⲉ'ⲙⲱⲛ, ⲁϥⲕⲉⲗⲉⲩⲉ' ⲉⲧⲣⲟⲩⲁⲁⲩ ⲛ̄ⲧⲟⲟⲩ' ⲛ̄ⲧⲁ-
ⲅⲙⲁ· ⲁⲩⲱ ϩⲟⲓ̈ⲛⲉ ⲛ̄ϩⲏⲧⲟⲩ ⲁⲩⲧ'ⲣⲟⲩϭⲓ ⲛ̄ⲧⲉⲥⲏⲡⲉ·' ϩⲉⲛⲕⲟⲟⲩⲉ ⲁⲩⲧⲣⲟⲩ'ⲣⲟⲕ-
ϩⲟⲩ ϩⲙ̄ⲡⲕⲱϩ̄ⲧ·' ϩⲛ̄ⲕⲟⲟⲩⲉ ⲁⲩⲧⲣⲟⲩⲡⲗⲩⲅⲏ ⲙ̄ⲙⲟⲟⲩ ϩⲙ̄'ⲡⲕⲉⲗⲉⲃⲓⲛ· ϩⲛ̄ⲕⲟ-'
ⲟⲩⲉ ⲁⲩⲧⲣⲟⲩⲥⲓⲙⲱ'ⲣⲉⲓ ⲙ̄ⲙⲟⲟⲩ ϣⲁⲛ'ⲧⲟⲩⲙⲟⲟⲩⲧⲟⲩ. ⲧⲁⲓ̈' ⲧⲉ ⲑⲉ ⲛ̄ⲧⲁⲩϫⲱⲕ
ⲉ'ⲃⲟⲗ ⲙ̄ⲡⲉⲩⲁⲅⲱⲛ' ⲙⲛ̄ⲧⲉⲩⲙⲁⲣⲧⲩⲣⲓⲁ' ⲙ̄ⲡⲉⲓ̈ϩⲟⲟⲩ ⲛ̄ⲟⲩⲱⲧ.' ⲁⲡⲉⲥⲧⲉⲣⲉⲱⲙⲁ
ⲧⲏ'ⲣϥ̄ ⲙⲟⲩϩ ⲛ̄ⲛⲁⲅⲅⲉ'ⲗⲟⲥ, ⲁⲩϫⲓ ⲛ̄ⲛⲉⲩ'ⲯⲩⲭⲏ ⲉϩⲣⲁⲓ̈ ⲉⲙⲡⲏⲩⲉ,' ϩⲛ̄ⲟⲩⲉⲓ-
ⲣⲏⲛⲏ, ϩⲁⲙⲏ(ⲛ).' ⲡϩⲁⲅⲓⲟⲥ ⲇⲉ ⲛⲉⲣⲉⲛⲉⲩ'ⲃⲁⲗ ϭⲱϣⲧ̄ ⲉⲣⲟⲟⲩ' ⲉⲩⲃⲏⲕ ⲉ-
ϩⲣⲁⲓ̈ ⲉⲧⲡⲉ·' ⲡⲙⲁⲕⲁⲣⲓⲟⲥ ⲇⲉ ⲁⲡⲁ ϣⲛ̄ⲟⲩϥⲉ ⲁⲩⲱ' ⲙ̄ⲡⲉⲓ̈ⲯⲁⲗⲙⲟⲥ' ϫⲉ
ⲁⲡⲁϩⲏⲧ ⲉⲩⲫ(ⲱ VII)ⲣⲁⲛⲉⲓ ⲉⲧⲃⲉⲛⲁⲥⲛⲏⲩ·' ⲁⲩⲱ ⲛⲉⲩⲟⲩⲱϣⲙ̄ ⲛ̄'ⲥⲱⲱ ⲛ̄ϭⲓ
ⲛⲉⲩⲥⲛⲏⲩ' ⲉⲩϫⲱ ⲙ̄ⲙⲟⲥ ϫⲉ ⲁⲕ'ⲥⲱⲧⲙ̄ ⲉⲣⲟⲛ ⲡⲣ̄ⲣⲟ ⲛ̄ⲛⲁⲧϩⲉ ⲙ̄ⲛ̄ⲁⲡⲕⲁϩ.'
ⲙ̄ⲡⲉⲕⲕⲁⲁⲛ ⲉϫⲓϣⲓⲡⲉ, ⲁⲗⲗⲁ ⲁⲕⲧⲉⲉⲟⲩ'ⲛⲁⲛ ⲁⲛ̄ⲟⲩⲟⲛ ⲛⲓⲙ' ⲉⲧⲥⲱⲧⲙ̄ ⲛ̄ⲥⲱⲕ'
ϫⲉ ⲛ̄ⲧⲟⲕ ⲡⲉ ⲡⲛⲟⲩⲧⲉ' ⲙⲁⲩⲁⲁⲕ ϩⲛ̄ⲧⲡⲉ ⲙⲛ̄'ϩⲓϫⲙ̄ⲡⲕⲁϩ ⲙⲛ̄'ⲡⲉⲕⲙⲉⲣⲓⲧ ⲛ̄ϣⲏ-

---

ρε̅ Ⲧⲉ ⲡⲉϫⲥ.' ⲁⲥϣⲱⲡⲉ ⲇⲉ ⲙ̅ⲛ̅ⲥⲁ'ⲛⲁⲓ ⲧⲏⲣⲟⲩ ⲁⲁⲣⲓⲁⲛⲟⲥ ⲡϩⲏⲅⲉⲙⲱⲛ' ⲉⲓ
ⲉⲃⲟⲗ ϩⲙ̅ⲙⲏⲃⲉ ⲙ̅ⲡⲉϩⲟⲟⲩ ⲉⲧⲙ̅ⲙⲁⲩ,' ⲛ̅ⲧⲟⲩ ⲙ̅ⲛ̅ⲧⲉⲩⲧⲁϫⲓⲥ' ⲧⲏⲣⲥ̅· ⲁⲩⲕⲉⲗⲉⲩ
ⲉ ⲉⲧ'ⲣⲟⲩⲉⲓⲛⲉ ⲛⲁⲩ ⲙ̅ⲙⲁ'ⲕⲁⲣⲓⲟⲥ ⲁⲡⲁ ϣ̅ⲛⲟⲩϥ̅ⲉ ⲙ̅ⲛ̅ⲛⲉⲩⲕⲉⲥⲛⲏⲩ ⲧⲏⲣⲟⲩ,
ⲛ̅ⲥⲉⲛⲟϫⲟⲩ' ⲉⲡⲉⲥⲏⲧ ⲉⲡⲟⲩⲉⲛⲧ' ⲙ̅ⲡⲁϣⲟⲓ, ⲉⲣⲉϩⲉⲛⲕⲟⲗ'ⲗⲁⲣⲓⲟⲛ ϩⲛ̅ⲛⲉⲩⲙⲟⲧⲉ,
ⲉⲣⲉϩⲉⲛⲡⲉⲇⲉⲥ ϩⲛ̅ⲛⲉⲩϭⲓϫ ⲙ̅ⲛ̅ϩⲛ̅ϫⲓⲣⲟ'ⲡⲉⲇⲏⲥ ⲉⲛⲉⲩⲟⲩⲉⲣⲏⲧⲉ. (112 R i) ⲛ̅
ⲧⲉⲩⲛⲟⲩ ⲁⲩϩⲱⲧ ⲉⲣⲏⲥ.' ⲡϩⲁⲅⲓⲟⲥ ⲇⲉ ⲁⲡⲁ ϣ̅ⲛⲟⲩϥⲉ ⲙ̅ⲛ̅ⲛⲉⲩⲥⲛⲏⲩ' ⲛⲉⲩ
ϩⲉϫϩⲱϫ ⲡⲉ, ⲁⲩⲱϣⲗⲏⲗ ⲇⲉ ⲉⲩϫⲱ' ⲙ̅ⲙⲟⲥ ϫⲉ ⲥⲱⲧⲙ̅' ⲉⲣⲟⲛ ⲡⲉⲛϫⲟⲉⲓⲥ ⲓ̅ⲥ̅'
ⲡⲉϫⲥ̅, ⲡⲉⲛⲧⲁⲩ'ⲛⲟⲩϩⲙ̅ ⲛ̅ⲓⲱⲛⲁⲥ' ⲉⲩⲛ̅ϩⲏⲧϥ̅ ⲙ̅ⲡⲕⲩⲧⲟⲥ,' ⲁⲩⲱ ⲁⲕⲛⲟⲩϩⲙ̅ ⲛ̅
ⲓⲱ'ⲥⲏϥ ⲉⲧⲃⲟⲣⲃⲥ̅ ⲛ̅ⲧⲉⲥ'ϩⲓⲙⲉ ⲛ̅ⲣⲙ̅ⲛ̅ⲕⲏⲙⲉ,' ⲁⲩⲱ ⲁⲕⲧⲟⲩϫⲟⲩ ϩⲛ̅'ⲛⲉⲩⲑⲗⲓ
ⲯⲓⲥ ⲧⲏⲣⲟⲩ,' ⲁⲩⲱ ⲁⲩϭⲟⲓⲡⲟⲙⲉⲛⲉ' ϣⲁⲛⲧⲉⲩⲣ̅ⲣ̅ⲣⲟ·' ⲛ̅ⲧⲉⲓϩⲉ ⲟⲛ ⲡⲉⲛϫⲟⲉⲓⲥ'
ⲉⲕⲉϯⲧⲟⲟⲧⲕ̅ ⲛⲙ̅ⲙⲁ(ⲛ)' ϩⲛ̅ⲛⲉⲛⲑⲗⲓⲯⲓⲥ ⲧⲏ'ⲣⲟⲩ, ϫⲉ ⲛ̅ⲧⲟⲕ ⲡⲉ' ⲡⲉⲛⲃⲟⲏⲑⲟⲥ
ⲁⲩⲱ' ⲡⲉⲕⲕⲁⲙ̅ⲡⲱⲧ' ⲁⲩⲱ ⲧⲛ̅ϩⲉⲗⲡⲓⲥ. ⲛⲁⲓ ⲇⲉ ⲉⲩϫⲱ' ⲙ̅ⲙⲟⲟⲩ' ⲛ̅ϭⲓ ⲛ̅ϩⲁⲅⲓ
ⲟⲥ, ⲉⲓⲥ' ⲡϫⲟⲉⲓⲥ ⲓ̅ⲥ̅ ⲁⲩⲉⲓ ⲉⲡⲉ'ⲥⲏⲧ ⲉⲃⲟⲗ ϩⲛ̅ⲧⲡⲉ' ⲙ̅ⲛ̅ⲙⲓⲭⲁⲏⲗ ⲡⲁⲣ'ⲭⲁⲅ
ⲅⲉⲗⲟⲥ ⲙ̅ⲛ̅ⲅⲁⲃ'ⲣⲓⲏⲗ ⲙ̅ⲛ̅ϩⲛ̅ⲙⲏ'ⲛ̅ϣⲉ ⲛ̅ⲁⲅⲅⲉⲗⲟⲥ.' ⲁⲩϣⲁϫⲉ ⲙ̅ⲛ̅ⲛⲉⲧⲟⲩ(Ri i)
ⲁⲁⲃ ⲉⲩϫⲱ ⲙ̅ⲙⲟⲥ'ϫⲉ ϫⲣⲟ ⲙ̅ⲙⲱⲧⲛ̅,' ⲙ̅ⲡⲣ̅ⲣ̅ϩⲟⲧⲉ· ϯϣⲟⲟⲡ' ⲛⲁⲙⲏⲧⲛ̅ ϩ̅ⲙⲁ
ⲛⲓⲙ ⲉⲧⲟⲩⲛⲁϫⲓⲧⲏⲩ'ⲧⲛ̅ ⲉⲣⲟⲟⲩ, ⲉⲓ'ϯϭⲟⲙ' ⲛⲏⲧⲛ̅ ϣⲁⲛⲧⲉⲧⲛ̅'ϯϣⲓⲡⲉ ⲛ̅ⲁⲣⲓⲁⲛⲟⲥ'
ⲡϩⲏⲅⲉⲙⲱⲛ ⲙ̅ⲛ̅'ⲛⲉⲩⲛⲟⲩⲧⲉ ⲉⲧⲟⲩⲉⲓⲧ.' ⲛⲁⲓ ⲇⲉ ⲛ̅ⲧⲉⲣⲉⲥⲱ'ⲧⲏⲣ ϫⲟⲟⲩ
ⲛⲁⲩ, ⲁⲩ'ϯ ⲛⲁⲩ ⲛ̅ⲧⲣⲏⲛⲏ,' ⲁⲩⲃⲱⲕ ⲉϩⲣⲁⲓ̈ ⲉⲙ̅ⲡⲏ'ⲩⲉ ⲉⲣⲉⲛ̅ⲁⲅⲅⲉⲗⲟⲥ ⲙ̅ⲡⲉ
ⲟⲟⲩ ϩⲩⲙⲛⲉⲩⲉ'ϩⲁⲧⲉⲩϩⲉ, ϩⲛ̅ⲟⲩⲉⲓⲣⲏ'ⲛⲏ, ϩⲁⲙⲏⲛ.' ⲛ̅ϩⲁⲅⲓⲟⲥ ⲇⲉ ⲛ̅ⲧⲉⲣⲟⲩ
ⲛⲁⲩ ⲉⲡϫⲟⲉⲓⲥ, ⲁⲡⲉⲩ'ϩⲏⲧ ⲣⲁϣⲉ, ⲁⲩⲱ'ⲡⲉ ⲉⲩⲧⲁⲗⲗⲉⲓ ⲙ̅'ⲡⲉϩⲟⲟⲩ ⲙ̅ⲛⲧⲉ
ⲩⲉ' ϣⲁⲛⲧⲟⲩⲡⲱϩ' ⲉⲧⲗⲟϭ. ⲡϩⲏⲅⲉ'ⲙⲱⲛ ⲇⲉ ⲛ̅ⲧⲉⲣⲉϥ'ⲧⲁϩⲉϯⲗⲟϭ ⲉⲣⲏⲥ'ⲁⲩ
ⲕⲉⲗⲉⲩⲉ ⲉⲧⲣⲉⲩⲙⲟ'ⲟⲛⲉ ⲉⲡⲉⲕⲣⲟ, ⲉϥⲟⲩ'ⲱϣ ⲉⲃⲱⲕ ⲉϩⲣⲁⲓ̈' ⲉⲧⲛⲟϭ ⲙ̅ⲡⲟⲗⲓⲥ
ⲁⲣ'ⲥⲓⲛⲟⲏ, ⲉⲧⲉⲧⲡⲟⲗⲓⲥ (Vi) ⲙ̅ⲡⲓⲟⲙ ⲧⲉ, ϫⲉⲕⲁⲥ' ⲉϥⲉϫⲓ ⲙ̅ⲡⲉⲡⲣⲟⲥⲧⲁⲅⲙⲁ
ⲉϩⲟⲩⲛ ⲉⲣⲟⲥ, ⲁⲩⲱ' ⲛ̅ϥ̅ⲧⲣⲟⲩϭⲱⲡⲉ ⲛ̅'ⲛⲉⲭⲣⲏⲥⲧⲓⲁⲛⲟⲥ ⲉⲧϩⲛ̅ⲡⲧⲟⲩ ⲉⲧⲙ̅ⲙⲁⲩ' ⲛ̅ϥ̅
ⲧⲣⲉⲩⲑⲩⲥⲓⲁ.' ⲛⲁⲓ ⲇⲉ ⲉⲩⲙⲉⲉⲩⲉ ⲉⲣⲟⲟⲩ' ⲛ̅ϭⲓ ⲡϩⲏⲅⲉⲙⲱⲛ,'ⲉⲓⲥ ⲣⲱⲙⲉ ⲥⲛⲁⲩ ⲁⲩ'
ⲉⲓ ⲉⲃⲟⲗ ϩⲛ̅ⲧⲗⲟϭ,' ⲁⲩⲥⲱⲧⲙ̅ ⲉⲡⲁⲩⲕⲁⲕ· ⲛⲉⲛⲣⲱⲙⲉ· ⲡⲉϫⲁⲩ'ϫⲉ ⲟⲩ ⲡⲉⲧϣⲟⲟⲡ
ϩⲛ̅ϯ̅ϥ̅ⲧⲣⲱ ⲙ̅ⲡⲟⲟⲩ,'· ⲁⲩⲧⲁⲙⲟⲟⲩ ϫⲉ ϩⲉⲛ'ⲭⲣⲏⲥⲧⲓⲁⲛⲟⲥ ⲛⲉ ⲛ̅'ⲧⲁⲡϩⲏⲅⲉⲙⲱⲛ' ⲉⲛ
ⲧⲟⲩ ⲉⲣⲏⲥ. ⲛ̅ⲧⲉ'ⲣⲟⲩⲥⲱⲧⲙ̅ ⲉⲛⲁⲓ ⲛ̅ϭⲓ ⲡⲣⲱⲙⲉ ⲥⲛⲁⲩ,' ⲡⲉϫⲁⲩ ϫⲉ ⲉⲛⲛⲁ'ⲧⲱⲛ ⲛⲉ;
ⲁⲩⲧⲁⲙⲟ'ⲟⲩ ϫⲉ ⲁⲡⲁ ϣ̅ⲛⲟⲩϥⲉ' ⲡⲉ ⲉⲃⲟⲗ ϩⲛ̅ⲛ̅ⲡⲁ'ⲓ̈ⲁⲧ. ⲡⲣⲱⲙⲉ ⲇⲉ' ⲥⲛⲁⲩ ⲛⲉ ⲛⲁⲓ

ΝΕ ΝΕΥΡΑΝ· ΖΗΛΙΑΣ ΜΝ ΠΑΜΟΥΝ· ΝΕΖΝ ΡΜΜΑΟ ΕΜΑΤΕ ΚΑΤΑΠΙΚΟCΜΟC ΝΕ·
ΕΥΟ ΜΜΑΪΝΟΥΜΝΟ (112 V ii) ΜΜΑΪΑΓΑΠΗ ΝΡΕΥ ΥΜΥΕΝΟΥΤΕ· ΝΤΕ ΡΟΥCΩΤΜ
ΕΤΒΕ ΠΜΑ ΚΑΡΙΟC ΑΠΑ ΥΝΟΥΓΕ ΖΕ ΥΙΧΕΝΤΜΡΩ ΜΠΝΕΥCΝΗΥ, ΑΥ ΤΩΟΥΝ,
ΑΥΕΙ ΝΖΝ ΟΕΙΚ ΕΥΤΒΒΗΥ ΜΝ ΠΕΝΥΑΓΟΥΟΜΥ ΖΝΟΥΤΒΒΟ· ΝΤΕΡΟΥ CΩΤΜ
ΕΤΒΕ ΠΜΑΚΑΡΙΟC ΑΠΑ ΥΝΟΥΓΕ· ΑΥΕΙ ΥΑΡΟΥ ΕΧΕΝΤΜΡΩ· ΑΥΩ ΝΕΡΕΑΡΙΑ-
ΝΟC ΠΖΗΓΕΜΩΝ ΜΜΑΥ ΠΕ· ΑΥΠΕΥΟΥΟΪ ΑΠΕCΝΑΥ, ΖΗΛΙΑC ΜΝ ΠΑΜΟΥΝ,
ΑΥΑCΠΑΖΕ ΝΝΕΤΟΥΑΑΒ, ΑΥΖΩΝΖ ΕΡΟΟΥ ΕΤ ΡΟΥΟΥΩΜ ΝΟΥΚΟΥΪ ΝΟΕΙΚ.
ΠΕΧΕ ΠΜΑΚΑΡΙΟC ΑΠΑ ΥΝΟΥΓΕ ΝΑΥ ΖΕ CΩΤΜ ΤΑΤΑΜΩΤΝ ΝΑCΝΗΥ ΕΠΕ-
ΤΝΒΙΟC ΤΗΡΥ· ΑΥΟΥΩ ΓΑΡ ΕΥΕΖΩ ΜΠΕΤΡΑ(Ν) ΕΤΠΕ ΝΝΕΜΑΡΤΥΡΟC,
ΕΠΙΔΗ ΑΤΕΤΝ ΖΩΚ ΕΒΟΛ ΝΝΕΕΝΤΟΛΗ ΜΠΕΥΑΓΓΕΛΙΟΝ ΕΤΟΥΑΑΒ ΖΕ ΝΕΙ-
Ζ(113 Ri) ΚΑΕΙΤ ΑΤΕΤΝ ΤΜΜΟΪ· ΝΕΙΟΒΕ ΑΤΕΤΝ ΤCΟΪ· ΝΕΙΟ ΝΥΜΜΟ ΑΤΕ ΤΝ
ΥΟΠΤ ΕΡΩΤΝ· ΝΕΙΚΗ ΚΑΖΗΥ ΑΤΕ ΤΝ Τ ΕΖΙΩΤ· ΝΕΙ ΥΩΝΕ ΑΤΕΤΝ ΜΠΑ-
ΥΙΝΕ· ΕΙCΖΗΝΤΕ ΔΕ Ω ΝΑΥΗΡΕ ΑΤΕΤΝ ΖΩΚ ΕΒΟΛ Ν ΤΕΚΡΑΦΗ ΕΤΟΥΑΑΒ·
ΠΔΡΟΜΟC ΑΤΕΤΝ ΖΟΚΥ ΕΒΟΛ· ΤΠΙCΤΙC ΑΤΕΤΝ ΖΑΡΕΖ ΕΡΟC· ΛΟΙΠΟΝ ΥΚΗ
ΝΗΤΝ ΕΖΡΑΪ ΝΟΙ ΠΕΚΛΟΜ· ΕΤΕΤΝ ΝΑΧΙΤΥ· ΑΥΩ ΜΠΟΟΥ ΤΕΤΝ ΝΑΡΥΑ ΖΝ-
ΤΜΝΤΡΡΟ ΜΠΝΟΥΤΕ ΝΤΕ ΤΝCΕΙ ΖΝ ΑΓΑΘΟΝ ΝΤΠΕ ΥΑΕΝΕΖ· ΑCΥΩΠΕ Ν-
ΤΕΡΟΥ CΩΤΜ ΕΝΑΪ ΕΡΕ ΠΖΑΓΙΟC ΑΠΑ ΥΝΟΥ ΓΕ ΖΩ ΜΜΟΟΥ, ΑΥ ΤΠΕΥΟΥΟΪ Ν-
ΟΙ ΠΑΜΟΥ(Ν) ΜΝ ΖΗΛΙΑC, ΑΥΩΥ ΕΒΟΛ ΖΕ ΑΝΟΝ ΖΕΝ ΧΡΗCΤΙΑΝΟC ΠΑΡ-
ΡΗCΙΑ· ΟΥΑ ΠΕ ΠΝΟΥΤΕ ΝΙΖΑΓΙΟC ΜΜΑΡ(Rii)ΤΥΡΟC· ΝΤΕΡΕΥ CΩΤΜ Ε-
ΝΑΪ ΝΟΙ ΑΡΙΑΝΟC ΠΖΗΓΕΜΩΝ, ΑΥ CΩΝΤ ΕΜΑΤΕ, ΑΥ ΚΕΛΕΥΕ ΕΤΡΟΥ CΩΠΕ
ΜΜΟΟΥ· ΠΕΧΑΥ ΝΑΥ ΖΕ ΝΤΩΤΝ ΝΡΑΤ ΩΝ; ΑΥΟΥ ΩΥΒ ΖΕ ΑΝΟΝ ΖΝ ΡΜ-
ΤΛΟΟ. ΠΕΧΑΥ ΝΑΥ ΖΕ ΝΙΜ ΝΕ ΝΕΤΝΡΑΝ; ΠΕΧΕ ΟΥΑ ΝΑΥ ΖΕ ΖΗΛΙΑC
ΠΕ ΠΑΡΑΝ· ΑΥΩ ΠΕΪΚΕΟΥΑ ΠΕ ΠΑΜΟΥΝ. ΠΕΧΑΥ ΝΑΥ ΖΕ ΑΡΙΘΥCΙΑ.
ΠΕΧΑΥ ΝΑΥ ΖΕ ΝΤΝΝΑ ΡΘΥCΙΑ ΑΝ· ΠΕΤΚ ΟΥΑΥΥ, ΑΡΙΥ ΝΑΝ· ΖΝ-
ΤΕΥΝΟΥ ΕΤΜΜΑΥ· ΑΥΚΕΛΕΥΕ ΕΤΡΟΥΤΑ ΜΙΟ ΜΠΒΗΜΑ ΖΙ ΧΕ ΝΤΕΜΡΩ Ν-
ΤΛΟΟ· ΑΥΤ ΝΑΥ ΝΟΥΜΗΝΥΕ ΝΒΑCΑΝΟC. ΑΥΥΙ ΖΡΑΪ ΕΖΡΑΪ ΕΤΠΕ, ΑΥ
ΤΩΒΖ ΜΠΝΟΥΤΕ ΕΥ ΖΩ ΜΜΟC ΖΕ ΑΜΟΥ ΥΑΡΟΝ ΙC ΠΡΡΟ ΝΝ ΕΩΝ ΤΗΡΟΥ,
ΑΡΙ ΠΜΕΕΥΕ ΖΕ ΑΝΚΩ ΝCΩΝ ΜΠΕΤΝΤΑΝ (Vi) ΤΗΡΥ, ΑΝΥΕΙ ΜΠΕΝCΤΑΥ-
ΡΟC, ΑΝΟΥΑΖΕ(Ν) ΝCΩΚ· ΝΤΟΚ ΔΕ ΖΩΩΚ Τ ΟΜ ΝΑΝ· ΑΙΕΤΕ ΔΕ ΕΥ ΖΩ

112 V ii 9. l. ΠΕΤ ΕΥΑΓΟΥΟΜΥ. 113 R i 6. Ε added; superfluous. 11. = ΓΡΑΦΗ. ii 8.
l. ΖΕΝ ΡΜΤΩΝ. 30. = -ΩΩΝ. V i 5. = ΕΤΙ

ⲛ̄ⲛⲁⲓ, ⲉⲓⲥ ⲡϫⲟⲉⲓⲥ ⲓ̅ⲥ̅' ⲁϥⲉⲓ ⲉⲃⲟⲗ ϩⲓⲧⲡⲉ,' ⲁϥϣⲁϫⲉ ⲛⲙ̄ⲙⲁⲩ' ⲉϥϫⲱ ⲙ̄ⲙⲟⲥ
ϫⲉ ϫⲣⲟ¹⁰ ⲙ̄ⲙⲱⲧⲛ̄, ⲙ̄ⲡⲣ̄ⲣ̄²ϩⲟⲧⲉ, ⲛⲁϣⲟⲉⲓϫ' ⲉⲧⲥⲙⲁⲙⲁⲁⲧ · ⲙ̄ⲡⲟⲟⲩ ⲅⲁⲣ ⲧⲉ-
ⲧⲛ̄ⲛⲁ'ϣⲱⲡⲉ ⲛⲙ̄ⲙⲁⲓ¹⁵ ϩⲛ̄ⲧⲁⲙⲛ̄ⲧⲣ̄ⲣⲟ.' ⲡⲅⲉⲛⲛⲁⲓⲟⲥ ⲇⲉ ⲟⲛ' ⲛ̄ⲧⲉⲣⲉϥϣⲁϫⲉ
ⲛ̄ⲙ̄ⲙⲁⲩ, ⲁⲡⲉⲩϩⲏⲧ' ⲧⲁϫⲣⲟ, ⲁⲩⲕⲓⲙ²⁰ ⲉⲣⲟⲟⲩ ϩⲓⲧⲛ̄ⲧϭⲟⲙ' ⲙ̄ⲡⲉⲡ̄ⲛ̄ⲁ ⲉⲧⲟⲩⲁ-
ⲁⲃ·' ⲁⲩⲛⲉϫⲉⲓⲧⲛ̄ ⲉϩⲟⲩⲛ' ϩⲙ̄ⲡϩⲟ ⲙ̄ⲡϩⲏⲅⲉ'ⲙⲱⲛ, ⲁⲩϭⲁϫⲟⲩ²⁵ ⲙ̄ⲙⲟⲩ ⲙⲛ̄ⲛⲉⲩϭ-
ⲛⲟⲩⲧⲉ ⲙⲛ̄ⲛⲉⲩⲣ̄'ⲣⲱⲟⲩ. ⲁϥϭⲱⲛⲧ̄' ⲛ̄ϭⲓ ⲁⲣⲓⲁⲛⲟⲥ ⲡϩⲏⲅⲉ'ⲙⲱⲛ, ⲁϥϯ ⲛ̄ⲧⲉⲩ-³⁰
ⲁⲡⲟⲫⲁⲥⲓⲥ ⲉⲣⲟⲟⲩ ⲉⲧ'ⲣⲟⲩϥⲓ ⲛ̄ⲧⲉⲩⲁⲡⲉ' ϩⲛ̄ⲧⲥⲏϥⲉ. ⲁⲩⲉⲓ (113 V ii) ⲛ̄ϭⲓ ⲟⲩ-
ⲕⲉⲥⲧⲟⲛⲁⲣⲓⲟⲥ,'ⲁⲩϥⲉⲓ ⲛ̄ⲧⲉⲩⲁⲡⲉ· ⲧⲁⲓ' ⲧⲉ ⲑⲉ ⲛ̄ⲧⲁⲩϫⲱⲕ ⲉⲃⲟⲗ' ⲛ̄ⲧⲉⲩⲙⲁⲣⲧⲩ-
ⲣⲓⲁ ⲛ̄ϭⲓ⁵ ⲛ̄ϩⲁⲅⲓⲟⲥ ⲙ̄ⲙⲁⲣⲧⲩⲣⲟⲥ' ⲛ̄ⲥⲟⲩⲙⲛ̄ⲧⲁⲥⲉ ⲛ̄ⲑⲟⲟⲩⲧ,' ϩⲛ̄ⲟⲩⲉⲓⲣⲏⲛⲏ, ϩⲁ-
ⲙⲏ(ⲛ).' ⲙⲛ̄ⲛⲥⲱⲥ ⲁⲩⲧⲣⲟⲩⲉⲓ'ⲛⲉ ⲉⲑⲏ ⲛ̄ⲁⲗⲁ ϣⲛⲟⲩ'ϥⲉ¹⁰ ⲙⲛ̄ⲛⲉⲩⲥⲛⲏⲩ,' ⲡⲉϫⲁⲩ
ⲛⲁⲩ ϫⲉ ⲥⲱⲧⲙ̄' ⲛ̄ⲥⲱⲓ, ⲁⲣⲓⲑⲩⲥⲓⲁ' ⲁⲩⲱ ⲧⲉⲧⲛ̄ⲁⲣ̄ⲃⲟⲗ ⲉϩⲉⲛ̄ⲃⲁⲥⲁⲛⲟⲥ ⲙⲛ̄ϩⲉⲛ-¹⁵
ⲇⲓⲙⲱⲣⲉⲓⲁ ⲉⲩⲟⲩⲏ.' ⲡⲉϫⲉⲡϩⲁⲅⲓⲟⲥ ⲁⲡⲁ ϣⲛ'ⲟⲩϥⲉ ⲛⲁⲩ ϫⲉ ϣⲁⲣⲉ'ⲟⲩϣⲁϫⲉ
ⲣⲁⲩⲧⲟⲩⲥⲁ'ⲃⲉ ⲛ̄ⲣⲱⲙⲉ · ⲡⲥⲟϭ²⁰ ⲇⲉ ⲉⲕϣⲁⲛϣⲁϫⲉ' ⲛⲙ̄ⲙⲁⲩ, ⲙⲉϥϭⲓⲥⲃⲱ.' ⲧⲉⲛⲟⲩ ϭⲉ ⲙⲁⲣⲉⲡⲉⲓ'ϣⲁ'ϫⲉ ⲣⲱϥⲉ ⲉⲣⲟⲕ ϫⲉ' ⲟⲩⲇⲉ ⲛ̄ⲧⲟⲕ ⲟⲩⲇⲉ ⲛⲉⲕ'ⲛⲟⲩⲧⲉ²⁵
ⲛ̄ⲧⲛ̄ⲛⲁⲥⲱ'ⲧⲙ̄ ⲛ̄ⲥⲱⲕ ⲁⲛ· ⲁⲛⲏ'ⲡ ⲉⲡϫⲟⲉⲓⲥ ⲓ̅ⲥ̅ ⲡⲉⲭ̅ⲥ̅' ⲡⲛⲟⲩⲧⲉ ⲙ̄ⲙⲉ.' ⲛ̄ⲧⲉ-
ⲣⲉϥⲥⲱⲧⲙ̄ ⲉⲛⲁⲓ³⁰' ⲛ̄ϭⲓ ⲁⲣⲓⲁⲛⲟⲥ ⲡϩⲏⲅⲉ'ⲙⲱⲛ ⲁϥϭⲱⲛⲧ̄,' ⲡⲉϫⲁⲩ ϫⲉ ⲟⲩ(114 R i)
ⲕⲟⲩⲛ ⲉⲕⲉⲓⲣⲉ ⲙ̄ⲙⲟⲓ' ⲛ̄ⲥⲟϭ. ⲁⲩⲕⲉⲗⲉⲩⲉ ⲉⲧ'ⲣⲟⲩϫⲉⲣⲟ ⲛ̄ϩⲉⲛⲡⲉⲛⲓⲡⲉ ⲛ̄ⲥⲉⲕⲁ-
ⲁⲩ ϩⲁⲛⲉⲩ⁵ⲥⲡⲓⲣⲟⲩⲉ, ϩⲱⲥⲧⲉ' ⲛ̄ⲥⲉⲃⲱⲗ ⲛ̄ϭⲓ ⲛ̄ⲅⲁⲁⲣ ⲙ̄ⲡⲉⲩⲥⲱⲙⲁ·' ⲡϩⲁⲅⲓⲟⲥ
ⲇⲉ ⲁⲡⲁ ϣⲛ'ⲟⲩϥⲉ ⲡⲉϫⲁⲩ ϫⲉ ⲥⲱⲧⲙ̄ ⲉⲣⲟⲛ ⲡⲉⲛϫⲟⲉⲓⲥ' ⲓ̅ⲥ̅ ⲡⲉⲭ̅ⲥ̅, ⲙ̄ⲡⲣ̄ⲕⲁ-
ⲁⲛ' ⲛ̄ⲥⲱⲕ· ⲁⲩⲕⲟⲧⲩ̄' ⲉⲛⲉⲩⲕⲉⲥⲛⲏⲩ, ⲡⲉ'ϫⲁⲩ ⲛⲁⲩ ϫⲉ ϩⲩⲡⲟⲙⲉⲓ'ⲛⲉ. ⲉⲓⲧⲁ
ⲁⲩⲕⲉⲗⲉ'ⲩⲉ ⲛ̄ϭⲓ ⲁⲣⲓⲁⲛⲟⲥ ⲡϩⲏ'ⲅⲙⲱⲛ ⲉⲧⲣⲟⲩⲉⲓ'ⲛⲉ ⲛ̄ϩⲉⲛⲛⲱⲛⲉ' ⲛ̄ⲥⲉⲕⲁⲁⲩ
ⲉϫⲛ̄ϩⲏⲧⲟⲩ²⁰'ⲛ̄ⲛⲉϩⲁⲅⲓⲟⲥ ⲛ̄ⲥⲉ'ⲛⲱϩⲧ ⲛ̄ⲟⲩϩⲏ̅ⲥ̅' ⲙ̄ⲛⲟⲩⲕⲱⲛⲓⲁ ⲉⲡⲉⲥⲏⲧ ⲉⲩϫⲁⲁ-
ⲧⲟⲩ ⲉⲧ'ⲧⲏϩ ⲙⲛ̄ⲛⲉⲩⲉⲣⲏⲩ,²⁵' ⲉⲣⲉⲡⲁⲛⲟⲙⲟⲥ ϫⲱ' ⲙ̄ⲙⲟⲥ ϫⲉ ⲙ̄ⲡⲣ̄ⲙⲉ'ⲉⲩⲉ ϫⲉ
ⲁⲛ̄ⲃⲁⲥⲁⲛⲟⲥ' ⲟⲩⲱ. ⲟⲩⲛ̄ⲃⲁϩⲁ'ⲛⲟⲥ ⲉϥⲟⲩⲟⲧⲩ̄ ⲉⲛⲁⲓ³⁰' ⲉⲧⲉⲧⲛ̄ⲙ̄ⲙⲉⲧⲁⲛⲟⲓ'
ⲛ̄ⲧⲉⲧⲛ̄ⲑⲩⲥⲓⲁⲍⲉ.' ⲛ̄ϩⲁⲅⲓⲟⲥ ⲇⲉ ⲁⲩⲉⲓ ϩ(R ii)ⲣⲁⲩ ⲉϩⲣⲁⲓ̈ ϩⲛ̄ⲟⲩⲥⲙⲏ' ⲛ̄-
ⲟⲩⲱⲧ ⲉⲩϫⲱ ⲙ̄ⲙⲟⲥ ϫⲉ ⲁⲙⲟⲩ ϣⲁ'ⲣⲟⲛ, ⲡⲁⲅⲅⲉⲗⲟⲥ ⲙ̄'ⲡⲉⲛϫⲟⲉⲓⲥ ⲓ̅ⲥ̅ ⲡⲉ-⁵
ⲭ̅ⲥ̅,' ⲛ̄ϥϯϭⲟⲙ ⲛⲁⲛ.' ⲛ̄ⲧⲉⲩⲛⲟⲩ ⲉⲓⲥ ⲙⲓⲭⲁ'ⲏⲗ ⲡⲁⲣⲭⲁⲅⲅⲉⲗⲟⲥ' ⲁⲩⲉⲓ ⲉⲃⲟⲗ
ϩⲛ̄ⲧⲡⲉ,¹⁰ ⲁⲩⲉⲓ ϣⲁⲛ̄ϩⲁⲅⲓⲟⲥ,' ⲁⲩϫⲱϩ ⲉⲣⲟⲟⲩ ⲙ̄'ⲡⲉⲩϩⲣⲁⲩⲧⲟⲥ, ⲁⲩⲧⲁⲗ-
ϭⲟⲟⲩ· ⲁⲩⲱ' ⲁⲛⲱⲛⲉ ⲥⲕⲟⲣⲕⲣ̄¹⁵ ⲙ̄ⲙⲁⲩ ⲁⲁⲩ ⲉⲃⲟⲗ ϩⲛ̄'ⲧⲉⲩⲕⲁⲗⲁϩⲏ, ⲁⲡ'ϩⲙ̄ⲙⲉ
ⲣ̄ⲑⲉ ⲛ̄ⲟⲩⲉⲓⲱ'ⲧⲉ ⲉⲥⲛⲟⲧⲙ̄ ⲉⲥⲛⲏⲩ' ⲉϣⲉⲛϣⲁⲁⲧⲟⲩ.²⁰' ⲁⲩⲃⲟϭⲧⲟⲩ ⲉϩⲣⲁⲓ̈ ⲛ̄ϭⲓ'

_____

113 V ii 15. = -ⲧⲓⲙⲱⲣⲓⲁ.   26. ⲗ. ⲉⲛⲏⲡ.

ⲛ̄ⲍⲁⲅⲓⲟⲥ ⲉⲙ̄ⲡⲧⲁⲕⲟ· ϣⲟⲟⲡ ⲙ̄ⲙⲟⲟⲩ· ⲛ̄ⲧⲉⲣⲉⲇⲙⲏⲏϣⲉ ⲛⲁⲩ· ⲉⲡⲉⲓⲛⲟϭ ⲛ̄ϣⲡⲏⲣⲉ, ⲁⲩⲱϣ ⲉⲃⲟⲗ ⲉⲧⲙ̄ⲡϩⲏⲅⲉⲙⲱⲛ· ⲁⲗⲉⲝ·ⲣⲏⲧⲱⲣ ⲕⲓⲙ ⲛ̄ⲧⲉⲩϭⲓⲝ ⲉⲣⲟⲟⲩ, ⲁⲩⲕⲁⲣⲱⲟⲩ. ⲁⲩⲕⲉⲗⲉⲩⲉ ⲛ̄ϭⲓ ⲡϩⲏⲅⲉⲙⲱⲛ ⲉⲧⲣⲟⲩϭⲱⲕ ⲛ̄ϩⲛ̄ϩⲧⲱⲱⲣ ⲛⲁⲩ ϫⲉ ⲉⲩⲉⲁⲗⲉ ⲉ(114 Vi)ⲣⲟⲟⲩ ⲛ̄ⲧ̄ⲃⲱⲕ ϩⲁⲃⲟⲗ ⲙ̄ⲡⲁϩⲁⲗ ⲙ̄ⲡⲙⲏⲏϣⲉ. ⲁⲩⲱϣ ⲉⲃⲟⲗ ⲛ̄ϭⲓ ⲛ̄ⲍⲁⲅⲓⲟⲥ ϩⲛ̄ⲟⲩⲥⲙⲏ ⲛ̄ⲟⲩⲱⲧ ϫⲉ ϯⲟⲛϩ̄ ⲛ̄ϭⲓ ⲡϫⲟⲉⲓⲥ ⲡ·ⲛⲟⲩⲧⲉ ⲡⲉⲧϫ̄ϭⲟⲙ ⲛⲁⲛ ϣⲁⲛⲧⲛ̄ ϯ·ϣⲓⲡⲉ ⲛⲁⲕ ⲙⲛ̄ⲛⲉⲕⲃⲁⲍⲁⲛⲟⲥ ⲙⲛ̄ⲛⲉⲕⲉⲓⲇⲱⲗⲟⲛ ⲛ̄ⲕⲟⲩⲣ ϫⲉ ⲛ̄ⲕⲛⲁⲥⲉⲛⲧⲡⲉⲓⲙⲁ ⲉⲃⲟⲗ ⲁⲛ ⲙ̄ⲡⲉⲕϯ ⲛ̄ⲧⲉⲛⲁⲡⲟⲫⲁⲥⲓⲥ· ⲁⲩⲱ ⲁⲩⲁⲙⲁϩⲧⲉ ⲛ̄ⲛⲉⲙⲟⲩⲥ ⲛ̄ⲛⲉϩⲧⲱⲱⲣ, ⲙ̄ⲡⲟⲩⲕⲁⲁⲩ ⲉⲙⲟⲟϣⲉ. ⲁⲩⲉⲓ ⲇⲉ ϫⲉ ⲉⲩⲛⲁϯ ⲁⲡⲟⲫⲁⲥⲓⲥ· ⲉⲣⲟⲟⲩ ⲛ̄ϩⲟⲧⲃⲟⲩ· ⲛ̄ϩ̄ⲛⲟⲕⲟⲩ ⲉⲡⲉⲓⲣⲣⲟ· ϩⲓⲧⲛ̄ⲡϣⲱⲛⲧ ⲙ̄ⲡⲑⲩⲙⲟⲥ ⲉⲧϩⲓⲱⲱⲩ· ϊⲟⲩⲗⲓⲟⲥ ⲇⲉ ⲡⲕⲱⲙⲉⲛⲧⲁⲣⲏⲥⲓⲟⲥ ⲡⲣⲁⲕⲃⲁⲍⲉ ⲁⲩⲱ ⲑⲉⲟⲫⲁⲛⲟⲓⲥ ⲡⲧⲱⲙⲉⲥⲧⲓⲕⲟⲥ ⲁⲩϯⲡⲉⲩⲟⲩⲟⲓ ⲉⲡϩⲏⲅⲉⲙⲱⲛ, ⲡⲉϫⲁⲩ ⲛⲁⲩ ϫⲉ ⲡⲉⲛϫⲟⲉⲓⲥ, ⲙⲁⲣⲉⲛϫⲓⲧⲟⲩ (Vii) ⲛⲙ̄ⲙⲁⲛ ⲉϩⲣⲁⲓ ⲉⲁⲣⲥⲓⲛⲟⲏ ⲧⲛⲟϭ ⲙ̄ⲡⲟⲗⲓⲥ, ⲙⲏⲡⲟⲧⲉ ⲛ̄ⲥⲉⲛⲁⲩ ⲉⲛⲉⲓⲉⲓⲇⲱⲗⲟⲛ ⲛ̄ⲥⲉⲟⲩⲱϣⲧ ⲛⲁⲩ· ⲡⲁⲛⲧⲟⲥ ⲉⲩϣⲓⲡⲉ ⲉⲧⲃⲉⲡⲙⲏⲏϣⲉ ⲉⲧⲕⲱⲧⲉ ⲉⲣⲟⲟⲩ· ⲁⲩⲱ ϯⲥⲟⲟⲩⲛ̄· ⲁⲛⲁⲡⲉⲓⲧⲟⲩ ϫⲉ ϩⲛ̄ⲥⲧⲁⲥⲓⲁⲥⲧⲏⲥ ⲛ̄ⲧⲟⲗⲙⲏⲣⲟⲥ ⲛⲉ· ⲛ̄ⲥⲉⲛⲁⲧⲥⲟ ⲉⲣⲟⲛ ⲁⲛ, ⲟⲩⲇⲉ ⲛ̄ⲥⲉ·ⲛⲁⲕⲁⲁⲛ ⲁⲛ ⲉⲧⲁⲡⲟⲫⲁⲥⲓⲥ ⲉⲣⲟⲟⲩ ⲙ̄ⲡⲉⲓⲙⲁ· ⲁⲩⲕⲉⲗⲉⲩⲉ ⲇⲉ ⲉⲧⲣⲟⲩ·ⲥⲱⲛϩ̄ ⲙ̄ⲙⲟⲟⲩ ⲛ̄ⲥⲉ·ϫⲓⲧⲟⲩ ϩⲁⲧⲉⲩϫⲏ ⲉϩⲟⲩⲛ ⲉⲧⲡⲟⲗⲓⲥ ⲙ̄ⲡⲓⲟⲙ· ⲛ̄ⲧⲉⲣⲉϥⲃⲱⲕ ⲉϩⲟⲩⲛ ⲉⲧⲡⲟⲗⲓⲥ, ⲁⲩϭⲛ̄ⲧⲟⲩ· ⲉⲩⲉⲓⲣⲉ ⲛ̄ⲟⲩⲛⲟϭ ⲛ̄ϣⲁ· ⲙ̄ⲡⲉϩⲟⲟⲩ ⲉⲧⲙ̄ⲙⲁⲩ, ⲉⲡⲉⲓⲇⲏ ⲧⲉⲗⲉⲩⲑⲉⲣⲓⲁ· ⲛ̄ⲧⲉⲩⲡⲟⲗⲓⲥ ⲧⲉ· ⲁⲩⲱ ⲕⲁⲧⲁ ⲥⲁϣϥⲉ ⲛ̄ⲣⲟⲙⲡⲉ ⲉⲡⲥⲟⲡ ϣⲁⲣⲉⲛⲁⲣⲭⲱⲛ ⲉⲓⲛⲉ· ⲉⲃⲟⲗ ⲛ̄ϩⲁϩ ⲙ̄ϩⲁⲗ ⲛ̄ⲧⲁⲩ ⲛ̄ⲥⲉⲁⲁⲩ ⲛ̄ⲣⲙ̄ϩⲉ· ⲁⲣⲓⲁⲛⲟⲥ ⲇⲉ ⲡⲍⲏⲅⲉ·ⲙⲱⲛ ⲁϥⲡⲱⲧ ϫⲉ· ⲉⲩⲛⲁⲥⲱⲧⲙ̄ ⲛ̄ⲍⲁⲅⲓⲟⲥ ⲙ̄ⲙⲁⲣⲧⲩⲣⲟⲥ· ⲁ(115 Ri)ⲛⲁ·ⲧⲡⲟⲗⲓⲥ ⲱϣ ⲉⲃⲟⲗ· ϫⲉ ⲙ̄ⲡⲱⲣ, ⲙ̄ⲡⲣⲧⲁ·ⲕⲉⲧⲉⲗⲉⲩⲑⲉⲣⲓⲁ ⲛ̄ⲧⲉⲛⲡⲟⲗⲓⲥ, ⲁⲗⲗⲁ ⲕⲁⲁⲩ ϣⲁⲛⲧⲉⲩⲟϣⲱ· ⲛ̄ϭⲓ ⲡⲏⲁ ⲛ̄ⲧⲉⲛⲡⲟⲗⲓⲥ· ⲁⲩⲱ ⲕ̄ⲛⲁⲥⲱⲧⲙ̄ ⲉⲣⲟⲟⲩ· ⲁⲩ·ⲕⲉⲗⲉⲩⲉ ⲉⲧⲣⲟⲩϫⲓ ⲛ̄ⲛⲉⲧⲟⲩⲁⲁⲃ ⲉⲧⲉⲫⲩⲗⲁ·ⲕⲏ, ⲁⲩⲁϩⲉⲣⲁⲧⲟⲩ, ⲁⲩ·ϣⲗⲏⲗ· ⲡ·ⲍⲁⲅⲓⲟⲥ· ⲇⲉ ⲁⲡⲁ ϣⲡⲟⲩϭⲉ· ⲁⲩⲁⲟⲩⲱⲛ ⲛ̄ⲣⲱϥ· ⲁⲩϫⲱ ⲙ̄ⲡⲉⲓϣⲗⲏ·ⲛⲟⲥ, ⲉⲩⲟⲩⲱϩⲙ̄ ⲛ̄ⲥⲱϥ, ϫⲉ ⲧⲥⲙⲟⲩ·ⲉⲣⲟⲕ ⲓ̅ⲥ̅ ⲡⲉⲧⲉⲛⲟⲩϥ ⲛⲉ ⲥⲙⲟⲩ ⲛⲓⲙ· ⲧⲥⲙⲟⲩ ⲉⲣⲟⲕ ⲓ̅ⲥ̅ ⲡⲙⲟⲛⲟⲅⲉⲛⲏⲥ ⲙ̄ⲡⲉⲓⲱⲧ· ⲧⲥⲙⲟⲩ ⲉⲣⲟⲕ ⲓ̅ⲥ̅ ⲧⲃⲱ· ⲛ̄ⲉⲗⲟⲟⲗⲉ ⲙ̄ⲙⲉ ⲉⲧⲟ· ⲛ̄ⲟⲩⲕⲗⲟⲙ ⲉϫⲛ̄ⲡⲉⲑⲣⲟⲛⲟⲥ ⲙ̄ⲡⲉⲓⲱⲧ· ⲧⲥⲙⲟⲩ ⲉⲣⲟⲕ ⲓ̅ⲥ̅ ⲡⲉⲛⲧⲁⲩⲙⲟⲟⲩϣⲉ ϩⲓϫⲛ̄ⲛ̄ⲙⲟⲟⲩ, ⲙ̄ⲡⲟⲩ·ϩⲱⲣⲡ̄ ⲛ̄ϭⲓ ⲛⲉϥⲟⲩⲉⲣⲏⲧ· ⲧⲥⲙⲟⲩ ⲉⲣⲟⲕ ⲓ̅ⲥ̅ ⲡⲉⲛⲧⲁⲩⲧⲣⲉⲡⲗⲩⲅⲏ· ⲉⲧⲥⲁϣⲉ ϩⲗⲟϭ· ⲧⲥⲙⲟⲩ ⲉⲣⲟⲕ ⲓ̅ⲥ̅ ⲡϭⲉ(Rii)ⲣⲱⲃ ⲉⲧ̄ϩⲛ̄ⲧⲙⲏ·

---

114 Vi 27. ⲗ. ⲑⲉⲟⲫⲁⲛⲏⲥ. ii 6. = ⲡⲁⲛⲧⲱⲥ. 32. ⲗ. ⲉⲛ̄ⲍⲁⲅⲓⲟⲥ. 115 Rii 28. ⲗ. ⲟ̄ⲩⲉⲣⲏⲧⲉ.

ⲧⲉ ⲙ̄ⲡⲉⲓⲱⲧ· ⳿ⲧⲥⲙⲟⲩ ⲉⲣⲟⲕ ⲓ̅ⲥ̅ ⲧⲡⲉⲧⲣⲁ ⲛ̄ⲁⲧⲕⲓⲙ· ⳿ⲧⲥⲙⲟⲩ ⲉⲣⲟⲕ ⲓ̅ⲥ̅ ⲙ̄ⲡⲛⲉ⳿ⲕⲁⲅ-
ⲅⲉⲗⲟⲥ ⲧⲏⲣⲟⲩ· ⳿ⲧⲥⲙⲟⲩ ⲉⲣⲟⲕ ⲓ̅ⲥ̅ ⲙ̄ⲛ̄ⲡⲉⲕⲉⲓⲱⲧ ⲛ̄ⲁⲅⲁⲑⲟⲥ, ⳿ⲡⲁⲓ ⲉⲧⲉⲣⲉⲡⲉⲛⲛⲓ̈ⲃⲉ
ⲥ̄ⲙⲛⲉⲩⲥⲓ̈ⲥ, ⳿ⲁⲩⲱ ⲉϥⲧ ⲙ̄ⲡⲱⲛϩ̅ ⲛⲁⲛ· ϫⲉ ⲧⲱⲕ⳿ ⲧⲉ ⲧϭⲟⲙ ⲙ̄ⲛⲡⲉⲟⲟⲩ⳿ ϣⲁⲉⲛⲉϩ,
ϩⲁⲙⲏⲛ.ⁱ⁵ ⲛ̄ⲧⲉⲩⲛⲟⲩ ⲁⲙⲙⲁ ⲉ⳿ⲧⲟⲩⲁϩⲉⲣⲁⲧⲟⲩ ⲛ̄ϩⲏⲧϥ̄⳿ ⲣⲟⲩⲟⲉⲓⲛ· ⲁⲡϫⲟⲉⲓⲥ⳿
ⲟⲩⲱⲛϩ̅ ⲛⲁⲩ ⲉⲃⲟⲗ,⳿ ⲡⲉϫⲁⲩ ⲛⲁⲩ ϫⲉ ⲭⲉⲣⲉ²⁰ ⲛⲁⲙⲉⲣⲓⲧ ⲉⲧⲟⲩⲁⲁⲃ,⳿ ⲛⲁⲩⲃⲏⲣ ⲛ̄-
ⲕⲗⲏⲣⲟ⳿ⲛⲟⲙⲟⲥ, ⳿ⲧⲣⲏⲛⲏ ⲛⲏⲧⲛ̄,⳿ ⲙ̄ⲡⲣ̄ⲣϩⲟⲧⲉ, ⲧϥⲟⲟⲣ⳿ ⲛ̄ⲁⲙⲏⲧⲛ̄ ϣⲁⲛ⳿ⲧⲉⲧⲛ̄ϫⲱⲕ
ⲉⲃⲟⲗ ⲙ̄⳿ⲡⲉⲧⲛ̄ⲁⲅⲱⲛ·⳿ ⲁⲩⲱ ⲁϥⲧ ⲛⲁⲩ ⲛ̄ϩⲛ̄ⲁ⳿ⲅⲁⲑⲱⲛ ⲛ̄ⲧⲉⲡⲏⲓ⳿ ⲁⲩⲟⲩⲱⲙ, ⲁ-
ⲡⲉⲩ³⁰ϩⲏⲧ ⲧⲁⲭⲣⲟ· ⲁϥⲥϥ⳿ⲣⲁⲅⲓⲍⲉ ⲙ̄ⲙⲟⲟⲩ, ⲁⲩ⳿ⲃⲱⲕ ⲉϩⲣⲁⲓ̈ ⲉⲙ̄ⲡⲏⲩⲉ, (115 V i)
ⲉⲣⲉⲛ̄ϩⲁⲅⲓⲟⲥ ϭⲱϣⲧ⳿ ⲛ̄ⲥⲱⲟⲩ, ϩⲛ̄ⲟⲩⲉⲓⲣⲏ⳿ⲛⲏ, ϩⲁⲙⲏⲛ.⳿ ⲡϩⲁⲅⲓⲟⲥ ⲇⲉ ⲁⲡⲁ ⲯⲛ̄ⁱ⁵ⲟⲩ-
ϭⲉ ⲁⲩⲧⲉⲩⲅⲉ ⲧⲏⲓⲣϥ̄ ⲉϥⲥⲟⲗⲥⲗ̄ ⲙ̄ⲙⲟⲟⲩ⳿ ϣⲁⲛⲧⲉⲡⲟⲩⲟⲉⲓⲛ⳿ ⲉⲓ ⲉϩⲣⲁⲓ̈· ⲯⲱⲣⲡ⳿
ⲇⲉ ⲛ̄ⲧⲉⲣⲉϥϣⲱⲡⲉ¹⁰ ⲛⲉⲩ̄ⲛⲟⲩⲣⲱⲙⲉ⳿ ⲛ̄ϩⲟⲩⲛ ⲉⲧⲉϥⲩⲗⲁ⳿ⲕⲏ ⲉⲟⲩⲛⲟⲩⲡⲛ̄ⲁ⳿ ⲛ̄ⲁⲅⲁ-
ⲑⲁⲣⲧⲟⲛ ⲛⲙ̈ⲙⲁⲩ· ⲁⲩⲱϣ ⲉⲃⲟⲗ¹⁵ ϫⲉ ⳿ⲧⲛⲁⲡⲱⲧ ⲉⲃⲟⲗ⳿ ⲛ̄ⲑⲉⲟⲱⲇⲱⲣⲟⲥ⳿ ⲡϣⲏⲣⲉ ⲛ̄-
ⲇⲓⲟⲛⲏ⳿ⲡⲧⲁ ⲡⲗⲟⲅⲓⲥⲧⲏⲥ⳿ ⲛ̄ⲧⲡⲟⲗⲓⲥ, ⲱ ⲡϩⲁ²⁰ⲅⲓⲟⲥ ⲁⲡⲁ ⲯⲛⲟⲩϭⲉ,⳿ ⲉⲧⲃⲉⲃⲟⲧⲉ ⲙ̄-
ⲡⲉⲭⲥ̅,⳿ ⲡⲁⲓ̈ ⲛ̄ⲧⲁϥⲉⲓ ⲯⲁ⳿ⲣⲟⲕ ⲉⲧⲉⲫⲩⲗⲁⲕⲏ⳿ ⲛ̄ⲧⲉⲓ̈ⲟⲩϣⲏ.²⁵ ⲛ̄ⲧⲉⲩⲛⲟⲩ ⲁⲡⲇⲁⲓ̈ⲙⲱ-
ⲛⲓⲟⲛ ⲣⲉϩⲧ⳿ⲡⲣⲱⲙⲉ, ⲁϥⲉⲓ ⲉⲃⲟⲗ⳿ ⲛ̄ϩⲏⲧϥ̄, ⲁϥⲡⲱⲧ·⳿ ⲁϥⲡⲁϩⲧϥ̄ ϩⲁⲣⲁⲧⲟⲩ·³⁰ ⲛ̄ⲛⲉⲟ-
ⲟⲩⲉⲣⲏⲧⲉ ⲛ̄ⲛⲉⲧⲟⲩⲁⲁⲃ, ⲁϥ⳿ϣⲱⲡⲉ ⲉϥⲡⲓ ⲉⲣⲟ(V ii)ⲟⲩ. ⲡⲉⲡⲣⲟⲥⲑⲩⲣⲟⲥ⳿ ⲇⲉ ⲉⲧ-
ϩⲓⲕⲁⲡⲉⲩⲧⲉ⳿ⲕⲟ ⲛ̄ⲧⲉⲣⲉϥⲛⲁⲩ ⲉⲧ⳿ϭⲟⲙ ⲛ̄ⲧⲁⲥϣⲱⲡⲉ⁵ⲉⲃⲟⲗ ϩⲓⲧⲛ̄ϩⲁⲅⲓⲟⲥ,⳿ ⲛ̄ⲧⲟϥ
ⲇⲉ ϩⲱⲱϥ⳿ ⲛⲉⲟⲩⲛ̄ⲧϥ̄ⲟⲩϣⲉⲉⲣⲉ⳿ ⲙ̄ⲙⲟⲛⲟⲅⲉⲛⲏⲥ ⲉⲥⲉ⳿ⲉⲧ, ⲉⲁⲥⲉⲓ ⲉϩⲣⲁⲓ̈ ⲉⲡⲉⲥ¹⁰ⲉ-
ⲃⲟⲧ ⲙ̄ⲙⲓⲥⲉ,⳿ ⲉⲁⲡⲉⲥϣⲏⲣⲉ ⲡⲱϩϥ̄⳿ ϩⲛ̄ⲧⲉⲥⲕⲁⲗⲁϩⲏ, ⲉⲁⲥⲣ̄ⲙⲛ̄ⲧⲟⲩⲉ ⲛ̄ϩⲟⲟⲩ· ⲉⲥ-
ϩⲁⲃⲁⲥⲁⲛⲟⲥ· ⲉⲁⲩⲉⲓ⳿ⲛⲉ ⲉⲣⲟⲥ ⲛ̄ⲟⲩⲙⲏⲏϣⲉ⳿ ⲛ̄ⲥⲁⲉⲓⲛ ⲙ̄ⲛ̄ⲟⲩⲙⲏ⳿ⲏϣⲉ ⲛ̄ⲉⲝⲟⲣⲅⲓⲥ-
ⲧⲏⲥ,⳿ ⲙ̄ⲡⲟⲩⲉϣϭⲙ̄ϭⲟⲙ⳿ ⲉⲑⲩⲣⲁⲡⲉⲩⲉ ⲙ̄ⲙⲟⲥ.²⁰ ⲡⲉϫⲁⲩ ⲙ̄ⲡϩⲁⲅⲓⲟⲥ ⳿ⲁⲡⲁ ⲯⲛⲟⲩϭⲉ ϫⲉ ⲧ⳿ⲥⲟⲡⲥ̄ ⲙ̄ⲙⲟⲕ, ⲩⲛ̄ϩ̄⳿ⲧⲏⲕ ϩⲁⲧⲁⲙⲟⲛⲟⲅⲉ⳿ⲛⲏⲥ ⲛ̄ϣⲉⲉⲣⲉ ϫⲉ ⲥ̄ⲙⲟⲕϩ̄
ⲉⲙⲁⲧⲉ.⳿ ⲡⲉⲭⲉⲡϩⲁⲅⲓⲟⲥ ⲛⲁⲩ⳿ ϫⲉ ⲁⲛⲉⲓⲛⲉ ⲛⲁⲓ̈ ⲛ̄ⲟⲩ⳿ⲕⲟⲩⲓ̈ ⲛ̄ⲛⲉϩ, ⲧⲁⲩⲗⲏⲗ
ⲉϫⲱϥ, ⲧⲁⲣⲉⲡⲉⲟⲟⲩ³⁰ ⲛ̄ⲓ̅ⲥ̅ ⲟⲩⲱⲛϩ̅ ⲉⲃⲟⲗ.⳿ ⲛ̄ⲧⲉⲩⲛⲟⲩ ⲁⲩⲉⲓⲛⲉ ⲙ̄ⲡ⳿ⲕⲟⲩⲓ̈ ⲛ̄ⲛⲉϩ,
ⲁϥϫⲓⲧϥ̄ (116 Ri) ⲛ̄ϭⲓ ⲡϩⲁⲅⲓⲟⲥ, ⲁϥⲥϥ⳿ⲣⲁⲅⲓⲥ ⲙ̄ⲙⲟϥ, ⲁϥ⳿ϣⲗⲏⲗ ⲉϩⲣⲁⲓ̈ ⲉ-
ϫⲱϥ,⳿ ⲁϥⲙⲟⲟⲩϭⲉ ⲉϩⲟⲩⲛ ⲉ⳿ⲛⲉⲩⲥⲛⲏⲩ, ⲁϥⲧⲣⲟⲩ⳿ⲥⲫⲣⲁⲅⲓⲍⲉ ⲙ̄ⲙⲟⲩ⳿ ϩⲱⲟⲩ·
ⲁϥϫⲓⲧϥ̄⳿ ⲛ̄ⲧⲉⲩⲛⲟⲩ, ⲁϥⲧⲱϩⲥ̄⳿ ⲛ̄ⲧⲉϥϣⲉⲉⲣⲉ ⲛ̄ϩⲏⲧϥ̄·¹⁰ ⲁⲩⲱ ⲛ̄ⲧⲉⲩⲛⲟⲩ ⲁⲥ⳿ⲙⲓⲥⲉ
ⲛ̄ⲟⲩϣⲏⲣⲉ ⲛ̄⳿ϩⲟⲟⲩⲧ, ⲁⲥⲙⲟⲩⲧⲉ⳿ ⲉⲣⲟϥ ϫⲉ ⲯⲛⲟⲩϭⲉ⳿ ⲕⲁⲧⲁⲡⲣⲁⲛ ⲙ̄ⲡϩⲁ¹⁵ⲅⲓⲟⲥ
ⲁⲡⲁ ⲯⲛⲟⲩϭⲉ.⳿ ⲛ̄ⲧⲉⲩⲛⲟⲩ ⲁⲟⲩⲛⲟϭ⳿ ⲛ̄ⲣⲁϣⲉ ϣⲱⲡⲉ⳿ ϩⲙ̄ⲡⲏⲓ̈ ⲛ̄ⲛⲉⲥⲉⲓⲟⲧⲉ.⳿

---

115 R ii 28. l. ⲁⲧⲉⲧⲛⲉ. V i 32-ii 1. l. ⲉⲣⲱⲟⲩ. ii 29. -ⲉⲟⲟⲩ: second o
added. 116 R i 1 f. l. -ⲥⲫⲣⲁⲅⲓⲍⲉ.

ⲁⲩⲱ ⲡⲣⲱⲙⲉ ⲛ̄ⲧⲁⲡⲇⲁⲓⲙⲱⲛ ⲉⲓ ⲉⲃⲟⲗ ⲛ̄ⲅ̄ⲏⲧϥ ⲁϥⲉⲓ ⲉⲃⲟⲗ ϩⲛ̄ⲧⲡⲟⲗⲓⲥ ⲧⲏⲣⲉ
ⲉϥϯ ⲙ̄ⲡⲥⲟⲉⲓⲧ ⲛ̄ⲛⲉⲧⲟⲩⲁⲁⲃ ⲉⲧⲃⲉⲛ̄ϭⲟⲙ ⲙⲛ̄ⲛⲉϣⲡⲏⲣⲉ ⲉⲧⲟⲩⲉⲓⲣⲉ ⲙ̄ⲙⲟⲟⲩ ⲛ̄-
ϩⲟⲩⲛ ⲉⲧⲉⲫⲩⲗⲁⲕⲏ· ϩⲱⲥⲧⲉ ⲣⲱⲙⲉ ⲛⲓⲙ ⲉⲣⲉϣⲱⲛⲉ ϩⲓⲱⲱϥ ⲉⲩⲙⲟⲕⲥ̄ ⲁⲩⲃⲓ-
ⲧⲟⲩ ⲉⲧⲉⲫⲩⲗⲁⲕⲏ· ⲁⲩⲧⲁⲗϭⲟⲟⲩ ⲧⲏⲣⲟⲩ· (116 R ii) ⲓ̈ⲟⲩⲗⲓⲟⲥ ⲇⲉ ⲡⲃⲟⲏⲑⲟⲥ ⲡ-
ⲕⲟⲙⲙⲉⲛⲧⲁⲣⲏⲥⲓⲟⲥ· ⲛ̄ⲧⲉⲣⲉϥⲛⲁⲩ ⲉⲛⲉϭⲟⲙ ⲉⲧⲉⲣⲉⲛⲉⲧⲟⲩⲁⲁⲃ ⲉⲓⲣⲉ ⲙ̄ⲙⲟⲟⲩ
ⲛ̄ϩⲟⲩⲛ ⲉⲧⲉⲫⲩⲗⲁⲕⲏ, ⲁϥⲧⲱⲟⲩⲛ, ⲁϥⲃⲱⲕ ϣⲁⲣⲟⲟⲩ ⲛ̄ϩⲟⲩⲛ ⲉⲧⲉⲫⲩⲗⲁⲕⲏ ϩⲛ̄-
ⲟⲩⲱⲡ, ⲉⲡⲓⲇⲏ ⲛ̄ⲧⲟⲩ ϩⲱⲱϥ ⲛⲉⲩϩⲟⲩⲛⲟϭ ⲛ̄ϩⲓⲥⲉ ⲙ̄ⲡⲟⲩⲙⲟⲕⲥ̄ ϩⲓⲱⲱϥ, ⲉ-
ⲣⲉⲟⲩⲧϥ̄ⲕⲁⲥ ϩⲓϫⲛ̄ⲛⲉϥϭⲓϫ ⲙⲛ̄ⲛⲉⲩⲟⲩⲉⲣⲏⲧⲉ· ⲕⲁⲧⲁⲕⲁⲓⲣⲟⲥ, ⲉⲛⲉ ⲁϥⲣⲟⲩⲙⲏ-
ⲛⲏϭⲉ ⲛ̄ϩⲟⲟⲩ ⲉϥϩⲁⲃⲁⲥⲁⲛⲟⲥ· ⲉϥϯⲕⲣⲁⲅⲅⲏ· ⲛ̄ⲧⲉⲣⲉϥⲃⲱⲕ ⲉϩⲟⲩ(ⲛ) ϣⲁⲛⲉ-
ⲧⲟⲩⲁⲁⲃ, ⲁϥⲡⲁⲣⲁⲕⲁⲗⲉⲓ ⲙ̄ⲙⲟⲟⲩ ⲉϥϫⲱ ⲙ̄ⲙⲟⲥ· ϫⲉ ⲉϣⲱⲡⲉ ⲁⲧⲉⲧⲛ̄ϣⲁⲛⲉⲓ-
ⲣⲉ ⲛⲙⲁⲓ̈ ⲙ̄ⲡⲉⲓ̈ⲛⲟϭ ⲛ̄ϩⲙⲟⲧ, ⲁⲛⲟⲕ ϩⲱ ϯⲛⲁⲣ ⲧⲁϭⲟⲙ ⲛⲙ̄ⲙⲏⲧⲛ̄ ⲙ̄ⲡⲉⲧⲉ-
ⲧⲛ̄ⲁⲁⲓⲧⲉⲓ ⲙ̄ⲙⲟⲓ ⲙ̄ⲙⲟϥ· ⲡⲣⲟⲥⲧⲉⲭⲣⲓⲁ ⲉⲡⲓⲕⲟⲥⲙⲟⲥ· ⲉϣⲱⲡⲉ (Vi) ⲧⲉⲧⲛ̄ⲟⲩⲱϣ
ⲉⲧⲣⲁⲕⲁⲧⲏ ⲧⲛ̄ ⲉⲃⲟⲗ ⲛ̄ⲧⲉⲧⲛ̄ⲃⲱⲕ ⲉⲡⲉⲧⲛ̄ⲏⲓ̈ ϩⲛ̄ⲟⲩⲉⲓⲣⲏⲛⲏ· ϣⲁⲉϩⲣⲁⲓ ⲉⲥⲁⲩ-
ϭⲉ ⲛ̄ⲗⲓⲧⲣⲁ ⲛ̄ⲛⲟⲩⲃ, ϯⲛⲁ ⲧⲁⲁⲩ ⲉⲝⲛ̄ⲧⲏⲩⲧⲛ̄· ⲙⲟⲛⲟⲛ ⲁⲣⲓⲣⲉ ⲛⲙ̄ⲙⲁⲓ ⲙ̄ⲡⲉⲓ̈-
ⲛⲟϭ ⲛ̄ⲁⲅⲁⲑⲱⲛ. ⲡⲉϫⲉ ⲡϩⲁⲅⲓⲟⲥ ⲁⲡⲁ ϣⲛⲟⲩϭⲉ ⲛⲁⲩ ϫⲉ ⲛ̄ⲧⲛ̄ⲟⲩⲱϣ ⲁⲛ ⲉ-
ⲧⲣⲉⲕ ⲕⲁⲁⲛ ⲉⲃⲟⲗ, ⲟⲩⲇⲉ ⲛ̄ⲣⲱⲙⲉ ⲁⲛ ⲡⲉⲛⲧⲁϥⲁⲛⲁⲅⲕⲁⲍⲉ ⲙ̄ⲙⲟⲛ ⲁⲩⲛⲧⲟⲛ ⲉ-
ⲡⲓⲙⲁ· ⲁⲗⲗⲁ ⲧⲟⲓⲕⲟⲛⲟⲙⲓⲁ ⲙ̄ⲡϫⲟⲉⲓⲥ ⲧⲛ̄ⲧⲁⲥⲛ̄ⲧⲛ̄ ⲉⲡⲓⲙⲁ, ⲉⲡⲓⲇⲏ ⲁⲩⲧⲁⲙⲟⲛ
ⲙ̄ⲡⲉⲧⲛⲁⲛⲟⲩⲟⲩ ⲉⲧⲕⲉⲓⲣⲉ ⲙ̄ⲙⲟⲟⲩ ⲙⲛ̄ⲛⲉⲧⲟⲩⲁⲁⲃ ⲧⲏⲣⲟⲩ· ⲡⲉⲓ̈ϩⲱⲃ ⲙ̄ⲙⲁⲧⲉ
ⲡⲉⲧⲛ̄ⲃ̄ⲭⲣⲓⲁ ⲙ̄ⲙⲟⲕ ⲛ̄ϩⲏⲧϥ̄· ⲁⲛⲟⲩⲱϣ ⲉⲧⲣⲉⲕⲁϩⲉⲣⲁⲧⲕ̄ ⲉⲣⲟⲛ ⲛ̄ⲅ̄ϭⲓⲛⲉ[ⲣ]ⲡⲣⲟ-
ⲟⲩϣ ⲙ̄ⲡⲉⲛⲥⲱⲙⲁ ⲉⲩϣⲁ(ⲛ)ϯ ⲛ̄ⲧⲛ̄ⲁⲡⲟⲫⲁⲥⲓⲥ, (V ii) ⲉⲙⲙⲟⲛ ⲉⲛϩⲛ̄ⲟⲩⲕⲁϩ
ⲛ̄ϣⲙⲙⲟ, ⲉⲙⲙ̄ⲡⲣⲱⲙⲉ ⲛ̄ⲧⲁⲛ ⲙ̄ⲡⲉⲓ̈ⲙⲁ ⲉϥⲛⲁϥⲓ ⲡⲉⲛⲡⲣⲟⲟⲩϣ· ⲡⲉϫⲉⲓ̈ⲟⲩⲗⲓⲟⲥ
ⲛⲁⲩ ϫⲉ ⲡⲉⲓ̈ϩⲱⲃ ϯⲥⲉⲧⲱⲧ ⲉⲓⲁⲁϥ, ⲉⲡⲓⲇⲏ ⲁⲩⲟⲩⲱ ⲉⲩⲧⲁⲙⲁ ⲙ̄ⲙⲟⲓ ϩⲓⲧⲛ̄
ⲟⲩⲁⲅⲅⲉⲗⲟⲥ ⲛ̄ⲧⲉ ⲡⲛⲟⲩⲧⲉ ϩⲛ̄ⲟⲩϩⲟⲣⲟⲙⲁ ⲛ̄ⲧⲉⲩϣⲉ· ⲁⲩⲱ ⲛⲉⲧⲛ̄ⲕⲉ[ⳝ]ϩⲟⲓⲡⲟ-
ⲙⲛⲏⲙⲁ ϯⲛⲁϩⲁⲓⲥⲟⲛ ⲛ̄ⲧⲁⲕⲁⲁⲩ ⲛ̄ϩⲟⲩⲛ ⲉⲡⲁϩⲏⲓ̈, ϫⲉⲕⲁⲥ ⲉⲣⲉⲡⲉⲧⲛ̄ⲥⲙⲟⲩ
ϣⲱⲡⲉ ϩⲙ̄ⲡⲁϩⲏⲓ̈ ϣⲁⲉⲛⲉϩ. ⲁⲗⲗⲁ ⲥⲙⲟⲩ ⲉⲣⲟⲓ̈ ϩⲱ, ⲁⲣⲓⲡⲁ ⲙⲉⲉⲩⲉ ϩⲛ̄ⲛⲉⲛ-
ⲧⲟⲡⲟⲥ ⲉⲧⲉⲛⲁⲃⲱⲕ ⲉⲣⲟⲟⲩ. ⲁⲩⲟⲩⲱⲛ ⲛ̄ⲣⲱϥ ⲛ̄ϭⲓ ⲡϩⲁⲅⲓⲟⲥ ⲁⲡⲁ ϣⲛⲟⲩϭⲉ, ⲁϥⲥⲙⲟⲩ ⲉⲓⲟⲩⲗⲓⲟⲥ ⲉϥϫⲱ ⲙ̄ⲙⲟⲥ ϫⲉ ⲉⲣⲉⲡⲛⲟⲩⲧⲉ ⲥⲙⲟⲩ ⲉⲣⲟⲕ ⲙ̄ⲡ-
ⲡⲉⲕⲏⲓ ⲛ̄ⲛⲁⲧⲙⲟⲩⲛ̄ϥ ⲛ̄ϭⲓϫ ⲛ̄ⲧⲁⲩⲥⲃ̄ⲧⲱ ⲧⲃ̄ ⲛⲁⲕ, ⲁⲩⲱ ⲡⲉⲕⲏⲓ ⲉⲧϩⲓϫⲙ̄ⲡ-
ⲕⲁϩ· ⲉⲣⲉⲡⲉⲥⲙⲟⲩ ⲙ̄ⲡⲛⲟⲩⲧⲉ ϣⲱⲡⲉ ⲛ̄ϩⲏⲧϥ ϣⲁⲉ(117 R i) ⲛⲉϩ, ⲁⲩⲱ ϣⲁ-

---

116 R ii 19. = -ⲕⲣⲁⲅⲅⲏ. 24 f. l. ⲉⲧⲉⲧⲛ̄ϣⲁⲛⲉⲓⲣⲉ. V i 20. l. ⲧⲉ ⲁⲧⲁⲥ-. 22 f.
l. ⲁⲛⲉⲧⲛⲁⲛⲟⲩⲟⲩ. 28 f. l. ⲉⲛⲟⲩⲱϣ. ii 2. l. ⲉⲙⲛ-. 8. l. ⲉⲩⲧⲁⲙⲟ. 19 f. l.
ϩⲛ̄ⲛ̄ⲧⲟⲡⲟⲥ.

ⲛ̄ⲅⲉⲛⲉⲁ ⲧⲏⲣⲟⲩ ⲙ̄ⲡⲕⲁϩ· ⲛ̄ⲛⲉϥⲉⲃⲃⲱⲱⲛ ⲟⲩⲇⲉ ⲗⲟⲓⲙⲟⲥ ϣⲱⲡⲉ ϩⲙ̄ⲡⲉⲕⲙⲁ·
ⲛ̄ϣⲱⲡⲉ· ϣⲁⲅⲉⲛⲉⲁ ⲧⲏⲣⲟⲩ ⲙ̄ⲡⲕⲁϩ· ⲛ̄ⲛⲉⲥⲡⲉⲣⲙⲁ ⲉⲃⲟⲗ ⲛ̄ϩⲏⲧⲕ̄ ⲛⲁⲩ·
ⲉⲧⲉⲕⲣⲓⲥⲓⲥ ϣⲁϣⲟⲙⲧⲉ ⲉⲓⲉ ϣⲧⲟ ⲛ̄ⲅⲉⲛⲉⲁ· ⲉⲕⲉⲱⲛ ⲅⲣⲉⲭⲟⲣⲟⲥ ⲛ̄ⲛⲉⲙⲙⲁⲣⲧⲩ-
ⲣⲟⲥ ⲙ̄ⲡⲉⲭ̅ⲥ̅· ⲉⲕⲉⲭⲓⲕⲗⲏⲣⲟⲛⲟⲙⲁⲓ· ⲙ̄ⲛ̄ⲛⲉⲧⲟⲩⲁⲁⲃ ⲧⲏⲣⲟⲩ ⲙ̄ⲡⲉϩⲟⲟⲩ ⲙ̄ⲡϣⲟ
ⲛ̄ⲣⲟⲙⲡⲉ, ⲉⲩⲥϩⲁⲓ ⲙ̄ⲡⲉⲕⲣⲁⲛ ⲉⲡϫⲱⲱⲙⲉ ⲙ̄ⲡⲱⲛϩ̄, ⲛ̄ⲧⲟⲕ· ⲙ̄ⲛ̄ⲡⲉⲕⲕⲉⲥⲡⲉⲣⲙⲁ
ⲧⲏⲣϥ̄· ⲟⲩⲱϣⲧ̄ ⲙ̄ⲡⲉⲕⲣⲣⲟ ϩⲛ̄ⲟⲩϩⲟ ⲉⲙ̄ⲛϣⲓⲡⲉ ⲛ̄ϩⲏⲧϥ̄, ϩⲛ̄ⲟⲩⲉⲓⲣⲏⲛⲏ, ϩⲁⲙⲏⲛ·
ⲁϥⲟⲩⲱϣϥ̄ ⲛ̄ϭⲓ ⲡⲕⲉⲙⲛ̄ⲧⲟⲩⲉ ⲛ̄ⲥⲟⲛ· ⲛ̄ϩⲁⲅⲓⲟⲥ ⲉⲩϫⲱ ⲙ̄ⲙⲟⲥ· ϫⲉ ϩⲁⲙⲏⲛ, ⲉⲥⲉ-
ϣⲱⲡⲉ· ⲙ̄ⲛ̄ⲥⲁⲛⲁⲓ ⲁⲡϩⲁⲅⲓⲟⲥ ⲁⲡⲁ ϣ̄ⲛⲟⲩϥⲉ ϫⲟⲟⲥ ⲛ̄ⲉⲓⲟⲩⲗⲓⲟⲥ ⲉⲧⲣⲟⲩⲉⲓⲛⲉ
ⲛⲁⲩ ⲛ̄ⲟⲩⲕⲟⲩⲓ̈ ⲛ̄ⲛⲉϩ, ⲁϥϫⲓⲧϥ̄, ⲁⲩ(117 R ii)ϣⲗⲏⲗ ⲉϫⲱϥ ⲛ̄ϭⲓ ⲛ̄ϩⲁⲅⲓⲟⲥ ⲁⲡⲁ
ϣ̄ⲛⲟⲩϥⲉ· ⲉϥϫⲱ ⲙ̄ⲙⲟⲥ ϫⲉ ⲉⲣⲉⲡⲁϫⲟⲉⲓⲥ ⲓ̅ⲥ̅ ⲡⲉⲭ̅ⲥ̅ ⲡⲉⲧⲉⲣⲉⲡⲧⲁⲗϭⲟ ⲙ̄ⲛ̄ⲡⲱⲛϩ̄
ϣⲟⲟⲡ ⲉⲃⲟⲗ· ϩⲓⲧⲟⲟⲧϥ̄, ⲡⲉⲛⲧⲁϥⲟⲩⲱⲛ ⲛ̄ⲛ̄ⲃⲁⲗ ⲛ̄ⲛ̄ⲃⲗ̄ⲗⲉ, ⲁϥⲧⲣⲉⲛⲉⲉⲙ ⲡⲟ ϣⲁϫⲉ, ⲁϥⲧⲣⲉⲛ̄ⲕⲟⲩⲣ ⲥⲱⲧⲙ̄, ⲛⲉⲧ̄ⲕⲏⲕ ⲉⲡⲥⲱⲃϩ̄ ⲁϥⲧⲃⲃⲟⲟⲩ, ⲁⲩⲧⲣⲉⲛ̄ϩⲁⲗⲉ ⲙⲟⲟⲩⲉ, ⲛⲉⲧⲥⲏϭ ⲁⲩⲥⲟⲟⲩⲧⲛ̄, ⲉⲕⲉⲣ̄ⲡⲁϩⲣⲉ ϩⲱⲱⲕ ⲉⲡⲉⲕϩⲙ̄ϩⲁⲗ ⲓ̈ⲟⲩⲗⲓⲟⲥ· ⲡⲁⲓ
ⲉⲧϥⲓ ⲙ̄ⲡⲣⲟⲟⲩϣ ⲛ̄ⲛⲉⲕϩⲙ̄ϩⲁⲗ ⲙ̄ⲙⲁⲣⲧⲩⲣⲟⲥ· ϫⲉ ⲛ̄ⲧⲟⲕ ⲡⲉⲧⲉⲣⲉⲡⲧⲁⲗϭⲟ ⲙ̄ⲛ̄
ⲡⲱⲛϩ̄ ϣⲟⲟⲡ ⲉⲃⲟⲗ ϩⲓⲧⲟⲟⲧⲕ̄· ⲛ̄ⲧⲉⲩⲛⲟⲩ ⲁⲡϩⲁⲅⲓⲟⲥ· ⲧⲱϩⲥ̄ ⲙ̄ⲡⲥⲱⲙⲁ ⲛ̄ⲉⲓⲟⲩ-
ⲗⲓⲟⲥ, ⲁⲩⲃⲱϣ ⲛ̄ϭⲓ ⲙ̄ⲙⲟⲕϩⲥ̄ ⲙ̄ⲡⲧⲓⲧⲕⲁⲥ ⲉⲧϩⲙ̄ⲡⲉϥⲥⲱⲙⲁ, ⲁⲩⲱ ⲛⲉⲙⲟⲩⲧ
ⲛ̄ⲧⲓⲧⲕⲁⲥ· ⲉⲧϩⲛ̄ⲛⲉϥϭⲓϫ ⲙ̄ⲛ̄ⲛⲉϥⲟⲩⲉⲣⲏⲧⲉ ⲁⲩⲣⲟⲟⲩⲧ (V i) ⲛ̄ⲑⲉ ⲛ̄ⲧⲥⲁⲣϩ̄ ⲛ̄-
ⲟⲩϣⲏⲣⲉ ⲕⲟⲩⲓ̈, ⲉⲡⲓⲇⲏ ⲛⲉⲁⲩⲗⲱⲱⲙ ϩⲓⲧⲙ̄ⲡⲛⲟϭ ⲛ̄ⲧⲓⲧⲕⲁⲥ ⲉⲧϩⲓϫⲱϥ· ⲁⲩⲙⲟⲟⲩ-
ϣⲉ ⲉⲡⲉⲓⲥⲁ· ⲙ̄ⲛ̄ⲡⲁⲓ ϩⲛ̄ⲧⲉⲫⲩⲗⲁⲕⲏ ⲉⲩⲥⲙⲟⲩ ⲉⲡⲛⲟⲩⲧⲉ ⲛ̄ⲛⲁⲗⲁ ϣ̄ⲛⲟⲩϥⲉ ⲙ̄ⲛ̄ⲛⲉϥ-
ⲥⲛⲏⲩ· ⲁⲩⲧⲉ'ⲟⲟⲩ ⲙ̄ⲡⲛⲟⲩⲧⲉ ⲛ̄ⲛⲉⲭⲣⲏⲥⲧⲓⲁⲛⲟⲥ ⲡⲉϫⲉ ⲅⲉ· ⲓ̈ⲟⲩⲗⲓⲟⲥ ⲇⲉ ⲁϥⲉⲓ ⲉⲃⲟⲗ
ϩⲓⲧⲛ̄ⲛⲉⲧⲟⲩⲁⲁⲃ ⲉϥⲥⲙⲟⲩ ⲉⲡϫⲟⲉⲓⲥ ⲡⲛⲟⲩⲧⲉ, ⲁⲩⲱ ⲙ̄ⲡⲉϩⲓⲥⲉ ⲟⲩⲇⲉ ⲙⲟⲕ ϩⲥ̄ ϣⲱⲡⲉ ϩⲙ̄ⲡⲉϥⲥⲱⲙⲁ ⲉϫⲓⲛⲡⲉϩⲟⲟⲩ ⲉⲧⲙ̄ⲙⲁⲩ· ⲁⲥϣⲱⲡⲉ ⲙ̄ⲛ̄ⲥⲁⲛⲁⲓ ⲧⲏⲣⲟⲩ ⲁⲩⲥⲱ-
ⲧⲙ̄ ⲛ̄ϭⲓ ⲁⲣⲓⲁⲛⲟⲥ ⲡϩⲏⲅⲉⲙⲱⲛ ⲉⲧⲃⲉⲛϭⲟⲙ ⲙ̄ⲛ̄ⲛⲉϣⲡⲏⲣⲉ ⲉⲧϣⲟⲟⲡ ⲉⲃⲟⲗ ϩⲓⲧⲛ̄ⲛⲉ-
ⲧⲟⲩⲁⲁⲃ ⲛ̄ϩⲟⲩⲛ ⲉⲧⲉⲫⲩⲗⲁⲕⲏ, ⲁⲩⲱⲛⲧ̄ ⲛ̄ϭⲓ ⲡϩⲏⲅⲉⲙⲱⲛ, (V ii) ⲁϥⲕⲉⲗⲉⲩⲉ ⲉ-
ⲧⲣⲟⲩⲧⲁⲙⲉⲓⲟ ⲙ̄ⲡⲃⲏⲙⲁ ⲛ̄ϩⲟⲩⲛ ⲉⲡⲉⲑⲉⲁⲇⲣⲟⲛ, ⲁⲩⲧⲣⲟⲩⲉⲓⲛⲉ ⲛⲁⲩ ⲛ̄ⲛⲉⲧⲟⲩⲁ-
ⲁⲃ ⲉϩⲣⲁⲓ ⲉϫⲙ̄ⲡⲃⲏⲙⲁ, ⲁⲩⲧⲣⲟⲩⲉⲓⲕⲉ ⲙ̄ⲙⲟⲟⲩ ⲛⲁⲩ ⲉⲩⲟⲛϩ̄· ⲛⲉⲣⲉⲡϩⲁⲅⲓⲟⲥ ⲁⲡⲁ
ϣ̄ⲛⲟⲩϥⲉ ϩⲓϫⲏ ⲙ̄ⲙⲟⲟⲩ· ⲛ̄ϩⲟⲥⲟⲛ ⲇⲉ ⲉⲩⲙⲟⲟⲩϣⲉ· ϩⲛ̄ⲧⲉⲡⲗⲁⲧⲓⲁ ⲛ̄ⲧ̄ⲡⲟⲗⲓⲥ ⲉⲩⲛⲁϫⲓ-
ⲧⲟⲩ· ⲉⲭⲙ̄ⲡⲃⲏⲙⲁ,· ⲉⲓⲥ ⲛⲉϩⲧⲱⲣ ⲙ̄ⲡⲁ'ⲅⲱⲛ ⲁⲩⲛ̄ⲧⲟⲩ ⲉⲃⲟⲗ· ⲉⲩⲛⲁϣⲟⲕⲙⲟⲩ ϩⲛ̄·
ⲑⲱⲛⲉ ⲛ̄ⲥⲉⲕⲩⲙⲛⲁ'ⲍⲉ ⲙ̄ⲙⲟⲟⲩ, ⲉⲡⲓⲇⲏ ⲁⲩⲱⲛ ⲉϩⲟⲩⲛ ⲛ̄ϭⲓ· ⲡⲁⲅⲱⲛ. ⲛⲉϩⲧⲱⲱⲣ

ⲇⲉ ⲛⲉⲩⲧⲱⲙ ⲛ̅ⲥⲱⲟⲩ ⲛ̅ϭⲓ ⲛⲉⲥⲧⲁⲩ'ⲗⲓⲧⲏⲥ ⲉⲧϫⲓⲭⲱⲟⲩ,' ⲁⲩϭⲱⲙ ⲉϩⲣⲁⲓ̈ ⲉⲝⲛ̅ⲟⲩ
ϭⲏⲣⲉ ϣⲏⲙ, ⲁⲩ'ϩⲟⲧⲃⲉϥ ⲉϥⲙⲟⲟⲩⲉ' ϩⲛ̅ⲛⲉⲡⲗⲁⲧⲓⲁ ⲛ̅ⲧ'ⲡⲟⲗⲓⲥ, ⲁⲩⲕⲁⲧⲁⲧⲥⲓ(ⲛ)'
ⲙ̅ⲙⲟϥ, ⲁⲛⲉϥⲙⲁϩⲧ̅ ⲉⲓ ⲉⲃⲟⲗ, ⲁϥⲙⲟⲩ.' ⲁⲙⲙⲏⲛⲩⲉ ⲕⲱⲧⲉ' ⲉⲣⲟϥ ⲁⲛⲑⲉⲱⲣⲉⲓ
ⲙ̅ⲙⲟϥ (118 Ri) ⲉⲩⲣⲓⲙⲉ, ⲁⲩⲱ ⲁⲩⲥⲉⲡ'ⲡϩⲁⲅⲓⲟⲥ ⲁⲡⲁ ⲯ̅ⲛⲟⲩϥⲉ' ⲉⲧⲣⲉϥⲃⲱⲕ
ϣⲁⲣⲟϥ.' ⲛ̅ⲧⲉⲣⲉϥⲡⲱⲧ ⲇⲉ ϣⲁ'ⲣⲟϥ, ⲡⲉϫⲁϥ ⲛ̅ⲙ̅ⲙⲏⲛⲩⲉ ⲉⲧⲕⲱⲧⲉ ⲉⲣⲟϥ ϫⲉ ⲥⲁ
ϩⲉⲧⲏⲩⲧⲛ̅ ⲉϩⲣⲁⲓ̈' ⲛ̅ⲧⲁⲣⲉⲡⲉⲟⲟⲩ ⲛ̅ⲧⲉ ⲟⲩⲱⲛϩ̅ ⲉⲃⲟⲗ, ⲡⲁⲛⲓⲉⲟⲟⲩ ⲧⲏⲣⲟⲩ ⲙ̅ⲛ̅ⲓⲥⲟⲙ.'
ⲛ̅ⲧⲉⲩⲛⲟⲩ ⲛ̅ⲧⲁⲙⲙⲏⲛⲩⲉ ⲥⲁϩⲱⲟⲩ ⲉϩⲣⲁⲓ̈,' ⲁⲡϩⲁⲅⲓⲟⲥ ⲁⲡⲁ ⲯ̅ⲛⲟⲩϥⲉ ⲣⲁⲕⲧϥ̅ ⲉ-
ⲡⲉⲥⲏⲧ ⲉⲝⲙ̅ⲡϣⲏ'ⲣⲉ ⲕⲟⲩⲓ̈, ⲁⲩϭⲉⲓ ⲛ̅'ⲛⲉϥⲙⲁϩⲧ̅, ⲁⲩⲧⲁⲁⲩ' ⲉϩⲟⲩⲛ ⲛ̅ϩⲏⲧϥ̅,' ⲁⲩ
ⲥⲫⲣⲁⲅⲓⲍⲉ ⲙ̅ⲙⲟϥ,' ⲁⲩⲗⲉϭⲗⲱϭⲡⲉϥ'ⲥⲱⲙⲁ, ⲁⲧⲉϥⲥⲁⲣⲝ' ⲧⲱϭⲉ ⲉⲡⲉⲥⲉⲣⲏⲩ,' ⲁϥ
ⲛⲓϥⲉ ⲉϩⲟⲩⲛ ⲉϩⲣⲁⲩ' ⲛ̅ⲩⲟⲙⲛ̅ⲧ ⲛ̅ⲥⲟⲡ' ϩⲁⲡⲣⲁⲛ ⲙ̅ⲡⲉⲓⲱⲧ' ⲙ̅ⲡϣⲏⲣⲉ ⲙ̅ⲛ̅ⲡⲉ
ⲡ̅ⲛ̅ⲁ̅ ⲉⲧⲟⲩⲁⲁⲃ,' ⲁⲡϩⲁⲅⲓⲟⲥ ⲁⲡⲁ ⲯ̅ⲛⲟⲩϥⲉ ⲁⲙⲁϩⲧⲉ ⲛ̅'ⲧⲉϥϭⲓϫ, ⲁϥⲧⲁⲁⲩ' ⲛ̅-
ⲛⲉϥⲉⲓⲟⲧⲉ ⲉϥϫⲱ' ⲙ̅ⲙⲟⲥ ϫⲉ ⲙⲟⲟⲩⲉ (R ii) ⲛⲏⲧⲛ̅ ⲉⲡⲉⲧⲛⲏⲓ, ϯⲉⲟⲟⲩ ⲙ̅ⲡⲛⲟⲩ-
ⲧⲉ.' ⲁⲙⲙⲏⲛⲩⲉ ⲛ̅ⲧⲡⲟⲗⲓⲥ' ⲣ̅ϣⲡⲏⲣⲉ, ⲁⲩϯⲉⲟⲟⲩ ⲙ̅ⲡⲛⲟⲩⲧⲉ ⲛ̅ⲁⲡⲁ' ⲯ̅ⲛⲟⲩϥⲉ.
ⲁⲩⲱ' ⲉⲓⲥ ⲡϫⲉϩⲙⲉ ⲥⲁϣϥ̅ ⲛ̅'ⲣⲱⲙⲉ ⲉⲃⲟⲗ ϩⲙ̅ⲡⲙⲏ'ⲛⲏⲩⲉ ⲁⲩϣⲱ ⲉⲃⲟⲗ' ⲉⲩϯⲉⲟⲟⲩ
ⲙ̅ⲡⲛⲟⲩⲧⲉ' ⲙ̅ⲡϩⲁⲅⲓⲟⲥ ⲁⲡⲁ ⲯ̅ⲛⲟⲩϥⲉ, ⲁⲩⲡⲱⲧ' ⲉⲑⲏ ⲙ̅ⲡϩⲏⲅⲉⲙⲱ(ⲛ),' ⲁⲩⲱ ϣ
ⲉⲃⲟⲗ ϫⲉ ⲁ'ⲛⲟⲛ ϩⲉⲛⲭⲣⲏⲥⲧⲓⲁ'ⲛⲟⲥ ϩⲱⲱⲛ ⲡⲁⲣ'ⲣⲏⲥⲓⲁ. ⲁⲡϩⲏ'ⲅⲉⲙⲱⲛ ϣⲧⲟⲣⲧⲣ̅
ϩⲓⲧⲙ̅ⲡⲁϣⲁⲓ̈' ⲛ̅ⲛⲉⲣⲱⲙⲉ,' ⲡⲉϫⲁϥ ⲛⲁⲩ ⲉⲃⲟⲗ ϩⲓⲧⲙ̅ⲡϩⲉⲣⲙⲏⲛⲉⲩ'ⲧⲏⲥ ϫⲉ ⲧⲉ
ⲧⲛ̅ⲡⲁⲣϩⲏ'ⲥⲓⲁ ⲇⲉ ϫⲉⲛⲙ̅ⲙⲟⲛ' ⲛ̅ⲧⲁ.ϯ ⲛⲏⲧⲛ̅ ⲛ̅ⲧⲉ'ⲧⲛ̅ⲁⲡⲟⲫⲁⲥⲓⲥ; ⲁⲩⲟⲩⲱϣϥ̅ ⲛ̅ϭⲓ
ⲡϫⲉϩⲙⲉ ⲥⲁϣϥ̅ ⲛ̅ⲣⲱ'ⲙⲉ ϩⲛ̅ⲟⲩⲧⲁⲡⲣⲟ' ⲛ̅ⲟⲩⲱⲧ ϫⲉ ϥⲟⲛϩ̅' ⲛ̅ϭⲓ ⲡⲛⲟⲩⲧⲉ ⲡⲉϫⲉ
ⲓ̅ⲥ̅ ϫⲉ ⲡⲙⲟⲩ ⲉⲧⲉⲣⲉ(V i)ⲡϩⲁⲅⲓⲟⲥ ⲁⲡⲁ ⲯ̅ⲛⲟⲩϥⲉ ⲛⲁⲙⲟⲩ ⲛ̅ϩⲏⲧϥ̅ ⲧⲛ̅ⲛⲁⲙⲟⲩ'
ⲛ̅ϩⲏⲧϥ̅ ϩⲱⲱⲛ,' ϫⲉⲕⲁⲥ ⲉⲛⲛⲁϣⲱ'ⲡⲉ ⲛⲙ̅ⲙⲁϥ ϩⲙ̅'ⲡⲏⲓ̈ ⲙ̅ⲡⲛⲟⲩⲧⲉ.' ⲛ̅ⲧⲉⲩⲛⲟⲩ
ⲁⲩⲣ̅ϩⲟⲧⲉ' ⲛ̅ϭⲓ ⲡϩⲏⲅⲉⲙⲱⲛ' ⲉⲧⲃⲉⲧⲁⲥⲫⲩⲙⲓⲁ ⲛ̅ⲧⲡⲟⲗⲓⲥ, ⲉϥϫⲱ' ⲙ̅ⲙⲟⲥ ϩⲙ̅ⲡⲉϥ
ϩⲏⲧ' ϫⲉ ⲙⲏⲡⲟⲥ ϩⲛ̅ⲉⲃⲟⲗ' ⲛⲉ ϩⲁⲧⲡⲟⲗⲓⲥ ⲙ̅ⲡⲓⲟⲙ' ⲛϥ̅ⲥⲱⲧⲙ ⲉⲣⲟⲟⲩ' ⲛ̅ϩⲟⲩⲛ ⲉ-
ⲧⲡⲟⲗⲓⲥ' ⲛ̅ⲧⲉⲛⲁⲧⲡⲟⲗⲓⲥ' ⲕⲱⲗⲩ ⲙ̅ⲙⲟϥ.' ⲁϥⲕⲉⲗⲉⲩⲉ ⲛ̅ⲥⲉϫⲓⲧⲟⲩ' ⲉϩⲟⲩⲛ ϩⲉⲡⲧⲟ-
ⲟⲩ ⲛ̅ⲥⲉϫⲉⲓ ⲛ̅ⲧⲉⲩⲁⲡⲉ.' ⲁⲩⲧⲁⲁⲩ ⲉⲧⲟⲟⲧϥ̅ ⲛ̅ⲥⲩⲙⲁⲭⲟⲥ ⲡϥⲉⲇ'ⲣⲁⲁⲣⲭⲏⲥ ⲡⲁⲕⲉⲥ'
ⲇⲱⲛⲁⲣⲓⲟⲥ ⲙ̅ⲛ̅ⲟⲩⲛⲟϭ ⲛ̅ⲃⲟⲏⲑⲓⲁ' ⲙ̅ⲙⲁⲧⲟⲓ̈, ⲁⲩⲥⲟⲟⲣⲟⲩ' ⲉⲃⲟⲗ, ⲁⲩⲁⲁⲩ ⲛ̅ⲧⲁⲅ'
ⲙⲁ ⲧⲁⲅⲙⲁ· ⲁϥⲉⲓ' ϣⲁⲣⲟⲩ ⲛ̅ϭⲓ ⲥⲩⲙⲁⲭⲟⲥ' ⲡⲁⲕⲉⲥⲧⲱⲛⲁⲣⲓⲟⲥ·' ϩⲟⲓⲛⲉ ⲛ̅ϩⲏⲧⲟⲩ
ⲁⲩ(V ii)ϫⲁⲗⲁ ⲛⲁⲩ ⲉⲛⲉⲩⲕⲗⲓⲥ,' ϩⲉⲛⲕⲟⲟⲩⲉ ⲁⲩⲥⲱⲗ' ⲛ̅ⲛⲉⲩⲙⲟⲩⲧ, ϩⲛ̅'ⲕⲟⲟⲩⲉ ⲁⲩ

---

117 Vii 28. – ⲧⲁⲧⲥⲓ(ⲛ): a more correct Saʿidic form would be ⲧⲁⲃⲥⲉ; the superlineation (/ⲛ ⲛ) is a mistake. 118 Vi 10. l. ⲉⲧⲃⲉⲧⲉⲃⲗⲁⲥⲫⲩⲙⲓⲁ; see commentary. 13. =
ⲙⲏⲛⲱⲥ. 14. ⲓ̈ added. 20. ϩ added; mistakenly, or as incomplete correction to ϩⲛ̅ⲛⲧⲟⲟⲩ?
23-5. l. ⲥⲩⲙⲙⲁⲭⲟⲥ ⲡⲧⲉⲧⲣⲁⲣⲭⲏⲥ ⲡⲕⲉⲥⲧⲓⲱⲛⲁⲣⲓⲟⲥ.   ii. 1. l. ⲛ̅ⲛⲉⲩⲕⲗⲉⲓⲥ.

ΠΑΖΖΗΤΟΥ· ΑΥΖΙCΕ, ΑΥΜΟΟC ΝΟΥ'ΚΟΥΪ ΖΕ ΕΥΝΑΜΙΚΕ' ΜΜΟΥ. ΕΙC ΟΥΑ ΕΒΟΛ'
ΖΑΠΜΗΗΨΕ ΝΝΕ'ΤΟΥΑΑΒ ΕΠΕΥΡΑΝ ΠΕ ΚΑΛΛΙΝΙΧΟC' ΠΕΧΑΥ ΜΠΑΚΕCΔΩΝΑ'ΡΙΟC ΖΕ CΗΜΑΧΟC' ΠΑΨΗΡΕ ΖΩ ΕΡΟΚ' ΤΕΝΟΥ ΝΓΖΡΟΚ Μ'ΜΟΚ, ΖΩ ΕΡΟΚ ΕΚ-'ΠΗΤ ΕΧΠΠΕCΝΟΥ' ΝΝΕΤΟΥΑΑΒ ΝΤΕΪΖΕ·' ΜΜΟΝ ΟΥΝΟ6 ΠΕ' ΠΕΥΝΟΥΤΕ, ΝΥΝΑ-ΑΝΕΧΕ ΜΜΟΚ ΑΝ.' ΑΥΟΥΩΨΒ Ν6Ι ΠΑ'ΚΕCΔΩΝΑΡΙΟC ΠΕΧΑΥ ΖΕ ΕΪΨΑΝΜΟΥ,' ΜΑΡΟΥΚΩ ΝΤΑΑΡΟΥ' ΝΟΥΝΑΜ ΖΑΤΠ'ΠΕΨΤΒC ΜΠΡΟ ΝΑ'ΜΝΤΕ. ΑΥΟΥΩΨΒ' Ν6Ι ΠCΕΕΠΕ ΝΝΕ'ΤΟΥΑΑΒ ΖΕ ΖΑΜΗΝ,' ΕCΕΨΩΠΕ, ΑΥΩ' ΠΕΝΤΑΚΧΟΟΥ ΕΥ'ΕΙ ΕΖΡΑΪ ΕΧΩΚ. (119 R i) ΑΥΒΟ6Υ ΕΖΡΑΪ Ν6Ι CΥΜΑ'ΧΟC ΖΝΟΥ6ΩΝΤ ΝΤΕ'ΠΔΙΑ-ΒΟΛΟC, ΑΥΧΙ' ΝΤCΗΥΕ, ΑΥΨΕΙ ΝΤΑΠΕ ΜΠCΕΕΠΕ ΝΝΕ'ΤΟΥΑΑΒ· ΑΥΨΩΚ'Ε-ΒΟΛ ΝΤΕΥΜΑΡΤΥΡΙΑ' ΝΟΥΖΟΟΥ ΝΟΥΩΤ' Ν6Ι ΠΨΕΖΜΕ CΑΨΥ'ΝΡΩΜΕ. ΑΠΕ-CΤ'ΡΕΩΜΑ ΤΗΡΥ ΜΟΥΖ Ν'ΝΑΓΓΕΛΟC, ΑΥΧΙ Ν'ΝΕΥΨΥΧΗ ΕΖΡΑΪ ΕΝ'ΜΠΗΥΕ Ε-ΑΥCΟΥ'ΛΩΛΟΥ ΝΖΕΝΜΑΠ'ΛΑ ΝΨΕΝC, ΕΥΟ Ν'ΘΕ ΝΖΕΝ6ΡΟΟΜΠΕ Ν'ΟΥΩΒΨ ΕΥΝΗΥ' ΕΒΟΛ ΖΝΝΜΕ6ΟΥ'ΗΛ, ΑΥΒΙΤΟΥ ΕΖΡΑΪ'ΕΤΠΕ, ΑΥΘΜCΟΟΥ ΖΙ'ΧΝΝΕΥ-ΘΡΟΝΟC,' ΑΥΩ ΑΥΤ ΕΚΩΟΥ ΜΠΕΚΛΟΜ ΝΑΤΖΟ6Β' ΕΒΟΛ ΖΙΤΝΙC ΠΕΧC' ΠΕΝΧΟ-ΕΙC, ΠΑΪ ΕΤΕ'ΠΟΥΥ ΠΕ ΠΕΟΟΥ' ΨΑΝΙΕΝΕΖ, ΖΑΜΗΝ.' ΜΝΝCΑΝΑΪ ΑΥΚΕΛΕΥΕ Ν6Ι ΑΡΙΑΝΟC ΠΖΗ'ΓΕΜΩΝ ΕΤΡΟΥΧΙ' ΝΑΥ ΜΠΖΑΓΙΟC ΑΠΑ (R ii) ΨΝΟΥΨΕ ΖΝΤΨΟΡΠΕ'ΝΕΞΕΤΕCΙC. ΠΕΧΑΥ' ΝΑΥ ΖΕ Ω ΠΑΠΟC'ΤΑΤΗC ΕΤCΟΟΥ ΜΜΑΓΟC,' ΟΥ ΝΕ ΝΕΙ-ΖΒΗΥΕ ΜΜΑΓΙΑ ΝΤΑΪCΩΤΜ ΖΕ' ΚΕΙΡΕ ΜΜΟΟΥ ΖΝΤΕ'ΦΥΛΑΚΗ ΖΝΝΕΚΜΝΤ-ΜΑΓΟC; ΠΕ'ΧΕΠΖΑΓΙΟC ΝΓΕΝΝΑΙΟC ΑΥΩ ΝΧΩΩΡΕ' ΑΠΑ ΨΝΟΥΨΕ ΜΠΖΗΓΕ-ΜΩΝ' ΖΕ ΝΕΖΒΗΥΕ ΝΤΑΚ'CΩΤΜ ΕΡΟΟΥ ΧΕ ΑΪ'ΑΑΥ, Ω ΠΑΝΖΟCΙΟC' ΕΤΑΖΜ,' ΝΤΑΪΑΑΥ' ΑΝ ΖΝΟΥΜΝΤΜΑ'ΓΟC, ΑΛΛΑ ΑΪΑΑΥ' ΖΙΤΝΤ6ΟΜ ΜΠΑΧΟ'ΕΙC ΙC ΠΕ-ΧC ΠΕΤΕ'ΡΕΠΝΙΒΕ ΝΟΥΟΝ ΝΙΜ' ΖΝΝΕΥCΙ6. ΚΑΙ' ΓΑΡ ΑΪCΩΤΜ ΕΤΒΕΟΥ'ΝΟ6 ΜΜΑΓΟC ΖΕ ΑΚ'ΤΡΑΤΩΛΗ, ΕΟΥΑΡΧΙ'ΕΡΕΥC ΝΤΕΥΜΟΥΝ' ΠΕ ΕΥΕΙΡΕ ΝΖΝΝΟ6' ΝΖΒΗΥΕ ΖΝΤΕΥΜΝΤ'ΜΑΓΟC· ΑΥΕΠΙΘΥΜΕΙ ΕΤΡΕΥΠΩΤ Ε'ΠΕCΗΤ ΕΤΨΩΤΕ (Vi)
ΜΠΝΟΥΝ ΕΤΡΕΥ'ΜΟΥΤΕ ΝΨΕΙΜΕ ΖΕ' ΕCΟ ΝΑΥ ΝΖΕ· ΑΥ'ΕΠΙΚΑΛΕΙ ΖΝΝΕΥ-'ΜΑΓΙΑ· ΑΤΨΩΤΕ' ΜΠΝΟΥΝ ΟΥΩΝ,' ΑΥΒΩΚ ΕΠΕCΗΤ·' ΑΤΨΩΤΕ ΤΩΜ ΕΡΟΨ ΝΤΕCΖΕ· ΑΝ'ΔΑΙΜΩΝ ΚΩΤΕ' ΕΡΟΨ· ΠΕΧΕΖΟΪΝΕ' ΝΖΗΤΟΥ ΖΕ ΜΑΡΕΝ'ΨΕΙ ΝΝ-ΤΕΨΑΠΕ·' ΖΝΚΟΟΥΕ ΔΕ ΖΕ ΜΑΡΕ(Ν)'ΖΙΤΕ ΜΠΕΨΨΑΑΡ' ΕΨΟΝΖ· ΖΝΚΟΟΥΕ ' ΖΕ ΜΑΡΕΝΨΙ ΝΝΕΨ'ΕΙΗΒ· ΖΑΠΛΩC' ΝΕΥΜΕΕΥΕ ΕΤ ΝΑΥ'ΖΝΖΝΝΟ6 ΝΔΙΜΟ'ΡΙΑ.

---

118 V ii 15f. l. εκπωζτ εβολ μπεcνου? So Erman. 24. l. νταλον. 31f. l. ευ-εει. 119 R i 10f. = -cτερεωμα. ii 2. = -εξεταcιc. 23. l. -διχ.

ⲁϥϭⲓⲥⲉ ⲉϥⲉⲡⲓⲕⲁⲗⲓ ⲛ̄ⲛⲉϩⲟⲩⲥⲓⲁ· ⲧⲏⲣⲟⲩ ⲉⲧϩⲁⲧⲡⲉ·' ϫⲡⲟⲩⲉⲩϭ̄ⲙ̄ϭⲟⲙ· ⲉⲛⲁϩⲙⲉϥ·
ⲙⲛ̄ⲛ̄ⲥⲱⲥ ⲁϥⲣ̄ⲙⲉⲉⲩⲉ ⲛ̄'ⲓ̄ⲥ̄ ⲡϣⲏⲣⲉ ⲙ̄ⲡⲛⲟⲩⲧⲉ·ⲉⲧⲟⲛϩ̄ ⲁⲩⲱ ⲡⲛⲟⲩⲧⲉ· ⲛ̄ⲛⲉⲭⲣⲏ-
ⲥⲧⲓⲁⲛⲟⲥ' ⲧⲏⲣⲟⲩ· ⲁⲡⲉϥϩⲏⲧ' ⲧⲱⲧ ϩⲣⲁⲓ ⲁϩⲏⲧϥ̄·' ⲡⲉϫⲁϥ ϩⲁⲡⲉⲩϩⲏⲧ (119 V ii)
ⲙⲁⲩⲁⲁⲩ ϫⲉ ⲉⲩϫⲉ ⲁⲓ̈'ⲣ̄ⲙⲉⲉⲩⲉ ⲛ̄ⲓ̄ⲥ̄ ⲡⲉϫⲉ ⲡ'ⲛⲟⲩⲧⲉ ⲛ̄ⲛⲉⲭⲣⲓⲥⲧⲓⲁ'ⲛⲟⲥ ϩⲙ̄-
ⲡⲁϩⲏⲧ ⲙ̄ⲙⲁⲧⲉ' ⲁⲩⲱ ⲁⲓ̈ϭ̄ⲙ̄ϭⲟⲙ ⲛ̄ⲧⲉⲓ̈ϩⲉ' ⲧⲏⲣⲥ̄, ⲉⲓⲉ ⲡⲟⲥⲟⲛ ⲙⲁⲗ'ⲗⲟⲛ ⲉⲓ̈ϣⲁⲛ-
ⲧⲁⲩⲉⲡⲉⲩ'ⲣⲁⲛ ⲉⲃⲟⲗ ϩⲛ̄ⲧⲁⲧⲁⲡ'ⲣⲟ, ⲟⲩ ⲡⲉⲧⲛⲁⲩϣⲱⲡⲉ' ⲙ̄ⲙⲟⲓ̈; ⲁⲩⲱ ⲛ̄ⲧⲉⲩ'ⲛⲟⲩ ⲁϥⲱϣ ⲉⲃⲟⲗ ϩⲛ̄ⲟⲩ'ⲛⲟϭ ⲛ̄ⲥⲙⲏ ⲛ̄ϭⲓ ⲁⲥⲧⲣⲁ'ⲧⲱⲗⲏ ϫⲉ ⲓ̄ⲥ̄ ⲡⲉϫⲥ̄· ⲡⲛⲟⲩⲧⲉ ⲛ̄ⲛⲉⲭⲣⲏⲥ-
ⲧⲓⲁⲛⲟⲥ, ⲉⲕϣⲁⲛⲛⲁ'ϩⲙⲉⲧ ϩⲛ̄ⲧⲉⲓⲛⲟϭ ⲛ̄ⲁ'ⲛⲁⲅⲕⲏ, ϯⲛⲁⲃⲱⲕ' ⲧⲁⲡⲉϩⲧⲡⲁⲥⲛⲟⲩ ⲉ-
ⲃⲟⲗ' ⲉⲭⲙ̄ⲡⲉⲕⲣⲁⲛ ⲉⲧⲟⲩ'ⲁⲁⲃ. ⲁⲩⲱ ⲛ̄ⲧⲉⲩ'ⲛⲟⲩ ⲁⲧⲩⲱⲧⲉ ⲟⲩⲱⲛ' ⲛⲁⲩ, ⲁϥⲉⲓ
ⲉϩⲣⲁⲓ̈, ⲁϥ'ⲃⲱⲕ, ⲁϥⲣ̄ⲙⲁⲣⲧⲩⲣⲟⲥ·' ϫⲉⲕⲁⲥ ⲉⲕⲉⲉⲓⲙⲉ ⲱ ⲡⲁ'ⲛⲟⲙⲟⲥ ⲛ̄ϩⲏⲅⲉ-
ⲙⲱⲛ· ϫⲉ ⲛ̄ⲧϭⲟⲙ ⲛ̄ⲗⲁⲁⲩ ⲙ̄'ⲙⲁⲅⲟⲥ ⲁⲛ ⲧⲉ ⲉⲡⲉⲓⲣⲁ(ⲛ)' ϫⲉ ⲓ̄ⲥ̄. ⲁⲩϭⲱⲛⲧ' ⲛ̄ϭⲓ
ⲡϩⲏⲅⲉⲙⲱⲛ,'ⲁϥⲕⲉⲗⲉⲩⲉ ⲉⲧⲣⲟⲩⲧ' ⲛⲁⲩ ⲛ̄ϩⲛ̄ⲃⲁⲥⲁⲛⲟⲥ· ⲛ̄ⲧⲟⲩ ⲙⲛ̄ⲛⲉⲩⲕⲉⲥⲛⲏⲩ.
(120 R i) ⲁⲩϩⲩⲡⲟⲙⲉⲓⲛⲉ ϩⲛ̄'ⲟⲩⲙⲛ̄ⲧⲅⲉⲛⲛⲁⲓⲟⲥ·' ⲁⲡⲉⲗⲁⲁⲩ ⲛ̄ⲃⲁⲍⲁ'ⲛⲟⲥ ⲉⲩ-
ϭ̄ⲙ̄ϭⲟⲙ ⲉⲣⲟⲩ, ⲉⲡⲓⲇⲏ ⲛⲉⲣⲉⲡⲛⲟⲩⲧⲉ' ϯϭⲟⲙ ⲛⲁⲩ ⲙ̄ⲡⲛⲁⲩ' ⲉⲧⲙ̄ⲙⲁⲩ. ⲡⲉϫⲉ-
ⲡ'ϩⲏⲅⲉⲙⲱⲛ ⲙ̄ⲡϩⲁ'ⲅⲓⲟⲥ ⲁⲡⲁ ⲯⲟⲧⲉ ϫⲉ ⲛⲉⲫⲁⲣⲙⲁⲅⲟⲥ ⲙⲛ̄'ⲛⲉⲣⲉⲩⲩⲁⲗⲉⲡⲉ,'
ⲛⲉⲛⲟⲙⲟⲥ ⲛ̄ⲛⲉⲣⲣⲱ'ⲟⲩ ⲕⲉⲗⲉⲩⲉ ⲉⲧⲣⲉⲩⲛⲟ'ϫⲟⲩ ⲉϩⲟⲩⲛ ⲉⲡⲙⲁⲛ'ⲧⲱⲕ ⲛ̄ⲧⲥⲓⲟⲟⲩⲛ·'
ⲧⲉⲛⲟⲩ ϭⲉ ⲧⲉⲕⲁⲡⲟⲫⲁ'ⲥⲓⲥ ⲧⲉ ⲧⲁⲓ̈, ⲛ̄ⲧⲟⲕ ⲙⲛ̄'ⲛⲉⲕⲉⲥⲛⲏⲩ,' ⲉⲧⲣⲟⲩⲛⲉϫⲧⲏⲩⲧⲛ̄ ⲉ-
ϩⲟⲩⲛ ⲉⲡⲙⲁⲛⲧⲱⲕ' ⲛ̄ⲧⲥⲓⲟⲟⲩⲛ, ϩⲱⲥ ⲉ'ⲁⲓ̈ⲉⲓⲙⲉ ⲉⲣⲟⲕ ϫⲉ ⲕⲣ̄'ϩⲱⲃ ϩⲛ̄ϩⲉⲛϩⲃⲏⲩⲉ'
ⲙ̄ⲙⲁⲅⲓⲁ, ⲉⲡⲓⲇⲏ'ⲁⲕⲣ̄ⲙⲁⲅⲓⲁ ⲉⲡⲓϣⲉϩⲙⲉ' ⲥⲁⲩϥ ⲛ̄ⲣⲱⲙⲉ, ⲁⲕ'ⲉⲓ ⲙ̄ⲡⲉⲩϩⲏⲧ
ⲙ̄ⲙⲁⲩ,' ⲟⲩⲙⲟⲩ ⲕⲁⲕⲱⲥ·' ⲁϥⲕⲉⲗⲉⲩⲉ ⲉⲧⲣⲟⲩⲉⲓⲛⲉ' ⲙ̄ⲡⲉⲓⲙⲛ̄ⲧⲥⲛⲟⲟⲩⲥ' ⲛ̄ϩⲁⲅⲓ-
ⲟⲥ ⲉⲩⲥⲱⲕ' ⲙ̄ⲙⲟⲟⲩ ⲉⲧⲥⲓⲟⲟⲩⲛ·' (R ii) ⲁⲩⲥⲟⲛϩⲟⲩ ⲛ̄ⲛⲉⲩϭⲓϫ' ⲙⲛ̄ⲛⲉⲩⲉⲣⲏⲧⲉ·
ⲁⲩ'ⲧⲣⲉⲛϩⲩⲡⲏⲣⲉⲧⲏⲥ' ⲧⲱⲕ ϩⲁⲣⲟⲟⲩ· ⲁⲇⲙⲁ'ⲧⲟⲓ̈ ⲧⲱⲱⲃⲉ ϫⲡⲣⲟ' ⲛ̄ⲧⲥⲓⲟⲟⲩⲛ, ⲁⲩ-

---

119 V ii 27. l πεϊραν. 120 R i 18. l. - ⲛⲉⲕⲥⲛⲏⲩ (or possibly -ⲛⲉⲕⲕⲉⲥⲛⲏⲩ).

119 V ii 29 - 32 : B may be restored from A's text as far as ⲛ̄ⲧⲟⲩ. 120 R i. B's text seems
to have been shorter. 5. ⲉⲡⲓⲇⲏ A; ϫⲉ B; where probably restore ⲛⲉⲣⲉⲡⲛ[ⲟⲩⲧⲉ]. 6. B
[ϯ]ϭⲟⲙ; so Sottas. ⲛⲁⲩ A; ⲛⲁⲩ B. 6 f. ⲙ̄ⲡⲛⲁⲩ ⲉⲧⲙ̄ⲙⲁⲩ A; [ϩⲛ̄ⲛ̄]ⲉⲧⲣⲓⲥⲉ B. 8 f. ⲙ̄ⲡϩⲁ-
ⲁⲡⲁ ⲯ. A; ⲛⲁⲩ B. 10 f. Restore B from Text of A. 13 f. ⲉⲧⲣⲟⲩⲛⲟϫⲟⲩ A; ⲛ̄ⲥⲉⲛ. B. 16. ϭⲉ A; ⲇⲉ B.
16 f. -ⲁⲡⲟⲫⲁⲥⲓⲥ A; -ⲇⲓⲙⲱⲣⲓⲁ B. 17. ⲛ̄ⲧⲟⲕ A; om. B. 19-21. ⲉⲧⲣⲟⲩⲛⲉϫⲑⲏⲧⲛ̄ — ⲛ̄ⲧⲥⲓⲟⲟⲩⲛ A;
om. B. 22. ⲉⲣⲟⲕ A; om. B. 23. ϩⲁϩⲉⲛϩⲃⲏⲩⲉ A; ϩⲛ̄ϩⲉⲛϩ. B. 24. ⲙ̄ⲙⲁⲅⲓⲁ A; ⲙ̄ⲙⲛ̄ⲧⲙⲁ-
ⲅⲟⲥ B. 25. ⲁⲕⲣ̄ⲙⲁⲅⲓⲁ A; ⲁⲕⲙⲁⲅⲉⲩⲉ B. ⲉⲡⲓϣⲉϩⲙⲉ A; ⲙ̄ⲡⲉⲓ̈ϣ. B. 26. ⲥⲁⲩϥ A;
ⲛ̄ϣⲉ B. 26 f. ⲁⲕⲉⲓ - ⲙ̄ⲙⲁⲩ A; om. B. 28. ⲁⲩⲙⲟⲩ A; ⲩⲁⲛⲧⲟⲩⲙⲟⲩ B. 29-31. ⲁⲩⲕⲉⲗⲉⲩⲉ — ⲛ̄ϩⲁⲅⲓⲟⲥ A; ⲁⲩⲟⲩⲉϩⲥⲁϩⲛⲉ ⲛ̄ⲥⲉⲧⲱⲕⲉ ⲛ̄ⲛⲉϩⲁⲅⲓⲟⲥ B. 31 f. ⲉⲩⲥⲱⲕ — ⲉⲧⲥⲓⲟⲟⲩⲛ A;
om. B. ii 1. ⲁⲩⲥⲟⲛϩⲟⲩ A; ⲛ̄ⲥⲉⲙⲟⲧⲣ B. 2-7. ⲁⲩⲧⲣⲉⲛϩⲩⲡⲏⲣⲉⲧⲏⲥ — ⲁⲩⲕⲁⲁⲩ A; ⲛ̄ⲥⲉⲛⲟ-
ϫⲟⲩ ⲉⲡⲉⲥⲏⲧ ⲉⲡⲏⲓ̈(?) ⲛ̄ⲧⲱⲕ ⲛ̄ⲥⲉⲧⲱⲕ ⲉϫⲱⲟⲩ ⲁⲩⲱ ⲛ̄ⲥⲉⲧⲱⲱⲃⲉ ϫⲡⲣⲟ ⲉⲣⲱⲟⲩ B.

ⲃⲱⲕ, ⲁ̄ⲩⲕⲁⲁⲩ. ⲡⲉⲁⲅⲓⲟⲥ ⲇⲉ ⲁⲡⲁ ⲯⲟⲩ̀ⲅⲉ ⲁ̄ϥϫⲓ ⲛⲁⲩ ⲛ̄ⲟⲩⲙ̄ⲛⲧ ⳟⲁⲣⲍⲏⲧ ⲛ̄ⲧⲉ̀ⲡⲉ-
ⲡⲛ̄ⲁ ⲉⲧⲟⲩⲁⲁⲃ, ⲁⲩⲧⲱⲃⲉ̄ ⲙ̄ⲡⲛⲟⲩⲧⲉ ⲍⲛ̄ⲧⲙⲏⲧⲉ ⲙ̄ⲡⲕⲱϩⲧ ⲉⲩϫⲱ ⲙ̄ⲙⲟⲥ ϫⲉ
ⲥⲱⲧⲙ̄ ⲉⲣⲟⲓ ⲡⲛⲟⲩⲧⲉ ⲡⲉⲓⲱⲧ ⲙ̄ⲡⲉⲛⲭⲟⲉⲓⲥ Ⲓⲥ ⲡⲉⲭⲥ, ⲡⲉⲛⲧⲁⲩⲥⲱⲧⲙ̄ ⲉⲡⲉⲛ̀ⲉⲓⲱⲧ
ⲁⲃⲣⲁϩⲁⲙ, ⲁⲩⲱϣⲙ̄ ⲙ̄ⲡⲕⲱϩⲧ ⲙ̄ⲡⲣ̄ⲣⲟ ⲥⲟⲃⲟⲭ ϩⲁⲣⲟϥ. ⲡⲉⲛⲧⲁⲩⲥⲱⲧⲙ̄ ⲉⲡⲉ̀ⲛⲉⲓⲱⲧ
ⲡⲁⲩⲗⲟⲥ ⲙ̄ⲛⲑⲉⲕⲗⲁ ⲁⲩⲱ̀ϣⲙ̄ ⲙ̄ⲡⲕⲱϩⲧ ⲛ̄ⲑⲁⲙⲉⲣⲓⲥ ϩⲁⲣⲟⲟⲩ. ⲡⲉⲛⲧⲁⲩⲥⲱⲧⲙ̄ ⲉ-
ⲡϣⲟⲙⲛ̄ⲧ ⲛ̄ⲅⲁⲅⲓⲟⲥ ⲁⲛⲁⲛⲓⲁⲥ ⲁⲍⲁⲣⲓⲁⲥ ⲙⲓⲥⲁⲏⲗ, ⲁⲩⲭⲟⲟⲩ ⲙ̄ⲡⲉⲩⲁⲅⲅⲉⲗⲟⲥ ϣⲁⲣⲟⲟⲩ ⲁⲩⲱϣⲙ̄ (120 Vi) ⲙ̄ⲡⲕⲱϩⲧ ⲛ̄ⲧⲕⲁⲙⲓⲛⲟⲥ ϩⲁⲣⲟⲟⲩ ⲁⲩ̀ⲛⲁⲍⲙⲟⲩ. ⲉⲕⲉⲥⲱ-
ⲧⲙ̄ ⲉⲣⲟⲛ ϩⲱⲱⲛ ⲙ̄ⲡⲟⲟⲩ ⲛ̄ⲛⲁϩⲙⲉⲛ · ϫⲉ ⲟⲩϭⲟⲟⲩ ⲛ̄ⲑⲗⲓⲯⲓⲥ ϩⲓⲟⲣⲅⲏ ⲡⲉ ⲡⲟⲟⲩ.
ⲛ̄ϩⲟⲥⲟⲛ ⲉⲣⲉ̀ⲡⲅⲁⲅⲓⲟⲥ ⲁⲡⲁ ⲯⲟⲩ̀ⲅⲉ ϫⲱ ⲛ̄ⲛⲁⲓ, ⲉⲓⲥϩⲏⲏⲧⲉ ⲉⲓⲥ ⲡⲁⲣ̀ⲭⲁⲅⲅⲉⲗⲟⲥ
ⲙⲓⲭⲁ̀ⲏⲗ ⲁϥⲉⲓ ⲉⲃⲟⲗ ϩⲛ̄ ⲧⲡⲉ ϣⲁ̀ⲡⲅⲁⲅⲓⲟⲥ ⲁⲡⲁ ⲯⲟⲩ̀ⲅⲉ ⲙ̄ⲛ̀ⲛⲉϥⲥⲛⲏⲩ ⲉϩⲟⲩⲛ
ⲉⲡⲙⲁⲛ̄ⲧⲱⲕ ⲛ̄ⲧⲥⲓⲟⲟⲩⲛ, ⲁⲩⲡⲱ̀ⲣϣ̄ ⲛ̄ⲛⲉⲩⲧⲏⲛⲉ̄ ⲛ̄ⲟⲩⲟⲉⲓⲛ ⲉⲃⲟⲗ ⲉϫⲱ̀ⲟⲩ, ⲁⲩⲁϩ
ⲙ̄ⲡⲕⲱϩⲧ ⲣ̄ⲑⲉ ⲛ̄ⲟⲩⲛⲉⲓⲃ ⲛ̄ⲉⲓⲱⲧⲉ. ⲡⲉⲭⲁⲩ ⲛ̄ⲛⲅⲁⲅⲓⲟⲥ ϫⲉ ϫⲣⲟ ⲁ̄ⲙⲱⲧⲛ̄ ⲱ
ⲛ̄ⲁ̀ⲑⲗⲏⲧⲏⲥ ⲙ̄ⲡⲉⲭⲥ · ⲁⲛⲟⲕ ⲡⲉ ⲙⲓⲭⲁⲏⲗ ⲉⲁⲩⲧⲛ̄ⲛⲟⲟⲩⲧ ϣⲁ̀ⲣⲱⲧⲛ̄, ⲧⲁϣⲟ̀ⲡⲉ
ⲉⲓ̀ⲇⲓⲁⲕⲟⲛⲉⲓ ⲉ̀ⲣⲱⲧⲛ̄, ⲉⲓ̀ⲧⲥⲟⲙ ⲛⲏⲧⲛ̄ ϣⲁⲛⲧⲉ (Vii) ⲧⲛ̄ϫⲱⲕ ⲉⲃⲟⲗ ⲙ̄ⲡⲉ̀ⲧⲛ̄ⲁ-
ⲅⲱⲛ. ⲁⲩⲱ ⲁ̀ⲡⲁⲅⲅⲉⲗⲟⲥ ⲙ̄ⲡⲛⲟⲩⲧⲉ ⲡⲱⲣϣ̄ ⲛ̄ⲧⲉϥⲥⲧⲟⲗⲏ ⲉⲃⲟⲗ ⲉⲥⲙⲉϩ ⲛ̄ⲕⲁⲣⲡⲟⲥ
ⲉⲃⲟⲗ ϩⲛ̄ⲛⲉⲛ ϣⲏⲛ ⲙ̄ⲡⲡⲁⲣⲁⲇⲓⲥⲟⲥ, ⲁⲩ̀ϯ ⲛ̄ⲛⲉⲧⲟⲩⲁⲁⲃ, ⲁⲩⲟⲩ̀ⲱⲙ, ⲁⲩⲡⲉⲩϩⲏⲧ
ⲧⲁϫⲣⲟ. ⲁⲩⲟⲩⲱⲛ ⲉⲣⲱⲟⲩ ⲛ̄ϭⲓ ⲡⲅⲁⲅⲓⲟⲥ ⲁⲡⲁ ⲯⲟⲩ̀ⲅⲉ, ⲁⲩ̀ϫⲱ ⲙ̄ⲡⲉⲓ̀ϩⲩⲙⲛⲟⲥ ⲉⲩ-
ⲟⲩⲱϣⲙ̄ ⲛ̄ⲥⲱⲟⲩ ⲛ̄ϭⲓ ⲡⲕⲉⲙⲛ̄ⲧⲟⲩⲉ ⲛ̄ⲅⲁⲅⲓⲟⲥ ϫⲉ ϯⲣⲏⲛⲏ ⲛⲁⲛ ϫⲉ ⲁⲡⲛⲟⲩⲧⲉ ⲣ̄ⲡⲉⲛ-
ⲙⲉⲉⲩⲉ · ⲙ̄ⲡⲟ̀ⲟⲩ ⲅⲁⲣ ⲁⲛⲉⲓⲙⲉ ϫⲉ ⲙ̄ⲡⲉ̀ⲡϫⲟⲉⲓⲥ ⲣ̄ⲡⲉⲛⲱ̀ϣϥ̄ ⲕⲁⲧⲁⲑⲉ ⲉⲧⲥⲏ ϩⲛ̄ⲧⲉ-
ⲕⲣⲁⲫⲏ ⲉⲧⲟⲩⲁⲁⲃ ϫⲉ ⲙ̄ⲡ̀ϫⲟⲉⲓⲥ ⲛⲁⲕⲱ̀ ⲛ̄ⲥⲱϥ ⲁⲛ ⲙ̄ⲡ̀ⲇⲓⲕⲁⲓ̀ⲟⲥ ϣⲁⲃⲟⲗ, ⲁⲩⲱ
ⲑⲩ̀ⲡⲟⲙⲟⲛⲏ ⲙ̄ⲡⲉϥ̀ϩⲏⲛ ⲛⲁϣⲉ ⲉⲃⲟⲗ ⲁⲛ ϣⲁ̀ⲡ̀ⲧⲏⲣϥ̄. ⲉⲧⲃⲉⲡⲁⲓ̀ ⲇⲉ ⲙ̄ⲡⲉ ⲛ̄ⲡⲛⲟⲩⲧⲉ

---

120 Vi 22. l. ⲛ̄ⲟⲩⲛⲓϣⲉ. ii 9. l. ⲁⲡⲉⲩϩⲏⲧ (or ⲁⲩϫⲱ ⲁⲡⲉⲩϩⲏⲧ?)

---

120 Rii 7. ⲡⲅⲁⲅⲓⲟⲥ A; ⲡⲡⲉⲧⲟⲩⲁⲁⲃ B. 8. ⲯⲟⲩϭⲉ A; ⲯⲟⲩⲧⲃⲉ B (and so throughout).
9–13. ⲁⲩϫⲓ — ⲙ̄ⲡⲕⲱϩⲧ A; ⲡⲉϫⲁⲩ ⲛⲁⲩ ϫⲉ ⲛⲁⲥⲛⲏⲩ ⲧⲱⲟⲩⲛ ⲛ̄ⲧⲉⲛⲱ̄ⲯⲗⲏⲗ· ⲁⲩⲧⲱⲟⲩⲛ ⲇⲉ ⲁⲩ-
ϣ̄ⲗⲏⲗ ⲛ̄ⲧⲉⲓ̀ϩⲉ B. 14. ⲉⲩϫⲱ A; ⲉⲧϫⲱ B. 15. ⲉⲣⲟⲓ A; ⲉⲣⲟⲛ B. 16 ff. Large lacuna in
B. 27 f. B may be restored from A's text. 28–30. B's text was shorter here; ⲛ̄ⲅⲁⲅⲓⲟⲥ
ⲛ̄ϣⲏⲣⲉ ϣⲏⲙ? 30 (end) f.: B may be restored from A's text. Vi f. ⲙ̄ⲡⲕⲱϩⲧ ⲛ̄ⲧⲕⲁⲙⲓ-
ⲛⲟⲥ A; [ⲛ̄ⲧⲕⲁⲙⲓⲛⲟⲥ ? ⲛ̄]ⲕ[ⲱϩ]ⲧ + ⲙ̄ⲡⲣ̄ⲣⲟ ⲛⲁⲃⲟⲭⲟⲇⲟⲛⲟⲥⲟⲣ B. 11. ⲉⲓⲥϩⲏⲏⲧⲉ A; om. —
B. 11 f. ⲡⲁⲣⲭⲁⲅⲅⲉⲗⲟⲥ A; om. B. 14. After ϩⲛ̄ⲧⲡⲉ, + ⲁⲩⲃⲱⲕ B. 15– 18. ⲁⲡⲁ —
ⲛ̄ⲧⲥⲓⲟⲟⲩⲛ A; om. B. 18–23. ⲁⲩⲡⲱⲣϣ̄ — ⲛ̄ⲉⲓⲱⲧⲉ A; ⲁⲩⲱϣⲙ̄ ⲙ̄ⲡⲓ[   ] ⲙ̄ⲡⲕⲱϩⲧ
ⲁⲩⲉⲓⲙⲉ] ⲛ̄ⲟⲩⲧⲏⲩ ⲛⲱⲧⲙ̄[   ] B (text much shorter). 23 f. ⲡⲉϫⲁⲩ ⲛ̄ⲛⲅⲁⲅⲓⲟⲥ A;
ⲡⲉϫⲉⲛ[ⲁⲣⲭⲁⲅ]ⲅⲉⲗⲟⲥ ⲛⲁⲩ B. 25–28. Text of B fragmentary; probably to be restored
much as in A. 29–32. ⲧⲁϣⲟⲡⲉ ⲉⲓ̀ⲇⲓⲁⲕⲟⲛⲉⲓ ⲉⲣⲱⲧⲛ̄ ⲉⲓ̀ϯⲥⲟⲙ ⲛⲏⲧⲛ̄ ϣⲁⲛⲧⲉⲧⲛ̄ϫⲱⲕ
(etc.) A; ? ϫⲉⲕⲁⲥ ⲉⲓⲉ]ⲥⲱ ⲉⲓ̀ⲇ[ⲓⲁⲕⲟⲛⲉⲓ ⲉⲣ]ⲱⲧⲛ̄ ⲁⲩ[B. After this, evidently much
lost from B.

ⲣⲡⲉⲛⲓⲱⲃϣ̄, ⲁⲗⲗⲁ ⲁ̅ⲩⲧⲁ'ⲟⲧⲟ ⲙ̅ⲡⲉⲩⲁⲅⲅⲉⲗⲟⲥ,'ⲁⲩⲃⲟⲏⲑⲓⲁ ⲉⲣⲟⲛ, (121 Ⲣ ⲓ)ⲕⲁⲧⲁ-
ⲑⲉ ⲉⲧⲥⲏ2 ϫⲉ' ⳛⲁⲣⲉⲡⲁⲅⲅⲉⲗⲟⲥ ⲙ̅'ⲡϫⲟⲉⲓⲥ ⲕⲱⲧⲉ ⲉⲛⲉⲧⲣ̅'2ⲟⲧⲉ 2ⲏⲧϥ̄ ⲛ̄ϥⲛⲁ2ⲙⲟⲩ.'
ϥ̄ϫⲱ ⲙ̅ⲙⲟⲥ ⲟⲛ ϫⲉ' ϫⲓⲛⲉ̈ⲓⲟ ⲣ̄ⲕⲟⲩⲓ̈ ⲉⲓⲥ'2ⲏⲏⲧⲉ ⲁⲓ̈ϥⲣⲁⲗⲟ ⲙ̅'ⲡⲉⲓ̈ⲛⲁⲩ ⲉⲇⲓⲕⲁⲓⲟⲥ'
ⲉⲁⲩⲕⲁⲁⲩ ⲛ̄ⲥⲱⲓ.' ⲁⲩⲱ ⲛⲉⲕⲉ2ⲁⲅⲓⲟⲥ ⲙ̄ⲡⲟⲩ'ⲕⲁⲧⲟⲟⲧⲟⲩ ⲉⲃⲟⲗ ⲉⲩ'ⲥⲙⲟⲩ ⲉⲡⲛⲟⲩⲧⲉ 2ⲛ̄'ⲧⲙⲏⲧⲉ ⲙ̄ⲡⲕⲱ2ⲧ̄,' ⲉⲣⲉⲡⲁⲅⲅⲉⲗⲟⲥ ⲙ̄ⲡ'ⲛⲟⲩⲧⲉ ϯⲟⲙ ⲛⲁⲩ.' 2ⲙ̄ⲡⲛⲁⲩ ⲇⲉ
ⲛ̄ϣⲁϯ' ⲙ̄ⲡⲉⲩⲣⲁⲥⲧⲉ ⲁ̄ⲩⲉⲓ ⲉ'ⲧⲥⲓⲟⲟⲩⲛ ⲛ̄ϭⲓ ⲁⲣⲓⲁⲛⲟⲥ' ⲡ2ⲏⲅⲉⲙⲱⲛ ϫⲉ' ⲉⲩⲛⲁ-
ϫⲱⲕⲙ̄· ⲁ̄ⲩⲣ̄'ⲡⲙⲉⲉⲩⲉ ⲛ̄ⲛⲉⲛ2ⲁ'ⲅⲓⲟⲥ· ⲛⲉⲩϫⲱ ⲅⲁⲣ' ⲙ̅ⲙⲟⲥ 2ⲙ̄ⲡⲉⲩ2ⲏⲧ' ϫⲉ ⲁⲟⲩⲱ
ⲉⲩⲣⲱⲕ2̄' ⲛ̄ϭⲓ ⲛⲉⲩⲕⲉⲉⲥ 2ⲙ̄'ⲡⲕⲱ2ⲧ̄. ⲁ̄ⲩⲱϣ' ⲉⲃⲟⲗ 2ⲛ̄ⲟⲩⲛⲟϭ ⲁ̄ⲥⲙⲏ' ⲉⲩϫⲱ ⲙ̅-
ⲙⲟⲥ ϫⲉ ⲁⲕ'ϫⲓ ⳛⲓⲛⲉ ⲙ̄ⲡⲟⲟⲩ' ⲱ ⲩⲛⲟⲩϭⲉ ⲙⲛ̄'ⲛⲉⲕⲣⲉϥ ϫⲏⲛⲏⲩ· ⲉⲩⲧⲱ(ⲛ)'ⲧⲉⲛⲟⲩ ⲓⲥ
ⲡⲉⲕⲛⲟⲩⲧⲉ (Ⲣ ⲓⲓ) ⲉⲧⲉⲕⲕⲱ ⲛ̄2ⲧⲏⲕ'ⲉⲣⲟϥ; ⲉⲧⲃⲉⲟⲩ ⲙ̄ⲡⲉϥ'ⲛⲁ2ⲙⲉⲕ ⲉⲃⲟⲗ 2ⲙ̄-
ⲡⲓ'ⲕⲱ2ⲧ̄; ⲁⲓⲧⲉⲓ ⲉⲣⲉ'ⲡ2ⲏⲅⲉⲙⲱⲛ ϫⲱ ⲛ̄'ⲛⲁⲓ̈, ⲁⲡⲁⲅⲅⲉⲗⲟⲥ' ⲙ̄ⲡⲛⲟⲩⲧⲉ ⲥⲱⲗ2̄'ⲉ-
ⲃⲟⲗ ⲛ̄ⲛⲉⲡⲗⲁ2' ⲛ̄ⲧⲥⲓⲟⲟⲩⲛ, ⲁ̄ⲩⲧⲁ'ⲗⲟ ⲁ̄ⲡⲙⲛ̄ⲧⲥⲛⲟⲟⲩⲥ' ⲛ̄2ⲁⲅⲓⲟⲥ ⲉⲭⲉⲛⲛⲉⲩ'ⲧⲏ-
ⲛ2̄ ⲛ̄ⲟⲩⲟⲉⲓⲛ,' ⲁⲩⲕⲁⲁⲩ ⲉⲡⲉⲥⲏⲧ' ⲉⲭⲉⲛⲡⲉⲑⲟⲗⲟⲥ ⲛ̄ⲧ'ⲥⲓⲟⲟⲩⲛ ⲙ̄ⲡⲉⲙⲧⲟ' ⲉⲃⲟⲗ
ⲙ̄ⲡ2ⲏⲅⲉⲙⲱ(ⲛ)' ⲉⲙⲡⲗⲁⲁⲩ ⲛ̄ⲧⲁⲕⲟ' ⳛⲟⲟⲡ ⲙ̄ⲙⲁⲩ·' ⲁⲩⲱ ⲟⲩⲕⲁⲛ ⲛ̄ⲃⲱ' ⲛ̄ⲧⲉ-
ⲧⲉⲩⲁⲡⲉ ⲙ̄ⲡⲉⲩ'ⲣⲱⲕ2̄. ⲛ̄ⲧⲉⲣⲉϥ'ⲛⲁⲩ ⲉⲣⲟⲟⲩ ⲛ̄ϭⲓ ⲡ2ⲏ'ⲅⲉⲙⲱⲛ, ⲁⲩϭⲱⲛ̄ⲧ ⲉⲙⲁⲧⲉ,
ⲁ̄ⲩⲕ'ⲧⲟⲩ ⲉⲃⲟⲗ, ⲙ̄ⲡⲉⲩϫⲱ'ⲕⲙ̄ ⲙ̄ⲡⲉ2ⲟⲟⲩ ⲉⲧⲙ̄ⲙⲁⲩ.'ⲧⲟⲧⲉ ⲡⲙⲛ̄ⲧⲥⲛⲟⲟⲩⲥ'ⲛ̄2ⲁ-
ⲅⲓⲟⲥ ⲁ̄ⲩⲉⲓ ⲉⲃⲟⲗ' 2ⲛ̄ⲧⲉⲡⲗⲁⲧⲓⲁ ⲛ̄ⲧ'ⲡⲟⲗⲓⲥ ⲉⲩⲟⲩⲏ2 ⲛ̄ⲥⲁ'ⲡ2ⲏⲅⲉⲙⲱⲛ, ⲁⲩⲱ' ⲉ-
ⲣⲉⲡⲙⲏⲏϣⲉ ⲛ̄ⲧⲡⲟⲗⲓⲥ (Ⲥ ⲓ) ⲕⲱⲧⲉ ⲉⲣⲟⲟⲩ ⲉⲩϯ'ⲉⲟⲟⲩ ⲙ̄ⲡⲛⲟⲩⲧⲉ ⲙ̄'ⲡ2ⲁⲅⲓⲟⲥ ⲁ-
ⲡⲁ ⲩⲛⲟⲩϭⲉ. ⲡ2ⲏⲅⲉⲙⲱ(ⲛ)' ⲇⲉ ⲙ̄ⲡⲉⲩⲃⲱⲕ ⲉⲡⲁ'ⲣⲓⲥⲧⲟⲛ ⲙ̄ⲡⲉ2ⲟⲟⲩ' ⲉⲧⲙ̄ⲙⲁⲩ,

---

121 Ⲣ ⲓ 21 ƒ ⲓ. ⲛ̄ⲛ2ⲁⲅⲓⲟⲥ. ⲓⲓ 4. =ⲉⲧⲓ; ⲓ added. 18. ⲓ. ⲙ̄ⲙⲟⲟⲩ

120 Ⲥ ⲓⲓ 31 ƒ. Ⲃ probably to be restored as A. 121 Ⲣ ⲓ 4–5. After ⲛ̄ϥⲛⲁ2ⲙⲟⲩ, + ⲁⲩⲱ
[ⲩⲁϥ]ⲣⲟⲉ[ⲓⲥ ⲉ]ⲣⲟⲟⲩ 2ⲉⲛⲧⲟⲛⲟⲥ ⲛⲉⲙ (= ⲙⲛ) ⲉⲩⲁⲩⲃⲱⲕ ⲉⲣⲟϥ Ⲃ. 5. ϥ̄ϫⲱ ⲙ̅ⲙⲟⲥ A;
ⲩⲁϥϫⲟⲟⲥ Ⲃ. 6. ϫⲓⲛⲉ̈ⲓⲟ A; ⲛⲉ̈ⲓⲟ Ⲃ. After ⲣ̄ⲕⲟⲩⲓ̈, + ⲡⲉ Ⲃ. 6 ƒ. ⲉⲓⲥ2ⲏⲏⲧⲉ A; ⲁⲩⲱ Ⲃ.
9. After ⲉⲇⲓⲕⲁⲓⲟⲥ, + ⲉⲛⲉ2 Ⲃ. 9 ƒ. After ⲛ̄ⲥⲱ, + ⲟⲩⲇⲉ ⲡⲉⲩⲥⲡⲉⲣⲙⲁ ⲙ̄ⲡⲉⲩϣⲓⲛⲉ ⲛ̄ⲥⲁ-
ⲟⲉⲓⲕ Ⲃ. 10. ⲁⲩⲱ A; om. Ⲃ. ⲛⲉⲕⲉ2ⲁⲅⲓⲟⲥ A; ⲛⲉ2 ⲇⲉ Ⲃ. 11 ƒ. Restore ⲉⲩⲥⲙⲟⲩ in Ⲃ,
as A. 12 ƒ. 2ⲛ̄ⲧⲙⲏⲧⲉ ⲙ̄ⲡⲕⲱ2ⲧ̄ A; [ⲛ̄ⲧⲉⲣ]ϫⲏ ⲧⲏⲣⲥ̄ Ⲃ. 15. -ⲛⲟⲩⲧⲉ A; -ϫⲟⲉⲓⲥ Ⲃ.
15. Restore ϯϭⲟⲙ in Ⲃ, as A. 16. 2ⲙ̄ⲡⲛⲁⲩ ⲇⲉ ⲛ̄ϣⲁϯ A; om. Ⲃ. 17. After ⲙ̄ⲡⲉⲩ-
ⲣⲁⲥⲧⲉ, + ⲇⲉ Ⲃ. 18. ⲁⲣⲓⲁⲛⲟⲥ A; om. Ⲃ. 19 ƒ. ϫⲉ ⲉⲩⲛⲁϫⲱⲕⲙ̄ A; ⲉ[ⲉⲓⲕⲁⲥ ⲉⲩⲉ]ϫ.
Ⲃ. 21 ƒ. ⲛ̄ⲛⲉⲛ2ⲁⲅⲓⲟⲥ A; ⲉⲛⲉ2. Ⲃ. After 22, much lost from Ⲃ; ⲓⲓ 9 ƒ., 15 ƒ. may
correspond to A's text, but rest seems different. ⲓⲓ 22. After ⲛ̄ⲧⲉⲣⲉϥⲛⲁⲩ, + ⲇⲉ Ⲃ.
ⲛ̄ϭⲓ in Ⲃ (Sottas) confirmed. 24 ƒ. ⲁⲩⲕⲧⲟⲩ A; ⲁⲩⲕⲟⲧⲩ Ⲃ. 25. After ⲉⲃⲟⲗ, + 2ⲉⲛ-
ⲧⲥⲓⲟⲟⲩⲛ Ⲃ. 27. ⲧⲟⲧⲉ A; om. Ⲃ. After ⲡⲙⲛ̄ⲧⲥⲛⲟⲟⲩⲥ, + ⲇⲉ Ⲃ. 29 ƒ. 2ⲛ̄ⲧⲉⲡⲗⲁⲧⲓⲁ
ⲛ̄ⲧⲡⲟⲗⲓⲥ A; om. Ⲃ. 30. ⲉⲩⲟⲩⲏ2 A; ⲁⲟⲩⲁ2ⲟⲩ Ⲃ. 31. ⲁⲩⲱ A; om. Ⲃ. 32. ⲛ̄ⲧⲡⲟⲗⲓⲥ
A; ⲧⲏⲣϥ̄ Ⲃ. Ⲥ ⲓ 1. After ⲉⲣⲟⲟⲩ, + ⲉⲩⲉⲣ ⲩⲙ ⲛⲏⲣⲉ Ⲃ. 2–4. ⲙ̄ⲡ2·ⲁ·ⲩ· A; ⲛ̄ⲛⲉⲭⲣⲏ-
ⲥⲧⲓⲁⲛⲟⲥ ⲡⲉϫⲉ ⲓⲥ Ⲃ. 6 ƒ. ⲙ̄ⲡⲉ2ⲟⲟⲩ ⲉⲧⲙ̄ⲙⲁⲩ A; om. Ⲃ.

ⲁⲗⲗⲁ'ⲛⲉⲩⲍⲁ̅ⲡⲉⲡⲣⲟⲃⲏ'ⲙⲁⲧⲟⲥ ⲁ̅ⲡⲉ2ⲟⲟⲩ¹⁰ ⲉⲧⲁ̅ⲙⲁⲩ 2ⲛ̅ⲧⲙⲏ'ⲧⲉ ⲛ̅ⲧⲁⲕⲟⲣⲁ. ⲁⲩ-
ⲧ'ⲣⲟⲩⲉⲓⲛⲉ ⲉⲑⲏ ⲛⲛ̅²ⲍⲁⲅⲓⲟⲥ ⲡ̅ⲙⲁⲣⲧⲩ'ⲣⲟⲥ ⲟⲩⲁ ⲟⲩⲁ, ⲁⲩⲱ¹⁵ ⲁⲩⲧⲣⲟⲩⲉⲓⲛⲉ ⲙ̅ⲙⲁⲧ'-
ⲥⲛⲟⲟⲩⲥ ⲛ̅2ⲉⲣⲙⲉⲧⲁ'ⲣⲓⲟⲛ, ⲁⲩⲧⲣⲟⲩⲁⲩ'ⲧⲟⲩ ⲉⲣⲟⲟⲩ ⲟⲩⲁ.ⲟⲩⲁ,' ⲁⲩⲧ ⲛ̅2ⲉⲛⲗⲁⲙⲡⲁⲥ²⁰
ⲛ̅ⲕⲱ2̅ⲧ 2ⲁⲛⲉⲩⲥ'ⲡⲓⲣⲟⲟⲩⲉ, ⲁⲩⲉⲓⲛⲉ' ⲛ̅2ⲉⲛⲩⲗⲓⲅ ⲙ̅ⲡⲉ'ⲛⲓⲡⲉ ⲉⲩⲗⲟⲃ̄ⲏ 2ⲛ̅'ⲡⲕⲱ2̅ⲧ,
ⲁⲩⲧⲁⲁⲩ' ⲉ2ⲟⲩⲛ ⲉⲛⲉⲩⲙⲁⲁ ̄ⲭⲉ,' ⲁⲩⲱ 2ⲛ̅ⲡⲉⲣⲓⲕⲉⲫⲁ'ⲗⲉⲁ ⲙ̅ⲡⲉⲛⲓⲡⲉ ⲁⲩ'ⲧⲁⲁⲩ
ⲉⲭⲉⲛⲧⲉⲩⲁⲡⲉ,' ⲁⲩⲧ ⲛ̅2⁰ⲛ̅ⲕⲱ2̅ⲧ' ⲉⲩⲙⲟⲩ2 2ⲁⲛ̅ⲥ̅ⲟⲡ' ⲛ̅ⲣⲁⲧⲟⲩ. ⲛ̅2ⲁⲅⲓ'ⲟⲥ ⲇⲉ ⲁⲗⲁ
ⲩ̅ⲛ̅ⲟⲩ ̄ϭⲉ (121 Vⲓⲓ) ⲁⲩⲥⲙⲟⲩ ⲉⲡⲛⲟⲩⲧⲉ ⲉⲩ'ϫⲱ ⲙ̅ⲙⲟⲥ ϫⲉ ⲧⲥⲙⲟⲩ' ⲉⲣⲟⲕ ⲡⲁⲗⲫⲁ
ⲙⲛ̅ⲡⲱ̅,' ⲧⲁⲣⲭⲏ ⲁⲩⲱ ⲡ̅ϫⲱⲕ.' ⲛⲉⲩⲟⲩⲱϣⲙ̅ ⲛ̅ⲥⲱⲥ ̄⁵ ⲛ̅'ϭⲓ ⲡⲕⲉⲙⲏ̅ⲧⲟⲩⲉ ⲛ̅ⲍⲁ'ⲅⲓⲟⲥ
ϫⲉ ⲧⲥⲙⲟⲩ ⲉⲣⲟⲕ' ⲓ̅ⲥ̅ ⲡ̅ⲙⲟⲛⲟⲅⲉⲛⲏⲥ ⲙ̅ⲡⲉⲓⲱⲧ, ⲡⲉⲧϣⲟⲟⲡ'¹⁰ 2ⲛ̅ⲧⲗⲉ2ⲥⲁⲩ ̄ϭⲉ ⲙ̅ⲡⲏ'
ⲉⲣⲉⲥⲁⲩ ̄ϭ ⲛ̅ⲕⲁⲧⲁⲡⲉⲧⲁⲥ'ⲙⲁ 2ⲱⲃⲉ ⲙ̅ⲡⲉⲩ2ⲟ.' ⲉⲛⲧⲱⲃⲉ ⲙ̅ⲙⲟⲕ ϫⲉ'ⲉⲕⲉϣⲱⲡⲉ
ⲛ̅ⲙ̅ⲙⲁⲛ¹⁵' 2ⲛ̅ⲛⲉⲛⲑⲗⲓⲯⲓⲥ ⲙ̅ⲛ̅ⲛⲉⲛⲇⲓⲟⲕⲙⲟⲥ, ϫⲉ ⲛ̅ⲧⲟⲕ ⲡⲉ ⲡⲥⲁⲉⲓⲛ ⲛ̅'ⲉⲛ̅ϭⲁⲉⲓⲛ
ⲧⲏⲣⲟⲩ' ⲉⲣⲉⲡⲧⲁⲗϭⲟ ⲙ̅ⲡⲗⲱⲛ̅ ̄²⁰ ϣⲟⲟⲡ ⲉⲃⲟⲗ 2ⲓⲧⲟⲟⲧ ̄.' ⲛ̅2ⲟⲥⲟⲛ ⲇⲉ ⲉⲣⲉⲛ̅2ⲁ-
ⲅⲓ'ⲟⲥ ϫⲱ ⲛ̅ⲛⲉⲓ̈ϣⲁϫⲛⲟⲩ' ⲉⲡⲛⲟⲩⲧⲉ ⲁⲩⲱ ⲉⲩ'ⲥⲙⲟⲩ ⲉⲣⲟϥ, ⲉⲓⲥ ⲙ̅ⲛ̅ⲧ'ⲥⲛⲟⲟⲩⲥ
ⲛ̅ⲇⲣⲟⲙⲡⲉ' ⲛ̅ⲟⲩⲃⲩ ⲁⲩⲉⲓ ⲉⲃⲟⲗ' 2ⲛ̅ⲧⲡⲉ, ⲁⲩⲟⲩⲱ2 ⲉ2ⲣⲁⲓ̈' ⲉⲭⲉⲛⲧⲁⲡⲉ ⲛ̅ⲛ̅2ⲁ'ⲅⲓⲟⲥ ⲉⲧⲟⲩⲁⲁⲃ ⲟⲩⲁ ̄³⁰ ⲟⲩⲁ ⲉⲛⲁϥ ⲉ2ⲣⲁⲓ̈.' ⲁⲙ̅ⲙⲏⲩϣⲉ ϭⲱ'ϣⲧ̄, ⲁⲩⲛⲁⲩ ⲉⲣⲟⲟⲩ,
(122 Rⲓ) ⲁⲩⲣ̅ϣⲡⲏⲣⲉ. ⲉⲓⲥ ⲡ'ϫⲟⲉⲓⲥ ⲓ̅ⲥ̅ ⲁϥⲉⲓ ⲉⲃⲟⲗ 2ⲛ̅ⲧⲡⲉ ⲙ̅ⲛ̅ⲙⲓⲭⲁⲏⲗ ⲙⲛ̅'
ⲅⲁⲃⲣⲓⲏⲗ, ̄⁵ ⲁϥϭⲱϣ ⲉⲡⲥⲱⲙⲁ' ⲛ̅ⲛⲉⲧⲟⲩⲁⲁⲃ,' ⲁϥⲛⲟⲩϫⲉ ⲉⲃⲟⲗ ⲛⲛ̅'ⲥⲟⲩ ̄ⲡ̅ⲗⲓⲛ ⲛ̅ⲕⲱ2̅ⲧ'
2ⲛ̅ⲛⲉⲩⲙⲁⲁⲭⲉ,'¹⁰ ⲁⲩⲱ ⲛⲉⲡⲉⲣⲓⲕⲉⲫⲁ'ⲗⲁⲓⲁ ⲛ̅ⲕⲱ2̅ⲧ' ⲁⲩϣⲱⲡⲉ ⲛ̅ⲑⲉ ⲛ̅2ⲉⲛⲕⲗⲟⲙ 2ⲓ-

---

121 Vⲓ 27 –ⲗⲉⲁ: ⲉ ⲁⲇⲇⲉⲇ. Vⲓⲓ 16. = -ⲇⲓⲱⲅⲙⲟⲥ. 122 Rⲓ 8. ⲁⲥ ⲉⲛⲇ, ⟨ⲉⲧ-⟩ (ⲥⲟ B).

121 Vⲓ 8-11. ⲛⲉⲩ2ⲁ̅ⲡⲉⲡ. – ⲛ̅ⲧⲁⲕⲟⲣⲁ A; ⲁⲩⲉⲙⲟⲟⲥ 2ⲛ̅ⲧⲁⲅⲟⲣⲁ B. 11-14. ⲁⲩⲧⲣⲟⲩⲉ-
ⲉⲓⲛⲉ — ⲁⲩⲱ A; ⲟⲙ. B. 15. ⲁⲩⲧⲣⲟⲩⲉⲓⲛⲉ A; ⲁⲩⲟⲩⲉ2ⲥⲁ2ⲛⲉ ⲁⲩⲉⲓⲛⲉ B. 17ⲋ. ⲁⲩⲧⲣⲟⲩ-
ⲁⲩⲧⲟⲩ A; ⲁⲩⲧⲁⲗⲟ ⲛ̅ⲛⲉ2ⲁⲅⲓⲟⲥ B. 19. ⲁⲩⲧ A; ⲉⲣ̅ⲧ B. 21. Aⲋⲧⲉⲣ ⲁⲩⲉⲓⲛⲉ, ⲧ ⲟⲛ B.
23ⲋ. ⲉⲩⲗⲟⲃ̄ⲏ 2ⲛ̅ⲡⲕⲱ2̅ⲧ A; ⲉⲩ ⲛ̅ⲕ. B. 27. ⲁ̅ⲡⲉⲛⲓⲡⲉ A; ⲛ̅ⲕⲱ2̅ⲧ B. 29. ⲁⲩⲧ
ⲛ̅2ⲛ̅ⲕⲱ2̅ⲧ A; ⲁⲩⲧ2ⲉⲛⲕ. B. 30ⲋ. 2ⲁⲛⲥⲟⲡ ⲛ̅ⲣⲁⲧⲟⲩ A; 2ⲁⲛⲉⲩⲟⲩⲉ̅ⲣⲏⲧⲉ B. ⲓⲓ 3.
Aⲋⲧⲉⲣ ⲉⲣⲟⲕ, ⲧ ⲓ̅ⲥ̅ B. ⲙⲛ̅ – A; ⲁ⳽ⲱ B. 4. Aⲋⲧⲉⲣ ⲡ̅ϫⲱⲕ, ⲧ ⲛ̅2ⲱⲃ ⲛⲓⲙ B. 5. ⲛⲉⲩⲟⲩⲱϣⲙ̅
ⲛ̅ⲥⲱϥ A; ⲛⲉⲩ2ⲱ ⲙ̅ⲙⲟⲥ B. 5-7. ⲛ̅ϭⲓ – ⲛ̅ⲍⲁⲅⲓⲟⲥ A; ⲧⲏⲣⲟⲩ 2ⲓⲟⲩⲥⲟⲡ B. 7. ⲧ ⲥⲙⲟⲩ A;
ⲧⲉⲛ⟨ⲥⲙⲟⲩ?⟩ B. 8. ⲡⲙⲟⲛⲟⲅⲉⲛⲏⲥ A; ⲡⲗⲟⲅ[ⲟⲥ B. 9-11. B ⲡⲣⲟⲃⲁⲃⲗⲩ ⲧⲟ ⲃⲉ ⲣⲉⲥⲧⲟⲣⲉⲇ ⲁⲥ
A; ⲑⲟⲩⲅ2 [2]ⲛ̅ⲛⲉⲓ̈ - ⲓⲥ ⲇⲓⲋⲋⲓⲥⲩⲗⲧ. 13. ⲉⲛⲧⲱⲃⲉ A; ⲧⲉⲛⲧ. B. ϫⲉ A; ϫⲉⲕⲁⲥ B. 18.
Aⲋⲧⲉⲣ ⲧⲏⲣⲟⲩ, ⲧ ⲁⲩⲱ B. 21. ⲛ̅2ⲟⲥⲟⲛ A; ⲉⲧⲉⲓ B. 21-23. ⲉⲣⲉⲛ2 – ⲛ̅ⲛⲉⲓ̈ϣⲁϫⲛⲟⲩⲥ
A; ⲉⲩⲥⲙⲟⲩ B. 23ⲋ. ⲁⲩⲱ ⲉⲩⲥⲙⲟⲩ ⲉⲣⲟϥ A; ⲟⲙ. B. 27. ⲉ2ⲣⲁⲓ̈ A; ⲟⲙ. B. 29ⲋ.
ⲉⲧⲟⲩⲁⲁⲃ ⲟⲩⲁ ⲟⲩⲁ A; ⲟⲙ. B. 30. ⲉ2ⲣⲁⲓ̈ A; ⲉⲫⲉⲣⲙⲏⲧⲁⲣⲓⲟⲛ ⲧ ⲁⲩⲱ B. 31. ⲁ̅-
ⲙ̅ⲙⲏⲩϣⲉ A; ⲁⲡⲛ̅. ⲧ ⲧⲏⲣϥ̅ B. 31ⲋ. ϭⲱϣⲧ̄ A; ⲟⲙ. B. 32. ⲁⲩⲛⲁⲩ A; ⲉⲧⲛⲁⲩ B.
122 Rⲓ 1. ⲁⲩⲣ̅ϣⲡⲏⲣⲉ A; ⲉⲣϣⲡ. B. 2. ⲓ̅ⲥ̅ A; ⲟⲙ. B. 4-6. ⲙ̅ⲛ̅ⲅⲁⲃⲣⲓⲏⲗ –
ⲛ̅ⲛⲉⲧⲟⲩⲁⲁⲃ A; ⲟⲙ. B. 7-9. ⲛ̅ⲛ̅ⲥⲟⲩⲡⲗⲓⲛ ⲛ̅ⲕⲱ2̅ⲧ 2ⲛ̅ⲛⲉⲩⲙⲁⲁⲭⲉ A; ⲛ̅ⲛⲉⲕⲱ-
2̅ⲧ ⲉⲧ2. ⲧ ⲙ̅ⲛ̅ⲧⲉⲧⲁⲡⲉ B. 10ⲋ. ⲛⲉⲡⲉⲣⲓⲕⲉⲫⲁⲗⲁⲓⲁ A; ⲁⲡⲉⲛ. B. 12. ⲁⲩϣⲱⲡⲉ A;
ϣⲱⲡⲉ B. ⲛ̅ⲑⲉ ⲛ̅- A; ⲛ̅- B. 13. Aⲋⲧⲉⲣ - 2ⲉⲛⲕⲗⲟⲙ, ⲧ ⲛ̅ⲟⲩⲟⲉⲓⲛ (Sⲟⲧⲧⲉⲥ) B. 13ⲋ.
2ⲓⲭⲉⲛⲛⲉⲩⲁⲡⲏⲩⲉ A; ⲉⲭⲉⲛⲛⲉⲩⲁⲡⲉ B.

ϫⲉⲛ'ⲛⲉⲩⲁⲡⲏⲅⲉ,¹⁵ⲁⲩⲱ ⲛ̄ⲗⲁⲙⲡⲁⲥ ⲛ̄'ⲕⲱϩⲧ̄ ⲙ̄ⲛ̄ⲕⲉⲃⲁ' ⲉⲧⲟⲩⲃⲁⲥⲁⲛⲓⲍⲉ ⲙ̄'ⲙⲟⲟⲩ
ⲛ̄ϩⲏⲧⲟⲩ'ⲁⲅⲕⲟⲧⲟⲩ ⲉⲡⲁϩⲟⲩ ⲁⲩ'ⲣⲟⲕϩ̄²⁰ⲛ̄ⲛ̄ⲣⲣⲱⲟⲩ ⲙ̄'ⲙⲟⲟⲩ· ⲁⲟⲩⲛⲟϭ ⲛ̄'ⲧⲁⲗϭⲟ
ϣⲱⲡⲉ ϩⲙ̄'ⲡⲥⲱⲙⲁ ⲛ̄ⲛⲉⲧⲟⲩ'ⲁⲁⲃ. ⲛ̄ⲧⲉⲩⲛⲟⲩ'ⲁⲩϭⲱϣⲧ̄ ⲛ̄ϭⲓ ⲡϫⲁ'ⲥⲓⲟⲥ ⲁⲡⲁ ϣⲛⲟⲩϥⲉ,'ⲁⲩⲛⲁⲩ ⲉⲡⲥⲱⲧⲏⲣ' ⲓ̄ⲥ ⲙ̄ⲛ̄ⲙⲓⲭⲁⲏⲗ' ⲙ̄ⲛ̄ⲅⲁⲃⲣⲓⲏⲗ ⲉⲩⲁ³⁰ϩⲉⲣⲁⲧⲟⲩ ⲥⲁⲡϣⲱⲓ' ⲙ̄-
ⲡⲇⲓⲕⲁⲥⲧⲏⲣⲓⲟ(ⲛ)' ⲁⲩϫⲓⲧϥ̄ ⲉⲡⲉⲥⲏⲧ ⲁⲩ(122 R ii)ϭⲱϣⲧ̄ ⲛ̄ⲧⲉ ⲉϥϫⲱ' ⲙ̄ⲙⲟⲥ ϫⲉ
ⲡⲁϫⲟⲉⲓⲥ,' ⲁⲛⲟⲛ ⲛⲓⲙ ⲁⲛⲟⲛ' ϫⲉ ⲉⲕⲉⲥⲕⲏⲗⲗⲓ ⲙ̄⁵'ⲙⲟⲕ ⲛ̄ϥⲉⲓ ϣⲁⲣⲟⲛ 'ⲛ̄ⲛⲉⲓⲥⲟⲡ
ⲧⲏⲣⲟⲩ' ⲡⲉϫⲉ ⲡⲥⲱⲧⲏⲣ ⲛⲁϥ' ϫⲉ ⲙ̄ⲡⲣ̄ⲣ̄ⲅⲟⲧⲉ ⲡⲁ'ⲥⲱⲧ̄ⲡ̄ ϣⲛⲟⲩϥⲉ,¹⁰ ⲛ̄ⲧⲛⲁⲕⲁ-
ⲁⲕ ⲛ̄ⲥⲱⲓ' ⲁⲛ· ⲁⲩϥⲱⲛⲧ̄ ⲛ̄ϭⲓ' ⲡⲉⲕⲗⲟⲙ ⲙ̄ⲡⲉⲕⲁ'ⲅⲱⲛ· ⲁⲓⲟⲩⲱ ⲅⲁⲣ' ⲉⲓⲥⲟⲩⲧⲉ ⲛ̄-
ⲛⲉⲧⲛ̄ⲕ'ⲗⲟⲙ ⲙ̄ⲙⲛⲉⲧⲛ̄ⲑⲣⲟ'ⲛⲟⲥ ϩⲛ̄ⲑⲓⲗⲏ̄ⲙ̄ ⲛ̄ⲧⲡⲉ.' ⲛ̄ⲧⲉⲩⲛⲟⲩ ⲁⲡⲥⲱⲧⲏⲣ' ⲙ̄ⲛ̄ⲡⲁⲣ-¹⁵
ⲭⲁⲅⲅⲉⲗⲟⲥ' ⲁⲥⲡⲁⲍⲉ ⲛ̄ⲛⲉⲧⲟⲩ'ⲁⲁⲃ, ⲁⲩⲃⲱⲕ ⲉϩⲣⲁⲓ'²⁰ ⲙ̄ⲡⲏⲩⲉ, ϩⲛ̄ⲟⲩⲉⲓⲣⲏ'ⲛⲏ, ϩⲁⲙⲏⲛ.'
ⲙ̄ⲛ̄ⲛ̄ⲥⲱⲥ ⲁⲩⲉϫⲉⲧⲁ'ⲍⲉ ⲙ̄ⲙⲟⲟⲩ ⲙ̄ⲡⲙⲉϩ²⁵'ϩⲟⲟⲩ ⲥⲛⲁⲩ ⲛ̄ϭⲓ ⲡϫⲏ'ⲧⲉⲙⲱⲛ, ⲁⲩⲧⲣⲟⲩ'ⲉⲓⲛⲉ
ⲛⲁⲩ ⲛ̄ⲟⲩⲑⲏⲛ' ⲙ̄ⲡⲟⲩⲗⲁⲙⲭⲁⲧ̄ⲡ̄'ⲉⲩϩⲏⲣⲃ̄ϥ̄, ⲁⲩⲡⲁⲍⲧⲩ̄³⁰'ⲉⲭⲉⲛⲧⲉⲩⲁⲡⲉ ⲙ̄ⲛ̄'ⲧⲉⲩⲧⲡⲉ·
ⲁⲩⲱ'ⲧⲙⲁⲕⲁⲣⲓⲁ ⲁⲙⲁ ⲥⲟ(V i)ⲫⲓⲁ ⲁⲩⲧⲣⲟⲩϩⲓⲧⲥ̄' ⲛⲁⲩ ⲉⲭⲉⲙⲡⲃⲏⲙⲁ,' ⲡⲉϫⲁⲩ ⲛⲁⲥ
ϫⲉ ⲛ̄ⲧⲟ' ϩⲱⲱⲧⲉ ⲛ̄ⲧⲉⲟⲩ' ⲧⲉⲓ'ⲙⲓⲛⲉ, ⲉⲓⲉ ⲛⲓⲙ' ⲡⲉ ⲡⲟⲩⲣⲁⲛ; ⲡⲉϫⲉ'ⲧⲙⲁⲕⲁⲣⲓⲟⲥ ⲛⲁⲩ' ϫⲉ⁵
ⲁⲛⲅ̄ⲟⲩⲭⲣⲏⲥⲧⲓⲁ'ⲛⲟⲥ, ⲁⲛⲅ̄ⲟⲩϩⲙ̄ϩⲁⲗ'¹⁰ ⲛ̄ⲧⲉⲡⲛⲟⲩⲧⲉ ⲡⲁ'ⲥⲱⲧⲏⲣ ⲡⲁⲛⲩⲙ'ⲫⲓⲟⲥ ⲛ̄ⲥⲁⲃⲉ

---

122 R ii 4. = -ⲥⲕⲩⲗⲗⲉⲓ. 122 V. In upper margin, representation of a female face, with legend
ⲥⲟⲫⲓⲁ. i 5. ℓ. ⲛ̄ⲧⲉⲓⲙⲓⲛⲉ. ℓ. ⲏ. 7. ℓ. -ⲧⲙⲁⲕⲁⲣⲓⲁ.

---

122 R i 15. ⲁⲩⲱ A; om. B. ⲛ̄ⲗⲁⲙⲡⲁⲥ A; ⲛ̄ⲕⲉⲗ. B. 16-21. ⲙ̄ⲛ̄ⲕⲉⲃⲁ — ⲙ̄ⲙⲟⲟⲩ A; ⲉⲧⲥⲁⲛⲉⲩ-
ⲥⲡⲓⲣⲟⲟⲩⲉ ⲁⲩⲱ ⲙ̄ B. 21 f. ⲛ̄ⲧⲁⲗϭⲟ A; ⲙ̄ⲟⲧⲛⲉⲥ B. 22-24. ϩⲙ̄ⲡⲥⲱⲙⲁ ⲁⲛⲉⲧⲟⲩⲁⲁⲃ A;
ⲛⲁⲩ B. 24-26. ⲛ̄ⲧⲉⲩⲛⲟⲩ — ⲡϫⲁⲥⲓⲟⲥ A; om. B. 26. After ϣⲛⲟⲩϥⲉ, + ⲇⲉ B. 27. ⲁⲩⲛⲁⲩ
A; ⲛ̄ⲧⲉⲣⲉⲩⲛⲁⲩ B. 28-30. ⲓ̄ⲥ — ⲉⲩⲁϩⲉⲣⲁⲧⲟⲩ A; om. B. 30. ⲥⲁⲡϣⲱⲓ A; ⲉⲩⲥ. B. 32.
ⲁⲩϫⲓⲧϥ̄ A; ⲁⲩⲡⲁϩⲧⲩ̄ B. ii 1 f. ⲛ̄ⲧⲉ ⲉϥϫⲱ ⲙ̄ⲙⲟⲥ A; ⟨ⲁⲩ⟩ϫⲟⲟⲥ? B. 4-6. ϫⲉ – ⲧⲏⲣⲟⲩ A;
perhaps restore in B: ϫⲉ] ⲁⲕ[ⲥⲕⲩⲗⲗⲉⲓ ⲙ̄ⲙⲟⲕ ⲁⲕⲉⲓ ϣⲁⲣⲟⲛ ⲛ̄ⲛⲉⲓ]ⲥⲟⲡ ⲧⲏⲣⲟⲩ]ⲣ. 7. -ⲡⲥⲱ-
ⲧⲏⲣ A; ⲡϫⲟⲉⲓⲥ + ⲇⲉ B. 9. After ϣⲛⲟⲩϥⲉ, + ϫⲉ B. 10. Restore B's text as A; ϩⲟ Sottas.
11. After ⲁⲛ, + ϩⲩⲡⲟⲙⲓⲛⲉ B. ⲁⲩϥⲱⲛⲧ̄ A; ⲁⲩϥⲱⲛ ⲉϩⲟⲩⲛ B. 12 f. ⲙ̄ⲡⲉⲕⲁⲅⲱⲛ A;
ⲙ̄ⲡⲉⲕⲥ̄ Joc B. 14. Sottas' restoration of B confirmed by A. 15. After -ⲕⲗⲟⲙ, lacuna of 4 letters indicated in B. 16. After -ⲑⲣⲟⲛⲟⲥ, + ⲉⲩⲙⲉϩ ⲛ̄ⲣⲁⲩϭⲉ ⲉⲩⲛⲉⲭⲟⲩⲉⲓⲛ ⲉⲃⲟⲗ
B. ϩⲛ̄ⲑⲓⲗⲏ̄ⲙ̄ ⲛ̄ⲧⲡⲉ A; ϩⲛ̄ⲧⲁⲡⲟⲗⲓⲥ ⲑⲓⲗⲏ̄ⲙ̄ B. 17. ⲛ̄ⲧⲉⲩⲛⲟⲩ A; ⲁⲩⲱ B. 18 f. ⲙ̄ⲛ̄ⲡⲁⲣⲭⲁⲅ-
ⲅⲉⲗⲟⲥ A; om. B. 19. ⲁⲥⲡⲁⲍⲉ A; ⲁⲥⲡ. B. 19 f. ⲛ̄ⲛⲉⲧⲟⲩⲁⲁⲃ A; ⲙ̄ⲙⲟⲟⲩ + ⲙ̄ⲛ̄ⲙⲓⲭⲁⲏⲗ
B. 21 f. -ⲉⲓⲣⲏⲛⲏ A; -ⲉⲟⲟⲩ B. 22. ϩⲁⲙⲏⲛ A; om. B. 23 f. ⲁⲩⲉϫⲉⲧⲁⲍⲉ A; ⲁⲡϫⲏⲅⲉ-
ⲙⲱⲛ ⲃⲁⲥⲁⲛⲓⲍⲉ B. 24 f. ⲙ̄ⲡⲙⲉϩϩⲟⲟⲩ ⲥⲛⲁⲩ A; ⲙ̄ⲡⲉⲩⲣⲁⲥⲧⲉ B. 25 f. ⲛ̄ϭⲓ ⲡϫⲏⲅ.
A; om. B. 26-28. ⲁⲩⲧⲣⲟⲩⲉⲓⲛⲉ ⲛⲁⲩ ⲛ̄ⲟⲩⲑⲏⲛ ⲙ̄ⲡⲟⲩⲗⲁⲙⲭⲁⲧ̄ⲡ̄ A; ⲁⲩⲧⲣⲟⲩⲡⲉⲝⲧ-
ⲑⲏⲛ [ⲙ̄]ⲗ. B. 29. ⲁⲩⲡⲁⲍⲧⲩ̄ A; om. B. 30. ⲉⲭⲉⲛⲧⲉⲩⲁⲡⲉ A; ⲉⲭⲉⲙⲡⲉⲩⲥⲱⲙⲁ
B. 30 f. ⲙ̄ⲧⲉⲩⲧⲡⲉ A; om. B. 31. ⲁⲩⲱ A; ⲡⲉϫⲁⲩ ⲛ̄- B. V i 1-3. ⲁⲩⲧⲣⲟⲩϩⲓⲧⲥ̄
— ⲛⲁⲥ A; om. B. 5. ⲧⲉⲓⲙⲓⲛⲉ A; ⲛ̄ⲧⲉⲓϩⲉ B. 5 f. ⲉⲓⲉ ⲛⲓⲙ ⲡⲉ ⲡⲟⲩⲣⲁⲛ A; om.
B. 7. -ⲧⲙⲁⲕⲁⲣⲓⲟⲥ (sic) A; ⲧⲡⲁⲣⲑⲉⲛⲟⲥ B. 8 f. ⲁⲛⲅ̄- (bis) A; ⲁⲛⲟⲕ (bis) B. 10
f. -ⲛⲟⲩⲧⲉ ⲡⲁ- A; om. B. 12. ⲛ̄ⲥⲁⲃⲉ B; ⲡⲉ ⲡⲉϫⲉ ⲓ̄ⲥ B.

καταθε ´ ⲛ̄ⲧⲁⲡⲥⲟⲫⲟⲥ ⲡⲁⲩ´ⲗⲟⲥ ⲭⲟⲟⲥ ⲭⲉ ⲁⲓ̈ⲥⲃ̄ⲧⲱⲧ¹⁵ ⲉⲡⲁⲣⲍⲓⲥⲧⲁ ⲛ̄ⲛⲉⲧⲛ̄´ⲥⲱⲙⲁ ⲛ̄-
ⲟⲩⲡⲁⲣⲑⲉ´ⲛⲟⲥ ⲉⲥⲟⲩⲁⲁⲃ ⲛ̄ⲟⲩ´ⲍⲁⲓ ⲛ̄ⲟⲩⲱⲧ ⲡⲉⲭ̄ⲥ´ ⲁⲩⲱ ⲥⲟⲫⲓⲁ ⲡⲉ ⲡⲁ´ⲣⲁⲛ. ⲡⲉⲭⲉ-
ⲡⲍⲏⲅⲉ´ⲙⲱⲛ ⲛⲁⲥ ⲭⲉ ⲟⲩ´ ⲍⲱⲱⲩ ⲡⲉ ⲥⲟⲫⲓⲁ´ ⲡⲉⲭⲉⲧⲡⲁⲣⲑⲉⲛⲟⲥ´ ⲛⲁⲩ ⲭⲉ ⲧⲥⲟⲫⲓⲁ ⲙ̄-´²⁵
ⲡⲛⲟⲩⲧⲉ ⲧⲉ ⲧⲍⲉⲣ´ⲙⲏⲛⲓⲁ ⲙ̄ⲡⲁⲣⲁⲛ,´ ⲕⲁⲧⲁⲑⲉ ⲉⲧⲥⲏⲍ ⲍⲛ̄´ⲧⲉⲅⲣⲁⲫⲏ ⲭⲉ ⲉⲩⲛⲁ´ⲥⲃ̄ⲧⲉⲡⲉ
ⲛⲉⲓ̈ⲙ̄ⲙⲁⲩ³⁰ ⲛ̄ⲙⲁⲩ ⲡⲉ, ⲁⲩⲱ´ ⲉⲩⲛⲁⲥⲃ̄ⲧⲉ ⲙ̄ⲡⲉⲩ´ⲑⲣⲟⲛⲟⲥ ⲍⲓⲭⲉⲛⲛⲉ(122 V ii) ⲥⲏⲡⲉ
ⲛ̄ⲧⲡⲉ, ⲁⲛⲟⲕ· ⲡⲉⲧⲩⲟⲭⲛⲉ ⲛ̄ⲙⲁⲩ.´ ⲁⲥⲩⲱⲡⲉ ⲇⲉ ⲛ̄ⲧⲉⲣⲉⲥ´ⲭⲉⲛⲁⲓ̈ ⲁⲩⲧⲱⲛⲧ̄´⁵ ⲛ̄ϭⲓ
ⲡⲍⲏⲅⲉⲙⲱⲛ,´ ⲁⲩⲧⲣⲟⲩⲡⲉⲍⲍⲏⲧⲉ´ ⲙ̄ⲛⲛⲉⲥⲉⲕⲓⲃⲉ, ⲁⲩ´ⲣⲟⲩⲅⲉⲛⲉ ⲛ̄ⲟⲩⲡⲓⲡⲉ´ⲣⲟⲥ ⲙ̄ⲛⲟⲩⲍⲙⲟⲩ
ⲙ̄ⲛ´ⲟⲩⲅⲉⲗⲧⲏⲙ ⲙ̄ⲛ´ⲟⲩⲍⲙⲙⲉ¹⁰ ⲉⲩⲭⲏ´ⲩ, ⲁⲩⲧⲣⲟⲩⲧ ⲉⲍⲣⲁⲓ̈ ⲉⲍⲏⲧⲉ´ ⲙ̄ⲛⲛⲉⲥⲉⲕⲓⲃⲉ. ⲁⲩⲱ´
ⲍⲓⲧⲛ̄ⲧϭⲟⲙ ⲙ̄ⲡⲛⲟⲩ´ⲧⲉ¹⁵ ⲁⲛⲉⲥⲕⲓⲃⲉ ⲗⲟ ⲉⲩ´ⲧⲁⲟⲩⲉⲥⲛⲟⲩ ⲉⲃⲟⲗ, ⲁⲩ´ⲧⲁⲟⲩⲉⲉⲣⲱⲧⲉ ⲉⲃⲟⲗ,´
ⲁⲩⲛⲉⲭⲛ̄ⲕⲉⲥⲧⲱⲛⲁ´ⲣⲓⲟⲥ ⲉⲧⲃⲁⲍⲁⲛⲓⲍⲉ²⁰ ⲙ̄ⲙⲟⲥ. ⲁⲡⲙⲏⲏⲩⲉ´ ⲛ̄ⲧⲡⲟⲗⲓⲥ ⲣ̄ⲩⲡⲏⲣⲉ,´ ⲁⲩ-
ⲉⲟⲟⲩ ⲙ̄ⲡⲛⲟⲩⲧⲉ.´ ⲙ̄ⲛ̄ⲛⲥⲱⲥ ⲁⲡⲍⲏⲅⲉ´ⲙⲱⲛ ⲕⲟⲧⲩ ⲉⲛⲉⲧⲟⲩ²⁵ⲁⲁⲃ, ⲡⲉⲭⲁⲩ ⲛⲁⲩ ⲭⲉ·ⲧⲉ-
ⲧⲛ̄ⲁⲣⲑⲩⲥⲓⲁ ⲭⲉⲛⲙ̄´ⲙⲟⲛ ⲧⲁⲧⲁⲕⲉⲧⲏⲩⲧⲛ̄. ⲡⲉⲭⲉⲍⲁ´ⲧⲓⲟⲥ ⲛⲁⲩ ⲭⲉ ⲛⲉⲛⲥⲱ³⁰ⲙⲁ ⲙⲉⲛ
ⲕⲟ ⲛ̄ⲉⲍⲟⲩ´ⲥⲓⲁ ⲉⲣⲟⲟⲩ· ⲛⲉⲛⲯⲩ´ⲭⲏ ⲇⲉ ⲙ̄ⲙⲛ̄ⲧⲕⲉⲍⲟⲩ(123 R i)ⲥⲓⲁ ⲉⲍⲟⲩⲛ ⲉⲣⲟⲟⲩ ⲉ-
[ⲃⲟⲗ]´ⲃⲟⲗ ⲭⲉ ⲁⲡⲉⲛⲥⲱⲧⲏⲣ´ⲟⲩⲉⲍⲥⲁ2ⲛⲉ ⲛⲁⲛ ⲍⲛ̄´ⲡⲉⲩⲉⲟⲩⲁⲅⲅⲉⲗⲓⲟⲛ⁵ ⲉⲧⲟⲩⲁⲁⲃ ⲭⲉ
ⲙ̄ⲡⲣ̄´ⲣ̄ⲍⲟⲧⲉ ⲍⲏⲧⲟⲩ ⲛ̄ⲛⲉⲧ´ⲛⲁⲙⲟⲩⲟⲩⲧ ⲛ̄ⲛⲉⲧⲛ̄´ⲥⲱⲙⲁ· ⲁⲣⲓ2ⲟⲧⲉ´ ⲛ̄ⲧⲟⲩ ⲛ̄ⲍⲏⲧⲩ̄ ⲙ̄-´¹⁰
ⲡⲉⲧⲉⲟⲩⲛ̄ϭ̄ϭⲟⲙ´ ⲙ̄ⲙⲟⲩ ⲉⲧⲁⲕⲟ ⲛ̄´ⲧⲉⲯⲩⲭⲏ ⲙⲛ̄ⲡⲥⲱ´ⲙⲁ ⲍⲛ̄ⲧⲅⲉⲍⲉⲛⲛⲁ´ ⲛ̄ⲥⲁⲧⲉ. ⲧⲉ-

---

122 V ii 15. ℓ. ⲁⲛⲉⲥⲉⲕⲓⲃⲉ.   18. ℓ. ⲁⲩⲛⲉⲭⲛ̄ⲕⲉⲥⲧ.

---

122 V i 13. ⲛ̄ⲧⲁⲡⲥⲟⲫⲟⲥ ⲡⲁⲩⲗⲟⲥ ⲭⲟⲟⲥ A; ⲉⲧⲥⲏⲍ B.   15f. ⲛ̄ⲛⲉⲧⲛ̄ⲥⲱⲙⲁ A; ⲙ̄ⲙ[ⲱ]ⲧⲛ̄ B.
23. -ⲧⲡⲁⲣⲑⲉⲛⲟⲥ A; -ⲧⲙⲁⲕⲁⲣⲓⲁ B.   24. Probably [ⲛⲁⲩ] in B, as in A.   24f. B's
text lost; it must have differed from A's; see 26, below.   25f. Restore ⲧⲍⲉⲣⲙⲏⲛ-
[ⲛⲓ]ⲁ in B, as A.   26. After ⲙ̄ⲡⲁⲣⲁⲛ, + [ⲧⲉ] ⲧⲥⲟⲫⲓⲁ ⲙ̄ⲡⲛⲟⲩⲧⲉ B.   28. After ⲧⲉⲅⲣⲁ-
ⲫⲏ, + ⲉⲧⲟⲩⲁⲁⲃ B.   28. – ii 2. ⲉⲩⲛⲁⲥⲃ̄ⲧⲉⲡⲉ — ⲛ̄ⲙⲁⲩ A; ⲛⲉⲓ̈ⲟ ⲛ̄ⲙⲁⲩ ⲡⲉ ⲉⲩ[ⲛⲁ-
ⲥ]ⲃⲉⲧⲉⲙ̄ⲡⲏⲩⲉ ⲁ[ⲩⲱ] ⲉⲩⲛⲁⲡⲱⲣ̄ϫ ⲉⲃⲟⲗ ⲙ̄ⲡⲉⲩⲑⲣⲟⲛⲟⲥ [ⲍⲓ]ⲭⲛ̄ⲛ̄ⲧⲏⲩ? ⲛⲉⲓ̈ⲟ?]ⲛ̄ⲙⲁⲩ
ⲡⲉ B.   3f. ⲁⲥⲩⲱⲡⲉ — ⲁⲩⲧⲱⲛⲧ̄ A; ⲁ[ⲩⲱ ⲁⲩⲕⲉⲗ]ⲉⲩⲉ B.   6f. ⲁⲩⲧⲣⲟⲩⲡⲉⲍⲍⲏⲧⲉ
ⲙ̄ⲛⲛⲉⲥⲉⲕⲓⲃⲉ A; ⲁⲩⲡⲱⲧⲉ ⲛ̄ⲧⲉⲥⲕⲓⲃⲉ ⲥⲛ̄ⲧⲉ ⲙ̄ⲡⲍⲏⲧⲉ B.   8f. -ⲛ̄ⲟⲩⲡⲓⲡⲉⲣⲟⲥ A;
ⲛ̄ⲍⲙ̄ⲡⲓⲡⲣⲉ B.   9f. ⲙ̄ⲛⲟⲩⲅⲉⲗⲧⲏⲙ A; om. B.   11. After ⲉⲩⲭⲏⲩ, + ⲛ̄ⲥⲉⲧⲁⲍⲟⲩ ⲙ̄ⲡⲁⲛⲉⲩ-
ⲉⲣⲏⲩ B.   12f. ⲁⲩⲧⲣⲟⲩⲧ — ⲙ̄ⲛⲛⲉⲥⲉⲕⲓⲃⲉ A; ⲛ̄ⲥⲉⲡⲁⲍⲧⲟⲩ ⲉⲍⲣⲁⲓ̈ ⲉⲭⲱⲟⲩ B.   16–22.
ⲁⲩⲧⲁⲟⲩⲉⲉⲣⲱⲧⲉ — ⲙ̄ⲡⲛⲟⲩⲧⲉ A; ⲁⲩⲱ ⲁⲛⲉⲕⲉⲥⲧ[ⲱ]ⲛⲁⲣⲓⲟⲥ ⲕⲁⲧⲟⲟⲧⲟⲩ ⲉⲃⲟⲗ B.   23f.
ⲁⲡ2. ⲕⲟⲧⲩ ⲉⲛⲉⲧⲟⲩⲁⲁⲃ A; ⲡⲉⲭⲉⲡ2. ⲛ̄ⲛⲉⲧⲟⲩ. B.   25. ⲡⲉⲭⲁⲩ ⲛⲁⲩ A; om. B.   26.-ⲣ̄-
ⲑⲩⲥⲓⲁ A; -ⲑⲩⲥⲓⲁⲍⲉ B.   27f. ⲧⲁⲧⲁⲕⲉⲧⲏⲩⲧⲛ̄ A; ⲛ̄ⲧⲉⲧⲛ̄ⲁⲙⲟⲩ ⲕⲁⲕⲱⲥ B.   30f.
ⲕⲟ ⲛ̄ⲉⲍⲟⲣⲥⲓⲁ A; ⲟⲩⲛ̄ⲧⲁⲕⲉⲍ. ⲉⲍⲟⲩⲛ B.   31–123 R i 1. ⲛⲉⲛⲯⲩⲭⲏ — ⲉⲣⲟⲟⲩ A; om.
B (by homoteleuton).   1–3. ⲉⲃⲟⲗ ⲭⲉ — ⲟⲩⲉⲍⲥⲁ2ⲛⲉ A; ⲛ̄ⲑⲉ ⲛ̄ⲧⲁⲡⲉⲛⲭⲟⲉⲓⲥ ⲭⲟⲟⲥ B.
3f. ⲍⲛ̄ⲡⲉⲩⲉⲟⲩⲁⲅⲅⲉⲗⲓⲟⲛ A; ⲍⲛ̄ⲡⲉⲩ. B.   8. After - ⲥⲱⲙⲁ, +ⲁⲗⲗⲁ B.   9. ⲛ̄ⲧⲉⲩ A;
om. B.   ⲛ̄ⲍⲏⲧⲩ̄ A; ⲍⲏⲧⲩ̄ B.   10. -ϭⲟⲙ A; -ϭⲟⲙ B.   11–13. ⲛ̄ⲧⲉⲯⲩⲭⲏ ⲙⲛ̄ⲡⲥⲱ-
ⲙⲁ A; ⲛ̄ⲧⲉⲧⲉⲛⲩ̄ ⲙ̄ⲛ̄ⲡⲉⲧⲉⲛⲥ. B.   13. After - ⲥⲱⲙⲁ, + 2ⲣⲁⲓ̈ B.   14. If ⲛ̄ⲍⲁⲧⲉ
in fact stood in B, it should be corrected to ⲛ̄ⲥⲁⲧⲉ, as in A.

ⲚⲞⲨ ⲅ̄ⲉ ⲡⲉⲛⲭⲟⲉⲓⲥ ⲓ̅ⲥ̅ ⲡⲉⲧⲟ ⲛ̅ⲭⲟⲉⲓⲥ ⲉⲛⲉⲛⲥⲱⲙⲁ ⲙ̅ⲛ̅ⲛⲉⲛⲯⲩⲭⲏ ⲙ̅ⲛ̅ⲛⲉⲛⲡ̅ⲛ̅ⲁ̅ ⲍⲣⲁⲓ
ⲇⲉ ⲍ̅ⲛ̅ⲛⲉⲍⲟⲟⲩ ⲉⲧ̅ⲙ̅ⲙⲁⲩ ⲛⲉⲣⲉⲫⲣⲁⲛ̅ⲧⲓⲟⲥ ⲟ ⲇⲉⲡⲁⲣⲭⲟⲥ ⲉⲧⲡⲟⲗⲓⲥ ⲡⲓⲟⲙ ⲙ̅ⲛ̅ ⲡⲉⲥⲧⲟⲟⲩ,
ⲉⲣⲉⲫⲓⲗⲓ̅ⲡⲡⲟⲥ ⲟ ⲛ̅ⲍⲣⲏⲡⲁⲣⲓ̅ⲟⲥ ⲉⲁⲗⲉⲍⲁⲛⲇⲣⲟⲩ ⲡⲟⲗⲓⲥ ⲉⲧⲉⲧⲡⲟⲗⲓⲥ ⲙ̅ⲡⲓⲟⲙ ⲧⲉ, ⲉⲣⲉⲗⲉⲱ̅ⲛⲧⲓⲟⲥ ⲟ ⲛ̅ⲗⲟⲅⲓⲥ̅ⲧⲏⲥ ⲉⲕⲁⲙⲏ ⲡⲟⲗⲓⲥ. ⲧⲟⲧⲉ ⲁⲩⲟⲩⲱⲛ ⲛ̅ⲣⲱⲟⲩ ⲛ̅ϭⲓ ⲓⲟⲩⲗⲓⲟⲥ ⲡ-
ⲕⲟⲩⲣ̅ⲥⲟⲛ, ⲁⲩⲧⲗⲓⲃⲓⲗⲗⲟⲥ (123 R ii) ⲍⲁⲛ̅ⲍⲁⲅⲓⲟⲥ ⲙ̅ⲙⲁⲣ̅ⲧⲩⲣⲟⲥ· ⲡⲉⲭⲁⲩ ⲙ̅ⲡ̅ⲍⲏⲅⲉⲙⲱⲛ ⲭⲉ ⲡⲁⲭⲟ̅ⲉⲓⲥ ⲡ̅ⲍⲏⲅⲉⲙⲱⲛ, ⲥ̅ⲱⲧⲙ̅ ⲉⲣⲟⲓ ⲛ̅ⲧⲁ̅ⲩⲁⲭⲉ ⲙ̅ⲛ̅ⲧⲉⲕⲁ̅ⲣⲉⲧⲏ ⲉⲩⲱⲡⲉ ⲉⲕⲱⲁⲛⲕⲁⲛⲉⲓ̅ⲣⲱ̅ⲙⲉ ⲉⲧⲉⲓⲣⲉ ⲛ̅ⲛⲉⲓ̅ⲍ̅ⲃⲏⲩⲉ ⲉⲙⲁⲅⲓⲁ ⲍ̅ⲛ̅ⲧⲉⲓⲡⲟⲗⲓⲥ, ⲥⲉⲛⲁ̅ⲡⲓⲥⲧⲉⲩⲉ
ⲉⲣⲟⲟⲩ ⲧⲏⲣⲟⲩ ⲛ̅ⲥⲉⲩⲙ̅ⲯⲉ ⲙ̅ⲡⲉⲩ̅ⲛⲟⲩⲧⲉ. ⲁⲗⲗⲁ ⲥⲱⲧⲙ̅ ⲉⲣⲟⲓ ⲛ̅ⲧⲁⲭⲱ̅ ⲛⲁⲕ ⲙ̅ⲡⲉⲓ̅ⲩⲁⲭⲉ. ⲟⲩⲛ̅ⲟⲩⲕⲟⲩⲓ̅ ⲙⲡⲟ̅ⲗⲓⲥ ⲛ̅ⲥⲁ ⲡⲉⲙ̅ⲛ̅ⲧ̅ ⲙ̅ⲙⲟⲛ, ⲉⲟⲩⲛ̅ⲍ̅ⲛ̅ⲣⲡⲉ ⲉⲩⲉ ⲛ̅ⲍⲏⲧⲥ̅, ⲉⲥ-
ⲍⲓⲭⲉⲛⲟⲩⲡⲅⲏ ⲙ̅ⲙⲟⲟⲩ ⲛ̅ⲩⲁⲩ̅ⲙⲟⲩⲧⲉ ⲉⲣⲟⲥ ⲭⲉ ⲫⲁ̅ⲗⲉⲍ, ⲍ̅ⲛ̅ⲟⲩⲧⲙⲉ ⲛ̅̅ⲩⲁⲩ̅ⲙⲟⲩⲧⲉ
ⲉⲣⲟⲩ̅ⲭⲉ ⲡⲟⲩⲃⲉⲥⲧ· ⲙⲁ̅ⲣⲉⲛⲭⲓⲧⲟⲩ ⲉⲡⲙⲁ̅ⲉⲧⲙ̅ⲙⲁⲩ ⲍⲁⲃⲟⲗ ⲛ̅ⲧⲉⲓⲡⲟⲗⲓⲥ ⲛ̅ⲧⲁⲅⲉⲓ̅ⲣⲉ
ⲛ̅ⲛⲉⲓ̅ⲍⲃⲏⲩⲉ ⲧⲏ̅ⲣⲟⲩ ⲛ̅ⲍⲏⲧⲥ̅· ⲡⲉⲧ̅ⲉⲍⲛⲁⲕ ⲧ̅ⲛ̅ⲁⲁⲁⲩ (V i) ⲛⲁⲩ ⲍ̅ⲛ̅ⲡⲙⲁ ⲉⲧⲙ̅ⲙⲁⲩ.
ⲉⲓ̅ⲉ ⲛ̅ⲥⲉⲟⲩⲱ̅ⲯ̅ ⲛ̅ⲛⲉⲛⲛⲟⲩⲧⲉ ⲉⲧⲧⲁⲓ̅ⲏⲩ ⲓ̅ⲉ ⲛ̅ⲥⲉ̅ⲭⲓ ⲛ̅ⲧⲉⲩⲁⲡⲟⲫⲁⲥⲓⲥ· ⲧ̅ⲥⲟⲟⲩⲛ̅ ⲅⲁⲣ
ⲭⲉ ⲙ̅ⲛ̅ⲗⲁⲁⲩ ⲛⲁ̅ⲩⲁⲩⲧ̅ⲛ̅ ⲍ̅ⲛ̅ⲡⲙⲁ ⲉⲧⲙ̅ⲙⲁⲩ. ⲩⲁⲛⲧⲉⲛⲉⲓⲣⲉ ⲙ̅(ⲛ̅)ⲛⲉⲓ̅ⲁⲡⲟⲥⲧⲁⲧⲏⲥ
ⲛ̅ⲑⲉ ⲉⲧⲉⲍⲛⲁⲛ· ⲍ̅ⲣⲁⲓ ⲇⲉ ⲍ̅ⲛ̅ⲡⲉⲍⲟⲟⲩ ⲉⲧⲙ̅ⲙⲁⲩ ⲁⲩⲕⲉⲗⲉ̅ⲩⲉ ⲛ̅ϭⲓ ⲡ̅ⲍⲏⲅⲉⲙⲱ(ⲛ) ⲉ-
ⲧⲣⲟⲩⲥⲱⲛ̅ⲍ̅ ⲛ̅ⲛ̅ⲍⲁⲅⲓⲟⲥ ⲙ̅ⲙⲁⲣⲧⲩ̅ⲣⲟⲥ ⲛ̅ⲥⲁ ⲡⲁⲍⲟⲩ ⲛ̅ⲛⲉⲍ̅ⲧⲱⲣ, ⲁⲡⲁ ⲯⲛ̅ⲟⲩ̅ϥⲉ ⲙ̅ⲛ̅-
ⲛⲉⲩ̅ⲥⲛⲏⲩ· ⲁⲩⲕⲉⲗⲉ̅ⲩⲉ ⲛ̅ⲥⲉ̅ⲭⲓⲧⲟⲩ ⲉⲧⲉ̅ⲫⲩⲗⲁⲕⲏ ⲩⲁⲛ̅ⲧⲉⲩⲕⲟⲧϥ̅ ⲉⲍⲣⲁⲓ ⲉⲧ̅ⲡⲟⲗⲓⲥ.
ⲡ̅ⲍⲁⲅⲓⲟⲥ ⲇⲉ ⲁⲡⲁ ⲯⲛ̅ⲟⲩϥⲉ ⲙ̅ⲛ̅ⲛⲉϥ̅ⲥⲛⲏⲩ ⲉⲩⲛⲁⲭⲓⲧϥ̅ ⲉⲃⲟⲗ ⲁⲩⲡⲉⲩⲟⲩⲟⲓ̅ ⲉⲣⲟϥ

---

123 R i 20 f. l. <ⲉⲧ>ⲫⲣⲁⲛⲧⲓⲟⲥ?   24 f. = -ⲍⲣⲓⲡⲁⲣⲓⲟⲥ, *riparius*.   31. = - ⲕⲟⲩⲣⲥⲱⲣ, *cursor*. 32. = -ⲗⲓⲃⲉⲗⲗⲟⲥ, *libellus*.   ii 20. Second ⲉ added.   V i 2. l. ⲏ (so B.)   4. l. ⲏ (so B).

123 R i 15. ⲡⲉⲛⲭⲟⲉⲓⲥ A; ⲡⲭ̅ B.   15 f. ⲡⲉⲧⲟ ⲛ̅ⲭⲟⲉⲓⲥ A; so, one suspects, B (Munier ⲡⲉⲧⲛ̅ⲕ̅., Sottas ⲡⲉⲧⲣ̅ⲕ̅.)   18-29. ⲙ̅ⲛ̅ⲉⲧⲡ̅ⲛ̅ⲡⲁ −ⲡⲟⲗⲓⲥ A; om. B.   30. ⲁⲩⲟⲩⲱⲛ ⲛ̅ⲣⲱⲟⲩ A; ⲁⲩⲟⲩⲱⲩⲃ̅ B.   31. ⲡⲕⲟⲩⲣⲥⲟⲛ A; ⲡⲕⲟⲩⲥⲟⲛ (*sic*) B.   32 - ii 2. ⲁⲩⲧⲗⲓⲃⲓⲗⲗⲟⲥ — ⲙ̅ⲙⲁⲣⲧⲩⲣⲟⲥ A; om. B (but see next n.).   3. After ⲙ̅ⲡ̅ⲍⲏⲅⲉⲙⲱⲛ, +ⲉⲩⲧⲗⲓⲃⲉⲗⲗⲟⲥ ⲍⲁ-ⲛⲉⲧⲟⲩⲁⲁⲃ B.   3 f. ⲡⲁⲭⲟⲉⲓⲥ ⲡ̅ⲍⲏⲅ. A; om. B.   5. After ⲉⲣⲟⲓ, +ⲡⲁⲭⲟⲉⲓⲥ B.   5-7. ⲛ̅ⲧⲁⲩⲁⲭⲉ ⲙ̅ⲡⲧⲉⲕⲁⲣⲉⲧⲏ A; om. B.   7 ⲉⲩⲱⲡⲉ A; ⲭⲉ B.   9 f. ⲉⲧⲉⲓⲣⲉ −ⲉⲙⲁⲅⲓⲁ A; om. B (but see next n.).   11. After ⲍ̅ⲛ̅ⲧⲉⲓⲡⲟⲗⲓⲥ, +ⲉⲧⲉⲓⲣⲉ ⲛⲛⲉⲍⲃⲏⲩⲉ (*sic*) ⲙ̅ⲫⲁⲛⲧⲁⲥⲓⲁ ⲍ̅ⲛ̅ⲧⲉⲩⲙⲁⲧⲙⲁⲍⲟⲥ B.   12. After ⲉⲣⲟⲟⲩ, +ⲛ̅ϭⲓ ⲛⲁⲧⲉⲓⲡⲟⲗⲓⲥ B.   13 f. ⲛ̅ⲥⲉⲩⲙ̅ⲯⲉ ⲙ̅ⲡⲉⲩⲛⲟⲩⲧⲉ A; om. B.   18. ⲛ̅ⲥⲁ − A; ⲥⲁ − B.   19 f. ⲉⲩⲟⲩⲍ̅ⲛ̅ⲣⲡⲉⲉⲩⲉ A; ⲉⲣⲉⲍⲉⲛ-ⲉⲣⲡⲉ B.   22. ⲛ̅ − A; ⲉ− B.   24. ⲍ̅ⲛ̅ⲟⲩⲧⲙⲉ A; ⲍⲉⲛⲟⲩⲙⲁ B. ⲛ̅ − A; ⲉ− B.   28. ⲍⲁⲃⲟⲗ A; ⲛ̅ⲥⲁⲃⲟⲗ B.   29 f. ⲛ̅ⲧⲁⲅⲉⲓⲣⲉ ⲛ̅ − A; ⲛ̅ⲧⲁⲅⲉⲣ− B.   31. After ⲛ̅ⲍⲏⲧⲥ̅, + ⲁⲩⲱ B.   32. ⲧ̅ⲛ̅ⲁⲁⲁⲩ A; ⲁⲣⲓⲩ B.   V i 2. ⲉⲓ̅ⲉ A; ⲏ B.   3. ⲛ̅ⲛⲉⲛⲛⲟⲩⲧⲉ A; ⲛ̅ⲛⲉⲛ. B.   4. ⲓ̅ⲉ A; ⲏ B.   4 f. ⲛ̅ⲥⲉⲭⲓ ⲛ̅ⲧⲉⲩⲁⲡⲟⲫⲁⲥⲓⲥ A; ⲛ̅ⲥⲉⲧⲁⲡⲟⲫⲁⲥⲓⲥ ⲉⲣⲟⲟⲩ ⲙ̅ⲙⲁⲩ B.   6. ⲅⲁⲣ A; ⲁⲛⲟⲕ B.   7. ⲛⲁⲩⲁⲩⲧ̅ⲛ̅ A; ⲛⲁⲕⲱⲗⲩ ⲙ̅ⲙⲟⲕ B.   8 ff. Loss of text from B.   21 f. ⲉⲧⲉⲫⲩⲗⲁⲕⲏ A; [ⲉ]ⲡⲡⲱⲁ ⲉⲧⲙ̅ⲙⲁⲩ B.   23. -ⲕⲟⲧϥ A; -ⲕⲧⲟⲩ+ ⲉⲍⲣⲁⲓ B.   From 24 to 124 R ii 18 no text in B corresponding to A's; whether this is due to scribal omission in B (the two passages begin almost identically) or loss of a folio there seems uncertain.

ⲡⲉⲝⲁⲩ ⲛⲁⲩ ⳉⲉ ⳙ̄ⲡⲉⲕⲟⲩⳉⲁⲓ̈ ⲱ ⲡⲉⲛⲏ̇ⲉⲓⲱⲧ ⳙ̄ⲡⲉⲣⲡⲱⲧ ⲛ̄ⲅ̄ⲕⲁⲁⲛ ⳉⲥⲱⲕ · (123
V ii) ⲁⲣⲓⲡⲉⲛⲙⲉⲉⲩⲉ ⳉⲉⲕⲁⲥ ⳙ̄ⲛⲉⲛⲡⲱⲣⳝ ⲉⲛⲉ̇ⲛⲉⲣⲏⲩ ⳅⳜⲡⲏⲓ̈ ⳙ̄ⲡ̇ⲛⲟⲩⲧⲉ. ⲡⳉⲁⲅⲓⲟⲥ ⲇⲉ ⲁⲡⲁ ⲩⲛ̅ⲟⲩϥⲉ ⲁⲩϥⲉⲓ̇ⲛⲉⲩⲃⲁⲗ ⲉⳉⲣⲁⲓ̇, ⲁⲩⲥⲟⲡ̄ⲥ̄ ⳙ̄ⲡ̅ⲛⲟⲩⲧⲉ ⲉϥ̅ϫⲱ ⳙ̄ⲙⲟⲥ ⳉⲉ
ⲥⲱⲧ̅ⳙ̄ ⲉⲣⲟⲓ̈ ⲡⲁⳉⲟⲉⲓⲥ ⲓ̅ⲥ̅ ⲡⲉⳉⲥ̅ ⲛ̄ⲑⲉ ⲛ̄ⲧⲁⲛⲉⲓ̇ⲣⲱⲙⲉ ⲡⲓⲥⲧⲉⲩⲉ ⲉⲡⲉⲕ̇ⲣⲁⲛ ⲉⲧⲟⲩⲁⲁⲃ ⲉⲃⲟⲗ ⳉⲓⲧⲟⲟⲧ, ⲛ̄ⲧⲉⲓ̈ⳅⲉ ⳙ̄ⲡⲣⲁⲁⲩ ⲛ̄ⲛⲙⲙⲟ ⲉⲣⲟⲛ. ⳉⳉⲟⲥⲟⲛ ⲇⲉ ⲉⲣⲉⲡⳉⲁⲅⲓⲟⲥ
ⲁⲡⲁ ⲩⲛ̅ⲟⲩϥⲉ ⳉⲱ ⲛ̄ⲛⲁⲓ̈, ⲁⲛ̅ⲟⲩⲉⲣⲏ̄ⲧⲉ ⳙ̄ⲡⲉⳉ̇ⲧⲟ ⲉⲧⲉⲣⲉⲡⳉⲏⲅⲉⲙⲱⲛ ⳟ ⲧⲁⲗⲏⲩⲉⲣⲟⲩ
ⲁⲩⲧⲱⲗⳝ̄ ⲉⳉⲟⲩⲛ ⲉⲣⲟϥ, ⳙ̄ⲡⲉϥⲉϣⳛⳜϭⲟⲙ ⲉⲕⲓⲙ ⲉⲡⲓⲥⲁ ⲙ̄ⲛ̄ⲡⲁⲓ̈. ⲡⳉⲁⲅⲓⲟⲥ ⲇⲉ ⲁⲡⲁ
ⲩⲛ̅ⲟⲩϥⲉ ⲡⲉⳉⲁϥ ⳙ̄ⲡⳉⲏⲅⲉⲙⲱⲛ ⳉⲉ ⳟ ⲩⲉ ⲡⲉⲅⲣⲁⲧⲟⲥ ⳙ̄ⲡⲁⳉⲟⲉⲓⲥ ⲓ̅ⲥ̅ ⲡⲉⳉⲥ̅, ⲛ̄ⲑⲉ ⲛ̄ⲧⲁ-
ⲛⲉⲓ̈ⲣⲱⲙⲉ ⲡⲓⲥⲧⲉⲩⲉ ⲉⲡⲉⲩⲣⲁⲛ ⲉⲃⲟⲗ ⳉⲓⲧⲟⲟⲧ, ⲛ̄ⲧⲟⲕ ⳉⲱⲱⲕ ⲱ ⲡⳉⲏⲅⲉ (124 Ri) ⲙⲱⲛ
ⲛ̄ⲅ̄ⲛⲁⲥⲛ̄ⲧ ⲡⲉⲓ̈ⲙⲁ ⲉⲃⲟⲗ ⲁⲛ ⳙ̄ⲡⲉ̇ⲕⲉⲓⲛⲉ ⲛ̄ⲛⲁⲕⲉⲥⲛⲏⲩ ⲛⲙ̄ⲙⲁⲓ̈ ⲉⲡⲙⲁ ⲉⲧⲕ̇ⲛⲁⳉⲓⲧ
ⲉⲣⲟϥ, ⳉⲉⲕⲁⲥ ⳙ̄ⲛⲉⲛⲡⲱⲣⳝ ⲉⲛⲉ̇ⲛⲉⲣⲏⲩ ⳅⳜⲡⲏⲓ̈ ⳙ̄ⲡⲛⲟⲩⲧⲉ. ⲁϥⲕⲉⲗⲉ̇ⲩⲉ ⲛ̄ϭⲓ ⲡⳉⲏⲅⲉ-
ⲙⲱⲛ ⲉⲧⲣⲟⲩⲥⲱⳉ̄ ⳙ̄ⲡ̇ⲥⲉⲉⲡⲉ ⲛ̄ⲛⲉⲧⲟⲩⲁⲁⲃ ⳙ̄ⲙⲁⲣⲧⲩⲣⲟⲥ ⲉⳉⲟⲩ(ⲛ) ⲉⲛⲉⲩⲉⲣⲏⲩ, ⲁⲩⳉⲓ-
ⲧⲟⲩ ⳉⲁⲧⲉⲩⳅⲏ ⲉⳉⲟⲩ(ⲛ) ⲉⲕⲟⲙⲏ ⲡⲟⲗⲕ. ⲛ̄ⳉⲁⲅⲓⲟⲥ ⲇⲉ ⳙ̄ⲙⲁⲣ̇ⲧⲩⲣⲟⲥ ⲛⲉⲩⳉⲓⲟⲩⲁ ⲉⲁⲣⲓⲁ-
ⲛⲟⲥ ⲡⳉⲏⲅⲉ̇ⲙⲱⲛ ⲉⲩⳉⲱ̇ ⳙ̄ⲙⲟⲩ ⲙⲛ̄ⲛⲉⲩ̇ⲛⲟⲩⲧⲉ ⲉⲩϫⲱ ⳙ̄ⲙⲟⲥ ⳉⲉ ⲛ̄ⳉⲉⲛⲛⲟⲩⲧⲉ
ⲁⲛ ⲛⲉ, ⲁⲗⲗⲁ ⳅⲛ̄ⲃⲉⲗⲗⲉⲉⲩ ⲛ̄ⲕⲟⲩⲣ ⲛⲉ. ⲡⳉⲁⲅⲓⲟⲥ ⲇⲉ ⲁⲡⲁ ⲩⲛ̅ⲟⲩϥⲉ ⲛ̄ⲧⲉⲣⲉϥⲥⲱ̇-
ⲧⳙ̄ ⲉⲛ̄ⳉⲁⲅⲓⲟⲥ ⲉⲩϫⲱ̇ⳟ ⲛ̄ⲛⲉⲉⲓⲇⲱⲗⲟ(ⲛ), ⲁϥⲣ̄ⲙⲉⲉⲩⲉ ⳙ̄ⲡⳟⳉⲁϫⲉ ⲉⲧⲉⳉ̄ⲥ ⳅⳜⲡⳉⲓⲉⲣⲟ-
ⲯⲁⲗⲧⲏⲥ ⲇⲁⲩⲉⲓⲇ ⳉⲉ ⲛ̄ⲉⲓⲁⲩ (Rii) ⲗⲟⲛ ⲛ̄ⲉⲛ̄ⳉⲉⲑⲛⲟⲥ ⳅⲛ̄ⳅⲁⲧ ⳅⲓⲛⲟⲩ ⲛⲉ, ⳅⲛ̄ⳅⲃⲏⲩⲉ
ⲛ̄ϭⲓⳝ ⳟ̄ⲣⲱⲙⲉ ⲛⲉ· ⲟⲩⲛ̄ⲃⲁⲗ ⳙ̄ⲙⲟⲟⲩ, ⲛ̄ⲥⲉⲛⲁⲩ ⲉⲃⲟⲗ ⲁⲛ· ⲟⲩⳙ̄ⲙⲁ̇ⲁϫⲉ ⳙ̄ⲙⲟⲟⲩ, ⲛ̄-
ⲥⲉ̇ⲥⲱⲧⳙ̄ ⲁⲛ· ⲣⲱⲟ̇ⳙ̄ⲙⲟⲟⲩ, ⲙⲉⲩⳉⲁϫⲉ· ⳉⲁⲁⲧⲟⲩ ⳙ̄ⲙⲟⲟⲩ, ⲙⲉⲩⳉⲱⲗⳙ̄· ⲛⲉⲩ̇-
ϭⲓϫ ⳙ̄ⲙⲟⲟⲩ, ⲙⲉⲩϭⲟⲙ̇ϭⳙ̄· ⲛⲉⲩⲟⲩⲉⲣⲏⲧⲉ ⳙ̄ⲙⲟⲟⲩ, ⲙⲉⲩⲙⲟⲟϣⲉ· ⲉⲩⲉⲣⲧⲉⲩⳅⲉ ⲛ̄ϭⲓ
ⲛⲉⲛ̇ⲧⲁⲩⲧⲁⲙⲓⲟⲟⲩ ⲙⲛ̄ⲟⲩⲟⲛ ⲛⲓⲙ ⲉⲧⲛⲁⳉ̇ⲧⲉ ⲉⲣⲟⲟⲩ. ⲡⳉⲁⲅⲓ̇ⲟⲥ ⲇⲉ ⲁⲡⲁ ⲩⲛ̅ⲟⲩϥⲉ
ⲁϥⲥⲱⲕ ⳉⲁⳉⲱⲟⲩ ⲛ̄ⲛⲉⲧⲟⲩⲁⲁⲃ ⲛ̄ⲑⲉ ⲛ̄ⲟⲩⳉⲱⲥ ⲉⲛⲁ̇ⲛⲟⲩⲩ ⲉϥⲥⲱⲕ ⳉⲓ̇ⳅⲏ ⳟⲛⲉⲩ-
ⲉⲥⲟⲟⲩ· ⲁⲩⲱ ⲛⲉⲩϫⲱ ⳙ̄ⲡⲓ̇ⲯⲁⲗⲙⲟⲥ ⲛ̄ⲧⲉ̇ⲇⲁⲇ ⲉⲩϫⲱ ⳙ̄ⲙⲟⲥ ⳉⲉ ⲁⲙⲏⲓ̈ⲧ̄ⲛ̄ ⲛⲁϣⲏ̇ⲣⲉ
ⲛ̄ⲧⲉⲧⲛ̄ⲥⲱⲧⳙ̄ ⲉⲣⲟⲓ̈ ⲧⲁ⳨ⲥⲃⲱ ⲛⲏⲧⲛ̄ ⲉⲑⲟⲧⲉ ⳙ̄ⲡ̇ϫⲟⲉⲓⲥ· ⲛⲓⲙ ⲡⲉ ⲡⲣⲱⲙⲉ ⲉⲧ(ⲱ̇)ⲟⲩ-
ⲉϣⲡⲱⲛ̄ⳉ ⲛ̄ⲧ̇ⲙⲉ ⲛⲁⲩ ⲉⲛ̄ⳅⲟⲟⲩ ⲉⲧ̇ⲛⲁⲛⲟⲩⲟⲩ; ⲙⲁⲣⲉϥ̇ⲧⲁⲗϭⲉⲡⲉϥⲗⲁⲥ ⲉⲃⲟⲗ ⳅⳜ-
ⲡⲡⲉⲑⲟⲟⲩ, ⲁⲩⲱ̇ⲛⲉϥⲥⲡⲟⲧⲟⲩ ⲉⲧⳙ̄ϫⲱ ⲛ̄ⲟⲩⲕⲣⲟϥ· ⲙⲁⲣⲉϥϣⲓⲛⲉ ⲛ̄ⲥⲁ̇⳨ⲣⲏⲛⲏ ⲛⳟ̄ⲡⲱⲧ

---

124 Ri 15. l. ⲉⲕⲟⲙⲏ n. 22. ⲛ̄ⳉⲉⲛⲛ.: first ⲛ added. 27. ⲉⲛ̄ⳅ.: ⲉ added. ii 13.
ⲛⲉⲩ-: ⲩ added. Vi 1 f. l. ⲉⲧⲙⲉ ⲛ̄ⲛⲁⲩ.

124 Rii 20. ⲁⲩⲥⲱⲕ A; ⲛⲉⲩⲥⲱⲕ B. 21. ⲛ̄ⲛⲉⲧⲟⲩⲁⲁⲃ A; om. B. 22 f. ⲉⲛⲁⲛⲟⲩⲩ A;
om. B. 23 f. ⳉⲓ⳽ⳅⲏ A; ⳉⲁⳉⲱⲟⲩ B. 25. ⲁⲩⲱ A; om. B. 25–27. ⲛⲉⲩϫⲱ – ⲇⲁⲇ
A; ⲛⲉⲩⲯⲁⲗⲗⲉⲓ B. 27. ⲉⲩϫⲱ A; ⲉϥϫⲱ B. 31. ⲉⲑⲟⲧⲉ A; ⳅⲉⲛⲑ. B. Vi 1 f. ⲛⲧⲙⲉ
(ⲥⲓⲥ) A; ⲉⲧⲙⲉ B. 5. ⳅⳜ- A; ⳙ̄- B. 9. After -⳨ⲣⲏⲛⲏ, †ⲁⲩⲱ B.

ⲛⲥⲱⲥ· ⲭⲉ ⲉⲣⲉⲛ̄ⲃⲁⲗ' ⲙ̄ⲡϫⲟⲉⲓⲥ ϭⲱϣⲧ' ⲉⲭⲛ̄ⲛ̄ⲇⲓⲕⲁⲓⲟⲥ,' ⲁⲩⲱ ⲉⲣⲉⲡⲉϥⲙⲁⲁϫⲉ
ⲣⲟⲕⲉ ⲉⲡⲉⲩⲥⲟⲡⲥ̄[15] ϣⲁⲉⲛⲉϩ, ϩⲁⲙⲏⲛ.' ⲁⲩⲱ ⲁⲩⲟⲩⲱϣϥ' ⲛ̄ϭⲓ ⲛ̄ⲛⲉⲧⲟⲩⲁⲁⲃ' ϫⲉ
ϩⲁⲙⲏⲛ.' ⲛⲉⲩⲙⲟⲟϣⲉ ϩⲓⲧⲉϩⲓⲏ[20] ⲛ̄ϭⲓ ⲛ̄ϩⲁⲅⲓⲟⲥ ⲙ̄ⲙⲁⲣ'ⲧⲩⲣⲟⲥ ϣⲁⲛⲧⲟⲩ'ⲡⲱϩ ⲉ-
ⲕⲁⲙⲏ ⲡⲟ'ⲗⲓⲥ ϫⲉ ⲡⲟⲩⲃⲉⲥⲧ.' ⲛ̄ⲧⲉⲣⲉϥⲡⲱϩ ⲉⲡⲟⲩ'ⲃⲉⲥⲧ̄ ⲛ̄ϭⲓ ⲡϩⲏⲅⲉ'ⲙⲱⲛ, ⲁϥⲃⲱⲕ' ⲉϩⲟⲩⲛ Ⲓ·Ⲓ ⲉⲡⲉⲣⲡⲏ,' ⲁⲩⲟⲩⲱϣⲧ̄. ⲁϥ'ⲟⲩⲉϩⲥⲁϩⲛⲉ ⲉⲧⲣⲟⲩ'ⲉⲓⲛⲉ ⲉϩⲟⲩⲛ[30]
ⲛⲉⲧⲟⲩ'ⲁⲁⲃ ⲧⲏⲣⲟⲩ, ⲉⲩⲉⲓⲣⲉ' ⲛ̄ⲩⲧⲉⲩϭⲟⲩⲱⲧ (124 V ii) ⲙ̄ⲛ̄ϣⲟⲙⲧⲉ, ⲭⲱⲣⲓⲥ' ⲡ-
ⲙ̄ⲛ̄ⲧⲥⲛⲟⲟⲩⲥ ⲛ̄ϩⲁ'ⲅⲓⲟⲥ ⲁⲡⲁ ⲩⲛⲟⲩϭⲉ' ⲙ̄ⲛ̄ⲛⲉⲩⲥⲛⲏⲩ.'[5] ⲡⲉϫⲉ ⲡϩⲏⲅⲉⲙⲱⲛ' ⲛⲁⲩ
ϫⲉ ⲁⲙⲏⲓⲧⲛ̄, ⲟⲩⲱϣⲧ̄ ⲙ̄ⲡⲁⲡⲟⲗ'ⲗⲱⲛ ⲙ̄ⲛ̄ⲧⲁⲣⲇⲉ'ⲙⲓⲥ ⲙ̄ⲛ̄ⲥⲉⲉⲡⲉ[10] ⲛ̄'ⲛⲉⲛⲟⲩⲧⲉ ⲉⲩⲉⲓⲣⲉ ⲛ̄'ⲩϥⲏ. ⲁⲩⲟⲩⲱϣϥ' ⲛ̄ϭⲓ ⲛ̄ϩⲁⲅⲓⲟⲥ ϩⲛ̄ⲟⲩⲥ'ⲙⲏ ⲛ̄ⲟⲩⲱⲧ ⲧⲏⲣⲟⲩ' ⲉⲩϫⲱ ⲙ̄ⲙⲟⲥ
ϫⲉ ⲙ̄'ⲙⲛ̄ⲛⲟⲩⲧⲉ ⲛ̄ⲥⲁⲓⲥ̄' ⲡⲉⲭ̄ⲥ̄ ⲡⲛⲟⲩⲧⲉ ⲙ̄'ⲙⲉ ⲙⲁⲅⲁⲁⲩ, ⲡⲁⲓ' ⲉⲧⲛ̄ⲙⲙⲏⲩⲉ ⲛⲁⲩ,'
ⲁⲩⲱ ⲉⲣⲉⲡⲉⲛⲛⲓⲃⲉ'[20] ϩⲛ̄ⲛⲉⲩⲥⲓⲭ, ⲉϥⲥⲟⲩ' ⲛⲁⲛ ϣⲁⲛⲧⲉⲛ ϥ'ⲩⲓⲡⲉ ⲛ̄ⲛⲉⲕⲛⲟⲩⲧⲉ.'
ⲧⲟⲧⲉ ⲡϩⲏⲅⲉⲙⲱⲛ' ⲁϥϭⲱⲛⲧ̄ ϩⲛ̄ⲟⲩⲟⲣ'ⲅⲏ, ⲁϥⲕⲉⲗⲉⲩⲉ ⲛ̄ⲥⲉ'ⲥⲟⲣⲟⲩ ⲉⲃⲟⲗ ⲛ̄ⲥⲁⲗⲁⲩ'
ⲛ̄ⲧⲁⲅⲙⲁ ⲧⲁⲅⲙⲁ' ⲛ̄ⲥⲉⲃⲁⲍⲁⲛⲓⲍⲉ ⲙ̄'ⲙⲟⲟⲩ. ϩⲟⲓⲛⲉ ⲛ̄ϩⲏⲧⲟⲩ[30]' ⲁⲩⲧⲣⲟⲩⲕⲟⲛⲥⲟⲩ ϩⲛ̄'
ⲧⲥⲏⲃⲉ· ϩⲛ̄ⲕⲟⲟⲩⲉ' ⲁⲩⲧⲗⲁⲙⲡⲁⲥ ⲛ̄ⲕⲱϩⲧ̄ (125 R i) ϩⲁⲣⲟⲟⲩ ϣⲁⲛⲧⲉⲛⲉⲩ'ⲥⲡⲓⲣⲟⲟⲩⲉ ϩⲉ ⲉⲭⲙ̄ⲡⲕⲁϩ·' ϩⲛ̄ⲕⲟⲟⲩⲉ ⲁⲩⲧⲣⲟⲩⲧⲥⲟⲩ'ⲡⲗⲓⲛ ⲛ̄ⲕⲱϩⲧ̄ ⲉϩⲟⲩ(ⲛ)' ⲉⲛⲉⲩⲕⲁ-
ⲁϫⲉ ϣⲁⲛ'ⲧⲉⲡⲕⲁⲡⲛⲟⲥ ⲙ̄ⲡⲉⲩ'ⲁⲛⲕⲉⲫⲁⲗⲟⲥ ϫⲓⲥⲉ' ⲉⲙⲁⲧⲉ· ϩⲛ̄ⲕⲟⲟⲩⲉ' ⲁⲩ-
ⲧⲣⲟⲩⲥⲫⲉⲛⲧⲏⲣⲓ'ⲍⲉ ⲙ̄ⲙⲟⲟⲩ ϣⲁⲛⲧⲟⲩ'ⲣⲕⲗⲏⲡⲓⲥⲑⲉ ⲛ̄ⲥⲉϩⲉ' ⲉⲭⲙ̄ⲡⲉϩⲟ· ϩⲁⲡ.'
ⲗⲱⲥ ⲁⲩϯ ⲛⲁⲩ ⲛ̄ⲟⲩ'ⲙⲏⲏϣⲉ[15] ⲛ̄ⲃⲁⲍⲁⲛⲟⲥ. ⲛⲉⲁⲣⲟⲩϩⲉ ⲇⲉ' ϣⲟⲡⲉ ⲙ̄ⲡⲉϩⲟⲟⲩ ⲉⲧⲙ̄-
ⲙⲁⲩ· ⲁⲩⲕⲉⲗⲉⲩⲉ ⲇⲉ ⲛ̄ϭⲓ ⲗⲉⲱⲛⲧⲓ'ⲟⲥ ⲡⲗⲟⲅⲓⲥⲧⲏⲥ ⲉⲧ'ⲣⲟⲩϩⲁⲣⲉϩ ⲉⲣⲟⲟⲩ ϣⲁ'ⲡⲉⲩ-

---

124 V i 18. ⲗ. ϩⲁⲙⲏⲛ.   30 ϥ. ⲗ. ⲛ̄ⲛⲉⲧ.   125 R i 7 = -ⲉⲅⲕⲉⲫⲁⲗⲟⲥ.   9. = -ⲥⲫⲓⲅⲕⲧⲏⲣⲓ ⲍⲉ.
11 = -ⲉⲕⲗⲉⲓⲡⲉⲥⲑⲁⲓ (sic); ⲗ. ⲉⲕⲗⲉⲓⲡⲉ(ⲓⲛ)?

---

124 V i 15–18. ϣⲁⲉⲛⲉϩ—ϩⲁⲙⲏⲛ (sic) A; om. B.   19. ϩⲓⲧⲉϩⲓⲏ A; ⲇⲉ B.   20 ϥ. ⲙ̄ⲙⲁⲣ-
ⲧⲩⲣⲟⲥ A; ⲉⲩⲥⲙⲟⲩ ⲉⲡⲛⲟⲩⲧⲉ B.   23. ϫⲉ ⲡⲟⲩⲃⲉⲥⲧ A; ⲉⲧⲉⲛ. ⲡⲉ B.   24. ⲛ̄ⲧⲉⲣⲉϥⲡⲱϩ
A; ⲛ̄ⲧⲉⲣⲟⲩⲡⲱϩ + ⲇⲉ B.   25 ϥ. ⲛ̄ϭⲓ ⲡϩⲏⲥ. A; om. B.   27–31. B's text may probably be restored from A.   32. ⲉⲩⲉⲓⲣⲉ A; ? ⲉⲩⲉⲓⲣⲉ] ⲉ + ⲅⲁⲣ B.   32 – 11 1. ⲛ̄ⲩⲧⲉⲩ-
ϭⲟⲩⲱⲧ ⲙ̄ⲛ̄ϣⲟⲙⲧⲉ A; ⲛ̄ϩ[ⲉ]ⲙⲉ ϣⲁⲧⲛ̄ϩⲧⲟⲩ B.   2 ϥ. ⲡⲙ̄ⲛ̄ⲧⲥⲛⲟⲟⲩⲥ ⲛ̄ϩⲁⲅⲓⲟⲥ A; om. B.
6. After ⲁⲙⲏⲓⲧⲛ̄, + ⲧⲉⲛⲟⲩ ⲛ̄ⲧⲉⲧⲛ̄– B.   9. –ⲛⲥⲉⲉⲡⲉ A; –ⲛⲕⲉⲥ. B.   10 ϥ. ⲉⲩⲉⲓⲣⲉ ⲛ̄ⲩϥⲏ A;
om. B.   14. ⲉⲩϫⲱ ⲙ̄ⲙⲟⲥ A; om. B.   16 ϥ. ⲡⲛⲟⲩⲧⲉ ⲙ̄ⲙⲉ ⲙⲁⲅⲁⲁⲩ A; om. B.   19. ⲁⲩⲱ A;
ⲡⲁⲓ B.   22. ⲛ̄ⲛⲉⲕⲛⲟⲩⲧⲉ A; ⲛⲁⲕ ⲙ̄ⲛ̄ⲉⲕⲛⲟⲩⲧⲉ ⲙ̄ⲙⲟⲩⲛⲅ̄ ⲛ̄ϭⲓⲭ B.   23–25. ⲧⲟⲧⲉ —
ϩⲛ̄ⲟⲩⲟⲣⲅⲏ A; ⲁϥϭⲱⲛⲧ̄ ⲇⲉ ⲛ̄ϭⲓ ⲡϩⲏⲅ. B.   25. ⲛ̄ⲥⲉⲥⲟⲣⲟⲩ A; ⲉⲧⲣⲉⲩⲥ. B.   27. ⲛ̄-
ⲧⲁⲅⲙⲁ ⲧⲁⲅⲙⲁ A; ⲛ̄ⲩⲟⲉⲓⲙ ϣⲟⲉⲓⲙ B.   29. ⲛ̄ϩⲏⲧⲟⲩ A; om. B.   ⲁⲩⲧⲣⲟⲩⲕⲟⲛⲥⲟⲩ A;
ⲁⲩⲕⲱⲛⲥ̄ ⲙ̄ⲙⲟⲟⲩ B.   30 ϥ. ϩⲛ̄ⲧⲥⲏⲃⲉ A; om. B.   31. ϩⲛ̄ⲕⲟⲟⲩⲉ A; ϩⲟⲓⲛⲉ B.   32.
ⲁⲩϯ- A; ⲁⲩ+- B.   125 R i 1. ϩⲁⲣⲟⲟⲩ A; ϩⲁⲛ[B. Some loss of text here in B.
8. ⲉⲙⲁⲧⲉ A; ϫⲉⲓ B.   9 ϥ. ⲁⲩⲧⲣⲟⲩⲥⲫⲉⲛⲧⲏⲣⲓⲍⲉ A; ⲁⲩⲥⲫ[.]ⲧⲉⲣⲓⲍⲉ (–ⲥϥⲓ[ⲛ]ⲧⲉⲣⲓⲍⲉ?)
B.   11. –ⲣ̄ⲕⲗⲏⲡⲓⲥⲑⲉ A; –ⲥⲕⲟⲑⲟⲩ B. ⲛ̄ⲥⲉϩⲉ probable in B; Some loss of text.   18 ϥ.
B's text probably to be restored much as in A.   20 ϥ. ϣⲁⲡⲉⲩⲣⲁⲥⲧⲉ A; ϣⲁⲩϣⲱⲣⲡ̄ B.

ραϲτε. ⲛ̄ⲧⲉⲣⲟⲩⲛ̄ⲧⲟⲩ ⲇⲉ ⲉϩⲟⲩⲛ ⲉⲩϩⲁⲃⲁⲍⲁⲛⲟⲥ ⲉⲩⲙⲟⲕϩ̄ ⲉⲙⲁⲧⲉ ϩⲓⲧⲙ̄ⲡⲁ⳿ⲅⲁⲓ

ⲛ̄ⲛⲃⲁⲍⲁⲛⲟⲥ, ⳿ⲡϩⲁⲅⲓⲟⲥ ⲇⲉ ⲁⲡⲁ ϣⲏⲛⲟⲩϥⲉ ⲛⲉⲩⲧⲧⲱⲕ ⲛ̄ϩⲏⲧ ⲛⲁⲩ ⲉⲩϫⲱ⳿ⲙ̄ⲙⲟⲥ

ϫⲉ ⲧⲱⲕ ⲛ̄ϩⲏⲧ ⲛⲁⲥⲛⲏⲩ, ⳿ⲙ̄ⲡⲣ̄ⲣ̄ⲅⲟⲧⲉ· ⲡⲕⲱϩⲧ̄ ⲅⲁⲣ ⲛ̄ⲛⲓⲁⲛⲟⲙⲟⲥ (125 R ii)

ⲉϥⲉⲓⲛⲉ ⲛ̄ⲟⲩⲙⲟⲟⲩ⳿ ⲉϥⲕⲏⲃ· ⲙ̄ⲡⲣ̄ⲧⲣⲉⲛ⳿ⲉⲓ ⲉⲡⲁϩⲟⲩ ϩⲓⲧⲙ̄ⲡⲉⲛ⳿ⲁⲅⲱⲛ, ϫⲉ ⲛ̄ⲛⲉⲛ⳿ⲡⲱ-

ⲣ̄ϣ̄ ⲉⲛⲉⲛⲉⲣⲏⲩ⳿ ϩⲓⲧⲙ̄ⲡϩ̄ ⲙ̄ⲡⲛⲟⲩⲧⲉ· ⳿ⲱ ⲛⲉⲥⲛⲏⲩ, ⲁⲣⲓ⳿ⲡⲙⲉⲉⲩⲉ ⲙ̄ⲡϣⲁϫⲉ⳿ ⲛ̄ⲧⲁ-

ⲡⲉⲛⲉⲓⲱⲧ ⲇⲁⲇ⳿ ϫⲟⲟⲩ ϫⲉ ⲟⲩ ⲡⲉⲧⲛⲁⲛⲟⲩⲩ ⲏ ⲟⲩ ⲡⲉⲧⲛⲁⲧⲙ̄ ⲛ̄ⲥⲁϩⲉⲛⲥ⳿ⲛⲏⲩ ϩⲛ̄

ⲟⲩⲙⲁ ⲛ̄ⲟⲩ⳿ⲱⲧ ⲉⲣⲉⲧⲣⲏⲛⲙ ⲙ̄⳿ⲡⲛⲟⲩⲧⲉ ϩⲓⲧⲉⲩ⳿ⲙⲏⲧⲉ; ⲉⲩⲛⲁⲣⲑⲉ⳿ ⲙ̄ⲡⲥⲟⲟϩⲛ ⲉⲧϩⲓ-

ϫⲉⲛ̄ⲧⲁⲗⲉ ⲛ̄ⲁⲁⲣⲱⲛ⳿ ⲉⲧⲛⲏⲩ ⲉⲡⲉⲥⲏⲧ ⲉ⳿ϫⲉⲛⲧⲉⲩⲙⲟⲣⲧ⳿ ⲉⲡⲉⲥⲏⲧ ⲉϫⲉⲛⲛⲉ⳿ⲥⲱϫⲉ

ⲛ̄ⲛⲉⲩϩⲟⲓⲧⲉ·⳿ⲉⲩⲛⲁⲣⲑⲉ ⲛ̄ⲧⲱⲧⲉ⳿ ⲛ̄ⲁⲣⲙⲱⲛ ⲉⲧⲛⲏⲩ⳿ⲉⲡⲉⲥⲏⲧ ⲉϫⲉⲛⲛ̄ⲛⲧⲟⲟⲩ ⲛ̄-

ⲥⲓⲱⲛ·⳿ϫⲉ ⲛ̄ⲧⲁⲡⲭⲟⲉⲓⲥ⳿ϩⲱⲛ ⲙ̄ⲙⲁⲩ ⲙ̄⳿ⲡⲉⲩⲥⲙⲟⲩ ⲉⲟⲧⲱⲛϩ̄⳿ ϣⲁⲉⲛⲉϩ. ⲡⲙⲁ⳿ⲕⲁ-

ⲣⲓⲟⲥ ⲇⲉ ⲁⲡⲁ ϣⲏⲛⲟⲩϥⲉ ⲁϥⲕⲟⲧϥ̄ (V i) ⲉⲛⲉⲧⲟⲩⲁⲁⲃ, ⲡⲉϫⲁⲩ⳿ ⲛⲁⲩ ϫⲉ ⲛⲁⲥⲛⲏⲩ⳿

ⲙⲁⲣⲉⲛⲧ̄ ⲛ̄ⲛⲉⲛ⳿ⲩⲯⲓⲭⲏ ⲉⲡⲛⲟⲩⲧⲉ⳿ ϩⲓⲧⲉⲓⲟⲩϣⲏ, ⲧⲁ⳿ⲣⲉⲛⲁⲡⲁⲛⲧⲁ ⲉⲡⲁϩ⳿ⲟⲉⲓⲥ ⲛ̄ⲧⲃ̄-

ⲃⲏⲣ, ⲛ̄ⲧⲙ̄ⲙ̄ⲡϣⲁ⳿ ⲛ̄ⲉⲣϣ̄ⲃⲏⲣ⳿ ⲉⲣⲟϥ ϩⲓⲧⲉⲩⲙ̄ⲛ̄⳿ⲧ̄ⲣ̄ⲣⲟ. ⲁⲩⲧⲱⲟⲩⲛ⳿ ⲇⲉ ⲧⲏⲣⲟⲩ, ⲁⲩ-

ⲡⲣ̄ϣ̄⳿ⲛⲉⲩϭⲓϫ ⲉⲃⲟⲗ ϩⲓⲟⲩ⳿ⲥⲟⲡ ⲉⲩϫⲱ ⲙ̄ⲙⲟⲥ⳿ ϫⲉ ⲧⲛ̄ⲡⲱⲣϣ̄ ⲛ̄⳿ⲛⲉⲛϭⲓϫ ⲉϩⲣⲁⲓ ⲉ-

ⲣⲟⲕ⳿ ⲡⲛⲟⲩⲧⲉ ⲛ̄ⲛⲟⲩⲧⲉ⳿ ⲁⲧⲛ̄ⲯⲩⲭⲏ⳿ ⲉⲓⲃⲉ ⲙ̄ⲙⲟⲕ ⲛ̄ⲑⲉ⳿ ⲛ̄ⲟⲩⲕⲁϩ ⲛ̄ⲁⲧⲙⲟⲟⲩ·

ⲧⲛ̄ⲛⲁⲟⲩⲱⲛϩ̄⳿ⲛⲁⲕ ⲉⲃⲟⲗ, ⲡⲡⲉⲧⲟⲩ⳿ⲁⲁⲃ, ⲧⲁⲣⲉⲛⲛⲁⲩ⳿ ⲉⲧⲉⲕϭⲟⲙ ⲙ̄ⲡⲉ⳿ⲕⲉⲟⲟⲩ·

ⲁⲥϣⲱⲡⲉ ⲇⲉ ⲉⲣⲉⲡ̄⳿ϩⲁⲅⲓⲟⲥ ⲩⲗⲏⲗ, ⲁⲡ⳿ⲩⲏⲣⲉ ⲙ̄ⲡⲛⲟⲩⲧⲉ⳿ ⲉⲓ ⲉⲧⲉⲩⲙⲏⲧⲉ ⲉϥ⳿ⲣⲟⲩⲉ

ⲉϥⲧⲉⲗⲏⲗ⳿ ⲡⲉϫⲁⲩ ⲛⲁⲩ ϫⲉ ϯ⳿ⲣⲏⲛⲏ ⲛⲏⲧⲛ̄ ⲧⲏⲣ⳿ⲧⲛ̄ ⲛⲁⲩⲃⲉⲉⲣ ⲉⲧ(V ii)ⲧⲁⲓⲏⲩ· ⲁϥ-

ϩⲓⲟⲧⲉ ⲛ̄⳿ⲧⲉϥϭⲓϫ ⲉⲡⲉⲩⲥⲱⲙⲁ⳿ ϫⲉ ⲛ̄ⲛⲉⲃⲁⲍⲁⲛⲟⲥ ϣⲛ̄ϭⲟⲙ ⲉⲣⲟϥ ⲙ̄ⲛ̄ⲛⲉⲩⲕⲉ⳿ⲥⲛⲏⲩ.

ⲁⲥϣⲱⲡⲉ⳿ ⲙ̄ⲛ̄ⲥⲁⲛⲁⲓ⳿ ⲁⲡⲟⲩⲟⲉⲓⲛ ⲉⲓ ⲉⲃⲟⲗ ⲛ̄ⲥⲟⲩ⳿ⲥⲟⲟⲩ ⲙ̄ⲡⲁϣⲱⲡⲉ,⳿ ⲁⲩⲧⲱⲟⲩⲛ ⲛ̄ϭⲓ

---

125 R ii ii. l. – ⲛⲟⲧⲙ.   V i 16 f.   l. ⲡⲛ. ⲡⲉⲛⲛⲟⲩⲧⲉ (so B).

125 R i 22. – ⲛ̄ⲧⲟⲩ A ; – ⲟⲧⲁ[ⲟⲩ] B. 23. ⲉⲩϩⲁⲃⲁⲍⲁⲛⲟⲥ ⲉⲩⲙⲟⲕϩ̄ A ; ⲉⲛⲉⲩⲑⲗ[ⲓⲃ]ⲉ B. 24 f.
ϩⲓⲧⲙ̄ⲡⲁⲅⲁⲓ A ; ϩⲁⲧⲓⲧⲩⲏ B. 25. + ⲛ̄ⲧⲁⲩⲧⲟⲟⲩ ⲛⲁⲩ B. 29 f. ⲧⲱⲕ ⲛ̄ϩⲏⲧ A ; ⲟⲙ. B. 32 – ii 2
ⲡⲕⲱϩⲧ̄ — ⲉϥⲕⲏⲃ A ; ⲟⲩⲇⲉ ⲙ̄ⲡⲉⲣⲉⲣϩⲁⲃ2ⲏⲧ ⲟⲩⲇⲉ B. 2 f. ⲙ̄ⲡⲣ̄ⲧⲣⲉⲛⲉⲓ A ; ⲙ̄ⲡⲉⲣⲉⲓ B. 3 f. ϩⲓⲧⲙ̄-
ⲡⲉⲛⲁⲅⲱⲛ A ; ϩⲓⲧⲙⲡⲉⲛⲁ. B. 4. ϫⲉ A ; ϫⲉⲕⲁⲥ B. 7. ⲱ – ⲙ̄ⲡϣⲁϫⲉ A ; ⲁⲣⲓⲡⲁⲙⲉⲉⲩⲉ
(sic) ⲱ ⲛⲉⲥⲛⲏⲩ [ϩ]ⲙ̄ⲡϣ. B. 15 f. Restore in B ϩⲓⲧⲉ[ⲩⲙⲏⲧⲉ], as A. Text in B corresponding to A 125 R ii 20 – 27 seems to have been shorter ; its readings uncertain. At A's 28
– 30 it may be restored as A. From A's 31 – V i 9 it is again impossible to suggest restorations
in B.   V i 11 f. ⲁⲩⲡⲣ̄ϣ̄ⲛⲉⲩϭⲓϫ A ; ⲁⲩⲛⲱⲣ̄ϣ̄ ⲛ̄ⲛⲉⲧⲟ. B. 12 f. ϩⲓⲟⲩⲥⲟⲡ A ; ⲁⲩⲩⲗⲏⲗ B.
16 f. ⲛ̄ⲛⲟⲩⲧⲉ A ; ⲡⲉⲛⲛ. B. 20. ⲧⲛ̄ⲛⲁⲟⲩⲱⲛϩ̄ A ; ⲧⲉⲛⲟⲩ. B. 22. ⲧⲁⲣⲉⲛⲛⲁⲩ A ; ⲉⲛⲁⲣ
B. 23 f. ⲙ̄ⲡⲉⲕⲉⲟⲟⲩ A ; ⲟⲙ. B. 25. ⲁⲥϣⲱⲡⲉ A ; ⲉⲧⲉⲓ B. 25 f. – ⲛ̄ϩⲁⲅⲓⲟⲥ A ;
– ⲛⲉⲓⲍ. B. 26. After ⲩⲗⲏⲗ, + ⲉⲓⲥ B. 26 f. ⲁⲡⲩⲏⲣⲉ A ; ⲡ.ⲩ. B. 28. ⲉⲓ A ; ⲁⲩⲉⲓ B.
ⲉⲧⲉⲩⲙⲏⲧⲉ A ; ⲉϫⲛ̄ⲙ̄[   ]B. 29. ⲉϥⲧⲉⲗⲏⲗ A ; ⲟⲙ. B. 31 f. ⲧⲏⲣⲧⲛ̄ A ; ⲟⲙ. B. 32 ii 1. Restore [ⲉⲧⲧⲁⲓⲏⲩ in B, as A.   ii 1. ⲁϥϩⲓⲟⲧⲉ A ; ⲁϥⲥⲟⲟⲩⲧⲛ̄ ⲉⲃⲟⲗ B. 2. ⲉⲡⲉⲩⲥⲱⲙⲁ A ; ⲁⲩ-
ϫⲟϩ ⲙ̄ⲡⲉⲩⲥ. B. 3. ϫⲉ A ; ϫⲉⲕⲁⲥ B. 4. ⲉⲣⲟϥ A ; ⲉⲡⲉⲩⲥⲱⲙⲁ B. 4 f. ⲙ̄ⲛ̄ⲛⲉⲩⲕⲉⲥⲛⲏⲩ A ; ⲟⲙ.
B. 5 f. ⲁⲥϣⲱⲡⲉ ⲙ̄ⲛ̄ⲥⲁⲛⲁⲓ A ; ⲁⲩⲱ ⲛ̄ⲧⲉⲓϩⲉ B. 7. ⲉⲃⲟⲗ A ; ⲉϩⲣⲁⲓ B.

ⲡ̄ⲍ̄ϩⲏⲅⲉⲙⲱⲛ, ⲁϥⲃⲱⲕ ⲉϩⲟⲩⲛ ⲉⲡⲣ̅ⲡⲉ ⲉⲟⲩⲱϣⲧ· ⲁⲩⲕⲉⲗⲉⲩⲉ ⲉⲉⲓⲛⲉ ⲛⲁⲩ ⲛ̄ⲛⲉⲭⲣⲏⲥ-
ⲧⲓⲁⲛⲟⲥ, ϫⲉⲕⲁⲥ ⲉⲩⲉⲟⲩⲱϣⲧ̄ ⲛ̄ⲛⲉⲛⲟⲩⲧⲉ ⲉⲧⲙⲟⲟⲩⲧ.· ⲡⲉϫⲉⲡⲍ̄ϩⲏⲅⲉⲙⲱⲛ· ⲛⲁⲩ ϫⲉ
ⲁⲣⲓⲑⲩⲥⲓⲁ·ⲛⲁⲩ.· ⲁⲩⲟⲩⲱϣⲃ̄ ⲧⲏⲣⲟⲩ ϩⲛ̄ⲟⲩⲥⲙⲏ ⲛ̄ⲟⲩⲱⲧ· ⲉⲩϫⲱ ⲙ̄ⲙⲟⲥ ϫⲉ ⲛ̄ⲧⲛ̄ⲛⲁ-
ⲣⲑⲩⲥⲓⲁ ⲁⲛ·· ⲡⲉⲧⲉϩⲛⲁⲕ ⲁⲣⲓϥ· ⲛⲁⲛ· ⲁⲙⲟⲛ ⲙⲛ̄ⲛⲟⲩⲧⲉ ⲛ̄ⲥⲁⲡⲉⲭ̄ⲥ̄ ⲓ̄ⲥ̄ ⲡⲉⲛϫⲟⲉⲓⲥ·
ⲁⲩⲟⲩⲛⲧ ⲛ̄ϭⲓ ⲡ̄ⲍ̄ϩⲏⲅⲉⲙⲱⲛ, ⲁϥⲕⲉⲗⲉⲩⲉ ⲉⲧⲣⲟⲩⲃⲁⲍⲁⲛⲓⲍⲉ ⲙ̄ⲙⲟⲟⲩ. ⲁⲩⲥⲟⲟⲩⲣ ⲉⲃⲟⲗ
ⲛ̄ϭⲓ ⲛ̄ⲕⲉⲥ(126 R i)ⲇⲱⲛⲁⲣⲓⲟⲥ, ⲁⲩⲉⲓⲛⲉ ⲛ̄ϩⲉⲛⲭⲁⲗⲕⲓⲟⲛ· ⲙ̄ⲙⲟⲟⲩ ⲉⲩⲃⲏⲣⲃⲣ̄·ϩⲓⲱⲧ
ⲛ̄ⲧⲉⲛⲏ ϩⲓ·ϩⲙ̄ⲝ̄ ϩⲓⲕⲱⲛⲓⲁ· ϩⲓⲁⲥⲫⲁⲗⲧⲱⲛ· ϩⲓⲧⲁϩⲧ̄ ⲉⲩⲃⲏⲣⲃⲣ̄·· ϩⲟⲓⲛⲉ ⲛ̄ϫⲏⲧⲟⲩ ⲁⲩ·
ⲡⲱϩⲧ ⲉϫⲉⲛ̄ⲛⲉⲩⲥⲡⲗⲁⲭⲛⲟⲛ·· ϩⲛ̄ⲕⲟⲟⲩⲉ ⲉϫⲉⲛⲛⲉ·ⲛ̄ϭⲟⲡ
ⲛ̄ⲣⲁⲧⲟⲩ· ⲙⲛ̄ⲛⲉⲩⲛⲁϩⲃⲉ· ϩⲛ̄ⲕⲟⲟⲩⲉ ⲟⲛ ⲁⲩ·ⲧⲁⲗⲟⲟⲩ ⲉϫⲉⲛϩⲉⲛ·ⲩϩⲛ, ⲁⲩⲛⲉϫⲥⲟ·ⲧⲉ
ⲉⲣⲟⲟⲩ.· ⲁⲡⲁ ⲯ̄ⲛⲟⲩϭⲉ ⲇⲉ ⲙⲛ̄·ⲛⲉⲩⲥⲛⲏⲩ ⲁⲩϭⲁⲗⲁ· ⲙ̄ⲙⲟⲟⲩ ⲉⲡⲉⲥⲏⲧ ⲉⲩⲭⲁⲗⲕⲓⲟⲛ
ⲛ̄ⲧⲁϩⲧ̄·ⲉⲩⲃⲏⲣⲃⲣ̄.· ⲡϩⲁⲅⲓⲟⲥ ⲇⲉ ⲁⲡⲁ ⲯ̄ⲛⲟⲩϭⲉ ⲁϥⲧⲱⲃϩ̄ ⲙ̄ⲡⲛⲟⲩⲧⲉ ⲉϥϫⲱ·ⲙ̄ⲙⲟⲥ
ϫⲉ ϩⲙ̄ⲡⲉⲕ·ⲣⲁⲛ ⲡϫⲟⲉⲓⲥ ⲙⲁⲣⲉ·ⲡⲕⲱϩⲧ̄ ϫⲛⲁ·· ⲛ̄ⲧⲉⲑⲁⲗⲁⲥⲥⲁ ϣⲟⲟⲩⲉ·· ⲛ̄ⲧⲉⲛⲧⲟⲟⲩ
ⲃⲱⲗ ⲉ·ⲃⲟⲗ, ⲛ̄ⲧⲉⲙ̄ⲡⲉⲧⲣⲁ (R ii) ⲟⲩⲱϣϥ̄· ⲛ̄ϥⲟⲩⲟⲥϥ̄· ⲛ̄ⲙⲡⲟⲗⲉⲙⲟⲥ.· ⲡϫⲟⲉⲓⲥ ⲡ-
ⲛⲟⲩⲧⲉ, ⲙ̄·ⲡⲉⲣⲕⲧⲉⲡⲉⲕϩⲟ ⲉⲃⲟⲗ· ⲙ̄ⲙⲟⲛ· ϣⲱⲡⲉ· ⲛⲁⲛ ⲛ̄ⲃⲟⲏⲑⲟⲥ·, ⲛ̄ϥ̄ϭⲟⲙ ⲛⲁⲛ·,
ⲡⲉⲥⲕⲉⲡⲁⲥⲧⲏⲥ ⲛ̄ⲛ̄ⲇⲓⲕⲁⲓⲟⲥ ⲧⲏⲣⲟⲩ·· ϫⲉ ⲧⲱⲕ ⲧⲉ ⲧϭⲟⲙ· ⲙⲛ̄ ⲡⲉⲟⲟⲩ ϣⲁⲉ·ⲛⲉϩ, ϩⲁⲙⲏⲛ.· ⲛ̄ⲧⲉⲩⲛⲟⲩ ⲉⲓⲥ ⲙⲓⲭⲁ·ⲏⲗ ⲡⲁⲣⲭⲁⲅⲅⲉⲗⲟⲥ· ⲁϥⲉⲓ ⲉⲃⲟⲗ ϩⲛ̄ⲧⲡⲉ,· ⲁϥϣⲁϫⲉ
ⲙⲛ̄ⲛⲉ·ⲧⲟⲩⲁⲁⲃ ⲉϥϫⲱ ⲙ̄·ⲙⲟⲥ ϫⲉ ϫⲣⲟ ⲁⲩⲱ· ⲑⲙ̄ϭⲟⲙ· ⲁⲩⲱ ⲛ̄·ⲧⲉⲩⲛⲟⲩ ⲁⲡⲧⲁϩⲧ̄·
ⲣ̄ⲑⲉ ⲛ̄ⲟⲩⲙⲟⲟⲩ ⲉϥ·ⲕⲏⲃ· ⲁⲛ̄ϩⲁⲅⲓⲟⲥ· ⲉⲓ ⲉϩⲣⲁⲓ ϩⲛ̄ⲛ̄ⲭⲁⲗ·ⲕⲓⲟⲛ ⲉⲙⲛ̄ⲧⲁⲕⲟ· ϣⲟⲟⲡ ⲛ̄-

---

126 R i 2. -ⲭⲁⲗⲕⲓⲟⲛ: ⲟ ⲁⲇⲇⲉⲇ. 11. = -ⲥⲡⲗⲁⲅⲭⲛⲟⲛ. ii 1. ℓ. ⲛ̄ϥⲟⲩⲱⲥϥ̄

125 V ii 13. ⲉⲉⲓⲛⲉ A; ⲉⲧⲣⲉⲩⲉⲓⲛⲉ B. 13 f. ⲛ̄ⲛⲉⲭⲣⲏⲥⲧⲓⲁⲛⲟⲥ A; ⲛ̄ⲛⲉⲧⲟⲩⲁⲁⲃ ⲧⲏⲣⲟⲩ B.
16. ⲛ̄ⲛⲉⲛⲟⲩⲧⲉ ⲉⲧⲙⲟⲟⲩⲧ A; ϩⲙ̄ⲡⲣ̄ⲡⲉ B. 18 f. ⲁⲣⲓⲑⲩⲥⲓⲁ ⲛⲁⲩ A; ⲑⲩⲥⲓⲁⲍⲉ B. 20. ⲁⲩⲟⲩⲱ-
ϣⲃ̄ A; ⲡⲉϫⲁⲩ B. After this, some text lost in B. 30 f. In B restore -ⲃⲁϭⲁⲛⲓⲍⲉ, as in
A. 31– 126 R i 1. ⲁⲩⲥⲟⲟⲣⲟⲩ — ⲛ̄ⲕⲉⲥⲇⲱⲛⲁⲣⲓⲟⲥ A; ⲁⲩⲱ ⲛ̄ⲧⲉⲩⲛⲟⲩ B. 2. + ⲉⲩⲃⲏⲣⲃⲣ̄ B. 3.
ⲉⲩⲃⲏⲣⲃⲣ̄ A; ⲉⲩⲃ. + ϩⲓⲗⲁⲩϩⲁⲡ B. 4 f. ϩⲓϩⲙ̄ⲝ̄ ϩⲓⲕⲱⲛⲓⲁ A; om. B. 8. ⲛ̄ϫⲏⲧⲟⲩ A; ⲛ̄ⲛⲉ-
ⲧⲟⲩⲁⲁⲃ B. 10. ϩⲛ̄ⲕⲟⲟⲩⲉ ⲟⲛ A; ϩⲟⲓⲛⲉ B. 12–14. ϩⲛ̄ⲕⲟⲟⲩⲉ — ⲙⲛ̄ⲛⲉⲩⲛⲁϩⲃⲉ A; om. B.
15. ϩⲛ̄ⲕⲟⲟⲩⲉ ⲟⲛ A; ϩⲟⲓⲛⲉ B. 15–18. ⲁⲩⲧⲁⲗⲟⲟⲩ ⲉϫⲉⲛϩⲉⲛ ⲩϩⲛ ⲁⲩⲛⲉϫⲥⲟⲧⲉ ⲉⲣⲟⲟⲩ A; ⲁⲩⲧⲁⲗⲟⲟⲩ ⲛ̄ϩⲉⲛⲩϩⲉ ⲁⲩⲛⲉϫⲥⲁⲧⲉ ⲉⲣⲟⲟⲩ B. 19 f. ⲙⲛ̄ⲛⲉⲩⲥⲛⲏⲩ A; ϩⲱⲱϥ B. 20–22. ⲁⲩϭⲁⲗⲁ
ⲙ̄ⲙⲟⲟⲩ ⲉⲡⲉⲥⲏⲧ ⲉⲩⲭⲁⲗⲕⲓⲟⲛ A; [ⲛⲉϥ]ϩⲛⲟⲩ ϫ. B. (So Sottas). 22. ⲛ̄ⲧⲁϩⲧ̄ A; om. B. 23.
After ⲉⲩⲃⲏⲣⲃⲣ̄, + ⲙⲛ̄ⲛⲉⲩⲥⲛⲏⲩ B. 24 f. ϩ. ϩⲙ̄ - ⲯ̄ⲛⲟⲩϭⲉ A; ⲁⲩ ⲃ. 25 f. ⲁϥⲧⲱⲃ̄ϩ̄
ⲙ̄ⲡⲛⲟⲩⲧⲉ A; ⲁϥϣⲗⲏⲗ ⲉⲡϩ. B. 28. ⲡϫⲟⲉⲓⲥ A; ⲡⲁϫ. B. 29. ϫⲛⲁ A; ϣⲟⲩⲙ B. ii 1. ⲟⲩⲟ-
ϣϥ̄ A; ⲡⲱϩ B. ⲛ̄ϥⲟⲩⲟⲥϥ̄ (sic) A; ⲛ̄ϥⲟⲩⲱϣϥ̄ (sic, = -ⲟⲩⲱⲥϥ̄? -ⲟⲩⲱϣϥ̄? -ⲱϣⲧ̄?) B.
4. -ⲕⲧⲉⲡⲉⲕϩⲟ A; -ⲕⲱⲧⲉ ⲙ̄ⲡⲉⲕϩⲟ B. ⲉⲃⲟⲗ A; ⲛ̄ⲥⲁⲃⲟⲗ B. 6–8. B's text probably to be restored as A. 11 ff. The corresponding text in B is very fragmentary; it varies so widely from A's that it is not easy to relate the two. The passage in B corresponding
to A's 19–25 might be restored:]ⲭⲁⲗⲕⲓⲟⲛ] ⲁⲩⲧⲣⲉ[ⲩ(ⲧⲁⲗⲟ?)] ⲙ̄ⲙⲟⲟⲩ ⲧⲏⲣⲟⲩ ϩⲛ̄ⲛⲉⲩ-
ϩⲓⲥⲉ ⲁⲩϩⲉⲣⲁⲧⲟⲩ ⲉⲙⲉⲛⲗⲁⲁⲩ ⲛ̄ⲧⲁⲕⲟ ϣⲟⲟⲡ ⲛ̄ϩⲏⲧⲟⲩ.

ⲌⲎⲦⲞⲨ Ⲉ'ⲠⲦⲎⲢϤ· ⲀⲨⲰ ⲀⲚ'ⲌⲀⲄⲒⲞⲤ ⲦⲎⲢⲞⲨ ⲦⲀ'ϬⲞ ⲌⲒⲦⲚ̄ⲦϬⲞⲘ Ⲙ̄ⲘⲒ'ⲬⲀⲎⲖ. Ⲛ̄ⲦⲈⲢⲈⲚⲈ-
ⲦⲞⲨⲀⲀⲂ ⲦⲎⲢⲞⲨ ⲦⲀ'ϬⲞ ⲌⲚ̄ⲚⲈⲨⲌⲒϬⲈ, ⲀⲨ'ⲚⲀⲨ ⲈⲘⲒⲬⲀⲎⲖ ⲈϤ(126 Ⅵ)ⲌⲀⲌⲦⲎⲨ ⲈϤⲦ-
ϬⲞⲘ ⲚⲀⲨ¦ⲀⲚⲈⲨⲤⲰⲘⲀ ⲞⲨⲞⲘ.'ⲠⲈⲬⲀⲨ ⲚⲀⲨ ⲬⲈ Ⲙ̄ⲠⲞ'ⲞⲨ ⲄⲀⲢ ⲦⲈⲦⲚ̄ϪⲒ Ⲙ̄'ⲠⲈ-
ⲔⲖⲞⲘ Ⲙ̄ⲠⲰⲚ̄Ⲍ̄' ⲘⲀⲈⲚⲈⲌ, ⲌⲀⲘⲎⲚ.'Ⲛ̄ⲦⲈⲦⲚ̄ϢⲰⲠⲈ ⲌⲚ̄'ⲦⲠⲞⲖⲒⲤ Ⲙ̄ⲠⲈⲬⲤ̄' ⲐⲒⲖⲎⲘ̄
Ⲛ̄ⲦⲠⲎ'. ⲦⲞⲨⲚ̄ⲐⲎⲨⲦⲚ̄ ϬⲈ, ⲂⲰⲔ' ⲈⲢⲀⲦϤ̄ Ⲙ̄ⲠⲌⲎⲄⲈ'ⲘⲰⲚ Ⲛ̄ⲦⲈⲦⲚ̄ϪⲰⲔ' ⲈⲂⲞⲖ Ⲙ̄ⲠⲈ-
ⲦⲚ̄ⲀⲄⲰ(Ⲛ).' ⲚⲀⲒ ⲆⲈ Ⲛ̄ⲦⲈⲢⲈϤϪⲞⲞⲨ'ⲚⲀⲨ Ⲛ̄ϬⲒ ⲘⲒⲬⲀⲎⲖ'ⲀϤⲂⲰⲔ ⲈⲌⲢⲀⲒ̈ Ⲙ̄ⲠⲎ'ⲨⲈ ⲌⲚ̄'
ⲞⲨⲈⲒⲢⲎⲚⲎ.' Ⲛ̄ⲦⲈⲨⲚⲞⲨ ⲀⲨⲂⲰⲔ' Ⲛ̄ϬⲒ ⲚⲈⲦⲞⲨⲀⲀⲂ ⲌⲚ̄ⲞⲨϬⲰⲚⲦ̄ ⲈⲌⲢⲀⲒ̈ ⲈⲬⲘ̄'ⲠⲌⲎⲄⲈⲘⲰⲚ·
ⲀⲨ'ⲰϢ ⲈⲂⲞⲖ ϪⲈ ⲀⲚⲞⲚ' ⲌⲈⲚⲬⲢⲎⲤⲦⲒⲀⲚⲞⲤ'ⲠⲀⲢⲢⲎⲤⲒⲀ, ⲀⲨⲰ' ⲈⲚⲎⲠ ⲈⲒⲤ. Ⲡ̄ⲌⲎ'ⲄⲈ-
ⲘⲰⲚ ⲆⲈ ⲀⲞⲨⲌⲞⲦⲈ' ϪⲒⲦϤ̄, Ⲙ̄ⲠⲈϤⲯⲨⲬⲀ'ϪⲈ ⲌⲀⲢⲞⲞⲨ· ⲀⲨⲦ'ⲚⲈⲨⲞⲨⲞⲒ ⲈⲬⲘ̄ⲠⲂⲎ'ⲘⲀ,
ⲀⲨⲠⲰⲰⲚⲈ' Ⲙ̄ⲠⲈϤⲐⲢⲞⲚⲞⲤ ϨⲀ'ⲢⲞϤ, ⲀϤⲚⲞⲞⲚⲈ ⲈⲬ̄Ⲙ̄.(Ⅶ)ⲠⲈϤⲌⲞ. ⲀⲠⲘⲎⲎⲨⲈ'
ⲦⲎⲢϤ̄ ⲰϢ ⲈⲂⲞⲖ ⲈⲚ'ϪⲀⲔ Ⲛ̄ⲚⲈⲨϬⲒϪ' ⲈⲨⲰϢ Ⲙ̄ⲘⲞⲤ ϪⲈ ⲬⲒⲰⲒⲠⲈ ⲚⲀⲔ Ⲙ̄ⲠⲞ'ⲞⲨ Ⲱ
ⲠⲀⲚⲞⲘⲞⲤ Ⲛ̄ⲌⲎⲄⲈⲘⲰⲚ. ⲀⲨⲦⲦⲞ'ⲞⲦⲞⲨ Ⲛ̄ϬⲒ ⲚⲈⲨⲚⲞϬ,'ⲀⲨⲦⲀϨⲞϤ ⲈⲢⲀⲦϤ̄.' Ⲛ̄ⲦⲈⲨⲚⲞⲨ
ⲀⲨϬⲰⲚⲦ' Ⲛ̄ϬⲒ ⲠⲌⲎⲄⲈⲘⲰⲚ,'ⲀϤⲔⲈⲖⲈⲨⲈ ⲌⲚ̄ⲞⲨϬⲰ'Ⲛ̄Ⲧ ⲈϤ Ⲛ̄ⲦⲈⲨⲀⲠⲞⲫⲀ'ⲤⲒⲤ ⲈⲢⲞ-
ⲞⲨ Ⲛ̄ⲦⲈⲒ̈Ⲍ̄Ⲉ' ϪⲈ ⲀⲚⲞⲔ ⲠⲈ ⲀⲢⲒⲀⲚⲞⲤ' ⲠⲌⲎⲄⲈⲘⲰⲚ †ⲔⲈ'ⲖⲈⲨⲈ Ⲛ̄ⲤⲈⲢⲰⲔⲌ̄ Ⲙ̄Ⲡ[Ⲉ]-
Ϥ'ⲦⲈⲨϪⲞⲨⲰⲦ Ⲙ̄Ⲛ̄ⲦⲨⲞⲘ[Ⲛ̄Ⲧ]'ⲦⲈ Ⲙ̄ⲘⲀⲢⲦⲨⲢⲞⲤ Ⲛ̄ⲤⲈ'ⲚⲞⲬⲞⲨ ⲈⲌⲈⲚⲪⲞⲤⲤⲀ'ⲀⲨⲰ
ⲠⲒⲔⲈⲘⲚ̄ⲦⲤⲚ̄'ⲞⲞⲨⲤ Ⲛ̄ⲤⲞⲠ ⲀⲠⲀ Ϣ'Ⲛ̄ⲞⲨϤⲈ Ⲙ̄ⲠⲚⲈϤⲤⲚⲎⲨ' ⲀⲤⲈⲦ ⲚⲀⲨ Ⲛ̄ϨⲈⲚⲘⲎ'Ⲏ-
ϢⲈ Ⲛ̄ⲂⲀⲤⲀⲚⲞⲤ.' ⲀⲨⲈⲒ ⲆⲈ Ⲛ̄ϬⲒ Ⲛ̄ⲔⲈⲤⲦⲰ'ⲚⲀⲢⲒⲞⲤ, ⲀⲨⲤⲰⲔ Ⲛ̄'Ⲛ̄Ⲍ̄ⲀⲄⲒⲞⲤ, ⲀⲨⲬⲀⲖⲀ'
ⲚⲀⲨ ⲈⲚⲈⲨⲔⲖⲒⲤ· ⲌⲚ̄'ⲔⲞⲞⲨⲈ ⲀⲨϤⲒ Ⲛ̄ⲦⲈⲨⲀ'ⲠⲈ· ⲌⲚ̄ⲔⲞⲞⲨⲈ ⲀⲨ'ⲠⲖⲎⲄⲎ Ⲙ̄ⲘⲞⲞⲨ ⲌⲚ̄-'

---

126 R ii 30 f. l. ⲦⲀⲖϬⲞ. Ⅴ i 26. ⲀⲞⲨ-: ⲟ added. 28. l. ⲌⲀⲢⲰⲞⲨ (so B). 32. l. ⲀⲨⲚⲞⲞⲚⲈⲨ.
ii 4. A couple of words erased; ⲈⲨⲰϢ – ⲠⲌⲎⲄⲈⲘⲰⲚ added, perhaps by original hand. ii 15.
ⲘⲀⲦ-: Ⲧ added, wrongly. 29 f. l. ⲌⲚ̄ⲠⲔⲈⲖⲈⲂⲒⲚ.

A long passage in A (126 R ii 26 – Ⅴ i 2) is not represented in B. After this
(cf. 3–6): ⲀⲨⲰ ⲠⲈⲬⲀⲨ ⲚⲀⲨ ϪⲈ ⲬⲢⲞ Ⲙ̄ⲘⲰⲦⲚ̄ Ⲱ Ⲛ̄ⲌⲀⲄⲒⲞⲤ ⲈⲦⲦⲀⲒ̈ⲎⲨ, ϪⲈ ⲀϤϪⲰⲚ ⲈⲌⲞⲨⲚ
ⲈⲢⲰⲦⲚ̄ Ⲛ̄ϬⲒ ⲠⲈⲦⲚ̄ⲔⲖⲞⲘ; (10–13): ⲦⲈⲚⲞⲨ ⲆⲈ (l. ⲆⲈ ?) ⲂⲰⲔ ϢⲀⲠⲌⲎⲄⲈⲘⲰⲚ Ⲛ̄ⲦⲈⲦⲚ̄-
ⲀⲠⲞⲖⲞⲄⲒⲌⲈ ⲚⲀϤ; (18–25): Ⲛ̄ⲦⲞⲞⲨ ⲆⲈ ⲀⲨⲀⲌⲈⲢⲀⲦⲞⲨ <verb of motion missing?> Ⲉ-
ⲠⲌⲎⲄⲈⲘⲰⲚ ⲀⲨⲰϢ Ⲙ̄ⲘⲞⲨ Ⲙ̄ⲠⲈⲨⲚⲞⲨⲦⲈ. From 25 it again becomes possible to
compare the MSS.: 25–27.: ⲠⲌ. ⲆⲈ ⲀⲞⲨⲌⲞⲦⲈ ϪⲒⲦϤ̄ A; ⲠⲌ. ⲆⲈ ⲀϤⲈⲢⲌⲞⲦⲈ B. 27 f.
Ⲙ̄ⲠⲈϤⲯⲨⲬⲀϪⲈ A; Ⲙ̄ⲠⲈϤⲯⲀϪⲈ B. 28. ⲌⲀⲢⲞⲞⲨ (sic) A; ⲌⲀⲢⲰⲞⲨ † Ⲛ̄ⲦⲞⲞⲨ ⲆⲈ B. 31
f. ⲌⲀⲢⲞϤ ⲀⲨⲠⲞⲞⲚⲈ (sic) A; om. B. 32. ⲈⲬⲘ̄- A; ⲀⲬⲘ̄- (sic; = ⲈⲬⲘ̄- Sottas) B.
ii 1–3. ⲀⲠⲘⲎⲎⲨⲈ – ⲠⲌⲎⲄⲈⲘⲰⲚ A; om. B. 4 f. ⲀⲨⲦⲦⲞⲞⲦⲞⲨ Ⲛ̄ϬⲒ ⲚⲈⲨⲚⲞϬ; ⲚⲈⲨ-
ⲚⲞϬ ⲆⲈ B. 6. After ⲈⲢⲀⲦϤ̄, + · · · · Ⲛ̄ⲔⲈⲤⲞⲠ B. .7–12. Ⲛ̄ⲦⲈⲨⲚⲞⲨ — Ⲛ̄ⲦⲈⲒ̈Ⲍ̄Ⲉ ϪⲈ A;
[ ] ⲆⲈ ⲀⲨϬⲰⲚⲦ, and then perhaps [ⲀϤⲦ Ⲛ̄ⲦⲈⲨⲀⲠⲞ[ⲫⲀⲤⲒⲤ] Ⲉ[Ϥ]ϪⲰ Ⲙ̄ⲘⲞ[ⲤⲚ̄]
ϪⲈ B. 12. ⲀⲚⲞⲔ ⲠⲈ ⲀⲢⲒⲀⲚⲞⲤ ⲠⲌⲎⲄⲈⲘⲰⲚ; om. B. 14. Ⲛ̄ⲤⲈⲢⲰⲔⲌ̄ A; ⲈⲦⲢⲈⲨ
B. After this, a considerable loss of text from B. 27 f. ⲀⲨϤⲒ Ⲛ̄ⲦⲈⲨⲀⲠⲈ A, so
probably to be restored in B. 28. ⲌⲚ̄ⲔⲞⲞⲨⲈ A; [ⲌⲈⲚ]ⲔⲰ (sic ?) B. 29 f. ⲌⲚ̄Ⲙ̄ⲠⲔⲈ-
ⲖⲈⲂⲒⲚ (sic) A; ⲌⲚ̄Ⲍ̄ⲈⲚⲔ· B.

ⲙ̄ⲡⲕⲉⲗⲉⲃⲓⲛ.' ⲁⲩϭⲓⲕⲉ ⲛ̄ϫⲉⲛⲛⲟϭ' ⲙ̄ⲫⲟⲥⲥⲁ, ⲁⲩⲛⲟⲭⲟⲩ (127 R i) ⲉϩⲣⲁⲓ̈ ⲉⲣⲟⲟⲩ, ⲁⲩⲛⲉⲝ'ⲕⲱⲧϩ̄ ⲉⲭⲱⲟⲩ.' ⲧⲁⲓ ⲧⲉ ⲑⲉ ⲛ̄ⲧⲁⲩϫⲱⲕ'ⲉⲃⲟⲗ ⲛ̄ⲧⲉⲩⲙⲁⲣⲧⲩⲣⲓⲁ' ⲛϭⲓ
ⲡ̄ϣⲧⲉⲩϫⲟⲩⲱⲧ' ⲙ̄ⲛ̄ⲧⲥ̄ⲟⲙⲧⲉ ⲛ̄ϫⲁⲅⲓⲟⲥ· ⲁⲩϭⲓ ⲛ̄ⲛⲉⲩⲯⲩⲭⲏ ⲉϩⲣⲁⲓ̈ ⲉⲛⲁⲡⲏⲩⲉ
ⲉⲣⲉⲡϫⲁⲅⲓⲟⲥ ⲁⲡⲁ ⲩⲛ̄ⲟⲩϭⲉ ⲥⲱⲩⲧ̄' ⲉⲥⲱⲟⲩ, ⲛ̄ⲧⲟⲩ ⲙ̄ⲛ̄'ⲛⲉⲩⲕⲉⲥⲛⲏⲩ, ⲉⲩⲃⲏⲕ'ⲉ-
ϩⲣⲁⲓ̈ ⲉⲁⲡⲏⲩⲉ ⲛ̄ⲥⲟⲩ'ⲥⲟⲟⲩ ⲙ̄ⲡⲁⲱⲡⲉ ⲛ̄ⲧ'ⲭ̄ⲡ̄ⲥⲁⲩϭⲉ ⲙ̄ⲡⲉϩⲟⲟⲩ.' ⲁⲩϭⲓ ⲙ̄ⲡⲉⲕⲗⲟⲙ
ⲛ̄ⲁⲧ'ⲧⲁⲕⲟ ⲩⲁⲉⲛⲉϩ, ϩⲁⲙⲏⲛ.' ⲁ̄ⲛⲁⲅⲅⲉⲗⲟⲥ ⲙ̄ⲛ̄ⲛ̄'ⲇⲓⲕⲁⲓⲟⲥ ⲁⲥⲡⲁⲍⲉ' ⲙ̄ⲙⲟⲟⲩ ϩⲛ̄-
ⲧⲡⲁⲣⲁ'ⲇⲓⲥⲟⲥ, ⲁⲩⲱ ⲥⲉⲕⲓϩ'ⲙⲟⲧ ⲉⲭⲱⲛ ϩⲁⲧⲙ̄'ⲡⲉⲓⲱⲧ.' ⲙ̄ⲛ̄ⲥⲁⲛⲁⲓ̈ ⲁⲡ̄ϩⲏ'ⲅⲉⲙⲱⲛ
ⲕⲟⲧϥ̄ ⲙ̄ⲁ̄' ⲉⲡϫⲁⲅⲓⲟⲥ ⲁⲡⲁ ⲩⲛ̄ⲟⲩ'ϭⲉ, ⲡⲉⲭⲁⲩ ⲛⲁⲩ ϫⲉ' ⲁ̄ⲡⲁⲧⲉⲕⲗⲓⲑⲉ ⲟⲛ' ⲛ̄ϥ-
ⲑⲩⲥⲓⲁⲍⲉ ⲱ ⲡⲁⲛ'ϩⲟⲥⲓⲟⲥ; ⲁⲩⲟⲩⲱϣϥ̄' ⲛ̄ϭⲓ ⲡⲙⲁⲕⲁⲣⲓⲟⲥ ⲁⲡⲁ' ⲩⲛ̄ⲟⲩϭⲉ, ⲡⲉⲭⲁⲩ
ⲙ̄(ⲣ ii)ⲡϩⲏⲅⲉⲙⲱⲛ ϫⲉ ⲁⲓ̈'ϫⲟⲟⲥ ⲛⲁⲕ ⲛ̄ⲕⲉⲥⲟⲡ' ϫⲉ ⲛ̄ⲧⲛⲁⲑⲩⲥⲓⲁ ⲁⲛ'ⲛⲛⲉⲕ-
ⲙⲟⲩⲛϥ̄ ⲛ̄ϭⲓϫ'ⲧⲁⲕⲱ ⲛ̄ⲥⲱⲓ̈ ⲙ̄ⲡⲁ'ⲛⲟⲩⲧⲉ ⲓ̄ⲥ̄ ⲡⲉⲭ̄ⲥ̄·' ⲕⲁⲓ ⲅⲁⲣ ⲁⲗⲉⲛⲥⲱⲧⲏⲣ' ⲟⲩⲱ
ⲉⲩⲧⲁⲙⲟ ⲙ̄ⲙⲟⲛ' ϫⲉ ⲙ̄ⲡⲉⲣⲧ̄ ⲛ̄ⲛⲉⲧⲛ̄'ⲡⲉⲧⲟⲩⲁⲁⲃ ⲛ̄ⲛⲉⲩϩⲟⲱ'ⲱⲣ, ⲟⲩⲇⲉ ⲙ̄ⲡⲉⲣ-'
ⲛⲟⲩϫⲉ ⲛ̄ⲛⲉⲧⲛ̄ⲉⲛⲉ'ⲛⲉⲙⲙⲉ ϩⲁⲣⲟⲟⲩ ⲛ̄'ⲛⲉϣⲁⲩ. ⲁⲩϭⲱⲛⲧ̄' ⲇⲉ ⲛ̄ϭⲓ ⲡϩⲏⲅⲉⲙⲱⲛ'
ⲡⲉⲭⲁⲩ ϫⲉ ⲟⲩⲕⲟⲩⲛ' ⲉⲕⲧⲟⲛⲧⲛ̄ ⲙ̄ⲙⲟⲓ̈' ⲉⲛⲉϣⲁⲩ ⲙ̄ⲛ̄ⲛⲉⲩ'ϩⲟⲱⲣ; ⲡⲉⲭⲉⲡϫⲁ'ⲅⲓⲟⲥ
ⲛⲁⲩ ϫⲉ ⲕ̄ϩⲟⲟⲩ' ⲉϩⲟⲩⲉ ⲉⲣⲟⲟⲩ· ⲕⲁⲓ ⲅⲁⲣ' ⲛ̄ⲑⲩⲣⲓⲟⲛ ⲙ̄ⲛ̄ⲛ̄'ϩⲁⲧⲃⲉ ⲉⲩϣⲁⲛ'ⲥⲱⲧⲙ̄
ⲉⲡⲣⲁⲛ ⲙ̄ⲡ'ⲛⲟⲩⲧⲉ, ϣⲁⲩⲱⲙⲕ̄' ⲛ̄ⲧⲉⲩⲙⲁⲧⲟⲩ· ⲛ̄ⲧⲟⲕ' ⲇⲉ ⲕⲥⲱⲟⲩ ⲙ̄ⲙⲟⲩ.' ⲁⲩϭⲱⲛⲧ̄
ⲛ̄ϭⲓ ⲡϩⲏⲅⲉ'ⲙⲱⲛ, ⲁⲩⲕⲉⲗⲉⲩⲉ' ⲉⲧⲣⲟⲩⲑ̄ⲥⲟⲟⲩ ϩⲓϫⲉⲛ'ϩⲉⲛⲙⲁⲛ̄ⲛ̄ⲕⲟⲧⲕ̄' ⲙ̄ⲡⲉⲛⲓⲡⲉ
ⲛ̄ⲥⲉⲥⲁϩⲧⲉ (ⲣ̄ i)ϩⲁⲣⲟⲟⲩ ⲩⲁⲛⲧⲉⲛ̄'ⲩⲁⲁⲣ ⲙ̄ⲡⲉⲩⲥⲱ'ⲙⲁ ⲃⲱⲗ· ⲁⲩⲧⲣⲟⲩ'ⲧ̄ ⲛ̄ϩⲉⲛⲥⲫⲏ-
ⲣⲁ ⲛ̄'ⲕⲱⲧ ⲉⲛⲉⲩϭⲓⲝ.'ⲛ̄ϫⲁⲅⲓⲟⲥ ⲇⲉ ⲉⲛⲉⲩ'ⲭⲱ ⲙ̄ⲙⲟⲥ ϫⲉ ⲥⲱ'ⲧⲙ̄ ⲉⲣⲟⲛ ⲡⲉⲧⲥⲱⲧⲙ̄

---

127 R i 2. First ⲧ added, wrongly. 11. ℓ. ⲛ̄ⲥⲟⲩⲟⲩ. 20. ℓ. ϩⲙⲡⲛ. V i 4. = -ⲥⲫⲁⲓⲣⲁ.

126 V ii 31 – 127 R i 2. ⲁⲩϭⲓⲕⲉ — ⲉⲭⲱⲟⲩ A; ⲁⲩⲱ ⲁⲩⲣⲟⲕϩⲟⲩ ⲁⲩⲛⲟⲭⲟⲩ ⲉⲩⲛⲟϭ ⲙ̄-
ⲫⲟⲥⲥⲁ ⲛ̄ⲕⲱⲧϥ̄ ⲁⲩⲱ B.   5 ϥ. ⲡ̄ϣⲧⲉⲩϫⲟⲩⲱⲧ ⲙ̄ⲛ̄ⲧⲥⲟⲙⲧⲉ A; ⲡϩⲉ ⲩⲁⲧⲛ̄ⲩⲧⲟⲟⲩ B.
7. After ⲛ̄ϫⲁⲅⲓⲟⲥ, + ⲛ̄ⲥⲟⲩⲥⲟⲟⲩ ⲙ̄ⲡⲟⲟⲡⲉ B.   7. ⲁⲩϭⲓ A; ⲉⲁⲩϭⲓ B.   8. After
-ⲯⲩⲭⲏ, + ϩⲓⲧⲛ̄ⲛ̄ⲁⲅⲅⲉⲗⲟⲥ B.   8ϥ. ⲉϩⲣⲁⲓ̈ ⲉⲛⲁⲡⲏⲩⲉ A; ⲉⲧⲙ̄ⲧⲉⲣⲣⲟ ⲛ̄ⲁⲡⲏⲩⲉ B.
9. ⲉⲣⲉⲡϫⲁⲅⲓⲟⲥ ⲁⲡⲁ A; ⲉⲣⲉⲁⲡⲁ B.   11. ⲉⲥⲱⲟⲩ (sic) A; ⲉⲣⲟⲟⲩ B.   11-23. ⲛ̄ⲧⲟⲩ
— ϩⲁⲧⲙ̄ⲡⲉⲓⲱⲧ A; [ⲉⲩⲡⲁ]ⲩϭ (so Sottas) ϩ̄ⲛ̄ⲟⲩⲉⲓⲣⲏⲛⲏ ⲛ̄ⲧⲉⲡⲛⲟⲩⲧⲉ, ϩⲁⲙⲏⲛ
B.   24- 27. ⲁⲡ̄ϩⲏⲅ. —ⲛⲁⲩ A; ⲡⲉⲭⲉⲡϩⲏⲅ. ⲛ̄ⲁⲡⲁ ⲩⲛ̄ⲟⲩⲃⲉ B. 28. - ⲡⲓⲑⲉ A;
So B? (ⲧⲉⲑⲉ Munier; ϯⲑⲉ Sottas.) 29. ⲛϥ̄ⲑⲩⲥⲓⲁⲍⲉ A; ⲛ̄ⲉⲣⲟⲩⲥⲓⲁ B. 31.- ⲡⲙⲁⲕⲁⲣⲓⲟⲥ A; om. B.   32- ii 1. ⲡⲉⲭⲁⲩ ⲁⲡ̄ϩⲏⲅ. A; om. B.   1-3. ⲁⲓ̈ϫⲟⲟⲥ — ϫⲉ A;
om. B.   3. ⲛ̄ⲧⲛⲁⲑⲩⲥⲓⲁ A; ⲛ̄ⲧⲉⲛ[ⲛⲁ]ⲑⲩⲥⲓⲁⲍⲉ (sic) B. 4. ⲛ̄ⲛⲉⲕⲙⲟⲩⲛϥ̄ A;
ⲛⲉⲓⲙ. B.   6. -ⲛⲟⲩⲧⲉ A; -[ⲭ]ⲟⲉⲓⲥ B. 7. [ⲕⲁⲓ ⲅⲁⲣ ⲁⲗⲉⲛⲥⲱⲧⲏⲣ may be restored
in B, as A. 8. ⲟⲩⲱ ⲉⲩⲧⲁⲙⲟ ⲙ̄ⲙⲟⲛ A; [   ]ⲟⲩⲛⲁⲣⲓ[B. 9-12. B probably to be
restored as A. After 13, some loss of text from B. 23ϥ. B probably to be restored as A.
25 ϥ. ⲩⲁⲩⲱⲙⲕ̄ ⲛ̄ⲧⲉⲩⲙⲁⲧⲟⲩ A; ⲩⲁⲩⲉⲣϩⲟ[ⲧⲉ] B. 27. ⲕⲥⲱⲟⲩ A; ⲥⲱⲩ (sic) B. 30ϥ.
ϩⲓϫⲉⲛϩⲉⲛⲙⲁⲛ̄ⲛ̄ⲕⲟⲧⲕ̄ A; ϩⲓϩⲉⲛⲙⲁⲛ̄ϩ̄ⲙⲟⲟⲥ B. 32-Vi 4. ⲛ̄ⲥⲉⲥⲁϩⲧⲉ — ⲁⲩⲧⲣⲟⲩⲧ̄ A;

εογον νιμ ετωγ εzραϊ εpoy· σωyϯ εzραϊ εσω(ν)· νϯνα ναν zπ'νενzι-
ce μππε'νzιμωρια νϥ'τπνooγ ναν μμι'χαηλ παρχαγγελoc νyϥσom
ναν.' αγω εic μιχαηλ παρχαγγελoc αϥ'ει εβoλ zπτπε, αϥ'yωπε εyϯ-
σom' πνετoγααB, αγϥ'θε εyχε μπoγδωz' εpooy επτηρϥ.' αγBωσoy εzραϊ
zι'oγcoπ, αγϥ'πεp'oνoϊ επzηγεμω(ν),' πεχαγ ναγ χε oγ'πσηBε πτooτπ' zικωzτ zικελεBι(ν)' zιBαζανoc νιμ.' πετεzνακ αριϥ να(ν), (127 V ii) εν-
zocoν εyϥσom να(ν)' πσι πσoεic ιc, αγω'ϥνατσom ναν oν.' αϥσωπτ πσι
πzη'γεμων, αϥκελεγ'ε' ετpoγνoχoy εzoγν' εoγμα πκακε yα'πεγpαcτε
πcετμ'ϯoεικ ναγ oγδε μooγ' yαντoγμoγ. πτεγ'νoγ απzηγεμων' ανα-
χωpι ναγ·' πzαγιoc δε πτεpoγ'νoχoy εzoγν επκα'κε αγτpεzπκεμα'τoϊ
poεic εpooy.' zpαϊ δε zπτπαyε' πτεγyη εic oγ'νoσ πoγoειν αϥ'yα zπ-
πμα ενεγ'πzητϥ.' αγω εic πσoεic ιc' αϥει εβoλ zπτπε' μπoγμηηyε'
παγγελoc, αϥ'Bωκ yανετoγα'αB, πεχαϥ ναγ χε' σpo μμωτπ τηp'τπ, ω
ναμεpoc' ετoγααB· εic νετπ'θpoνoc αϊτazooγ' εpατoγ, αϊcτεϥα (128 R i)-
νoγ πνετπκλoμ' μπνετπcτoλη.' zγπoμεινε, αγω' μππpzoτε, χε oγπ zπ-
νoσ πσom μπ'zπyπηpε να'yωπε εβoλ zιτπ'τηγτπ πpαcτε·' cεναϯ νητπ πoγ'μηηyε πBαζα'νoc· cεναcικε π'νετπcωμα πθε νoγ'coγo, πcε-
νoχoγ εzενφocca,' χε ενε'ωχπ μπετπρμεεγε·' αλλα μπpcαoy'νoσ π-
oγoειy cενα'oγωνz εBoλ πσι' νετπcωμα· αγω' πμα ετoγνακω' πνετπ-
cωμα π'zητϥ, oγπzεν'νoσ πσom μπzπ'yπηpε ναyωπε πzητϥ, πcε-'
ϯεooγ νητπ ετBεπ'zice πτατετπyo'oγ οπ εχμπαpαν' ετoγααB.' ναϊ
δε πτεpεπcω'τηp χooγ ναγ, αϥc'παzε μμooγ, αϥ'Bωκ εzραϊ ελπηγε,
(R ii) εpεπαγγελoc π'πεooy zγμνεγε za'τεϥzη, zπoγειpη'νη, zαμην.'
νετoγααB δε αγεγϥ'pανε' πτεpoγναγ' επσoεic πθε πνετ'ταzε zππpπ,
αγ'oγνoϥ, αγcμoγ'επνoγτε yαντε'πoγoειν σι εzραϊ.' cτooγε δε πτεpεϥ-'

---

127 V ii 29. l. ναμελoc. 128 R? 13. Line erased, and -coγo — ενεωκπ substituted, apparently by same hand; - ωκπ in margin of 14. 26 f. l. -yonoγ.

127 V i 10. εpoγ A; ovθηγ B. 14. -διμωρια A; -διωγμoc B. 18. εic A; πτεγ-
noγ B. μιχαηλ A; au. B. 19 f. αyει A; ει B. 20. εBoλ zπτπε A; yαρo-
oγ B. 20-22. αyyωπε εyσom πνετoγααB A; nyσom nay B. 23 f.
-δωz εpooγ A; -BacanizE μμooγ B. 28 f. Restore ovπjcηγε in B, as A.
29 f. πτooτπ zικωzτ A; om. B. 30. zικελεBιν A; ovπκ. B. 31. zιBαζανoc
νιμ A; om. B. 32. After ναν, B breaks off.

ϥϣⲱⲡⲉ, ⲁϥⲟⲩⲉϩⲥⲁϩⲛⲉ ⲛ̄ϭⲓ ⲡⲁⲛⲟⲙⲟⲥ ⲛ̄ϩⲏⲅⲉⲙⲱⲛ ⲉⲧⲣⲟⲩⲥⲟⲃⲧⲉ ⲙ̄ⲡⲃⲏⲙⲁ ⲍⲛ̄-
ⲧⲁⲅⲟⲣⲁ. ⲁϥⲕⲉⲗⲉⲩⲉ ⲉⲧⲣⲟⲩⲉⲓⲛⲉ ⲛⲁϥ ⲙ̄ⲡⲁⲅⲓⲟⲥ ⲁⲡⲁ ⲯⲛⲟⲩϥⲉ ⲙⲛ̄ⲛⲉϥⲥⲛⲏⲩ.
ⲛ̄ⲧⲉⲣⲟⲩⲉⲓ ⲇⲉ ⲁϥϭⲱϣⲧ̄, ⲁϥⲛⲁⲩ ⲉⲣⲟⲟⲩ ⲉⲣⲉⲧⲉⲭⲁⲣⲓⲥ ⲙ̄ⲡⲛⲟⲩⲧⲉ ⲍⲙ̄ⲡⲉⲩϩⲟ, ⲉⲩ-
ⲣⲟⲩⲟⲉⲓⲛ ⲧⲏⲣⲟⲩ, ⲙⲛ̄ⲧⲙⲁⲕⲁⲣⲓⲁ ⲙ̄ⲡⲁⲣⲑⲉⲛⲟⲥ ⲁⲙⲁ ⲥⲟⲫⲓⲁ. ⲁϥⲩⲧⲟⲣⲧ̄ⲣ̄ ⲍⲙ̄-
ⲡⲉⲩⲡⲛ̄ⲁ ⲉϩⲣⲁⲓ ⲉⲝⲱⲟⲩ. ⲡⲉⲭⲁϥ ⲙ̄ⲡⲁⲅⲓⲟⲥ (128 V i) ⲁⲡⲁ ⲯⲛⲟⲩϥⲉ ⲙⲛ̄ⲛⲉϥ-
ⲥⲛⲏⲩ, ⲙⲁⲗⲓⲥⲧⲁ ⲧⲡⲁⲣⲑⲉⲛⲟⲥ ⲁⲙⲁ ⲥⲟⲫⲓⲁ ϫⲉ ⲥⲱⲧⲙ̄ ⲛ̄ⲥⲱⲓ ⲧⲉⲛⲟⲩ, ⲁⲣⲓ ⲑⲩⲥⲓⲁ,
ϫⲉ ϯ ⲯⲉⲛⲍ ⲧⲏⲓ ϩⲁⲧⲉⲧⲛ̄ⲙⲛ̄ⲧⲥⲁⲃⲉ, ⲉⲡⲓⲇⲏ ⲁⲧⲉⲧⲛ̄ϭⲛ̄ϫⲁⲣⲓⲥ ⲛⲁϩⲣⲁⲓ. ⲁⲩⲱ ⲛ̄-
ⲕⲉⲃⲁⲥⲁⲛⲟⲥ ⲛ̄ⲧⲁⲓⲧⲁⲁⲩ ⲛⲏⲧⲛ̄, ⲛ̄ⲧⲁⲓⲧⲁⲁⲩ ⲛⲏⲧⲛ̄ ⲛ̄ⲑⲉ ⲛ̄ⲟⲩⲉⲓⲱⲧ ⲉϥ ϯⲥⲃⲱ ⲛ̄ⲛⲉϥ-
ϣⲏⲣⲉ ⲉⲡⲱⲛϩ̄. ⲛⲁⲓ ⲇⲉ ⲛ̄ⲧⲉⲣⲟⲩⲥⲱⲧⲙ̄ ⲉⲣⲟⲟⲩ, ⲁⲩⲥⲱⲃⲉ. ⲡⲉⲭⲉⲁⲗⲁ ⲯⲛⲟⲩϭⲉ ⲡ-
ⲇⲓⲕⲁⲓⲟⲥ ⲛⲁϥ ⲉϥⲥⲱⲃⲉ ⲛ̄ⲥⲱϥ ϫⲉ ⲉⲕⲟⲩⲱϣ ⲧⲁⲥⲱⲧⲙ̄ ⲛ̄ⲥⲱⲕ ϩⲛ̄ⲟⲩ. ⲁϥⲣⲁⲩⲉ ⲇⲉ
ⲛ̄ϭⲓ ⲡⲍ̄ϩⲏⲅⲉⲙⲱⲛ, ⲡⲉⲭⲁϥ ⲛⲁϥ ϫⲉ ⲉⲓ̈ⲟⲩⲱϣ ⲛ̄ⲧⲉⲧⲛⲁϩⲏⲧ ⲛ̄ⲣⲟⲩⲱϣⲧ̄ ⲙ̄ⲁⲡⲟⲗ-
ⲗⲟ(ⲛ) ⲡⲛⲟϭ ⲛ̄ⲛⲟⲩⲧⲉ, ⲙⲁⲗⲗⲟⲛ ⲇⲉ ⲧⲁⲫⲣⲟⲇⲓⲇⲏ ⲙⲛ̄ⲧⲁⲣⲧⲩⲙⲓⲥ ⲙⲛ̄ (V ii)ⲥⲉⲩⲥ
ⲙⲛ̄ⲥⲉⲣⲁⲡⲓⲥ, ⲛ̄ⲧⲉⲧⲛ̄ⲧⲁⲗⲉⲟⲩⲕⲟⲩⲓ ⲛ̄ⲗⲓⲃⲁⲛⲟⲥ ⲉϩⲣⲁⲓ ⲛ̄ⲧⲁⲕⲁⲑⲏⲧⲛ̄ ⲉⲃⲟⲗ ⲛ̄-
ⲧⲉⲧⲛ̄ⲃⲱⲕ ⲉⲛⲉⲧⲛ̄ⲏⲓ ϩⲛ̄ⲟⲩⲉⲓⲣⲏⲛⲏ, ⲧⲁϯ ⲛⲏⲧⲛ̄ ⲛ̄ϩⲉⲛⲕⲉⲛⲟϭ ⲛ̄ⲧⲁⲓⲟ. ⲡⲉⲉⲛ-
ⲛⲁⲓⲟⲥ ⲇⲉ ⲁⲡⲁ ⲯⲛⲟⲩϥⲉ ⲡⲉⲭⲁϥ ⲙ̄ⲡ ϩⲏⲅⲉⲙⲱⲛ ϫⲉ ⲙⲁⲣⲉⲛⲛⲁⲩ ⲉⲧⲟⲙ ⲛ̄ⲛⲉⲕ-
ⲛⲟⲩⲧⲉ ⲛ̄ⲧⲛ̄ⲇⲟⲕⲓⲙⲁⲍⲉ ⲙ̄ⲙⲟⲟⲩ. ⲡⲉⲭⲉⲡ ϩⲏⲅⲉⲙⲱⲛ ⲛ̄ⲛⲉϥⲙⲁⲧⲟⲓ ϫⲉ ϭⲉ ⲡⲏ, ⲁ-
ⲛⲓⲥⲟⲩ ⲛⲁⲓ ⲉⲡⲓⲙⲁ. ⲁⲩⲡⲱⲧ ⲛ̄ϭⲓ ⲛⲟⲩⲏⲏⲃ, ⲁⲩⲉⲓⲛⲉ ⲛ̄ⲛⲉⲩⲛⲟⲩⲧⲉ ⲉⲧⲁⲅⲟⲣⲁ, ⲁⲩ-
ⲧⲁϩⲟⲟⲩ ⲉⲣⲁⲧⲟⲩ ϩⲓϫⲉⲛ ⲛⲉⲩⲃⲁⲥⲓⲥ. ⲡ̄ⲁⲅⲓⲟⲥ ⲇⲉ ⲛ̄ⲧⲉⲣⲟⲩⲛⲁⲩ ⲉⲛⲉⲉⲓⲇⲱⲗⲟⲛ, ⲁⲩ-
ⲃⲟⲥⲧⲟⲩ ⲉϩⲣⲁⲓ ⲛ̄ϭⲓ ⲁ̇ⲡⲁ ⲯⲛⲟⲩϥⲉ ⲙⲛ̄ ⲁⲛⲇⲣⲉⲁⲥ ⲙⲛ̄ⲡⲉⲧⲣⲟⲥ ⲙⲛ̄ⲫⲓⲗⲏⲙⲙ(ⲛ)
ⲙⲛ̄ⲛⲉϥⲥⲛⲏⲩ· ⲁⲡⲟⲩⲁ ⲡⲟⲩⲁ ⲛⲉⲭ ⲡⲉⲩⲉⲓⲇⲱⲗⲟⲛ ⲉ(129 R i)ⲡⲙⲛ̄ⲕⲁϩ, ⲁⲩⲁⲁⲩ ⲛ̄ⲕⲟⲩⲓ
ⲕⲟⲩⲓ· ⲁⲩⲱ ⲛⲥⲉⲉⲡⲉ ⲛ̄ⲛⲉⲧⲟⲩⲁⲁⲃ ⲁⲩϫⲓⲱⲛⲉ ⲁⲩⲥⲓⲧⲉ ⲉⲝⲉⲛⲛⲟⲩⲏⲏⲃ ⲙⲛ̄ⲡ ϩⲏⲅⲉⲙⲱⲛ.
ⲁⲩⲱ ⲁⲡ ϩⲏⲅⲉⲙⲱⲛ ϭⲱⲛⲧ̄ ⲉⲙⲁⲧⲉ ϩⲛ̄ⲟⲩⲟⲣⲅⲏ, ⲁϥⲟⲩⲉϩⲥⲁϩⲛⲉ ⲉⲧⲣⲟⲩⲭⲉⲣⲱ ⲛ̄ϩⲉⲛ-
ⲧⲣⲓⲣ ⲛ̄ⲕⲱϩⲧ̄ ⲛ̄ⲥⲉⲥⲱⲛϩ̄ ⲛ̄ⲛⲁϩⲁⲡⲓⲟⲥ ⲛ̄ⲥⲉⲛⲟϫⲟⲩ ⲉϩⲟⲩⲛ ⲉⲣⲟⲥ ⲛ̄ⲥⲉ ⲧⲱⲕ ⲉϩⲟⲩⲛ
ϣⲁ(ⲛ)ⲧⲉⲛⲉⲩⲕⲉⲉⲥ ⲣⲱⲕϩ̄. ⲁⲩⲉⲓⲣⲉ ⲕⲁⲧⲁⲡⲉⲩϫⲁ ϫⲉ, ⲁⲩⲙⲟⲩϩ ⲛ̄ⲛⲉⲧⲣⲓⲣ ⲛ̄ⲕⲱϩⲧ̄.
ⲛⲉϥϫⲟⲥⲉ ⲡⲉ ⲛ̄ϭⲓ ⲡϩⲁϫ ⲛ̄ⲛⲉⲧⲣⲓⲣ ⲛ̄ⲕⲱϩⲧ̄ ⲉⲝⲁⲡⲧⲩⲙⲟⲥ ⲧⲏⲣϥ̄ ⲛ̄ⲛⲁⲁϫⲟⲩⲱⲧ ⲙ̄-
ⲙⲁⲍⲉ ⲛ̄ϫⲓⲥⲉ. ⲡϩⲁⲅⲓⲟⲥ ⲇⲉ ⲁⲡⲁ ⲯⲛⲟⲩϥⲉ ⲙⲛ̄ⲛⲉϥⲥⲛⲏⲩ ⲛⲉⲩⲥⲟⲡⲥ̄ ⲙ̄ⲡⲛⲟⲩⲧⲉ ⲉⲩ-
ϩⲓⲡⲉⲥⲏⲧ ⲛ̄ⲛⲉⲧⲣⲓⲣ ⲉⲩϫⲱ ⲙ̄ⲙⲟⲥ ϫⲉ ⲥⲱⲧⲙ̄ ⲉⲣⲟⲛ ⲡⲛⲟⲩⲧⲉ ⲡⲉⲓⲱⲧ (R ii) ⲙ̄ⲡⲉⲛ-
ϫⲟⲉⲓⲥ ⲓ̅ⲥ̅ ⲡⲉⲭ̅ⲥ̅· ϩⲙ̄ⲡⲉⲕⲣⲁⲛ ϣⲁⲣⲉ ⲑⲁⲗⲁⲥⲥⲁ ϩⲣⲟⲕ ⲙ̄ⲙⲟⲥ ⲛ̄ⲧⲉⲡⲕⲱϩⲧ̄ ⲱϣⲙ̄ ⲛ̄-
ⲧⲉ ⲧⲅⲉϩⲉⲛⲛⲁ ⲕⲁⲧⲟⲟⲧⲥ̄ ⲉⲃⲟⲗ ⲛ̄ⲧⲉ ⲡⲕⲱϩⲧ̄ ⲃⲱⲗ ⲉⲃⲟⲗ. ⲛⲉⲧϣⲏⲩ ϩⲛ̄ⲛⲉⲩⲁⲛⲁⲅⲕⲏ

---

128 V i 26–29. Lines short; hole in parchment. ii 1. = -ⲍⲉⲩⲥ. 30. ⲙⲛ̄- seems superfluous. 129 R i 14. l. ⲉⲣⲟⲟⲩ. 22. = -ⲇⲏⲙⲟⲥ. 23. l. ⲛ̄ⲁϫⲟⲩⲱⲧ. This column is
a line short, owing to a hole in the parchment.

ϣⲁⲕⲥⲉⲗ⸗ⲥⲱⲗⲟⲩ· ⲛⲉⲧⲙⲟⲕⲍ̄' ϣⲁⲕⲉⲣⲡⲁϩⲣⲉ ⲉⲣⲟⲟⲩ·' ⲛⲉⲧⲥⲟⲣⲙ̄ ϩⲛ̄ⲑⲁⲗⲁⲥⲥⲁ
ϣⲁⲕⲃⲟⲏⲑⲓⲁ ⲉ'ⲣⲟⲟⲩ· ⲛ̄ⲧⲉⲓϩⲉ ⲟⲛ' ⲡⲁⲭⲟⲉⲓⲥ ⲉⲕⲉⲃⲟⲏⲑⲓⲁ' ⲉⲣⲟⲛ ϩⲱⲛ, ⲛⲅ̄-'
ⲛⲁϩⲙⲉⲛ ϩⲛ̄ⲧⲉⲓⲁ'ⲛⲁⲅⲕⲏ· ϫⲉ ⲛ̄ⲧⲟⲕ' ⲡⲉ ⲡⲛⲟⲩⲧⲉ ⲙ̄ⲙⲉ,' ⲧⲃⲟⲏⲑⲓⲁ ⲛ̄ⲟⲩⲟⲛ' ⲛⲓⲙ
ⲉⲧϩⲏⲩ ϩⲛ̄'ⲛⲉⲩⲑⲗⲓⲯⲓⲥ· ϫⲉ' ⲧⲱⲕ ⲧⲉ ⲧϭⲟⲙ ⲙⲛ̄'ⲡⲉⲟⲟⲩ ϣⲁⲉⲛⲉϩ,' ϩⲁⲙⲏⲛ.'

ⲁⲓⲧⲉⲓ Δⲉ ⲉⲣⲉⲛ̄ⲍⲁⲅⲓⲟⲥ' ϫⲱ ⲛ̄ⲛⲁⲓ ⲉⲩⲧⲱⲃⲍ̄' ⲙ̄ⲡⲛⲟⲩⲧⲉ, ⲉⲓⲥϩⲏⲧⲉ ⲉⲓⲥ ⲟⲩⲕⲗⲟⲟ-
ⲗⲉ' ⲛ̄ⲉⲉⲓⲱⲧⲉ ⲁⲥⲡⲱⲣ'ϣ ⲉⲃⲟⲗ ⲉϫⲛ̄ⲡⲉⲧ'ⲣⲓⲣ, ⲁⲥϭⲟⲩⲉⲉⲓⲱⲧ (129 Vi) ⲉⲡⲉⲥⲏⲧ
ⲉϫⲱⲟⲩ,' ⲁⲥⲱϣⲙ̄ ⲙ̄ⲡⲕⲱϩⲧ̄·' ⲁⲩⲱ ⲙ̄ⲙⲉⲉⲣⲉ ⲉⲧⲉⲣⲉⲛ̄ⲍⲁⲅⲓⲟⲥ ⲥⲱⲛϩ̄ ⲛ̄ϩⲏⲧⲟⲩ
ⲁⲩⲃⲱⲗ ⲉ'ⲃⲟⲗ ϩⲓⲧⲙ̄ⲡⲁⲅⲅⲉⲗⲟⲥ ⲙ̄ⲡⲛⲟⲩⲧⲉ,' ⲁⲩⲧⲟⲟⲧⲟⲩ ⲁⲩⲛ̄'ⲧⲟⲩ ⲉϩⲣⲁⲓ ϩⲛ̄ⲛⲉ-
ⲧ'ⲣⲓⲣ, ⲁⲩⲁϩⲉⲣⲁⲧⲟⲩ' ⲉϫⲙ̄ⲡⲃⲏⲙⲁ ⲉⲙ̄'ⲛⲗⲁⲁⲩ ⲛ̄ⲧⲁⲕⲟ' ϣⲟⲟⲡ ⲙ̄ⲙⲁⲩ.' ⲁⲡⲙⲏⲏϣⲉ
ⲧⲏⲣ'ϥ̄ ⲣ̄ϣⲡⲏⲣⲉ, ⲁⲩⲧⲉⲟⲟⲩ' ⲙ̄ⲡⲛⲟⲩⲧⲉ ⲛ̄ⲛⲉ'ⲭⲣⲓⲥⲧⲓⲁⲛⲟⲥ ⲡⲉϫⲉ ⲓⲥ̄.' ⲡϩⲁⲅⲓⲟⲥ
Δⲉ ⲁⲡⲁ' ⲫⲓⲗⲓⲡⲡⲉ ⲛ̄ⲉⲟⲩ'ⲛⲉⲱⲇⲉⲣⲓⲥ ⲛ̄ϣⲱ'ⲱⲣⲉ ⲡⲉ ϩⲙ̄ⲡⲉϥ'ⲥⲱⲙⲁ, ⲉϥϩⲟⲥⲉ ⲉ-
ϫⲛ̄ⲛⲉϥⲥⲛⲏⲩ ⲧⲏ'ⲣⲟⲩ ⲛ̄ⲟⲩϭⲓⲛ ⲛ̄'ⲛⲁϩⲃⲉ ⲉⲛϣⲱⲓ·' ⲁⲩϫⲓ ⲛⲁⲩ ⲛⲟⲩ'ⲙⲛ̄ⲧⲥⲁⲣϩⲏⲧ
ⲛ̄ⲧⲉⲗⲉ ⲡⲕⲁ, ⲁⲩ'ⲥⲟⲩⲧⲛ̄ⲧⲟⲟⲧⲟⲩ ⲉⲃⲟⲗ' ⲉϫⲛ̄ⲛⲉϥⲥⲛⲏⲩ' ⲧⲏⲣⲟⲩ, ⲁϥⲃⲱⲡⲉ' ⲛ̄ⲛⲉⲉⲓⲡⲗⲱⲛ
ⲉ(Vii)ⲧⲉⲣⲉⲡⲗⲓⲙⲏⲛ ⲛ̄ⲡⲣ̄'ⲣⲱⲟⲩ ⲥⲏϩ ⲉⲣⲟⲟⲩ, ⲁⲩ'ⲁⲁⲩ ⲛ̄ⲕⲟⲩⲓ̈ ⲕⲟⲩⲓ.' ⲙⲛ̄ⲛⲥⲱⲥ ⲁⲩ-
ϯⲡⲉⲩ'ⲟⲩⲟⲓ ⲉⲡϩⲏⲅⲉⲙⲱⲛ' ⲁⲩⲡⲉⲉⲛⲉⲡⲉⲩⲑⲣⲟ'ⲛⲟⲥ ϩⲁⲣⲟϥ, ⲡⲁⲓ ⲉⲛϥ̄'ϩⲙⲟⲟⲥ ϩⲓϫⲱϥ,'
ⲁⲩⲱ ⲛⲉⲩϩⲓⲟⲩⲉ ⲉϩⲟⲩⲛ' ϩⲙ̄ⲡⲉϥϩⲟ ⲛⲟⲩⲙⲏ'ⲏϣⲉ ⲛ̄ⲛⲟⲩⲁϫⲉ' ⲙ̄ⲙⲛ̄ⲧⲁⲧϫⲓ ⲛ̄ϭⲟⲛⲥ·
ⲉⲃⲟⲗ Δⲉ ⲡⲕⲟⲥ' ⲛ̄ϩⲧⲟⲡ ⲛ̄ⲧⲁⲩϫⲓⲧϥ̄' ⲁⲩⲧⲟⲟⲧϥ̄ ⲛ̄ϭⲓ ⲛⲉⲩ'ⲛⲟϭ ⲉⲧⲁϩⲉⲣⲁⲧⲟⲩ, ⲁⲩ-'
ⲑⲙ̄ⲥⲟϥ ⲉⲕⲉⲛⲡⲉⲩ'ⲑⲣⲟⲛⲟⲥ ⲛ̄ⲧⲉⲩϩⲉ·' ⲁⲩⲱ ⲡϩⲁⲅⲓⲟⲥ ⲁⲡⲁ' ⲫⲓⲗⲓⲡⲡⲉ ⲁⲩⲥⲟⲩ'ⲁⲩ-
ⲥⲟⲛϥ̄ ⲛ̄ⲧⲟⲟⲧϥ̄' ⲙ̄ⲛⲣⲁⲧϥ̄.' ⲡϩⲏⲅⲉⲙⲱⲛ Δⲉ ⲉ'ⲃⲟⲗ ϩⲓⲧⲙ̄ⲡⲛⲟϭ' ⲛ̄ϣⲓⲡⲉ ⲛ̄ⲧⲁⲩϫⲓⲧϥ̄
ϩⲛ̄ⲧⲙⲏⲧⲉ ⲙ̄'ⲡⲙⲏⲏϣⲉ, ⲁⲩ'ϩⲱⲥ ⲙ̄ⲡⲁⲩ ⲉⲧ'ⲙ̄ⲙⲁⲩ, ⲁϥⲥϩⲟⲩⲉⲣ'ⲡⲅⲉⲛⲟⲥ ⲧⲏⲣϥ̄ ⲛ̄ⲛⲉ-
ⲭⲣⲓⲥⲧⲓⲁⲛⲟⲥ' ϩⲓⲭⲙ̄ⲡⲕⲁϩ. (130 Ri) ⲡϩⲁⲅⲓⲟⲥ Δⲉ ⲁⲡⲁ' ϣⲛⲟⲩϭⲉ ⲡⲉϫⲁϥ' ⲙ̄ⲡ-
ϩⲏⲅⲉⲙⲱⲛ' ϫⲉ ⲉⲡⲓⲇⲏ ⲁⲕⲧⲟⲗⲟ'ⲙⲁ ⲉϫⲓⲟⲩⲁ ⲉⲡⲣⲁⲛ' ⲙ̄ⲡⲁⲛⲟⲩⲧⲉ, ⲡⲁⲓ ⲉ'ⲛⲅ̄ⲙⲡ-
ϣⲁ ⲙ̄ⲙⲟϥ' ⲁⲛ ⲙ̄ⲡⲉϥⲉⲟⲟⲩ' ⲉⲧⲟⲩⲁⲁⲃ, ⲉϥⲉⲧⲱ'ⲃⲉ ⲛⲁⲕ ϩⲛ̄ⲟⲩϭⲉ'ⲡⲏ, ⲉϥⲉϩⲟⲣⲓ-
ⲍⲉ' ⲉϫⲱⲕ ⲛⲟⲩⲙⲛ̄ⲧ'ⲁⲡⲟ, ⲛ̄ⲧⲉⲡⲉⲕϣⲓⲡⲉ ⲟⲩⲱⲛϩ̄ ⲉⲃⲟⲗ' ϩⲛ̄ⲧⲙⲏⲧⲉ ⲙ̄ⲡⲓⲧⲩ'ⲙⲟⲥ
ⲧⲏⲣϥ̄, ϫⲉⲕⲁⲥ' ⲉⲩⲉⲉⲉⲓⲙⲉ ϫⲉ ⲟⲩⲛⲟⲩ'ⲧⲉ ⲉⲟⲩⲛ̄ϭⲟⲙ ⲙ̄ⲙⲟⲩ ⲡⲉ ⲓⲥ̄ ⲡⲉϫⲥ̄' ⲉϩⲟⲩ-
ⲉⲛⲉⲕⲛⲟⲩⲧⲉ' ⲉⲧⲙⲟⲟⲩⲧ. ⲁⲩⲱ' ⲛ̄ⲧⲉⲩⲛⲟⲩ ⲁⲩⲱⲗϩ̄' ⲛ̄ϭⲓ ⲛⲉⲥⲡⲟⲧⲟⲩ ⲙ̄ⲡϩⲏⲅⲉⲙⲱⲛ'
ⲙ̄ⲡⲉϥⲗⲁⲥ ⲛ̄ϩⲟⲩ(ⲛ) ⲉⲣⲱϥ, ⲁⲡⲉϥϣ̄'ϭⲁϫⲉ ⲉⲡⲧⲏⲣϥ̄.' ⲁⲩϭⲱⲛⲧ ⲛ̄ϭⲓ ⲡϩⲏ'ⲅⲉⲙⲱⲛ,
ⲁⲩϭⲱⲣⲙ̄' ⲉⲛⲁⲧⲉⲩⲧⲁϫⲓⲥ ϩⲛ̄'ⲧⲙⲏⲧⲉ ⲙ̄ⲡⲙⲏ'ⲏϣⲉ. ⲙⲛ̄ⲛⲥⲱⲥ (Rii) ⲁⲩⲧⲱⲟⲩⲛ ⲉϥ-
ϩⲙⲟ'ⲟⲥ, ⲁⲩⲃⲱⲕ ϣⲁ'ⲓ̈ⲟⲩⲗⲓⲟⲥ ⲡⲣⲙ̄ⲕⲃⲉϩⲥ̄,' ⲁⲩϭⲱ ⲉϥϭⲱⲣⲙ̄ ⲟⲩⲃⲏⲩ ⲉⲡϩⲁⲅⲓⲟⲥ'

---

129 R ii 26. =ⲉⲧⲓ. 32. l.ⲉⲓⲱⲧⲉ. V i 4. l.ⲥⲟⲛϩ. 5f. l. ⲉⲃⲟⲗ. 9. l. ⲉϩⲣⲁⲓ. 13. l. ⲙⲙⲟⲟⲩ.
20. =-ⲛⲉⲱⲧⲉⲣⲟⲥ. 32. l. ⲛ̄ⲛⲥⲓⲅⲛⲟⲛ; see commentary. ii 13. After Δⲉ, <ϩⲓⲧⲙ̄–>?
32. Hole in parchment. 130 R i 4f. =-ⲧⲟⲗⲙⲁ. 15f. =-Δⲏⲙⲟⲥ.

απα ψⲛοⲩϥε' ϫⲉⲕⲁⲥ ⲉϥⲉⲡⲁⲣⲁⲕⲁ'ⲗⲓ ⲙ̅ⲙⲟϥ ⲧⲁⲣⲉϥ'ⲟⲩⲱⲛ ⲛ̅ⲧⲉϥⲧⲁⲡ'ⲣⲟ· ⲓⲟⲩⲗⲓⲟⲥ
ⲇⲉ ⲡ'ⲃⲟⲏⲑⲟⲥ ⲡⲕⲱⲙⲏ'ⲧⲁⲣⲏⲥⲓⲟⲥ ⲡⲣ̅'ⲕⲍⲉⲋⲍ ⲁϥⲡⲉϥ'ⲟⲩⲟⲓ̈ ⲉⲡϩⲁⲅⲓⲟⲥ ⲁⲡⲁ'ψⲛⲟⲩϥⲉ, ⲁϥⲡⲁ'ⲣⲁⲕⲁⲗⲉⲓ ⲙ̅ⲙⲟϥ' ⲉⲧⲃⲉⲡϩⲏⲅⲉⲙⲱⲛ' ϫⲉ ⲉϥⲉⲑⲉⲣⲁⲡⲉⲩⲉ' ⲙ̅ⲙⲟϥ· ⲡϩⲁⲅⲓⲟⲥ' ⲇⲉ ⲁⲡⲁ ψⲛⲟⲩϥⲉ' ⲡⲉϫⲁϥ ⲛ̅ⲓⲟⲩⲗⲓⲟⲥ' ϫⲉ ⲉⲕⲟⲛⲱϣ ⲉⲧⲣⲁ'ϫⲟⲩ; ⲡⲉϫⲁϥ ⲱ
ⲡⲁ'ⲥⲟⲛ ⲁϥⲱ ⲛ̅ⲧⲛⲁ'ⲣⲁⲧⲥⲱⲧⲙ̅ ⲛ̅ⲥⲱⲕ' ⲁⲛ· ⲕⲁⲓ ⲅⲁⲣ ⲙ̅'ⲡⲛⲁⲩ ⲉⲣⲉⲡⲁϫⲟⲉⲓⲥ' ⲧⲁⲗⲏⲩ ⲉⲡⲉⲥϥⲟⲥ,' ⲉⲣⲉⲛⲉⲓⲟⲩⲇⲁⲓ ϯⲉⲓ'ⲃⲧ ⲛⲁⲩ, ⲉⲩⲛⲉϫ'ⲡⲁϭⲋ ⲉϩⲟⲩⲛ ⲉϩ'ⲣⲁⲩ, ⲁϥⲱϣ ⲉϩⲣⲁⲓ̈ (130 V i) ϣⲁⲡⲉϥⲉⲓⲱⲧ ⲉϥ'ϫⲱ ⲙ̅ⲙⲟⲥ ϫⲉ ⲁⲛⲟⲕ' ⲡⲉ ⲓⲥ̅ ⲡⲉⲧⲉⲙⲡⲉϥ'
ⲣⲁⲧⲥⲱⲧⲙ̅ ⲉⲛⲉϩ· ⲉⲩϫⲉ ⲡⲉⲛⲧⲁⲩⲧⲁ'ⲙⲓⲟ ⲛ̅ⲧⲡⲏ ⲙⲛ̅'ⲡⲕⲁϩ ⲙ̅ⲡⲉϥⲣⲁⲧ'ⲥⲱⲧⲙ̅ ⲉ-
ⲛⲉϩ, ⲉⲓⲉ' ϯⲛⲁⲣⲁⲧⲥⲱⲧⲙ̅ ⲉⲁ'ⲛⲟⲕ ⲡⲉ ⲡⲉϥϩⲙ̅ϩⲁⲗ' ⲁⲩⲱ ⲛ̅ⲧⲟϥ ⲡⲉⲛⲧ'ⲁϥⲧⲁⲙⲓⲟⲓ̈
ϩⲱ,' ⲁⲩⲱ ⲉⲣⲉⲡⲁⲛⲓⲃⲉ' ϩⲛ̅ⲛⲉϥϭⲓϫ; ⲧⲉ'ⲛⲟⲩ ϭⲉ ⲁⲛⲁⲩ ϫⲉ ⲟⲩ' ⲡⲉⲧ̅ⲕⲟⲩⲉϣⲧⲣⲁ'ⲁϥ
ⲱ ⲡⲁⲥⲟⲛ.' ⲡⲉϫⲉⲓⲟⲩⲗⲓⲟⲥ ϫⲉ ⲉⲓ'ⲟⲩⲱϣ ⲉⲧⲣⲉⲡⲓ'ⲁ'ⲛⲟⲙⲟⲥ ⲛ̅ϩⲏⲅⲉ'ⲙⲱⲛ ϣⲁϫⲉ'
ⲛ̅ⲥⲉⲟⲩⲱⲛ ⲛ̅ϭⲓ ⲧⲉϥ'ⲧⲁⲡⲣⲟ. ⲡⲉϫⲉ'ⲡϩⲁⲅⲓⲟⲥ ⲁⲡⲁ ψⲛⲟⲩϥⲉ ⲛ̅ⲓⲟⲩⲗⲓⲟⲥ'ϫⲉ ϯϭⲟⲛϩ̅
ⲛ̅ϭⲓ ⲡⲁ'ⲛⲟⲩⲧⲉ ⲓⲥ̅ ⲡⲉⲭⲥ̅' ϫⲉ ⲛ̅ϯⲛⲁⲩϣⲁϫⲉ ⲁⲛ ⲉⲓⲙⲏⲧⲉ' ⲛ̅ϫⲓ ⲛⲟⲩⲙⲉⲗⲁ'ⲙⲛ̅-
ⲟⲩⲕⲁϣ ⲙⲛ̅'ⲟⲩⲭⲁⲣⲧⲏⲥ ⲛ̅ϥⲥ̅(Vii)ϩⲁⲓ̈ ⲉϥⲧⲁⲉⲓⲟ ⲙ̅ⲡⲁ'ⲛⲟⲩⲧⲉ. ⲛ̅ⲧⲉⲩⲛⲟⲩ' ⲁⲡϩⲏ-
ⲅⲉⲙⲱⲛ ϫⲱ'ⲣⲙ̅ ⲉⲛⲁⲧⲧⲁⲝⲓⲥ,' ⲁⲩⲉⲓⲛⲉ ⲛⲁⲩ ⲛ̅ⲟⲩⲕⲁϣ' ⲙ̅ⲛ̅ⲟⲩⲙⲉⲗⲁ ⲙⲛ̅ⲟⲩ'ⲭⲁⲣ-
ⲧⲏⲥ, ⲁϥϫⲓⲧⲟⲩ,' ⲁϥⲥϩⲁⲓ̈ ⲛ̅ⲧⲉⲓϩⲉ ⲉϥ'ϫⲱ ⲙ̅ⲙⲟⲥ ϫⲉ ϯϩⲟ'ⲙⲟⲗⲟⲧⲓ ⲙ̅ⲙⲟⲕ ⲓⲥ̅' ⲡⲉⲭⲥ̅
ⲡⲛⲟⲩⲧⲉ' ⲛ̅ⲛⲉⲭⲣⲏⲥⲧⲓⲁⲛⲟⲥ·' ϯⲥⲟⲟⲩⲛ ϫⲉ ⲛ̅ⲧⲟⲕ' ⲡⲉ ⲡⲛⲟⲩⲧⲉ ϩⲛ̅ⲟⲩ'ⲡⲁⲣⲣⲏⲥⲓⲁ,
ⲁⲩⲱ ϫⲉ' ⲁⲙⲁⲣⲓⲁ ϫⲡⲟⲕ, ⲁⲕ'ⲁⲗⲉ ⲉϫⲙ̅ⲡⲉⲥⲧⲁⲩ'ⲣⲟⲥ, ⲁⲕⲙⲟⲩ, ⲁⲩⲱ' ⲁⲕⲱⲛϩ̅
ⲉⲧⲃⲉⲧⲉⲕ'ϩⲓⲕⲱⲛ· ⲁⲗⲗⲁ ⲛ̅ⲣ̅'ⲣⲱⲟⲩ ⲛⲉⲧⲟⲛⲁⲅ'ⲕⲁⲍⲉ ⲙ̅ⲙⲟⲛ· ⲙ̅ⲙⲟⲛ ⲛ̅ⲧⲟⲕ ⲡⲉ
ⲡ'ⲛⲟⲩⲧⲉ ⲙ̅ⲙⲉ. ⲛ̅ⲧⲉⲩ'ⲛⲟⲩ ⲁⲩϫⲓ ⲙ̅ⲡϫⲱ'ⲱⲙⲉ, ⲁⲩⲁϥϫ ⲛ̅ϭⲓ' ⲟⲩⲟⲛ ⲛⲓⲙ ⲉⲧⲥⲟⲟⲩ(ⲛ̅)'
ⲛ̅ⲥϩⲁⲓ̈, ⲁⲩⲱ ⲛⲉⲧⲛ̅'ⲥⲉⲥⲟⲟⲩⲛ ⲁⲛ ⲁⲩⲥⲱ'ⲧⲙ̅ ϩⲓⲧⲛ̅ⲛⲉⲧⲛⲟⲓ̈.' ϩⲛ̅ⲧⲉⲩⲛⲟⲩ ⲇⲉ ⲉⲧⲙ̅'-
ⲙⲁⲩ ⲁⲡϩⲁⲅⲓⲟⲥ ⲁⲡⲁ (131 R i) ψⲛⲟⲩϥⲉ ϥⲉⲓ ⲛ̅ⲛⲉϥ'ⲃⲁⲗ ⲉϩⲣⲁⲓ̈ ⲉⲧⲡⲉ, ⲁϥ'ϣⲗⲏⲗ
ⲉϥϫⲱ ⲙ̅ⲙⲟⲥ' ϫⲉ ⲥⲱⲧⲙ̅ ⲉⲣⲟⲓ̈ ⲡⲁϫⲟⲉⲓⲥ' ⲓⲥ̅ ⲡⲉⲭⲥ̅ ⲡⲉⲛⲧⲁϥⲉⲓ' ⲉⲡⲉⲥⲏⲧ ⲉⲡⲕⲟⲥ-
ⲙⲟⲥ,' ⲁϥϣⲱⲡⲉ ⲛ̅ⲟⲩⲥⲱ'ⲧⲏⲣⲓⲁ ⲙ̅ⲡⲅⲉⲛⲟⲥ' ⲧⲏⲣϥ̅ ⲛⲁⲇⲁⲙ·' ⲛⲉⲧϣⲱⲛⲉ ⲁⲕⲧⲁⲗ'-
ϭⲟⲟⲩ· ⲛⲉⲧⲙⲟⲕϩ̅' ⲁⲕⲣ̅ⲡⲁϩⲣⲉ ⲉⲣⲟⲟⲩ·' ⲛ̅ⲕⲟⲩⲣ ⲁⲕⲧⲣⲟⲩⲥⲱⲧⲙ̅·' ⲛ̅ⲃⲉⲗⲗⲉⲉⲩ ⲁⲕ'-
ⲧⲣⲟⲩⲛⲁⲩ ⲉⲃⲟⲗ· ⲛ̅'ϭⲁⲗⲉ ⲁⲕⲧⲣⲟⲩⲙⲟⲟϣⲉ·' ⲛ̅ⲉⲙⲡⲟ ⲁⲕⲧⲣⲟⲩϣⲁ'ϫⲉ· ⲓⲥ̅ ⲡⲁⲱⲛϩ̅'
ⲡⲉⲧⲉⲣⲉⲡⲁⲗϭⲟ ⲙⲛ̅'ⲡⲱⲛϩ̅ ϣⲟⲟⲡ ⲉⲃⲟⲗ' ϩⲓⲧⲟⲟⲧϥ̅, ⲉⲕⲉⲣ̅ⲡⲁϩ'ⲣⲉ ⲉⲡⲓⲁⲛⲟ-
ⲙⲟⲥ ⲛ̅ϩⲏ'ⲅⲉⲙⲱⲛ· ⲛ̅ⲧⲟⲕ ⲅⲁⲣ' ⲡⲁϫⲟⲉⲓⲥ ⲡⲉⲛⲧⲁⲕ'ϫⲟⲟⲥ ϫⲉ ⲙ̅ⲡⲣ̅ⲧⲱⲱ'ⲃⲉ ⲛ̅ⲟⲩ-

---

130 Rii 11f. ⲡⲕⲱⲙⲏ'ⲧⲁⲣⲏⲥⲓⲟⲥ, sic; no superlinear stroke over first ⲏ. 23. ⲡⲉϫⲁⲩ
cannot be right; some expression meaning 'Tell me' seems required. V i 9. ⲉⲁⲛⲟⲕ:
ⲉ added. 16f. l. -ⲧⲣⲁⲁⲁϥ. 22. l. ⲛ̅ⲉⲟⲩⲱⲛ. ii 20. = -ⲉⲓⲕⲱⲛ. 21f. l. ⲛⲉⲧⲁ-
ⲛⲁⲅⲕⲁⲍⲉ. 131 R i 12. ⲉⲣⲟⲟⲩ: first o added.

πεθοου επ'μα ⲛ̄ογπεθοου.' ⲁⲥⲟⲗⲟⲙⲱⲛ' ϫοος ⲅ̄ⲛ̄ⲛ̄'ⲗⲁⲣⲟⲓⲙⲓⲁ ϫⲉ' ⲉⲣϣⲁⲛⲡⲉⲕ-
ϫⲁ'ϫⲉ ⲉ2ⲕⲟ, ⲙⲁⲧ(131 R ii)ⲙⲟⲩ· ⲉϥϣⲁⲛⲉⲓϥⲉ' ⲙⲁⲧⲥⲟⲩ· ⲉ̄ⲕⲉⲓⲣⲉ' ⲅⲁⲣ ⲙ̄ⲡⲁⲓ,
ⲕ̄ⲛⲁⲡⲣ̄'ⲩ̄ϫ̄ⲛ̄ϫⲉⲉⲃⲉⲥ ⲛ̄ⲕⲱϩⲧ̄' ⲉϫⲉⲛⲧⲉϥⲁⲡⲉ.' ⲧⲉⲛⲟⲩ ⲇⲉ ⲡⲁϫⲟⲉⲓⲥ ⲓ̄ⲥ'ⲛ̄ⲧⲕ̄ⲟⲩ-
ϣⲉⲛⲥⲧⲏⲩ' ⲛ̄ⲣⲉϥⲕⲱ ⲉⲃⲟⲗ.' ⲡϩⲁⲅⲓⲟⲥ ⲇⲉ ⲛ̄ⲧⲉⲣⲉϥ'ⲟⲩⲱ ⲉϥϣⲗⲏⲗ, ⲁϥ'ⲕⲱ ⲉⲛⲉⲥⲡⲟⲧⲟⲩ ⲛ̄ⲡϫⲏⲅⲉⲙⲱⲛ ⲙⲛ̄'ⲧⲉϥⲧⲁⲡⲣⲟ ⲉϥϫⲱ'ⲙ̄ⲙⲟⲥ ϫⲉ ⲅⲛ̄ⲧⲉⲕ'ϭⲟⲙ ⲡⲁϫⲟⲉⲓⲥ
ⲓ̄ⲥ ⲡⲉ'ϫⲥ ⲡⲉⲛⲧⲁϥⲟⲩ'ⲱⲛ ⲉⲣⲱϥ ⲛ̄ϫⲁⲭⲁ'ⲣⲓⲁⲥ ⲛ̄ⲧⲉⲣⲉϥϫⲁⲓ̈ ⲉⲧ'ⲡⲉⲛⲁⲅⲓⲥ ϫⲉ
ⲓⲱ'ϩⲁⲛⲛⲏⲥ ⲡⲉ ⲡⲣⲁⲛ' ⲙ̄ⲡⲡϣⲏⲣⲉ ⲕⲟⲩⲓ̈,' ⲁϥϣⲁϫⲉ, ⲁϥⲥⲙⲟⲩ ⲉ'ⲡⲛⲟⲩⲧⲉ, ⲛ̄ⲧⲉⲓ̈ϩⲉ'
ⲟⲛ ⲡⲁϫⲟⲉⲓⲥ ⲓ̄ⲥ ⲡⲉϫⲉ' ⲙⲁⲣⲉⲡⲓⲁⲛⲟⲙⲟⲥ' ⲡ̄ϫⲏⲅⲉⲙⲱⲛ ϣⲁ'ϫⲉ ⲛϥ̄ϫⲱ ⲙ̄ⲡⲉⲧϥ̄-
ⲟⲩⲱϣ ⲉ'ϫⲟⲟϥ.' ⲛ̄ⲧⲉⲩⲛⲟⲩ ⲁϥⲕⲱϩ' ⲉⲧⲉϥⲧⲁⲡⲣⲟ ⲉϥ'ϫⲱ ⲙ̄ⲙⲟⲥ ϫⲉ ⲅⲙ̄'ⲡⲣⲁⲛ
ⲙ̄ⲡⲁϫⲟⲉⲓⲥ ⲓ̄ⲥ ⲡⲉ'ϫⲉ'(V i)ⲡⲉⲧⲉⲣⲉⲧϭⲟⲙ ⲙ̄'ⲡⲱⲛϩ ϣⲟⲟⲡ ⲉⲃⲟⲗ'2ⲓⲧⲟⲟⲧϥ̄,
ⲉⲕⲉⲣⲡⲁⲣ̄'ⲣⲉ ⲉⲡⲉⲓ̈ⲣⲱⲙⲉ.' ⲛ̄ⲧⲉⲩⲛⲟⲩ ⲛ̄ⲧⲁϥ'ⲕⲱϩ ⲉⲛⲉⲥⲡⲟⲧⲟⲩ' ⲙ̄ⲡϫⲏⲅⲉⲙⲱⲛ,'
ⲁⲡⲉϥⲗⲁⲥ ⲥⲟⲟⲩⲧⲛ̄,' ⲁϥϣⲁϫⲉ, ⲁϥⲱϣ ⲉⲃⲟⲗ ⲉϥϫⲱ ⲙ̄'ⲙⲟⲥ ϫⲉ ⲁⲧⲉⲧⲛ̄ⲣⲧⲉ'
ⲧⲛ̄ϭⲟⲙ ⲧⲏⲣⲥ̄ ⲛⲙ̄'ⲙⲁⲓ̈ ⲱ ⲛⲉⲁⲛⲥⲟ'ⲥⲓⲟⲥ ⲛ̄ⲧⲁⲗⲉⲡⲟⲣⲟⲥ.' ⲁⲗⲗⲁ ⲁⲛⲟⲕ ⲡⲉⲧ'ⲛⲁ-
ⲡⲉⲇⲉⲩⲉ ⲙ̄ⲙⲱ'ⲧⲛ̄. ⲁϥⲃⲱⲕ ⲛ̄'ϭⲓ ⲡϫⲏⲅⲉⲙⲱⲛ' ϫⲉ ⲉϥⲛⲁⲃⲁⲥⲁⲛⲓⲍⲉ ⲛ̄ⲛⲉⲧⲟⲩ-
ⲁⲁⲃ.' ⲁⲡⲙⲏⲏϣⲉ ⲱϣ'ⲉⲃⲟⲗ ⲉϩⲣⲁⲓ̈ ⲉϫⲱϥ,' ⲙ̄ⲡⲟⲩⲕⲁⲁⲩ ⲉⲃⲁⲥⲁ'ⲛⲓⲍⲉ ⲙ̄ⲙⲟⲟⲩ.'
ⲥⲱⲧⲏⲣⲓⲭⲟⲥ ⲇⲉ' ⲡⲇⲟⲙⲉⲥⲧⲓⲕⲟⲥ' ⲙⲛ̄ⲑⲉⲟⲫⲁⲛⲏⲥ' ⲡⲛⲟⲩⲙⲉⲣⲁⲣⲓⲟⲥ' ⲁⲩⲡⲉⲟⲩⲟⲓ̈
ⲉⲡ'ϫⲏⲅⲉⲙⲱⲛ, ⲁⲩ'ϣⲁϫⲉ ⲛⲙ̄ⲙⲁϥ' ⲉⲩϫⲱ ⲙ̄ⲙⲟⲥ ϫⲉ (V ii)ⲡⲉⲛϫⲟⲉⲓⲥ ⲡϫⲏⲅⲉⲙⲱⲛ, ⲥⲱⲧⲙ̄ ⲉⲣⲟⲛ.' ⲧⲁⲡⲟⲫⲁⲥⲓⲥ ⲉⲛⲉⲓ̈'ⲣⲱⲙⲉ, ⲛ̄ⲧⲛ̄ⲥⲕⲩⲗ'ⲗⲓ ⲙ̄ⲙⲟⲛ ⲛ̄ⲧⲛ̄ⲗⲟ' ⲅⲙ̄-
ⲡⲉⲓ̈ⲙⲁ· ⲙⲏ ⲛ̄ⲅ'ⲛⲁⲗⲟ ⲁⲛ ⲉⲕϫⲙⲟ'ⲟⲥ ⲛ̄ⲧⲉⲓ̈ϩⲉ ⲅⲛ̄ⲧⲙⲏⲧⲉ ⲛ̄ⲧⲉⲓ̈ⲥⲱϣⲉ;' ⲛⲉⲥⲣⲱⲙⲉ
ⲅⲁⲣ ⲅⲛ̄'ⲧⲩⲣⲁⲛⲟⲥ ⲛⲉ ⲙⲡⲟ'ⲛⲏⲣⲟⲥ, ⲛ̄ⲥⲉⲛⲁⲧⲥⲟ' ⲉⲣⲟⲛ ⲁⲛ· ⲥⲉⲛⲁ'ⲧⲱⲟⲩⲛ ⲉϩⲣⲁⲓ̈
ⲉϫⲱ(ⲛ)' ⲛ̄ⲥⲉⲣⲡⲟⲗⲉⲙⲉⲓ ⲛⲙ̄'ⲙⲁⲛ· ⲕⲁⲓ ⲅⲁⲣ ⲛⲟⲩ'ⲡⲟⲗⲓⲥ ⲁⲛ ⲧⲉ ⲉⲟⲩⲛ̄'ⲛⲟⲙⲟⲥ ϩⲓ-
ⲥⲃⲱ ⲛ̄'ϩⲏⲧⲥ̄, ⲁⲗⲗⲁ ⲟⲩ'ⲥⲱϣⲉ ⲧⲉ ⲛⲁⲧⲥⲃⲱ.' ⲡϫⲏⲅⲉⲙⲱⲛ ⲇⲉ' ⲁϥϣⲁϫⲉ ⲅⲁⲡⲉϥ'-
ϩⲏⲧ ⲙⲁⲅⲁϥ, ⲉϥ'ϫⲱ ⲙ̄ⲙⲟⲥ ϫⲉ ⲡⲁⲛ'ⲧⲟⲥ ⲣⲱ ⲅⲛ̄ⲙⲉ ⲛⲉ' ⲛ̄ⲩϣⲁϫⲉ ⲉⲧⲉⲣⲉ[.]·ⲧ̄'ⲛⲁⲧⲧⲁϫⲓⲥ ϫⲱ ⲙ̄ⲙⲟⲟⲩ· ⲉⲣϣⲁ'ⲛⲛⲉⲓ̈ⲣⲱ'ⲙⲉ ⲛ̄ⲧⲩⲣⲁ'ⲛⲟⲥ ⲣ̄ⲡⲟⲗⲉⲙⲟⲥ' ⲛⲙ̄ⲙⲁⲛ ⲅⲛ̄-
ⲧⲉⲓ̈(132 R i)ⲥⲱϣⲉ, ⲛⲓⲙ ⲡⲉⲧ'ⲛⲁⲧⲟⲟⲧⲩ̄ ⲛⲙ̄ⲙⲁⲛ ⲙ̄ⲡⲉⲓ̈ⲙⲁ;' ⲛⲟⲩⲡⲟⲗⲓⲥ ⲁⲛ ⲧⲉ'
ⲉⲥϩⲁⲧⲉⲥⲃⲱ ⲛ̄ⲣ̄'ⲣⲱⲟⲩ. ⲁϥϩⲁⲓ̈ ⲇⲉ ⲙ̄ⲡⲉⲩⲣⲁⲛ' ⲉⲟⲩⲭⲁⲣⲧⲏⲥ ⲛ̄ⲧⲉⲓ̈ϩⲉ ⲉϥⲧ̄-
ⲁⲡⲟⲫⲁⲥⲓⲥ' ⲉⲣⲟⲟⲩ ⲉϥϫⲱ ⲙ̄ⲙⲟⲥ'ϫⲉ ϣⲛ̄ⲟⲩϭⲉ ⲙⲛ̄'ⲫⲓⲗⲏⲙⲱⲛ ⲙⲛ̄'ⲁⲡⲁ ⲛⲓⲗⲓⲟⲥ
ⲙⲛ̄'ⲡⲉⲧⲣⲟⲥ ⲙⲛ̄'ⲁⲛⲇⲣⲉⲁⲥ ⲙⲛ̄ⲓ̈ⲱ'ϩⲁⲛⲛⲏⲥ ⲙⲛ̄'ⲫⲟⲓⲃⲁⲙⲱⲛ ⲙⲛ̄'ⲥⲟⲫⲓⲁ ⲙⲛ̄ⲭⲉ'ⲣⲏ-
ⲙⲱⲛ ⲙⲛ̄'ⲁⲛⲧⲱⲛⲓⲟⲥ ⲙⲛ̄'ⲫⲓⲗⲓⲡⲡⲟⲥ ⲙⲛ̄'ⲅⲉⲣⲙⲉⲓⲁ ⲛⲉⲉⲃⲟⲗ' ⲅⲛ̄ⲛ̄ⲡⲁⲓ̈ⲁⲧ' ⲛ̄ⲧⲉ-
ⲧⲡⲉⲇⲓⲛⲏ,' ⲉⲡⲓⲇⲏ ⲡⲉⲩⲟⲩ'ⲱϣ ⲡⲉ ⲡⲁⲓ̈ ⲉⲙⲟⲣ' ⲉϩⲣⲁⲓ̈ ⲉⲕ̄ⲙ̄ⲡⲓⲣⲁⲛ' ϫⲉ ⲓ̄ⲥ, ⲛ̄ⲧⲟⲟⲩ

131. R i 27-30. Lines short; hole in parchment. ii 19. = -ⲛⲓⲛⲁϩ. V i 14. = -Ταλαιπω-
ρος. 16. = - ⲛⲁⲓⲇⲉⲩⲉ. ii 4f. =-ⲥⲕⲩⲗⲗⲉⲓ. 28-31. Lines short; hole in parchment.

ⲙⲁⲁⲁⲩ ⲛⲉⲛⲧⲁⲩⲉⲓ ⲉϩⲣⲁⲓ ⲉϫⲙ̄ⲡⲃⲏⲙⲁ ⲉⲡⲗⲉⲣⲱⲙⲉ ⲁⲛⲁⲛ'ⲕⲁⲍⲉ ⲙ̄ⲙⲟⲟⲩ, ϫⲉ-
(132 R ii)ⲕⲁⲥ ⲉⲩⲉⲉⲓⲙⲉ ⲛ̄ϭⲓ' ⲟⲩⲟⲛ ⲛⲓⲙ ⲉⲧⲛⲁ'ⲥⲱⲧⲙ̄ ⲉⲧⲉⲩⲁⲡⲟ'ⲫⲁⲥⲓⲥ ϫⲉ ⲧⲟⲩⲁⲁⲃ' ⲉⲡⲉⲩⲥⲛⲟϥ· ⲁⲗⲗⲁ' ⲡⲉⲧⲉϣϣⲉ ⲡⲉ ⲉⲧⲣⲁϩⲣⲉ ⲛⲁⲩ ⲕⲁⲧⲁ'ⲧⲕⲉⲗⲉⲩⲥⲓⲥ ⲛ̄ⲛ̄ϫⲓ-
ⲥⲟⲟⲩⲉ ⲛ̄ⲛ̄ⲣ̄ⲣⲱⲟⲩ· ⲁⲛⲟⲕ ϩⲱ ϯⲕⲉⲗⲉⲩⲉ ⲉⲧⲣⲟⲩⲛⲟⲩϫⲉ ⲛ̄ⲛⲉⲩⲥⲱⲙⲁ ⲉϩⲟⲩⲛ
ⲍⲁⲍⲉⲛⲕⲟⲧ' ⲛ̄ⲥⲓⲕⲉ ⲛ̄ⲥⲉⲥⲓⲕⲉ ⲉϩⲣⲁⲓ ⲉϫⲱⲟⲩ' ϣⲁⲛⲧⲉⲛⲉⲩⲥⲁⲣⲝ ⲉⲣⲩⲏⲙ ⲩⲏⲙ·
ⲁⲩⲱ ⲛⲥⲉⲉⲡⲉ ⲛ̄ⲛⲉⲩ'ⲥⲱⲙⲁ ϯⲛⲁⲕⲉ'ⲗⲉⲩⲉ ⲉⲧⲣⲟⲩϣⲓⲕⲉ'ⲡⲟⲩⲛⲟϭ ⲙ̄ⲫⲟⲥⲥⲁ' ⲛ̄ⲥⲉϫⲓ-
ⲧⲟⲩ ⲉⲡⲉⲥⲏⲧ' ϫⲉⲕⲁⲥ ⲉⲛⲉⲩϩⲱⲡ' ⲙ̄ⲡⲉⲩⲣ̄ⲡⲙⲉⲉⲩⲉ· ⲧⲁⲓ ⲇⲉ ⲧⲉ ⲧⲁⲡⲟⲫⲁ'ⲥⲓⲥ
ⲛ̄ⲧⲁⲩⲧⲁⲁⲥ' ⲉⲣⲟⲟⲩ ⲙ̄ⲡⲉϩⲟⲟⲩ' ⲉⲧⲙ̄ⲙⲁⲩ. ⲧⲟⲧⲉ ⲛ̄ϩⲁⲅⲓⲟⲥ ⲙ̄'ⲙⲁⲣⲧⲩⲣⲟⲥ ⲉⲧⲟⲩ-
ⲁ'ⲁⲃ ⲛ̄ⲧⲉⲣⲟⲩⲥⲱ'ⲧⲙ̄ ⲉⲛⲉϩⲣⲟⲟⲩ ⲛ̄ⲧⲉⲩ(Ⅵ)ⲁⲡⲟⲫⲁⲥⲓⲥ, ⲁⲡⲉⲩ'ϩⲏⲧ ⲟⲩⲛⲟϥ ⲉⲣⲟⲟⲩ,'
ⲁⲩⲡⲱⲣϣ ⲛ̄ⲛⲉⲩ'ϭⲓϫ ⲉⲃⲟⲗ, ⲁⲩϣⲗⲏⲗ' ⲉⲡⲛⲟⲩⲧⲉ ⲉⲩϫⲱ' ⲙ̄ⲙⲟⲥ ϫⲉ ⲡⲁϫⲟⲉⲓⲥ'
ⲓ̄ⲥ̄ ⲡⲉϫⲉ ⲉⲕⲉⲁϩⲉ'ⲣⲁⲧⲕ̄ ⲛⲙ̄ⲙⲁⲛ' ϩⲛ̄ⲧⲉⲓⲟⲩⲛⲟⲩ ⲛ̄ⲁ'ⲛⲁⲅⲕⲏ. ⲡϩⲁⲅⲓⲟⲥ ⲇⲉ ⲁ-
ⲡⲁ ⲩⲛⲟⲩ'ϥⲉ ⲛ̄ⲧⲉⲣⲟⲩⲛ̄ⲧϥ' ⲉⲡⲙⲁ ⲛ̄ⲧⲉϥⲁⲡⲟ'ⲫⲁⲥⲓⲥ, ⲁϥⲁϩⲉⲣⲁ'ⲧϥ̄ ⲉϫⲙ̄ⲡⲕⲟⲧ
ⲛ̄'ⲥⲓⲕⲉ ⲁϥⲥⲙⲟⲩ ⲉⲡ'ⲛⲟⲩⲧⲉ ⲉϥϫⲱ ⲙ̄'ⲙⲟⲥ ϫⲉ' ϯⲥⲙⲟⲩ ⲉⲣⲟⲕ ⲡ̄ⲣ̄ⲣⲟ' ⲁⲩⲱ ⲡϣⲏⲣⲉ ⲙ̄ⲡ̄ⲣ̄ⲣⲟ·' ϯⲥⲙⲟⲩ ⲉⲣⲟⲕ ⲡⲁϩⲟ'ⲣⲁⲧⲟⲥ ⲡⲉⲧⲉⲙ̄ⲡϣ̄ϭⲟⲙ' ⲛ̄ⲗⲁⲁⲩ ⲉⲛⲁⲩ ⲉⲣⲟϥ'
ϩⲛ̄ⲃⲁⲗ ⲛ̄ⲧⲥⲁⲣⲝ·' ϯⲥⲙⲟⲩ ⲉⲣⲟⲕ ϩⲛ̄ⲧⲡⲉ' ⲙ̄ⲛ̄ϫⲓⲭⲙ̄ⲡⲕⲁϩ· ϯⲥⲙⲟⲩ ⲉⲣⲟⲕ ⲡ-
ϣⲟⲣⲡ̄' ⲛ̄ϫⲡⲟ, ⲡⲁⲅⲉⲛⲏ'ⲧⲟⲥ, ⲡⲁⲩⲙⲓⲟⲩⲣⲅⲟⲥ·' ϯⲥⲙⲟⲩ ⲉⲣⲟⲕ ⲡⲉⲛⲧⲁϥ'ⲧⲣⲉⲛⲉ-
ⲧⲉⲛ̄ⲥⲉⲩϣⲟⲟⲡ' ⲁⲛ ϣⲱⲡⲉ· (Ⅴ ii) ϯⲥⲙⲟⲩ ⲉⲣⲟⲕ ⲓ̄ⲥ̄ ⲡⲉⲧⲉ'ⲛⲟⲩⲩ ⲛⲉ ⲥⲙⲟⲩ ⲛⲓⲙ'
ϯⲥⲙⲟⲩ ⲉⲣⲟⲕ ⲓ̄ⲥ̄ ⲡⲉⲛⲧⲁ'ⲡϣⲟⲣⲡ̄ ⲛ̄ϩⲁⲓⲣⲉ ⲙ̄ⲡⲉⲓⲱⲧ ⲡⲱϩ ϣⲁⲣⲟϥ' ϯⲥⲙⲟⲩ ⲉⲣⲟⲕ
ⲓ̄ⲥ̄ ⲡⲉⲕⲗⲁ'ⲧⲟⲥ ⲛ̄ⲧⲁϥⲧⲟⲩⲱ ⲉⲃⲟⲗ' ϩⲙ̄ⲡϩⲏⲧ ⲙ̄ⲡⲉⲓⲱⲧ· ϯⲥⲙⲟⲩ ⲉⲣⲟⲕ ⲓ̄ⲥ̄ ⲡⲉⲥⲕⲉ-'
ⲡⲁⲥⲧⲏⲥ ⲛ̄ⲛ̄ⲇⲓⲕⲁⲓ'ⲟⲥ ⲧⲏⲣⲟⲩ·' ϯⲥⲙⲟⲩ ⲉⲣⲟⲕ ⲓ̄ⲥ̄ ⲡⲁⲡ'ϣⲟϫⲛⲉ ⲛ̄ⲁⲧⲕⲓⲙ' ⲁⲩⲱ
ⲛ̄ⲁⲧⲡⲱⲛⲉ·' ϯⲥⲙⲟⲩ ⲉⲣⲟⲕ ⲓ̄ⲥ̄ ⲑⲃ̄ⲥⲱ' ⲛ̄ⲛⲉⲧⲕⲏ ⲕⲁϩⲏⲩ' ⲁⲩⲱ ⲧⲉϩⲣⲉ ⲛ̄ⲛⲉⲧ-
ϩⲕⲁⲉⲓⲧ·' ϯⲥⲙⲟⲩ ⲉⲣⲟⲕ ⲓ̄ⲥ̄ ⲧⲕⲓⲑⲁ'ⲣⲁ ⲛ̄ⲛⲉⲧⲟⲩⲁⲁⲃ, ⲧϭⲓⲛ'ϩⲱⲥ ⲛ̄ⲛⲉⲭⲉⲣⲟⲩⲃⲓⲛ'
ⲙ̄ⲛ̄ⲛⲉⲥⲉⲣⲁⲫⲓⲛ ⲁⲩⲱ' ⲡϩⲩⲙⲛⲟⲥ ⲛ̄ⲛⲁⲅⲅⲉⲗⲟⲥ·' ϯⲥⲙⲟⲩ ⲉⲣⲟⲕ ⲓ̄ⲥ̄ ⲡⲉⲧϩ'ⲧⲏⲛ ⲍ̄
ⲉⲛⲉⲥⲉⲣⲁⲫⲓⲛ·' ϯⲥⲙⲟⲩ ⲉⲣⲟⲕ ⲓ̄ⲥ̄ ⲡⲉⲓⲉⲣⲟ' ⲙ̄ⲙⲟⲩ ⲛ̄ⲱⲛϩ̄ ⲉⲧⲧⲥⲟ ⲛ̄ⲛ̄ⲇⲓⲕⲁⲓⲟⲥ
ⲧⲏⲣⲟⲩ·' ϯⲥⲙⲟⲩ ⲉⲣⲟⲕ ⲓ̄ⲥ̄ ⲧⲕⲉⲫⲁ'ⲗⲓⲥ ⲙ̄ⲡⲟⲩϫⲁⲓ ⲁⲩⲱ ⲡⲉⲥⲧⲩⲗⲗⲟⲥ ⲙ̄ⲙⲁⲣ-'
ⲙⲁⲣⲟⲛ ⲛ̄ⲧⲁϥⲉⲓ ⲉⲃⲟⲗ' ϩⲙ̄ⲡⲉⲓⲱⲧ, ⲁϥⲣⲟⲩ(133 R i)ⲟⲉⲓⲛ ⲉⲛ̄ⲇⲓⲕⲁⲓⲟⲥ ⲧⲏⲣⲟⲩ·'
ϯⲥⲙⲟⲩ ⲉⲣⲟⲕ ⲓ̄ⲥ̄ ⲧⲡⲉⲧⲣⲁ ⲛ̄ⲁⲧⲕⲓⲙ ⲛ̄ⲧⲁⲥ'ϣⲱⲡⲉ ⲛ̄ⲧⲁϫⲣⲟ ⲛ̄ ⲛ̄ⲇⲓⲕⲁⲓⲟⲥ ⲧⲏⲣⲟⲩ·'
ϯⲥⲙⲟⲩ ⲉⲣⲟⲕ ⲓ̄ⲥ̄ ⲧⲡⲩⲅⲏ' ⲙ̄ⲙⲟⲩ ⲛ̄ⲱⲛϩ̄ ⲉⲧϩ̄ⲛ̄ⲉⲇⲉⲙ ⲉⲧⲧⲥⲟ ⲛ̄'ⲡⲩⲏⲛ ⲙ̄ⲡⲡⲁ-
ⲣⲁ'ⲇⲓⲥⲟⲥ ⲉⲧⲉⲛ̄ⲇⲓⲕⲁⲓ'ⲟⲥ ⲧⲏⲣⲟⲩ ⲛⲉ·' ϯⲥⲙⲟⲩ ⲉⲣⲟⲕ ⲓ̄ⲥ̄ ⲙⲛ̄'ⲡⲉⲕⲉⲓⲱⲧ ⲛ̄ⲁⲅⲁ'ⲑⲟⲥ,
ϫⲉⲕⲁⲥ ⲉⲕⲉⲉⲓ' ϣⲁⲣⲟⲓ ⲙ̄ⲡⲟⲟⲩ ⲙ̄ⲛ̄'ⲛⲁⲥⲛⲏⲩ ϩⲛ̄ⲧⲉⲓ'ⲟⲩⲛⲏ ⲛ̄ⲁⲛⲁⲅⲕⲏ' ⲛ̄ⲧⲛ̄-

---

132 R i 31. Last letter seems a compromise between Γ and N. ii 9. Final Y over o.
V i 22. y added.   ii 6 f. = -ⲕⲗⲁⲇⲟⲥ. 26. l. ⲙ̄ⲙⲟⲟⲩ.

ⲙⲡⲛⲅⲁ ⲛ̄ⲥⲱ'ⲧⲛ̄ ⲉⲧⲉⲕⲥⲙⲏ ⲛ̄'ⲛⲟⲩⲧⲉ ⲉⲕⲧⲟⲩⲣⲟⲧ'ⲛⲁⲛ. ⲁⲣⲓⲡⲉ(ⲛ)'ⲙⲉⲉⲩⲉ ⲍⲛ̄ⲧⲛ̄-
ⲥⲓⲛ'ⲉⲓ ϣⲁⲣⲟⲕ· ⲙⲁⲣⲉ'ⲛⲉⲧⲥⲁⲟⲩⲛⲁⲙ ⲁⲍⲉⲣⲁ'ⲧⲟⲩ ⲛⲁ̄ⲙⲁⲛ, ⲛ̄ⲧⲉ'ⲛ̄ⲅⲧ ⲍⲓⲃⲟⲩⲣ ⲥⲟ-
ⲕⲟⲩ'ⲛⲁⲩ. ⲙⲁⲣⲉⲡⲕⲁⲕⲉ'ⲁⲛⲁⲭⲱⲣⲓ ⲛ̄ⲧⲉⲡⲟⲩ'ⲟⲉⲓⲛ ϣⲁ ⲛⲁⲛ. ⲙⲁⲣⲉⲧⲁⲡⲓⲗⲏ ⲍⲣⲟⲕ'
ⲙ̄ⲙⲟⲥ· ⲙⲁⲣⲉⲡⲉⲭⲁ'ⲗⲁⲥⲥⲁ ⲱϫⲛ̄ ⲍⲁ(133 R ii)ⲧⲛ̄ⲍⲉ· ⲁⲟⲩⲱⲛ ⲛⲁ(ⲛ)' ⲛⲛⲉⲕⲡⲩ-
ⲗⲏ, ⲡⲣ̄ⲣⲟ,'ⲧⲁⲣⲉⲛⲉⲓ ⲉⲍⲟⲩⲛ ⲛ̄ⲍⲏⲧⲟⲩ.' ⲛ̄ⲁⲅⲅⲉⲗⲟⲥ ⲙⲡⲛⲟⲩ'ⲧⲉ, ⲁⲙⲏⲓⲧⲛ̄, ⲁⲍⲉⲣⲁⲧ'
ⲧⲏⲩⲧⲛ̄ ⲛⲁ̄ⲙⲁⲛ·' ⲛⲉ ⲭⲁⲓⲣⲟⲩⲃⲓⲛ ⲙ̄ⲡⲟⲩ'ⲟⲉⲓⲛ, ⲁⲍⲉⲣⲁⲧⲧⲏⲩⲧⲛ̄' ⲛⲁ̄ⲙⲁⲛ· ⲛⲛ̄-
ⲧⲟⲩⲣⲅⲟⲥ ⲙ̄ⲡⲟⲩⲟⲉⲓⲛ,' ⲁⲍⲉⲣⲁⲧⲧⲏⲩⲧⲛ̄ ⲛ̄ⲁ̄ⲙⲁⲛ.' ⲛⲉⲑⲏⲥⲁⲩⲣⲟⲥ ⲙ̄ⲡⲟⲩ'ⲟⲉⲓⲛ, ⲁⲍⲉ-
ⲣⲁⲧⲧⲏⲩⲧⲛ̄'ⲛⲁ̄ⲙⲁⲛ· ⲁⲟⲩ'ⲱⲛ ⲛⲁⲛ ⲛ̄ⲛⲁ'ⲡⲩⲗⲏ ⲛ̄ⲧⲡⲉ.' ⲛⲉⲡⲣⲉⲥⲃⲩⲧⲉⲣⲟⲥ ⲙ̄'ⲡⲟⲩⲟⲉⲓⲛ, ⲁⲍⲉⲣⲁⲧ'ⲧⲏⲩⲧⲛ̄ ⲛⲁ̄ⲙⲁ(ⲛ).' ⲛⲉⲉⲡⲓⲥⲕⲟⲡⲟⲥ ⲙ̄'ⲡⲟⲩⲟⲉⲓⲛ, ⲁⲍⲉⲣⲁⲧ'ⲧⲏⲩⲧⲛ̄
ⲛⲁ̄ⲙⲁⲛ·' ⲡⲉⲓⲱⲧ ⲛ̄ⲛⲉⲟⲩⲟ'ⲉⲓⲛ ⲧⲏⲣⲟⲩ ⲙⲛ̄'ⲡⲉϥϣⲏⲣⲉ ⲙ̄ⲙⲉⲣⲓⲧ ⲓ̄ⲥ ⲡⲉϫⲉ ⲙⲛ̄ⲡⲉ-
ⲡⲛ̄ⲁ ⲛ̄ⲍⲁⲅⲓⲟⲛ,' ⲁⲍⲉⲣⲁⲧⲧⲏⲩⲧⲛ̄' ⲛⲁ̄ⲙⲁⲛ· ⲁ'ⲙⲟⲩ ϣⲁⲣⲟⲓ̈ ⲓ̄ⲥ ⲡⲉⲭ̄ⲥ̄,' ⲧⲁⲁⲓⲧⲓ ⲙ̄-
ⲙⲟⲕ ⲙ̄(ⲛ)ⲡⲉⲧⲛⲙⲁ ⲛ̄ⲧⲁⲩ'ϫⲏ ⲙ̄ⲡⲁⲧⲁⲉⲓ ⲉⲃⲟⲗ'ⲍⲛ̄ⲥⲱⲙⲁ. ⲛ̄ⲍⲟ'ⲥⲟⲛ ⲇⲉ ⲉⲣⲉ-
ⲡⲍⲁⲅⲓ'ⲟⲥ ⲁⲡⲁ ϣⲛⲟⲩϥⲉ 'ⲭⲱ ⲛ̄ⲧⲉⲓ̈ⲍⲟⲙⲟⲗⲟ'ⲅⲓⲁ, ⲉⲓⲥ ⲍⲛ̄ⲍⲣⲟⲟⲩ' ⲛ̄ⲥⲁⲗⲡⲓⲅⲝ ⲁⲩⲉⲓ
ⲉⲃⲟⲗ ⲍⲛ̄ⲧⲡⲉ· ⲁⲩⲱ'ⲉⲓⲥ ⲡϫⲟⲉⲓⲥ ⲓ̄ⲥ ⲁⲩ'ⲉⲓ ⲉⲃⲟⲗ ⲍⲛ̄ⲧⲡⲉ ⲉⲩ'ⲧⲁⲗⲏⲩ ⲉⲭⲉⲛⲟⲩ'ⲍⲁⲣ-
ⲙⲁ ⲛ̄ⲟⲩⲟⲉⲓⲛ' ⲉⲣⲉⲛⲁⲅⲅⲉⲗⲟⲥ ⲙ̄'ⲡⲉⲟⲟⲩ ⲍⲩⲙⲛⲉⲩⲉ' ⲍⲁⲧⲉϥⲍⲏ· ⲁⲩⲧⲁ'ⲍⲉⲍⲍⲁⲣⲙⲁ
ⲉⲣⲁⲧϥ̄'ⲍⲓⲛⲩϣⲱⲓ̈ ⲙ̄ⲡⲇⲓ'ⲕⲁⲥⲧⲏⲣⲓⲟⲛ, ⲁϥ'ⲱϣ ⲉⲃⲟⲗ ϫⲉ ⲱ̄ⲛ̄'ⲟⲩϥⲉ, ⲡⲣⲁϣⲉ ⲛ̄ⲛⲁ-
ⲙ̄ⲡⲏⲩⲉ ⲁⲩⲱ'ⲡⲥⲟⲗⲥⲗ̄ ⲛ̄ⲛⲁⲡⲓ'ⲕⲁⲍ, ⲛ̄ⲧⲟⲕ ⲙⲛ̄'ⲛⲉⲕⲕⲉⲥⲛⲏⲩⲉ,' ⲁⲙⲏⲓⲧⲛ̄ ⲉⲍⲣⲁⲓ̈'
ϣⲁⲣⲟⲓ̈ ⲛⲁⲩⲃⲏⲣ'ⲛ̄ⲕⲗⲏⲣⲟⲛⲟⲙⲟⲥ' ⲧⲁⲧ ⲛⲏⲧⲛ̄ ⲙ̄ⲡⲃⲏ'ⲕⲉ ⲛ̄ⲛ̄ⲍⲓⲥⲉ ⲛ̄ⲧⲁ'ⲧⲉⲧⲛ̄-
ϣⲟⲡⲟⲩ ⲉⲭⲙ̄'ⲡⲁⲣⲁⲛ. ⲡⲍⲁⲅⲓ(V ii)ⲟⲥ ⲇⲉ ⲁⲡⲁ ϣⲛⲟⲩϥⲉ' ⲛ̄ⲧⲉⲣⲉϥⲥⲱⲧⲙ̄ ⲉⲧⲉ'-
ⲥⲙⲏ ⲙ̄ⲡⲥⲱⲧⲏⲣ,' ⲁⲡⲉϥⲍⲏⲧ ⲟⲩⲛⲟϥ ⲉ'ⲣⲟϥ· ⲡⲉϫⲁϥ ⲙ̄ⲡⲥⲱ'ⲧⲏⲣ ϫⲉ ⲡⲁϫⲟⲉⲓⲥ,
ⲉ'ϣⲱⲡⲉ ⲉⲍⲛⲁⲕ ⲡⲉ' ⲉⲓ'ⲟⲩⲱϣ ⲉⲧⲣⲉⲕⲡⲓ'ⲑⲉ ⲙ̄ⲙⲟⲓ̈ ⲙ̄ⲛ̄ⲛⲁⲕⲉ'ⲥⲛⲏⲩ ⲍⲙ̄ⲡⲁⲓ-
ⲇⲏ'ⲙⲁ ⲛ̄ⲧⲁⲩϫⲏ.' ⲡⲉϫⲉⲡⲥⲱⲧⲏⲣ ⲛⲁϥ' ϫⲉ ϣⲁϫⲉ ⲡⲁⲙⲉⲣⲓⲧ,' ⲁϫⲓⲡⲉⲧⲉ-
ⲍⲛⲁⲕ.' ⲡⲉϫⲉⲡⲍⲁⲅⲓⲟⲥ ⲛⲁϥ' ϫⲉ ⲉϣⲱⲡⲉ ⲉⲍⲛⲁⲕ' ⲡⲉ ⲡⲁⲥⲱⲧⲏⲣ, ⲙ̄'ⲡⲣ̄ⲕⲁ-
ⲡⲉⲛⲥⲱⲙⲁ' ⲉⲍⲱⲛ ⲍⲙ̄ⲡⲕⲁⲍ,' ϫⲉ ⲛ̄ⲛⲉⲡⲉⲛⲣ̄ⲡⲙⲉ'ⲉⲩⲉ ⲍⲱⲛ.' ⲡⲉϫⲉⲡⲥⲱⲧⲏⲣ
ⲛⲁϥ' ϫⲉ ⲁⲡⲁⲉⲓⲱⲧ ⲟⲩⲱ' ⲉϥⲥⲟⲃⲧⲉ ⲛⲁⲕ ⲛ̄ⲟⲩ'ⲧⲟⲡⲟⲥ ⲉⲛⲁⲛⲟⲩϥ' ⲉⲧⲣⲉⲛⲉⲧⲛ̄-
ⲥⲱⲙⲁ' ⲟⲩⲱⲍ ⲛ̄ⲍⲏⲧϥ̄ ⲍⲙ̄'ⲡⲓⲕⲟⲥⲙⲟⲥ· ⲁⲩⲱ' ⲡⲙⲁ ⲉⲧⲟⲩⲛⲁⲕⲁ'ⲛⲉⲧⲛ̄ⲥⲱⲙⲁ ⲛ̄-
ⲍⲏⲧϥ̄ ϯⲛⲁⲕⲱ ⲙ̄'ⲡⲉⲥⲙⲟⲩ ⲙⲛ̄'ϯⲣⲙ̄(134 R i)ⲛⲏ ⲛ̄ⲍⲏⲧⲩ ⲙⲛ̄'ⲍⲛ̄ⲍⲙⲟⲧ ⲛ̄ⲧⲁⲗ-
ϭⲟ.' ⲡⲉϫⲉⲡⲍⲁⲅⲓⲟⲥ ⲛⲁϥ' ϫⲉ ⲥⲱⲧⲙ̄' ⲉⲣⲟⲓ̈ ⲡⲁϫⲟⲉⲓⲥ ⲓ̄ⲥ ⲡⲉⲭ̄ⲥ̄·' ⲉϣⲱⲡⲉ ⲉⲣ'
ϣⲁⲛⲟⲩⲣⲱⲙⲉ ⲉⲓ' ⲉⲡⲧⲟⲡⲟⲥ ⲉⲧⲟⲩⲛⲁ'ⲕⲱ ⲙ̄ⲡⲁⲥⲱⲙⲁ' ⲛ̄ⲍⲏⲧϥ̄ ⲛ̄ϥϫⲉ' ⲍⲛ̄ⲟⲩⲡⲁ-

---

133 R i 19f. l. ⲉⲧⲛⲟⲧⲩ̄? 26. l. -ⲛⲉⲧⲍⲓⲃⲟⲩⲣ. 31f. l. ⲧⲉⲭⲁⲗⲁⲍⲁ? ii 1. l. -ⲍⲏ. 8;
11. ⲁⲍⲉⲣⲁⲧⲧⲏⲩⲧⲛ̄; second ⲧ added. 13. l. -θυρωρος; so Epim. V i 1. =-ⲁⲓⲧⲏⲙⲁ. 29.
l. -ⲃⲉⲕⲉ. 134 R i 4-7; lines short; hole in parchment.

ρανδωμα· ΜΠΝΟΥΝΟΒΕ· ΝϤΕΕΙ ΕϪΠΑCω̄μα Ν̄ϤΤωΒΖ̄ Μ̄ΜΟΝ Χ̄ΠΑΤΕΠΡΗ· Ζωτπ̄,
ΕΚΕΚω· ΝΑΥ ΕΒΟΛ Μ̄ΠΝΟ·ΒΕ Ν̄ΤΑϤΑΑΥ.²⁰ ΠΕϪΕΠCωΤΗΡ ΝΑΥ· ϪΕ ΕCΕϢωΠΕ Ν̄ΤΕΙ·
ΖΕ. ΠΕϪΕΠϪΑΓΙ·Οϲ ΝΑΥ ϪΕ ΠΕΤΝΑ·CΥΝΑΓΕ Ν̄ΟΥΠΡΟϲ·ΦΟΡΑ²⁵ Ζ̄Μ̄ΠΤΟΠΟϲ· ΕΤΟΥΝΑ·
Κω Ν̄Ζ̄Η·ΤϤ̄ Μ̄ΠΑCωΜΑ,· ΕΚΕCΥΝΑΓΕ Μ̄ΜΟϤ· Ζ̄ΝΤΕΠΡΟϲΦΟΡΑ³⁰ ᾹΠΕ· ΠΕΤΝΑ·
Κωωϲ Ν̄ΝΕΝCω·ΜΑ Ζ̄ΝΟΥΚΑΪCΕ,· ΕΚΕCΤΟΛΙΖΕ Ν̄ΝΕΥ(134 R ii)ΨΥΧΗ Ζ̄ΝΝΕΕΝ·
ΤΗΜΑ Μ̄ΠΟΥϪΑΪ·' ΠΕΤΝΑCϪΑΛᾹϪ Μ̄ΠϪω·ωΜΕ Ν̄ΤΕΝΜΑΡ·ΤΥΡΙΑ ΝϤΟΥωΝΖ̄ ΕΒΟΛ
Μ̄ΠΕΝΡ̄ΜΕ·ΕϤΕΤΕ, ΕΚΕCϪΑΪ Μ̄·ΠΕϤΡΑΝ ΕΠϪω·ωΜΕ Μ̄ΠωΝΖ̄·¹⁰ ΠΕΤΝΑΤ Ν̄ΝΕΝ·
ΡΑΝ ΕΝΕϤϢΗΡΕ· ΕΥΟΥωΝΖ̄ ΕΒΟΛ Ν̄ΝΕΝΡΑΝ, ΕΚΕΠΕΙ·ΘΕ Μ̄ΜΟΟΥ Ζ̄ΝΝΕΥ·ΕΠΙΘΕ¹⁵
Ν̄ϪΙ+Τ·' ΑΥω ΠΜΑ ΕΤΟΥΝΑ·Κω Μ̄ΠΕΝCωΜΑ· Ν̄Ζ̄ΗΤϤ̄, ΕΚΕΚΑ·ΠΕΚCΜΟΥ Μ̄Ν̄ΤΕΚ·²⁰
ΕΙΡΗΝΗ ΕΥΜΗΝ· ΕΒΟΛ Ν̄Ζ̄ΗΤϤ̄ ϢΑΕ·ΝΕΖ.· ΑϤΟΥωϢΒ̄ Ν̄ϬΙ Π·Cω ΤΗΡ, ΠΕϪΑϤ²⁵
Μ̄Π̄ϪΑΓΙΟϲ ΑΠΑ· ϢΝΟΥϤΕ ϪΕ ΑΛΗ·Θωϲ ΠΑΜΕΡΙΤ,· Ζ ωΒ ΝΙΜ Ν̄ΤΑΚΑΙ·ΤΙ Μ̄·
ΜΟΟΥ, ΑΠΑ·ΕΙωΤ ΟΥ ω ΕΥϪΑ·ΡΙΖΕ Μ̄ΜΟΟΥ ΝΑΚ.· ΑΥω ΑΠCωΤΗΡ· ΑΜΑΖΤΕ Ν̄·
ΝΕΝϬΙϪ (V i) Ν̄ΝΕΝϪΑΓΙΟϲ,· ΑϤΤΟΥΝΟCΟΥ Ζ̄ΙϪΜ̄·ΠΚΟΤ Ν̄CΙΚΕ·' ΑϤΑCΠΑΖΕ Μ̄·
ΜΟΟΥ,⁵ ΠΕϪΑϤ ΝΑΥ ϪΕ ΤωΚ· Ν̄Ζ̄ΗΤ, Μ̄ΠΡ̄Ρ̄ΖΟΤΕ·' ΤϤϢΟΟΠ ΝΜ̄ΜΗΤΝ̄·' ΕΙCΖΗΗΤΕ
ΓΑΡ ΑΪ·CΟΒΤΕ Ν̄ΝΕΤ̄Ν̄ΘΡΟ·ΝΟϲ Μ̄Ν̄ΕΤΝ̄Κ·ΛΟΜ Μ̄Ν̄ΕΤΕΝ·CΤΟΛΗ ΕΥΤΑΕΙΗΥ· Ε·
ΜΑΤΕ Ζ̄ΡΑΪ Ζ̄Ν̄ΤΜΕΖ·ϢΟΜΤΕ Μ̄ΠΕ.¹⁵ ΕΙCΖΗΗΤΕ Τ ωΡΚ̄· ΝΗΤΝ̄ Μ̄ΠΑΡΑΝ· ΕΤΟΥΑ·
ΑΒ Μ̄ΝΑ·ϪΑΓΙΟϲ Ν̄ΑΓΓΕΛΟϲ²⁰ ϪΕ Ρ ωΜΕ ΝΙΜ ΕΤΝΑ·ΠΙCΤΕΥΕ ΕΝΕΤΝ̄·ΡΑΝ Ζ̄ΝΟΥ·
ΖΗΤ Ν̄ΟΥ·ωΤ, Ζ ωΒ ΝΙΜ,· ΕΤΟΥΝΑΑΙΤΕΙ²⁵ Μ̄·ΜΟΟΥ Ζ̄ΜΠΡΑΝ Μ̄·ΠΑΕΙωΤ, ΤΝΑΤΑ·ΑΥ
ΝΑΥ· ΑΥω Ν̄·ΤΝΑΟΒῩΤ ΕΡΟΟΥ ΑΝ· Μ̄ΠΝΑΥ Ν̄ΤΕΥ·ΑΝΑΓΚΗ·³⁰ ΠΕΤ·ΝΑΡ̄Ρ̄ΗΤ Ν̄ΟΥ·
ΕΡΗΤ· ΕΠΕΤ̄ΤΟΠΟϲ· Ν̄ϤΑΜΕΛΕΙ ΕΤΜ̄·ϪΟΚϤ ΕΒΟΛ, ΤΝΑΕΙ(V ii)ΡΕ Μ̄ΠΕϤΚ̄ΖΒΑ
Ζ̄ΝΟΥ·CΗΠΕ· ΑΥω ΤΝΑ·ΤΡΕΠΕΤ̄ΡΑ(Ν)· Ρ̄ΟΕΙΤ, ω⁵ Π̄ϪΑΓΙΟϲ· ϢΝΟΥϤΕ· Μ̄ΝΝΕΚ·
ΚΕCΝΗΥ·' ΤΝΑΤΡΟΥΕΙΝΕ Ν̄Ζ̄Ν̄¹⁰ Δωρον ΕΠΕΚΤΟΠΟϲ· Ζ̄Μ̄ΠΑΡΑΝ· ΑΥω· ΠΜΑ Ε·
ΤΟΥΝΑΤ Ν̄ΤΕ·ΤΝ̄ΑΠΟΦΑCΙϲ Ν̄·Ζ̄ΗΤϤ̄, ΤΚω Ν̄Ζ̄Η¹⁵ΤϤ̄ Ν̄Ζ̄Ν̄Ζ̄ΜΟΟΥ Ν̄·ΤΑΛϬΟ. ΝΑΪ ΔΕ·
Ν̄ΤΕΡΕΠCωΤΗΡ· ϪΟΟΥ Ν̄Ν̄ϪΑΓΙΟϲ,· ΑϤΤ ΝΑΥ Ν̄ΤΡΗΝΗ,²⁰ ΑϤΒωΚ ΕΖ̄ΡΑΪ ΕΝΕΜ·ΠΗ·
ΥΕ ΕΡΕΝ̄ΑΓΓΕ·ΛΟϲ Ζ̄ΥΜΝΕΥΕ Ζ̄ΑΤΕϤ·ΖΗ.· ΤΟΤΕ ΤΜΑΚΑΡΙΑ Μ̄·ΠΑΡΘΕΝΟϲ ΑΜΑ
CΟΦΙΑ ΑCΠΕΡϢ̄ΝΕϲ·ϬΙϪ ΕΒΟΛ, ΑCΟΥΗΛ· ΕΠΝΟΥΤΕ ΕϲϪω· Μ̄ΜΟϲ ϪΕ ΠΑϪΟΕΙϲ³⁰
ῙC ΠΕΧ̄C, Ν̄ΘΕ Ν̄·ΤΑΚCωΤΜ̄ ΕΝΑϲ·ΝΗΥ ΕΥΤωΒΖ̄ Μ̄·ΜΟΚ, ΑΚϪΙ Ν̄ΤΕΥ(135 R i)·
ΘΥCΙΑ Ν̄ΤΟΟΤΟΥ,·Ν̄ΤΕΙϪΕ ΕΚΕCωΤΜ̄ Ε·ΡΟΪ Ζω ΕΪΤωΒΖ̄ Μ̄·ΜΟΚ. ΜΑΡῙΡ̄ΠΝΑ·⁵
Ζω Μ̄ΠΕΚΛΟΜ Ν̄ΤΑ·ΝΑϲΝΗΥ ϪΙΤϤ̄.· Ν̄ΤΕΡΕΠΖΗΓΕΜωΝ· ΔΕ ΝΑΥ ΕΤΜΑΚΑΡΙΑ·

---

134 R ii 1 f. = ΕΝΔΥΜΑ. 10 ff. Confusion between singular and plural. 15. = -ΠΕΙΘΕ?
30 - Vi 1. l. Π̄ΝΟϹΙΧ Ν̄Ν̄Ζ. 14. l. Μ̄ΠΕ. ii 2. l. -ϬΕΠΗ. 4-8. Lines short; hole
in parchment. 15. -Ζ ΜΟΟΥ; first o added; cf. 136 R i 5, below.

ⲉⲥⲁⲍⲉⲣⲁⲧⲥ̄ ⲉⲥϫⲏⲗ,¹⁰ ⲁϥⲕⲉⲗⲉⲩⲉ ⲉⲧⲣⲟⲩⲧⲁⲗⲟⲥ ⲉⲡϩⲉⲣⲙⲉⲧⲁⲣⲓⲟⲛ ⲛ̄ⲥⲉϩⲱⲕⲉ ⲙ̄-
ⲙⲟⲥ· ⲁⲩⲱ ϩⲛ̄ⲕⲉⲗⲁⲙⲡⲁⲥ ⲛ̄ⲕⲱϩⲧ̄ ⲱⲧⲁⲁⲩ¹⁵ ⲉϩⲟⲩⲛ ϩⲁⲛⲉⲥⲡⲓⲣⲟⲟⲩⲉ. ⲁⲥⲟⲩⲱϣⲃ̄
ⲛ̄ϭⲓ ⲧⲙⲁⲕⲁⲣⲓⲁ ⲁⲙⲁ ⲥⲟⲫⲓⲁ ⲡⲉϫⲁⲥ ϫⲉ· ⲛⲁⲓⲁⲧ ⲁⲛⲟⲕ ϫⲉ· ⲡⲉⲥⲕⲉⲟⲥ ⲛ̄ⲟⲩⲃ̄²⁰ ⲁⲩϣⲱⲡⲉ ⲛ̄ⲟⲩⲙⲉⲣⲓⲧ ⲙ̄ⲡⲇⲟⲝ²⁵ ϩⲛ̄ⲧⲙⲛ̄ⲧⲣ̄ⲣⲟ ⲛ̄ⲙ̄ⲡⲏⲩⲉ. ⲁⲩⲱ ⲛⲉⲥⲧⲁⲟⲩⲉϩⲁϩ ⲛ̄ⲅⲁ-
ϫⲉ ⲛ̄ϫⲓⲟⲩⲁ ⲉϩⲟⲩⲛ ϩⲁⲡϩⲟ ⲙ̄ⲡϩⲏⲅⲉ ⲙⲱⲛ. ⲡⲉϫⲉ ⲡϩⲏⲅⲉⲙⲱⲛ ⲛⲁⲥ³⁰ ϫⲉ ⲥⲟⲫⲓⲁ,
ⲧⲩⲉⲛⲉϩ ⲧⲏⲓ ϩⲁⲧⲟⲩⲙⲛ̄ⲧⲕⲟⲩⲓ ⲛ̄ϣⲏⲣⲉ· ⲙ̄ⲙⲟⲛ (135 R ii) ⲛ̄ⲧⲛⲁⲁⲛⲉⲭⲉ ⲙ̄ⲙⲟ ⲁⲛ
ⲛ̄ⲧⲉⲓϩⲉ ⲧⲏⲣⲥ̄· ⲡⲗⲏⲛ ⲁⲣⲓⲑⲩⲥⲓⲁ ⲙ̄ⲡⲁⲧⲉⲙⲟⲩ ⲕⲁⲕⲱⲥ·⁵ ⲁⲓϫⲓⲥⲉ ⲉⲓⲧϭⲟ ⲉⲣⲟ ⲩⲁϩ·
ϩⲟⲩⲛ ⲉⲧⲉⲛⲟⲩ. ⲁⲥⲟⲩⲱϣⲃ̄ ⲛ̄ϭⲓ ⲧⲙⲁⲕⲁⲣⲓⲁ ⲁⲙⲁ ⲥⲟⲫⲓⲁ ϫⲉ ⲙ̄ⲡⲣ̄ⲧⲣⲉⲡⲉⲓϩⲱⲃ¹⁰
ⲣⲣⲟⲟⲩϣ ⲛⲁⲕ ϫⲉ ⲣ̄ⲑⲩⲥⲓⲁ· ⲛ̄ⲧⲛⲁⲣ̄ⲑⲩⲥⲓⲁ ⲁⲛ, ϫⲉⲕⲁⲥ ⲉⲛⲛⲉ(ⲛ)ⲡⲱⲣϫ̄ ⲉⲛⲉ ⲛⲉ-
ⲣⲏⲩ· ϩⲙ̄ⲡⲏⲓ ⲙ̄ⲡⲛⲟⲩⲧⲉ¹⁵ ⲓ̄ⲥ̄ ⲡⲉⲭ̄ⲥ̄· ⲁⲗⲗⲁ ⲡⲙⲟⲩ ⲉⲧⲟⲩⲛⲁⲙⲟⲩ ⲛ̄ϩⲏⲧϥ̄ ⲉⲓⲛⲁⲙⲟⲩ
ⲛ̄ϩⲏⲧϥ̄ ϩⲱ, ϫⲉⲕⲁⲥ ⲟⲛ ⲉⲓⲉⲱⲛϩ̄²⁰ ⲛⲙ̄ⲙⲁⲩ ϩⲛ̄ⲛⲉⲱⲛ ⲛ̄ⲁⲧⲟⲩⲱ. ⲁⲩⲟⲩⲱϣϥ ⲛ̄ϭⲓ
ⲡϩⲏⲅⲉⲙⲱⲛ, ⲡⲉϫⲁϥ ⲛⲁⲥ ϫⲉ ⲁⲗⲏⲑⲱⲥ ⲱ²⁵ ⲥⲟⲫⲓⲁ ⲉⲣϣⲁⲛⲥⲱⲧⲙ̄ ⲛ̄ⲥⲱⲓ ⲛ̄ⲧⲉ-
ⲉⲓⲣⲉ ⲙ̄ⲡⲧⲱⲧ ⲛ̄ϩⲏⲧ ⲁⲛ̄ⲣ̄ⲣⲱⲟⲩ, ϯⲛⲁϫⲓⲧⲉ ⲉϩⲟⲩⲛ ⲉⲡⲁⲏⲓ·³⁰ ⲟⲩⲛⲧⲁⲓ ⲟⲩ ϣⲏⲣⲉ
ⲙ̄ⲙⲟⲛⲟⲅⲉⲛⲏⲥ· ϯⲛⲁϫⲓⲧⲉ ⲛⲁⲩ ⲛ̄ⲥ̄ϩⲓⲙⲉ, (Vi) ϯⲛⲁⲧⲣⲟⲩⲧⲁⲙⲉⲓⲟ ⲛⲉ ⲛⲟⲩ-
ⲥⲣⲏⲡⲉ· ⲉⲛⲁⲛⲟⲩⲥ ⲙ̄ⲡⲉⲗⲁⲁⲩ ⲛ̄ⲁⲣⲭⲱⲛ⁵ ⲧⲁⲙⲉⲓⲟⲥ ⲉⲛⲉϩ· ⲡⲉϫⲉ ⲧⲙⲁⲕⲁⲣⲓⲁ ⲙ̄
ⲡⲁⲣⲑⲉⲛⲟⲥ ⲛⲁⲩ ϫⲉ ϥⲥⲏϩ ϩⲛ̄ⲧⲉⲅⲣⲁⲫⲏ ⲉⲧⲟⲩⲁⲁⲃ¹⁰ ϫⲉ ⲡⲛⲟⲩⲃ ⲙⲛ̄ⲡϩⲁⲧ ⲥⲉ-
ⲛⲁⲣ̄ϭⲓⲃⲉ· ⲡⲥⲁ ϩⲱⲱⲥ ⲙ̄ⲡ̄ⲥⲱⲙⲁ ⲛⲁⲩϣⲡⲉ ⲛ̄ϭⲁⲓⲉ ϩⲁⲛⲉ(ⲛ)ⲧⲁⲫⲟⲥ· ⲡⲉⲧⲉⲓ-
ⲣⲉ· ⲇⲉ ⲛ̄ⲧⲟϥ ⲙ̄ⲡⲟⲩⲱϣ ⲙ̄ⲡⲛⲟⲩⲧⲉ ϥⲛⲁⲙⲟⲩⲛ ⲉⲃⲟⲗ ϣⲁⲉⲛⲉϩ· ⲡⲉϫⲉ ⲡϩⲏⲅⲉⲙⲱⲛ ⲛⲁⲥ ϫⲉ ⲧⲉⲟⲩⲱϣ ⲉⲧⲣⲁⲧ ⲛ̄ⲧⲟⲩⲁⲡⲟⲫⲁⲥⲓⲥ ⲛ̄ⲑⲉ ⲛ̄ⲛⲟⲩⲕⲉⲥⲛⲏⲩ ⲧⲏⲣⲟⲩ²⁵
ⲁⲥⲟⲩⲱϣⲃ̄ ⲛ̄ϭⲓ ⲧⲙⲁⲕⲁⲣⲓⲁ ⲁⲙⲁ³⁰ ⲥⲟⲫⲓⲁ ϫⲉ ϯⲩⲡ ϩⲙⲟⲧ ⲛ̄ⲧⲙ̄ⲡⲛⲟⲩⲧⲉ ⲉϫⲉⲛ-
ⲧⲉⲕⲁⲡⲟⲫⲁⲥⲓⲥ. ⲛ̄ⲧⲉⲩⲛⲟⲩ ⲁⲩⲧⲟⲩϫⲓ ⲛ̄ⲧⲕⲉⲟⲩⲉⲓ, ⲁⲩⲧⲁ(Vii)ⲗⲟⲥ ⲉϩⲣⲁⲓ ⲉ-
ϫⲙ̄ⲡⲕⲟⲧ ⲛ̄ⲥⲓⲕⲉ ϩⲁϩ ⲧ̄ⲙ̄ⲡⲛ̄ⲧⲟⲩⲉ ⲛ̄ϩⲁⲅⲓⲟⲥ· ⲁⲩⲥⲓⲧⲉ ⲛ̄ⲛⲉⲩⲥⲱⲙⲁ ϩⲁⲡⲕⲟⲧ⁵
ⲛ̄ⲥⲓⲕⲉ, ⲁⲩⲥⲓⲕⲉ ⲉϫⲱⲟⲩ ϣⲁⲛⲧⲉⲛⲉⲩⲕⲉⲉⲥ ⲟⲩⲱϣ̄ ⲉϫⲉ(ⲛ)ⲛⲉⲩⲉⲣⲏⲩ ⲛ̄ⲥⲉⲣ̄¹⁰
ϣⲏⲙ ϣⲏⲙ, ⲁⲡⲉⲩⲥⲛⲟϥ ⲙⲛ̄ⲡⲉⲩⲥⲱⲙⲁ ⲙⲛ̄ⲡⲉⲩϣⲁⲁⲣ ⲃⲱⲗⲝ̄ ⲉⲡⲕⲟⲧ ⲛ̄ⲥⲓⲕⲉ.
ⲁⲩⲥⲱⲟⲩϩ¹⁵ ⲛ̄ϭⲓ ⲟⲩⲛⲟϭ ⲙ̄ⲙⲏⲏϣⲉ ⲛ̄ⲧⲉⲡⲧⲟⲟⲩ ⲉⲧⲙ̄ⲙⲁⲩ, ⲁⲩⲉⲓ ϣⲁ ⲛⲉⲧⲟⲩⲁⲁⲃ,
ⲁⲩⲛⲁⲩ ⲉⲣⲟⲟⲩ·²⁰ ⲣⲱⲙⲉ ⲛⲓⲙ ⲉⲟⲩⲛ ϣⲱⲛⲉ ⲉⲩⲙⲟⲕϩ̄ ⲛ̄ϩⲏⲧⲟⲩ ⲕⲁⲧⲁ ⲥⲙⲟⲧ ⲛⲓⲙ,
ⲁⲩϫⲓ ⲉⲃⲟⲗ ϩⲙ̄ⲡⲉⲥⲛⲟϥ²⁵ ⲛ̄ⲛⲉⲧⲟⲩⲁⲁⲃ, ⲁⲩϯ ⲉⲛⲉⲩⲙⲉⲗⲟⲥ ⲉⲧⲙⲟⲕϩ̄· ⲛ̄ⲃⲉⲗ-
ⲗⲉⲉⲩ ⲁⲩⲛⲁⲩ ⲉⲃⲟⲗ· ⲛ̄ϭⲁⲗⲉ ⲁⲩⲙⲟⲟϣⲉ·³⁰ ⲛ̄ⲕⲟⲩⲣ ⲁⲩⲥⲱⲧⲙ̄· ⲛⲉⲙⲡⲟ ⲁⲩϣⲁϫⲉ (136 Ri) ⲛⲉⲧⲥⲟⲃϩ̄ ⲁⲩⲧⲃ̄ⲃⲟ, ⲕⲁⲧⲁ ⲡϣⲁϫⲉ ⲛ̄ⲧⲁ ⲡⲉⲛⲥⲱⲧⲏⲣ ϫⲟⲟϥ ⲛⲁⲩ

---

135 R i 15f. l. ϩⲁⲛⲉⲥⲡⲓⲣⲟⲟⲩⲉ. 20. =-ⲥⲕⲉⲩⲟⲥ. 22. ⲙ̄ⲡⲇⲟⲝ (sic); some expression containing Δοξα? ii 20. =-ⲁⲓⲱⲛ. V ii 20. At end of line, ink marks; apparently an offset.

ϫⲉ ϯⲛⲁⲕⲱ ⲛ̅ⲅ̅ⲛ̅ϩⲙⲟⲟⲩ ⲛ̅ⲧⲁⲗ'ϭⲟ ϩⲓⲡⲙⲁ ⲉⲧⲟⲩⲛⲁ'ⲕⲁⲛⲉⲧ̅ⲛ̅ⲥⲱⲙⲁ' ⲛ̅ϩⲏⲧϥ̅, ⲁⲩⲱ
ϩⲙ̅'ⲡⲙⲁ ⲉⲧⲉⲧⲛ̅ⲁϫⲱⲕ' ⲉⲃⲟⲗ ⲛ̅ⲧⲉⲧⲛ̅ⲟⲓⲕⲟ'ⲛⲟⲙⲓⲁ ⲛ̅ϩⲏⲧϥ̅.' ⲁⲩⲱ ⲧⲁⲓ ⲧⲉ ⲑⲉ ⲛ̅-
ⲧⲁⲩ'ϫⲱⲕ ⲉⲃⲟⲗ ⲛ̅ⲧⲉⲩ'ⲟⲓⲕⲟⲛⲟⲙⲓⲁ ⲙⲛ̅'ⲧⲉⲩⲙⲁⲣⲧⲩⲣⲓⲁ' ⲛ̅ϭⲓ ⲡⲙⲛ̅ⲧⲥⲛⲟⲟⲩⲥ' ⲛ̅ⲅⲉⲛ-
ⲛⲁⲓⲟⲥ ⲙ̅'ⲙⲁⲣⲧⲩⲣⲟⲥ' ⲁⲡⲁ ⲯⲟⲩⲯⲉ ⲙ̅ⲛ̅'ⲁⲡⲁ ⲫⲓⲗⲏⲙⲱⲛ' ⲙ̅ⲛ̅ⲁⲡⲁ ⲛⲓⲗⲓⲟⲥ' ⲙ̅ⲛ̅ⲁⲡⲁ
ⲡⲉⲧⲣⲟⲥ' ⲙ̅ⲛ̅ⲁⲡⲁ ⲁⲛⲇⲣⲉⲁⲥ' ⲙ̅ⲛ̅ⲁⲡⲁ ⲓ̈ⲱⲁⲛⲛⲓⲥ' ⲙ̅ⲛ̅ⲁⲡⲁ ⲫⲟⲓⲃⲁⲙⲱ(ⲛ)'ⲙ̅ⲛ̅ⲁⲡⲁ
ⲥⲟⲫⲓⲁ' ⲙ̅ⲛ̅ⲁⲡⲁ ⲁⲛⲧⲱⲛⲓⲟⲥ' ⲙ̅ⲛ̅ⲁⲡⲁ ϩⲉⲣⲙⲓⲁ'ⲙ̅ⲛ̅ⲁⲡⲁ ⲭⲉⲣⲉⲙⲱ(ⲛ)'ⲙ̅ⲛ̅ⲁⲡⲁ ⲫⲓⲗⲓⲡⲡⲟⲥ' ⲛ̅ⲥⲟⲩⲥⲁⲩϣ̅ ⲙ̅ⲡⲁⲟⲡⲉ,' ⲁⲩϫⲓ ⲙ̅ⲡⲉⲕⲗⲟⲙ ⲙ̅(136 R ii)ⲡⲱⲛϩ̅, ⲁⲛϭⲟⲉⲓⲥ'
ⲓ̅ⲥ̅ ϫⲓ ⲛ̅ⲛⲉⲩⲯⲩⲭⲟ'ⲟⲩⲉ, ⲁⲩⲁⲥⲡⲁⲍⲉ ⲙ̅'ⲙⲟⲟⲩ, ⲁⲩϭⲟⲁⲗⲟⲩ' ⲛ̅ϩⲉⲛⲙⲁⲡⲡⲁ ⲛ̅'ⲩⲉⲛϭ̅,
ⲁⲩⲧⲁⲗⲟⲟⲩ' ⲛ̅ⲙⲙⲁⲩ ⲉϫⲉⲙ'ⲡϫⲁⲣⲙⲁ, ⲁⲩϫⲓ'ⲧⲟⲩ ⲉϩⲣⲁⲓ̈ ⲙ̅ⲡⲏ'ⲩⲉ ⲉⲣⲉⲛ̅ⲁⲅⲅⲉ'ⲗⲟⲥ
ⲥⲱⲕ ϩⲓϩⲏ ⲙ̅'ⲙⲟⲟⲩ ϩⲉⲛϩⲛ̅'ⲕⲟⲩⲕⲙ̅ ⲙ̅ⲛ̅'ϩⲉⲛⲭⲟⲣⲟⲥ' ⲙ̅ⲛ̅ϩⲛ̅ⲇⲩⲕ'ⲡⲁⲛⲟⲛ ⲙ̅ⲛ̅ϩⲉⲛ-
ⲥⲁⲗⲡⲓⲅⲝ' ⲙ̅ⲛ̅ϩⲉⲛⲗⲟⲩⲗⲁⲓ̈.' ⲁⲡⲉⲭⲟⲣⲟⲥ ⲧⲏⲣϥ̅' ⲛ̅ⲛⲉⲧⲟⲩⲁⲁⲃ ⲥⲧⲟ'ⲗⲓⲍⲉ ⲙ̅ⲙⲟⲟⲩ,
ⲁⲡϫⲟⲉⲓⲥ ϯ ⲉϫⲉⲛⲧⲉⲩ'ⲁⲡⲉ ⲙ̅ⲡⲉⲕⲗⲟⲙ' ⲙ̅ⲡⲱⲛϩ̅, ⲁⲩⲑ̅ⲥ̅ⲥⲟⲟⲩ ϩⲓⲕⲉⲛⲛⲉⲩⲑⲣⲟ-
ⲛⲟⲥ, ⲁⲩⲣϣⲁ' ⲙ̅ⲛ̅ⲛⲉⲧⲟⲩⲁⲁⲃ' ⲧⲏⲣⲟⲩ, ⲉⲡⲓⲇⲏ ⲁⲩⲙⲓϣⲉ ϩ̅ⲙ̅ⲡⲁ'ⲅⲱⲛ ⲉⲧⲛⲁⲛⲟⲩϥ,'
ⲁⲩⲥⲉⲕⲗⲡⲱⲧ' ⲉⲃⲟⲗ, ⲁⲩϩⲁⲣⲉϩ (V i) ⲉⲧⲡⲓⲥⲧⲓⲥ, ⲁⲩ'ϫⲓ ⲙ̅ⲡⲉⲕⲗⲟⲙ' ⲉⲧⲕⲏ ⲛⲁⲉ-
ϩⲣⲁⲓ̈ ⲩⲁⲉⲛⲉϩ, ϩⲁⲙⲏⲛ.' ⲙ̅ⲛ̅ⲥⲁⲛⲁⲓ̈' ⲇⲉ ⲧⲏⲣⲟⲩ ⲁϥ'ⲕⲉⲗⲉⲩⲉ ⲛ̅ϭⲓ ⲡ'ϩⲏⲅⲉⲙⲱⲛ'
ⲉⲧⲣⲟⲩϭⲓⲕⲉ' ⲛ̅ⲟⲩⲛⲟϭ ⲙ̅'ⲫⲟⲥⲥⲁ ⲛ̅ⲥⲁⲣϩⲥ̅ ⲙ̅ⲡⲧⲙⲉ ⲛ̅ⲥⲉ'ⲛⲟⲩϫⲉ ⲛ̅ⲛⲉⲛⲥⲱⲙⲁ' ⲛ̅ϩⲁ-
ⲅⲓⲟⲥ' ⲓ̅ⲙⲁⲣⲧⲩⲣⲟⲥ' ⲉⲡⲉⲥⲏⲧ ⲉⲣⲟⲥ.' ⲁⲩⲱ ⲁⲩⲛⲟ'ϫⲟⲩ, ⲁⲩϩⲱⲥ' ⲉϫⲱⲟⲩ.' ⲡⲙⲁ ⲇⲉ
ⲛ̅ⲧⲁⲩ'ⲕⲱ ⲛ̅ⲛⲉⲩⲥⲱⲙⲁ' ⲛ̅ϩⲏⲧϥ̅ ⲁⲩⲕⲓⲙ' ⲛ̅ⲩⲟⲙⲛ̅ⲧ ⲛ̅ⲥⲟⲡ' ⲉⲡⲉⲓⲥⲁ ⲙ̅ⲛ̅ⲡⲁⲓ̈,' ⲁⲟⲩⲛⲟϭ ⲛ̅ϭⲟⲧⲉ' ⲙ̅ⲛ̅ⲟⲩⲛⲟϭ ⲛ̅ⲧⲁ'ⲣⲁⲭⲏ ⲛ̅ⲩⲧⲟⲣⲧⲣ̅' ϣⲱⲡⲉ ϩⲙ̅'ⲡⲧⲟⲩ ⲧⲏⲣϥ̅ ⲉⲧⲙ̅ⲙⲁⲩ'
ϩⲓⲧⲛ̅ⲧϭⲓⲛⲉⲓ ⲉⲃⲟⲗ' ϩⲛ̅ⲛⲥⲱⲙⲁ ⲛ̅ⲛⲉ(V ii) ⲛ̅ϩⲁⲅⲓⲟⲥ ⲁⲡⲁ ⲯⲟⲩϫⲉ ⲙ̅ⲛ̅ⲛⲉϥⲥⲛⲏⲩ. ⲛ̅-
ⲧⲟⲩ ϩⲱ'ⲟⲩ ⲟⲛ ⲡⲁⲛⲟⲙⲟⲥ' ⲛ̅ϩⲏⲅⲉⲙⲱⲛ ⲁϥ'ⲣϩⲟⲧⲉ, ⲁϥⲩⲧⲟⲣⲧⲣ̅,' ⲁϥⲥⲉⲕⲡⲟⲩϩⲏⲗⲟ(ⲛ),'
ⲁϥⲃⲟϭϥ̅ ⲉϩⲣⲁⲓ̈ ·' ⲁⲩⲱ ⲡⲥⲉⲉⲡⲉ ⲛ̅ⲛⲉ'ⲧⲟⲩⲁⲁⲃ ⲉⲧⲛ̅ⲧⲟⲟⲧϥ̅' ⲁϥⲥⲟⲛϩⲟⲩ ⲁⲩϫⲓ'ⲧⲟⲩ
ⲛ̅ⲙⲙⲁⲩ ⲉⲧⲡⲟⲗⲓⲥ ⲑⲉⲃⲁⲉⲓⲥ.' ⲁⲛⲟⲕ ⲇⲉ ⲓ̈ⲟⲩⲗⲓⲟⲥ' ⲁⲓ̈ⲥϩⲁⲓ̈ ⲛ̅ⲛⲉϩⲩⲡⲟ'ⲙⲛⲏⲙⲁ ⲛ̅-
ⲛⲉⲧ'ⲟⲩⲁⲁⲃ ⲁⲡⲁ ⲯⲟⲩϭⲉ ⲙ̅ⲛ̅ⲛⲉϥⲥⲛⲏⲩ' ⲛ̅ⲉⲉⲃⲟⲗ ϩⲛ̅ⲙ̅ⲡⲁ'ⲓ̈ⲁⲧ ⲛ̅ⲧⲉⲡⲉⲇⲓⲛⲏ,' ⲁⲓ̈-
ⲧⲁⲁⲩ ⲛ̅ⲧⲣⲁⲫⲁ'ⲛⲏⲥ ⲡⲁϩ̅ϩ̅ⲅⲁⲗ ⲛ̅ⲁ'ⲛⲁⲅⲕⲁⲓⲟⲛ, ⲁϥ'ϫⲓⲧⲟⲩ ⲉϩⲣⲁⲓ̈ ⲉⲡⲁⲏ'ⲓ̈ ⲉⲧϣⲟⲟⲡ
ⲛ̅ϩⲏⲧϥ̅' ϩⲛ̅ⲕⲃⲁϩⲥ̅, ⲁⲩⲕⲁⲁⲩ' ⲛ̅ϩⲏⲧϥ̅, ϩⲱⲙⲟⲥ' ⲉⲣⲉⲡⲉⲩⲥⲙⲟⲩ ⲙ̅ⲛ̅ⲡⲉⲩϩⲙⲟⲧ ϣⲱⲡⲉ' ⲉⲩⲙⲏⲛ ⲉⲃⲟⲗ ⲛⲙ̅'ⲙⲁⲛ ⲩⲁⲉⲛⲉϩ,' ϩⲁⲙⲏⲛ. ⲡⲛⲟⲩⲧⲉ (137 R i) ⲡⲉⲧⲟ ⲙ̅ⲙⲛ̅ⲧⲣⲉ
ⲙ̅ⲛ̅'ⲡⲁⲡ̅ⲛ̅ⲁ ⲁⲛⲟⲕ ⲡⲉ' ⲓ̈ⲟⲩⲗⲓⲟⲥ ϫⲉ ⲙ̅ⲡⲓⲟⲩ'ⲱϩ ⲉϫⲉⲛⲛⲉⲛⲃⲟⲙ' ⲛ̅ⲛⲉⲧⲟⲩⲁⲁⲃ ⲛ̅ϩⲁ'ⲅⲓⲟⲥ

---

136 R i 19-30; a numeral in margin against each name; cf. 106 R i, above.   ii 2 f. l.
-ψυχοογε. 7-17: short lines; hole in parchment. V i 6-21: short lines; hole in
parchment, patched on this side. 30. ΤΗΡϤ added. ii 7. = velum. 27.=ϩⲱⲙⲟⲥ;
l. Ⲣⲟⲛⲱⲉⲓ Ⲉⲣⲓⲙⲁ ϫⲉⲕⲁⲥ).

ⲁⲗⲗⲁ ⲩϩⲛⲟⲩϭⲉˈ ⲙ̄ⲛ̄ⲛⲉϥⲥⲛⲏⲩˌˈ ⲟⲩⲇⲉ ⲙ̄ⲡⲉⲓϭⲓ ⲛ̄ϫⲏⲧⲟⲩ, ⲁⲗⲗⲁ ⲛ̄ⲛⲉ(ⲛ)ˈⲧⲁⲧⲁⲁⲩ ⲙ̄ⲛ̄
ⲛⲉⲛⲧⲁⲓⲛⲁⲩ ⲉⲣⲟⲟⲩ ⲉⲃⲟⲗ ϩⲓⲧⲟⲟⲧⲟⲩ, ⲛⲁⲓ ⲛⲉ ⲛ̄ⲧⲁⲓⲥϫⲁⲓⲥⲟⲩˈ ⲙ̄ⲛ̄ⲛ̄ⲥⲱⲥ ⲁⲓⲕⲧⲟⲓ,
ⲁⲓⲃⲱⲕ ⲉⲣⲁⲕⲟⲧⲉ, ⲁⲓⲥⲱ ϩⲓⲝⲉⲛⲧⲉⲭⲣⲓⲁ ⲛ̄ⲧⲁⲩⲕⲁⲁⲧ ϩⲓϫⲱⲥˈ ⲉⲓϭⲓ ⲙ̄ⲡⲣⲟⲟⲩϣ ⲛ̄
ⲛⲉⲧⲟⲩⲁⲁⲃ ⲕⲁⲧⲁ ⲡ(ⲧ)ⲱϣ ⲙ̄ⲡⲛⲟⲩⲧⲉˈ ⲛ̄ⲧⲁⲩϭⲙⲟⲧ ⲙ̄ⲙⲟⲩˈ ⲛⲁⲓ ϣⲁⲗⲉϩⲟⲟⲩˈ ⲛ̄ⲧⲁⲩ-
ⲙⲟⲩ ⲛ̄ϭⲓ ⲡⲁⲛⲟⲙⲟⲥ ⲛ̄ⲣ̄ⲣⲟ ⲇⲓⲱⲕ(ⲗ)ⲏⲧⲓⲁⲛⲟⲥ, ⲁϥⲕⲱ ⲛ̄ⲛⲉⲧⲟⲩⲁⲁⲃ ⲉⲃⲟⲗ ⲉⲩⲧⲡ̄
ⲉϩⲟⲩⲛ ⲕⲁⲧⲁⲙⲁ· ⲁⲩⲱ ⲛⲉⲧⲟⲩⲁⲁⲃ ⲉⲧⲟⲧⲡ̄ ⲉϩⲟⲩ(ⲛ)ˈ ⲉⲧⲉⲫⲩⲗⲁⲕⲏ ⲛ̄ⲣⲁ̄ⲕⲟⲧⲉ ⲛⲉⲓ-
ϭⲓ ⲙ̄ⲡⲉⲩⲣⲟⲟⲩϣ ⲕⲁⲧⲁⲧⲉⲭⲣⲓⲁ (137 R ii) ⲙ̄ⲡⲓⲕⲟⲥⲙⲟⲥ ⲕⲁⲧⲁⲡⲉⲛⲩⲁⲅⲟⲩˈⲱ ⲙ̄ⲛ̄
ϩⲛ̄ⲟⲩⲧⲃ̄ⲃⲟ, ⲁⲩⲱ ⲛⲉⲓϫⲓ ⲛⲁⲩ ⲉϩⲟⲩⲛ ⲛ̄ⲟⲩⲕⲱⲧ ⲙ̄ⲟⲩⲙⲟⲟⲩ, ⲉⲡⲓⲇⲏ ⲛⲉⲩϫⲉ-
ϩⲱϫˈ ϩⲓⲧⲛ̄ⲡⲁϩⲩⲁⲓ ⲛ̄ⲛⲉⲛϩⲓⲥⲉ ⲛ̄ⲛ̄ⲃⲁⲍⲁⲛⲟⲥ. ⲛ̄ⲧⲉⲣⲓⲛⲁⲩˈ ⲉⲡⲉⲩϩⲓⲥⲉ ⲙ̄ⲛ̄ⲧⲉⲩ-
ⲑⲗⲓⲯⲓⲥ, ⲁⲓⲃⲱⲕˈ ϣⲁⲡⲉⲡⲁⲣⲭⲟⲥ, ⲁⲓ ⲡⲁⲣⲁⲕⲁⲗⲉⲓ ⲙ̄ⲙⲟⲩ ϫⲉⲕⲁⲥ ⲉϥⲉⲕⲁⲁⲩ ⲉ-
ⲃⲟⲗ. ⲡⲉϫⲉⲡⲉ ⲡⲁⲣⲭⲟⲥ ⲛⲁⲓ ϫⲉ ⲧ̄ⲣ̄ϩⲟⲧⲉ ⲁⲛⲟⲕ ⲙⲏ ⲛ̄ϩⲟ̄ⲇⲉ ⲛ̄ⲅ̄ⲧⲱⲟⲩ(ⲛ) ⲛ̄ϭⲓ ⲕⲉ-
ⲣ̄ⲣⲟ ⲛ̄ⲁⲛⲟⲙⲟⲥ ⲛ̄ϥⲩⲓⲛⲉ ⲛ̄ⲥⲱⲟⲩ, ⲧⲁⲧⲁϫⲉ ⲉⲣⲟⲟⲩ ⲧⲁⲧⲁⲁⲩ ⲛⲁⲩ, ⲧⲁⲩϣⲱⲡⲉ
ϩⲁⲟⲩ ⲕⲓⲛⲇⲩⲛⲟⲥ ⲉⲧⲃⲏ̄ⲏⲧⲟⲩ. ⲁⲛⲟⲕ ⲇⲉˈ ϩⲱ ⲡⲉϫⲁⲓ ⲙ̄ⲡⲉ ⲡⲁⲣⲭⲟⲥ ϫⲉ ⲁⲛⲟⲕˈ
ⲡⲉⲧⲛⲁϩⲙⲟⲟⲥ ϩⲛ̄ⲧⲉⲫⲩⲗⲁⲕⲏ ⲙ̄ⲛ̄ⲛⲁⲣⲱⲙⲉ ⲧⲏⲣⲟⲩˈ ϣⲁⲡⲉϩⲟⲟⲩ ⲉⲧⲉ(ⲩⲓ)ⲣⲉⲡ-
ⲛⲟⲩⲧⲉ ⲛⲁⲧ ⲟⲩⲧⲱϣ ⲉⲛⲁⲛⲟⲩ ⲉ ⲉⲛⲉⲧⲟⲩⲁⲁⲃ. ⲡⲉϫⲉⲡⲉⲡⲁⲣⲭⲟⲥ ϫⲉ ⲟⲩⲕⲟⲩⲛ
ⲃⲱⲕ, ⲁⲣⲓⲣⲉ ⲕⲁⲧⲁⲑⲉ ⲉⲧ ⲣⲁⲛⲁⲕ. ⲁⲓⲃⲱⲕ ⲇⲉ ⲉⲧⲉⲫⲩⲗⲁⲕⲏ, ⲁⲓϩⲙⲟⲟⲥ ϩⲙ̄-
ⲡⲙⲁ ⲉⲧⲙ̄ⲙⲁⲩ ⲙ̄ⲛ̄ⲉⲩⲥⲧⲟⲭⲓⲁ ⲧⲁϭⲓⲙⲉ ⲙ̄ⲛ̄ⲡⲁϣⲏⲣⲉ ⲉⲩⲭⲁⲣⲓⲥⲧⲟⲥ ⲙ̄ⲛ̄ⲧⲁⲥⲱ-
ⲛⲉ ⲉⲩⲭⲁⲣⲓⲥⲧⲓⲁ, ⲁⲛⲁϣⲙ̄ϫⲁⲗ ϣⲱⲡⲉ ⲉⲩⲇⲓⲁⲕⲟⲛⲉⲓ ⲉⲣⲟⲛ· ⲁⲛⲕⲱ ⲉⲃⲟⲗ ⲛ̄ⲛⲉ-
ⲧⲟⲩⲁⲁⲃ, ⲁⲡⲟⲩⲁ ⲡⲟⲩⲁ ⲡⲱⲧ ⲉⲡⲉϥⲙⲁ ϣⲱⲡⲉ ϩⲛ̄ⲟⲩⲉⲓⲣⲏⲛⲏ ⲉⲩⲧⲉⲟⲟⲩ ⲙ̄-
ⲡⲛⲟⲩⲧⲉ. ⲛ̄ⲧⲁⲛϣⲱ ⲛ̄ϩⲟⲩ(ⲛ) ⲉⲧⲉⲫⲩⲗⲁⲕⲏ ⲛ̄ⲣⲁⲕⲟⲧⲉ ⲉⲛ ⲟⲧⲡ̄ ⲉϩⲟⲩⲛ ϣⲁⲗⲉϩⲟ-
ⲟⲩ ⲛ̄ⲧⲁⲩⲣ̄ⲣⲟ ⲛ̄ϭⲓ ⲡⲙⲁⲓⲛⲟⲩⲧⲉ ⲛ̄ⲉⲣⲟ ⲕⲟⲥⲧⲁⲛⲧⲓⲛⲟⲥ, ⲁϥϫⲟⲟⲩ ⲉϩ(ⲣⲁⲓ) ⲉ-
ⲕⲏⲙⲉ, ⲁϥⲕⲱ ⲉⲃⲟⲗ ⲛ̄ⲛⲉⲫⲩⲗⲁⲕⲏ ⲧⲏⲣⲟⲩ ϫⲓⲛⲣⲁⲕⲟⲧⲉ ϣⲁⲡⲣⲏⲥ ⲛ̄ⲕⲏ̄ⲙⲉ ⲧⲏ-
ⲣⲩ̄. ⲁⲥϣⲱⲡⲉ ⲛ̄ⲧⲉⲣⲟⲩⲕⲱ ⲉⲃⲟⲗ ⲛ̄ⲧⲉⲫⲩⲗⲁⲕⲏ ⲛ̄ⲣⲁⲕⲟⲧⲉ, ⲁⲓⲉⲓ ⲉϩⲣⲁⲓ ⲉⲡⲁⲏⲓ
ⲁⲛⲟⲕ ⲙ̄ⲛ̄ⲛⲁϣⲙ̄ϫⲁⲗ ⲙ̄ⲛ̄ⲛⲁⲣⲱⲙⲉ ⲧⲏⲣⲟⲩ· ⲁⲩⲥⲱⲧⲙ̄ ϩⲱⲟⲩ ⲛ̄ϭⲓ ⲛⲉⲧⲟⲩⲁⲁⲃ ϫⲉ
ⲁⲓⲉⲓ ⲉϩⲣⲁⲓ ⲉⲡⲁⲏⲓ, ⲁⲩⲧⲱⲟⲩ(ⲛ) ϩⲓⲟⲩⲥⲟⲡ ⲛ̄ⲟⲩⲱⲧ, ⲁⲩⲉⲓ ϣⲁⲣⲟⲓ ⲛ̄ϩⲟⲩⲛ ⲉⲡⲁⲏⲓ.
ⲁⲩⲱ ⲧⲁⲥⲱⲛⲉ ⲉⲩⲭⲁⲣⲓⲥⲧⲓⲁ ⲁⲥⲉⲓⲛⲉ ⲛ̄ⲟⲩⲙⲟⲟⲩ, ⲁⲥⲉⲓⲱ ⲛ̄ⲛⲉⲩⲟⲩⲉⲣⲏⲧⲉ, ⲁⲩⲥⲛⲁⲅⲉ
ϩⲛ̄ⲛⲁⲙⲁ ⲛ̄ϣⲱ ⲡⲉ· ⲁⲓⲇⲡϩⲩⲁ ⲁⲩⲟⲩⲱⲙ ⲛ̄ⲟⲩⲟⲉⲓⲕ ϩⲛ̄ⲛⲁⲙⲁ ⲛ̄ϣⲱ ⲡⲉ· ϩⲟⲓⲛⲉ
ⲙⲉ(ⲛ) ⲛ̄ϩⲏⲧⲟⲩ ⲁⲩⲕⲁⲥⲱⲙⲁ ⲉϩⲣⲁⲓ ⲛ̄ϩⲟⲩⲛ ⲉⲡⲁⲏⲓ ⲉⲧⲃⲉⲡϩⲓⲥⲉ ⲛ̄ⲛⲉϩⲓⲟⲟⲩⲉ ⲙ̄ⲛ̄
ⲡⲁϩⲩⲁⲓ ⲛ̄ⲛⲉⲛⲃⲁ (138 R i) ⲍⲁⲛⲟⲥ· ⲁⲓⲧⲟⲙⲥⲟⲩ ⲛ̄ϩⲟⲩⲛ ⲛ̄ⲁⲁⲡⲟⲑⲩ̄ⲕⲏ ⲙ̄ⲛ̄ⲛⲁⲁⲣⲕⲁ-

---

137 R i 9 f. l. ⲛⲉⲛⲧⲁⲩⲁⲁⲩ. 26. ⲉⲃⲟⲗ makes poor sense and should probably be deleted. ii 1 ff. l. ⲕⲁⲧⲁⲗⲉ(ⲧ)ⲩⲁⲩⲟⲩⲟⲙϥ. vi 2. -ⲟⲣⲧⲱⲩ: ⲟⲩ added, in margin. 30. l. ⲛ̄ⲣ̄ⲣⲟ. 138 R i 2-4. l. ⲛ̄ⲛⲁⲁⲡⲟⲑⲏⲕⲏ ⲙ̄ⲛ̄ⲛⲁⲉⲣⲅⲁⲥⲧⲏⲣⲓⲟⲛ.

ⲥⲧⲏⲣⲓⲟⲛ, ϫⲉⲕⲁⲥ ⲉⲣⲉⲡⲉⲩⲥⲙⲟⲩ ⲙⲛⲡⲉⲩϩⲙⲟⲧ ϣⲱⲡⲉ ⲛⲙⲙⲁⲛ. ⲙⲛⲛⲥⲱⲥ ⲁⲡⲥⲉⲉⲡⲉ ⲛⲛⲉⲧⲟⲩⲁⲁⲃ ⲡⲱⲧ ⲉⲃⲟⲗ ϩⲓⲧⲟⲟⲧ, ⲉⲓⲡⲟϫ ⲙⲙⲟⲟⲩ ⲉⲃⲟⲗ ϩⲛⲟⲩⲉⲓⲣⲏⲛⲏ, ⲁⲡⲟⲩⲁ ⲡⲟⲩⲁ ⲃⲱⲕ ⲉⲡⲉⲩⲙⲁⲛϣⲱⲡⲉ ⲉⲩⲧⲉⲟⲟⲩ ⲙⲡⲛⲟⲩⲧⲉ. ⲁⲛⲟⲕ ⲇⲉ ⲓⲟⲩⲛⲟⲥ ⲉⲧⲃⲉⲛϭⲓⲥⲉ ⲛⲧⲁⲓⲛⲁⲩ ⲉⲛⲉⲧⲟⲩⲁⲁⲃ ⲛϩⲏⲧⲟⲩ, ⲛⲛⲁⲟⲩⲱϩ ⲉⲧⲟⲟⲧ ⲉⲥⲉⲡⲣ ⲟⲩⲇⲉ ⲉⲧⲱϩ ⲙⲡⲁⲥⲱⲙⲁ ⲛⲟⲩⲛⲉϫ ϣⲁⲡⲉϩⲟⲩ ⲙⲡⲁⲙⲟⲩ. ⲡⲛⲟⲩⲧⲉ ⲇⲉ ⲁϥⲭⲁⲣⲓⲍⲉ ⲛⲁⲓ ⲙⲡⲓⲛⲟϭ ⲛϩⲙⲟⲧ ⲙⲛⲧⲉⲓⲛⲟϭ ⲛⲇⲱⲣⲁⲓⲁ, ⲁϥⲧ ⲛⲟⲩⲃⲩϭ ⲉⲡϩⲏⲧ ⲙⲡⲁⲛⲟⲙⲟⲥ ⲛϩⲏⲅⲉⲙⲱⲛ, (138 Rⲓⲓ) ⲟⲩⲇⲉ ⲙⲡⲓⲅⲩⲥⲓⲁⲍⲉ ⲟⲩⲇⲉ ⲙⲡⲟⲩⲁⲛⲁⲅⲕⲁⲍⲉ ⲙⲙⲟⲓ, ⲁⲗⲗⲁ ⲁⲓϣⲱⲡⲉ ⲉⲓⲡⲣⲟⲥⲕⲁⲣⲧⲉⲣⲉⲓ ⲉⲡϩⲱⲃ ⲛⲛⲉⲧⲟⲩⲁⲁⲃ ⲉⲧⲃⲉⲧⲉⲩⲭⲣⲓⲁ· ⲁⲓⲕⲱ ⲛⲟⲩϩⲙϩⲁⲗ ⲛⲧⲁⲓ ⲕⲁⲧⲁⲇⲓⲕⲁⲥⲧⲏⲣⲓⲟⲛ ϫⲓⲛⲣⲁⲕⲟⲧⲉ ϣⲁⲡⲣⲏⲥ ⲛⲕⲏⲙⲉ ⲧⲏⲣϥ ⲉⲩⲥϩⲁⲓ ⲛⲛⲉϩⲟⲓⲡⲟⲙⲛⲏⲙⲁ ⲛⲛⲉⲧⲟⲩⲁⲁⲃ ⲕⲁⲧⲁⲡⲁⲗ ⲉⲩⲉⲓⲛⲉ ⲙⲙⲟⲟⲩ ⲛⲁⲓ. ⲁⲓϩⲙⲟⲟⲥ ⲉϩⲣⲁⲓ ⲁⲕⲣⲓⲃⲟⲥ ⲁⲓⲉϫⲁⲓⲥⲟⲩ ⲛⲥⲩⲙⲓⲟⲛ ⲛⲍⲣⲟⲙⲁⲓⲕⲟⲛ, ⲁⲓⲕⲁⲁⲩ ⲛϩⲟⲩⲛ ⲉⲡⲁⲏⲓ ϫⲉⲕⲁⲥ ⲉⲣⲉⲡⲉⲩⲥⲙⲟⲩ ⲙⲛⲡⲉⲩϩⲙⲟⲧ ϣⲱⲡⲉ ⲉϥϭⲙⲏⲛ ⲉⲃⲟⲗ ϩⲛⲁⲙⲁ ⲛϣⲱⲡⲉ ⲧⲏⲣⲟⲩ ϣⲁⲡⲉⲛⲉϩ ⲧⲏⲣⲟⲩ ⲙⲡⲕⲁϩ. ⲁⲩⲱ ϯⲡⲓⲥⲧⲉⲩⲉ ϫⲉ ⲡⲉⲩⲥⲙⲟⲩ ⲙⲛⲡⲉⲩϩⲙⲟⲧ ⲛⲁϣⲱⲡⲉ ⲉϥⲙⲏⲛ ⲉⲃⲟⲗ ⲙⲛ (Vⲓ) ⲡⲁⲕⲉⲥⲡⲉⲣⲙⲁ ⲧⲏⲣϥ ϣⲁⲡϫⲱⲕ ⲛⲧⲥⲩⲛⲧⲉⲗⲓⲁ ⲙⲡⲁⲓⲱⲛ. ⲡⲁⲓ ⲡⲉ ⲡϫⲱⲕ ⲛⲧⲙⲁⲣⲧⲩⲣⲓⲁ ⲙⲡⲙⲛⲧⲥⲛⲟⲟⲩⲥ ⲛⲁⲅⲓⲟⲥ ⲙⲙⲁⲣⲧⲉⲣⲟⲥ ⲛⲧⲉⲛⲉⲡⲁⲓⲁⲧ, ⲁⲡⲁⲩ ⲏⲟⲩϭⲉ ⲙⲛⲛⲉϥⲥⲛⲏⲩ, ⲉⲁⲩϫⲱⲕ ⲉⲃⲟⲗ ⲛⲧⲉⲩⲙⲁⲣⲧⲩⲣⲓⲁ ϩⲓ ⲕⲁⲙⲏ ⲡⲟⲗⲓⲥ ⲉⲧⲉⲡⲟⲩⲃⲉⲥⲧ ⲙⲡⲉⲓⲟⲙ ⲡⲉ. ⲁⲩⲱ ⲯⲩⲭⲏ ⲛⲓⲙ ⲛⲧⲁⲩⲣⲙⲁⲣⲧⲩⲣⲟⲥ ⲉⲃⲟⲗ ϩⲓⲧⲛⲁⲡⲁ ⲏⲟⲩϭⲉ ⲙⲛⲛⲉϥⲥⲛⲏⲩ ⲥⲉⲉⲓⲣⲉ ⲛϩⲙⲟⲩⲛⲉ ⲛϣⲉ ϥⲧⲉⲩϣⲟⲩⲱⲧ ⲙⲛⲧⲏ ⲙⲯⲩⲭⲏ, (Vⲓⲓ) ⲉⲁⲩϫⲓ ⲙⲡⲉⲕⲗⲟⲙ ⲙⲡⲱⲛϩ, ⲁⲩⲃⲱⲕ ⲉϩⲣⲁⲓ ⲙⲡⲏⲩⲉ ϩⲛⲟⲩⲉⲓⲣⲏⲛⲏ, ϩⲁⲙⲏⲛ. ϯⲣⲏⲛⲏ ⲛⲟⲩⲟⲛ ⲛⲓⲙ ⲛⲧⲁⲩⲣⲙⲁⲣⲧⲩⲣⲟⲥ ϩⲙⲡⲣⲁⲛ ⲙⲡⲉⲛϫⲟⲉⲓⲥ ⲓⲥ ⲡⲉⲭⲥ, ⲡⲁⲓ ⲉⲧⲉⲡⲱϥ ⲡⲉ ⲡⲉⲟⲟⲩ ⲙⲛⲧϭⲟⲙ ⲙⲛⲧⲉϩⲟⲩⲥⲓⲁ ⲙⲛⲡⲁⲙⲁϩⲧⲉ, ϩⲛⲟⲩⲧⲣⲓⲁⲥ ⲛϩⲟⲙⲟⲟⲩⲥⲓⲟⲛ ϩⲛⲟⲩⲡⲣⲟⲥⲕⲩⲛⲏⲥⲓⲥ ⲉⲛⲁⲛⲟⲩⲥ ⲛϣⲁⲉⲛⲉϩ ⲛⲛⲉⲛⲉϩ, ϩⲁⲙⲏⲛ.

_____

138 Rⲓ 10. ℓ. ⲉⲓϩⲡⲟ.   29. = -ⲇⲱⲣⲉⲁ.   ⲓⲓ 17f. = ⲁⲕⲣⲓⲃⲱⲥ.   19. = -ⲥⲏⲙⲉⲓⲟⲛ.
19 f. = -ϩⲣⲱⲙⲁⲓⲕⲟⲛ.   Vⲓ 1. = -ⲥⲡⲉⲣⲙⲁ.

For the colophon which follows this text, see Lantschoot, *Les colophons coptes des manuscrits sahidiques*, p. 13.

MARTYRDOM OF SS. APAIOULE AND PTELEME
FROM PIERPONT MORGAN CODEX M 583
T. 41, FF. 168–173

(168 R i) ΤΜΑΡΤΥΡΙΑ ⲙ̄ⲡ̄ⲍⲁⲅⲓⲟⲥˈⲛ̄ⲅⲉⲛⲛⲁⲓⲟⲥ ⲁⲩⲱ ⲙ̄ⲙⲁⲣˈⲧⲩⲣⲟⲥ ⲙ̄ⲡⲉ-
ⲭⲥ ⲁⲡⲁ ⲁ'ⲡⲁⲓⲟⲩⲗⲉ ⲙ̄ⲛ̄ⲁⲡⲁ ⲡⲧⲉˈⲗⲉⲙⲏˑ ⲉⲁⲩϭⲱⲕ ⲉˈⲃⲟⲗ ⲙ̄ⲡⲉⲩⲁⲅⲱⲛˈ
ⲉⲧⲛⲁⲛⲟⲩⲩ ⲛ̄'ⲥⲟⲩⲭⲟⲩⲧⲟⲩⲉ ⲙ̄ⲡⲉˈⲃⲟⲧ ⲧⲱⲃⲉ, ϩⲛ̄ⲟⲩˈⲉⲓⲣⲏⲛⲏ ⲛ̄ⲧⲉⲡⲛⲟⲩ'ⲧⲉ,
ϩⲁⲙⲏⲛˑ' ⲁⲥϣⲱⲡⲉ ⲇⲉˈϩⲛ̄ⲧⲙⲛ̄ⲧⲣ̄ⲣⲟ ⲛ̄ˈⲇⲓⲟⲕⲗⲏⲧⲓⲁⲛⲟⲥˈⲙ̄ⲛ̄ⲙⲁⲝⲓⲙⲓⲛⲓⲁ-'
ⲛⲟⲥ ⲛ̄ⲣ̄ⲣⲱⲟⲩ ⲛ̄ⲁ'ⲛⲟⲙⲟⲥ, ⲉⲣⲉⲕⲟⲩⲗ'ⲕⲓⲁⲛⲟⲥ ⲟ ⲛ̄ϩⲩⲡⲁ'ⲧⲟⲥ, ⲉⲣⲉⲍⲱⲧⲏ-'
ⲣⲓⲭⲟⲥ ⲟ ⲛ̄ⲉⲡⲁⲣ'ⲭⲟⲥ ⲉⲧⲉⲭⲱⲣⲁ ⲧⲏⲣⲥ̄ ⲩⲁⲡⲉϭⲟⲩⲩ,' ⲉⲣⲉϩⲣⲱⲙⲁⲛⲟⲥˈ
ⲟ ⲛ̄ⲥⲧⲣⲁⲧⲏⲗⲁⲧⲏⲥ ²⁵ ⲙ̄ⲛ̄ⲉⲩⲍⲓⲟⲥ ⲙ̄ⲛ̄(R ii) ⲃⲁⲥⲓⲗⲓⲧⲏⲥ, ⲛ̄ⲇⲓ'ⲁⲃⲟⲗⲟⲥ ⲇⲉ
ⲁⲩϭⲱⲣⲙ̄' ⲙ̄ⲡⲉⲩϩⲏⲧ ⲥⲁⲛ̄ⲃⲟⲗ' ⲙ̄ⲡⲛⲟⲩⲧⲉ ⲛ̄ⲧⲡⲉˑ' ⲇⲓⲟⲕⲗⲏⲧⲓⲁⲛⲟⲥ ⲇⲉ'
ⲁⲩⲟⲩⲱϣϥ̄, ⲡⲉⲝⲁⲩ'ⲛ̄ⲛⲁⲡⲡⲟⲗⲗⲁⲧⲓ'ⲟⲛ ϫⲉ ⲉⲓ̈ⲭⲉⲣⲱⲧⲛ̄'ⲛ̄ⲧⲱⲧⲛ̄ ⲛⲁⲡ-
ⲡⲟⲗ'ⲗⲁⲧⲓⲟⲛ, ⲉⲓⲥϩⲏ'ⲏⲧⲉ †ⲕⲉⲗⲉⲩⲉ ⲛⲏ'ⲧⲛ̄ ϫⲉ ⲣⲱⲙⲉ ⲛⲓⲙˈ ⲉⲟⲩⲛ̄ⲓ'ⲩⲉ
ⲛ̄ⲱⲛ̄ϩ̄' ⲛ̄ϩⲏⲧⲟⲩ, 'ⲉⲓⲧⲉ ⲕⲟⲩⲓ̈, ⲉⲓⲧⲉ' ⲛⲟϭ, ⲉⲓⲧⲉ ϩⲟⲟⲩⲧ, ' ⲉⲓⲧⲉ ⲥϩⲓⲙⲉ,
ⲉⲓⲧⲉ'ϩⲙ̄ϩⲁⲗ, ⲉⲓⲧⲉ ' ⲣⲙ̄ϩⲉ, ⲉⲓⲧⲉ ⲙⲁⲧⲟⲓ̈, ²⁰ ⲉⲓⲧⲉ ⲉⲝⲟⲩⲥⲓⲁ, ⲉⲓⲧⲉ' ⲡⲁⲅⲁⲛⲟⲥ,
ⲉⲓⲧⲉ' ⲉⲡⲓⲥⲕⲟⲡⲟⲥ, ⲉⲓⲧⲉ' ⲡⲣⲉⲥⲃⲩⲧⲉⲣⲟⲥ, ⲉⲓⲧⲉ 'ⲇⲓⲁⲕⲟⲛⲟⲥ, ⲉⲓⲧⲉ' ²⁵ ⲁⲛⲁ-
ⲅⲛⲟⲥⲧⲏⲥ,'ⲉⲓⲧⲉ ⲙⲟⲛⲁⲭⲟⲥ,' ⲉⲩⲉⲉⲓ ⲧⲏⲣⲟⲩ ⲛ̄ⲥⲉ'ⲟⲩⲱϣⲧ̄ ⲙ̄ⲡⲁ'ⲡⲟⲗⲗⲱⲛ
ⲙ̄ⲛ̄'ⲧⲁⲣⲧⲩⲙⲓⲥ ⲙ̄ⲛ̄'ⲧⲁⲑⲏⲛⲁ ⲙ̄ⲛ̄'ⲡⲍⲉⲩⲥˑ ⲡⲉⲧⲛⲁⲣⲁⲧ(V i)ⲥ̄ⲱⲧⲙ̄ ⲛ̄ⲥⲱⲓ̈'
ⲙ̄ⲛ̄'ⲡⲁⲇⲓⲁⲧⲁⲅⲙⲁ, †'ⲕⲩⲗⲉⲩⲉ ⲉⲧⲣⲉⲩⲃⲁ'ⲍⲁⲛⲓⲍⲉ ⲙ̄ⲙⲟⲩ, ⁵ ⲁⲩⲱ ⲛ̄ⲧⲉⲡⲉⲩ-
ⲏⲓ̈' ⲟ̄ⲩⲡⲉ ⲉⲩⲧⲱⲣⲡ̄ˑ' ⲁⲩⲱ ⲁⲩⲥϩⲁⲓ̈ ⲙ̄ⲡⲉ'ⲡⲣⲟⲥⲧⲁⲅⲙⲁ ⲛ̄ⲧⲉⲓ̈'ϩⲉˑ ϫⲉ ⲁ-
ⲛⲟⲕ' ¹⁰ ⲡⲉ ⲇⲓⲟⲕⲗⲏⲧⲓⲁⲛⲟⲥ'ⲡⲣ̄ⲣⲟ ⲉϥⲥϩⲁⲓ̈ ⲛ̄ⲛ̄'ϩⲏⲅⲉⲙⲱⲛ ⲕⲁⲧⲁ ⲡⲟⲗⲓⲥ,
ⲭⲁⲓⲣⲉⲧⲉˑ' †ⲧⲁⲙⲟ ⲙ̄ⲙⲱⲧⲛ̄ ϫⲉ ¹⁵ ⲁⲓ̈ⲧⲱϣⲉ ⲉⲃⲟⲗ ⲛ̄ⲟⲩ'ⲡⲣⲟⲥⲧⲁⲅⲙⲁ ⲙ̄-'
ⲡⲕⲁϩ ⲧⲏⲣϥ̄, 'ⲉⲧⲣⲉⲟⲩⲟⲛ ⲙ̄ⲙ̄' ⲑⲩⲥⲓⲁⲍⲉ ⲛ̄ⲛⲟⲩ'ⲧⲉ ²⁰ ⲛ̄ⲧⲁⲓ̈ⲧⲁⲙⲓⲟⲟⲩ.'
ⲛ̄ⲧⲉⲩⲛⲟⲩ ⲁϥⲧ̄ ⲙ̄ⲡⲉ'ⲡⲣⲟⲥⲇⲁⲅⲙⲁ ⲛ̄ⲥⲉ'ⲃⲁⲥⲧⲓⲁⲛⲟⲥ ⲡⲕⲟ'ⲙⲏⲥ. ²⁵ ⲁϥⲉⲓ ⲉⲣⲏⲥˈ
ϩⲛ̄ⲕⲏⲙⲉ ⲧⲏⲣϥ̄ˑ'ⲛ̄ⲧⲉⲣⲉϥⲉⲓ ⲇⲉ ⲉⲣⲁ'ⲕⲟⲧⲉ, ⲁϥⲧ̄ ⲛ̄ⲛⲉⲥϩⲁⲓ̈ ⲛ̄ⲕⲟⲩⲗⲕⲓⲁ'ⲛⲟⲥ ⲡ-
ϩⲏⲅⲉⲙⲱⲛˑ ³⁰ ⲛ̄ⲣⲁⲕⲟⲧⲉˑ ⲛ̄ⲧⲉⲩ'ⲛⲟⲩ ⲛ̄ⲧⲁⲩϫⲓ ⲛ̄ⲛⲉⲥϩⲁⲓ̈, ⲁϥⲁⲥⲡⲁ(V ii)ⲍⲉ ⲙ̄-
ⲙⲟⲟⲩ, ⲁϥⲕⲩ'ⲗⲉⲩⲉ ⲉⲧⲣⲉⲩⲥⲱⲟⲩϩ'ⲉϩⲟⲩⲛ ⲛ̄ⲛⲁⲧⲉⲩⲧⲁ'ⲍⲓⲥ ⲧⲏⲣⲟⲩ. ⁵ ⲁϥⲧ̄'ⲣⲉⲩ-
ⲱϣ ⲉⲣⲟⲟⲩ ⲛ̄ⲧⲉ'ⲡⲓⲥⲧⲟⲗⲏ ⲙ̄ⲡⲣ̄ⲣⲟ, 'ⲁⲩⲱ ⲁⲩⲑⲩⲥⲓⲁⲍⲉ 'ⲧⲏⲣⲟⲩ. ⲙ̄ⲛ̄'ⲥⲱⲥ ⲁϥϫⲓ ⲙ̄ⲡⲉⲡ'ⲣⲟⲥⲇⲁⲅⲙⲁ ⲛ̄ϭⲓ ⲥⲏ'ⲃⲁⲥⲧⲓⲁⲛⲟⲥ, ⲁϥⲉⲓ' ⲉⲣⲏⲥ ϩⲛ̄ⲕⲏⲙⲉ ⲧⲏⲣϥ̄,'ⲉⲣⲉ-
ⲟⲩⲙⲏⲏϣⲉ ⲙ̄ⲙⲁ'ⲧⲟⲓ̈ ⲟⲩⲏϩ ⲛ̄ⲥⲱϥ, ¹⁵ ϣⲁⲛⲧⲉϥ ⲡⲱϩ ⲉⲡ'ⲧⲟⲩ ϩⲛ̄ⲏⲥˑ ⲁϥⲉⲓ' ⲉ-
ϩⲣⲁⲓ̈ ⲉⲩⲧⲙⲉ ⲛ̄ⲩⲁⲣ'ⲙⲟⲛⲧⲉ ⲉⲣⲟⲩ ϫⲉ ⲡⲓ'ⲥⲟⲩⲧⲟⲩⲙⲏⲧ, ⲁⲩⲟⲩ'ⲉϩⲥⲁϩⲛⲉ ²⁰ ⲉⲧⲣⲉⲩ-

---

168 R i 12. Initial ⲁ very large and ornamental; remaining letters of the line
larger than normal. 19 f. l. -ⲥⲱⲧⲏⲣⲓⲭⲟⲥ. ii 1. l. -ⲃⲁⲥⲓⲗⲓⲇⲏⲥ. 25. l.
ⲁⲛⲁⲅⲛⲱⲥⲧⲏⲥ. 30. l. -ⲧⲁⲣⲧⲉⲙⲓⲥ; ⲇ for ⲧ passim in this Ms. V i 19. At
end of line, a mark; offset?

πω'ρϥ ⲙⲡⲃⲏⲙⲁ ϩⲓ'ⲭⲙⲡⲉïⲉⲣⲟ,ˈ ⲁ·ϥⲕⲩⲗⲉⲩⲉ ⲉⲧⲣⲉⲩ'ⲥⲱⲟⲩ² ⲉⲣⲟⲩ ⲛ̄ⲛⲉⲩ·²⁵
ⲙⲁⲧⲟï ⲧⲏⲣⲟⲩ, ⲁϥ'ⲧⲣⲉⲩⲱϣ ⲉⲣⲟⲟⲩ ⲙ̄'ⲡⲉ ⲡⲣⲟⲥⲧⲁⲅⲙⲁ' ⲙ̄ⲡⲣⲣⲟˑ ⲁⲩⲡⲁⲍ'ⲧⲟⲩ
ⲧⲏⲣⲟⲩ, ⲁⲅⲟⲩ'ⲱϣⲧ ⲛⲁⲩ ⲉⲩϭⲓ'ⲩⲕⲁⲕ ⲉⲃⲟⲗ ⲉⲛ'ⲭⲱ ⲙ̄ⲙⲟⲥ ⲭⲉ ⲙ̄ⲛ̄(169 Ri)·
ⲛⲟⲩⲧⲉ ⲛ̄ⲥⲁⲡⲁⲡⲟⲗ'ⲗⲱⲛ ⲙ̄ⲛ̄ ⲡⲍⲉⲩⲥˈ ⲙ̄ⲛ̄ⲧⲁⲣⲧⲉⲙⲓⲥ' ⲙ̄ⲛ̄ⲧⲁⲑⲏⲛⲁˑ ˈⲛⲉⲩⲛ̄·
ⲟⲩϣⲏⲣⲉ ϣⲏⲙ' ⲇⲉ ⲙ̄ⲙⲁⲧⲟï ⲛ̄ϩⲏⲧⲟⲩˈ ⲉⲩⲉⲩⲅⲉⲛⲏⲥ ⲡⲉ ⲛ̄'ⲥⲁⲃⲉ ⲛ̄ⲇⲓⲕⲁⲓ·
ⲟⲥ' ⲉⲡⲉⲩⲣⲁⲛ ⲡⲉ ⲡⲧⲉ'ⲗⲏ ⲙⲏ, ⲉϥϭⲙ̄'ⲙⲁⲃ ϭⲟⲙⲧⲉ ⲛ̄ⲣⲟⲙⲡⲉ, ˈⲉⲣⲉⲡⲉⲥⲧⲣⲁⲧⲉⲩ·
ⲙⲁ' ⲧⲏⲣϥ̄ ⲙ̄ⲙⲁⲧⲟï ⲙⲉ' ⲙ̄ⲙⲟϥ, ⲭⲉ ⲛⲉⲩ'ⲣ̄ⲛ̄ⲛⲟⲩⲧⲉ ⲡⲉ, ˈⲉϥⲥⲱⲧⲙ̄ ⲛ̄ⲥⲁ·
ⲕⲟⲩï ⲙ̄ⲛ̄ⲛⲟⲥˑ ˈ ⲡϣⲏⲣⲉ ⲕⲟⲩï ⲇⲉ 'ⲛⲉⲟⲩⲣⲙ̄ⲧⲉⲫⲟⲓⲛⲓⲕⲏ²⁰' ⲡⲉ ⲛ̄ⲧⲉⲧⲁⲛⲇⲓⲟⲭⲓⲁˑˈ
ⲡⲉⲭⲉ ⲡⲕⲟⲙⲏⲥ ⲛⲁⲩ' ⲭⲉ ⲁⲙⲟⲩ ϩⲱⲱⲕ 'ⲛ̄ⲟⲩⲱϣⲧ ⲙ̄'ⲡⲉ ⲡⲣⲟⲥⲇⲁⲅⲙⲁ²⁵ ⲙ̄ⲡⲣ·
ⲣⲟˑ ⲡⲉⲭⲉ'ⲡⲧⲉⲛⲛⲁⲓⲟⲥ ⲛⲁⲩ'ⲭⲉ ⲛ̄ⲧⲛⲁⲟⲩⲱϣⲧ 'ⲁⲛ ⲛ̄ϩⲉⲛⲉⲓⲇⲱⲗⲟⲛ' ⲙ̄·
ⲙⲟⲩⲛⲅ̄ ⲛ̄ϭⲓϫ³⁰' ⲙⲛ̄ⲟⲩⲣⲱⲙⲉ ⲛ̄'ⲧⲁⲍⲉ· ϥⲥⲏϩ ⲅⲁⲣ ϩⲙ̄'ⲡⲉⲡⲣⲟⲫⲏⲧⲏⲥ (R ii)
ïⲉⲣⲏⲙⲓⲁⲥ ⲭⲉ ⲟⲩⲟï 'ⲛⲟⲩⲣⲱⲙⲉ ⲉⲣⲉⲧⲉⲩϩⲉⲗⲡⲓⲥ ϩ̄ⲛ̄ⲟⲩⲣⲱⲙⲉ·ˈ ⲁⲗⲗⲁ ⲛⲁⲓⲁ·
ⲧϥ̄ ⲛ̄'ⲧⲟⲩ ⲛⲟⲩⲣⲱⲙⲉ ⲉⲣⲉ'ⲧⲉⲩϩⲉⲗⲡⲓⲥ ϩⲓⲛ̄'ⲛⲟⲩⲧⲉ ⲛ̄ⲧⲡⲉˑ ⲡⲉ·ⲧⲙ̄ⲙⲁⲩ ⲡⲉ
ⲙⲉⲩⲃⲱⲕ' ⲉⲡⲧⲁⲕⲟ ϣⲁⲉⲛⲉϩˑ ¹⁰ⲙⲏ ⲙ̄ⲡⲉⲕⲥⲱⲧⲙ̄ 'ⲛ̄ⲧⲟⲕ ⲉⲡⲣⲉϥϫⲁⲗ'ⲭⲉ ⲇⲁⲩ·
ⲉⲓⲇ ⲉϥϫⲱ 'ⲙ̄ⲙⲟⲥ ⲭⲉ ⲙⲏ ⲁⲛ'ⲣ̄ⲡⲱⲃϣ̄ ⲙ̄ⲡⲣⲁⲛ¹⁵ ⲙ̄ⲡⲉⲛⲛⲟⲩⲧⲉ [.]] 'ⲏ ⲁⲛ·
ⲡⲉⲣϭ̄ⲛⲉⲛ'ϭⲓϫ ⲉⲃⲟⲗ ⲉⲕⲉⲛⲟⲩⲧⲉ ⲛ̄ϣ̄ⲙⲙⲟ; 'ⲁ·ⲟⲩⲱϣϥ̄ ⲛ̄ϭⲓ ⲥⲏ'ⲃⲁⲥⲧⲓⲁⲛⲟⲥ
ⲡⲕⲟ'ⲙⲏⲥ ⲡⲉⲭⲁϥ ⲛⲁⲩ' ⲭⲉ ⲥⲱⲧⲙ̄ ⲛ̄ⲥⲱï,ˈ ⲙ̄ⲡⲣ̄ⲙⲟⲩ ⲕⲁⲕⲱⲥˑ ˈ ⲑⲩⲥⲓⲁⲍⲉ
ⲛ̄ⲛ̄ⲛⲟⲩ'ⲧⲉ²⁵ ⲉⲧⲧⲁïⲏⲩ, ⲧⲁⲣⲉ'ⲡⲟⲩⲭⲁï ϣⲱⲡⲉ'ⲛⲁⲕˑ ⲉⲩϣ'ⲡⲉ ⲙ̄ⲙⲟⲛ, ⲧ̄ⲛⲁ·
ϭⲓ'ⲙⲱⲣⲉⲓ ⲙ̄ⲙⲟⲕ³⁰' ⲕⲁⲕⲱⲥ ϩⲛ̄ϩⲉⲛⲃⲁ'ⲥⲁⲛⲟⲥ ⲉⲩⲛⲁϣⲧ̄ 'ⲉⲙⲁⲧⲉˑ ⲁⲩⲱ
ⲙ̄(ⲛ̄)ⲗⲁⲁⲩ ⲛⲁⲉϣⲛⲁϩ'ⲙⲉⲕ ⲉⲃⲟⲗ ϩⲛ̄ⲛⲁ'ϭⲓϫ. ⲁ·ⲟⲩⲱϣϥ̄ 'ⲛ̄ϭⲓ ⲡⲙⲁ·
ⲕⲁⲣⲓⲟⲥ⁵ ⲁⲡⲁ ⲡⲧⲉⲗⲏⲙⲏ ' ⲡⲉⲭⲁϥ ⲭⲉ ⲛ̄ⲧⲛⲁ'ⲑⲩⲥⲓⲁⲍⲉ ⲁⲛ ⲛ̄ϩⲉⲛ'ⲛⲉⲓⲇⲱ·
ⲗⲟⲛ ⲛ̄ⲇⲁï'ⲙⲱⲛⲓⲟⲛ, ⲧⲁ'ⲕⲱ ⲛ̄ⲥⲱï ⲙ̄ⲡⲉ' ⲡⲁⲟⲩⲭⲁïˑ ˈ ⲕⲁⲓ ⲅⲁⲣ ⲉⲕⲩⲁⲛϩⲟⲧ·
ⲃⲉⲧ, ⲓ̄ⲥ̄ ⲡⲁⲛⲟⲩⲧⲉ' ⲛⲁⲧⲁⲛϩⲟï ⲟⲛ. ¹⁵ϥⲥⲏϩ ϩⲙ̄ⲡⲉⲩⲁⲅⲅⲉ'ⲗⲓⲟⲛ ⲉⲧⲟⲩⲁⲁⲃ '
ⲭⲉ ⲡⲉⲧⲡⲓⲥⲧⲉⲩⲉ'ⲉⲣⲟï, ⲕⲁⲛ ⲉϥϣⲁ(ⲛ)'ⲙⲟⲩ, ϥⲛⲁⲱⲛϩ̄ ⲟⲛˑ²⁰ ⲁⲩⲱ ⲟⲛ
ⲭⲉ ⲟⲩⲟⲛ 'ⲛⲓⲙ ⲉⲧⲡⲓⲥⲧⲉⲩⲉ' ⲉⲣⲟï ⲛ̄ϥⲛⲁⲙⲟⲩ ⲁⲛ ⲙ̄ⲡⲙⲟⲩ ϣⲁⲉⲛⲉϩˑ ˈ
ⲛⲁï ⲇⲉ ⲛ̄ⲧⲉⲣⲉϥⲥⲟⲧ'ⲙⲟⲩ ⲛ̄ϭⲓ ⲡⲕⲟⲙⲓⲥ,ˈⲁⲩϭⲱⲛⲧ̄ ⲉⲙⲁⲧⲉˈ,'ⲁⲩⲱ ⲁⲩ·

---

168 V ii 22. Four marks at end of line (so below 169 R i 25; ii 27); apparently
ornamental space-fillers. 24. ⲱ of ⲥⲱⲟⲩ² large; apparently correction from ⲟ.
27. Mark in margin, either offset or beginning of large ⲡ which scribe
at first intended to set out in margin, but later decided not to do so. 31.
Mark at end of line: offset? 169 R ii 8. Writing at end of line small.
15. At end, letter (ⲁ of ⲁⲛ?) apparently cancelled. 28f. ϫ /ⲣ ⲇ: l.–ⲧⲓⲙⲱⲣⲉⲓ.
V i 7f. l. ⲛ̄ϩⲉⲛⲉⲓⲇ. 17. ⲡ and ⲓ ligated. 25 l.–ⲕⲟⲙⲏⲥ.

ⲍⲣⲟⲭⲣⲉⲭ ⲛ̄ⲛⲉⲩⲟⲃⲍⲉ ⲉⲍⲣⲁⲓ̈ ⲉϫⲱⲩ, ⲡⲉϫⲁⲩ [30] ⲛⲁⲩ ϫⲉ ϫⲉ ⲡⲟⲩ ϫⲁⲓ̈ ⲛ̄ⲡⲁ-
ⲡⲟⲗⲗⲱ(ⲛ), ⲉⲕⲧⲙ̄ⲥⲱⲧⲙ̄ ⲛ̄ (169 V ii) ⲥⲱⲓ ⲕ̄ⲛⲁⲙⲟⲩ ⲕⲁ ⲕⲱⲥ· ⲁⲩⲱ ⲉⲩϫⲉ
ⲁⲕⲣⲥⲟⲃ, ϯⲛⲁⲉⲓⲣⲉ ⲛⲁⲕ ⲕⲁⲧⲁⲧⲉⲕⲙ̄ⲛ̄ⲧⲥⲟⲃ· [5] ⲁⲩⲟⲩⲱϣⲃ̄ ⲛ̄ϭⲓ ⲡ̄ⲍⲁⲅⲓⲟⲥ
ⲁⲡⲁ ⲡⲇⲉⲗⲏⲙⲏ ϫⲉ ϥⲥⲏⲍ ϫⲛ̄ⲡⲁ ⲡⲟⲥⲧⲟⲗⲟⲥ ⲉⲧⲟⲩⲁⲁⲃ ϫⲉ ⲁⲛⲟⲛ ⲍⲉⲛ-
ⲥⲟⲃ ⲉⲧⲃⲉⲡⲉⲭ̄ⲥ̄· ⲡⲁⲗⲓⲛ ⲟⲛ ⲟⲛ ϥϫⲱ ⲙ̄ⲙⲟⲥ ϫⲉ ⲛ̄ⲥⲟⲃ ⲙ̄ⲡⲕⲟⲥⲙⲟⲥ
ⲛⲉⲛⲧⲁⲡⲛⲟⲩⲧⲉ ⲥⲟⲧⲡⲟⲩ ϫⲉⲕⲁⲥ [15] ⲉϥⲉϯϣⲓⲡⲉ ⲛ̄ⲛ̄ ⲥⲁⲃⲉⲉⲩ· ⲛⲁⲓ̈ ⲇⲉ ⲛ̄ⲧⲉ-
ⲣⲉϥⲥⲟⲧⲙⲟⲩ ⲛ̄ϭⲓ ⲥⲏⲃⲁⲥⲧⲓ ⲁⲛⲟⲥ ⲡⲕⲟⲙⲏⲥ, [20] ⲁϥⲕⲩⲗⲉⲩⲉ ⲉⲧⲣⲉⲩ ⲥⲱⲗⲡ̄ ⲛ̄-
ⲧⲉϥⲉⲛⲥⲱⲛⲏ, ⲁⲩⲱ ⲉⲧⲣⲉⲩ ⲕⲁⲁⲩ ⲕⲁϫⲏⲩ· ⲁⲩ ⲕⲁⲁⲩ ⲙ̄ⲙⲁⲧⲉ ⲉⲣⲉ [25] ⲡⲉⲩϥⲓ-
ⲙⲓⲧⲁⲗⲓⲟⲛ ϫⲛ̄ⲛⲉⲩⲟⲩⲉⲣⲏⲧⲉ ⲉⲩⲙⲏⲣ ⲉϫⲛ̄ⲧⲉϥ ϯⲡⲉ· ⲁⲩϯ ⲉⲧⲟⲟⲧⲩ̄ ⲙ(ⲛ̄)
ⲣⲁⲧⲩ̄ ⲛ̄ϫⲙ̄ⲙⲟⲩⲥ, [30] ⲁⲩⲭⲟⲗⲕⲩ̄ ⲉⲃⲟⲗ ⲙ̄ⲡⲉϥϫⲱⲧⲉ ⲉⲃⲟⲗ· ⲁⲩϯⲧⲣⲟⲩⲥⲱⲗⲡ̄ ⲛ̄-
ϫⲟⲩ (170 R i) ⲱⲧ ⲛ̄ⲃⲁ ϫⲛ̄ⲡⲉϥ ⲥⲱⲙⲁ ⲉⲩ ϫⲓⲟⲩⲉ ⲉⲣⲟϥ ⲥⲛⲁⲩ ⲥⲛⲁⲩ, ϣⲁⲛ-
ⲧⲉⲛⲉϥⲥⲛⲱⲱⲩ [5] ϩⲁⲧⲉ ⲉⲡⲉⲥⲏⲧ ⲉϫⲙ̄ⲡⲕⲁϩ ⲛ̄ⲑⲉ ⲛⲟⲩⲙⲟⲟⲩ· ⲡⲉϫⲉⲡⲕⲟⲙⲏⲥ
ⲛⲁⲩ ϫⲉ ⲁⲕⲛⲁⲩ ⲉ ⲧⲁⲣⲭⲏ ⲛ̄ⲛ̄ⲃⲁⲥⲁ [10] ⲛⲟⲥ, ϫⲉ ⲥⲉϫⲟⲟⲩ ⲉⲙⲁⲧⲉ· ⲁⲩⲟⲩⲱϣⲃ̄ ⲛ̄ϭⲓ
ⲡ̄ⲙⲁⲕⲁⲕⲁⲣⲓⲟⲥ ⲁⲡⲁ ⲡⲇⲉⲗⲏⲙⲏ ϫⲉ ϥⲥⲏⲍ ϫⲛ̄ⲛⲉⲡⲣⲁⲝⲓⲥ ⲛ̄ⲛⲉ [15] ⲉⲓⲟⲧⲉ ⲛⲁ-
ⲡⲟⲥⲧⲟⲗⲟⲥ ⲉⲧⲟⲩⲁⲁⲃ ϫⲉ ⲛⲉⲩ ϫⲓⲟⲧⲉ ⲉⲛⲁⲡⲟⲥⲧⲟⲗⲟⲥ ϫⲉ ⲙ̄ⲡⲣ̄ⲧⲁⲩⲉ ⲡⲣⲁⲛ
ⲛ̄ⲓ̄ⲥ̄ ⲉⲃⲟⲗ ϫⲛ̄ [20] ⲣⲱⲧⲛ̄· ⲁⲩⲱ ⲛⲉⲩ ⲙⲟⲟϣⲉ ⲉⲩⲧⲉⲗⲏⲗ ϫⲉ ⲁⲩⲙ̄ⲡϣⲁ ⲛ̄ⲥⲟϣⲟⲩ
ⲉϫⲙ̄ⲡⲣⲁⲛ ⲛ̄ⲓ̄ⲥ̄. ⲛⲁⲓ̈ ⲇⲉ [25] ⲛ̄ⲧⲉⲣⲉϥⲥⲟⲧⲙⲟⲩ ⲛ̄ϭⲓ ⲥⲏⲃⲁⲥⲧⲓⲁⲛⲟⲥ ⲡⲕⲟⲙⲏⲥ,
ⲁⲩ ⲙⲟⲩⲍ ⲉⲃⲟⲗ ϫⲛ̄ⲡϭⲱⲛⲧ ⲡⲉϥⲉⲓⲱⲧ ⲡⲇⲓ ⲁⲃⲟⲗⲟⲥ· ⲁⲩⲕⲩⲗⲉⲩⲉ ⲉⲧⲣⲉⲩⲛⲟ-
ϫⲩ̄ ⲉϩⲟⲩ(ⲛ) ⲉⲩⲣⲓ ⲛ̄ⲥⲟⲧ ⲉϥⲗⲏⲕ (R ii) ⲉⲥⲟ ⲛ̄ⲕⲁⲕⲉ, ⲛ̄ⲥⲉⲧⲙ̄ϯⲟⲉⲓⲕ ⲛⲁⲩ
ⲟⲩⲇⲉ ⲙⲟⲟⲩ ϣⲁⲛ ⲧⲉϥⲙⲟⲩ ϩⲁⲡⲉϩⲕⲟ [5] ⲙⲛ̄ⲡⲉⲓⲃⲉ. ⲛ̄ⲧⲟⲩ ⲇⲉ ⲛⲉϥⲟⲧⲛ̄ ⲉ-
ϩⲟⲩⲛ ⲛ̄ϭⲓ ⲡⲙⲁⲕⲁⲣⲓⲟⲥ ⲁⲡⲁ ⲡⲇⲉⲗⲏⲙⲏ, ⲁϥⲧⲱⲟⲩⲛ, ⲁϥⲁϩⲉ [10] ⲣⲁⲧⲩ̄, ⲁϥϣⲗⲏⲗ
ⲉϥϫⲱ ⲙ̄ⲙⲟⲥ ϫⲉ ⲡⲛⲟⲩⲧⲉ, ⲥⲱⲧⲙ̄ ⲉⲣⲟⲓ ⲉⲓ̈ϣϣ ⲉⲍⲣⲁⲓ̈ ⲉⲣⲟⲕ· ⲡⲁϫⲟⲉⲓⲥ ⲓ̄ⲥ̄. [15]
ⲙ̄ⲡⲣ̄ⲕⲁⲁⲧ ⲛ̄ⲥⲱⲕ, ⲁⲗⲗⲁ ⲁⲙⲟⲩ ϣⲁⲣⲟⲓ̈ ϩⲛ̄ⲟⲩϭⲉⲡⲏ, ⲡⲛⲟⲩ ⲉⲧⲉⲙⲛ̄ⲕⲉⲟⲩⲁ
ⲛ̄ⲥⲁ ⲃⲗⲗⲁⲩ, ϫⲉⲕⲁⲥ [20] ⲉⲕⲉϣⲱⲡⲉ ⲛⲙ̄ⲙⲁⲓ̈ ϣⲁⲛⲧⲉⲡⲁ ⲛⲟⲙⲟⲥ ⲉⲓⲙⲉ ϫⲉ ⲙⲛ̄
ⲕⲉⲛⲟⲩⲧⲉ ⲛ̄ⲥⲁⲃⲉⲗ ⲗⲁⲕ· ϫⲉ ⲧⲱⲕ ⲧⲉ [25] ⲧϭⲟⲙ ⲙ̄ⲡⲉⲟⲟⲩ ϣⲁⲉⲛⲉⲍ ⲛ̄ⲉⲛⲉⲍ,
ϩⲁⲙⲏⲛ. ⲛ̄ⲧⲉⲩ ⲛⲟⲩ ⲁⲡϫⲟⲉⲓⲥ ⲓ̄ⲥ̄ ⲉⲓ ⲉⲃⲟⲗ ϩⲛ̄ⲧⲡⲉ, ⲉⲣⲉⲛⲉϥ ⲁⲅⲅⲉⲗⲟⲥ ϩⲩⲙⲛⲉⲩⲉ ϩⲁⲧⲉϥϩⲏ· ⲁⲩⲱ ⲁⲩⲛⲟϭ ⲛ̄ⲟⲩⲟⲉⲓⲛ (V i) ϣⲁ ϩⲉⲛⲧⲣⲓ ⲉⲧⲉϥ ⲟⲧⲡ̄ ⲉϩⲟⲩⲛ
ⲉⲣⲟⲥ· ⲁⲩⲥⲙⲏ ϣⲱⲡⲉ ⲉⲃⲟⲗ ϩⲙ̄ⲡⲟⲩⲟⲉⲓⲛ [5] ⲉⲥϫⲱ ⲙ̄ⲙⲟⲥ ϫⲉ ⲛ̄ϯⲥⲟⲟⲩⲛ ⲁⲛ ⲱ
ⲡ̄ⲙⲁⲕⲁⲣⲓⲟⲥ ⲁⲡⲁ ⲡⲇⲉⲗⲉⲙⲏ ϫⲉ ⲛⲉⲧⲡⲓⲥⲧⲉⲩⲉ ⲉⲣⲟⲓ̈ [10] ⲛ̄ϯⲛⲁⲕⲁⲁⲩ ⲛ̄ⲥⲱⲓ̈ ⲁⲛ;

---

169 V ii 11. on, dittography. 21f. l. -ⲉⲛⲍⲱⲚⲎ. 25. l. -ⲪⲈⲘⲒⲚⲁⲗⲓⲟⲛ. 28f. l.
ⲁⲩϯⲧⲟⲟⲧⲩ̄ ⲙ̄ⲡⲣⲁⲧⲩ̄ ⲛ̄ϫⲉⲚⲘⲟⲩⲥ; superlineation (irregularly) over ⲙ. 170 R i 12.
l. -ⲙⲁⲕⲁⲣⲓⲟⲥ. 21. l. ⲙ̄ⲡⲉⲩⲉⲓⲱⲧ. 31. l. -ⲛⲟⲃⲩ̄. ii 17f. l. ⲡⲛⲟⲩⲧⲉ ⲉⲧⲉ-

ⲁⲛⲟⲕ ⲡⲉ ⲓ̅ⲥ̅ ⲡϣⲏⲣⲉ ⲙⲡⲛⲟⲩⲧⲉ ⲉⲧⲟⲛϩ· ϫⲣⲟ ⲙⲙⲟⲕ, ⲁⲩⲱ ⲛⲅϭⲙϭⲟⲙ· ⲙ-
ⲡⲣ̅ⲣ̅ϩⲟⲧⲉ· ϯϣⲟⲟⲡ ⲛⲙⲙⲁⲕ ϣⲁⲛⲧⲉⲕⲧⲱⲟⲩⲛ ϩⲁϩⲉⲛⲕⲟⲩⲓ ⲛⲃⲁⲥⲁⲛⲟⲥ
ϩⲙⲡⲕⲟⲥⲙⲟⲥ· ⲧⲁⲥⲁⲓ ⲙⲡⲉⲕⲣⲁⲛ ϩⲛⲛⲁⲓⲱⲛ ⲛⲁⲧⲧⲁⲕⲟ, ⲁⲩⲱ ϯⲛⲁⲁⲁⲕ ⲙ-
ⲙⲁⲧⲟⲓ ⲉⲩⲗⲉⲅⲉⲱⲛ ⲛⲁⲅⲅⲉⲗⲟⲥ ϩⲛⲛⲁⲓⲱⲛ ⲙⲡⲟⲩⲟⲉⲓⲛ, ⲉⲡⲓⲇⲏ ⲕⲉⲩⲁⲙⲛⲧ
ⲛ̅ϩⲟⲟⲩ ⲛⲉⲧⲉⲟⲩⲛⲧⲁⲕ ⲥⲟⲩ ϩⲙⲡⲓⲕⲟⲥⲙⲟⲥ· ⲙⲛⲛⲥⲱⲥ ⲧⲁϫⲓⲧⲕ ⲉⲛⲁⲓⲱⲛ ⲙ-
ⲡⲟⲩⲟ(170 V ii)ⲉⲓⲛ, ⲛⲁⲓ ⲉⲧⲉⲙⲛϭⲟⲙ ⲙⲙⲟⲕ ⲉⲧⲟⲩⲟⲛ ϩⲁⲛⲁⲕⲧⲓⲛ ⲙⲡⲉⲩ-
ⲟⲩⲟⲉⲓⲛ· ⲁⲓⲟⲩⲱ ⲅⲁⲣ ⲉⲓⲥⲟⲃⲧⲉ ⲙⲡⲉⲕⲑⲣⲟⲛⲟⲥ ϩⲛⲧⲙⲛⲧⲣⲣⲟ ⲛⲙⲡⲏⲩⲉ· ⲁⲓⲕⲱ ϩⲓϫⲱϥ ⲛⲟⲩⲕⲗⲟⲙ ⲛⲉⲟⲟⲩ ⲙⲛ ⲟⲩⲥⲧⲟⲗⲏ ⲉϥⲣⲟⲩⲟⲉⲓⲛ ⲛⲑⲉ ⲙⲡⲣⲏ·
ϯⲛⲁⲧⲛⲛⲟⲟⲩ ϣⲁⲣⲟⲕ ⲛⲟⲩϣⲃⲏⲣ ⲛⲧⲁⲕ ⲉⲩⲙⲟⲛⲁⲭⲟⲥ ⲡⲉ· ⲡⲧⲟⲡⲟⲥ ⲅⲁⲣ
ⲉⲧⲛⲁϫⲓⲧⲕ ⲉⲣⲟϥ, ⲉⲓⲛⲁϫⲓ ⲙⲡⲉⲧⲙⲙⲁⲩ ⲉⲣⲟϥ· ⲡⲉⲕⲗⲟⲙ ⲉⲧⲉⲕⲛⲁϫⲓⲧϥ,
ⲛⲧⲟϥ ⲡⲉⲧⲉⲣⲉⲡⲉⲧⲙⲙⲁⲩ ⲛⲁϫⲓⲧϥ· ⲉⲃⲟⲗ ϫⲉ ⲡⲣⲱⲙⲉ ⲉⲧⲙⲙⲁⲩ ⲟⲩⲥⲕⲉ-
ⲟⲥ ⲛⲥⲱⲧⲡ ⲛⲁⲓ ⲡⲉ· ϯⲣⲏⲛⲏ ⲛⲁⲕ· ⲙⲡⲣ̅ⲣ̅ϩⲟⲧⲉ· ⲛⲁⲓ ⲇⲉ ⲛⲧⲉⲣⲉϥϫⲟⲟⲩ ⲛϭⲓ
ⲡϫⲟⲉⲓⲥ ⲓ̅ⲥ̅ ⲁϥⲃⲱⲕ ⲉϩⲣⲁⲓ ⲉⲧⲡⲉ· ⲉⲣⲉⲛⲉϥⲁⲅⲅⲉⲗⲟⲥ ϩⲩⲙⲛⲉⲩⲉ ϩⲁⲧⲉϥϩⲏ·
ⲡⲙⲁⲕⲁⲣⲓⲟⲥ ⲇⲉ ⲁⲡⲁ ⲡⲇⲉⲗⲉⲙ ⲙⲡⲉϥ(171 R i)ⲕⲁⲧⲟⲟⲧϥ ⲉⲃⲟⲗ ⲉϥⲩⲗⲏⲗ
ϣⲁⲛⲧⲉⲡⲟⲩⲟⲉⲓⲛ ⲉⲓ ⲉϩⲣⲁⲓ· ⲉⲁϥⲣⲩⲟⲙⲛⲧ ⲛϩⲟⲟⲩ ⲙⲛ ϣⲟⲙⲛⲧⲉ ⲛⲟⲩϣⲏ
ⲙⲡⲉϥⲟⲩⲱⲙ ⲟⲩⲇⲉ ⲙⲡⲉϥⲥⲱ· ⲙⲛⲛⲥⲁⲛⲁⲓ ⲛⲉϥⲛⲟⲩⲙⲟⲛⲁⲭⲟⲥ ⲛⲁⲛⲁⲭⲱⲣⲓ-
ⲧⲏⲥ ⲁⲩⲱ ⲛⲁⲥⲕⲏⲧⲏⲥ, ⲉⲡⲉϥⲣⲁⲛ ⲡⲉ ⲁⲡⲁ ⲁⲡⲁⲓⲟⲩⲗⲉ, ⲉⲩⲣ̅ⲙ̅ϩⲁⲛⲉⲡⲓⲟⲟⲣ ⲡⲉ
ϩⲙⲡⲧⲟⲩϩ ϩⲛⲏⲥ· ⲉⲛⲉⲡⲁⲓ ⲅⲁⲣ ⲡⲉ ⲡⲉϥϩⲱⲃ· ⲥⲱⲙⲁ ⲛⲓⲙ ⲛⲧⲉⲙⲙⲁⲣⲧⲩⲣⲟⲥ
ⲉⲧⲟⲩⲛⲁϩⲟⲧⲃⲟⲩ ⲛⲉϥⲁⲩⲙⲟⲟⲩⲉ ⲛⲥⲱⲟⲩ ⲛϩⲟⲗⲟⲩ· ⲛⲧⲉⲣⲉϥⲥⲱⲧⲙ ⲇⲉ ⲉⲧⲃⲉ-
ⲡⲙⲁⲕⲁⲣⲓⲟⲥ ⲁⲡⲁ ⲡⲇⲉⲗⲉⲙ ϫⲉ ϥⲟⲧⲡ ⲉϩⲟⲩⲛ ϩⲙⲡⲥⲟⲩⲧⲟⲩⲙⲛⲧ, ⲁϥⲧⲱⲟⲩⲛ,
ⲁϥⲉⲓ ϣⲁⲣⲟϥ ϩⲛⲟⲩⲛⲟϭ ⲛⲣⲁϣⲉ ⲙⲛⲟⲩⲧⲉⲗⲏⲗ, ⲉⲃⲟⲗ ϫⲉ ⲁⲡⲉⲡⲛⲁ ⲙⲡⲛⲟⲩⲧⲉ
ⲧⲁⲙⲟϥ ϫⲉ ⲉⲕⲛⲁϫⲉⲕⲧⲉⲕⲟⲓⲕⲟⲛⲟ(R ii)ⲙⲓⲁ ⲉⲃⲟⲗ ⲛⲙⲙⲁϥ· ⲛⲧⲉⲣⲉϥⲃⲱⲕ
ⲇⲉ ϣⲁⲣⲟϥ, ⲁⲩⲕⲱⲗⲩ ⲙⲙⲟϥ ⲛϭⲓ ⲙⲙⲁⲧⲟⲓ ⲉⲧⲣⲟⲉⲓⲥ ⲉⲣⲟϥ, ⲙⲡⲟⲩⲕⲁⲁϥ
ⲉⲃⲱⲕ ⲉϩⲟⲩⲛ ϣⲁⲣⲟϥ· ⲙⲛⲛⲥⲱⲥ ⲁϥⲥⲱ ⲉϥⲥⲟⲡ ⲙⲙⲟⲟⲩ, ⲁⲩⲕⲁⲁϥ, ⲁϥⲃⲱⲕ ⲉϩⲟⲩⲛ· ⲛⲧⲉⲩⲛⲟⲩ ⲁⲩⲧⲱⲟⲩ ⲛϭⲓ ⲁⲡⲁ ⲡⲇⲉⲗⲉⲙ· ⲁⲩⲁⲥⲡⲁⲍⲉ ⲛⲛⲉⲩⲉⲣⲏⲩ, ⲁⲩⲙⲟⲟⲥ· ⲡⲉϫⲉⲁⲡⲁ ⲁⲡⲁⲓⲟⲩⲗⲉ ⲛⲁϥ ϫⲉ ⲭⲁⲓⲣⲉ ⲡϩⲟⲉⲓϫ ⲉⲧⲟⲩⲁⲁⲃ
ⲙⲡⲉⲭ̅ⲥ̅· ⲡⲉϫⲉⲡϩⲁⲅⲓⲟⲥ ⲁⲡⲁ ⲡⲇⲉⲗⲉⲙ ⲛⲁϥ ϫⲉ ⲭⲁⲓⲣⲉ ⲧⲉϫⲓⲏ ⲙⲡⲟⲩϫⲁⲓ
ⲛⲧⲁⲥⲡⲱϩ ϣⲁⲣⲟⲓ ⲙⲙⲟⲟⲩ· ϫⲉ ⲛⲧⲕⲟⲩⲣⲱⲙⲉ ⲉϥⲟⲩⲁⲁⲃ, ⲱ ⲡⲁϫⲟⲉⲓⲥ ⲛⲉⲓⲱⲧ·
ⲡⲉϫⲉ ⲡⲙⲁⲕⲁⲣⲓⲟⲥ ⲁⲡⲁ ⲓⲟⲩⲗⲉ ⲛⲁϥ ϫⲉ ⲙⲡⲣ̅ⲣ̅ϩⲟⲧⲉ ⲡⲁⲥⲟⲛ· ⲓ̅ⲥ̅ ⲛⲁⲕⲁⲁⲛ ⲛ-
ⲥⲱϥ ⲁⲛ· ⲁⲩⲱ (V i) ⲁⲩⲣ̅ⲡⲉϩⲟⲟⲩ ⲧⲏⲣϥ ⲉⲧⲙⲙⲁⲩ ⲉⲩⲧⲉⲧⲉⲗⲏⲗ ⲙⲙⲟⲟⲩ ⲙⲛ-

ⲛⲉⲩⲉⲣⲏⲩ· ⲁⲩⲱ ⲥⲩⲣⲁ̄ⲅⲉ,' ⲉⲩϭⲟⲗⲡ̄ ⲙ̄ⲡⲛⲟⲩⲧⲉ.' ⲧⲟⲧⲉ ⲁⲩⲃⲱⲕ ⲛ̄ϭⲓ 'ⲟⲩⲙⲁⲧⲟⲓ,
ⲁⲩⲧⲁ'ⲙⲉⲡⲕⲱⲙⲏⲥ· ϫⲉ ⲁϥⲉⲓ ⲉⲡⲓⲙⲁ' ⲛ̄ϭⲓ ⲟⲩⲙⲟⲛⲁⲭⲟⲥ, 'ⲁⲩⲃⲱⲕ ⲉϩⲟⲩⲛ 'ⲩⲁ
ⲡⲁⲉⲗⲉⲙⲏ.' ⲛ̄ⲧⲉⲣⲉϥⲥⲱⲧⲙ̄ ⲇⲉ ⲉ̄ⲛⲁⲓ ⲛ̄ϭⲓ ⲥⲉⲃⲁⲥⲧⲓⲁⲛⲟⲥ ⲡⲕⲱⲙⲏⲥ,'ⲁⲩⲕⲉ
ⲗⲉⲩⲉ ⲉⲧⲣⲉⲩ'ⲡⲱⲣϣ̄ ⲙ̄ⲡⲃⲏ'ⲙⲁ ϩⲓϫⲛ̄ⲧⲡⲣⲱ· ⲁⲩⲱ ⲁϥϫⲟⲟⲥ ⲉⲧⲣⲉⲩⲉⲛⲧⲟⲩ
ⲛⲁⲩ'ⲙⲡⲉⲥⲛⲁⲩ ⲉⲩⲙⲏⲣ' ⲉⲧⲉⲓⲣⲁ ⲙ̄ⲛⲛⲉⲩ'ⲉⲣⲏⲩ. ⲡⲉϫⲉⲡ̄'ⲕⲱⲙⲏⲥ ⲛⲁⲩ ϫⲉ'
ⲉⲧⲉⲧⲛ̄ⲕⲱ ⲙ̄ⲙⲟⲥ 'ⲇⲉ ⲟⲩ; ⲧⲉⲧⲛⲁⲣ̄'ⲥⲟⲥ ⲛ̄ⲧⲉⲧⲛ̄ⲙⲟⲩ' ⲕⲁⲕⲟⲥ ϫⲓⲛⲙ̄'ⲙⲟⲛ;
ⲁⲩⲟⲩⲱ'ϣⲃ̄ ⲛ̄ϭⲓ ⲡⲙⲁⲕⲁ'ⲣⲓⲟⲥ ⲁⲡⲁⲓⲟⲩⲗⲉ (171 V ii) ⲉⲩϫⲱ ⲙ̄ⲙⲟⲥ ϫⲉ' ⲉⲓⲉ
ⲛ̄ⲅⲥⲟⲟⲩⲛ ⲁⲛ,' ⲱ ⲡⲕⲱⲙⲏⲥ, ϫⲉ'ⲛⲁⲛⲟⲩⲥⲱⲧⲙ̄ ⲛ̄ⲥⲁⲡⲛⲟⲩⲧⲉ ⲡⲁⲣⲁⲁ̄ⲡⲣⲱⲙⲉ;
ϥⲥⲏϩ'ⲅⲁⲣ ϫⲉ ⲉⲣϣⲁⲛⲟⲩ'ⲣⲱⲙⲉ ⲣ̄ⲛⲟⲃⲉ ⲉⲩ'ⲣⲱⲙⲉ, ϣⲁⲩⲥⲟⲡⲥ̄ ⲙ̄ⲡⲛⲟⲩⲧⲉ ⲛϥ̄
ⲕⲱ'ⲛⲁⲩ ⲉⲃⲟⲗ· ⲧⲉⲛⲟⲩ'ϭⲉ ⲧⲛ̄ⲛⲁⲥⲱⲧⲙ̄ 'ⲛ̄ⲥⲁⲡⲛⲟⲩⲧⲉ ⲛ̄ϩⲟⲩⲟ ⲉⲣⲟⲕ. ⲛⲁⲓ
ⲇⲉ ⲛ̄ⲧⲉⲣⲉϥⲥⲟⲧ'ⲙⲟⲩ ⲛ̄ϭⲓ ⲡⲕⲱⲙⲏⲥ,'ⲁⲩϭⲱⲛⲧ̄ ϩⲛ̄ⲟⲩ'ⲟⲣⲅⲏ· ⲁϥⲕⲉⲗⲉⲩⲉ'ⲉⲧⲣⲉⲩ
ⲉⲓⲛⲉ ⲉⲃⲏ'ⲁⲡⲁ ⲁⲡⲁⲓⲟⲩⲗⲉ,'ⲁⲩⲑⲙ̄ⲥⲟⲩ ϩⲓϫⲛ̄'ⲟⲩⲙⲁⲛ̄ⲛ̄ⲕⲟⲧⲕ̄' ⲁ̄ⲡⲉⲛⲓⲡⲉ ⲛ̄
ⲥⲉ'ⲉⲓⲛⲉ ⲛ̄ⲟⲩⲟⲣⲅⲁⲛⲟ(ⲛ)'ⲛ̄ⲕⲱϩⲧ̄ ⲛ̄ⲥⲉⲧⲁ'ⲁⲁⲩ ⲉϩⲟⲩⲛ ⲉⲗⲉⲩ'ⲃⲁⲗ ⲛ̄ⲟⲩⲛⲁⲙ,'
ⲁⲩⲱ ⲁⲩⲧⲣⲉⲩϫⲓ'ⲧⲉ ⲛ̄ⲥⲱⲩ ϣⲁⲛ'ⲧⲉⲧⲉϥⲁⲗⲟⲩ ⲃⲟϭⲉ'ⲉⲃⲟⲗ ⲉϫⲙ̄ⲡⲕⲁϩ·' ⲛ̄ⲧⲟⲩ
ⲇⲉ ⲁϥⲗⲩⲡⲉⲓ, (172 R i) ⲁⲩⲱ ⲁⲩϭⲱϣⲧ̄ ⲉ'ϩⲣⲁⲓ ⲉⲧⲡⲉ, ⲁϥϫⲓ'ⲩⲕⲁⲕ ⲉⲃⲟⲗ
ⲉϥϫⲱ'ⲙ̄ⲙⲟⲥ ϫⲉ ⲡⲁϫⲟⲉⲓⲥ 'ⲓ̄ⲥ̄ ⲡⲉⲭ̄ⲥ̄, ϭⲱϣⲧ̄ ⲛⲅ̄'ⲛⲁⲩ ⲉⲡⲁⲟⲩⲟⲉⲓⲛ' ⲛ̄ⲧⲁⲓ
ⲟⲥⲉ ⲙ̄ⲙⲟⲩ ⲉⲧⲃⲉⲡⲉⲕⲣⲁⲛ ⲉⲧⲟⲩⲁⲁⲃ·' ⲁⲩⲱ ϯⲡⲓⲥⲧⲉⲩⲉ ⲉⲣⲟⲕ' ϫⲉ ⲟⲩⲛ̄ϭⲟⲙ
ⲙ̄ⲙⲟⲕ' ⲉϩⲱⲃ ⲛⲓⲙ.' ⲧⲟⲧⲉ ⲁⲩⲕⲩⲗⲉⲩⲉ ⲛ̄ϭⲓ'ⲡⲕⲱⲙⲏⲥ ⲉⲧⲣⲟⲩ'ⲉⲓⲛⲉ ⲉⲃⲟⲗ ⲙ̄
ⲡⲙⲁ'ⲕⲁⲣⲓⲟⲥ ⲁⲡⲁ ⲡⲁⲉⲗⲉ'ⲙⲏ· ⲡⲉϫⲁⲩ ⲛⲁⲩ'ϫⲉ ⲕ̄ⲛⲁⲣⲑⲩⲥⲓⲁ ϩⲱ'ⲱⲕ· ϫⲓⲛ
ⲙ̄ⲙⲟⲛ' ⲕ̄ⲛⲁⲙⲟⲩ ⲕⲁⲕⲟⲥ'ϩⲛ̄ϩⲉⲛⲃⲁⲥⲁⲛⲟⲥ' ⲉⲩϩⲟⲟⲩ. ⲧⲟⲧⲉ ⲁⲩ'ⲟⲩⲱϣϥ̄ ⲛⲁⲩ
ⲛ̄ϭⲓ 'ⲡⲙⲁⲕⲁⲣⲓⲟⲥ ⲁⲡⲁ'ⲡⲁⲉⲗⲉⲙⲏ ϫⲉ ⲛ̄'ϯⲛⲁⲑⲩⲥⲓⲁⲍⲉ ⲁⲛ' ⲛ̄ϩⲉⲛⲉⲓⲇⲱⲗⲟⲛ'
ⲉⲩⲙⲟⲟⲩⲧ. ⲧⲟⲧⲉ' ⲁⲩϭⲱⲛⲧ̄ ⲛ̄ϭⲓ ⲡ'ⲕⲱⲙⲏⲥ, ⲁϥⲕⲩ'ⲗⲉⲩⲉ ⲉⲧⲣⲉⲩⲉⲓⲛⲉ ⲛ̄ϩⲉⲛ
ⲟⲣⲅⲁⲛⲟⲛ ⲛ̄'ⲕⲱϩⲧ̄ ⲛ̄ⲥⲉⲧⲁⲁⲩ (R ii) ⲉϩⲟⲩⲛ ϩⲁⲛⲉϥⲥⲡⲓ'ⲣⲟⲟⲩⲉ ϣⲁⲛⲧⲟⲩ'ϭⲱ
ⲧϥ̄ ⲉϩⲟⲩⲛ ϩⲛ̄'ⲛⲉⲩⲉⲣⲏⲩ.' ⲁⲥϣⲱⲡⲉ ⲇⲉ ⲛ̄ⲧⲉ'ⲣⲉϥⲟⲩⲱ ⲉϥϯ ⲛⲁⲩ' ⲛ̄ⲧⲃⲁⲥⲁ
ⲛⲟⲥ, ⲁϥ'ⲕⲩⲗⲉⲩⲉ ϩⲛ̄ⲟⲩⲛⲟϭ' ⲛ̄ϭⲱⲛⲧ̄ ⲉⲧⲣⲉⲩϭⲓ'ⲛ̄ⲧⲉϥⲁⲡⲉ. ⲡⲙⲁ'ⲕⲁⲣⲓⲟⲥ ⲇⲉ
ⲁⲡⲁⲓⲟⲩⲗⲉ' ⲁⲩⲕⲩⲗⲉⲩⲉ ⲉⲧⲣⲉⲩ'ϫⲓⲧϥ̄ ⲉϩⲟⲩⲛ ⲉⲩⲣⲓ'ⲉⲥⲟ ⲛ̄ⲕⲁⲕⲉ ⲉϥϩⲁ'ⲃⲁⲥⲁ
ⲛⲟⲥ ϣⲁⲛ'ⲧⲉϥⲙⲟⲩ.' ⲡⲙⲁⲕⲁⲣⲓⲟⲥ ⲇⲉ ⲁⲡⲁ' ⲡⲁⲉⲗⲉⲙⲏ ⲛ̄ⲧⲉ'ⲣⲉϥⲥⲱⲧⲙ̄ ⲉ
ⲧⲉⲩⲁ'ⲡⲟⲫⲁⲥⲓⲥ, ⲁⲩⲣⲁ'ϣⲉ ⲉⲙⲁⲧⲉ,' ⲁϥⲕⲟⲧϥ̄ ⲉⲁⲡⲁⲓⲟⲩ'ⲗⲉ, ⲡⲉϫⲁⲩ ⲛⲁⲩ' ϫⲉ
ϯ̄ⲛⲉ ⲉⲣⲟⲕ,' ⲡⲁⲉⲓⲱⲧ, ⲙ̄ⲡⲣ̄'ⲣ̄ⲕⲟⲩⲓ ⲛ̄ϩⲏⲧ. ⲙ̄ⲙⲟⲛ ⲟⲩⲛ̄ⲧⲁⲛ ⲙ̄'ⲙⲁⲩ ⲛ̄ⲓ̄ⲥ̄
ⲛϥ̄ⲃⲟⲏ'ⲑⲉⲓ ⲉⲣⲟⲛ· ϫⲉ ⲡⲕⲉ'ⲛⲟⲟⲩ'ⲙ̄ⲙⲁⲧⲉ' ⲡⲉⲧⲉⲟⲩⲛ̄ⲧⲁⲕϥ̄' ϩⲙ̄ⲡⲉⲓ̈ⲕⲟⲥⲙⲟⲥ·

171 V i 29. l. ⲕⲁⲕⲱⲥ. ii 30. l. –ϥⲟⲟϭⲉ. 172 R ii 29 f. l. ⲡⲉⲓ̈ⲕⲉϩⲟⲟⲩ·
30. ⲙ̄ⲙⲁⲧⲉ added above, small.

(172 Vi) ⲙⲛⲛⲥⲱⲥ ⲡⲉⲓ̈ⲛⲁⲩ ⲡⲣⲁⲥⲧⲉ ⲕⲛⲁ̈ϣⲱⲡⲉ ⲛⲙⲙⲁⲓ̈ ⲍ̅ⲩⲡⲙⲁⲛϣⲉⲗⲉⲉⲧ [5]
ⲙⲡⲉⲭ̅ⲥ̅. ⲡⲉⲭⲉⲁ̈ⲡⲁⲓⲟⲩⲗⲉ ⲛⲁϥ ϫⲉ ⲥ̈ⲟⲡⲥ̅ ⲉⲭⲱⲓ̈ ⲡⲁ̈ⲥⲟⲛ ⲛ̅ⲛⲁⲍⲣ̅ⲡⲗⲉⲭ̅ⲥ̅,
ϫⲉ ⲕⲛⲁⲣ̅ϣⲟⲣⲡ̅ [10] ⲉⲣⲟⲓ̈ ⲉⲍⲟⲩⲛ ⲉⲧⲉϥⲙⲛⲧⲣ̅ⲣⲟ. ⲛⲁⲓ̈ ⲇⲉ ⲛ̅ⲧⲉⲣⲟⲩⲭⲟ̈ⲟⲩ ⲙⲛ
ⲛⲉⲩⲉⲣⲏⲩ, ⲁⲩⲉⲓⲛⲉ ⲙ̅ⲡⲙⲁⲕⲁ̈ⲣⲓⲟⲥ ⲁⲡⲁ ⲡ̅ⲇⲉⲗⲉ̈ⲙⲏ ⲉⲃⲟⲗ ⲕⲁⲧⲁ̈ ⲧⲕⲩⲗⲉⲩⲥⲓⲥ
ⲙⲡ̅ⲕⲱⲙⲏⲥ ⲉⲧⲣⲉⲩ̈ϫⲓ ⲛ̅ⲧⲉϥⲁⲡⲉ. [20] ⲛ̅ⲧⲟⲩ ⲇⲉ ⲁⲩϥⲓ ⲛ̅ⲛⲉϥⲃⲁⲗ ⲉⲍⲣⲁⲓ̈ ⲉⲧ̅ⲡⲉ,
ⲡⲉⲭⲁⲩ ϫⲉ ϯ̈ⲥⲟⲡⲥ̅ ⲙ̅ⲙⲟⲕ ⲓ̅ⲥ̅ [25] ⲧⲁⲍⲉⲗⲡⲓⲥ, ⲡ̅ ⲡⲁ̈ⲕⲗⲟⲙ ⲡⲉⲧϯⲕ̅ⲗⲟⲙ ⲉⲭⲛ̅
ⲛⲉⲧⲟⲩ̈ⲁⲁⲃ ⲧⲏⲣⲟⲩ ⲉⲧⲛⲁ̈ⲙⲟⲩ ⲉⲭⲙⲡⲉⲩ̈ⲣⲁⲛ ⲉⲧⲟⲩⲁⲁⲃ, [30] ⲙ̅ⲡⲣⲟⲃⲩⲕ̅ ⲉⲣⲟⲓ̈
ⲉⲓ̈ⲛⲏⲩ ⲉⲛⲉⲕⲥⲓⲝ, (Vii) ϫⲉ ⲧⲱⲕ ⲧⲉ ⲧϭⲟⲙ ⲙ̅ⲛⲡⲉⲟⲟⲩ ϣⲁⲉⲛⲉⲍ. ϩⲁⲙⲏⲛ.
ⲛⲁⲓ̈ ⲇⲉ ⲛ̅ⲧⲉⲣⲉⲩϫⲟⲟⲩ [5] ⲛ̅ϭⲓ ⲡⲙⲁⲕⲁⲣⲓⲟⲥ ⲁⲡⲁ ⲡ̅ⲇⲉⲗⲗⲉⲙⲏ ⲉⲣⲉⲡⲉⲩⲙⲁⲕϯ ⲥⲟⲩ
ⲧⲱⲛ ⲉⲃⲟⲗ, ⲁⲩϥⲓ (ⲛ̅)ⲛ̅ⲧⲉϥⲁⲡⲉ ⲛ̅ⲥⲟⲩ̈ [10] ϫⲟⲩⲱⲧ ⲙ̅ⲡⲉⲃⲟⲧ ⲧⲱⲃⲉ· ⲁⲩⲭⲱⲕ ⲉ
ⲃⲟⲗ ⲛ̅ⲧⲉϥⲙⲁⲣⲧⲩ̈ⲣⲓⲁ ϩⲛ̅ⲟⲩⲉⲓⲣⲏⲛⲏ ⲛ̅ⲧⲉⲡⲛⲟⲩⲧⲉ, ϩⲁ̈ [15] ⲙⲏⲛ. ⲡⲙⲁⲕⲁ
ⲣⲓⲟⲥ ⲇⲉ ⲁⲡⲁ̈ ⲁⲡⲁⲓⲟⲩⲗⲉ ⲛⲉϥⲟⲧ̈ ⲏ̅ ⲉⲍⲟⲩⲛ ⲉⲧⲣⲓ ⲉϥ̈ϣⲟⲟⲡ ϩⲁⲃⲁⲥⲁⲛⲟⲥ. [20]
ⲁⲩⲱ ⲛⲉϥⲥⲟⲡⲥ̅ ⲙ̅ⲡⲛⲟⲩⲧⲉ ⲛ̅ⲧⲉⲩ̈ϣⲏ ⲧⲏⲣⲉ̅ ⲉⲧⲙ̅ⲙⲁⲩ ⲉϥϫⲱ ⲙ̅ⲙⲟⲥ ϫⲉ
ⲡ̅ⲛⲟⲩⲧⲉ, ⲙ̅ⲡ̅ⲣⲁⲁⲧ̈ [25] ⲛ̅ϣⲙ̅ⲙⲟ ⲉⲡⲉⲕⲁ̈ⲅⲱⲛ ⲉⲧⲟⲩⲁⲁⲃ, ⲡⲁⲓ̈ ⲛ̅ⲧⲁⲩⲕⲗⲏ̈ⲣⲟⲩ
ⲉⲣⲟϥ ⲛ̅ϭⲓ ⲛⲁ̈ϣⲃⲏⲣ ⲙⲉⲣⲟⲥ, [30] ⲁⲗⲗⲁ ⲙⲁⲣⲉⲓⲛⲁⲩ (173 Ri) ⲉⲣⲟϥ ϩⲛ̅ⲟⲩ
ϭⲉⲡⲏ ϩⲛ̅ⲧⲉⲕⲙⲛⲧⲣ̅ⲣⲟ ⲉⲧⲟⲩⲁⲁⲃ, ⲡⲛⲟⲩⲧⲉ ⲉⲧⲥⲙⲁⲙⲁⲁⲧ ϣⲁ̈ⲉⲛⲉⲍ. [5]
ⲛⲁⲓ̈ ⲇⲉ ⲉϥϫⲱ ⲙ̅ⲙⲟⲟⲩ ⲛ̅ϭⲓ ⲡⲙⲁⲕⲁⲣⲓⲟⲥ ⲁⲡⲁⲓⲟⲩⲗⲉ, ⲁϩ̈ⲧⲟⲟⲩⲉ ϣⲱⲡⲉ, [10]
ϩⲧⲟⲟⲩⲉ ⲇⲉ ⲛ̅ⲥⲟⲩ̈ ϫⲟⲩⲧⲟⲩⲉ ⲛ̅ⲧⲱⲃⲉ· ⲁϥⲕⲩⲗⲉⲩⲉ ⲛ̅ϭⲓ ⲡ̅ⲕⲱⲙⲏⲥ ⲉⲧⲣⲉⲩ̈
ⲉⲓⲛⲉ ⲉⲃⲟⲗ ⲙ̅ⲡⲙⲁ̈ [15] ⲕⲁⲣⲓⲟⲥ ⲁⲡⲁⲓⲟⲩⲗⲉ̈ ⲉⲣⲉⲡⲉⲩϩⲟ ⲛⲉⲥⲁⲕ̈ⲧⲓⲛ ⲛ̅ⲟⲩⲟⲉⲓⲛ
ⲉ̈ⲃⲟⲗ. ⲡⲉⲭⲉⲡⲕⲱ̈ⲙⲏⲥ ⲛⲁϥ ϫⲉ ⲡⲁ(ⲛ)̈ϩⲟⲥⲓⲟⲥ ⲙ̅ⲙⲟⲛⲟⲭⲟⲥ, ⲁⲣⲁ ⲁⲕⲥⲙ̅
ⲡⲉⲕ̈ϩⲏⲧ; ⲉϥϣⲱⲡⲉ ⲁ̈ⲡⲉ, ⲧⲁⲡⲁⲓⲇⲉⲩⲉ̈ ⲙ̅ⲙⲟⲕ ⲕⲁⲕⲟⲥ. [25] ⲛ̅ⲧⲟⲩ ⲇⲉ ⲡⲙⲁ
ⲕⲁ̈ⲣⲓⲟⲥ ⲁⲡⲁⲓⲟⲩⲗⲉ̈ ⲙ̅ⲡⲉϥⲉϣϭⲙ̅ϭⲟⲙ (Rii) ⲉⲟⲩⲱϣϥ̅ ⲛⲁϥ, ⲉⲃⲟⲗ ϫⲉ ⲁ
ⲡⲉϥⲥⲱ̈ⲙⲁ ⲃⲁⲧϭⲟⲙ. ⲛ̅ⲧⲉⲩ̈ⲛⲟⲩ ⲁϥⲕⲩⲗⲉⲩⲉ ⲛ̅̈ϭⲓ [5] ⲡⲕⲱⲙⲏⲥ ⲉⲧ̈ⲣⲉⲩϫⲓ
ⲛ̅ⲧⲉϥⲁⲡⲉ· ⲁⲩⲱ ⲁⲩϫⲓⲧϥ̅ ⲛ̅ϭⲓ ⲙ̅ⲙⲁⲧⲟⲓ̈ ⲙ̅ⲡⲛⲁⲩ̈ ⲛ̅ϩⲧⲟⲟⲩⲉ ⲛ̅ⲥⲟⲩ̈ ϫⲟⲩ
ⲧⲟⲩⲉ ⲛ̅ⲧⲱⲃⲉ, ⲁⲩⲃⲓ ⲛ̅ⲧⲉϥⲁⲡⲉ· ⲛ̅ⲧⲉⲩⲛⲟⲩ ⲁⲩⲉⲓ̈ ⲛ̅ϭⲓ ⲛ̅ⲁⲅⲅⲉⲗⲟⲥ, ⲁⲩ
ϫⲓ ⲛ̅ⲧⲉϥ ⲯⲩⲭⲏ̈ [15] ⲉⲍⲣⲁⲓ̈ ⲛ̅ⲙⲡⲏⲩⲉ, ⲁⲩⲧⲣⲉϥ ⲁⲥⲡⲁⲍⲉ̈ ⲛ̅ⲛⲉⲧⲟⲩⲁⲁⲃ. ⲙⲛ
ⲛ̅ⲥⲱⲥ ⲁⲩⲁⲥ̈ⲡⲁⲍⲉ ⲛⲁⲡⲁ ⲡ̅ⲇⲉⲗⲉⲙⲏ ϩⲛ̅ⲧ̈ⲙⲛⲧⲣ̅ⲣⲟ ⲛ̅ⲓ̅ⲥ̅ ⲡⲉ̈ ⲭ̅ⲥ̅.
ⲁⲩⲱ̈ ⲡⲉⲭⲉⲁⲡⲁ ⲡ̅ⲇⲉⲗⲉ̈ⲙⲏ ⲛⲁϥ ϫⲉ ⲕⲁ̈ⲗⲱⲥ ⲁⲕⲉⲓ ⲡⲁⲉⲓ̈ⲱⲧ ⲉⲧⲟⲩⲁⲁⲃ
ⲁⲡⲁⲓⲟⲩⲗⲉ· ⲉⲓⲥϩⲏⲏⲧⲉ ⲅⲁⲣ ⲁⲩⲟⲩ(Vi)ⲱ ⲉⲩⲡⲱⲣϣ̅ ⲛ̅ⲡⲉⲕⲑⲣⲟⲛⲟⲥ ⲙ̅

172 V i 8. ñ added, small. ii 8 f. (ñ)'ñ : dittography.   173 R ii 6.
1 of -ϥⲓ small; added.   11. - B1; l. -ϥⲓ

ππαραδεικος ' μⲛⲛⲉⲧⲟⲩⲁⲁⲃ ᷓⲧⲏⲣⲟⲩ, ⲁⲩⲱ ' ⲁⲩⲥⲟⲃⲧⲉ ⲙⲡⲉⲕ'ⲕⲗⲟⲙ
ⲉⲩ ⲛⲡ̅ⲓⲱⲟⲩ ' ⲍⲛ̅ⲙ̅ⲡ[ⲏⲩⲉ ?̣] ' ⲁⲩⲱ ⲧⲉⲕⲥⲧⲟⲗⲏ ' ⲉⲥ ⲛⲡ̅ⲓⲱⲟⲩ ⲉⲥⲟⲩ'ⲃⲉ ⲩ
ⲛ̅ⲥⲉ · · · · ' ⲱⲛ ⲁⲩⲧⲣⲉ · · ' ⲣ̄ⲩⲁ ⲙⲛ̅ⲛ̅ ⲍⲁ'ⲅⲓⲟⲥ ⲛ̅ⲙⲁⲣⲧⲩ̅ⲣⲟⲥ ⲍⲛ̅ⲧⲉⲩ-
ⲙⲛ̅'ⲧⲣ̅ⲣⲟ ⲩ ⲁⲉ ⲛ ⲉⲍ ' ⲉⲃⲟⲗ ⲍⲓⲧⲛ̅ ⲓ̅ⲥ̅ ⲡⲉ'ⲭ̅ⲥ̅ ⲡⲉⲛ ⲭ ⲟⲉⲓⲥ, ' ⲡⲁⲓ̈ ⲉⲃⲟⲗ ⲍⲓ-
ⲧⲟⲟⲧϥ̄ ' ⲡⲉⲟⲟⲩ ⲛⲁⲩ ⲙⲛ̅'ⲡⲉ ⲩ ⲉⲓⲱⲧ ⲛ̅ⲁ ⲥⲁ'ⲑⲟⲥ ⲙⲛ̅ ⲡⲉ ⲛ̅ⲛ̅ⲁ ' ⲉⲧⲟⲩⲁⲁⲃ
ⲛ̅ⲩⲁ ⲉ'ⲛⲉ ⲍ, ⲍ ⲁⲙⲏⲛ.

---

173 V i 23 . *l.* ⲩⲁ-

For the colophon which follows this text, see Lantschoot, Les colophons des manuscrits sahidiques, p. 11 f.

APPENDIX: MS. PARIS COPTE 78, FOLS. 16 f.
(*COLUTHUS* II)

(Fol. 16 R i) ⲧⲙⲁⲣⲧⲩⲣⲓⲁ ⲙ̄ⲡ̄ⲙⲁⲣⲧⲩⲣⲟⲥ ⲉⲧⲧⲁⲓⲏⲩ 'ⲡⲍⲁⲅⲓⲟⲥ ⲁⲡⲁ ⲕⲟⲗⲟⲩ'ⲑⲟⲥ,
ⲛ̄ⲧⲁⲩϫⲱⲕ ⲉ'ⲃⲟⲗ ⲍ̄ⲛ̄ⲟⲩⲙⲛ̄ⲧⲙⲁⲣ'ⲣⲉ ⲛ̄ⲥⲟⲩϫⲟⲩⲧⲁⲩⲧⲉ' ⲙ̄ⲡⲉⲃⲟⲧ ⲡⲁⲩⲟⲛⲉ̄.'
ⲁⲥϣⲱⲡⲉ ⲇⲉ ⲍⲛ̄ⲧ'ⲙⲉⲍϫⲟⲩⲧⲟⲩⲉ ⲛ̄ⲣⲟⲙ'ⲡⲉ ⲛ̄ⲇⲓⲟⲕⲗⲏⲧⲓⲁ'ⲛⲟⲥ ⲙⲛ̄ⲙⲁⲍⲓⲙⲓⲛⲓ'
ⲁⲛⲟⲥ ⲛ̄ⲣ̄ⲣⲱⲟⲩ ⲙ̄ⲡⲁ'ⲣⲁⲛⲟⲙⲟⲥ ⲉⲩⲇⲓⲱⲕⲉ 'ⲛ̄ⲥⲁⲛⲉⲭⲣⲓⲥⲧⲓⲁⲛⲟⲥ, 'ⲍ̄ⲣⲁⲓ̈ ⲇⲉ
ⲍⲛ̄ⲥⲟⲩⲭⲟⲩⲧ'ⲟⲩⲉ ⲙ̄ⲡⲉⲃⲟⲧ ⲡⲁⲩⲟ'ⲛⲉ̄ ⲁⲩⲡⲁⲣⲍⲓⲥⲧⲁ' ⲙ̄ⲡⲍⲁⲅⲓⲟⲥ ⲁⲡⲁ'ⲕⲟⲗⲗⲟⲩⲑⲟⲥ ⲛ̄ⲁ'ⲣⲓⲁⲛⲟⲥ ⲡⲍⲏⲅⲉⲙⲱ(ⲛ)' ⲉⲩⲍⲙⲟⲟⲥ ⲍⲓⲡⲃⲏ'ⲙⲁ ⲛ̄ϫⲟⲩⲛ ⲉⲩⲙⲟⲩ(ⲛ).'
ⲁⲣⲓⲁⲛⲟⲥ ⲇⲉ ⲡⲍⲏⲅⲉ'ⲙⲱⲛ ⲛ̄ⲑⲏⲃⲁⲉⲓⲥ' ⲡⲉϫⲁⲩ ⲛ̄ⲁⲡⲁ ⲕⲟⲗ'[ⲗⲟ]ⲩⲑⲟⲥ ϫⲉ ⲕⲟⲩⲱⲩ' [ⲉⲥⲱⲧⲙ̄]; ⲛⲁⲓ ⲅⲁⲣ' [ⲧⲏⲣⲟ]ⲩ ⲉⲧⲁⲍⲉⲣ[ⲁ]ⲧⲟⲩ' [ⲙ̄ⲡⲉⲓ̈]ⲙⲁ, ⲥⲉⲩ[ⲱ]ⲛⲁ
ⲉ(ⲣⲓⲓ)ϫⲱⲕ ⲉⲧⲣⲉⲕⲣ̄ⲥⲁⲃⲉ. 'ⲉⲩϭⲉ ⲟⲩⲛ̄ⲟⲩϣⲓⲡⲉ' ⲁⲙⲁⲍⲧⲉ ⲙ̄ⲙⲟⲕ ⲕⲁ'ⲧⲁⲟⲩ-
ⲙⲛ̄ⲧϣⲟⲩϣⲟ 'ⲁⲩⲱ ⲕⲁⲧⲁⲡⲛⲟⲙⲟⲥ 'ⲛ̄ⲛⲉⲭⲣⲓⲥⲧⲓⲁⲛⲟⲥ,' ⲧⲉⲛⲟⲩ ⲇⲉ ⲍⲱⲱⲩ 'ⲙⲁ-
ⲣⲉⲟⲩϣⲓⲡⲉ ⲉⲛⲁ'ⲛⲟⲩⲩ ⲉⲓ ⲛⲁⲕ ⲉⲧⲣⲉⲕ'ⲟⲩϣⲙ̄ϣⲉ ⲛ̄ⲛ̄ⲛⲟⲩⲧⲉ ' ⲛ̄ⲛ̄ⲣ̄ⲣⲱⲟⲩ. ⲁⲩⲟⲩ'ⲱϣⲃ̄ ⲛ̄ϭⲓ ⲡⲍⲁⲅⲓⲟⲥ'ⲁⲡⲁ ⲕⲟⲗⲗⲟⲩⲑⲟⲥ 'ϫⲉ ⲛ̄ⲛⲉⲥϣⲱⲡⲉ ⲙ̄ⲙⲟⲓ̈ ⲉⲛⲉⲍ ⲉ-
ⲧⲣⲁⲕⲁ'ⲡⲁⲛⲟⲩⲧⲉ ⲛ̄ⲥⲱⲓ̈, ⲧⲁ'ⲩϣⲙ̄ϣⲉ ⲛ̄ⲍⲛ̄ⲉⲓⲇⲱ'ⲗⲟⲛ ⲉⲍⲉⲛⲍⲃⲏⲩⲉ ⲛⲉ 'ⲛ̄ϭⲓⲝ
ⲛ̄ⲣⲱⲙⲉ. ⲟⲩⲛ̄ⲃⲁⲗ ⲙ̄ⲙⲟⲟⲩ ⲛ̄ⲥⲉ'ⲛⲁⲩ ⲉⲃⲟⲗ ⲁⲛ· ⲟⲩⲛ̄'ⲙⲁⲁϫⲉ ⲙ̄ⲙⲟⲟⲩ ⲛ̄ⲥⲉ-'
ⲥⲱⲧⲙ̄ ⲁⲛ· ⲟⲩⲛ̄ⲧⲁ'ⲡⲣⲟ ⲙ̄ⲙⲟⲟⲩ ⲙⲉⲩⲅⲁ'ϣⲉ- ϣⲁⲩⲛⲧⲟⲩ ⲙ̄'ⲙⲟⲟⲩ ⲙⲉⲩϣⲱ-
ⲗⲙ̄·' ⲛⲉⲩϭⲓϫ ⲙ̄ⲙⲟⲟⲩ ⲙⲉⲩ'ϭⲟⲙϭⲙ̄· ⲛⲉⲩⲟⲩⲉⲣⲏ'ⲧⲉ ⲙ̄ⲙⲟⲟⲩ ⲙⲉⲩⲙⲟⲟ'ⲩⲉ·
ⲙⲉⲩⲙⲟⲩⲧⲉ ⲍⲁⲧⲉⲩ'ϣⲟⲩⲟⲃⲉ· (ⲃⲓ) ⲙⲛ̄ ⲡⲛⲁ ⲅⲁⲣ ⲛ̄ⲍⲏⲧⲟⲩ·' ⲉⲩⲉⲣⲡⲧⲉⲩⲍⲉ ⲛ̄ϭⲓ
ⲛⲉⲛ'ⲧⲁⲩⲧⲁⲙⲓⲟⲟⲩ ⲙⲛ̄'ⲟⲩⲟⲛ ⲛⲓⲙ ⲉⲧⲛⲁⲍⲧⲉ̄' ⲉⲣⲟⲟⲩ. ⲛ̄ⲧⲟⲕ ⲅⲁⲣ' ⲙ̄ⲛⲛⲉⲕ-
ⲣ̄ⲣⲱⲟⲩ ⲛ̄ⲁ'ⲛⲟⲙⲟⲥ, ⲁⲡⲇⲓⲁⲃⲟ'ⲗⲟⲥ ⲧⲱⲙ ⲛ̄ⲛⲉⲥⲑⲏ'ⲥⲓⲥ ⲧⲏⲣⲟⲩ ⲛ̄ⲧⲉⲧⲛ̄'ⲯⲩⲭⲏ, ⲛ̄ⲑⲉ ⲛ̄ⲛⲉⲧⲉ'ⲧⲛ̄ⲟⲩϣⲙ̄ϣⲉ ⲛⲁⲩ. ⲁⲩ'ϭⲱⲛⲧ ⲇⲉ ⲛ̄ϭⲓ ⲁⲣⲓⲁⲛⲟⲥ,'ⲁⲩⲕⲉⲗⲉⲩⲉ
ⲛ̄ⲙ̄ⲙⲁ'ⲧⲟⲓ̈ ⲉⲧⲣⲉⲩⲕⲱ ⲉⲍⲣⲁⲓ̈ 'ⲍⲓⲑⲏ ⲙ̄ⲡⲍⲁⲅⲓⲟⲥ ⲁⲡⲁ'ⲕⲟⲗⲗⲟⲩⲑⲟⲥ ⲛ̄ⲛⲉ-'
ⲍⲛⲁⲁⲩ ⲧⲏⲣⲟⲩ ⲉⲩⲁⲩ'ⲃⲁⲥⲁⲛⲓⲍⲉ ⲛ̄ⲛ̄ⲣⲱ'ⲙⲉ ⲛ̄ⲍⲏⲧⲟⲩ, ϫⲉ'ⲙⲉⲅⲁⲕ ⲉⲃⲟⲗ
ⲍⲓⲧⲛ̄'ⲧⲉⲩⲍⲟⲧⲉ ⲉϥⲉⲃ̄'ϭⲟⲙ ⲉⲡⲓⲑⲉ ⲙ̄ⲙⲟⲩ' ⲉⲑⲩⲥⲓⲁⲍⲉ ⲛ̄ⲛⲉⲓⲇⲱ'ⲗⲟⲛ·
ⲁⲩⲉⲓⲛⲉ ⲇⲉ ⲉⲧ'ⲙⲏⲧⲉ ⲛ̄ⲟⲩⲕⲱϫⲧ̄' ⲙ̄ⲛⲟⲩⲛⲟϭ ⲛ̄ⲱⲛⲉ' ⲉⲧⲣⲉⲩⲁⲩⲧⲩ ⲉⲡⲉϥⲙⲁ'ⲕⲏ̄ ⲙ̄ⲡⲙⲁⲕⲁⲣⲓⲟⲥ, 'ⲙ̄ⲛⲟⲩⲍⲱⲧ ⲉϥⲙⲉⲍ' ⲛ̄ⲏⲱ, ⲙ̄ⲛⲟⲩⲕⲁⲥⲓⲥ, (ⲃⲓⲓ)
ⲙ̄ⲛ̄ⲗⲕⲉⲥⲉⲉⲡⲉ ⲛ̄ⲕⲟ'ⲗⲁⲥⲧⲏⲣⲓⲟⲛ· ⲛⲁⲓ̈ ⲇⲉ ⲧⲏⲣⲟⲩ ⲛ̄ⲧⲉⲣⲟⲩ'ⲕⲁⲁⲩ ⲙ̄ⲡⲉϥ-
ⲙ̄ⲧⲟ ⲉ'ⲃⲟⲗ, ⲡⲉϫⲉⲡⲍⲏⲅⲉ'ⲙⲱⲛ ⲛⲁⲩ ϫⲉ ⲱ ⲕⲟ'ⲗⲟⲩⲑⲉ, ⲁⲣⲓⲍⲟⲧⲉ ⲍⲏ'ⲧⲟⲩ
ⲛ̄ⲛⲉⲓ̈ⲃⲁⲥⲁⲛⲟⲥ' ⲧⲏⲣⲟⲩ ⲉⲧⲕⲏ ⲉⲍ'ⲣⲁⲓ̈ ⲍⲓⲑⲏ ⲙ̄ⲙⲟⲕ ⲛ̄ⲅ̄'ⲑⲩⲥⲓⲁⲍⲉ· ⲛⲉⲓ̈-
ⲃⲁ'ⲥⲁⲛⲟⲥ ⲧⲏⲣⲟⲩ ⲙⲛ̄'ⲛⲉⲓ̈ⲙⲟⲕⲍ̄ ⲉⲩⲅⲟ'ⲟⲡ ⲉⲧⲃⲉⲛⲉⲧⲛⲁⲣ'ⲁⲧⲥⲱⲧⲙ̄ ⲛ̄ⲥⲁ-
ⲛ̄ⲣ̄'ⲣⲱⲟⲩ. ⲁⲩⲟⲩⲱϣⲃ̄' ⲇⲉ ⲛ̄ϭⲓ ⲁⲡⲁ ⲕⲟⲗⲗⲟⲩ'ⲑⲟⲥ ϫⲉ ϥⲥⲉⲏⲍ ϫⲉ ⲙ̄'ⲡⲣ̄ⲣ̄ⲍⲟⲧⲉ

Fol. 16 R ii 30a. ϣⲟⲩⲟⲃⲉ beneath end of l. 30.

ϩⲏⲧⲟⲩ ⲛ̄'ⲛⲉⲧⲛⲁⲙⲟⲩⲟⲩⲧ· ⲙ̄ⲡⲉⲧⲛ̄ⲥⲱⲙⲁ, ⲉⲙ̄'ⲃ̄ⲟⲙ ⲇⲉ ⲙ̄ⲙⲟⲟⲩ ⲉⲙⲟⲩ'ⲟⲩⲧ
ⲛ̄ⲛⲉⲧⲛ̄ⲯⲩⲭⲏ·'ⲁⲣⲓ̈ϩⲟⲧⲉ ⲛ̄ⲧⲟⲩ ϩⲏⲧⲟⲩ ⲙ̄ⲡⲉⲧⲉⲟⲩⲛ̄ϭⲟⲙ ⲙ̄'ⲙⲟⲩ ⲉⲧⲁⲕⲟ ⲛ̄-
ⲧⲉⲧ[ⲙ̄]'ⲯⲩⲭⲏ ⲙⲛ̄ⲡⲉ[ⲧⲛ̄]'ⲥⲱⲙⲁ ϩⲣⲁⲓ̈ ϩ[ⲛ̄ⲧⲅⲉ'ϩ]ⲉⲛⲛⲁ ⲛ̄ⲥⲁ[ⲧⲉ ϥ̄ϭ̄ϩ̄ϩ̄]
ⲇⲉ [ⲟⲛ] ϫⲉ ⲡ̣[ⲉⲧⲛⲁ̣ϩⲟϫ](17 Ri)ⲙⲟⲗⲟⲅⲓ ⲙ̄ⲙⲟⲓ̈ ⲙ̄ⲡ̄ⲁ'ⲧⲟ ⲉⲃⲟⲗ ⲛ̄ⲛ̄ⲣⲱⲙⲉ,'
ϯⲛⲁϩⲟⲙⲟⲗⲟⲅⲓ ϩⲱ'ⲛ̄ϩⲏⲧϥ̄ ⲙ̄ⲡⲁⲧⲟ ⲉ'ⲃⲟⲗ ⲙ̄ⲡⲁⲓⲱⲧ ⲉⲧϩⲛ̄'ⲙ̄ⲡⲏⲩⲉ ⲙⲛ̄-
ⲛⲉϥⲁⲅ'ⲅⲉⲗⲟⲥ ⲉⲧⲟⲩⲁⲁⲃ·'ⲁⲩⲱ ⲟⲛ ϫⲉ ⲡⲉⲧⲛⲁ'ⲁⲣⲛⲁ ⲙ̄ⲙⲟⲓ̈ ⲙ̄ⲡⲁ̄ⲧⲟ'ⲉ-
ⲃⲟⲗ ⲛ̄ⲛ̄ⲣⲱⲙⲉ, ϯⲁⲣ'ⲛⲁ ⲙ̄ⲙⲟⲩ ϩⲱ ⲙ̄ⲡⲁ̄'ⲧⲟ ⲉⲃⲟⲗ ⲙ̄ⲡⲁⲓ̈ⲱⲧ 'ⲉⲧϩⲛ̄ⲙ̄ⲡⲏ-
ⲩⲉ ⲙⲛ̄'ⲛⲉϥⲁⲅⲅⲉⲗⲟⲥ ⲉⲧⲟⲩⲁⲁⲃ·' ⲁϥⲟⲩⲱϣⲃ̄ ⲇⲉ ⲛ̄ϭⲓ ⲁⲣⲓ̈ⲁⲛⲟⲥ ⲡⲉϫⲁⲩ
ⲛ̄ⲁⲡⲁ' ⲕⲟⲗⲟⲩⲑⲟⲥ ϫⲉ ⲛ̄ⲧⲁⲩ'ⲙⲟⲩⲧⲉ ⲉⲣⲟⲕ ⲁⲛ ⲉϫⲉ'ⲟⲩⲙ̄ⲡⲏⲩⲉ ⲛ̄ⲩⲁϫⲉ·'
ⲉⲕⲩⲁⲛⲧⲟⲗⲙⲁ ⲛ̄ⲕⲉ'ⲥⲟⲡ ⲉⲩⲁϫⲉ ⲙ̄ⲡⲁⲇ̄'ⲧⲟ ⲉⲃⲟⲗ, ϯⲛⲁⲧⲣⲉⲩ'ⲡⲱⲣⲕ̄ ⲙ̄-
ⲡⲉⲕⲗⲁⲥ·'[ⲛⲁⲓ̈] ⲅⲁⲣ ⲧⲏⲣⲟⲩ ⲉⲧⲁ'[ϩ]ϩⲉⲣⲁ]ⲧⲟⲩ ⲙ̄ⲡⲉⲓⲙⲁ,'[ⲥⲉⲗⲧⲏ]ⲙ ⲉⲧ-
ⲃⲏⲏ[ⲧⲕ̄]'[. . . . . .].ⲉⲟⲛ·' (3 lines lost. At end of l. 30: ⲁϥⲟⲩⲱϣⲃ̄]
(Rii) ⲛ̄ϭⲓ ⲁⲡⲁ ⲕⲟⲗⲗⲟⲩⲑⲟⲥ·'ϫⲉ ⲡⲁϥⲟⲩⲅⲟⲩ ⲙⲛ̄'ⲡⲁⲕⲗⲟⲙ ⲡϫⲟⲉⲓⲥ ⲡⲉ·'
ϥ̄ϭ̄ϩ̄ ⲅⲁⲣ ϫⲉ ⲁⲛⲟⲛ ⲉⲣⲉ'ⲡⲉⲛⲡⲟⲗⲓⲧⲉⲩⲙⲁ ϩⲛ̄'ⲙ̄ⲡⲏⲩⲉ, ⲡⲙⲁ ⲉⲧⲛ̄'ϭⲱ-
ϣⲧ̄ ⲉⲃⲟⲗ ϩⲏⲧϥ̄·'ⲙ̄ⲡⲉⲛⲥⲱⲧⲏⲣ ⲡ̄ⲭⲟ̄ⲉⲓⲥ ⲓ̄ⲥ̄, ⲡⲁⲓ̈ ⲉⲧⲛⲁϫⲓ̈'ⲃⲉ ⲙ̄ⲡⲥⲱⲙⲁ
ⲙ̄ⲡⲉⲛ'ⲑ̄ⲃ̄ⲃⲓⲟ ⲉⲡⲉⲓⲛⲉ ⲙ̄ⲡ'ⲥⲱⲙⲁ ⲙ̄ⲡⲉϥⲉⲟⲟⲩ,'ⲉⲧⲣⲉⲛ̄ⲃⲱⲗ ⲙ̄ⲡⲉⲧⲛ̄'ϩⲏⲧ
ϫⲓⲟⲩⲟⲉⲓⲛ·' ⲁϥⲟⲩⲱϣⲃ̄ ⲛ̄ϭⲓ ⲁⲣⲓ̈'ⲁⲛⲟⲥ ⲡⲉϫⲁϥ ⲛⲁⲩ'ϫⲉ ⲙⲏ ⲛ̄ⲧⲟⲕ ⲟⲩ-
ⲇⲓ̈'ⲁⲕⲟⲛⲟⲥ ⲏ ⲟⲩⲡⲣⲉⲥ'ⲃⲩⲧⲉⲣⲟⲥ, ϫⲉ ⲕ̄ⲧⲁϫⲟ'ⲛ̄ⲛⲉⲓ̈ϣⲁϫⲉ; ⲙⲁⲧⲁ'ⲙⲟⲓ̈
ⲇⲉ ⲟⲛ ϫⲉ ⲟⲩ ⲧⲉ'ⲧⲉⲕⲉⲓⲟⲡⲉ· ⲡⲉϫⲉ'ⲁⲡⲁ ⲕⲟⲗⲟⲩⲑⲟⲥ ⲛⲁϥ'ϫⲉ ⲕⲁⲧⲁ-
ⲡⲉⲓ̈ⲕⲟⲥⲙⲟⲥ'ⲙⲉⲛ ⲁⲛ̄ⲅⲟⲩⲥⲁⲉⲓⲛ·'ϫⲓⲛⲧⲁⲙⲛ̄ⲧⲕⲟⲩⲓ̈,'[ϫⲉ] ϩⲓⲧⲙ̄ⲡⲛⲟⲩ-
ⲧⲉ'[ⲁⲩϫ]ⲁⲣⲓ̈ϩⲉ ⲛⲁⲓ̈'[ⲛ̄ⲧⲙⲛ̄]ⲧⲑⲉⲣⲁⲡⲉⲩⲉ'[. . . . . .].·ⲕⲁ[ⲧⲁ](Vi)ⲡ-
ⲛⲟⲩⲧⲉ ⲇⲉ ⲁⲛ̄ⲅⲟⲩ'ⲭⲣⲓⲥⲧⲓⲁⲛⲟⲥ, ⲉⲓ̈ϥⲙ̄'ϣⲉ ⲛ̄ⲓ̄ⲥ̄ ⲡⲉⲭ̄ⲥ̄ ⲡⲁϫⲟⲉⲓⲥ·'ⲁⲣⲓ̈-
ⲁⲛⲟⲥ ⲇⲉ ⲡⲉϫⲁϥ ⲛⲁⲩ'ϫⲉ ⲑⲩⲥⲓⲁⲍⲉ ⲱ ⲕⲟⲗ'ⲗⲟⲩⲑⲟⲥ ⲛ̄ⲅϣⲛ̄ϩ̄ⲧⲏⲕ·'
ϩⲁⲣⲟⲕ· ⲙⲁⲣⲉⲟⲩⲟⲛ'ⲛⲓⲙ ϭⲱϣⲧ̄ ⲛ̄ⲥⲱⲕ ⲕⲁ'ⲗⲱⲥ ϩⲛ̄ϩⲛ̄ⲥⲙⲟⲧ ⲉⲛⲁ-'
ⲛⲟⲩⲟⲩ· ⲛ̄ⲧⲟⲕ ⲅⲁⲣ'ⲙ̄ⲡⲉⲕϯⲗⲁⲁⲩ ⲛ̄ⲛⲉϩ'ⲣⲏⲧⲱⲣ ⲉⲧⲁϩⲉⲣⲁⲧⲟⲩ'ⲉⲧⲣⲉⲩ-
ⲙⲓϣⲉ ⲉϫⲱⲕ·'ⲛ̄ⲧⲟⲟⲩ ⲇⲉ ⲧⲏⲣⲟⲩ ⲉⲩ'ϩⲓⲛⲉⲩⲉⲣⲏⲩ ⲙ̄ⲡⲉⲕ'ϫⲓⲡⲉⲩϩⲕⲟⲧ
ⲛ̄ⲥⲉⲩⲁ'ϫⲉ ⲉϫⲱⲕ. ⲁϥⲟⲩⲱ'ⲩϣⲃ̄ ⲇⲉ ⲛ̄ϭⲓ ⲁⲡⲁ ⲕⲟⲗ'ⲗⲟⲩⲑⲟⲥ ϫⲉ ⲛ̄ϯⲭⲣⲓⲁ
ⲙ̄ⲙⲟⲟⲩ ⲁⲛ· ⲟⲩⲛ̄ⲧⲁⲓ̈'ⲅⲁⲣ ⲙ̄ⲙⲁⲩ ⲙ̄ⲡⲁϫⲟ'ⲉⲓⲥ ⲓ̄ⲥ̄ ⲡⲉϫⲉ ⲉϥⲙⲓϣⲉ'ⲉϩⲣⲁⲓ̈
ⲉϫⲱⲓ̈· ⲛⲉⲕ ⲃⲁ'ⲥⲁⲛⲟⲥ ⲅⲁⲣ ⲧⲏⲣⲟⲩ ⲉⲧ'ⲕ̄ⲙ ⲉϩⲣⲁⲓ̈ ϩⲛ̄ⲗⲁⲁⲩ ⲛⲉ'ⲙ̄ⲡⲁⲙ̄ⲧⲟ

_____

17 R i 10. l. ϯⲛⲁⲁⲣⲛⲁ, which Peyron prints. 28. [. . . . . .].ⲉⲟⲛ: o might,
less probably, be read as ⲑ. V i 19. l. ⲛ̄ϯⲭⲣⲓⲁ.

ⲉⲃⲟⲗ· ⲃⲁⲥⲁⲛⲟⲥ ⲇⲉ ⲛⲓⲙ [ⲉⲧⲉⲅ]ⲛⲁⲕ, ⲧⲁⲁⲩ ⲛ[ⲁ]ⲓ̈   ]ⲥⲟ ⲙ̄ⲙⲟⲓ̈ ⲉⲧ·[3ᵖ
ⲓ̓
[...].··[   ](17 Vii) ⲙⲉⲣⲉⲩⲟⲉⲓⲝ ϫⲓ ⲕⲗⲟⲙ' ⲉⲓⲙⲏⲧⲓ ⲛ̄ϥⲙⲓⲩⲉ' ⲕⲁⲗⲱⲥ. ⲁ̄ⲩⲕⲉⲗⲉⲩⲉ 'ⲛ̄ⲧⲉⲩⲛⲟⲩ ⲛ̄ϭⲓ ⲡ̄ⲅ̓ⲏ̓ⲅⲉⲙⲱⲛ ⲉⲧⲣⲉⲩⲧⲁ'ⲗⲟⲩ ⲉⲡϫⲉⲣⲙⲏ-
ⲧⲁⲣⲓ'ⲟⲛ ⲛ̄ⲥⲉϩⲱⲕⲉ ⲙ̄ⲙⲟⲩ' ⲁⲩⲱ ⲛ̄ⲥⲉϯϩⲃⲟⲕ ⲛⲁⲩ. 'ⲛ̄ⲧⲉⲣⲟⲩⲧⲁⲗⲟⲩ ⲇⲉ ¹⁰
ⲉⲡϫⲉⲣⲙⲏⲧⲁⲣⲓⲟⲛ, 'ⲁⲩⲥⲫⲣⲁⲅⲓⲍⲉ ⲙ̄ⲙⲟⲩ' ⲛ̄ⲧⲉⲩⲛⲟⲩ ⲛ̄ϭⲓ ⲡϫⲁ'ⲅⲓ̓ⲟⲥ ⲁ-
ⲡⲁ ⲕⲟⲗⲟⲩⲑⲟⲥ·' ⲁⲡϫⲉⲣⲙⲏⲧⲁⲣⲓⲟⲛ¹⁵' ⲟⲩⲱϭⲡ ⲁⲩⲣ̄ⲥⲛⲁⲩ. ' ⲡⲉϫⲁⲩ ⲇⲉ ⲛ̄ϭⲓ
ⲁⲣⲓⲁ'ⲛⲟⲥ ϫⲉ ⲁⲛⲁⲩ ⲉⲧⲙⲁ'ⲅⲓⲁ ⲛ̄ⲛⲉⲭⲣⲓⲥⲧⲓⲁⲛⲟⲥ' ϫⲉ ⲟⲩⲁⲩ ⲛ̄ϭⲟⲧ ⲧⲉ·' ²⁰
ⲁⲩⲕⲉⲗⲉⲩⲉ ⲇⲉ ⲛ̄ϭⲓ ⲡ'ϩⲏⲅⲉⲙⲱⲛ ⲉⲧⲣⲉⲩ'ⲉⲓⲛⲉ ⲛ̄ⲕⲉϫⲉⲣⲙⲏⲧⲁ'ⲣⲓⲟⲛ ⲛ̄ⲥⲉⲧⲁ-
ⲗⲉⲁⲡⲁ'ⲕⲟⲗⲟⲩⲑⲟⲥ ⲉⲣⲟ[ϥ ⲛ̄]'ⲥⲉϩⲱⲱⲕⲉ ⲙ̄[ⲙⲟⲩ]' [ϩⲛ̄ⲟⲩ]ⲕⲁⲥⲓⲥ·[   ]'   ²⁵
[ⲁⲡⲁ] ⲕⲟⲗⲗⲟⲩⲑⲟⲥ   ]' (3 lines lost.)

———

17 V ii 18. Peyron read ⲧⲓ as ⲡ.

S. COLUTHUS

(**88 V i**) The *martyrology* of the holy *martyr* of *Christ* Coluthus, and the physician and *healer*[1] of every one who partakes of the *body* and blood of *Christ* in purity; he fulfilled his *contest* on the twenty-fourth day of Pashons;[2] in God's *peace*, *Amen*.

It happened in the twentieth year of the emperors Diocletian and Maximinian (*sic*), the *transgressors*, and in the third year of Constantine,[3] on the twenty-fourth day of Pashons, that the *holy* Coluthus was set (**88 V ii**) upon the *tribunal* of Antinoou.[4] Arianus[5] the *governor* said to the *holy* Coluthus, 'If you want to be saved, do *sacrifice*, and you shall live. All these people present are praying for you to see sense. If shame is what restrains you, *arising from* vanity, well, now, show some shame before me; do *sacrifice*, and you will be saved. *For* so far you have shown no shame before any one worth your shame. Coluthus, reverence the Emperor's gods, so that you do not perish *miserably*.'[6] The *holy* Coluthus answered, 'The glory of this *world* is tempor*al*, (**89 R i**) but the glory of the Kingdom of Heaven is eternal life.' The *governor* said to him, 'The *tortures* of the *lawcourt* are many; and if there were some one present today *accusing* you, you would do your best not to be defeated in any argument; do not *accuse* your own self, and kill yourself. *For* your own people who are present are *grieved* for your sake.[7] Let them see you *sacrifice*, and rejoice with you. Moreover, the administrator of judgment—that is, myself—has won no credit for his place of giving judgment for this matter. Let every one see your good sense and admire (**89 R ii**) you.[8] Moreover, if there is any affair or consideration between you and any one, that other person will *certainly* be present

---

[1] In *Coluthus* II, fol. 17 R ii 15–29 (see above, p. 13), the governor is made to ask Coluthus what is his profession. On our assumption that the text of 88 V ii ff. is a genuine transcript of proceedings which, as in the case of Phileas (see V. Martin, *Pap. Bodmer XX (Phileas)*, p. 24) were only one (in this case the last) of a series, such a question would have been out of place here, since it will have been made at the first hearing.

[2] = May 19th; in *Synax.* it is Bashons 25th.

[3] Pashons of the twentieth year of Diocletian and Maximian would be May 304; the earliest known date for Arianus as *praeses* of the Thebaid is 305/6; see P. Oxy. 2665. The mention of 'the third year of Constantine' hardly inspires confidence in the writer's chronology; but the Oxyrhynchus text shows that Arianus has by 305/6 had time to try and condemn at least one Christian victim, the disposal of whose goods is under discussion; so 304 will not be impossibly early.

[4] *Coluthus* II (16 R i 22) makes the scene of the trial Shmoun (Hermopolis Magna).

[5] For Arianus, see our Introduction, p. 7.

[6] 88 V ii 6–27: cf. *Coluthus* II, 16 R i 26–ii 11.

[7] 89 R i 20–22: cf. *Coluthus* II, 17 R i 24–26.

[8] 89 R i 30–33: cf. *Coluthus* II, 17 V i 7–10.

to your *discomfiture*;[9] do not spite your own self. *For* when death comes peacefully and naturally, people console themselves, *for* they call it "the *(lot) of mankind*", since it is the fate of every one; but in this place where you are now *sentence* is passed upon *murderers* and temple robbers and violators of graves and *debauchees* and adulterers and villains—no respectable person is brought out from here and destroyed.[10] But if there is any one (**89 V i**) who has *flouted* the *law*, it is evident to every one that what has *betrayed* such a person is not *wisdom*, but an *insanity* of conceit; just as robbers are *reckless of* death for robbery's sake. *Now* I have been lenient with you so far, so that you may see sense and live a life of *liberty* like any free man. . . . Coluthus, why don't you speak to me when I am speaking to you?' The *holy* Coluthus said, 'It is not fitting for me to make a long speech[11] before a *governor*.' The *governor* said (**89 V ii**) to him, 'Do *sacrifice*, Coluthus!' The saint said, 'I will not *sacrifice*.' The *governor* said to him, '*Indeed* you have not obeyed me and *sacrificed* to the gods about whom the Emperor has written to me. I shall *consume* your *body* by fire. *But* this shall not happen yet, *in case* you wish to *consider* with yourself.' The saint answered, 'I have already *considered* with myself before I came here to you.'[12] The *advocates*[13] said to him, 'Grant him a few days, if you please.' Arianus said to the *advocates*,'He looks to me as if he wants to, and has changed his mind.' (**90 R i**) The *governor* said to him, 'Do you want to wait a few days, to think the matter over? For I can see it in your face—it shows me that you want to be saved.' The *saint* made no answer at all . . . The *governor* said to him, '*Are* you ashamed to *admit* it?' The *saint* said to him, 'A word is enough to the wise.'[14]

---

[9] In the text published by Till, *KHML* I, p. 170, there is mention of Coluthus' enemies and accusers; one of them is evidently alluded to here. It might be suggested that ⲙ̄ⲙⲟⲕ here is a mistake for ⲉⲧⲃⲏⲏⲧⲕ̄, and that the passage should read '. . . *surely* that man *grieves* for your sake'; i.e., even Coluthus' adversary is more concerned for his fate than he is himself. Possibly the Coptic translator misunderstood the Greek original.

[10] 89 R ii 19–32: similar arguments in Delehaye, *Mart. Ég.*, p. 191 (Paphnutius, *graece*); cf. Eusebius, *HE* viii 6, 9.

[11] In the 'epic' martyrologies the governor frequently accuses the martyr of loquacity (e.g. Bal. - Hyv. *AM* I, p. 16 (Lacaron)); cf. 92 R i 14 ff.; *Coluthus* II, 17 R i 15 ff.

[12] Cf. *Phileas*, p. 51; and in the 'epic' martyrologies, e.g., Hyv. *Actes*, p. 101 (Apater); Bal. - Hyv. *AM* I, p. 18 (Lacaron); Drescher, *Mena*, pp. 53 f.; Krumbacher, *Abh. d. kgl. bayer. Akad., philos. - philolog. Kl.* 24, 3 (1907), 39 (Menas, *graece*).

[13] Cf. *Coluthus* II, 17 V i 10–17; also the δικολόγοι in *Phileas*, p. 50; they also occasionally feature in the 'epic' martyrologies.

[14] See our Introduction, p. 10. The saying is frequent in the 'epic' martyrologies, often with considerable and tedious expansions; e.g., *P. & T.* 81 V i 5 ff.; *Sh.* 113 V ii 17 ff.; *Epima* (ed. Mina), p. 19; Hyv. *Actes*, p. 157 (Piroou & Athom); Bal. - Hyv. *AM* I, p. 234 (Anoub); E. W. *Macarius*, p. 95 (Thomas of Shentalolet). This might be taken as an example of the way in which stereotyped phrases were copied from one of these

The *governor* had the fire[15] laid before the *blessed* Coluthus. The
governor said to him (*sic*),[16] 'Stop, don't do him any *harm* yet.' *Then*
the *governor* turned to the *holy* Coluthus and said to him, 'Be sensible
now, and do as you are told. (**90 R ii**) (There was) Apollonius, the
bishop of Siout;[17] his people were most understanding about him,
and took a *dignified* view of his *prudence, since* he did not wish to be
disobedient, *or* to be brought to *court* and hear all this rigmarole, *but*
he proceeded of his own accord into the temple and *sacrificed* in *full
view* of every one, with the *vessels* of libation in his hand, standing
there and offering up *sacrifice*; he is not at all ashamed, and every
one honours him. . . . *Well now*, speak to me, Coluthus, and you shall
(**90 V i**) be in especial *honour*. . . . Then (there was) P(l)utarchus, the
bishop of Sbeht;[18] this man for the excellence of his *wisdom* and[19]
(*sic*) is worthy of all respect. He was *prudent* and reverenced the
Emperor's gods, and offered up *sacrifice* to them; and look at him
now! He is alive, with every one who *sacrificed* with him, and is *bishop*
over them. As for you, Coluthus, it is a *governor* who is pleading with
you, and *advising* you! The *governor*ship has humbled itself for you.
Let it be enough to have done what you have in the matter of the
books, when you were *persuaded* by your God and did not burn
them.[20] There was a man here today on a *charge* (**90 V ii**) of murder.

---

compositions to another, the present instance being the original occurrence. But we
believe rather that it was part of the regular Christian repertoire of stock answers to
stock questions. On the origin of the saying, see H. Chadwick, *JTS*, N. S. 20 (1969),
645, where he points out that σοφῶ τὸ νεῦμα in *Barsenouphis and John* (Answer 69),
ed. J. Chitty, *PO* 31, 3 (1966), p. 96, is an unrecognized citation from New Comedy,
and compares *dictum sapienti sat* in Plautus, *Persa* 729; Terence, *Phormio* 541. This
version of the saying has passed, with a small mutation, into universal parlance as
verbum sapienti sat (*verb. sap.*); see *Oxford English Dictionary*, s.v. It would appear
that νεῦμα in the Greek form of the citation discussed by Chadwick, which must surely
be original, has at some early stage been replaced by the more colourless ῥῆμα. For the
kind of compendium of moral maxims current in Egypt from which this citation may
well have been drawn, see D. Hagedorn–M. Weber, 'Die griechisch-koptische Rezension
der Menandersentenzen', *Ztschr. f. Papyrologie u. Epigraphik* 3 (1968), 50 ff.

[15] 90 R i 18–22: cf. *Coluthus* II, 16 V i 24 f.
[16] Read 'them'.
[17] Apollonius, bishop of Siout (= Lycopolis, Asyut) is the recipient of a letter attributed to
Peter of Alexandria, the beginning of which is preserved in Ms. Paris Copt. 131, fol. 1,
in which he is reproached for his defection. This text, mentioned by C. Schmidt in
Text. u. Unters. N. F. V, p. 46, and Crum, *Byz.Ztschr.* xxx, p. 326, is as yet unpublished;
see our Introduction, p. 10.
[18] This person is otherwise unknown. For Sbeht ('Απολλώνος κάτω, Kôm Isfaḥt), see
Amélineau, *Géographie de l' Égypte a l' époque copte*, p. 463; Munier, *Recueil des
listes épiscopales de l' église copte*, p. 57; Calderini, *Dizionario geografico dell' Egitto*
I (2), pp. 170 ff.; Gardiner, *Ancient Egyptian Onomastica* II, pp. 56* ff.
[19] 'And' is superfluous.
[20] References to the requirement to burn Christian books are not common in texts from
Egypt; but it is expressly mentioned in the Sermon of Isaac of Antinoë on Coluthus; and
cf. *Epima*, p. 2; Till, *KHML* I, p. 42 (Besamon).

This man wants to live; but as for you, Coluthus, something evil
possesses you, *to* make you destroy yourself with murderers! Don't
you see the beauty of this pleasant *weather*?[21] There will be no
pleasure to come your way if your kill your own self. *But* listen to
me and you will be saved.' The *holy* Coluthus said to him, 'The
death which is coming to me is more pleasant *than* the life which
you would give me.' The *governor* said to him, 'So you do not realize
that I have *authority* to *chastise* you? Come now, use your *reason*
like a sensible man, and listen to me.' The *holy* Coluthus said to him,
'Whoever **(91 R i)** listens to you will bring his own death upon himself. *But* I will not forsake my Lord Jesus *Christ*.' The *governor* said
to him, 'Look at all these people with their tears streaming down as
they see you standing on the *tribunal*—and you have shown no pity
on your own self,[22] *but* you are disobedient. *Now*, listen to me and
sacrifice, and you shall live.' The *saint* said to him, 'This life is indeed
no life to me, *but* death.'

    And straightway he *ordered* him to be set up on the *rack*.[23] The
governor said to him, 'You do not *need* any one **(91 R ii)** to ask you—
do you want me to grant you some more days?' Bēsamōn the *advocate* said, 'Yes, that is his wish.' The *governor* said to him, 'What do
you want? (Say), and I will do it for you.' Jeremias[24] the chief
advocate said, 'My lord, this is indeed what he wishes—that you
should *bear with* him for a few days more; for his silence tells us
this; (we know) from his demeanour.' The *governor* said, 'Coluthus,
why don't you speak? Which do you want me to do—to *sentence*
you, or to be lenient with you?' The *righteous* man said to him, 'Do
what you like.' The *governor* said **(91 V i)** to him, '*Thus far* till now
I have been lenient with you. If you for your part will only be lenient
with yourself, then I shall be all the more pleased.' The *saint* said to
him, 'Your kindness constrains me to say a word more.'[25] The
governor said to him, 'Now I have *begun* to hear a good word from
you. *For* this kind of speech tells me that you want me to leave you
for a few more days.' The *holy* Coluthus said to the *governor*, 'What

---

[21] Cf. (e.g.) Hyv. *Actes*, p. 121 (Pisoura); E. W. *Macarius*, p. 110 (Kradjon & Amoun). For
ἀήρ in this sense, cf. P. Merton II, 82, 15 (2nd. cent.); *Apophthegmata Patrum*, ed. Chaîne
(*Le manuscrit copte*, etc.), p. 55 (No. 210).

[22] 91 R i 15–17: cf. *Coluthus* II, 17 V i 6 f.; Krumbacher, *Abh. d. kgl. bayer. Akad.* 24, 3
(1907), 35 (Menas, *graece*); Rossi, *Un nuovo codice copto* . . . . *Torino*, p. 74 (Philemon).

[23] 91 R i 27–29: cf. *Coluthus* II, 17 V ii 4 ff. For the nature of the ἑρμητάριον, see the
very full discussion by Vergote, *Ztschr. f. NT. Wiss.* 37 (1939), pp. 239 ff., where classical
sources and previous articles are cited. The definition in Lampe, *Patr. Gr. Lex.*, p. 549,
as 'stake' is misleading, since it is evidently a rather elaborate machine, which in the
martyrdoms is often made to fall apart by superhuman agency; so *Coluthus* II, 17 V ii 9 ff.

[24] The name suggests a person of Christian (or Jewish) origin or connections.

[25] This passage reminds us of places in the 'epic' martyrologies in which the martyr appears
to weaken, only to disappoint his persecutors (Delehaye *Mart. Ég.*, p. 154); cf. 92 R ii
26–V i 5, below; also *P. & T.* 74 R ii 16 ff.; 75 V ii 16 ff.

are these words of comfort which you are saying? I will *no longer*
listen to you and be *misled so as to* forsake **(91 V ii)** my God; *but* I
am *rather* confirmed in His *Faith*. And I am ready to bear anything
for the sake of His holy Name; for the *torments* of this *world* are
nothing, *but* the *torments* of God are great, and eternal, and there is
none who shall be able to hide in His presence.'[26]

The *governor ordered* a great stone to be hung upon his neck.[27]
The *governor* said to him, 'Coluthus, do not say a word to me about
anything but the matter which we are *hoping for*—that you will obey
the *law* of the Emperors.' *But* the saint spoke no word at all.

The *governor* said **(92 R i)** to him, '*Think scorn of* this vain glory
which will be of no profit to you! Turn now, man, and take for
yourself a glory worthy of respect.' The *saint* said to him, 'The glory
of my Lord Jesus *Christ* will preserve me for ever.' The *governor*
said to him, 'We are not *demanding* from you a contest of words
with us, *but* we are *demanding* from you an *urgent* matter—that you
should be *persuaded* by us and *sacrifice* to the gods.[28] *Well*, then,
consider with yourself.' The *holy* Coluthus said to him, 'Do not *detain*
me any more.'[29] The *governor* said **(92 R ii)** to him, 'You have been
ordered to be wise and not *show contempt of* the *court*.' The *holy*
Coluthus said to him, 'I have been wise all the time; and I came here
in pursuit of the wisdom of my Lord Jesus *Christ*.'[30] The *governor*
said to the members of the *entourage*, 'There, you see; I have used
every possible means with him in the hope of saving him; and you see
how he would not listen and be saved. I am *just* not going to *tolerate*
him for another single moment.' The members of the *entourage* said,
'*Sentence* him; he deserves to die, *for* he has *dared* to *mislead* us,
(92 V i) and he made us a promise and broke it, when he mocked us
and did not *sacrifice*.' The *holy* Coluthus said to them, 'I said no word
which it was not proper to say.' The *governor* said to him, '*Sacrifice*
and be sensible.' The *saint* said to him, 'I will not *sacrifice, neither* will
I listen to your stupid *arguments*.' The *governor* was angry, and said
to him, 'If you will not *sacrifice*, hear your *sentence*, which you have
earned: I *order* you to be burned alive.' The *holy* Coluthus said, 'I
thank Thee, my Lord Jesus *Christ*, **(92 V ii)** that I have been deemed
worthy of Thy grace, to die for the sake of Thy holy Name.'[31] And
he was taken out to be burned.

[26] 91 V ii 7–15: cf. *Coluthus* II, 17 V i 23–28; E. W. *Macarius*, p. 100 (Thomas of
Shentalolet).
[27] 91 V ii 16–19: cf. *Coluthus* II, 16 V i 26.
[28] 92 R i 14 ff.: cf. *Coluthus* II, 17 R i 15–23.   [29] Cf. *Phileas*, p. 48 f.
[30] Cf. Budge, *Mart.*, p. 38 (Victor); *PSBA* 32 (1910), 200 (Psote); Bal.-Hyv. *AM* I, p. 20
(Lacaron); Hyv. *Actes*, p. 61 (Macarius).
[31] Note that the final words of the martyr are not to be found in B.

Now [32] that day was the twenty-fourth of the month Pashons, and
the *holy* Coluthus fulfilled his *martyrdom*, and his *soul* was taken up
to heaven in glory, and he made festival with the *angels*, and all the
saints rejoiced with him through the *grace* and compassion of our
Lord Jesus *Christ*; with whom is the glory of the Father and the Holy
Spirit, for ever and ever, *Amen*.

[32] Here, as often in Coptic and contemporary Greek, γάρ does not mean 'for', but rather
'now, . . .'; this use is fairly frequent in the present group of texts.

SS. PAESE AND THECLA

(**49 R i**) The *martyrdom* of the *holy martyr* of *Christ*, the *holy* Apa Paēse, the man of Pousire,[1] and the *holy* Thecla his sister,[2] who fulfilled the *exercise* of their *contest* on the eighth day of the month Choiach, in God's *peace*, *Amen*.

It befell in the reign of Diocletian, the *lawless* emperor, who had provoked God and His *angels*, when Armenius[3] was *duke* in Alexandria, and Eutychianus[4] was *duke* in the Thebaid, that there was a man at the north of Shmoun,[5] in a 'hill called Pousire, whose name was Paēse. He was a (**49 R ii**) *good* man, performing great acts of charity to the poor people and the *orphans* and *widows* who were in that place. And that man had a great *household* in this *world*, and much lands and numerous cattle and asses and camels and sheep, and great wealth. That man, whenever he sheared his sheep yearly, was wont to assign a hundred sheep for wool for the *widows* and *orphans* and the poor and destitute who were in his village; and also at the second time of shearing his (**49 V i**) sheep he was wont to assign another hundred sheep for wool to those who were in his village, the poor and those in his neighbourhood. And again, in the time of harvest time (*sic*) he was wont to give a sheaf each to the *widows* and the strangers who were (employed) in his harvesting *every* two days. And his father Elias and his mother Mariam kept *urging* him, saying, 'Let us take a wife for thee, that we may see joy of thee before we die.' *But* he would not *endure* (this) at all, saying, 'I care not for a wife; *for* my sister married a husband, and behold, she has become a widow. (**49 V ii**) *Now*, she has borne a son; he together with her will suffice me.' And after some few days, his father fell asleep in a good old age; and his mother also fell asleep, being sixty-five years old, before the *persecution* came to pass.

But when the *lawless* emperor Diocletian began to reign, he published an *edict* throughout all the *countries*, saying: 'Whosoever shall not *sacrifice* to my gods shall die by the sword.' It befell that when the letters arrived at Alexandria, they were given to Armenius, the *count* of Alexandria. He read them out; the whole *city* was troubled (**50 R i**) because of what had happened. And many of the

---

[1] Βουσίρις is attested as the name of a village in a Hermopolite papyrus, P. Herm. Rees, 21, 9 (A.D. 346).

[2] The saints are found in the *Synaxary* under Kihak 8th.

[3] See Vandersleyen, pp. 86 ff. (especially p. 92) (cf. Lallemand, p. 255); Jones–Martindale–Morris, p. 108.

[4] See Vandersleyen, p. 89 f.; Jones–Martindale–Morris, p. 319.   [5] Hermopolis Magna.

Christians offered their *bodies* to death (*sic*)[6] and fire and sword and
divers manners of death; and the prisons were filled in *each* place
with men and women for the sake of the Name of *Christ*. And the
letters were bróught south to the Thebaid and were given to the
governor Eutychianus, and he *persecuted* the *Christians*. And great
numbers were cast into the prisons in *each* place. And Paēse the man
of Pousire would arise, and go into Shmoun and Antinoou, and cook
great meals, and prepare (**50 R ii**) wine, and load it upon his *labourers*
and servants, and journey and go to the prisons, and *urge* the saints
to eat of his *repast*. *And* the saints would see a shining crown
hovering over his head, and they knew that he too was a saint like
themselves; wherefore they would partake of his *repast*, and eat; and
they would[7] bless him, saying, 'May the Lord *grant* to thee the
imperishable crown in the heavenly Jerusalem; *for* behold, today thou
hast fulfilled the *charge* (**50 V i**) of *Christ*, (wherein) He says: 'I was
sick, and ye visited Me; I was in prison, and ye came unto Me';[8] and
again: 'Whosoever shall give to drink unto one of these little ones a
cup of cold water only in the name of a *Disciple, verily* I say unto
you, he shall not lose his re*ward*,'[9] *Now* thus he did for many days,
going to Shmoun and Antinoou and eating with the saints.

And he had a sister whose name was Thecla, who had married a
husband in the *city* of Antinoou; and she bore a son, and called his
name Apollonius; and she (**50 V ii**) sent him to school before the
persecution took place. And the husband of Thecla fell asleep; he
was a very rich man, and he fell asleep while he[10] was young. Thecla,
then, became a *widow*; and this woman was very well favoured in
her beauty. She was wont to go to the *church* and hear the words of
the *Scripture* with her son; and Thecla was wont to send and buy
much clothing and bedding, and load it upon her servants and send
them throughout the whole *city* and distribute them to the poor and
destitute. And thus she did until the completion of three years.
(**51 R i**) And from the time that the *persecution* began she was
ministering to the saints, *comforting* them; and her *charity* continued
in the prisons, as she cooked meals, taking them in to the saints, while
they ate from her hands. And whenever she saw one naked, she would
take him into her house and clothe him, and she would give him to
eat. And the *angel* of the Lord would appear to her often, and speak
with her; *and* often she would speak with him, saying, 'My lord, *help*
me'; and he would say to her, 'Even as thou hast clothed the naked,
(**51 R ii**) I will make thee also to be clothed, both thy *body* and thy

[6] Read 'water'?
[8] Mt. xxv, 36.
[10] The father, or the son?

[7] Till, *Kopt. Grammatik*, ed.[3], § 307.
[9] Mt. x, 42; Mk. ix, 41.

soul, in the *garments* of light; and whosoever shall give graveclothes to your *bodies*, I will *cover* their *souls* with the *garments* of light, that no *power* of darkness prevail over them.' *And* Thecla meditated within herself upon the word of the *angel* which he had said to her, 'Your *bodies* shall be clothed', saying,[11] 'What *then* will happen to me? Perhaps poverty is coming upon me, or the *wild beasts* are to devour me, and my *body* is to be buried in *charity*. But the will of God (51 V i) will be done.' *And* many rich men of the *city urged* her, saying 'We wish to take thee to wife'; but she was not *persuaded*, but *resolutely devoted* herself to the saints, binding up their wounds; to their *bodies*, subjected to *tortures*, she applied oil and wine.[12] The saints would hear her saying (*sic*)[13] 'May the Lord save you, thee and thy little son and thy brother, and may you come into the *number* of the saints and receive *inheritance* in the heavenly Jerusalem.'

It befell after this, that there was a man in the *city* of Shmoun who was a great *merchant* (51 V ii) in his (*sic*) *family*, being a kinsman (of theirs). And this man had much *wealth*; and it was he who bought the *flax fibre* of that whole nome;[14] and the name of that man was Paul.[15] And he was a God-fearing man, performing very many charities secretly. And that man was friendly with Paēse, *since* the latter sowed a great plantation of flax. *And* Paēse was *noble* and *rich* and famous in that whole nome. He would load the camels for the (*goods for*) *disposal*, (52 R i) and arise and go to the *city* of Shmoun to Paul the *merchant*; and Paul was glad whenever he saw Paēse, and he would keep him with him for a month at a time, while they ate and drank together, rejoicing exceedingly and conversing together upon the word of God. And it befell that in the month Parmhot (Parmoute) Paul the *merchant* arose and went off to Alexandria with his *merchandise*; and when he went into the *city*, he fell sick, (52 R ii) and he languished and came to the point of death. He wrote to the south to his servants, saying '*Quick*, join me, for behold, I am sick, and *perchance* I shall die; and say to my brother Paēse, 'If thou art willing to come, that I may see thee before I die, then come! Otherwise, I bid thee farewell.' It befell that when the letter came to the south, Paēse was informed. Straightway as soon as Paēse heard, his heart was very sorrowful, and he arose and took about the amount of one *pound* of gold, and (*goods for*)

---

[11] I.e. thinking.   [12] Cf. Lk. x, 34.
[13] Read 'would bless her, saying: . . .'
[14] On the cultivation of flax in the Hermopolite nome, see *P. Herm. Rees,* p. 41. On the word οἴππιον, see W. Girgis, *BSAC* 19 (1967–8), 60.
[15] O'Leary, *Saints,* p. 221; *Synax.* Amshir 9.

disposal, and boarded the boat. He left his *steward* set over his lands, and (**52 V i**) *managers* over his house, and went into Antinoou, and he went into the house of Thecla his sister, and said to her, 'Thecla, my sister, behold, my friend Paul has written to us, saying, "Come and let me see thee before I die." Now therefore, my sister, remember me in they prayers, for thou art a *devout* woman.' She said to him, 'My brother, I know that if thou goest away from me, and I do not come with thee, I shall not be able to endure (it) because of thee; indeed, *in general*, if ever I pass a *week* without seeing thee, I am most *afflicted*, (**52 V ii**) and I send my son Apollonius to thee in Pousire to bring me news of thee. If thou goest to this distant place and I do not hear news of thee, I shall die because of thee. Thou thyself knowest, my brother, that I have no brother *or* sister on earth beside thee.' He said to her, 'Do not be faint-hearted, my sister; *but* I shall go and satisfy him, for he is my friend; and if it is the will of God, I shall come to thee in *peace*.' Thecla loved him very much. She said to him, 'If *then* this is the way it is, go in *peace*, (**53 R i**) and come again in *peace*, that I may see thee before I die. And by thy health, my brother—*for* I know that thou wilt go into the prison of Alexandria to visit the saints—*please* to remember me and my little son, and perhaps God will count me also in their *number*.' Paēse answered, 'As the Lord lives, my sister, I will make them to bless thee before myself.' And she let him go with a kiss. *And* Paēse went into the prison of Antinoou, the place in which the saints were. They blessed him, saying, 'Go (**53 R ii**) in *peace*, our beloved brother!' One of the saints said to him, 'My brother Paēse, if we shall go before thee, we shall come to thee; if thou shalt go before us, come to us ourselves, and we will greet thee; for we shall not see one another again in the *flesh* until we go to the heavenly Jerusalem.' *But* Paēse did not understand the word which he said to him.

And thus Paēse came out, and when he had come out he went on board the boat, and sailed north till he came to Alexandria. And *while* he was on the way, God restored Paul to health; (**53 V i**) *since* (*sic*) *for* this thing came to pass from God, that He might separate the *persons* of the saints from their home. And when he came into Alexandria with the servants of Paul, they went into the house, and found him recovered from his sickness; and their hearts were relieved, and they *greeted* one another, he and his servants, and he said to them, 'Is he well, my friend Paēse, and his God-loving sister Thecla?' They said, 'Here is Paēse, outside the door.' He was angry with his servants, and he arose and came out, and cast himself down on (**53 V ii**) the ground and did him reverence upon his face. *And* Paēse was much moved, and they fell upon each other's necks and wept

for a great while. Paul said to Paēse, 'Come in; why dost thou stand
outside? Come in, thou man worthy to be loved by God and men.'
Paēse said, '*Verily*, my brother, I was glad when I found thee well.'
Paul said to him, 'God has given me a little chastisement for my sins;
I thank God and the prayers of the saints—(God) Who has given me
strength and healed me.' And he took him into his (**54 R i**) house,
and he himself rejoiced with him, and they ate and drank together.
And on the morrow Paēse came through the *city* with his servants,
and he went into the prison and sought after the saints. And one of
the saints said to him, '*Hail*, Paēse, thou man of God, and *blessed*
Thecla thy God-loving sister, and Apollonius her little son, *according
to* the oath which thou didst swear to her when thou wast about to
leave her, saying, "I will remember thee, and will cause thee to be
blessed before me"; may the Lord remember her and bless her and
her little son, (**54 R ii**) and may He count you in the *number* of the
saints.' And it befell that when he heard these words, he wondered
greatly at what he had heard from the holy *martyrs*; and Paēse said
to him who was speaking with him, 'Whence dost thou know me, my
holy father?' He said to him, 'Since this night when I arose, performing my *devotions*,[16] the *angel* of God told me that thou wast
coming to me, and (that) He had counted thee in the number of
the saints, thee and thy sister and her little son, and Paul, the man
with whom thou art lodging.' He came (**54 V i**) away from him,
with his servant, and he cast himself down before the saints, and
they blessed him, and he came away from them, he and his servant,
wondering at the words which the saint had said to him. And he
went into the house of Paul, and he said to him, 'I desire, my brother,
that thou do this little thing for me.' Paul said to him,' Tell me what
thou wilt, and I will do it for thee.' Paēse said to him, '<I> wish that
thy servants go with me, since I am a stranger in this *city*, that I may
buy a little wine and some few articles of food, and let them (**54 V ii**)
cook it for me, that I may load them with it, and they may come
with me to the prison, so that I may eat with the saints before I come
home to the south.' *And* Paul was very glad when he heard this. He
gave orders to his servants, and they went straightway and bought
everything which he ordered them. And Paēse made a great *expen-
diture* upon bread and wine and oil, as much as a hundred articles of
food; he himself bought them, and when the servants of Paul had
cooked the food, he loaded them with it and took it into the prisons
that day, and he *urged* the saints to eat (**55 R i**) from his hands; and
Paēse had his loins girt up, *ministering* to the saints. On the morrow
again he went into another of the prisons, and he informed us

16 See Lampe, *Patr. Gr. Lex.*, s. v.

concerning (*sic*)[17] the imprisoned saints, and gave them to drink.
And after he had spent fifteen days in Alexandria, visiting the sick
and the saints daily, and (*sic*)[18] he said to Paul, 'Let me go off to the
south; for thou knowest that it is the *season* to work on the land;
and I know that my sister is troubled concerning me.' Paul said, 'I
myself will come with thee. Why art thou (**55 R ii**) thus troubled
and faint-hearted? *But* stay for this *week*, and we will[19] go off
together; why shouldst thou go and leave me?' And Paul himself
devoted two days to the saints in the prison, and Paēse was going
with him and his servants, he *ministering* to them, since Paul was
afraid to go to the prison lest he should be spoken about to the
duke, and he should seize him and *sacrifice* (*sic*).[20]

After this, on the twentieth day of Parmoute, the emperor
Diocletian *sent into exile* a (**55 V i**) youth whose name was Victor,[21]
who was the son of a great *general* of the emperor. He was brought
into Alexandria bound hand and foot in *chains* of iron, and there
was a *gag*[22] in his mouth. The *courier*[23] gave the letters to the *duke*,
and he had them read to the whole *city*. He *ordered* him to be taken
into the prison. The *citiz*ens wondered, saying, 'If he has not spared
the son of the great *general* of his empire, then will he spare the
poor people of the *cities*? And the whole multitude of the *city*
(**55 V ii**) was troubled about the saintly youth, the *holy* Victor,
since he was very fair of face, and he was the only son of his father.
On the morrow the *duke* sat in the *theatre* to hear (the case of) the
holy Apa Victor. The *citiz*ens heard, and assembled together, men
and women, rich and poor, so that they might see the son of the
general. It befell that when Paēse heard the things which the multitude
was saying, that he wondered; and he too was walking with the
people, (**56 R i**) desiring to see the youth Victor. The *duke* gave
orders for severe *punishments* and *tortures* to be inflicted upon him,
and he did not *feel* them at all. And straightway the eyes of the *holy*
Apa Paēse were opened, and he saw the *angel* of the Lord standing
by him, giving him strength so that he could endure the *tortures*.
The *duke ordered* him to be cast into the stoke-hole of the bath, and

---

[17] Read 'he fed the saints'.   [18] 'And' is superfluous.
[19] Till, *Kopt. Grammatik*, ed.[3], § 304.
[20] Perhaps 'and <should make him> sacrifice'.
[21] The hero of a considerable body of Coptic hagiographical literature; see O'Leary, *Saints*,
pp. 278 ff.; *Synax.*, Barmoudeh 27.
[22] χάμος is frequently found in the martyrologies; not in L&S[9], but cited in Sophocles and
Lampe.
[23] The regular word is βερεδ άριος (*veredarius*); the form **ΒЄΡЄⲀⲰⲚ** perhaps arises from
confusion with βέρεδον: Sophocles s.v. 'a body of infantry'.

a fire was stoked over him with *axle* (*sic*) wood[24] and vine wood. And
an *angel* of the Lord came from heaven, and unloosed the iron *chains*
which were upon his hands (**56 R ii**) and feet, and gave him strength.
And when the *duke* saw, he was very angry, and *ordered* him to be
beheaded. And the *citi*zens would not allow them, saying, 'We will
not allow the son of the *general* to be killed in our *city*.' He *ordered*
him to be *sent into exile* south to the Thebaid. As for Paēse, when
he saw the great miracles which the holy Apa Victor was performing,
the Holy *Spirit* descended upon him, and he said within himself,
'Behold, the son of the great *general* of the emperor has renounced
his great (**56 V i**) *dignity* and all his *possessions*, and has offered up
his *body* as a *sacrifice* to our Lord Jesus *Christ*; and he has not obeyed
the *ordinance* of the emperor, *but* has taken up his *cross* and followed
his Lord,[25] having fulfilled that which is written in the Holy *Gospel*,
which says: 'Whoso shall forsake father, and mother, and daughter
(*sic*), and wife, and house, and lands, shall receive them manifold, and
shall *inherit* eternal life.'[26] Now therefore, how long do I sit still
watching these great honours being received by the saints? *But* now
I myself will arise (**56 V ii**) and take up my *cross* and follow my Lord
Jesus *Christ*. *Am* I myself as good as[27] this royal youth?' As the
blessed Apa Paēse was saying this in his heart, he came into the house
of Paul, and they ate together at noontide. And Paul said to Paēse,
'My brother, dost (*sic*)[28] thou see this great man today, how he has
endured these great *tortures* for the Name of *Christ*?' Paēse said to
him, 'Yes, my brother, I was greatly moved.' They continued talking
together about his honour. And the Holy *Spirit* descended upon the
holy Apa (**57 R i**) Paēse. He was up betimes on the morrow, and
came out with his young servant, and he gave him twenty *solidi* and
set him free, and said to him, 'Take these for thyself and live on
them, for they are all that remains of the gold which I brought with
me.' And straightway he went to the *praetorium*, and cried out,

---

[24] The word is very variably spelt in the martyrologies. Till (following Jernstedt) translates
ϥⲉ ⲛⲁⲍⲱⲛ in *KHML* I, p. 97 (Panesnew) as 'Feuerbohrer'. It is plain, however,
from other contexts where it is mentioned in parallel with other kinds of wood or
vegetable tinder (e.g., Hyv. *Actes*, p. 49 (**ⲁⲣⲍⲱⲛ**); ib. 310 f., with vine-wood and
σφονδύλιον) that a particular species of wood is meant. Its occurrence in Hyv. *Actes*,
p. 311,1 (**ⲟⲍⲓⲛⲟⲛ**); 323, 1 (**ⲟⲍⲓⲟⲛ**) show it to be 'beech', *Fagus silvatica*; see
L&S[9] s. v. ὀξύα (var. ὀξέα); Hyvernat (*Actes*, p. 323) had already deduced this,
translating 'hêtre'. For the properties of beechwood as fuel, see MacGregor Skene,
Trees (Home University Library, 1927), p. 142.

[25] Cf. Mt. xvi, 24; Mk. viii, 34; Lk. ix, 23.

[26] Mt. xix, 29; Mk. x, 29 f.; Lk. xviii, 29 f.

[27] It might at first seem that we should insert **ⲁⲛ** here and read 'Am I myself <not> as
good as . . .?' But B's text reads 'Am I as good as a single servant of . . .'; which makes
good sense.

[28] Read 'didst'.

saying, 'I am a *Christian, confessedly*!' The *duke* said to him, *'Evil wretch*! Whence art thou, *and* what is thy name?' The *blessed* man answered, 'If thou dost enquire my name, Paēse is my **(57 R ii)** name, and I am a man of Pousire in the nome of Shmoun.' The *duke* said to him, 'And why hast thou come here?' The *blessed* man said to him, 'It is God who has brought me here, that I may enter into His holy *contest.*' The *duke* said to him, *'Sacrifice,* do not perish *miserably*! Hast thou not heard about the son of the emperor's *general*? If I did not spare that man, shall I spare thee?' The *blessed* Apa Paēse said to him, 'Thou hast *well* said; if the son of the *general* did not *sacrifice* to thy gods, but has followed **(57 V i)** the God of heaven, Jesus *Christ*, mayest thou know what thy gods are not gods, *but inanimate* (*things*). *But* my Lord Jesus *Christ* has power in all things.' When the *duke* heard this, he was very angry, and said to him, 'Thou hast contemned (our) lords the emperors and their revered gods. By the *fortune* of (our) lords the emperors and their revered gods and the health of Apollo, I will make thy *body* ashes and cast it into the *sea*, and then will I know what god it is that has power to save thee from my hands.' **(57 V ii)** The *blessed* Apa Paēse answered and said to him, 'I know that my Lord Jesus *Christ* is with me; and as for thee, He will give thee great *punishments* in hell in the day of the true judgment.' The duke hearing this *ordered* him to be stripped of his clothes and bound hand and foot and placed upon the *rack* and scraped by eight *tormentors*, four and four by turns, until the bones of his *body* were laid bare. Afterwards he had six flaming *torches* brought and placed under **(58 R i)** his sides, until the odour of his *flesh* was diffused exceedingly. And straightway he lifted up his eyes to heaven, and cried out, saying, 'My Lord Jesus *Christ*, Lord God *Almighty*, Who dost save those who *hope* in Thee, hear me, and send me Thine *angel*, that he may give me strength until I fulfil my *contest* and put this *lawless* one and his *unlawful* emperor too to shame. Glory to Thee for ever and ever, *Amen.*' As he said this, lo, the *angel* Raphael came from heaven, and he shattered **(58 R ii)** the *rack*, and the *chains* which were fastened to his hands and feet were unloosed, and the *torches* were quenched. And the hands of the *tormentors* stiffened and became like stone.[29] The *angel* said to him, 'Fear not, Paēse; God has sent me to thee, that I may give thee strength and save thee until thou fulfil thy *contest* in *peace*. Furthermore, the place wherein thy *body* shall be laid, I will *minister* to it for ever.' The *angel* stretched forth his hand and stroked his whole *body*; **(58 V i)** and straightway he was healed *as if* he had never been *tortured* at all. And the hands of the

[29] Cf. I Kings xiii, 4.

tormentors were bent upon themselves, and they were unable to extend them; and the *tormentors entreated* him, saying, 'Be thou *pleased* to heal our hands.' And straightway he *signed* them (with the Cross), saying, 'In the Name of the Father, and of the Son, and of the Holy *Spirit*; may He (*sic*)[30] *grant* you healing.' And straightway they were healed.[31] And the holy Apa Paēse said to the *duke*, 'Be shamed, *lawless* one, for (**58 V ii**) my Lord Jesus *Christ* is with me, and behold, He has sent His *angel* to me, and he has healed me from thy *torture* which thou didst inflict upon me.' Armenius the *duke* was angry, and said to him, 'O Paēse, *wilt* thou also perform works of *magic* even as this *unholy* man Victor, who has disgraced his *dignity*? And his *magic* has not been able to save him from my hands.' The *blessed* Apa Paēse said to him, 'Hold thy peace, thou *impious* one, and cease blaspheming against the living God.' Armenius was very angry; he said to the *blessed* (**59 R i**) Apa Paēse, 'By the seventy[32] revered gods, I will make thy *flesh* into little pieces.' The *duke ordered* him to be bound and laid upon his belly and dragged upon by twenty men, and he made the soldiers flog him with thongs of raw hide until the earth was drenched with his blood, and his *body* was all torn, and the bones of his elbows and his back were wrenched apart with the dragging upon him. Further, the *duke ordered* unslaked *lye* to be brought and put upon his *body*, and (**59 R ii**) vinegar to be poured upon him, and his whole *body* was set on fire and burned like a *torch*, so that they said[33] that he was dead. And as he was lying on the earth, he was unable to raise his head for the pain of the *tortures* which were in his *body*; and he was weeping, saying, 'God, my God, why hast Thou forsaken me? me?'[34] *And* the *duke* cried out, 'Thou hast been shamed, O Paēse; why has not Jesus come to *help* thee and save thee from my hands? *Since* there is no god who is powerful like Apollo.' As the *duke* was saying this, (**59 V i**) lo, the *Archangel* Raphael came from heaven and stood over the *body* of the *blessed* Apa Paēse, and he said to him, 'Be strong, O Paēsə, and fear not; I am with thee. Arise, and stand upon thy feet, and go and confront this *lawless* one, and shame him and his creations of (men's) hands.' *And* the *angel* of the Lord stretched forth his hand over the *body* of the *blessed* Apa Paēse; and he arose in strength *as if* he had not been *tortured* at all. *And* the whole multitude, when they saw what had happened, wondered (**59 V ii**) exceedingly, seeing the *blessed* Apa Paēse with no hurt in his *body*, and they cried out, saying, 'Great is the God of the *Christians*, Who gives strength to those who *hope* in Him.' The *duke*

[30] This type of formula, with its confused construction, occurs several times in our texts.
[31] Cf. I Kings xiii, 4–6.   [32] The traditional number in the martyrologies.
[33] I.e., thought.   [34] Ps. xxii, 1; Mt. xxvii, 46; Mk. xv, 34.

when he saw what had happened was greatly troubled, and *ordered* the *blessed* man to be cast into prison until he had *considered* what he should do to him. And straightway he was taken to the prison, with his young servant following him, weeping. When he was taken to the prison, the saints saw him (**60 R i**) and they *saluted* him, saying, 'Thou art *well* come to us today; we see thee daily, *but* today we rejoice the more with thee because thou hast come into the bridechamber of *Christ* with they whole heart.'

Paul was in his house, and he did not know what had befallen Paēse. *But* his servant went weeping, and told him what had befallen him. *And* Paul when he heard this laid hands upon his clothes and rent them, and wept with sore weeping, saying, 'O that I had let him go home! *For* he was distressed, *entreating* (**60 R ii**) me (and) saying, "Let me go away", and I did not let him. I would rather have lost twenty *pounds* of gold today than that this should have happened. What use is *wealth* of gold and silver to me compared with a friend who is sweet and good? There is another great *sorrow* in my heart because of his sister; she will say "This befell him because of thee." ' All his servants rent their clothes, and they wept, for they loved him greatly. Paul arose, and went to the prison. He saw Paēse with the (*marks of*) *torture* upon his *body*, and he cried out, weeping, and saying, (**60 V i**) 'The pain of my heart is great today, O my brother; O that I had lost all that I had rather than that this should have befallen thee. I do not know what I shall say to thy sister.' Paēse said to him, 'Dost thou *then* hate me, because I have been counted to the *lot* of the saints? This is my joy, for which I seek, that God has redeemed me from my sins.' And thus he and the saints consoled him. He went to his house *peace*ably. He did not eat *or* drink for three days and three nights, and he fell sick of *bilious humour* because of Paēse. His servants came back and told (**60 V ii**) Paēse: 'If Paul comes to thee to visit thee, let him eat with thee; for lo, these three days he has not eaten *or* drunk because of thee.' And when Paul came to the prison to visit his friend Paēse, Paēse said to Paul, 'Constrain thyself to eat a little bread with the saints today.' And when Paul heard this, he went in haste to his house, and prepared a *repast*, and brought it into the prison, and ate with the saints. When they had finished eating, Paēse said to Paul, 'I (**61 R i**) wish to see Thecla my sister before I die.' Paul said to him, 'My brother, lo, thy servant is here; I myself will send another servant of mine with him, and they shall go south and tell thee (*sic*)[35] what has befallen thee...'[36] Paēse said to him, 'No, my brother, we will wait

---

[35] Read 'her' (with D).

[36] The omission here is supplied by D, which reads: '. . . what has happened; and if she hears that this has befallen thee, she will die'; if Thecla is not informed by a reliable and tactful messenger, the shock of the news about her brother will be fatal.

here until the Lord brings her here to us; and if it be yet the will of
the Lord to separate us from one another, then let His will be done.'
And in that night the *angel* Raphael appeared to him, and he said to
him, '*Hail*, thou man worthy to be loved by God **(61 R ii)** and men.'
It befell that when Paēse saw the *angel* of the Lord, he fell down
upon his face; and he raised him up, and gave him strength. The
whole prison shone like the sun; the saints saw the light, and were
amazed. The *angel* said to them, '*Peace* (be) to you all.' And they
cast themselves down and did reverence to Paul, and he [37] gave his
blessing. The *holy* Apa Paēse said to the *angel*, 'My lord, I wish to
see my sister before I die.' The *angel* said to him, 'It will be seven
days *yet* before thy sister comes to thee here and thou seest her;
and I will fill her **(61 V i)** with power through the power of *Christ*;
and your *souls* and *bodies* shall not be separated from one another.
When thou risest in the morning, the *duke* will send for thee and
set thee upon the iron bed and kindle fire underneath thee; and I
will quench the fire, and overshadow thy *body* so that the flame
of the fire shall not *vex* thee. Be strong, and play the man; for thou
shalt be in the *lawcourt* of this *lawless* one, and shalt shame him for
seven months.' The *blessed* Apa Paēse answered and said to the *angel*,
'I am ready, my lord, to **(61 V ii)** bear any suffering for the Name of
my Lord Jesus *Christ*.' And the *angel gave salutation* to the *blessed*
Apa Paēse, and went up to heaven in glory.

And on the morrow, Armenius sat on the *tribunal* in the *theatre*;
and he *ordered* the *blessed* Apa Paēse and all the saints to be brought
to him bound hand and foot in iron *chains*, with *collars* on their
necks, the *tormentors* going with them till they brought them on to
the *tribunal*. When the *duke* saw them, he said to the *blessed* **(62 R i)**
Apa Paēse, 'O *magician*, thou hast tasted the *tortures* of the *lawcourt*,
and hast learned that they are evil. Now therefore *sacrifice* to the
revered gods;[38] do not perish *miserably*.' The *blessed* man said to
him, 'Thou hast been shamed, thou and thine abominable gods.'
Hearing these words, the *duke* was very angry. He *ordered* him to be
set upon the iron bed, and fire to be kindled underneath him by
eight *tormentors*. And straightway the *angel* Raphael came from
heaven, and overshadowed him with his shining wings, and remained
speaking with him of the **(62 R ii)** heavenly *mysteries*; and the fire
did not *harm* him at all. The *tormentors* were kindling the fire underneath him from the second hour of the day until the sixth. *And* when
the *duke* arose to *withdraw*, he *gave orders*, saying, 'Take up his ashes
and cast them into the *sea*'; for he thought that he was already dead.

---

[37] The angel; see D's fuller text here.
[38] 62 R i 2–9: cf. Till, *KHML* I, p. 95 (Panesnew).

But the *holy* Apa Paēse came out of the midst of the fire by the
power of the Holy *Spirit*, with the *angel* of the Lord standing by
him, holding his hand, as he stood in the midst of the multitude,
with no hurt (**62 V i**) upon him. When the multitude saw this great
wonder which had come to pass, they cried out, saying, 'One is the
God of the holy Apa Paēse, and there is none beside Him!' And the
number of the people who *believed* on that day was twenty-four
souls; they stood and contemned the *duke* and also the *lawless*
emperor and his abominable gods. *And* the *duke ordered* them to
be taken outside the *city* and beheaded. And thus they fulfilled their
martyrdom on the second day (**62 V ii**) of the month Pashons, in
peace, *Amen. And* the *duke* turned to the *blessed* Apa Paēse and said
to him, 'Art thou satisfied now that this has happened, and all these
have died on thine *account*?' The blessed Apa Paēse answered and
said to him, 'When thou goest to thy *lawless* king, *art* thou not wont
to send before thee some presents? So it is with myself; I have sent
these before me as presents to my King, *Christ.*'[39] The *duke* said to
him, 'Once *again* thou dost contemn (our) lords the emperors. By the
health of Apollo, (**63 R i**) I will not eat and I will not drink until I
have destroyed thy *sorceries*.' And he *ordered* a furnace to be stoked
from noon time till evening time, and he had pitch brought, and his
whole *body* was smeared with it up to his head; and he had him
fettered with iron *chains*, and his feet were bound to his neck, and
he was cast into the bottom of the fiery furnace; and it was burning
fiercely, inspiring fear and amazement. And the *duke ordered* them
to cover up the furnace and seal it, and to *withdraw* until the morrow.
(**63 R ii**) *And* the *blessed* Apa Paēse prayed at the bottom of the
furnace, saying, 'Hearken to me today, my Lord Jesus *Christ*, and
help me; Thou Who didst save the three *Saints* in the burning fiery
furnace,[40] mayest Thou hear me also, me, Thy servant, in this hour
of *necessity*. Thou Who didst hear the *prophet* Daniel when he was
in the lions' pit,[41] mayest Thou save me today! Thou Who didst
send Thine *angel*, and he saved Thy servant Victor from the stoke-
hole of the bath,[42] mayest Thou send him now again today, that
he may save me (**63 V i**) from these great *tortures*.' While the *blessed*
Apa Paēse was saying this, Raphael the *angel* of the Lord came down
from heaven, and stood at his right hand, and made the flame of the
furnace like a dewy breeze blowing at morning time upon the earth.[43]
And the holy Apa Paēse was sitting in the midst of the fire like one
who has come out of the *burning sun* and has sat upon a cool (*stone*)

[39] 62 V ii 9–27: cf. (e.g.) Hyv. *Actes*, p. 58 (Macarius).   [40] Cf. Dan. iii, 19 ff.
[41] Cf. Dan. vi, 16 ff.   [42] See above, 56 R i f.
[43] Cf. Song 3 Holy Ch. 26 f.

slab, by reason of the power of the *angel* who was watching over him; and the *chains* which were bound to him were loosed; and the pitch dropped from his *body* . . . [44] was *cleansed* (**63 V ii**) like one who has washed in a bath before going to a *banquet. And* the *angel* of the Lord made <the> walls of the furnace to burst open, and he brought the *righteous* Apa Paēse out of the midst of the fiery furnace with no hurt upon him at all. The *angel* of the Lord said to him, 'Fear not, O my beloved Paēse, these tempo*ral tortures*; for I am with thee, giving thee strength.' The *angel* of the Lord walked with him. It was midnight, and he took him into the house of Paul, to the *bedchamber* in which he was sleeping; (**64 R i**) and the *angel gave* him *salutation*, and went up to heaven in glory. *Now* Paul was sleeping, grieving for Paēse, not knowing what had befallen him. *And* the *blessed* Apa Paēse awakened Paul; *and* Paul, when he opened his eyes and saw his friend Paēse, was amazed, because a *bright light* was glowing at him within his *bedchamber* continuously; and *since* he did not understand the thing which had befallen him, the *blessed* Apa Paēse said to him, 'Fear not, my brother; I am Paēse.' And it befell that when Paul heard (**64 R ii**) the voice of his friend Paēse, he arose straightway in haste, and cast himself at his feet, and reverenced him joyfully; and straightway he raised him up, and they both embraced one another. Paul said to Paēse, 'I have learned today that God saves those who *hope* in Him.' And they sat down, and talked together of the great (works) of God, and the miracles which He performs for His saints. The *blessed* Apa Paēse said to Paul, 'By thy health, my brother, if I had known that God is with His (**64 V i**) *Christian* saints like this, then I had been numbered among them since the first day that the *persecution* came to pass. *But* this is the time at which it has pleased my Lord Jesus *Christ* to summon me to His holy bridechamber. *For* it is written, that he who came at the eleventh hour has received the wages of the whole day.'[45] Paul said to him, 'By thy health, my brother, since the time when thou wast taken to the *tribunal* yesterday, I have neither eaten bread *nor* drunk water.' And straightway he aroused his servants; and when they had seen the *blessed* Apa Paēse, they reverenced him, (bowing) down (**64 V ii**) to the ground, and *greeted* him. *And* Paul gave orders to his servants, and they prepared a *table*; and they ate and drank together, and they slept until the light spread abroad. The holy Apa Paēse arose, and went to the prison. The saints saw him, and were glad, and *greeted* him. He told them how the *angel* of the Lord had saved him from the fiery furnace. *And* the man who was set over the prison,

[44] Omission in A; supply (from D): 'like cool water; and his *body* . . .'   [45] Mt. xx, 9 ff. .

when he saw the holy Apa Paēse, arose and cast himself down and reverenced him, saying, '*Verily* there is no other god with power save Jesus *Christ*. (**65 R i**) Remember me also, and may your grace attend me.' And the saints blessed him, saying, 'May the Lord call thee to the *number* of the saints who are in heaven.'

When morning was come on the morrow, the *duke* said to those of the *entourage*, 'Go and see whether the furnace is sealed as before, and open it and see whether this *lawless Christian* is alive; *for* he said, "My God has power to deliver me from thine hands." ' *And* they went and did as the *duke* commanded them; and they found the furnace sealed as before. They uncovered it, and the fumes of it (**65 R ii**) rushed up and burned the heads of the *tormentors* who were around the furnace, and all three of them died.[46] And no one could approach the furnace, for it was burning very fiercely. The *duke* was informed about what had happened. He said, 'By Apollo the great god, the fire has *consumed* his bones. Let him come now and contemn (our) lords the emperors and their revered gods.' *And while* he was *yet* speaking, lo, one of the *tormentors* came and said in the presence of the *duke*, 'Lo, Paēse is within the prison with no hurt (**65 V i**) upon him at all; *but* he is like one *rejoicing* in good wine.'[47] Armenius was amazed. He said to the *tormentor*, '*Evil wretch*! Perhaps it is one who is like him; the bones of that man have become ashes altogether.' The *tormentor* said, 'Dost thou desire me to go and bring him into thy presence, that thou mayest know whether it is indeed he?' He said to him in anger, 'Go, bring him! By the health of Apollo, if it is not he, I will cut out thy tongue, that thou mayest not *dare* to utter (such) words in my presence again.' And accordingly (**65 V ii**) the *tormentor* went to the prison, and he cast himself down before the *blessed* Apa Paēse and *entreated* him, saying, 'May thy mercy attend me, O my lord and father, and do thou come with me to this *lawless duke* and shame him. *For* as for me, I *believe* and *confess* that there is no god save Jesus *Christ*.' As he was saying this, the *holy* Apa Paēse arose and walked with him, and came and stood in the presence of the *duke*. The *duke* when he saw him made a loud noise with his nose,[48] and smote his hands together and said to those around him, '*Verily* (**66 R i**) I have heard (the cases of) many *Christians*, (but) I have not seen such *magic* as the *magic* of this man Victor, and Paēse, this *Christian magician*.' The *holy* Apa Paēse answered, 'Dost thou not know that thy *tortures* will have no power over me, while my Lord Jesus *Christ* is with me?' The *duke* said to

---

[46] Cf. Dan. iii, 22; Song 3 Holy Ch. 25.   [47] Cf. Zech. x, 7.
[48] I.e., snorted. See Drescher, *Le Muséon* 82, 90 ff.

him, in anger, 'Behold, thou hast *dared* to contemn me! By the health
of Apollo, I will make thy *flesh* into little pieces. For I know that it is
by reason of thy *sorceries* that thou hast escaped from the furnace.
But I will *chastise* thee *sorely*.' *And* the *duke* (**66 R ii**) was saying,[49]
'If I *torture* him again and he escapes, he will shame me in the midst
of the multitude.' *And* the *duke ordered* him to be cast into prison
until he decided what to do to him.

And in that night the *angel* of the Lord came to him, and spoke
with him, saying, '*Hail*, thou man worthy to be loved!' *And* the holy
Apa Paēse when he saw the *angel* reverenced him. And the *angel* gave
him his hand, and raised him up, and said, 'Be strong, and play the
man,[50] and contend for thy (**66 V i**) Lord; and it will be four more
days before I bring thee Thecla thy sister, this (woman) strong of
soul; and she shall *satisfy* thine heart, and shall shame the *duke* and
his *lawcourt* and his abominable gods; and she shall perform great
miracles, and great multitudes shall be converted to God by reason
of her.' Apa Paēse said to the *angel*, 'My lord, thou hast relieved me,
if my sister is not to be separated from me.' The *angel* said to him,
'I shall go to this *lawless duke*, and bring upon him a great sickness,
(**66 V ii**) so that he will not seek after thee until thy sister has come;
and he shall not be relieved from the sickness till thou shalt come in
to him and heal him.' When the *angel* Raphael had said this, he bade
him *peace*, and came away from him. He went and brought a great
sickness upon the *duke*, and he went up to heaven in glory. When
morning came, the saints arose to bring (*sic*)[51] their *devotions*; and
they saw the holy Apa Paēse with great *grace* in his countenance,
and they all knew that it was an *angel* of God who (**67 R i**) had
appeared to him.

On the morrow, the *duke* fell sick with a great sickness. He cried
out, saying, 'It is this *lawless* one Paēse who has bewitched me with
his *sorceries*, so that I have fallen sick.' His wife[52] said to him, 'I said
to thee, Have nothing to do with the *Christians*, and thou didst not
listen to me. *For* it is their God Who fights for them; he has power
to save them.' He answered and said to her, 'If Apollo the great god
gives me healing, and I rise (from my sickness), I shall know what
to do to that *unholy* one.' (**67 R ii**) And the *duke ordered* them to
raise him up and lay him down beneath the *plinth* of the (statue of)
Apollo; and he commanded them to anoint him with sweet-smelling
oil. Thereafter, he made them offer up *incense* on the altar. And he
vowed him a vow, saying, 'Apollo, if thou heal me from the *magic*

---

[49] I.e. thinking.
[50] Cf. I Sam. iv, 9; I Kings ii, 2; I Cor. xvi, 13.
[51] Read 'make'.
[52] The Bohairic text names her Dorothea; see above, p.72.

of this *magician* Paēse, I will *present* great *gifts* to thy temple; *for* I
know that thou art able to *chastise* him.'

It befell after all this that Thecla was very sore at heart for her
brother (**67 V i**) Paēse. She said, 'Perhaps my brother is no more. It
is now a full month and a half since he went, and he has not returned,
neither has he sent me news of himself. I will arise and go to the saints
in the prison and enquire about him from them.' The God-loving
Thecla arose, and went to the prison to receive blessing from the
saints. One of the saints said to her, 'Thecla!' She said, 'Bless me, my
father.' He said to her, 'Why hast thou not gone to the wedding feast
of thy brother Paēse? *For* behold, (**67 V ii**) the wedding feast is
celebrated with great rejoicing. *For* it is an *angel* of the Lord who has
said to me: 'Say to thee (*sic*)[53] : "Go to the wedding feast of thy
brother." ' *And* Thecla said to him, 'Perhaps my brother has died,
my father. If so, tell us, that I may go and bring his *body* home; for
I have no brother or sister, *but only* him, and my little son.' The
holy man said to her, 'As the Lord lives, he has not died, *but* is alive;
and now today he is in great joy. And lo, a multitude of people have
assembled for his wedding. (**68 R i**) Arise, *then*, and go in *peace*; and
if it is the will of God, then we too will come to the rejoicing of thy
brother, for he is our friend.' The God-loving Thecla did not understand the *import* of his speech; *but* she arose and came out upon the
quay of Antinoou. She found a little ship with the *angel* Raphael
standing upon it, and Gabriel sitting (there), and *Saint* Mary, the
Holy *Virgin*, and Elizabeth the mother of John the *Baptist* sitting
in the prow of the ship. *Now*, she thought that the *angels* were
sailors, (**68 R ii**) and that the ladies were *gentle*women. *And* she
said, 'My brethren, whither are you thus bound?' They answered,
'With God's will we are bound for the *city* of Alexandria.' Thecla
said to them, 'Can you *please* take me on board with you, that I
may seek my brother?' They said to her, 'Go and bring thy *baggage
quickly*; come, let us sail with this southerly wind.' *And* Thecla said
to them, 'My brethren, let one of you see to my *baggage*.' *And* they
said to her 'Go, bring it; we will settle with thee; lo, these other
*gentle*women (**68 V i**) are embarked with us; do thou pay the fare
thyself as they will.' *And* Thecla loaded the *baggage* upon her servants,
and she brought about the amount of a *pound* of gold, saying, 'I will
spend a little upon the saints, and will give a little beside as a gift to
my brother.' She took the keys of her house, and gave them to
Apollonius her little son, and she said to him, 'My son, be not faint-
hearted till I return; and do not neglect the saints, but go and take

[53] Read 'her'

care of them; *even* as thou seest me doing, do thou also.' Apollonius
said (68 V ii) to her, 'By thy health, O my mother, if thou goest to
the saints who are imprisoned, and seekest them out, let them bless
me also.' She said to him, 'By thy health, O my son, if God and the
prayers of the saints protect me until I see my brother Paēse safe,
I will cause them to bless thee before me.' And she *gave* him
salutation, and came away from him, her servants following her and
giving her farewell. And the *angels* put all her *baggage* on board, and
she embarked with one serving-woman of hers only. (69 R i) The
angels put the ship out, and set sail northwards, for the south wind
was blowing. *And* Thecla thought that the *angels* were sailors; and
she said to them, 'My brethren, take a little wine for yourselves, and
a few pieces of bread, and a little fish, and eat, because you have
taken trouble with me.' *But* they said to her, 'What thou thyself
carest to give with thine hands, give it to us; for we will not touch
any of thy *baggage*, lest thou say "These men have undone my
baggage." ' *And* Thecla bade her serving-maid give them what they
needed—for she thought (69 R ii) that they were men in the *flesh*.
And when evening came, she saw the ladies sitting with their countenances sad. Thecla said to them, 'My sisters, why are your
countenances so sad?' Elizabeth answered, 'My sister, I do not wish
to be sad; (but?) my husband [54] and my son have been beheaded for
this Name of Jesus; and, behold, they have come for me, saying, 'Let
us go to a wedding in Alexandria.' Thecla said to her, 'And this (our)
sister too?' The holy *Virgin* Mary said to her, 'My Son was set upon
a wooden *cross* for the *race* (69 V i) of men.' Thecla said to her,
'*Verily*, my sisters, you have received great sorrow. To what *city* do
you belong? I indeed do not know you.' They said to her, 'No; we
are from Jerusalem.' The holy *Virgin* Mary said to her, 'I was
dwelling in the *city* of Shmoun,[55] I and my little Son feeding at my
breast; and I left that place, and my Son grew up, till He was thirty
years old; and the Jews *crucified* Him; and behold, I am going to a
wedding in Alexandria.' Thecla said to them, 'Sisters, tell (69 V ii)
me, whom are you going to visit in Alexandria?' They said, 'We
are going to visit Paul the *merchant*, who holds a marriage feast for

---

[54] On the traditions in Christian apocryphal literature about the violent end of Zacharias, hus-
band of Elizabeth and father of St. John the Baptist, based on the identification of him
with Zacharias the son of Barachias (Mt. xxiii, 35; Lk. xi, 51; cf. the tradition of II Chron.
XXIV, 20–22?), see A. Berendts, *Studien über Zacharias-Apokryphen und Zacharias-
Legenden*, Leipzig, 1895; ibid., *Die handschriftliche Überlieferung der Zacharias- und
Johannes-Apokryphen*, Texte u. Untersuchungen XXVI, 3 (Berlin 1904); Hennecke-
Schneemelcher, *Neutestamentliche Apokryphen* I, pp. 255; 279; 290; II 534; 565;
C. C. Torrey, *The Lives of the Prophets*, J. B. L. Monograph Series I (Philadelphia 1948),
pp. 29 ff.; with the present passage cf. Till, *KHML* I, p. 6 (Nahrow). (We owe these
references to Mr. J. -D. Dubois of The Queen's College Oxford.)
[55] The tradition of the sojourn of the Holy Family in Hermopolis was generally familiar to
early Christianity, and not confined to Egypt. For some sources, see M. Jullien,
'Traditions et légendes coptes sur le voyage de la Sainte Famille en Égypte', *Les*

a man named Paēse, from Pousire.' Raphael said to her, 'I know that thou art Thecla, the daughter of Elias. It was for this reason that we took thee on board; otherwise we should not have taken thee on board.' And the ladies embraced Thecla, and kissed her mouth and her head; and they said to her, 'If thou art the sister of Paēse, we rejoice with thee.' She arose forthwith, and made ready a *table*, and she laid upon it many *dainties*, and wine; (**70 R i**) *for* she thought that they were people in the *flesh. And* Thecla was attending and *ministering* to them; for they appeared *as if* eating. They said to her, 'Listen to me (*sic*),[56] Thecla; we speak with thee; *for* even as thou hast attended upon us, and *ministered* to us, who are strangers whom thou dost not know, it behoves us also to attend upon thee and thy brother and thy little son.' She said to them, 'Forgive me, my brethren; I am *quite* unworthy to sit down with you.' *Now* it was the night when there was no moonlight. And (*sic*)[57] the light of God was filling (**70 R ii**) the whole ship; and the sail sped the whole (*sic*) ship exceedingly. Thecla said to them, '*Verily*, I have never seen a night like this.' . . . [58] They said to her, 'Hast thou not heard that "the night shall be clear as the day?"'[59] And again: "When the *Saviour* went up into the ship with His *Disciples*, there arose a great commotion; and the *Saviour* arose, and He *rebuked* the winds and the *sea*; and there was a great calm."[60] *Now* we are *disciples* of that One.' And the *Virgin* Mary brought out a *vessel* of green hue, full of sweet-smelling oil of great price; and she poured it (**70 V i**) upon the head of Thecla, and anointed her whole *body*. The God-loving Thecla said to her, 'Forgive me, my Lady Mother; I am not worthy of this great honour which thou hast given to me.' The Holy *Virgin* said to her, 'If thou wert not worthy of it, it would not be poured upon thee. *For* this is the oil of the wedding of my Son, which I have brought for the wedding of thy brother.' Thecla said, 'What hast thou added to this oil? *Verily*, I have never seen any like this.' The Holy *Virgin* said to her, 'None will find this ever (*sic*)[61] save those who are worthy of the wedding of my Son.' And Thecla slept; (**70 V ii**) she was lulled by reason of the odour of the oil. The Holy *Virgin* Mary said to Gabriel and Raphael, 'Moor the ship here, and bid this other friend to the wedding.' And they moored the ship at Tammah,[62] in the nome of Memphis, and went into the house of

---

Missions Catholiques 19 (1887), 9–12; 20–24; O. Meinardus, *In the Steps of the Holy Family from Bethlehem to Upper Egypt* (Cairo 1963), pp. 45 ff.

[56] Read 'us'.   [57] Read 'But'?

[58] There has evidently been a substantial omission here in A; D continues: 'As the sail was bearing the ship along, and (*sic*) the *angels* were sitting in the stern of the ship; they did not move an oar backward or forward, and the ship sailed northward steadily. Thecla said to them, '*Verily*, I have never seen a ship like this ship.'

[59] Ps. cxxxix, 11 f.   [60] Mt. viii, 24 ff.; Mk. iv, 37 ff; Lk. viii, 23 f.
[61] Read 'oil'.   [62] See Amél. *Géogr.*, p. 474 f.

the chief *presbyter* of the village. They saw his little daughter, about twelve years old, whose name was Heraei.[63] And the *God-bearing One* put her hand upon her head, and blessed her, saying, 'Hasten, meet me at the wedding; *for* I have already prepared for thee thy *bridegroom*.'[64] When she had said this, they (71 **R i**) came out of the house, filled with joy of the Holy *Spirit*, and they sailed northward. Thecla said, 'My Lady, why didst thou not tell her parents, so that they might send her with us? How shall the young maiden come alone?' The Holy *Virgin* Mary said to her, 'Hast thou not heard what is written in the *Gospel*: 'Whoso shall not leave father and mother and brother and sister, he cannot be My disciple''?'[65] *But* as for Thecla, her *mind* did not penetrate (the meaning of) these words.

They reached a little village called Sheremoun,[66] and saw the river vexing it. The *Virgin* said to it, 'Leave this village alone, (71 **R ii**) and do not vex it; for it is written, "If a grape is found in the cluster, they are wont to say, Do not spoil it, for there is a blessing of the Lord in it; blessed be the Lord for ever".'[67] And lo, there came a voice from heaven over the river, saying, 'There is no *foundation course* surrounding it.' The Holy *Virgin* Mary answered, 'My Son has already prepared the bricks; lo, another four months, and a *foundation course* will be built for it, and a wall for three generations.'[68]

And they sailed northward. *And* early on the morrow they moored at the *city* of Alexandria, and they arose and came to the shore. Thecla said to them, 'My brethren, do you (71 **V i**) know the house of Paul? If so, go and have the *goodness* to call my brother to load up my *baggage*; for I do not know the place, because I have never come to this *city*.' They said to her, 'Leave thy serving-maid with thy *baggage*; come, and let us show thee the place where thy brother is.' And she walked with them, and they brought her to where the prison was, and they stood by; and the *Virgin* said, 'Thecla, hast thou not recognized me?' She said, 'No, my Lady.' She said, 'I am Mary, the Holy *Virgin*, who bore God, the *Word*, Whom the Jews *crucified*; and this one whom thou seest (71 **V ii**) is Elizabeth, the mother of John the *Baptist*; and these two other people whom thou

---

[63] Heraei (= 'Ἡραΐς) of Tammah is the young virgin martyr, the heroine of the martyrology published by Rossi, *I papiri copti del museo egizio di Torino* I, v, pp. 32 ff., where she is said to be not yet fourteen years old. She is also prominent, as a historical figure, in Hyv. *Actes*, pp. 78 ff. (Apater & Irai). We hear no more of her later in the present text.

[64] Cf. Rossi, op. cit., p. 37 f.   [65] Lk. xiv, 26. Cf. Rossi, loc. cit.

[66] See Amél. *Géogr.*, p. 425 (s. n. ϪⲈⲘⲘⲞⲨⲚ); the locality cannot now be traced; this, as A. observes, might be because the river eventually overwhelmed and obliterated it.

[67] Isaiah lxv, 8.

[68] The point of this story is somewhat obscure. This is regrettable, since it has the flavour of genuine local tradition.

seest, who (were) on board the ship, are Gabriel and Raphael, who
stand in the presence of God.' When Thecla heard this, she fell down
upon the ground on her face, and became as one dead. The Holy
Virgin reached out and raised her up, and said to her, 'Hast thou
not heard what is written in the Holy *Gospel*, where my Son says
to His *Apostles*, "It is not ye that have chosen <Me>, *but* it is I
that have (72 **R** i) chosen you"?[69] Now, therefore, it is my Son
Who has chosen thee. Be not faint-hearted, *but* courageous; and,
behold, I have already prepared for you your houses and your
thrones and your crowns in the holy *city* of my Son, the heavenly
Jerusalem. *For* behold, I have anointed thee with the holy oil,
which flows down to the *lamp* of the firstborn;[70] and I have given
thee strength thyself; and, lo, I have appointed the *Archangel*
Raphael to watch over you and give you strength until you have
fulfilled your *contest*. Go in *peace*; be strong, fear not!' And she
gave her *salutation*, (72 **R** ii) and she went into the prison. The Holy
God-bearer Mary and Elizabeth went up to heaven, while Thecla
gazed after them.[71]

When she went into the prison, she made a great *banquet* for the
saints, and sought after her brother. She found him fettered with
the saints, with great *grace* in his countenance like an *angel* of God.
She approached him, and kissed him, and said to him, 'My lord and
my brother, dost thou wish to go to the Kingdom of Heaven and
leave thy *wretched* sister in the *torments*? Why didst thou not send
for me (72 **V** i) and my little son? If it were I that found distinction,
I should tell thee first.' Paëse answered and said, 'By thy health, O
my sister, I went to send for thee; (but) the *angel* of the Lord would
not allow me; *for* he said to me, 'It is I who will bring her here to
thee.' And he appeared to me this night, saying that thou comest
here today.' When he had said this, she came away from him, and
put up her *baggage*, and took it to the prison; and she made a great
banquet <for the> saints that day. (72 **V** ii) And she told them
everything she had seen in the ship, and what the Holy *Virgin* Mary
had said to her; and the saints of God all wondered, and gave glory
to *Christ* Jesus. And Thecla said to her brother Paëse, 'My brother,
what dost thou wish me to do with the small *bounty* which I have
brought with me?' He said, 'Send it south to thy son Apollonius,
and he shall spend it upon the poor and the saints. Lo, Paul will go
south; and write to him to care for his[72] house; for this is the way
in which the Lord has ordained for us.'

---

[69] Jn. xv, 16.   [70] Cf. Zech. iv?
[71] Cf. Acts i, 9 f.; a regular cliché in the martyrologies.
[72] Apollonius'; see 82 V i 22, below.

(**73 R i**) It befell after this that the *duke* suffered, sleeping in the
temple of Apollo, and he was not relieved. His wife went to him and
said to him, 'How long wilt thou sleep here? Behold, thou hast not
been relieved of thy sickness. Arise, and come home, and I will send
for the holy Apa Paēse, that he may pray for thee, and thou wilt be
relieved.' The *duke* was angry, and said, 'Come, and *sacrifice* to
Apollo, and *entreat* him, and he will *grant* me healing.' *But* she said
to him, 'I will not *sacrifice*, *neither* am I sorry for thee.' When the
duke saw that (**73 R ii**) he got no relief, he had himself taken home;
and he *urged* his wife, saying, 'Send for this *Christian*, Paēse; perhaps
he will heal me from (?)[73] his *sorceries*.' *And* she sent for the holy
Apa Paēse; and when he came, his wife came out to meet him, and
cast herself at his feet; and she raised him up (*sic*)[74] and she
entreated him, saying, 'My lord, have pity on this *wretch*, and *give*
him *remission* from this sickness until the day when the Lord shall
require him and his *lawless* emperor, and reward them *according to*
their works.' (**73 V i**) *And* the *duke* said to the holy Apa Paēse, 'I
know that thou art angry with me because I have inflicted all these
tortures upon thee; *but* I know that thou art merciful, and all thy
brethren; come, and lay thine hand upon me, and I shall be whole.'
And the holy Apa Paēse laid his hand upon him, and said, 'In the
Name of my Lord Jesus *Christ*, mayest Thou (*sic*)[75] give this *wretch*
remission from his sickness until he shall come into Thine hands,
and Thou shalt chastise him.' And he *signed* him (with the Cross),
and came away from him, and went to the prison. The *duke ordered*
a great present to be borne behind Apa (**73 V ii**) Paēse to the prison.
And the saints did not eat of it, because it was a portion of *idol*
(*sacrifice*); they gave it to those who were imprisoned. The saints
themselves ate of the *dainties* which Thecla had brought with her.
On the morrow, the *duke* arose from his sick (bed). His wife said
to him, 'Behold, the God of the *Christians* has given thee health.
Set them free; thou hast no concern with them; *lest* they be angry
with thee, and thou die, even as thy son who died on thine account.'[76]
The *duke* was angry, and said to her, '*Evil wretch*! Shall we *then* set
at naught (**74 R i**) the *commandment* of the emperor for *magicians*?'
His wife was angry, *for* her mind was in God, and she said to him,
'I shall see thee again being shamed by the *Christians*.' The *duke*
sent for the *blessed* Apa Paēse, and said to him, 'If I send for thee,
saying "*Sacrifice* to the gods", say "I will *sacrifice*", and give me

---

[73] ⲉⲃⲟⲗ ⲍⲛ̄⁻ = 'from'; hardly 'by'. In 76 V ii the duke accuses Paēse of bringing his
illness upon him by sorcery.

[74] Read 'he raised her up'.   [75] See p. 159, n. 30.

[76] There is no reference to this incident elsewhere in this text.

honour in the presence of the whole multitude and the *entourage*; and
I will cease from anger against thee for the sake of this word only,
since thou dost disgrace me in the presence of the *entourage*; for, by
the health of Apollo, I do love thee in my *soul*. And I will write south
to the *duke* of (**74 R ii**) the Thebaid concerning thee, that he set thee
over ten villages *besides* thine own; and as for all thy lands, I will have
all their *public charges* remitted for thee. *For* I am informed that
thou art a great man and rich, a *wealthy public tax* payer, and *noble*,
and of a most esteemed *family*.' The *blessed* man said to him, 'I will
obey thee even as thou hast said.'[77] He came away from him, and
went to the prison. Presents were brought him from the *duke*. And
he told the saints about the *purport* of the speech, and they gave
glory to God, Who saves those who *hope* in Him.

On the morrow, the *duke* sat (**74 V i**) on the *tribunal*, and he
ordered the *blessed* Apa Paēse to be brought to him. And the *tormentors* bound him hand and foot, and put a *collar* on his neck, and
brought him out of the prison. *And* his sister arose, and spread out
her hands to heaven, and prayed, saying, 'O God *Almighty*, Who
didst send Thy beloved Son to the *world*, so that He ransomed us
through His *Body* and His holy Blood, and set us free from the
slavery of the *Devil*; mayest Thou give strength (**74 V ii**) to me and
my brother, that we may fulfil Thy salvation and Thy will; for
Thine is the glory and the power, with Thy beloved Son Jesus *Christ*
and Thine (*sic*)[78] Holy *Spirit*, for ever and ever, Amen.' The *blessed*
Thecla arose, and walked with her brother in great fortitude. *And*
when they reached the *tribunal*, they stood in the presence of the
duke. The *duke* said to him, 'O Paēse, come and *sacrifice* to Apollo
the great god, and go home in *peace*.' This brave-*souled* (woman)
answered, 'If thy god has power, why (**75 R i**) was he not able to
heal thee of thy sickness?' The *duke* was *confounded* by reason of
this speech; he said, 'Who is this who *argues with* me thus?' They
said to him, 'It is the sister of Paēse.' The *duke* said, 'I have said
myself that it is an impudent *breed*.' And he said to her, '*Sacrifice*!
Do not perish *miserably*!' She answered, 'I will not *sacrifice*.' He
ordered her to be set up on the *rack* and scraped until her rib bones
were laid bare. *And* this *blessed* woman endured this *torture* with
great fortitude. Thereupon he had both her breasts slashed, and he
(**75 R ii**) had four burning *torches* brought, and they were put under
her sides. The *blessed* Thecla endured these *tortures* with fortitude.
She lifted up her eyes to heaven, and said, 'My Lady Mary, thou
Holy *Virgin*, thou and thy beloved Son Jesus *Christ* have called us

[77] Cf. p. 148, n. 25. Note, however, that D's reading has the opposite sense.
[78] Read 'the', with D.

to this *contest*, and thou didst covenant with us to give us strength till
we fulfil our *contest*; now therefore give us strength in this great
necessity!' And straightway the *Archangel* Raphael came from heaven,
and he stood at her right hand and said to her, 'Fear not!' And he
quenched the *torches* (**75 V i**) which were under her sides, and he
healed her breasts *as if* she had never been *tortured* at all; and he
broke the *rack* and it fell into two pieces. She stood with great fortitude in the presence of the *duke*, and said to him, 'These are thy
tortures; the Lord Jesus *Christ* shames thee and thy *lawless* emperor
too.' The *duke* was very angry; he said to her, 'By the *sovereignty* of
the Romans, I will make thy *body* into pieces and give it to the *wild
beasts* and the birds,[79] and then will I see what god will be able to
save thee from my hands.' Thecla answered and said to him, 'He
Who (**75 V ii**) gave me strength the first time, He also it is Who will
save me from thy *tortures*.' *And* those of the *entourage*, when they
saw her with no hurt in her *person*, cried out, giving glory to the
God of the *Christians*, Who saves those who *hope* in Him. The *duke*
said to the *blessed* Apa Paēse, '*But* as for thee, thou hast given me
a *word*, and thou canst not *cheat* it.' The *Saint* said to him, 'Thou
art godless, thou and thy father the *Devil*.'[80] The *duke ordered*
their heels to be pierced, and *chains* to be inserted into them, and
a stone to be bound to their necks, (**76 R i**) and that they be hung
up head downward till their blood dripped from their mouths and
noses. The *duke withdrew*, and left them hanging up under *torture*.
And lo, the *angel* Raphael came from heaven, and he brought slumber
upon those who guarded the saints. He took them down, and broke
their bonds, and took their hands and brought them to the prison.
And the saints saw them, and were very glad; *for* they were praying
for them. And when the soldiers arose, and (could) not see the saints,
they were dismayed, and rent their garments. They went and told
(**76 R ii**) the *duke*, saying, 'Lord, these *magicians* brought slumber
upon us, and while we slept, they fled; and we do not know where
they have gone.' The *duke* was angry, and sent to the prison, and
he found the saints with no hurt upon their *persons* at all. *And* on
the morrow the *duke ordered* the saints to be brought to him upon
the *tribunal*. The *duke* said to them, 'These works of *magic* will not
be able to save you from my hands. *Now*, *sacrifice* to the revered
gods.' The *blessed* Thecla said to the *duke*, 'Let Apollo (**76 V i**)
walk, and come to me here, and I will worship him.' The *duke* said
to her, 'I will make the priests raise him up and bring him to him
(*sic*).'[81] The holy Thecla answered, 'I never yet saw a god raised up

---

[79] Cf. I Sam. xvii, 44.   [80] Cf. Jn. viii, 14.
[81] Read 'thee'.

and brought to men; *but* our Lord Jesus *Christ* is wont to go to every one and save those who *hope* in Him. If Apollo is a god, let him hold back the sun and the moon in the sky,[82] and say to the *sea*, "Be divided", and it be divided.'[83] As the *duke* heard this, he was filled with anger, and he said to her, 'Apollo too is a *magician* (**76 V ii**) like[84] the *Christians; for* he is a *world-ruling* god.' The holy woman said to him, 'If Apollo is a living god, when thou art sick again, let him heal thee.' The *duke* was angry, and said, '*Evil wretch*! Dost thou *then* wish me to be sick again? *For indeed* thou and thy brother have bewitched me, so that I was sick; *but* the great god Apollo *helped* me, and healed me.' *And* the *duke ordered* them to be seated upon an iron *chair*, and he had the skin of their heads chafed; *and* he *ordered also* their heads to be pierced with a carpenter's awl, and boiling pitch to be poured (**77 R i**) down on to their *brains. Furthermore* the *duke ordered* olive wood to be brought, smeared with bitumen; and he had it laid out on the ground till it was two cubits higher than their heads, and he *ordered* it to be kindled with fire; and it burned fiercely, *so that* a great flame arose, and none could bear to stay near it.[85] And lo, the Holy *Virgin* Mary came from heaven, with Gabriel and Raphael, and they came to the saints. She said to them, 'Be firm and strong; my Son is with you.' And she *signed* them (with the Cross), in the Name (**77 R ii**) of *Christ*. All the (*marks of*) *torture* which were on their *persons* were healed; and she made the fire to be like a dewy breeze[86] blowing at the time of early morning; and she blessed them, and went up to heaven in great glory. Those of the *entourage* said to the *duke*, 'Our lord, their bones are burned up.' And he laughed and said, 'Now let this worthless woman come and *argue* with me again. *For* there is no god powerful like Apollo and Artemis.' *While* he was saying this, lo, the *angel* Raphael came from heaven, and brought the saints out of the fire, with no hurt upon them, *neither* (**77 V i**) did their *bodies* smell of fire.[87] They cried out, saying, 'Be shamed, thou and thy *lifeless* Apollo.' The whole multitude saw what had happened, and they gave glory to the God of the *Christians, Christ* Jesus, Who saves those who *hope* in Him. And the number of those who *believed* on that day was forty people, with eight soldiers of the *entourage*. And the *duke ordered* them to be taken outside the *city* and beheaded; and they fulfilled their *martyrdom* on the twentieth day of the month Epēp, in (**77 V ii**) *peace, Amen*.

And the *duke ordered* the saints to be taken to the prison until the morrow. *And* it befell that at midnight the *angel* of the Lord

[82] Cf. Josh. x, 12.
[83] Cf. Ex. xiv.
[84] I.e., 'as good as'?
[85] Cf. Dan. iii, 22; Song 3 Holy Ch. 25.
[86] Cf. Song 3 Holy Ch. 27.
[87] Cf. Dan. iii, 27.

came to him (*sic*), and set the holy Apa Paēse upon his shining wings, and took him to heaven, and showed him the holy *city*, the heavenly Jerusalem; and all the saints came out to meet him, and they *greeted* him, and showed him the *city* of *Christ*, with its *streets* encrusted with precious stones, it being brighter than the sun. The *angel* of the Lord took him and showed him a house exceedingly spacious; (**78 R i**) *and* that house was encrusted with stones of divers hues, emitting *rays* of light, the *pillars* being firmly set; and that house was (built) *colonnade* upon *colonnade*, with twenty *pillars* supporting each of the *colonnades*, emitting *rays* of light; the *pillars* which were upon the south side of the house numbering sixty-five, and the rest (*sic*) on the north side; and the other thirty *pillars* on the west side, and above (*sic*) the house, there being established upon it a hundred *pillars*, very precious; *for* it was built like a *church*.[88] 'And I looked to the east (he[89] said), and I saw a great *throne*, with twelve (**78 R ii**) steps therein leading up to the *throne*. *Now*, great was the splendour of that *throne*, with great trees forming a crown round about it, laden with *fruit*, and their fragrance was diffused exceedingly. And I saw a royal diadem above the *throne*; and I saw garments of linen, their *panels* (?)[90] hung with *pearls*, above the throne. And I saw four *thrones* under each *pillar*, one on each side, spread with great splendour, with a crown of *pearl* upon each *throne*, and a tree growing *at each pillar*, with (**78 V i**) the *branches* of each one spread out over the *thrones*. And I, Paēse, saw a great *laver* of the colour of fire, with a golden *pillar* beneath it, and four golden *pipes* under the *laver*, on *each* side, and the four *pipes* flowing at all times like a *fountain* of water, and *bowls* of gold and *pearl* in the *laver*. And there were soldiers in the house, even to the number of a hundred soldiers, *wearing* gold and fine linen, with golden *torques* upon their necks, and with golden girdles girt upon their loins, each of them measuring five cubits in length; no man on earth could *wear* their like; (**78 V ii**) it was a wonder to see them. I said to the *angel*, 'My lord, what is the fashion of this house? There is no king of this *world* who will be able to build such a house as this.' The *angel* said to me, 'By thy health, O my beloved Paēse, all the kingdoms of the world are not worth a single *pillar* in this house.' I answered and said to him, 'My lord, to

---

[88] This passage (78 R i 9–28) contains two serious corruptions, and is so confused as to be hardly translatable. The Bohairic version is clearer: '. . . the *pillars* on the south side numbering 65, and (read **ⲟⲩⲟⲍ**) another 65 being on the north side, and another 65 on the east of the house; on the under side of the house there being established 100 *pillars*, which were precious; it was built like a *church*.' A's first error is **ⲛⲕⲉⲥⲉⲉⲛⲉ** for **ⲛⲕⲉⲥⲉⲧⲏ** ; the second is **ⲍⲓⲧⲛⲉ ⲙ̄ -** , behind which probably lies misunderstanding of **ⲍⲣⲁⲓ̈** as 'up' instead of 'down' in a previous version.

[89] Sc. Paēse.　　[90] No comparable use of πλάκιον is cited in the lexica.

whom does this house belong?' The *angel* said to me, 'This is the
house of Apa Victor, the son of Romanus the *general*, who
renounced his *dignity* and all his *possessions*, and having taken up
his *cross* followed his Lord; wherefore so great an honour has been
given to him.' **(79 R i)** *And* I said to him, 'My lord, tell me about the
fashion of this house, and all these *thrones*, and these trees which
are spread out over them, laden with *fruit*.' He said to me, 'Thou
seest all these *thrones* and these trees which are spread out over them;
these are the resting-places of every man who shall glorify a saint
upon earth.' *And* I said to him, 'My lord, how (is this)? Tell me about
this fashion.' And he answered and said to me, 'If a man build a
martyr-shrine in the name of a saint, *or* one clothe the *body* of one
in graveclothes, *or* one give an *offering* on the day of a saint, **(79 R ii)**
or give an alms to the poor and the strangers on the day of his commemoration, *or* give a *gift* to the house of a saint, *or* produce a book
for the house of God in his name, *or* buy a *Gospel* and place it in his
martyr-shrine for a memorial to him—*in short*, as much as a single
piece of bread which a man shall give, he will find it (repaid), when
he comes out of the *body*, through the *bodies* of the saints. *For
indeed* the *martyr* is wont to go to the *Almighty*, and cast himself
down and worship, saying, 'My Lord, grant me this *soul*, because it
comforted me in this *world*.' *Now* if it is defiled **(79 V i)** by many
sins, the utterance is wont to come from the mouth of Michael,
saying, 'The Lord *Almighty* has said, "Give it a few severe *punishments*, (and) afterwards I will *grant* it to thee"'.' And straightway it
is delivered to the *tormentors*, and they plunge it in severe *punishments*; and afterwards they bring it up as white as *snow*, and it is
given to the saint who had obtained grace for it, and he takes it into
his house and clothes it in a splendid garment, and seats it upon the
throne, and sets upon it the imperishable crown, and it eats of the
good things of the trees **(79 V ii)** and enjoys everlasting rest.[91] Thus
it is with every one who shall glorify a saint upon earth; wherefore
are these *thrones* and these trees in the houses of all the saints, and
these four *fountains* of water which flow into this *laver* which is in the
houses of the saints, so that they may drink from them.' *And* I said
to the *angel*, 'My lord, they are mingled together.' *And* he said to me,
'They cannot be mingled; *but* the one which each one desires comes
to him.' *And* I said to him, 'My lord, who are these soldiers who *wear*
such great splendours as these?' The *angel* said **(80 R i)** to me, 'Thou
seest these soldiers; they are *angels* attending and *ministering* to the
saints; and when the lord of the house comes through the *city*, they

---

[91] This very express account of the doctrine of purgatory is perhaps not without interest.

go before and behind him, glorifying him.' *And* I wondered greatly
that man of *flesh* and blood should *inherit* these great splendours for
the sake of a little suffering which he will receive on earth for the
Name of the Lord. I said to him again, 'My lord, tell me concerning
this thing also: If a *presbyter* or a *deacon* be in the house of a saint,
and waste the *offering* which is given to the *shrine* in **(80 R ii)**
profligacy, what of him?' The *angel* said to me, 'Listen, and I will
tell thee. If any one in the *city* or in the village give an *offering* to
the *shrine* of a saint for the salvation of his *soul*, he[92] will require it
of the *administrator*; *for charity* is given without asking of questions.
And if the *presbyter* or the *deacon* or the *administrator* performs the
service of the saints *properly* without *neglectfulness*, and he is
zealous for it with (true) *zeal*, when he comes out of the *body*, the
saint takes him into his house, and makes him to sit upon a *throne*,
and sets upon him **(80 V i)** a crown, and has him *ministered to well*.
If, however, he keeps eating and drinking in profligacy, wasting the
offerings which are given to him in the name of the saint, the saint
causes him to be taken into severe and unrelieved *punishments*. This
is what awaits the *administrator* who does not practise uprightness
in the house of God.'[93] *And* when I, Paēse, heard this, I was greatly
troubled, and I wondered. The *angel* said to me, 'Hast thou not
heard concerning the sons of Eli, what befell them?'[94] The *angel*
took my hand again, and took me, and showed me another **(80 V ii)**
house like the first one, there being a hundred *pillars* under that
house, and four *thrones at each pillar*, and a *laver* in the midst of
the house, and a tree growing *at each pillar*; and the *laver* which was
in the midst of the house was filled from the four rivers.[95] And I
saw three *thrones* exceedingly lofty and splendid, with trees round
about them, laden with *fruit*, and a crown of *pearl* upon each of the
thrones. The *angel* said to me, 'Thou seest this house; it is thine, and
thy sister's and thy friend Paul's. Lo, your three crowns are prepared
for you; one for your lot as a stranger,[96] **(81 R i)** one for your blood
which shall be shed for the Name of *Christ*, and another one because
of your *chastity*. *And* your *bodies* shall be in a single *shrine* on *earth*.'
And I said to the *angel*, 'My lord, thou hast honoured me exceedingly
(and) *beyond* measure. *But* my house is small *in comparison with* the
first one.' He answered and said to me, 'Dost thou not know that the
honour of a king is one thing, and the honour of a *magistrate* another?'

---

[92] The Saint, presumably. [93] Cf. Hyv. *Actes*, p. 67 (Macarius).
[94] Cf. I Sam. ii, 4.   [95] Is the reference to conduits, or to the four rivers of Paradise?
[96] Cf. (e.g.) Hyv. *Actes*, p. 170 (Pirou & Athom). Egyptians of every age regarded exile
   from home, even in another part of Egypt, as great hardship; hence its prominence here,
   as a trial which wins the martyr especial merit.

And after this he took my hand, and brought me to the place from which he had taken me. And I was wondering at the *blessings* which God will give to His saints in reward for the sufferings which they shall endure on earth.'

And it befell that when the *angel* had brought Apa Paēse into the prison, he *gave* him *salutation* and went up to heaven (**81 R ii**) while the *blessed* man gazed after him.

And it befell that when the saints arose in the morning, they saw the holy Apa Paēse with his countenance full of joy, and his garments were diffusing a sweet odour; and they knew that he had seen a vision. And they adjured him, saying, 'Thou must tell us of all that thou hast seen, and not hide anything from us.' *And* the holy Apa Paēse told them about all that he had seen; *and* the saints when they heard this gave glory to God for the *blessings* which they were to receive from the Lord.

And it befell after this that the *duke* sat on the *tribunal* in the *theatre.* He *ordered* the saints to be brought to him, and he said, (**81 V i**) 'Will you *sacrifice* or not?' The saints answered, 'A single word is wont to suffice a wise man;[97] but as for the fool, thou art wearied in teaching him; he does not *perceive.* For so says Solomon the *sage*: 'Reprove a wise man, and he will love thee; (but) teach not a fool.'[98] *But* if thou wert a wise man, thou wouldst not say this word another time.' When the *duke* heard this, he said, 'Art thou (*sic*)[99] *then* stupid and a fool?' He *ordered* straightway that their tongues should be cut out, and their eyes plucked out and put upon their hands; and he had stakes brought and fixed in the ground, and the saints stretched (**81 V ii**) toward them till their bones were wrenched apart. After this, he *ordered* to be brought tar and pitch and *bitumen* and *lye*, and they were put into a *cauldron*, and fire was kindled under them until their boiling rose up exceedingly high; and he had the mouths of the saints opened with iron tongs, and (it) was poured down into their mouths. And straightway the *Archangel* Raphael came from heaven, and made the *cauldron* like cool water, and he made it sweet in the mouths of the saints like honey. *And* the *duke* arose, and *withdrew* and left the saints lying in the *theatre.* The *angel* (**82 R i**) of the Lord touched the saints, and he raised them up and healed them from their *tortures*; and he gave sight to their eyes, and their tongues were set right, and they spoke, and blessed God. And he *signed* them (with the Cross), and went up to heaven in glory. The holy Apa Paēse and his sister Thecla hastened and met the *duke* coming out from the bath, being

[97] See p. 146, n. 14, above.   [98] Prov. ix, 8.
[99] Read 'Am I . . . ?'

about to go to *breakfast*. They said to him, 'Thy *tortures* have been put to shame; behold, the *angel* of the Lord has come and *granted* us healing in all our *members.*' When the multitude saw the [*members*] of the saints (**82 R ii**) healed, and their eyes open, and their tongues speaking, they cried out, saying, 'Great is the God of Apa Paēse . . .'[100] The *duke* went home; he did not eat *or* drink, from *bilious humour*. *And* his wife said to him, 'Why dost thou not eat *or* drink? *Perchance* the *Christians* have performed some miracles in thy presence, and thou hast been *confounded.*' *And* the *duke* said to her, '*Evil wretch*! *Now* I know that thou art serving Jesus; wherefore thou speakest for these *Christian magicians*. By the health of Apollo the great god, I will behead thee with the sword on their (**82 V i**) *account.*' *And* she answered and said, 'Would indeed that I were worthy of this great honour.'[101]

And the *duke* had the saints brought into the *prison; and* Thecla was bearing the (*marks of the*) *tortures* which were upon her *body*, and she was *ministering to* the saints with what was hers. *And* the holy Apa Paēse said to Thecla, 'Why hast thou not written a *letter* to thy son Apollonius, that he may take care of his house and may not continue expecting us? I for my part have given what belongs to me to Paul, that he may give it as charity, since I do not know the day when the Lord will require me.' And Thecla took *paper*, (**82 V ii**) and wrote to her son, saying thus:[102] 'Before all else I ask concerning thy health, O Apollonius, my sweet little son. *Just as* I left thee on my way to Alexandria, now, then, lo, our Lord has called us to His holy *contest*. Do not be faint-hearted, O my son. I wander through the strange land; and all our fathers were strangers; *for* our father David has said, 'I am a sojourner, sojourning *as* all my fathers did.'[103] Do not say that I have died; it is the death of the *Apostles* and *Prophets* that I have died. By thy health, O my son, do not forsake the *Faith* of *Christ* (**83 R i**) Jesus our Lord; and regard the saints, that they may pray for thee that thou mayest be saved. *Now* it is some holy writings which will be brought to thee. By thy health, O my son, see to thy young servants, and give them each an *ounce* of gold for the sake of their livelihood; and distribute my clothing to the naked; and perhaps God will put it into the heart of someone to wrap my own *body* when the Lord visits me. And go down to the

---

[100] There seems to have been an omission here in A. The Bohairic reads: '. . . and Thecla his sister. The holy Paēse and his sister went away to the prison; and . . .'

[101] The Bohairic here has a passage which, though hardly essential to the narrative, seems a sensible enough addition: 'She also said: 'I am weary of entreating thee to leave the *Christians* alone; for their God fights for them; He has more power than thy deaf Apollo of stone. [. . .' (The duke's reply probably followed.)

[102] The letter begins and ends with normal Coptic epistolary formulae.   [103] Ps. xxxix, 12.

cave; thou wilt find (there) the property of thy father. By thy health, O my son, I have not wasted anything of the property of thy father; *but* every one (*sic*)[104] I have spent has been (**83 R ii**) my parents' property. Turn not thy face from a stranger, or a *widow*, or an *orphan*, that God may be a *wall* (*of defence*) to thee from the snares of the *Devil*. And if I find *liberty to speak* before the Lord, thou art the first for whom I (shall) obtain grace. Do not be distressed, O my son, that our *bodies* were separated from one another; *for* it is well for us if we are separated from one another in this *world* that we may be together in Jerusalem, the *city* of *Christ*. I greet thee, my little son, *for* I shall not see thee again in the *flesh*. And thy father (*sic*) Paēse greets thee. I *salute* thee in my (**83 V i**) *soul* and my *spirit*. Farewell in the Lord, my beloved son.' And when Thecla had finished writing this *epistle*, she gave it to a young servant of hers, and sent it to Antinoou.

And after this, the *duke* delayed and did not enquire for the saints in the prison. *Now* they thought that the *duke* would not *torture* them again. *But* it befell that after twenty days the priests of the temple came and said to the *duke*, 'The whole *city* has gone after these two *magicians*, and they are healing the sick through their *sorceries*, and have drawn all the *city* to them; and the people are no longer allowed (**83 V ii**) to come to the temple.' The *duke* was angry; he said to them, 'Enquire from the gods, and let them tell me of some severe *tortures* to give them; for I have been powerless against them, and they have *afflicted* me exceedingly; and if I leave them thus, the whole *city* will rise against me. And my wife too they have *bewitched*, and she has *denied* the gods.' *And* the priests went, and agreed upon one counsel. They came to the *duke* and said to him, 'Our gods have told us of severe *tortures*; *for* they have said to us: "Take these *magicians*, and bind them in iron *chains*, and put them upon a *boat* (**84 R i**) and tie a great stone to their necks, and let them be borne out and cast into the *depths* of the *sea*, so that no man see them (again) for ever".' When the *duke* heard this, he *ordered* the saints to be brought to him on the morrow. And he said (to himself) '*Verily*, this is the *torture* by which I shall be able to prevail against them.' He sat (in judgment) on the saints *before the tribunal*, and said to them 'You have (had) all these days (to) *consider* whether to *sacrifice* to the revered gods.' Thecla answered and said to him, (**84 R ii**) 'Like a woman who will be foolish, and her parents and kinsfolk are wearied with teaching her, and she does not hearken to them and feel shame;[105] and like a dog which returns to his vomit

---

[104] Read 'thing'?   [105] Perhaps a loose paraphrase of Ecclus. xxii, 3.

and is abhorred;[106] so it is with thee also.' *And* when the *duke* heard this, he was very angry, and he burned like a fire, and gnashed his teeth and said to those of the *entourage*, 'Do you not hear this vile woman comparing me to *harlots* and dogs?' The holy woman an answered, 'Perhaps indeed thou art worse than the dogs; for the *beasts* know God; *but* thou **(84 V i)** hast not known Him.' The *duke* leapt up in anger. He had them fettered with iron *chains*, and had a great stone tied to their necks, and they were put upon a *boat*, and they were taken out to *sea* and cast into the *deep*. And straightway the *Archangel* Raphael came from heaven and overshadowed them, and loosed them from the bonds with which they were bound; and a great *whale* came and took them up (on its back), and brought them to the shore. *And* when the multitude saw the saints with no hurt upon them, they all cried **(84 V ii)** out, 'One is the God of Apa Paēse and his sister Thecla, *Christ* Jesus!' When the *duke* heard the *clamour* of the multitude, he enquired what was afoot. He was told that it was the saints who had come to the shore. When the *duke* heard, he wondered, and *withdrew*, fearing the multitude. *And* as for the saints, they went to the prison, and *greeted* their fellow *martyrs*, and told them how the Lord had saved them from the *sea*. And on the morrow he *ordered* the saints to be brought to him. And the whole multitude was **(85 R i)** crying out, 'One is the God of Apa Paēse and his sister Thecla!' And the *duke* in anger *ordered* them to be taken outside the *city* and beheaded. And on that day there were slain one hundred and forty *souls*; and they fulfilled their *martyrdom* on the eighth day of the month Hathor, in *peace*, *Amen*.

The *duke* had the saints taken to the prison while he *considered* what he should do to them. And it befell that at midnight, lo, the Lord Jesus *Christ* came down from heaven with His holy *angels*, and He came **(85 R ii)** to the saints Apa Paēse and his sister, and He said to them, '*Hail*, my fellow *inheritors* of the Kingdom of Heaven! *Hail*, ye who have *striven well* for your Lord! *Hail*, ye blessed of My Father, who shall *inherit*[107] the *blessings* of the *fruits* of the Tree of Life!' When the *holy* Apa Paēse and his sister Thecla heard this, their hearts were very glad. The Lord said to them, 'Fear not, *but* be strong and firm, for I am with you.' *And* Thecla cast herself down at the feet of **(85 V i)** the *Saviour*, and said to Him, 'My Lord, let Thy mercy attend us; and do Thou *protect* our *bodies*, so that the *impious* may not cast them to the *wild beasts*, and our bones be not found.' The Saviour said to them, 'Fear not; it is I Who will *protect* your *bodies*, and I will cause a *martyr-shrine* to be built for you in My Name; and whoso shall give an *offering* to your *shrine*. I will fill his

---

[106] Prov. xxvi, 11; II Pet. ii, 22.   [107] Cf. Mt. xxv, 34.

house with every *good thing* on earth; and I will cause My *angels* to *protect* their (*sic*) *bodies* and their (*sic*) *souls* in the *aeons* of the light. (**85 V ii**) Whoso shall write the book of your *martyrdom*, I will write his name in the Book of Life. And I will set My blessing and My *peace* in the place where your *bodies* shall be laid. And behold, I have set the *angel* Raphael to *minister to* your *shrine*; and great numbers of sick people suffering from divers diseases shall come to your *shrine*, and obtain healing, and go home in *peace*. And whoso shall give alms to a poor person, or a stranger, or a *widow* on the day of your commemoration, I will not leave him lacking for any *good thing* for ever.[108] (**86 R i**) Fear not, *but* be strong and firm; *for* I am with you. *For* you have another full month on earth before you come to Me, and rest from your sufferings, and find your rest for ever.' When the *Saviour* had said this to them, He gave them *salutation* and went up to heaven in glory.

And it befell after this that an *officer of the bodyguard* of the emperor came into Alexandria, having been sent by him (to go) throughout all Egypt, and he brought (there) all the *governors* of the *several cities*, that he might read them the *ordinance* of the emperor. *And* there came (**86 R ii**) also Eutychianus the *duke* of the Thebaid; and the letter of the emperor was read to them. And after they had been in Alexandria for sixteen days, the *general* dismissed them to go each to his *city*. And Armenius the *count* of Alexandria *urged* Eutychianus the *duke* of the Thebaid, saying, 'Take these two *magicians*, and do me this favour: take them to the south with thee, and *exile* them; and let them *sacrifice*, or cast them to the *wild beasts*; for they have contemned the *lawcourt*. And I have had trouble, wishing to destroy them, and I have not been (**86 V i**) able. And they have stirred up the whole *city* against me, and have carried away a multitude of people from me through their *sorceries*.' So saying, the *count* Armenius commanded the saints to be brought out from the prison, and they were *presented* to Eutychianus the *duke*, and he had them cast down into the hold of the ship; and they went on board, and he sailed south. And he came to a bend in the river, to the north of Tepôt;[109] and the wind left them, and they moored the

---

[108] For the whole preceding passage, cf. (e.g.) Hyv. *Actes*, p. 169 f. (Piroou & Athom); p. 220 (Ari).

[109] In the Bohairic martyrdom of Anoub (Bal.–Hyv. *AM* I, pp. 200 ff.) occurs the following passage (p. 225 f.):

ⲘⲈⲚⲈⲚⲤⲀⲚⲀⲒ̈ ⲆⲈ ⲚⲀⲨⲨⲤⲎⲢ ⲈⲢⲎⲤ ⲠⲈ ⲅⲁⲧⲟⲨϥⲟⲍ Ⲉⲟⲩⲧⲁⲓ ⲝⲈ ⲩⲈⲧⲚⲟⲩⲅⲓ, ⲟⲩⲟⲍ ⲁⲩⲧⲁⲥⲃⲟ ⲈϩⲎⲧ ϩⲈⲚϥⲓⲁⲢⲟ ⲚⲈⲙⲈⲚⲦ· ϩⲈⲚⲚⲓⲝⲱⲕ ⲆⲈ Ⲛϥ ⲚⲈⲍⲟⲟⲩ ⲁⲩⲁⲙⲟⲚⲒ Ⲉⲟⲩⲧⲁⲓ ⲝⲈ Ⲧⲟⲩϥⲱⲧ, ⲁⲩⲝⲓⲙⲓ ⲙⲠⲒⲍⲎⲦⲈⲙⲱⲚ Ⲉϥⲧⲁⲛⲟⲫⲁⲥⲓⲥ ⲈⲚⲒⲈⲂⲓⲁⲓⲕ ⲚⲦⲈⲠⲬ̅Ⲥ̅ ϩⲈⲚⲦⲔⲟⲧⲤⲒ ⲚⲦⲈⲦⲟⲩϥⲱⲧ ⲍⲓⲛⲭⲟ, Ⲉⲧⲉⲛⲓⲁⲧⲓⲟⲥ ⲚⲀⲎⲤⲒ ⲛⲈ ⲚⲈⲙⲐⲈⲔⲗⲁ ⲦⲈⲨⲤⲱⲚⲒ ⲚⲈⲙⲔⲈϩⲈⲗⲗⲟ ⲙⲠⲢⲈⲤⲂⲨⲦⲈⲢⲟⲥ· ⲈⲧⲁⲩⲔⲎⲚ ⲈⲩⲱⲗⲒ ⲚⲦⲟⲩⲁϥⲈ ⲈⲐⲟⲩⲁⲃ, ⲈⲢⲉⲛⲟⲩⲤⲱ

ship at the shore, at a hamlet; that day being the eighth of Choiach.
Eutychianus *ordered* the *tribunal* to be set out, and he had the saints
brought (**86 V ii**) to the shore, and they were brought up from the
hold of the ship, with a great *grace* in their countenance; it being the
eighth day since they had eaten *or* drunk. Eutychianus said to them,
'Come and *sacrifice* to the gods of the emperor; *for*, behold, no one
will see you here.'[110] The *blessed* Apa Paēse said to him, 'It is
written: "Whosoever shall *confess* Me before men, him will I *confess*
also before My Father Which is in heaven, and His holy *angels*."[111] It
is written also: "Where two or three are gathered together (**87 R i**)
in My Name, I am with them."[112] Do we *therefore* fear men? No; *but*
we fear God, Who will preserve us from thy *tortures*.' Hearing this,
the *duke* Eutychianus was angry, and he gave *sentence* upon them
that they should be beheaded. And he had them taken into some
reeds and thorns, that the *wild beasts* should devour their *flesh*. And
when the saints had been taken to the place of their *condemnation*,
they turned their faces to the east, saying, 'Lord God *Almighty*, the
Father of our Lord Jesus *Christ*, Who didst give strength to Thy
(**87 R ii**) *Prophets* and Thine holy *Apostles*, Thou Who hast given
strength to Thine holy *Martyrs*, mayest Thou give strength to us
also, and *protect* our *bodies*, and take to Thyself our *souls* with face
unashamed! To Thee be glory, and to Thy beloved and holy Son
Jesus *Christ* and the Holy *Spirit*, for ever and ever, *Amen*!' The *holy*
Thecla cried out, saying, 'I greet thee, my little son, for I shall not
see thee again in the *flesh*.' *And* when the saints had said this, the
tormentors fitted the *gag* to them (*sic*)[113] (**87 V i**) and beheaded
them.

I, Julius,[114] was staying in Alexandria, writing the *records* of the
saints. God knows that what I have seen in respect of these saints, I
have neither added to *nor* taken therefrom.[115] And I was on board
with the *duke* until the saints fulfilled their *contest* on the eighth day
of the month Choiach; and I saw the *angel* Raphael, (how) having

---

ⲙⲁ ⲥⲁϥ ⲉⲃⲟⲗ ϩⲉⲛⲑⲙⲏϥ ⲛⲛⲓⲕⲁⲙ ⲛⲉⲙⲛⲓⲥⲟⲩⲣⲓ, ⲙⲙⲟⲛ ⲩⲝ̄ⲟⲙ ⲛⲧⲉⲭⲗⲓ ⲟ̄ⲧ ⲛⲉⲙⲛⲟⲩ-
ⲥⲱⲙⲁ ⲉⲑⲃⲉϥⲍⲟϥ ⲛⲛⲓ ⲍ̄ⲩⲡⲉⲣⲉⲧⲏⲥ ⲉⲑⲣⲱⲓⲥ ⲉⲣⲱⲟⲩ.

ⲧⲟⲩⲫⲱⲧ (see Amél. *Géogr*., p. 526 f.) is evidently identical with ⲧⲉⲛⲱⲧ here.
It is mentioned also ibid., p. 227, and would appear to lie north of Shetnoufe, on the
western (Canopic) branch of the Nile (ⲫⲓⲁⲡⲟ ⲛⲉⲙⲉⲛⲧ), at a point where there
is a bend (ⲕⲟⲧⲉ̄ / ⲕⲟⲧⲥⲓ) in the stream.
ⲧⲉⲡⲱⲧ occurs among place names in the Hermopolite nome in a seventh-century Greek
document, *Stud. Pal.* 25, 27.

[110] Cf. (e.g.) Hyv. *Actes*, p. 53.   [111] Mt. x, 32; Lk. xii, 8.
[112] Mt. xviii, 20.   [113] Read 'to their mouths'.
[114] For Julius, see our Introduction, pp. 3; 6, n. 20, above; O'Leary, *Saints*, p. 174 f.;
Delehaye, *Mart. Ég*., p.138; *Synax*. Tout 22.
[115] Cf. Deut. iv, 2; xii, 32; Rev. xxii, 18 f.

stretched forth his hands he gathered up the blood of these saints, and did not let it sink to the ground; and I saw the whole *firmament* filled with *angels*; (87 **V ii**) and I saw crowns and *robes* of great price put upon the saints.

And there were some flocks of sheep being pastured in that hamlet, with six great dogs among them, very powerful; they spent that whole night watching over the *bodies* of the saints, without letting any one touch them.[116] *And* the *duke* was troubled, and those who were with him. He *ordered* the *tormentors* to go and cast the *bodies* of the saints into the water; *but* when the *tormentors* approached (88 **R i**) the *bodies* of the saints, the dogs leapt up and *wounded* them sorely.

There was an old man in Shetnoufe,[117] *and* he was a saint; his name was Arē.[118] And the *angel* of the Lord appeared to him in the night, and said to him, 'Arē! Arē!' He answered 'Here am I, lord.' The *angel* of the Lord said to him, 'Arise, come and *protect* the *bodies* of these saints.' He said to him, 'My lord, I do not know the place where they are.' The *angel* of the Lord walked with him; and the man brought (88 **R ii**) some few graveclothes; and when they came upon the *bodies* of the saints, the man of God saw them, and he said, 'I thank Thee, God, that Thou hast deemed me worthy to have seen the *bodies* of these saints.' And he wrapped them in the graveclothes, and took them upon a high place,[119] and buried them until the day when it pleased God to reveal them.[120]

And the number of the people who were *martyred* on that day with the saints was a hundred and thirty-seven *souls*.

Glory to the Father, and to the Son, and to the Holy *Spirit*, for ever, *Amen.*

[116] Cf. (e.g.) Rossi, p. 90 (Apa Dios).
[117] See Amél. *Géogr.*, p. 424 f.
[118] For Arē of Shetnoufe, see O'Leary, *Saints*, p. 85; he must be identical with Arius, separately entered ibid., p. 86; *Synax.* Mesorē 9; his martyrology, Hyv. *Actes*, pp. 202 ff.
[119] For the burial of saints in hill country, see Cauwenbergh, *Étude sur les moines de l' Égypte*, p. 164.
[120] Cf. Rossi, loc. cit.

S. SHENOUFE AND HIS BRETHREN

(103 R i) This is the *martyrdom* of the holy *Saint* Apa Shenoufe[1] and his brethren, on the seventh day of Paōpe, in *peace*, *Amen*.

This is the first *written account* which was made in the land of Egypt concerning the saints in the days of Diocletian,[2] the *lawless* emperor, when he was reigning in Antioch; Antiochus[3] being *governor* over Phoenicia, and Culcianus[4] being *governor* over Alexandria, and Pompeius[5] being *governor* over Peremoun,[6] and Hierocleianus[7] being *governor* over Heracleopolis,[8] and the *city* of Arsinoē,[9] and also over the *city* of Oxyrhynchus,[10] and Arianus being *governor* over the Thebaid.

The emperor Diocletian was sitting in the midst (103 R ii) of his *palace*, surrounded by all his *courtiers* and *counts* and *henchmen* and *bodyguards*. *And* the emperor Diocletian spoke with his notables, saying, 'Hearken to me, all of you, my friends; *for* you all know that I love you.' They said to him, 'Speak, our lord.' He said to them, 'You know that the emperor is not wont to lie. While I was *yet* sleeping this night, the great god Apollo came in to me, with seventy gods besides; and they said to me in their sweet language, "Behold, we have honoured thee, and have given thee might in *war*, and have given thee the crown of *victory*. Do thou for thy part honour (103 V i) us in thy whole empire." What then would you that I should do for them?' Romanus the *general*, who was the father of Apa Victor,[11] said to him, 'Hearken to me, O King! Even as it befell in the land of Egypt in the days of Pharaoh, when they (?) put their trust in the

[1] For the martyr's name, see p. 190, n. 48, below.
[2] 103 R i–13; cf. Mina; *Epima*, p. 1.
[3] Perhaps (allowing for some geographical inaccuracy) cf. Jones–Martindale–Morris, p. 71.
[4] For this notorious persecutor, see Vandersleyen, pp. 73 ff.; 85 ff.; 93; Lallemand, p. 23; Jones–Martindale–Morris, p. 233 f.; Frend, pp. 505; 531; 534. For his trial of Phileas, see Martin, *P. Bodmer XX (Phileas)*, *passim*.
[5] Another persecutor; see (e.g.) Bal.-Hyv. *AM* I, pp. 89 ff. (Apa Til).
[6] For Peremoun (Pelusium, Tell-el-Farama), see Amél. *Géogr.*, p. 317 f.; Munier, *BSAC* 5, 235; ibid., *Recueil*, p. 55, 1. 82.
[7] This official, who figures in several martyrologies, is to be identified with Sossianus Hierocles, a well-known doctrinaire anti-Christian (cf. Frend, pp. 497f.; 505f.; 515) who became Prefect of Egypt in 307; see Lallemand, p. 239 f.; Vandersleyen, pp. 80 ff.; Jones–Martindale–Morris, p. 432; and above, Introd., p. 7.
[8] Heracleopolis (Hnês, Ihnasîya el-Medina): see Amél. *Géogr.*, pp. 196 ff.; Munier, *Recueil*, p. 56, 1. 95; Gardiner, *AEO* II, p. 116* f.
[9] Elsewhere 'the city of Piom' (Medînet el-Fayûm); Amél. *Géogr.*, pp. 337 ff.; Munier, *Recueil*, p. 56, 1. 95; Gardiner, *AEO* II, p. 116* f.
[10] For Pemdje (Oxyrhynchus, El-Behnasa), see Amél. *Géogr.*, pp. 90 ff.; Munier, *BSAC* 5, 235; *Recueil*, p. 56.
[11] See p. 156, n. 21, above.

gods whom they had fashioned, thus let it be done again. Arise, O
King, and write an *edict* to Egypt, from Romania the first *city*,[12] as
far as the furthermost *city* in the south of (*sic*) Pilak,[13] bordering
upon the Ethiopians,[14] that the temples be built up, and the revered
gods be placed in them; and let gods of gold and silver be fashioned
for them, and let them be served by the priests, **(103 V ii)** and let
care be taken of them, and *sacrifices* offered up to them, with
unmixed wine and finely kneaded flour; as for the priests, let their
lands be made *free of taxes*, that they may live *delicately* and take
care for the revered gods; and let the *magistrates* and *governors* be
established in the *several cities* and the *several provinces*, that each
one may seize the *Christians* who are in his nome, so that they may
come and worship the gods of the emperor, and offer up *sacrifice*;
and whosoever shall be disobedient, let them be killed with fire and
sword and divers forms of death. As for the *governors* in the *cities*
which are in Egypt, write to Egypt for them, and let them be brought
to thee here; give them the *ordinance*, and let each one **(104 R i)**
take it to his *own country* and his *province*; and charge them that
they do *according to* thy command.' Diocletian answered, saying,
'By the health of Apollo the great god, I will do thus, and will not
be remiss.' And Diocletian wrote letters, and published them from
the *palace,* saying, 'Any men soever who are soldiers and *generals*, any
race of men soever who dwell in my whole empire, let me not hear this
name of Jesus, but let them turn their faces to the west, and worship
the revered gods, and offer up *incense* to them.'[15] And the *edict* was
published from the *palace.*

And there was a youth who was the son of a *general* **(104 R ii)**
named Basilides;[16] and the name of the young man was Eusebius.[17]
When he saw the letter published from the *palace*, he was much *distressed*, and cried out, 'Jesus *Christ, help* me, and kindle my lamp
within me, that I may have power to speak with this shameless
governor (*sic*)[18] who insults Thy holy Name!' *And* when he had said
this, he stripped off his armour, and left only his *kerchief* (*sic*)[19]

---

[12] It is not easy to see what precisely is meant by this expression, which occurs in parallel
passages in other martyrologies; see Mina's remarks, *Epima*, p. 40, n. 2.

[13] For Pilak(h) (Philae), see Amél. *Géogr.*, p. 347; Munier, *BSAC* 5, 226; *Recueil*, p. 57,
1. 119; Mina, *Epima*, p. xxvi.

[14] 103 R ii 8–V i 24: cf. *Epima*, pp. 1 f.; also Hyv. *Actes*, p. 284 (Didymus).

[15] 104 R i 5–27: cf. Hyv. *Actes*, p. 285 (Didymus).

[16] A personality with whom a large body of martyr literature is connected; see O'Leary,
Saints, pp. 19; 100 ff.

[17] See *Synax*. Amshir 23. A son of Basilides named Christophorus occupies the same place
in the doublet of this passage in *Epima*; see below.

[18] Read 'king'; so in the corresponding place in the *Epima* doublet.

[19] ϥⲁⲕⲓⲁⲗⲓⲟⲛ, 'turban' or 'kerchief' (see Girgis, *BSAC* 19, 1967–8), 58; but cf.
Epima, and similar passages in AI. & Pt. 109 V ii 25; Till, *KHML* I, p. 43 (Besamon);

upon him, and he went in to the emperor and stood before him. The emperor said to him, 'Who is this?' He said to him, 'I am Eusebius, the son of Basilides.' The emperor said to him 'And why art thou standing here in undress? Thou hast disgraced the *dignity* of thy father.' The young (**104 V i**) man said to him, 'I shall not be a soldier for thee from now onward, since the root (?)[20] of the *Devil* has taken root in thy heart; *but* I will be a soldier for my Lord Jesus *Christ*,[21] Who created heaven and earth, the *sea* and the rivers and all that are in them;[22] and it is He Who has created me also, and my breath is in His Hands.'[23] When the young man had said this,[24] he replied again, and said to the emperor, '*Well*, then, what god wouldst thou have me serve, that I should forsake the living God?' The emperor said to him 'I desire thee to serve Apollo, the great god.' The young man said to him, 'Let him be brought here to me, and let me (**104 V ii**) see him myself, that the glory of Jesus may be made manifest; to Whom belong all glory and power.' *And* the emperor *commanded* the priests, and they brought the (image of) Apollo, and set it before him. And the young man arose, and stood up, and extended his arms in the *form* of the *Cross*, and he blessed God, saying, 'My Lord Jesus *Christ*, give me aid, for this is the time for Thy Name to be glorified, Thou *Only Begotten* of the Father.' Straightway he spurned the Apollo with his foot, and it rolled down upon the ground until it came to where the *throne* of Diocletian was. He seized a sword which was in the hand of a soldier, and thrust it into the belly of the young man and cleft his *body*; *and* the soldiers saw (it), and (**105 R i**) surrounded the young man, and cut him *limb* from *limb* with the sword. And he fulfilled his *martyrdom* on the fourteenth day of Epēp, and he received the crown of Jesus *Christ*, in *peace*, *Amen*.[25]

And it befell after this, that Diocletian sent the *ordinance* into Alexandria first, to be given to Eutychianus,[26] the *count* of Alexandria, that he might send it up to Egypt, and that the *governors* of the *several provinces* should be brought to him, and taken to Armenius.[27] And the *governors* of the *several provinces* and the *several cities* gathered together, and they went in to Antioch to

---

read 'loincloth'. The stripping off of armour as a gesture of renunciation of imperial allegiance and service is a commonplace in the *Acta* of recusant soldier martyrs.

[20] In *Epima*, 'heart'; see textual n. Elsewhere (e.g., Rossi, *I papiri copti. . . Torino* I, v, p. 51), ⲡⲛ̄ⲁ, 'spirit'.

[21] Cf. (e.g.) Till, *KHML* I, p. 42 f. (Besamon).

[22] Cf. Ex. xx, 11; Ps. cxlvi, 6; Acts iv, 24; xiv, 15.

[23] Cf. Job xii, 10; Dan. v, 23; a frequent cliché in this text.

[24] 104 R i 8–V i 18: cf. *Epima*, p. 2 f.   [25] 104 V ii 26–105 R i 8: cf. *Epima*, p. 3.

[26] See p. 151, n. 3, above.   [27] See p. 151, n. 2. above.

to Diocletian; and he had them all *sacrifice* to the gods. And all those
who worshipped on that day (were these): eight (**105 R ii**) thousand
soldiers worshipped, together with thirty thousand *civilians*; the small
and the great, men and women, every person in the *city* in whom was
the *spirit* of life, he made them all to worship; and they numbered
two hundred and seventy thousand people.[28] Thereafter he wrote
letters,[29] and gave them to Arianus the *governor* of the Thebaid, and
he first sent him to Alexandria, and he gave them to Eutychianus the
duke of Alexandria; he *ordered* him to give a large *force* of soldiers,
and the *ordinance*, to take them up to Egypt and *reproduce* them[30]
in the *several cities*; *and* Eutychianus the *duke* of Alexandria called
Julius the *assistant* and *commentariensis*,[31] and gave him a (**105 V i**)
force of soldiers to go with Arianus the *governor*, so that they might
do *according to* the *orders* of Diocletian. *And* Arianus went on board
a ship, he and Julius the *assistant* and the *guard* of soldiers, and he
came south to Egypt in the quays and *harbours* of the *several cities*
and *several* villages, until he came to a *city* called Chortasa;[32] and the
governor moored there. And many men and women and little
children forsook all that they had and went to the *governor* and
cried out, 'We are *Christians, confessedly*!' And he sat (in judgment)
on them *before the tribunal* at that (*sic*) river. And there were seized
(**105 V ii**) for him all the *leading persons* who were in that nome, the
bishops and the *presbyters*, Philemon[33] the *bishop* of Thmouis,[34] and
Antony[35] the *bishop* of Natho,[36] and Plasse[37] the *bishop* of Atripe,[38]

---

[28] We do not see how this figure was arrived at.   [29] 105 R i 30–ii 3: cf. *Epima*, p. 3.

[30] Cf. *Epima*, p. 3.

[31] See pp. 3; 10; 183, n. 114, above; and Crum, *Cat. Copt. B.M.*, p. 146.

[32] See Ball, *Egypt in the Classical Geographers*, p. 170, for a mention of Chortasō in
Stephen of Byzantium. There an absurd Greek etymology of the name is given; even
so, it is not valueless in so far as it suggests that Chortasō was a place of some size. The
present passage suggests that it was in the region of Alexandria. A village so named is
mentioned in a papyrus from the Heracleopolite nome, *Stud. Pal.* X, 233 B (5th cent.).

[33] For Philemon, doubtless to be identified with the Phileas of Eusebius, *HE* VIII, ix 7–
x. 11 and *P. Bodmer XX*, see our Introduction, p. 8 f.

[34] See Amél. *Géogr.*, pp. 500 ff.; Munier, *Recueil*, p. 55, 1. 77; Gardiner, *AEO* II, p. 151*.

[35] Otherwise unknown.

[36] For the place name Ⲛⲁⲃⲱ/Leontopolis, see Amél. *Géogr.*, p. 269 f.; Munier, *BSAC* 5,
234; *Recueil*, p. 55, 1. 106; and for the problem of identification and locality, Gardiner,
AEO II, pp. 146* ff.

[37] Unknown. With the name, perhaps cf. ⳡⲗⲁⲥ, Preisigke, *Nb.* s. n. (exx. of Roman and
early Byzantine date).

[38] The place name ⲁⲧⲣⲓⲛⲉ has given rise to some dispute. Gardiner (*AEO* II, p. 46*;
JEA 31 (1945), 108 ff.) denies the propriety of applying the name of Athribis in
Lower Egypt (Tell Atrîb; for which see Amél. *Géogr.*, p. 69 f.; Munier, *Recueil*, p. 55
(1. 67); Ball, pp. 122, etc.; Calderini, *Diz. geogr.* I (1), p. 32 f.) to the locality ⲁⲧⲣⲓⲛⲉ
near Shenute's White Monastery at Sohag, which he attributes to confusion. If so, we
here see the confusion working in the opposite direction; ⲁⲧⲣⲓⲛⲉ as the seat of a
bishopric can only be the Lower Egyptian Athribis.

and Eisidimus[39] the *bishop* of the Birthplace (?) of the *Encampment*,[40] who were in the nome of Alexandria; and he inflicted upon them many *tortures; and* great miracles and wonders were done through them.

But hear now, you to whom has been given the (gift of) hearing, and pay heed, you to whom instruction has been given—*since* there is nothing sweeter than this Name of Jesus, and nothing more precious than this name of *Christian*;[41] even as the scholar of the *Apostles* has said: 'There is laid up for us a great thing'[42] because of these *martyrs*; **(106 R i)** all this befell that the glory of the *Church* should be made manifest.

There were eleven men from Empaiat,[43] who were all members of a single *family*; these are their names: Shenoufe, and Philemon, and Apa Nile, and Peter, and John, Andrew, Phoebam(m)on, Antony, Philip, and Chaeremon, and Hermini (*sic*),[44] and a woman, a sister of theirs, named Sophia; they were *Christians*, far removed from any evil; they were prudent, hospitable and charitable, loving their *religious assemblies* and devoted to the *Sacrament*; their house was a lodging for the strangers, since they were very rich *in respect of* this *world's* (goods); and they were protectors **(106 R ii)** of all the *widows* and *orphans* who were in their nome. They had a great *church* over which they presided. And the *noble* and *holy* ones, when they heard about the miracles which the saints were performing at the *tribunal* of Arianus, they too *longed for* the crown of *martyrdom*; and they were enquiring daily how they could go to the *governor*, so that they might receive the crown of *Christ. And* the *holy* Apa Shenoufe was sleeping within his *church* on this day, as an *act of self-discipline*, not being in his bed. And lo, a man all radiant came to him, having a *rod* in his right hand, and stood over him, and touched his right side, **(106 V i)** saying, 'Shenoufe, Shenoufe, open thine eyes, and know Me, Who I am! I am Jesus, Whose star did arise; I am He concerning Whom Gabriel proclaimed to the shepherds; I am Jesus, Whom the *Virgin* Mary bore; I am Jesus, the Bearer of good tidings. Behold, I

---

[39] A name Εἰσίδιλμος occurs in an Alexandrian tomb inscription at Hadra (Breccia, *Rapport sur la marche du Service du Musée en 1912* (Alexandria, 1913), p. 21 = Preisigke, *Sb.* I 5841), in an evidently pagan context, of Roman date, in company with names which are mostly Greek.

[40] The form of the place name is puzzling, but its identity and location seem indicated by comparison with ϭⲓⲛⲙⲉϭⲧⲏⲗⲟ : | ⲧⲃⲁⲕⲓ ⲥⲟⲩⲁⲛ in Munier, *Recueil*, p. 51, 11. 11 ff.; cf. also Amél. *Géogr.*, p. 467; Ball, p. 145. The occurrence of παρεμβολή in connection with the name is hardly surprising in a town situated in a frontier region. This list as a whole has a look of authenticity.

[41] 105 V ii 20–28: cf. *Epima*, p. 4.   [42] Col. i, 5? II Tim. iv, 8?

[43] Amél. *Géogr.*, p. 242; Munier, *BSAC* 5, 241; Drescher, *Mena*, pp. 2; 36 f.; 101; equated, or associated, with Μαρεώτης, Maryût; elsewhere in this text (108 R ii 25; 132 R i 24; 136 V ii 20) spoken of as belonging to a district called 'The Plainland' (Πεδ ι(ει)νή).

[44] Elsewhere (132 R i 22; 136 R i 28) ⲍⲉⲣⲙⲓⲁⲥⲥ.

proclaim to thee and to thy brethren. For this cause (sic) therefore [45] do you sit thus *careless*, while the *contest* is spread abroad, and while your crowns are laid up (for you).[46,47] *For since* (sic) thou shalt receive a great *inheritance*. Thou and thine eleven brethren have yourselves received the *type* of My twelve *Disciples*; *and* as for thee, moreover, O my beloved, (106 V ii) thy name shall no more be called Shenoute (Son of God),[48] but thou shalt be called Shenoufe (Good Tidings);[49] for this is the first *greeting* which Gabriel proclaimed to Mary My Mother; he proclaimed to her, "Lo, the Son of God shall come, and shall become *incarnate* in thee, and thou shalt bring Him forth, and He shall be the *salvation* of the whole *world*."[50] Arise then, go to the *governor*, thou and thy brethren, submit your *bodies* to *martyrdom* for My Name. Great miracles and wonders shall come to pass through you, *since* I have appointed for you Michael the *Archangel* to be *ministrant* upon you, giving strength to you until you fulfil your *contest*. Your *bodies* shall stay a long (107 R i) while hidden in the earth; afterwards they shall be revealed, and (in) the place where your *bodies* shall be laid, Michael the *Archangel* shall be *ministrant* upon them. *For* your end shall be fulfilled in a strange *city*, in a place called Poubaste;[51] *so that* you shall receive two crowns, one for your condition as strangers, and another for your *martyrdom* which you shall fulfil. Your *bodies* shall be in a single *shrine* in the *world*, *but* your *souls* shall be in a single place, in the heavenly Jerusalem. *Now*, I have appointed Julius the *assistant* and *commentariensis*, the man of Kbahs, to take care of you[52] until the day when you shall fulfil your *contest*; and your (107 R ii) *records* he shall write down and keep in his house until the day when it shall please My Father to reveal them.' When the *Saviour* had said this to the *holy* Apa Shenoufe, He *gave* him *salutation* and bade him *peace*,

---

[45] Read 'Why therefore' (ⲈⲦⲂⲈⲞⲨ ⲄⲈ) as in the corresponding passage in *Epima*; cf. Hyv. *Actes*, p. 288 (Didymus).

[46] Cf. II Tim. iv, 8.   [47] 106 V i 17–22: cf. *Epima*, p. 5.

[48] In Hyv. *Actes*, p. 100 (Apater) we find in a list of saints in prison the name of ⲤⲈⲚⲞⲨⲐⲒ ⲚⲒⲢⲈⲙⲂⲞⲨⲀⲤⲦ , who may be presumed to be our saint; but whether he is there called designedly by his original name, or by mistake for 'Shenoufe', we cannot say.

[49] This will be simply a pun on his name, rather than a serious etymology of it; *Šri-nfr* is found from the New Kingdom onwards; see Ranke, *Äg. Personennamen* I, p. 329.

[50] Cf. Lk. i, 26 ff.

[51] See Amél. *Géogr.*, p. 89 (ⲂⲞⲨⲀⲤⲦ); where, however, the reference is taken to be to the northern city of Bubastis. Bubastis (-os) is well known as a village of the division of Heraclides in the Arsinoite nome. It is expressly identified in 138 V i ff., below, with ⲔⲀⲘⲒ ⲚⲞⲖⲒⲤ. Χωρ/Καμη.[in *Stud. Pal.* x 53 (7th–8th cent.) has been taken (e.g., by Preisigke, *Wb.* III, p. 303) as a variant of Κάμωοι; but the latter village is in the division of Polemon (see Grenfell–Hunt–Goodspeed, *Tebtunis Papyri* II, p. 382); so Kamē polis and Kaminoi can hardly be identical. Καμη also occurs as a place name in P. Oxy. 1972, 10.

[52] 107 R i 25–29: cf. *Epima*, p. 6.

and departed from him to his other *martyr* brethren, and appeared to them also in a *vision*, and proclaimed to them these words; and He went up to heaven with the *angels* of glory *singing hymns* before Him, in *peace*, *Amen*.

And the *holy* Apa Shenoufe was not *remiss* at all, *but* he arose and came out of that *church* and came into his house; and he sent and called these other ten *saints* and also the woman, their sister; and he made a great *banquet* (**107 V i**) for them within his house that day. *And* when they had eaten and drunk and enjoyed themselves, the *holy* Apa Shenoufe said to them, 'My brethren, I saw a *vision* this night, in which Jesus crowned the twelve of us.' The other eleven *saints* answered with one voice, '*Verily*, that which thou hast seen, we saw also; and the words which were said to thee were said to us also.' The *holy* Apa Shenoufe said to them, 'And what is in your mind concerning the words which were said to you?' The saints answered, 'As God lives, the place whither thou shalt go, we will follow thee; and the death which thou shalt die, we will die (**107 V ii**) by it also, that even as we have not been separated from one another on earth, so we shall not be separated in the house of God.'

The *saints* arose, and they stood and prayed together. And after they had drunk and enjoyed themselves, they returned from the *banquet*, and each went home; and they gave charge of their households to their people and their children; *but* they did not tell the *secret* to any *save* themselves alone.

And when the *holy* Apa Shenoufe had slept in his house, lo, the Lord came to him, and said to him, '*Hail*, Shenoufe, My fellow *member*; thou hast made the *banquet* with thy brethren in this *world*; now therefore prepare thyself that thou mayest make it for them in My *city*, the heavenly Jerusalem, thou being at their head in My Kingdom which is in heaven. (**108 R i**) May the *peace* of My Father be with you for ever and ever, *Amen*.' And the *Saviour* went up to heaven, while the *holy* Apa Shenoufe gazed after Him, even up to heaven.[53]

And the *holy* Apa Shenoufe bestirred himself early in the morning, before any had yet arisen, and he went and awakened the other eleven *saints*, and they came to the east side of their house,[54] and prayed together, and they travelled together until they came down beside the quay of Chortasa, the place where the *governor* was. They saw him sitting *before the tribunal*, *judging* the multitude of the *Christians*; and they made their way up to the *tribunal*, and cried out 'O *lawless governor*, how long dost thou trouble the (**108 R ii**)

[53] Cf. Acts i, 9 f.; a commonplace in the martyrologies.
[54] 108 R i 14–16: cf. *Epima*, p. 6.

servants of *Christ*, *constraining* them to forsake the living God and
serve dead gods? *Now* as for us, we are *Christians*, and we are servants
of the living God, Jesus *Christ*!' The *governor* said to them through
the *interpreter*, 'Whence are you, *or* from what *country*, *or* whence
have you come here?' The *holy* Apa Shenoufe answered and said to
the *governor*, 'Why indeed dost thou enquire about our village? We
are from Empaiat of the *Plainland*;[55] and we are brethren together,
and our true *city* is the heavenly Jerusalem from this day forth,
whose sun never sets, (**108 V i**) *neither* does its moon wane; but it is
our Lord Jesus Who shines upon it at all times.'[56] When Arianus the
governor heard this, he was very angry, and he *ordered* them to be
struck[57] in the mouth until their teeth fell out. The *courier* cried
out, 'Shut your mouths! Be silent! Let me not hear this name of
Jesus from your mouths!' The athlete of *piety* answered and said to
the *governor*, 'Why indeed dost thou strike us in the mouth?' The
governor said to him, '*Since* thou hast said many words before me,
and hast *argued* for these others, while they do not speak.' The saints
answered with one voice, saying, (**108 V ii**) 'We came here with one
intent—to shed our blood for the Name of *Christ* Jesus.' Straightway
the *governor* looked upon the multitude which surrounded him, and
he saw them ready to *conflict* with him, and take the *saints* away
from him, and he was afraid, and *ordered* the *martyrs* to be seized
and cast down into the hold of the ship; and they sailed southward,
till they approached the *city* of Memphis.[58] The *governor ordered*
the ship to be moored at the shore; and he went into the temple of
the *city*, and he worshipped, and came out, and *ordered* the saints to
be brought to him in the house. The holy Apa Shenoufe was leading
them, reciting this *psalm*, thus: 'Let God (**109 R i**) arise, and let His
enemies be scattered.'[59] And the troop of the saints was repeating
(it) after him. *While* they were walking along the *street*, lo, the pillars
took human voice, saying, '*Hail*, Apa Shenoufe, thou of the name of
gladness![60] *Hail* to his (*sic*) reverend brethren also! Blessed are we
today that thou hast come to us; thou hast brought the good tidings
to us in our *city*! Blessed is any place soever whither thou shalt be
taken! Blessed is the place where your *bodies* shall be laid!' *And*
when the multitude heard the pillars saying this, they glorified the
passing by of the saints, and they cast themselves down and reverenced
them and the *blessed* Apa Shenoufe, saying, 'Blessed are we, that we
have been counted worthy that you should have *passed* our way.'
Straightway, lo, a (**109 R ii**) blind man who was sitting in the *street*,

---

[55] See p. 189, n. 34, above.
[57] For ⲔⲞⲨⲘⲛⲟⲥ, see Girgis, *BSAC* 19, p. 58.
[59] Ps. lxviii, 1.

[56] Cf. Isaiah lx, 20.
[58] Here spelt ⲘⲎⲂⲈ.
[60] Cf. p. 190, n. 49, above.

when he heard what the crowd was saying, cast away his garments and the *vessels* in which he was receiving alms, and came running, and cast himself at the feet of the saints, and *entreated* them that they might enlighten his eyes. *And* the *holy* Apa Shenoufe prayed, saying, 'Hear me, my Lord Jesus *Christ*, Who didst spit upon the earth and didst make clay, and didst anoint the eyes of him who was blind from birth, and he received sight;[61] mayest Thou open the eyes of this poor man, that he may do his work and live through Thy charity!' Straightway he breathed thrice into his face, in the Name of the Father, and of the Son, and of the Holy *Spirit*; (**109 V i**) and straightway his eyes were opened, and he received sight.[62]

Moreover, lo, there was another man, whose hand was withered, and his right side; and he was walking in the *street* bowed together, and could not lift himself up; when he saw the miracle which befell the blind man, he made his way to the *holy* Apa Shenoufe, and *entreated* him to *heal* him also. *And* the *holy* Apa Shenoufe traced a *Cross* on his hand and his side, saying, 'In the Name of my Lord Jesus *Christ*, through Whom are healing and life, may Thy (*sic*) glory and Thy power be manifested in this man!' Straightway his *flesh* became sound like (**109 V ii**) that of a little child,[63] and he walked hither and thither in the *street* of the *city*, glorifying the God of the *holy* Apa Shenoufe, the man from Empaiat, and his brethren.

And after they had been taken to him upon the *tribunal*, the *governor* said to them, 'Thou art Shenoufe, the man of Empaiat. Come, worship the gods with thy brethren *according to* the commandment of the emperors!' The holy Apa Shenoufe said to him, 'It is written: "Thou shalt not worship any *save* God alone, Whom thou shalt serve";[64] now, therefore, may it not befall that we should worship another god *save* God the Father, and His beloved Son Jesus *Christ*, and the Holy *Spirit*.' (**110 R i**) The *governor* was angry, and he *ordered* them to be *seared* with iron *awls*[65] made red hot in a fire, till their hearts and ribs within them were pierced, and their sides pierced; and he had them cast down upon their bellies, and boiling oil was poured upon their bellies until their skin peeled off. *And* the *blessed* Apa Shenoufe was reciting this *psalm*: 'Come, let us rejoice in the Lord, and let us exult in God our salvation; for the Lord our God is great, and a great King above all the mighty ones of the earth.'[66] Thereupon he turned to the saints and said to them, 'Fear not, my brethren; the Lord will not (**110 R ii**) forsake us. *For* I see Michael

---

[61] Cf. Jn. ix, 6.
[62] 109 R i 32—V i 3: cf. *Epima*, p. 14 f.
[63] Cf. II Kings v, 14.
[64] Deut. vi, 13; Mt. iv, 10; Lk. iv, 8.
[65] ϭⲟⲩⲛⲗⲓⲛ = σουβλίον, 'awl'; see Sobhy, *Mart. St. Hélias*, p. 109, with refs.
[66] Ps. xcv, 1–3.

the *Archangel*, with crowns in his hands, about to *garland* us with them.' The *governor* said to them, 'You shall reply, or else perish *miserably*.' The saints said to him, 'May it not befall that we should forsake our God and serve dead gods; for our Lord has said: "Whosoever shall *deny* Me, him will I *deny* also; and whosoever shall *confess* Me, him will I *confess* also before My Father."[67] *And* the *holy* Apa Shenoufe was a fair person, more than them all; he was ruddy, with beautiful eyes,[68] and hair entwined like clusters of henna (?)[69] blossom, and of blushful hue (**110 V i**) in his *person* like roses, being *well* formed in his shape and his *bodily habit*.[70] He had him called, and said to him, 'Shenoufe! *Now* I see the *condition* in which thou art, and thy wisdom, that it is that of a *prudent* man; hearken therefore, and *sacrifice*, and I will set thee free; and *ask* a *boon* of me, and I will grant it to thee; *since* I sympathize with thee, because thou art wise.' The *saint* said to him, laughing, 'But what is the *boon* which thou wilt grant me?' The *governor* said to him, 'I will write to my lord and emperor Diocletian concerning thee, and he will give thee great *dignity* with the emperors, and will *grant* thee a hundred soldiers (**110 V ii**) to be under thine *authority*, thou being appointed over them.' The *saint* said to him, 'So this is thy *boon* which thou wilt give to me! As my Lord Jesus *Christ* lives, if thou shouldst give me a hundred soldiers, and each one should spend a hundred and five years under me, they will not find a single day in the Kingdom of my Lord Jesus *Christ*.'[71,72] The *governor* was angry, and he *ordered* the *holy* Apa Shenoufe to be seated upon an iron couch, him and his brethren, and fire to be kindled under them. The *governor* said to him, 'Shenoufe, listen to me! Do not perish *miserably*!' The *blessed* Apa Shenoufe said, 'Thanks to God, Who has called me to His holy calling.'[73] (**111 R i**) Straightway the *Archangel* Michael stretched forth his hand over the fire, and it became like dew. And the *persons* of the saints were as that of one sitting on cool (*stone*) *slabs* in the days of winter. *And* the *holy* Apa Shenoufe was reciting this *psalm*: 'I have put my trust in Thee, O Lord; let me never be shamed.'[74] And his brethren repeated (it) after him in the midst of the fire. And he said to Arianus the *governor*, 'Tell thy soldiers to make thy *tortures properly*; for they are (too) cold.' When the *governor* heard

---

[67] Mt. x, 32 f.; cf. Lk. xii, 8 f.; II Tim. ii, 12.   [68] 110 R ii 26–29: cf. *Epima*, p. 9.
[69] See Crum, *CD*, p. 114a.
[70] Cf. I Sam. xvi, 12; xvii, 42. 100 R ii 26–V i 4: cf. Till, *KHML* I, p. 32 (Ptolemy of Dendera); Budge, *Mart.*, p. 237 (Mercurius).
[71] Cf. Ps. lxxxiv, 10.
[72] 110 V i 15–ii 14: cf. *Epima*, p. 19; also (110 V i 5–ii 14) Till, *KHML* I, p. 35 f. (Heraclides).
[73] Cf. II Tim. i, 9.   [74] Ps. xxxi, 1 f.; cf. xxv, 2; lxxi, 1.

this, he was *angry* with the *attendants*, thinking that it was true; and
he himself arose and (**111 R ii**) went over to the fire, desiring to
ascertain the matter. *And* the *holy* Apa Shenoufe took a handful of
fire, and cast it into the face of the *governor*, and straightway his face
was consumed. And the whole multitude cried out, 'One is the God
of these *saints*, giving strength to those who obey Him!' Straightway
eighteen men leapt in from the multitude, and cried out, 'We are
Christians, confessedly! *For* the death by which these *holy martyrs*
shall die, we will die by it also!' The *governor* said to them, 'Listen
to me! *Sacrifice*, do not perish *miserably*!' They answered, 'We will
not *sacrifice, but* we belong to Jesus *Christ*!' And they cursed him
(**111 V i**) and his *idols* and his emperors. The *governor* was angry,
and *ordered* them to be made into four *bands*; and some of them he
had beheaded; others he had burned in the fire; others he had
smitten with *axes*; others he had *tortured* to death. Thus they fulfilled their *contest* and their *martyrdom* on this same day. And the
whole *firmament* was filled with *angels*; and their *souls* were taken
up to heaven, in *peace, Amen. And* as for the *saints*, their eyes
beheld them going up to heaven; and the *blessed* Apa Shenoufe sang
this *psalm*: 'My heart *was glad* (**111 V ii**) for my brethren's sakes';[75]
and his brethren were repeating (it) after him, saying, 'Thou hast
heard us, O King of those in heaven and earth; Thou hast not suffered
us to be shamed; *but* Thou hast glorified us, and every one who
hearkens to Thee; for Thou art God alone in heaven and earth,[76]
and Thy beloved Son Jesus *Christ*.'

And it befell after all this, that Arianus the *governor* came out
from Memphis on that day, he and his whole *entourage*; and he
ordered the *blessed* Apa Shenoufe to be brought to him, with all his
brethren, and cast down into the hold of the ship, with *collars* upon
their necks, and *shackles* on their hands, and *manacles* (*sic*) on their
feet. (**112 R i**) Straightway they sailed southward. *And* the *holy* Apa
Shenoufe and his brethren were distressed, *and* they prayed, saying,
'Hearken to us, our Lord Jesus *Christ*, Who didst save Jonah when
he was in the belly of the *whale*,[77] and didst save Joseph from the
snare of the Egyptian woman,[78] and didst preserve him in all his
tribulations; and he *endured* until he became king. Even so too, our
Lord, mayest Thou succour us in all our *tribulations*; for Thou art
our *Helper* and our refuge and our hope.' As the *saints* were saying
this, lo, the Lord Jesus came from heaven, with Michael the *Archangel*,
and Gabriel, and multitudes of *angels*, and He spoke with the saints,

---

[75] Ps. cxxii, 1; 8.   [76] Cf. II Kings xix, 15; Isaiah xxxvii, 16.
[77] Cf. Jonah i, 17–ii.
[78] Cf. Gen. xxxix. Cf. Rossi, *Pap. copt. Torin.* I, p. 50 (Pteleme).

(**112 R ii**) saying, 'Be strong, fear not! I am with you in every place
to which you shall be taken, giving you strength, till you shame
Arianus the *governor* and his vain gods.' When the *Saviour* had said
this to them, He bade them *peace*, and went up to heaven with the
angels of glory *singing hymns* before Him, in *peace, Amen. And*
when the *saints* had seen the Lord, their hearts rejoiced, and they
fell to *chanting psalms* day and night until they reached Tilog.[79]
And the *governor* when he had arrived southward at Tilog, *ordered*
them to moor at the bank, purposing to go to the great *city* Arsinoē,
which is the (chief) *city* (**112 V i**) of the Fayûm, that he might take
the *ordinance* thither, and have the *Christians* who were in that nome
seized and made to *sacrifice*. And as the *governor* was considering
this, lo, two men came from Tilog; they heard the outcry of the
people, and they said, 'What is happening at the quay today?' They
were told, 'It is some *Christians* whom the *governor* has brought
south.' When the two men heard this, they said, 'Whence are they?'
They were told, 'It is Apa Shenoufe from Empaiat.' *And* the two
men, whose names were Elias and Pamoun,[80] were very rich *in
respect of* this *world*('s goods); they were hospitable (**112 V ii**) and
charitable, men of Godly piety. When they heard about the *blessed*
Apa Shenoufe, that he was at the quay with his brethren, they arose,
and took some loaves of pure bread and what is wont to be eaten in
purity. When they heard about the *blessed* Apa Shenoufe (*sic*),[81] they
came to him on the quay. And Arianus the *governor* was there. Elias
and Pamoun made their way together, and they *greeted* the saints
and exhorted them to eat a little bread. The *blessed* Apa Shenoufe
said to them, 'Listen, and I will tell you, my brethren, about your
whole *career*; *for* your names are already written among the number
of the *martyrs, since* you have fulfilled the *commandments* of the
holy *Gospel*, which says: "I was (**113 R i**) hungry, and ye fed Me; I
was thirsty, and ye gave Me to drink; I was a stranger, and ye took
Me in; I was naked, and ye clothed Me; I was sick, and ye visited
Me."[82] Behold then, my sons, you have fulfilled the Holy *Scripture*;
the *course* you have finished, the *Faith* you have kept; *henceforth*
there is laid up for you the crown[83] which you will receive; and
today you shall hold festival in the Kingdom of God, and be filled
with the *good things* of heaven for ever.' It befell, that after they
heard these things which the *holy* Apa Shenoufe was saying,

---

[79] For Tilog (Nilopolis, Dallâs), see Amél. *Géogr.*, pp. 136 ff.; Munier; *BSAC* 5, 240;
[80] *Recueil*, p. 55; Ball, p. 172; Mina, *Epima*, p. xxxii; Gardiner, *AEO* II, p. 140*.
[80] The names Elias and Pamoun are not found together in the *Synaxary*.
[81] A meaningless repetition of 2 ff., above.   [82] Mt. xxv, 35 f.
[83] Cf. II Tim. iv, 7 f.

Pamoun and Elias approached, and cried out, 'We are *Christians, confessedly*! One is the God of the *holy martyrs*!' **(113 R ii)** When Arianus the *governor* heard this, he was very angry, and he *ordered* them to be seized, and said to them, 'Whence are you?' They answered 'We are men of Tilog.' He said to them, 'What are your names?' One (of them) said to him, 'My name is Elias, and this other is Pamoun.' He said to them, 'Do *sacrifice*!' They said to him, 'We will not *sacrifice*; do to us what you wish.' Thereupon straightway he *ordered* the *tribunal* to be prepared on the quay of Tilog; and he inflicted upon them many *tortures*. They lifted up their cry to heaven and besought God, saying, 'Come to us, Jesus, King of all the *ages*! Remember that we have forsaken all that we had, **(113 V i)** and have carried our *cross* and followed Thee;[84] *and* do Thou give us strength.' While they were *yet* saying this, lo, the Lord Jesus came from heaven and spoke with them, saying, 'Be ye strong, and fear not, My blessed athletes! *For* today you shall be with Me in My Kingdom.'[85] When the *Noble* One had spoken with them, their hearts were strengthened, and they were moved by the power of the Holy *Spirit*. They cast earth in the face of the *governor*, and cursed him and his gods and his emperors. Arianus the *governor* was angry, and pronounced *sentence* upon them, that they should be beheaded with the sword. **(113 V ii)** A *tormentor* came and beheaded them. Thus the *holy martyrs* fulfilled their *martyrdom* on the sixteenth day of Thout, in *peace, Amen*.

Thereafter he had Apa Shenoufe and his brethren brought forward, and he said to them, 'Listen to me! Do *sacrifice*, and you shall escape numerous *tortures* and *punishments*.' The *holy* Apa Shenoufe said to him, 'A word is wont to suffice a wise man;[86] *but* as for the fool, if thou speak with him, he is not taught.[87] Now, therefore, let this word suffice thee: that *neither* thee *nor* thy gods will we obey thee (*sic*); we belong to the Lord Jesus *Christ*, the true God.' When Arianus the *governor* heard this, he was angry, and said, **(114 R i)** 'Dost thou *then* treat me as a fool?' He *ordered* some irons to be heated and put under their sides, *so that* the skin of their *bodies* peeled off. The *holy* Apa Shenoufe said, 'Hear us, our Lord Jesus *Christ*, and do not forsake us!' He turned to his brethren also, and said to them, 'Endure!' *Then* Arianus the *governor ordered* stones to be brought and placed upon the bellies of the *saints*, and vinegar and *lye* mixed together to be poured down into their nostrils; the *lawless* one saying the while, 'Do not think that the *tortures* are come to an end; there are *tortures* surpassing these, if you do not *repent* and *sacrifice*.' And the *saints* lifted up **(114 R ii)** their cry with one voice, saying, 'Come to us, thou

---

[84] Cf. Mt. xix, 27; Mk. x, 28; Lk. xviii, 28; also Mt. xvi, 24; Mk. viii, 34; Lk. ix, 23.
[85] Cf. Lk. xxiii, 43.   [86] See p. 146, n. 14, above. Cf. *Epima*, p. 19.
[87] Cf. Ecclus. xxi, 12.

angel of our Lord Jesus *Christ*, and give us strength.' Straightway, lo,
Michael the *Archangel* came from heaven, and came to the *saints*, and
touched them with his *rod* and healed them; and the stones rolled of
themselves from off their bellies, and the vinegar became like a sweet
dew coming upon their nostrils. The *saints* sprang up, with no hurt
upon them. When the multitudes saw these great wonders, they cried
out against the *governor*. The *advocate* signed to them with his hand,
and they were silent. The *governor ordered* horses to be harnessed
for him, so that he might mount them, (**114 V i**) and avoid the
clamour of the multitude. The *saints* cried out with one voice, 'As
the Lord lives, it is God Who gives us strength, till we shame thee,
and thy *torments* and thy deaf *idols*; for thou shalt not pass from
this place without passing *sentence* upon us.' And they seized the
harness straps of the horses, and would not allow them to go. *And*
he came, ready to pass *sentence* upon them and kill them and cast
them into the river, by reason of the fury of *rage* which was upon
him. *But* Julius the *commentariensis*, the man of Kbahs, and
Theophanes the *domesticus*, approached the *governor* and said to
him, 'Our lord, let us take them (**114 V ii**) with us to Arsinoë, the
great *city*; *perchance* they will (?) see these *idols* and worship them;
doubtless they are ashamed because of the multitude around them.
And I know the people of this nome, that they are *impudent
rebels*;[88] they will give us no peace, *neither* will they let us pass
sentence upon them here.' *And* he *ordered* them to be bound, and
taken before him into the *city* of the Fayūm.

When he went into the *city*, he found a great festival being celebrated that day, *since* it was the *freedom day* of their *city*; and
once every seven years the *rulers* were wont to bring out servants of
theirs and make them free men. *And* Arianus the *governor* hastened
to hear (the case of) the *holy martyrs*. (**115 R i**) The *citi*zens cried
out 'No! Do not spoil the *freedom day* of our *city*; *but* leave them
until the festival of our *city* is over, and (then) thou shalt hear
(their case).'[89] He *ordered* the saints to be taken to the *prison*.
They stood and prayed; *and* the *holy* Apa Shenoufe opened his
mouth and sang this *hymn*, while they repeated (it) after him: 'I
bless Thee, Jesus, to Whom belong all blessings. I bless Thee, Jesus,
Thou *Only Begotten* of the Father.[90] I bless Thee, Jesus, Thou true
Vine,[91] Which is a crown upon the *throne* of the Father. I bless Thee,
Jesus, Who didst walk upon the waters,[92] and Thy Feet became not
wet. I bless Thee, Jesus, Who didst make the bitter waters sweet.[93]

[88] 114 V ii 9–11: cf. *Epima*, p. 29.　　　[89] Cf. *Epima*, p. 13.
[90] Cf. Jn. i, 14.　　　[91] Cf. Jn. xv, 1.
[92] Cf. Mt. xiv, 22 ff.; Mk. vi, 45 ff.　　　[93] Cf. Ex. xv, 23 f.

I bless Thee, Jesus, Thou Staff (**115 R ii**) Which is in the midst with
the Father. I bless Thee, Jesus, Thou Rock unshakable.[94] I bless Thee,
Jesus, and all Thine *angels*. I bless Thee, Jesus, and Thy *good* Father,
in Whose Hands is our breath,[95] and He gives us life. For Thine is the
power and the glory, for ever, *Amen*.' Straightway the place wherein
they stood became illuminated, and the Lord appeared to them. He
said to them, '*Hail*, My beloved saints, My fellow *heirs*, *peace* be unto
you! Fear not! I am with you until you fulfil your *contest*.' And He
gave them *goodly sustenance* from heaven, and they ate, and their
hearts were strengthened. And He *signed* them (with the Cross), and
went up to heaven, (**115 V i**) while the saints gazed after Him,[96] in
peace, Amen.

And the *holy* Apa Shenoufe spent the whole night comforting
them until the dawn came up. *And* when it was early morning, there
was a man in the *prison* who had an *unclean spirit* upon him. It cried
out, 'I will flee away from Theodorus the son of Dionēpta (*sic*)[97] the
logistes[98] of the *city*, O thou *holy* Apa Shenoufe, for fear of *Christ*,
Who has come to thee in the *prison* this night.' Straightway the *demon*
struck the man, and came out of him; and he ran, and cast himself
down at the feet of the saints, and fell to kissing them. (**115 V ii**) *And*
when the *janitor* who was set over the prison saw the miracle which
came to pass through the *saints*, he also had an *only* daughter who
was pregnant, having come to the month of her delivery; and the
child was hindered in her womb, and she had spent eleven days in
torment; and (though) many physicians and[99] many *exorcists* had
been brought to her, they were unable to *treat* her.[100] He said to
the *holy* Apa Shenoufe, 'I beseech thee, have compassion upon my
only daughter, for she suffers exceedingly.' The *saint* said to him,
'Bring me a little oil, and I will pray over it, that the glory of Jesus
may be made manifest.' Straightway they brought the little portion
of oil; and the *saint* took it, (**116 R i**) and *signed* it (with the Cross),
and prayed over it; and he went in to his brethren and had them *sign*
it also. And he[101] took it straightway, and anointed his daughter

---

[94] Cf. Mt. vii, 24 ff.; Lk. vi, 47 ff.   [95] Cf. Job xii, 10; Dan. v, 23.
[96] Cf. Acts i, 9 f.
[97] See Introduction, p. 3, n. 9. This individual is named ΔΙΟΝΗΚΤΛ in Winstedt, *CTST*,
p. 178 (Gamoul); but ibid., p. 185, he appears as ΔΙΟΝΥϹΙΟϹ. *Epima*, p. 14, makes
him ΔΙΟΝΗϹΙΟϹ. It would appear that these strange spellings are simply due to
corruption, copied from text to text.
[98] For the λογιστής and his competence, see B. R. Rees, *Journal of Juristic Papyrology*
VII–VIII, 83 ff.; his judicial powers are illustrated in 125 R i, below.
[99] 115 V i 4–ii 16: cf. Winstedt, *CTST*, p. 178 (Gamoul).
[100] 115 V i 10–ii 19: cf. *Epima*, p. 13 f.
[101] The father. The change of person is awkward; in the corresponding place in *Epima*
(see below) the third person plural is used; perhaps the text should be so emended here.

with it; and straightway she brought forth a man child; and she called him Shenoufe, *after* the name of the *holy* Apa Shenoufe. And straightway there was great rejoicing in the house of her parents.[102] And the man from whom the *demon* came out came through all the *city* spreading the fame of the saints, because of the miracles and wonders which they were performing in the *prison*, *so that* every one who had a disease and was distressed was taken to the *prison*; and they were all healed. **(116 R ii)** *And* when Julius the *assistant* and *commentariensis* saw the miracles which the saints were performing within the *prison*, he arose and went to them in the *prison* secretly, *since* he himself-was in great suffering and affliction, there being a painful disease upon his hands and feet *at certain seasons*; and he had spent many days *crying out* in *torment*. When he went in to the saints, he *entreated* them, saying, 'If you will only do this great favour for me, I for my part will do my utmost for you in whatever you may *ask in respect of* this *world's needs*. If **(116 V i)** you wish me to set you free to go home in *peace*, I will pay as much as seven *pounds* of gold on your behalf; *only* do me this great *favour*.'[103] The *holy* Apa Shenoufe said to him, 'We do not wish thee to set us free, *neither* is it man who has *constrained* us and brought us here, *but* it is the *dispensation* of the Lord which has brought us here, *since* we have been told of the good which thou dost to all the saints. This thing only do we *require* of thee: we have desired that thou attend to us and take care for our *bodies* when *sentence* has been passed **(116 V ii)** upon us, since we are in a strange land and there is no kin of ours here to take care for us.' Julius said to them, 'This thing I am ready to do, *since* I have already been told it by an *angel* of God in a *vision* this night; and your *records* too I will write down, and will keep them in my house, so that your blessing may be in my house for ever. *But* bless me also; remember me in the places to which you will go.' The *holy* Apa Shenoufe opened his mouth, and he blessed Julius, saying, 'May God bless thee and thine house not made with hands which has been prepared for thee; and as for thine house on earth, may the blessing of God be within it for ever **(117 R i)** and unto all earthly *generations*. Let not famine *or pestilence* happen in thy dwelling-place unto all earthly *generations*. Let the *seed* which proceeds from thee not see the *judgment* into the third or fourth *generation*.[104,105] Mayest thou

---

[102] 115 V ii 26–116 R i 15: cf. *Epima*, p. 14. Cf. also Munier, *Ann. Serv.* 19 (1920), 72 (Till, *KHML* I. p. 12: Nahrow). With the whole text 115 V ii 1–116 R i 18, cf. Hyv. *Actes*, p. 293 (Didymus); Bal. - Hyv. *AM* I, p. 167 f. (Apa Til).
[103] 116 R ii 24–V i 6: cf. Till, *KHML* I, p. 35 (Heraclides).
[104] Cf. Ex. xx, 5; xxxiv, 7; Num. xiv, 18; Deut. v, 9.
[105] For a much shorter version of 116 V i 25–117 R i 10, see Hyv. *Actes*, p. 299 (Didymus).

be counted unto the *chorus* of *martyrs* of *Christ*,[106] and mayest thou
receive *inheritance* with all the saints in the day of the thousand
years,[107] thy name being written in the Book of Life,[108] thou and all
thy *seed*; worship thy King with a face unashamed; in *peace, Amen.*'
The eleven *holy* brethren also answered, saying, '*Amen*, so be it.'
Thereafter the *holy* Apa Shenoufe said to Julius that they should
bring him a little oil; and he took it, and (**117 R ii**) the *holy* Apa
Shenoufe prayed over it, saying, 'May (*sic*)[109] My Lord Jesus *Christ*,
by Whom are healing and life, Who didst open the eyes of the blind,
and make the deaf to hear, and didst cleanse the lepers, and make the
lame to walk, and didst make straight those who were deformed;
mayest Thou work a cure also upon Thy servant Julius, who takes
care for Thy servants the *martyrs*; for Thou art He by Whom is healing
and life.' Straightway the *holy* man anointed the *body* of Julius; and
the pains of the affliction which was in his *body* were relieved, and
the afflicted sinews in his hands and feet became sound, (**117 V i**)
like the *flesh* of a little child[110] —*for* they had withered through the
grievous affliction which was upon him. He walked hither and thither
in the *prison*, blessing the God of Apa Shenoufe and his brethren;
and they glorified the God of the *Christians, Christ* Jesus. *And* Julius
came away from the saints blessing the Lord God; and no pain *or*
suffering was in his *body* from that day onward.[111]

It befell after all this that Arianus the *governor* heard about the
miracles and wonders which came to pass through the saints in the
prison. The *governor* was angry, (**117 V ii**) and he *ordered* the
tribunal to be set up in the *theatre*. He had the saints brought upon
the *tribunal*; he had them brought to him bound. The *holy* Apa
Shenoufe was leading them; *and while* they were walking in the
street of the *city*, as they were about to be taken on to the *tribunal*,
lo, the *race*horses were brought out in readiness to be washed in the
canal and *exercised, since* the (racing) *contest* was at hand. *And* the
horses were being urged on by the *grooms* who were riding them,
and they trod upon a little boy, and killed him as he was walking in
the *street* of the *city*, and they trampled him, and his bowels came
out, and he died. The multitudes gathered round him, and *looked
upon* him, (**118 R i**) weeping. And they besought the *holy* Apa
Shenoufe to go to him. *And* when he had hastened to him, he said
to the multitudes which surrounded him, 'Draw back, that the glory

---

[106] 116 R ii 27–117 R i 12: cf. *Epima*, p. 16; also von Lemm, *Bruchstücke kopt.
Martyrerakten*, p. 25 (Heraclides), may be compared with 116 V ii 21 ff.
[107] Cf. Rev. xx; see von Lemm, *Br. k. Mart.*, p. 66; E. W. *Macarius*, pp. 16 ff.
[108] Cf. Ps. lxix, 28; Phil. iv, 3; Rev. iii, 5; xiii, 8; xx, 12; 15; xxi, 27; xxii, 19.
[109] Superfluous.   [110] Cf. II Kings v, 14.
[111] 116 R ii 1–117 V i 22: cf. Till, *KHML* I, p. 98 f. (Panesnew).

of Jesus may be made manifest, to Whom belong all glory and power!'
Straightway as the multitudes drew back, the *holy* Apa Shenoufe
bent down over the little boy, and he picked up his bowels and put
them into him; and he *signed* him (with the Cross), and rubbed his
body, and his *flesh* came together. He breathed into his face thrice,
in the Name of the Father, and of the Son, and of the Holy *Spirit*.
And the *holy* Apa Shenoufe took his hand, and gave him to his
parents, saying, 'Go (118 R ii) home, and give glory to God.' The
multitudes of the *city* wondered, and glorified the God of Apa
Shenoufe. And lo, one hundred and forty-seven men came out of
the multitude and cried out, glorifying the God of the *holy* Apa
Shenoufe, and they hastened before the *governor* and cried out, 'We
are *Christians, confessedly*!' The *governor* was troubled by the
outcry of the men. He said to them through the *interpreter*, 'Will
you then do *sacrifice*, or will you not, that I pass *sentence* upon you?'
The hundred and forty-seven men answered (as) with one mouth, 'As
God lives, (Who is) *Christ* Jesus, the death (118 V i) by which the
holy Apa Shenoufe shall die, we also will die by it, that we may be
with him in the house of God.' Straightway the *governor* was afraid
of the *obloquy*[112] of the *city*, saying in his heart that *perhaps* they
were inhabitants of the *city* of the Fayūm, and if he heard (their
case) in the *city*, the people of the *city* would *hinder* him. He *ordered*
them to be taken into hill country and beheaded. He handed them
over to Sym(m)achus the *tetrarch* (and) *tormentor*, with a large *force*
of soldiers, and they were divided into *bands*; and Symmachus the
tormentor came to them; (118 V ii) he *dislocated* the *joints* of some,
and severed the necks of others, and ripped open the bellies of
others. He became exhausted, and sat down for a little while to rest
himself. And lo, one of the multitude of the saints, named Callinicus,
said to the *tormentor*, 'Symmachus, my son, let this be enough for
thee now; have done! Let it be enough for thee, that thou art rushing
upon (*sic*)[113] the blood of the saints thus; for their God is great; He
will not *suffer* thee.' The *tormentor* answered and said, 'When I die,
may the pupil of my right eye be set under the hinge of the gate of
Hell!'[114] The rest of the saints answered, '*Amen*! So be it! And may
that which thou hast said come upon thee!' (119 R i) Symmachus
leapt up with *devilish* rage, and he took the sword, and beheaded the
rest of the saints. The hundred and forty-seven men fulfilled their
martyrdom in a single day. The whole *firmament* became full of the

[112] Cf. *Epima*, p. 26.   [113] Read 'that thou art shedding . . .'; so *Epima*.
[114] See Mina, *Epima*, p. 71, n. 4 on the striking correspondence of the parallel passage
there (p. 26) with the Demotic Setne Romance II (Griffith, *Stories of the High Priests
of Memphis*, p. 151).

angels, and their *souls* were taken up to heaven, having been wrapped
in *sheets* of fine linen, they being like white doves coming from the
dovecotes, and they were taken up to heaven and seated upon their
thrones and crowned with the crown which fades not, by Jesus *Christ*
our Lord,[115] to Whom belongs glory for ever, *Amen*.

After this, Arianus the *governor ordered* the *holy* Apa Shenoufe to
be taken to him (**119 R ii**) in the first *examination*. He said to him,
'O filthy *renegade* and *magician*, what are these works of *magic* which
I have heard thou doest in the *prison*, through thy *magical* arts?' The
holy, *noble* and strong Apa Shenoufe said to the *governor*, 'The
works which thou hast heard that I have done, O *unholy* and defiled
one, not by *magician's* art have I done them, but I have done them
through the power of my Lord Jesus *Christ*, in Whose Hands is the
breath of every one.[116] *For indeed* I have heard about a great *magician*
called Astratolē,[117] who was a *high priest* of Shmoun, doing great
things with his *magician's* art. He desired to go down to the pit
(**119 V i**) of the abyss to inspect it and find out what it was like. He
made invocation with his *magic arts*, and the pit of the abyss opened,
and he went down; and the pit closed up as it was (before). The
demons surrounded him, and some of them said, 'Let us behead him!'
Others said, 'Let us flay him alive!' Others said, 'Let us remove his
nails!' *In short*, they were contemplating giving him great *punishments*. He wearied himself with *invoking* all the *powers* under heaven,
and they were unable to deliver him. Thereupon he remembered
Jesus, the Son of the living God and the God of all the *Christians*;
and his heart was confirmed within him. He said in his own heart,
(**119 V ii**) 'If I have remembered Jesus *Christ*, the God of the
Christians, in my heart only, and have found strength like this, then
how much more if I utter His Name with my mouth—what will
happen to me?' And straightway Astratolē cried out with a loud
voice, 'Jesus *Christ*, Thou God of the *Christians*, if Thou deliver me
from this great *plight*, I will go and shed my blood for Thy holy
Name.' And straightway the pit opened for him, and he came up;
and he went and became a *martyr*. (This I say) so that thou mayest
know, O thou *lawless governor*, that it is no power of any *magician*,
this Name of Jesus.'[118] The *governor* was angry, and he *ordered*

---

[115] 118 V i 19–119 R i 26: cf. *Epima*, p. 25 f.   [116] Cf. Job xii, 10; Dan. v, 23.

[117] See Mina, *Epima*, p. 62, n. 1; Till, *KHML* I, p. 120 (Timotheus); also in E. W. *Macarius*,
p. 102 f., where he features in a martyrology possibly devoted to him, but perhaps
more probably to Ginousi. He is mentioned (though not by name) in *Synax*. (Thomas,
Baounah 27). For the name, see Crum, *Short Coptic Texts*, no. 52, 1.5; cf. Ἀστρατόλιος
in P. Lond. V 1703, 4; 5; ibid. 1787, 24 (both 6th cent.); Ἀστρατόλαος in P. Oxy.
1965 (6th cent.).

[118] 119 R ii 2–V ii 28: cf. *Epima*, p. 18 f. With 119 R ii 7–21, cf. Till, *KHML* I, p. 35
(Heraclides).

tortures to be inflicted upon him and his brethren too. (**120 R i**)
He *endured* with *nobility*; no *torture* could prevail over him, *since*
God was giving him strength in that hour. The *governor* said to the
holy Apa Shenoufe, 'The *wizards* and temple robbers the *laws* of the
emperors *order* to be cast into the stoke-hole of the bath. Now therefore, this is thy *sentence*, and thy brethren's too: that you be cast into
the stoke-hole of the bath, *forasmuch as* I have learned of thee that
thou dost work through *magical* practices, since thou hast practised
magic upon these hundred and forty-seven men, and didst take away
their senses, and they perished *miserably*.' He *ordered* these twelve
saints to be brought and dragged to the bath; (**120 R ii**) they were
bound hand and foot, and the *attendants* were made to kindle fire
under them; the soldiers sealed the door of the bath, and went and
left them. *And* the *holy* Apa Shenoufe took to himself fortitude
from the Holy *Spirit*, and he besought God in the midst of the fire,
saying, 'Hear me, God, Thou Father of our Lord Jesus *Christ*, Who
didst hear our father Abraham, and didst quench the fire of King
Soboch (*sic*)[119] under him; Thou Who didst hear our father Paul and
Thecla, and didst quench the fire of Thamyris under them;[120] Thou
Who didst hear the three *saints* Ananias, Azarias and Misael, and
didst send Thine *angel* to them, and didst quench (**120 V i**) the fire
of the *furnace* under them, and save them;[121,122] mayest Thou hear
us also today, and save us; for today is a day of *tribulation* and
wrath.' *While* the *holy* Apa Shenoufe was saying this, lo and behold,
the *Archangel* Michael came from heaven to the *holy* Apa Shenoufe
and his brethren, into the stoke-hole of the bath. He spread out his
shining wings over them, and the flame of the fire became like a
dewy breeze.[123] He said to the *saints*, 'Be strong, O ye *athletes* of
Christ; I am Michael, who have been sent to you to be *ministrant*
upon you, giving you strength until (**120 V ii**) you fulfil your *contest*.'
And the *angel* of God opened his *robe*, which was full of *fruits* from
the trees of *Paradise*; he gave to the saints, and they ate, and their
hearts were strengthened. The *holy* Apa Shenoufe opened his mouth
and sang this *hymn*, with the other eleven *saints* repeating (it) after
him: '*Peace* to us, for God has remembered us; *for* today we have
learned that God has not forgotten us, *even as* it is written in the

---

[119] The forms of the name in *Epima* are respectively **ⲃⲟⲥⲟⲕ** in Saʿidic (Mina, *Epima*,
p. 23) and **ⲃⲟⲥⲟⲝ** in Bohairic (Bal.-Hyv. *AM* I, p. 143). No such character is known
from Biblical or apocryphal sources. We would suggest, with all reserve, that in an
original passage which has been repeated from martyrology to martyrology the
reading may have been **ⲛ̄ϥ̄ⲣ̄ⲕ̄ⲥⲟⲇⲟⲙⲁ**; cf. Gen. xix.
[120] Cf. *Acta Pauli & Theclae*, § 22; see Mina, *Epima*, p. 68, n. 1.
[121] Cf. Dan. iii; Song 3 Holy Ch. 26 f.   [122] 120 R ii 17–V i 3: cf. *Epima*, p. 23.
[123] Cf. Song 3 Holy Ch. 27.

Holy *Scripture*: "The Lord will not forsake the *righteous* for ever, and the *patient abiding* of the meek shall not perish altogether."[124] Wherefore then God has not forgotten us, *but* He has sent His *angel* and he has helped us, (121 R i) *even as* it is written: "The *angel* of the Lord tarrieth round about them that fear Him, and delivereth them."[125] Further, he[126] says: "Since I was young, (and) behold, I have grown old, I have not seen a *righteous* man whom He had forsaken."[127] And the other *saints* did not cease blessing God in the midst of the fire, the *angel* of God giving them strength.

And at the fifth hour on the morrow Arianus the *governor* came to the bath to wash himself; and he remembered the *saints*; *for* he was saying in his heart, 'They are already burned up in the fire.' And he cried out with a loud voice, saying, 'Thou hast been shamed today, O Shenoufe, thou and thy brethren. Where now is Jesus, thy God (121 R ii) in Whom thou dost trust? Why has He not saved thee from this fire?' While the *governor* was *yet* saying this, the *angel* of God burst open the (*stone*) *slabs* of the bath, and raised up the twelve *saints* on his shining wings, and set them down upon the *dome* of the bath in the presence of the *governor*,[128] with no hurt upon them; and not a hair of their head was singed.[129] When the *governor* saw them, he was very angry; and he turned away, and did not take a bath that day. *Then* the twelve *saints* came through the *street* of the *city*, following after the *governor*, and with the multitude of the *city* (121 V i) surrounding them,[130] glorifying the God of the *holy* Apa Shenoufe. *And* the *governor* did not go to *breakfast* that day; *but* he was sitting *before the tribunal* that day in the midst of the *marketplace*. He had the *holy martyrs* brought forward one by one, and he had twelve *racks* brought, and he had them hung upon them, one upon each; and burning *torches* were put under their sides, and red hot iron spikes were brought and thrust into their ears, and iron *helmets*[131] were put upon their heads, and burning fires were put under the soles of their feet. And the *holy* Apa Shenoufe (121 V ii) blessed God, saying, 'I bless Thee, Thou *Alpha* and *O*(*mega*), the *beginning* and the end.'[132] The other eleven *saints* were repeating after him: 'I bless Thee, Jesus, Thou *Only Begotten* of the Father, Thou Who art in the seventh heaven, with seven *veils* covering Thy Face;[133] we beseech Thee that Thou wilt be with us in our *tribulations*

---

[124] Ps. ix, 18.   [125] Ps. xxxiv, 7.
[126] The Psalmist.   [127] Ps. xxxvii, 25.
[128] 121 R ii 6–16: cf. Till, *KHML* I, p. 96 f. (Panesnew); Hyv. *Actes*, p. 50 (Macarius).
[129] Cf. Dan. iii, 27   [130] 120 V ii 10–121 V i 1: cf. *Epima*, p. 23 f.
[131] These too were evidently red hot; cf. 122 R i 10, below.
[132] Cf. Rev. xxi, 6; xxii, 13.
[133] 121 V ii 2–12: cf. *BIFAO* 15 (1918), 247 (Nabraha). For the significance of the number seven, see Hastings, *Dictionary of the Bible*, III, pp. 562 ff.; Kittel, *Theologisches Wörterbuch zur N. T.* II, pp. 623 ff.

and our *persecutions*, for Thou art the physician of all physicians, and through Thee is healing and life.' *And while* the *saints* were singing these *hymns* to God, and blessing Him, lo, twelve white doves came from heaven, and settled upon the heads of the holy *saints*, where each one hung. The multitudes looked, and saw them, (122 R i) and wondered. And lo, the Lord Jesus came from heaven with Michael and Gabriel, and He touched the *bodies* of the saints, and he loosed the fiery *awls* from their ears, and the fiery *helmets* became like crowns upon their heads, and the fiery *torches* and the other tools (?)[134] with which they were *tormented* were turned back, and the princes were burned by them; and a great healing was wrought upon the *bodies* of the saints. Straightway the *holy* Apa Shenoufe looked, and saw the *Saviour* Jesus with Michael and Gabriel, standing above the *lawcourt*; and he cast himself down and (122 R ii) worshipped Jesus, saying, 'My Lord, who are we that Thou shouldst *trouble* Thyself to come to us all these times?' The *Saviour* said to him, 'Fear not, My elect Shenoufe; I will not forsake thee; the crown of thy *contest* is at hand; *for* already I have prepared your crowns and your *thrones* in the heavenly Jerusalem.' Straightway the *Saviour* and the *Archangels gave salutation* to the saints, and they went up to heaven, in *peace, Amen.*

After this the *governor examined* them the second day; he had *sulphur* brought, and boiling pitch, and he poured it upon their heads and their loins. And the *blessed* Ama Sophia (122 V i) he had taken to him on the *tribunal*, and he said to her, 'As for thyself, of what sort art thou,[135] and what is thy name?' The *blessed* one said to him, 'I am a *Christian*, and I am a servant of God my *Saviour*, my wise *Bridegroom*; *even* as the *sage* Paul has said: "I have prepared to *present* your *bodies* as a chaste *virgin* to a single husband, *Christ*";[136] and Sophia is my name.' The *governor* said to her, 'But what is Sophia?' The *virgin* said to him, ' "The *wisdom* of God" is the *interpretation* of my name, *even as* it is written in the *Scripture*: "When He was about to prepare the heaven, I was there with Him; and when He was about to prepare His *throne* upon the (122 V ii) clouds of heaven, it was I who took counsel with Him".'[137] It befell that when she had said this, the *governor* was angry, and he caused her belly and her breasts to be cleft open; and he had *pepper* and salt and mustard and acrid vinegar brought, and he had (them) applied to her belly and

---

[134] Crum, *CD*, p. 28 a?

[135] The correction suggested by Sottas, *Rev. Ég.* N. S. I (1919), 264, seems unnecessary.

[136] II Cor. xi, 2.

[137] Prov. viii, 27 f. The text is somewhat approximate. Possibly $-$ ⲩⲟⲝⲛⲉ has at some stage been corruptly substituted for $-$ⲥⲟⲃⲧⲉ.

her breasts. And through the power of God her breasts ceased bleeding, and they issued forth milk, and sprinkled the *tormentors* who were *torturing* her. The multitude of the *city* wondered, and glorified God. Thereupon the *governor* turned to the saints, and said to them, 'You shall do *sacrifice*, or else I will destroy you.'[138] The *saints* said to him, 'As for our *bodies*, thou art in *authority* over them; but as for our *souls*, thou hast no *authority* (**123 R i**) over them, since our *Saviour* has enjoined upon us in His Holy *Gospel*, "Fear not them which shall kill your *body*, but rather fear him which is able to destroy both *soul* and *body* in the *Gehenna* of fire."[139] Now therefore it is our Lord Jesus Who is Lord over our *bodies* and *souls* and *spirits*.'

In those days Phrantius[140] was *commander* in the *city* of the Fayūm and its nome, and Philip was *riparius*[141] for Alexandrou *polis*,[142] which is the (*sic*) *city* of the Fayūm, and Leontius was *logistes* for Kamē *polis*.[143] Then Julius the *cursor*[144] opened his mouth, and he submitted a *document* (**123 R ii**) in respect of the *holy martyrs*; he said to the *governor*, 'My lord, listen to me, and let me speak with thine *excellency*. If thou leavest these persons performing these works of *magic* in this *city*, they[145] will all *believe*, and serve their God. *But* listen to me, and I will tell thee this thing. There is a small *city* to the west of us, in which are some temples; it is beside a *spring* of water which is called Phalex,[146] in a village called Poubesti; let us take them there, away from this *city* in which they have done all these works; and we will do to them whatever pleases thee (**123 V i**) there. Let them worship the[147] revered gods, or let them receive their *sentence*. *For* I know that no one will hinder us there from doing as we please to these *renegades*.'

---

[138] So Sottas, p. 265: a statement rather than a question.   [139] Mt. x, 28; Lk. xii, 4 f.

[140] Read ⳡⲉⲣⲧⲫⲣⲁⲛⲧⲓⲟⲥ? This name occurs in P. Oxy. 2415 (3rd cent.); P. Lond. I 113 (p. 204); Stud. Pal. X 153 (both 6th cent.).

[141] For this office, see Oertel, *Die Liturgie*, pp. 284 f.; Rouillard, *Adm. civ.*, pp. 156; 163.

[142] If, as seems probable, this is to be identified with 'A. νῆσος, 'A. χώριον, it is in the division of Themistes.

[143] See p. 190, n. 51, above.

[144] See Girgis, *BSAC* 19, 65. The word seems to be confused (here and often elsewhere) with κοῦρσον, 'marauding party' (see Sophocles, *Lex. Byz. Gr.*, s. v.). This Julius is evidently not identical with Julius of Aqfahs, the βοηθός and *commentariensis*, who is already a secret sympathizer with the martyrs.

[145] The people.

[146] It might be suggested that the name is connected with a word ⲍⲁⲗⲉ (Crum, *CD*, p. 667 a) occurring as part of a place name (for which see E. W. *Macarius*, pp. 79; 85; Crum, *Cat. Copt. Ryl.*, p. 99), preceded by the definite article. It is, however, difficult to account for the final ⲝ, which is found in both Mss here. Another possibility seems suggested by a reference to 'Sénourès, Haris son hameau, et ses roseaux' in 'Abd el-Latif, *Relation d' Egypte*, ed. de Sacy, p. 683, whose situation would seem to be in the same part of the northern Fayûm as the geographical feature mentioned here.

[147] Or 'our'.

And on that day the *governor ordered* the *holy martyrs* to be
bound behind the horses, Apa Shenoufe and his brethren, and he
ordered them to be taken to the *prison* until he returned to the *city*.
As for the *holy* Apa Shenoufe and his brethren, when they were about
to take him away, they approached him and said to him, 'By thy
health, O our father, do not hasten away and forsake us; (123 V ii)
remember us, that we may not be separated from one another in
the house of God.' *And* the *holy* Apa Shenoufe lifted up his eyes,
and besought God, saying, 'Hear me, my Lord Jesus *Christ*! Even as
these men have *believed* in Thy holy Name through me, even so
make them not to be estranged from us.' *While* the *holy* Apa Shenoufe
was saying this, the legs of the horse on which the *governor* sat clave
to him, and he was unable to move hither or thither. *And* the *holy*
Apa Shenoufe said to the *governor*, 'By the *might* of my Lord Jesus
Christ, even as these men have *believed* in His Name through me,
thou thyself, O *governor*, (124 R i) shalt not pass from this place
without bringing my brethren with me too to the place whither thou
wilt bring me, that we may not be separated from one another in the
house of God.' The *governor ordered* the rest of the holy *martyrs* to
be bound to each other, and they were taken before him to Kamē
polis. *And* the *holy martyrs* were reviling Arianus the *governor*, and
mocking him and his gods, saying, 'They are not gods, *but* are blind
and deaf things.' *And* when the *holy* Apa Shenoufe heard the *saints*
mocking the *idols*, he remembered the speech which is written in the
holy Psalmist David: 'The *idols* (124 R ii) of the *heathen* are silver
and gold, works of men's hands; they have eyes, and see not; they
have ears, and hear not, they have mouths, and speak not; noses have
they, and smell not; hands have they, and handle not; feet have they,
and walk not; they that have made them are like unto them, and
every one that putteth his trust in them.'[148] *And* the *holy* Apa
Shenoufe led the saints like a good shepherd leading his sheep. And
they were singing this *psalm* of David, saying: 'Come ye, my children,
and hearken unto me, and I will teach you the fear of the Lord. What
man is he that (124 V i) lusteth to live, and would fain see good days?
Let him hold his tongue from evil, and his lips that they speak no
guile; let him seek after *peace*, and ensue it; for the Eyes of the Lord
look upon the *righteous*, and His Ears are inclined unto their prayers;[149]
for ever, *Amen*.' And the saints answered, '*Amen*.'.

The *holy martyrs* walked upon the road till they reached Kamē *polis*,
which is called Poubesti. And when the *governor* reached Poubesti, he
went into the temple, and worshipped. He commanded all the saints

---

[148] Ps. cxv, 4–8.   [149] Ps. xxxiv, 11–15.

to be brought in, numbering eighty- (124 V ii) three, *apart from* the
twelve *saints* Apa Shenoufe and his brethren. The *governor* said to
them, 'Come in, worship Apollo and Artemis and the rest of the gods,
numbering seventy.' The *saints* all answered with one voice, saying,
'There is no god save Jesus *Christ* the only true God, Whom we serve,
and in Whose Hands is our breath,[150] He giving us strength until we
put thy gods to shame!' *Then* the *governor* was *furiously* angry, and
ordered them to be divided and made into *bands* and *tortured.* Some
of them he had slaughtered with the sword; under others he placed
flaming *torches* (125 R i) until their ribs dropped on the ground; he
had red hot *awls* thrust into the ears of others until the *smoke* from
their *brains* rose up exceedingly; others he had *sphincterized*[151] until
they *fainted*[152] and fell upon their faces; *in short*, he inflicted a great
number of *tortures* upon them.

    And the evening of that day had come; *and* Leontius the *logistes*
ordered them to be kept until the morrow. *And* when they were
brought in, being under *torture* and exceedingly distressed by the
multitude of the *tortures*, the *holy* Apa Shenoufe was encouraging
them, saying, 'Courage, my brethren! Fear not! *For* the fire of these
lawless ones (125 R ii) is like cool water; let us not retreat from our
contest, that we may not be separated from one another in the house
of God. O our brethren, remember the word which our father David
has said: "What is a good thing, or a pleasant, more than brethren
(dwelling) in one place, with the *peace* of God in the midst of them?
They shall be like the ointment upon the head of Aaron, that runs
down upon his beard, even down unto the hems of his garments; they
shall be like the dew of Hermon which comes down upon the hills of
Sion; for there the Lord bade His blessing for everlasting life".'[153]
And the *blessed* Apa Shenoufe turned (125 V i) to the saints, and
said to them, 'My brethren, let us give our prayers to God this night,
that we may *meet* the Lord pure, and be counted worthy to be
companions with Him in His Kingdom.' *And* they all arose, and
stretched forth their hands together, saying, 'We stretch forth our
hands unto Thee, O God of Gods; our *soul* hath thirsted for Thee
like a waterless land.[154] We shall appear to Thee, Thou Holy One,[155]

---

[150] Cf. Job xii, 10; Dan. v, 23.
[151] σφιγκτηρίζειν: *add. lex.*; cf. the treatment of the martyr Ischyrion, Eusebius, *HE* VI
xiii, 1; and see our Introduction, p. 2, n. 7, above. (Where the reading dependent upon one
Ms. alone, σφαιρίζειν 'buffet like a ball' (see Lampe, *Patr. Gr. Lex.* s.v.) might be
suggested, and would suit the present context very well; it is also found elsewhere in
martyrologies. But the τ in both Mss. in this text seems conclusive.)
[152] Apparently ἐκλείπειν; see L & S[9] s. v. (II, 3). B's ⲤⲔⲟⲐⲟⲨ must be for σκοτοῦ(σθαι),
with the sense 'swoon'.
[153] Ps. cxxxiii.   [154] Ps. cxliii, 6; and cf. Ps. lxiii, 1 f.
[155] So Sottas, *Rev. Ég.* N. S. I, p. 266.

that we may behold Thy power and Thy glory.' *And* it befell, that as
the *saints* were praying, the Son of God came into their midst, joyful
and exulting; He said to them, '*Peace* (be) to you all, My honoured
friends.' (**125 V ii**) He cast His Hand upon his[156] *body*, so that no
torture should have power over him, and his brethren also.

It befell after this, that (when) the light dawned on the sixth day
of Paōpe, the *governor* arose and went into the temple to worship;
and he *ordered* the *Christians* to be brought to him, that they should
worship the dead gods. The *governor* said to them, 'Do *sacrifice* to
them!' They answered with a single voice, saying, 'We will not do
sacrifice; do to us what thou wilt; for there is no god save *Christ* Jesus
our Lord.' The *governor* was angry, and he *ordered* them to be
tortured. The *tormentors* (**126 R i**) divided them up, and they brought
cauldrons of boiling water, and fat of beasts, and vinegar, and *lye*, and
bitumen, and boiling lead; some of them had (it) poured on their
bellies, and other on their *intestines*, and others on the soles of their
feet and their shoulders; others again he set up on trees, and arrows
were shot at them.[157] *And* Apa Shenoufe and his brethren were
lowered into a *cauldron* of boiling lead. *And* the *holy* Apa Shenoufe
besought God, saying, 'Through Thy Name, O Lord, the fire is
quenched, and the *sea* dried up, and the hills melted,[158] and the
rocks (**126 R ii**) shattered, and Thou makest *wars* to cease.[159] O Lord
God, turn not Thy Face from us; be to us a *helper*, and give us strength,
Thou *protector* of all the *righteous*; for Thine is the power and the
glory, for ever, *Amen*.' Straightway, lo, Michael the *Archangel* came
from heaven, and he spoke with the saints, saying, 'Be firm and
strong!' And straightway the lead became like cool water; the *saints*
came up out of the *cauldrons* with no hurt upon them at all; and all
the *saints* were healed through the power of Michael. When all the
saints were healed from their sufferings, they saw Michael (**126 V i**)
beside them, giving them strength, and their *bodies* became strong.
He said to them, '*Now* today you shall receive the crown of life for
ever, *Amen*; and you shall dwell in the *city* of *Christ*, the heavenly
Jerusalem. Arise ye, therefore, go to the *governor* and fulfil your
contest!' And when Michael had said this to them, he went up to
heaven, in *peace*.

Straightway the saints went against the *governor* in anger, and
cried out, 'We are *Christians*, *confessedly*, and we belong to Jesus!'

---

[156] Shenoufe's
[157] B's text has 'they set them in (?) some pieces of wood (ⲩⲉ) and set fire (ⲥⲁⲧⲉ) to
them.' Our reading seems supported by Till, *KHML* I, p. 118, 13; cf. Hyv. *Actes*,
p. 308. Cf. Lam. iii, 12.
[158] Cf. Ps. xcvii, 5.   [159] Cf. Ps. xlvi, 9.

As for the *governor*, fear seized him, and he was unable to speak concerning (*sic*)[160] them. They advanced on to the *tribunal*, and overturned his *throne* from under him, and overturned <him> upon
(**126 V ii**) his face. The whole multitude cried out, clapping their
hands and saying, 'Be thou shamed today, O thou *lawless governor*!'
His nobles came to (his) assistance, and raised him to his feet. Straightway the *governor* was angry,[161] and he *ordered* in anger that their
sentence be passed upon them thus: 'I, Arianus the *governor*, *order*
these eighty-three *martyrs* to be burned and cast into *trenches*; and
as for these twelve brethren, Apa Shenoufe and his brethren, they
are to be subjected to numerous *tortures.' And* the *tormentors* came
and dragged off the *saints*; they *dislocated* their *joints*: others they
beheaded; others they smote with the *axe. And* they dug great
trenches, and cast them (**127 R i**) down into them, and cast fire upon
them. Thus the eighty-three *saints* fulfilled their *martyrdom*; and
their *souls* were taken up to heaven, while the *holy* Apa Shenoufe
gazed after them, he and his brethren, as they went up to heaven,[162]
on the sixth day of Paōpe, at the seventh hour of the day; they
received the imperishable crown, for ever, *Amen*; and the *angels* and
the *righteous greeted* them in *Paradise*; and they intercede for us
with the Father.

After this, the *governor* turned to the *holy* Apa Shenoufe, and
said to him, 'Art thou not yet *persuaded* to *sacrifice*, O *unholy* one?'
The *blessed* Apa Shenoufe answered and said to (**127 R ii**) the
governor, 'I have told thee at another time[163] that I will not do
sacrifice to thy creations of (men's) hands, and forsake my God Jesus
Christ; for indeed our *Saviour* has already told us, 'Give not your
holy things unto the dogs, *neither* cast ye your jewels before the
swine.'[164] The *governor* was angry, and said, 'Dost thou *then* compare
me to the swine and the dogs?' The *saint* said to him, 'Thou art worse
than they; *for indeed* the *wild beasts* and creeping things, if they hear
the Name of God, are wont to swallow their poison;[165] but thou dost
scorn it!'[166] The *governor* was angry, and he *ordered* them to be
seated upon iron couches, and fire to be kindled (**127 V i**) under
them, until the skin of their *bodies* peeled off; and he had red hot
balls put into their hands. *And* the *saints* were saying, 'Hear us, Thou
Who hearest every one who cries out to Thee! Look down upon us,

---

[160] Read ⲌⲀⲢⲰⲞⲨ , 'to them', with B; see Sottas, p. 266.
[161] 126 V i 28–ii 8: cf. *Epima*, p. 31 (and 129 V ii of the present text).
[162] Cf. Acts i, 9 f.   [163] That is, 'before'.
[164] Mt. vii, 6.   [165] This of course applies only to the reptiles.
[166] 127 R ii 21–26: cf. *Epima*, p. 8; also Bal. - Hyv. *AM* I, p. 115 (Paphnutius);
Delehaye, *Mart. Ég.*, p. 187, 25 ff. (Paphnutius, *graece*); Budge, *Misc.*, p. 1153 f.
(Psote, *aethiopice*).

and have pity on us in our sufferings and *torments*, and send to us
Michael the *Archangel* to give us strength!' And lo, Michael the
Archangel came from heaven, and fell to giving strength to the
saints, and they became as if they had not been touched at all.
They sprang up together, and approached the *governor*, and said to
him, 'Thou hast sword with thee, and *axe*, and all manner of *torment*;
do to us what thou wilt, (127 V ii) *while* the Lord Jesus gives us
strength; and He will give us strength again.' The *governor* was angry,
and he *ordered* them to be cast into a dark place till the morrow,
and not to be given bread *or* water until they died. Straightway the
governor withdrew; *and* when the *saints* were cast into the darkness,
soldiers also were made to watch over them. *And* at midnight, lo, a
great light shone in the place where they were;[167] and lo, the Lord
Jesus came from heaven with a multitude of *angels*, and He went to
the saints, and said to them, 'Be strong, all of you, O My holy
members! Lo, I have established your *thrones*, and have *garlanded*
(128 R i) your crowns and your *robes* (*sic*); *endure*, and fear not; for
great miracles and wonders shall come to pass through you tomorrow;
many *tortures* will be inflicted upon you; your *bodies* will be ground
like wheat, and will be cast into *trenches,* that your memorial may be
destroyed; but after a great while your *bodies* shall be revealed, and
in the place wherein your *bodies* shall be laid, great miracles and
wonders shall come to pass; and you will be glorified because of
the pains which you have suffered for My Holy Name.' When the
Saviour had said this, He *gave* them *salutation,* and went up to
heaven, (128 R ii) with the *angels* of glory *singing hymns* before
Him, in *peace, Amen. And* the saints *were merry* after they
had seen the Lord, even as those who are drunken with wine; they
rejoiced and blessed God until the light dawned. *And* when morning
came, the *lawless governor* commanded the *tribunal* to be made
ready in the *market-place*; and he *ordered* the *holy* Apa Shenoufe to
be brought with his brethren. *And* when they came, he looked, and
saw them with the *grace* of God in their countenance, all shining,
with the *blessed virgin* Ama Sophia, and he was troubled in his *spirit*
about them. He said to the *holy* (128 V i) Apa Shenoufe and his
brethren, and *especially* to the *virgin* Ama Sophia, 'Listen to me now!
Do *sacrifice*, for I feel compassion for your prudence, *since* you have
found favour with me; and moreover the *tortures* which I have
inflicted upon you, I have inflicted upon you as a father educating
his children for life.' When they heard this, they laughed. Apa
Shenoufe, the *righteous* man, said to him, laughing at him, 'In what
dost thou wish me to obey thee?' The *governor* was pleased, and
[167] Cf. Acts xii, 7.

said, 'I wish thee to satisfy me and worship Apollo the great god—*nay more*, Aphrodite and Artemis and (**128 V ii**) Zeus and Serapis, and to offer up a little *incense*, and then I will set you free to go home in *peace*, and I will give you great gifts also.' *And* the *noble* Apa Shenoufe said to the *governor*, 'Let us see the power of thy gods, and *prove* them.' The *governor* said to the soldiers, 'Quick, bring them here to me.' The priests hastened, and they brought their gods to the *market-place* and set them on their *plinths*. When the *saints* saw the *idols*, they sprang up, Apa Shenoufe and Andrew and Peter and Philemon and (*sic*)[168] his brethren; and each one cast down his *idol* (**129 R i**) upon the ground, and broke it into little pieces; and the rest of the saints took up stones and pelted the priests and the *governor*. And the *governor* was very *furiously* angry, and he commanded that fiery furnaces be lit, and the *saints* bound and cast into it (*sic*), and fire to be stoked over them till their bones were burned up. It was done according to his word; the fiery furnaces were kindled, and the flames of the fiery furnaces rose up above the whole *populace* to a height of about twenty cubits.[169] And the *holy* Apa Shenoufe and his brethren were beseeching God in the bottom of the furnaces, saying, 'Hear us, O God, the Father (**129 R ii**) of our Lord Jesus *Christ*! Through Thy Name the *sea* becomes calm, and the fire is quenched, and *Gehenna* ceases, and the fire is brought to naught; those who are oppressed in their *plight* Thou dost comfort; those who are suffering Thou dost heal; those who are lost in the *sea* Thou dost *aid*; thus also, my Lord, mayest Thou *aid* us too, and deliver us from this *plight*; for Thou art the true God, the *aid* of those who are oppressed in their *tribulation*, for Thine is the power and the glory, for ever, *Amen*.' While the *saints* were *yet* saying this, as they entreated God, lo and behold, a cloud of dew spread abroad over the furnaces and showered dew (**129 V i**) down upon them, and quenched the fire; and the bonds in which the saints were bound were unloosed by the *angel* of God, and he came to their assistance and brought them up from the furnaces, and they stood upon the *tribunal* with no hurt upon them. The whole multitude wondered, and glorified the God of the *Christians, Christ* Jesus. *And* the *holy* Apa Philip was a *stripling* vigorous in *body*, head and shoulders taller than his brethren; he received fortitude of the *Spirit*, and he stretched forth his hand over all his brethren, and he seized the *standards*[170] (**129 V ii**) on which the portraits[171] of the emperors were depicted, and he broke them in little pieces. Thereupon he advanced to the *governor*, and overturned his *throne*, on which he sat, from under him, and struck him in the face a number

[168] Superfluous.   [169] Cf. Song 3 Holy Ch. 24.
[170] Roman military standards, *signa*.
[171] On this mysterious word, see Crum, *CD*, p. 143 a.

of buffets, (though) without violence. *And* because of the great fall
which he had sustained, his nobles who were standing by came to his
assistance, and they seated him upon his *throne* as he was (before);[172]
and the *holy* Apa Philip they seized, and bound him hand and foot.
And the *governor* by reason of the great humiliation he had received
in the midst of the multitude was discomfited in that moment, and he
cursed the whole *race* of *Christians* on earth. (**130 R i**) And the *holy*
Apa Shenoufe said to the *governor*, '*Since* thou hast *dared* to blas-
pheme the Name of my God, of which, and of His holy glory, thou
art not worthy, may He be revenged upon thee quickly;[173] may He
ordain dumbness upon thee, so that thy shame may be manifest in
the midst of all this *populace*, that they may know that Jesus *Christ*
is a God more powerful than thy dead gods.' And straightway the
lips of the *governor* and his tongue within his mouth clave together,
and he could not speak at all. The *governor* was angry, and he made
signs to those of his *entourage* in the midst of the multitude. Thereupon (**130 R ii**) he arose from where he was sitting, and went to
Julius, the man of Kbahs, and continued making signs to him for the
holy Apa Shenoufe, that he might *entreat* him to open his mouth.[174]
And Julius the *assistant* and *commentariensis*, the man of Kbahs,
approached the *holy* Apa Shenoufe and *entreated* him on behalf of
the *governor*, that he should heal him. *And* the *holy* Apa Shenoufe
said to Julius, 'What dost thou wish me to do', he said,[175] 'O my
brother? And I will not disobey thee. *For indeed* at the hour when
the Lord was lifted up on the Cross, while the Jews nailed Him
(there) and spat in His Face, He cried out (**130 V i**) to His Father,
saying, "I am Jesus, Who never was disobedient." If He Who made
heaven and earth was never disobedient, then shall I be disobedient,
seeing that I am His servant, and it is He Who created myself, and my
breath is in His Hands?[176] Now therefore, see what thou desirest me
to do, O my brother.' Julius said to him, 'I wish for this *lawless*
governor to speak, and his mouth to be opened.' The *holy* Apa
Shenoufe said to Julius, 'As my God Jesus *Christ* lives, he shall not
be able to speak *unless* he takes *ink* and pen and *paper*, and writes
(**130 V ii**) honouring my God.' Straightway the *governor* made signs
to those of the *entourage*, and they brought him pen and *ink* and
paper; he took them, and wrote after this manner, saying: 'I *acknow-*
ledge Thee, Jesus *Christ*, God of the *Christians;* I know that Thou art

---

[172] 129 V i 26–ii 18: cf. *Epima*, p. 31.   [173] 130 R i 1–11: cf. *Epima*, p. 21.
[174] 130 R ii 2–10: cf. *Epima*, p. 21.
[175] ⲡⲉϫⲁⲩ seems otiose. The clause is elliptical, as in the corresponding place in *Epima*;
understand '(Tell me) . . .'
[176] Cf. Job xii, 10; Dan. v, 23.

God, *confessedly*, and that Mary bore Thee, and that Thou wast raised upon the *Cross*, and didst die, and live (again) for the sake of Thy *likeness*;[177] *but* it is the emperors who *constrain* us. For Thou art the true God.' *And* straightway they took the document, and they read it, every one who knew writing; and those who did not know it, heard (it) from those who *understood*.[178] *And* at that moment the *holy* Apa (131 **R** i) Shenoufe lifted up his eyes to heaven, and prayed, saying, 'Hear me, my Lord Jesus *Christ*, Thou Who didst come down to the *world*, and didst become the *salvation* of the whole *race* of Adam. The sick Thou hast healed; the suffering Thou hast cured; the deaf Thou hast made to hear; the blind Thou hast made to see; the lame Thou hast made to walk; the dumb Thou hast made to speak; Jesus my Life, through Whom are healing and life, mayest Thou cure this *lawless governor*; *for* it is Thou, my Lord, Who didst say, "Recompense not evil for evil".[179] Solomon has said in the *Proverbs,* "If thine enemy hunger, feed (131 **R** ii) him; if he thirst, give him to drink; for in doing so thou shalt heap coals of fire upon his head."[180] Now therefore, my Lord Jesus, Thou art compassionate and forgiving.' When the *saint* had done praying, he touched the lips of the *governor*, saying, 'By Thy power, my Lord Jesus *Christ*, Who didst open the mouth of Zacharias, who when he had written on the *tablet*, "John is the name of the little child", spoke and blessed God;[181] even so also, my Lord Jesus *Christ*, let this *lawless governor* speak, and say what he wishes to say.'[182] Straightway he touched his mouth, saying, 'In the Name of my Lord Jesus *Christ*, (131 **V** i) through Whom are power and life, mayest Thou (*sic*) cure this man.' Straightway as soon as he touched the lips of the *governor*, his tongue was loosed, and he spoke; and he cried out, saying, 'You have wrought your power to the utmost upon me, O *unholy wretches*! *But* it is I who will *chastise* you.'[183] The *governor* went, purposing to *torture* the saints. The multitude cried out against him, and would not suffer him to *torture* them. And Soterichus the *domesticus* and Theophanes the *numerarius*[184] approached the *governor*, and spoke with him, saying, (131 **V** ii) 'O lord our *governor*, hear us; pass *sentence* upon these men, and we will *bestir* ourselves and quit this place; wilt thou not cease staying thus in the midst of this country? *For* its people are *villainous brutes*; they will give us no peace. They will rise up against

---

[177] I.e., man, who is made in God's image.
[178] 130 R ii 19–V ii 30: cf. *Epima*, p. 21 f.; a much shorter version of the whole incident in Hyv. *Actes*, p. 298 f. (Didymus).
[179] Mt. v, 44; cf. Rom. xii, 17; I Thess. v, 15; I Pet. iii, 9.
[180] Prov. xxv, 21 f.; so Rom. xii, 20.   [181] Cf. Lk. i, 62–4.
[182] 131 R ii 16–28: cf. *Epima*, p. 22.   [183] 131 V i 9–17: cf. *Epima*, p. 22.
[184] For this office, see Rouillard, *Adm. civ.*, pp. 43 ff.

us and *contend* with us;[185] *for indeed* it is not a *city* in which there is
law and civilization, *but* it is an uncivilized country.' *And* the *governor*
spoke in his own heart, saying, '*Surely*, indeed, the words which those
of the *entourage* say are true; if these *brutal* people *contend* with us
in this (132 **R** i) country, who will come to our assistance here? It is
not a *city* which is under the civilizing influence of the emperors.'
And he wrote their names upon a *paper* thus, passing *sentence* upon
them, and saying: 'Shenoufe and Philemon and Apa Nilius and Peter
and Andrew and John and Phoebammon and Sophia and Chaeremon
and Antony and Philip and Hermias, from Empaiat of the *Plainland*,
since it is their desire to die for this Name of Jesus, have of themselves
come up on to the *tribunal*, without any man having *constrained*
them; that (132 **R** ii) every man who may hear their *sentence* may
understand that I am pure from their blood; *but* it is fitting that I
should do to them according to the *order* of our lords the emperors.
As for me, I *order* that their *bodies* be cast under mill-wheels, and
ground down until their *flesh* is ground small; and as for what remains
of their *bodies*, I shall *order* that a great *trench* be dug, and they be
cast down (into it), that their memorial may be hidden away.' This
then was the *sentence* which he passed upon them that day. *Then*
the *holy martyr* saints when they heard the pronouncement of their
(132 **V** i) *sentence*, their hearts rejoiced within them, and they spread
out their hands and prayed to God, saying, 'My Lord Jesus *Christ*,
mayest Thou stand with us in this hour of *necessity*.' *And* the *holy*
Apa Shenoufe, after he was brought to the place of his *sentence*,
stood upon the mill-wheel and blessed God, saying, 'I bless Thee,
Thou King, and Son of the King. I bless Thee, Thou *Invisible* One,
Whom none can see with the eyes of the *flesh*. I bless Thee, in heaven
and on earth. I bless Thee, Thou First Begotten, Thou *uncreated*
Creator. I bless Thee, Thou Who didst cause to be those things which
were not. (132 **V** ii) I bless Thee, Jesus, to Whom belong all blessings.
I bless Thee, Jesus, to Whom the first '*All hail*' of the Father came.[186]
I bless Thee, Jesus, the *Branch*[187] which sprang forth from the Heart
of the Father. I bless Thee, Jesus, the *Protector* of all the *righteous*.
I bless Thee, Jesus, Thou of the immovable and unchangeable counsel.
I bless Thee, Jesus, Thou clothing of the naked, and sustenance of the
hungry. I bless Thee, Jesus, the *lyre* of the saints, and the lay of the
Cherubim and *Seraphim*, and the *hymn* of the *angels*. I bless Thee,
Jesus, Who givest wings to the *Seraphim*. I bless Thee, Jesus, Thou
river of water of life,[188] Who givest all the *righteous* to drink. I bless

---

[185] 131 V i 25–ii 14: cf. von Lemm, *Mart. Victor & Stephanou*, p. 33; and *Epima*,
p. 29, where Theophanes is named as *domesticus* and Soterichus as *symboulos*.
[186] Cf. Lk. i. 28.   [187] Cf. Isaiah xi, 1; Jer. xxiii, 5; Zech. iii, 8; vi, 12.
[188] Cf. Rev. xxii, 1

Thee, Jesus the *column-head* of salvation, and the *pillar* of *marble*[189] which came forth from the Father, and enlightened **(133 R i)** all the *righteous*. I bless Thee, Jesus, Thou immovable *Rock* which has become the strength of all the *righteous*. I bless Thee, Jesus, Thou *spring* of the water of life which is in Eden, which watereth the trees of *Paradise*,[190] which are all the *righteous*. I bless Thee, Jesus, and Thy *good* Father, that Thou mayest come to me today and to my brethren in this night of *necessity*, that we may be counted worthy to hear Thy Divine (*sic*)[191] Voice, Thou gladdening us. Remember us in our coming to Thee; let those who are on the right hand stand with us, and those on the left hand depart;[192] let the darkness *withdraw*, and let the light shine for us.[193] May the *menace* desist; may the *hailstorm* (?)[194] cease **(133 R ii)** before us; open to us Thy *gates*, O King, that we may come within them. Ye *angels* of God, come ye, and stand with us! Ye *Cherubim* of the light, stand ye with us![195] Ye *ministers* of the light, stand ye with us! Ye *treasuries* (*sic*)[196] of the light, stand ye with us! Open to us the *gates* of heaven! Ye *elders* of the light, stand ye with us![197] Ye *overseers* of the light, stand ye with us! Thou Father of all Lights, and Thy beloved Son Jesus *Christ*, and the Holy *Spirit*, stand Ye with us! Come to me, Jesus *Christ*,[198] and I will *require* of Thee **(133 V i)** the *boon* that my *soul* (desires), ere I come forth from the *body*.' *While* the *holy* Apa Shenoufe was pronouncing this *profession*, lo, sounds of *trumpets* came from heaven; and lo, the Lord Jesus came from heaven, mounted upon a shining *chariot*, with the *angels* of glory *singing hymns* before Him; He made the *chariot* to stand still over the *lawcourt*, and He cried out, 'Shenoufe, thou joy of those in heaven, and comfort of those in earth, thou and thy brethren, come ye up to Me, My fellow *heirs*, that I may give you the wages for the pains which you have suffered for My Name's sake.' *And* when the *holy* **(133 V ii)** Apa Shenoufe heard the voice of the *Saviour*, his heart rejoiced within him, and he said to the *Saviour*, 'My Lord, if it please Thee,[199] I will that Thou *assure* me and my brethren of the *boon* which my *soul* (desires).' The *Saviour* said to him, 'Speak, My beloved, say what is thy pleasure.' The *saint* said to Him, 'If it please Thee, my *Saviour*, let not our *bodies* be

[189] Or 'crystal'; see L & S[9], s. v.
[190] Cf. Gen. ii, 10; Rev. xxii, 1.
[191] Read 'sweet'.
[192] Cf. Mt. xxv, 33.
[193] 133 R i 23–29: cf. *Epima*, p. 32 f.; von Lemm, *Br. kopt. Mart.*, p. 28 (Heraclides).
[194] = χάλαξα. Or θάλασσα? If the latter, perhaps cf. Ex. xiv. But the former seems preferable.
[195] 133 R ii 1–9: cf. *Epima*, p. 32 f. Also (133 R ii 1–12), von Lemm, *Br. kopt. Mart.*, p. 28 (Heraclides).
[196] Read Ⲑⲣⲱⲡⲟⲥ, 'doorkeepers'; so *Epima*.
[197] 133 R ii 13–20: cf. *Epima*, p. 32; Budge, *Mart. Isaac of Tiphre*, p. 32.
[198] 133 R ii 30 f.: cf. *Epima*, p. 33.
[199] 133 V i 24–ii 16: cf. *Epima*, p. 33.

hidden in the earth, that our memorial be hidden away.' The *Saviour*
said to him, 'My Father has already prepared a goodly *shrine*, that your
bodies may be laid therein in this *world*; and the place where your *bodies*
shall be laid, I will lay blessing therein, and *peace*, (**134 R i**) and graces of
healing.' The *saint* said to Him, 'Hear me, my Lord Jesus *Christ*! If a man
should come to the *shrine* where my *body* shall be laid, and he fall by a
transgression and a sin, and shall come to my *body* and entreat us
before the sun sets, mayest Thou forgive him the sin which he has
done.'[200] The *Saviour* said to him, 'Be it even so.' The *saint* said to
Him, 'Whoso shall *gather* an *offering* in the *shrine* where my *body*
shall be laid, mayest Thou *gather* him in the heavenly *offering*.
Whoso shall enshroud our *bodies* in graveclothes, mayest Thou *array*
their (**134 R ii**) *souls* in the *garments* of salvation.[201] Whoso shall
write the book of our *martyrdom*, and show forth our memorial,
mayest Thou write his name in the Book of Life.[202] Whoso shall
give our names to their children, showing forth our names, mayest
Thou *assure* them in their heart's *assurance* (?)[203] And in the place
where our *bodies* shall be laid, mayest Thou lay Thy blessing and
Thy *peace* enduring therein for ever.' The *Saviour* answered and said
to the *holy* Apa Shenoufe, '*Verily*, My beloved, everything which
thou hast *requested*, My Father has already *granted* thee.'[204] And
the Saviour took the hands (**134 V i**) of the *saints*, and raised them
up on the mill-wheel. He *gave* them *salutation*, and said to them,
'Courage! Fear not! I am with you; *for* behold, I have prepared your
thrones and your crowns and your *raiment*, very precious, in the
third heaven.[205] Behold, I adjure you by My Holy Name, and My
holy *angels*, that all men who shall *believe* in your name with a
single heart, every thing that they shall *ask* in the Name of My
Father, I will give it to them; and I will not forget them in the hour
of their *necessity*. And whoso shall vow a vow upon your *shrine*, and
shall *neglect* to fulfil it, I will take (**134 V ii**) vengeance upon him
swiftly. And I will make your names to be famous, O thou *holy*
Shenoufe and thy brethren; I will cause *presents* to be brought to
thy shrine in My Name; and in the place where your *sentence* shall
be passed, I set graces of healing.' When the *Saviour* had said this to
the *saints*, He bade them *peace*, and went up to heaven, with the
angels singing hymns before Him.[206]

[200] 134 R i 7–19: cf. *Epima*, p. 33.   [201] Cf. Isaiah lxi, 10.
[202] Cf. Ps. lxix, 28; Phil. iv, 3; Rev. iii, 5; xiii, 8; xx, 12; 15; xxi, 27; xxii, 19.
[203] Corrupt?   [204] 134 R ii 3–31: cf. *Epima*, p. 33 f.
[205] Cf. II Cor. xii, 2.
[206] Requests by the martyr about his future commemoration, and the Saviour's promises,
are a commonplace in the martyrologies; see (e.g.) Budge, *Mart. Isaac of Tiphre*,
pp. 32 ff.; Bal. - Hyv. *AM* I, pp. 20 ff. (Lacaron); ibid., pp. 84 ff. (Sarapion), as well
as *P. & T.* 85 V i.

Then the *blessed virgin* Ama Sophia spread out her hands and prayed to God, saying, 'My Lord Jesus *Christ*, even as Thou hast heard my brethren entreating Thee, and hast accepted their (**135 R i**) *sacrifice* at their hands, even so mayest Thou hear me also when I entreat Thee; may I too be counted worthy of the crown which my brethren have received.' When the *governor* saw the *blessed* one standing praying, he *ordered* her to be set up on the *rack* and scraped; and flaming *torches* were applied to her sides. And the *blessed* Ama Sophia answered and said, 'Blessed am I, even I, that the weak *vessel*[207] has become a beloved of the *duke (sic)*[208] in the Kingdom of Heaven.' And she uttered many despiteful words in the face of the *governor*. The *governor* said to her, 'Sophia, I feel compassion for thy youth; else (**135 R ii**) I should not *bear with* thee even thus; *but* do *sacrifice* before thou perish *miserably*! I have been at pains to spare thee until now.' The *blessed* Ama Sophia answered, 'Let not this matter concern thee, to say "Do *sacrifice*"; I will not do *sacrifice*, that we may not be separated from one another in the house of God, Jesus *Christ*; *but* the death which they shall die, I will die by it also, that I may also live with them in endless *ages*.' The *governor* answered and said to her, '*Verily*, O Sophia, if thou wilt hearken to me, and satisfy the emperors, I will receive thee into my house; I have an *only* son, and I will take thee as wife for him, (**135 V i**) and I will have fashioned for thee a fair diadem, (such as) no *ruler* ever fashioned.' The *blessed virgin* said to him, 'It is written in the Holy *Scripture*:[209] "Gold and silver shall change,[210] and likewise shall the beauty of the *body* be marred in the *tombs*;[211] *but* he who doeth the will of God shall endure for ever".'[212] The *governor* said to her, 'Dost thou wish that I pass upon thee thy *sentence*, as upon all thy brethren?' The *blessed* Ama Sophia answered, 'I thank God for thy *sentence*.' Straightway he had this one also taken, and she (**135 V ii**) was set upon the mill-wheel beside the eleven *saints*. Their *bodies* were cast under the mill-wheel, and they were ground down until their bones were broken one upon another into little pieces; and their blood and their *bodies* and their skin clave to the mill-wheel. A great multitude of that nome gathered together, and they came to the saints, and saw them. Every person who was sick of a grievous illness *of* any sort, they took

---

[207] Cf. I Pet. iii, 7.
[208] Evidently corrupt; ⲆⲞⲨⲌ perhaps misread for ⲆⲞⲌⲀ; if so, cf. II Tim. ii, 21?
[209] The passage which follows is not to be found, as a whole, in any canonical scripture, or in any apocryphon known to us. Other citations of it in Budge, *Mart.*, p. 6; 17 f. (Victor); Bal. - Hyv. *AM* I, p. 68 (Sarapion); ibid., p. 77 (Paphnutius); ibid. p. 204 (Anoub); Delehaye, *Mart. Ég.*, p. 190 (Paphnutius, *graece*).
[210] Cf. James v, 3?   [211] Cf. Ps. xlix, 14.
[212] I Jn. ii, 17.

of the blood of the saints, and put (it) upon their *members* which
were diseased; the blind received sight, the lame walked, the deaf
received hearing, the dumb spoke, (**136 R i**) and the lepers were
cleansed, *according to* the word which our *Saviour* had said to
them: 'I will set graces of healing in the place where your *bodies*
shall be laid, and in the place where you shall fulfil your *dispensation.*' And thus they fulfilled their *dispensation* and their *martyrdom*, the twelve *noble martyrs*, Apa Shenoufe and Apa Philemon
and Apa Nilius and Apa Peter and Apa Andrew and Apa John and
Apa Phoebammon and Ama Sophia and Apa Antony and Apa
Hermias and Apa Chaeremon and Apa Philip, on the seventh day of
Paōpe; and they received the crown of (**136 R ii**) life, and the Lord
Jesus received their *souls*, and He *greeted* them, and wrapped them
in *sheets* of fine linen, and set them with Him on the *chariot*, and
took them up to heaven,[213] with the *angels* leading them with tabors
and *choirs* and *drums* and *trumpets* and shouting; the whole *choir* of
the saints *arrayed* them, and the Lord set upon their heads the crown
of life, and He seated them upon their *thrones*, and they made
festival with all the saints,[214] *since* they had contended in the good
fight, and had finished the course, and had kept (**136 V i**) the *Faith*;
and they received the crown which was laid up for them[215] for ever,
Amen.

After all this, the *governor ordered* a great *trench* to be dug on the
south side of the village, and the *bodies* of the *holy martyrs* to be
cast into it; and they were cast (in), and covered up. *And* the place
where their *bodies* were laid was shaken thrice on this side and that;[216]
and there was great terror, and great *confusion* and disturbance
wrought in all that nome by the coming out from the *body* of the
(**136 V ii**) *holy* Apa Shenoufe and his brethren. As for the *lawless
governor* himself, he was afraid and troubled; and he hoisted *sail*,[217]
and rose up in haste; and the rest of the saints who were in his hand
he bound, and took them with him to the *city* (of) the Thebaid.

And I, Julius, wrote the *records* of the holy Apa Shenoufe and his
brethren, from Empaiat of the *Plainland*; and I gave them to Traphanes,
my *personal* servant, and he took them up to my house where I dwelt
in Kbahs, and left them there, *however* (*sic*)[218] their blessing and
grace might be with us continually for ever, *Amen.* God (**137 R i**) is
witness, and my *spirit*, that I, Julius, have not added to the mighty

---

[213] 136 R ii 1–10: cf. *Epima*, p. 34.   [214] 136 R ii 24–28: cf. *Epima*, p. 34.
[215] Cf. II Tim. iv, 6 (and I Tim. vi, 12).   [216] 136 V i 21–25: cf. *Epima*, p. 34.
[217] See Girgis, *BSAC* 19, 63; cf. Sophocles, *Lex. Byz. Gr.* s. v.; also Lampe, *Patr. Gr. Lex.*
(but not in the sense of 'sail').
[218] Read 'in order that . . .'; see textual n.

deeds of the holy *saints* Apa Shenoufe and his brethren, *nor* have I
taken away (aught) from them;[219] *but* the things which they did,
and those which I saw (done) by them, these things I have written
down.[220] Thereafter I returned, and went to Alexandria; and I continued in charge of the *duty* for which I had been made responsible,
taking care of the saints *according to* the ordinance of God with
which He had favoured me until the day when the *lawless* emperor
Diocletian died. He left (?) the saints imprisoned in *divers* places; and
as for the saints who were shut up in the *prison* of Alexandria, I was
taking care of them *in respect of* the *needs* (137 **R ii**) of this *world*,
according to what they ate in purity; and I took them fire and water,
since they were afflicted by the multitude of the(ir) sufferings and
tortures. When I had seen their sufferings and *tribulation*, I went to
the *commander*, and *entreated* him to set them free. The *commander*
said to me, 'I fear for my part *lest* another *lawless* emperor should
arise, and enquire for them, and I fail to find them and deliver them
to him, and so find myself in *peril* on their account.' And I for my
part said to the *commander*, 'I will abide in the *prison* with all my
people until the day when (137 **V i**) God shall give a good ordinance
concerning the saints.' The *commander* said, 'Go *then*, and do *as* thou
dost please.' And I went to the *prison*, and abode there with Eustochia
my wife, and my son Eucharistus, and my sister Eucharistia; and my
servants were *attending* upon us; we released the saints, and each
departed to his dwelling-place in *peace*, glorifying God. And we
remained within the *prison* of Alexandria, shut in there until the day
when the God-loving emperor Constantine become emperor; and he
sent (word) (137 **V ii**) to Egypt, and threw open all the *prisons*,
from Alexandria to all the south of Egypt. It befell that when the
prison of Alexandria was thrown open, I came up to my house, I and
my servants and all my people; and the saints also heard that I had
come up to my house, and they arose all together, and came to me
in my house. And my sister Eucharistia brought water, and washed
their feet;[221] and they *congregated* in my dwelling-places, and I was
counted worthy that they ate bread in my dwelling-places. *And* some
of them laid down the *body*[222] in my house, by reason of the hard-
ships of the(ir) journeyings and the multitude of the(ir) *tortures*;
(138 **R i**) and I buried them within my *storehouses* and *workshops*,[223]
that their blessing and their grace might be with us. Thereafter, the
rest of the saints departed from me, I letting them go in *peace*, and

[219] Cf. Deut. iv, 2; xii, 32; Rev. xxii, 18 f.   [220] 138 V ii 14–137 R i 13: cf. *Epima*, p. 35.
[221] Cf. I Tim. v, 10.   [222] I.e., died.
[223] For the keeping of martyrs' bodies in private houses, often unburied, see Schmidt, *ZÄS*
     32, 54 ff.; Amélineau, *Actes des Mart.*, p. 236; Schmitz, *ZÄS* 65, 6.

they went each to his dwelling-place, glorifying God.[224] *And* I, Julius, by reason of the pains which I saw the saints suffering, will never again drink wine, *or* anoint my *body* with oil, till the day of my death. *And* God has *granted* me this great grace and this great *boon*, that he put forgetfulness in the heart of the *lawless governor*, (**138 R ii**) and I have *neither sacrificed, nor* been *constrained*,[225] *but* I have *per-severed* in the work for the saints, for the sake of their *needs*; and I placed a servant of mine in *each lawcourt* from Alexandria unto all the south of Egypt, writing the *records* of the saints[226] in *each* place, and bringing them to me. And I have sat down and *accurately* have I written them in the *Roman*[227] *character*, and have preserved them in my house, that their blessing and their grace might be continually with (**138 V i**) all my *seed* until the *consummation* of the *age.*[228]

This is the end of the *martyrdom* of thre twelve *holy martyrs* of Empaiat, Apa Shenoufe and his brethren, who fulfilled their *martyr-dom* in Kamē *polis*, which is Poubesti of the Fayūm. And all the *souls* who became *martyrs* through Apa Shenoufe and his brethren number eight hundred and ninety-five *souls*; (**138 V ii**) they received the crown of life, and they went up to heaven, in *peace, Amen.*

Peace (be) to all who have become *martyrs* in the Name of our Lord Jesus *Christ*; to Whom belongs the glory and the power, the *authority* and the might, in a *consubstantial Trinity*; in fair *adoration*, for ever and ever, *Amen.*[229,230]

---

[224] 137 R i 22–138 R i 16: cf. *Epima*, p. 35 f.   [225] 138 R i 26–ii 3: cf. *Epima*, p. 35.
[226] I.e., of their trials.   [227] I.e., Latin.
[228] 138 R ii 7–V i 4: cf. *Epima*, p. 36 f. Also, less exactly, the whole passage from 136 V ii 14 to here, Winstedt, *CTST*, pp. 186–8.
[229] Cf. Jude 25.   [230] 138 V ii 6–18: cf. *Epima*, p. 37.

SS. APAIOULE AND PTELEME

(168 R i) The *martyrdom* of the *noble saint* and *martyr* of *Christ* Apa Apaioule, and Apa Pteleme;[1] they having fulfilled their good *contest* on the twenty-first day of the month Tōbe, in God's *peace, Amen.*

It befell in the reign of Diocletian and Maximinian (*sic*), the *lawless* emperors, when Culcianus[2] was *consul*, and Soterichus[3] *prefect* over the whole *country* as far as the Ethiopians, and Romanus[4] was *general* with Euhius[5] and (168 R ii) Basilides,[6] that the *Devil* perverted their hearts from the God of heaven; *and* Diocletian answered and said to those of the *Palace*, 'I say to you of the *Palace*, behold, I *order* you that every person in whom is the breath of life, *whether* small *or* great, *whether* male *or* female, *whether* bond *or* free, *whether* soldiers *or authorities or civilians*[7] *or bishops or presbyters or deacons or lectors or monks*,[8] they must all come and worship Apollo and Artemis and Athena and Zeus. Any one who shall disobey (168 V i) me and my *edict*, I *order* to be *tortured*, and his house shall be for plunder.' And he wrote the *ordinance* in this sort: 'I, the emperor Diocletian, write to the *governors* of the *several cities*: *Greeting*! I inform you that I have published an *ordinance* in the whole earth, that every one is to *sacrifice* to the gods which I have made.' Straightway he gave the *ordinance* to Sebastianus[9] the *count*. He came south through all Egypt; *and* when he came to Alexandria, he gave the despatches to Culcianus the *governor* of Alexandria. Straightway as soon as he received the despatches, he *saluted* (168 V ii) them; and he *ordered* all those of his *entourage* to be assembled, and he had the *epistle* of the emperor read to them, and they all *sacrificed*. Thereupon

---

[1] Neither Saint is identifiable in the *Synaxary*. In the designation of the former, the title Apa has become so inseparable from the personal name that it must be regarded as part of it (cf., e.g., ⲁⲛⲁⲛⲟⲩⲃ (= ⲁⲛⲁ ⲛⲟⲩⲃ), ⲁⲛⲁⲛⲟⲗⲓ, ⲁⲛⲟⲗⲓ (= ⲁⲛⲁ ⲛⲟⲗⲓ), ⲁⲛⲁⲡⲏ (= ⲁⲛⲁ ⲁⲡⲏ). We have treated it accordingly throughout.
[2] See p. 185, n. 4, above.
[3] There is no documentary record of a Prefect of Egypt of this name.
[4] Well known from martyr literature; a military commander with Antiochene connections, the impious father of the famous Victor; see p. 156, above.
[5] Another general, also connected with Antioch, whose name occurs in the martyrologies; he is one of the principal villains in the martyrdom of Anoub (Bal. - Hyv. *AM* I, pp. 200 ff.); in Budge, *Mart.*, p. 3 (Victor), his name is spelt ⲉⲩⲍⲁⲓⲟⲥ; Εὔαιος is cited (doubtfully) as a proper name by Pape, *Wb. d. gr. Eigennamen*, p. 299.
[6] See p. 186, n. 16, above.
[7] See Till, *KHML* I, p. 44.
[8] This enumeration is a commonplace in the martyrologies; cf. (e.g.) Till, *KHML* I, p. 159 (Cosmas & Damian).
[9] A personage so named (though variously designated) features in other martyrologies (e.g. *Epima*), but is not identifiable from Greek documents.

Sebastianus took the *ordinance*, and came south through all Egypt
with a large force of soldiers attendant upon him, until he reached
the nome of Hnēs.[10] He came up to a village called Psoutoumēt,[11]
and commanded the *tribunal* to be set out beside the river;[12] and he
ordered all his soldiers to be assembled around him, and had the
ordinance of the emperor read out to them. They all cast themselves
down and worshipped it, crying out and saying,'There is no (**169 R i**)
god save Apollo and Zeus and Artemis and Athena.'

But there was among them a young soldier, *of gentle birth*, wise
and *righteous*, whose name was Pteleme; he was thirty-three years
old, and the whole *host* of soldiers loved him; for he was a man of
God, attentive to both small and great; *and* the youth was a
Phoenician of Antioch. The *count* said to him, 'Do thou also come
and worship the *ordinance* of the emperor.' The *noble* man said to
him, 'I will not worship *idols* made with hands, and (one who is but)
a man like myself; for it is written in the *Prophet* (**169 R ii**) Jeremias:
"Woe to a man whose *hope* is in man; *but* blessed is a man whose *hope*
is in the God of heaven;"[13] that man shall never go to destruction.
Hast thou not heard the *Psalm*ist David saying: "Have we forgotten
the Name of our God, *or* holden out our hands to another strange
god?" '[14] Sebastianus the *count* answered and said to him, 'Hearken
to me! Do not perish *miserably*! *Sacrifice* to the revered gods, and it
shall be well with thee. If not, I shall *punish* thee *sorely* with very
severe *torments*, and no (**169 V i**) one will be able to save thee from
my hands.' The *blessed* Apa Pteleme answered and said to him, 'I
will not *sacrifice* to *idol images* of *fiends* and forsake Jesus, my
Salvation. *For indeed* if thou kill me, Jesus my God will make me to
live again. It is written in the holy *Gospel*: "He that *believeth* in
Me, though he were dead, yet shall he live."[15] And again: "Every
one that *believeth* in Me, he shall never taste of death." '[16] When
the *count* heard this, he was very angry, and he gnashed his teeth
upon him, and said to him, 'By the health of Apollo, if thou dost
not obey (**169 V ii**) me, thou shalt perish *miserably*. And if thou hast
played the fool, I will deal with thee *according to* thy folly.' The *holy*
Apa Pteleme answered, 'It is written in the holy *Apostle*: "We are

---

[10] = Heracleopolis; see above, p. 185, n. 8.

[11] See Amél. *Géogr.*, p. 363 (s.n. ⲡⲟⳓⲟⲧⲟⲙⲉⲛⲧ); Sedment el- Gebel. A place Σουτμει is
mentioned in a papyrus (*Sb.* 4309, 7) of the 3rd century B.C., found in the area of
Alexandria. 'Ηρακλει[in 1. 2 of this document has been taken to refer to the division
of Heraclides in the Fayûm; it might be suggested, however, that it refers instead to the
Heracleopolite nome.

[12] This will be the Bahr Yussuf.   [13] Jer. xvii, 5; 7;

[14] Ps. xliv, 20.   [15] Jn. xi, 25.

[16] Jn. viii, 52; xi, 26.

fools for *Christ's* sake."[17] *Further*more he says: "The foolish of the
world are they whom God hath chosen to confound the wise." '[18]
When Sebastianus the *count* heard this, he *ordered* his *accoutrement*[19]
to be torn off, and himself to be stripped naked; he was left with only
his *loincloth*[20] between his legs, girt upon his loins, and straps were
put on his hands and feet, and he was stretched out in his presence;
and he had them break twenty (**170 R i**) palm staves on his *body*,
they beating him two at a time until his blood flowed down on the
ground like water. The *count* said to him, 'Thou hast seen (but) the
beginning of the *tortures*, that they are very sore.'[21] The *blessed* Apa
Pteleme answered, 'It is written in the *Acts* of our holy fathers the
Apostles that they beat the *Apostles*, saying, "Do not utter the Name
of Jesus with your mouths"; and they went their way rejoicing that
they had been counted worthy to suffer humiliation for the Name
of Jesus.'[22] When Sebastianus the *count* heard this, he was filled with
the anger of his father the *Devil*; and he *ordered* him to be cast into
a cell (full) of fresh dung, (**170 R ii**) which was all dark, and to be
given neither bread *nor* water till he should die of hunger and thirst.[23]
And the *blessed* Apa Pteleme was shut in. He arose, and stood and
prayed, saying, 'God, hearken to me when I cry to Thee; my Lord
Jesus, forsake me not, *but* come to me quickly, Thou God beside
Whom there is none other, that Thou mayest be with me until this
lawless one shall know that there is none other god beside Thee; for
Thine is the power and the glory, for ever and ever, *Amen*.'[24] Straightway the Lord Jesus came from heaven, with His *angels singing hymns*
before Him; and a great light (**170 V i**) shone in the cell in which he
was shut up, and a voice came from the light, saying, 'Dost thou not
know, O *blessed* Apa Pteleme, that those who *believe* in Me I will not
forsake? I am Jesus, the Son of the living God. Be strong and firm!
Fear not! I am with thee, until thou endure some few *torments* in the
world; and I will write thy name among the imperishable *aeons*, and
will make thee a soldier for a *legion* of *angels* among the *aeons*[25] of
the light; *since* thou hast three days more (to live) in this *world*; and
thereafter I will receive thee into the *aeons* of the light, (**170 V ii**)
the *rays* of whose light thou art not able to bear. *For* already have I
prepared thy *throne* in the Kingdom of Heaven, and have placed upon

---

[17] I Cor. iv, 10.   [18] I Cor. i, 27.
[19] On this word, and its claim to separate existence, see Girgis, *BSAC* 19, p. 72 f.
[20] This is one of many misspellings of φεμινάλιον.
[21] 170 R i 8–10: cf. Till, *KHML* I, p. 95 (Panesnew).   [22] Acts v, 40 f.
[23] This treatment is a commonplace in the martyrologies; e.g., *BIFAO* 15 (1918),
    p. 236 (Nabraha); *PSBA* 32 (1910), p. 286 (Psote).
[24] Cf. Mt. vi, 13.
[25] Perhaps in the sense cited by Lampe, *Patr. Gr. Lex.*, p. 56 b (I).

it a crown of glory, and *raiment* shining like the sun. And I will send thee a companion (to be) thine, who is a *monk*; *now*, the *shrine* to which I shall take thee, I will take that man there also; and the crown which thou shalt receive, the same that one also shall receive; for that man is a chosen *vessel* for Me.[26] *Peace* (be) to thee! Fear not!' When the Lord Jesus had said this, He went up to heaven, with His *angels singing hymns* before Him. *And* the *blessed* Apa Pteleme did not (171 R i) cease praying until the dawn came; he spent three days and three nights not having eaten *or* drunk.

After this, there was a *monk*, an *anchorite* and *ascetic*, whose name was Apa Apaioule; he was a man of Hanepioor,[27] in the nome of Hnēs. *Now* this was his occupation: all the *bodies* of the *martyrs*, whosoever would be slain, he would go for them and collect them. *And* when he heard about the *blessed* Apa Pteleme, that he was imprisoned in Psoutoumēt, he arose and came to him in great gladness and rejoicing, because the *Spirit* of God had told him, 'Thou shalt fulfil thy *ministration* (171 R ii) with him.' *And* when he went to him, the soldiers who were guarding him *prevented* him, and would not allow him to go in to him. Thereupon he persistently besought them, and they allowed him, and he went in. Straightway Apa Pteleme arose, and they *greeted* one another, and sat down. Apa Apaioule said to him, '*Hail*, thou holy athlete of Christ!' The *holy* Apa Pteleme said to him, '*Hail*, thou way of salvation[28] which has reached me this day! For thou art a holy man, O my lord and father.' The *blessed* Apaioule said to him, 'Fear not, my brother; Jesus will not forsake us.' And (171 V i) they spent that whole day in mutual jubilation and rejoicing, and in entreating God.

Then a soldier went and told the *count*, 'A *monk* has come here and has gone in to Pteleme.' *And* when Sebastianus the *count* heard this, he *ordered* the *tribunal* to be set out on the quay, and he said that they were both to be brought bound together by the *rope*. The *count* said to them, 'What do you say? Will you be fools, and perish *miserably*, or not?' The *blessed* Apaioule answered, (171 V ii) saying, 'Dost thou not know, O *count*, that it is good to obey God *rather than* men?[29] For it is written: "If a man sin against an(other) man, entreaty is made to God, and He forgives him."[30] Now therefore we will obey God rather than thee.' When the *count* heard this, he was *furiously* angry, and he *ordered* Apaioule to be brought forward; he

[26] Cf. Acts ix, 15.
[27] Aυιπιαρ occurs as the name of an ἐποίκιον in the Heracleopolite nome in Stud. Pal. XX 137, 9 (A.D. 522); see Calderini, *Diz. geogr.* I (2), p. 46.
[28] Cf. Acts xvi, 17.   [29] Cf. Acts v, 29.
[30] I Sam. ii, 25.

was seated upon an iron bed, and that a red hot *instrument* be (*sic*)[31] brought and thrust into his right eye; and he had it stirred up until its pupil sprang out on to the ground. And he was *distressed,* (172 **R i**) and he looked up to heaven, and cried out, saying, 'My Lord Jesus *Christ*, look, and see my light which I have lost for Thy Holy Name's sake. And I *believe* in Thee, that Thou hast power to (do) anything.'[32] *Then* the *count ordered* the *blessed* Apa Pteleme to be brought out, and he said to him, 'Thou too, wilt thou do *sacrifice*? If not, thou shalt perish *miserably* through sore *tortures.*' *Then* the *blessed* Apa Pteleme answered him, 'I will not *sacrifice* to dead *idols.*' *Then* the *count* was angry, and he *ordered* red hot *instruments* to be brought, and thrust (172 **R ii**) in under his sides until they penetrated in amongst one another. *And* it befell that after he had finished inflicting this *torture* upon him, he *ordered* in a great rage that he should be beheaded. As for the *blessed* Apaioule, he *ordered* him to be taken into a cell which was all dark, to be under *torture* until he died. *And* the *blessed* Apa Pteleme when he heard his *sentence* rejoiced greatly. He turned to Apaioule and said to him, 'I salute thee, my father; be not faint-hearted; for we have Jesus to *help* us. For this one day more is all that thou hast left in this *world*; (172 **V i**) hereafter, at this time tomorrow, thou shalt be with me in the bridechamber of *Christ*.' Apaioule said to him, 'Entreat for me, my brother, before *Christ*, since thou wilt go before me into His Kingdom.'

When they had thus spoken together, the *blessed* Apa Pteleme was brought out *according to* the *orders* of the *count* to be beheaded. And he lifted up his eyes to heaven and said, 'I entreat Thee, Jesus, my *hope*, Jesus, my crown, Thou Who crownest all the saints whoso shall die for Thine Holy Name, do not forget me, who am about to come into Thine Hands; (172 **V ii**) for Thine is the power and the glory, for ever, *Amen.*'[33] When the *blessed* Apa Pteleme had said this, his neck being stretched out, he was beheaded, on the twentieth day of the month Tōbe; and he fulfilled his *martyrdom*, in God's *peace*, *Amen.*

And the *blessed* Apa Apaioule was shut up in the cell, being under *torture*; and he was entreating God all that night, saying, 'God, estrange me not from Thine holy *contest*, which has fallen to the *lot* of my fellow *member*; *but* may I see (173 **R i**) him soon in Thine holy Kingdom, O God Who art blessed for ever!' As the *blessed* Apaioule was saying this, morning came, the morning of the

---

[31] Conjunctive, continuing ⲁⲩⲕⲉⲗⲉⲩⲉ ⲉⲧⲡⲉⲩⲉⲓⲛⲉ of 18 f., irrespective of the fact that ⲁⲩⲑⲩⲟⲩ intervenes.
[32] 171 V ii 23–172 R i 11: cf. *BIFAO* 15, 245 (Nabraha).
[33] Cf. Mt. vi, 13.

twenty-first day of Tōbe. The *count ordered* the *blessed* Apaioule to be brought out, with his countenance emitting *rays* of light. The *count* said to him, '*Abominable monk*! *Well*, hast thou found thy senses? If not, I will *chastise* thee *sorely*.' *But* as for the *blessed* Apaioule, he was unable (**173 R ii**) to answer him, because his *body* had become powerless. Straightway the *count ordered* him to be beheaded. And the soldiers took him at morning time on the twenty-first day of Tōbe, and beheaded him. Straightway the *angels* came and took his *soul* up to heaven, and they caused him to *greet* the saints. Thereafter he *greeted* Apa Pteleme in the Kingdom of Jesus *Christ*. And Apa Pteleme said to him, 'Thou art *well* come, my holy father Apaioule; *for* behold, already (**173 V i**) has thy *throne* been set out in *Paradise* with all the saints; and thy shining crown has been prepared in [heaven (?)], and thy shining white *raiment* [. . . they (?) were caused (?)] to make festival with the *holy martyrs* in His Kingdom for ever by Jesus *Christ* our Lord; through Whom be the glory to Him (*sic*) and His *good* Father and the Holy *Spirit* for ever, *Amen*.

I. PROPER NAMES: PERSONAL AND RELIGIOUS.

Apollonius ⲁⲡⲟⲗⲗⲱⲛⲓⲟⲥ (*bishop*) 90 R ii 1.
Arianus ⲁⲣⲓⲁⲛⲟⲥ (*governor*) 88 Vii 3; 89 Vii 28.
Besamon ⲃⲏⲥⲁⲙⲱⲛ (*advocate*) 91 Rii 4.
Christus ⲬⲤ 88 V i 4; 9; 92 R i 12; ii 13; V i 30; ii 24.
Coluthus ⲕⲟⲗ(ⲗ)ⲟ(ⲩ)ⲑⲟⲥ 88 V i 4; 30; ii 5; 23; 29; 89 V i 23; 27; ii
2; 90 R i 22; 29; ii 32; V i 19; ii 4; 16; 31; 91 R ii 22; V i 24; ii
21; 92 R i 27; ii 6; V i 6; 28; ii 14.
Constantinus ⲕⲱⲛⲥⲧⲁⲛⲧⲓⲛⲟⲥ (*emperor*) 88 V i 25.
Diocletianus ⲇⲓⲟⲕⲗⲏⲧⲓⲁⲛⲟⲥ (*emperor*) 88 V i 19.
Jeremias ⲉⲓⲏⲣⲏⲙⲓⲁⲥ (*advocate*) 91 R ii 11.
Jesus ⲓⲥ 92 R i 12; ii 12; V i 30; ii 24.
Maximianus ⲙⲁⲝⲓⲙⲓⲛⲓⲁⲛⲟⲥ (sic) (*emperor*) 88 V i 21.
Plutarchus ⲡⲟⲩⲧⲁⲣⲭⲟⲥ (sic) (*bishop*) 90 V i 3.

II. GEOGRAPHICAL AND ETHNICAL.

Antinoou ⲁⲛⲧⲓⲛⲱⲟⲩ (=Antinoöpolis) 88 Vii 2
Sieht ⲥⲃⲉⲝⲧ (= Apollonopolis Parva) 90 V i 4.
Siout ⲥⲓⲟⲟⲩⲧ (= Asyût, Lycopolis) 90 R ii 3.

III. GENERAL: (a) COPTIC

ⲁⲙⲁϩⲧⲉ 88 Vii 12; 90 V ii 5
ⲁⲛ, passim.
ⲁⲧ-, *privative*, 90 R ii 10.
ⲁⲩⲁⲓ̈ (n.) ⲁⲩⲏ (-ⲉ) 90 R ii 15.
ⲁϩⲉⲣⲁⲧ⸗, see ⲱϩⲉ.
ⲁϩⲣⲟ= 91 R ii 22.
ⲃⲱⲗ:
    ⲉⲃⲟⲗ, passim.
    ⲛ̄ⲥⲁⲃⲏⲗ 91 Vii 23.
ⲃⲟⲗⲃⲗ̄ (ⲃⲟⲣⲃⲣ̄):
    ⲣⲉⲩⲃⲉⲣⲃⲉⲣⲕⲱⲱⲥ 89 R ii 26.
ⲃⲟⲣⲃⲣ̄: see last.
ⲉⲃⲟⲧ 92 Vii 8
ⲉⲛⲉϩ:
    ϣⲁⲉ. 89 R i 4; 91 Vii 12; 92 R i 13
    ϣⲁⲉ. ⲛ̄ⲉ. 92 Vii 28
ⲉⲭⲧ:
    ⲉⲛⲉ. 91 R i 12.
ⲉⲧⲉ-, passim.
ⲉⲧⲃⲉ-, passim.

ⲉⲟⲟⲩ 88 Vii 31; 89 R i 1; 92 R i 2; 7; 11; 92 V ii 17; 25
ϯⲉ. 89 R i 28; 90 R ii 28.
ⲉⲩϫⲉ 88 Vii 11; 92 V i 20.
ⲉ: 89 R ii 12; Vii 22; 92 R ii 10.
ⲉⲓⲉ 90 Vii 23; 91 V i 6.
ⲉⲓⲛⲉ 90 R ii 12; 91 R i 2.
ⲉⲓⲡⲉ, passim.
ⲉⲓⲥϩⲙⲏⲧⲉ 90 V i 13; 92 R ii 16; 20
ⲉⲓⲱⲧ 92 Vii 25
ⲉⲓⲩϫ 91 Vii 18
ⲕⲉ, passim
ⲕⲟⲩⲓ 89 Vii 26; 90 R i 3; 91 V i 27
ⲕⲱ 90 R i 3; 91 V i 22
    ⲕ.ⲉϩⲣⲁⲓ̈ 90 R i 19
    ⲕ.ⲛ̄ⲥⲁ- 91 R i 4; V i 32.
ⲕⲁ-ⲣⲟ: (ⲛ)ⲕⲁⲣⲱⲟⲩ 91 R ii 17

ⲕⲱⲡϥ̄ 90 V i 21
ⲕⲱⲱⲥ: (n.) 89 R ii 26
ⲕⲱⲧⲉ 90 R i 28; 92 R i 5.
ⲕⲱϯ 89 Vii 14; 90 R i 20
ⲗⲁⲁⲩ 88 Vii 21; 89 R i 15; ii 30; 90 R i 25; 91 V ii 9; 13; 22; 30; 92 V i 8
ⲙⲁ 89 R ii 19; 31; Vii 22; 90 V i 31
ⲙⲁⲛ̄ϯϩⲁⲛ 89 R i 29
ⲙⲉ 'love':
    ⲙⲁⲓⲣⲱⲙⲉ: ⲙ̄ⲛⲧⲙ. 91 V i 9; 92 Vii 23
ⲙⲟⲩ 92 Vii 3
    (n.) 89 R ii 11; V i 13; 90 V i 18; 91 R i 26; 92 R ii 29
ⲙⲁⲕⲉ̄ 91 V i 19
ⲙⲙⲁⲩ 90 Vii 25
ⲙ̄ⲙⲓⲛ (ⲙ̄ⲙⲟ=) 91 R i 17
ⲙ̄ⲙⲟⲛ 'not' 91 R ii 26
ⲙⲓⲛⲉ 91 V i 19.

229

ⲧⲉⲛⲟⲩ. see ⲟⲩⲛⲟⲩ.

ⲧⲏⲣ=, *passim*

  ⲉⲛⲧⲏⲣϥ 90 R i 10; ii 27,
  91 V ii 31

ⲧⲱⲣⲉ:

  ⲛ̄ⲧⲟⲟⲧ=, ϩⲓⲧⲟⲟⲧ=, *pas-
  sim*

+ⲧⲱⲛ, see ⲧⲱⲛ

ⲧⲱⲩ:

  (ⲛ.) 91 V ii 24

ⲧⲁϩⲟ 90 V ii 12

  ⲧ. ⲉⲣⲁⲧ= 88 V i 29

ⲑⲃ̄ⲃⲓⲟ 90 V i 24

ⲧⲟⲩⲝⲟ 92 R i 13

ⲧⲁⲭⲣⲟ 91 V ii 2

ⲟⲩ (*interrog.*), *passim*

ⲟⲩⲁ ' one ' 89 R i 9; ii 5;
  6; 33; 90 V i 31; 91 R i
  32

  ⲟⲩⲱⲧ 92 R ii 25

ⲟⲩⲟⲉⲓ:

  +ⲟⲩ. 90 R ii 16

ⲟⲩⲱ 'cease' 89 V ii 20

ⲟⲩⲁⲁⲃ, see ⲟⲩⲟⲡ

ⲟⲩⲟⲛ 'one' 88 V i 6; 89 R
  i 31; ii 18; V i 5; 90 R
  i 20; ii 28; V i 15

ⲟⲩⲛ̄ⲧⲁ= 90 V ii 25

ⲟⲩⲛⲟⲩ 92 R ii 24

  ⲛ̄ⲧⲉⲩⲛⲟⲩ 91 R i 27
  ⲧⲉⲛⲟⲩ 88 V ii 15; 89 V
  ii 16; 90 R i 26; 31; V i
  14; ii 27; 91 V i 15
  ⲩⲁⲧ. 88 V ii 19; 89 V i
  17; 91 V i 1
  ⲝⲓⲛⲧ. 92 R i 30

ⲟⲩⲱⲛϩ̄ 89 V i 4; 90 R i
  6

ⲟⲩⲟⲡ:

  ⲟⲩⲁⲁⲃ : ⲉⲧⲟⲩ. 88 V i 3;
  91 V ii 6; 92 V ii 27
  ⲛⲉⲧⲟⲩ. (ⲛ.) 91 V i 8; ii
  29; 92 V ii 18

ⲟⲩⲱⲧ, see ⲟⲩⲁ

ⲟⲩⲱⲧⲛ̄:

  ⲟⲩ. ⲉⲃⲟⲗ (ⲛ.) 90 R ii 23

ⲟⲩⲟⲉⲓⲩ 92 R ii 8

ⲡⲣⲟⲥⲟⲩ. 88 V ii 32

ⲟⲣⲱⲩ 88 V ii 6; 89 V ii 17;
  31; 90 R i 2; ii 10; 14;
  V ii 2; 91 R ii 1; 9; 14;
  24; 30; V i 21; 92 R
  ii 18
  (ⲛ.) 91 R ii 6

ⲟⲩⲱⲩⲃ̄ 88 V ii 28; 89
  V ii 19; 90 R i 10

ⲟⲩⲱⲧ̄ 88 V ii 24; 90 V
  i 10

ⲟⲩⲭⲁⲓ 88 V ii 7; 18; 90
  R i 8; V ii 15; 92 R ii
  19; 22

ⲱⲛⲉ 91 V ii 19

ⲱⲛϩ̄ 88 V ii 8; 89 V i 19;
  90 V i 14; ii 3; 91 R i
  22; 92 V i 26
  (ⲛ.) 89 R i 4; V i 20;
  90 V ii 20; 91 R i 24
  (ⲃⲓⲥ)

ⲱϣⲉ:

  ⲁϩⲉⲣⲁⲧ= 88 V ii 9; 89
  R i 10; 21; ii 6; 20; 90
  R ii 24; 91 R i 13

ⲩⲁ :

  ⲣ̄ⲩⲁ 92 V ii 18

ⲩⲱⲗ:

  ⲩⲁⲗⲣ̄ⲡⲉ 89 R ii 25

ⲩⲗⲏⲗ 88 V ii 10

ⲩⲟⲙⲛ̄ⲧ:

  ⲩⲟⲙⲧⲉ 88 V i 24

ⲩⲓⲛⲉ 92 R ii 10

ⲩⲛ̄ϩⲏⲧ 91 R i 16

ⲩⲓⲛⲉ 88 V ii 16; 20; 90
  R i 13; ii 26
  (ⲛ.) 88 V ii 12; 90 V i
  8

ⲩⲟⲣⲩ. 88 V ii 22; 92
  R i 8

ⲩⲱⲡⲉ 88 V i 17; 89 V i 3;
  17; ii 15; 90 R i 30; V
  i 11; 90 V i 9
  ⲉⲩ. 88 V ii 6; 89 R ii 1;
  33; V ii 27; 91 V i 4

ⲩⲏⲣⲉ :

  ⲡ̄ⲩ. 89 R i 33

ⲩⲁⲩ:

  ⲩⲟⲩ- 'worthy of' 88 V
  ii 22; 92 R i 8
  ⲩⲟⲩ-. see last
  ⲩⲟⲩⲟ 91 R i 11
  (ⲉⲧ)ⲩⲟⲩⲉⲓⲧ 92 R i 3

ⲩⲟⲩⲩⲟ:

  ⲙ̄ⲛ̄ⲧ⳨ⲩ. 88 V ii 4; 89
  V i 10
  ⳩ⲛⲩⲉ 89 V i 29; 92 V i 9

ⲩⲟⲩⲩⲧ:

  ⲩⲁⲩⲧⲉ 89 R ii 29
  ⲩⲁⲭⲉ 89 V i 24; 25; 90
  R ii 30; 91 R ii 23
  (ⲛ.) 89 R i 15; V i 30;
  90 R i 16; ii 16; 91 V i
  16; 27; ii 23; 31; 92 R
  i 11; V i 8
  ⲩⲟⲭⲛⲉ 90 R i 4
  (ⲛ.) 89 R ii 3
  91. 91 V ii 5

ⲩⲧⲟⲟⲩ:

  ⲭⲟⲩⲧⲁⲩⲧⲉ 88 V i 13; 27;
  92 V ii 7

ϩⲉ 'way':

  ⲛ̄ⲑⲉ, *passim*

ϩⲏ 'front':

  21ⲑⲏ ⲛ̄- 89 V i 31; 90
  R i 21

ϩⲏ 'belly':

  ⲛ̄ϩⲏⲧ=, *passim*

ϩⲟ 90 R i 6

ϩⲱ 'suffice' 90 V i 25

ϩⲱⲱ= 90 R ii 31

  ϩⲱⲱϥ as particle 88 V
  ii 16; 89 R ii 20; 91 V
  i 4

ϩⲱⲃ 89 R ii 3; 90 V i 26;
  ii 4; 91 V ii 5; 92 R i
  21.

ϩⲁⲕ 89 R ii 31

ϩⲙⲟⲧ 92 V ii 2

ϩⲛⲁ= 89 V ii 27

ϩⲁⲡ:

  +ϩ. : ⲡⲉⲩ+ϩ. 89 R i 28
  ⲙⲁⲛ+ϩ. 89 R i 29

ϩⲱⲡ 91 V ii 9

(b) GREEK

Words not in Liddell-Scott-Jones marked *

I. PROPER NAMES: PERSONAL AND RELIGIOUS

Apollo ΑΠΟΛΛΩΝ 57 V i 24; 59 R ii 30; 62 Vii 33; 65 R ii 15; V i 24; 66 R i
24; 67 R i 26; ii 6; 19; 73 R i 5; 23; 74 R i 29; Vii 25; 76 R ii 32; V
i 21; 32; ii 7; 20; 77 R ii 21; V i 6; 82 R ii 28

Apollonius ΑΠΟΛΛΩΝΙΟϹ 50 V i 32; 52 Vii 2; 54 R i 20; 68 V i 19, 32; 72 V
ii 22; 82 V i 20; ii 6

Arē ΑΡΗ 88 R i 11; 16 (bis)

Armenius ΖΑΡΜΕΝΙΟϹ (count (or duke) of Alexandria) 49 R i 21; V ii 29;
58 V ii 9; 30; 61 V ii 12; 65 V i 6; 86 R ii i 13; V i 8

Artemis ΑΡΔΥΜΙϹ 77 R ii 23

Christus χϲ, passim

Daniel ΔΑΝΙΗΛ 63 R ii 19

David ΔΑΔ 82 V ii 22

Diocletianus ΔΙΟΚΛΗΤΙΑΝΟϹ 49 R i 16; Vii 16; 55 R i 31

Eli 2ΗΛΙ 80 V i 28

Elias 2ΗΛΙΑϹ 49 V i 17; 69 V ii 4

Elizabeth ΕΛΖΑΒΗΘ 68 R i 26; 69 R ii 13; 17; Vii 7; 72 R ii 5

Eutychianus ΕΥΤΥΧΙΑΝΟϹ (etc.) (governor (or duke)) 49 R i 24; 50 R i 16;
86 R ii 1; 16; V i 15; 30; ii 11; 87 R i 11

Gabriel ΓΑΒΡΙΗΛ 68 R i 22; 70 Vii 5; 71 V ii 8; 77 R i 24

Hēraei 2ΗΡΑΕΙ 70 Vii 22

Jesus χϲ, passim

Johannes (Baptist) ΙΩΖΑΝΝΗϹ 68 R i 28; 71 V ii 2

Julius ΙΟΥΛΟϹ 87 V i 2

Maria ΜΑΡΙΑ (B.V.) 68 R i 24; 69 R ii 28; V ii 15; 70 R ii 28; Vii 5; 71 R
i 14; ii 16; V i 26; ii 22; 72 R ii 4; Vii 6; 75 R ii 12; 77 R i 22

Mariam ΜΑΡΙΖΑΜ 49 V i 18

Michael ΜΙΧΑΗΛ 79 V i 3

Paëse ΠΑΗϹΕ, passim

Paulus ΠΑΥΛΟϹ 51 Vii 11; 52 R i 4; 8; 22; V i 10; 53 R ii 32; V ii 11; ii 9; 22;
54 R ii 31; V i 14; 19; ii 7; 24; 55 R i 21; 30; ii 11; 19; 56 Vii 6; 60 R i 12;
22; ii 26; Vii 2; 12; 16; 21; 33; 61 R i 4; 63 Vii 31; 64 R i 6; 13; 33; ii 13; 28;
V i 19; ii 3; 69 Vii 5; 71 V i 2; 72 Vii 27; 80 Vii 28; 82 V i 26

Raphael 2ΡΑΦΑΗΛ 58 R i 30; 59 V i 1; 61 R i 29; 62 R i 28; 63 V i 8; 66 Vii 10;
68 R i 19; 69 V ii 10; 70 Vii 6; 71 Vii 9; 72 R i 22; 75 R ii 27; 76 R i 11;
77 R i 25; ii 25; 81 Vii 20; 84 V i 18; 85 Vii 13; 87 V i 21

Romanus 2ΡΩΜΑΝΟϹ 78 Vii 21

Solomon ϹΟΛΟΜΩΝ 81 V i 12

Thecla ΘΕΚΛΑ, passim

Victor ΒΙΚΤΩΡ 55 V i 2; ii 4; 15; 56 R i 2; ii 23; 58 Vii 19; 63 R ii 27;
66 R i 7; 78 V ii 20

II. GEOGRAPHICAL AND ETHNICAL

Antinoou ⲁⲛⲧⲓⲛⲱⲟⲩ (Antinoöpolis) 50 R i 29; V i 21; 28; 52 V i 3; 53
    R i 27; 68 R i 16.

Jerusalem ⲑⲓⲗⲏⲙ 50 R ii 30; 51 V i 26; 53 R ii 18; 69 V ii 3; 72 R i 14; 77 V ii
    17; 83 R ii 24

Judaeus ⲓⲟⲩⲇⲁⲓ ò 9 V i 26; 71 V i 31

Kême ⲕⲏⲙⲉ (= Egypt) 86 R i 27

Mefi(ò)e ⲙⲃ̄ⲃⲉ, ⲙⲏⲃⲉ (= Memphis) 70 V ii 14

Pousine ⲡⲟⲩⲥⲓⲣⲉ (= Busiris) 49 R i 29; 50 R i 25; 52 V ii 4; 57 R ii 2;
    69 V ii 9

Rakote ⲣⲁⲕⲟⲧⲉ (= Alexandria) 49 R i 23; V ii 28; 31; 52 R i 25; 53 R i
    8; ii 29; V i 9; 55 R i 15; V i 7; 68 R ii 10; 69 R ii 24; V i 31; ii 3; 71
    R ii 29; 82 V ii 11; 86 R i 23; ii 8; 14; 87 V i 3

Romaios ⲣⲱⲙⲁⲓⲟⲥ (Romanus) 75 V i 23

Sheremoun ϣⲉⲣⲉⲙⲟⲩⲛ 71 R i 28

Shelnoufe ϣⲉⲗⲛⲟⲩϥⲉ 88 R i 8

Shmoun ϣⲙⲟⲩⲛ (= Hermopolis Magna) 49 R i 27; 50 R i 28; V i 20;
    51 V i 30; 57 R ii 3; 69 V i 18

Tammah ⲧⲁⲙⲙⲁⲍ 70 V ii 13

Tepôt ⲧⲉⲡⲱⲧ 86 V i 22

Thebaïs ⲑⲏⲃⲁⲓⲥ 49 R i 25; 50 R i 15; 56 R ii 17; 74 R ii 1; 86 R ii 3

III. GENERAL (a) COPTIC

a- 'about' 70 V ii 20

ⲁⲗⲉ 52 R ii 29; 53 R ii 26;
    68 V ii 30; 70 R ii 14

ⲁⲙⲟⲩ, ⲙⲏⲛ 52 R ii 15; V i
    12; 53 R ii 11; V ii 10; 13;
    68 R ii 21; 71 V i 14; 73 R
    i 22; V i 10; 74 V ii 23;
    86 V ii 12; 88 R i 22

ⲁⲙⲛ̄ⲧⲉ 57 V ii 10

ⲁⲙⲣϩⲉ 77 R i 7

ⲁⲙⲁⲍⲧⲉ 52 R i 10; 55 R ii
    24; 62 R ii 30; 69 V ii 19;
    76 R i 9; 80 V i 30; 81 R
    i 19
    (n.) 74 V ii 6

ⲁⲛ 'not', passim

ⲁⲛⲁ =:
    ⲡⲁⲛⲁ = 64 V i 9

ⲁⲛ ⲍⲏⲃ 50 V ii 1

ⲁⲛⲁⲩ 54 R i 22

ⲁⲛⲁ, passim

ⲁⲛⲉ 50 R ii 16; 56 R ii 7; 62

V i 24; 63 R i 14; 65 R ii 2;
    69 R ii 17; 18; V ii 22; 70
    V i 1; ii 26; 76 V ii 27; 30;
    77 R i 11; V i 27; 82 R ii
    30; 85 R i 9; 87 R i 16;
    V i 1

ⲁⲡⲏⲩ 51 R ii 25; 53 R i 14;
    55 V i 10; 67 V i 2; ii 10;
    73 R ii 9; 83 R i 16; 84
    R ii 28

ⲁⲣⲉⲓ, see next

ⲁⲣⲁⲛ 70 R ii 29; 78 V i 6

ⲁⲣⲉⲓ a. 78 R i 3

ⲁⲩ (interrog.) 57 V i 29; 69
    V i 7; 70 R i 9; 75 V i 28;
    79 R i 20

ⲁⲍⲉ, see ⲉⲍⲉ, 'yes'

ⲁⲍⲣ̄ⲟ = 69 R ii 9

ⲁⲍⲏⲩ, see ⲕⲱⲕ

ⲁⲝⲱ 81 V ii 16

ⲃⲱⲕ 'go', passim.

ⲃⲉⲕⲉ 50 V i 16; 64 V i 17

ⲃⲁⲗ 56 R i 12; 58 R i 6; 64
    R i 16; 75 R ii 10; 81 V i
    28; 82 R i 7; ii 2

ⲃⲱⲗ :
    B. ⲉⲃⲟⲗ 56 R i 21; 58 R
    ii 6; 63 R i 3; V i 29; 69
    R i 28; 84 V i 21
    ⲉⲃⲟⲗ, passim
    ⲉⲛⲃⲟⲗ ⲛ̄- 62 V i 26
    ϫⲓⲛⲃⲟⲗ ⲛ̄- 52 V i 28
    ⲛ̄ⲃⲗ̄ⲗⲁ = 62 V i 12
    ⲛ̄ⲥⲁⲃⲏⲗ- 52 V ii 14
    ⲛ̄ⲥⲁⲃⲟⲗ 53 V i 7
    ϩⲓⲛⲥⲁ ⲛ̄ⲃⲟⲗ 53 V ii 13

ⲃⲗ̄ⲃⲓⲗⲉ 71 R ii 3

ⲃⲉⲛⲓⲛⲉ (ⲛⲉⲛ.) 55 V i 9; 56
    R i 32; 61 V i 11; ii 23; 62
    R i 21; 63 R i 17; 76 V ii
    25; 81 V ii 17; 83 V ii 32;
    84 V i 2

ⲃ̄ⲣ̄ⲃ̄ⲣ 77 R i 1
    (n.) 81 V ii 13

ⲥⲧⲛⲟⲩⲅⲉ 67 R ii 10; 70
R ii 31; 78 R ii 10; 81 R
ii 9
ⲛⲉⲍ ꞌoil' 51 V i 13; 54 V ii
20; 67 R ii 10; 70 R ii
31; V i 18; 23; 30 (ⲉⲛⲉⲍ,
sic); ii 3; 72 R i 16
ⲛⲟⲩⲍⲉ 59 R i 24; 69 R i
3; 81 V ii 2
ⲛⲟⲩⲍⲙ̄ 51 V i 18; 57 V i 31;
58 R i 14; ii 19; 58 V ii
21; 59 R ii 26; 63 R ii
9; 26; 33; 64 R ii 16;
V ii 20; 65 R i 24; 66
R i 27; ii 4; 67 R i 23;
68 V ii 14; 74 R ii 30; 75
V i 30; ii 4; 14; 76 R ii
25; V i 18; 77 V ii 19; 83
R i 5; 84 V ii 26
ⲛⲉⲍⲥⲉ 64 R i 13; V i 28
ⲛⲟⲩⲭⲉ 50 R i 32; 56 R i 22;
57 V i 27; 59 R ii 8; V ii
19; 62 R ii 16; 63 R i 21;
66 R ii 9; 78 R i 4; 12;
81 V ii 10; 32; 84 R i 4;
V i 14; 85 V i 7; 86 R ii
27; V i 17; 87 V ii 26
ⲛⲁⲭ(ⲍ)ⲉ 78 V ii 30
ⲛⲟⲃ, passim
ⲙ̄ⲛ̄ⲧⲛ̄. 64 R ii 21; 72 V
i 4
ⲡⲛ̄: 69 V i 25
ⲛ̄ⲟⲓ, passim
ⲛⲟⲩⲥⲉ (ⲛⲟⲩⲭⲉ) 73 V ii 24
ⲟⲃⲍⲉ 84 R ii 19
ⲟⲉⲓⲕ 54 V ii 19; 60 V ii 19;
64 V i 25; 69 R i 14; 79
R i 17
ⲟⲛ, passim
ⲟⲥⲉ:
ⲧⲟ. 58 V ii 18; 60 R ii 6;
V i 4
ⲟⲟⲍ 70 R i 30; 76 V i 23
ⲟⲍⲉ 87 V ii 7
ⲡⲉ ꞌheaven', passim
ⲉⲧⲡⲉ ꞌup', passim
ⲙ̄ⲡⲉⲧⲡⲉ ⲛ̄- 50 R ii 15;

78 R ii 13
ⲡⲓ:
ⲧⲡⲓ 53 R i 24; 69 V ii 21;
72 R ii 22
ⲛ̄ⲱ=, passim
ⲛⲱⲗ̄ⲧ 68 R ii 31
ⲡⲉⲛⲓⲛⲉ, see ⲃⲉⲛⲓⲛⲉ
ⲛⲱⲡⲕ̄ 81 V i 27
ⲡⲁⲣⲙⲟⲩⲧ 52 R i 21; 55
R ii 30
ⲛⲱⲡⲏ̄ϥ 74 V i 15; 78 R ii
26; V i 2; 79 R i 6; 12;
86 V i 31
ⲡⲣⲏ̄ⲩ 50 V ii 23
ⲛⲱⲡⲕ̄ 61 R i 22; V i 5; 66
V i 25; 76 V i 25; 26; 83
R ii 18; 20
ⲛⲓⲥⲉ 50 R i 31; 51 R i 9;
54 V ii 1; 25
ⲛⲱⲧ 61 V ii 26; 76 R ii 6; 82
R ii 8
ⲛ̄ⲟⲩⲧⲉ 75 R i 32
ⲛⲱⲩ:
ⲛⲁⲩⲉ 63 V ii 28; 77 V ii
8; 85 R i 27
ⲛⲁⲩⲟⲛⲉ 62 V ii 1
ⲛⲱⲍ ꞌcleave' 60 R i 26; ii
21; 63 V ii 7; 76 R i 31
(n.) 59 R i 20 (bis)
ⲛⲱⲍ ꞌreach' 71 R i 25; 74
V ii 18; 78 R ii 2
ⲛⲱⲍⲧ 53 V i 32; ii 5; 54
R ii 3; 59 R i 33; 61 R
ii 17; 64 R ii 5; V ii 28;
65 V ii 3; 70 R ii 33; V
i 16; 73 R ii 18; 79 R ii
26; 81 R i 2; V ii 17; 85
R ii 32
ⲛⲁⲍⲟⲩ:
ⲍⲓⲛ. 73 V i 33; 80 R i 11
ⲛⲉⲭⲉ-, passim
ⲡⲏ 6! R ii 10; 76 V i 23;
77 V ii 27
ⲡⲟ 53 V i 28; 55 V ii 13; 69
V ii 21; 72 R ii 23; 76 R
i 5; 81 V ii 15; 18; 26
ⲡⲱ 52 V i 28; 69 V i 9; 82

V i 3; 25; 84 R ii 29
ⲡⲱⲕⲍ 65 R ii 2; 77 R ii 14.
ⲡⲓⲙⲉ 53 V ii 7; 59 R ii 14;
V ii 29; 60 R i 19; 27; ii
22; 32
(n.) 60 R i 28
ⲡⲱⲙⲉ, passim
ⲡⲙ̄-, with place names,
49 R i 5; 50 R i 25; 57
R ii 2; 69 V i 13; ii 9
ⲡⲙ̄ⲕⲁ2 78 V i 32
ⲡⲙ̄ⲙⲁⲟ, see s.v.
ⲡⲙ̄ⲛ̄ⲧⲱⲛ 57 R i 26
ⲡⲙ̄ⲡⲁⲓⲧⲉ 51 V ii 2
ⲡⲙ̄-, see last
ⲡⲙ̄ⲙⲁⲟ 50 V ii 6; 51 V i 2;
55 V ii 20; 74 R ii 11.
ⲙ̄ⲛ̄ⲧⲣ. 49 R ii 26
ⲡⲟⲙⲛⲉ 49 R ii 24; V ii 11;
50 V ii 33; 69 V i 26; 70
V ii 21
ⲡⲙ̄ⲍⲉ 57 R i 9; 74 V i 29
ⲡⲁⲛ, passim
ⲡⲛⲉ 67 R ii 25; 73 R i 4;
83 V i 24; ii 2
ⲡ̄ⲣⲟ, passim
ⲙ̄ⲛ̄ⲧⲣ̄. 49 R i 16; 55 V
i 28; 72 R ii 27; 78 V ii
11; 85 R ii 7; V i 22
ⲡⲏⲥ 50 R i 15; 52 R ii 3;
19; 54 V ii 6; 56 R ii 17;
61 R i 10; 72 V ii 22; 28;
74 R i 33; 78 R i 15; 86
R ii 23; V i 20
ⲙⲁⲣⲏⲥ 55 R i 23
ⲧⲟⲩⲣⲏⲥ 68 R ii 23; 69
R i 4
ⲡⲟⲉⲓⲥ 63 V i 27; 72 R i
25; 76 R i i 15; 87 V ii 17
ⲡⲁⲥⲧⲉ 54 R i 4; 55 R i 6;
V ii 9; 57 R i 2; 61 V ii
10; 63 R i 33; 65 R i 12;
67 R i 3; 71 R ii 27; 73
V ii 13; 74 R ii 33; 76 R
ii 17; 77 V ii 6; 84 R i
14; V ii 28
ⲡⲁⲧ= 61 V ii 21

ⲥⲱⲟⲩ 'strike':
  ⲥⲁⲟⲩ 'wound' 51 Vi 10
ⲥⲱⲟⲩ 'scorn' 65 R ii 21; 74
  R i 26
  (n.)
  + c. 57 Vi 15; 62 Vi 19;
  ii 29; 66 R i 22; 86 R ii
  29
ⲥⲱⲟⲩⲉ 49 R ii 14; 51 Vii 23;
  26; 52 R ii 32; 55 R i 26;
  56 V i 21; 74 R ii 5
ⲥⲱⲟⲩⲧ 76 V i 22
ⲥⲁⲟⲩⲏ̄ 61 R ii 28; V i 28; 88
  R i 29
ⲩⲩⲉ 59 R i 2
ⲥⲁⲟⲩ 64 V i 24
ⲥⲏⲟⲩⲉ 49 Vii 25; 50 R i 7;
  82 R ii 31
ⲥⲓⲟⲩⲉ 81 Vii 6
ⲥⲱ2ⲉ 67 R i 15; 71 R i 32
ⲥ?ⲁⲓ 49 Vii 18; 52 R ii 3;
  V i 11; 56 V i 14; 64 V i
  14; 71 R i 16; ii 2; Vii
  26; 72 Vii 29; 74 R i
  32; 82 V i 18; ii 1; 83
  V i 6; 85 Vii 1; 4; 86
  Vii 20; 31; 87 V i 4
  (n.) 49 Vii 27; 50 R i
  14; 55 V i 15; 83 R i 5;
  86 R ii 5
ⲥ2ⲓⲙⲉ 49 V i 22; 30; 50
  R i 12; V i 25; 51 V i 6;
  52 V i 18; 55 Vii 19;
  56 V i 20; 67 R i 13; 68
  R ii 2; 33; Vii 31; 69
  R ii 5; Vii 19; 73 R i 7,
  ii 5; 16; Vii 17; 74 R i
  3; 82 R ii 12; 83 Vii 18;
  84 R ii 1
ⲥⲁ2ⲛⲉ, ⲥⲉⲉⲟⲩⲱ2
ⲥⲁ2ⲧⲉ 54 Vii 21; 61 V i 11;
  62 R i 22; ii 6; 81 Vii 11
ⲥⲟⲟ̄ 81 V i 23
  ⲡ̄ⲥ. 84 R ii 2
ⲥⲟ̄ⲏⲣ 53 R ii 27; 68 R ii 22;
  71 R i 4; ii 26
ⲧⲁⲉⲓⲟ 57 V i 18; 22; 59

R i 3; 62 R i 9; 65 R ii 24;
  74 R ii 15; 76 R ii 29;
  78 R i 25; 79 V i 26; 80
  Vii 17; 84 R i 30
  (n.) 56 V i 30; ii 30; 62
  Vii 22; 26; 68 V i 16; 70
  V i 10; 73 V i 32; 74 R
  ii 23; 78 R ii 4; 27; V
  ii 32; 79 Vii 31; 80 R i
  18; 82 V i 5
+ 'give', passim
+ 21- 'clothe' 51 R i 18;
  79 V i 24
+ⲟⲥⲉ 58 Vii 18; 60 R ii
  6; V i 4
+ⲛ̄ 53 R i 24; 69 Vii 21;
  72 R ii 22
+ⲥⲟ 55 V i 24; 29
+ⲥⲃⲱ 73 V i 24; 81 V i
  9; 14; 84 R ii 5
+ⲧⲟⲟⲧ= 60 R i 23; 66 R
  ii 25
+ⲟⲣⲟⲉⲓ 72 R ii 21
+2ⲏⲧ 83 R i 2
ⲧⲱ(ⲱ)ⲃⲉ 'brick' 71 R ii 19
ⲧⲱⲱⲃⲉ 'seal' 63 R i 30;
  65 R i 16; 31
ⲧⲃ̄ⲛⲏ 49 R ii 14
+ⲃ̄ⲉ̄ 75 V ii 30
ⲧⲃ̄ⲧ 69 R i 15
ⲧⲱⲕ 'kindle' 56 R i 24;
  63 R i 6
  ⲙⲁⲛⲧ. 56 R i 23; 63 R
  ii 29
ⲧⲁⲕⲟ 71 R ii 5; 80 R i 30;
  V i 7; 83 R i 28; 86 R ii
  32
  (n.) 59 Vii 4; 62 R ii 33;
  63 Vii 13; 65 R ii 33; 75
  Vii 8; 76 R ii 14; 77 R
  ii 31; 84 V i 31
  ⲁⲧⲧ. 50 R i 29; 79 V
  i 29
ⲧⲱⲕⲉ̄ (ⲧⲱⲧⲉ̄, ⲧⲱⲟ̄ⲉ̄) 71 V
  ii 24; 78 R i 2; 81 V i 32
ⲧⲁⲗⲟ 50 R ii 2; Vii 24; 54
  Vii 1; 26; 56 V i 3; 57

Vii 20; 59 R i 31; 61 V i
  9; 62 R i 20; 67 R ii 13;
  68 R ii 14; V i 1; ii 28;
  69 R ii 31; Vii 15; 17;
  70 Vii 24; 71 V i 6; ii
  17; 72 V i 26; 73 V i 11;
  15; 75 R i 21; 77 Vii
  11; 83 Vii 33; 84 V i 10;
  26; 86 V i 19; 87 V i 13
ⲧⲱⲗⲙ̄ 79 R ii 33
ⲧⲁⲗϭⲟ 53 Vii 31; 58 V i 3;
  15; 27; ii 6; 66 Vii 8; 67
  R ii 20; 73 R ii 10; 75 R
  i 2; V i 3; 76 Vii 10; 21;
  77 R ii 3; 82 R i 4; ii 1;
  83 V i 29
  (n.) 58 V i 25; 67 R i 29;
  73 R i 27; 82 R i 28;
  85 V ii 22
ⲧⲱⲙ 'shut' 58 Vii 25
ⲧⲁⲙⲓⲟ 79 R ii 8
ⲧⲁⲙⲟ 52 R ii 19; 54 R ii
  24; 60 R i 20; V i 33;
  61 R i 11; 64 Vii 18; 65
  R ii 12; 67 Vii 14; 69
  Vii 1; 71 V i 14; 72 V i
  5; 74 R ii 9; 26; 76 R
  i 32; 79 R i 3; 20; 80
  R i 24; ii 4; 81 R ii 14;
  19; 83 Vii 7; 26; 84 Vii
  11; 24
+ⲙⲉ 49 R ii 31; V i 4; 70
  Vii 18; 71 R i 26; 33; 74
  R ii 4; 80 R ii 7
ⲧⲙ̄- (negative), passim
ⲧⲙ̄ⲟ 55 R i 9 (ⲧⲁⲙⲟ, sic)
ⲧⲱⲙ̄ⲉ 88 R ii 19
ⲧⲱⲛ 54 R ii 16; 57 R i 27
  ⲉⲧ. 76 R ii 8
ⲧⲛ̄ⲛⲟⲟⲩ 50 Vii 19; 25; 52
  Vii 1; 58 R i 17; ii 16;
  Vii 3; 61 R i 8; V i 8; 62
  Vii 24; 63 R ii 24; 31;
  67 V i 8; 71 R i 8; 72 R
  ii 32; V i 11; 73 R i 16; ii
  7; 12; 74 R i 12; 16; V i
  21; 76 R ii 11; 86 R i 25

oron :
  oγaaB 83 Ri6
  ETOγ., passim
  πEToγaaB as n., 'saint',
  passim
  oγHMB 76Vi6; 83Vi
  24; 83 Vii 21
oγEpHTE 55 Vi 11; 56Rii
  1; 57Vii 19; 58Rii 5;
  59 Vi 13; 63 Ri 19; 64
  Rii6; 73Rii 19; 74V
  i9; 85 Rii 33
oγwcγ 73 Vii 33
oγwT 'raw' 59 R i 15
oγwT 'single', 'same'
  55 Vii 7; 78Vii14; 79
  Rii 17; 81 Ri8; Vi6;
  83 Vii 23
oγw(w)TE:
  oγET 81 Ri 16; 17
oγoEiγ 49 Vi 7; 8
  πpocoγ. 63 Vii 22
oγwϣ 51 Vi 5; 52Rii 12;
  53 Vii 15; 54Vi 16;21;
  25; 56 R i i; 60 Rii5; 61
  Ri 1; ii 23; 65Vi16; 69
  Ri 20; ii 15; 72 Rii 26;
  Vii 16; 76Vii 14; 79 Vii
  25; 86 Rii 31
  (n.)51 Rii 32; 52Vii23;
  61 Ri 20; 23; 68Rii 8; 74
  Vii 4
  πγoγ(oγ)aϣ= 61Ri32;
  66 Rii 20; 68 Ri 4
oγγH 54 Rii 19; 60 Vi 29;
  61 Ri 26; 63 Vii 29; 66
  Rii 13; 70 Ri 28; ii7; 11;
  72 Vi 20; 77 Vii 8; 85R
  i 27; 87 Vii 15; 88 Ri 14
oγwϣB 53 Ri 17; 57 Ri 29;
  Vi 33; 61 Vi 28; 62 Vii 13;
  66 Ri 10; 67 Ri 24; 68R
  ii 7; 69 Rii 12; 71 Rii 14;
  72 Vi 7; 74 Vii 29; 75
  Rii 8; Vi 31; 76 Vi 9;
  78 Vii 15; 79 Ri 22; 81
  Ri 14; Vi 3; 82 Vii; 84

Ri 30; ii 26; 88 Ri 17
oγwγE 77 Vii 31
oγwγT 53 Vii 1; 61 Rii 18;
  64 Rii 6; Vi 32; ii 28;
  66 Rii 24; 76 Vi 3; 79R
  ii 27
oγwϣγ 58 Ri 33
oγwZ 87 Vi 10
  oγ.ñca- 56 Vi 11; ii 2;
  57 Rii 33; 59 Vii 28; 68
  Vii 24; 78 Vii 29; 83
  Vi 27
  (n.) 86 Vi 26; 87 Vii 10
  oγEZca2NE 54 Vii 10;
  15; 56 Ri 4; 64 Vii 3;
  65 Ri 28; 67 Rii 7; 69
  Ri 30; 86 Vi 10
oγZop 84 Rii 8; 26; 29;
  87 Vii 12; 88 Ri 4
oγxaï 53 Vi 14; 21; ii 21;
  68 Vii 17; 73 Vi 13; 83 V
  i 2
  (n.)53 Ri5; ii 32; 57V
  i 23; 62 Vii 32; 64 Rii 30;
  Vi 20; 65 Vi 24; 66 Ri
  23; 68 Vii 1; 10; 72 Vi 9;
  73 Vii 20; 74 Ri 29; V
  ii 3; 78 Vii 9; 82 Rii 27;
  Vii 6; 31; 83 Ri 8; 26
oγwōñ 75 Vi 7
wBγ 70 Vii 1 (wγB, sic)
wküi 69 Rii 7; 11; 16
wλ 87 Vi 24
wλK 58 Vi 8
wλm 64 Rii 10
wmE 79 Vi 14
wNE 58 Rii 11; 75 Vii 33;
  78 R i 3; 84 Ri 2; Vi 9
  w. ΣmE 77 Vii 25
wNK 84 Vi 3; 88 Ri 3
wNZ 53 Ri 18; 57 Ri 11; 58
  Vii 29; 65 Ri 20; 67 Vii
  23; 26; 76 Vii 7
  (n.)56 Vi 25; 85 Rii 18;
  Vii 6
ōiNw. 83 Ri 13
wπ 53 Ri 15; 54 Rii 1; 26;

60 Vi 14; 64 Vi 3
HπE 54 Rii 26; 62 Vii 13;
  78 Vi 21; 88 Rii 23
wpK 54 Ri 23; 81 Rii 12
wpγ 50 Vi 10
wcK 83 Vi 12
wTπ 51 Vii 32; 54 Ri i 10;
  68 Vii 5; 73 Vii 7; 78R
  ii 8; 79 Ri 8; 80 Vii 19
wγ 49 Vii 31; 55 Vi 17;
  58 Ri 8; 62 Vi 6; 67 Ri-
  6; 75 Vii 11; 77 Vi 3; 82
  Ri 4; 86 Ri 31; ii 4
wγπ 58 Rii 8; 61 Vi 13; 75
  Rii 33
aTw. 59 Ri 30
w2E:
  a2EpaT= 53 Vii 12; 56
  Ri 15; 59 Vi 4; 12; 14;
  62 Rii 28; 30; Vi 18; 63
  Vi 10; 65 Vii 23; 68 Ri
  20; 70 Ri 4; 13; 19; 71 V
  i 19; ii 10; 74 Vii 19; 75
  Rii 29; Vi 9; 80 Ri 4
w2E :
  (n.)49 Vi 9; 14
wōB 63 Vi 24
ϣ- 'be able', passim
ϣa- (prep.), passim
ϣa 'nose' 65 Vii 28; 76 R
  i 6
ϣE 'go' 54 Vi 27
ϣE 'wood' 56 Ri 25; 27;
  69 Rii 31
ϣ. ñ2aoEiT 77 Ri 6
ϣE 'hundred' 49 Rii 25;
  Vi 2; 54 Vii 21; 78 Ri
  24; Vi 21; 80 Vii 2; 85
  Ri 12; 88 Rii 8
ϣE 'by' (in oaths) 57 Vi 19;
  59 Ri 1; 62 Vii 32; 64 R
  ii 29; Vi 20; 65 Rii 15;
  Vi 24; 66 Ri 23; 68 Vii
  10; 72 Vi 9; 74 Ri 29; 75
  Vi 22; 78 Vii 9; 82 Rii
  27
ϣHi 'pit' 63 Rii 20

(ⲛ.)63Rⅈ26
ϣⲁⲩ 'worth' 52Rⅈⅈ26; 68V
i9
ⲁⲧⲩ. 77Rⅈⅈ17; 84Rⅈⅈ
23
ⲛ̄ϣⲟⲩ(ⲟⲩ)ⲁϥ= 61Rⅈ32;
66Rⅈⅈ20
ϣⲁⲩ 'piece' 75Vⅈ25
ϣⲏⲣⲉ 67Rⅈⅈ15
ϣⲟⲣⲟ 76Vⅈⅈ32
ϣⲱϣ 58Rⅈ3; 78Rⅈⅈ11; 81
Rⅈⅈ9
ϣⲟⲩ⳨ 68Vⅈⅈ7
ϣⲁⳅ 61Vⅈ17; 63Vⅈ12; 77
Rⅈ17
ϣⲁϫⲉ 51Rⅈ24; 27; 52Rⅈ
16; 54Rⅈⅈ14; 56Vⅈⅈ28;
62Rⅈ32; 64Rⅈⅈ14; 65
Rⅈⅈ25; 66Rⅈⅈ17; 70Rⅈ
11; 82Rⅈ9; 82Rⅈⅈ3; 24
(ⲛ.) 51Rⅈⅈ18; 52Rⅈ18;
53Rⅈⅈ21; 54Rⅈⅈ6; Vⅈ
10; 55Vⅈⅈ27; 65Vⅈ31;
68Rⅈ13; 71Rⅈ25; 74R
ⅈ25; ⅈⅈ28; 75Rⅈ5; 81V
ⅈ5; 18
ϣⲟⲝⲛⲉ (ϣⲁ-)83Vⅈⅈ22
ϣⲃⲏⲣ, see ⲥⲟⲃⲏⲣ
ϥⅈ 51Rⅈ17; Vⅈⅈ22; 52Rⅈⅈ25;
56Rⅈⅈ6; Vⅈ10; ⅈⅈ1; 57R
ⅈ10; 58Rⅈ6; 59Rⅈⅈ10; 61
Vⅈⅈ1; 62Vⅈ26; 28; 68Vⅈ
17; 69Rⅈ11; ⅈⅈ7; 72V
ⅈⅈ30; 73Vⅈ31; 75Rⅈⅈ9;
77Vⅈ25; 27; 78Vⅈⅈ28;
82Rⅈⅈ30; Vⅈ9; 21; 84R
ⅈ3; 85Rⅈ9; 86Vⅈ3; 87R
ⅈ15; Vⅈ1; 12
ϥⲁⅈ ⲇⲏⲙⲟⲥⲓⲟⲛ 74Rⅈⅈ11
ϥⲧⲟⲟⲩ 57Vⅈⅈ25(ⲃⅈⲥ); 66Vⅈ
2; 71Rⅈⅈ20; 75Rⅈⅈ11; 78
Rⅈⅈ21; Vⅈ9; 17; 79Vⅈⅈ
10; 80Vⅈⅈ4; 13
-ⲁϥⲧⲉ 62Vⅈ17; 85Rⅈ12
ϥⲱϭⲉ 65Rⅈⅈ1
Ⳅⲁⅈ 49Vⅈ32; 50Vⅈ28; ⅈⅈ
4; 52Rⅈⅈ19; 69Rⅈⅈ18

2ⲉ 'fall' 61Rⅈⅈ5; 71Vⅈⅈ15
2ⲉⲉ-53Vⅈ13; 65Rⅈ30;
70Vⅈ29; 71Rⅈⅈ3; 72R
ⅈⅈ15; 79Rⅈⅈ19; 85Vⅈ8
2ⲉ 'way', passim
ⲣⲟ̄ⲉ ⲛ̄- 58Rⅈⅈ11; 63V
ⅈ13; 77Rⅈⅈ5; 81Vⅈⅈ23
2ⲏ 'front':
(ⲛ̄)2ⲏⲧ=, passim
2:ⲑⲏ ⲛ̄- 62Vⅈⅈ21; 25;
65Rⅈⅈ28; 68Rⅈ30; 80
Rⅈ10
2ⲏ 'belly' 59Rⅈ9
2ⅈⲏ 53Rⅈⅈ31
2ⲟ 'face' 53Vⅈⅈ2; 55Vⅈⅈ
6; 61Rⅈⅈ6; 66Vⅈⅈ29; 69
Rⅈⅈb; 11; 71Vⅈⅈ17; 72
Rⅈⅈ18; 81Rⅈⅈ7; 83Rⅈⅈ
2; 87Rⅈ26; ⅈⅈ12
2ⲱⲱ=, passim
2ⲱⲱϥ (as particle) 55R
ⅈⅈ11; 80Vⅈ4; 86Rⅈⅈ1
2ⲱⲃ 53Vⅈ2; 54Vⅈⅈ18; ⅈⅈ
14; 57Vⅈ10; 58Vⅈⅈ14;
64Rⅈ25; 69Vⅈⅈ16; 72
Vⅈⅈ2; 73Rⅈⅈ33; Vⅈⅈ22;
76Rⅈⅈ23; 80Rⅈ25; ⅈⅈ
2; 82Vⅈⅈ4
ⲣ̄2. 55Rⅈ25; 58Vⅈⅈ13
2ⲁⲉⅈⲃⲉ 61Vⅈⅈ15; 62Rⅈ
29
ⲣ̄2. 84Vⅈ20
2ⲱⲃⲉ 51Rⅈ32; ⅈⅈ2; 21;
63Rⅈ28; 79Rⅈ28; 83
Rⅈ19
2ⲃⲱ 78Rⅈⅈ15; 79V
ⅈ25
2ⅈⲕ:
ⲣ̄2. 67Rⅈ10; 76Vⅈⅈ17
2ⲏⲕⲉ, see 2ⲕⲟ
2ⲱⲱⲕⲉ 49Rⅈⅈ23; 57Vⅈⅈ
22; 75Rⅈ22
(ⲛ.) 49Rⅈⅈ33
2ⲕⲟ:
2ⲏⲕⲉ 49Rⅈⅈ4; 29; Vⅈ
4; 50Vⅈⅈ28; 55Vⅈ30;
ⅈⅈ21; 72Vⅈⅈ25; 79Rⅈⅈ

2; 85Vⅈⅈ26
ⲙⲛ̄ⲧ2. 51Rⅈⅈ26
2ⲗ̄ⲟ 88Rⅈ7
ⲙⲛ̄ⲧ2. 49Vⅈⅈ7
2ⲁⲗⲏⲧ 75Vⅈ27
2ⲗⲟϭ 60Rⅈⅈ13; 81Vⅈⅈ25;
82Vⅈⅈ8
2ⲁⲙⲟ̈ⅈ 60Rⅈ29; Vⅈ3; 83
Vⅈ3
2ⅈⲙⲉ, see ⲥ2ⅈⲙⲉ
2ⲙⲉ 77Vⅈ9
2ⅈⲙⲉ:
+2. 68Vⅈ3
2ⲙⲟⲟⲥ 50Vⅈ27; 55Rⅈⅈ4;
Vⅈⅈ10; 56Vⅈ28; 61Rⅈ
16; Vⅈⅈ11; 63Vⅈ19; 23;
64Rⅈⅈ19; 68Rⅈⅈ22; 29;
69Rⅈⅈ5; 70Rⅈ26; 74
Rⅈⅈ33; 81Rⅈⅈ28; 84Rⅈ
20
2ⲙⲟⲧ 65Rⅈ2; 86Rⅈⅈ21
ϣⲡ̄2. 53Vⅈⅈ26; 88Rⅈⅈ8
ϫⅈ2. 79Vⅈ22; 83Rⅈⅈ14
2ⲁⲙϣⲉ 76Vⅈⅈ31
2ⲧ̄2ⲁⲗ 50Rⅈⅈ4; Vⅈⅈ25;
52Rⅈⅈ4; 53Vⅈ10; 19;
30; 54Rⅈ7; Vⅈ2; 8; 26;
ⅈⅈ11; 23; 55Rⅈⅈ19; 57R
ⅈ5; 59Vⅈⅈ28; 60Rⅈⅈ9;
ⅈⅈ20; Vⅈ33; 61Rⅈⅈb; 8;
63Rⅈⅈ15; 27; 64Vⅈ29;
ⅈⅈ5; 68Vⅈ7; ⅈⅈ24; 31;
69Rⅈ31; 71Vⅈ12; 83
Rⅈ10; Vⅈ9
ⲙⲛ̄ⲧ2. 74Vⅈ30
2ⲧ̄ⲝ̄ 59Rⅈⅈ1
2ⲟⲩⲛ: in ⲉ2., ⲛ̄2., etc.,
passim
2ⲱⲛ 'approach' 65Rⅈⅈ8;
87Vⅈⅈ31
2ⲛⲁ=:
ⲣ̄2. 88Rⅈⅈ20
2ⅈⲛⲏⲃ 76Rⅈ14; ⅈⅈ4
2ⲁⲛ 57Vⅈⅈ11
2ⲟ(ⲱ)ⲡ 67Vⅈ30; ⅈⅈ8
ⲣ̄2. 67Vⅈⅈ1
2ⲱⲛ 81Rⅈⅈ16

ⲟ̅ⲉ̅, passim
ⲥⲱ 52 V i 26; 56 V ii 27; 62
R i 32; 77 R i 19; 80 V i 5;
82 V i 23
ⲥⲃⲃⲉ:
ⲥⲁⲃⲍⲏⲧ 72 R i 5
ⲥⲟⲉⲓⲗⲉ 54 R ii 32; 82 V ii 24
ⲣⲱⲛⲥ̅. 82 V ii 23
ⲥⲱⲗⲏ 65 R i 32
(ⲛ.) ⲥ. (ⲉⲃⲟⲗ) 81 R ii 11
ⲥⲗⲟⲟϥ 61 V i 10; 62 R i 21
ⲥⲟⲙ 56 R ii 21; 61 V i 1 (bis);
62 R ii 24; 63 V i 25, 64
R ii 23; 66 V i 16; 82 R ii
18
ⲟⲩⲛⲥ̅. 57 V i 9; 30; 59 R i
29; 55 R i 23; 57 R i 22;
ii 26; 74 V ii 32; 77 R i 20
ⲙⲛ̅ⲥ̅. 71 R i 20; 75 V ii
21; 79 V ii 22
ϯⲟ̅. 53 V ii 30; 56 R i 17;
ii 2; 58 R i 19; ii 18; V ii
11; 61 R ii 7; 63 V ii 24; 72
R i 21; 26; 74 V i 32; 75
R ii 19; 22; V ii 1; 87 R
i 33; ii 4; 6
(ⲧⲏ̅) ⲥⲛⲥ̅. 51 V ii 14; 52 V
i 25; 58 V i 9; 59 R ii 9;

61 V i 19; 64 V ii 32; 66
R i 4; 16; ii 28; 72 R i 31;
75 R ii 1; 77 R ii 18; 28;
83 V ii 10; 84 R i 18; 85 R
ii 29; 86 R i 2; ii 33; 87
V ii 4
ⲥⲁⲙⲟⲩⲗ 49 R ii 17; 51 V ii
33
ⲥⲓ̈ⲛ-
ⲥⲓ̈ⲛⲟⲩⲱⲙ 50 R i 32; 51
R i 9; 54 V ii 25
ⲥⲓ̈ⲛⲱⲛⲍ 83 R i 13
ⲥⲓ̈ⲛⲉ 68 R i 17; 76 R ii 12;
83 R i 24; 83 R ii 10
ⲥⲓ̈ⲥⲟⲙ, see s.v. ⲥⲟⲙ
ⲥⲓ̈ⲡⲏⲩⲓⲛⲉ 56 V i 4; 55
R i 6; 60 V ii 3; 12; 83
R i 21
ⲁⲧⲥⲓⲡⲏⲩ. 80 V i 14
ⲥⲟⲛⲥ̅:
ⲥⲓⲛ̅ⲥ̅. 60 V ii 17
ⲥⲱⲛⲧ̅ 53 V i 29; 56 R ii 4;
57 V i 13; 58 V ii 9; 31;
62 R i 18; 73 V i 4; ii 29;
74 R i 4; 24; 75 V i 20; 76
R ii 9; V ii 10; 83 V ii 3; 84
R ii 15; 87 R i 13
(ⲛ.) 65 V i 22; 66 R i 20;

76 V i 29; 84 V i 4; 85 R
i 6
ϯⲥ̅. 49 R i 19
ⲥⲉⲡⲏ 70 V ii 28
2ⲛ̅ⲟⲩⲥ̅. 60 V ii 24; 64 R ii
4; 69 V ii 28
ⲥⲣⲏⲡⲉ 78 R ii 12
ⲥⲱⲣⲙ̅ 'to snare':
ⲥⲟⲣⲥ̅ⲉ 83 R ii 8
ⲥⲟⲥ 67 V i 5
ⲥⲟⲧ 78 V ii 32; 79 V ii 32
ⲥⲱⲧⲙ̅ 71 R i 24; 75 V ii 29
(ⲥⲱⲧⲙ̅, sic); 76 V ii 29
ⲥⲟⲩⲟ 'push' 69 R i 1
ⲥⲱⲟⲩⲧ̅ 72 R ii 8; 78 R i 29; 81
R ii 2; 82 V i 23
ⲥⲓ̈ⲭ 51 R ii 13; 55 R ii 1; V i
10; 56 R i 33; 57 V i 32;
ii 18; 58 R ii 5; 9; 31; V
i 6; 16; ii 22; 59 R ii 27;
V i 21; 62 R ii 30; 65 R i
25; V ii 30; 69 R i 22;
70 V ii 25; 73 V i 12;
16; 23; 74 V i 8; 16; 75
V i 31; 76 R i 20; ii 26;
80 V i 31; 81 R i 20; V
i 29; 87 V i 24
ⲙⲟⲩⲛϥ̅ ⲛ̅ⲥ̅. 59 V i 18

(b) GREEK
Words not in Liddell - Scott - Jones marked *

ἀγαθός 49 R ii 1
- όν, as n., 69 V ii 32; 73
V ii 10; 79 V i 31; 81 R i 23;
ii 24; 85 R ii 16; V i 26;
85 V ii 32
ἀγάπη 51 R i 6; ii 31; 53 R i
11; 58 V i 14; 68 R ii 13; 71
V i 4; 80 R ii 14
ἄγγελος 49 R i 21; 51 R i
21; ii 18; 54 R ii 22; 56 R
i 14; 29; 58 R i 18; 31; ii
12; 29; V ii 4; 59 V i 19;
61 R i 29; ii 3; 14; 22; 27;
V i 31; ii 14; 62 R i 28; ii 26;
63 R ii 25; V i 8; 26; ii 5;
16; 25; 64 R ii 1; V ii 19; 66

R ii 15; 23; 26; V i 21;
27; ii 11; 31; 67 V ii 3; 58;
R i 20; 33; V ii 27; 69 R i
18; 72 R ii 19; V i 13; 76 R i
12; 77 R ii 26; V ii 10; 28;
78 V ii 2; 8; 18; 79 V ii 17;
80 R i 1; 3; ii 3; V i 25; 31;
ii 25; 81 R i 9; 29; V ii 21;
33; 82 R i 26; 85 R i 31; V
i 29; ii 14; 86 V ii 29; 87
V i 21; 32; 88 R i 12; 20; 29
ἅγιος, passim
ἁγία 49 R i 6; 68 R ii 23;
87 R ii 21
ἁγνεία 81 R i 5
ἀγών 49 R i 10; 57 R ii 12;

58 R i 21; ii 22; 72 R i 29;
75 R ii 17; 21; 82 V ii 14;
87 V i 17
ἀγωνίζεσθαι 85 R ii 9
*ἄθλησις 49 R i 9
αἰσθάνεσθαι 56 R i 8; 81 V
i 9
αἰών 85 V i 32
ἀκρίβεια 68 R i 12
ἀκτίς (ⲁⲕⲧⲓⲛ) 78 R i 13
ἀληθῶς 53 V ii 18; 54 V ii 30;
65 V ii 33; 69 V i 3; 70 R
ii 6; V i 23; 84 R i 16
ἀλλά, passim
ἅλυσις 55 V i 9; 56 R i 32;
58 R ii 3; 61 V ii 22; 63

*ἑρμητάριον 57 Vii 21;58 Rii 1; 75 Ri 21; Vi 8	-ῶς 57 Rii 27; 60 Ri 3; 80 Rii 23; Vi 3; 85 R ii 10	30; 86 Rii 14; Vi 9
εὐαγγέλιον 56 Vi 15; 71 Ri 16; Vii 26; 79 Riii 2	καρπός 78 Rii 9; 79 Ri 8; 80 Vii 20; 85 Rii 17	κονία 59 Ri 30; 81 Vii 9
εὐγενής 51 Vii 27; 74 Rii 14	κατά, passim	*κόριος (corius, -um?) 71 Ri ii 13; 22
εὐλογία 72 Vii 18	καταφρονεῖν 80 Rii 23	κοσμοκράτωρ 76 Vii 3
εὐφραίνειν 65 Vi 3	καῦμα 63 Vi 22	κόσμος 49 Rii 11; 78 Vii 6; 12; 79 Rii 32; 83 R ii 22
ἡγεμών 50 Ri 17	κελεύειν 55 Vi 18; 56 Ri 20; ii 6; 15; 57 Vii 14; 59 Ri 6; 27; Vii 18; 61 Vii 15; 62 Ri 19; ii 14; Vi 24; 63 Ri 5; 27; 66 Rii 8; 67 Rii 2; 73 Vi 30; 74 V i 2; 75 Ri 20; Vii 28; 76 Rii 18; V ii 23; 28; 77 Ri 3; 12; V i 23; ii 3; 81 Rii 31; Vi 24; ii 4; 84 Ri 11; Vii 29; 85 Ri 5; 86 Vi 30; 87 Vii 23.	κράτος 75 Vi 22
θάλασσα 57 Vi 27; 62 Rii 17; 70 Rii 21; 76 V i 25; 84 Ri 6; Vi 13; ii 27		κραυγή 84 Vii 7
θάλπειν 51 Ri 5		λαμπάς 57 Vii 32; 58 R ii 8; 59 Rii 5; 75 Rii 2; 33
θέατρον 55 Vii 12; 61 Vii 14; 81 Rii 30; Vii 33	κέλευσις 74 Ri 1	λίβανος 67 Rii 13
θεοτόκος (Blessed Virgin Mary) 70 Vii 24; 72 R ii 3	*κεστιονάριος (quaestionarius) 57 Vii 24; 58 Rii 9; Vi 7; 11; 61 Vii 27; 62 Ri 24; ii 7; 65 Rii 3; 26; Vi 8; 15; ii 2; 74 Vi 6; 87 Rii 31; Vii 29	λ/τρα 52 Rii 20; 60 R ii 7; 68 Vi 9
θηρίον 51 Rii 28; 75 V i 26; 84 Rii 30; 85 Vi 7; 86 Rii 28; 87 Ri 20		λόγος 71 Vi 30; 75 Vii 20
θλίβειν 52 Vi 32; 83 Vii 12		λοιπόν 50 Vii 10; 68 Ri 1; 76 Rii 27
θρόνος 72 Ri 10; 78 Ri 31; ii 3; 5; 14; 22; 30 (bis); Vi 3; 79 Ri 4; 10; Vi 27; ii 7; 80 Rii 32; Vii 4; 15; 23	κεφαλή : κακὴ κ. 57 Ri 25; 65 Vi 10; 73 Vii 32; 76 Vii 12; 82 Rii 21	λουτήρ 78 Vi 5; 10; 18; 79 Vii 12; 80 Vii 6; 10
θυσία 56 Vi 5	λῆτος 84 Vi 25	λύπη 60 Rii 14
θυσιάζειν 49 Vii 22; 55 Rii 25; 57 Rii 15; 31; 62 Ri 8; 73 Ri 23; 29; 74 Ri 17; 19; Vii 24; 75 Ri 16; 19; 76 Rii 27; 81 Vi 1; 84 Ri 28; 86 Rii 24; Vii 13	κλάδος 78 Vi 1	λυχνία 72 Ri 19
	κληρονομεῖν 56 Vi 24; 80 Ri 17; 85 Rii 14	μαγεία 58 Vii 15; 20; 63 Ri 4; 66 Ri 4; 6; 29; 67 Rii 11; Vi 21; 73 Rii 11; 76 Rii 24; 83 Vi 31; 86 V i 6
	κληρονομία 51 Vi 25	
καθαρίζειν 63 Vi 33	κληρονόμος 85 Rii 5	μαγεύειν 83 Vii 18
καθέδρα 76 Vii 24	κλῆρος 60 Vi 14	μάγος 62 Ri 2; 66 Ri 8; 67 Rii 22; 74 Ri 3; 76 R ii 3; Vi 31; 82 Rii 25; 83 Vi 28; ii 30; 86 Rii 20
καιρός 55 Ri 25	κοιτών 64 Ri 22	
κακός : κακὴ κεφαλή 57 Ri 25; 65 Vi 9; 73 Vii 31; 76 V ii 12; 82 Rii 21	κόλασις 57 Vii 9; 72 Rii 30; 79 Vi 7; 15; 80 Vi 13	μαθητής 50 Vi 12; 70 Rii 16; 25; 71 Ri 22
-ῶς 57 Rii 16; 62 Ri 10; 66 Ri 32; 75 Ri 17	κολλάριον (collarium) 61 Vii 24; 74 Vi 10	μακάριος, passim -ία 54 Ri 17; 74 Vii 14; 75 Ri 26; ii 5; 76 R ii 30
		μανιάκης 78 Vi 24
		μαργαρίτης 78 Kii 18; 28; Vi 17; 80 Vii 21
καλός :	κόμης (comes) 49 Vii	μαρτυρία 49 Ri 1; 62 V i 31; 77 Vi 29; 85 Ri 15; Vii 3
		μαρτύριον 'martyr shrine'

ii 13; 80 Vii 2; 5; 9
στύπνιον: see σίππ(ι)ον
συγχωρεῖν 73 Rii 26; Viiq
σύναξις 54 Rii 21; 66Vii24;
σφραγίζειν 58Vi 17; 73 Vi
25; 77Ri 31; 82 Rii 11
σωλήν 78 Viq; 12
σῶμα 50 Ri 5; 51 Rii 3; 8;
22; 30; Vi 11; 53 Vi 5;
56 Vi 4; 57 Vi 25; ii
28; 58 Rii 26; 33; 58 R
i 19; 59 Ri 32; ii 2; 13;
Vi 5; 22; ii 6; 60 Rii 30;
61 Vi 4; 16; 63 Ri 13; V
i 33; 67 Vii 16; 70 Vi
3; 74 Vi 26; 75 Vi 24;
ii 10; 76 Rii 15; 77 Rii
3; 79 Ri 29; ii 20; 21;
80 Rii 28; 81 Ri 6; 82 V
i 11; 83 Ri 19; ii 17; 85 V
i 5; 13; 31; ii 11; 87 Rii 9;
Vii 17; 27; 88 Ri 1; 24;
ii 4; 13
σωτήρ 70 Rii 14; 19; 85
Vi 1; 10; 86 Ri 16
Ταλαίπωρος 72 Rii 28;
73 Rii 24; Vi 20
τάξις 65 Ri 14; 74 Ri 23;
28; 75 Vii 6; 77 Rii 11; V
i 22; 84 Rii 20

τάχα 82 Rii 15
ταχύ (ταχη) 52 Rii 5; 68 R
ii 21
τιμωρία 56 Ri 6
τολμᾶν 55 Vi 29; 66 Ri 22
τόπος 80 Ri 33; ii 8; 81 Ri
8; 85 Vi 25; ii 16; 21
τράπεζα 64 Vii 6; 69 vii 29
τύχη 57 Vi 19
ὑπάρχοντα 56 Vi 2; 78
Vii 26
ὑπηρεσία 49 Rii 10
ὑπόμνημα 87 Vi 5
φανός 54 Ri 20
φιάλη 78 Vi 16
φορεῖν 78 Vi 22; 33; 79
V ii 30
φυλακή 82 Vi 8
χαίρειν: χαῖρε (greeting)
54 Ri 14; 61 Ri 31; 66 R
ii 19; 85 Rii 4; 8; 12
χαλκεῖον 81 Vii 10; 22
Χάμος 55 Vi 12; 87 Rii 33
χαρίζεσθαι 50 Rii 27;
58 Vi 24; 67 Rii 23; 73
Ri 26; 79 Rii 29; Viq;
82 Ri 27; 85 Vi 20
χάρις 66 Vii 28; 72 Rii π;
86 Vii 5
χάρτης 82 Vi 33

χήρα 49 Rii 6; 27; Vi
17; 33; 50 Vii 11; 83 R
ii 4; 85 Vii 28
χιών 79 Vi 18
χολή 60 Vi 30; 82 Rii 11
χρεία 69 Ri 33
χρῆμα 51 Vii 4; 60 Rii
10
Χριστιανός 50 Ri 3; 20;
57 Ri 22; 59 Vii 10; 64
Vi 1; 65 Ri 21; 66 Ri
2; 9; 67 Ri 16; 73 Rii
8; Vii 19; 74 Ri 9; 75
Vii 13; 76 Vii 1; 77 Vi
12; 82 Rii 16; 26
χώρα 49 Vii 20
χωρίς 74 Rii 4
ψυχή 51 Rii 4; 10; 61 Vi
3; 62 Vi 18; 66 Vi 76
74 Ri 31; Vii 31; 79
Rii 30; 80 Rii 11; 83
Vi 1; 85 Ri 13; Vi 32;
87 Rii 11; 88 Rii 30
ὦ, passim
ὡς 58 Vi 3
ὥστε 59 Rii 6; 77 Ri
16.

IV. SCRIPTURE CITATIONS AND ALLUSIONS

Ex. xiv	76 Vi	Prov. ix, 8	81 Vi	Mt. viii, 24 f.	70 Rii
Deut. (iv, 2)	87 Vi	xxvi, 11	84 Rii	x, 32	86 Vii
(xii, 32)	87 Vi	Isa. lxv, 8	71 Rii	x, 42	50 Vi
Josh. (x, 12)	76 Vi	Dan. (iii, 19 ff.)	63 Rii	xviii, 20	86 Vii - 87 Ri
I Sam (ii-iv)	80 Vi	(iii, 22)	65 Rii	(xvi, 24)	56 Vi
(iii)	88 Ri		77 Ri	xix, 29	56 Vi
(iv q)	66 Rii	(iii, 27)	77 Rii-Vi	xx, 9 ff.	64 Vi
(xvii, 44)	75 Vi	(vi, 16 ff.)	63 Rii	xxv, 34	85 Rii
I Kings (ii, 2)	66 Rii	Zech (iv?	72 Ri	xxv, 36	50 Vi
(xiii, 4)	58 Rii	(x, 7)	65 Vi	xxvii, 46	59 Rii
(xiii, 4-6)	58 Vi	Song 3 ch. (25	65 Rii	Mk. iv, 37 ff.	70 Rii
Ps. xxii, 1	59 Rii	Ecclus. (22, 3?)	77 Ri	(viii, 34)	56 Vi
xxxix, 12	82 Vii	(26 f.)	63 Vi	ix, 41	50 Vi
cxxxix, 11 f.	70 Rii	(27)	77 Rii	x, 29 f.	56 Vi

I. PROPER NAMES : PERSONAL AND RELIGIOUS

II GEOGRAPHICAL AND ETHNICAL

Eden (Edem) ⲉⲇⲉⲙ 133 R i 8
Empaiat ⲙ̄ⲡⲁⲓⲁⲧ, ⲛⲉⲡ. (Mareotis) 106 R i 6; 108 R ii 25; 109 V ii 7; 14;
    112 V i 25; 132 R i 23; 136 V ii 19; 139 V i 9
Heracleos polis ⲡ.ϩⲏⲣⲁⲕⲗⲁⲓⲟⲥ 103 R i 25
Hermon ⲁⲣⲙⲱⲛ 125 R ii 24
Jerusalem ⲍ̄ⲓⲗ̄ⲏ̄ⲙ 107 R i 24; V ii 30; 108 R ii 29; 122 R ii 16; 126 V i 9
Judaeus ⲓ̈ⲟⲩⲇⲁⲓ̈ 103 R ii 29
Kame polis ⲕⲁⲙⲏ ⲡⲟⲗⲓⲥ 123 R i 29; 124 R i 15; V i 22; 138 V i 14
Kbahs ⲕⲃⲁⲍⲉ̄ (Agfahs) 107 R i 28; 114 V i 26; 130 R ii 13; 136 V ii 26
Keme (Egypt) 103 R ii 10; V i 12; 19; ii 27; 105 R i 17; V i 13; 137 V ii 1; 4; 138 R ii 11
    ⲡ̄ⲕ̄ⲙ̄ⲕ̄. 112 R i 13
Mebe ⲙⲏⲃⲉ (= Memphis) 108 V ii 19; 111 V ii 19
Natho ⟨ⲛ⟩ⲁⲑⲱ (= Leontopolis) 105 V ii 8
Oxyrhynchus ⲍⲉⲡⲓⲭⲟⲥ 103 R i 27
Parembole: ⲧⲥⲓⲙⲓⲥⲉ ⲛ̄ⲧⲡ., see s. v. ⲥⲓⲙⲓⲥⲉ
Pedine ⲧⲡⲉⲧⲓⲛⲏ 108 R ii 25; 132 R i 24; 136 V ii 20
Peremoun ⲡⲉⲣⲉⲙⲟⲩⲛ (= Pelusium) 103 R i 22
Phalex ⲫⲁⲗⲉⲍ 123 R ii 23
Phoenice ⲫⲩⲛⲉⲓⲕⲏ 103 R i 17
Pilakh ⲡⲓⲗⲁⲭ (= Philae) 103 V i 23
Piom ⲡⲓⲟⲙ (= Fayûm) 112 V i 1; 123 R i 26; 138 V i 15
    ⲧⲡⲟⲗⲓⲥ ⲙ̄ⲡ. 114 V ii 18; 118 V i 14; 123 R i 22
Poubaste ⲡⲟⲩⲃⲁⲥⲧⲉ, -ⲃⲉⲥⲧ (Butastis) 107 R i 13; 123 R ii 26; 124 V i 24; 138 V i 15
Rakote ⲣⲁⲕⲟⲧⲉ (= Alexandria) 103 R i 20; 105 R i 16; ii 16; 19; 28; V ii 14; 137 R i
    15; 30; V i 27; ii 3; 8; 138 R ii 20
Romaikos ϩⲣⲱⲙⲁⲓ̈ⲕⲟⲥ 138 R ii 19
Romania ϩⲣⲱⲙⲁⲛⲓⲁ 103 V i 20
Shmoun ϣⲙⲟⲩⲛ (= Hermopolis Magna) 119 R ii 27
Simise: ⲧⲥ. ⲛ̄ⲧⲡⲁⲣⲉⲃⲟⲗⲏ (in district of Syene/Aswan) 105 V ii 12
Sion ⲥⲓⲱⲛ 125 R ii 28
Thebais ⲑⲏⲃⲁⲓ̈ⲥ 103 R i 29; 105 R ii 15; 136 V ii 13
Thmuis ⲑⲙⲟⲩⲓ̈ 105 V ii 6
Tilog ⲧⲗⲟϭ (= Nilopolis) 112 R ii 25; 27; V ii 1; 113 R ii 10
Xerichos ⲍⲉⲣⲓⲭⲟⲥ, see Oxyrhynchus

III GENERAL (a) COPTIC

ⲁ-, 'about', 129 R i 23

ⲁⲗ, see s. v. ⲱⲏ

ⲁⲗⲉ 105 V i 7; 114 R ii 32; 130
    V i 7

ⲁⲗⲟⲩ (ⲁⲣⲟⲩ) 118 V ii 24

ⲁⲙⲁ 122 R ii 32; 128 R ii
    29; V i 3; 134 V ii 25;
    135 R i 17; ii 8; 26

ⲁⲙⲟⲩ 109 V ii 15; 110 R i

20; 113 R ii 28; 114 R ii
3; 124 R ii 28; V ii 6;
133 R ii 5; 30; V i 26

ⲁⲙⲛ̄ⲧⲉ 118 V ii 26

ⲁⲙⲁϩⲧⲉ 114 V i 16; 118 R
    i 29; 134 R ii 33
(n.) 138 V ii 13

ⲁⲛ (negative), passim

ⲁⲛⲁⲓ: ⲡⲁⲛⲕ = 137 V i 7

ⲁⲛⲁ, passim

ⲁⲛⲉ 106 R ii 5; 107 V ii 31;
    111 V i 8; 113 V i 31; ii 2;
    118 V i 21; 119 R i 4; V i
    13; 121 R ii 20; V i 28;
    ii 28; 122 R i 14; ii 30;
    125 R ii 18; 126 V ii 27;
    131 R ii 5; 136 R ii 23

ⲁⲣⲟⲩ, see ⲁⲗⲟⲩ

ΜΕϤ⳦ΒΕ 118 V ii 26
ΜΟΥⳌ 'fill' 111 R ii 5; Vi 22; 119 R i 11; 120 V ii 5
ΜΕⳅ-, in ordinals, 121 V ii 10; 122 R ii 2⳨; 134 V i 13
ΜΟΥⳌ 'burn' 121 V i 30; 129 R i 18
ΜΑⳅΕ 'cubit' 129 R i 24
ΜΑⳅⳞ 117 V ii 29; 118 R ii 17
ΜΑⳌΟΥⲀⲖ (ΜϬΟΥΗⲖ) 119 R ii 19
ΜΑⲀⳄΕ 121 V i 25; 122 R i 9; 124 R ii 6; V i 13; 125 R i 5
ΝⲀ 'pity' 109 R ii 28; 127 V i 12
ΜⲚ̄ΤΝⲀ 'alms' 109 R ii 8
ΝΟΥ: ΝΗΥ 106 V ii 11; 114 R ii 18; 119 R i 18; 125 R ii 19; 24
ΝΟΥⲂ 103 V i 30; 116 V i 6; 124 R ii 2; 135 V i 10
ΝΟΒΕ 134 R i 13; 18
Ν̄ΚΟΤⲔ 103 R ii 19; 106 R ii 22; 107 V ii 20
ΜⲀⲏ̄. 106 R i 26; 110 V ii 19; 127 R ii 31
ΝΙⲘ (interrog.), passim
ΝΙⲘ 'every', passim
ΝΟΥΝ 119 V i 1; 6
ΝΑΝΟΥ- 116 V i 23; 124 R ii 22; V i 3; 125 R ii 11; 133 V ii 25; 135 V i 3; 136 R ii 30; 137 V i 2; 138 V ii 16
ΝΟΥΝΕ 104 V i 4
ⳜΙΝ. 104 V i 5
ΝΕϬΕ- 110 R ii 29
ΝⲀϊⲀⳆ =, see ΕΙⲀ
ΝΟΥ⳦Ε (pagan), passim
ⲡⲚ.(Christian), passim
ΜⲀⲏ̄Ν. 137 V i 30
ΠΕϤϢⲘϢΕΝ. 112 V ii 1
Ν̄⳦Ⲁ =, possessive, 106 R i 19; 113 R ii 32; 114 V ii 28; 116 V ii 3; 138 R ii 8
ΝΟΥ⳦Ε 103 R ii 25; 114 R ii 18; 125 R ii 12; 133 R i 20(?) (ΝΟΥ⳦Ε, sic)
Ν̄⳦ΟϤ (as adversative part.)

123 R i 9; 135 V i 16
ΝⲀΥ 'see', passim
ΝⲀΥ 'time' 104 V i 3; ii 16; 106 V ii 2; 108 V i 4; 120 R i 8; 121 R ii 6; 130 R ii 27; 134 V i 28
Ν̄ϢΟ⳦: ΝⲀϢ⳦Ε 106 R i 32
ΝΙϤΕ 109 R ii 29; 118 R i 23; 120 V i 22
(ⲛ.) 104 V ii 6; 115 R ii 9; 119 R ii 22; 124 V ii 19; 130 V i 13
ΝΟΥϤⳞ̄
ϢΕΝΟΥϤΕ 'good news' 106 V i 14
ΝΕⳌ 110 R i 13; 115 V ii 28; 32; 117 R ii 32; 138 R i 23
ΝΟΥⳅΕ 122 R i 7
ΝⲀⳌΒ(Ε) 126 R i 14; 129 V i 25
ΝΟΥⳌⲘ̄ 112 R i 9; 11; 119 V i 25; ii 15; 120 V i 3; 5; 121 R i 4; ii 3; 129 R ii 17
ΝΕⳌϬΕ 108 R i 13
ΝⲀⳌⳅΕ 124 R i 17
ΝΟΥⳄΕ 108 V ii 15; 109 R ii 6; 19; 111 R ii 6; V ii 26; 113 V i 22; 114 V i 22; 120 R i 13; 19; 126 R i 17; V ii 17; 32; 127 R i 1; ii 12; V ii 6; 14; 128 R i 12a; V ii 32; 129 R i 13; 130 R ii 30; 132 R ii 11; 136 V i 13; 18
ΝΟΥⳅⲔ 122 V ii 18
ΝΟϬ, passim
(ⲛ.) 'great one', 126 V ii 5; 129 V ii 16
Ν̄ϬΙ, passim
ⲞΒ⳨Ϭ, see ⲰΒϢ
ⲞΒⳌΕ 108 V i 11
ⲞΕΙⲔ 112 V ii 8; 22; 127 V ii 9; 137 V ii 25
ⲞⲘΕ 109 R ii 21
ⲞⲚ, passim
ⲞΕΙⲨ: see ⲦⲀⳌⲨⲞ
ⲡⲀϊ, ⲦⲀϊ, ⲚⲀϊ, passim
ⲡΕ, 'heaven', passim
Ε⳦ⲡΕ 113 R ii 26

ⲡⲏ, demonstr. 109 V ii 6
ⲡⲒ:
 ⳦ⲡⲒ 115 V i 32
ⲡⲰⲰⲚΕ 126 V i 30; 32; 129 V ii 6
 Ⲁ⳦ⲡ. 132 V ii 14
ⲡΕⲚΙⲚΕ, see ΒΕⲚΙⲚΕ
ⲡⲀⲰⲚΕ 103 R i 5; 125 V ii 8; 127 R i 14; 136 R i 31
ⲡⲢⲰ 111 R i 10
ⲡⲰⲢϤ 104 V ii 11; 106 V i 26; 120 V i 18; ii 4; 125 V i 11; 14; 129 R ii 30; 131 R ii 3; 132 V i 3; 134 V ii 26
ⲡⲰⲢⳄⳞ 107 V ii 2; 4; 123 V ii 2; 124 R i b; 125 R ii 5
ⲡⲰ⳦ 109 R ii 9; 114 V ii 31; 115 V ii 15; 28; 118 R i 4; ii 12; V ii 16; 119 R ii 31; 123 V i 31; 124 V i 9; 128 V ii 18; 137 V i 21; 138 R i 9 (ⲛ.) 136 R ii 31
 ⲘⲀ⳦ⲡ. 112 R i 23
ⲡⲰⲨ:
 ⲡⲀⲨΕ 127 V ii 17
ⲡⲰⳌ 'cleave', 104 V ii 31; 118 V ii 4; 122 V ii 6
ⲡⲰⳌ 'reach' 112 R ii 24; 124 V i 22; 132 V ii 5
ⲡⲀⳌⲢΕ:
 ⲡⳞ. 117 R ii 16; 129 R ii 11; 131 R i 12; 21; V i 3
ⲡⲰⳌΕ 115 V ii 11
ⲡⲀⳌⳞ 108 V ii 3; 109 R i 25; ii 9; 110 R i 11; 12; 114 R i 21; 115 V i 29; 119 V ii 18; 122 R ii 29; 125 R i 9
ⲡⲀⳌⲞⲨ:
 Εⲡ. 122 R i 19; 125 R ii 3
 Ν̄ϬⲀⲡ. 123 V i 17
ⲡΕⳄΕ-, passim
ⲡⲰϬΕ:
 ⲡⲀⳄϬΕ: ⲚΕⳄⲡ. 109 R ii 20; 130 R ii 31
ⲡⲏ 108 R ii 32; 134 R i 16
ⲡⲞ 108 V i 17; 23; 115 R i 13; 116 V ii 22; 118 V ii 26; 120

ογω 'cease' 112 V ii 27;
115 R i 5; 116 V ii 8; 121
R i 24; 122 R ii 13; 127
R ii 8; 131 R ii 10; 133 V
ii 23; 134 R; 30
ⲁⲧⲟγω 135 R ii 21
ογω 'grow':
ϯⲟγω 132 V ii 7
ⲟγⲁⲁⲃ, ⲟγⲏⲏⲃ, see ⲟⲣⲟⲛ
ⲟγⲃⲉ - 130 R ii 5
ⲟγⲃⲁϣ 119 R i 18; 121 V ii
26
ⲟγⲱⲙ 107 V i 3; 112 V ii
9; 21; 115 R ii 29; 120
V ii 9; 137 R ii 2; V ii
25
ⲟⲩⲟⲛ 'he', passim
ⲟⲩⲟⲛ 'one', passim
ⲟγⲟⲉⲓⲛ 106 R ii 28; 108
V i 3; 109 R ii 3; 115 V
i 7; 120 V i 20; 121 R
ii 12; 125 V ii 6; 127 V
ii 19; 128 R ii 11; 133
R; 28; ii 7; 10; 13; 19;
22; 24; V i 13
ⲣⲟγⲟⲉⲓⲛ 115 R ii 17; 128
R ii 26; 132 V ii 32
ⲟγⲱⲛ 'open' 106 V i 3;
109 R ii 24; V i 3; 115 R
i 13; 116 V ii 21; 117 R
ii 8; 119 V i 6; 120 V ii
10; 123 R i 30; 130 R ii
9; V i 22; 131 R ii 17; 133
R ii 1; 15
ⲟγⲛⲁⲙ 106 R ii 30; V i 1;
109 V i 6; 118 V ii 25;
133 R i 24
ⲟγⲛⲧ 108 V ii 16; 111 V ii 27
ⲟγⲛ̄ⲧⲁ= 115 V ii 7; 135 R
ii 30
ⲟγⲛⲟγ 113 R ii 20; 132 V
i 9
ⲛ̄ⲧⲉγⲛⲟγ, passim
ⲧⲉⲛⲟγ, passim
ⲟγⲛⲟγ 107 V i 4; ii 9; 128
R i 9; 132 V i 2
ⲟγⲱⲛ̄ϩ̄ 104 V ii 2; 106 R

i 4; 107 R i 2; ii 5; 14;
109 V i 29; 115 R ii 18;
V ii 30; 118 R i 8; 125
R ii 29; V i 20; 128 R
i 17; 130 R i 14; 134
R ii 5; 12
ⲟⲣⲟⲛ
ⲟγⲁⲁⲃ: ⲉⲧⲟγ. 132 R ii
4
ⲛⲉⲧⲟγ., passim
ⲟγⲏⲏⲃ 103 V i 32; ii
6; 104 V ii 6; 128 V ii
19; 129 R i 5
ⲟγⲣⲟⲧ 109 V i 32; 117 R
ii 32
(n.) 133 R i 20
ⲟγⲣ̄ⲧ 110 V i 2
ⲟγⲉⲣⲏⲧⲉ 109 R ii 10; 111 V
ii 32; 115 R i 28; V i 30;
116 R ii 15; 117 R ii 32;
120 R ii 2; 123 V ii 18;
124 R ii 13; 137 V ii 21
ⲩⲛⲟγ. 104 V ii 2
ⲟγⲱⲥϥ̄ 126 R ii 1
ⲟγⲱⲧ, see ⲟⲩⲁ
ⲟγⲧⲉ (ⲟγⲁⲉ) 'among'
110 R ii 27
ⲟγⲱⲧⲃ̄ 114 R i 29
ⲟγⲟⲉⲓⲱ 107 R i 1; 128 R
i 16
ⲟγⲱⲱⲩ 103 V i 3; 104 V i
21; 26; 107 V i 11; 112 R
ii 29; 113 R ii 19; 116 V
i 1; 13; 26; 124 V i 1;
128 V i 21; 25; 130 R ii
22; V i 16; 19; 131 R ii
28; 135 V i 21
(n.) 132 R i 25; 133 V ii
8; 135 V i 16
ⲟγⲱⲱⲩⲉ 111 R ii 9
ⲟγⲱⲏ 103 R ii 20; 107 V
i 9; 112 R ii 23; 115 V i
5; 24; 116 V ii 11; 125 V
i 5; 127 V ii 18; 133 R
i 17
ⲟγⲱⲩⲃ̄ 103 V i 4; 104 R i
5; V i 19; 25; 108 R ii

18; V ii 17; 30; 110 V ii 26;
111 R ii 2; 28; 113 R ii 8;
117 R i 24; 27; 118 R ii
27; V ii 21; 27; 124 V
i 16; ii 11; 125 V ii 20;
127 R i 30; 134 R ii 23;
135 R i 16; 135 R ii 7;
22; V i 25
ⲟγⲱⲩⲙ̄ 103 V ii 5
ⲟγⲱⲩⲧ 103 V ii 19; 104 R
i 24; 105 R i 30; ii 1; 9;
108 V ii 24; 109 R i 26;
V ii 15; 20; 26; 114 V i
5; 117 R i 20; 122 R ii
1; 123 V i 2; 124 V i 28;
ii 6; 125 V ii 12; 15; 128
V i 27
ⲟγⲱⲩⲩ̄ 126 R ii 1
ⲟγⲱ2 121 V ii 27; 133 V ii
27; 137 R i 3
ⲟγⲱ2 ⲉⲧⲟⲟⲧ= 138 R i 21
ⲟγⲱ2 ⲛ̄ⲥⲁ- 107 V i 29;
113 V i 2; 121 R ii 30
ⲟγⲉ2ⲥⲁ2ⲛⲉ 104 R i 5;
123 R i 3; 124 V i 29; 128
R ii 13; 129 R i 9
ⲟγⲱ2 (n.) 109 V ii 17
ⲟγⲱ2ⲩ̄ 111 R i 17; V ii 2;
115 R i 15; 120 V ii 14;
121 V ii 5
ⲟγⲵⲟⲣ 127 R ii 10; 18
ⲟγⲁⲝⲉ 129 V ii 11
ⲟγⲭⲁⲓ:
(n.) 110 R i 23; 123 V i
30; 132 V ii 29; 134
R ii 2
ⲟγⲱⲝⲛ̄, see next
ⲟγⲱϭⲛ̄ 135 V ii 8
ⲱⲱ 115 V ii 8
ⲱⲃⲩ̄ 134 V i 27
(n.) ⲡⲛⲱ. 120 V ii 20;
29
ⲟⲃⲩⲉ̄ (n.) 138 R i 3
ⲱⲙⲕ 127 R ii 25
ⲱⲛⲉ 114 R i 18; ii 14;
129 R i 4
ⲉⲛⲉⲙⲙⲉ 127 R ii 12

ϣⲱⲥ 106 Vi9; 124 Rii 22

ϣⲱⲧⲉ 'pit' 119 Rii 32; Vi5; 8; 119 Vii 21

ϣⲧⲉⲕⲟ 115 Vii 2

ϣⲧⲟⲣⲧⲣ 118 Rii 18; 128 Rii 30; 136 Vii6 (n.) 136 V i 28

ϣⲟⲟⲣⲉ 109 Vi5; 112 Rii10; 126 R i 30

ϣⲟⲩⲟ 129 Rii 32

ϣ̅ⲏⲉ 132 Rii 6

ϣⲱϣⲧ, see ⲥⲱⲱⲧ

ϣϥⲉ, see ⲥⲁϣϥ̄

ϣⲱϥⲧ:
  ⲣⲉϥϣ. 138 Vii 22

ϣⲁϩ:
  (n.) 'flame' 120 Vi 21; 129 R i 20

ϣⲁϫⲉ, passim
  (n.), passim

ϣⲱϫⲉ:
  ϫⲟⲉⲓϫ 108 Vi18; 113 Vi11

ϣⲟϫⲛⲉ 122 Vii 2; 132 Vii 13

ϥⲓ 103 Vii 1; 108 Vii 11; 111V i8; 113 Rii 25; Vi1; 31; ii 2; 114 Ri 32; 118 Ri16; V i 21; 119Ri4; Vi 13; 17; 120 Ri 27; 123 Vii5; 126 Vii 27; 137 Ri 8
  ϥⲓⲡⲟⲟⲣⲉ 104 Ri 29; 116 V i 30; ii 4; 117 Rii 18; 129 Ri 4; 137 Ri 18; 31
  ϥⲁⲓⲩⲉⲛⲟⲩϥⲉ 106 Vi 13

ϥⲱ 110 Rii 30; 121 Rii 19

ϥⲧⲟⲟⲩ 111 Vi5; 117 Ri 10
  ϥⲧⲉⲩ- 126 Vii 14; 127 R i5; 138 Vi 22
  ⲙⲛ̄ⲧⲁϥⲧⲉ 105 R i 5

ϥⲱϭⲉ 111 Rii 14; 114 Rii 20; 119 Ri 1; 127 Vi 25; 128 Vii 26; 136 Vii 8

ϩⲁⲉ 103 Vi 22

ϩⲁⲓ 'husband' 122 Vii 18

ϩⲉ 'fall' 108 Vi 12; 125 R i 2; 11; 134 Ri 11; 137 Rii 22
  ϩ. ⲉⲃⲟⲗ 120 Vii 27

ϩⲉ 'way', passim
  ⲛ̄ⲧⲉⲓϩⲉ, passim
  ⲛ̄ⲑⲉ, passim
  ⲕⲁⲧⲁⲑⲉ 105 Vii21; 120 V ii 21; 122 V i 12; 27
  ⲣ̄ⲑⲉ ⲛ̄- 114 Rii 17; 120 V i 22; 121 Ri 1; 124 Rii 15; 125 R ii 16; 125 Rii 23; 126 Rii 21; 127 Vi 23

ϩⲏ 'front' 103 Vii 31
  ⲉⲑⲏ 113 Vii 9; 118 Rii 13; 121 Vi 12
  ϩⲁⲑⲏ ⲛ̄- 107 Rii 21; 112 Rii 17; 114 Vii 17; 124 R i 14; 128 Rii 3; 133 Rii 1; Vi 16; 134 Vii 22
  ϩⲓⲑⲏ ⲛ̄- 104 Rii 22; 108 Vii 28; 117 V ii 9; 124 R ii 24; 126 Rii 11

ϩⲏ 'belly' 110 R i 12; 14; 112 Rii 10; 114 Rii 19; 118 Ri 18; 122 Vii 6; 12; 126 R i 9
  ⲛ̄ϩⲏⲧ=, passim

ϩⲏ 'Season':
  ϩⲉⲃⲃⲱⲛ 117 Ri 3

ϩⲓⲏ 124 Vi 19; 137 Vii 31

ϩⲟ 104 Ri 22; 109 Rii 30; 111 Rii 7; 8; 113 Vi23; 117 Ri 21; 121 Vii 12; 125 Ri 12; 126 Vii 1; 128 Rii 26; 129 Vii 10; 130 Rii 31; 135 Ri 27

ϩⲱ 'suffice' 118 Vii 13; 15

ϩⲱⲱ=, passim
  ϩⲱⲱϥ, as particle, 105 V ii 20

ϩⲱⲃ (n.) 105 Vi 24; ii 31; 111 Rii 3; 116 Vi 26; ii6; 119 Rii 5; 14; 29; 120 Ri 23; 123 Rii 9; ii30; 134 Rii 28; 135 Rii 9
  p̄2. 120 R i 22; 124 Rii 3; 134 Vi 22

ϩⲃⲟⲩⲣ 133 Ri 26

ϩⲏⲃⲉ̄ 104 Rii 9

ϩⲱⲃⲉ̄ 121 Vii 12

ϩⲃⲥⲱ 132 Vii 15

ϩⲱⲕ 104 Rii 29; 114 Rii 31
  (n.) 104 Rii 17 (20k)

ϩⲱⲕⲉ 135 Ri 12

ϩⲕⲟ 112 Vii 32; 131 Ri 32; 132 Vii 17

ϩⲏⲕⲉ 109 Rii 25

ϩⲗⲗⲟ:
  p̄2. 121 Ri 7

ϩⲗⲟϭ 105 Vii 25; 115 Ri 31

ϩⲱⲙ 117 Vii 24

ϩⲓⲙⲉ: see ⲥϩⲓⲙⲉ

ϩⲙⲉ 'forty' 118 Rii 7; 28; 119 Ri 9; 120 Ri 25

ϩⲙⲟⲩ 122 Vii 9

ϩⲙⲟⲟⲥ 103 Ri 32; 105 Vi 29; 106 Vi 18; 108 Rii 23; 109 Rii 1; 111 Ri 8; 118 Vii 5; 129 Vii 8; 130 Rii 1; 131 Vii 17; 137 Rii 29; Vi 9; 138 Rii 17

ϩⲙⲟⲧ 110 Vii 29; 116 Rii 26; 134 Ri 2; Vii 15; 136 Ri 5; Vii 29; 138 Ri 6; 28; ii 23; 31
  p̄2. 137 Ri 21
  ϣ̄p̄2. 135 Vi 27
  ϣ̄ⲓⲧ2. 127 Ri 21

ϩⲙ̄ϩⲁⲗ 108 Rii 1; 9; 114 V ii 28; 117 Rii 17; 19; 122 V i 9; 130 Vi 10; 136 Vii 22; 137 Vi 16; ii 10; 138 Rii 8

ϩⲙ̄ϭ 114 Ri 21; ii 17; 122 V ii 11; 125 Ri 5

ϩⲟⲩⲛ:
  ⲉϩ., passim
  ϩⲓϩ. 104 Rii 9

ϩⲱⲛ 'approach' 108 Vii 18; 112 Vii 20; 117 Vii 19

ϩⲱⲛ 'order' 104 Ri 3; 125 Rii 28

ϩⲟⲓ̈ⲛⲉ 111 Vi 6; 118 Vi 32; 119 Vii 11; 124 Vii 29; 126 R i 8; 137 Vii 27

ϩⲉⲛ-, passim

ϩⲱⲛⲉ 117 Vii 17

ϭ 137 R i 16; V i 25
ϭⲃⲃⲉ :
  ϭⲱⲃ 135 R i 20
ϭⲟⲗ 103 R ii 18
ϭⲱⲗ 107 V ii 10; 110 R i 16;
  114 R i 6; 127 V i 3
ϭⲁⲗⲉ 117 R ii 13; 131 R i 16;
  135 V ii 28
ϭⲟⲉⲓⲗⲉ :
  ⲙⲁⲛϭ. 106 R i 23
ϭⲱⲱⲗⲉ 136 R ii 4
ϭⲱⲗⲛ̄ 121 R ii 7
ϭⲱⲗⲝ̄ 123 V ii 21; 130 R i 22;
  135 V ii 13
ϭⲟⲙ 104 V ii 4; 105 V ii 17;
  106 R ii 8; V ii 22; 109 V
  i 9; ii; 29; 113 V i 20; 115
  R ii 13; V ii 3; 116 R i 25;
  ii 3; 117 V i 27; 118 R i 10;
  119 R ii 20; V ii 26; 122 V ii
  14; 125 V i 23; 126 R ii 10;
  28; 128 R i 5; 22; V ii 12;
  129 R ii 23; 131 R ii 15; V i
  1; 137 R i 4; 138 V ii 11
  ⲣϭ. 116 R ii 27; 124 V ii 20;
  131 V i 12
  ϯϭ. 106 V ii 29; 111 R ii 12;
  112 R ii 6; 113 V i 4

ϭⲙ̄ϭ. 104 R ii 11; 119 V ii 5;
  125 V ii 4; 126 V i 2
  ϭϭⲟⲙ 132 V i 22
ϭⲟⲙϭⲙ 124 R ii 2
ϭⲓⲛ-, passim
ϭⲓⲛⲉ 110 V ii 12; 114 V ii 20
  ϭⲙ̄ϭⲟⲙ, seo s. v. ϭⲟⲙ
ϭⲟⲛϭ :
  ϭⲓ ⲛ̄ϭ. : ⲁⲧϭⲓ ⲛ̄ϭ. : ⲙⲛ̄ⲧⲁ.
  129 V ii 12
ϭⲱⲛⲧ 108 V ii 8; 109 V ii 32;
  110 V ii 15; 111 R i 29; V i 3;
  113 R ii 4; V i 27; ii 31; 117
  V i 31; 119 V ii 28; 121 R ii
  23; 122 V ii 4; 124 V ii 24;
  125 V ii 28; 126 V ii 7; 127
  R ii 14; 28; V ii 4; 129 R i 8;
  130 R i 28
  (n.) 114 V i 23; 119 R i 2; 121
  V i 20; ii 9
ϭⲟⲡ 121 V i 30; 126 R i 13
ϭⲉⲡⲏ 128 V ii 16
  (n.) 2ⲡⲟⲩϭ. 130 R i 10; 134
  V ii 2
ϭⲏⲡⲉ 122 V ii 1
ϭⲱⲡⲉ 103 V ii 16; 26; 105 V i
  32; 108 V ii 14; 112 V i 4;
  113 R ii 5; 129 V i 31

ϭⲉⲣⲱⲃ 115 R i 32
ϭⲣⲟⲟⲙⲡⲉ 119 R i 17; 121 V ii 25
ϭⲣⲏⲡⲉ 135 V i 2
ϭⲱⲣϭ :
  ϭⲟⲣϭⲉ 112 R i 12
ϭⲟⲧ 110 V i 4
ϭⲱⲧⲍ̄ 110 R i 7; 10
ϭⲱⲱϥⲧ 108 R i 7; V ii 6; 111
  V i 27; 115 V i 1; 121 V ii
  31; 122 R i 25; 124 V i
  11; 127 R i 10; V i 11; 128
  R ii 23
ϭⲓⲝ 104 V i 16; ii 11; 27;
  106 R ii 30; 109 V i 5;
  22; 110 R ii 5; 111 R i
  4; ii 5; 114 R ii 28; 115
  R ii 10; 116 R ü 14; V ii
  28; 117 R ii 31; 118 R i
  30; 119 R ii 23; 120 R ii
  1; 124 R ii 3; 12; V ii
  20; 125 V i 12; 15; ii 2;
  126 V ii 3; 127 V i 5; 130
  V i 14; 132 V i 4; 134
  R ii 33; V ii 27
ϭⲱⲝⲃ̄ 108 V i 2

(b). GREEK   (Words not in Liddell - Scott - Jones marked ✱)

ἀγαθός 115 R i 8; 133 R i 13
  -ον (as n.) 113 R i 21; 115
  R ii 27; 116 V i 9
ἀγάπη :
  ⲙⲁⲓⲁ. 112 V ii 1
ἄγγελος 107 R ii 19; 111 V i 22;
  112 R i 32; 112 R ii 15; 114
  R ii 4; 115 R ii 6; 116 V ii 9;
  119 R i 12; 120 R ii 31; V ii
  3; 31; 121 R i 2; ii 6; 127 R
  i 18; V ii 25; 128 R ii 1; 129
  V i 6; 132 V ii 22; 133 R ii 4;
  V i 14; 134 V i 18; ii 21; 136
  R ii 10
ἀγέννητος 132 V i 28
ἅγιος, passim

ἀγορά 121 V i 11; 128 R ii 17;
  V ii 21
ἀγών 106 V i 20; ii 31; 107
  R i 32; 111 V ii 18; 115 R ii
  26; 117 V ii 14; 20; 120 V ii
  2; 122 R ii 12; 125 R ii 4;
  126 V i 13; 136 R ii 29
ἀθλητής 120 V i 25
αἰτεῖν 110 V i 15; 116 R ii 29;
  133 R ii 32; 134 R ii 28;
  V i 23
αἴτημα 110 V i 16; 22; ii 5;
  133 V i 1; ii 10
αἰών 113 R ii 30; 135 R ii 20;
  138 V i 3
ἀκάθαρτος 115 V i 13

ἄκρατον 103 V ii 3
ἀκριβής :
  -ῶς 138 R ii 17
ἀληθής :
  -ῶς 107 V i 14; 134 R ii 26;
  135 R ii 24
ἀλλά, passim
ἄλφα 121 V ii 3
ἀμελεῖν 107 R ii 24; 134 V i
  32
ἀμελής 106 V i 19
  ⲣⲁ. 104 R i 11
ἀμήν 103 R i 6; 105 R i 8; 107
  R ii 22; 108 R i 3; 111 V i 25;
  112 R ii 18; 113 V ii 7; 115
  R ii 14; V i 3; 117 R i 23;

107 R ii 21; 108 R ii 1; 111 V ii 25;
112 R ii 17; 113 V ii 7; 115 R ii 32;
V i 2; 116 V i 4; 117 R i 22; 120
V ii 11; 122 R ii 21; 124 V i 9;
125 R ii 14; V i 30; 126 V i 17;
128 R ii 3; V ii 6; 133 V ii 32;
134 R ii 20; 137 V i 23; 138 R
i 12; V ii 4; 6
†εἰ. 107 R ii 11; 112 R ii 13;
134 V ii 19
εἶτα 114 R i 15
ἐκκλησία 106 R i 3; ii 5; 23;
107 R ii 27
ἐκλείπειν (ⲣⲕⲗⲏⲡⲓⲥⲑⲉ) 125
R i 11
ἐλευθέρια 114 V ii 23; 115 R i 3
ἐλπίς 112 R i 24
ἔνδυμα 134 R ii 1
ἐντολή 112 V ii 30
ἐξετάζειν 122 R ii 23
ἐξέτασις 119 R ii 2
ἕξις 110 V i 4
*ἐξκουβίτωρ (ⲥⲕⲟⲩⲃⲓⲧⲱⲣ;
excubitor) 103 R ii 5
ἐξορκιστής 115 V ii 15
ἐξουσία 110 V ii 1; 119 V i 22;
122 V ii 30; 32; 138 V ii 12
ἐπειδή, passim
ἐπιθυμεῖν 106 R ii 12; 119 R ii
30
ἐπικαλεῖν 119 V i 4; 21
ἐπίσκοπος 105 V ii 3; 6; 7. 9;
11; 133 R ii 21
ἐργαστήριον (ⲁⲣⲕⲁⲥⲧⲏⲣⲓⲟⲛ)
138 R i 3
ἑρμηνεία 122 V i 25
ἑρμηνευτής 108 R ii 13; 118
R ii 22
*ἑρμητάριον 121 V i 16; 135 R
i 11
ἔτι 103 R ii 19 (αιτει); 113 V
i 5 (αιετε); 121 R ii 4; 129
R ii 26

εὐαγγέλιον 112 V ii 31; 128 R i 4
εὐσεβής:
μήτε. 108 V i 19
εὐφραίνειν 111 V i 32; 128 R ii
5
ἡγεμών, passim
θάλασσα 104 V i 10; 126 R i
30; 129 R ii 3; 12
θέατρον 117 V ii 3
θεῖον (ⲑⲏⲛ) 122 R ii 27
θεραπεύειν 109 V i 17; 115 V
ii 19; 130 R ii 18
θεωρεῖν 117 V ii 32
θηρίον 127 R ii 22
θησαυρός 133 R ii 13 (read
θυρωρός)
θλῖψις 112 R i 15; 20; 120 V i
7; 121 V ii 15; 129 R ii 22;
137 R ii 2
θόλος 121 R ii 14
θρόνος 104 V ii 24; 115 R i 24;
119 R i 22; 122 R i 15; V i 32;
126 V i 31; 127 V ii 31; 129
V ii 6; 18; 134 V i 9; 136 R ii
25
θυμός 114 V i 24
θυρωρός (ⲑⲏⲥⲁⲩⲣⲟⲥ, sic)
133 R ii 13
θυσία 103 V ii 2; 21; 135 R i
(used as verb) 112 V i 7
ⲣⲑ. 113 R ii 16; 18; V ii 12;
118 R ii 23; 122 V ii 26; 125
V ii 18; 23; 127 R ii 3; 128 V
i 6; 135 R ii 3; 10; 11
θυσιάζειν 105 R i 28; 110 V i
13; 111 R ii 27; 30; 114 R i 31;
127 R i 29; 138 R ii 1
ἱεροφύλαξ 124 R i 31
καὶ (γάρ) 119 R ii 23; 127 R
ii 21
καιρός 116 R ii 16
κακός:
- ὡς 110 R ii 10; V ii 26; 111
R ii 28; 120 R ii 28; 135 R ii 4
καλός:
- ⲱ̄s 103 V ii 8; 110 V i 3; 111
R i 25

κάμινος 120 V i 1
καπνός 125 R i 6
καρπός 120 V ii 5
κατά, passim
καταπέτασμα 121 V ii 11
κατάστασις 110 V i 8
καυτηριάζειν 110 R i 2
κελεύειν 104 V ii 5; 104 R ii
20; 108 V i 9; ii 13; 20; 25;
110 R i 2; V ii 16; 111 V i 4; ii 2;
112 R ii 28; 113 R ii 5; 21; 114
R i 2; 15; ii 29; V ii 15; 115
R i 8; 117 V ii 1; 118 V i 19; 119
R i 29; V ii 30; 120 R i 13; 29;
123 V i 13; 20; 124 R i 8; V
ii 25; 125 R i 7; V ii i 2; 29;
126 V ii 9; 13; 127 R ii 29; V
ii 5; 128 R ii 18; 132 R ii 10; 19;
135 R i 10; 136 V i 7
κέλευσις 105 V i 5; 132 R ii 8
*κεστιονάριος (quaestio-
narius) 113 V ii 1; 118 V i
24; 31; ii 11; 22; 122 V ii
18; 125 V ii 32; 126 V ii 23
κεφαλίς 132 V ii 28
κῆτος 112 R i 10
κιθάρα 132 V ii 18
κίνδυνος 137 R ii 25
κλάδος 132 V ii 6
κλείς 118 V ii 1; 126 V ii 26
κληρονομία 106 V i 24; 117
R i 13
κληρονόμος 115 R ii 22; 133
V i 28
κολλάριον (collarium) 111
V ii 28
κόμης (comes) 103 R ii 4;
105 R i 15
*κομμενταρήσιος (com-
mentariensis) 105 R ii 31;
107 R i 27; 114 V i 25; 116
R ii 2; 130 R ii 11
κονία 114 R i 22; 126 R i 5
κόσμος 106 R i 31; V ii 15;
107 R i 21; V ii 27; 112 V i
31; 116 R ii 32; 131 R i 6;
133 V ii 28; 137 R ii 1

IV. SCRIPTURE CITATIONS AND ALLUSIONS

	xxv, 35f. 112 Vii-113Ri		127 Ri	(iii, 9)	131 Ri
Mk.	(iii, 1ff.) 109 Vi-ii	(iv, 24) 104 Vi		I Jn. ii, 17	135 Vi
	(vi, 45ff) 115 Ri	(xii, 7) 127 Vii		Jude (25)	138 Vii
	(viii, 34) 113Rii-Vi	(xiv, 15) 104 Vi		Rev. (iii, 5)	117 Ri
	(x, 28) 113 Rü-Vi	Rom. (xii, 17) 131 Ri			134 Rii
Lk.	(i, 26ff.) 106 Vii	(xii, 20) 131 Ri-ii		(xlii, 8)	117 Ri
	(i, 28) 132 Vii	II cor. xi, 2 122 Vi			134 Rii
	(i, b2-4) 131 Rii	(xii, 2) 134 Vi		(xx, 12)	117 Ri
	iv, 8 109 Vii	Phil. (iv, 3) 117 Ri			134 Rii
	(Vi, bff) 109 Vi-ii	134 Rii		(xx, 15)	117 Ri
	(Vi, 47ff.) 115 Rii	Col. i, 5(?) 105 Vii			134 Rii
	(ix, 23) 113 Rii-Vi	I Thess. (v, 15) 131 Ri		(xxi, 6)	121 Vii
	xii, 4f. 123 Ri	I Tim. (V, 10) 137 Vii		(xxi, 27)	117 Ri
	(xii, 8f.) 110 Rii	(Vi, 12) 136 Rii-Vi			134 Rii
	(xlii, 11ff.) 109 Vi-ii	II Tim. (i, 9) 110 Vii		(xxii, 1)	132 Vii
	Lxviii, 28) 113 Rii-Vi	(ii, 12) 110 Rii			133 Ri
	(xxii, 43) 113 Vi	(iv, 6) 136 Rii-Vi		(xxii, 13)	121 Vii
Jn.	(i, 14) 115 Ri	(iv, 7f.) 113 Ri		(xxii, 18f)	137 Ri
	(ix, 6) 109 Rii	iv, 8 (?) 105 Vii		(xxii, 19)	117 Ri
	(xv, 1) 115 Ri	(iv, 8) 106 Vi			134 Rii
Acts	(i, 9f.) 108 Ri	James (v, 3?) 135 Vi		Act. Paul. et Thecl. (§22)
	115 Rii-Vi	I Pet. (iii, 7) 135 Ri			120 Rii

I. PROPER NAMES: PERSONAL AND RELIGIOUS

II. GEOGRAPHICAL AND ETHNICAL

GENERAL: (a) COPTIC

274

Eⲟⲟⲩ 168 R i 22; see Geoᴦⲛ.
Hi 168 Vi 5
Ei 'come', passim
Eiⲁ: ⲛⲁⲉiⲁⲧ= 169 R ii 4
Eiⲉ ⲛi Vii 2
EiBE:
  (n.) 170 R ii 5
Eiⲙⲉ 170 R ii 22
Eiⲛⲉ ⲛi Vi 21; ii 19; 24;
  172 R i 14; 30; Vi 14; 173
  R i 14
Eiⲟⲟⲣ:
  Eiⲉⲣⲟ 168 Vii 22
Eiⲣⲉ, passim
EiⲥⳅHHⲧⲉ, passim
Eiⲱⲧ 170 R ii 15; 29; 171 R ii
  27; 172 R ii 25; 173 R ii
  25; Vi 21
KE, passim
Koⲩi; passim
  ⲡ̄K. ⲛ̄ⲌHⲦ 172 R ii 26
Kⲱ 169 Vii 24; 170 Vii 8; 171
  R ii 6; 10
  K. EBoⲗ 171 Vii 10
  K. ⲛ̄ⲥⲁ- 169 Vi 10; 170 R ii
  15; Vi 10; 171 R ii 31
  Kⲁⲧⲟⲟⲧ= EBoⲗ ⲛi R i 1
  Kⲱ KⲁⳅHⲩ, see next
KⲱK: K. ⲁ2Hⲩ (as if Kⲱ
  Kⲁ2Hⲩ) 169 Vii 23
KⲀKE 170 R ii 1; 172 R ii 14
Kⲗoⲙ 170 Vii 9; 18; 172 Vi
  25; 26; 173 Vi 7
Kⲱⲧⲉ 172 R ii 22
Kⲁ2 168 Vi 17; 170 R i 6;
  171 Vii 31
Kⲱ2ⲧ 171 Vii 25; 172 R i 32
ⲗⲁⲁⲩ 169 Vi 1
ⲙⲁ 171 Vii 10
  ⲙⲁⲛ̄ⲛ̄Koⲧⲕ 171 Vii 22
  ⲙⲁⲛⳅⲩⲉⲗⲉⲉⲧ 172 Vi 4
ⲙoⲩ 169 R ii 23; Vi 19; ii 1;
  170 R ii 4; 171 Vi 28; 172
  R ii 9; 27; ii 16; Vi 28
  (n.) 169 Vi 23
ⲙⲁ(ⲁ)B 169 R i 11
ⲙⲁKⲌ 172 Vii 7

ⲙ̄ⲙoⲛ 'not' 169 R ii 28
  Ⲍiⲛⲙ̄. ⲛi Vi 29; 172 R ii 18
ⲙ̄ⲙoⲛ 'for' 172 R ii 26
ⲙ̄ⲙⲁⲩ, passim
ⲙ̄ⲛ̄- 'is not', passim
ⲙ̄ⲛ̄- (ⲛ̄ⲙ̄ⲙⲁ=), passim
ⲙoⲩⲛK:
  (n.) ⲙ. ⲛ̄Ϭiⲝ 169 R i 29
ⲙ̄ⲛ̄ⲧ-
  ⲙ̄ⲛ̄ⲧ̄ⲣ̄ⲣⲟ 168 R i 13; 170 Vii 6;
  172 Vi 11; 173 R i 2; ii 21; Vii 5
  ⲙ̄ⲛ̄ⲧⲥⲟϭ 169 Vii 4
ⲧⲙ̄ⲡⲉ 'not': ⲉⳅⲱⲡⲉ ⲙ̄. 'if
  not' 173 R i 23
ⲧⲛ̄ⲛⲩⲁ 170 R i 22
ⲁⲧⲙ̄. 173 Vii 21
ⲙoⲣⲡ 169 Vii 27; 171 Vi 22
ⲙ̄ⲣⲱ 171 Vi 19
ⲙoⲩⲥ 169 Vii 29
ⲙⲁⲧⲉ 'very': Eⲙ., passim
ⲙⲁⲧⲉ 'only': ⲙⲙ. 169 Vii 24
ⲙⲁⲧoi 168 R ii 19; Vii 13; 25;
  169 R i 6; 13; 170 Vi 24; 171
  R ii 4; Vi 8; 173 R ii 8
ⲙoⲣⲧⲉ 168 Vii 18
ⲁ̄ⲧo: ⲙ̄. EBoⲗ 169 Vii 31
ⲙoⲟⲩ 170 R i 6; ii 3
ⲙHHⳅⲉ 168 Vii 13
ⲙoⲟⲩⳅⲉ 170 R i 21; 171 R ii 13
ⲙoⲩ2 'fill' 170 R i 28
ⲛⲁ:
  (n.) 173 Vii 10
ⲛoⲩ-ⲛHⲩ 172 Vi 31
ⲛoBE:
  ⲣ̄ⲛ̄. ⲛi Vii 18
ⲛ̄Koⲧⲕ:
  ⲙⲁⲛ̄ⲛ̄. 171 Vii 22
ⲛiⲙ 'every', passim
ⲛⲁⲛoⲩ- 168 R i 7; 171 Vii 4
ⲛⲁ(E)iⲁⲧ=, see Eiⲁ
ⲛoⲩⲧⲉ (pagan) 168 Vi 19;
  169 R ii 1; ii 17; 24
  ⲛⲛ. (Christian), passim
  ⲡ̄ⲛ̄ⲛ̄. 169 R i 15
ⲛ̄ⲧⲁ= (possessive) 170 Vii 13
ⲛⲁⲩ 'see' 170 R i 8; 172 R i 6;
  Vii 30

ⲛⲁⲩ 'time' 172 Vi 2; 173 R ii 8
  ⲛ̄ⲏoⲧ: ⲛⲁⲩⲧ 169 R ii 31
ⲛHⲩE 168 R ii 13
ⲛoⲩⲌⲙ̄ 169 Vi 1
ⲛⲁ2ⲣⲛ̄- 172 Vi 8
ⲛoⲩ2E 170 R i 31; 173 R i 16
ⲛoϭ, passim
ⲛ̄ϭi, passim
oB2E 169 Vi 28
oEiK 170 R ii 2
oⳅⲉ:
  ⲧo. 172 R i 7
ⲛⲁi, ⲧⲁi, ⲛⲁi, passim
ⲛⲉ 'heaven' 168 R ii 4; 169 R
  ii 7; 170 R ii 29; Vii 7; 28;
  172 R i 2; Vi 22; 173 R ii
  8; 15
ⲛⲉⲱ= 170 R ii 24; 172 Vii 1
ⲛⲉⲛiⲛⲉ, see BEⲛiⲛE
ⲛEiⲣE 173 Vi 7; 10
ⲛⲱⲣ̄ⳡ 168 Vii 20; 169 R ii 16
  171 Vi 18; 173 Vi 1
ⲛⲱ2 'reach' 168 Vii 15; 171
  R ii 23
ⲛⲱ2ⲧ 168 Vii 28
ⲛEⲝE-, passim
ⲡH 170 Vii 11
ⲡi 170 R i 32; Vi 1; 172 R ii 13
  Vii 8
ⲡo 'mouth' 170 R i 20
ⲡⲱⲙE 169 R i 30; ii 2; 3; 5;
  170 Vii 22; 171 R ii 25; V
  ii 6; 8; 9
  ⲡ̄ⲙ̄ⲛ̄ⲛoⲩⲧⲉ 169 R i 5
  ⲡⲙ̄-+place name 169 R i
  19; 171 R i 13
  ⲣⲉⲩϥⲁⲗⲗⲉi 169 R ii 11
ⲡⲙ̄-, see last
ⲡoⲙⲛE 169 R i 1
ⲡⲙ̄2E 168 R ii 19
ⲡⲁⲛ 169 R i 9; ii 14; 170 R
  i 19; 23; Vi 21; 171 R i 2;
  172 R i 8; Vi 29; 173 Vii 2
ⲣ̄ⲣⲟ 168 R i 16; Vi 11; ii 6; 28;
  169 R i 25
  ⲙ̄ⲛ̄ⲧ̄ⲣ̄. 168 R i 13; 170 Vii 6;
  172 Vi 11; 173 R i 2; ii 21;

ϫⲓϥ · ⲉⲃⲟⲗ 168 Vii 31; 172
R i 3
ⲩⲗⲏⲗ 170 Rii 10; 171 R i 2
ϣⲉⲗⲉⲉⲧ :
  ⲙⲁⲏⲩ. 172 Vi 4
ϣⲏⲙ 169 R i 5
ϣⲏⲙⲟ 169 Rii 18; 172 Vii 25
ϣⲟⲙⲛⲧ, ϣⲟⲙⲧⲉ 169 R ii 1;
  170 V i 28; 171 R i 4; 5
ϣⲓⲛⲉ 172 R ii 24
ϣⲓⲛⲉ :
  (n.) ϯϣ. 169 Vii 15
ϣⲱⲡⲉ, passim
  ⲉϣ. 169 R ii 27; 173 R i 22
ϣⲏⲣⲉ 169 R i 5; 18; 170 V i
  12
ϣⲱⲣⲡ :
  ϣⲟⲣⲡ. ⲣ̄ϣ. 172 Vi 9
ϣⲱϫⲉ :
  ϣⲟⲉⲓϣ 171 R ii 18
ϥⲓ 172 R ii 9; V i 19; 20; ii 8;
  173 R ii 6; 11
ϥⲱϭⲉ ⲡⲓ Vii 30
ϩⲉ 'way', passim
ϩⲏ 'front':
  ⲉⲑⲏ 171 Vii 19
  ϩⲁⲑⲏ ⲛ̄- 170 R ii 31, Vii 30
ϩⲏ 'belly':
  ⲛ̄ϩⲏⲧⲉ, etc., passim
ϩⲏ ⲡⲓ R ii 22
ϩⲟ 173 R ii 6
ϩⲱⲱ=, passim

ϩⲱⲃ ⲡⲓ R i 16; 172 R ii 11
ϩⲕⲟ :
  (n.) 170 R ii 4
ϩⲙⲟⲟⲥ 171 R ii 15
ϩⲙ̄ϫⲁⲗ 168 R ii 18
ϩⲟⲩⲛ : ⲉϩ., passim
ϩⲣⲟϣⲣⲉϣ 169 V i 27
ϩⲏⲧ 168 R ii 3
  ⲥⲙ̄(ⲡⲉϥ) 2. 173 R i 21
  ⲣ̄ⲕⲟⲩⲓ ⲛ̄ϩ. 172 R ii 26
ϩⲁⲧⲉ ⲡⲟ R i 5
ϩⲓⲧⲉ ⲡⲓ Vii 28
ϩⲟⲧⲉ :
  ⲣ̄2. 170 V i 16; 25; 171 R ii
  30
ϩⲱⲧⲃ 169 V i 12; 171 R i 18
ϩⲧⲟⲟⲩⲉ 173 R i 8; 10; ii 9
ϩⲟⲟⲩ 'day' 170 V i 29;
  171 R i 4; V i 1
  ⲡⲟⲟⲩ 172 R ii 29
  ⲙⲛ. 171 R ii 24
ϩⲟⲟⲩ 'evil' 170 R i 10; 172
  R i 21
ϩⲓⲟⲩⲉ 170 R i 2; 17
ϩⲟⲩⲟ : ⲛ̄2. 171 Vii 14
ϩⲟⲟⲩⲧ 168 R ii 16
ϫⲉ, passim
ϫⲓ, 'take', passim
ϫⲓⲧⲛⲉ 169 V i 22
ϫⲱ 'say', passim
ϫⲱ 'head', in compounds,
  ϫⲓϫⲛ̄, etc., passim

ϫⲱⲕ : ϫ. ⲉⲃⲟⲗ 168 R i 5; 171
  R i 32; 172 Vii 12
ϫⲉⲕⲁⲥ, passim
ϫⲱⲗⲕ 169 Vii 30
ϫⲓⲛ- 'or': ϫⲓⲛⲙⲙⲟⲛ 171 V
  i 29; 172 R i 18
ϫⲣⲟ 170 V i 14
ϫⲟⲉⲓⲥ 170 R ii 14; 28; Vii
  27; 171 R ii 26; 172 R i 4;
  173 V i 18
ϫⲟⲩⲱⲧ 169 Vii 22; 172 Vii 10
  ϫⲟⲩⲧ- 168 R i 8; 173 R ii 1; ii 10
ⲥⲉ, passim
ⲥⲱ 171 R ii 8
ⲥⲟⲙ 170 R ii 25; 172 Vii 1
  ⲟⲩⲛⲥ. 172 R ii 10
  ⲙⲛⲥ. 170 Vii 2
  ⲁⲧⲥ. : ⲣ̄ⲁⲧⲥ. 173 R ii 3
  ϭⲟⲙⲥ. 170 V i 15; 173 R i 27
ⲥⲓⲛⲉ :
  ⲥⲁ(ⲡⲉϥ) ϩⲏⲧ 173 R i 21
  ϭⲙ̄ϭⲟⲙ 170 V i 15; 173 R i 27
ⲥⲱⲛⲧ 169 V i 26; 171 Vii 17; 172
  R i 28
  (n.) 170 R i 28; 172 R ii 9
ⲥⲉⲡⲏ :
  (n.) 2ⲛⲟⲩⲉ. 170 R ii 17; 173
  R i 1
ⲥⲱⲧⲉ 171 R ii 3
ⲥⲱⲟⲩϩ 172 R i i; 5
ⲥⲓϣ 169 R i 29; ii 17; V i 3;
  172 V i 31

(b) GREEK   (Words not in Liddell-Scott-Jones marked *)

ἀγαθός 173 V i 21
ἄγγελος 170 R ii 30; V i 25; ii
  29; 173 R ii 13
ἅγιος, passim
ἀγων 168 R i 6; 172 Vii 25
αἰών 170 V i 22; 26; 32
ἀκτίς (ⲁⲕⲧⲓⲛ) 170 Vii 3; 173 R
  i 16
ἀλλά, passim
ἀμήν 168 R i 11; 170 R ii 27;
  172 Vii 3; 15
ἀναγνώστης 168 R ii 25.
ἀναχωρητής 171 R i 10

ἄνομος 168 R i 16; 170 R ii 21
ἀνόσιος 173 R i 19
ἀπόστολος 169 Vii 7; 170
  R i 15; 17
ἀπόφασις 172 R ii 19
ἀρχή 170 R i 9
ἀσκητής 171 R i 11
ἀσπάζεσθαι 168 V i 32; 171 R
  ii 14; 173 R ii 18
βασανίζειν 168 V i 3
βάσανος 169 R ii 30; 170 R i 9;
  V i 19; 172 R i 20; ii 7; 15; V
  ii 19

βῆμα 168 Vii 21; 171 V i 18
βοηθεῖν 172 R ii 28
γάρ, passim
  καὶ γάρ 169 V i 12
γενναῖος 168 R i 2; 169 R i 26
δαιμόνιον 169 V i 8
δέ, passim
διάβολος 168 R ii 1; 170 R i 29
διάκονος 168 R ii 24
διάταγμα 168 V i 2
δίκαιος 169 R i 8
εἴδωλον 169 R i 28; V i 8; 172 R i
  26

IV. SCRIPTURE CITATIONS AND ALLUSIONS

OTHER TITLES IN THIS HARDBACK REPRINT PROGRAMME FROM
SANDPIPER BOOKS LTD (LONDON) AND POWELLS BOOKS (CHICAGO)